WEBSTER'S
NEW WORLD™

ITALIAN
DICTIONARY

POCKET EDITION

WEBSTER'S
NEW WORLD™

ITALIAN
DICTIONARY

POCKET EDITION

MACMILLAN • USA

First published in Great Britain as *Harrap's Pocket
Italian Dictionary* by Chambers Harrap Publishers Ltd.,
43-45 Annandale Street, Edinburgh, Scotland EH7 4AZ

First Webster's New World™ Book edition 1996

Macmillan General Reference
A Simon & Schuster Macmillan Company
1633 Broadway
New York, NY 10019-6785

A Webster's New World™ Book

ISBN: 0-02-861413-5

Manufactured in the United States of America

10   9   8   7   6   5   4   3   2   1

Preface to the Italian-English Section

1. The information contained in this part of the dictionary is designed to help the English-speaking user. The Italian alphabet is described and the rules of Italian pronunciation and accentuation are set out. The preface provides a list of irregular Italian verbs and some common irregular plurals of nouns. A similar introduction is provided for the Italian-speaking user of the dictionary.

2. Since Italian presents particular problems with its verbs, we have provided a list of irregular verbs in general use. We have not included their compounds as they are conjugated in the same way. Those verbs which take *essere* as an auxiliary are indicated by means of a single star. Those which take *essere* when used intransitively and *avere* when used transitively have a double star.

   With the past definite tense, we have shown the 1st person singular only, since the 3rd person singular and the 3rd person plural follow the same pattern, while the 2nd person singular and plural are regular in form eg: *prendere* – **presi**, *prendesti*, **prese**, *prendemmo*, *prendeste*, **presero**.

3. There are two points concerning the current use of verbs which the student of Italian may well find helpful:

   a) there is a tendency in modern Italian towards a more frequent use of the perfect tense to represent completed past action (though such irrefutable statements as, for example, *Dante died in 1321* would still always be translated as *Dante morì* ...);

   b) though the polite form in the singular, with *Lei* and the 3rd person of the verb, is regularly used eg: *Lei scrive in inglese?* (Are you writing in English?), the plural form addressed to more than one person is now more frequently the 2nd person plural with *Voi*, instead of the 3rd person plural with *Loro* eg: *Voi scrivete in inglese?* rather than *Loro scrivono in inglese?*

4. As some Italian nouns have irregular plurals or do not change their form in the plural, we have included a list of the more commonly used ones.

5. In illustrating the possible alternative translations for the Italian words listed, the following symbols have been adopted:

   a) a double line (||) after the initial translation or translations indicates a grammatical change from, for example, an adjective to a noun or a pronoun to an adverb;

   b) a lozenge (♦) indicates something more than just an alternative translation, showing, for example, a figurative or idiomatic use;

   c) the numbers printed in large type (**1.**, **2.**, **3.**, etc.) indicate the various alternative meanings;

   d) the small numbers (^{1}, ^{2}, ^{3} etc.) indicate words of identical form but different meaning.

The Alphabet

The Italian alphabet consists of 21 letters only. **j** (*i lunga*), **k** (*cappa*), **w** (*doppio vu*), **x** (*ics*), **y** (*ipsilon*) do not occur in the alphabet, though they are used for the spelling of foreign words eg: *judo, kimono, watt, xenofobia, yacht*. In some cases, **y** is replaced by **i** eg *raion* for rayon. **ch** replaces **k** eg *chilogrammo* for kilogram. **ph** is represented by **f** eg *fobia* for phobia. **x** occurs in certain expressions such as *ex-presidente, extraterritoriale* etc.

Letter	Name	Letter	Name
a	*a*	m	*emme*
b	*bi*	n	*enne*
c	*ci*	o	*o*
d	*di*	p	*pi*
e	*e*	q	*cu*
f	*effe*	r	*erre*
g	*gi*	s	*esse*
h	*acca*	t	*ti*
i	*i*	u	*u*
l	*elle*	v	*vu*
		z	*zeta*

Pronunciation

Since Italian is a phonetic language, once the rules of pronunciation are learnt, it is possible to pronounce most words correctly, though it is not always easy to tell on which syllable the tonic stress falls.

The Vowels

Italian vowels are pure sounds and should be pronounced well forward in the mouth:

	A	like a in far	*gala*
close	E	like a in fate	*seta*
open	E	like e in ten	*pelle*
	I	like i in machine	*vino*
close	O	like o in store	*corte*
open	O	like o in spot	*motto*
	U	like oo in spoon	*uso*

The Consonants

In the case of double consonants, each consonant is sounded, with the voice rising on them and falling on the following vowel.

The consonants B, D, F, L, M, N, P, Q, T and V are pronounced very much as in English. The rest are as follows:

C   1. before a, o, u and consonants, including h: like c in cat, as in *casa, crema, chilo*;
    2. before e or i: like ch in chip, as in *cena, cibo*.
G   1. before a, o, u and consonants, including h but not including l and n: like g in gap, as in *gala, grido, ghiro*;
    2. before e or i: like g in gem, as in *gente, gita*.
gli   like lli in billion, as in *figlia*; (a few exceptions have the gli pronounced as in English, eg *anglicano, negligente*).
gn   like ni in onion, as in *signore*.
H   is always silent and occurs in very few words, except as shown above to harden the c and g sounds before e and i.
Q   is always followed by u, like qu in quick, as in *quinto*.
R   is rolled, rather as in rr Scottish pronunciation, as in *pera, serra*.
S   1. is voiced, like s in rose, as in *rosa, esatto*, or when followed by b, d, g, l, m, n, r, v, the voiceless consonants, as in *sdegno, svelto*;
    2. is unvoiced like s in sap, at the beginning of a word, or when it is doubled, as in *sega, rosso*.
sc   1. before e or i is like sh in shot, as in *scena*;
    2. before a, o and u is like sk in skate, as in *scarpa, scopo, scudo*;
    3. an h after it and before e or i makes it like sk, as in *schema, schiena*;
    4. an i after it and before a, o or u makes it like sh, as in *scialle, sciocco, sciupare*.
Z   1. voiced like ds in treads, as in *zio*;
    2. unvoiced like ts in wits, as in *forza*.

Accentuation

In printed and written Italian, an accent is used to indicate when the tonic stress falls on a final vowel such as in *città* or *caffè*. It is also used to distinguish between two words which are spelt and pronounced alike but which have different meanings:

$$è = \text{is} \qquad dà = \text{he gives}$$
$$e = \text{and} \qquad da = \text{from, by, of etc.}$$

It also occurs on some monosyllabic words as in *già* and *più*.

In print, the acute accent is used to indicate a stress on a final e as in *perché* or *né*, though in handwriting the grave accent is more usual. In modern Italian, the grave accent is normally used elsewhere and we have followed this practice.

As a general rule, the tonic stress is on the penultimate syllable, but this is not by any means always so. The grave and acute accents have been used to show where the stress falls when it does not fall on the penultimate syllable. The open and close e are distinguished in the accepted way, by means of è and é, eg *créscere*, *crédere*, *fèstival*, *fèrvido* and the grave accent is used everywhere else eg *càndido*, *moltitùdine*.

Irregular Italian Verbs

accendere   *p. def.* accesi; *p.p.* acceso
accludere   see **alludere**
addurre   *pres.* adduco; *p. def.* addussi; *fut.* addurrò; *p.p.* addotto
affliggere   *p. def.* afflissi; *p.p.* afflitto
alludere   *p. def.* allusi; *p.p.* alluso
andare*   *pres.* vado, vai, va, andiamo, andate, vanno; *fut.* andrò
annettere   *p. def.* annettei (annessi); *p.p.* annesso
apparire*   *pres.* apparisco; *p. def.* apparii (apparvi, apparsi); *p.p.* apparso
appendere   *p. def.* appesi; *p.p.* appeso
ardere   *p. def.* arsi; *p.p.* arso
aspergere   *p. def.* aspersi; *p.p.* asperso
assalire   *pres.* assalgo (assalisco), assalgono
assolvere   *p. def.* assolsi (assolvei, assolvetti); *p.p.* assolto
assumere   *p. def* assunsi; *p.p.* assunto

bere   *pres.* bevo; *p. def* bevvi; *fut.* berrò

cadere*   *p. def.* caddi; *fut.* cadrò
cedere   *p. def.* cedei
chiedere   *p. def.* chiesi; *p.p.* chiesto
chiudere   *p. def.* chiusi; *p.p.* chiuso
cingere   *p. def.* cinsi; *p.p.* cinto
cogliere   *pres.* colgo, colgono; *p. def.* colsi; *p.p.* colto
comprimere   *p. def.* compressi; *p.p.* compresso
conoscere   *p. def.* conobbi; *p.p.* conosciuto
consumare   *p. def.* consumai (consunsi); *p.p.* consumato (consunto)
correre**   *p. def.* corsi; *p.p.* corso
costruire   *p.p.* costruito (costrutto)
crescere*   *p. def* crebbi; *p.p.* cresciuto
cucire   *pres.* cucio
cuocere   *pres.* cuocio, cuoci, cuoce, cociamo, cocete, cuociono; *p.def.* cossi; *p.p.* cotto

dare   *pres.* do, dai, dà, diamo, date, danno; *p.def.* diedi (detti), desti; *fut.* darò; *p.p.* dato
decidere   *p. def.* decisi; *p.p.* deciso
difendere   *p. def.* difesi; *p.p.* difeso
dipendere**   *p. def.* dipesi; *p.p.* dipeso
dipingere   *p. def.* dipinsi; *p.p.* dipinto
dire   *pres.* dico, dite; *p. def.* dissi; *fut.* dirò; *p.p.* detto
dirigere   *p. def.* diressi; *p.p.* diretto
discutere   *p. def.* discussi; *p.p.* discusso
dissolvere   *p.def* dissolsi (dissolvei); *p.p.* dissolto
distinguere   *p. def* distinsi; *p.p.* distinto
dividere   *p. def.* divisi; *p.p.* diviso
dolersi   *pres.* mi dolgo, ti duoli, si duole, ci doliamo, vi dolete, si dolgono; *p.def.* mi dolsi; *fut.* mi dorrò
decidere   *pres.* devo (debbo), devi, deve, dobbiamo, dovete, devono (debbono); *fut.* dovrò

eccellere   *p.def.* eccelsi; *p.p.* eccelso
emergere*   *p.def.* emersi; *p.p.* emerso

ix

ergere	*p.def.* ersi; *p.p.* erto
erigere	*p.def.* eressi; *p.p.* eretto
esigere	*p.p.* esatto
espellere	*p.def.* espulsi; *p.p.* espulso
esplodere**	*p.def.* esplosi; *p.p.* esploso
evadere	*p.def.* evasi; *p.p.* evaso
fare	*pres.* faccio (fo), fai, fa, facciamo, fate, fanno; *imper.* facevo; *p. def.* feci; *fut* farò; *p.p.* fatto
fendere	*p.def.* fendei (fendetti); *p.p.* fesso (fendutto)
figgere	*p.def.* fissi; *p.p.* fisso (fitto)
fingere	*p.def.* finsi; *p.p.* finto
fondere	*p.def.* fusi; *p.p.* fuso
frangere	*p.def.* fransi; *p.p.* franto
friggere	*p.def.* frissi; *p.p.* fritto
giacere*	*pres.* giaccio, giacciono; *p.def.* giacqui; *p.p.* giaciuto
giungere*	*p. def.* giunsi; *p.p.* giunto
godere	*fut.* godrò
incutere	*p.def.* incussi (incutei); *p.p.* incusso
indulgere	*p.def.* indulsi; *p.p.* indulto
intridere	*p.def.* intrisi; *p.p.* intriso
invadere	*p.def.* invasi; *p.p.* invaso
ledere	*p.def.* lesi; *p.p.* leso
leggere	*p.def.* lessi; *p.p.* letto
mettere	*p.def.* misi; *p.p.* messo
mordere	*p.def.* morsi; *p.p.* morso
morire*	*pres.* muoio, muori, muore, moriamo, morite, muoiono; *fut.* morrò; *p.p.* morto
mungere	*p.def.* munsi; *p.p.* munto
muovere	*pres.* moviamo, movete; *p.def.* mossi; *p.p.* mosso
nascere*	*p.def.* nacqui; *p.p.* nato
nascondere	*p.def.* nascosi; *p.p.* nascosto
nuocere	*pres.* noccio, nociamo, nocete, nocciono; *p.def.* nocqui; *p.p.* nociuto
offrire*	*p.def.* offrii (offersi); *p.p.* offerto
parere*	*pres.* paio, paiamo, paiono; *p.def.* parvi; *fut.* parrò; *p.p.* parso
percuotere	*p.p.* percosso
perdere	*p.def.* persi (perdei, perdetti); *p.p.* perduto (perso)
persuadere	*p.def.* persuasi; *p.p.* persuaso
piacere*	*pres.* piaccio, piaci, piace, piacciamo, piacete, piacciono; *p. def.* piacqui; *p.p.* piaciuto
piangere	*p.def.* piansi; *p.p.* pianto
piovere**	*p.def.* piovve, piovvero
porgere	*p.def.* porsi; *p.p.* porto
porre	*pres.* pongo, poni, pone, poniamo, ponete, pongono; *p.def.* posi; *fut.* porrò; *p.p.* posto
potere	*pres.* posso, puoi, può, possiamo, potete, possono; *fut.* potrò
prediligere	*p.def.* predilessi; *p.p.* prediletto
prendere	*p. def.* presi; *p.p.* preso
proteggere	*p.def.* protessi; *p.p.* protetto
pungere	*p.def.* punsi; *p.p.* punto
radere	*p. def.* rasi; *p.p.* raso
redimere	*p.def.* redensi; *p.p.* redento
reggere	*p. def.* ressi; *p.p.* retto

rendere	*p.def.* resi; *p.p.* reso
ridere	*p.def.* risi; *p.p.* riso
rifulgere**	*p. def.* rifulsi; *p.p.* rifulso
rispondere	*p.def.* risposi; *p.p.* risposto
rodere	*p.def.* rosi; *p.p.* roso
rompere	*p.def.* ruppi; *p.p.* rotto
salire**	*pres.* salgo, salgono
sapere	*pres.* so, sai, sa, sappiamo, sapete, sanno; *p. def.* seppi; *fut.* saprò
scegliere	*pres.* scelgo, scelgono; *p. def.* scelsi; *p.p.* scelto
scendere**	*p. def.* scesi; *p.p.* sceso
scindere	*p.def.* scissi; *p.p.* scisso
sciogliere	*pres.* sciolgo, sciolgono; *p.def.* sciolsi; *p.p.* sciolto
scrivere	*p. def.* scrissi; *p.p.* scritto
scuotere	*p. def.* scossi; *p.p.* scosso
sedere*	*pres.* siedo (seggo), siedi, siede, sediamo, sedete, siedono (seggono)
soddisfare	*pres.* soddisfo (soddisfaccio, soddisfò), soddisfi (soddisfai), soddisfa, soddisfiamo (soddisfacciamo), soddisfate, soddisfano (soddisfanno); *p. def.* soddisfeci; *p.p.* soddisfatto
sorgere*	*p. def.* sorsi; *p.p.* sorto
spargere	*p.def.* sparsi; *p.p.* sparso
spegnere	*p.def.* spensi; *p.p.* spento
spendere	*p. def.* spesi; *p.p.* speso
spingere	*p. def.* spinsi; *p.p.* spinto
stare*	*pres.* sto, stai, sta, stiamo, state, stanno; *imperf.* stavo; *p. def.* stetti; *p.p.* stato
stringere	*p. def.* strinsi; *p.p.* stretto
svellere	*pres.* svello (svelgo), svellono (svelgono); *p. def.* svelsi; *p.p.* svelto
svenire*	*p.def.* svenni
tacere	*pres.* taccio, taci, tace, taciamo, tacete, tacciono; *p. def.* tacqui; *p.p.* taciuto
tendere	*p.def.* tesi; *p.p.* teso
tenere	*pres.* tengo, tieni, tiene, teniamo, tenete, tengono; *p. def.* tenni; *fut.* terrò
tingere	*p. def.* tinsi; *p.p.* tinto
togliere	*pres.* tolgo, tolgono; *p. def.* tolsi; *p.p.* tolto
torcere	*p. def.* torsi; *p.p.* torto
trarre	*pres.* traggo, trai, trae, traiamo, traete, traggono; *imperf.* traevo; *p. def.* trassi; *fut.* trarrò; *p.p.* tratto
uccidere	*p.def.* uccisi; *p.p.* ucciso
udire	*pres.* odo, odi, ode, udiamo, udite, odono; *fut.* udrò (udirò)
ungere	*p.def.* unsi; *p.p.* unto
uscire*	*pres.* esco, esci, esce, usciamo, uscite, escono
valere**	*pres.* valgo, valgono; *p. def.* valsi; *fut.* varrò; *p.p.* valso
vedere	*pres.* vedo (veggo), vedono (veggono); *p. def.* vidi; *fut.* vedrò; *p.p.* visto, veduto
venire*	*pres.* vengo, vieni, viene, veniamo, venite, vengono; *p. def.* venni; *fut.* verrò
vilipendere	*p. def.* vilipesi; *p.p.* vilipeso
vincere	*p.def.* vinsi; *p.p.* vinto
vivere**	*p. def.* vissi; *p.p.* vissuto
volere	*pres.* voglio, vuoi, vuole, vogliamo, volete, vogliono; *p. def.* volli; *fut.* vorrò
volgere	*p. def.* volsi; *p.p.* volto

Irregular Plurals
of Some Common Nouns

l'autobus	gli autobus
il bar	i bar
il caffè	i caffè
la città	le città
la frutta	le frutta
il re	i re
il braccio	le braccia
il bue	i buoi
il centinaio	le centinaia
il dito	le dita
il ginocchio	le ginocchia
la guancia	le guance
il labbro	le labbra
il lenzuolo	le lenzuola
la mano	le mani
il migliaio	le migliaia
l'orecchio	le orecchie
il paio	le paia
l'uomo	gli uomini

Abbreviations Used in the Dictionary
Elenco delle abbreviazioni

abbreviazione	*abbr.*	abbreviation
aeronautica	*(aer.)*	aviation
aggettivo	*agg.*	adjective
agricoltura	*(agr.)*	agriculture
americano, americanismo	*(amer.)*	American
amministrativo, amministrazione	*amm.*	administrative
anatomia	*(anat.)*	anatomy
anticamente, antiquato	*(ant.)*	archaic
architettura	*(arch)*	architecture
articolo	*art.*	article
arte, artistico	*(arte)*	art
assoluto	*assol.*	absolute
astronomia	*(astr.)*	astronomy
attributo, attributivo	*attr.*	attribute
ausiliare	*aus.*	auxiliary
automobilismo	*(auto)*	motoring
avverbio	*avv.*	adverb
biologia	*(biol.)*	biology
botanica	*(bot.)*	botany
chimica	*(chim.)*	chemistry
chirurgia	*(chir.)*	surgery
cinematografia	*(cine)*	cinematography
collettivo	*coll.*	collective
commercio, commerciale	*(comm.)*	commerce
comparativo	*comp.*	comparative
complemento	*compl.*	complement
condizionale	*condiz.*	conditional
congiunzione	*cong.*	conjunction
costruzioni	*(costr.)*	building
cucina	*(cuc.)*	cooking
dialettale	*(dial.)*	dialect
difettivo	*dif.*	defective
diminutivo	*dim.*	diminutive
dimostrativo	*dimostr.*	demonstrative
eccetera	*ecc., etc.*	et cetera
ecclesiastico	*(eccl.)*	ecclesiastical
economia	*(econ.)*	economics
edilizia	*(edil.)*	building industry
elettricità, elettrotecnica	*(elettr.)*	electricity
esclamativo, in esclamazione	*escl.*	exclamation
femminile	*f.*	feminine

Abbreviazioni   Abbreviations

familiare	*(fam.)*	familiar
farmacia, farmaceutico	*(farm.)*	pharmaceutical
ferrovia	*(ferr.)*	railway
figurato	*(fig.)*	figurative
filosofia	*(fil.)*	philosophy
fisica	*(fis.)*	physics
fotografia	*(foto)*	photography
futuro	*fut.*	future
genitivo	*gen.*	genitive
generalmente	*general.*	generally
geografia	*(geogr.)*	geography
geologia	*(geol.)*	geology
geometria	*(geom.)*	geometry
gerundio	*ger.*	gerund
gergo, gergale	*(gergo)*	jargon, slang
giornalismo, giornalistico	*(giorn.)*	journalism
giuridico	*(giur.)*	legal
grammatica	*(gramm.)*	grammar
intransitivo	*i.*	intransitive
idem	*id.*	idem
impersonale	*imp.*	impersonal
imperativo	*imperat.*	imperative
imperfetto	*imperf.*	imperfect
indicativo	*ind.*	indicative
indefinito	*indef.*	indefinite
infinito	*inf.*	infinitive
interrogativo	*int.*	interrogative
interiezione, interiettivo	*inter.*	interjection
ironico	*(iron.)*	ironic
irregolare	*irr.*	irregular
ittiologia	*(itt.)*	ichthyology
latino, latismo	*(lat.)*	Latin, Latinism
letteratura, letterario	*(lett.)*	literature
locuzione avverbiale	*loc. avv.*	adverbial phrase
locuzione congiuntiva	*loc. cong.*	conjunctive phrase
locuzione prepositiva	*loc. prep.*	prepositional phrase
maschile	*m.*	masculine
marina, marittimo, marinaresco	*(mar.)*	naval, maritime
matematica	*(mat.)*	mathematics
meccanica	*(mecc.)*	mechanics
medicina	*(med.)*	medicine
metallurgia	*(metal.)*	metallurgy
militare	*(mil.)*	military
mineralogia, minerario	*(min.)*	mineralogy
mitologia	*(mit.)*	mythology
musica	*(mus.)*	music
negazione, negativo	*neg.*	negative
neologismo	*(neol.)*	neologism

	Abbreviazioni		Abbreviations

oggetto	ogg.	object
ottica	(ott.)	optics
participio	p.	participle
passato	pass.	past
passato remoto	p. def.	past definite
persona, personale	pers.	personal
pittura	(pitt.)	painting
plurale	pl.	plural
poetico	(poet.)	poetical
politica	(pol.)	political
popolare	(pop.)	popular
possessivo	poss.	possessive
participio passato	p.p.	past participle
preposizione	prep.	preposition
predicato, predicativo	pred.	predicate
presente	pres.	present
pronome, pronominale	pron.	pronoun
proverbio, proverbiale	prov.	proverbial
psicologia	psicol	psychology
qualcosa	qc.	something
qualcuno	. qu.	someone
riflessivo	r.	reflexive
radiofonia	(radio)	radio
reciproco	rec.	reciprocal
regolare	reg.	regular
relativo	rel.	relative
religione	(relig.)	religion
sostantivo	s.	noun
sostantivo maschile e femminile (dall'italiano)	s.	masculine and feminine noun
scherzoso	(scherz.)	humorous
scolastico	(scol.)	scholastic
scultura	(scult.)	sculpture
semidifettivo	semidif.	partly defective
sostantivo femminile	sf.	feminine noun
singolare	sing.	singular
sostantivo maschile	sm.	masculine noun
someone	so.	someone
soggetto	sogg.	subject
sostantivato	sost.	noun
specialmente	spec.	especially
sport, sportivo	(sport)	sport
spregiativo	(spreg.)	pejorative
something	sthg.	something
storia	(stor.)	history
superlativo	superl.	superlative
transitivo	t.	transitive
teatro	(teat.)	theatre
tecnica	(tec.)	technical

Abbreviazioni		Abbreviations
telefonia, telefono	*(tel)*	telephony
teologia	*(teol.)*	theology
tipografia	*(tip.)*	typography
televisione	*(tv.)*	television
uso, usato	*(us.)*	usage
verbo	*v.*	verb
vedi	*V.*	cf.
verbo difettivo	*v. dif.*	defective verb
vezzeggiativo	*(vezz.)*	diminutive
verbo intransitivo	*vi.*	intransitive verb
verbo irregulare	*(v. irr.)*	irregular verb
volgare	*(volg.)*	vulgar
verbo riflessivo	*vr.*	reflexive verb
verbo semidifettivo	*v. semidif.*	partially defective verb
verbo transitivo	*vt.*	transitive verb
zoologia	*(zool.)*	zoology

ITALIAN – ENGLISH
ITALIANO – INGLESE

A

a, ad *prep.* **1.** (*termine*) to: *l'ho dato a te*, I gave it to you **2.** (*moto a luogo*) *vado alla stazione*, I am going to the station **3.** (*stato in luogo*) in, at: *vivo a Milano*, I live in Milan; *sono a casa*, I am at home **4.** (*tempo determinato*) at, on, in: *al mio arrivo*, on my arrival **5.** (*iterativo*): *due, tre volte al giorno*, twice, three times a day.

àbaco (*arch.*) *sm.* abacus.

abate *sm.* abbot.

abbacchiare *vt.* (*di frutta*) to beat (*v. irr.*) down. ♦ **abbacchiarsi** *vr.* to feel (*v. irr.*) down-hearted.

abbacchiato *agg.* down-hearted.

abbacinare *vt.* to dazzle.

àbbaco *sm.* elementary arithmetic book.

abbagliante *agg.* dazzling: *fari abbaglianti*, dazzling beams.

abbagliare *vt.* to dazzle, to blind (with).

abbaglio *sm.* **1.** dazzling **2.** (*errore*) blunder.

abbaiare *vi.* to bark.

abbaino *sm.* garret.

abbandonare *vt.* **1.** to leave (*v. irr.*), to forsake (*v. irr.*), to abandon **2.** (*rinunciare*) to give (*v. irr.*) up.

abbandonato *agg.* **1.** (*trascurato*) neglected **2.** (*di casa*) deserted **3.** (*di persona*) forsaken.

abbandono *sm.* **1.** (*di persona che viene abbandonata*) forsaking **2.** (*rinuncia*) giving up.

abbarbicare *vi.* to take (*v. irr.*) root. ♦ **abbarbicarsi** *vr.* to cling (*v. irr.*) (*anche fig.*).

abbaruffarsi *vr.* to quarrel.

abbassamento *sm.* lowering ‖ — *di temperatura*, fall (in temperature).

abbassare *vt.* **1.** to lower, to pull down ‖ — *la testa*, to bend (*v. irr.*) one's head **2.** (*ridurre*) to reduce. ♦ **abbassarsi** *vr.* to stoop (down).

abbasso *avv.* **1.** (*al di sotto*) below **2.** (*giù*) down **3.** (*al piano terreno, dopo aver sceso le scale*) downstairs. ♦ **abbasso!** *inter.* down with!

abbastanza *avv.* **1.** enough **2.** (*discretamente*) quite.

abbàttere *vt.* to pull down. ♦ **abbàttersi** *vr.* to be discouraged.

abbattimento *sm.* **1.** throwing down **2.** (*morale*) dejection.

abbattuto *agg.* disheartened.

abbazìa *sf.* abbey.

abbecedario *sm.* primer.

abbellimento *sm.* embellishment.

abbellire *vt.* to embellish.

abbeverare *vt.* to water. ♦ **abbeverarsi** *vr.* to water.

abbeveratoio *sm.* trough.

abbiccì *sm.* **1.** alphabet **2.** (*principi elementari*) primer.

abbiente *agg.* well-to-do, wealthy.

abbigliamento *sm.* clothes ‖ *industria dell'—*, clothing industry.

abbigliare *vt.* to dress.

abbinare *vt.* to couple.

abbindolare *vt.* to cheat.

abbisognare *vi.* to need, to be necessary.

abboccamento *sm.* interview.

abboccare *vt. e vi.* **1.** to bite (*v. irr.*) **2.** (*fig.*) to be taken in. ♦ **abboccarsi** *vr.* to confer (with).

abbonacciarsi *vi.* **1.** (*di vento*) to drop **2.** (*di mare*) to smooth down.

abbonamento *sm.* **1.** subscription **2.** (*ferr.*) season-ticket.

abbonare *vt.* **1.** to make (*v. irr.*) (*so.*) a subscriber **2.** (*defalcare*) to make a discount. ♦ **abbonarsi** *vr.* to subscribe (to).

abbonato *sm.* **1.** subscriber **2.** (*ferr.*) season-ticket holder.

abbondante *agg.* plentiful.

abbondanza *sf.* plenty.

abbondare *vi.* to have plenty (of), to be plentiful.

abbonire *vt.* to calm.

abbordàbile *agg.* accessible.

abbordaggio *sm.* boarding.

abbordare *vt.* **1.** (*mar.*) to board **2.** (*una persona*) to open conversation (with).

abborracciare *vi.* to bungle.

abbottonare *vt.* to button (up). ♦ **abbottonarsi** *vr.* to button one's clothes (up).

abbottonatura *sf.* **1.** button-holes **2.** (*l'abbottonarsi*) buttoning.

abbozzare *vt.* to sketch ‖ — *un sorriso*, to smile faintly.

abbozzo *sm.* sketch.

abbozzolarsi *vr.* to cocoon.

abbracciare *vt.* **1.** to embrace **2.** (*comprendere*) to include **3.** (*afferrare*) to grasp **4.** (*con lo sguardo*)

to take (*v. irr.*) in. ♦ **abbracciarsi** *vr.* to embrace.
abbraccio *sm.* embrace.
abbrancare *vt.* to grasp. ♦ **abbrancarsi** *vr.* to cling (*v. irr.*) (to).
abbreviare *vt.* to shorten, to abridge.
abbreviazione *sf.* abbreviation.
abbrivare *vt.* to get (*v. irr.*) under way.
abbrivo *sm.* freshway.
abbronzare *vt.* 1. to bronze 2. (*al sole*) to tan. ♦ **abbronzarsi** *vr.* to get (*v. irr.*) tanned.
abbronzatura *sf.* tanning.
abbruciacchiare *vt.* to scorch.
abbrustolire *vt.* to toast, to roast.
abbrutimento *sm.* brutalization.
abbrutire *vt.* to brutalize.
abbuffarsi *vr.* to stuff oneself.
abbuiarsi *vr.* to get (*v. irr.*) dark.
abbuono *sm.* allowance.
abburattare *vt.* to sift.
abdicare *vi.* to abdicate.
abdicazione *sf.* abdication.
aberrare *vi.* to stray.
aberrazione *sf.* aberration.
abetaia *sf.* fir-wood.
abete *sm.* fir-tree.
abietto *agg.* abject, base.
abiezione *sf.* abjection.
abigeato *sm.* cattle-stealing.
àbile *agg.* 1. able, skilful 2. (*a fare qc.*) clever at.
abilità *sf.* ability, skill.
abilitare *vt.* to qualify.
abilitazione *sf.* qualification || *esame di —*, qualifying examination.
abisso *sm.* abyss.
abitàbile *agg.* inhabitable.
abitàcolo *sm.* (*aer.*) cockpit.
abitante *sm.* inhabitant.
abitare *vi.* to inhabit, to live in.
abitato *sm.* inhabited place.
abitazione *sf.* habitation, house.
àbito *sm.* 1. (*da uomo*) suit 2. (*da donna*) dress.
abituale *agg.* usual, customary.
abituare *vt.* to accustom. ♦ **abituarsi** *vr.* to get (*v. irr.*) used (to).
abitudinario *agg.* methodical. ♦ **abitudinario** *sm.* routinist.
abitùdine *sf.* habit, custom.
abituro *sm.* slum dwelling.
abiura *sf.* abjuration.
abiurare *vt.* to abjure.
ablazione *sf.* ablation.

abluzione *sf.* ablution.
abnegazione *sf.* self-denial.
abnorme *agg.* abnormal.
abolire *vt.* to abolish.
abolizione *sf.* abolition, repeal.
abominare *vt.* to loathe.
abominévole *agg.* abominable.
aborìgeni *sm. pl.* the natives.
aborrimento *sm.* abhorrence.
aborrire *vt.* to hate, to loathe.
abortire *vi.* to miscarry.
aborto *sm.* miscarriage.
abrasione *sf.* abrasion.
abrogare *vt.* 1. to abrogate 2. (*giur.*) to repeal.
abrogazione *sf.* 1. abrogation 2. (*giur.*) repeal.
àbside *sf.* apse.
abulìa *sf.* (*fig.*) lack of will-power.
abùlico *agg.* (*fig.*) lacking in will-power.
abusare *vi.* to abuse.
abusivo *agg.* abusive.
abuso *sm.* abuse.
acacia *sf.* acacia.
acanto *sm.* acanthus.
acca *sf.* letter *H*.
accademia *sf.* academy.
accadèmico *agg.* academical. ♦ **accadèmico** *sm.* academician.
accademismo *sm.* academism.
accadere *vi.* to happen.
accaduto *sm.* event.
accagliarsi *vr.* 1. to curdle 2. (*del sangue*) to coagulate.
accalappiacani *sm.* dog-catcher.
accalappiare *vt.* 1. to catch (*v. irr.*) 2. (*fig.*) to ensnare.
accalcarsi *vr.* to crowd.
accaldarsi *vi.* 1. to get (*v. irr.*) heated 2. (*fig.*) to get excited.
accaldato *agg.* hot.
accalorarsi *vr.* to get (*v. irr.*) excited.
accampamento *sm.* camp.
accampare *vt.* to camp: — *diritti*, to lay (*v. irr.*) claims (to).
accanimento *sm.* 1. fury 2. (*tenacia*) tenacity.
accanirsi *vr.* 1. (*infierire*) to rage 2. (*ostinarsi*) to persist.
accanito *agg.* 1. (*senza pietà*) relentless 2. obstinate.
accanto *avv.* beside, near, by || *accanto a*, by, near, at the side of.
accantonare *vt.* to set (*v. irr.*) aside.
accaparrare *vt.* to buy (*v. irr.*) up.

accapigliarsi *vr.* to come (*v. irr.*) to blows, to quarrel.

accappatoio *sm.* bath-gown.

accapponarsi *vr.* to get (*v. irr.*) goose-flesh.

accarezzare *vt.* **1.** to caress, to stroke **2.** (*fig.*) to entertain.

accartocciare *vt.* **1.** to wrap up **2.** (*spiegazzare*) to crumple.

accasare *vt.* to marry, to give (*v. irr.*) in marriage. ♦ **accasarsi** *vr.* to get (*v. irr.*) married.

accasciarsi *vi.* **1.** to fall (*v. irr.*) to the ground **2.** (*fig.*) to lose (*v. irr.*) heart.

accatastare *vt.* to heap up.

accattivarsi *vi.* to win (*v. irr.*).

accattonaggio *sm.* begging.

accattone *sm.* beggar.

accavallare *vt.* to overlap: — *le gambe*, to cross one's legs.

accecamento *sm.* **1.** blinding **2.** (*fig.*) lack of perception.

accecare *vt.* to blind. ♦ **accecarsi** *vr.* to blind oneself.

accèdere *vi.* **1.** to approach **2.** (*entrare*) to enter **3.** (*comm.*) to comply (with).

accelerare *vt.* **1.** to quicken **2.** (*di velocità*) to accelerate.

accelerato *sm.* (*ferr.*) slow train.

acceleratore *sm.* accelerator.

accelerazione *sf.* acceleration.

accèndere *vt.* **1.** to light **2.** (*di fiammiferi*) to strike (*v. irr.*) **3.** (*di radio, luce ecc.*) to switch on **4.** (*fig.*) to inflame. ♦ **accèndersi** *vr.* **1.** to light up **2.** (*prender fuoco*) to catch (*v. irr.*) fire || — *in volto*, to blush.

accendino *sm.* **accendisìgaro** *sm.* (cigarette)-lighter.

accennare *vi.* **1.** to make (*v. irr.*) a sign **2.** (*menzionare*) to mention **3.** (*alludere*) to allude.

accenno *sm.* **1.** sign **2.** (*fig.*) hint.

accensione *sf.* **1.** lighting **2.** (*mecc.*) ignition || *chiavetta d'*—, ignition-key.

accentare *vt.* to accent, to stress.

accentazione *sf.* accentuation, stressing.

accento *sm.* **1.** accent **2.** (*tonico*) stress.

accentramento *sm.* centralization.

accentrare *vt.* to centralize.

accentuare *vt.* to accentuate, to stress. ♦ **accentuarsi** *vr.* to get (*v. irr.*) worse, to increase.

accerchiamento *sm.* surrounding.

accerchiare *vt.* to surround.

accertamento *sm.* **1.** assurance **2.** (*controllo*) verification.

accertare *vt.* **1.** to assure **2.** (*verificare*) to verify.

acceso *agg.* **1.** lit up **2.** (*in volto*) blushing **3.** (*d'ira*) in a temper.

accessìbile *agg.* **1.** open to **2.** (*di persona*) approachable.

accesso *sm.* **1.** admission **2.** (*di malattia, passione*) fit.

accessorio *agg.* accessory. ♦ **accessori** *sm. pl.* fittings.

accetta *sf.* hatchet.

accettare *vt.* **1.** to accept **2.** (*consentire*) to consent.

accetto *agg.* welcome.

accezione *sf.* meaning.

acchiappare *vt.* to catch (*v. irr.*).

acchito *sm. di primo* —, at first sight, at once.

acciacco *sm.* infirmity.

acciaieria *sf.* steel-mill.

acciaio *sm.* steel.

acciarino *sm.* **1.** flint-lock **2.** (*di fucile*) gun-lock.

accidentale *agg.* accidental.

accidentato *agg.* uneven.

accidente *sm.* chance, accident.

accidenti *inter.* damn.

accidia *sf.* sloth.

accigliarsi *vr.* to frown.

accingersi *vr.* to set (*v. irr.*) about (doing).

acciottolare *vt.* to cobble.

acciottolato *sm.* cobbled paving.

acciottolìo *sm.* clatter.

acciuffare *vt.* to catch (*v. irr.*), to seize.

acciuga *sf.* anchovy.

acclamare *vt.* **1.** to acclaim **2.** (*applaudire*) to applaud.

acclamazione *sf.* acclamation, applause.

acclimatazione *sf.* acclimatization.

acclùdere *vt.* to enclose.

accluso *agg.* enclosed.

accoccolarsi *vr.* to squat down.

accodarsi *vr.* to follow.

accogliente *agg.* comfortable, hospitable.

accoglienza *sf.* reception, welcome.

accògliere *vt.* **1.** to receive **2.** (*fare buona accoglienza*) to welcome **3.** (*una richiesta*) to grant.

accòlito *sm.* acolyte.

accollatura *sf.* neckline.

accoltellare *vt.* to stab.

accomiatare *vt.* **1.** to give (*v. irr.*) leave **2.** (*licenziare*) to dismiss. ◆ **accomiatarsi** *vr.* to take (*v. irr.*) leave (of).

accomodamento *sm.* **1.** adjustment **2.** (*conciliazione*) conciliation.

accomodante *agg.* yielding.

accomodare *vt.* **1.** (*riparare*) to repair **2.** (*sistemare*) to settle **3.** (*far comodo*) to suit.

accompagnamento *sm.* **1.** (*l'accompagnare*) accompanying **2.** (*seguito*) retinue **3.** (*mus.*) accompaniment.

accompagnare *vt.* **1.** to accompany **2.** (— *qu. alla stazione*) to see (*v. irr.*) so. off **3.** (*mus.*) to accompany.

accompagnatore *sm.* **1.** companion **2.** (*mus.*) accompanist.

accomunare *vt.* to join, to associate. ◆ **accomunarsi** *vr.* to join.

acconciare *vt.* **1.** to adjust, to adorn **2.** (*capelli*) to dress.

acconciatura *sf.* hair-style.

acconsentire *vi.* **1.** to consent **2.** (*annuire*) to assent.

accontentare *vt.* to satisfy. ◆ **accontentarsi** *vr.* to be content (with).

acconto *sm.* account.

accoppare *vt.* to kill.

accoppiamento *sm.* **1.** coupling **2.** (*di buoi al giogo*) yoking **3.** (*mecc.*) connection.

accoppiare *vt.* **1.** to couple **2.** (*fig.*) to match. ◆ **accoppiarsi** *vr.* to couple, to mate.

accoppiata *sf.* (*ippica*) fourecast.

accorato *agg.* sorrowful.

accorciare *vt.* to shorten.

accordare *vt.* **1.** to grant **2.** (*mus.*) to tune **3.** (*armonizzare*) to match. ◆ **accordarsi** *vr.* to agree (upon).

accordatore *sm.* tuner.

accordo *sm.* **1.** agreement ‖ *come d'—*, as agreed **2.** (*mus.*) chord **3.** (*fig.*) harmony.

accorgersi *vr.* **1.** (*percepire*) to perceive **2.** (*rendersi conto*) to realize.

accorgimento *sm.* **1.** sagacity **2.** (*stratagemma*) clever device.

accòrrere *vi.* to run (*v. irr.*), to hasten: — *in aiuto*, to rush to the help.

accortezza *sf.* sagacity.

accorto *agg.* shrewd.

accostare *vt.* **1.** to draw (*v. irr.*) near **2.** (*porte, finestre ecc.*) to set

(*v. irr.*) ajar. ◆ **accostarsi** *vr.* to come (*v. irr.*) near.

accotonare *vt.* to raise.

accotonatura *sf.* raising.

accozzaglia *sf.* huddle: *un'— di gente*, a motley crowd.

accozzare *vt.* to huddle. ◆ **accozzarsi** *vr.* to huddle.

accreditamento *sm.* (*comm.*) crediting.

accreditare *vt.* to credit. ◆ **accreditarsi** *vr.* to gain credit.

accréscere *vt.* to increase.

accrescimento *sm.* increase.

accrescitivo *agg.* e *sm.* augmentative.

accucciarsi *vr.* to crouch.

accudire *vi.* to look after: — *alla casa*, to do (*v. irr.*) the housewok.

accumulare *vt.* to heap up.

accumulatore *sm.* accumulator.

accuratezza *sf.* accuracy, care.

accurato *agg.* careful, precise.

accusa *sf.* charge.

accusare *vt.* **1.** to accuse, to charge (with) **2.** (*sentire*) to feel (*v. irr.*) **3.** (*comm.*) to acknowledge.

accusativo *agg.* e *sm.* accusative.

accusato *sm.* accused.

accusatore *sm.* prosecutor: *pubblico —*, public prosecutor.

acerbo *agg.* **1.** unripe **2.** (*acido*) sour.

àcero *sm.* maple.

acetilene *sm.* acetylene.

aceto *sm.* vinegar.

acetone *sm.* acetone.

acidità *sf.* **1.** acidity **2.** (*di stomaco*) hyperchlorhydria.

àcido *agg.* sour. ◆ **àcido** *sm.* acid.

acìdulo *agg.* acidulous.

àcino *sm.* (*di uva*) grape.

acme *sf.* **1.** acme **2.** (*di malattia*) crisis (*pl.* -ses).

acne *sf.* acne.

aconfessionale *agg.* nondenominational.

acqua *sf.* **1.** water: — *marina*, sea water; — *piovana*, rain water; — *potabile*, drinking water **2.** (*pioggia*) rain: — *a catinelle*, heavy rain.

acquaforte *sf.* etching.

acquaio *sm.* sink.

acquamarina *sf.* aquamarine.

acquaragia *sf.* turpentine.

acquario *sm.* aquarium.

acquasanta *sf.* holy water.

acquasantiera *sf.* stoup.

acquàtico *agg.* aquatic.

acquattarsi *vr.* **1.** to crouch **2.** (*nascondersi*) to hide (*v. irr.*).

acquavite *sf.* brandy.

acquazzone *sm.* downpour.

acquedotto *sm.* aqueduct.

acquerellista *sm.* water-colourist.

acquerello *sm.* water-colour.

acquerùgiola *sf.* drizzle.

acquiescente *agg.* acquiescent.

acquiescenza *sf.* acquiescence.

acquirente *sm.* buyer.

acquisire *vt.* to acquire.

acquistare *vt.* **1.** (*comperare*) to buy (*v. irr.*) **2.** (*ottenere*) to get (*v. irr.*) **3.** (*fig.*) to gain ‖ — *terreno*, to make (*v. irr.*) progress.

acquisto *sm.* purchase ‖ *fare acquisti*, to go (*v. irr.*) shopping.

acquitrino *sm.* marsh.

acquolina *sf.* drizzle: *far venire l'— in bocca*, to make (*v. irr.*) so.'s mouth water.

acre *agg.* **1.** sour **2.** (*fig.*) sarcastic **3.** (*pungente*) pungent.

acrèdine *sf.* **1.** acridity **2.** (*fig.*) acrimony.

acrimonia *sf.* acrimony.

acròbata *s.* acrobat.

acrobàtico *agg.* acrobatic.

acrobazia *sf.* acrobatics (*pl.*) ‖ *fare delle acrobazie*, to perform stunts.

acròpoli *sf.* acropolis.

acuire *vt.* to sharpen: — *l'interesse*, to stimulate interest.

acùleo *sm.* **1.** (*bot.*) prickle **2.** (*zool.*) sting.

acume *sm.* insight.

acuminare *vt.* to sharpen.

acùstica *sf.* acoustics.

acutezza *sf.* **1.** sharpness **2.** (*di mente*) perspicacity.

acutizzare *vt.* to make (*v. irr.*) acute. ♦ **acutizzarsi** *vr.* to grow (*v. irr.*) acute.

acuto *agg.* **1.** sharp **2.** (*di angoli, accenti*) acute **3.** (*intenso*) intense **4.** (*di suono*) shrill. ♦ **acuto** *sm.* (*mus.*) high note.

adagiare *vt.* to lay (*v. irr.*) down with care. ♦ **adagiarsi** *vr.* to lie (*v. irr.*) down.

adagio[1] *avv.* **1.** slowly **2.** (*con cautela*) cautiously **3.** (*con delicatezza*) gently.

adagio[2] *sm.* proverb, saying.

adamantino *agg.* adamantine.

adamìtico *agg.* adamic.

adattàbile *agg.* adaptable.

adattamento *sm.* **1.** adaptation **2.** (*assestamento*) adjustment.

adattare *vt.* to adapt, to fit. ♦ **adattarsi** *vr.* **1.** to adapt oneself **2.** (*attagliarsi*) to fit.

adatto *agg.* **1.** fit, proper **2.** (*che va bene*) suitable (for).

addebitare *vt.* to debit.

addébito *sm.* charge: *fare un — a qu. per qc.*, to charge so. with sthg.

addendo *sm.* addendum (*pl.* -da).

addensamento *sm.* **1.** thickening **2.** (*di persone*) crowding.

addensare *vt.* **1.** to thicken. ♦ **addensarsi** *vr.* **1.** to thicken **2.** (*di folla*) to crowd.

addentare *vt.* to bite (*v. irr.*).

addentellato *sm.* **1.** (*arch.*) toothing **2.** (*fig.*) stepping-stone.

addentrarsi *vr.* to penetrate: — *in una questione*, to probe a question.

addentro *avv.* inside.

addestramento *sm.* **1.** training **2.** (*mil.*) drilling.

addestrare *vt.* **1.** to train **2.** (*mil.*) to drill.

addetto *agg.* employed (in). ♦ **addetto** *sm.* attaché.

addietro *avv.* **1.** (*di spazio*) behind **2.** (*di tempo*) before, ago ‖ *era venuto due giorni —*, he had come two days before.

addìo *inter.* good-bye.

addirsi *vr.* to become (*v. irr.*).

addirittura *avv.* **1.** quite **2.** (*in esclamazioni*) really!

additare *vt.* to point at.

addizionale *agg.* additional.

addizionare *vt.* to sum up.

addizionatrice *sf.* adding-machine, adder.

addizione *sf.* addition.

addobbare *vt.* to adorn.

addobbo *sm.* **1.** decoration **2.** (*eccl.*) sacred ornaments (*pl.*).

addolcire *vt.* **1.** to sweeten **2.** (*fig.*) to soften. ♦ **addolcirsi** *vr.* to become (*v. irr.*) soft(er).

addolorare *vt.* to grieve. ♦ **addolorarsi** *vr.* to be grieved.

addolorato *agg.* grieved, sorry.

addome *sm.* abdomen.

addomesticare *vt.* to tame.

addominale *agg.* abdominal.

addormentare *vt.* **1.** to send (*v. irr.*) to sleep **2.** (*med.*) to anaesthetize. ♦ **addormentarsi** vr. **1.** to fall (v. irr.) asleep **2.** (fig.) to go (v. irr.) to sleep.

addossare vt. **1.** to lean **2.** (attribuire) to lay (v. irr.). ♦ **addossarsi** vr. **1.** (affollarsi) to crowd **2.** (prendere su di sé) to take (v. irr.) upon oneself.

addosso avv. prep. **1.** on, upon: mettere qc. —, to put (v. irr.) sthg. on; togliere qc. d'—, to take (v. irr.) sthg. off **2.** (vicino a) close to: la casa è — alla montagna, the house is close to the mountain ‖ dare —, to assault, to contradict.

addottrinare vt. to instruct. ♦ **addottrinarsi** vr. to instruct oneself.

addurre vt. **1.** to put (v. irr.) forward: — una scusa, to plead **2.** (citare) to quote.

adeguamento sm. **1.** proportionment **2.** (adattamento) adaptation.

adeguare vt. **1.** to proportionate **2.** (adattare) to conform. ♦ **adeguarsi** vr. to conform oneself, to adapt oneself.

adeguato agg. **1.** proportionate **2.** (adatto) convenient, fit **3.** (giusto) fair.

adémpiere vt. **1.** (compiere) to fulfil **2.** (eseguire) to carry out. ♦ **adémpiersi** vr. (avverarsi) to come (v. irr.) true.

adempimento sm. **1.** fulfilment **2.** (esecuzione) carrying out.

adenòidi sf. pl. adenoids.

adepto sm. **1.** adept **2.** (seguace) follower.

aderente agg. **1.** adherent **2.** (di abito) close-fitting.

aderenza sf. **1.** adherence **2.** (med.) adhesion **3.** (pl.) connections.

aderire vi. **1.** (stare vicino e fig.) to adhere, to stick **2.** (consentire) to comply with **3.** (partegiare per) to take sides (with).

adescamento sm. **1.** enticement **2.** (seduzione) seduction.

adescare vt. **1.** to entice **2.** (sedurre) to seduce.

adesione sf. adhesion: dare la propria — ad un partito, to join a party.

adesivo agg. adhesive.

adesso avv. now, at present, at the moment.

adiacente agg. adjacent.

adibire vt. to use as.

àdipe sm. fat.

adiposo agg. adipose.

adirarsi vr. to get (v. irr.) angry.

adirato agg. angry.

adire vt. (giur.) to apply to: — le vie legali, to take (v. irr.) legal steps.

àdito sm. entry: dare —, to give (v. irr.) rise.

adocchiare vt. **1.** to glance **2.** (scorgere) to catch (v. irr.) sight of.

adolescente agg. teen-aged, adolescent. ♦ **adolescente** sm. teen-ager.

adolescenza sf. adolescence.

adombrare vt. **1.** to shade **2.** (nascondere) to conceal **3.** (simboleggiare) to symbolize. ♦ **adombrarsi** vr. **1.** to resent **2.** (di cavallo) to shy.

adoperare vt. to use. ♦ **adoperarsi** vr. to endeavour.

adoràbile agg. charming.

adorare vt. to adore, to worship.

adorazione sf. adoration, worship.

adornare vt. to adorn.

adorno agg. adorned.

adottare vt. to adopt.

adottivo agg. adoptive.

adozione sf. adoption: patria d'—, adopted country.

adrenalina sf. adrenalin.

adulare vt. to flatter.

adulatore agg. flattering. ♦ **adulatore** sm. flatterer.

adulazione sf. flattery.

adùltera sf. adulteress.

adulterare vt. **1.** to adulterate **2.** (fig.) to falsify.

adulterino agg. adulterine.

adulterio sm. adultery.

adùltero agg. adulterous. ♦ **adùltero** sm. adulterer.

adulto agg. e sm. grown-up, adult.

adunanza sf. meeting.

adunco agg. hooked.

aerare vt. **1.** to air **2.** (chim.) to aerate.

aerazione sf. **1.** airing **2.** (chim.) aeration.

aèreo agg. aerial ‖ per via aerea, by air. ♦ **aèreo** sm. **1.** plane **2.** (radio) aerial.

aerodinàmica sf. aerodynamics.

aeròdromo sm. aerodrome.

aerolito sm. aerolite.

aeromodello sm. model aircraft.

aeronàuta sm. aeronaut.

aeronàutica sf. aeronautics.

aeronave *sf.* airship.

aeronavigazione *sf.* air navigation

aeroplano *sm.* (aero)plane, aircraft || — *a razzo*, rocket plane; — *passeggeri*, passenger plane; — *da bombardamento*, bomber.

aeroporto *sm.* airport.

aerosòl *sm.* aerosol.

aerostàtica *sf.* aerostatics.

aeròstato *sm.* aerostat.

aerostazione *sf.* air-terminal.

aerotassì *sm.* airtaxi.

aerotraspòrtare *vt.* to air-bear.

afa *sf.* sultriness.

afasìa *sf.* aphasia.

affàbile *agg.* affable.

affabilità *sf.* affability, kindness.

affaccendarsi *vr.* to busy oneself.

affaccendato *agg.* busy.

affacciare *vt.* **1.** to show (*v. irr.*) **2.** (*un dubbio*) to raise. ◆ **affacciarsi** *vr.* **1.** to show oneself **2.** (*su un luogo*) to face.

affamare *vt.* to starve (out).

affamato *agg.* **1.** hungry **2.** (*fig.*) eager. ◆ **affamato** *sm.* starveling.

affamatore *sm.* starver.

affannare *vt.* to trouble, to worry. ◆ **affannarsi** *vr.* **1.** to worry oneself **2.** (*affaccendarsi*) to busy oneself.

affanno *sm.* **1.** breathlessness **2.** (*pena*) worry.

affannoso *agg.* **1.** breathless || *respiro* —, difficult breathing **2.** (*ansioso*) anxious.

affare *sm.* **1.** affair, business: — *di cuore*, love affair; *questo è* — *nostro*, this is our business **2.** (*comm.*) business: *fare affari*, to do (*v. irr.*) business || (*pol.*) *affari esteri*, foreign affairs; (*in Gran Bretagna*) *Ministero degli Affari Esteri*, Foreign Office.

affarista *sm.* speculator.

affascinante *agg.* charming.

affascinare *vt.* to charm.

affaticamento *sm.* weariness.

affaticare *vt.* to tire. ◆ **affaticarsi** *vr.* **1.** to get (*v. irr.*) tired **2.** (*lavorare molto*) to work hard.

affatto *avv.* **1.** completely, quite **2.** (*in frasi negative*) at all: *niente* —, not at all.

affatturare *vt.* to bewitch.

affermare *vt.* **1.** to affirm **2.** (*fig.*) to assert. ◆ **affermarsi** *vr.* to make (*v. irr.*) a name for oneself.

affermativo *agg.* affirmative.

affermazione *sf.* **1.** statement **2.** (*successo*) achievement.

afferrare *vt.* to grasp **2.** (*fig.*) to seize. ◆ **afferrarsi** *vr.* to grasp at, to clutch at.

affettare[1] *vt.* (*tagliare a fette*) to slice.

affettare[2] *vt.* (*ostentare*) to affect.

affettato[1] *agg.* sliced.

affettato[2] *agg.* (*ostentato*) affected.

affettatrice *sf.* slicing machine.

affettazione *sf.* affectation, show.

affettivo *agg.* emotional.

affetto[1] *sm.* affection: *portare* — *a qu.*, to set (*v. irr.*) one's affection on so.

affetto[2] *agg.* affected (with).

affettuosità *sf.* tenderness.

affettuoso *agg.* tender, affectionate.

affezionarsi *vr.* to grow (*v. irr.*) fond of.

affezione *sf.* **1.** affection **2.** (*med.*) affection, disease.

affiancare *vt.* to flank. ◆ **affiancarsi** *vr.* to line up (with).

affiatamento *sm.* concord.

affiatare *vt.* **1.** to bring (*v. irr.*) together **2.** (*mus.*) to tune. ◆ **affiatarsi** *vr.* to become (*v. irr.*) familiar (with).

affibbiare *vt.* **1.** to buckle **2.** (*fig.*) to shift (upon).

affidamento *sm.* trust, confidence: *dare* —, to inspire confidence.

affidare *vt.* **1.** to entrust **2.** (*consegnare*) to commit. ◆ **affidarsi** *vr.* to rely upon.

affievolire *vt.* to weaken. ◆ **affievolirsi** *vr.* to grow (*v. irr.*) weak.

affiggere *vt.* to post up: — *lo sguardo*, to fix one's eyes (on).

affilare *vt.* to sharpen. ◆ **affilarsi** *vr.* (*dimagrire*) to thin.

affilato *agg.* **1.** sharp **2.** (*di naso, viso*) thin.

affiliare *vt.* to affiliate.

affiliato *sm.* member, associate.

affiliazione *sf.* affiliation.

affinamento *sm.* **1.** refining **2.** (*fig.*) sharpening.

affinare *vt.* **1.** to refine **2.** (*assottigliare*) to make (*v. irr.*) thin. ◆ **affinarsi** *vr.* **1.** to refine, to improve **2.** (*assottigliarsi*) to become (*v. irr.*) thin.

affinché *cong.* so that, in order that.

affine *agg.* like, similar.

affinità *sf.* affinity.

affiorare *vi.* to appear on the surface.

affissare *vt.* to affix.

affissione *sf.* bill-posting.

affisso *sm.* 1. (*avviso*) bill 2. (*cartello*) placard 3. (*manifesto*) poster.

affittacàmere *sm.* e *sf.* landlord, landlady.

affittare *vt.* 1. (*dare in affitto*) to let (*v. irr.*) 2. (*prendere in affitto*) to rent 3. (*noleggiare*) to hire.

affitto *sm.* rent.

afflato *sm.* afflatus.

affliggere *vt.* 1. to distress 2. (*di malattie*) to afflict. ♦ **affliggersi** *vr.* to worry.

afflitto *agg.* sad, sorrowful.

afflizione *sf.* 1. affliction 2. (*flagello*) calamity.

afflosciarsi *vr.* 1. to become (*v. irr.*) flabby 2. (*fig.*) to weaken.

affluente *sm.* affluent.

affluenza *sf.* 1. (*di acque*) flow 2. (*di persone*) crowd 3. (*abbondanza*) plenty.

affluire *vi.* 1. (*di acque*) to flow 2. (*di persone*) to crowd 3. (*di cose*) to pour in.

afflusso *sm.* afflux.

affogamento *sm.* drowning.

affogare *vt.* 1. to drown 2. (*fig.*) to smother. ♦ **affogarsi** *vr.* to drown oneself.

affogato *agg.* 1. drowned 2. (*fig.*) oppressed || *uova affogate*, poached eggs.

affollamento *sm.* overcrowding, throng.

affollare *vt.* 1. to crowd 2. (*fig.*) to overwhelm. ♦ **affollarsi** *vr.* to press up.

affollato *agg.* crowded.

affondare *vt.* 1. (*sommergere*) to sink (*v. irr.*) 2. (*immergere*) to plunge.

affossamento *sm.* ditching.

affossare *vt.* to ditch. ♦ **affossarsi** *vr.* to become (*v. irr.*) hollow.

affrancamento *sm.* release.

affrancare *vt.* 1. to release 2. (*con francobollo*) to stamp. ♦ **affrancarsi** *vr.* to free oneself.

affrancato *agg.* 1. free 2. (*con francobollo*) stamped.

affrancatura *sf.* postage.

affranto *agg.* broken-hearted || (*dalla fatica*) worn out.

affratellarsi *vr.* to fraternize.

affresco *sm.* fresco.

affrettare *vt.* 1. to hasten 2. (*anticipare*) to anticipate. ♦ **affrettarsi** *vr.* to make (*v. irr.*) haste.

affrettatamente *avv.* hastily.

affrettato *agg.* 1. hasty 2. (*trascurato*) careless.

affrontare *vt.* 1. to face 2. (*fig.*) to deal (*v. irr.*) with. ♦ **affrontarsi** *vr.* (*venire alle mani*) to come (*v. irr.*) to blows.

affronto *sm.* insult.

affumicare *vt.* 1. to fill with smoke 2. (*cuc.*) to smoke.

affumicato *agg.* 1. blackened by smoke 2. (*cuc.*) smoked || *lenti affumicate*, sun-glasses.

affusolare *vt.* to taper.

afonìa *sf.* aphonia.

àfono *agg.* voiceless.

aforisma *sm.* aphorism.

afoso *agg.* sultry.

africano *agg.* e *sm.* African.

afroasiàtico *agg.* Afro-Asiatic.

afta *sf.* aphtha.

àgata *sf.* agate.

àgave *sf.* agave.

agenda *sf.* note-book.

agente *sm.* agent.

agenzìa *sf.* agency.

agevolare *vt.* to make (*v. irr.*) easy.

agevolazione *sf.* facilitation.

agévole *agg.* 1. easy 2. (*di strada*) smooth.

agevolmente *avv.* easily.

agganciare *vt.* 1. to hook 2. (*ferr.*) to couple up.

aggeggio *sm.* device.

aggettare *vi.* to jut out.

aggettivo *sm.* adjective.

agghiacciare *vt.* to freeze (*v. irr.*). ♦ **agghiacciarsi** *vr.* to freeze.

agghindare *vt.* to array. ♦ **agghindarsi** *vr.* to dress (oneself) up.

aggiogare *vt.* to yoke.

aggiornamento *sm.* 1. (*rinvio*) adjournment 2. (*di un libro*) revision.

aggiornare *vt.* 1. (*rinviare*) to adjourn 2. (*mettere al corrente*) to bring (*v. irr.*) up to date. ♦ **aggiornarsi** *vr.* to brush up one's knowledge.

aggiornato *agg.* up-to-date.

aggirare *vt.* to go (*v. irr.*) round || — *l'ostacolo*, to avoid an obstacle. ♦ **aggirarsi** *vr.* to wander about, to go about.

aggiudicare *vt.* to award. ♦ **ag-**

giudicarsi *vr.* to win (*v. irr.*).
aggiudicazione *sf.* award.
aggiùngere *vt.* to add. ♦ **aggiùngersi** *vr.* to join.
aggiunta *sf.* 1. addition 2. (*aumento*) increase.
aggiunto *agg.* added, joined. ♦ **aggiunto** *sm.* assistant.
aggiustare *vt.* 1. (*riparare*) to mend 2. (*sistemare*) to arrange. ♦ **aggiustarsi** *vr.* (*accomodarsi*) to make (*v. irr.*) oneself comfortable.
agglomerato *sm.* agglomerate.
agglutinare *vt.* to agglutinate.
aggraffare *vt.* to seize.
aggranchire *vt.* to benumb.
aggrapparsi *vr.* to cling (*v. irr.*) (to), to get (*v. irr.*) hold (of).
aggravante *agg.* aggravating. ♦ **aggravante** *sf.* (*giur.*) aggravating circumstance.
aggravare *vt.* to aggravate, to overburden. ♦ **aggravarsi** *vr.* to grow (*v. irr.*) worse.
aggravato *agg.* 1. overburdened 2. (*med.*) worse.
aggraziare *vt.* to make (*v. irr.*) graceful.
aggredire *vt.* to assault.
aggregare *vt.* to associate. ♦ **aggregarsi** *vr.* to join.
aggressione *sf.* aggression, assault.
aggressività *sf.* aggressiveness.
aggressivo *agg.* aggressive.
aggressore *sm.* aggressor.
aggrottare *vt.* to frown.
aggrovigliare *vt.* to entangle.
aggrovigliarsi *vr.* to get (*v. irr.*) entangled.
aggruppare *vt.* to group.
agguantare *vt.* to catch (*v. irr.*).
agguato *sm.* ambush.
agguerrire *vt.* to inure (for war). ♦ **agguerrirsi** *vr.* to get (*v. irr.*) inured.
agiatamente *avv.* in ease and comfort.
agiato *agg.* well-to-do.
àgile *agg.* nimble.
agilità *sf.* nimbleness.
agio *sm.* comfort, ease, leisure.
agiografia *sf.* hagiography.
agire *vi.* to act.
agitare *vt.* 1. to agitate 2. (*scuotere*) to shake (*v. irr.*) 3. to stir (*anche fig.*). ♦ **agitarsi** *vr.* to be agitated.
agitatore *sm.* 1. agitator 2. (*mecc.*) stirrer.

agitazione *sf.* 1. agitation 2. (*eccitazione*) excitement 3. (*di folla*) tumult.
aglio *sm.* garlic.
agnello *sm.* lamb.
agnosticismo *sm.* agnosticism.
ago *sm.* 1. needle 2. (*mecc.*) tongue.
agognare *vt.* to long (for sthg.).
agonìa *sf.* agony, pangs (*pl.*) of death.
agonismo *sm.* athletic spirit.
agonizzante *agg.* dying.
agonizzare *vi.* to be in one's death agony.
agorafobìa *sf.* agoraphobia.
agosto *sm.* August.
agraria *sf.* agriculture.
agrario *agg.* agrarian. ♦ **agrario** *sm.* 1. land-owner 2. (*esperto*) agriculturist.
agreste *agg.* agrestic, rustic.
agretto *agg.* sourish.
agrìcolo *agg.* agricultural.
agricoltore *sm.* farmer.
agricoltura *sf.* agriculture.
agrifoglio *sm.* holly.
agrimensore *sm.* land-surveyor.
agro *agg.* sour. ♦ **agro** *sm.* sourness.
agrodolce *agg.* bitter-sweet, sourish.
agronomìa *sf.* agronomy.
agronòmico *agg.* agronomical.
agrònomo *sm.* agronomist.
agrumi *sm. pl.* citrus fruit (*sing.*).
aguzzare *vt.* to sharpen.
aguzzino *sm.* 1. gaoler, jailer 2. (*fig.*) torturer.
aguzzo *agg.* sharp, pointed.
ahimè *inter.* alas.
aia *sf.* threshing-floor.
aio *sm.* tutor.
airone *sm.* heron.
aitante *agg.* vigorous, stout.
aiuola *sf.* flower-bed.
aiutante *sm.* 1. assistant 2. (*mil.*) adjutant: — *di campo*, aide-de-camp.
aiutare *vt.* to help. ♦ **aiutarsi** *vr.* (*ingegnarsi*) to make (*v. irr.*) shift. ♦ **aiutarsi** *vr. rec.* to help (one another).
aiuto *sm.* 1. help: *chiedere* —, to call for help 2. (*chi aiuta*) help, helper 3. (*pl.*) (*mil.*) reinforcements.
aizzare *vt.* to incite, to rouse.
ala *sf.* wing.
alabarda *sf.* halberd.

alabastro *sm.* alabaster.

àlacre *agg.* brisk, industrious.

alacrità *sf.* alacrity.

alamaro *sm.* frog.

alambicco *sm.* still.

alano *sm.* Great Dane.

alba *sf.* dawn.

albanese *agg.* e *sm.* Albanian.

àlbatro *sm.* albatross.

albeggiare *vi.* to dawn.

alberare *vt.* 1. to plant with trees 2. (*mar.*) to mast.

alberato *agg.* planted with trees.

alberatura *sf.* (*mar.*) masting.

albergatore *sm.* hotel-keeper.

alberghiero *agg.* hotel (*attributivo*): *industria alberghiera.* hotel trade.

albergo *sm.* hotel.

àlbero *sm.* 1. tree 2. (*mar.*) mast 3. (*mecc.*) shaft.

albicocca *sf.* apricot.

albino *agg.* e *sm.* albino.

albo *sm.* 1. list, roll: — *degli avvocati,* Law List; — *d'onore,* roll of honour 2. (*per fotografie ecc.*) album 3. (*tavola per affissione*) notice-board.

album *sm.* album.

albume *sm.* albumen.

albumina *sf.* albumin.

alca *sf.* auk.

alcalino *agg.* e *sm.* alkaline.

alce *sm.* elk.

alchimìa *sf.* alchemy.

alcòlico *agg.* alcoholic.

alcolismo *sm.* alcoholism.

alcolizzato *agg.* e *sm.* alcoholic.

alcool *sm.* alcohol.

alcova *sf.* alcove.

alcunché *pron.* anything, something.

alcuno *agg.* 1. (*frasi affermative*) some, a few 2. (*frasi negative*) any. ♦ **alcuno** *pron.* 1. (*frasi affermative*) somebody, someone 2. (*frasi negative*) anybody, anyone.

aldilà *sm.* hereafter.

aleatorio *agg.* aleatory.

aleggiare *vi.* 1. to flutter 2. (*fig.*) to hover (about).

alettone *sm.* aileron.

alfa *sf.* alpha.

alfabeto *sm.* alphabet.

aliiere *sm.* 1. ensign 2. (*scacchi*) bishop.

alga *sf.* seaweed.

àlgebra *sf.* algebra.

algèbrico *agg.* algebraic, algebraical.

aliante *sm.* glider.

àlibi *sm.* alibi.

alienare *vt.* to alienate, to estrange. ♦ **alienarsi** *vr.* to alienate oneself, to become (*v. irr.*) estranged.

alienato *agg.* lunatic, mad; estranged, alienated. ♦ **alienato** *sm.* 1. lunatic, madman (*pl.* -men) 2. alienated person, estranged person.

alienazione *sf.* alienation, estrangement.

alienista *sm.* alienist, psychiatrist.

alieno *agg.* averse, opposed.

alimentare[1] *vt.* to feed (*v. irr.*), to nourish.

alimentare[2] *agg.* alimentary || *generi alimentari,* foodstuffs; *negozio di generi alimentari,* grocery store.

alimentazione *sf.* nourishment, feeding.

alimento *sm.* food.

alìnea *sf.* paragraph.

aliquota *sf.* aliquot, rate.

aliscafo *sm.* hydrofoil boat.

aliseo *sm.* trade-wind.

àlito *sm.* breath.

allacciare *vt.* 1. to lace, to connect 2. (*fig.*) to establish. ♦ **allacciarsi** *vr.* 1. (*abbracciarsi*) to embrace 2. (*aggrovigliarsi*) to get (*v. irr.*) entangled, to be entangled.

allagare *vt.* to flood, to inundate.

allampanato *agg.* lean, lanky.

allargamento *sm.* widening, enlargement.

allargare *vt.* to widen, to enlarge, to extend. ♦ **allargarsi** *vr.* to widen, to extend, to spread (*v. irr.*).

allarmante *agg.* alarming.

allarmare *vt.* to alarm. ♦ **allarmarsi** *vr.* to get (*v. irr.*) frightened.

allarme *sm.* alarm, warning, alert.

allattamento *sm.* breast-feeding, nursing.

allattare *vt.* to suckle, to nurse.

alleanza *sf.* alliance.

allearsi *vr.* to ally, to become (*v. irr.*) allies.

alleato *agg.* allied. ♦ **alleato** *sm.* ally.

allegare *vt.* 1. to allege 2. (*accludere*) to enclose.

allegato *sm.* enclosure.

alleggerimento *sm.* lightening, relief.

alleggerire *vt.* to lighten, to relieve, to unburden. ♦ **alleggerirsi** *vr.* to relieve oneself.

allegorìa *sf.* allegory.

allegòrico *agg.* allegoric(al).

allegramente *agg.* cheerfully, merrily.

allegrìa *sf.* cheerfulness, mirth.

allegro *agg.* merry, cheerful, jolly.

allegrone *sm.* jolly fellow.

allenamento *sm.* · training.

allenare *vt.* to train. ♦ **allenarsi** *vr.* to train (oneself).

allenatore *sm.* trainer; (*di squadre*) coach.

allentamento *sm.* 1. loosening 2. (*di velocità*) slackening.

allentare *vt.* to slacken, to loosen, to relax: — *il freno*, to release the brake. ♦ **allentarsi** *vr.* to slacken.

allergìa *sf.* allergy.

allèrgico *agg.* allergic.

allestimento *sm.* preparation, fitting out || — *scenico*, staging.

allestire *vt.* to prepare, to fit out.

allettamento *sm.* enticement, allurement.

allettante *agg.* alluring, enticing.

allettare *vt.* to allure, to entice.

allevamento *sm.* 1. breeding, raising || (*di bambino*) bringing up 2. (*luogo*) stock-farm || — *di cavalli*, stud-farm.

allevare *vt.* 1. (*bambini*) to bring (*v. irr.*) up 2. (*animali*) to breed (*v. irr.*), to rear.

allevatore *sm.* breeder.

alleviare *vt.* to relieve, to alleviate.

allibire *vi.* to be left speechless, to be struck dumb.

allibito *agg.* struck dumb, speechless.

allibratore *sm.* bookmaker.

allietare *vt.* to cheer. ♦ **allietarsi** *vr.* to cheer up.

allievo *sm.* 1. pupil 2. (*mil.*) cadet.

alligatore *sm.* alligator.

allineamento *sm.* 1. alignment || (*tip.*) — *di caratteri*, ranging of characters 2. (*mil.*) dressing.

allineare *vt.* 1. to line up, to align: — *delle cifre*, to tabulate figures 2. (*mil.*) to dress; (*in ordine di marcia*) to form up. ♦ **allinearsi** *vr.* 1. to get (*v. irr.*) into line 2. (*mil.*) to dress || *allineatevi*, draw up! 3. (*pol.*) to be aligned with.

allocco *sm.* 1. owl 2. (*fig.*) fool.

allocuzione *sf.* allocution: *fare un'—*, to deliver a speech.

allòdola *sf.* skylark, lark.

allogare *vt.* to lodge.

allogazione *sf.* lease.

alloggiare *vt.* 1. to lodge, to house, to put (*v. irr.*) up 2. (*mil.*) to quarter; (*in casa privata*) to billet. ♦ **alloggiare** *vi.* 1. to lodge, to live 2. (*mil.*) to quarter; (*in casa privata*) to be billeted.

alloggio *sm.* · 1. lodging || *indennità di —*, living-out allowance 2. (*mil.*) quarters (*pl.*).

allontanamento *sm.* 1. removal 2. (*licenziamento*) dismissal.

allontanare *vt.* 1. to remove, to drive (*v. irr.*) away: — *un pericolo*, to evert a danger 2. (*licenziare*) to dismiss, to turn out. ♦ **allontanarsi** *vr.* to go (*v. irr.*) away, to depart.

allora *avv.* 1. then 2. (*quindi*) so.

allorché *cong.* when.

alloro *sm.* laurel.

àlluce *sm.* big toe.

allucinare *vt.* 1. to dazzle 2. (*dare allucinazioni*) to hallucinate.

allucinato *agg.* hallucinated.

allucinazione *sf.* hallucination.

allùdere *vi.* to allude (to), to hint (at).

alluminio *sm.* aluminium.

allunaggio *sm.* mooning.

allunare *vi.* to moon.

allungàbile *agg.* extensible.

allungamento *sm.* lengthening, stretching.

allungare *vt.* 1. to lengthen, to extend, to stretch || — *il passo*, to quicken one's steps || — *il collo*, to stretch one's neck || — *gli orecchi*, to strain one's ears || (*fig.*) — *le mani su qc.*, to lay (*v. irr.*) hands on sthg. ♦ **allungarsi** *vr.* to lengthen, to grow (*v. irr.*) longer, to draw (*v. irr.*) out.

allusione *sf.* allusion, hint.

allusivo *agg.* allusive.

alluvionato *agg.* flooded || *zone alluvionate*, flood-areas. ♦ **alluvionato** *sm.* flood-victim.

alluvione *sf.* flood.

almanaccare *vi.* to fantasticate.

almanacco *sm.* almanac.

almeno *avv.* at least.

alno *sm.* alder-tree.

aloè *sm.* aloe.

alone *sm.* halo.

alpaca *sm.* alpaca.

alpe *sf.* alp.

alpestre *agg.* alpine.

alpinismo *sm.* (mountain-)climbing, mountaineering.

alpinista *s.* (mountain-)climber.

alpino *agg.* Alpine.

alquanto *avv.* somewhat, rather.

altalena *sf.* swing.

altana *sf.* roof-terrace.

altare *sm.* altar.

alterare *vt.* to alter; (*salute*) to impair; (*cibo*) to adulterate. ◆ **alterarsi** *vr.* 1. to alter, to change 2. (*andare a male*) to go (*v. irr.*) bad 3. (*turbarsi*) to be upset || *la sua voce si alterò*, his voice faltered.

alterazione *sf.* 1. alteratiòn 2. (*deteriorazione*) deterioration 3. (*turbamento*) emotion; (*della voce*) faltering.

alterco *sm.* altercation.

alterigia *sf.* haughtiness.

alternanza *sf.* alternation.

alternare *vt.* to alternate. ◆ **alternarsi** *vr.* to alternate.

alternativa *sf.* alternative.

alterno *agg.* alternate.

altero *agg.* lofty, proud.

altezza *sf.* 1. height 2. (*di tessuto*) width 3. (*di suono*) pitch 4. (*fig.*) *essere all'— di qc.*, to be equal to sthg.; to be up to sthg. 5. (*titolo*) highness.

altezzoso *agg.* haughty.

alticcio *agg.* tight, tipsy.

altimetro *sm.* altimeter.

altitùdine *sf.* altitude.

alto *agg.* 1. high, tall: *un uomo —,* a tall man || *alta direzione*, top management 2. (*di suono*) loud || *ad alta voce*, aloud, loudly 3. (*profondo*) deep: *acqua alta*, deep water 4. (*geogr.*) northern, upper 5. (*stor.*) early. ◆ **alto** *sm.* height || *alti e bassi*, ups and downs. ◆ **alto** *avv.* high, up || *mani in —,* hands up.

altoforno *sm.* blast-furnace.

altolocato *agg.* high-ranking, high--class.

altoparlante *sm.* loud-speaker.

altopiano *sm.* plateau.

altresì *avv.* likewise, also.

altrettanto *agg. correlativo* as much (...as); (*pl.*) as many (...as) || (*neg.*) as (o so) much (...as); (*pl.*)

as (o so) many... (as): *egli ha altrettante possibilità quanto me*, he has as many chances as I. ◆ **altrettanto** *pron.* 1. as much; (*pl.*) as many 2. (*lo stesso*) the same: *— a voi!*, the same to you!. ◆ **altrettanto** *avv.* 1. (*con agg. e avv.*) as (...as); (*neg.*) as (o so) ...as) 2. (*coi verbi*) as much (as).

altrimenti *avv.* otherwise. ◆ **altrimenti** *cong.* otherwise, else.

altro *agg. indef.* 1. other || *un —,* another 2. (*differente*) different 3. (*con pronomi int.*) else: *chi altro?*, who else? 4. (*in più*) more: *leggerò altri due libri*, I shall read two more books 5. (*susseguente*) next: *verrò l'altra domenica*, I shall come next Sunday 6. (*antecedente*) last: *andai l'altro mese*, I went last month.

altronde 1. (*nella loc. avv.*) *d'—,* on the other hand 2. (*tuttavia*) however.

altrove *avv.* elsewhere, somewhere else.

altrùi *agg.* other people's, someone else's. ◆ **l'altrùi** *sm.* the property of others.

altruismo *sm.* unselfishness.

altruìstico *agg.* unselfish.

altura *sf.* height.

alunno *sm.* pupil.

alveare *sm.* beehive.

àlveo *sm.* river-bed.

alzàia *sf.* towing-line || *strada d'—,* towing-path.

alzare *vt.* 1. to lift, to raise 2. (*erigere*) to build (*v. irr.*) 3. (*mar.*) to hoist. ◆ **alzarsi** *vr.* (*dal letto*) to get (*v. irr.*) up 2. (*in piedi*) to stand (*v. irr.*) up 3. (*in altezza*) to grow (*v. irr.*) tall.

alzata *sf.* 1. raising 2. (*l'alzarsi*) rising.

amàbile *agg.* amiable.

amabilità *sf.* amiability.

amaca *sf.* hammock.

amàlgama *sm.* amalgam.

amalgamare *vt.* to amalgamate.

amante *s.* 1. lover 2. (*fig.*) fond.

amanuense *sm.* copyist.

amaranto *sm.* amaranth.

amare *vt.* 1. to love, to be fond of 2. (*richiedere*) to require.

amareggiare *vt.* 1. to make (*v. irr.*) bitter 2. (*fig.*) to sadden. ◆ **amareggiarsi** *vr.* to worry.

amarena *sf.* sour black cherry.

amaretto *sm.* macaroon.

amarezza *sf.* 1. bitterness 2. (*fig.*) sorrow.

amaro *agg.* bitter. ◆ **amaro** *sm.* (*liquore*) bitters (*pl.*).

amatore *sm.* 1. lover 2. (*chi si occupa d'arte per diletto*) amateur.

amàzzone *sf.* 1. Amazon 2. (*fig.*) masculine woman.

ambage *sf.* ambages (*pl.*) || *senza ambagi*, plainly.

ambasciata *sf.* 1. embassy 2. (*messaggio*) message.

ambasciatore *sm.* ambassador.

ambedue *agg.* e *pron.* both.

ambientare *vt.* 1. to acclimatize 2. (*fatti, personaggi ecc.*) to place. ◆ **ambientarsi** *vr.* to get (*v. irr.*) accustomed.

ambiente *sm.* 1. ambient 2. (*fig.*) milieu 3. (*stanza*) room.

ambiguità *sf.* ambiguity.

ambiguo *agg.* ambiguous.

ambio *sm.* amble.

ambire *vt.* to desire.

àmbito *sm.* ambit.

ambivalente *agg.* ambivalent.

ambivalenza *sf.* ambivalence.

ambizione *sf.* ambition.

ambizioso *agg.* ambitious.

ambo *sm.* ambo.

ambra *sf.* amber.

ambrosia *sf.* ambrosia.

ambulante *agg.* itinerant || *venditore* —, pedlar.

ambulanza *sf.* ambulance.

ambulatorio *sm.* surgery.

ameba *sf.* amoeba.

amebìasi *sf.* amoebiasis (*pl.* -ses).

amenità *sf.* 1. amenity 2. (*facezia*) joke.

ameno *agg.* 1. pleasant 2. (*divertente*) funny: *un tipo* —, a funny chap.

americanismo *sm.* Americanism.

americano *agg.* e *sm.* American.

ametista *sf.* amethyst.

amianto *sm.* amianthus.

amichévole *agg.* friendly.

amicizia *sf.* friendship || *fare* —, to make (*v. irr.*) friends with.

amico *sm.* friend.

amidatura *sf.* starching.

àmido *sm.* starch.

ammaccare *vt.* to bruise.

ammaccatura *sf.* bruise.

ammaestramento *sm.* 1. (*addestramento*) training 2. (*insegnamento*) teaching 3. (*di animali*) taming.

ammaestrare *vt.* 1. (*addestrare*) to train 2. (*insegnare*) to teach (*v. irr.*) 3. (*di animali*) to tame.

ammainare *vt.* to furl.

ammalarsi *vr.* to fall (*v. irr.*) ill.

ammalato *agg.* 1. (*pred.*) ill 2. (*attr.*) sick. ◆ **ammalato** *sm.* sick person, patient.

ammaliare *vt.* to bewitch.

ammaliatrice *sf.* bewitcher.

ammanco *sm.* shortage || — *di cassa*, deficit.

ammanettare *vt.* to handcuff.

ammannire *vt.* to prepare.

ammansire *vt.* 1. to tame 2. (*fig.*) to calm. ◆ **ammansirsi** *vr.* 1. to become (*v. irr.*) tamed 2. to calm down.

ammarare *vi.* 1. to alight (on water) 2. (*di capsule spaziali*) to splash down.

ammassare *vt.* to heap. ◆ **ammassarsi** *vr.* to gather.

ammasso *sm.* heap.

ammattire *vi.* to get (*v. irr.*) mad.

ammazzare *vt.* to kill.

ammazzatoio *sm.* slaughter-house.

ammenda *sf.* amends (*pl.*).

amméttere *vt.* 1. (*lasciar entrare*) to admit, to receive 2. (*concedere, supporre*) to acknowledge, to suppose.

ammezzato *sm.* mezzanine.

ammezzire *vi.* to become (*v. irr.*) over-ripe.

ammiccare *vi.* to wink (at).

ammina *sf.* amine.

amministrare *vt.* 1. to manage 2. (*giur.; eccl.*) to administer.

amministrativo *agg.* administrative.

amministratore *sm.* manager.

amministrazione *sf.* management.

ammiràbile *agg.* admirable.

ammiraglio *sm.* admiral.

ammirare *vt.* to admire.

ammiratore *sm.* 1. admirer 2. (*di attori ecc.*) fan.

ammirazione *sf.* admiration.

ammirévole *agg.* admirable.

ammissìbile *agg.* admissible.

ammobiliamento *sm.* furnishing.

ammobiliare *vt.* to furnish.

ammodernare *vt.* to modernize.

ammodo *agg.* nice, proper.

ammogliare *vt.* to marry. ◆ **ammogliarsi** *vr.* to get (*v. irr.*) married.

ammollare vt. **1.** to soak **2.** (am-morbidire) to soften.

ammollire vt. to soften.

ammonìaca sf. ammonia.

ammonire vt. **1.** to admonish **2.** (avvisare) to warn.

ammonizione sf. **1.** admonition **2.** (rimprovero) reproof **3.** (avvertimento) warning.

ammontare vi. to amount.

ammonticchiare vt. to heap (up).

ammorbare vt. to taint.

ammorbidire vt. to soften.

ammortamento sm. redemption ‖ quota d'—, depreciation allowance.

ammortire vt. to numb.

ammortizzare vt. to redeem.

ammosciare vt. to become (v. irr.) flabby.

ammucchiare vt. to heap (up).

ammuffire vi. **1.** to grow (v. irr.) musty **2.** (fig.) to languish: — in casa, to languish at home.

ammutinamento sm. mutiny.

ammutinarsi vr. to mutiny.

ammutinato agg. mutinous. ♦ **ammutinato** sm. mutineer.

ammutolire vi. **1.** to become (v. irr.) dumb **2.** (essere ammutolito da altri) to be struck dumb.

amnesìa sf. loss of memory.

amnistìa sf. amnesty.

amnistiare vt. to amnesty.

amo sm. fish-hook.

amorale agg. amoral.

amoralità sf. amorality.

amore sm. **1.** love ‖ — di sé, selfishness **2.** (persona o cosa amata) beloved ‖ per amore di, for the sake of.

amoreggiare vi. to flirt.

amoretto sm. flirtation.

amorévole agg. loving.

amorevolezza sf. lovingness.

amorfo agg. amorphous.

amorino sm. Cupid.

amoroso agg. **1.** loving **2.** (fig.) amorous: poesia —, amorous verse.

amovìbile agg. movable.

amperòmetro sm. amperometer.

ampiezza sf. width, (anche fig.) breadth.

ampio agg. **1.** wide **2.** (di abito) comfortable.

amplesso sm. embrace.

ampliamento sm. amplification.

ampliare vt. **1.** to amplify **2.** (aumentare) to increase. ♦ **ampliar-**

si vr. to widen.

amplificare vt. **1.** to enlarge **2.** (fig.; fis.) to amplify.

amplificatore sm. amplifier.

amplificazione sf. amplification.

ampolla sf. **1.** phial **2.** (per olio, aceto ecc.) cruet.

ampollosità sf. pomposity.

ampolloso agg. pompous: stile —, bombastic style.

amputare vt. to amputate.

amputazione sf. amputation.

amuleto sm. amulet.

anabbaglianti sm. pl. lower beams

anabolismo sm. anabolism.

anacoreta sm. anchorite.

anacronismo sm. anachronism.

anacronìstico agg. anachronistic.

anàgrafe sf. registry office.

anagramma sm. anagram.

analcòlico agg. soft.

anale agg. anal.

analfabeta sm. illiterate.

analfabetismo sm. illiteracy.

analgèsico agg. e sm. analgesic.

anàlisi sf. analysis (pl. -ses).

analìtico agg. analytical.

analizzare vt. to analyse.

analogamente avv. likewise.

analogìa sf. analogy.

anàlogo agg. similar.

ànanas sm. pine-apple.

anarchìa sf. anarchy.

anàrchico agg. anarchic. ♦ **anàrchico** sm. anarchist.

anatema sm. anathema.

anatomìa sf. anatomy.

anatòmico agg. anatomic.

anatomista sm. anatomist.

ànatra sf. duck.

anatròccolo sm. duckling.

anca sf. hip.

ancestrale agg. ancestral.

anche avv. **1.** (pure) also, too **2.** (in frasi neg.) either: anch'io non verrò, I will not come either **3.** (con comp.) even, still: ciò è anche peggio, it is still worse **4.** (persino) even. ♦ **anche** cong. (anche se) even if, even though

ancheggiare vi. to waddle.

anchilosato agg. ankylosed.

anchilosi sf. ankylosis.

àncora sf. **1.** anchor: levar l'—, to weigh anchor **2.** (fig.) hope: — di salvezza, last hope.

ancora avv. **1.** (tuttora) still **2.** (in frasi neg.) yet **3.** (di nuovo) again **4.** (davanti a comp.) still, even

5. (*con pron. e agg. quantitativi*)
more: — *molte persone*, many
more people **6.** (« *di più* » *in frasi
affermative*) some more: *voglio ancora caffè*, I want some more coffee **7.** (« *di più* » *in frasi neg. e
dubitative*) any more: *hai ancora
caffè?*, have you any more coffee?
8. (*più a lungo*) longer: *leggi ancora un po'*, read a little longer.

ancoraggio *sm.* anchorage.

ancorare *vt.* to anchor.

ancorché *cong.* even if, even though.

andamento *sm.* **1.** (*tendenza*) trend
2. (*procedimento*) proceeding.

andante *agg.* **1.** (*scadente*) plain **2.**
(*comm.*) current **3.** (*mus.*) andante.

andare *vi.* **1.** (*anche fig.*) to go (*v.
irr.*): — *a cavallo*, to go on horseback; — *a far compere*, to go
shopping; — *a piedi*, to go on
foot; — *a zonzo*, to lounge about;
— *e venire*, to come (*v. irr.*) and
go; — *in bicicletta*, to ride (*v.
irr.*) a bicycle; — *in treno*, to go
by train; — *a male*, to go bad **2.**
(*essere molto venduto*) to be in
demand **3.** (— *bene, di indumen-
to*) to fit || — *avanti* (*di orologi*),
to be fast; — *indietro* (*di orologi*),
to be slow. ♦ **andàrsene** *vr.* to
go away.

andata *sf.* going: — *e ritorno*,
going there and back || *biglietto
di sola* —, single ticket || *biglie-
to di* — *e ritorno*, return ticket.

andatura *sf.* **1.** gait **2.** (*velocità*)
pace.

andazzo *sm.* habit, custom.

andicappare *vt.* to handicap.

andirivieni *sm.* coming and going.

àndito *sm.* passage.

andrògino *agg.* androgynous. ♦ **andrògino** *sm.* androgyne.

androne *sm.* lobby.

aneddòtico *agg.* anecdotic.

anèddoto *sm.* anecdote.

anelare *vi.* **1.** to gasp **2.** (*fig.*) to
long for.

anèlito *sm.* **1.** gasp **2.** (*fig.*) longing
for.

anello *sm.* ring: — *di fidanzamento*,
engagement ring; — *di matri-
monio*, wedding ring || — *di ca-
tena*, link of a chain.

anemìa *sf.* anaemia.

anèmico *agg.* anaemic.

anèmone *sm.* anemone.

anestesìa *sf.* anaesthesia.

anestesista *s.* anaesthetist.

anestètico *agg.* e *sm.* anaesthetic.

anestetizzare *vt.* to anaesthetize.

anfibio *agg.* amphibious. ♦ **anfibio** *sm.* (*zool.; mil.*) amphibian.

anfiteatro *sm.* amphitheatre.

anfitrione *sm.* amphitryon.

ànfora *sf.* amphora (*pl.* -ae).

anfrattuoso *agg.* anfractuous.

angèlico *agg.* angelic(al).

àngelo *sm.* angel.

angherìa *sf.* vexation.

angina *sf.* angina.

angioma *sm.* angioma.

anglicano *agg.* e *sm.* Anglican.

angolare *agg.* angular.

àngolo *sm.* **1.** corner **2.** (*fis.; geom.*)
angle.

angoloso *agg.* angular.

angoscia *sf.* anguish.

angosciare *vt.* to anguish.

angoscioso *agg.* **1.** (*che dà angoscia*) distressing **2.** (*pieno di angoscia*) full of anguish.

anguilla *sf.* **1.** eel **2.** (*fig.*) elusive
person.

anguria *sf.* water-melon.

angustia *sf.* **1.** narrowness **2.** (*tribolazione*) distress.

angustiare *vt.* to afflict. ♦ **angu-
stiarsi** *vr.* to worry.

angusto *agg.* **1.** narrow **2.** (*fig.*)
mean.

ànice *sm.* anise.

anidride *sf.* anhydride.

anilina *sf.* aniline.

ànima *sf.* **1.** soul || *esalare l'*—, to
die || *vender l'*— *a caro prezzo*, to
sell (*v. irr.*) one's life dearly. **2.**
(*parte centrale, nerbo*) soul, heart
3. (*cuore, sentimento*) feeling, heart
4. (*persona*) person: *Torino ha oltre un milione di anime*, Turin
has over one million persons.

animale *sm.* e *agg.* animal.

animalesco *agg.* beastly.

animare *vt.* to enliven, to give
(*v. irr.*) life. ♦ **animarsi** *vr.* to
become (*v. irr.*) lively.

animatamente *avv.* animatedly.

animato *agg.* **1.** living **2.** (*vivace*)
lively.

animatore *sm.* animator.

animazione *sf.* briskness.

animismo *sm.* animism.

ànimo *sm.* **1.** mind: *ho in animo
di fare ciò*, I have a mind to do
that **2.** (*coraggio*) courage **3.** (*inclinazione*) disposition.

animosità sf. animosity.
animoso agg. 1. brave 2. (ostile) malevolent.
anisetta sf. anisette.
ànitra sf. duck.
annacquare vt. 1. to water 2. (fig.) to moderate.
annaffiare vt. to water.
annaffiatoio sm. watering-can.
annali sm. pl. annals.
annaspare vi. to grope.
annaspìo sm. groping.
annata sf. 1. year 2. (raccolto) crop.
annebbiare vt. 1. to dim 2. (fig.) to dull. ♦ **annebbiarsi** vr. (della vista) to blur.
annegamento sm. drowning.
annegare vt. to drown. ♦ **annegarsi** vr. to drown oneself.
annegato agg. drowned.
annerimento sm. blackening.
annerire vt. to blacken.
annessione sf. annexation.
annesso agg. 1. connected 2. (accluso) enclosed.
annèttere vt. to annex.
annichilazione sf. annihilation.
annichilimento sm. annihilation.
annichilire vt. to annihilate.
annidarsi vr. 1. to nestle 2. (nascondersi) to hide (v. irr.).
annientamento sm. 1. destruction 2. (di desideri) frustration.
annientare vt. to destroy.
anniversario agg. e sm. anniversary.
anno sm. 1. year: — bisestile, leap-year || Capo d'—, New Year's Day || durante tutto l'—, all the year round 2. (periodo lungo e indeterminato) a long time 3. (nell'indicare l'età) to be ... years old: ho 10 anni, I am 10 years old.
annodare vt. to knot: — amicizie, to make friends.
annoiare vt. to bore, to tire. ♦ **annoiarsi** vr. to be bored.
annoiato agg. bored.
annoiatore sm. tiresome person.
annoso agg. old.
annotare vt. 1. (corredare di note) to annotate 2. (prendere nota) to take (v. irr.) a note (of).
annotazione sf. note.
annottare vi. to grow (v. irr.) dark.
annuale agg. yearly.
annuario sm. year-book.
annuire vi. to nod.
annullamento sm. cancellation.

annullare vt. 1. to annul 2. (comm.) to cancel.
annunciare vt. 1. to announce 2. (predire) to foretell (v. irr.).
annunciatore sm. announcer.
annuncio sm. 1. notice 2. (presagio) presage.
ànnuo agg. yearly.
annusare vt. 1. to smell 2. (tabacco) to take (v. irr.) snuff.
annuvolarsi vr. 1. to get (v. irr.) cloudy 2. (fig.) to become (v. irr.) gloomy.
ano sm. anus.
anòdino agg. anodyne.
ànodo sm. anode.
anomalìa sf. anomaly.
anòmalo agg. anomalous.
anònima sf. joint-stock company.
anònimo agg. anonymous. ♦ **anònimo** sm. anonym.
anormale agg. abnormal.
anormalità sf. abnormality.
ansa sf. 1. (insenatura) creek 2. (di fiume) bend 3. (manico) handle.
ansante agg. panting.
ansare vi. to pant.
ansia sf. anxiety.
ansietà sf. anxiety.
ansimare vi. to pant.
ansioso agg. 1. anxious 2. (desideroso) eager.
ànsito sm. panting.
anta sf. 1. shutter 2. (di armadio) door.
antagonismo sm. antagonism.
antagonista s. antagonist.
antàrtico agg. Antarctic.
antecedente agg. previous. ♦ **antecedente** sm. antecedent.
antecessore sm. predecessor.
antefatto sm. antecedent fact.
anteguerra sm. pre-war time.
antenato sm. ancestor.
antenna sf. 1. (zool.) antenna (pl. -nae) 2. (radio) aerial.
anteporre vt. to place before, to put (v. irr.) before.
anteprima sf. preview.
anteriore agg. 1. (nello spazio) fore 2. (nel tempo) previous, former.
antiabbaglianti sm. pl. anti-dazzle.
antiaèreo agg. anti-aircraft.
antibattèrico agg. e sm. antibacterial.
antibiòtico agg. e sm. antibiotic.
anticaglia sf. worthless antique.
anticamente avv. in ancient times.
anticàmera sf. ante-room || fare —,

to be kept waiting.
anticarro *agg.* anti-tank.
antichità *sf.* 1. antiquity 2. (*oggetti antichi*) antiques (*pl.*).
anticipare *vt.* 1. to anticipate 2. (*di danaro*) to pay in advance.
anticipatamente *avv.* in advance.
anticipato *agg.* 1. advanced 2. (*comm.*) in advance.
anticipazione *sf.* anticipation.
anticipo *sm.* advance: *essere in —*, to be before time 2. (*caparra*) earnest money.
anticlericale *agg. e s.* anticlerical.
anticlericalismo *sm.* anticlericalism.
antico *agg.* 1. ancient 2. (*all'antica*) old-fashioned.
anticonformista *s.* nonconformist.
anticongelante *sm.* anti-freeze.
anticorpo *sm.* antibody.
anticostituzionale *agg.* anticonstitutional.
antidatare *vt.* to antedate.
antidiluviano *agg. e sm.* antediluvian.
antìdoto *sm.* antidote.
antiestètico *agg.* antiaesthetic.
antifascismo *sm.* antifascism.
antifascista *s. e agg.* antifascist.
antifebbrile *sm.* febrifuge.
antifecondativo *sm.* anti-conceptive.
antìfona *sf.* antiphon: *capire l'—* to take (*v. irr.*) a hint.
antifurto *sm.* antitheft device.
antigàs *agg.* anti-gas: *maschera —*, gas-mask.
antigiènico *agg.* unhealthy.
antìlope *sf.* antelope.
antimilitarismo *sm.* antimilitarism.
antincendio *agg.* antifire: *pompa —*, fire-pump.
antinebbia *agg.* *faro —*, fog-light.
antinevràlgico *agg.* antineuralgic.
antinomìa *sf.* antinomy.
antiparticella *sf.* antiparticle.
antipasto *sm.* hors-d'oeuvre.
antipatìa *sf.* dislike.
antipàtico *agg.* disagreeable.
antìpodi *sm. pl.* antipodes.
antiquariato *sm.* antique-dealing.
antiquario *sm.* antique-dealer.
antiquato *agg.* old-fashioned.
antireumàtico *agg.* antirheumatic.
antirùggine *agg.* anti-rust.
antisemitismo *sm.* anti-Semitism.
antisèttico *agg. e sm.* antiseptic.
antispàstico *agg.* antispasmodic.

antistante *agg.* before, in front of.
antìtesi *sf.* antithesis (*pl.* -ses).
antitetànico *agg.* antitetanic.
antitètico *agg.* antithetic(al).
antitòssico *agg.* antitoxic.
antivigilia *sf.* the day before the eve.
antologìa *sf.* anthology.
antològico *agg.* anthological.
antonomasia *sf.* antonomasia || *per —*, antonomastically.
antracite *sf.* anthracite.
antro *sm.* 1. cave 2. (*tana*) den.
antropocentrismo *sm.* anthropocentrism.
antropofagìa *sf.* anthropophagy.
antropòfago *agg.* anthropophagous.
♦ **antropòfago** *sm.* cannibal.
antropologìa *sf.* anthropology.
antropòlogo *sm.* anthropologist.
antropomorfo *agg.* anthropomorphous.
anulare *agg.* annular. ♦ **anulare** *sm.* ring-finger.
anzi *cong.* 1. (*al contrario*) on the contrary 2. (*in più*) moreover || *— che*, rather than; *— che no*, rather.
♦ **anzi** *avv.* before: *— tempo*, before time.
anzianità *sf.* seniority.
anziano *agg.* 1. elderly 2. (*in cariche, uffici ecc.*) senior.
anziché *cong.* 1. rather than 2. (*invece di*) instead of.
anzidetto *agg.* above-mentioned.
anzitempo *avv.* before time.
aorta *sf.* aorta.
apartìtico *agg.* non-sectarian.
apatìa *sf.* apathy, indifference.
apàtico *agg.* listless.
ape *sf.* bee.
aperitivo *sm.* aperitif.
apertamente *avv.* openly.
aperto *agg.* open.
apertura *sf.* 1. opening 2. (*di mente*) broad-mindedness 3. (*ampiezza di un arco*) span: *— alare*, wing-span.
àpice *sm.* apex.
apicoltura *sf.* bee-keeping.
apnea *sf.* apnoea.
apocalisse *sf.* apocalypse.
apocalìttico *agg.* apocalyptic(al).
apòcrifo *agg.* apocryphal || *libri apocrifi*, Apocrypha.
apòfisi *sf.* apophysis.
apogeo *sm.* apogee.
apòlide *agg.* stateless. ♦ **apòlide** *sm.* stateless person.

apolìtico *agg.* non-political.

apologìa *sf.* apologia.

apologista *s.* apologist.

apòlogo *sm.* apologue.

apoplessìa *sf.* apoplexy.

apoplèttico *agg.* apoplectic: *colpo —*, apoplectic fit.

apostasìa *sf.* apostasy.

apòstata *sm.* apostate.

apòstolo *sm.* apostle.

apostrofare *vt.* to apostrophize.

apòstrofe *sf.* apostrophe.

apòstrofo *sm.* apostrophe.

apoteòsi *sf.* apotheosis.

appagare *vt.* **1.** to satisfy, to gratify **2.** (*la sete*) to quench one's thirst.

appaiare *vt.* **1.** to couple **2.** (*armonizzare colori, vestiario ecc.*) to match.

appallottolare *vt.* to roll into a ball.

appaltare *vt.* to give (*v. irr.*) out by contract.

appaltatore *sm.* contractor.

appalto *sm.* contract, bid.

appannaggio *sm.* apanage.

appannamento *sm.* **1.** (*di metalli*) tarnishing **2.** (*di vetri ecc.*) clouding **3.** (*di vista*) dimming.

appannare *vt.* **1.** (*di metalli*) to tarnish **2.** (*di vetri ecc.*) to cloud **3.** (*di vista*) to dim.

apparato *sm.* **1.** apparatus **2.** (*mostra*) display.

apparecchiare *vt.* to prepare: *— la tavola*, to lay (*v. irr.*) the table.

apparecchio *sm.* **1.** set **2.** (*aereoplano*) aeroplane || *— fotografico*, camera; *— telefonico*, telephone; *— radio*, radio set.

apparentare *vt.* to relate.

apparente *agg.* **1.** (*illusorio*) seeming **2.** (*chiaro*) apparent, obvious.

apparentemente *avv.* seemingly.

apparenza *sf.* **1.** appearance **2.** (*aspetto*) look **3.** (*pompa*) show.

apparire *vi.* **1.** to appear **2.** (*aver l'aspetto*) to look **3.** (*risultare*) to result.

appariscente *agg.* **1.** striking **2.** (*vistoso*) showy.

apparizione *sf.* apparition.

appartamento *sm.* flat.

appartarsi *vr.* to retire.

appartenenza *sf.* belonging.

appartenere *vi.* **1.** to belong (to) **2.** (*essere membro*) to be a member (of).

appassionare *vt.* to impassion. ♦ **appassionarsi** *vr.* to become (*v. irr.*) fond of.

appassionato *agg.* **1.** passionate **2.** (*di musica, arte ecc.*) keen (on).

appassire *vi.* to wither.

appellare *vt.* to name, to call. ♦ **appellarsi** *vr.* to appeal.

appellativo *sm.* appellative.

appello *sm.* **1.** (*giur.*) appeal **2.** (*chiamata*) call **3.** (*esortazione*) appeal.

appena *avv.* **1.** (*a fatica*) hardly **2.** (*molto poco*) very little **3.** (*da poco*) just: *ero — arrivato*, I had just arrived || *non —*, as soon as.

appèndere *vt.* to hang (*v. irr.*).

appendice *sf.* appendix || *romanzo d'—*, serial.

appendicite *sf.* appendicitis.

appesantire *vt.* to make (*v. irr.*) heavy. ♦ **appesantirsi** *vr.* to grow (*v. irr.*) heavy.

appestare *vt.* **1.** to infect **2.** (*spargere odore*) to stink (*v. irr.*).

appestato *agg.* **1.** plague-stricken **2.** (*fig.*) tainted. ♦ **appestato** *sm.* plague-stricken person.

appetenza *sf.* **1.** appetite **2.** (*desiderio*) longing (for sthg.).

appetìbile *agg.* pleasing.

appetire *vt.* to desire.

appetito *sm.* appetite.

appezzamento *sm.* plot of land.

appianare *vt.* **1.** to level **2.** (*fig.*) to smooth.

appiattarsi *vr.* **1.** to crouch **2.** (*stare in agguato*) to lie (*v. irr.*) in wait **3.** (*nascondersi*) to hide (*v. irr.*).

appiattire *vt.* to flatten.

appiccare *vt.* (*il fuoco*) to set (*v. irr.*) fire.

appiccicare *vt.* **1.** to stick (*v. irr.*) **2.** (*appioppare*) to palm off.

appiccicoso *agg.* sticky.

appiè *prep.* **1.** (*al di sotto*) below **2.** (*ai piedi*) at the foot: *— del letto*, at the foot of the bed.

appiedare *vt.* to dismount.

appiedato *agg.* dismounted.

appieno *avv.* fully.

appigliarsi *vr.* to get (*v. irr.*) hold of: *— ad un pretesto*, to take (*v. irr.*) a pretext.

appiglio *sm.* **1.** support **2.** (*fig.*) pretext.

appiombo *sm.* perpendicularity.

appioppare *vt.* **1.** to give (*v. irr.*)

‖ — *uno schiaffo*, to slap 2. (*affibbiare*) to palm off.

appisolarsi *vr.* to doze off.

applaudire *vt. e vi.* to applaud.

applauditore *sm.* applauder.

applàuso *sm.* 1. applause (*solo sing.*) 2. (*fig.*) praise.

applicare *vt.* 1. to apply 2. (*giur.*) to carry out 3. (*accostare*) to set (*v. irr.*). ♦ **applicarsi** *vr.* to apply oneself.

applicazione *sf.* 1. application 2. (*fig.*) care 3. (*guarnizione*) trimming.

appoggiare *vt.* 1. to lean (*v. irr.*) 2. (*posare*) to lay (*v. irr.*) 3. (*fig.*) to back. ♦ **appoggiarsi** *vr.* 1. to lean (*v. irr.*) 2. (*fig.*) to rely (on).

appoggio *sm.* 1. support 2. (*fig.*) assistance 3. (*colui che dà* —) supporter.

appollaiarsi *vr.* to perch.

apporre *vt.* to affix.

apportare *vt.* 1. to bring (*v. irr.*) 2. (*produrre*) to produce.

apporto *sm.* contribution.

appositamente *avv.* on purpose.

appòsito *agg.* 1. special 2. (*adatto*) fit.

apposizione *sf.* 1. (*gramm.*) apposition 2. (*l'apporre*) affixing.

apposta *avv.* expressly.

appostare *vt.* (*mil.*) to place. ♦ **appostarsi** *vr.* to lie (*v. irr.*) in ambush.

apprèndere *vt.* to learn (*v. irr.*).

apprendista *sm.* apprentice.

apprendistato *sm.* apprenticeship.

apprensione *sf.* 1. concern 2. (*l'apprendere*) learning.

appresso *avv.* near, close by. ♦ **appresso** *prep.* near, close to.

apprestamento *sm.* preparation.

apprestare *vt.* to prepare.

apprettare *vt.* to dress.

apprezzàbile *agg.* appreciable.

apprezzamento *sm.* 1. appreciation 2. (*giudizio*) opinion.

apprezzare *vt.* 1. to appreciate 2. (*valutare*) to value.

approdare *vi.* 1. to land 2. (*fig.*) to be of use.

approfittare *vi.* to profit (by). ♦ **approfittarsi** *vr.* 1. to avail oneself 2. (*abusare*) to take (*v. irr.*) undue advantage.

approfondire *vt.* 1. to make (*v. irr.*) deeper 2. (*fig.*) to examine closely.

approntare *vt.* to make (*v. irr.*) ready.

appropriarsi *vr.* to take (*v. irr.*) possession of.

appropriato *agg.* fit, suitable.

appropriazione *sf.* appropriation: — *indebita*, embezzlement.

approssimarsi *vr.* 1. to come (*v. irr.*) near 2. (*di tempo*) to draw (*v. irr.*) near.

approssimativamente *avv.* approximately.

approssimativo *agg.* approximative.

approssimazione *sf.* approximation.

approvare *vt.* 1. to approve (of) 2. (*promuovere*) to pass.

approvazione *sf.* approval.

approvvigionamento *sm.* 1. (*l'approvvigionare*) supplying 2. (*provviste*) supplies.

approvvigionare *vt.* to supply provisions (to).

appuntamento *sm.* appointment.

appuntare *vt.* 1. to sharpen 2. (*prender nota*) to note 3. (*biasimare*) to blame.

appuntellare *vt.* 1. to prop 2. (*fig.*) to support.

appuntino *avv.* nicely.

appuntito *agg.* pointed.

appunto¹ *sm.* 1. note 2. (*critica*) blame.

appunto² *avv.* exactly, just.

appurare *vt.* to verify.

apribottiglie *sm.* bottle-opener.

aprile *sm.* April: *pesce d'*—, April fool.

aprire *vt.* to open: — *le braccia a qc.*, to welcome so.

apriscàtole *sm.* tin-opener.

àquila *sf.* eagle.

aquilino *agg.* aquiline.

aquilone *sm.* 1. (*vento del nord*) north wind 2. (*giocattolo*) kite.

aquilotto *sm.* eaglet.

arabescare *vt.* to decorate with arabesques.

arabesco *sm.* arabesque.

aràbico *agg.* Arabic.

aràbile *agg.* arable.

àrabo *agg. e sm.* Arab.

aràchide *sf.* peanut.

aragosta *sf.* lobster.

aràldico *agg.* heraldic

araldo *sm.* herald.

arancia *sf.* orange.

aranciata *sf.* orange squash.
aranciera *sf.* orangery.
arancio *agg.* (*colore*) orange. ♦ **arancio** *sm.* orange-tree.
arancione *agg.* orange-coloured.
arare *vt.* to plough.
aratore *sm.* ploughman (*pl.* -men).
aratro *sm.* plough.
aratura *sf.* ploughing.
arazzo *sm.* arras.
arbitraggio *sm.* **1.** (*sport*) umpirage **2.** (*comm.*) arbitrage.
arbitrare *vt.* **1.** to arbitrate **2.** (*calcio, boxe*) to referee.
arbitrario *agg.* arbitrary.
arbitrio *sm.* **1.** will: *libero —, free will* **1.** (*atto arbitrario*) arbitrary act.
àrbitro *sm.* **1.** (*sport*) umpire **2.** (*calcio, boxe*) referee **3.** (*giur.*) arbitrator.
arboricoltore *sm.* arboriculturist.
arboricoltura *sf.* arboriculture.
arboscello *sm.* shrub.
arbusto *sm.* shrub.
arca *sf.* ark || *— di scienza,* eminent scholar.
arcàdico *agg.* e *sm.* Arcadian.
arcàico *agg.* **1.** archaic **2.** (*di parole, stile*) obsolete.
arcaismo *sm.* **1.** archaism **2.** (*parola arcaica*) obsolete word.
arcàngelo *sm.* archangel.
arcano *agg.* mysterious.
archeologìa *sf.* archaeology.
archeològico *agg.* archaeologic(al).
archeòlogo *sm.* archaeologist.
archètipo *sm.* archetype.
archetto *sm.* **1.** small arch **2.** (*mus.*) bow.
architettare *vt.* **1.** to draw (*v. irr.*) the plans **2.** (*fig.*) to devise.
architetto *sm.* architect.
architettònico *agg.* architectonic.
architettura *sf.* architecture.
architrave *sm.* architrave.
archiviare *vt.* **1.** to place in the archives **2.** (*comm.*) to file.
archivio *sm.* **1.** archives (*pl.*) **2.** (*comm.*) file.
archivista *sm.* archivist.
arciduca *sm.* archduke.
arciere *sm.* archer.
arcigno *agg.* gruff.
arcimiliardario *sm.* multimillionaire.
arcipèlago *sm.* archipelago (*pl.* -goes).
arcivescovado *sm.* archbishopric.

arcivéscovo *sm.* archbishop.
arco *sm.* **1.** (*arma*) bow **2.** (*geom.*) arc **3.** (*arch.*) arch **4.** (*mus.*) bow.
arcobaleno *sm.* rainbow.
arcolaio *sm.* wool-winder.
arcuare *vt.* **1.** to arch **2.** (*piegare*) to bend (*v. irr.*).
ardente *agg.* **1.** burning **2.** (*fig.*) passionate.
ardentemente *avv.* ardently.
àrdere *vt.* to burn (*v. irr.*).
ardesia *sf.* slate.
ardire *vi.* **1.** to dare **2.** (*avere l'impudenza*) to have the impudence.
ardito *agg.* **1.** bold **2.** (*rischioso*) risky.
ardore *sm.* **1.** fierce heat **2.** (*fig.*) passion.
àrduo *agg.* **1.** hard **2.** (*erto*) steep.
àrea *sf.* **1.** area **2.** (*sfera d'azione*) sphere.
arena *sf.* **1.** (*sabbia*) sand **2.** (*arch.*) arena.
arenarsi *vr.* to get (*v. irr.*) stranded (*anche fig.*).
arengario *sm.* tribune.
areòpago *sm.* Areopagus.
àrgano *sm.* **1.** (*mar.*) capstan **2.** (*mecc.*) windlass.
argentare *vt.* to silver.
argènteo *agg.* silvery.
argenterìa *sf.* silver ware.
argentino *agg.* silvery.
argento *sm.* silver.
argilla *sf.* clay.
argilloso *agg.* clayey.
arginare *vt.* **1.** to dam **2.** (*fig.*) to check.
àrgine *sm.* bank.
argomentare *vt.* to infer. ♦ **argomentare** *vi.* to argue.
argomentazione *sf.* reasoning.
argomento *sm.* **1.** subject **2.** (*prova a sostegno*) argument.
arguire *vt.* to deduce.
argutezza *sf.* shrewdness.
arguto *agg.* **1.** sharp **2.** (*faceto*) witty.
arguzia *sf.* wit.
aria *sf.* **1.** air: *— condizionata,* air conditioning || *corrente d'—,* draught || *camera d'—,* inner tube || *andare all'—,* to fall (*v. irr.*) through **2.** (*aspetto*) look **3.** (*mus.*) tune.
ariano *agg.* e *sm.* Aryan.
aridità *sf.* **1.** aridity **2.** (*di cuore*) lack of feeling.
àrido *agg.* **1.** arid **2.** (*di cuore*)

lacking feeling.

arieggiare vt. **1.** to air **2.** (rasso-migliare) to look like **3.** (imitare) to imitate.

arieggiato agg. aired.

ariete sm. ram.

aringa sf. herring.

arioso agg. airy.

aristocràtico agg. aristocratic. ♦ **aristocràtico** sm. aristocrat.

aristocrazìa sf. aristocracy.

aristotèlico agg. e sm. Aristotelian.

aritmètica sf. arithmetic.

aritmètico agg. arithmetic(al).

arlecchinata sf. harlequinade.

arlecchino sm. harlequin.

arma sf. weapon, arm: armi bianche, side-arms; armi da fuoco, fire--arms ǁ galleria d'armi, armoury.

armadietto sm. **1.** (per medicinali, strumenti ecc.) cabinet **2.** (per abiti) locker.

armadio sm. **1.** (per stoviglie) cupboard **2.** (per abiti) wardrobe.

armaiolo sm. armourer.

armamentario sm. **1.** instruments (pl.) **2.** (armeria) armoury.

armamento sm. arming.

armare vt. to arm.

armata sf. army.

armatore sm. **1.** shipbuilder **2.** (chi possiede una nave) shipowner.

armatura sf. **1.** armour **2.** (impalcatura) scaffolding.

armeggiare vi. **1.** to handle arms **2.** (darsi da fare) to busy oneself **3.** (tramare) to manoeuvre.

armeggìo sm. **1.** handling of arms **2.** (l'affaccendarsi) bustling **3.** (intrigo) manoeuvre.

armento sm. herd.

armerìa sf. armoury.

armiere sm. gunsmith.

armistizio sm. armistice.

armonìa sf. harmony.

armònica sf. (a bocca) mouth-organ.

armònico agg. harmonic.

armonio sm. harmonium.

armonioso agg. harmonious.

armonista s. harmonist.

armonizzare vt. to harmonize. ♦ **armonizzare** vi. **1.** to harmonize **2.** (di colori) to match.

arnese sm. **1.** (strumento) tool **2.** (aggeggio) gadget.

arnia sf. beehive.

aroma sm. flavour.

aromàtico agg. aromatic.

aromatizzare vt. to flavour.

arpa sf. harp.

arpeggiare vi. to play the harp.

arpeggio sm. arpeggio.

arpista s. harpist.

arra sf. earnest.

arrabattarsi vr. to bestir oneself.

arrabbiare vi. **1.** to become (v. irr.) angry **2.** (di cane) to be affected with rabies. ♦ **arrabbiarsi** vr. to get (v. irr.) angry.

arrabbiato agg. **1.** angry **2.** (di cane) rabid.

arrabbiatura sf. rage.

arraffare vt. to grasp.

arrampicarsi vr. to climb.

arrampicata sf. climb.

arrampicatore sm. **1.** mountain climber **2.** (fig.) social climber.

arrancare vi. **1.** to plod along **2.** (zoppicare) to limp **3.** (affaticarsi) to get (v. irr.) tired.

arrangiamento sm. arrangement.

arrangiare vt. to arrange. ♦ **arrangiarsi** vr. to manage.

arrecare vt. **1.** to bring (v. irr.) **2.** (causare) to cause.

arredamento sm. furnishing.

arredare vt. to furnish.

arredatore sm. internal decorator.

arredo sm. piece of furniture.

arrèndersi vr. **1.** to surrender **2.** (fig.) to give (v. irr.) it up.

arrendévole agg. **1.** pliant **2.** (fig.) docile.

arrestare vt. **1.** to stop **2.** (trarre in arresto) to arrest. ♦ **arrestarsi** vr. to stop.

arresto sm. arrest.

arretrare vt. **1.** to pull back **2.** (ritirare) to withdraw (v. irr.).

arretrato agg. backward.

arricchimento sm. enrichment.

arricchire vt. to enrich. ♦ **arricchirsi** vr. to grow (v. irr.) rich.

arricciare vt. to curl: — il naso, to turn up one's nose.

arrìdere vi. to be favourable.

arringare vt. to harangue.

arringatore sm. haranguer.

arrischiare vt. to risk. ♦ **arrischiarsi** vr. to venture.

arrivare vi. **1.** to arrive (at), (in) **2.** (fig.) to attain.

arrivato agg. (fig.) successful.

arrivederci inter. goodbye.

arrivismo sm. social climbing.

arrivista sm. social climber.

arrivo sm. arrival.

arrogante *agg.* arrogant.

arroganza *sf.* arrogance.

arrogarsi *vr.* to arrogate to oneself.

arrossire *vi.* to blush.

arrostire *vt.* 1. to roast 2. (*di pane*) to toast.

arrosto *sm.* roast.

arrotare *vt.* to grind (*v. irr.*): — i denti, to grind one's teeth.

arrotino *sm.* knife-grinder.

arrotolare *vt.* to roll up.

arrotondare *vt.* 1. to round 2. (*di cifre*) to make (*v. irr.*) a round figure.

arrovellarsi *vr.* to worry.

arroventare *vt.* to make (*v. irr.*) red-hot.

arruffare *vt.* to ruffle.

arruffone *sm.* muddler.

arrugginire *vi.* to rust.

arruolare *vt.* to enrol.

arsenale *sm.* 1. (*cantiere*) ship-yard 2. (*deposito di armi*) arsenal.

arsènico *sm.* arsenic.

arsura *sf.* 1. (*siccità*) drought 2. (*sete*) parching thirst.

arte *sf.* art || *belle arti*, fine arts.

artefatto *agg.* adulterated.

artéfice *sm.* maker.

arteria *sf.* 1. artery 2. (*di traffico*) thoroughfare.

arteriosclerosi *sf.* arteriosclerosis.

artesiano *agg.* artesian.

àrtico *agg.* arctic.

articolare *vt.* to articulate.

articolazione *sf.* articulation.

artìcolo *sm.* 1. (*gramm.; di giornale*) article || — *di fondo*, editorial 2. (*comm.*) item.

artificiale *agg.* artificial.

artificio *sm.* 1. device 2. (*astuzia*) cunning.

artigianato *sm.* handicraft.

artigiano *sm.* craftsman (*pl.* -men).

artigliere *sm.* gunner.

artiglierìa *sf.* artillery.

artiglio *sm.* claw.

artista *sm.* artist.

artìstico *agg.* artistic(al).

arto *sm.* limb: — *artificiale*, artificial limb.

artrite *sf.* arthritis (*pl.* -ides).

artrosi *sf.* arthrosis.

arzigògolo *sm.* subtlety.

arzillo *agg.* lively, brisk.

ascella *sf.* armpit.

ascendente *sm.* 1. ascendancy 2. (*antenato*) ancestor.

ascendenza *sf.* ancestry.

ascéndere *vi.* (*anche fig.*) to rise (*v. irr.*).

ascensione *sf.* 1. ascension 2. (*scalata*) climb.

ascensore *sm.* lift.

ascesa *sf.* ascent.

ascesi *sf.* mystical practice.

ascesso *sm.* abscess.

asceta *sm.* ascetic.

ascètico *agg.* ascetical.

ascetismo *sm.* asceticism.

ascia *sf.* axe.

ascissa *sf.* abscissa (*pl.* -sae).

asciugacapelli *sm.* hair-drier.

asciugamano *sm.* towel.

asciugare *vt.* 1. to dry 2. (*con un panno*) to wipe. ◆ **asciugarsi** *vr.* to dry up.

asciugatoio *sm.* towel.

asciutto *agg.* 1. (*anche fig.*) dry 2. (*magro*) thin.

ascoltare *vt.* 1. to listen (to) 2. (*assistere*) to attend: — *le lezioni*, to attend classes.

ascolto *sm.* listening.

ascrivere *vt.* 1. to count 2. (*attribuire*) to ascribe. ◆ **ascrìversi** *vr.* to claim.

asepsi *sf.* asepsis.

asessuale *agg.* asexual.

asèttico *agg.* aseptic.

asfaltare *vt.* to asphalt.

asfalto *sm.* asphalt.

asfissìa *sf.* 1. asphyxia 2. (*da gas*) gassing.

asfissiare *vt.* 1. to asphyxiate 2. (*con gas*) to gas.

asiàtico *agg.* e *sm.* Asiatic.

asilo *sm.* 1. shelter 2. (*scuola materna*) infant-school.

asimmetrìa *sf.* asymmetry.

asimmètrico *agg.* asymmetrical.

asinerìa *sf.* stupidity.

asinità *sf.* asininity.

àsino *sm.* 1. ass 2. (*fig.*) jackass.

asma *sf.* asthma.

asmàtico *agg.* asthmatical.

asociale *agg.* asocial.

àsola *sf.* buttonhole.

aspàrago *sm.* asparagus.

aspèrgere *vt.* to sprinkle.

asperità *sf.* 1. asperity 2. (*di superfici*) unevenness 3. (*di carattere*) harshness.

aspersorio *sm.* aspergillum.

aspettare *vt.* to wait (for). ◆ **aspettarsi** *vr.* to expect.

aspettativa *sf.* 1. expectation 2.

(*esonero temporaneo*) temporary retirement.

aspetto *sm.* look || *di bell'aspetto*, good-looking || *sala d'—*, waiting--room.

àspide *sm.* asp.

aspirante *agg.* aspirant. ♦ **aspirante** *sm.* candidate, applicant.

aspirapòlvere *sm.* vacuum cleaner, hoover.

aspirare *vt.* to inspire. ♦ **aspirare** *vi.* to aspire (to).

aspiratore *sm.* aspirator.

aspirazione *sf.* 1. aspiration 2. (*mecc.*) suction.

aspirina *sf.* aspirin.

asportare *vt.* 1. to remove 2. (*med.*) to extirpate.

asportazione *sf.* 1. removal 2. (*med.*) extirpation.

asprezza *sf.* 1. sourness 2. (*fig.*) harshness.

asprigno *agg.* sourish.

aspro *agg.* 1. sour 2. (*fig.*) harsh.

assaggiare *vt.* to taste.

assaggio *sm.* 1. tasting 2. (*campione*) sample.

assai *avv.* 1. (*con agg. e avv.*) very 2. (*con comp.*) much: — *meglio*, much better.

assalire *vt.* 1. to assail 2. (*di malattia*) to attack.

assalitore *sm.* assailer.

assaltare *vt.* to assault.

assalto *sm.* assault, attack.

assaporare *vt.* 1. to savour 2. (*fig.*) to enjoy.

assassinare *vt.* to murder.

assassinio *sm.* murder.

assassino *sm.* murderer.

asse *sf.* 1. (*tavola di legno*) board 2. (*geom.*) axis (*pl.* axes) 3. (*stor.*) Axis.

assecondare *vt.* to favour.

assediare *vt.* to besiege.

assedio *sm.* siege.

assegnamento *sm.* assignment || *fare — su qualcuno*, to rely on so.

assegnare *vt.* 1. to assign 2. (*un premio*) to award.

assegno *sm.* cheque: — *al portatore*, cheque to bearer; — *circolare*, banker's draft; — *sbarrato*, crossed cheque.

assemblea *sf.* 1. meeting 2. (*corpo deliberante*) assembly.

assembramento *sm.* concourse of people.

assembrarsi *vr.* to assemble.

assennatezza *sf.* common sense.

assennato *agg.* sensible.

assenso *sm.* assent.

assentarsi *vr.* to go (*v. irr.*) away.

assente *agg.* absent.

assenteismo *sm.* absenteeism.

assentire *vi.* 1. to assent (to) 2. (*col capo*) to nod (in assent).

assenza *sf.* absence.

assenzio *sm.* absinth.

asserire *vt.* to affirm.

asserragliarsi *vr.* to barricade oneself.

asserto *sm.* assertion.

assertore *sm.* 1. assertor 2. (*difensore*) defender, champion.

asservimento *sm.* enslavement.

asservire *vt.* to enslave, to subdue.

asserzione *sf.* statement.

assessorato *sm.* assessorship.

assessore *sm.* 1. (*alle imposte*) assessor 2. (*comunale*) councillor responsible for a municipal region.

assestamento *sm.* 1. adjustment 2. (*definitivo*) settlement 3. (*del terreno*) settling.

assestare *vt.* to arrange: — *un colpo*, to deal (*v. irr.*) a blow. ♦ **assestarsi** *vr.* to settle (down).

assetato *agg.* 1. thirsty 2. (*fig.*) eager (for).

assetto *sm.* order.

assicurare *vt.* 1. (*legare*) to fasten 2. (*promettere*) to assure 3. (*affermare*) to affirm 4. (*comm.*) to insure.

assicurata *sf.* registered letter.

assicurato *agg.* insured, assured. ♦ **assicurato** *sm.* insurant.

assicuratore *sm.* insurer.

assicurazione *sf.* 1. assurance 2. (*comm.*) insurance.

assideramento *sm.* frost-bite.

assiduità *sf.* assiduity.

assìduo *agg.* assiduous.

assieme *avv.* V. *insieme*.

assieparsi *vr.* to crowd (round).

assillante *agg.* urging.

assillare *vt.* to urge.

assillo *sm.* 1. urge 2. (*fig.*) worry.

assimilàbile *agg.* assimilable.

assimilare *vt.* to assimilate, to absorb.

assimilazione *sf.* assimilation.

assioma *sm.* axiom.

assiomàtico *agg.* axiomatic.

assise *sf. pl.* assizes.

assistente *sm.* assistant.

assistenza *sf.* assistance.

assistenziale *agg.* charitable.

assistere *vt.* 1. to assist 2. (*curare*) to nurse. ♦ **assìstere** *vi.* to attend (sthg.).

assito *sm.* 1. (*curare*) wooden partition 2. (*pavimento*) plank floor.

asso *sm.* 1. (*carte*) ace 2. (*sport*) champion || *piantare in* —, to leave (*v. irr.*) in the lurch.

associare *vt.* to join. ♦ **associarsi** *vr.* to associate.

associato *sm.* member.

associazione *sf.* association.

assodare *vt.* 1. to consolidate 2. (*accertare*) to ascertain.

assoggettare *vt.* to subject. ♦ **assoggettarsi** *vr.* to submit oneself.

assolato *agg.* sunny.

assoldare *vt.* to recruit.

assolo *sm.* (*mus.*) solo.

assolutamente *avv.* absolutely.

assolutismo *sm.* absolutism.

assolutista *agg. e sm.* absolutist.

assoluto *agg. e sm.* absolute.

assoluzione *sf.* 1. (*eccl.*) absolution 2. (*giur.*) discharge.

assòlvere *vt.* 1. (*teol.*) to absolve 2. (*giur.*) to discharge 3. (*eseguire*) to accomplish.

assomigliante *agg.* like.

assomigliare *vi.* to look like.

assommare *vt. e vi.* to add, to amount (to).

assonanza *sf.* assonance.

assonnarsi *vr.* to fall (*v. irr.*) asleep.

assonnato *agg.* sleepy.

assopimento *sm.* dozing.

assopire *vt.* to make (*v. irr.*) dozy. ♦ **assopirsi** *vr.* to doze off.

assorbente *agg.* absorbing || *càrta* —, blotting-paper.

assorbimento *sm.* absorption.

assorbire *vt.* to absorb.

assordante *agg.* deafening.

assordare *vt.* to deafen.

assortimento *sm.* assortment.

assortire *vt.* 1. to stock 2. (*fig.*) to match.

assorto *agg.* absorbed.

assottigliamento *sm.* 1. thinning 2. (*riduzione*) reduction.

assottigliare *vt.* 1. to thin 2. (*diminuire*) to reduce. ♦ **assottigliarsi** *vr.* to grow (*v. irr.*) thin.

assuefare *vt.* to accustom. ♦ **assuefarsi** *vr.* to accustom oneself.

assuefazione *sf.* custom.

assùmere *vt.* 1. to assume 2. (*in servizio*) to employ 3. (*informazioni*) to make (*v. irr.*) inquiries.

assunzione *sf.* 1. (*ascesa*) accession 2. (*impiego*) engagement 3. (*teol.*) Assumption.

assurdamente *avv.* absurdly.

assurdità *sf.* absurdity.

assurdo *agg.* absurd. ♦ **assurdo** *sm.* absurdity.

assùrgere *vi.* to rise (*v. irr.*).

asta *sf.* 1. pole 2. (*di bandiera*) flagstaff 3. (*di occhiali*) bar 4. (*di bilancia*) arm (of balance) 5. (*vendita all'asta*) auction(-sale).

astante *agg.* present. ♦ **astante** *sm.* on-looker.

astemio *agg.* abstemious. ♦ **astemio** *sm.* teetotaller.

astenersi *vr.* to abstain.

astenìa *sf.* asthenia.

astensione *sf.* abstention.

astensionista *sm.* abstentionist.

asterisco *sm.* asterisk.

asteròide *sm.* asteroid.

asticciola *sf.* pothook.

astigmàtico *agg.* astigmatic.

astigmatismo *sm.* astigmatism.

astinenza *sf.* abstinence.

astio *sm.* resentment.

astiosamente *avv.* resentfully.

astioso *agg.* resentful.

astracàn *sm.* astrakhan.

astràgalo *sm.* 1. (*bot.*) astragalus (*pl.* -li) 2. (*arch.*) astragal.

astrale *agg.* astral.

astrarre *vt.* to abstract. ♦ **astrarsi** *vr.* to think (*v. irr.*) about sthg. else.

astrattismo *sm.* (*arte*) abstractionism.

astratto *agg.* abstract.

astrazione *sf.* abstraction.

astringente *agg. e sm.* astringent.

astro *sm.* star.

astrolabio *sm.* astrolabe.

astrologìa *sf.* astrology.

astròlogo *sm.* astrologer.

astronàuta *sm.* astronaut.

astronave *sf.* space-ship.

astronomìa *sf.* astronomy.

astronòmico *agg.* astronomic(al).

astrònomo *sm.* astronomer.

astrusità *sf.* abstruseness.

astruso *agg.* abstruse.

astuccio *sm.* case, box: — *per occhiali*, spectacle-case.

astuto *agg.* cunning.

astuzia *sf.* 1. (*qualità*) cunning 2. (*atto*) trick.

atassìa *sf.* ataxy.

atàvico *agg.* atavic.

atavismo *sm.* atavism.

ateismo *sm.* atheism.

àteo *agg.* atheistic. ♦ àteo *sm.* atheist.

atleta *sm.* athlete.

atlètica *sf.* athletics.

atlètico *agg.* athletic.

atmosfera *sf.* atmosphere.

atollo *sm.* atoll.

atòmico *agg.* atomic.

atomismo *sm.* atomism.

atomìstica *sf.* atomic theory.

atomizzatore *sm.* atomizer.

àtomo *sm.* (*anche fig.*) atom.

atonìa *sf.* atony.

àtono *agg.* atonic.

atrio *sm.* (entrance-)hall.

atroce *agg.* dreadful.

atrocità *sf.* atrocity.

atrofìa *sf.* atrophy.

atrofizzare *vt.* to atrophy.

atrofizzato *agg.* atrophic.

atropina *sf.* atropine.

attaccabottoni *sm.* buttonholer.

attaccabrighe *sm.* quarrelsome fellow.

attaccamento *sm.* attachment: *avere dell'—*, to entertain an attachment (for).

attaccante *sm.* attacker.

attaccapanni *sm.* cloak-stand.

attaccare *vt.* 1. (*unire*) to attack 2. (*appiccicare*) to stick (*v. irr.*) 3. (*cucire*) to sew (*v. irr.*) 4. (*assalire*) to attack 5. (*mus.*) to open. ♦ attaccarsi *vr.* 1. (*appigliarsi*) to cling (*v. irr.*) 2. (*affezionarsi*) to become (*v. irr.*) fond of.

attaccatura *sf.* junction: *— della manica*, arm-hole.

attacchino *sm.* bill-poster.

attacco *sm.* 1. (*mil.*) attack 2. (*med.*) fit 3. (*mecc.*) connection || *— elettrico*, connecting plug.

attagliarsi *vr.* to suit.

attanagliare *vt.* to pinch.

attardarsi *vr.* to delay.

attecchire *vi.* 1. to take (*v. irr.*) root 2. (*aver fortuna*) to find (*v. irr.*) favour.

atteggiamento *sm.* attitude.

atteggiarsi *vr.* to assume an attitude: *— a vittima*, to pose as a victim.

attempato *agg.* elderly.

attendente *sm.* orderly.

attèndere *vt.* 1. (*aspettare*) to wait for 2. (*aspettarsi*) to expect 3. (*accudire, frequentare*) to attend.

attendìbile *agg.* reliable.

attenere *vi.* to concern. ♦ attenersi *vr.* 1. to cling (*v. irr.*) (on), (to) 2. (*seguire*) to conform.

attentamente *avv.* 1. attentively 2. (*con cura*) carefully.

attentare *vi.* to attempt. ♦ attentarsi *vr.* to dare.

attentato *sm.* attempt (upon).

attenti *sm.* attention: *stare sull'—*, to stand (*v. irr.*) at attention.

attento *agg.* attentive, careful.

attenuante *agg.* extenuating.

attenuare *vt.* 1. to attenuate 2. (*giur.*) to extenuate.

attenuazione *sf.* 1. attenuation 2. (*di colpa*) extenuation.

attenzione *sf.* 1. attention 2. care: *fate —*, take care 3. (*riguardo*) regard.

atterraggio *sm.* landing.

atterrare *vt.* to knock down. ♦ atterrare *vi.* (*aer.*) to land.

atterrire *vt.* to terrify. ♦ atterrirsi *vr.* to take (*v. irr.*) fright.

attesa *sf.* wait.

attestare *vt.* to attest.

attestato *sm.* 1. certificate 2. (*prova*) proof.

atticciato *agg.* sturdy.

àttico *sm.* attic.

attiguo *agg.* adjoining.

attillarsi *vr.* to spruce oneself up.

attillato *agg.* close-fitting.

àttimo *sm.* moment.

attinente *agg.* pertaining.

attinenza *sf.* relationship.

attìngere *vt.* to draw (*v. irr.*): *— acqua da un pozzo*, to draw water from a well; *— denaro da qu.*, to draw on so. for money.

attirare *vt.* to attract, to draw (*v. irr.*) (*anche fig.*).

attitùdine *sf.* turn, disposition.

attivare *vt.* to make (*v. irr.*) active.

attivista *s.* activist.

attività *sf.* 1. activity 2. (*comm.*) profit: *— e passività*, assets and liabilities.

attivizzare *vt.* to make (*v. irr.*) active.

attivo *agg.* active.

attizzare *vt.* to stir up.

attizzatoio *sm.* poker.

atto[1] *sm.* 1. act 2. (*azione*) action 3. (*fatto*) deed: *un — buono*, a good deed.

atto² *agg.* fit.

attònito *agg.* astonished.

attore *sm.* actor: — *cinematografico*, screen actor.

attorniare *vt.* to surround.

attorno *avv.* e *prep.* about, round, around: *non c'è nessuno* —, there is nobody about; — *alla tavola*, round the table; *le colline* — *al villaggio*, the hills around the village || *darsi d'*—, to busy oneself.

attraccàggio *sm.* mooring.

attraccare *vi.* to moor.

attraente *agg.* charming, attractive.

attrarre *vt.* to attract, to draw (*v. irr.*) (*anche fig.*).

attrattiva *sf.* attraction, appeal.

attraversamento *sm.* crossing.

attraversare *vt.* 1. to cross 2. (*ostacolare*) to thwart.

attraverso *avv.* 1. (*di luogo*) across, through: — *il fiume*, across the river 2. (*di tempo*) through.

attrazione *sf.* attraction, appeal.

attrezzare *vt.* to equip.

attrezzatura *sf.* equipment.

attrezzista *sm.* (*teat.*) property-man.

attrezzo *sm.* tool.

attribuire *vt.* 1. to attribute 2. (*assegnare*) to assign 3. (*addossare*) to put (on).

attributo *sm.* attribute.

attribuzione *sf.* attribution.

attrice *sf.* actress: — *cinematografica*, screen actress.

attrito *sm.* 1. friction 2. (*fig.*) dissension.

attruppamento *sm.* trooping

attrupparsi *vr.* to troop.

attuàbile *agg.* feasible.

attuale *agg.* present.

attualità *sf.* the moment: *cosa d'*—, topical question.

attualmente *avv.* at present.

attuare *vt.* to carry out.

attutire *vt.* to mitigate: — *un rumore*, to deaden a noise.

audace *agg.* bold.

audacia *sf.* boldness.

audiovisivo *agg.* audiovisual.

auditore *sm.* listener.

auditorio *sm.* 1. auditorium 2. (*pubblico*) audience.

audizione *sf.* 1. (*fisiol.*) hearing 2. (*teat.*) performance.

àuge *sm.* summit: *essere in* —, to enjoy great favour.

augurale *agg.* augural.

augurare *vt.* to wish.

augurio *sm.* wish || *auguri di Natale e Capodanno*, season's greetings.

augusto *agg.* august.

àula *sf.* hall, room: — *di scuola*, school-room.

aumentare *vt.* to increase.

aumento *sm.* increase.

àureo *agg.* 1. gold 2. (*dorato*) golden.

aurèola *sf.* halo.

aurìcola *sf.* auricle.

auricolare *agg.* auriculaı.

aurìfero *agg.* auriferous.

aurora *sf.* dawn (*anche fig.*).

auscultare *vt.* to auscultate.

auscultazione *sf.* auscultation.

ausiliare *agg.* auxiliary.

ausilio *sm.* 1. help 2. (*difesa*) defence.

auspicare *vt.* to augur.

auspicio *sm.* 1. (*stor.*) auspice, omen: *di buon*, *cattivo* —, of good, ill omen 2. (*augurio*) wish.

austerità *sf.* austerity.

austero *agg.* austere.

australe *agg.* austral.

australiano *agg.* e *sm.* Australian.

austrìaco *agg.* e *sm.* Austrian.

autarchìa *sf.* autarky.

autenticare *vt.* to certify.

autenticazione *sf.* authentication.

autenticità *sf.* authenticity.

autèntico *agg.* 1. authentic 2. (*genuino*) genuine.

autista *sm.* driver: — *di piazza*, taxi-driver.

àuto *sf.* car: — *da corsa*, racing car; — *aperta*, open car; — *di serie*, production-model car; — *fuori serie*, special-body car.

autoambulanza *sf.* ambulance.

auto-attrezzi *sf.* breakdown-lorry.

autobiografìa *sf.* autobiography.

autobiògrafo *sm.* autobiographer.

autoblinda *sf.* armoured car.

autobotte *sf.* tank truck.

àutobus *sm.* (motor-) bus.

autoclave *sf.* autoclave.

autocontrollo *sm.* self-control.

autòcrate *sm.* autocrat.

autocrazìa *sf.* autocracy.

autocrìtica *sf.* self-criticism.

autòctono *agg.* autochthonous. ◆ **autòctono** *sm.* native.

autodafé *sm.* auto-da-fé (*pl.* autos--da-fé).

autodeterminazione sf. self-determination.

autodidatta s. self-taught person.

autòdromo sm. motor-racing track.

autoeducazione sf. self-education.

autofinanziamento sm. self-financing.

autògeno agg. autogenous.

autogoverno sm. self-government.

autografare vt. to autograph.

autògrafo agg. autographic(al). ♦ **autògrafo** sm. autograph.

autolesione sf. self-injury.

autolesionismo sm. self-injuring.

autolettiga sf. ambulance.

autolìnea sf. bus line.

automa sm. automaton, robot.

automàtico agg. automatic: *pistola, fucile* —, automatic pistol, gun || *distributore* —, slot machine.

automatismo sm. automatism.

automazione sf. automation.

automòbile sf. V. *auto.*

automobilismo sm. motoring.

automobilista sm. motorist.

automotrice sf. rail-car.

autonoleggio sm. car rental.

autonomìa sf. autonomy: — *di volo,* flight range.

autonomismo sm. self-government.

autònomo agg. self-governing.

autoparco sm. car-park.

autopilota sm. automatic pilot.

autopompa sf. fire-engine.

autoposteggio sm. parking.

autopsìa sf. autopsy.

autoradio sf. car radio-set.

autore sm. author.

autorespiratore sm. aqualung.

autorévole agg. authoritative.

autorevolezza sf. authoritativeness.

autorimessa sf. garage.

autorità sf. authority.

autoritario agg. authoritative.

autoritratto sm. self-portrait.

autorizzare vt. 1. (*dare autorità*) to empower 2. (*permettere*) to permit.

autorizzazione sf. permission, consent.

autoscuola sf. driving school.

autostazione sf. filling station.

autostòp sm. hitch-hiking.

autostoppista sm. hitch-hiker.

autostrada sf. motor-way.

autosuggestione sf. auto-suggestion.

autotreno sm. motor-lorry.

autrice sf. authoress.

autunnale agg. autumnal.

autunno sm. autumn.

ava sf. 1. grandmother 2. (*antenata*) ancestress.

avallare vt. to guarantee.

avallo sm. guarantee.

avambraccio sm. forearm.

avamposto sm. outpost.

avanguardia sf. vanguard: *essere all'*—, to be in the van.

avannotto sm. fry.

avanscoperta sf. scouting party: *andare all'*—, to scout.

avanspettàcolo sm. introductory variety turn.

avanti avv. 1. (*di luogo*) forward: *andare* —, to move forward 2. (*a chi bussa*) « come in » 3. (*di tempo*) before || (*di orologio*) fast: *il mio orologio è avanti di 20 minuti,* my watch is twenty minutes fast. ♦ **avanti** prep. before. ♦ **avanti che** cong. before (*con ger.*).

avantieri avv. the day before yesterday.

avanzamento sm. 1. advancing 2. (*progresso*) advancement 3. (*promozione*) promotion.

avanzare vt. 1. to advance 3. (*fig.*) to put (*v. irr.*) forward 3. (*promuovere*) to promote. ♦ **avanzare** vi. to advance. ♦ **avanzarsi** vr. to advance.

avanzata sf. advance.

avanzato agg. 1. advanced 2. (*promosso*) promoted.

avanzo sm. remnant || — *di galera,* jail-bird || — *di stoffa,* scrap of cloth.

avarìa sf. damage.

avariato agg. damaged.

avarizia sf. avarice.

avaro agg. avaricious.

avena sf. oats (*p*).

avere vt. 1. (*general. e come v. ausiliare*) to have: *ho molti libri,* I have many books; *ho letto questo giornale,* I have read this newspaper 2. (*possedere*) to own, to have got: *ha una grande casa,* he owns, has got a big house 3. (*ottenere*) to get (*v. irr.*): *ebbi quell'impiego,* I got that job 4. (*indossare*) to wear (*v. irr.*): *aveva (indosso) un abito rosso,* she was wearing a red dress 5. (*dovere*) to have to: *ho molte cose da fare,*

I have many things to do 6. (*di anni*) to be ... years old: *ho 10 anni*, I am ten years old.

aviatore *sm.* airman (*pl.* -men), pilot.

aviazione *sf.* 1. aviation 2. (*arma*) Air Force.

avicoltura *sf.* bird-rearing.

avidità *sf.* 1. avidity 2. (*ingordigia*) greed 3. (*brama*) eagerness.

àvido *agg.* 1. avid 2. (*ingordo*) greedy 3. (*desideroso*) eager.

aviere *sm.* airman (*pl.* -men).

aviogetto *sm.* jet(-plane).

aviolìnea *sf.* airline.

aviotrasportare *vt.* to air-bear (*v. irr.*).

aviotrasporto *sm.* air-transport.

avitaminosi *sf.* avitaminosis.

avito *agg.* ancestral.

avo *sm.* 1. grandfather 2. (*antenato*) ancestor 3. (*pl.*) forefathers.

avorio *sm.* ivory.

avulso *agg.* uprooted.

avvalersi *vr.* to avail oneself.

avvaloramento *sm.* strengthening.

avvalorare *vt.* 1. to give (*v. irr.*) value to 2. (*rafforzare*) to strengthen.

avvampare *vi.* to flare up (*anche fig.*).

avvantaggiare *vt.* to advantage, to better. ♦ **avvantaggiarsi** *vr.* to profit (by).

avvedersi *vr.* to perceive.

avvedutamente *avv.* shrewdly.

avvedutezza *sf.* shrewdness.

avveduto *agg.* shrewd.

avvelenamento *sm.* poisoning.

avvelenare *vt.* to poison.

avvelenatore *sm.* poisoner.

avvenente *agg.* charming, pretty.

avvenenza *sf.* charm, loveliness.

avvenimento *sm.* event.

avvenire[1] *vi. imp.* to happen.

avvenire[2] *sm.* future.

avventarsi *vr.* to throw (*v. irr.*) oneself.

avventatamente *avv.* rashly.

avventatezza *sf.* rashness.

avventato *agg.* rash.

avventizio *agg.* 1. temporary 2. (*giur.*) adventitious.

avvento *sm.* 1. (*eccl.*) Advent 2. arrival 3. (*assunzione al trono*) accession.

avventore *sm.* customer.

avventura *sf.* adventure.

avventurarsi *vr.* to venture.

avventuriero *sm.* adventurer.

avventuroso *agg.* adventurous.

avverarsi *vr.* to come (*v. irr.*) true.

avverbiale *agg.* adverbial.

avverbio *sm.* adverb.

avversare *vt.* to oppose.

avversario *agg.* contrary. ♦ **avversario** *sm.* opponent.

avversione *sf.* aversion, dislike.

avversità *sf.* adversity, misfortune.

avverso *agg.* unfavourable.

avvertenza *sf.* 1. (*avviso*) warning 2. (*attenzione, cura*) attention, care.

avvertìbile *agg.* perceptible.

avvertimento *sm.* warning.

avvertire *vt.* 1. (*avvisare*) to inform 2. (*mettere in guardia*) to warn 3. (*osservare*) to notice.

avvezzare *vt.* to accustom.

avvezzo *agg.* accustomed, used.

avviamento *sm.* starting.

avviare *vt.* to start.

avvicinamento *sm.* approach.

avvicinare *vt.* to approach. ♦ **avvicinarsi** *vr.* 1. to approach 2. (*essere simile*) to be similar.

avvicendare *vt.* to alternate. ♦ **avvicendarsi** *vr.* to alternate.

avvicendamento *sm.* alternation.

avvilente *agg.* 1. discouraging 2. (*umiliante*) humiliating.

avvilimento *sm.* 1. dejection 2. (*umiliazione*) humiliation.

avvilire *vt.* 1. (*scoraggiare*) to dishearten 2. (*umiliare*) to humiliate. ♦ **avvilirsi** *vr.* 1. to lose heart 2. (*umiliarsi*) to abase oneself.

avvilito *agg.* 1. downcast 2. (*umiliato*) humbled.

avviluppare *vt.* 1. to wrap up 2. (*aggrovigliare*) to entangle. ♦ **avvilupparsi** *vr.* 1. to wrap oneself up 2. (*aggrovigliarsi*) to get (*v. irr.*) entangled.

avvinazzarsi *vr.* to get (*v. irr.*) drunk.

avvinazzato *agg.* tipsy.

avvincente *agg.* engaging.

avvincere *vt.* to enthral.

avvinghiarsi *vr.* to cling (*v. irr.*).

avvìo *sm.* start: *prendere l'—*, to start off.

avvisaglia *sf.* (*primo segno*) foreshadowing.

avvisare *vt.* 1. to inform, to let (*v. irr.*) know 2. (*mettere in guardia*) to warn.

avviso *sm.* 1. notice 2. (*consiglio*) warning 3. (*manifesto*) poster 4.

(*opinione*) opinion.

avvistare *vt.* to sight.

avvitamento *sm.* spin.

avvitare *vt.* 1. (*mecc.*) to screw 2. (*aer.*) to spin.

avviticchiarsi *vr.* to twist round.

avvocato *sm.* 1. lawyer 2. (*civilista*) solicitor.

avvocatura *sf.* legal profession.

avvòlgere *vt.* 1. to wrap (*anche fig.*) 2. (*arrotolare*) to roll up.

avvolgimento *sm.* 1. winding 2. (*di pacchi*) wrapping up 3. (*elettr.*) winding.

avvoltoio *sm.* vulture (*anche fig.*).

azalea *sf.* azalea.

azienda *sf.* firm, concern: — *industriale*, manufacturing concern; — *agricola*, farm.

aziendale *agg.* firm, concern.

àzimut *sm.* azimuth.

azimutale *agg.* azimuthal.

azionamento *sm.* working.

azionare *vt.* to set (*v. irr.*) in action, to work.

azionario *agg.* share: *capitale* —, share capital.

azione *sf.* 1. action 2. (*comm.*) share.

azionista *s.* shareholder.

azotare *vt.* to azotize.

azoto *sm.* azote.

azteco *agg.* e *sm.* Aztec.

azzannare *vt.* to seize in the jaws.

azzardare *vt.* to risk, to venture.

azzardo *sm.* hazard || *gioco d'*—, game of chance.

azzeccare *vt.* to guess, to hit (*v. irr.*) the mark.

àzzimo *agg.* unleavened: *pane* —, unleavened bread.

azzoppare *vt.* to lame. ♦ **azzopparsi** *vr.* to become (*v. irr.*) lame.

azzuffarsi *vr.* to come (*v. irr.*) to blows.

azzurro *agg.* blue.

azzurrògnolo *agg.* bluish.

B

babbeo *sm.* blockhead.

babbo *sm.* father, daddy.

babbuccia *sf.* slipper.

babbuino *sm.* baboon.

babele *sf.* babel.

bacare *vi.* **bacarsi** *vr.* to rot.

bacato *agg.* rotten.

bacca *sf.* berry.

baccalà *sm.* stockfish.

baccanale *sm.* bacchanal.

baccano *sm.* uproar.

baccante *sf.* Bacchante.

baccarà *sm.* baccarat.

baccellierato *sm.* bachelorship.

baccelliere *sm.* bachelor.

baccello *sm.* pod.

bacchetta *sf.* 1. rod 2. (*di direttore d'orchestra*) baton 3. (*di tamburo*) drumstick.

bacchettata *sf.* rod stroke.

bacchettone *sm.* bigot.

bacchiare *vt.* to beat (*v. irr.*) down.

bàcchico *agg.* Bacchic.

bacheca *sf.* show-case.

bachelite *sf.* bakelite.

bacherozzo *sm.* 1. (*scarafaggio*) cockroach 2. (*bruco*) maggot.

bachicoltura *sf.* silkworm breeding.

baciamano *sm.* hand-kissing.

baciapile *sm.* bigot.

baciare *vt.* to kiss. ♦ **baciarsi** *vr. rec.* to kiss each other.

bacile *sm.* basin.

bacillo *sm.* bacillus (*pl.* -li).

bacinella *sf.* basin.

bacino *sm.* 1. basin 2. (*anat.*) pelvis 3. (*mar.*) dock: — *di carenaggio*, dry dock.

bacio *sm.* kiss.

baciucchiare *vt.* to kiss repeatedly.

baco *sm.* worm: — *da seta*, silkworm.

bada *sf.* (*nella loc.*) tenere a — *qu.*, to hold (*v. irr.*) so. at bay.

badare *vi.* to mind (so., sthg.): *senza* — *a spese*, regardless of expense.

badessa *sf.* abbess.

badìa *sf.* abbey.

badilante *sm.* navvy.

badile *sm.* shovel.

baffo *sm.* 1. moustache: *portare i baffi*, to wear (*v. irr.*) a moustache || *ridere sotto i baffi*, to laugh in one's sleeve 2. (*sgorbio*) smear.

bagagliaio *sm.* luggage van.

bagaglio *sm.* luggage (*solo sing.*) || *fare i bagagli*, to pack || *disfare i bagagli*, to unpack.

bagarinaggio *sm.* cornering.

bagattella *sf.* trifle.

baggianata *sf.* 1. (*azione*) foolish action 2. (*discorso*) nonsense.

bagliore *sm.* flash.

bagnante *sm.* bather.

bagnare *vt.* 1. to wet 2. (*immergere*) to dip 3. (*di mare, fiume*) to wash. ♦ **bagnarsi** *vr.* 1. to get (*v. irr.*) wet 2. (*fare bagni in mare ecc.*) to bathe.

bagnato *agg.* wet.

bagnino *sm.* bathing attendant.

bagno *sm.* 1. bath: *far un —*, to take (*v. irr.*) a bath; *— di sole*, sun-bath 2. (*in mare ecc.*) bathe || *fare il —*, to bathe || *costume da —*, bathing-costume.

bagnomaria *sm.* bain-marie.

bagordo *sm.* revelry.

baia¹ *sf.* (*scherzo*) joke || *dare la — a qu.*, to make (*v. irr.*) fun of so.

baia² *sf.* (*geogr.*) bay.

baionetta *sf.* bayonet.

bàita *sf.* Alpine hut.

balaustrata *sf.* balustrade.

balbettare *vt.* e *vi.* to stammer.

balbettìo *sm.* stammer.

balbuzie *sf.* stammer.

balbuziente *agg.* stammering. ♦ **balbuziente** *s.* stammerer.

balconata *sf.* balcony.

balcone *sm.* balcony.

baldacchino *sm.* canopy.

baldanza *sf.* boldness.

baldanzoso *agg.* bold.

baldo *agg.* bold.

baldoria *sf.* revel: *far —*, to make (*v. irr.*) merry.

balena *sf.* whale: *stecca di —*, whalebone.

balenare *vi.* 1. to lighten 2. (*di idea*) to flash.

baleno *sm.* lightning || *in un —*, in the twinkling of an eye.

balestra *sf.* 1. crossbow 2. (*mecc.*) leaf spring.

balia *sf.* wet nurse: *— asciutta*, dry-nurse.

balìa *sf.* mercy: *in — di*, at the mercy of.

balìstica *sf.* ballistics.

balla *sf.* 1. (*di cotone, di lana*) bale 2. (*volg.; fandonia*) tall story 3. (*fig.; mucchio*) heap.

ballare *vt.* e *vi.* to dance.

ballata *sf.* ballad.

ballatoio *sm.* gallery.

ballerina *sf.* 1. dancer 2. (*classica*) ballerina.

ballerino *sm.* 1. dancer 2. (*classico*) ballet-dancer.

balletto *sm.* ballet.

ballo *sm.* 1. dance 2. (*festa*) ball || *essere in —*, to be on the go; *tirare in —*, to call in question.

ballottaggio *sm.* second ballot.

balneare *agg.* bathing || *stazione —*, seaside resort.

balocco *sm.* toy.

balordàggine *sf.* 1. dullness 2. (*azione*) foolish action 3. (*discorso*) nonsense.

balordo *agg.* e *sm.* stupid.

balsàmico *agg.* balmy.

bàlsamo *sm.* balm.

baluardo *sm.* bulwark.

balza *sf.* 1. cliff 2. (*di vestito*) flounce.

balzano *agg.* 1. queer 2. (*di cavallo*) white-footed.

balzare *vi.* to jump.

balzo *sm.* jump: *cogliere la palla al —*, to seize an opportunity.

bambagia *sf.* cotton-wool.

bambina *sf.* 1. little girl, child (*pl.* children) 2. (*in fasce*) baby.

bambinaia *sf.* nurse.

bambino *sm.* 1. little boy, child (*pl.* children) 2. (*in fasce*) baby || *dare alla luce un —*, to bring (*v. irr.*) forth a child.

bamboccio *sm.* 1. (*bambola*) rag-doll 2. (*fig.*) simpleton.

bàmbola *sf.* doll.

bambù *sm.* bamboo.

banale *agg.* banal.

banalità *sf.* banality.

banana *sf.* banana.

banano *sm.* banana-tree.

banca *sf.* bank.

bancarella *sf.* stall.

bancario *agg.* bank: *libretto —*, passbook. ♦ **bancario** *sm.* bank clerk.

bancarotta *sf.* bankruptcy: *fare —*, to go (*v. irr.*) bankrupt.

banchetto *sm.* banquet.

banchiere *sm.* banker.

banchina *sf.* 1. (*molo*) wharf 2. (*terrapieno*) bank.

banchisa *sf.* ice-pack.

banco *sm.* 1. bench 2. (*di chiesa*) pew 3. (*di negozio*) counter 4. (*di nebbia, di sabbia, di gioco*) bank.

banconota *sf.* banknote.

banda *sf.* 1. (*lato*) side 2. (*mus.; striscia di stoffa*) band 3. (*di delinquenti*) gang.

banderuola *sf.* weathercock.

bandiera *sf.* flag, colours (*pl.*).

bandire *vt.* 1. to proclaim 2. (*esi-*

liare, eliminare) to banish.
bandito *sm.* outlaw.
bando *sm.* 1. ban 2. (*esilio*) banishment || *essere al* —, to be banished 3. (*annunzio*) announcement.
bar *sm.* bar.
bara *sf.* coffin.
baracca *sf.* hut.
baraccone *sm.* booth.
baraonda *sf.* chaos.
barare *vi.* to cheat.
bàratro *sm.* abyss.
barattare *vt.* to exchange.
baratto *sm.* barter.
baràttolo *sm.* 1. jar 2. (*di metallo*) tin.
barba *sf.* beard: *fare, farsi la* —, to shave || (*fig.*) *in* — *a*, in spite of.
barbabiètola *sf.* beet-root.
barbarie *sf.* 1. barbarousness 2. (*crudeltà*) barbarity.
bàrbaro *agg. e sm.* barbarian.
barbiere *sm.* barber.
barbone *sm.* 1. (*straccione*) tramp 2. (*cane*) poodle.
barbuto *agg.* bearded.
barca *sf.* boat: *andare in* —, to go (*v. irr.*) boating.
barcaiolo *sm.* boatman (*pl.* -men).
barcamenarsi *vr.* to wangle.
barcollare *vi.* to stagger.
barcone *sm.* long boat.
bardare *vt.* to harness. ◆ **bardarsi** *vr.* to dress up.
barella *sf.* stretcher.
barile *sm.* barrel.
barista *sm.* barman (*pl.* -men). ◆ **barista** *sf.* barmaid.
baritonale *agg.* baritone.
barìtono *sm.* baritone.
barlume *sm.* glimmer.
baro *sm.* cheat.
barocco *agg. e sm.* baroque.
baromètrico *agg.* barometric(al).
baròmetro *sm.* barometer.
barone *sm.* baron.
baronessa *sf.* baroness.
barra *sf.* 1. bar 2. (*mar.*) helm.
barricare *vt.* to barricade.
barricata *sf.* barricade.
barriera *sf.* 1. barrier 2. (*fig.*) obstacle.
barrire *vi.* to trumpet.
barrito *sm.* trumpet.
barroccio *sm.* cart.
baruffa *sf.* quarrel.
barzelletta *sf.* joke.
basalto *sm.* basalt.

basamento *sm.* base.
basare *vt.* to base.
basco *agg. e sm.* Basque. ◆ **basco** *sm.* (*berretto*) beret.
base *sf.* base.
basette *sf. pl.* whiskers.
bàsico *agg.* basic.
basilare *agg.* basic.
basìlica *sf.* basilica.
basìlico *sm.* basil.
basilisco *sm.* basilisk.
bassezza *sf.* baseness.
basso *agg.* 1. low 2. (*di statura*) short 3. (*abietto*) base. ◆ **basso** *avv.* low. ◆ **basso** *sm.* 1. bottom 2. (*mus.*) bass.
bassofondo *sm.* shallow || *i bassifondi della società*, the underworld.
bassopiano *sm.* lowland.
bassorilievo *sm.* bas-relief.
bassotto *agg.* thick-set. ◆ **bassotto** *sm.* (*cane*) dachshund.
bassoventre *sm.* belly.
basta *inter.* stop it!: — *con*, enough of.
bastardo *agg. e sm.* 1. bastard 2. (*di animali*) mongrel.
bastare *vi.* to be enough.
bastimento *sm.* ship.
bastione *sm.* 1. rampart 2. (*mil.*) bastion.
basto *sm.* pack-saddle.
bastonare *vt.* to cane.
bastonata *sf.* blow with a cane.
bastonatura *sf.* caning.
bastone *sm.* stick, staff.
batacchio *sm.* clapper.
batisfera *sf.* bathysphere.
batista *sf.* batiste.
batosta *sf.* blow.
batrace *sm.* batrachian.
battaglia *sf.* battle, fight || (*fig.*) *cavallo di* —, favourite subject, favourite piece.
battagliare *vi.* to battle, to fight (*v. irr.*), to struggle.
battagliero *agg.* 1. warlike 2. (*fig.*) fierce.
battaglione *sm.* battalion.
battelliere *sm.* boatman (*pl.* -men).
battello *sm.* boat.
battente *sm.* 1. (*picchiotto*) knocker 2. (*di porta*) wing.
bàttere *vt.* 1. to beat (*v. irr.*), to strike (*v. irr.*) (*anche delle ore*) 2. (*scrivere a macchina*) to type || — *le mani*, to clap hands; — *i piedi*, to stamp; *in un batter d'oc-*

chio, in the twinkling of an eye.
♦ **bàttere** *vi.* 1. to knock 2.
(*pulsare*) to throb. ♦ **bàttersi**
vr. to fight (*v. irr.*).
batterìa *sf.* 1. battery 2. (*da cucina*) kitchen utensils.
batterìo *sm.* bacterium (*pl. -ia*).
batteriologìa *sf.* bacteriology.
battésimo *sm.* baptism: *nome di —*, Christian name.
battezzare *vt.* to baptize.
battibaleno *sm.* (*nella loc. avv.*) *in un —*, in a twinkling.
battibecco *sm.* squabble.
batticuore *sm.* 1. throb 2 (*fig.*) fear.
battimano *sm.* clap.
battipanni *sm.* carpet-beater.
battistero *sm.* baptistery.
battistrada *sm.* 1. outrider 2. (*di pneumatico*) tread || *fare da —*, to lead (*v. irr.*) the way.
bàttito *sm.* 1. beat 2. (*mecc.*) knock.
battitore *sm.* 1. beater 2. (*cricket, baseball*) batsman (*pl. -men*).
battitura *sf.* thrashing.
battuta *sf.* 1. beating: *— di caccia*, beating 2. (*di spirito*) witty remark 3. (*mus.*) bar 4. (*teat.*) cue 5. (*tennis*) service.
batùffolo *sm.* flock.
baule *sm.* trunk.
bauxite *sf.* bauxite.
bava *sf.* 1. slaver 2. (*di lumaca*) slime.
bavaglino *sm.* bib.
bavaglio *sm.* gag: *mettere il — a qu.* (*fig.*), to gag so.
bàvero *sm.* collar.
bazàr *sm.* bazaar.
bazza *sf.* slipper-chin.
bazzècola *sf.* trifle.
bazzicare *vt.* e *vi.* to frequent.
bazzotto *agg.* soft-boiled.
be' *inter.* well.
beare *vt.* to make (*v. irr.*) so. happy.
♦ **bearsi** *vr.* to rejoice (at).
beatificazione *sf.* beatification.
beatitùdine *sf.* beatitude.
beato *agg.* 1. happy 2. (*relig.*) blessed.
beccaccia *sf.* woodcock.
beccaccino *sm.* snipe.
beccare *vt.* 1. to peck 2. (*fam. per acchiappare*) to catch (*v. irr.*). ♦
beccarsi *vr.* 1. (*procurarsi*) to get (*v. irr.*) 2. (*litigare*) to quarrel.
beccata *sf.* peck.

beccheggiare *vi.* to pitch.
beccheggio *sm.* pitching.
becchime *sm.* birdseed.
becchino *sm.* grave-digger.
becco *sm.* 1. beak 2. (*caprone*) billy-goat 3. (*fig.*) cuckold.
beccuccio *sm.* (*di teiera ecc.*) spout.
beduino *agg.* e *sm.* Bedouin.
befana *sf.* 1. "befana" 2. (*fig. fam.*) hag.
beffa *sf.* mockery: *farsi — di*, to laugh at; (*ingannare*) to make (*v. irr.*) a fool of.
beffardo *agg.* mocking. ♦ **beffardo** *sm.* mocker.
beffare *vt.* to mock. ♦ **beffarsi** *vr.* to laugh at.
beffeggiare *vt.* V. *beffare*.
bega *sf.* 1. quarrel 2. (*problema intricato*) entangled affair.
beghina *sf.* bigot.
begonia *sf.* (*bot.*) begonia.
belare *vi.* to bleat.
belato *sm.* bleat.
belga *agg.* e *sm.* Belgian.
bella *sf.* 1. beauty 2. (*innamorata*) sweetheart || *copiare in —*, to make (*v. irr.*) a fair copy.
belladonna *sf.* (*bot.; farm.*) belladonna.
belletto *sm.* rouge.
bellezza *sf.* beauty: *istituto di —*, beauty parlour.
bellicismo *sm.* warlikeness.
bèllico *agg.* 1. war (*attributivo*) 2. (*del tempo di guerra*) wartime.
bellicoso *agg.* warlike.
belligerante *agg.* e *sm.* belligerent.
belligeranza *sf.* belligerence.
bellimbusto *sm.* dandy.
bello *agg.* 1. fine, beautiful 2. (*di uomo*) handsome || *nel bel mezzo*, right in the middle. ♦ **bello** *sm.* 1. (*la bellezza*) beauty 2. (*innamorato*) sweetheart || *sul più —*, at the right moment; *ora viene il —*, now you'll hear the best of it.
belva *sf.* wild beast.
belvedere *sm.* 1. observation post 2. (*arch.*) belvedere.
bemolle *sm.* (*mus.*) flat.
benché *cong.* though.
benda *sf.* bandage.
bendaggio *sm.* bandage.
bendare *vt.* to bandage.
bene *sm.* good: *per il tuo —*, for your sake; *voler —*, to love. ♦

beni *sm. pl.* property || *— immobili*, real estate; *— di consumo*, consumer goods. ✦ **bene** *avv.* **1.** well **2.** (*molto*) very **3.** (*nientemeno*) no less than || *star —*, to be well; *andar —*, to suit.

benedetto *agg.* blessed.

benedire *vt.* to bless.

benedizione *sf.* blessing.

benefattore *sm.* benefactor.

beneficare *vt.* to help.

beneficenza *sf.* charity.

beneficiario *agg. e sm.* beneficiary.

beneficiata *sf.* benefit.

beneficio *sm.* **1.** benefit **2.** (*eccl.; giur.*) benefice.

benèfico *agg.* **1.** beneficent **2.** (*vantaggioso*) beneficial.

benemerenza *sf.* merit.

benemèrito *agg.* well-deserving.

beneplàcito *sm.* consent: *a tuo —*, as you like.

benèssere *sm.* welfare.

benestante *agg.* well-off. ✦ **benestante** *s.* well-to-do person.

benestare *sm.* assent.

benevolenza *sf.* benevolence.

benèvolo *agg.* benevolent.

bengala *sm.* Bengal light.

beniamino *sm.* darling.

benignità *sf.* **1.** benignity **2.** (*di clima*) mildness.

benigno *agg.* **1.** benign **2.** (*di clima*) mild.

beninteso *avv.* of course.

benpensante *agg.* sensible || *i benpensanti*, the right thinking.

benservito *sm.* testimonial.

bensì *cong.* but.

benvenuto *agg. sm. inter.* welcome || *dare il — a qu.*, to welcome so.

benvolere *vt.* to like: *farsi —*, to make (*v. irr.*) oneself liked.

benzina *sf.* petrol.

benzinaio *sm.* filling station attendant.

benzolo *sm.* benzol.

beone *sm.* drunkard.

beota *agg. e sm.* Bœotian.

bèrbero *agg. e sm.* Berber.

berciare *vi.* to bawl.

bere *vt.* to drink (*v. irr.*) || *darla a — (fig.)*, to tell (*v. irr.*) tall stories.

bergamotto *sm.* (*bot.; farm.*) bergamot.

berillo *sm.* beryllium.

berlina *sf.* **1.** (*carrozza*) berline **2.** (*automobile*) limousine **3.** (*gogna*) pillory: *mettere alla —*, to pillory.

bernòccolo *sm.* bump.

berretta *sf.* cap.

berretto *sm.* cap.: *— con visiera*, peaked cap.

bersagliare *vt.* **1.** to shoot (*v. irr.*) (at) **2.** (*fig.*) to torment.

bersaglio *sm.* target: *tiro al —*, target-shooting || *colpire il —*, to hit (*v. irr.*) the mark.

besciamella *sf.* cream-sauce.

bestemmia *sf.* swear.

bestemmiare *vi.* to swear (*v. irr.*).

bestia *sf.* beast || *montare in —*, to lose (*v. irr.*) one's temper.

bestiale *agg.* beastly.

bestialità *sf.* **1.** beastliness **2.** (*fig.*) foolishness || *dire —*, to talk nonsense; *fare —*, to make (*v. irr.*) blunders.

bestiame *sm.* cattle.

béttola *sf.* tavern.

betulla *sf.* birch.

bevanda *sf.* drink.

beveraggio *sm.* beverage.

bevitore *sm.* drinker.

bevuta *sf.* **1.** draught **2.** (*il bere*) drinking.

biada *sf.* fodder.

biancastro *agg.* whitish.

biancheggiare *vi. e vt.* **1.** (*essere bianco*) to be white **2.** (*diventare, far diventare bianco*) to whiten.

biancheria *sf.* linen.

bianco *agg.* white || *in —*, blank; *di punto in —*, suddenly.

biancore *sm.* whiteness.

biancospino *sm.* hawthorn.

biascicare *vt.* to mumble.

biasimare *vt.* to blame.

biasimévole *agg.* blamable.

biàsimo *sm.* blame.

Bibbia *sf.* Bible.

bìbita *sf.* drink.

bìblico *agg.* biblical.

bibliografia *sf.* bibliography.

bibliogràfico *agg.* bibliographic(al).

biblioteca *sf.* **1.** library **2.** (*scaffale*) bookcase.

bibliotecario *sm.* librarian.

bica *sf.* stack.

bicamerale *agg.* (*pol.*) bicameral.

bicarbonato *sm.* bicarbonate.

bicchiere *sm.* glass.

bicèfalo *agg.* V. *bicipite*.

bicicletta *sf.* bicycle: *andare in —*, to cycle.

bicìpite *agg.* two-headed. ✦ **bicìpite** *sm.* biceps.

bicocca *sf.* hut.
bicolore *agg.* two-coloured.
bidè *sm.* bidet.
bidello *sm.* porter.
bidente *sm.* pitchfork.
bidone *sm.* 1. can 2. (*fam.*) swindle.
bieco *agg.* sinister.
biella *sf.* (*mecc.*) connecting rod.
biennale *agg.* biennial.
biètola *sf.* beet.
biennio *sm.* biennium (*pl.* -nia).
bifase *agg.* (*elettr.*) two-phase.
bifolco *sm.* boor.
biforcarsi *vr.* to fork.
biforcazione *sf.* fork.
biforcuto *agg.* forked.
bigamìa *sf.* bigamy.
bìgamo *agg.* bigamous. ◆ **bìgamo** *sm.* bigamist.
bighellonare *vi.* to lounge.
bighellone *sm.* lounger.
bigio *agg.* grey.
bigiotterìa *sf.* trinkets (*pl.*).
biglia *sf.* (biliard-)ball.
bigliettaio *sm.* 1. conductor 2. (*di stazione*) booking-clerk.
biglietterìa *sf.* 1. booking-office 2. (*di teatro*) box-office.
biglietto *sm.* 1. card: — *di visita*, visiting card 2. (*di tram ecc.*) ticket: — *di andata e ritorno*, return ticket; *mezzo* —, half-fare ticket 3. (*banconota*) bank-note.
bigodino *sm.* (hair-)curler.
bigotto *agg.* bigoted. ◆ **bigotto** *sm.* bigot.
bikini *sm.* bikini.
bilancia *sf.* balance, scales (*pl.*).
bilanciare *vt.* to balance.
bilanciere *sm.* 1. balance-wheel 2. (*mar.*) outrigger.
bilancio *sm.* budget: *fare il* —, to strike (*v. irr.*) the balance.
bilaterale *agg.* bilateral.
bile *sf.* 1. bile 2. (*ira*) anger.
biliardo *sm.* billiards (*pl.*).
bilico *sm.* 1. balance 2. (*fig.*) uncertainty || *mettere in* —, to balance; *stare in* —, to be balanced.
bilingue *agg.* bilingual.
bilione *sm.* billion.
bilioso *agg.* bilious.
bimba *sf.* V. *bambina.*
bimbo *sm.* V. *bambino.*
bimensile *agg.* fortnightly.
bimestrale *agg.* bimestrial.
bimestre *sm.* (period of) two months.

bimotore *agg.* two-engined: *aereo* —, two-engined plane.
binario *sm.* track: — *morto*, dead-end track.
binòcolo *sm.* binoculars (*pl.*).
binomio *sm.* binomial.
biòccolo *sm.* flock: — *di neve*, snow-flake.
biochìmica *sf.* biochemistry.
biofìsica *sf.* biophysics.
biografìa *sf.* biography.
biogràfico *agg.* biographic(al).
biògrafo *sm.* biographer.
biologìa *sf.* biology.
biològico *agg.* biologic(al).
biòlogo *sm.* biologist.
biondo *agg.* fair.
biosfera *sf.* biosphere.
biòssido *sm.* dioxide.
bipartizione *sf.* bipartition
bipede *agg.* e *sm.* biped.
biplano *sm.* biplane.
bipolare *agg.* bipolar.
birba *sf.* scapegrace.
birbante *s.* rogue.
birbonata *sf.* knavery.
birbone *sm.* rogue.
bireattore *sm.* two-engined jet.
birichino *sm.* urchin. ◆ **birichino** *agg.* naughty.
birillo *sm.* skittle.
biro *sf.* ball-point pen.
biroccio *sm.* cart.
birra *sf.* beer.
birrerìa *sf.* 1. beer-house 2. (*fabbrica*) brewery.
bisaccia *sf.* packsack.
bisbètico *agg.* cantankerous.
bisbigliare *vt.* to whisper.
bisbiglio *sm.* whisper.
bisboccia *sf.* spree: *far* —, to revel.
bisca *sf.* gambling-house.
biscia *sf.* snake.
biscotto *sm.* biscuit.
bisessuale *agg.* bisexual.
bisestile *agg.* *anno* —, leap year.
bisettimanale *agg.* bi-weekly.
bisettrice *sf.* bisector.
bisillabo *agg.* disyllabic. ◆ **bisillabo** *sm.* disyllable.
bislacco *agg.* odd.
bislungo *agg.* oblong.
bismuto *sm.* bismuth.
bisnipote *s.* great-grandchild (*pl.* -children).
bisnonna *sf.* great-grandmother.
bisognare *vi. imp.* to be necessary, must.
bisnonno *sm.* great-grandfather.

bisogno *sm.* 1. need 2. (*povertà*) necessity || *aver —,* to need.

bisognoso *agg.* needy.

bisonte *sm.* bison.

bissare *vt.* to give (*v. irr.*) an encore (of sthg.).

bistecca *sf.* beefsteak.

bisticciare *vi.* to squabble.

bisticcio *sm.* 1. squabble 2. (*gioco di parole*) pun.

bistrattare *vt.* to ill-treat.

bistro *sm.* bistre.

bisturi *sm.* lancet.

bitòrzolo *sm.* bump.

bitume *sm.* bitumen.

bivacco *sm.* bivouac.

bivalente *agg.* bivalent.

bivio *sm.* 1. fork 2. (*fig.*) alternative.

bizantino *agg.* e *sm.* Byzantine.

bizza *sf.* freak || *fare le bizze,* to be peevish.

bizzarria *sf.* 1. peculiarity 2. (*cosa*) curiosity 3. (*atto, detto*) extravagance.

bizzarro *agg.* strange.

bizzoso *agg.* 1. freakish 2. (*irascibile*) irascible.

blandire *vt.* to soothe.

blandizia *sf.* blandishment.

blando *agg.* bland.

blasone *sm.* 1. blazon 2. (*nobiltà*) nobility.

blaterare *vi.* e *vt.* to prate.

bleso *agg.* lisping || *pronuncia blesa,* lisp. ♦ **bleso** *sm.* lisper.

blindare *vt.* (*mil.*) to armour.

bloccare *vt.* to block, to stop. ♦ **bloccarsi** *vr.* to jam.

blocco *sm.* 1. block 2. (*mil.*) blockade.

blu *agg.* e *sm.* blue.

bluff *sm.* bluff.

blusa *sf.* blouse.

boa¹ *sf.* (*mar.*) buoy.

boa² *sm.* (*zool.*) boa.

bobina *sf.* bobbin.

bocca *sf.* mouth: *— da incendio,* fire-plug; *— dello stomaco,* pit of the stomach; *chiudere la — a qu.,* to silence so.

boccaccia *sf.* grimace.

boccale *sm.* jug.

boccaporto *sm.* hatchway.

boccata *sf.* mouthful.

boccheggiare *vi.* to gasp.

bocchino *sm.* mouthpiece.

boccia *sf.* 1. water-bottle 2. (*sport*) bowl.

bocciare *vt.* 1. (*respingere*) to reject 2. (*agli esami*) to fail.

bocciatura *sf.* failure.

boccio *sm.* bud.

boccone *sm.* 1. bit 2. (*boccata*) mouthful 3. (*esca*) bait.

bocconi *avv.* lying face downwards.

boia *sm.* executioner.

boicottare *vt.* to boycott.

bolgia *sf.* 1. (*fig.*) bedlam 2. (*di inferno*) pit.

bòlide *sm.* (*astr.*) bolide.

bolla *sf.* 1. bubble 2. (*vescica*) blister 3. (*eccl.*) bull.

bollare *vt.* 1. (*timbrare*) to stamp 2. (*a fuoco e fig.*) to brand.

bollato *agg.* 1. stamped: *carta bollata,* stamped paper 2. (*a fuoco e fig.*) branded.

bollente *agg.* boiling.

bolletta *sf.* 1. bill 2. (*ricevuta*) receipt || *essere in —* (*fig.*), to be (*v. irr.*) penniless.

bollettario *sm.* counterfoil-book.

bollettino *sm.* 1. bulletin 2. (*comm.*) list, note.

bollire *vi.* e *vt.* to boil.

bollito *sm.* boiled meat.

bollitore *sm.* 1. boiler 2. (*bricco*) kettle.

bollitura *sf.* boiling.

bollo *sm.* stamp.

bollore *sm.* 1. boil 2. (*fig.*) excitement.

bolscevico *agg.* e *sm.* Bolshevist.

bolscevismo *sm.* Bolshevism.

boma *sm.* (*mar.*) boom.

bomba *sf.* bomb.

bombardamento *sm.* bombardment.

bombardare *vt.* to bombard; (*generalmente da aereo*) to bomb.

bombardiere *sm.* 1. (*soldato*) bombardier 2. (*aereo*) bomber.

bombetta *sf.* bowler.

bòmbola *sf.* bottle.

bomboniera *sf.* candy-box.

bonaccia *sf.* dead calm.

bonaccione *agg.* good-natured. ♦ **bonaccione** *sm.* good-natured man (*pl.* men).

bonarietà *sf.* good nature.

bonario *agg.* good-natured, friendly.

bonìfica *sf.* reclamation.

bonificare *vt.* 1. to reclaim 2. (*comm.*) to grant an allowance.

bonomìa *sf.* good nature.

bontà *sf.* goodness.

bonzo *sm.* bonze.

borbottare *vi.* e *vt.* 1. to mumble

2. (*lamentarsi*) to grumble.

borbottìo *sm.* **1.** mumbling **2.** (*protesta*) grumbling.

bordare *vt.* to border.

bordeggiare *vi.* to tack.

bordello *sm.* bawdyhouse.

bordo *sm.* **1.** edge **2.** (*mar.*) board: *a —*, on board.

bordura *sf.* border.

bòrea *sf.* Boreas.

boreale *agg.* boreal: *aurora —*, aurora borealis.

borgata *sf.* village.

borghese *agg.* **1.** middle-class **2.** (*comune*) plain **3.** (*civile*) civilian: *in —*, in civilian dress. ♦ **borghese** *s.* middle-class person.

borghesìa *sf.* middle class(es): *l'alta —*, the upper middle class(es); *la piccola —*, the lower middle class(es).

borgo *sm.* village.

borgomastro *sm.* burgomaster.

boria *sf.* arrogance.

bòrico *agg.* boric.

borioso *agg.* arrogant.

borotalco *sm.* talcum powder.

borraccia *sf.* flask.

borsa[1] *sf.* bag || *— per documenti*, brief case; *— di studio*, scholarship.

borsa[2] *sf.* (*comm.*) Stock Exchange.

borsaiolo *sm.* pickpocket.

borseggiare *vt.* to pick pockets.

borsellino *sm.* purse.

borsetta *sf.* (hand-)bag.

boscaglia *sf.* brushwood.

boscaiolo *sm.* woodman (*pl.* -men).

boschetto *sm.* grove.

bosco *sm.* wood.

boscoso *agg.* woody.

bòssolo *sm.* cartridge-case.

botànica *sf.* botany.

bòtola *sf.* trap-door.

botta *sf.* **1.** blow **2.** (*battuta*) sarcastic remark || *dare un sacco di botte a qu.*, to whack so.

botte *sf.* barrel.

bottega *sf.* shop.

bottegaio *sm.* shop-keeper.

bottiglia *sf.* bottle.

bottiglierìa *sf.* wine shop.

bottino *sm.* booty: *far —*, to plunder.

botto *sm.* blow || *di —*, suddenly.

bottone *sm.* button || *attaccare un —* (*fig.*), to buttonhole.

bovaro *sm.* cowherd.

bovini *sm. pl.* cattle (*sing.*).

bozza *sf.* **1.** (*gonfiore*) swelling **2.** (*tip.*) proof **3.** (*abbozzo*) draft || *correggere le bozze*, to proofread.

bozzetto *sm.* sketch.

bòzzolo *sm.* cocoon.

braccare *vt.* to hunt.

braccetto (*nella loc. avv.*) *a —*, arm-in-arm.

bracciale *sm.* **1.** (*fascia che si porta al braccio*) arm-band **2.** (*braccialetto*) bracelet.

braccialetto *sm.* bracelet.

bracciante *sm.* labourer.

bracciata *sf.* **1.** armful **2.** (*di nuoto*) stroke.

braccio *sm.* arm: *essere in — a qu.*, to be in so.'s arms || *— di mare*, sound.

bracco *sm.* hound.

bracconaggio *sm.* poaching.

bracconiere *sm.* poacher.

brace *sf.* embers (*pl.*).

brache *sf. pl.* **1.** trousers **2.** (*mutande*) drawers.

brachicèfalo *agg.* brachycephalous.

braciere *sm.* brazier.

braciola *sf.* chop.

bradicardìa *sf.* (*med.*) bradycardia.

brado *agg.* wild.

brama *sf.* longing.

bramare *vt.* to long for (sthg.).

bramosìa *sf.* covetousness.

bramoso *agg.* eager for (sthg.).

branca *sf.* **1.** claw **2.** (*settore*) branch.

branchia *sf.* gill.

branco *sm.* **1.** herd **2.** (*di pecore*) flock **3.** (*di pesci*) shoal **4.** (*di lupi e fig.*) pack.

brancolare *vi.* to grope.

branda *sf.* **1.** camp-bed **2.** (*mar.*) bunk.

brandello *sm.* **1.** rag **2.** (*pezzetto*) bit || *coi vestiti a brandelli*, in rags; *fare a brandelli*, to tear (*v. irr.*) up.

brandire *vt.* to brandish.

brano *sm.* piece.

brasato *sm.* braised beef.

brasiliano *agg. e sm.* Brazilian.

bravata *sf.* bravado.

bravo *agg.* clever, good || *—!*, well done!; *su, da —!*, be a good boy!

bravura *sf.* **1.** cleverness **2.** (*coraggio*) bravery || (*mus.*) *pezzo di —*, bravura.

breccia *sf.* breach: *essere sulla —*, to stand (*v. irr.*) in the breach.

brefotrofio *sm.* foundling hospital.

bretella *sf.* brace.
breve *agg.* short.
brevettare *vt.* to patent.
brevetto *sm.* patent.
breviario *sm.* breviary.
brevità *sf.* brevity.
brezza *sf.* breeze.
bricco *sm.* kettle, pot.
bricconata *sf.* roguish trick.
briccone *sm.* rogue.
briciola *sf.* crumb.
briciolo *sm.* bit.
briga *sf.* 1. trouble 2. (*lite*) quarrel: *attaccar* —, to pick a quarrel.
brigadiere *sm.* 1. « brigadiere » 2. (*uficiale nell'Esercito Britannico assegnato al comando di brigata*) brigadier.
brigante *sm.* robber.
brigantino *sm.* (*mar.*) brig.
brigare *vi.* to intrigue.
brigata *sf.* 1. party 2. (*mil.*) brigade.
briglia *sf.* bridle || *a — sciolta*, at full gallop.
brillante *agg.* e *sm.* brilliant.
brillantina *sf.* brilliantine.
brillare *vi.* to shine (*v. irr.*). ◆ **brillare** *vt.* 1. (*riso ecc.*) to hull 2. (*una mina*) to blast.
brillo *agg.* tipsy.
brina *sf.* hoarfrost.
brinare *vi. imp.*: *ha brinato*, there has been a frost.
brinata *sf.* hoarfrost.
brindare *vi.* to toast: — *a qu.*, to toast so.
brindello *sm.* rag.
brindisi *sm.* toast.
brio *sm.* liveliness.
brioso *agg.* lively.
britannico *agg.* British.
brivido *sm.* 1. shiver 2. (*di paura, orrore*) shudder.
brizzolato *agg.* grizzled.
brocca *sf.* jug.
broccato *sm.* brocade.
bròccolo *sm.* broccoli.
brodaglia *sf.* slops (*pl.*).
brodo *sm.* broth.
broglio *sm.* intrigue: — *elettorale*, gerry-mander.
bromo *sm.* bromine.
bromuro *sm.* bromide.
bronchiale *agg.* bronchial.
bronchite *sf.* bronchitis.
broncio *sm.* pout || *fare il* —, to pout.
bronco *sm.* bronchus (*pl.* -chi).

broncopolmonite *sf.* bronchopneumonia.
brontolare *vi.* e *vt.* to grumble.
brontolìo *sm.* grumbling.
brontolone *sm.* grumbler.
brontosàuro *sm.* brontosaurus.
brònzeo *agg.* 1. bronze (*attributivo*) 2. (*simile a bronzo*) bronzy.
bronzo *sm.* bronze || *faccia di* —, brazen-faced person.
brossura *sf.* paper-back binding || *in* —, paper-bound.
brucare *vt.* to browse (on).
bruciacchiare *vt.* to scorch.
bruciacchiatura *sf.* scorching.
bruciapelo (*nella loc. avv.*) *a* —, point-blank.
bruciare *vt.* e *vi.* to burn (*v. irr.*).
bruciatore *sm.* burner.
bruciatura *sf.* burn.
bruciore *sm.* burning, smart (*anche fig.*).
bruco *sm.* caterpillar.
brùffolo *sm.* pimple.
brughiera *sf.* heath.
brulicare *vi.* to swarm (with).
brulichìo *sm.* swarm.
brullo *agg.* bare.
bruma *sf.* mist.
brumoso *agg.* misty.
brunire *vt.* to burnish.
brunitura *sf.* burnishing.
bruno *agg.* brown.
bruscamente *avv.* roughly.
brusco *agg.* 1. rough 2. (*di sapore*) sour.
brusìo *sm.* buzz.
brutale *agg.* brutal.
brutalità *sf.* brutality.
bruto *agg.* e *sm.* brute.
bruttezza *sf.* ugliness.
brutto *agg.* 1. ugly 2. (*cattivo*) bad.
bruttura *sf.* 1. ugly thing 2. (*azione*) base action.
bùbbola *sf.* lie.
bubbone *sm.* bubo.
bubbònico *agg.* bubonic.
buca *sf.* hole: — *delle lettere*, letter-box.
bucaneve *sm.* snowdrop.
bucaniere *sm.* buccaneer.
bucare *vt.* 1. to pierce 2. (*una gomma*) to puncture 3. (*biglietti*) to punch.
bucato *sm.* 1. washing 2. (*i panni*) laundry.
buccia *sf.* peel.
bucherellare *vt.* to riddle.

buco *sm.* hole.
bucòlico *agg.* bucolic.
buddismo *sm.* Buddhism.
buddista *s.* Buddhist.
budello *sm.* **1.** bowel **2.** (*strada stretta*) alley **3.** (*tubo*) narrow tube.
budino *sm.* pudding.
bue *sm.* ox (*pl.* oxen): *carne di —*, beef.
bùfalo *sm.* buffalo.
bufera *sf.* **1.** storm **2.** (*di vento*) gale.
buffetto *sm.* fillip: *dare un —*, to fillip.
buffo *agg.* funny || *opera buffa*, comic opera.
buffonata *sf.* buffoonery.
buffone *sm.* **1.** clown, fool **2.** (*di corte*) court jester **3.** (*fig.*) unreliable person.
bugìa *sf.* **1.** lie **2.** (*portacandela*) flat candlestick.
bugiardo *agg.* false. ♦ **bugiardo** *sm.* liar.
bugigàttolo *sm.* lumber-room.
buio *agg.* e *sm.* dark: *— pesto*, pitch dark.
bulbo *sm.* **1.** bulb **2.** (*di occhio*) eyeball.
bùlgaro *agg.* e *sm.* Bulgarian.
bulinare *vt.* to engrave.
bulino *sm.* burin.
bullonare *vt.* (*mecc.*) to bolt.
bullone *sm.* bolt.
buonanotte *sf.* good night.
buonasera *sf.* good evening.
buoncostume *sm.*: *squadra del —*, vice squad.
buongiorno *sm.* **1.** (*di mattina*) good morning **2.** (*di pomeriggio*) good afternoon **3.** (*a ogni ora incontrandosi, fam.*) hullo **4.** (*a ogni ora lasciandosi*) goodbye.
buongustaio *sm.* gourmet.
buongusto *sm.* good taste.
buono *agg.* **1.** good **2.** (*di tempo*) fine || *alla buona*, informal; *a buon diritto*, by right; *di buon grado*, willingly. ♦ **buono** *sm.* **1.** good **2.** (*persona*) good person **3.** (*comm.*) bond **4.** (*tagliando*) coupon.
buonsenso *sm.* (common) sense.
buontempone *sm.* merry fellow.
buonumore *sm.* V. *umore*.
buonuomo *sm.* **1.** good-natured man (*pl.* men) **2.** simple man (*pl.* men).

burattinaio *sm.* puppet showman (*pl.* -men).
burattino *sm.* puppet.
burbanzoso *agg.* haughty.
bùrbero *agg.* gruff.
burla *sf.* trick || *per —*, in fun.
burlare *vt.* to play a trick on (so.). ♦ **burlarsi** *vr.* to make (*v. irr.*) fun of.
burlesco *agg.* farcical.
burlone *sm.* joker.
buròcrate *sm.* bureaucrat.
burocràtico *agg.* bureaucratic.
burocrazìa *sf.* bureaucracy; (*in Inghilterra*) Civil Service.
burrasca *sf.* storm.
burrascoso *agg.* stormy.
burrificio *sm.* dairy.
burro *sm.* butter.
burrone *sm.* ravine.
burroso *agg.* buttery.
buscarsi *vr.* to get (*v. irr.*) || *buscarle*, to get a thrashing.
bussare *vi.* to knock: *— alla porta*, to knock at the door.
busse *sf. pl.* blows: *prendere le —*, to get (*v. irr.*) a thrashing.
bùssola *sf.* compass: *perdere la — (fig.)*, to lose (*v. irr.*) one's head.
bussolotto *sm.* dice-box || *fare il giuoco dei bussolotti* (*anche fig.*), to juggle.
busta *sf.* **1.** envelope **2.** (*astuccio*) case.
bustarella *sf.* bribe.
bustina *sf.* (*mil.*) service cap.
busto *sm.* **1.** bust **2.** (*indumento per donna*) corset.
butano *sm.* (*chim.*) butane.
buttare *vt.* **1.** to throw (*v. irr.*) **2.** (*sprecare*) to waste || *— all'aria*, to upset (*v. irr.*); *— a terra*, to knock down.
butterato *agg.* pitted.
buzzo *sm.* belly || *di — buono*, very eagerly.

C

càbala *sf.* cab(b)ala.
cabalìstico *agg.* cab(b)alistic(al).
cabina *sf.* **1.** box, hut: *— balneare*, bathing hut; *— telefonica*, telephone box **2.** (*aer.; mar.*) cabin.
cablogramma *sm.* cable.

cabotaggio *sm.* cabotage: *nave di piccolo* —, coasting vessel.

cacao *sm.* **1.** (*bot.*) cacao **2.** (*polvere, bevanda*) cocoa.

cacare *vi.* to evacuate one's bowels.

cacarella *sf.* diarrhoea.

cacatoa, cacatùa *sm.* cockatoo.

cacca *sf.* excrement.

caccia *sf.* hunt, hunting || — *grossa*, big game || *cane da* —, sporting dog; *stagione di* —, shooting season; *andare a* —, to go (*v. irr.*) hunting; *andare a* — *di uccelli*, to go shooting. ♦ **caccia** *sm.* (*aer.*) fighter.

cacciagione *sf.* game.

cacciare *vt.* **1.** to hunt **2.** (*mil.; mar.*) to chase **3.** (*scacciare*) to expel **4.** (*mettere*) to put (*v. irr.*).

cacciatore *sm.* hunter (*anche fig.*).

cacciatorpediniere *sf.* (torpedo-boat) destroyer.

cacciavite *sm.* screwdriver.

cachi *sm.* persimmon.

cacio *sm.* cheese || *essere alto come un soldo di* —, to be very short.

cacofonìa *sf.* cacophony.

cactus *sm.* cactus (*pl.* cacti).

cadauno *agg.* e *pron. indef.* each.

cadàvere *sm.* corpse.

cadavèrico *agg.* **1.** corpse-like **2.** (*pallido*) deadly pale.

cadente *agg.* **1.** falling **2.** (*di astri*) setting || *stella* —, shooting star || *età* —, decrepit old age.

cadenza *sf.* **1.** cadence **2.** (*ritmo*) rhythm **3.** (*accento*) accent.

cadere *vi.* **1.** to fall (*v. irr.*) (*anche fig.*): — *bocconi*, to fall flat on one's face; — *in mare*, to fall overboard; — *addormentato*, to fall asleep; — *a proposito*, to fall in the nick of time; — *dal sonno*, to be overcome by sleep; — *nell'errore*, to fall into error || *far* —, to knock down; (*fig.*) to bring (*v. irr.*) about the fall of **2.** (*tramontare, di astri*) to set (*v. irr.*) **3.** (*calare*) to drop **4.** (*far fiasco*) to fail.

cadetto *agg.* e *sm.* cadet.

caducità *sf.* caducity.

caduco *agg.* perishable, decaying.

caduta *sf.* **1.** fall, falling **2.** (*fig.*) downfall, ruin **3.** (*fis.*) drop.

caffè *sm.* **1.** coffee: — *macinato*, ground coffee; — *nero*, black coffee **2.** (*locale*) coffee-house.

caffeina *sf.* caffeine.

caffettiera *sf.* coffee-pot.

cafone *sm.* boor.

cagionévole *agg.* sickly, weak.

cagliarsi *vr.* to curdle.

cagna *sf.* bitch.

cagnara *sf.* **1.** furious barking **2.** (*fig.*) uproar.

cagnesco *agg. in* —, surlily || *guardare in* —, to scowl at.

cagnolino *s.m.* **1.** (*cucciolo*) puppy **2.** (*cane piccolo*) small dog.

caimano *sm.* cayman.

cala *sf.* **1.** creek **2.** (*mar.*) hold.

calabrone *sm.* hornet.

calamaio *sm.* ink-stand.

calamaro *sm.* calamary.

calamita *sf.* magnet (*anche fig.*).

calamità *sf.* calamity, misfortune.

calamitare *vt.* to magnetize (*anche fig.*).

calamitoso *agg.* calamitous.

calandra *sf.* **1.** (*zool.*) wood-lark **2.** (*mecc.*) calender.

calare *vt.* to lower, to drop || *cala la tela*, the curtain drops. ♦ **calare** *vi.* **1.** to descend **2.** (*di astri*) to set (*v. irr.*) **3.** (*di febbre*) to abate **4.** (*comm.*) to fall (*v. irr.*). ♦ **calarsi** *vr.* to let (*v. irr.*) oneself down.

calata *sf.* descent.

calca *sf.* crowd.

calcagno *sm.* heel || *stare alle calcagna di qu.*, to follow so. closely.

calcare[1] *vt.* **1.** to tread (*v. irr.*) **2.** (*premere*) to press down || — *la mano* (*fig.*), to exaggerate.

calcare[2] *sm.* limestone.

calcàreo *agg.* calcareous.

calce *sf.* lime || *in* — (*loc. avv.*), at the foot.

calcestruzzo *sm.* concrete.

calciare *vi.* to kick.

calciatore *sm.* footballer.

calcificare *vt.* to calcify.

calcificazione *sf.* calcification.

calcina *sf.* lime.

calcinaccio *sm.* debris (*solo sing.*).

calcinare *vt.* to calcine.

calcio[1] *sm.* **1.** kick **2.** (*giuoco*) football || — *d'inizio*, kick-off; — *di rigore*, penalty **3.** (*di arma*) butt.

calcio[2] *sm.* (*chim.*) calcium.

calco *sm.* **1.** (*scult.*) cast **2.** (*di disegno*) drawing.

calcolàbile *agg.* computable.

calcolare *vt.* **1.** to calculate, to compute **2.** (*prevedere*) to estimate.

calcolatore *sm.* (electronic) computer || *regolo* —, slide-rule.

calcolatrice *sf.* calculating machine.

càlcolo *sm.* **1.** calculation **2.** (*med.*) stone.

calcomanìa *sf.* transfer.

caldaia *sf.* **1.** kier **2.** (*per produzione di vapore*) boiler.

caldamente *avv.* warmly.

caldeggiare *vt.* to favour.

caldeggiatore *sm.* supporter.

calderaio *sm.* tinker.

calderone *sm.* **1.** cauldron **2.** (*fig.*) medley.

caldo *agg.* **1.** warm; (*molto caldo*) hot **2.** (*fig.*) ardent. ♦ **caldo** *sm.* heat || *far* —, to be warm, to be hot.

caleidoscopio *sm.* kaleidoscope.

calendario *sm.* calendar.

calende *sf. pl.* kalends || *rimandare alle* — *greche*, to put off till doomsday.

calesse *sm.* gig, calash.

calessino *sm.* gig.

calibrare *vt.* to calibrate.

calibratura *sf.* calibration.

càlibro *sm.* **1.** calibre **2.** (*di persona*) caliber, importance.

càlice *sm.* **1.** (*eccl.*) chalice **2.** (*bicchiere*) goblet, drinking-cup.

calìgine *sf.* thick fog, smog.

callìfugo *sm.* corn-plaster.

calligrafìa *sf.* handwriting.

calligràfico *agg.* calligraphic.

callìgrafo *sm.* calligrapher: *perito* —, handwriting expert.

callista *sm.* chiropodist.

callo *sm.* corn.

callosità *sf.* callosity.

calloso *agg.* callous.

calma *sf.* calm.

calmante *agg.* calming, soothing. ♦ **calmante** *sm.* (*farm.*) sedative.

calmare *vt.* **1.** to calm **2.** (*metter pace*) to appease.

calmo *agg.* calm, quiet.

calo *sm.* **1.** shrinkage **2.** (*comm.*) drop.

calore *sm.* **1.** (*forte*) heat; (*moderato*) warmth **2.** (*fig.*) warmth, eagerness.

calorìa *sf.* calory.

calorìfero *sm.* heating apparatus, radiator.

caloroso *agg.* **1.** warm, hearty **2.** (*che non sente freddo*) not feeling the cold.

calotta *sf.* **1.** cap: — *cranica*, skull-cap **2.** (*geom.*) bowl.

calpestare *vt.* to tread (*v. irr.*):

vietato — *l'erba*, keep off the grass.

calpestìo *sm.* trampling (of feet).

calunnia *sf.* slander.

calunniare *vt.* to slander.

calunniatore *sm.* slanderer.

calvizie *sf.* baldness.

calvo *agg.* bald.

calza *sf.* **1.** (*corta*) sock; (*da donna*) stocking **2.** (*lavoro a maglia*) knitting || *fare la* —, to knit.

calzamaglia *sf.* tights (*pl.*).

calzare *vt.* to put (*v. irr.*) on. ♦ **calzare** *vi.* to fit.

calzatura *sf.* shoe || *negozio di calzature*, shoe-shop.

calzaturificio *sm.* boot factory.

calzettone *sm.* heavy sock.

calzino *sm.* sock.

calzolaio *sm.* shoemaker.

calzolerìa *sf.* shoemaker's shop.

calzoni *sm. pl.* trousers.

camaleonte *sm.* chameleon (*anche fig.*).

cambiale *sf.* bill (of exchange): — *a vista*, bill at sight; *emettere una* —, to issue a bill; *girare una* —, to endorse a bill; *protestare una* —, to note a bill || — *pagherò*, promissory note.

cambiamento *sm.* change.

cambiare *vt.* to change (*anche fig.*). ♦ **cambiarsi** *vr.* to change.

cambio *sm.* **1.** change **2.** (*econ.*) exchange **3.** (*mecc.*) change-gear **4.** (*auto*) gear || *in* —, in exchange for, instead of.

camelia *sf.* (*bot.*) camellia.

càmera *sf.* **1.** room: — *da letto*, bedroom; — *dei bambini*, nursery; — *degli ospiti*, guest-room || *musica da* —, chamber music **2.** (*pol.*) Chamber House: *camera dei deputati*, Chamber of Deputies **3.** (*tec.*) chamber || — *oscura*, dark room; — *d'aria*, inner tube.

camerata[1] *sm.* comrade, mate.

camerata[2] *sf.* dormitory.

cameratismo *sm.* comradeship.

cameriera *sf.* **1.** maid **2.** (*di albergo*) chambermaid **3.** (*di ristorante*) waitress.

cameriere *sm.* **1.** man-servant (*pl.* men-) **2.** (*di ristorante*) waiter.

càmice *sm.* **1.** overall **2.** (*eccl.*) surplice.

camicetta *sf.* blouse.

camicia *sf.* **1.** (*da uomo*) shirt || — *da notte* (*da uomo*), night-shirt

2. (*da donna*) chemise || — *da notte* (*da donna*), night-dress 3. (*tec.*) jacket || *è nato con la* —, he was born with a silver spoon in his mouth.

caminetto *sm.* fireplace.

camino *sm.* 1. (*focolare*) fireplace 2. (*comignolo*) chimney.

camion *sm.* lorry.

camioncino *sm.* van.

camionista *sm.* lorry-driver.

cammello *sm.* camel.

cammeo *sm.* cameo.

camminare *vi.* 1. to walk || — *a grandi passi*, to stride (*v. irr.*) along; — *in punta di piedi*, to walk on tiptoe 2. (*di meccanismi*) to go (*v. irr.*), to work 3. (*discorsi, affari ecc.*) to proceed.

camminata *sf.* 1. walk 2. (*andatura*) gait.

camminatore *sm.* walker.

cammino *sm.* way.

camomilla *sf.* (*bot.*) camomile: *una tazza di* —, a cup of camomile-tea.

camoscio *sm.* chamois: *pelle di* —, chamois leather.

campagna *sf.* 1. country: *casa di* —, country-house; *andare in* —, to go (*v. irr.*) into the country; *essere in* —, to be in the country 2. (*tenuta*) estate 3. (*mil.*) campaign 4. (*villeggiatura*) holidays.

campana *sf.* bell.

campanaro *sm.* bell-ringer.

campanello *sm.* door-bell: — *d'allarme*, alarm-bell.

campanile *sm.* bell-tower.

campanilismo *sm.* parochialism.

campare *vi.* to live.

campeggiatore *sm.* camper.

campeggio *sm.* camping.

campestre *agg.* rural, rustic || *corsa* —, cross-country race.

campionario *sm.* set of samples, sample case || *fiera campionaria*, trade fair.

campionato *sm.* championship.

campione *sm.* 1. champion 2. (*comm.*) sample.

campo *sm.* 1. (*mil.*) field 2. (*sport*) sport ground || — *da tennis*, tennis court 3. (*terreno*) field || — *di battaglia*, battle-field.

camuffare *vt.* to disguise.

canadese *agg. e sm.* Canadian.

canaglia *sf.* 1. rabble 2. (*di persona malvagia*) rascal.

canale *sm.* 1. canal 2. (*braccio di mare*) channel 3. (*condotto*) pipe 4. (*tv.*) channel.

cànapa *sf.* hemp.

canarino *sm.* canary.

cancellare *vt.* 1. (*a penna*) to cross out; (*con una gomma*) to rub out; (*con un panno*) to wipe out 2. (*fig.*) efface.

cancellatura *sf.* 1. erasure 2. (*fig.*) effacement.

cancelleria *sf.* 1. (*pol.*) chancellery 2. (*materiale di* —) stationery articles 3. (*giur.*) record-office.

cancelliere *sm.* 1. (*pol.*) chancellor 2. (*giur.*) recorder.

cancello *sm.* gate.

cancrena *sf.* gangrene.

cancro *sm.* cancer.

candeggina *sf.* chloride.

candela *sf.* 1. candle: — *di sego*, tallow candle; *al lume di* —, by candle-light 2. (*auto*) sparking plug.

candelabro *sm.* branched candlestick.

candeliere *sm.* candlestick.

candelotto *sm.* short thick candle: — *fumogeno*, smoke candle.

candidato *sm.* candidate.

candidatura *sf.* candidature.

càndido *agg.* 1. snow-white 2. (*innocente*) innocent.

candito *agg.* candied. ◆ **candito** *sm.* sugar candy.

candore *sm.* 1. whiteness 2. (*innocenza*) innocence.

cane *sm.* 1. dog: — *da caccia*, sporting dog; — *pastore*, sheep dog; — *da guardia*, watch-dog 2. (*persona spietata*) brute 3. (*di fucile*) cock.

cànfora *sf.* camphor.

canguro *sm.* kangaroo.

canìcola *sf.* the height of summer.

canile *sm.* kennel.

canino *agg.* canine: *dente* —, canine tooth.

canna *sf.* 1. reed 2. (*coltivata*) cane || — *da zucchero*, sugar cane 3. (*tubo*) pipe 4. (*di arma*) barrel 5. (*da pesca*) (fishing-)rod.

cannella *sf.* 1. (*bot.*) cinnamon 2. (*di botte*) spout.

cannello *sm.* 1. torch 2. (*chim.*) pipe.

canneto *sm.* canebrake.

cannìbale *sm.* cannibal.

cannocchiale *sm.* binoculars (*pl.*) || — *da campagna*, field glasses; — *da teatro*, opera glasses.

cannone *sm.* **1.** gun: — *antiaereo,* anti-aircraft gun; — *anticarro,* anti-tank gun **2.** (*fig.*) ace.

cannuccia *sf.* **1.** thin cane: — *per sorbire bibite,* straw.

canone *sm.* canon: — *d'affitto,* rent; — *della radio,* radio-licence fee.

canònica *sf.* rectory.

canònico *agg.* canonical ‖ *diritti canonici,* canon law. ♦ **canònico** *sm.* canon.

canonizzare *vt.* to canonize.

canoro *agg.* singing.

canottaggio *sm.* **1.** rowing, boating **2.** (*come attività*) boating.

canottiera *sf.* vest.

canotto *sm.* small boat.

canovaccio *sm.* **1.** (*per asciugare stoviglie*) dish-cloth; **2.** (*per ricamo*) canvas **3.** (*trama di un'opera*) plot.

cantante *sm.* singer.

cantare *vt.* **1.** to sing (*v. irr.*) **2.** (*del gallo*) to crow **3.** (*fare la spia*) to squeal.

cantata *sf.* song.

canterellare *vt. e vi.* to sing (*v. irr.*) softly, to hum.

càntico *sm.* hymn.

cantiere *sm.* yard.

cantilena *sf.* sing-song.

cantina *sf.* cellar.

cantiniere *sm.* cellarman (*pl.* -men).

cantino *sm.* chanterelle.

canto[1] *sm.* singing.

canto[2] *sm.* (*angolo*) corner ‖ *dal* — *mio,* for my part; *da un* —, on one hand.

cantonata *sf.* corner: *prendere una* —, to make (*v. irr.*) a blunder.

cantone *sm.* **1.** corner **2.** (*geogr.*) canton.

cantoniera *sf.* **1.** (*mobile*) corner cupboard **2.** (*casa*) roadman's house **3.** (*ferr.*) signalman's house.

cantoniere *sm.* signalman (*pl.* -men).

canuto *agg.* hoary.

canzonare *vt.* to make (*v. irr.*) fun of.

canzone *sf.* song.

canzonetta *sf.* **1.** short song **2.** (*poet.*) canzonet.

canzonettista *s.* **1.** music-hall singer **2.** (*autore di canzoni*) songwriter.

caolino *sm.* kaolin.

caos *sm.* chaos.

capace *agg.* **1.** able **2.** (*idoneo*) fit **3.** (*abile*) clever.

capacità *sf.* **1.** ability, cleverness **2.** (*capienza*) capacity.

capanna *sf.* hut.

capanno *sm.* **1.** (*da caccia*) shooting-box **2.** (*per bagnanti*) bathing-box.

caparbieria *sf.* stubbornness.

caparbio *agg.* stubborn.

caparra *sf.* caution-money.

capeggiare *vt.* to lead (*v. irr.*).

capello *sm.* hair (*solo sing.*) ‖ *acconciatura dei capelli,* hairdress; *farsi tagliare i capelli,* to have one's hair cut; *avere un diavolo per* —, to be furious.

capezzale *sm.* bolster.

capézzolo *sm.* nipple.

capienza *sf.* capacity.

capigliatura *sf.* hair.

capillare *agg.* capillary.

capillarità *sf.* capillarity.

capinera *sf.* blackcap.

capire *vt.* to understand (*v. irr.*).

capitale *sm.* capital. ♦ **capitale** *agg.* **1.** (*che riguarda la vita*) capital **2.** (*principale*) main.

capitalismo *sm.* capitalism.

capitalista *s.* capitalist.

capitalizzare *vt.* to capitalize. ♦ **capitalizzare** *vi.* (*accumulare denaro*) to save.

capitano *sm.* captain, leader.

capitare *vi.* **1.** (*giungere*) to arrive **2.** (*accadere*) to happen, to befall (*v. irr.*).

capitello *sm.* (*arch.*) capital.

capitolare *vi.* to capitulate.

capitolare *sm.* capitulary. ♦ **capitolare** *agg.* capitular.

capitolo *sm.* chapter.

capitómbolo *sm.* tumble.

capo *sm.* **1.** head ‖ *avere mal di* —, to have a headache; *senza* — *né coda,* without rhyme or reason **2.** (*estremità*) end ‖ *da un* — *all'altro,* from end to end; *andare a* —, new line; *in* — *a un anno,* within a year; *Capo d'Anno,* New Year's day **3.** (*geogr.*) cape **4.** (*chi comanda*) leader.

capobanda *sm.* **1.** (*mus.*) bandmaster **2.** (*di una banda di criminali*) ringleader.

capocuoco *sm.* head cook.

capocordata *sm.* first man on the rope.

capodanno *sm.* New Year's day.

capofamiglia *s.* head of a family.

capofila *sm.* file-leader.

capofitto (*nella loc. avv.*) *a* —, headlong || *cadere, tuffarsi a* —, to fall (*v. irr.*), to dive head first.

capogiro *sm.* dizziness.

capolavoro *sm.* masterpiece.

capolìnea *sm.* terminus (*pl.* -ni).

capolino *sm.* small head || *far* —, to peep in.

capoluogo *sm.* main town.

caporale *sm.* corporal.

caporedattore *sm.* editor in chief.

caposaldo *sm.* **1.** datum point **2.** (*mil.*) stronghold **3.** (*fondamento*) main point.

caposcuola *sm.* leader of a movement.

capostazione *sm.* station-master.

capotare *vi.* **1.** (*di aerei*) to somersault **2.** (*di auto*) to turn over.

capoufficio *sm.* head-clerk.

capoverso *sm.* **1.** (*in poesia*) beginning of a line **2.** (*in prosa*) beginning of a paragraph.

capovòlgere *vt.* to turn upside down. ✦ **capovòlgersi** *vr.* to capsize.

cappa *sf.* **1.** (*mantello*) cloak **2.** (*di prete*) cape **3.** (*fig.*) vault || — *del camino*, chimney.

cappella *sf.* chapel.

cappellano *sm.* chaplain.

cappello *sm.* **1.** hat: — *a cilindro*, top-hat; — *di paglia*, straw hat; **2.** (*introduzione*) preamble.

càppero *sm.* caper.

cappone *sm.* capon.

cappotto *sm.* **1.** coat **2.** (*di gioco*) capot.

cappuccino *sm.* **1.** (*eccl.*) capuchin **2.** (*bevanda*) white coffee.

cappuccio *sm.* hood.

capra *sf.* goat.

capretto *sm.* kid.

capriccio *sm.* whim: *fare i capricci*, to be naughty.

caprino *agg.* goatish.

capriola[1] *sf.* caper: *far capriole*, to cut (*v. irr.*) capers.

capriola[2] *sf.* (*femmina del capriolo*) doe.

capriolo *sm.* roe-deer.

càpsula *sf.* **1.** capsule **2.** (*di dente*) crown.

captare *vt.* (*radio*) to pick up.

capzioso *agg.* captious.

carabina *sf.* carabine.

carabiniere *sm.* carabineer.

caracollare *vi.* to caracole.

caraffa *sf.* **1.** (*per acqua*) carafe **2.** (*per vino*) decanter.

caràmbola *sf.* cannon: *far* —, to cannon.

carambolare *vi.* to cannon.

caramella *sf.* sugar-drop, toffee.

caramellare *vt.* to coat with burnt sugar.

caramello *sm.* caramel.

carato *sm.* carat.

caràttere *sm.* **1.** character, temper **2.** (*caratteristica*) character **3.** (*tip.*) type.

caratterista *s.* character actor (actress).

caratterìstico *agg.* characteristic. ✦ **caratterìstica** *sf.* characteristic.

caravella *sf.* caravel.

carbonaio *sm.* coal merchant.

carbone *sm.* coal || — *di legna*, charcoal; — *fossile*, pit coal; *miniera di* —, coal-mine.

carbonerìa *sf.* Carbonarist movement.

carbonìfero *agg.* carboniferous.

carbonio *sm.* carbon.

carbonizzare *vt.* **1.** to carbonize **2.** (*di legno*) to char.

carburante *sm.* fuel.

carburatore *sm.* carburettor.

carburazione *sf.* carburation.

carcassa *sf.* carcass.

carcerazione *sf.* imprisonment.

càrcere *sm.* prison, jail.

carceriere *sm.* jailer.

carciofo *sm.* artichoke.

cardano *sm.* (*mecc.*) cardan joint.

cardare *vt.* to card.

cardìaco *agg.* cardiac || *disturbi cardiaci*, heart-disease.

cardinale *agg. e sm.* cardinal.

càrdine *sm.* **1.** hinge, pivot **2.** (*fig.*) foundation.

cardiòlogo *sm.* cardiologist.

cardiopatìa *sf.* cardiopathy.

cardo *sm.* **1.** (*bot.*) thistle **2.** (*cuc.*) cardoon **3.** (*mecc.*) carding machine.

carena *sf.* **1.** (*mar.*) keel **2.** (*aer*) hull **3.** (*zool.*) càrina (*pl.* -nae).

carenza *sf.* want, lack.

carestìa *sf.* famine.

carezza *sf.* caress.

carezzévole *agg.* caressing.

cariàtide *sf.* caryatid.

cariato *agg.* decayed.

càrica *sf.* **1.** (*pubblico ufficio*) office: *entrare in* —, to take (*v.*

irr.) office **2.** (*mil.*) charge **3.** (*di arma da fuoco; elettr.*) charge **4.** (*di orologio*) winding up.

caricare *vt.* **1.** to load **2.** (*mil.; elettr.*) to charge **3.** (*di orologio*) to wind (*v. irr.*) up.

caricatore *sm.* **1.** loader **2.** (*di arma*) magazine.

caricatura *sf.* caricature.

càrico[1] *agg.* **1.** loaded, laden (*anche fig.*) **2.** (*di caffè*) strong **3.** (*elettr.*) charged.

càrico[2] *sm.* **1.** (*di nave*) freight; (*di veicolo*) load; (*di animale da soma*) burden **2.** (*fig.*) load, weight **3.** (*accusa*) charge || (*comm.*) *essere a — di qu.*, to be charged to so.

carie *sf.* decay.

carino *agg.* pretty, nice.

carità *sf.* **1.** (*amore; teol.*) charity **2.** (*elemosina*) alms.

carlinga *sf.* cockpit.

carlona (*nella loc. avv.*) *alla —*, carelessly.

carminio *agg.* carmine.

carnagione *sf.* complexion.

carnale *agg.* carnal.

carne *sf.* **1.** flesh **2.** (*come alimento*) meat || *— di manzo*, beef; *— di vitello*, veal; *— in scatola*, tinned meat; *— congelata*, frozen meat.

carnéfice *sm.* executioner.

carneficina *sf.* slaughter.

carnevale *sm.* carnival.

carnìvoro *agg.* carnivorous.

caro *agg.* **1.** dear **2.** (*costoso*) dear, expensive.

carogna *sf.* carrion.

carosello *sm.* carousel.

carota *sf.* carrot.

caròtide *sf.* carotid.

carovana *sf.* caravan.

carovita *sm.* high cost of living.

carpa *sf.* carp.

carpentiere *sm.* carpenter.

carpire *vt.* **1.** to snatch **2.** (*con astuzia*) to swindle.

carponi *avv.* on all fours.

carràbile *agg.* cart: *passo —*, driveway.

carreggiata **1.** (*solco*) track **2.** (*strada*) cartway.

carrellata *sf.* dolly shot.

carrello *sm.* **1.** (*ferr.*) wag(g)on **2.** (*aer.*) landing gear **3.** (*cine; tv.*) dolly **4.** (*di macchina per scrivere*)

carriage.

carriera *sf.* career || *di gran —*, at full speed.

carriola *sf.* wheelbarrow.

carrista *sm.* (*mil.*) tankman (*pl. -men*).

carro *sm.* **1.** (*a due ruote*) cart **2.** (*a quattro ruote*) wag(g)on || *— armato*, tank.

carrozza *sf.* carriage: *— diretta*, through coach; *— viaggiatori*, passenger car.

carrozzàbile *agg.* practicable.

carrozzella *sf.* **1.** cab **2.** (*per bambini*) perambulator; (*fam.*) pram.

carrozzerìa *sf.* body.

carrozziere *sm.* body-maker.

carrozzone *sm.* **1.** lumbering coach **2.** (*di zingari*) caravan.

carruba *sf.*, **carrubo** *sm.* carob.

carrùcola *sf.* pulley.

carta *sf.* paper: *— da lettere*, writing-paper; *— carbone*, carbon paper; *— d'identità*, identity card; *— stradale*, road-map.

cartaio *sm.* paper-maker.

cartamodello *sm.* dressmaker's pattern.

cartamoneta *sf.* paper-money.

cartapesta *sf.* paper-pulp.

cartavetrata *sf.* sand-paper.

carteggio *sm.* **1.** correspondence **2.** (*collezione di lettere*) collection of letters.

cartella *sf.* **1.** (*da scuola*) satchel **2.** (*di cuoio*) brief-case.

cartello *sm.* **1.** bill **2.** (*pubblicitario*) poster **3.** (*stradale*) traffic sign **4.** (*econ.*) cartel.

cartellone *sm.* **1.** (*pubblicitario*) poster **2.** (*teat.*) bill.

cartellonista *sm.* commercial artist.

cartiera *sf.* paper-mill.

cartilàgine *sf.* cartilage.

cartoccio *sm.* paper-bag.

cartografìa *sf.* cartography.

cartolerìa *sf.* stationer's shop.

cartolina *sf.* postcard: *— illustrata*, picture postcard.

cartoncino *sm.* thin card.

cartone *sm.* cardboard || *cartoni animati*, cartoons.

cartuccia *sf.* cartridge || *mezza —* (*fig.*), shrimp.

casa *sf.* **1.** (*abitazione*) house **2.** (*ambiente familiare*) home || *amico di —*, family friend; *donna di —*, housewife; *nostalgia di —*, home-sickness; *andare a —*, to go (*v. irr.*) home; *restare a —*, to stay at home; *essere in —*, to be in **3.** (*stirpe*) house, dynasty, family.

casacca *sf.* coat.

casaccio (*nella loc. avv.*) *a —*, at random.

casalinga *sf.* housewife.

casalingo *agg.* homely: *cucina casalinga*, **plain** cooking.

càsato *sm.* **1.** (*cognome*) surname **2.** (*origine, nascita*) birth.

cascame *sm.* waste.

cascamorto *sm.* spoon: *fare il —*, to run (*v. irr.*) after.

cascante *agg.* **1.** (*debole*) weak **2.** (*floscio*) flabby (*anche fig.*).

cascare *vi.* **1.** to fall (*v. irr.*) **2.** (*con rumore*) to crash || *— dalle nuvole*, to be struck with amazement; *— dal sonno*, to be overcome with sleep.

cascata *sf.* **1.** (*caduta*) fall **2.** (*d'acqua*) waterfall **3.** (*fig.*) cascade.

cascina *sf.* **1.** dairy farm **2.** (*cascinale*) farmstead.

casco *sm.* **1.** helmet **2.** (*per asciugare i capelli*) dryer.

casella *sf.*: *— postale*, post-box.

casellante *sm.* **1.** (*ferr.*) signalman (*pl.* -men) **2.** (*di passaggio a livello*) crossing keeper.

casellario *sm.* **1.** set of pigeon-holes **2.** (*giur.*) *— penale*, records-office.

casereccio *agg.* homely: *pane —*, home-made bread.

caserma *sf.* barracks (*pl.*).

caso *sm.* **1.** chance **2.** (*fatto*) case **3.** (*possibilità*) way, possibility || *a —*, at random; *per —*, by chance.

càspita *inter.* good gracious!

cassa *sf.* **1.** case, box **2.** (*comm.*) cash || *libro di —*, cash-book; *pagamento per —*, cash-payment; *sportello di —*, cashier's window **3.** (*mus.*) case || *gran —*, bass-drum.

cassaforte *sf.* safe.

cassapanca *sf.* chest.

cassazione *sf.* (*giur.*) cassation.

casseruola *sf.* saucepan.

cassetto *sm.* drawer.

cassettone *sm.* chest of drawers.

cassiere *sm.* cashier.

casta *sf.* caste.

castagna *sf.* chestnut.

castagnaccio *sm.* chestnut-tart.

castagno *sm.* chestnut-tree.

castano *agg.* nut-brown.

castellano *sm.* lord of a castle.

castello *sm.* castle.

castigare *vt.* to punish.

castigatezza *sf.* moderation.

castigato *agg.* **1.** (*casto*) chaste **2.** (*emendato*) castigated.

castigo *sm.* punishment.

castità *sf.* chastity.

casto *agg.* chaste.

castoro *sm.* beaver.

castrare *vt.* to castrate.

castrato *sm.* (*cuc.*) mutton.

castronerìa *sf.* stupidity.

casuale *agg.* casual.

casualità *sf.* casualness.

cataclisma *sm.* cataclysm (*anche fig.*).

catacomba *sf.* catacomb.

catafalco *sm.* catafalque.

catafascio (*nella loc. avv.*) *andare a —*, to go (*v. irr.*) to rack and ruin; *a —*, topsyturvy.

catalessi *sf.* catalepsy.

catalizzatore *sm.* catalyst.

catalogare *vt.* to catalogue.

catàlogo *sm.* catalogue.

catapecchia *sf.* hovel.

catapulta *sf.* catapult.

catarifrangente *sm.* reflector.

catarro *sm.* catarrh.

catarsi *sf.* catharsis.

catasta *sf.* pile, heap.

catasto *sm.* cadastre.

catàstrofe *sf.* catastrophe.

catastròfico *agg.* catastrophic(al).

catechismo *sm.* catechism.

catechizzare *vt.* **1.** to catechize **2.** (*fig.*) to persuade.

catecùmeno *sm.* catechumen.

categorìa *sf.* category, class.

categòrico *agg.* categorical, absolute.

catena *sf.* **1.** chain **2.** (*fig.*) bond.

catenaccio *sm.* bolt.

cateratta *sf.* cataract.

caterva *sf.* **1.** (*di persone*) crowd **2.** (*di cose*) great quantity.

catino *sm.* basin.

catione *sm.* (*fis.*) cation.

càtodo *sm.* cathode.

catramare *vt.* to tar.

catrame *sm.* tar.

càttedra *sf.* **1.** desk **2.** (*l'ufficio dell'insegnare*) teaching post **3.** (*di università*) chair.

cattedrale *sf.* cathedral.

cattiveria *sf.* wickedness.

cattività *sf.* captivity.

cattivo *agg.* e *sm.* bad || — *scrittore*, poor writer.

cattolicésimo *sm.* catholicism.

cattòlico *agg.* catholic.

cattura *sf.* 1. capture 2. (*arresto*) arrest: *mandato di* —, warrant of arrest.

catturare *vt.* 1. to capture 2. (*arrestare*) to arrest.

caucciù *sm.* india-rubber.

càusa *sf.* 1. cause 2. (*giur.*) law suit || *far* — *a qu.*, to sue so. (for).

causare *vt.* to cause.

càustico *agg.* caustic (*anche fig.*)

cautela *sf.* caution.

cautelare *vt.* to protect. ♦ **cautelarsi** *vr.* to take (*v. irr.*) precautions.

cauterizzare *vt.* to cauterize.

càuto *agg.* cautious, prudent.

cauzione *sf.* 1. guarantee 2. (*per essere rilasciato dalla polizia*) bail.

cava *sf.* quarry.

cavalcare *vt.* to ride (*v. irr.*). ♦ **cavalcare** *vi.* to ride on horseback.

cavalcavìa *sm.* fly-over bridge.

cavalcioni (a) *loc. avv.* astride.

cavaliere *sm.* 1. rider 2. (*di ordine cavalleresco*) knight.

cavalla *sf.* mare.

cavalleresco *agg.* knightly.

cavallerìa *sf.* 1. (*mil.*) cavalry 2. (*stor.*) chivalry.

cavalletta *sf.* grasshopper.

cavalletto *sm.* 1. trestle 2. (*foto*) tripod 3. (*per pittori*) easel.

cavallo *sm.* 1. horse: — *da corsa*, racehorse; — *a dondolo*, rocking-horse; — *da soma*, pack-horse; *ferro di* —, horse-shoe 2. (*ginnastica*) vaulting-horse 3. (*cavallo vapore*) horse-power (*abbr.* H.P.).

cavallone *sm.* (*maroso*) billow.

cavare *vt.* to take (*v. irr.*) off || — *un dente*, to pull out a tooth || *cavarsela*, to get (*v. irr.*) off.

cavatappi, cavaturàccioli *sm.* cork-screw.

caverna *sf.* cave.

cavernoso *agg.* cavernous || *voce cavernosa*, very deep voice.

cavezza *sf.* halter.

cavia *sf.* cavy.

caviale *sm.* caviar.

caviglia *sf.* ankle.

cavillare *vi.* to cavil (at).

cavillo *sm.* cavil.

cavità *sf.* cavity.

cavo *agg.* hollow, empty. ♦ **cavo** *sm.* cable, rope.

cavolfiore *sm.* cauliflower.

càvolo *sm.* cabbage.

cazzotto *sm.* punch || *fare a cazzotti*, to come (*v. irr.*) to blows.

cazzuola *sf.* trowel.

cece *sm.* chick-pea.

cecità *sf.* blindness (*anche fig.*).

cecoslovacco *agg.* e *sm.* Czechoslovak.

cèdere *vt.* e *vi.* 1. (*dare*) to give (*v. irr.*) 2. (*trasferire*) to hand over 3. (*vendere*) to dispose of. ♦ **cèdere** *vi.* 1. to surrender 2. (*venir meno*) to subside 3. (*essere inferiore*) to be second to.

cedimento *sm.* 1. yielding 2. (*fig.*) giving up.

cèdola *sf.* coupon.

cedrata *sf.* citron syrup.

cedrina *sf.* lemon-scented verbena.

cedro *sm.* 1. citron-tree 2. (*frutto*) citron.

cedrone *agg.* e *sm.* (*gallo*) capercaillie.

cefalea *sf.* cephalea.

cefalgìa *sf.* cephalalgy.

ceffone *sm.* slap in the face.

celare *vt.* to conceal, to hide (*v. irr.*).

celebrare *vt.* to celebrate || — *un anniversario*, to keep (*v. irr.*) an anniversary.

celebrazione *sf.* celebration.

cèlebre *agg.* celebrated.

celebrità *sf.* celebrity.

cèlere *agg.* quick, swift.

celerità *sf.* quickness.

celeste *agg.* 1. light-blue 2. (*del cielo*) heavenly.

celia *sf.* jest.

celiare *vi.* to jest.

celibato *sm.* bachelorhood.

cèlibe *agg.* e *sm.* single. ♦ **cèlibe** *sm.* bachelor.

cella *sf.* cell.

cèllula *sf.* cell.

cellulare *agg.* cellular || *segregazione* —, close confinement.

cellulite *sf.* cellulitis.

cellulòide *sf.* celluloid.

cellulosa *sf.* cellulose.

celta *sm.* Celt.

cèltico *agg.* Celtic.

cèmbalo *sm.* 1. (*tamburello*) tambourine 2. (*spinetta*) spinet.

cementare *vt.* to cement (*anche fig.*).

47 **cerino**

cementazione *sf.* cementation.
cementificio *sm.* cement-factory.
cemento *sm.* cement: — *armato*, reinforced concrete.
cena *sf.* **1.** (*pasto serale leggero*) supper **2.** (*pranzo*) dinner || *far* —, to have supper.
cenàcolo *sm.* **1.** supper-room **2.** (*di artisti*) artistic coterie || *il — di Leonardo da Vinci*, Leonardo's Last Supper.
cenare *vi.* to have (*v. irr.*) supper.
cenciaio *sm.* ragman (*pl.* -men).
cencio *sm.* **1.** rag **2.** (*vestito logoro*) tatters (*pl.*).
cencioso *agg.* ragged, tattered.
cénere *sf.* ash (*general. al pl.*).
cenno *sm.* **1.** (*segno*) sign **2.** (*allusione*) hint **3.** (*breve notizia*) notice || *fare un — col capo*, to nod || *a un vostro — (comm.*), on hearing from you.
cenobio *sm.* coenobium (*pl.* -ia).
cenone *sm.* **1.** (*di Natale*) Christmas eve dinner **2.** (*di Capodanno*) New Year's eve dinner.
censimento *sm.* census.
censire *vt.* **1.** to take (*v. irr.*) a census of **2.** (*di proprietà*) to assess.
censo *sm.* **1.** (*stor.*) census **2.** (*ricchezza*) wealth.
censore *sm.* **1.** censor **2.** (*fig.*) critic.
censorio *agg.* censorial.
censura *sf.* **1.** (*ufficio di censore*) censorship **2.** (*azione di censura*) censure.
censurare *vt.* **1.** to censor **2.** (*fig.*) to censure.
centàuro *sm.* **1.** centaur **2.** (*fig., motociclista*) motorcyclist.
centellinare *vt.* to sip.
centenario *agg. e sm.* **1.** centennial **2.** (*di persona*) centenarian. ♦ **centenario** *sm.* (*commemorazione*) centenary.
centesimale *agg.* centesimal.
centèsimo *agg.* (the) hundredth. ♦ **centèsimo** *sm.* (*one*) hundredth (of sthg.) **2.** (*di dollaro*) cent **3.** (*di franco*) centime || *non avere un —*, to be penniless.
centigrado *agg.* centigrade.
centigrammo *sm.* centigramme.
centilitro *sm.* centilitre.
centimetro *sm.* centimetre.
centinaio *sm.* hundred.
cento *agg. e num. card.* hundred || *— di questi giorni*, many happy

returns of the day.
centrale *agg.* central. ♦ **centrale** *sf.* **1.** — *elettrica*, power station **2.** — *telefonica*, exchange.
centralinista *s.* operator.
centralino *sm.* telephone exchange.
centralismo *sm.* centralism.
centrare *vt.* to hit (*v. irr.*) the centre.
centrifuga *sf.* centrifuge.
centrifugo *agg.* centrifugal.
centrino *sm.* doily.
centripeto *agg.* centripetal.
centrismo *sm.* centrism.
centro *sm.* **1.** centre **2.** (*istituto*) institute.
centuplicare *vt.* **1.** to centuplicate **2.** (*fig.*) to increase.
centuplo *agg. e sm.* centuple.
centuria *sf.* (*stor.*) century.
centurione *sm.* (*stor.*) centurion.
ceppo *sm.* **1.** stump **2.** (*fig.*) stock.
cera *sf.* **1.** wax **2.** (*aspetto*) look || *avere bella —*, to look well.
ceralacca *sf.* sealing-wax.
ceràmica *sf.* **1.** (*arte*) ceramics **2.** (*pezzo*) piece of pottery.
ceramista *sm.* ceramist.
cerato *agg.* waxed || *tela cerata*, wax-cloth.
cerbiatto *sm.* fawn.
cerbottana *sf.* **1.** blowgun **2.** (*giocattolo*) pea-shooter.
cercare *vt.* **1.** to look for **2.** (*per consultazione*) to look up **3.** (*a tentoni*) to fumble for **4.** (*chiedere*) to ask (for). ♦ **cercare** *vi.* to try.
cercatore *sm.* seeker: — *d'oro*, gold-digger; (*amer.*) prospector.
cerchia *sf.* circle.
cerchiare *vt.* to hoop.
cerchiatura *sf.* hooping.
cerchietto *sm.* **1.** small ring **2.** (*gioco*) quoit.
cerchio *sm.* **1.** circle **2.** (*gioco*) hoop.
cerchione *sm.* rim.
cereale *sm.* cereals (*pl.*).
cerebrale *agg.* cerebral.
cèreo *agg.* waxen.
ceretta *sf.* **1.** boot polish **2.** (*per depilare*) wax.
cerimonia *sf.* **1.** ceremony **2.** (*pompa*) pomp.
cerimoniale *sm.* ceremonial.
cerimoniere *sm.* Master of Ceremonies.
cerimonioso *agg.* ceremonious
cerino *sm.* match.

cerniera *sf.* **1.** (*di occhiali, porte, finestre*) hinge **2.** (*di borsetta*) clasp **3.** (*lampo*) zipper.

cèrnita *sf.* choice, selection.

cero *sm.* large candle.

cerone *sm.* make-up.

cerotto *sm.* plaster.

certamente *avv.* certainly, undoubtedly.

certezza *sf.* certainty.

certificare *vt.* to certify, to attest.

certificato *sm.* certificate.

certo[1] *agg. indef.* **1.** certain: *un — Mr. Smith*, a (certain) Mr. Smith **2.** (*qualche*) some: *certe persone lo riconobbero*, some people recognized him; *dopo un — tempo*, after some time **3.** (*tale, di tal genere*) such. ♦ **certi** *pron. indef. pl.* some people.

certo[2] *agg.* certain. ♦ **certo** *avv.* certainly.

certuni *pron. indef.* some.

cerùleo *agg.* sky-blue.

cerva *sf.* (*zool.*) hind.

cervella *sf.* brain.

cervelletto *sm.* cerebellum.

cervello *sm.* **1.** brain **2.** (*intelligenza, mente*) understanding, mind.

cervellòtico *agg.* far-fetched.

cervicale *agg.* cervical.

cervice *sf.* nape.

cèrvidi *sm. pl.* cervidae.

cervo *sm.* deer (*inv. al pl.*).

cesàreo *agg.* Caesarean || *taglio —*, Caesarean operation.

cesarismo *sm.* Caesarism.

cesellare *vt.* to chisel (*anche fig.*).

cesellatura *sf.* chisel work.

cesello *sm.* chisel.

cesoia *sf.* shears (*pl.*).

cespuglio *sm.* bush, thicket.

cespuglioso *agg.* bushy.

cessare *vt.* e *vi.* to cease, to stop.

cessazione *sf.* cessation.

cessione *sf.* transfer.

cesso *sm.* lavatory.

cesta *sf.* basket.

cestaio *sm.* **1.** basket-maker **2.** (*chi vende*) basket-vendor.

cestinare *vt.* (*fig.*) to refuse.

cestino *sm.* small basket: *— da lavoro*, work-basket; *— da viaggio*, luncheon-basket; *— per la carta straccia*, waste-paper basket.

cesto *sm.* (*sport*) basket.

cesura *sf.* caesura.

cetàceo *agg.* e *sm.* cetacean.

ceto *sm.* class, rank.

cetra *sf.* cithern, lyre.

cetriolino *sm.* gherkin.

cetriolo *sm.* cucumber.

che[1] *pron. rel.* **1.** (*sogg., riferito a persone*) who, that: *l'uomo — mi parlò*, the man who (that) spoke to me **2.** (*sogg., riferito a cose e animali*) which, that: *ecco il cane — mi fu regalato*, here is the dog which (that) was given to me **3.** (*ogg., riferito a persone*) whom: *è la ragazza più graziosa — abbia mai incontrato*, she is the prettiest girl whom I ever met **4.** (*ogg., riferito a cose e animali*) which: *questo è il libro — le darò*, this is the book which I shall give her **5.** *il —*, which **6.** (*riferito a tempo*) when.

che[2] *agg. int.* **1.** what: *— musica preferisci?*, what music do you prefer? **2.** which: *— libro scegli?*, which book do you choose? ♦ **che** *pron. int.* what: *— è questo?*, what is this? ♦ **che** *agg. escl.* what, what a. ♦ **che** *pron. ind.* something.

che[3] *cong.* **1.** that **2.** (*comparativo*) than: *è più bella che intelligente*, she is more beautiful than intelligent **3.** (*correlativo*) whether: *— tu venga o no*, whether you come or not. ♦ **che** *inter.* what!

checché *pron. indef.* whatever.

checchessìa *pron. indef.* anything.

chepì *sm.* (*mil.*) kepi.

cherosene *sm.* kerosene.

cherubino *sm.* cherub.

chetamente *avv.* quietly, secretly.

chetare *vt.* to quiet. ♦ **chetarsi** *vr.* to quiet down.

chetichella (*nella loc. avv.*) *alla —*, on the sly, secretly.

cheto *agg.* quiet.

chi *pron. rel.* **1.** (*colui che*) he (*ogg.* him) who (*ogg.* whom) **2.** (*colei che*) she (*ogg.* her) who (*ogg.* whom) **3.** (*coloro che*) they (*ogg.* them) who (*ogg.* whom) **4.** (*gen.*) those, the person who(m). ♦ **chi** *pron. indef.* **1.** whoever, anyone **2.** (*qualcuno che*) someone who. ♦ **chi** *pron. int.* **1.** (*sogg.*) who **2.** (*ogg.*) whom **3.** which: *— di voi?*, which of you? **4.** (*specificazione poss.*) whose: *di — è questa casa?*, whose house is this?

chiàcchiera *sf.* chatter.

chiacchierare *vi.* to chat.

chiacchierata *sf.* chat.
chiacchierone *sm.* chatterbox.
chiamare *vt.* to call || *mandare a —*, to send (*v. irr.*) for; *— al telefono*, to call up. ♦ **chiamarsi** *vr.* to be called || *come ti chiami?*, what's your name?
chiamata *sf.* call, appeal.
chiara *sf. — d'uovo*, white (of an egg).
chiaretto *sm.* (*vino*) claret.
chiarezza *sf.* 1. clearness 2. (*fig.*) evidence.
chiarificare *vt.* to clarify.
chiarificazione *sf.* 1. clarification 2. (*fig.*) frank explanation.
chiarimento *sm.* explanation.
chiarire *vt.* 1. to clarify, to clear up 2. (*spiegare*) to explain.
chiaro *agg.* 1. clear, evident 2. (*di luce*) light.
chiarore *sm.* 1. light 2. (*luce tenue*) faint light.
chiaroscuro *sm.* light and shade.
chiaroveggente *agg.* 1. clear-sighted 2. (*che ha facoltà divinatorie*) clairvoyant.
chiassata *sf.* row.
chiasso *sm.* noise, uproar.
chiassone *sm.* noisy person.
chiassoso *agg.* 1. noisy 2. (*fig.*) showy.
chiatta *sf.* barge.
chiavarda *sf.* bolt.
chiave *sf.* 1. key 2. (*mus.*) clef.
chiavistello *sm.* latch, bolt.
chiazza *sf.* spot, stain.
chicchessìa *pron. indef.* anyone.
chicco *sm.* 1. grain 2. (*di grandine*) hailstone 3. (*di caffè*) coffee-bean 4. (*di uva*) grape.
chièdere *vt.* 1. to ask: *— qc. a qu.*, (*per sapere*) to ask so. sthg., (*per avere*) to ask ɔ. for sthg. 2. (*riferito a un prezzo*) to charge.
chierichetto *sm.* altar boy.
chiesa *sf.* church.
chiglia *sf.* (*mar.*) keel.
chilo[1] *sm.* (*med.*) chyle || *fare il —*, to take (*v. irr.*) a nap.
chilo[2] *sm.* kilo.
chilogrammo *sm.* kilogram.
chilometraggio *sm.* distance in kilometres.
chilòmetro *sm.* kilometre.
chìlowatt *sm.* kilowatt.
chimera *sf.* chimera.
chìmica *sf.* chemistry.
chìmico *agg.* chemical. ♦ **chìmico**

sm. chemist.
china *sf.* slope.
chinare *vt.* to bend (*v. irr.*), to bow. ♦ **chinarsi** *vr.* to bend (*v. irr.*) down.
chincaglierìa *sf.* 1. small fancy articles (*pl.*) 2. (*negozio*) fancy goods shop.
chinino *sm.* quinine.
chioccia *sf.* brooding-hen.
chiòcciola *sf.* snail || *scala a —*, spiral staircase.
chiodato *agg.* nailed.
chiodo *sm.* 1. nail 2. (*fig.*) fixed idea.
chioma *sf.* hair.
chiosco *sm.* 1. kiosk 2. (*per giornali, frutta e verdura*) stand.
chiostro *sm.* cloister.
chiromante *s.* chiromancer.
chiromanzìa *sf.* chiromancy.
chirurgìa *sf.* surgery.
chirurgo *sm.* surgeon.
chissà *inter.* goodness knows.
chitarra *sf.* guitar.
chiùdere *vt.* 1. to shut (*v. irr.*) || *— a chiave*, to lock 2. (*terminare*) to close 3. (*rinchiudere*) to shut (*v. irr.*) up.
chiunque *pron.* 1. (*sogg.*) anyone who, whoever 2. (*ogg.*) whomever, anyone 3. (*specificazione possessiva*) *di —*, whosever.
chiuso *agg.* closed, shut || *— a chiave*, locked.
chiusura *sf.* closing.
ci *pron.* 1. (*ogg.*) us: *essi — amano*, they love us 2. (*riflessivo*) ourselves: *noi — laviamo*, we wash ourselves 3. (*rec. fra due persone*) each other: *mia madre ed io — guardammo*, my mother and I looked at each other 4. (*rec. fra più persone*) one another 5. (*dimostrativo*) this, that, it: *non badarci*, pay no attention to it. ♦ **ci** *avv. di luogo* there (*là*), here (*qui*).
ciabatta *sf.* slipper.
ciambella *sf.* ring-shaped cake.
ciambellano *sm.* chamberlain.
ciancia *sf.* idle talk || *ciance!*, nonsense!
cianciare *vi.* to chatter.
cianografìa *sf.* blueprint.
cianuro *sm.* cyanide.
ciao *inter.* 1. (*incontrandosi*) hullo 2. (*congedandosi*) bye-bye.
ciarla *sf.* 1. loquacity 2. (*notizia*

falsa) false report.
ciarlare *vi.* to talk idly.
ciarlatano *sm.* charlatan.
ciascuno *agg.* every. ♦ **ciascuno**
pron. **1.** (*con valore distributivo*)
each **2.** (*tutti*) everybody, everyone.
cibernètica *sf.* cybernetics.
cibo *sm.* food.
ciborio *sm.* ciborium (*pl.* -ia).
cicala *sf.* cicada.
cicatrice *sf.* scar.
cicatrizzare *vt.* to cicatrize, to heal.
♦ **cicatrizzarsi** *vr.* to cicatrize, to
heal.
cicerone *sm.* guide.
ciclamino *sm.* cyclamen.
ciclico *agg.* cyclic.
ciclismo *sm.* cycling.
ciclista *s,* cyclist.
ciclo *sm.* **1.** cycle **2.** (*di malattia*)
course.
ciclone *sm.* hurricane.
ciclòpico *agg.* Cyclopean.
ciclostilare *vt.* to mimeograph.
ciclostile *sm.* cyclostyle.
ciclotrone *sm.* cyclotron.
cicogna *sf.* stork.
cicuta *sf.* hemlock.
cieco *agg.* blind (*anche fig.*). ♦
cieco *sm.* blind man.
cielo *sm.* **1.** sky **2.** (*aria*) air **3.**
(*paradiso*) Heaven.
cifra *sf.* **1.** figure, number **2.** (*segno di cifrario*) cipher.
cifrare *vt.* **1.** to cipher **2.** (*ricamare
in cifra*) to mark.
ciglio *sm.* **1.** eyelash **2.** (*bordo*)
edge.
cigno *sm.* swan.
cilecca *sf.* failure || *far* —, to miss
fire, (*fig.*) to fail.
cileno *agg.* Chilean.
cilicio *sm.* **1.** hairshirt **2.** (*relig.*)
cilice.
ciliegia *sf.* cherry.
ciliegio *sm.* cherry-tree.
cilindrata *sf.* (*auto*) displacement.
cilindro *sm.* **1.** (*geom.; auto*) cylinder **2.** (*cappello*) top-hat.
cima *sf.* **1.** top, summit: *in* —,
at the top **2.** (*fig.*) genius.
cimbali *sm.* *pl.* *essere in* —, to be
tipsy.
cimentare *vt.* to put (*v. irr.*) to
the test. ♦ **cimentarsi** *vr.* to venture upon.
cimitero *sm.* cemetery, graveyard.
cinabro *sm.* cinnabar.
cincillà *sf.* chinchilla.

cineasta *sm.* cinematographer.
cinecàmera *sf.* cine-camera.
cinedilettante *sm.* film-amateur.
cinegiornale *sm.* news-reel.
cinema *sm.* **1.** cinema, pictures
(*pl.*) **2.** (*locale*) cinema **3.** (*amer.*)
movies (*pl.*).
cinemàtica *sf.* kinematics.
cinematografia *sf.* cinematography.
cinematògrafo *sm.* cinema.
cinèreo *agg.* cinereous, ashen-grey.
cinese *agg.* e *sm.* Chinese.
cineteca *sf.* film library.
cinètica *sf.* kinetics.
cìngere *vt.* **1.** to engird **2.** (*circondare*) to surround.
cinghia *sf.* **1.** strap **2.** (*mecc.*) belt.
cinghiale *sm.* (*zool.*) wild boar.
cinico *agg.* cynical. ♦ **cinico** *sm.*
cynic.
cinismo *sm.* cynicism.
cinocèfalo *sm.* cynocephalus (*pl.*
-ali).
cinòdromo *sm.* greyhound racing-
-track.
cinofilia *sf.* dog-love.
cinquanta *agg.* fifty.
cinquantenario *sm.* fiftieth anniversary.
cinque *agg.* five.
cinquecento *agg.* five hundred.
cinta *sf.* town-walls (*pl.*): *muro di*
—, boundary walls.
cinto *sm.* belt. ♦ **cinto** *agg.*
surrounded.
cintola *sf.* waist: *dalla* — *in giù*,
below the waist; *dalla* — *in su*,
above the waist.
cintura *sf.* belt.
cinturone *sm.* belt.
ciò *pron.* that, this, it.
ciocca *sf.* (*di capelli*) lock.
cioccolata *sf.* chocolate.
cioccolatino *sm.* chocolate.
cioccolato *sm.* chocolate.
cioè *cong.* that is.
ciondolare *vi.* **1.** to dangle **2.**
(*fig.*) to lounge.
ciòndolo *sm.* pendant.
ciondoloni *avv.* dangling.
ciòtola *sf.* cup, bowl.
ciòttolo *sm.* pebble.
cipolla *sf.* onion.
cipresso *sm.* cypress.
cipria *sf.* powder: *piumino per* —,
powder puff.
circa *prep.* e *avv.* about, nearly ||
— *a*, as to.
circo *sm.* circus.

circolante *agg.* circulating: *moneta* —, currency.

circolare¹ *agg.* circular. ♦ **circolare** *sf.* circular letter.

circolare² *vi.* to circulate.

circolatorio *agg.* circulatory.

circolazione *sf.* **1.** circulation **2.** (*traffico*) traffic **3.** (*comm.*) currency.

cìrcolo *sm.* **1.** circle **2.** (*associazione*) club.

circoncìdere *vt.* to circumcise.

circoncisione *sf.* circumcision.

circondare *vt.* to surround (*anche fig.*).

circonferenza *sf.* circumference.

circonflesso *agg.* circumflex.

circonlocuzione *sf.* circumlocution.

circonvallazione *sf.* ring-road.

circonvenire *vt.* to circumvent.

circonvoluzione *sf.* circumvolution.

circoscrìvere *vt.* to circumscribe.

circoscrizione *sf.* **1.** circumscription **2.** (*territorio*) area.

circospetto *agg.* circumspect.

circospezione *sf.* circumspection.

circostante *agg.* **1.** surrounding **2.** (*attr.*) neighbouring.

circostanza *sf.* circumstance, occasion: *in queste circostanze*, under these circumstances; *in quella* —, on that occasion.

circostanziale *agg.* circumstantial.

circostanziare *vt.* to detail.

circuire *vt.* **1.** to surround **2.** (*fig.*) to circumvent.

circùito *sm.* circuit.

cirìllico *agg.* cyrillic.

cirrosi *sf.* cirrhosis.

cisalpino *agg.* cisalpine.

cisposo *agg.* blear.

ciste *sf.* cyst.

cisterna *sf.* **1.** cistern **2.** (*serbatoio*) tank.

cistifèllea *sf.* gall-bladder.

cistite *sf.* cystitis.

citare *vt.* **1.** (*menzionare*) to mention **2.** (*da un libro o da un discorso ecc.*) to quote **3.** (*giur.*) to summon.

citazione *sf.* **1.** (*da un discorso, un libro ecc.*) quotation **2.** (*giur.*) summons (*pl.*).

citòfono *sm.* interphone.

citologìa *sf.* (*biol.*) cytology.

citrato *sm.* citrate.

cìtrico *agg.* citric.

città *sf.* **1.** town: — *di provincia*, country town; — *natale*, home

town; *gente di* —, townspeople; *vita di* —, town life **2.** (*metropoli*) city.

cittadella *sf.* **1.** citadel **2.** (*baluardo*) stronghold.

cittadina *sf.* **1.** small town **2.** (*donna che abita in città*) woman citizen.

cittadinanza *sf.* **1.** (*abitanti*) people of the city **2.** (*nazionalità*) citizenship: *diritto di* —, right of citizenship.

cittadino *sm.* **1.** (*che abita in città*) town-dweller **2.** (*che appartiene a uno stato*) citizen. ♦ **cittadino** *agg.* town.

ciuffo *sm.* **1.** forelock **2.** (*di penne, peli, erba*) tuft.

ciurma *sf.* crew.

civetta *sf.* **1.** owl **2.** (*fig.*) coquette.

civetterìa *sf.* coquetry.

cìvico *agg.* civic.

civile *agg.* **1.** civil **2.** (*che riguarda la civiltà*) civilized **3.** (*gentile*) polite **4.** (*non ecclesiastico o non militare*) civilian.

civilizzare *vt.* to civilize.

civilizzazione *sf.* civilization.

civiltà *sf.* **1.** civilization **2.** (*cortesia*) politeness.

civismo *sm.* civic virtues (*pl.*).

clamore *sm.* uproar.

clamoroso *agg.* noisy.

clandestino *agg.* clandestine, secret.

clarinetto, clarino *sm.* clarinet.

classe *sf.* class ‖ *di* — (*qualità*) first-rate.

classicismo *sm.* classicism.

clàssico *agg.* classical. ♦ **clàssico** *sm.* classic.

classifica *sf.* **1.** classification **2.** (*sport*) position.

classificare *vt.* to classify.

classificazione *sf.* classification.

claudicare *vi.* to limp.

clàusola *sf.* **1.** clause **2.** (*riserva*) reserve.

claustrofobìa *sf.* claustrophobia.

clava *sf.* club.

clavicémbalo *sm.* harpsichord.

clavìcola *sf.* collar-bone.

clemente *agg.* clement, mild.

clemenza *sf.* clemency, mildness.

cleptòmane *agg. e sm.* kleptomaniac.

cleptomanìa *sf.* kleptomania.

clericale *agg.* clerical.

clero *sm.* clergy.

cliente *sm.* **1.** customer **2.** (*di medico, avvocato*) client.

clientela *sf.* **1.** customers (*pl.*) **2.** (*di medico, avvocato*) practice **3.** (*comm.*) connection.

clima *sm.* climate.

clìnica *sf.* nursing-home.

clìnico *agg.* clinical. ♦ **clìnico** *sm.* clinician.

clistere *sm.* enema.

cloaca *sf.* cloaca.

cloro *sm.* chlorine.

clorofilla *sf.* chlorophyll.

cloroformio *sm.* chloroform.

cloruro *sm.* chloride.

coabitare *vi.* to cohabit.

coabitazione *sf.* cohabitation.

coadiuvante *agg.* coadjuvant.

coadiuvare *vt.* to help.

coagulare *vt.* **1.** to coagulate **2.** (*del latte*) to curdle.

coagulazione *sf.* coagulation.

coàgulo *sm.* **1.** curd **2.** (*di sangue*) blood-clot.

coalizione *sf.* alliance, coalition.

coalizzare *vt.* to unite. ♦ **coalizzarsi** *vr.* to form a coalition.

coartare *vt.* to force.

coatto *agg.* forced: *domicilio* —, forced residence.

cobalto *sm.* cobalt.

cobelligerante *agg. e sm.* co-belligerent.

cobra *sm.* cobra.

cocaina *sf.* cocaine.

cocainòmane *s.* cocainist.

coccarda *sf.* cockade.

cocchiere *sm.* coachman (*pl.* -men).

cocchio *sm.* coach.

còccige *sm.* cocyx (*pl.* -yges).

coccinella *sf.* ladybird.

cocciniglia *sf.* cochineal.

coccio *sm.* **1.** (*terracotta*) crock, pot **2.** (*pezzo rotto*) fragment of pottery.

cocciutàggine *sf.* stubbornness.

cocciuto *agg.* stubborn.

cocco *sm.* **1.** (*frutto*) coconut **2.** (*albero*) coconut-tree **3.** (*fam. vezz.*) darling.

coccodrillo *sm.* crocodile.

coccolare *vt.* to pet, to fondle.

cocente *agg.* **1.** hot, scalding **2.** (*fig.*) deep, bitter.

cocòmero *sm.* water-melon.

cocùzzolo *sm.* **1.** crown **2.** (*vetta*) top.

coda *sf.* **1.** tail **2.** (*fila*) queue: *fare la* —, to queue up.

codardo *agg.* cowardly. ♦ **codardo** *sm.* coward.

codesto *agg.* **1.** that (*pl.* those) **2.** (*come « tale »*) such. ♦ **codesto** *pron.* that one (*pl.* those ones).

còdice *sm.* **1.** code: — *civile*, Civil Law **2.** (*manoscritto antico*) codex.

codificare *vt.* to codify.

coefficiente *sm.* coefficient.

coercìtivo *agg.* coercive.

coercizione *sf.* compulsion.

coerente *agg.* coherent.

coerenza *sf.* coherence.

coesione *sf.* cohesion.

coesistenza *sf.* coexistence.

coesìstere *vi.* to coexist.

coetàneo *agg. e sm.* contemporary || *Carlo ed io siamo coetanei*, Charles and I are the same age.

cofanetto *sm.* casket: — *di gioielli*, jewel box.

còfano *sm.* **1.** coffer **2.** (*auto*) bonnet.

cògliere *vt.* **1.** to pick up, to pluck **2.** (*sorprendere*) to catch (*v. irr.*) **3.** (*colpire*) to hit (*v. irr.*) **4.** (*afferrare*) to seize: — *la palla al balzo*, to seize the opportunity.

cognata *sf.* sister-in-law.

cognato *sm.* brother-in-law.

cognizione *sf.* **1.** knowledge **2.** (*giur.*) cognizance.

cognome *sm.* surname.

coincidenza *sf.* **1.** coincidence **2.** (*ferr.*) connection.

coincìdere *vi.* to coincide, to clash.

coinvòlgere *vt.* to involve.

còito *sm.* coition.

colabrodo *sm.* strainer.

colaggio *sm.* **1.** (*di liquidi*) leakage **2.** (*metal.*) casting.

colare *vt.* **1.** to strain **2.** (*fondere*) to cast (*v. irr.*). ♦ **colare** *vi.* to drip.

colata *sf.* **1.** (*metal.*) casting **2.** (*quantità di metallo fuso*) cast **3.** (*di lava*) flow.

colato *agg.* strained, filtered.

colazione *sf.* **1.** (*del mattino*) breakfast **2.** (*di mezzogiorno*) lunch.

colbacco *sm.* busby.

colei *pron. dimostr.* **1.** (*sogg.*) she; (*ogg.*) her **2.** — *che*, she who, she whom (*sogg.*); her who, her whom (*ogg.*): — *che viene qui è mia sorella*, she who is coming here is my sister; — *che vedi è Maria*, she whom you see is Mary; *vedi* — *che viene?*, can you see her who is coming?; *sono stata aiutata da* —

che odiavo, I have been helped by her whom I hated.

coleòttero *sm.* coleopter.

colera *sm.* cholera.

colesterolo *sm.* cholesterol.

còlica *sf.* colic.

colino *sm.* strainer.

colite *sf.* colitis.

colla *sf.* glue || *— di farina,* paste.

collaborare *vi.* to collaborate.

collaboratore *sm.* collaborator.

collaborazione *sf.* collaboration.

collaborazionismo *sm.* collaborationism.

collaborazionista *sm.* collaborationist.

collana *sf.* 1. necklace 2. *(raccolta)* collection 3. *(di libri)* series.

collare *sm.* collar.

collasso *sm.* breakdown: *— cardiaco,* heart failure.

collaterale *agg.* collateral.

collaudare *vt.* to test.

collaudatore *sm.* 1. tester 2. *(aer.)* test pilot 3. *(auto)* test-driver.

collàudo *sm.* test: *fare un — di qc.,* to put *(v. irr.)* sthg. to the test.

collazionare *vt.* to collate.

colle *sm.* hill.

collega *sm.* colleague.

collegamento *sm.* 1. connection 2. *(mecc.)* linkwork || *essere in —,* to be in touch.

collegare *vt.* to connect, to link.

collegiale *agg.* collegial. ♦ **collegiale** *sm.* boarder.

collegio *sm.* 1. college 2. *(scuola con convitto)* boarding-school.

còllera *sf.* anger || *essere in —,* to be angry.

collèrico *agg.* hot-tempered.

colletta *sf.* collection.

collettivismo *sm.* collectivism.

collettività *sf.* collectivity.

collettivizzare *vt.* to collectivize.

collettivizzazione *sf.* collectivization.

collettivo *agg.* collective.

colletto *sm.* collar.

collettore *agg.* collecting. ♦ **collettore** *sm.* 1. *(esattore; raccoglitore)* collector 2. *(mecc.)* manifold 3. *(elettr.)* commutator.

collezionare *vt.* to collect.

collezione *sf.* collection.

collezionista *sm.* collector.

collimare *vi.* 1. *(essere d'accordo)* to agree (with) 2. *(coincidere)* to coincide.

collina *sf.* hill.

collinoso *agg.* hilly.

collirio *sm.* eye-wash.

collisione *sf.* collision *(anche fig.),* impact.

collo *sm.* 1. neck: *allungare il —,* to crane one's neck || *a rotta di —,* at breakneck speed; *tra capo e —,* unexpectedly 2. *(pacco)* parcel, package.

collocamento *sm.* 1. placing 2. *(impiego)* employment || *agenzia di —,* employment bureau 3. *(comm.)* disposal.

collocare *vt.* 1. to place 2. *(impiegare)* to employ 3. *(comm.)* to sell *(v. irr.),* to dispose of (sthg.). ♦ **collocarsi** *vr.* 1. to place oneself 2. *(impiegarsi)* to get a situation.

collocazione *sf.* 1. placing 2. *(comm.)* sale 3. *(di libri in biblioteche)* press-mark.

colloidale *agg.* colloidal.

colloquio *sm.* 1. conversation, talk 2. *(intervista)* interview.

collusione *sf.* collusion.

colluttazione *sf.* scuffle: *venire a —,* to come *(v. irr.)* to grips.

colmare *vt.* 1. to fill up 2. *(fig.)* to fill, to overwhelm.

colmo *agg.* full, brimful. ♦ **colmo** *sm.* top, summit, climax || *per — di sfortuna,* as a crowning misfortune; *è il —!,* that beats everything.

colomba *sf.* dove.

colombaia *sf.* dove-cot.

colombo *sm.* pigeon: *— viaggiatore,* carrier-pigeon.

colonia *sf.* colony.

coloniale *agg.* colonial.

colonialismo *sm.* colonialism.

colonialista *sm.* colonialist.

colonizzare *vt.* to colonize.

colonizzatore *sm.* colonizer.

colonizzazione *sf.* colonization.

colonna *sf.* column *(anche fig.),* pillar || *— d'acqua,* fall of water.

colonnato *sm.* colonnade.

colonnello *sm.* colonel.

colono *sm.* 1. farmer 2. *(abitante di una colonia)* settler.

colorante *agg.* colouring. ♦ **colorante** *sm.* dye.

colorare *vt.* to colour. ♦ **colorarsi** *vr.* 1. to colour 2. *(di persona)* to blush, to flush.

colorazione *sf.* colouring.

colore *sm.* 1. colour || *biancheria di* —, coloured linen; *gente di* —, coloured people; *colori a olio*, oil-paints 2. *(aspetto)* look.

colorire *vt.* to colour.

colorito *sm.* complexion.

coloritura *sf.* colouring.

coloro *pron. dimostr.* 1. they *(sogg.)*; them *(compl.)* 2. — *che*, they who, they whom *(sogg.)*; them who, them whom *(compl.)*: — *studiano saranno premiati*, they who study will be given a prize; — *tu vedi sono i miei amici*, they whom you see are my friends; *amerò sempre* — *mi amano*, I shall always love them who love me; *ti presenterò a* — *hai visto ieri*, I shall introduce you to them whom you saw yesterday.

colossale *agg.* colossal.

colosso *sm.* colossus *(pl. -si)*.

colpa *sf.* 1. fault 2. *(colpevolezza)* guilt.

colpévole *agg.* guilty.

colpevolezza *sf.* guilt, guiltiness.

colpire *vt.* 1. to hit *(v. irr.)*, to strike *(v. irr.; anche fig.)* 2. *(di arma da fuoco)* to shoot *(v. irr.)*.

colpo *sm.* 1. blow, stroke *(anche fig.)*: — *di fortuna*, stroke of luck; — *apoplettico*, stroke of apoplexy || — *d'aria*, draught; *a* — *d'occhio*, at a glance; *a* — *sicuro*, without any risk; *senza* — *ferire*, without resistance *(di arma da fuoco)* shot.

colposo *agg.* unpremeditated: *omicidio* —, manslaughter.

coltellata *sf.* stab.

coltello *sm.* knife: — *a serramanico*, jack-knife; *affilare un* —, to sharpen a knife.

coltivàbile *agg.* cultivable.

coltivare *vt.* to cultivate *(anche fig.)*, to till, to farm.

coltivatore *sm.* 1. tiller, farmer 2. *(di patate, tabacco ecc.)* grower.

coltivazione *sf.* 1. tilling, farming 2. *(di patate, tabacco ecc.)* growing.

colto *agg.* *(istruito)* learned.

coltre *sf.* blanket, coverlet.

colui *pron. dimostr.* 1. he *(sogg.)* him *(compl.)* 2. — *che*, he who, he whom *(sogg.)*; him who, him whom *(compl.)*: — *che ti ha salutato è mio fratello*, he who has greeted you is my brother; — *che vedesti ieri è un mio vecchio ami-*

co, he whom you saw yesterday is an old friend of mine; *daranno il premio a* — *che studierà*, they will give the prize to him who studies; *fui aiutata da* — *che avevo aiutato*, I was helped by him whom I had helped.

coma *sm.* coma.

comandamento *sm.* 1. command, precept 2. *(relig.)* commandment.

comandante *sm.* commander.

comandare *vt.* 1. to order, to command 2. *(essere al comando)* to command, to be in command of.

comando *sm.* 1. *(ordine)* order 2. *(autorità)* command 3. *(sede del comandante)* headquarters *(pl.)*.

comatoso *agg.* comatose.

combaciare *vi.* to fit together.

combattente *sm.* 1. fighting man 2. *(soldato)* soldier, service man.

combattentìstico *agg.* soldier (like) *(attr.)*.

combàttere *vt. e vi.* to fight *(v. irr.)* *(anche fig.)*.

combattimento *sm.* 1. combat, fight, battle 2. *(boxe)* match.

combattività *sf.* pugnacity.

combattivo *agg.* pugnacious.

combinare *vt.* 1. to combine 2. *(di colori)* to match 3. *(concludere)* to conclude 4. *(progettare)* to plan.

combinazione *sf.* 1. combination 2. *(sistemazione)* arrangement 3. *(caso, coincidenza)* chance, coincidence.

combrìccola *sf.* 1. band 2. *(comitiva)* party.

combustìbile *agg.* combustible. ◆ **combustìbile** *sm.* fuel.

combustione *sf.* combustion.

combutta *sf.* 1. gang: *essere in* —, to be hand in glove 2. *(congiura)* plot.

come *avv.* 1. *(simile a)* like: *è proprio* — *suo padre*, he is just like his father 2. *(in qualità di, modale)* as: *ti parlo* — *amico*, I am speaking to you as a friend 3. *(in comp.)* as ... as; so ... as: *Carlo è studioso* — *me*, Charles is as studious as I; *Carlo non è studioso* — *me*, Charles is not so studious as I 4. *(int.)* how: — *va?*, How are you? 5. *(escl.)* how: — *è interessante questo libro!*, How interesting this book is! ◆ **come** *prep.* 1. *(tempo-*

rale) as, as soon as: — *sentii la sua voce lo riconobbi*, as soon as I heard his voice I recognized him 2. (*come se*) as if: *mi guarda — se mi conoscesse*, he is looking at me as if he knew me || — *Dio volle*, in God's good time; — *segue*, as follows; — *d'accordo*, as agreed.

cometa *sf.* comet.

comicità *sf.* comicality.

còmico *agg.* comical, funny. ♦ **còmico** *sm.* comedian.

comìgnolo *sm.* chimney-pot.

cominciare *vt.* to begin (*v. irr.*), to start.

comitato *sm.* committee.

comitiva *sf.* party, company.

comizio *sm.* meeting.

comma *sm.* paragraph.

commedia *sf.* 1. comedy, play 2. (*fig.*) pretence || *recitare la* —, to play a part.

commediante *sm.* 1. player 2. (*fig.*) shammer.

commediògrafo *sm.* playwright.

commemorare *vt.* to commemorate.

commemorativo *agg.* memorial.

commemorazione *sf.* commemoration.

commendàbile *agg.* commendable.

commendatizia *sf.* letter of recommendation.

commensale *sm.* table-companion.

commentare *vt.* to comment (on).

commentario *sm.* (*lett.*) commentary.

commentatore *sm.* commentator.

commento *sm.* commentary.

commerciàbile *agg.* negotiable.

commerciale *agg.* commercial.

commercializzare *vt.* to commercialize.

commerciante *sm.* 1. trader 2. (*uomo d'affari*) business-man (*pl.* -men) || — *all'ingrosso*, wholesale dealer; — *al minuto*, retailer.

commerciare *vi.* to trade, to deal (*v. irr.*) (in).

commercio *sm.* 1. commerce, trade 2. (*affari*) business || — *all'ingrosso*, wholesale trade; — *al minuto*, retail trade; — *d'importazione, esportazione*, import, export trade; *essere in* —, to be on sale; *essere fuori* —, to be out of sale; *essere in* — (*di un commerciante*), to be in business.

commessa *sf.* shop assistant, shop-girl.

commesso *sm.* clerk, shopman (*pl.* -men), shop assistant || — *viaggiatore*, commercial traveller.

commestìbile *agg.* eatable. ♦ **commestìbili** *sm. pl.* foodstuffs.

comméttere *vt.* 1. to commit, to do (*v. irr.*), to make (*v. irr.*) 2. (*ordinare*) to order.

commiato *sm.* 1. (*preso*) leave 2. (*dato*) dismissal.

commilitone *sm.* fellow-soldier.

comminatoria *sf.* commination.

comminatorio *agg.* comminatory.

commiserare *vt.* to pity.

commiserazione *sf.* pity.

commissariato *sm.* 1. (*carica di commissario*) commissaryship 2. (*ufficio*) commissary's office.

commissario *sm.* commissary.

commissionare *vt.* (*comm.*) to order.

commissionario *sm.* (*comm.*) commission agent.

commissione *sf.* 1. errand: *fare una* —, to go (*v. irr.*) on an errand 2. (*comm.*) commission, order 3. (*comitato*) commission, committee.

commisurare *vt.* to compare.

committente *sm.* purchaser, buyer.

commosso *agg.* moved, affected.

commovente *agg.* moving, touching, affecting.

commozione *sf.* 1. emotion 2. (*med.*) concussion: — *cerebrale*, concussion of the brain.

commuòvere *vt.* to move, to touch. ♦ **commuòversi** *vr.* to be moved.

commutàbile *agg.* commutable.

commutare *vt.* to commute.

commutativo *agg.* commutative.

commutatore *sm.* commutator.

comò *sm.* chest of drawers.

comodino *sm.* night-table.

comodità *sf.* convenience, comfort.

còmodo *agg.* 1. useful 2. (*conveniente*) convenient 3. (*confortevole*) comfortable 4. (*maneggevole*) handy.

compagnìa *sf.* 1. company: *tener* —, to keep (*v. irr.*) company 2. (*gruppo di persone*) party 3. (*società*) company.

compagno *sm.* companion, mate, comrade || — *di giuochi*, playmate; — *di stanza*, room-mate; — *di studi*, fellow-student.

compagnone sm. jolly good fellow.

comparàbile agg. comparable.

comparare vt. to compare.

comparativo agg. (gramm.) comparative.

comparato agg. comparative.

compare sm. 1. (compagno) comrade, partner 2. (padrino) godfather 3. (testimone di matrimonio) witness 4. (complice) accomplice.

comparire vi. 1. to appear 2. (sembrare) to show (v. irr.) oneself 3. (far bella mostra) to show (v. irr.) off.

comparizione sf. appearance: (giur.) mandato di —, summons.

comparsa sf. 1. appearance 2. (teat.; cine) supernumerary 3. (giur.) appearance.

compartecipare vi. to share in.

compartimento sm. 1. compartment 2. (circoscrizione) department.

compartizione sf. distribution.

compassato agg. 1. stiff, formal 2. (di discorso) restrained.

compassione sf. pity, commiseration.

compasso sm. compasses (pl.).

compatibile agg. consistent.

compatibilità sf. consistency.

compatimento sm. pity, compassion.

compatire vt. to pity.

compatriota sm. fellow-countryman (pl. -men). ♦ **compatriota** sf. fellow-countrywoman (pl. -women).

compattezza sf. 1. compactness 2. (di associazione, partito) unity.

compatto agg. compact, solid.

compendiare vt. to abridge, to sum up.

compendio sm. 1. abridgement, summary.

compenetrare vt. to penetrate.

compensàbile agg. remunerable.

compensare vt. 1. to compensate 2. (ricompensare) to reward.

compensato sm. ply-wood.

compensazione sf. 1. compensation, indemnity 2. (comm.) clearing.

compenso sm. 1. compensation 2. (rimunerazione) reward, retribution.

còmpera sf. purchase.

competente agg. competent.

competenza sf. 1. competence 2. (onorario) fee.

compètere vi. 1. (gareggiare) to vie 2. (spettare) to be due, to belong.

competitivo agg. competitive.

competitore sm. competitor, rival.

competizione sf. competition.

compiacente agg. obliging.

compiacenza sf. 1. kindness 2. (soddisfazione) satisfaction.

compiacere vt. to please, to gratify. ♦ **compiacersi** vr. 1. to be pleased (with), to congratulate 2. (degnarsi) to condescend.

compiacimento sm. 1. satisfaction 2. (congratulazione) congratulation.

compiàngere vt. 1. to pity, to sympathize (with) 2. (disprezzare) to despise.

compianto agg. regretted. ♦ **compianto** sm. regret.

còmpiere vt. 1. (finire) to finish 2. (eseguire) to accomplish 3. (adempiere) to do (v. irr.): — il proprio dovere, to do one's duty 4. (di età) ho compiuto 30 anni, I am now 30 years old.

compilare vt. to compile: — un documento, to draw (v. irr.) up a document; — una lista, to make (v. irr.) a list.

compilazione sf. 1. compilation 2. (comm.) drawing up.

compimento sm. 1. (il compire) completion 2. (conclusione) achievement.

compitare vt. to spell (v. irr.).

compitezza sf. politeness, refinement.

compito agg. polite.

còmpito sm. 1. task, duty 2. (scolastico, a casa) homework; (a scuola) class-work.

compiutamente avv. completely.

compiutezza sf. completeness.

compiuto agg. complete.

compleanno sm. birthday: buon —!, happy birthday!.

complementare agg. complementary.

complemento sm. 1. complement 2. (gramm.) — indiretto, indirect object 3. (mil.) truppe di —, reserve.

complessato agg. neurotic.

complessione sf. constitution.

complessità sf. complexity.

complessivamente avv. on the whole.

complessivo agg. total, inclusive.

complesso agg. complex, complicated. ♦ **complesso** *sm.* **1.** whole **2.** (*industriale*) plant, set **3.** (*mus.*) band.

completamente *avv.* completely.

completare *vt.* to complete, to finish.

completezza *sf.* completeness.

completo *agg.* **1.** complete, whole **2.** (*pieno*) full. ♦ **completo** *sm.* (*vestito*) suit.

complicare *vt.* to complicate.

complicato *agg.* complicated.

complicazione *sf.* complication: *salvo complicazioni*, if no complications set in.

còmplice *s.* accomplice.

complicità *sf.* accomplicity.

complimentare *vt.* to compliment. ♦ **complimentarsi** *vr.* to congratulate (so.).

complimento *sm.* **1.** compliment **2.** (*congratulazione*) congratulation.

complottare *vi.* to plot.

complotto *sm.* plot, conspiracy.

compluvio *sm.* (*arch.*) compluvium (*pl.* -ia).

componente *agg.* component. ♦ **componente** *sm.* **1.** member **2.** (*chim.*) component.

componimento *sm.* **1.** (*lett.; mus.; scol.*) composition **2.** (*giur.*) settlement.

comporre *vt.* **1.** to compose: — *una poesia*, to write (*v. irr.*) a poem; — *un numero telefonico*, to dial a number **2.** (*chim.*) to compound **3.** (*assestare*) to arrange.

comportamento *sm.* behaviour.

comportare *vt.* to involve, to require. ♦ **comportarsi** *vr.* to behave (oneself).

compòsito *agg.* composite.

compositore *sm.* **1.** (*mus.*) composer **2.** (*tip.*) compositor.

composizione *sf.* **1.** composition **2.** (*conciliazione*) composition, agreement **3.** (*tip.*) composing.

composta *sf.* compote.

compostezza *sf.* **1.** composure **2.** (*dignità*) self-respect.

composto *agg.* **1.** compound **2.** (*ordinato*) tidy **3.** (*calmo*) calm ‖ *stare* —, to sit (*v. irr.*) still. ♦ **composto** *sm.* compound.

comprare *vt.* **1.** to buy (*v. irr.*): — *a credito*, to buy on credit; — *per contanti*, to buy for cash; — *all'ingrosso*, to buy wholesale **2.** (*corrompere*) to bribe.

compratore *sm.* buyer, purchaser.

compravéndita *sf.* marketing.

comprèndere *vt.* **1.** (*includere*) to include, to take (*v. irr.*) in **2.** (*capire*) to understand (*v. irr.*) **3.** (*rendersi conto*) to realize.

comprensìbile *agg.* intelligible.

comprensibilità *sf.* intelligibility.

comprensione *sf.* **1.** comprehension, understanding **2.** (*compassione*) sympathy.

comprensivo *agg.* **1.** comprehensive **2.** (*che capisce*) comprehending **3.** (*che prova simpatia*) sympathetic.

compressa *sf.* **1.** tablet **2.** (*di garza*) compress.

compressibilità *sf.* compressibility.

compressione *sf.* compression.

comprìmere *vt.* **1.** to compress **2.** (*fig.*) to restrain, to repress.

compromesso *sm.* compromise.

compromettente *agg.* compromising.

compromèttere *vt.* to compromise, to involve.

comproprietà *sf.* joint ownership.

comproprietario *sm.* joint owner.

comprovare *vt.* to prove.

compunto *agg.* filled with compunction, contrite.

computare *vt.* to compute.

computisterìa *sf.* book-keeping.

còmputo *sm.* reckoning.

comunale *agg.* communal, municipal.

comunardo *sm.* (*stor.*) Communard.

comune[1] *agg.* **1.** common **2.** (*abituale*) frequent, usual.

comune[2] *sm.* **1.** commune **2.** (*edificio*) Town Hall.

comunella *sf.* cabal: *far — con qu.*, to consort.

comunemente *avv.* commonly, usually.

comunicàbile *agg.* communicable.

comunicabilità *sf.* communicability.

comunicante *agg.* communicating.

comunicare *vt.* **1.** to communicate, to transmit **2.** (*relig.*) to communicate. ♦ **comunicarsi** *vr.* to receive Holy Communion.

comunicativa *sf.* communicativeness.

comunicativo *agg.* communicative.

comunicato *sm.* bulletin.

comunicazione *sf.* communication.

comunione *sf.* **1.** communion: —

di idee, similarity of ideas 2. (*relig.*) Holy Communion.

comunismo *sm.* communism.

comunista *s.* communist.

comunità *sf.* community.

comunque *avv.* however, anyhow.

con *prep.* 1. (*compagnia, unione, strumento*) with: *venne — me,* he came with me; *scrivo — questa penna,* I write with this pen 2. (*stato, condizione*) in: *— il freddo sto meglio,* in cold weather I feel better 3. (*mezzo di trasporto*) by: *arriverò col treno delle 3,* I shall arrive by the three o'clock train 4. (*per mezzo di*) by means of.

conato *sm.* effort || *avere conati di vomito,* to feel (*v. irr.*) sick.

conca *sf.* 1. basin, pot 2. (*valle*) valley.

concatenamento *sm.* concatenation.

concatenare *vt.* to concatenate.

concatenazione *sf.* concatenation.

còncavo *agg.* concave, hollow.

concèdere *vt.* 1. to grant, to bestow 2. (*permettere*) to allow.

concentramento *sm.* concentration: *campo di —,* concentration camp.

concentrare *vt.* to concentrate. ♦ **concentrarsi** *vr.* to concentrate.

concentrato *agg.* concentrated. ♦ **concentrato** *sm.* concentrated food.

concentrazione *sf.* concentration.

concèntrico *agg.* concentric.

concepìbile *agg.* conceivable.

concepimento *sm.* conception.

concepire *vt.* 1. to conceive 2. (*nutrire speranze, timori*) to entertain 3. (*formulare*) to express.

concerìa *sf.* tannery.

concèrnere *vt.* to concern, to relate to.

concertare *vt.* 1. (*mus.*) to harmonize 2. (*stabilire*) to plan, to arrange.

concertato *agg.* concerted (*anche mus.*), arranged.

concertista *s.* concert artist.

concertìstico *agg.* concert.

concerto *sm.* concert.

concessionario *sm.* concessionary agent.

concessione *sf.* 1. concession 2. (*permesso*) permission.

concetto *sm.* concept.

concettuale *agg.* conceptual.

concezionale *agg.* conceptional.

concezione *sf.* conception.

conchiglia *sf.* shell.

concia *sf.* 1. (*di pelli*) tanning 2. (*di tabacco*) curing.

conciare *vt.* 1. (*pelli*) to tan 2. (*tabacco*) to cure 3. (*fig.*) to ill-treat 4. (*insudiciare*) to soil. ♦ **conciarsi** *vr.* to get (*v. irr.*) dirty.

conciatore *sm.* tanner.

conciatura *sf.* tanning.

conciliàbile *agg.* compatible, consistent.

conciliabilità *sf.* compatibility.

conciliàbolo *sm.* conventicle, secret talk.

conciliante *agg.* conciliatory.

conciliare *vt.* 1. to reconcile 2. (*procacciare*) to win (*v. irr.*), to gain. ♦ **conciliarsi** *vr.* to win (*v. irr.*).

conciliare *agg.* conciliar.

conciliatore *agg.* conciliatory. ♦ **conciliatore** *sm.* peacemaker || *giudice —,* Justice of the Peace.

conciliazione *sf.* conciliation.

concilio *sm.* Council.

concimaia *sf.* dung-hill, dung-pit.

concimare *vt.* to dung.

concimazione *sf.* dunging.

concime *sm.* 1. (*organico*) dung 2. (*chimico*) fertilizer.

concio *sm.* dung.

concionare *vi.* to harangue.

concione *sf.* harangue.

concisione *sf.* concision.

conciso *agg.* concise, brief.

concistoro *sm.* (*eccl.*) concistory.

concitare *vt.* to excite, to stir (up).

concitazione *sf.* excitement, agitation.

concittadino *sm.* fellow-citizen.

conclamare *vt.* to acclaim.

conclave *sm.* (*eccl.*) conclave.

concludente *agg.* 1. conclusive 2. (*di persona*) energetic.

conclùdere *vt.* 1. to conclude, to finish 2. (*dedurre*) to infer 3. (*fare*) to do (*v. irr.*).

conclusionale *sf.* (*giur.*) pleadings (*pl.*).

conclusione *sf.* 1. conclusion 2. (*risultato*) issue, result.

conclusivo *agg.* conclusive.

concomitante *agg.* concomitant.

concomitanza *sf.* concomitance.

concordanza *sf.* agreement.

concordare *vi.* to agree. ♦ **concordare** *vt.* 1. to agree upon 2.

(mettere d'accordo) to reconcile 3. *(gramm.)* to put *(v. irr.)* in concord.

concordatario *agg.* 1. *(eccl.)* of concordat 2. *(giur.; comm.)* composition.

concordato *sm.* 1. convention 2. *(eccl.)* concordat 3. *(giur.; comm.)* agreement, composition.

concorde *agg.* concordant, agreeing: *volontà* —, unanimous will.

concordemente *avv.* concordantly.

concordia *sf.* concord, agreement.

concorrente *agg.* 1. concurrent 2. *(rivale)* competing. ♦ **concorrente** *sm.* 1. candidate 2. *(rivale)* competitor.

concorrenza *sf.* 1. *(affluenza)* concourse 2. *(comm.)* competition ‖ *fare* —, to compete with; — *sleale*, unfair competition.

concorrenziale *agg.* competitive.

concòrrere *vi.* 1. to come *(v. irr.)* together 2. *(contribuire)* to concur, to contribute 3. *(partecipare)* to share in 4. *(mettersi in gara)* to compete.

concorso *sm.* 1. *(affluenza)* rush, crowd, concourse 2. *(gara)* competition 3. *(sport)* contest.

concretare *vt.* 1. to make *(v. irr.)* concrete 2. *(concludere)* to realize.

concretezza *sf.* concreteness.

concreto *agg.* 1. concrete, real 2. *(solido)* solid.

concrezione *sf.* concretion.

concubina *sf.* concubine.

concubinaggio, concubinato *sm.* concubinage.

conculcare *vt.* to trample on.

concupire *vt.* to covet, to lust after.

concupiscenza *sf.* concupiscence, lust.

concussione *sf.* *(giur.)* concussion.

condanna *sf.* 1. condemnation 2. *(sentenza)* sentence: — *a morte*, death sentence 3. *(pena)* penalty.

condannàbile *agg.* condemnable.

condannare *vt.* 1. to sentence 2. *(fig.)* to condemn 3. *(riprovare)* to blame.

condannato *agg.* sentenced. ♦ **condannato** *sm.* condemned man.

condensàbile *agg.* condensable.

condensabilità *vt.* condensability.

condensazione *sf.* condensation.

condensare *vt.* to condense.

condensatore *sm.* condenser.

condimento *sm.* seasoning, dressing.

condire *vt.* to season; *(anche fig.)* to flavour.

condirettore *sm.* joint manager.

condiscendente *agg.* complying.

condiscendenza *sf.* 1. compliance 2. *(degnazione)* condescension.

condiscèndere *vi.* 1. to comply with 2. *(degnarsi)* to condescend.

condiscépolo *sm.* schoolfellow.

condivìdere *vt.* to share *(anche fig.)*.

condizionale *agg.* e *sm.* conditional. ♦ **condizionale** *sf.* *(giur.)* conditional sentence.

condizionamento *sm.* conditioning.

condizionare *vt.* to condition.

condizione *sf.* 1. condition: *a — che*: on condition that 2. *(ceto)* rank, station.

condoglianza *sf.* condolence.

condominio *sm.* joint ownership.

condòmino *sm.* joint-owner.

condonare *vt.* to remit.

condono *sm.* remission.

condotta *sf.* 1. conduct, behaviour.

condotto *agg. medico* —, doctor employed by the local authority. ♦ **condotto** *sm.* 1. conduit, pipeline 2. *(anat.)* duct.

conducente *sm.* driver.

conducibilità *sf.* *(fis.)* conductibility.

condurre *vt.* 1. *(guidare)* to lead *(v. irr.)* 2. *(accompagnare)* to take *(v. irr.)* 3. *(governare, trattare)* to manage: — *i propri affari*, to manage one's business 4. *(vivere)* to lead *(v. irr.)*: — *una vita triste*, to lead a sad life. ♦ **condurre** *vi.* to lead *(v. irr.)*: *questa strada conduce a Milano*, this route leads to Milan. ♦ **condursi** *vr.* to behave.

conduttività *sf.* conductivity.

conduttivo *agg.* conducting. ♦ **conduttore** *agg.* conducting. ♦ **conduttore** *sm.* 1. leader, guide 2. *(di veicoli)* driver 3. *(fis.)* conductor.

conduttura *sf.* 1. duct, conduit 2. *(di tubazioni)* piping.

conduzione *sf.* 1. management 2. *(fis.)* conduction.

confabulare *vi.* to confabulate.

confacente *agg.* suitable, proper.

confarsi *vr.* to suit, to become *(v. irr.)*.

confederale *agg.* confederal.

confederare *vt.* to confederate.

confederazione sf. 1. Confederation 2. (alleanza) confederacy.

conferenza sf. 1. lecture 2. (assemblea) conference.

conferenziere sm. lecturer.

conferimento sm. bestowal.

conferire vt. to confer, to bestow. ♦ **conferire** vi. 1. to have an interview 2. (giovare) to be useful.

conferma sf. confirmation.

confermare vt. to confirm. ♦ **confermarsi** vr. to prove oneself.

confermazione sf. confirmation.

confessare vt. 1. to confess 2. (riconoscere, ammettere) to admit. ♦ **confessarsi** vr. (eccl.) to go (v. irr.) to confession.

confessionale agg. confessional. ♦ **confessionale** sm. confessional.

confessione sf. 1. confession 2. (ammissione) admission 3. (memorie) memoirs (pl.).

confessore sm. confessor.

confetterìa sf. confectionery.

confettiere sm. confectioner.

confetto sm. comfit.

confettura sf. 1. (confetti) sweetmeats (pl.) 2. (marmellata) jam || — d'arance, marmalade.

confezionare vt. 1. to make (v. irr.) up 2. (di piatti) to prepare 3. (di pacchi) to pack up.

confezione sf. 1. manufacture 2. (preparazione) preparation 3. (pl.) (abiti) ready-to-wear clothes 4. (imballaggio) packing.

conficcare vt. to hammer, to drive (v. irr.). ♦ **conficcarsi** vr. to run (v. irr.) into.

confidare vt. to confide. ♦ **confidare** vi. 1. to confide, to trust 2. (fare assegnamento) to rely (on).

confidente agg. trustful. ♦ **confidente** sm. 1. confidant 2. (di polizia) police spy.

confidenza sf. 1. (fiducia) confidence 2. (cosa confidata) secret 3. (familiarità) familiarity || essere in — con qu., to be on familiar terms with so.

confidenziale agg. confidential: strettamente —, strictly confidential.

confidenzialmente avv. confidentially.

configgere vt. to drive (v. irr.) in.

configurare vt. to configure, to shape.

configurazione sf. configuration, shape.

confinante agg. 1. neighbouring 2. (fig.) bordering.

confinare vi. to border on. ♦ **confinare** vt. 1. to banish 2. (fig.) to confine.

confinario agg. border.

confinato agg. interned.

confine sm. 1. border, frontier 2. (fig.) limit, boundary.

confino sm. internment, political confinement.

confisca sf. confiscation.

confiscàbile agg. confiscable.

confiscare vt. to confiscate.

confitto agg. 1. nailed, driven in 2. (fig.) fixed.

conflagrare vi. to break (v. irr.) out.

conflagrazione sf. 1. conflagration 2. (fig.) sudden out-break (of war).

conflitto sm. 1. conflict 2. (fig.) clash.

confluente sm. confluent.

confluenza sf. confluence.

confluire vi. to flow together.

confòndere vt. 1. to confuse 2. (scambiare una persona per un'altra) to mistake (v. irr.) 3. (turbare) to confound. ♦ **confòndersi** vr. 1. to get (v. irr.) mixed up 2. (mescolarsi) to mingle 3. (turbarsi) to be disconcerted.

confondìbile agg. liable to be confused.

conformare vt. to conform. ♦ **conformarsi** vr. to conform.

conformato agg. shaped.

conformazione sf. conformation.

conforme agg. 1. conforming 2. (simile) similar 3. (fedele) true || — a, in conformity with. ♦ **conforme** a loc. avv. in conformity with.

conformismo sm. time-serving.

conformista s. 1. time-server 2. (relig.) conformist.

conformìstico agg. conformist.

conformità sf. conformity.

confortàbile agg. consolable.

confortante agg. consoling.

confortare vt. 1. to comfort 2. (incoraggiare) to encourage.

confortatore agg. comforting. ♦ **confortatore** sm. comforter.

confortatorio agg. comforting.

confortévole agg. 1. comforting 2. (comodo) comfortable.

confortevolmente *avv.* comfortably.

conforto *sm.* **1.** comfort, solace **2.** (*incoraggiamento*) encouragement.

confratello *sm.* brother (*pl.* brethren).

confratèrnita *sf.* brotherhood.

confrontàbile *agg.* comparable.

confrontare *vt.* **1.** to compare **2.** (*giur.*) to confront.

confronto *sm.* **1.** comparison **2.** (*giur.*) confrontation || *nei confronti di*, to, towards; *in — a*, in comparison with.

confucianésimo *sm.* confucianism.

confusamente *avv.* confusedly.

confusionario *agg.* blundering, unmethodical. ♦ **confusionario** *sm.* bungler, muddler.

confusione *sf.* confusion, medley.

confusionismo *sm.* general confusion.

confuso *agg.* **1.** confused, mixed, vague **2.** (*indistinto*) indistinct **3.** (*imbarazzato*) embarrassed.

confutàbile *agg.* confutable.

confutare *vt.* to confute.

confutazione *sf.* confutation.

congedare *vt.* **1.** to dismiss **2.** (*mil.*) to discharge. ♦ **congedarsi** *vr.* to take (*v. irr.*) one's leave.

congedato *sm.* dischargee.

congedo *sm.* **1.** (*commiato*) leave **2.** (*mil.*) leave, discharge || *essere in —*, to be on leave.

congegnare *vt.* **1.** (*mecc.*) to assemble **2.** (*fig.*) to devise.

congegno *sm.* **1.** device, gear **2.** (*fig.*) device, scheme.

congelamento *sm.* **1.** freezing **2.** (*med.*) congelation.

congelare *vt.* to freeze (*v. irr.*), to congeal.

congelato *agg.* congealed, frozen (*anche comm.*).

congelatore *sm.* freezer.

congènere *agg.* **1.** akin (*attr.*) **2.** similar (*pred.*).

congeniale *agg.* congenial.

congènito *agg.* congenital, innate.

congestionare *vt.* to congest.

congestionato *agg.* congested: *viso —*, flushed face.

congestione *sf.* congestion.

congettura *sf.* conjecture, supposition.

congetturare *vt.* to conjecture.

congiùngere *vt.* **1.** to join **2.** (*collegare*) to connect.

congiuntiva *sf.* conjunctiva.

congiuntivite *sf.* conjunctivitis.

congiuntivo *agg.* conjunctive. ♦ **congiuntivo** *sm.* (*gramm.*) subjunctive.

congiunto *agg.* **1.** joined, united **2.** (*collegato*) connected. ♦ **congiunto** *sm.* relative.

congiuntura *sf.* **1.** point of junction **2.** (*circostanza, situazione*) circumstance, situation **3.** (*econ.*) trend, trade cycle.

congiunzione *sf.* **1.** connection **2.** (*gramm.; astr.*) conjunction.

congiura *sf.* conspiracy, plot.

congiurare *vi.* to conspire, to plot.

congiurato *sm.* conspirator, plotter.

conglobamento *sm.* conglobation.

conglobare *vt.* **1.** to conglobate **2.** (*di tasse, debiti ecc.*) to combine.

conglobazione *sf.* conglobation.

conglomerato *sm.* **1.** (*geol.*) conglomerate **2.** (*etnico; pol.*) grouping.

congratularsi *vr.* to congratulate.

congratulazione *sf.* congratulation.

congregazione *sf.* assembly, congregation (*anche eccl.*).

congressista *s.* member of a congress.

congresso *sm.* congress.

congruo *agg.* **1.** (*coerente*) congruous **2.** (*adeguato*) adequate.

conguagliare *vt.* **1.** to equalize **2.** (*comm.*) to balance.

coniare *vt.* to coin (*anche fig.*).

cònico *agg.* conic(al).

conìfera *sf.* conifer.

coniglio *sm.* **1.** rabbit **2.** (*fig.*) faint-hearted.

conio *sm.* **1.** (*attrezzo per coniare*) minting die **2.** (*impronta*) coin, brand **3.** (*invenzione di nuove parole*) coinage.

coniugale *agg.* conjugal: *vita —*, married life.

coniugare *vt.* **1.** to conjugate **2.** (*unire in matrimonio*) to marry.

coniugato *agg.* married.

coniugazione *sf.* conjugation.

còniuge *sm.* husband. ♦ **còniuge** *sf.* wife.

connaturale *agg.* connatural, innate.

connaturato *agg.* deeply rooted.

connazionale *sm.* fellow-countryman (*pl.* -men). ♦ **connazionale** *sf.* fellow-countrywoman (*pl.* -women).

connessione sf. connection.

connesso agg. connected.

connèttere vt. 1. (unire) to connect, to join 2. (fig.) to associate, to link || non connettere, to talk at random.

connettivo agg. connective.

connivente agg. conniving (at).

connotato sm. description, feature || i connotati, description.

connubio sm. 1. marriage 2. (fig.) union.

cono sm. cone: — gelato, ice-cream cone.

conoscente sm. acquaintance.

conoscenza sf. 1. knowledge || venire a — di qc., to become (v. irr.) acquainted with sthg. 2. (persona) acquaintance 3. (sensi) consciousness.

conòscere vt. 1. to know (v. irr.): — di vista, to know by sight; — di fama, to know by reputation; — dalla voce, to recognize by one's voice 2. (fare la conoscenza) to meet (v. irr.).

conoscìbile agg. 1. knowable 2. (riconoscibile) recognizable.

conoscitivo agg. cognitive.

conoscitore sm. expert, good judge.

conosciuto agg. well-known, renowned.

conquista sf. conquest.

conquistare vt. 1. to conquer 2. (fig.) to win (v. irr.).

conquistatore sm. 1. conqueror 2. (rubacuori) lady-killer.

consacrare vt. 1. (eccl.) to consecrate 2. (dedicare) to devote.

consacrazione sf. consecration.

consanguineità sf. consanguinity.

consanguineo agg. consanguine, akin. ♦ **consanguineo** sm. kinsman (pl. -men).

consapévole agg. aware, conscious.

consapevolezza sf. 1. consciousness 2. (conoscenza) knowledge.

conscio agg. conscious.

consecutivo agg. 1. following 2. (di seguito) running: per due giorni consecutivi, for two days running 3. (gramm.) consecutive.

consegna sf. 1. (comm.) delivery: — contro assegno, cash on delivery; — mancata, nondelivery; ordine di —, delivery-note; effettuare la —, to effect delivery 2. (deposito) consignment 3. (mil.) orders (pl.) || — in caserma, confi-

nement to barracks.

consegnare vt. 1. to deliver 2. (mil.) to confine to barracks.

conseguente agg. consequent.

conseguenza sf. consequence.

conseguìbile agg. attainable.

conseguimento sm. attainment.

conseguire vt. to attain, to achieve, to get (v. irr.).

consenso sm. 1. consent 2. (matrimoniale) licence.

consensuale agg. by mutual consent.

consentire vi. to consent, to agree. ♦ **consentire** vt. to allow.

consenziente agg. consenting.

conserto agg. interwoven, folded: a braccia conserte, with folded arms.

conserva sf. preserve || — di frutta, jam; — di pomodoro, tomato sauce.

conservare vt. to preserve ♦ **conservarsi** vr. to keep (v. irr.).

conservativo agg. conservative.

conservatore agg. 1. preserving 2. (pol.) conservative. ♦ **conservatore** sm. 1. preserver 2. (pol.) conservative.

conservatorio sm. academy of music.

conservazione sf. preservation || istinto di —, instinct of self-preservation.

considerare vt. 1. to consider, to think (v. irr.) of 2. (reputare) to deem, to judge. ♦ **considerarsi** vr. to consider oneself.

considerato agg. considerate || — che, considering that.

considerazione sf. 1. consideration 2. (stima) esteem, regard || avere — per qu., to have regard for so.

considerévole agg. considerable.

consigliare vt. to advise. ♦ **consigliarsi** vr. to ask so.'s advice, to consult (with).

consigliere sm. 1. counsellor 2. (membro di un consiglio) councillor.

consiglio sm. 1. advice (solo sing.) 2. (corpo di persone) council.

consiliare agg. of a council.

consìmile agg. similar.

consistente agg. firm, substantial.

consistenza sf. 1. consistence 2. (comm.) on hand: — di cassa, cash on hand.

consìstere vi. to consist.

consociare *vt.* to associate.

consociato *agg.* associated.

consociazione *sf.* association.

consocio sm. co-partner.

consolante *agg.* cheering.

consolare[1] *vt.* to console, to comfort. ♦ **consolarsi** *vr.* to be comforted.

consolare[2] *agg.* consular.

consolato sm. consulate.

consolatore *agg.* consoling. ♦ **consolatore** sm. consoler.

consolazione *sf.* consolation, solace.

cònsole sm. consul.

consolidamento sm. consolidation.

consolidare *vt.* to consolidate, to strengthen.

consolidato *agg.* consolidated.

consonante *sf.* consonant.

consonanza *sf.* consonance (*anche fig.*).

cònsono *agg.* in accordance (with).

consorella *sf.* (*eccl.*) sister.

consorte sm. consort, husband. ♦ **consorte** *sf.* consort, wife.

consorterìa *sf.* faction.

consorzio sm. society: — *agrario*, agricultural union.

constare *vi.* 1. (*essere composto*) to consist 2. (*risultare*) to be within one's knowledge ‖ *da quanto mi consta*, as far as I know.

constatare *vt.* V. *costatare*.

constatazione *sf.* V. *costatazione*.

consueto *agg.* usual, customary.

consuetudinario *agg.* customary, consuetudinary.

consuetùdine *sf.* 1. custom, habit 2. (*comm.*) rule.

consulente sm. adviser.

consulenza *sf.* advice.

consulta *sf.* 1. consultation 2. (*corpo consultivo*) council.

consultare *vt.* 1. to consult 2. (*esaminare*) to examine.

consultazione *sf.* consultation: *libro di* —, reference book.

consultivo *agg.* consultative.

consulto sm. consultation.

consumare *vt.* 1. to consume 2. (*di abiti*) to wear (*v. irr.*) 3. (*dissipare*) to waste 4. (*compiere*) to commit.

consumato *agg.* 1. (*perfetto*) accomplished 2. (*logoro*) worn out 3. (*divorato*) consumed.

consumatore sm. consumer.

consumazione *sf.* 1. consumption 2. (*giur.*) consummation 3. (*bibi-*

ta) drink.

consumo sm. consumption ‖ *per proprio uso e* —, for one's private use.

consuntivo *agg.* final: *bilancio* —, final balance.

consunzione *sf.* consumption.

contàbile *agg.* bookkeeping. ♦ **contàbile** sm. bookkeeper.

contabilità *sf.* bookkeeping.

contachilòmetri sm. speedometer.

contadino sm. countryman (*pl. -men*), peasant. ♦ **contadino** *agg.* rustic.

contado sm. countryside.

contagiare *vt.* to infect.

contagio sm. contagion (*anche fig.*), infection.

contagioso *agg.* contagious, infectious (*anche fig.*).

contagiri sm. revolution counter.

contagocce sm. dropper.

contaminare *vt.* 1. to pollute, to infect 2. (*un testo letterario*) to corrupt.

contaminazione *sf.* contamination (*anche fig.*), pollution.

contante *agg.* ready. ♦ **contante** sm. ready money ‖ *pagare in contanti*, to pay cash.

contare *vt.* 1. to count, to number 2. (*considerare*) to consider 3. (*proporsi*) to think (*v. irr.*) of ‖ *conto di andare a Milano domani*, I think of going to Milan tomorrow 4. (*aspettarsi*) to expect. ♦ **contare** *vi.* 1. (*avere importanza*) to count, to be important 2. (*fare assegnamento*) to rely on.

contatore sm. meter: — *del gas*, gas-meter; — *dell'acqua*, water-meter; — *della luce*, electric power-meter.

contatto sm. 1. contact, touch: *essere in* —, to be in touch 2. (*elettr.*) contact.

conte sm. 1. Count 2. (*in Gran Bretagna*) Earl.

contea *sf.* 1. earldom 2. (*divisione territoriale*) county.

conteggiare *vt.* to count.

conteggio sm. computation.

contegno sm. 1. behaviour 2. (*atteggiamento*) attitude.

contegnoso *agg.* 1. dignified 2. (*altero*) stiff.

contemperamento sm. adaptation.

contemperare *vt.* to adapt.

contemplare *vt.* 1. to behold (*v.*

irr.), to admire 2. (*giur.*) to consider.

contemplativo *agg.* contemplative.

contemplatore *sm.* contemplator.

contemplazione *sf.* contemplation.

contempo (*nella loc. avv.*) nel —, in the meantime.

contemporaneamente *avv.* at the same time.

contemporaneità *sf.* contemporaneousness.

contemporàneo *agg.* e *sm.* contemporary.

contendente *agg.* contending, opposing. ♦ **contendente** *sm.* opponent, rival.

contèndere *vt.* to contend, to refuse. ♦ **contèndersi** *vr. rec.* to contend.

contenere *vt.* 1. to contain, to hold (*v. irr.*) 2. (*trattenere*) to repress. ♦ **contenersi** *vr.* 1. (*comportarsi*) to behave 2. (*dominarsi*) to contain oneself.

contenitore *sm.* container.

contentare *vt.* to content. ♦ **contentarsi** *vr.* to be content (with).

contentezza *sf.* pleasure, joy.

contento *agg.* content, pleased.

contenuto *sm.* contents (*pl.*).

contenzioso *agg.* contentious.

conterìe *sf. pl.* glass beads.

conterràneo *sm.* fellow-countryman (*pl.* -men) || (*femm.*) fellow-countrywoman (*pl.* -women).

contesa *sf.* 1. contest 2. (*litigio*) quarrel.

contessa *sf.* countess.

contestàbile *agg.* questionable.

contestare *vt.* 1. to contest, to challenge, to deny 2. (*notificare*) to declare.

contestazione *sf.* dispute, objection: *sollevare contestazioni*, to raise objections.

contesto *sm.* context.

contiguità *sf.* contiguity.

contiguo *agg.* neighbouring.

continentale *agg.* continental.

continente *agg.* moderate. ♦ **continente** *sm.* continent.

continenza *sf.* continence.

contingentamento *sm.* allotment.

contingentare *vt.* to allot.

contingenza *sf.* 1. emergency 2. (*circostanza*) circumstance 3. (*fil.*) contingency.

continuamente *avv.* continuously.

continuare *vt.* e *vi.* 1. to go (*v.*

irr.) on (with) 2. (*riprendere*) to resume.

continuativo *agg.* continuative.

continuato *agg.* 1. (*ininterrotto*) continuous 2. (*che si ripete*) continual.

continuatore *sm.* continuator.

continuazione *sf.* continuation.

continuità *sf.* continuity.

continuo *agg.* 1. (*ininterrotto*) continuous 2. (*che si ripete*) continual.

conto *sm.* 1. (*anche comm.*) account: *fare i conti*, to make (*v. irr.*) up accounts 2. (*di albergo ecc.*) bill 3. (*assegnamento*) reliance: *far — su*, to rely on 4. (*stima*) regard || *persona di poco —*, person of little account; *rendere — di*, to answer for; *rendersi —*, to realize; *mettersi per proprio —*, to set (*v. irr.*) for oneself.

contòrcere *vt.* to twist. ♦ **contòrcersi** *vr.* to twist.

contorcimento *sm.* twisting.

contornare *vt.* 1. to surround 2. (*con guarnizioni*) to trim.

contorno *sm.* 1. outline 2. (*orlo*) border 3. (*cuc.*) vegetables (*pl.*).

contorsione *sf.* contortion.

contorsionismo *sm.* writhing.

contorsionista *s.* contorsionist.

contorto *agg.* twisted.

contrabbandare *vt.* to smuggle.

contrabbandiere *sm.* smuggler.

contrabbando *sm.* smuggling.

contrabbassista *sm.* double-bass player.

contrabbasso *sm.* double-bass.

contraccambiare *vt.* to return.

contraccambio *sm.* return || *rendere il —*, to retaliate (upon).

contraccolpo *sm.* 1. counterblow 2. (*fig.*) reaction.

contraccusa *sf.* countercharge.

contrada *sf.* 1. quarter 2. (*paese*) country.

contraddanza *sf.* country-dance.

contraddire *vt.* to contradict. ♦ **contraddirsi** *vr.* to contradict oneself. ♦ **contraddirsi** *v. rec.* to contradict one another, each other.

contraddistìnguere *vt.* to mark.

contraddittore *sm.* opposer.

contraddittorio *agg.* contradictory. ♦ **contraddittorio** *sm.* debate.

contraddizione *sf.* contradiction, discrepancy.

contraente *agg.* contracting. ♦

contraente *sm.* contractor.

contraèrea *sf.* anti-aircraft artillery.

contraèreo *agg.* anti-aircraft.

contraffare *vt.* to counterfeit.

contraffatto *agg.* counterfeit.

contraffattore *sm.* 1. (*falsificatore*) counterfeiter 2. (*imitatore*) imitator.

contrafforte *sm.* buttress.

contraggenio *sm.* dislike || *a* (*di*) —, unwillingly.

contràlbero *sm.* (*mecc.*) countershaft.

contralto *sm.* contralto.

contrammiraglio *sm.* rear-admiral.

contrappasso *sm.* retaliation.

contrappello *sm.* second roll-call.

contrappesare *vt.* to counterbalance.

contrappeso *sm.* counterbalance.

contrapporre *vt.* to oppose, to contrast || — *qc. a qu.*, to set (*v. irr.*) sthg. against so.

contrapposizione *sf.* contraposition.

contrapposto *agg.* opposite || *per* —, on the contrary. ♦ **contrapposto** *sm.* opposite.

contrappunto *sm.* counterpoint.

contrariamente *avv.* on the contrary || — *ad ogni aspettativa*, contrary to all expectation.

contrariare *vt.* 1. to oppose 2. (*irritare*) to annoy.

contrarietà *sf.* 1. opposition 2. (*avversità*) misfortune.

contrario *agg.* 1. contrary, opposed 2. (*nocivo*) harmful 3. (*riluttante*) unwilling || *al* —, on the contrary. ♦ **contrario** *sm.* contrary.

contrarre *vt.* to contract.

contrassegnare *vt.* to mark.

contrassegno *sm.* 1. countersign 2. (*segno*) mark 3. (*distintivo*) badge.

contrastare *vi.* to be in contrast. ♦ **contrastare** *vt.* to oppose.

contrastato *agg.* opposed.

contrasto *sm.* 1. contrast 2. (*dissidio*) conflict.

contrattaccare *vt.* to counterattack.

contrattacco *sm.* counterattack.

contrattare *vt.* to negotiate: — *il prezzo*, to haggle about the price.

contrattazione *sf.* dealing, negotiation.

contrattempo *sm.* 1. (*incidente*) mishap 2. (*inconveniente*) inconvenience.

contràttile *agg.* contractile.

contratto *sm.* contract.

contratto *agg.* contracted.

contrattuale *agg.* contractual.

contravveleno *sm.* antidote.

contravvenire *vi.* to infringe.

contravventore *sm.* transgressor.

contravvenzione *sf.* 1. violation 2. (*multa*) fine.

contrazione *sf.* contraction.

contribuente *sm.* taxpayer.

contribuire *vi.* to contribute.

contributo *sm.* contribution.

contribuzione *sf.* contribution.

contristarsi *vr.* to grieve.

contrito *agg.* contrite.

contrizione *sf.* contrition.

contro *prep.* 1. against 2. (*in opposizione a*) contrary to || — *assegno*, cash on delivery.

controbàttere *vt.* (*confutare*) to disprove, to confute.

controbilanciare *vt.* to counterbalance.

controcampo *sm.* (*cine*) reverse shot.

controcorrente *sf.* counter-current. ♦ **controcorrente** *loc. avv.* against the stream.

controffensiva *sf.* counter-offensive.

controfigura *sf.* double.

controfirmare *vt.* to countersign.

controindicare *vt.* (*med.*) to contra-indicate.

controindicazione *sf.* (*med.*) contra-indication.

controllare *vt.* 1. to control 2. (*verificare*) to verify, to check 3. (*ispezionare*) to inspect 4. (*comm.*) to audit.

controllo *sm.* 1. control 2. (*verifica*) check, verification 3. (*ispezione*) inspection 4. (*comm.*) audit.

controllore *sm.* 1. controller 2. (*ferr.*) ticket-inspector.

controluce *avv.* against the light. ♦ **controluce** *sf.* counterlight.

contromarca *sf.* pass-out check (ticket).

controparte *sf.* counter-party.

contropartita *sf.* 1. (*comm.*) counter-item 2. (*compenso*) compensation.

contropelo *sm.* wrong way of the hair || *fare il* —, to shave against the lie of the hair.

controproducente *agg.* having opposite effect.

controproposta *sf.* counter-proposal.

controprova *sf.* 1. countercheck 2. (*giur.*) counter-evidence.

contròrdine *sm.* counter-order: *dare un —*, to countermand an order.

controriforma *sf.* counter-reformation.

controrivoluzione *sf.* counter-revolution.

controsenso *sm.* self-contradiction, absurdity.

controspionaggio *sm.* counter-espionage.

controstòmaco *avv.* reluctantly.

controvelaccio *sm.* (*mar.*) main royal.

controvento *avv.* against the wind.

controversia *sf.* controversy.

controverso *agg.* controversial.

controvertìbile *agg.* controvertible.

controvoglia *avv.* unwillingly.

contumace *agg.* guilty of default.

contumacia *sf.* default.

contumaciale *agg.* (*giur.*) judgment by default.

contumelia *sf.* insult, abuse.

contundente *agg.* blunt: *corpo —*, blunt instrument.

conturbare *vt.* 1. to perturb 2. (*eccitare*) to thrill.

contusione *sf.* bruise.

contuso *agg.* bruised.

convalescente *agg.* e *sm.* convalescent.

convalescenza *sf.* convalescence.

convalidare *vt.* to ratify, to confirm.

convegno *sm.* meeting.

convenévole *agg.* convenient, proper. ♦ **convenévoli** *sm. pl.* compliments.

conveniente *agg.* 1. convenient (for) 2. (*economicamente vantaggioso*) profitable.

convenienza *sf.* 1. convenience 2. (*vantaggio economico*) profit 3. (*buona creanza*) propriety.

convenire *vi.* 1. to convene 2. (*essere d'accordo*) to agree 3. (*essere utile*) to be convenient.

convento *sm.* 1. convent 2. (*di suore*) nunnery.

conventuale *agg.* conventual.

convenuto *agg.* agreed upon. ♦ **convenuto** *sm.* 1. agreement 2. *i convenuti*, the persons present.

convenzionale *agg.* conventional.

convenzionare *vt.* to make (*v. irr.*) an agreement.

convenzione *sf.* convention.

convergente *agg.* convergent.

convergenza *sf.* convergence.

convèrgere *vi.* to converge.

conversare *vi.* to talk.

conversatore *sm.* talker.

conversazione *sf.* conversation, talk.

conversione *sf.* 1. (*anche fig.*) conversion 2. (*mil.*) wheel.

convertìbile *agg.* convertible.

convertire *vt.* 1. (*pol.; relig.*) to convert 2. (*mutare*) to turn, to change. ♦ **convertirsi** *vr.* to be converted.

convessità *sf.* convexity.

convesso *agg.* convex.

convìncere *vt.* to convince, to persuade.

convinto *agg.* convinced, persuaded.

convinzione *sf.* persuasion, firm belief.

convitato *sm.* guest.

convito *sm.* banquet.

convitto *sm.* boarding-school.

convivente *agg.* cohabiting.

convivenza *sf.* cohabitation, life in common.

convivere *vi.* to live together.

convocare *vt.* to convene, to summon.

convocazione *sf.* convocation, summoning.

convogliare *vt.* 1. (*scortare*) to escort 2. (*trasportare*) to carry awe 3. (*indirizzare*) to address.

convoglio *sm.* 1. (*treno*) train 2. (*mil.; mar.*) convoy.

convolare *vi.* to fly (*v. irr.*) together: *— a giuste nozze*, to get (*v. irr.*) married.

convulsione *sf.* convulsion.

convulso *agg.* convulsive.

cooperare *vi.* to co-operate, to collaborate.

cooperativa *sf.* 1. co-operative society 2. (*di consumo*) co-operative store.

cooperativo *agg.* co-operative.

cooperatore *sm.* co-operator.

cooperazione *sf.* co-operation, collaboration.

coordinamento *sm.* co-ordination.

coordinare *vt.* to co-ordinate.

coordinata *sf.* co-ordinate.

coordinativo *agg.* co-ordinative.

coordinato *agg.* co-ordinate.

coordinatore *agg.* co-ordinative. ♦
coordinatore *sm.* co-ordinator.
coordinazione *sf.* co-ordination.
coorte *sf.* 1. (*mil.*) cohort 2. (*folla*) crowd.
copale *sf.* 1. copal 2. (*pelle*) patent leather.
copeco *sm.* copeck.
coperchio *sm.* lid, cover (*anche mecc.*).
coperta *sf.* 1. blanket: — *da viaggio*, rug; — *scozzese*, plaid 2. (*mar.*) deck.
copertina *sf.* cover: — *di libro*, book-cover.
coperto *agg.* 1. (*riparato*) covered, sheltered || — *di ferro*, iron-clad; *mettere al* —, to shelter from 2. (*di cielo*) overcast 3. (*nascosto*) hidden. ♦ **coperto** *sm.* cover.
copertone *sm.* tyre.
copertura *sf.* 1. covering 2. (*di mobili*) cover.
copia *sf.* 1. copy 2. (*foto*) print.
copiare *vt.* to copy.
copiativo *agg.* *matita copiativa*, copying pencil.
copiatura *sf.* copying.
copione *sm.* script.
copiosamente *avv.* plentifully.
copioso *agg.* plentiful.
copista *sm.* copyist.
coppa *sf.* 1. cup 2. (*auto*) pan.
coppella *sf.* (*metal.*) cupel.
coppellare *vt.* (*metal.*) to cupel.
coppia *sf.* 1. (*di persone e cose*) couple 2. (*di animali*) pair || *una* — *di buoi*, a yoke.
copricapo *sm.* hat.
coprifuoco *sm.* curfew.
copriletto *sm.* coverlet.
coprire *vt.* 1. to cover 2. (*nascondere*) to conceal 3. (*coprire un suono*) to drown.
copto *agg.* coptic. ♦ **copto** *sm.* copt.
copulativo *agg.* (*gramm.*) copulative.
copulazione *sf.* copulation.
coraggio *sm.* 1. courage, bravery, heart 2. (*sfrontatezza*) impudence.
coraggiosamente *avv.* bravely.
coraggioso *agg.* brave, bold.
corale *agg.* choral.
corallifero *agg.* coralliferous.
corallo *sm.* coral.
corazza *sf.* 1. cuirass 2. (*bot.; zool.*) armour, carapace.
corazzare *vt.* 1. to armour 2. (*fig.*)

to strengthen. ♦ **corazzarsi** *vr.* to harden oneself.
corazzata *sf.* (*mar.*) battleship.
corazziere *sm.* cuirassier.
corbellerìa *sf.* 1. foolish action 2. (*sciocchezza*) nonsense.
corda *sf.* 1. rope 2. (*mus.*) string.
cordaio *sm.* 1. (*chi fabbrica corde*) rope-maker 2. (*chi vende corde*) rope-seller.
cordame *sm.* cordage.
cordata *sf.* rope: *in* —, on the rope.
cordiale *agg.* cordial, hearty. ♦ **cordiale** *sm.* (*liquore*) cordial.
cordialità *sf.* cordiality.
cordialmente *avv.* cordially.
cordicella *sf.* string.
cordigliera *sf.* cordillera.
cordite *sf.* cordite.
cordoglio *sm.* deep sorrow.
cordone *sm.* 1. cord 2. (*mil.*) cordon.
coreano *agg. e sm.* Korean.
coreografia *sf.* choreography.
coreogràfico *agg.* 1. choreographic 2. (*fig.*) spectacular.
coreògrafo *sm.* choreographer.
coriàceo *agg.* coriaceous, tough.
coriàndolo *sm.* confetti (*pl.*).
coricare *vt.* to lay (*v. irr.*) down. ♦ **coricarsi** *vr.* to lie (*v. irr.*) down.
corifeo *sm.* coryphaeus (*pl.* -aei).
corinzio *agg. e sm.* Corinthian.
corista *sm.* chorus-singer.
cormorano *sm.* (*zool.*) cormorant.
cornacchia *sf.* rook, crow.
cornamusa *sf.* bagpipe.
cornata *sf.* butt.
còrnea *sf.* cornea.
cornetta *sf.* cornet.
cornice *sf.* frame.
cornicione *sm.* 1. (*arch.*) cornice 2. (*di finestre, porte*) label 3. (*di gronda*) eaves (*pl.*).
cornificare *vt.* 1. (*di moglie*) to cuckold 2. (*di marito*) to be unfaithful to.
corno *sm.* horn || (*inter.*) *un* —, not at all.
cornuto *agg.* horned. ♦ **cornuto** *sm.* (*fig.*) cuckold.
coro *sm.* 1. chorus 2. (*eccl.*) choir.
corolla *sf.* corolla.
corollario *sm.* corollary.
corona *sf.* 1. crown: — *del rosario*, rosary crown; — *del dente*, crown 2. (*mecc.*) rim 3. (*relig.*) (*tonsura*) tonsure.

coronamento *sm.* **1.** crowning **2.** (*completamento*) fulfilment.

coronare *vt.* to crown (*anche fig.*).

coronario *agg.* coronary.

corpo *sm.* **1.** body || *a — morto*, desperately; *combattere a — a —*, to fight (*v. irr.*) hand to hand; *passare sul — di qu.*, to pass over so. **2.** (*cadavere*) corpse **3.** (*collettività*) corps || *— insegnante*, teaching staff.

corporale *agg.* corporal.

corporativismo *sm.* (*econ.*) corporative system.

corporativo *agg.* (*econ.*) corporative.

corporatura *sf.* build, size.

corporazione *sf.* corporation.

corpòreo *agg.* corporeal.

corpulento *agg.* corpulent, stout.

corpulenza *sf.* stoutness.

corpuscolare *agg.* corpuscular.

corpùscolo *sm.* corpuscle.

corredare *vt.* **1.** to equip **2.** (*accompagnare*) to accompany.

corredino *sm.* baby's outfit.

corredo *sm.* **1.** outfit **2.** (*di sposa*) trousseau **3.** (*bagaglio*) wealth, store: *— di cultura*, store of knowledge.

corrèggere *vt.* **1.** to correct **2.** (*di bevande*) to lace. ♦ **corrèggersi** *vr.* to amend, to correct oneself.

correggia *sf.* leather strap.

correlativo *agg.* correlative.

correlazione *sf.* correlation.

corrente[1] *agg.* **1.** (*che scorre*) running **2.** (*circolante*) current **3.** (*comm.*) inst. (*abbrev. di instant*) || *conto —*, current account **4.** (*andante*) common.

corrente[2] *sf.* **1.** current (*anche fig.*), stream **2.** (*di aria*) draught.

correntemente *avv.* fluently.

còrrere *vi.* **1.** to run (*v. irr.*): *— dietro a qu.*, to run after; *— a gambe levate*, to run as hard as one can || *lasciar —*, to take (*v. irr.*) no notice of sthg. **2.** (*di tempo*) to pass **3.** (*di voci*) to be abroad.

corresponsàbile *agg.* jointly responsible.

corresponsione *sf.* payment.

correttezza *sf.* **1.** correctness **2.** (*onestà*) honesty **3.** (*decoro, educazione*) propriety, politeness.

correttivo *agg. e sm.* corrective.

corretto *agg.* **1.** correct, exact **2.** (*irreprensibile*) faultless **3.** (*di bevanda*) laced.

correttore *sm.* corrector || *— di bozze*, proof-reader.

correzionale *agg.* correctional.

correzione *sf.* correction || *— di bozze*, proof-reading; *casa di —*, house of correction.

corridoio *sm.* **1.** passage **2.** (*di treno*) corridor.

corridore *sm.* **1.** runner **2.** (*sport*) racer.

corriera *sf.* coach.

corriere *sm.* **1.** messenger **2.** (*chi trasporta merci*) carrier **3.** (*posta*) mail.

corrimano *sm.* handrail.

corrispettivo *agg.* correlative. ♦ **corrispettivo** *sm.* **1.** equivalent **2.** (*compenso*) compensation.

corrispondente *agg. e sm.* correspondent.

corrispondenza *sf.* correspondence.

corrispòndere *vi.* **1.** to correspond (with) **2.** (*ricambiare sentimenti ecc.*) to return. ♦ **corrispòndere** *vt.* to pay.

corrisposto *agg.* **1.** (*contraccambiato*) returned **2.** (*pagato*) paid.

corroborante *agg. e sm.* corroborant.

corroborare *vt.* to strengthen.

corròdere *vt.* to corrode.

corròmpere *vt.* **1.** to corrupt (*anche fig.*), to pollute **2.** (*con denaro*) to bribe.

corrosione *sf.* corrosion.

corrosivo *agg. e sm.* corrosive.

corrucciarsi *vr.* to get (*v. irr.*) angry.

corrucciato *agg.* angry, worried.

corruccio *sm.* anger, worry.

corrugamento *sm.* corrugation: *— della fronte*, wrinkling of the forehead.

corrugare *vt.* to wrinkle.

corruttìbile *agg.* corruptible.

corruttore *agg.* corrupting. ♦ **corruttore** *sm.* **1.** corrupter **2.** (*con denaro*) briber.

corruzione *sf.* **1.** corruption **2.** (*con denaro*) bribery.

corsa *sf.* **1.** run **2.** (*sport*) race **3.** (*su veicolo pubblico*) trip || *prezzo della —*, fare; (*ferr.*) *perdere la —*, to miss the train.

corsaro *sm.* corsair.

corsetto *sm.* corset.

corsìa *sf.* **1.** passage **2.** (*di ospedale*) ward **3.** (*di strada*) lane.

corsiero *sm.* steed.
corsivo *agg.* cursive. ♦ **corsivo** *sm.* (*tip.*) italics (*pl.*).
corso *sm.* 1. course (*anche fig.*) 2 (*di acque*) water-course.
corte *sf.* 1. court 2. (*cortile*) court-yard 3. (*corteggiamento*) courtship.
corteccia *sf.* 1. bark 2. (*anat.*) cortex.
corteggiare *vt.* 1. to woo 2. (*adulare*) to flatter.
corteggiatore *sm.* suitor, lover.
corteo *sm.* train, procession: — *funebre*, funeral train.
cortese *agg.* kind.
cortesìa *sf.* 1. kindness, politeness 2. (*favore*) favour || *per* —, please.
cortigiano *sm.* 1. courtier 2. (*adulatore*) flatterer.
cortile *sm.* courtyard || *animali da* —, poultry.
cortina *sf.* curtain: — *di ferro* (*pol.*), iron curtain.
cortisone *sm.* cortisone.
corto *agg.* short: *a* — *di*, short of.
cortocircùito *sm.* short circuit.
cortometraggio *sm.* short (film).
corvetta *sf.* (*mar.*) corvette.
corvino *agg.* 1. corvine 2. (*nero*) raven(-black).
corvo *sm.* raven.
cosa *sf.* 1. thing 2. (*faccenda*) matter || *nessuna* —, nothing; *ogni* —, everything; *che* —?, what?.
cosacco *agg. e sm.* Cossack.
coscia *sf.* 1. thigh 2. (*cuc.*) leg.
cosciente *agg.* 1. conscious 2. (*conscio*) aware.
coscienza *sf.* 1. conscience 2. (*consapevolezza*) consciousness.
coscienziosamente *avv.* conscientiously.
coscienzioso *agg.* conscientious.
cosciotto *sm.* leg: — *di manzo*, leg of beef.
coscritto *sm.* recruit.
coscrizione *sf.* conscription.
cosecante *sf.* cosecant.
coseno *sm.* (*mat.*) cosine.
così *avv.* so: *e* — *via*, and so on; — *come*, — *pure*, as well as; — ... *come*, — ... *quanto*, as ... as; — *da*, so ... as: *non è* — *sciocco da farlo*, he is not so foolish as to do that.
cosicché *cong.* so that.
cosiddetto *agg.* so-called.
cosiffatto *agg.* such, similar.

cosmesi *sf.* beauty culture.
cosmètico *agg. e sm.* cosmetic.
còsmico *agg.* cosmic.
cosmo *sm.* cosmos.
cosmogonìa *sf.* cosmogony.
cosmografìa *sf.* cosmography.
cosmògrafo *sm.* cosmographer.
cosmologìa *sf.* cosmology.
cosmonàuta *s.* astronaut.
cosmonàutica *sf.* astronautics.
cosmopolita *agg. e sm.* cosmopolitan.
cosmopolitismo *sm.* cosmopolitanism.
coso *sm.* (*fam.*) 1. (*cosa*) thing 2. (*individuo*) fellow.
cospàrgere *vt.* 1. to strew (*v. irr.*) 2. (*sale, zucchero ecc.*) to sprinkle.
cospetto *sm.* presence: *al* — *di*, in the presence of.
cospicuità *sf.* conspicuousness.
cospicuo *agg.* 1. (*visibile*) conspicuous 2. (*notevole*) remarkable.
cospirare *vi.* to plot.
cospiratore *sm.* plotter.
cospirazione *sf.* plot.
costa *sf.* 1. coast, shore 2. (*venatura*) rib 3. (*di monte*) side 4. (*di libro*) back.
costà *avv.* there.
costaggiù *avv.* down there.
costale *agg.* costal.
costante *agg.* steady. ♦ **costante** *sf.* constant.
costanza *sf.* 1. firmness 2. (*perseveranza*) perseverance || *con* —, steadily.
costare *vi.* to cost (*v. irr.*).
costassù *avv.* up there.
costata *sf.* chop.
costatare *vt.* 1. (*accertare*) to ascertain 2. (*notare*) to notice.
costatazione *sf.* 1. ascertainment 2. (*osservazione*) remark.
costato *sm.* chest.
costeggiare *vt.* 1. to follow the coast of 2. (*per terra*) to skirt. ♦ **costeggiare** *vi.* to coast along.
costei *pron.* 1. (*sogg.*) she 2. (*compl.*) her 3. this woman, that woman.
costellare *vt.* to scatter.
costellazione *sf.* constellation.
costernare *vt.* to dismay. ♦ **costernarsi** *vr.* to be dismayed (at).
costernazione *sf.* dismay.
costì *avv.* there.
costiera *sf.* stretch of coast.
costiero *agg.* coastal || *nave costiera*, coaster.

costipare vt. 1. (un terreno) to tamp 2. (ammassare) to amass. ♦ **costiparsi** vr. 1. (raffreddarsi) to catch (v. irr.) a cold 2. (di intestino) to become (v. irr.) constipated.

costipato agg. essere —, to have a cold.

costipazione sf. 1. (raffreddore) cold 2. (intestinale) constipation 3. (di terreno) tamping.

costituente agg. constituent.

costituire vt. 1. to constitute, to form 2. (nominare) to appoint. ♦ **costituirsi** vr. (consegnarsi) to give (v. irr.) oneself up.

costituito agg. constituted.

costitutivo agg. constitutive.

costituto sm. (giur.) interrogation of the accused.

costituzionale agg. constitutional.

costituzionalismo sm. constitutionalism.

costituzionalità sf. constitutionality.

costituzione sf. 1. establishment 2. (pol.; med.) constitution.

costo sm. cost: ad ogni —, at all cost; a nessun —, in no case.

còstola sf. rib || stare alle costole, to watch over.

costoletta sf. cutlet.

costone sm. side.

costoro pron. 1. (sogg.) they 2. (compl.) them 3. these people, those people.

costoso agg. expensive, dear.

costrìngere vt. 1. (stringere) to press 2. (obbligare) to compel.

costrizione sf. 1. (restringimento) constriction 2. (obbligo) compulsion.

costruire vt. to build (v. irr.).

costruttivo agg. constructive.

costruttore agg. building. ♦ **costruttore** sm. builder.

costruzione sf. construction, building.

costui pron. 1. (sogg.) he 2. (compl.) him 3. this man, that man.

costumato agg. 1. (virtuoso) virtuous 2. (educato) polite.

costume sm. 1. (usanza) custom 2. (personale) habit 3. (condotta) morals (pl.) 4. (vestito) costume.

costumista sm. costume-designer.

cotangente sf. (mat.) cotangent.

cotenna sf. 1. pigskin 2. (del cranio) scalp 3. (del lardo) rind.

còtica sf. V. cotenna.

cotogna sf. quince.

cotognata sf. quince jam.

cotoletta sf. cutlet.

cotone sm. cotton.

cotoniere sm. cotton-spinner.

cotoniero agg. cotton.

cotonificio sm. cotton-mill.

cotonina sf. calico.

cotta[1] sf. (eccl.) surplice.

cotta[2] sf. 1. (cottura) cooking 2. (infornata) batch 3. (fam.) prendere una — per, to have a crush on.

cottimista sm. pieceworker.

còttimo sm. piecework: lavorare a —, to work by the job; lavoro a —, job-work; contratto a —, job contract.

cotto sm. brickwork.

cottura sf. 1. cooking 2. (in forno) baking.

coturno sm. cothurnus (pl. -ni).

cova sf. 1. (il covare) brooding 2. (nido) nest.

covare vt. 1. to brood 2. (fig.) to brood over 3. (di fuoco; passioni) to smoulder 4. (di malattia) to be latent.

covata sf. brood.

covo sm. den.

covone sm. sheaf (pl. sheaves).

cozza sf. mussel.

cozzare vi. 1. to strike (v. irr.) 2. (venire in collisione) to collide.

cozzo sm. 1. clash, collision 2. (conflitto) conflict.

crampo sm. cramp.

cranio sm. skull.

crasso agg. crass, gross: ignoranza crassa, gross ignorance.

cratere sm. crater.

cràuti sm. pl. sauerkraut (sing.)

cravatta sf. neck-tie.

creanza sf. politeness.

creare vt. 1. to create 2. (causare) to cause 3. (nominare) to appoint 4. (costituire) to form.

creativo agg. creative.

creato sm. creation.

creatore agg. creating. ♦ **creatore** sm. creator.

creatura sf. creature.

creazione sf. creation.

credente sm. believer.

credenza[1] sf. belief.

credenza[2] sf. (buffet) sideboard.

credenziale agg. credential: lettera —, credential.

crédere *vt.* e *vi.* 1. (*pensare*) to think (*v irr.*) 2. (*prestar fede*) to believe. ♦ crédersi *vr.* to think (*v. irr.*) oneself.

credìbile *agg.* 1. credible 2. (*di persona*) trustworthy.

credibilità *sf.* credibility.

creditìzio *agg.* credit.

crédito *sm.* 1. (*comm.*) credit: *a* —, on credit 2. (*stima*) esteem.

creditore *sm.* creditor.

credo *sm.* creed.

credulità *sf.* credulity.

credulone *agg.* credulous.

crema *sf.* cream.

cremagliera *sf.* rack: *ferrovia a* —, rack-railway.

cremare *vt.* to cremate.

crematorio *agg.* crematory: *forno* —, crematory.

cremazione *sf.* cremation.

cremeria *sf.* creamery.

crèmisi *agg.* e *sm.* crimson.

crèolo *agg.* e *sm.* creole.

crepa *sf.* crack.

crepaccio *sm.* crevasse.

crepacuore *sm.* heart-break: *morire di* —, to die of a broken heart.

crepapelle (*nella loc. avv.*) *ridere a* —, to roar with laughter; *mangiare a* —, to eat to excess.

crepare *vi.* to crack.

crepella *sf.* crepoline.

crepitare *vi.* to crackle.

crepitìo *sm.* crackle.

crepuscolare *agg.* crepuscular.

crepùscolo *sm.* twilight.

crescente *agg.* growing.

crescenza *sf.* growth.

créscere *vi.* 1. to grow (*v. irr.*) 2. (*aumentare*) to increase.

crescione *sm.* (*bot.*) water-cress.

créscita *sf.* 1. growth 2. (*aumento*) increase.

crèsima *sf.* confirmation.

cresimare *vt.* to confirm.

creso *sm.* Croesus.

crespo *agg.* crisp.

cresta *sf.* 1. crest 2. (*di gallo*) comb.

crestina *sf.* maid-servant's cap.

creta *sf.* clay.

cretineria *sf.* 1. idiocy 2. (*azione*) foolish action 3. (*detto*) nonsense.

cretinismo *sm.* idiocy.

cretino *agg.* e *sm.* idiot.

cricca *sf.* gang.

cricco *sm.* jack.

criminale *agg.* e *sm.* criminal.

criminalista *s.* 1. (*avvocato*) criminal lawyer 2. (*studioso*) criminologist.

criminalità *sf.* criminality.

crìmine *sm.* crime.

criminologìa *sf.* criminology.

criminosità *sf.* criminality.

criminoso *agg.* criminal.

crine *sm.* horse-hair.

criniera *sf.* mane.

crinolina *sf.* crinoline.

criolite *sf.* cryolite.

cripta *sf.* crypt.

crisàlide *sf.* chrysalid.

crisantemo *sm.* chrysanthemum.

crisi *sf.* 1. crisis (*pl.* -ses) 2. (*med.*) fit.

crisma *sm.* 1. (*eccl.*) chrism 2. (*fig.*) approval || *con tutti i crismi*, approved, praised.

cristallerìa *sf.* 1. crystal-ware 2. (*fabbrica*) crystal manufactory.

cristalliera *sf.* glass case.

cristallino *agg.* e *sm.* crystalline.

cristallizzare *vt.* e *vi.*, cristallizzarsi *vr.* to crystallize.

cristallizzazione *sf.* crystallization.

cristallo *sm.* 1. crystal 2. (*lastra di vetro*) plate glass.

cristallografìa *sf.* crystallography.

cristianésimo *sm.* Christianity.

cristiania *sm.* (*sport*) Christiania.

cristianità *sf.* 1. (*i cristiani*) Christendom 2. (*cristianesimo*) Christianity.

cristiano *agg.* e *sm.* Christian.

criterio *sm.* 1. principle 2. opinion 3. (*buon senso*) sense.

crìtica *sf.* 1. criticism 2. (*saggio*) critical essay 3. (*i critici*) the critics (*pl.*).

criticamente *avv.* critically.

criticare *vt.* 1. to criticize 2. (*biasimare*) to blame.

criticismo *sm.* 1. criticism 2. (*stor.*) critical philosophy.

crìtico *agg.* critical. ♦ crìtico *sm* critic.

criticone *sm.* fault-finder.

crittògama *sf.* (*bot.*) cryptogam.

crittografìa *sf.* cryptography.

crittogramma *sm.* cryptogram.

crivellare *vt.* to riddle.

crivellatura *sf.* riddling.

crivello *sm.* riddle.

croato *agg.* e *sm.* Croatian.

croccante *agg.* crisp. ♦ croccante *sm.* almond sweetmeat.

crocchetta *sf.* croquette.

crocchia *sf.* bun.

crocchio *sm.* group.

croce *sf.* cross.

crocerossina *sf.* Red Cross nurse.

crociata *sf.* crusade.

crociato *sm.* crusader.

crocicchio *sm.* cross-road.

crociera *sf.* 1. cruise 2. (*arch.*) cross-vault.

crocifiggere *vt.* to crucify.

crocifissione *sf.* crucifixion.

crocifisso *sm.* crucifix.

croco *sm.* (*bot.*) crocus.

crogiuolo *sm.* crucible.

crollare *vi.* to fall (*v. irr.*) down.

crollo *sm.* 1. breakdown 2. (*caduta*) falling down.

croma *sf.* (*mus.*) quaver.

cromare *vt.* to chromium-plate.

cromàtico *agg.* chromatic.

cromatismo *sm.* chromatism.

cromatografìa *sf.* chromatography.

cromatura *sf.* chromium plating.

cromo *sm.* chromium.

cromolitografìa *sf.* chromolithography.

cromosoma *sm.* chromosome.

crònaca *sf.* 1. chronicle 2. (*di giornale*) news.

crònico *agg.* chronic. ♦ **crònico** *sm.* chronic invalid.

cronista *sm.* reporter.

cronistoria *sf.* chronicle.

cronologìa *sf.* chronology.

cronològico *agg.* chronological.

cronometraggio *sm.* time-study.

cronometrare *vt.* to time.

cronometrìa *sf.* timing.

cronòmetro *sm.* stop watch.

crosta *sf.* 1. crust 2. (*tec.*) coating.

crostàcei *sm. pl.* Crustacea.

crostata *sf.* (*cuc.*) tart.

cròtalo *sm.* rattlesnake.

crucciare *vt.*, **crucciarsi** *vr.* to worry.

cruciale *agg.* crucial.

cruciverba *sm.* cross-word puzzle.

crudele *agg.* cruel.

crudeltà *sf.* cruelty.

crudezza *sf.* 1. (*di stagione*) harshness 2. (*di parole*) coarseness 3. (*di cibo*) rawness.

crudo *agg.* 1. raw 2. (*poco cotto*) underdone 3. (*aspro, rigido*) harsh 4. (*rozzo*) coarse.

cruento *agg.* bloody.

crumiro *sm.* blackleg.

cruna *sf.* needle's eye.

crusca *sf.* bran.

cruscotto *sm.* dashboard.

cubaggio *sm.* cubage.

cubano *agg. e sm.* Cuban.

cubatura *sf.* cubature.

cubetto *sm.* — *di ghiaccio*, ice cube.

cùbico *agg.* cubic.

cubismo *sm.* cubism.

cubitale *agg. a caratteri cubitali*, in very large letters.

cùbito *sm.* 1. (*misura*) cubit 2. (*avambraccio*) forearm.

cubo *sm.* cube.

cuccagna *sf.* abundance || *albero della* —, greasy pole.

cuccetta *sf.* berth.

cucchiaiata *sf.* spoonful.

cucchiaino *sm.* 1. tea-spoon, coffee-spoon 2. (*il contenuto*) tea-spoonful.

cucchiaio *sm.* spoon.

cuccia *sf.* dog-house.

cùcciolo *sm.* puppy.

cùccuma *sf.* kettle.

cucina *sf.* 1. kitchen 2. (*modo di cucinare*) cooking 3. (*culinaria*) cookery 4. (*stufa*) stove.

cucinare *vt.* to cook.

cuciniere *sm.* man-cook.

cucire *vt.* 1. to sew (*v. irr.*) 2. (*med.*) to stitch.

cucito *sm.* needlework.

cucitrice *sf.* 1. seamstress 2. (*macchinetta*) stapler.

cucitura *sf.* 1. seam 2. (*di fogli*) stapling.

cucù *sm.* (*zool.*) cuckoo.

cucùrbita *sf.* gourd.

cuffia *sf.* 1. cap. 2. (*radio*) headphone.

cugina *sf.* cousin.

cugino *sm.* cousin.

cui *pron. rel.* 1. (*di possesso*) whose; (*di possesso, solo per animali e cose*) of which: *l'uomo la — casa*, the man whose house; *il libro le — pagine*, the book the pages of which 2. (*altri casi, per persone*) whom; (*altri casi, per animali e cose*) which: *l'uomo con — parlai*, the man to whom I spoke; *il libro di — parlai*, the book about which I spoke || *in — (dove)*, where; *in — (quando)* when.

culaccio *sm.* rump.

culatta *sf.* breech.

culinaria *sf.* cookery.

culinario *agg.* culinary.

culla *sf* cradle.

cullare *vt* to rock, to lull (*anche fig.*).

culminante *agg.* culminant: *momento* —, climax.

culminare *vi.* to culminate.

cùlmine *sm.* **1.** summit **2.** (*fig.*) apex.

culo *sm.* bottom; (*volg.*) ass.

culto *sm.* **1.** cult **2.** (*religione*) religion **3.** (*adorazione*) worship.

cultore *sm.* lover.

cultura *sf.* culture.

culturale *agg.* cultural.

cumulare *vt.* to heap up.

cumulativo *agg.* cumulative.

cumulatore *sm.* hoarder.

cumulazione *sf.* hoarding.

cùmulo *sm.* **1.** heap **2.** (*nube*) cumulus (*pl.* -li).

cuna *sf.* cradle.

cuneiforme *agg.* cuneiform, wedge-shaped.

cùneo *sm.* wedge.

cunetta *sf.* **1.** (*stradale*) road bump **2.** (*scolo*) gutter.

cunìcolo *sm.* underground passage, shaft.

cuòcere *vt.* **1.** to cook **2.** (*in forno, fornace*) to bake.

cuoco *sm.* cook.

cuoiame *sm.* leather and hides.

cuoio *sm.* leather || — *capelluto*, scalp.

cuore *sm.* heart.

cupezza *sf.* **1.** darkness **2.** (*tristezza*) gloom.

cupidigia *sf.* cupidity, greed.

cùpido *agg.* greedy.

cupo *agg.* **1.** dark **2.** (*triste*) gloomy **3.** (*profondo*) deep.

cùpola *sf.* dome.

cùpreo *agg.* cupreous.

cùprico *agg.* cupric.

cura *sf.* **1.** care **2.** (*med.*) treatment || *casa di* —, nursing-home.

curàbile *agg.* curable.

curante *agg. medico* —, attending physician.

curare *vt.* **1.** (*aver cura di*) to take (*v. irr.*) care of **2.** (*med.*) to treat **3.** (*una pubblicazione*) to edit. ♦ **curarsi** *vr.* (*seguire una cura*) to follow a treatment.

curaro *sm.* curare.

curato *sm.* vicar.

curatore *sm.* trustee.

curdo *agg.* Kurdish. ♦ **curdo** *sm.* Kurd.

curia *sf.* **1.** (*eccl.*) see **2.** (*giur.*) court of justice.

curie *sm.* curie.

curiosare *vi.* to pry.

curiosità *sf.* **1.** curiosity **2.** (*stranezza*) oddity.

curioso *agg.* curious.

currìculum *sm.* curriculum (*pl.* -la).

cursore *sm.* **1.** messenger **2.** (*mecc.*) slider.

curva *sf.* bend.

curvare *vt.* to bend (*v. irr.*). ♦ **curvarsi** *vr.* **1.** to bend (*v. irr.*) **2.** (*inclinarsi*) to bow.

curvatura *sf.* **1.** bending **2.** (*arch.*) sweep.

curvilìneo *agg.* curvilinear.

curvo *agg.* bent.

cuscinetto *sm.* small cushion || — *a sfera*, ball bearing.

cuscino *sm.* **1.** cushion **2.** (*guanciale*) pillow **3.** (*mecc.*) pillow.

custode *sm.* keeper.

custodia *sf.* **1.** care **2.** (*tutela*) guardianship **3.** (*astuccio*) case.

custodire *vt.* **1.** to keep (*v. irr.*) **2.** (*aver cura di*) to look after.

cutàneo *agg.* skin: *malattia cutanea*, skin disease.

cute *sf.* skin.

D

da *prep.* **1.** (*provenienza*) from: *vengo* — *Milano*, I come from Milan **2.** (*moto a luogo*) to: *andremo* — *loro*, we shall go to their house **3.** (*stato in luogo*) at: *vivo* — *mia zia*, I live at my aunt's **4.** (*moto per luogo*) through: *passai* — *Roma*, I passed through Rome **5.** (*tempo, durata*) for: *siamo qui* — *due mesi*, we have been here for two months; (*a partire da*) since: *lo conosco dal 1955*, I have known him since 1955 **6.** (*agente*) by: *fu aiutato* — *sua sorella*, he was helped by his sister **7.** (*come*) like: *si comportano* — *bambini*, they are behaving like children || *fare* —, to act as.

dabbasso *avv.* **1.** below, down below **2.** (*al piano inferiore*) downstairs.

dabbenàggine sf. ingenuousness.
dabbene agg. honest.
daccapo avv. over again, from the beginning.
dacché cong. since.
dadaismo sm. dadaism.
dado sm. **1.** die (pl. dice) **2.** (cuc.) cube **3.** (mecc.) nut.
daffare sm. work || darsi —, to be on the go.
dagherrotipìa sf. daguerreotypy.
dagherròtipo sm. daguerreotype.
dàgli, dài inter. go on.
dàino sm. fallow-deer (invariato al pl.).
dalia sf. dahlia.
daltònico agg. colour-blind.
daltonismo sm. colour-blindness.
d'altronde avv. on the other hand.
dama sf. **1.** lady of rank **2.** (al ballo) partner **3.** (giuoco) draughts (pl.).
damasco sm. damask.
damerino sm. dandy.
damiere sm. draughtboard.
damigella sf. maid of honour.
damigiana sf. demijohn.
danaroso agg. wealthy.
danese agg. Danish. ♦ **danese** sm. Dane.
dannare vt. to damn || far —, to drive (v. irr.) so. mad. ♦ **dannarsi 1.** to be damned **2.** (fig.) to strive (v. irr.) hard.
dannato agg. damned. ♦ **dannato** sm. damned soul.
dannazione sf. damnation: —!, damn!
danneggiamento sm. damage.
danneggiare vt. **1.** to damage **2.** (di persone) to injure.
danno sm. **1.** damage **2.** (a persona) injury || recare — a qu., to do (v. irr.) so. harm.
dànnoso agg. harmful.
dantesco agg. Dantesque.
danza sf. dance.
danzante agg. dancing: trattenimento —, dance.
danzare vt. e vi. to dance.
danzatore sm. dancer.
dappertutto avv. everywhere.
dappocàggine sf. ineptitude.
dappoco agg. inept.
dappresso avv. near-by.
dapprima avv. at first.
dardeggiare vt. e vi. to dart.
dardo sm. dart.
dare sm. debit. ♦ **dare** vt. to give

(v. irr.): — origine, luogo a qc., to give rise; — a bere a qu. che, to give so. to believe that; — ad intensère, to give to understand; — a pensare, to give food for thought || — atto di qc., to acknowledge; può darsi, maybe; — àla testa, to go (v. irr.) to one's head; — nell'occhio, to stand (v. irr.) out. ♦ **darsi** vr. to devote oneself || — al bere, to take (v. irr.) to drink; — ammalato, to pretend to be ill; — da fare, to busy oneself; darsela a gambe, to take (v. irr.) to one's heels.
dàrsena sf. wet dock.
darvinismo sm. Darwinism.
data sf. date: in — d'oggi, under to-day's date.
datare vt. to date.
dativo sm. dative.
dato agg. **1.** given **2.** (stabilito) stated **3.** (dedito) addicted || e non concesso, supposing that. ♦ **dato** sm. datum (pl. -ta). ♦ **dato che** cong. since, as.
datore sm. giver || — di lavoro, employer.
dàttero sm. **1.** date **2.** (albero) date-palm.
dattilografare vt. to typewrite.
dattilografìa sf. typewriting.
dattilògrafo sm. typist.
dattiloscritto agg. typewritten. ♦ **dattiloscritto** sm. typescript.
dattorno avv. round, about.
davanti avv. before, in front. ♦ **davanti** sm. front. ♦ **davanti** agg. front. ♦ **davanti a** (loc. prep.) before.
davantino sm. ruffle.
davanzale sm. window-sill.
davvero avv. really, indeed.
daziario agg. toll.
daziere sm. exciseman (pl. -men).
dazio sm. **1.** toll, duty **2.** (ufficio daziario) toll-house **3.** (di consumo) excise.
dea sf. goddess.
deambulare vi. to walk about.
deambulatorio agg. e sm. deambulatory.
deambulazione sf. deambulation.
debellare vt. **1.** to defeat **2.** (fig.) to overcome (v. irr.).
debilitante agg. weakening.
debilitare vt. to weaken.
debilitazione debilitation.

debitamente *avv.* duly.
débito *agg.* due, proper. ♦ **débito**
sm. debt: *fare un —*, to run (*v.
irr.*) into debt.
debitore *sm.* debtor.
débole *agg.* weak.
debolezza *sf.* weakness.
debosciato *agg.* debauched.
debuttante *sm.* 1. novice 2. (*di
ragazza in società*) debutante.
debuttare *vi.* 1. to make (*v. irr.*)
one's debut 2. (*di ragazza in società*) to come (*v. irr.*) out.
debutto *sm.* 1. debut 2. (*di ragazza
in società*) coming out.
dècade *sf.* 1. (*di giorni*) ten days
2. (*di anni*) ten years.
decadente *agg.* 1. decaying 2.
(*lett.*) decadent.
decadenza *sf.* decay, decline.
decadere *vi.* to decline || *— da
un diritto*, to lose (*v. irr.*) a right.
decaduto *agg.* impoverished.
decaedro *sm.* decahedron.
decagrammo *sm.* decagram.
decalcare *vt.* to transfer.
decalcificare *vt.* to decalcify.
decàlitro *sm.* decalitre.
decàlogo *sm.* decalogue.
decàmetro *sm.* decametre.
decampare *vi.* 1. to decamp 2.
(*fig.*) to recede.
decano *sm.* 1. senior 2. (*eccl.*)
dean.
decantare *vt.* 1. to extol 2. (*chim.*)
to decant.
decantazione *sf.* (*chim.*) decantation.
decapitare *vt.* to behead.
decappottàbile *agg.* (*auto*) convertible.
decasìllabo *agg.* decasyllabic. ♦
decasìllabo *sm.* decasyllable.
decatissaggio *sm.* decatizing.
decèdere *vi.* to die.
decelerare *vt.* to decelerate.
decennale *agg.* decennial.
decenne *agg.* 1. ten years old (*predicativo*) 2. ten-year-old (*attributivo*).
decennio *sm.* ten-year period.
decente *agg.* decent, proper.
decentramento *sm.* decentralization.
decentrare *vt.* to decentralize.
decenza *sf.* decency.
decesso *sm.* death.
decìdere *vt.* to decide. ♦ **decì-
dersi** *vr.* to make (*v. irr.*) up one's

mind.
decifrare *vt.* 1. to decipher 2.
(*fam.*) to make (*v. irr.*) out.
decifrazione *sf.* deciphering.
decigrammo *sm.* decigram.
decìlitro *sm.* decilitre.
decimale *agg.* e *sm.* decimal.
decimare *vt.* to decimate.
decimazione *sf.* decimation.
decìmetro *sm.* decimetre.
dècimo *agg.* tenth.
decina *sf.* ten, half-a-score.
decisione *sf.* decision.
decisivo *agg.* decisive.
deciso *agg.* 1. resolute, firm 2. (*definito*) decided.
declamare *vt.* e *vi.* to declaim.
declamatorio *agg.* declamatory.
declamazione *sf.* declamation.
declassare *vt.* to degrade.
declinàbile *agg.* declinable.
declinante *agg.* declining.
declinare *vt.* 1. to decline || *— le
proprie generalità*, to say (*v. irr.*)
one's name and surname. ♦ **declinare** *vi.* 1. (*del sole*) to set
(*v. irr.*) 2. (*degradare*) to slope
3. (*venir meno*) to decline.
declinazione *sf.* (*gramm.*) declension.
declino *sm.* decline.
declivio *sm.* declivity.
decollaggio *sm.* (*aer.*) take-off.
decollare *vi.* to take (*v. irr.*) off.
decollo *sm.* take-off.
decolorante *agg.* decolorating. ♦
decolorante *sm.* decolorant.
decolorare *vt.* to decolorate.
decolorazione *sf.* decoloration ||
— dei capelli, hair bleaching.
decomponìbile *agg.* decomposable.
decomporre *vt.* to decompose.
decomposizione *sf.* 1. decomposition 2. (*putrefazione*) putrefaction.
decongelare *vt.* to defrost.
decongestionare *vt.* to decongest.
decorare *vt.* to decorate: *— al valore*, to decorate for bravery.
decorativo *agg.* decorative.
decoratore *sm.* decorator.
decorazione *sf.* decoration.
decoro *sm.* dignity.
decoroso *agg.* decorous, proper.
decorrenza *sf.* expiration: *con —
da*, beginning from.
decòrrere *vi.* 1. to pass || *a — da*,
to begin (*v. irr.*) from 2. (*comm.*)
to run (*v. irr.*), to have effect.
decorso *sm.* 1. period 2. (*il passa-*

re) passing.

decrepitezza *sf.* decrepitude.

decrèpito *agg.* decrepit.

decréscere *vi.* to decrease.

decretare *vt.* 1. to decree 2. (*concedere*) to confer.

decreto *sm.* decree: — *legge*, Order in Council.

decuplicare *vt.* to decuple.

dècuplo *sm.* decuple, ten times as much.

decurtare *vt.* to ·reduce.

dèdalo *sm.* maze.

dèdica *sf.* dedication.

dedicare *vt.* to dedicate. ♦ **dedicarsi** *vr.* to devote oneself.

dedicatorio *agg.* dedicatory.

dèdito *agg.* 1. given up 2. (*a vizio*) addicted.

dedizione *sf.* devotion.

dedurre *vt.* 1. to infer, to deduce 2. (*defalcare*) to deduct.

deduttivo *agg.* deductive.

deduzione *sf.* deduction.

defalcare *vt.* to deduct.

defalco *sm.* deduction.

defecare *vi.* to defecate.

defenestrare *vt.* 1. to throw (*v. irr.*) out of the window 2. (*fig.*) to dismiss.

defenestrazione *sf.* defenestration.

deferente *agg.* deferential.

deferenza *sf.* compliance, deference.

deferire *vt.* 1. to submit 2. (*giur.*) to remit.

defezionare *vi.* to desert.

defezione *sf.* 1. defection 2. (*mil.*) desertion.

deficiente *agg.* 1. insufficient 2. (*idiota*) mentally deficient. ♦ **deficiente** *sm.* idiot.

deficienza *sf.* 1. deficiency, lack 2. (*idiozia*) mental deficiency.

dèficit *sm.* deficit.

definìbile *agg.* definable.

definire *vt.* 1. to define 2. (*determinare, risolvere*) to determine.

definitivo *agg.* final.

definito *agg.* definite.

definizione *sf.* 1. definition 2. (*risoluzione*) settlement.

deflagrante *agg.* deflagrating.

deflagrare *vi.* to deflagrate.

deflagrazione *sf.* deflagration.

deflazione *sf.* deflation.

deflèttere *vi.* to deflect.

deflettore *sm.* baffle.

deflorare *vt.* to deflower.

deflorazione *sf.* defloration.

defluire *vi.* to flow down.

deflusso *sm.* 1. downflow 2. (*di marea*) ebb-tide.

deformante *agg.* deforming.

deformare *vt.* 1. to deform, to disfigure 2. (*alterare*) to alter. ♦ **deformarsi** *vr.* 1. (*mecc.*) to warp 2. to get (*v. irr.*) deformed.

deformazione *sf.* 1. deformation 2. (*mecc.*) buckling.

deforme *agg.* deformed.

deformità *sf.* deformity.

defraudare *vt.* to defraud.

defunto *agg.* e *sm.* dead.

degenerare *vi.* to degenerate.

degenerazione *sf.* degeneration.

degènere *agg.* degenerate.

degente *sm.* patient.

degenza *sf.* stay in hospital.

deglutizione *sf.* swallowing.

degnarsi *vr.* to condescend.

degnazione *sf.* condescension.

degno *agg.* worthy, deserving.

degradante *agg.* degrading.

degradare *vt.* to degrade.

degradazione *sf.* degradation.

degustare *vt.* to taste.

deiezione *sf.* dejection.

deificare *vt.* to deify.

deismo *sm.* deism.

deità *sf.* deity.

delatore *sm.* delator.

delazione *sf.* delation, informing.

delèbile *agg.* erasable.

dèlega *sf.* 1. delegation 2. (*procura*) proxy.

delegare *vt.* to delegate.

delegato *sm.* delegate.

delegazione *sf.* 1. delegation 2. (*commissione*) committee.

deleterio *agg.* harmful.

delfino *sm.* 1. (*zool.*) dolphin 2. (*fig.*) probable successor 3. (*stor.*) dauphin.

deliberare *vt.* to decide.

deliberazione *sf.* deliberation.

delicatezza *sf.* delicacy.

delicato *agg.* 1. delicate 2. (*scrupoloso*) scrupulous 3. (*discreto*) discreet, tactful.

delimitare *vt.* to delimit.

delimitazione *sf.* delimitation.

delineare *vt.* to outline.

delineazione *sf.* delineation.

delinquente *sm.* delinquent.

delinquenza *sf.* criminality.

delinquere *vi.* to commit an offence.

deliquio *sm.* swoon.

delirare *vi.* to rave.
delirio *sm.* delirium, frenzy (*anche fig.*).
delitto *sm.* crime.
delittuoso *agg.* criminal.
delizia *sf.* delight.
deliziare *vt.* to delight.
delizioso *agg.* 1. delightful 2. (*di sapore, profumo*) delicious.
delta *sm.* delta.
deltòide *agg. e sm.* deltoid.
delucidare *vt.* to explain.
delucidazione *sf.* explanation.
delùdere *vt.* to disappoint.
delusione *sf.* disappointment.
demagogìa *sf.* demagogy.
demagògico *agg.* demagogic.
demagogo *sm.* demagogue.
demandare *vt.* to commit.
demaniale *agg.* (owned by the) State.
demanio *sm.* State property.
demarcare *vt.* to mark the boundaries of.
demarcazione *sf.* demarcation.
demente *agg.* insane. ♦ **demente** *sm.* madman (*pl.* -men).
demenza *sf.* insanity.
demeritare *vt.* to forfeit. ♦ **demeritare** *vi.* to deserve censure.
demèrito *sm.* demerit.
demiurgo *sm.* demiurge.
democràtico *agg.* democratic. ♦ **democràtico** *sm.* democrat.
democratizzare *vt.* to democratize.
democrazìa *sf.* democracy.
democristiano *sm.* christian-democrat.
demografìa *sf.* demography.
demogràfico *agg.* demographic(al).
demolire *vt.* to demolish.
demolitore *sm.* 1. demolisher 2. (*fig.*) iconoclast.
demolizione *sf.* 1. demolition 2. (*fig.*) destruction.
dèmone *sm.* 1. demon 2. (*diavolo*) devil.
demonìaco *agg.* demoniac(al).
demonio *sm.* 1. devil 2. (*fig.*) demon.
demonologìa *sf.* demonology.
demoralizzare *vt.* to demoralize. ♦ **demoralizzarsi** *vr.* to lose (*v. irr.*) heart.
demoralizzazione *sf.* demoralization.
denaro *sm.* 1. money 2. (*moneta antica*) denarius (*pl.* -rii).
denaturare *vt.* to denature.

dendrologìa *sf.* dendrology.
denegare *vt.* to deny.
denicotinizzare *vt.* to denicotinize.
denigrare *vt.* to denigrate.
denigratore *sm.* denigrator.
denigrazione *sf.* denigration.
denominare *vt.* to name.
denominativo *agg.* denominative.
denominatore *sm.* denominator.
denominazione *sf.* denomination.
denotare *vt.* to signify.
densità *sf.* density.
denso *agg.* thick.
dentale *agg.* dental.
dentario *agg.* dental, tooth (*attr.*).
dentato *agg.* toothed.
dentatura *sf.* 1. set of teeth 2. (*di ingranaggio*) toothing.
dente *sm.* tooth (*pl.* teeth).
dentellare *vt.* to indent.
dentellatura *sf.* indentation.
dentello *sm.* 1. (*mecc.*) tooth 2. (*arch.*) dentil 3. (*tacca*) notch.
dentiera *sf.* dental plate.
dentifricio *agg.* tooth (*attr.*) ♦ **dentifricio** *sm.* tooth-paste.
dentina *sf.* dentine.
dentista *sm.* dentist.
dentìstico *agg.* dental: *gabinetto* —, dentist's surgery.
dentizione *sf.* teething.
dentro *avv.* in, inside. ♦ **dentro** *prep.* 1. in, inside 2. (*di tempo*) (with)in.
denudare *vt.* 1. to strip 2. (*scoprire*) to lay (*v. irr.*) bare. ♦ **denudarsi** *vr.* to strip.
denudazione *sf.* denudation.
denuncia *sf.* 1. denunciation 2. (*dichiarazione*) statement: — *dei redditi*, statement of one's income.
denunciare *vt.* 1. to denounce 2. (*dichiarare*) to report 3. (*giur.*) — *qu.*, to inform against so.
denutrito *agg.* underfed.
denutrizione *sf.* underfeeding.
deodorante *agg.* deodorizing. ♦ **deodorante** *sm.* deodorant.
deodorare *vt.* to deodorize.
deontologìa *sf.* deontology.
depauperamento *sm.* impoverishment.
depauperare *vt.* to impoverish.
depennare *vt.* to cross out.
deperìbile *agg.* perishable.
deperimento *sm.* 1. (*di salute*) wasting away 2. (*per un dolore*) pining away 3. (*di cose*) deterioration.

deperire vi. 1. (di salute) to waste away 2. (per un dolore) to pine. away 3. (di cose) to deteriorate.
depilare vt. to remove hair (from).
depilatore sm. hair-remover.
depilatorio agg. hair-removing.
depilazione sf. hair-removal.
deplorábile agg. deplorable.
deplorare vt. 1. (essere spiacenti) to deplore 2. (lagnarsi di) to complain of.
deplorazione sf. 1. (biasimo) blame 2. (rimpianto) regret.
deplorévole agg. 1. deplorable 2. (biasimevole) blamable.
deporre vt. 1. to lay (v. irr.) 2. (da una carica) to remove from (an) office 3. (depositare) to deposit 4. (giur.) to witness. ♦ **deporre** vi. (giur.) to give (v. irr.) evidence.
deportare vt. to deport.
deportato agg. deported. ♦ **deportato** sm. convict.
deportazione sf. deportation.
depositante sm. depositor.
depositare vt. to deposit: — merci, to store goods.
depositario sm. trustee.
depòsito sm. 1. deposit 2. (luogo in cui depositare) warehouse 3. (per bagagli) left-luggage room.
deposizione sf. deposition.
depravare vt. to corrupt.
depravazione sf. corruption.
deprecábile agg. deprecable.
deprecare vt. to deprecate.
deprecativo agg. deprecatory.
deprecazione sf. deprecation.
depredamento sm. plunder.
depredare vt. to plunder, to ravage.
depressione sf. depression.
depressivo agg. depressing.
depresso agg. depressed.
depressore sm. depressor.
deprezzamento sm. depreciation.
deprezzare vt. to depreciate.
deprimente agg. depressing.
deprìmere vt. to depress.
depurare vt. to depurate.
depurativo agg. depurative.
depuratore sm. 1. depurator 2. (mecc.) cleaner.
depurazione sf. purification, depuration.
deputare vt. to depute.
deputato sm. deputy.
deputazione sf. deputation.

deragliamento sm. derailment.
deragliare vi. to go (v. irr.) off the rails.
derattizzare vt. to clear by derattization.
derattizzazione sf. deratization.
derelitto agg. forlorn.
deretano sm. posterior.
derìdere vt. to laugh at, to make (v. irr.) fun of.
derisìbile agg. laughable.
derisione sf. mockery.
derisorio agg. derisory.
deriva sf. drift.
derivare vi. 1. to derive 2. (originarsi) to rise (v. irr.). ♦ **derivare** vt. to derive.
derivativo agg. derivative.
derivato agg. derived. ♦ **derivato** sm. 1. derivative 2. (sottoprodotto) by-product.
derivazione sf. 1. derivation 2. (elettr.) shunt.
derma sm. derm.
dermatologìa sf. dermatology.
dermatològico agg. dermatological.
dermatòlogo sm. dermatologist.
dèroga sf. derogation.
derogare vi. to derogate.
derrata sf. 1. victual 2. (alimentare) food-stuff.
derubare vt. to rob (so. of).
desco sm. dinner table.
descrittivo agg. descriptive.
descrìvere vt. to describe.
descrivìbile agg. describable.
descrizione sf. description.
desèrtico agg. desert.
deserto agg. e sm. desert.
desideràbile agg. desirable.
desiderare vt. 1. to wish 2. (desiderare di avere) to wish for.
desiderio sm. wish.
desideroso agg. desirous, eager (for).
designare vt. to appoint.
designazione sf. designation.
desinare vi. to dine, to have dinner. ♦ **desinare** sm. dinner.
desinenza sf. ending.
desìstere vi. to cease, to leave (v. irr.) off.
desolare vt. 1. to desolate 2. (addolorare) to distress.
desolato agg. (spiacente) sorry.
desolazione sf. 1. desolation 2. (dolore) grief, sorrow.
dèspota sm. despot.
destare vt. 1. to wake (v. irr.) 2.

(*suscitare*) to rouse. ♦ **destarsi** *vr.* to wake (*v. irr.*) up.

destinare *vt.* 1. to destine 2. (*devolvere*) to assign.

destinatario *sm.* addressee.

destinazione *sf.* destination.

destino *sm.* 1. destiny 2. (*sorte*) lot.

destituire *vt.* to dismiss.

destituzione *sf.* dismissal.

desto *agg.* awake.

destra *sf.* 1. right hand 2. (*parte destra*) right, right side: *alla tua* —, on your right; *tenere la* —, to keep (*v. irr.*) right.

destramente *avv.* skilfully.

destreggiarsi *vr.* to manage.

destrezza *sf.* dexterity.

destriero *sm.* steed.

destrina *sf.* dextrine.

destro *agg.* 1. right 2. (*abile*) clever. ♦ **destro** *sm.* opportunity.

desueto *agg.* unusual, obsolete.

desuetùdine *sf.* disuse.

desùmere *vt.* 1. to infer 2. (*trarre*) to draw (*v. irr.*).

detenere *vt.* 1. to hold (*v. irr.*) 2. (*tener prigioniero*) to keep (*v. irr.*) in prison.

detentore *sm.* holder.

detenuto *agg.* imprisoned. ♦ **detenuto** *sm.* prisoner.

detenzione *sf.* 1. possession 2. (*il detenere*) holding 3. (*galera*) detention.

detergente *agg. e sm.* detergent.

detèrgere *vt.* to cleanse.

deterioramento *sm.* deterioration.

deteriorare *vt.* 1. to deteriorate 2. (*danneggiare*) to damage.

deteriore *agg.* worse.

determinàbile *agg.* determinable.

determinante *agg.* determinant.

determinare *vt.* 1. to determine 2. (*causare*) to cause.

determinativo *agg.* determinative || *articolo* —, definite article.

determinato *agg.* 1. determinate 2. (*particolare*) special 3. (*deciso*) resolute.

determinazione *sf.* determination.

determinismo *sm.* determinism.

deterrente *sm.* deterrent.

detersivo *agg. e sm.* detersive.

detestàbile *agg.* detestable.

detestare *vt.* to loathe.

detettore *sm.* detector.

detonante *agg.* explosive.

detonare *vi.* to detonate.

detonatore *sm.* detonator.

detonazione *sf.* explosion.

detrarre *vt.* to deduct.

detrattore *sm.* detractor.

detrazione *sf.* 1. deduction 2. (*fig.*) detraction.

detrimento *sm.* detriment.

detrìtico *agg.* detrital.

detrito *sm.* rubble, debris.

detronizzare *vt.* to depose.

detronizzazione *sf.* dethronement.

detta (*nella loc. avv.*) *a* — *di qu.*, according to what so. says.

dettagliante *sm.* retailer.

dettagliare *vt.* to detail.

dettagliatamente *avv.* in detail.

dettaglio *sm.* 1. detail 2. (*comm.*) retail.

dettame *sm.* dictate.

dettare *vt.* 1. to dictate 2. (*suggerire*) to suggest || — *la legge*, to lay (*v. irr.*) down the law.

dettato *sm.* dictation.

detto *agg.* 1. called 2. (*sopraddetto*) said, above-mentioned. ♦ **detto** *sm.* saying.

deturpare *vt.* to disfigure.

deturpazione *sf.* disfigurement.

devalutazione *sf.* depreciation.

devastare *vt.* to ravage, to ruin.

devastatore *agg.* ravaging. ♦ **devastatore** *sm.* ravager.

devastazione *sf.* devastation.

deviare *vi.* to deviate || *non* —! (*non cambiare discorso*), stick to the point! ♦ **deviare** *vt.* to divert.

deviazione *sf.* 1. deviation 2. (*stradale*) detour || — *ferroviaria*, shunting.

deviazionismo *sm.* deviationism.

devoluzione *sf.* devolution.

devòlvere *vt.* 1. (*giur.*) to devolve, to assign 2. (*adoperare*) to employ.

devoto *agg.* 1. devout, affectionate 2. (*relig.*) pious, religious.

devozione *sf.* devotion, piety.

di *prep.* 1. of 2. (*partitivo*) some, any: *dammi del pane*, give me some bread; *hai dello zucchero?*, have you any sugar? 3. (*tempo*) in, during: — *mattina*, in the morning 4. (*argomento*) of, about 5. (*paragone coi comparativi*) than: *è più graziosa* — *sua sorella*, she is prettier than her sister 6. (*nei superl.*) of, in 7. (*modo*) with, in.

dì *sm.* day.

diabete *sm.* diabetes.

diabètico *agg. e sm.* diabetic.

diabòlico *agg.* diabolic(al).

diàcono *sm.* deacon.

diadema *sm.* diadem.

diàfano *agg.* diaphanous.

diaframma *sm.* diaphragm.

diàgnosi *sf.* diagnosis (*pl.* -ses).

diagnosticare *vt.* to diagnose.

diagnòstico *agg.* diagnostic.

diagonale *agg.* diagonal. ◆ **diagonale** *sf.* diagonal.

diagonalmente *avv.* diagonally.

diagramma *sm.* diagram.

dialettale *agg.* dialectal.

dialèttica *sf.* dialectics.

dialèttico *agg.* dialectic. ◆ **dialèttico** *sm.* dialectic.

dialetto *sm.* dialect.

diàlisi *sf.* dialysis (*pl.* -ses).

dialogare *vi.* to hold (*v. irr.*) a dialogue.

diàlogo *sm.* dialogue.

diamante *sm.* diamond.

diametralmente *avv.* diametrically.

diàmetro *sm.* diameter.

diàmine *inter.* good heavens!

dianzi *avv.* just, just now.

diapositiva *sf.* slide.

diarchìa *sf.* diarchy.

diario *sm.* diary.

diarrea *sf.* diarrhoea.

diaspro *sm.* jasper.

diatonìa *sf.* diatony.

diatriba *sf.* diatribe.

diavolerìa *sf.* **1.** devilry **2.** (*fam.*) trick.

diavoletto *sm.* imp.

diàvolo *sm.* devil.

dibàttere *vt.* to debate. ◆ **dibàttersi** *vr.* to struggle.

dibàttito *sm.* debate, discussion.

dibattuto *agg.* controversial.

diboscamento *sm.* deforestation.

diboscare *vt.* to deforest.

dicastero *sm.* office.

dicembre *sm.* December.

dicerìa *sf.* gossip, rumour.

dichiarare *vt.* to declare.

dichiarato *agg.* declared.

dichiarazione *sf.* declaration.

diciannove *agg.* nineteen.

diciannovenne *agg.* **1.** nineteen years old (*pred.*) **2.** nineteen-year-old (*attr.*).

diciannovèsimo *agg.* nineteenth.

diciassette *agg.* seventeen.

diciassettenne *agg.* **1.** seventeen years old (*pred.*) **2.** seventeen-year-old (*attr.*).

diciassettèsimo *agg.* seventeenth.

diciottenne *agg.* **1.** eighteen years old (*pred.*) **2.** eighteen-year-old (*attr.*).

diciottèsimo *agg.* eighteenth.

diciotto *agg.* eighteen.

dicitore *sm.* speaker.

dicitura *sf.* wording.

didascalìa *sf.* **1.** explanation **2.** (*cine*) subtitles (*pl.*).

didàscàlico *agg.* didactic.

didàttica *sf.* didactics.

didàttico *agg.* didactic(al).

didentro *sm.* inside.

didietro *sm.* back.

dieci *agg.* ten.

diecina *sf.* ten, half a score.

diedro *sm.* dihedral.

dielèttrico *agg.* dielectric.

diesis *sm.* sharp.

dieta *sf.* diet.

dietètico *agg.* dietetic.

dietòlogo *sm.* dietician.

dietro *avv.* behind. ◆ **dietro** *prep.* behind, after. ◆ **dietro** *sm.* back, rear.

dietrofrònt *sm.* about turn!

difatti *avv.* as a matter of fact.

difèndere *vt.* to defend.

difendìbile *agg.* defensible.

difensiva *sf.* defensive.

difensivo *agg.* defensive.

difensore *agg.* defending. ◆ **difensore** *sm.* **1.** defender **2.** (*giur.*) defending counsel **3.** (*di un'idea ecc.*) supporter.

difesa *sf.* defence.

difettare *vi.* to be wanting.

difettivo *agg.* defective.

difetto *sm.* defect.

difettoso *agg.* defective.

diffamare *vt.* to defame.

diffamatore *sm.* defamer.

diffamatorio *agg.* defamatory.

diffamazione *sf.* defamation.

differente *agg.* unlike, different.

differentemente *avv.* differently.

differenza *sf.* difference.

differenziale *agg.* e *sm.* differential.

differenziare *vt.* to differentiate.

differenziato *agg.* differentiated.

differenziazione *sf.* differentiation.

differìbile *agg.* that can be deferred.

differimento *sm.* deferment.

differire *vi.* (*essere diverso*) to differ (from). ◆ **differire** *vt.* to delay.

difficile *agg.* difficult.
difficilmente *avv.* with difficulty.
difficoltà *sf.* difficulty.
difficoltoso *agg.* difficult.
diffida *sf.* warning, intimation.
diffidare *vi.* to distrust. ♦ **diffidare** *vt.* to give (*v. irr.*) warning.
diffidente *agg.* suspicious.
diffidenza *sf.* 1. distrust 2. (*sospetto*) suspicion.
diffóndere *vt.* to diffuse, to spread (*v. irr.*). ♦ **diffóndersi** *vr.* to spread (*v. irr.*).
difforme *agg.* 1. different 2. shapeless.
difformità *sf.* difference, deformity.
diffrazione *sf.* diffraction.
diffusamente *avv.* diffusely.
diffusione *sf.* 1. diffusion, spreading 2. (*di giornale*) circulation.
diffuso *agg.* diffuse.
diffusore *sm.* diffusor.
difilato *avv.* straight.
diftèrico *agg.* diphtheric.
difterite *sf.* diphtheria.
diga *sf.* dam.
digerente *agg.* digestive.
digerìbile *agg.* digestible.
digeribilità *sf.* digestibility.
digerire *vt.* to digest.
digestione *sf.* digestion.
digestivo *agg. e sm.* digestive.
digesto *sm.* digest.
digitale *agg.* digital ‖ *impronte digitali*, finger-prints. ♦ **digitale** *sf.* digitalis, (*fam.*) foxglove.
digiunare *vi.* to fast.
digiunatore *sm.* faster.
digiuno[1] *agg.* 1. fasting 2. (*fig.*) lacking (in).
digiuno[2] *sm.* fast.
dignità *sf.* dignity.
dignitario *sm.* dignitary.
dignitosamente *avv.* with dignity.
dignitoso *agg.* dignified.
digradante *agg.* 1. sloping 2. (*pitt.*) shading.
digradare *vi.* 1. to slope down 2. (*pitt.*) to shade off.
digressione *sf.* digression.
digressivo *agg.* digressive.
digrignare *vt.* to gnash.
digrossamento *sm.* 1. reducing 2. (*sbozzo*) rough-hewing.
digrossare *vt.* 1. to reduce 2. (*sbozzare*) to rough-hew.
dilacerare *vt.* to tear (*v. irr.*).
dilagare *vi.* to spread (*v. irr.*).
dilaniare *vt.* to tear (*v. irr.*) to

pieces.
dilapidare *vt.* to squander.
dilapidatore *sm.* squanderer.
dilapidazione *sf.* squandering.
dilatàbile *agg.* dilatable.
dilatabilità *sf.* dilatability.
dilatare *vt.*, **dilatarsi** *vr.* 1. to dilate 2. (*fis.*) to expand.
dilatazione *sf.* dilatation.
dilatorio *agg.* dilatory.
dilavamento *sm.* washing away.
dilavare *vt.* to wash away.
dilazionare *vt.* to defer.
dilazione *sf.* delay, respite.
dileggiare *vt.* to mock.
dileggio *sm.* mockery.
dileguare *vt.* to disperse. ♦ **dileguarsi** *vr.* to disappear.
dilemma *sm.* dilemma.
dilettante *sm.* amateur.
dilettantismo *sm.* amateurism.
dilettare *vt.* to delight. ♦ **dilettarsi** *vr.* to take (*v. irr.*) delight (in).
dilettévole *agg.* delightful.
diletto *agg.* beloved. ♦ **diletto** *sm.* delight.
diligente *agg.* diligent.
diligenza *sf.* 1. diligence 2. (*carrozza*) stage-coach.
dilucidare *vt.* V. *delucidare*.
dilucidazione *sf.* V. *delucidazione*.
diluente *sm.* diluent.
diluire *vt.* 1. to dilute 2. (*fig.*) to water down.
diluizione *sf.* dilution.
dilungarsi *vr.* to speak (*v. irr.*) diffusely.
diluviale *agg.* 1. torrential 2. (*geol.*) diluvial.
diluviano *agg.* diluvial.
diluviare *vi.* 1. to pour 2. (*fig.*) to shower.
diluvio *sm.* deluge, flood.
dimagramento *sm.* thinning.
dimagrante *agg.* slimming.
dimagrare *vi.* to thin.
dimagrire *vi.* V. *dimagrare*.
dimenare *vt.* 1. (*la coda*) to wag 2. to wave. ♦ **dimenarsi** *vr.* move about restlessly.
dimensione *sf.* dimension, size.
dimenticanza *sf.* 1. (*svista*) oversight 2. (*oblio*) oblivion.
dimenticare *vt.*, **dimenticarsi** *vr.* to forget (*v. irr.*).
diméntico *agg.* forgetful.
dimesso *agg.* 1. modest 2. (*trasandato*) shabby.

dimestichezza *sf.* familiarity.

dìmetro *sm.* dimeter.

diméttere *vt.* to dismiss || — *dall'ospedale*, to discharge. ♦ **diméttersi** *vr.* to resign.

dimezzamento *sm.* halving.

dimezzare *vt.* to halve.

diminuendo *sm.* 1. (*mat.*) minuend 2. (*mus.*) diminuendo.

diminuìbile *agg.* diminishable.

diminuire *vt.* e *vi.* to lessen, to diminish.

diminutivo *agg.* e *sm.* diminutive.

diminuzione *sf.* lessening, reduction.

dimissionare *vt.* to oblige (so.) to resign.

dimissionario *agg.* resigning.

dimissione *sf.* resignation || *dare le dimissioni*, to resign.

dimissoria *sf.* dimissory letter.

dimodoché *cong.* so that.

dimora *sf.* residence, lodgings (*pl.*).

dimorare *vi.* to stay, to live.

dimorfismo *sm.* dimorphism.

dimorfo *agg.* dimorphic.

dimostràbile *agg.* demonstrable.

dimostrabilità *sf.* demonstrability.

dimostrante *sm.* demonstrant.

dimostrare *vt.* 1. to show (*v. irr.*) 2. (*provare*) to demonstrate. ♦ **dimostrarsi** *vr.* to show oneself.

dimostrativo *agg.* e *sm.* demonstrative.

dimostratore *sm.* demonstrator.

dimostrazione *sf.* demonstration.

dina *sf.* dyne.

dinàmica *sf.* dynamics.

dinamicamente *avv.* dynamically.

dinamicità *sf.* dynamism, energy.

dinàmico *agg.* 1. dynamic 2. (*fig.*) energetic.

dinamismo *sm.* 1. dynamism 2. (*fig.*) energy.

dinamitardo *sm.* dynamiter.

dinamite *sf.* dynamite.

dìnamo *sf.* dynamo.

dinamòmetro *sm.* dynamometer.

dinanzi *prep.* before, in front of. ♦ **dinanzi** *avv.* before, in front, forward.

dìnaro *sm.* dinar.

dinasta *sm.* dynast.

dinastìa *sf.* dynasty.

dinàstico *agg.* dynastic(al).

dindo *sm.* turkey.

diniego *sm.* denial.

dinoccolato *agg.* slouching.

dinosàuro *sm.* dinosaur.

dintorni *sm. pl.* surroundings.

dintorno *avv.* e *prep.* 1. round, round about 2. (*circa*) about.

dio *sm.* god: *Marte, il — della guerra*, Mars, the god of war. ♦ **Dio** *sm.* God: — *ci assista!*, — *non voglia!*, God help us, God forbid.

diocesano *agg.* diocesan.

diòcesi *sf.* diocese.

dìodo *sm.* diode.

dionea *sf.* dionaea.

dionisìaco *agg.* Dionysiac.

diorama *sm.* diorama.

diorite *sf.* diorite.

diottrìa *sf.* diopter.

diòttrica *sf.* dioptrics.

diòttrico *agg.* dioptric.

dipanamento *sm.* winding into a ball.

dipanare *vt.* 1. to wind (*v. irr.*) into a ball 2. (*fig.*) to disentangle.

dipanatoio *sm.* skein-winder.

dipartimentale *agg.* departmental.

dipartimento *sm.* department.

dipartire *vi.* to depart. ♦ **dipartirsi** *vr.* 1. to go (*v. irr.*) away 2. (*morire*) to pass away.

dipartita *sf.* 1. departure 2. (*morte*) death.

dipendente *agg.* dependent (on). ♦ **dipendente** *sm.* employee.

dipendenza *sf.* dependence (on).

dipèndere *vi.* 1. (*derivare*) to be due 2. (*essere subordinato, vivere a carico*) to depend (on).

dipìngere *vt.* to paint.

dipinto *agg.* painted. ♦ **dipinto** *sm.* painting.

diplegìa *sf.* diplegia.

diplococco *sm.* diplococcus (*pl.* -ci).

diploma *sm.* diploma.

diplomare *vt.* to confer a diploma (upon so.). ♦ **diplomarsi** *vr.* to get (*v. irr.*) a diploma.

diplomàtica *sf.* diplomatics.

diplomaticamente *avv.* diplomatically.

diplomàtico *agg.* diplomatic. ♦ **diplomàtico** *sm.* diplomat.

diplomato *agg.* holding a diploma. ♦ **diplomato** *sm.* graduate.

diplomazìa *sf.* diplomacy.

diplopìa *sf.* diplopia.

dipnoi *sm. pl.* Dipnoi.

dipodìa *sf.* dipody.

dipoi *avv.* then.

diporto *sm.* recreation, diversion ||

viaggiare per —, to travel on pleasure.

dipresso (*nella loc. avv.*) *a un* —, approximately.

dìptero *agg.* dipteral.

diradamento *sm.* 1. thinning 2. (*di nebbia, gas*) rarefaction.

diradare *vt.* 1. to thin out 2. (*rendere meno frequente*) to do (*v. irr.*) less frequent. ♦ **diradarsi** *vr.* 1. to clear away 2. (*divenire meno frequente*) to become (*v. irr.*) less frequent.

diramare *vt.* to issue, to spread (*v. irr.*).

diramazione *sf.* 1. branching 2. (*diffusione*) diffusion 3. (*per radio*) broadcasting.

dire *vt.* 1. (*nel senso di enunciare e quando introduce il discorso diretto*) to say (*v. irr.*): *dice che ha sonno*, he says he is sleepy; «*venite*», *ci disse*, «come», he said to us 2. (*nel senso di raccontare e quando è enunciata la persona cui si parla*) to tell (*v. irr.*): *gli dissi di venire*, I told him to come *li si dice*, they say; *mi si dice*, I am told; *inutile* — *che*, it goes without saying that; *vale a* —, that is to say; *sentir* —, to hear (*v. irr.*); *voler* —, to mean (*v. irr.*).

dire *sm.* words (*pl.*), speech.

direttamente *avv.* directly.

direttìssima *sf. per* —, summarily.

direttìssimo *sm.* (*ferr.*) fast train.

direttiva *sf.* directions (*pl.*).

direttìvo *agg.* 1. leading 2. (*comm.*) managing.

diretto *agg.* direct, straight.

direttore *sm.* 1. (*comm.; amm.*) manager 2. (*di scuola*) headmaster.

direttoriale *agg.* directorial.

direttorio *sm.* executive board.

direttrice *sf.* 1. (*comm.; amm.*) manageress 2. (*di scuola*) headmistress.

direzionale *agg.* directional || *centro* —, office district.

direzione *sf.* 1. direction, course 2. (*di società*) management 3. (*di giornale*) editorship 4. (*di scuola*) headmastership 5. (*sede*) administrative office.

dirigente *agg.* directing, leading. ♦ **dirigente** *sm.* director, manager, leader.

dirìgere *vt.* 1. (*indirizzare*) to direct 2. (*guidare*) to lead (*v. irr.*) 3. (*sovraintendere*) to supervise. ♦ **dirigersi** *vr.* to turn one's steps towards.

dirigìbile *sm.* airship.

dirigismo *sm.* state planning.

dirigista *sm.* supporter of state planning.

dirimente *agg.* diriment.

dirìmere *vt.* to settle.

dirimpettaio *sm.* person living just opposite.

dirimpetto *avv.* face to face, opposite.

diritta *sf.* right, right-hand: *a* —, on the right.

dirittamente *avv.* straight.

diritto *agg.* straight, upright || *rigare* —, to behave properly. ♦ **diritto** *sm.* 1. right 2. (*tassa, tributo*) due 3. (*legge*) law.

dirittura *sf.* 1. straight line 2. (*rettitudine*) uprightness 3. (*sport*) — *d'arrivo*, home stretch.

dirizzare *vt.* 1. to direct 2. (*erigere*) to raise 3. (*raddrizzare; fig.*) to put (*v. irr.*) right, to straighten.

dirizzone *sm.* inconsiderate action.

diroccamento *sm.* demolition.

diroccare *vt.* to demolish.

diroccato *agg.* 1. (*demolito*) dismantled 2. (*in rovina*) crumbled.

dirompente *agg.* disruptive.

diròmpere *vt.* 1. (*di lino, canapa ecc.*) to scutch 2. (*rompere*) to break (*v. irr.*).

dirottare *vt.* to divert. ♦ **dirottare** *vi.* to change course.

dirotto *agg.* excessive: *pianto* —, desperate crying; *piove a* —, it is pouring.

dirozzamento *sm.* 1. (*lo sbozzare*) rough-hewing 2. (*fig.*) refinement.

dirozzare *vt.* 1. (*sbozzare*) to rough-hew 2. (*fig.*) to refine.

dirugginire *vt.* to remove the rust from.

dirupamento *sm.* 1. falling down 2. (*di luogo*) abruptness.

dirupato *agg.* 1. abrupt 2. (*roccioso*) rocky.

dirupo *sm.* precipice.

disabbellire *vt.* to spoil the beauty of. ♦ **disabbellirsi** *vr.* to lose (*v. irr.*) one's beauty.

disabitato *agg.* 1. uninhabited 2. (*abbandonato*) deserted.

disabituare *vt.* to disaccustom. ♦ **disabituarsi** *vr.* to give (*v. irr.*)

up the habit of.

disaccordo *sm.* disagreement.

disacerbare *vt.* to appease.

disadatto *agg.* 1. unfit 2. (*che non si addice*) unbecoming.

disadornare *vt.* to disadorn.

disadorno *agg.* 1. unadorned 2. (*spoglio*) bare.

disaffezionarsi *vr.* to lose (*v. irr.*) one's affection (for).

disaffezionato *agg.* estranged.

disaffezione *sf.* estrangement.

disagévole *agg.* uncomfortable.

disagiatamente *avv.* uncomfortably.

disagiato *agg.* 1. uncomfortable 2. (*povero*) needy.

disagio *sm.* 1. uneasiness || *essere a* —, to be uneasy 2. (*disturbo*) inconvenience 3. (*pl.; privazioni*) privations.

disamare *vt.* to cease to love.

disàmina *sf.* examination.

disaminare *vt.* to examine carefully.

disancorarsi *vr.* 1. to weigh anchor 2. (*fig.*) to break (*v. irr.*) all connections (with).

disanimarsi *vr.* to lose (*v. irr.*) heart.

disappetenza *sf.* lack of appetite.

disapprèndere *vt.* to forget (*v. irr.*).

disapprovare *vt.* to disapprove (of).

disapprovazione *sf.* disapproval.

disappunto *sm.* disappointment.

disarcionare *vt.* to unsaddle.

disarmare *vt.* to disarm.

disarmato *agg.* disarmed.

disarmo *sm.* disarmament.

disarmonìa *sf.* discord.

disarmonicamente *avv.* discordantly.

disarmònico *agg.* discordant.

disarmonizzare *vt.* to disharmonize.

disarticolare *vt.* to disjoint.

disarticolazione *sf.* disjointing.

disastro *sm.* disaster.

disastroso *agg.* disastrous.

disattento *agg.* inattentive.

disattenzione *sf.* inattention: *errore di* —, a slip of the pen.

disavanzo *sm.* deficit.

disavveduto *agg.* heedless.

disavventura *sf.* 1. mishap 2. (*sfortuna*) misfortune.

disavvertenza *sf.* inadvertence.

disavvezzo *agg.* unaccustomed.

disazotare *vt.* to remove nitrogen from.

disborso *sm.* disbursement.

disbrigo *sm.* dispatch.

disbrogliare *vt.* to disentangle.

discacciare *vt.* to turn out.

discapitare *vi.* to suffer damage.

discàpito *sm.* disadvantage.

discàrico *sm.* 1. discharge 2. (*scusa*) defence.

discendente *agg.* descending. ♦ **discendente** *sm.* descendant.

discendenza *sf.* 1. descent 2. (*discendenti*) offspring.

discéndere *vt.* 1. to descend, to go (*v. irr.*) down 2. (*di astri*) to sink (*v. irr.*) 3. (*di prezzi*) to fall (*v. irr.*).

discépolo *sm.* disciple.

discèrnere *vt.* 1. to discern 2. (*distinguere*) to distinguish.

discernìbile *agg.* discernible.

discernimento *sm.* discernment.

discesa *sf.* 1. descent 2. (*declivio*) slope 3. (*caduta*) fall 4. (*invasione*) invasion.

dischiùdere *vt.* to disclose.

dischiuso *agg.* disclosed.

discinto *agg.* ungirt.

disciplina *sf.* 1. (*materia di studio*) doctrine 2. (*regola*) discipline.

disciplinàbile *agg.* disciplinable.

disciplinare[1] *vt.* to discipline.

disciplinare[2] *agg.* disciplinary.

disciplinarmente *avv.* with discipline.

disciplinatamente *avv.* with discipline.

disciplinato *agg.* disciplined.

disco *sm.* 1. disk 2. (*mus.*) record 3. (*sport*) discus 4. (*ferr.*) disk signal.

discòbolo *sm.* discus-thrower.

discòide *agg.* discoid.

dìscolo *sm.* wild boy, little scamp.

discolpa *sf.* excuse.

discolpare *vt.* to clear.

disconoscente *aff.* ungrateful.

disconoscenza *sf.* ungratitude.

disconòscere *vt.* to refuse to recognize.

disconoscimento *sm.* 1. refusal to recognize 2. (*ingratitudine*) ingratitude.

discontinuità *sf.* discontinuity.

discontinuo *agg.* discontinuous.

discordante *agg.* 1. discordant 2. (*diverso*) different 3. (*di colori*) clashing.

discordanza *sf.* discordance.

discordare *vi.* 1. to disagree 2. (*di colori*) to clash 3. (*di suoni*) to jar.

discorde *agg.* discordant (with).

discordemente *avv.* discordantly.

discordia *sf.* discord.

discòrrere *vi.* to talk.

discorsivo *agg.* talkative.

discorso *sm.* speech.

discostare *vt.* to shift.

discosto *agg.* far, distant. ♦ **discosto** *avv.* at some distance.

discoteca *sf.* record library.

discreditare *vt.* to discredit.

discrédito *sm.* discredit.

discrepante *agg.* differing.

discrepanza *sf.* discrepancy.

discretamente *avv.* 1. (*con discrezione*) discreetly 2. (*sufficientemente*) fairly 3. (*piuttosto*) rather.

discreto *agg.* 1. (*che ha discrezione*) discreet 2. (*moderato*) moderate 3. (*abbastanza buono*) fairly good.

discrezionale *agg.* discretionary.

discrezione *sf.* discretion.

discriminante *agg.* discriminating.

discriminare *vt.* to discriminate.

discriminazione *sf.* discrimination.

discussione *sf.* discussion.

discusso *agg.* discussed.

discùtere *vt.* to discuss.

discutìbile *agg.* questionable.

disdegnare *vt.* to disdain.

disdegno *sm.* disdain.

disdegnosamente *avv.* disdainfully.

disdegnoso *agg.* disdainful.

disdetta *sf.* 1. (*giur.*) notice of leave 2. (*sfortuna*) bad luck.

disdettare *vt.* to give (*v. irr.*) notice.

disdicévole *agg.* unbecoming.

disdire *vt.* 1. (*ritrattare*) to take (*v. irr.*) back, to retract 2. (*annullare*) to cancel.

disegnare *vt.* 1. to draw (*v. irr.*) 2. (*progettare*) to plan.

disegnatore *sm.* designer.

disegno *sm.* 1. drawing 2. (*di tessuto*) pattern 3. (*di edificio*) plan 4. (*schizzo*) sketch 5. (*fig.*) design, plan.

diseredare *vt.* to disinherit.

diseredato *agg.* 1. poor, destitute 2. (*privato di eredità*) disinherited.

disertare *vt.* 1. to desert 2. (*abbandonare*) to leave (*v. irr.*).

disertore *sm.* deserter.

diserzione *sf.* desertion.

disfacimento *sm.* 1. (*il disfare*) undoing 2. (*decadimento*) decay.

disfare *vt.* 1. to undo (*v. irr.*) 2. (*slegare*) to untie.

disfasìa *sf.* dysphasia.

disfatta *sf.* defeat.

disfattismo *sm.* defeatism.

disfattista *agg. e s.* defeatist.

disfatto *agg.* 1. (*distrutto*) ruined 2. (*slegato*) undone 3. (*molto stanco*) worn out.

disfavore *sm.* disfavour.

disfida *sf.* challenge.

disfunzione *sf.* disorder.

disgelare *vt. e vi.* to thaw.

disgelo *sm.* thaw.

disgiùngere *vt.* to disjoin.

disgiungimento *sm.* disjoining.

disgiuntamente *avv.* separately.

disgiuntivamente *avv.* disjunctively.

disgiuntivo *agg.* disjunctive.

disgiunto *agg.* disjoined.

disgiunzione *sf.* disjunction.

disgrazia *sf.* 1. misfortune 2. (*sfavore*) disfavour || cadere in —, to lose (*v. irr.*) so.'s favour 3. (*fatto involontario*) accident.

disgraziatamente *avv.* unfortunately.

disgraziato *agg.* 1. unlucky, wretched 2. (*deforme*) misshapen.

disgregamento *sm.* disintegration.

disgregare *vt.* to disgregate, to break (*v. irr.*) up.

disgregazione *sf.* disgregation.

disguido *sm.* miscarriage.

disgustare *vt.* to disgust, to sicken. ♦ **disgustarsi** *vr.* to become (*v. irr.*) disgusted (with).

disgusto *sm.* 1. disgust 2. (*avversione*) dislike.

disgustoso *agg.* disgusting.

disidratare *vt.* to dehydrate.

disidratazione *sf.* dehydration.

disillùdere *vt.* to undeceive.

disillusione *sf.* disillusion.

disilluso *agg.* undeceived, disappointed.

disimballaggio *sm.* unpacking.

disimballare *vt.* to unpack.

disimpacciare *vt.* to disembarrass.

disimparare *vt.* to forget (*v. irr.*).

disimpegnare *vt.* 1. to redeem 2. (*liberare da un impegno*) to release. ♦ **disimpegnarsi** *vr.* **1.** to disengage oneself **2.** (*cavarsela*) to manage.

disimpegno *sm.* **1.** redemption **2.** (*il liberarsi da un impegno*) disengagement.

disincagliare *vt.* to get (*v. irr.*) afloat.

disincantare *vt.* to disenchant.

disincantato *agg.* disenchanted.

disincanto *sm.* disenchantment.

disinfestare *vt.* to disinfest.

disinfettante *sm.* disinfectant.

disinfettare *vt.* to disinfect.

disinfezione *sf.* disinfection.

disingannare *vt.* to undeceive.

disinganno *sm.* **1.** undeceiving **2.** (*delusione*) disappointment.

disinnescare *vt.* to defuse.

disinnestare *vt.* to disengage.

disinnesto *sm.* disengagement, release.

disinserire *vt.* to disconnect.

disintegrare *vt.* to disintegrate.

disintegratore *sm.* disintegrator.

disintegrazione *sf.* disintegration.

disinteressare *vt.* **1.** to disinterest **2.** (*comm.*) to buy (*v. irr.*) out. ♦ **disinteressarsi** *vr.* to take (*v. irr.*) no interest (in).

disinteressato *agg.* **1.** disinterested **2.** (*altruistico*) unselfish.

disinteresse *sm.* **1.** indifference **2.** (*altruismo*) unselfishness.

disintossicare *vt.* to unpoison.

disintossicazione *sf.* unpoisoning.

disinvolto *agg.* unconstrained, free--and-easy.

disinvoltura *sf.* unconstraint, free--and-easy way.

disistima *sf.* disesteem.

disistimare *vt.* to disesteem.

dislivello *sm.* **1.** difference of level **2.** (*di acque*) rise **3.** (*di strade*) gradient **4.** (*ineguaglianza*) inequality.

dislocamento *sm.* **1.** displacement **2.** (*mil.*) dislocation.

dislocare *vt.* **1.** to displace **2.** (*mil.*) to dislocate.

dislocazione *sf.* removal, dislocation.

dismisura *sf.* excess ‖ *a* —, excessively.

disobbedire *vi.* V. *disubbidire*.

disobbligare *vt.* to release from duty. ♦ **disobbligarsi** *vr.* to free oneself from duty.

disoccupato *agg.* unemployed. ♦

disoccupato *sm.* unemployed person.

disoccupazione *sf.* unemployment.

disonestà *sf.* **1.** dishonesty **2.** (*atto disonesto*) fraud.

disonesto *agg.* dishonest, fraudulent.

disonorante *agg.* shameful.

disonorare *vt.* to dishonour.

disonore *sm.* dishonour, shame.

disonorévole *agg.* dishonourable.

disopra *avv.* **1.** above, over **2.** (*in cima*) on top **3.** (*ai piani superiori*) upstairs. ♦ **disopra** *sm.* top, upper part. ♦ **al disopra di, disopra a** *prep.* above.

disordinare *vt.* to disorder.

disordinatamente *avv.* untidily.

disordinato *agg.* untidy, disorderly.

disòrdine *sm.* **1.** disorder, untidiness **2.** (*sregolatezza*) disorderliness **3.** (*tumulto*) disorder, tumult.

disorgànico *agg.* inorganic.

disorganizzare *vt.* to disorganize.

disorganizzato *agg.* disorganized.

disorganizzazione *sf.* disorganization.

disorientamento *sm.* disorientation, confusion.

disorientare *vt.* **1.** to disorientate **2.** (*sconcertare*) to bewilder.

disorientato *agg.* bewildered, puzzled.

disormeggiare *vt.* to unmoor.

disossare *vt.* to bone.

disossidante *sm.* deoxidizer.

disossidare *vt.* to deoxidize.

disossidazione *sf.* deoxidation.

disotto *avv.* **1.** below, underneath **2.** (*al piano inferiore*) downstairs. ♦ **disotto** *sm.* underside, lower part. ♦ **al disotto di, disotto a** *prep.* under, beneath, below.

dispaccio *sm.* dispatch.

disparato *agg.* disparate.

disparere *sm.* difference of opinion.

dìspari *agg.* odd.

disparità *sf.* disparity.

disparte *avv.* aside, apart: *starsene in* —, to stand (*v. irr.*) aside; (*fig.*) to stand aloof; *mettere in* —, to put (*v. irr.*) aside; (*per uno scopo*) to put by.

dispendio *sm.* **1.** heavy expense **2.** (*di forza, tempo*) waste.

dispendioso *agg.* expensive.

dispensa *sf.* **1.** pantry **2.** (*mobile*) sideboard **3.** (*pubblicazione perio-*

dica) number **4.** (*esenzione; eccl.*) dispensation.

dispensare *vt.* **1.** (*distribuire*) to deal (*v. irr.*) out **2.** (*esentare*) to exempt, to dispense.

dispensario *sm.* dispensary.

dispensato *agg.* exempted.

dispensatore *sm.* distributor, dispenser.

dispepsìa *sf.* dyspepsia.

dispèptico *agg.* dyspeptic.

disperare *vi.* to despair, to lose (*v. irr.*) all hope. ♦ **disperarsi** *vr.* to give (*v. irr.*) oneself up to despair.

disperatamente *avv.* desperately.

disperato *agg.* **1.** despairing **2.** (*senza speranza*) hopeless || *essere — (di malato)*, to be far gone. ♦ **disperato** *sm.* **1.** (*miserabile*) destitute **2.** (*forsennato*) madman (*pl.* -men).

disperazione *sf.* despair.

dispèrdere *vt.* to disperse **2.** (*consumare*) to waste.

dispersione *sf.* **1.** dispersion **2.** (*elettr.*) leak.

dispersivo *agg.* dispersive.

disperso *agg.* missing, lost.

dispetto *sm.* **1.** spite: *a — di*, in spite of **2.** (*stizza*) vexation.

dispettoso *agg.* spiteful.

displacere [1] *vi.* **1.** to dislike || *mi dispiace*, I am sorry; (*in espressioni di cortesia*) *se non vi dispiace*, if you please **2.** (*essere sgradevole*) to be disagreeable.

displacere [2] *sm.* **1.** regret **2.** (*disapprovazione*) displeasure **3.** (*fastidio*) tròuble.

dispiegare *vt.* **1.** (*allargare*) to spread (*v. irr.*) out **2.** (*le vele*) to unfurl.

displuvio *sm.* **1.** watershed || *linea di —*, ridge **2.** (*arch.*) hip.

disponìbile *agg.* available.

disponibilità *sf.* availability.

disporre *vt.* **1.** to arrange **2.** (*preparare*) to dispose **3.** (*deliberare*) to order.

dispositivo *sm.* (*mecc.*) device.

disposizione *sf.* **1.** disposition, arrangement **2.** (*ordine*) order, direction || *a —*, at one's disposal **3.** (*inclinazione*) bent.

disposto *agg.* **1.** ready, willing **2.** (*ben disposto fisicamente*) strong.

dispòtico *agg.* despotic.

dispotismo *sm.* despotism.

dispregiativamente *avv.* disparagingly.

dispregiativo *agg.* depreciative. ♦ **dispregiativo** *sm.* (*gramm.*) pejorative.

dispregiatore *sm.* contemner.

dispregio *sm.* contempt.

disprezzàbile *agg.* despicable.

disprezzare *vt.* **1.** to despise **2.** (*considerare di poco conto*) to look down on.

disprezzo *sm.* contempt.

dìsputa *sf.* discussion.

disputàbile *agg.* disputable.

disputare *vi.* e *vt.* to discuss.

disquisizione *sf.* disquisition.

dissaldare *vt.* to unsolder.

dissanguamento *sm.* **1.** bleeding **2.** (*fig.*) impoverishment.

dissanguare *vt.* **1.** to bleed **2.** (*fig.*) to impoverish. ♦ **dissanguarsi** *vr.* (*fig.*) to become (*v. irr.*) impoverished.

dissanguato *agg.* **1.** bloodless **2.** (*fig.*) impoverished.

dissanguatore *sm.* (*fig.*) blood--sucker.

dissapore *sm.* disagreement.

dissecare *vt.* to dissect.

disseccamento *sm.* drying up.

disseccante *agg.* drying up. ♦ **disseccante** *sm.* desiccative.

disseccare *vt.* **1.** to dry up **2.** (*cibo*) to desiccate.

disselciare *vt.* to unpave.

disseminare *vt.* to disseminate.

disseminato *agg.* strewn.

disseminante *agg.* disseminating. ♦ **disseminatore** *sm.* disseminator.

disseminazione *sf.* dissemination.

dissennatamente *avv.* madly.

dissennatezza *sf.* **1.** madness **2.** (*avventatezza*) rashness.

dissennato *agg.* **1.** mad **2.** (*avventato*) rash.

dissensione *sf.* dissension.

dissenso *sm.* dissent.

dissenterìa *sf.* dysentery.

dissentèrico *agg.* dysenteric.

dissentire *vi.* to dissent.

dissenziente *agg.* dissenting. ♦ **dissenziente** *sm.* dissenter.

disseppellimento *sm.* disinterment.

disseppellire *vt.* **1.** to disinter **2.** (*fig.*) to revive.

disserrare *vt.* to unfasten.

dissertare *vi.* to dissertate (on).

dissertatore *sm.* dissertator.

dissertazione *sf.* dissertation.

dissestare *vt.* 1. (*finanziariamente*) to ruin 2. (*mettere fuori posto*) to derange.

dissestato *agg.* (*di persona*) ruined.

dissesto *sm.* 1. trouble 2. (*fallimento*) bankruptcy.

dissetante *agg.* refreshing: *bibita* —, refreshing drink.

dissetare *vt.* to quench the thirst of. ♦ **dissetarsi** *vr.* 1. to quench one's thirst 2. (*bere*) to drink (*v. irr.*); (*di animali*) to water.

dissezione *sf.* dissection.

dissidente *agg.* e *sm.* dissident.

dissidenza *sf.* dissidence.

dissidio *sm.* 1. dissension, disagreement 2. (*litigio*) quarrel.

dissigillare *vt.* to unseal.

dissimile *agg.* unlike.

dissimmetrìa *sf.* dissymmetry.

dissimulare *vt.* to dissemble.

dissimulatamente *avv.* dissemblingly.

dissimulatore *sm.* dissimulator.

dissimulazione *sf.* dissimulation.

dissipare *vt.* to dissipate. ♦ **dissiparsi** *vr.* to dissipate, to vanish.

dissipatezza *sf.* dissipation.

dissipatore *sm.* waster.

dissipazione *sf.* dissipation.

dissociàbile *agg.* dissociable.

dissociare *vt.* to dissociate.

dissociazione *sf.* dissociation.

dissodamento *sm.* tillage.

dissodare *vt.* to till.

dissolùbile *agg.* dissoluble.

dissolubilità *sf.* dissolubility.

dissolutezza *sf.* dissoluteness.

dissoluto *agg.* dissolute.

dissoluzione *sf.* dissolution.

dissolvente *agg.* e *sm.* dissolvent.

dissòlvere *vt.* 1. to dissolve 2. (*disperdere*) to dispel. ♦ **dissòlversi** *vr.* to dissolve.

dissolvimento *sm.* dissolution.

dissomigliante *agg.* dissimilar (to).

dissomiglianza *sf.* dissimilarity.

dissomigliare *vi.* to be unlike. ♦ **dissomigliarsi** *vr.* to differ from.

dissonante *agg.* dissonant.

dissonanza *sf.* 1. dissonance 2. (*fig.*) discordance.

dissonare *vi.* 1. to be out of tune 2. (*fig.*) to discord (with).

dissotterramento *sm.* disinterment.

dissotterrare *vt.* to disinter.

dissuadere *vt.* to dissuade.

dissuasione *sf.* dissuasion.

distaccamento *sm.* 1. detaching 2. (*mil.*) detachment.

distaccare *vt.* to detach. ♦ **distaccarsi** *vr.* to come (*v. irr.*) off.

distacco *sm.* 1. detaching 2. (*partenza*) leaving 3. (*indifferenza*) unconcern.

distante *agg.* distant. ♦ **distante** *avv.* far, far off, far away.

distanza *sf.* distance.

distanziare *vt.* 1. to space 2. (*lasciare indietro*) to distance.

distanziato *agg.* 1. spaced 2. (*sport*) outdistanced.

distare *vi.* to be far: *quanto dista?*, how far is it?

distèndere *vt.* 1. (*allungare*) to stretch 2. (*spalmare*) to spread (*v. irr.*) 3. (*porre, stendere*) to lay (*v. irr.*). ♦ **distèndersi** *vr.* 1. to spread (*v. irr.*) 2. (*sdraiarsi*) to lie (*v. irr.*) down 3. (*rilassarsi*) to relax.

distensione *sf.* 1. (*di nervi, tensione*) relaxation 2. (*pol.*) distension.

distensivo *agg.* relaxing.

distesa *sf.* expanse || *a* —, continuously.

distesamente *avv.* diffusely.

disteso *agg.* 1. (*teso*) extended 2. (*giacente*) lying 3. (*esteso*) extensive || *per* —, diffusely.

distico *sm.* couplet.

distillare *vt.* to distil.

distillato *agg.* distilled. ♦ **distillato** *sm.* distillate.

distillatoio *sm.* still.

distillatore *sm.* distiller.

distillazione *sf.* distillation.

distillerìa *sf.* distillery.

distinguere *vt.* 1. to distinguish 2. (*contrassegnare*) to mark.

distinta *sf.* list.

distintivo *agg.* distinctive. ♦ **distintivo** *sm.* badge.

distinto *agg.* 1. distinct 2. (*garbato*) distinguished.

distinzione *sf.* 1. distinction 2. (*riguardo*) regard 3. (*raffinatezza*) refinement.

distògliere *vt.* 1. (*dissuadere*) to dissuade 2. (*distrarre*) to divert. ♦ **distògliersi** *vr.* to be distracted.

distorsione *sf.* distortion.

distrarre *vt.* 1. (*distogliere*) to divert 2. (*divertire*) to entertain.

distrattamente *avv.* 1. absent-mindedly 2. (*inavvertitamente*) inadvertently.

distratto *agg.* 1. absent-minded 2. (*disattento*) inattentive.

distrazione *sf.* 1. absent-mindedness 2. (*disattenzione*) inattention 3. (*divertimento*) recreation.

distretta *sf.* urgent need.

distretto *sm.* district || — *militare*, recruiting centre.

distrettuale *agg.* district.

distribuìbile *agg.* distributable.

distribuire *vt.* to distribute.

distributivo *agg.* e *sm.* distributive.

distributore *agg.* distributing. ♦ **distributore** *sm.* distributor || — *di benzina*, petrol pump.

distribuzione *sf.* distribution.

districare *vt.* to disentangle.

distrùggere *vt.* 1. to destroy 2. (*struggere*) to consume. ♦ **distrùggersi** *vr.* (*consumarsi*) to pine (away).

distruggìbile *agg.* destroyable.

distruttivo *agg.* destroying.

distrutto *agg.* destroyed.

distruttore *agg.* destroying. ♦ **distruttore** *sm.* destroyer.

distruzione *sf.* destruction.

disturbare *vt.* to disturb.

disturbato *agg.* 1. disturbed 2. (*indisposto*) unwell.

disturbatore *sm.* disturber.

disturbo *sm.* 1. trouble, inconvenience 2. (*malattia*) trouble, illness 3. (*radio*) disturbance.

disubbidiente *agg.* disobedient.

disubbidienza *sf.* disobedience.

disubbidire *vi.* to disobey.

disuguaglianza *sf.* 1. inequality 2. (*di terreno*) unevenness.

disuguale *agg.* 1. unequal 2. (*irregolare*) irregular 3. (*differente*) different.

disumanamente *avv.* inhumanly.

disumanare *vt.* to divest of humanity.

disumanità *sf.* inhumanity.

disumano *agg.* inhuman.

disumidire *vt.* to dry.

disunione *sf.* disunion.

disunire *vt.* to disunite. ♦ **disunirsi** *vr.* to become (*v. irr.*) disunited.

disunito *agg.* disunited.

disusare *vt.* to disuse.

disusato *agg.* disused.

disuso *sm.* disuse.

ditale *sm.* thimble.

ditata *sf.* finger-mark.

ditiràmbico *agg.* dithyrambic.

ditirambo *sm.* dithyramb.

dito *sm.* 1. finger 2. (*del piede*) toe.

ditta *sf.* firm.

dittàfono *sm.* dictaphone.

dittatore *sm.* dictator.

dittatoriale *agg.* dictatorial.

dittatorio *agg.* dictatorial.

dittatura *sf.* dictatorship.

dìttico *sm.* diptych.

dittongo *sm.* diphthong.

diuresi *sf.* diuresis.

diurètico *agg.* diuretic.

diurno *agg.* diurnal, daytime.

diuturnamente *avv.* for a long time.

diuturno *agg.* diuturnal.

diva *sf.* 1. goddess 2. (*cine*) star.

divagare *vi.* to wander 2. (*divertire*) to amuse. ♦ **divagarsi** *vr.* 1. to be distracted 2. (*divertirsi*) to amuse oneself.

divagazione *sf.* digression.

divampare *vi.* to blaze.

divano *sm.* divan, sofa.

divaricamento *sm.* straddle.

divaricare *vt.* to open wide || — *le gambe*, to part one's legs wide.

divario *sm.* difference.

divedere *vt.* 1. (*nella loc. avv.*) *dare a* —, to show (*v. irr.*) clearly 2. (*dar a credere*) to make (*v. irr.*) believe.

divèllere *vt.* to uproot.

divenire[1] *vi.* 1. to become (*v. irr.*) 2. (*mutarsi lentamente*) to grow (*v. irr.*).

divenire[2] *sm.* becoming: *l'essere e il* —, being and becoming.

diverbio *sm.* quarrel.

divergente *agg.* divergent.

divergenza *sf.* divergence.

divèrgere *vi.* 1. to diverge 2. (*scostarsi*) to wander.

diversamente *avv.* 1. differently 2. (*altrimenti*) otherwise.

diversificare *vt.* to diversify. ♦ **diversificarsi** *vr.* to differ.

diversione *sf.* diversion.

diversità *sf.* diversity.

diversivo *agg.* 1. deviating 2. (*che distrae*) diverting. ♦ **diversivo** *sm.* diversion, distraction.

diverso *agg.* different.

divertente *agg.* amusing.

divertimento *sm.* amusement.

divertire *vt.* to amuse, to entertain
♦ **divertirsi** *vr.* to enjoy oneself,
to have a good time.

divezzamento *sm.* weaning.

divezzare *vt.* to wean.

dividendo *sm.* dividend.

dividere *vt.* 1. to divide 2. (*condividere*) to share.

divieto *sm.* prohibition.

divinamente *avv.* divinely.

divinare *vt.* to divine.

divinatore *sm.* diviner.

divinatorio *agg.* divinatory.

divinazione *sf.* divination.

divincolarsi *vr.* to wriggle.

divinità *sf.* divinity.

divinizzare *vt.* to deify.

divino *agg.* divine.

divisa *sf.* 1. uniform 2. (*valuta*) currency.

divisare *vt.* to plan.

divisibile *agg.* divisible.

divisibilità *sf.* divisibility.

divisionale *agg.* divisional.

divisione *sf.* 1. division 2. (*amm.*) department.

divisionismo *sm.* pointillism.

divisionista *s.* pointillist.

divismo *sm.* stardom, star worship.

diviso *agg.* 1. divided 2. (*separato*) separated 3. (*condiviso*) shared.

divisore *sm.* divisor.

divisorio *agg.* dividing.

divo *sm.* 1. deity 2. (*cine*) star.

divorare *vt.* to devour.

divoratore *agg.* devouring.

divorziare *vi.* to divorce, to be divorced.

divorziato *agg.* divorced. ♦ **divorziato** *sm.* divorcee.

divorzio *sm.* divorce (*anche fig.*).

divulgàbile *agg.* that may be divulged.

divulgare *vt.* to spread (*v. irr.*).

divulgativo *agg.* divulging.

divulgatore *sm.* divulger.

divulgazione *sf.* divulgation, spreading.

dizionario *sm.* dictionary.

dizionarista *s.* lexicographer.

dizione *sf.* 1. diction 2. (*pronuncia*) pronunciation.

do *sm.* (*mus.*) C.

doccia *sf.* shower.

docente *agg.* teaching. ♦ **docente** *sm.* teacher ‖ *libero* —, fully established university lecturer.

docenza *sf.* teaching.

dòcile *agg.* docile.

docilità *sf.* docility.

documentare *vt.* to document.

documentario *sm.* documentary.

documentarista *s.* documentary film-maker.

documentato *agg.* documented.

documentazione *sf.* 1. documentation 2. *pl.* (*documenti*) papers.

documento *sm.* document.

dodecaedro *sm.* dodecahedron.

dodecafonìa *sf.* dodecaphony.

dodecafònico *agg.* dodecaphonic.

dodecàgono *sm.* dodecagon.

dodecasìllabo *sm.* dodecasyllable.

dodicèsimo *agg.* twelfth.

dòdici *agg.* twelve.

doga *sf.* stave.

dogana *sf.* customs (*pl.*).

doganale *agg.* customs (*attr.*): *dichiarazione* —, customs entry.

doganiere *sm.* customs officer.

doge *sm.* doge.

doglia *sf.* 1. sharp pains 2. (*pl., med.*) throes.

dogma *sm.* dogma.

dogmàtico *agg.* dogmatic(al).

dogmatismo *sm.* dogmatism.

dolce *agg.* 1. sweet 2. (*mite*) mild 3. (*tec.*) soft. ♦ **dolce** *sm.* 1. sweet 2. (*torta*) cake.

dolcezza *sf.* 1. sweetness 2. (*di clima*) mildness.

dolciario *agg.* confectionary.

dolciastro *agg.* sweetish.

dolcificare *vt.* 1. to sweeten 2. (*fig.*) to mitigate.

dolcificazione *sf.* sweetening.

dolciumi *sm. pl.* sweets.

dolente *agg.* 1. afflicted, grieved 2. (*spiacente*) sorry.

dolere *vi.* 1. to ache 2. (*rincrescere*) to regret. ♦ **dolersi** *vr.* to regret.

dolicocèfalo *agg.* dolichocephalic.

dòllaro *sm.* dollar.

dolmen *sm.* dolmen.

dolo *sm.* fraud.

dolomite *sf.* dolomite.

dolomìtico *agg.* dolomitic.

dolorante *agg.* aching.

dolore *sm.* 1. pain, ache 2. (*fig.*) sorrow, grief.

dolorosamente *avv.* 1. painfully 2. (*morale*) sadly.

doloroso *agg.* 1. painful 2. (*che causa dolore*) grievous.

doloso *agg.* fraudulent.

domàbile *agg.* tamable.

domanda *sf.* 1. question, request

2. (*richiesta scritta*) application.
domandare *vt.* to ask (so. for sthg.). ♦ **domandarsi** *vr.* to wonder.

domani *avv.* tomorrow.

domare *vt.* **1.** to tame **2.** (*sottomettere*) to subdue.

domatore *sm.* tamer.

domattina *avv.* tomorrow morning.

doménica *sf.* Sunday.

domenicale *agg.* Sunday (*attr.*).

domenicano *agg.* dominican.

domèstica *sf.* maid.

domèstico *agg.* e *sm.* domestic ‖ *lavori domestici*, household duties.

domiciliare *agg.* domiciliary.

domiciliarsi *vr.* to settle (in).

domiciliato *agg.* resident, living.

domicilio *sm.* **1.** house, dwelling **2.** (*giur.*) domicile.

dominante *agg.* dominant.

dominare *vt.* to dominate.

dominatore *sm.* ruler.

dominazione *sf.* domination.

dominio *sm.* **1.** domination **2.** (*territorio*) dominion **3.** (*giur.*) domain ‖ *di — pubblico*, known to everybody.

dòmino *sm.* domino.

donare *vt.* to give (*v. irr.*) ♦ **donare** *vi.* (*addirsi*) to suit.

donatore *sm.* donor.

donazione *sf.* **1.** donation **2.** (*somma elargita per uno scopo*) grant.

donchisciottesco *agg.* quixotic.

donde *avv.* whence, from where ‖ *ne ha ben —*, he has good reason for it.

dondolamento *sm.* swinging.

dondolare *vt.* e *vi.* to swing (*v. irr.*). ♦ **dondolarsi** *vr.* to swing, to rock.

dondolìo *sm.* swinging.

dòndolo *sm.* **1.** (*altalena*) swing ‖ *a —*, rocking.

donna *sf.* woman (*pl.* women).

donnaiolo *sm.* ladies' man (*pl.* men).

donnesco *agg.* womanlike.

dònnola *sf.* weasel.

dono *sm.* gift.

donzella *sf.* damsel.

dopo *avv.* **1.** (*di luogo*) after, next **2.** (*dietro*) behind **3.** (*di tempo*) after, then **4.** (*più tardi*) later. ♦ **dopo** *prep.* (*di luogo e tempo*) after.

dopodomani *avv.* the day after tomorrow.

dopoguerra *sm.* post-war period.

dopopranzo *sm.* afternoon.

dopotutto *avv.* after all.

doppiaggio *sm.* (*cine*) dubbing.

doppiamente *avv.* **1.** doubly **2.** (*con inganno*) deceitfully.

doppiare *vt.* **1.** to double **2.** (*cine*) to dub.

doppiato *agg.* **1.** doubled **2.** (*cine*) dubbed.

doppiatura *sf.* doubling.

doppietta *sf.* double-barrelled gun.

doppiezza *sf.* **1.** doubleness **2.** (*ambiguità*) double-dealing.

doppio *agg.* **1.** double **2.** (*ambiguo*) double-faced. ♦ **doppio** *sm.* twice as much, twice as many.

doppiofondo *sm.* double bottom.

doppione *sm.* **1.** double **2.** (*di parola*) doublet.

doppiopetto *sm.* double-breasted.

dorare *vt.* to gild.

dorato *agg.* **1.** gilded **2.** (*color oro*) golden.

doratore *sm.* gilder.

doratura *sf.* gilding.

dòrico *agg.* doric.

dorìfora *sf.* potato-beetle.

dormicchiare *vi.* to doze.

dormiente *agg.* sleeping. ♦ **dormiente** *sm.* sleeper.

dormiglione *sm.* sleepy-head.

dormire *vi.* **1.** to sleep (*v. irr.*) ‖ *— tra due guanciali*, to set (*v. irr.*) one's mind at rest **2.** (*fig.*) to remain inactive.

dormita *sf.* sleep.

dormitorio *sm.* dormitory.

dormiveglia *sm.* drowsiness.

dorsale *agg.* dorsal: *spina —*, backbone.

dorso *sm.* **1.** back **2.** (*di monte*) ridge.

dosàbile *agg.* measurable.

dosaggio *sm.* dosage.

dosare *vt.* to proportion: *— le parole*, to weigh one's words.

dosatura *sf.* dosage.

dose *sf.* dose: *una buona — di*, a good deal of.

dossale *sm.* dossal.

dosso *sm.* back: *togliersi di —*, to take (*v. irr.*) off.

dotare *vt.* **1.** to give (*v. irr.*) a dowry **2.** (*fornire di una rendita*) to endow **3.** (*fornire*) to provide (with).

dotato *agg.* **1.** gifted (with) **2.** (*e-*

quipaggiato) provided (with).

dotazione *sf.* endowment.

dote *sf.* 1. dowry 2. (*qualità*) endowment.

dotto[1] *agg.* learned. ♦ **dotto** *sm.* scholar.

dotto[2] *sm.* (*anat.*) duct.

dottorale *agg.* doctoral.

dottorato *sm.* doctorate.

dottore *sm.* 1. doctor 2. (*laureato*) graduate.

dottoressa *sf.* 1. (*laureata*) graduate 2. (*in medicina*) lady doctor.

dottrina *sf.* doctrine.

dottrinale *agg.* doctrinal.

dottrinario *sm.* doctrinaire.

dottrinarismo *sm.* doctrinairism.

dove *avv.* where.

dovere[1] *vi.* 1. (*obbligo*) must (*v. dif.*): *devi lavorare*, you must work 2. to have to 3. (*possibilità, predestinazione*) to be to: *doveva diventare un grande scrittore*, he was to become a great writer 4. (*devo?, dobbiamo?, nel senso di: vuoi che?*) shall (*v. dif.*): *devo aprire la finestra?*, shall I open the window? 5. (*al condizionale*) ought to, should (*v. dif.*): *dovresti essere gentile*, you ought to be kind; *dovremmo partire*, we should leave 6. (*al congiuntivo*) should, were to: *se dovesse venire*, if he should come, if he were to come 7. (*essere obbligati*) to be obliged, to be forced 8. (*essere da attribuire, dover arrivare*) to be due: *lo si deve al mio ritardo*, this is due to my being late; *il treno deve arrivare alle 4*, the train is due at 4 a.m. ♦ **dovere** *vt.* (*essere debitore in tutti i sensi*) to owe: *ti devo 1000 lire*, I owe you one thousand lire; *ti devo la vita*, I owe you my life.

dovere[2] *sm.* duty: *fare il proprio —*, to do (*v. irr.*) one's duty.

doverosamente *avv.* dutifully.

doveroso *agg.* dutiful.

dovizia *sf.* plenty.

dovizioso *agg.* abundant.

dovunque *avv.* 1. everywhere 2. (*seguito da verbo*) wherever.

dovuto *agg.* 1. due 2. (*equo*) fair. ♦ **dovuto** *sm.* due.

dozzina *sf.* dozen.

dozzinale *agg.* cheap, common.

draconiano *agg.* draconian.

draga *sf.* dredger.

dragaggio *sm.* dredging.

dragamine *sm.* mine-sweeper.

dragare *vt.* to dredge.

draglia *sf.* stay.

drago *sm.* dragon.

dragona *sf.* sword-knot.

dragone *sm.* dragon.

dramma *sm.* drama.

drammàtica *sf.* dramatics.

drammaticamente *avv.* dramatically.

drammaticità *sf.* tragicalness.

drammàtico *agg.* dramatic.

drammatizzare *vt.* to dramatise.

drammaturgìa *sf.* dramaturgy.

drammaturgo *sm.* dramatist.

drappeggiare *vt.* to drape.

drappeggio *sm.* draping.

drappello *sm.* squad.

drapperìa *sf.* drapery.

drappo *sm.* cloth.

dràstico *agg.* drastic.

drenaggio *sm.* drainage.

drenare *vt.* to drain.

drìade *sf.* 1. (*mit.*) dryad 2. (*bot.*) dryas (*pl.* -ades).

dribblare *vt.* to dribble.

dritta *sf.* 1. right hand, right 2. (*mar.*) starboard.

dritto *agg.* 1. (*non storto*) straight 2. (*eretto, onesto*) upright. ♦ **dritto** *sm.* right side.

drizza *sf.* halyard.

drizzare *vt.* to straighten.

droga *sf.* 1. drug 2. (*spezia*) spices (*pl.*).

drogare *vt.* 1. to drug 2. (*condire*) to spice.

drogherìa *sf.* grocery.

droghiere *sm.* grocer.

dromedario *sm.* dromedary.

drùido *sm.* druid.

drupa *sf.* drupe.

dualismo *sm.* dualism.

dualità *sf.* duality.

dubbiezza *sf.* dubiousness.

dubbio *sm.* doubt: *mettere in —*, to question. ♦ **dubbio** *agg.* dubious.

dubbioso *agg.* doubtful.

dubitare *vi.* to doubt.

dubitativo *agg.* dubitative.

duca *sm.* duke.

ducale *agg.* ducal.

ducato *sm.* 1. dukedom 2. (*moneta*) ducat.

duchessa *sf.* duchess.

due *agg.* two.

duecentèsimo *agg.* two hundredth.

duecentesco *agg.* thirteenth century (*attr.*).

duecento *sm.* two hundred || *il —*, the thirteenth century.

duellare *vi.* to duel.

duello *sm.* duel: — *all'ultimo sangue*, duel to the death.

duetto *sm.* duet.

duna *sf.* dune.

dunque *cong.* **1.** (*perciò*) therefore **2.** (*rafforzativo*) well, then. ♦ **dunque** *sm. venire al —*, to come (*v. irr.*) to the point.

duodenale *agg.* duodenal.

duodeno *sm.* duodenum.

duomo *sm.* cathedral.

duplicare *vt.* to duplicate.

duplicato *sm.* duplicate.

dùplice *agg.* twofold.

duplicità *sf.* double-dealing.

durabilità *sf.* durability.

duralluminio *sm.* duralumin.

durante *prep.* during.

durare *vi.* **1.** to last **2.** (*perseverare*) to persist **3.** (*resistere*) to hold (*v. irr.*) out. ♦ **durare** *vt.* to endure || *chi la dura la vince*, slow and steady wins the race.

durata *sf.* **1.** duration, length **2.** (*periodo*) term **3.** (*di un oggetto*) endurance.

duraturo *agg.* lasting.

durévole *agg.* durable.

durezza *sf.* **1.** hardness **2.** (*rigidità*) stiffness.

duro *agg.* **1.** hard **2.** (*di voce*) harsh || *avere il sonno —*, to sleep (*v. irr.*) like a log; *avere la testa dura*, to be a block-head, to be stubborn.

durone *sm.* hard skin.

dùttile *agg.* ductile.

duttilità *sf.* ductility.

E

e *cong.* and: *e... e*, both... and.

ebanista *sm.* cabinet-maker.

ebanisterìa *sf.* **1.** (*bottega*) cabinet-maker's shop **2.** (*arte*) cabinet-making.

ebanite *sf.* ebonite.

èbano *sm.* ebony.

ebbene *cong.* well: *—?*, what about it?

ebbrezza *sf.* **1.** drunkenness **2.** (*fig.*) elation.

ebbro *agg.* **1.** drunken **2.** (*fig.*) mad.

ebdomadario *agg.* weekly. ♦ **ebdomadario** *sm.* weekly paper.

èbete *agg.* idiotic. ♦ **èbete** *sm.* idiot.

ebollizione *sf.* boiling.

ebràico *agg.* Hebrew.

ebreo *agg.* Hebrew, Jewish. ♦ **ebreo** *sm.* Hebrew, Jew.

ecatombe *sf.* massacre.

eccedente *agg.* excessive, in excess (*pred.*). ♦ **eccedente** *sm.* (*comm.*) exceeding.

eccedenza *sf.* excess, surplus: — *di peso*, overweight.

eccèdere *vt.* to exceed. ♦ **eccèdere** *vi.* to go (*v. irr.*) too far.

eccellente *agg.* excellent.

eccellenza *sf.* **1.** excellence **2.** (*titolo*) excellency.

eccèllere *vi.* to excel.

eccelso *agg.* sublime.

eccentricità *sf.* eccentricity.

eccèntrico *agg.* eccentric.

eccepire *vi.* to object.

eccessivo *agg.* excessive.

eccesso *sm.* excess.

eccètera *sm.* et cetera (*abbr.* etc.), and so on.

eccetto *prep.* except, but, save. ♦ **eccetto che** *cong.* **1.** except that **2.** (*purché*) provided that.

eccettuare *vt.* to except.

eccettuato *agg.* excluded.

eccezionale *agg.* exceptional.

eccezione *sf.* exception.

ecchìmosi *sf.* bruise.

eccidio *sm.* bloodshed.

eccitàbile *agg.* excitable.

eccitabilità *sf.* excitability.

eccitamento *sm.* excitement.

eccitante *agg. e sm.* excitant.

eccitare *vt.* to excite. ♦ **eccitarsi** *vr.* to get (*v. irr.*) excited.

eccitatore *agg.* excitative. ♦ **eccitatore** *sm.* exciter.

eccitazione *sf.* excitement.

ecclesiàstico *agg.* ecclesiastical.

ecco *avv.* here, there (*in unione con le voci del verbo fa al pres. ind.*): — *il mio cappello!*, here is my hat! || — *tutto*, that's all; *quand' —*, when suddenly.

eccome *inter.* and how!

echeggiare *vi.* to echo (with sthg.).

echinoderma *sm.* echinoderm.

eclèttico *agg. e sm.* eclectic.

eclettismo *sm.* eclecticism.

eclissare *vt.* 1. to eclipse 2. (*fig.*) to overshadow.

eclisse, eclissi *sf.* eclipse.

eclìttica *sf.* ecliptic.

eclìttico *agg.* ecliptic.

eco *sf.* echo.

economato *sm.* 1. steward's office 2. (*in università*) bursar's office.

economìa *sf.* 1. economy 2. (*scienza*) economics.

econòmico *agg.* 1. economic 2. (*a buon prezzo*) cheap.

economista *s.* economist.

economizzare *vt.* to economize.

ecònomo *agg.* economical. ♦ **ecònomo** *sm.* 1. steward 2. (*di università*) bursar.

ecumènico *agg.* ecumenical.

eczema *sm.* eczema.

edema *sm.* oedema.

eden *sm.* Eden.

èdera *sf.* ivy.

edìcola *sf.* newspaper kiosk.

edicolista *sm.* news-agent.

edificante *agg.* edifying.

edificare *vt.* 1. to build (*v. irr.*) (up) 2. (*fig.*) to edify.

edificatore *sm.* 1. builder 2. (*fig.*) edifier.

edificazione *sf.* 1. building 2. (*fig.*) edification.

edificio *sm.* building.

edile *agg.* building: *perito —,* master-builder. ♦ **edile** *sm.* (*stor. romana*) aedile.

edilizia *sf.* building industry.

edilizio *agg.* building (*attr.*).

èdito *agg.* published.

editore *sm.* publisher.

editorìa *sf.* book industry.

editoriale *agg.* e *sm.* editorial.

editrice *agg.:* *casa —,* publishing house.

editto *sm.* edict.

edizione *sf.* edition, issue.

edonismo *sm.* hedonism.

edonista *s.* hedonist.

edotto *agg.* aware: *rendere —,* to inform.

educanda *sf.* boarding-school girl.

educandato *sm.* girls' boarding-school.

educare *vt.* 1. to educate 2. (*allevare*) to bring (*v. irr.*) up.

educativo *agg.* educational.

educato *agg.* well-bred, polite.

educatore *sm.* educator.

educazione *sf.* 1. education 2.

(*buone maniere*) good manners (*pl.*).

edulcorare *vt.* to edulcorate.

efebo *sm.* ephebe.

efèlide *sf.* freckle.

effemèride *sf.* ephemeris (*pl.* -ides).

effeminare *vt.* to effeminate. ♦ **effeminarsi** *vr.* to become (*v. irr.*) effeminate.

effeminatezza *sf.* effeminacy.

efferatezza *sf.* brutality.

efferato *agg.* brutal.

effervescente *agg.* sparkling.

effervescenza *sf.* effervescence.

effettivamente *avv.* actualy, indeed.

effettivo *agg.* actual.

effetto *sm.* 1. effect, result || *in effetti,* as a matter of fact 2. (*comm.*) bill.

effettuàbile *agg.* feasible.

effettuare *vt.* to carry out: *— un piano,* to carry out a plan. ♦ **effettuarsi** *vr.* (*aver luogo*) to take (*v. irr.*) place.

effettuazione *sf.* accomplishment.

efficace *agg.* effective, efficacious.

efficacia *sf.* efficacy.

efficiente *agg.* efficient.

efficienza *sf.* efficiency.

effigiare *vt.* to portray.

effigie *sf.* image.

effìmera *sf.* (*fam.*) mayfly.

effìmero *agg.* ephemeral.

effluvio *sm.* exhalation.

effòndere *vt.* to pour forth. ♦ **effòndersi** *vr.* to spread (*v. irr.*) (about).

effrazione *sf.* (*giur.*) house-breaking, burglary.

effusione *sf.* 1. shedding 2. (*cordialità*) cordiality 3. (*pl., manifestazioni*) effusions.

effusivo *agg.* effusive.

egemonìa *sf.* hegemony.

egemònico *agg.* hegemonic.

ègida *sf.* 1. aegis 2. (*fig.*) protection.

egiziano *agg.* e *sm.* Egyptian.

egli *pron.* he: *— stesso,* he himself.

ègloga *sf.* eclogue.

egocèntrico *agg.* egocentric. ♦ **egocèntrico** *sm.* egocentric man.

egocentrismo *sm.* egocentrism.

egoismo *sm.* selfishness.

egoista *agg.* e *sm.* egoist.

egotismo *sm.* self-conceit.

egregiamente *avv.* eminently.

egregio *agg.* eminent || (*nelle lettere*) *— Signore,* Dear Sir.

eguaglianza, eguagliare, eguale
  ecc. V. *uguaglianza, uguagliare,*
  uguale ecc.
egualità *sf.* equality.
eiaculare *vi.* to ejaculate.
eiaculazione *sf.* ejaculation.
eiezione *sf.* ejection.
elaborare *vt.* to elaborate.
elaborato *agg.* elaborate.
elaborazione *sf.* 1. elaboration 2.
  (*di piano*) formulation.
elargire *vt.* to lavish.
elargizione *sf.* donation.
elasticità *sf.* 1. elasticity 2. (*agilità*)
  nimbleness.
elasticizzare *vt.* to make (*v. irr.*)
  elastic.
elàstico *agg.* 1. elastic 2. (*agile*)
  nimble. ♦ **elàstico** *sm.* rubber
  band.
elce *sm.* ilex.
elefante *sm.* elephant.
elefantesco *agg.* elephantine.
elefantìasi *sf.* elephantiasis.
elegante *agg.* elegant, smart.
eleganza *sf.* smartness.
elèggere *vt.* 1. to elect 2. (*nomina-*
  re) to appoint.
eleggìbile *agg.* eligible.
eleggibilità *sf.* eligibility.
elegìa *sf.* elegy.
elegìaco *agg.* elegiac.
elementare *agg.* elementary: *scuo-*
  la —, primary school.
elemento *sm.* 1. element 2. (*com-*
  ponente) component 3. (*pl., rudi-*
  menti) rudiments 4. (*persona*)
  person.
elemòsina *sf.* alms: *chiedere l'—*,
  to beg.
elemosinare *vt.* e *vi.* to beg (for).
elencare *vt.* to list.
elenco *sm.* list: *— telefonico*, telephone directory.
elettivo *agg.* elective.
eletto *agg.* elect, chosen.
elettorale *agg.* electoral.
elettorato *sm.* electorate.
elettore *sm.* voter.
elettràuto *sm.* 1. (*officina*) car
  electrical repairs (*pl.*) 2. (*meccani-*
  co) car electrician.
elettricista *sm.* electrician.
elettricità *sf.* electricity.
elèttrico *agg.* electric.
elettrificare *vt.* to electrify.
elettrificazione *sf.* electrification.
elettrizzare *vt.* to electrify.
elettrocalamita *sf.* electro-magnet.

elettrocardiogramma *sm.* electrocardiogram.
elettrodinàmica *sf.* electrodynamics.
elèttrodo *sm.* electrode.
elettrodomèstici *sm. pl.* electrical
  household appliances.
elettrògeno *agg.* generating electricity.
elettròlisi *sf.* electrolysis.
elettromagnètico *agg.* electro-mag-
  netic.
elettromotore *sm.* dynamo.
elettromotrice *sf.* electric rail
  car.
elettrone *sm.* electron.
elettrònica *sf.* electronics.
elettrònico *agg.* electronic.
elettrotècnica *sf.* electrical technology.
elettrotreno *sm.* electric train.
elevamento *sm.* elevation.
elevare *vt.* 1. to elevate 2. (*erigere*)
  to erect 3. (*mat.*) to raise. ♦ **ele-**
  varsi *vr.* to rise (*v. irr.*).
elevatezza *sf.* loftiness.
elevato *agg.* elevated, high.
elevatore *sm.* elevator.
elevazione *sf.* 1. elevation 2. (*l'ele-*
  vare) rising 3. (*mat.*) raising.
elezione *sf.* election.
èlica *sf.* 1. (*aer.*) propeller 2. (*mar.*)
  screw.
elicoidale *agg.* helicoidal.
elicòttero *sm.* helicopter.
elìdere *vt.* to annul. ♦ **elìdersi**
  vr. rec. to annul each other.
eliminare *vt.* to eliminate. ♦ **eli-**
  minarsi *vr.* to be eliminated.
eliminatoria *sf.* preliminary heat.
eliminazione *sf.* elimination, expulsion.
elio *sm.* helium.
eliocèntrico *agg.* heliocentric.
eliografìa *sf.* heliography.
elioterapìa *sf.* heliotherapy.
eliotipìa *sf.* heliotypy.
eliporto *sm.* heliport.
elisione *sf.* elision.
elisìr *sm.* elixir.
èlitra *sf.* elytrum (*pl.* -ra).
ella *pron.* she: *— stessa*, she herself.
ellènico *agg.* Hellenic.
ellenismo *sm.* Hellenism.
ellenista *s.* Hellenist.
ellisse *sf.* ellipse.
ellissi *sf.* ellipsis (*pl.* -ses).
ellìttico *sm.* elliptic(al).
elmetto *sm.* helmet.

elmo *sm.* helmet.

elocuzione *sf.* elocution.

elogiàbile *agg.* praiseworthy.

elogiare *vt.* to eulogize, to praise.

elogiatore *sm.* eulogist.

elogio *sm.* eulogy, praise.

eloquente *agg.* eloquent.

eloquenza *sf.* eloquence.

elucubrare *vt.* to lucubrate: — *su*, *intorno a qc.*, to lucubrate on, about sthg.

elucubrazione *sf.* lucubration.

elùdere *vt.* to elude.

elusivo *agg.* elusive.

elvètico *agg.* Helvetic.

elzeviro *sm.* 1. elzevir 2. (*giorn.*) leading literary article.

emaciare *vt.* to emaciate. ♦ **emaciarsi** *vr.* to become (*v. irr.*) emaciated.

emaciato *agg.* emaciated.

emanare *vt.* 1. to issue 2. (*vapori*, *profumi*) to exhale.

emanazione *sf.* emanation.

emancipare *vt.* to emancipate.

emancipato *agg.* emancipated.

emancipazione *sf.* emancipation.

emàtico *agg.* haematic.

ematoma *sm.* haematoma (*pl.* -ata).

ematosi *sf.* haematosis.

embargo *sm.* embargo.

emblema *sm.* 1. emblem 2. (*simbolo*) symbol.

emblemàtico *agg.* emblematic.

embolìa *sf.* embolism.

èmbolo *sm.* embolus (*pl.* -li).

embrionale *agg.* embryonic.

embrione *sm.* embryo.

emendamento *sm.* 1. amendment 2. (*correzione*) emendation.

emendare *vt.* 1. to amend 2. (*correggere*) to emend.

emergenza *sf.* emergency.

emèrgere *vi.* 1. to emerge 2. (*fig.*) to emerge, to appear.

emèrito *agg.* emeritus.

emeroteca *sf.* newspaper library.

emersione *sf.* emersion.

eméttere *vt.* 1. to emit 2. (*di suono*) to utter 3. (*emanare*) to deliver 4. (*banconote*) to issue.

emiciclo *sm.* hemicycle.

emicrania *sf.* headache.

emigrante *agg.* e *sm.* emigrant.

emigrare *vi.* to emigrate.

emigrato *sm.* emigrant.

emigrazione *sf.* emigration.

eminente *agg.* outstanding, eminent.

eminenza *sf.* eminence.

emiro *sm.* emir.

emisfèrico *agg.* hemispheric(al).

emisfero *sm.* hemisphere.

emissario *sm.* emissary.

emissione *sf.* 1. emission 2. (*econ.*) issue.

emistichio *sm.* hemistich.

emittente *agg.* issuing || *stazione* — (*radio*), broadcasting station.

emofilìa *sf.* haemophilia.

emoglobina *sf.* haemoglobin.

emolliente *agg.* emollient.

emolumento *sm.* emolument.

emorragìa *sf.* haemorrhage.

emorròidi *sf. pl.* haemorrhoids.

emòstasi *sf.* haemostasis.

emostàtico *agg.* haemostatic.

emoteca *sf.* blood bank.

emotività *sf.* emotionality.

emotivo *agg.* emotional.

emottisi *sf.* haemoptysis.

emozionante *agg.* touching, exciting, thrilling.

emozionare *vt.* to move. ♦ **emozionarsi** *vr.* to get (*v. irr.*) excited.

emozione *sf.* emotion, thrill.

empiastro *sm.* plaster.

empietà *sf.* impiety.

empio *agg.* impious.

empire *vt.* to fill.

empìrico *agg.* e *sm.* empiric.

empirismo *sm.* empiricism.

emporio *sm.* department store.

emulare *vt.* to emulate.

emulazione *sf.* emulation.

èmulo *sm.* rival.

emulsionare *vt.* to emulsify.

emulsione *sf.* emulsion.

encefalite *sf.* encephalitis.

encèfalo *sm.* encephalon (*pl.* -ala).

encìclica *sf.* encyclic.

enciclopedìa *sf.* encyclopaedia.

enciclopèdico *agg.* encyclopaedic.

enclìtico *agg.* enclitic.

encomiàbile *agg.* praiseworthy.

encomiare *vt.* to commend.

encomio *sm.* panegyric.

endecasìllabo *agg.* hendecasyllabic. ♦ **endecasìllabo** *sm.* hendecasyllable.

endèmico *agg.* endemic.

endocardio *sm.* endocardium.

endocardite *sf.* endocarditis.

endòcrino *agg.* endocrine.

endocrinologìa *sf.* endocrinology.

endovenoso *agg.* intravenous. ♦ **endovenosa** *sf.* intravenous injection.

energètico agg. e sm. tonic.
energìa sf. energy.
energicamente avv. energetically.
enèrgico agg. energetic(al).
energùmeno sm. energumen.
ènfasi sf. emphasis.
enfàtico agg. emphatic.
enfiagione sf. swelling.
enfisema sm. emphysema.
enfitèusi sf. emphyteusis.
enigma sm. enigma, puzzle.
enigmàtico agg. puzzling.
enigmista sm. enigmatographer.
enigmìstica sf. enigmatography.
enigmìstico agg. puzzle (attr.).
ennèsimo agg. nth: *ennesima potenza*, nth power.
enologìa sf. oenology.
enòlogo sm. oenologist.
enorme agg. huge.
enormità sf. 1. hugeness 2. (fig.) absurdity.
ente sm. 1. being 2. (comm.) body, corporation.
enterite sf. enteritis.
enteroclisma sm. enema.
enterocolite sf. enterocolitis.
entità sf. entity.
entomologìa sf. entomology.
entomòlogo sm. entomologist.
entrambi pron. e agg. both.
entrante agg. (con espressioni di tempo) next, coming.
entrare vi. to enter, to come (v. irr.) in, to go (v. irr.) in || *non c'entra*, this has got nothing to do with it; — *correndo*, to run (v. irr.) in; — *in carica*, to come (v. irr.) into office; —*in società*, to go into partnership (with); — *precipitosamente*, to rush in; — *in giuoco*, to come into play; — *in vigore*, to come into force.
entrata sf. 1. entrance, entry 2. (rendita) income.
entratura sf. entrance.
entro prep. 1. (luogo) inside 2. (tempo) in, within, by: — *due giorni*, within two days; — *lunedì*, by Monday.
entrobordo sm. inboard.
entroterra sm. inland.
entusiasmante agg. exciting.
entusiasmare vt. to raise enthusiasm in. ♦ **entusiasmarsi** vr. to become (v. irr.) enthusiastic.
entusiasmo sm. enthusiasm.
entusiasta agg. enthusiast: *essere — di qc.*, to be crazy about sthg.

entusiàstico agg. enthusiastic(al).
enucleare vt. to enucleate.
enucleazione sf. enucleation.
enumerare vt. to enumerate.
enumerazione sf. enumeration.
enunciare vt. to state: — *un teorema*, to enunciate a theorem.
enunciato sm. proposition, terms (pl.).
enunciazione sf. enunciation.
enuresi sf. enuresis.
enzima sm. enzyme.
eòlico agg. Aeolian.
epàtico agg. hepatic.
epatite sf. hepatitis.
èpica sf. epic.
epicentro sm. epicentre.
èpico agg. epic.
epicureìsmo sm. 1. epicurism 2. (fil.) epicureanism.
epicureo agg. e sm. Epicurean.
epidemìa sf. epidemic.
epidèmico agg. epidemical.
epidèrmico agg. epidermic.
epidèrmide sf. epidermis, skin.
Epifanìa sf. Epiphany, Twelfth Night.
epìgono sm. imitator, follower.
epìgrafe sf. epigraph.
epigrafìa sf. epigraphy.
epigramma sm. epigram.
epigrammista s. epigrammatist.
epilessìa sf. epilepsy.
epilèttico agg. e sm. epileptic.
epìlogo sm. epilogue.
episcopale agg. episcopal.
episcopato sm. episcopacy.
episòdico agg. episodic(al).
episodio sm. episode.
epìstola sf. epistle.
epistolare agg. epistolary.
epistolario sm. letters (pl.).
epitaffio sm. epitaph.
epitalamio sm. epithalamium (pl. -ia).
epitelio sm. epithelium.
epìteto sm. epithet.
epìtome sf. epitome.
època sf. 1. epoch 2. (età) age 3. (data) date || *far —*, to mark an epoch.
epopea sf. 1. epopee 2. (serie di fatti eroici) epos.
eppure cong. yet.
epulone sm. glutton.
epurare vt. to purge.
epurazione sf. purge.
equamente avv. fairly.
equànime agg. equanimous.

equanimità sf. equanimity, impartiality.
equatore sm. equator.
equatoriale agg. equatorial.
equazione sf. equation.
equestre agg. equestrian.
equidistante agg. equidistant.
equidistanza sf. equidistance.
equilàtero agg. equilateral.
equilibrare vt. to balance.
equilibrato agg. 1. balanced 2. (fig.) well-balanced.
equilibrio sm. balance, equilibrium.
equilibrismo sm. acrobatics (pl.).
equilibrista s. acrobat.
equino agg. equine.
equinozio sm. equinox.
equipaggiamento sm. equipment, outfit.
equipaggiare vt. to equip, to fit out.
equipaggio sm. (mar.; aer.) crew.
equiparàbile agg. comparable.
equiparare vt. to equalize.
equiparazione sf. equalization.
equipollente agg. equipollent.
equipollenza sf. equipollence.
equità sf. equity, fairness.
equitazione sf. riding.
equivalente agg. equivalent.
equivalenza sf. equivalence.
equivalere vi. to be equivalent. ♦ **equivalersi** vr. to be equivalent.
equivocàbile agg. mistakable.
equivocare vi. to misunderstand (v. irr.).
equìvoco agg. equivocal, ambiguous. ♦ **equìvoco** sm. equivocation.
equo agg. fair.
era sf. era, epoch.
erariale agg. fiscal.
erario sm. Treasury.
erba sf. grass ‖ in —, green; (fig.) budding: un poeta in —, a budding poet.
erbaccia sf. weed.
erbàceo agg. herbaceous.
erbaggio sm. vegetable.
erbario sm. herbarium.
erbetta sf. new grass.
erbivéndolo sm. greengrocer.
erbìvoro agg. herbivorous.
erborista s. herborist.
erboso agg. grassy.
èrcole sm. Hercules.
ercùleo agg. Herculean.
erede sm. heir. ♦ **erede** sf. heiress.
eredità sf. inheritance.

ereditare vt. to inherit.
ereditarietà sf. hereditariness.
ereditario agg. hereditary.
ereditiera sf. heiress.
eremita sm. hermit.
eremitaggio sm. hermitage.
èremo sm. hermitage.
eresia sf. heresy.
erètico agg. heretical.
erèttile agg. erectile.
eretto agg. 1. upright 2. (costruito) built.
erezione sf. 1. erection 2. (costruzione) building.
ergastolano sm. convict (serving a life sentence).
ergàstolo sm. life imprisonment.
èrgere vt. to raise. ♦ **èrgersi** vr. to rise (v. irr.).
èrica sf. heather.
erìgere vt. to erect, to build (v. irr.). ♦ **erìgersi** vr. to set up (for).
erma sf. herma (pl. -ae).
ermafrodito agg. hermaphrodite.
ermellino sm. ermine.
ermenèuta sm. hermeneut.
ermenèutica sf. hermeneutics.
ermètico agg. 1. (tec.) airtight 2. (oscuro) obscure.
ermetismo sm. obscurity.
ernia sf. hernia.
erniario agg. hernial.
erodere vt. to wear (v. irr.) away.
eroe sm. hero.
erogare vt. 1. to distribute 2. (elett.; idraulica) to deliver.
erogazione sf. 1. distribution 2. (elettr.; idraulica) delivery.
eròico agg. heroic.
eroina sf. 1. heroine 2. (farm.) heroin.
eroismo sm. heroism.
eròmpere vi. to burst (v. irr.) forth.
erosione sf. erosion.
erosivo agg. erosive.
eròtico agg. erotic.
erotismo sm. eroticism.
erotòmane s. erotomaniac.
èrpete sm. herpes.
èrpice sm. harrow.
errabondo agg. wandering.
errante agg. errant.
errare vi. 1. (vagare) to wander 2. (sbagliare) to err.
erràtico agg. erratic.
errato agg. wrong.
erròneo agg. erroneous.

errore sm. error, mistake.

erta sf. steep || stare all'—, to be on the look-out.

erto agg. steep.

erudire vt. to teach (v. irr.). ♦ **erudirsi** vr. to get (v. irr.) educated.

erudito agg. learned. ♦ **erudito** sm. scholar.

erudizione sf. erudition, learning.

eruttare vt. to erupt.

eruttivo agg. eruptive.

eruzione sf. eruption.

esacerbare vt. to embitter.

esacerbazione sf. embitterment.

esaedro sm. hexahedron.

esagerare vt. to exaggerate. ♦ **esagerare** vi. to go (v. irr.) too far, to exceed.

esagerato agg. 1. exaggerated 2. (di prezzo) exorbitant.

esagerazione sf. exaggeration.

esagitare vt. to stir violently.

esagonale agg. hexagonal.

esàgono sm. hexagon.

esalare vt. to exhale. ♦ **esalare** vi. to exhale, to rise (v. irr.).

esalazione sf. exhalation.

esaltare vt. to exalt. ♦ **esaltarsi** vr. 1. (vantarsi) to boast 2. (infervorarsi) to become (v. irr.) excited.

esaltato agg. excited. ♦ **esaltato** sm. hot-head.

esaltazione sf. 1. exaltation 2. (eccitazione) excitement.

esame sm. examination: dare un —, to take (v. irr.) an examination; essere respinto ad un —, to fail in an examination.

esàmetro sm. hexameter.

esaminando sm. candidate.

esaminare vt. to examine.

esaminatore sm. examiner.

esangue agg. bloodless.

esànime agg. lifeless.

esasperare vt. to exasperate. ♦ **esasperarsi** vr. to become (v. irr.) irritated.

esasperato agg. exasperated.

esasperazione sf. exasperation.

esattamente avv. exactly, just.

esattezza sf. exactitude.

esatto agg. exact, right.

esattore sm. collector.

esattorìa sf. collector's office.

esaudimento sm. satisfaction.

esaudire vt. to grant.

esauriente agg. exhaustive.

esaurimento sm. exhaustion.

esaurire vt. to exhaust. ♦ **esaurirsi** vr. to get (v. irr.) exhausted.

esaurito agg. 1. exhausted 2. (di persona) worn out 3. (che ha l'esaurimento nervoso) suffering from a nervous breakdown 4. (di libro) out of print.

esàusto agg. exhausted.

esautorare vt. to deprive of authority.

esazione sf. collection.

esborso sm. outlay.

esca sf. 1. bait 2. (materiale infiammabile) tinder 3. (di esplosivo) fuse.

escandescenza sf. outburst of rage || dare in escandescenze, to lose (v. irr.) one's temper.

escatologìa sf. eschatology.

escavatore sm. digger.

escavatrice sf. digger.

escavazione sf. digging out.

eschimese agg. e sm. Eskimo.

esclamare vi. to exclaim.

esclamativo agg. exclamatory: punto —, exclamation mark.

esclamazione sf. exclamation.

esclùdere vt. to exclude, to leave (v. irr.) out.

esclusione sf. exclusion || ad — di, except.

esclusiva sf. 1. patent 2. (diritto esclusivo) sole right.

esclusività sf. exclusiveness.

esclusivo agg. exclusive, sole.

escluso agg. 1. excluded 2. (eccettuato) excepted.

escogitare vt. to contrive.

escoriare vt. to graze.

escoriazione sf. abrasion.

escremento sm. excrement.

escrescenza sf. excrescence.

escursione sf. excursion, trip.

escursionista s. excursionist.

escussione sf. examination.

esecràbile agg. execrable.

esecrare vt. to execrate.

esecrazione sf. execration.

esecutivo agg. executive.

esecutore sm. 1. executor 2. (di musica) performer 3. (carnefice) executioner.

esecuzione sf. 1. execution 2. (mus.) performance.

esedra sf. exedra (pl. -ae).

esegesi sf. exegesis (pl. -ses).

esegeta s. exegete.

eseguìbile agg. feasible.

eseguire *vt.* **1.** to execute, to carry out **2.** (*mus.*) to perform.

esempio *sm.* **1.** example, instance **2.** (*modello perfetto*) pattern.

esemplare *agg.* exemplary. ♦ **esemplare** *sm.* **1.** pattern, specimen **2.** (*di libro*) copy.

esemplificare *vt.* to exemplify.

esemplificazione *sf.* exemplification.

esentare *vt.* to exempt.

esente *agg.* exempt, free.

esenzione *sf.* exemption.

esequie *sf. pl.* exequies.

esercente *sm.* shop-keeper.

esercire *vt.* to manage (a business) || — *un negozio*, to keep (*v. irr.*) a shop.

esercitare *vt.* **1.** to exercise **2.** (*una professione*) to practice **3.** (*addestrare*) to train. ♦ **esercitarsi** *vr.* to practice.

esercitazione *sf.* **1.** exercise **2.** (*allenamento*) training **3.** (*mil.*) drill.

esèrcito *sm.* army.

esercizio *sm.* **1.** exercise **2.** (*negozio*) shop **3.** (*comm.*) — *finanziario*, financial year.

esibire *vt.* to exhibit, to show (*v. irr.*).

esibizione *sf.* exhibition, show.

esibizionismo *sm.* exhibitionism, showing-off.

esibizionista *s.* exhibitionist.

esigente *agg.* exacting.

esigenza *sf.* **1.** demand, exigence **2.** (*pretesa*) pretension.

esigere *vt.* **1.** (*comm.*) to collect **2.** (*richiedere con autorità*) to insist on **3.** (*pretendere*) to exact.

esigibile *agg.* **1.** exigible **2.** (*riscuotibile*) collectable.

esiguità *sf.* exiguity.

esiguo *agg.* exiguous, scanty.

esilarante *agg.* exhilarating.

esilarare *vt.* to exhilarate.

èsile *agg.* slender.

esiliare *vt.* to exile. ♦ **esiliarsi** *vr.* to go (*v. irr.*) into exile.

esiliato *agg.* banished. ♦ **esiliato** *sm.* exile.

esilio *sm.* exile.

esìmere *vt.* to free, to excuse. ♦ **esìmersi** *vr.* to evade (sthg.).

esimio *agg.* excellent.

esistente *agg.* **1.** existing **2.** (*di cose*) extant.

esistenza *sf.* existence.

esistenziale *agg.* existential.

esistenzialismo *sm.* existentialism.

esistenzialista *agg. e s.* existentialist.

esistere *vi.* to exist.

esitante *agg.* hesitating: *voce* —, faltering voice.

esitare *vi.* **1.** to hesitate **2.** (*di voce*) to falter.

esitazione *sf.* hesitation: *senza* —, unhesitatingly.

èsito *sm.* result, outcome.

esiziale *agg.* ruinous.

èsodo *sm.* exodus.

esòfago *sm.* oesophagus.

esògeno *agg.* exogenous.

esonerare *vt.* to exonerate.

esònero *sm.* exoneration.

esorbitante *agg.* exorbitant.

esorbitanza *sf.* exorbitance.

esorbitare *vi.* to exceed.

esorcismo *sm.* exorcism.

esorcista *sm.* exorcist.

esorcizzare *vt.* to exorcize.

esorcizzatore *sm.* exorcizer.

esordiente *agg.* beginning. ♦ **esordiente** *sm.* beginner.

esordio *sm.* preamble, beginning.

esordire *vi.* **1.** to begin (*v. irr.*) **2.** (*in arte*) to make (*v. irr.*) one's debut.

esortare *vt.* to exhort.

esortativo *agg.* exhortative.

esortazione *sf.* exhortation.

esosità *sf.* greediness.

esoso *agg.* greedy.

esotèrico *agg.* esoteric.

esotèrmico *agg.* exothermic.

esòtico *agg.* exotic.

esotismo *sm.* exoticism.

espàndere *vt.* to spread (*v. irr.*) (out). ♦ **espàndersi** *vr.* to spread.

espansione *sf.* expansion.

espansionismo *sm.* expansionism.

espansività *sf.* effusiveness.

espansivo *agg.* effusive.

espatriare *vi.* to emigrate.

espatrio *sm.* expatriation.

espediente *sm.* expedient.

espèllere *vt.* to expel.

esperanto *sm.* Esperanto.

esperienza *sf.* experience.

esperimento *sm.* **1.** experiment **2.** (*esame*) test **3.** (*tentativo*) trial.

esperire *vt.* to try.

esperto *agg. e sm.* expert.

espettorante *agg. e sm.* expectorant.

espettorare *vt.* to expectorate.

espettorazione *sf.* expectoration.

espiare *vt.* to expiate.

espiatorio *agg.* expiatory: *capro* —, scapegoat.

espiazione *sf.* expiation.

espirare *vt.* e *vi.* to expire.

espirazione *sf.* expiration.

espletare *vt.* to dispatch.

espletazione *sf.* dispatching.

esplicare *vt.* to explicate: — *un'attività,* to have an activity.

esplicativo *agg.* explanatory.

esplicazione *sf.* explication.

esplìcito *agg.* explicit.

esplòdere *vi.* to explode, to burst (*v. irr.*).

esplorare *vt.* 1. to explore 2. (*mil.*) to scout.

esploratore *sm.* 1. explorer 2. (*mil.*) scout.

esplorazione *sf.* 1. exploration 2. (*mil.*) scouting expedition.

esplosione *sf.* 1. explosion, blast 2. (*fig.*) outbreak.

esplosivo *agg.* e *sm.* explosive.

esponente *sm.* exponent.

esporre *vt.* 1. to show (*v. irr.*) 2. (*a rischio*) to venture 3. (*spiegare*) to expound 4. (*mettere in vista*) to display. ♦ **esporsi** *vr.* to expose oneself.

esportare *vt.* to export.

esportatore *agg.* exporting. ♦ **esportatore** *sm.* exporter.

esportazione *sf.* export, exportation.

esposìmetro *sm.* exposure-meter.

espositore *sm.* exhibitor.

esposizione *sf.* 1. exposure 2. (*mostra*) exhibition 3. (*eloquio*) exposition.

esposto *sm.* petition.

espressamente *avv.* 1. expressly 2. (*appositamente*) on purpose.

espressione *sf.* expression.

espressionismo *sm.* expressionism.

espressionista *s.* expressionist.

esprescivo *agg.* expressive.

espresso *agg.* express.

esprìmere *vt.* to express.

esprimìbile *agg.* expressible.

espropriare *vt.* to dispossess.

espropriazione *sf.* expropriation.

espugnare *vt.* to conquer.

espugnatore *sm.* conqueror.

espugnazione *sf.* conquest.

espulsione *sf.* expulsion.

espulsivo *agg.* e *sm.* expulsive.

espulsore *sm.* ejector.

espùngere *vt.* to expunge.

espurgare *vt.* 1. to expurgate 2. (*un libro*) to bowdlerize.

espurgazione *sf.* 1. expurgation 2. (*un libro*) to bowdlerize.

essa *pron.* 1. (*sogg.*) she, (*compl.*) her 2. (*riferito a cose o animali*) it.

esse *sf.* letter S.: *a* —, S-shaped.

essenza *sf.* essence.

essenziale *agg.* essential.

essenzialità *sf.* essentiality.

èssere *vi.* to be ‖ *c'è, ci sono,* there is, there are.

èssere *sm.* 1. being 2. (*esistenza*) existence.

essi *pron.* (*sogg.*) they, (*compl.*) them.

essiccare *vt.* to dry.

essiccatoio *sm.* drier.

essiccazione *sf.* drying process.

esso *pron.* 1. (*sogg.*) he, (*compl.*) him 2. (*per cose o animali*) it.

essudato *sm.* exudate.

essudazione *sf.* exudation.

est *sm.* east.

èstasi *sf.* ecstasy: *andare in* —, to go (*v. irr.*) into ecstasies; *mandare in* —, to throw (*v. irr.*) into ecstasies.

estasiare *vt.* to enrapture. ♦ **estasiarsi** *vr.* to be enraptured.

estate *sf.* summer.

estàtico *agg.* ecstatic.

estemporàneo *agg.* extempore.

estèndere *vt.* to extend.

estendìbile *agg.* extensible.

estensione *sf.* 1. extension 2. (*distesa*) expanse, extent 3. (*mus.*) range.

estensivo *agg.* extensive.

estensore *sm.* 1. compiler 2. (*giur.*) drafts-man (*pl.* -men) 3. (*sport*) chest-expander.

estenuante *agg.* exhausting.

estenuare *vt.* to tire out.

estenuazione *sf.* exhaustion.

esteriore *agg.* outward. ♦ **esteriore** *sm.* exterior, outside.

esteriorità *sf.* outward appearance.

esternamente *avv.* externally, outside.

esternare *vt.* to express, to utter.

esterno *agg.* outer, external.

èstero *agg.* foreign. ♦ **èstero** *sm.* foreign countries (*pl.*) ‖ *all'*—, abroad.

esterofilìa *sf.* xenomanìa.

esterrefatto *agg.* aghast, amazed.

esteso *agg.* large, wide || *per* —, in detail.

esteta *s.* aesthete.

estètica *sf.* aesthetics.

estètico *agg.* aesthetic.

estetismo *sm.* aestheticism.

èstimo *sm.* estimate.

estìnguere *vt.* 1. to put (*v. irr.*) out 2. (*saldare*) to extinguish || — *la propria sete*, to slake one's thirst. ♦ **estìnguersi** *vr.* (*finire*) to die.

estinguìbile *agg.* extinguishable.

estinto *agg.* 1. extinct 2. (*morto*) dead. ♦ **estinto** *sm.* deceased man.

estintore *sm.* extinguisher.

estinzione *sf.* 1. extinction 2. (*di sete*) quenching 3. (*di debito*) paying off.

estirpare *vt.* 1. to extirpate 2. (*di denti*) to pull out.

estirpazione *sf.* 1. extirpation 2. (*di denti*) extraction.

estivo *agg.* summer (*attr.*).

estòrcere *vt.* to extort.

estorsione *sf.* extortion.

estradare *vt.* to extradite.

estradizione *sf.* extradition.

estràneo *agg.* extraneous, alien. ♦ **estràneo** *sm.* stranger.

estraniare *vt.* to estrange. ♦ **estraniarsi** *vr.* to get (*v. irr.*) estranged.

estrarre *vt.* to draw (*v. irr.*) out: — *a sorte*, to draw by lot.

estrattivo *agg.* extractive.

estratto *sm.* 1. extract 2. (*riassunto*) excerpt 3. (*comm.*) — *conto*, statement of account.

estrattore *sm.* extractor.

estrazione *sf.* 1. extraction 2. (*di lotteria*) drawing.

estremamente *avv.* extremely.

estremismo *sm.* extremism.

estremista *s.* extremist: — *di destra*, extreme rightist; — *di sinistra*, extreme leftist.

estremità *sf.* extremity, end.

estremo *agg.* 1. utmost 2. (*eccessivo*) intense 3. (*drastico*) drastic. ♦ **estremo** *sm.* extreme.

estrinsecare *vt.* to express. ♦ **estrinsecarsi** *vr.* to be expressed.

estrinsecazione *sf.* expression.

estrìnseco *agg.* extrinsic(al).

estro *sm.* 1. inspiration 2. (*capriccio*) whim.

estromèttere *vt.* to turn out.

estromissione *sf.* expulsion.

estroso *agg.* 1. (*ispirato*) inspired 2. freakish.

estroverso *agg.* extroverted.

estuario *sm.* estuary.

esuberante *agg.* exuberant.

esuberanza *sf.* exuberance.

esulare *vi.* 1. to go (*v. irr.*) into exile 2. (*fig.*) to be beyond.

esulcerare *vt.* to exulcerate.

esulcerazione *sf.* exulceration.

èsule *sm.* 1. exile 2. (*profugo*) refugee.

esultante *agg.* rejoicing.

esultanza *sf.* exultation.

esultare *vi.* to rejoice.

esumare *vt.* to exhume.

esumazione *sf.* exhumation.

età *sf.* age || *che* — *hai?*, how old are you?; *avere la stessa* —, to be the same age; *una persona di mezza* —, a middle-aged person.

ètere *sm.* ether.

etèreo *agg.* ethereal.

eternare *vt.* to make (*v. irr.*) eternal.

eternità *sf.* eternity.

eterno *agg.* eternal, everlasting.

eteròclito *agg.* 1. heteroclite 2. (*fig.*) irregular.

eterodossìa *sf.* heterodoxy.

eterodosso *agg.* heterodox.

eterogeneìtà *sf.* heterogeneity.

eterogèneo *agg.* heterogeneous.

ètica *sf.* ethics.

etichetta *sf.* 1. label 2. (*galateo*) etiquette.

etichettare *vt.* to stick (*v. irr.*) a label (on).

ètico *agg.* ethical.

etilene *sm.* ethylene.

etìlico *agg.* ethylic.

etilismo *sm.* alcoholism.

etimologìa *sf.* etymology.

etimològico *agg.* etymologic(al).

ètnico *agg.* ethnic(al).

etnografìa *sf.* ethnography.

etnologìa *sf.* ethnology.

etnòlogo *sm.* ethnologist.

etrusco *agg.* e *sm.* Etruscan.

ettàgono *sm.* heptagon.

èttaro *sm.* hectare.

etto *sm.* hectogram.

ettògrammo *sm.* hectogram.

ettòlitro *sm.* hectolitre.

ettòmetro *sm.* hectometre.

eucalipto *sm.* eucalyptus.

eucaristìa *sf.* Eucharist, Holy Communion.

eucarìstico *agg.* Eucharistic.
eufemismo *sm.* euphemism.
eufonìa *sf.* euphony.
eufònico *agg.* euphonic(al).
euforbia *sf.* Euphorbia.
euforìa *sf.* euphoria.
eufòrico *agg.* euphoric.
eunuco *sm.* eunuch.
euritmìa *sf.* eurhythmy.
europeismo *sm.* Europeanism.
europeo *agg.* e *sm.* European.
eurovisione *sf.* Eurovision.
eutanasìa *sf.* euthanasia.
evacuare *vt.* to evacuate.
evacuazione *sf.* evacuation.
evàdere *vi.* to escape. ♦ evàdere
   vt. (*burocratico*) 1. to dispatch 2.
   (*eludere*) to evade.
evanescente *agg.* vanishing.
evangèlico *agg.* evangelic(al).
evangelista *sm.* evangelist.
evangelizzare *vt.* to evangelize.
evaporare *vi.* to evaporate.
evaporazione *sf.* evaporation.
evasione *sf.* 1. escape 2. (*comm.*)
   dare — a una pratica, to dispatch
   a business.
evasivo *agg.* evasive.
evaso *sm.* runaway.
evasore *sm.* evader: *— fiscale,* tax
   evader.
evenienza *sf.* event, occurrence:
   per ogni —, for any occasion.
evento *sm.* event.
eventuale *agg.* possible.
eventualità *sf.* eventuality.
eventualmente *avv.* in case.
evidente *agg.* evident, obvious,
   clear.
evidenza *sf.* evidence.
evincere *vt.* (*giur.*) to evict.
evirare *vt.* to evirate.
evitàbile *agg.* avoidable.
evitare *vt.* 1. to avoid 2. (*sfuggire*)
   to escape.
evo *sm.* age: *il Medio Evo,* the
   Middle Ages.
evocare *vt.* to evoke, to recall.
evocativo *agg.* evocative.
evocazione *sf.* evocation.
evolutivo *agg.* evolutive.
evoluto *agg.* well-developed, modern.
evoluzione *sf.* evolution.
evoluzionismo *sm.* evolutionism.
evòlvere *vt.* to evolve.
evviva *inter.* hurray.
ex libris *sm.* ex libris.
extra *agg.* extra.

extraterritoriale *agg.* extraterritorial.
eziologìa *sf.* aetiology.

F

fa¹ *sm.* (*mus.*) F.
fa² *avv.* ago: *un anno —,* a year ago.
fabbisogno *sm.* needs (*pl.*).
fàbbrica *sf.* 1. factory || *— di au-
   tomobili,* motor works; *— di
   mattoni,* brickyard; *— di carta,*
   paper-mill; *capo —,* fore-man (*pl.*
   -men); *marchio. di —,* trade-mark
   2. (*fabbricazione*) manufacture.
fabbricàbile *agg.* manufacturable ||
   area —, housing area.
fabbricante *sm.* manufacturer.
fabbricare *vt.* 1. (*produrre*) to
   manufacture 2. (*costruire*) to build
   (*v. irr.*) 3. (*fare*) to make (*v. irr*).
fabbricato *sm.* building || *imposta
   sui fabbricati,* house tax.
fabbricazione *sf.* 1. manufacture,
   make 2. (*costruzione*) building.
fabbro *sm.* blacksmith.
fabbroferraio *sm.* blacksmith.
faccenda *sf.* matter; business (*solo
   sing.*) || *— di stato,* state affair
   2. (*lavori domestici*) housework
   (*solo sing.*).
faccendiere *sm.* busybody.
faccetta *sf.* little face 2. (*geom.*)
   facet.
facchinaggio *sm.* porterage.
facchino *sm.* porter.
faccia *sf.* 1. face: *che — tosta!,*
   what a face!; *a — a —,* face to face
   2. (*aspetto*) look, expression 3. (*lato, superficie*) face, side.
facciale *agg.* facial.
facciata *sf.* 1. front, façade 2. (*pagina*) page.
face *sf.* torch.
faceto *agg.* facetious, witty.
facezia *sf.* witty remark, joke: *dire delle facezie,* to crack jokes.
fachiro *sm.* fakir.
fàcile *agg.* 1. easy 2. (*trattabile*)
   docile 3. (*pronto*) ready 4. (*incline*) inclined 3. (*probabile*) likely
facilità *sf.* 1. facility 2. (*attitudine*) aptitude.
facilitare *vt.* to make (*v. irr.*)
   easier

facilitazione *sf*. 1. facilitation 2. (*agevolazione*) facility.

facilone *sm*. slipshod fellow.

facinoroso *agg*. lawless. ♦ **facinoroso** *sm*. lawless man.

facoltà *sf*. faculty.

facoltativo *agg*. facultative: *fermata facoltativa*, request stop.

facoltoso *agg*. wealthy.

facondia *sf*. eloquence.

facondo *agg*. eloquent.

facsimile *sm*. facsimile.

factotum *sm*. factotum

faggeto *sm*. beech-wood.

faggio *sm*. beech.

fagiano *sm*. pheasant.

fagiolino *sm*. French bean.

fagiolo *sm*. bean.

fagocita, fagocito *sm*. phagocyte.

fagocitare *vt*. 1. to phagocyte 2. (*fig*.) to absorb.

fagocitosi *sf*. phagocytosis.

fagotto[1] *sm*. bundle.

fagotto[2] *sm*. (*mus*.) bassoon.

faina *sf*. beech-marten.

falange *sf*. phalanx (*pl*. -nges).

falcata *sf*. 1. curvet 2. (*di persona*) stride.

falce *sf*. 1. sickle 2. (*da fieno*) scythe 3. (*di luna*) crescent.

falciare *vt*. 1. to mow (*v. irr.*) 2. (*fig*.) to mow down.

falciatore *sm*. mower.

falciatrice *sf*. mowing-machine.

falciatura *sf*. mowing.

falcidiare *vt*. to reduce.

falco *sm*. hawk: *avere occhi di —*, to be hawk-eyed.

falconeria *sf*. falconry.

falconiere *sm*. hawker.

falda *sf*. 1. (*strato*) stratum (*pl*. -ta) 2. (*di neve*) flake 3. (*di cappello*) brim 4. (*di monte*) slope.

falegname *sm*. joiner.

falegnameria *sf*. 1. joinery 2. (*bottega*) joiner's shop.

falena *sf*. moth.

falla *sf*. leak.

fallace *agg*. false, disappointing.

fallacia *sf*. fallacy.

fallibile *agg*. liable to make mistakes.

fallico *agg*. phallic.

fallimentare *agg*. bankruptcy.

fallimento *sm*. 1. bankruptcy 2. (*fig*.) failure.

fallire *vi*. 1. to fail 2. (*comm*.) to go (*v. irr.*) bankrupt 3. (*fam*.) to go under.

fallito *agg*. 1. (*comm*.) bankrupt 2. (*fig*.) unsuccessful. ♦ **fallito** *sm*. 1. (*comm*.) bankrupt 2. (*fig*.) failure.

fallo *sm*. 1. fault: *senza —*, without fail 2. (*anat*.) phallus (*pl*. -li).

falò *sm*. bonfire.

falpalà *sm*. furbelow.

falsare *vt*. 1. to misrepresent 2. (*falsificare*) to falsify.

falsariga *sf*. 1. ruling paper 2. (*fig*.) pattern, model.

falsario *sm*. 1. forger 2. (*di monete*) coiner.

falsetto *sm*. falsetto.

falsificàbile *agg*. falsifiable.

falsificare *vt*. to falsify, to counterfeit.

falsificatore *sm*. 1. falsifier 2. (*di monete*) coiner.

falsificazione *sf*. falsification, forgery.

falsità *sf*. 1. falseness 2. (*menzogna*) falsehood 3. (*ipocrisia*) insincerity.

falso *agg*. 1. false 2. (*falsificato*) forged.

fama *sf*. fame, renown, reputation: *acquistarsi —*, to win (*v. irr.*) fame; *avere cattiva —*, to have a bad reputation.

fame *sf*. 1. hunger: *avere —*, to be hungry: *far morire di —*, to starve 2. (*carestia*) famine.

famèlico *agg*. ravenous.

famigerato *agg*. ill-famed.

famiglia *sf*. family.

familiare *agg*. 1. domestic, homely 2. (*intimo, anche fig*.) familiar 3. (*senza cerimonie*) informal. ♦ **familiare** *sm*. relative.

familiarità *sf*. familiarity: *avere — con qu*., to be familiar with so.

famoso *agg*. famous, celebrated.

fanale *sm*. 1. lamp 2. (*auto*) light: *— anteriore*, head-light; *— di coda*, (*aer*.) tail light, (*auto*) rear lamp; *— di posizione*, parking lights (*pl*.).

fanàtico *agg*. fanatical. ♦ **fanàtico** *sm*. 1. fanatic 2. (*fam*.) fan.

fanatismo *sm*. fanaticism.

fanatizzare *vt*. to fanaticize.

fanciulla *sf*. young girl.

fanciullàggine *sf*. 1. childishness 2. (*azione infantile*) childish action.

fanciullesco *agg*. childish.

fanciullezza *sf*. childhood.

fanciullo *sm.* young boy, child (*pl.* children).

fandonia *sf.* lie.

fanello *sm.* linnet.

fanfara *sf.* 1. brass band 2. (*suono di trombe*) fanfare.

fanfaronata *sf.* boasting.

fanfarone *sm.* boaster.

fangaia *sf.* muddy road.

fanghiglia *sf.* slush.

fango *sm.* 1. mud: *gettare del — addosso a qu.*, to throw (*v. irr.*) mud at so.; *cadere nel —*, to fall (*v. irr.*) very low 2. (*med.*) mud-baths (*pl.*).

fangoso *agg.* muddy.

fannullone *sm.* idler.

fanone *sm.* whalebone.

fantaccino *sm.* foot-soldier.

fantascienza *sf.* science fiction.

fantasìa *sf.* 1. imagination, fancy 2. (*inventiva*) inventiveness 3. (*articoli fantasia*) fancy goods.

fantasioso *agg.* fanciful.

fantasma *sm.* ghost.

fantasmagorìa *sf.* phantasmagoria.

fantasmagòrico *agg.* phantasmagoric.

fantasticare *vt.* to daydream.

fantasticherìa *sf.* daydream.

fantàstico *agg.* 1. fanciful 2. (*bizzarro*) queer 3. (*fam.*) extraordinary.

fante *sm.* 1. infantryman (*pl.* -men) 2. (*delle carte*) knave, jack.

fanterìa *sf.* infantry.

fantesca *sf.* maid-servant.

fantino *sm.* jockey.

fantoccio *sm.* puppet (*anche fig.*).

fantomàtico *agg.* mysterious.

farabutto *sm.* blackguard.

faraona *sf.* guinea-hen.

faraone *sm.* Pharaoh.

farcire *vt.* to stuff.

farcito *agg.* stuffed.

fardello *sm.* 1. bundle 2. (*fig.*) burden.

fare *vt.* 1. (*in senso generale*) to do (*v. irr.*): *cosa fai?*, what are you doing?; *ecco fatto!*, that's done!; *— del proprio meglio*, to do one's best; 2. (*fabbricare, produrre*) to make (*v. irr.*): *— amicizia*, to make friends; *— un errore*, to make a mistake; *— in fretta*, to make haste 3. (*essere, esercitare una professione*) to be: *faccio l'insegnante*, I am a teacher 4. (*reputare*) to think (*v. irr.*): *la facevo*

più intelligente, I thought she was more intelligent 5. (*segnare le ore*): *che ora fa il tuo orologio?*, what time is it by your watch? 6. (*praticare*) to go (*v. irr.*) in for || *— le carte*, to shuffle; *— fagotto*, to pack up; *— una passeggiata*, to go for a walk; *— colazione*, to have breakfast; *— bella, brutta figura*, to cut (*v. irr.*) a fine, a poor figure; *— compassione*, to rouse compassion; *— aspettare qu.*, to keep (*v. irr.*) so. waiting; *— avere, sapere, vedere a qu.*, to let (*v. irr.*) so. have, know, see. ♦ **fare** *vi.* 1. (*di condizioni atmosferiche*): *che tempo fa?*, what is the weather like? 2. (*far caldo, freddo*) to be hot, cold 3. (*essere adatto*) to suit. ♦ **farsi** *vr.* to become (*v. irr.*), to grow (*v. irr.*) || *— animo*, to take (*v. irr.*) courage.

fare *sm.* manners (*pl*).

faretra *sf.* quiver.

farfalla *sf.* butterfly.

farfugliare *vt.* to mumble.

farina *sf.* meal, flour.

farinàceo *agg.* farinaceous.

faringe *sf.* pharynx (*pl.* -nges).

faringite *sf.* pharyngitis.

farinoso *agg.* mealy, floury.

fariseo *agg.* e *sm.* Pharisee.

farmacèutico *agg.* pharmaceutic.

farmacìa *sf.* 1. pharmacy 2. (*negozio*) chemist's shop.

farmacista *sm.* chemist.

fàrmaco *sm.* medicine, remedy (*anche fig.*).

farmacologìa *sf.* pharmacology.

farmacopea *sf.* pharmacopoeia.

farneticare *vi.* to rave.

faro *sm.* 1. lighthouse 2. (*auto*) headlight.

farràgine *sf.* medley, mixture.

farraginoso *agg.* confused.

farsa *sf.* farce.

farsesco *agg.* farcical.

fascetta *sf.* 1. small band 2. (*med.*) bandage 3. (*edit.*) wrapper.

fascia *sf.* 1. band 2. (*med.*) bandage 3. (*dei bambini*) swaddling-band.

fasciame *sm.* planking.

fasciare *vt.* 1. to bind (*v. irr.*) (up) 2. (*dei neonati*) to swaddle.

fasciatura *sf.* 1. dressing 2. (*di neonato*) swaddling.

fascìcolo *sm.* booklet.

fascina *sf.* faggot.

fàscino *sm.* charm, fascination.

fascio *sm.* 1. bundle 2. (*geom.*) sheaf 3. (*di luce*) beam.

fascismo *sm.* Fascism.

fascista *agg.* e *s.* Fascist.

fase *sf.* 1. stage 2. (*elettr.*) phase 3. (*auto*) stroke.

fastello *sm.* faggot.

fastidio *sm.* 1. trouble: *dare — a qu.*, to give (*v. irr.*) so. trouble 2. (*contrarietà*) annoyance.

fastidioso *agg.* tiresome.

fastigio *sm.* 1. pediment 2. (*fig.*) height.

fasto *sm.* pomp.

fastosità *sf.* pomp, splendour.

fastoso *agg.* magnificent.

fasullo *agg.* false.

fata *sf.* fairy.

fatale *agg.* fatal, inevitable.

fatalismo *sm.* fatalism.

fatalista *agg.* e *s.* fatalist.

fatalità *sf.* fatality.

fatica *sf.* weariness, fatigue.

faticare *vi.* to toil, to work hard.

faticata *sf.* drudgery.

faticoso *agg.* hard, tiring.

fatìdico *agg.* fatidical.

fato *sm.* 1. fate, destiny 2. (*sorte*) lot.

fatta *sf.* kind, sort.

fattibile *agg.* practicable.

fattispecie *sf.* case in point: *nella —*, in this case.

fattivo *agg.* 1. effective 2. (*attivo*) busy.

fatto *sm.* 1. fact 2. (*azione*) deed 3. (*avvenimento*) event || *sapere il — proprio*, to know (*v. irr.*) one's business; *venire al` —*, to go (*v. irr.*) to the point; *in — di*, as regards.

fattore *sm.* 1. factor 2. (*agr.*) farmer.

fattorìa *sf.* farm.

fattorino *sm.* errand-boy.

fattucchiere *sm.* wizard.

fattura *sf.* 1. making 2. (*lavorazione*) work 3. (*comm.*) invoice 4. (*stregoneria*) sorcery.

fatturare *vt.* 1. to adulterate 2. (*comm.*) to invoice.

fatturazione *sf.* (*comm.*) invoicing.

fatuità *sf.* fatuity.

fatuo *agg.* 1. fatuous 2. (*vanitoso*) vain || *fuoco —*, will-o'-the-visp.

fàuci *sf. pl.* 1. jaws 2. (*di persona*) throat (*sing.*).

fàuna *sf.* fauna.

fàuno *sm.* faun.

fàusto *agg.* propitious.

fautore *sm.* supporter.

fava *sf.* broad bean || *pigliare due piccioni con una —*, to kill two birds with one stone.

favella *sf.* speech.

favellare *vi.* to speak (*v. irr.*).

favilla *sf.* spark (*anche fig.*).

favo *sm.* 1. honeycomb 2. (*med.*) favus.

fàvola *sf.* 1. fable 2. (*frottola*) idle story 3. (*oggetto di pettegolezzo*) byword.

favoloso *agg.* fabulous.

favore *sm.* favour.

favoreggiamento *sm.* favouring.

favoreggiare *vt.* to favour.

favoreggiatore *sm.* abettor.

favorévole *agg.* favourable.

favorire *vt.* 1. to favour 2. (*aiutare*) to help 3. (*promuovere*) to foster.

favoritismo *sm.* favouritism.

favorito *agg.* e *sm.* favourite.

fazione *sf.* faction.

fazioso *agg.* factious.

fazzoletto *sm.* 1. handkerchief 2. (*da collo*) neckerchief.

febbraio *sm.* February.

febbre *sf.* fever.

febbricitante *agg.* feverish.

febbrìfugo *agg.* febrifugal. ♦ febbrìfugo *sm.* febrifuge.

febbrile *agg.* feverish.

fecale *agg.* fecal.

feccia *sf.* dregs (*pl.*) (*anche fig.*).

feci *sf. pl.* excrement (*sing.*).

fècola *sf.* starch.

fecondare *vt.* to fecundate.

fecondazione *sf.* fecundation.

fecondità *sf.* fecundity.

fecondo *agg.* fecund.

fede *sf.* 1. faith, belief 2. (*fiducia*) trust.

fedele *agg.* faithful.

fedeltà *sf.* fidelity.

fèdera *sf.* pillow-case.

federale *agg.* federal.

federalismo *sm.* federalism.

federativo *agg.* federative.

federato *agg.* federate.

federazione *sf.* federation.

fedìfrago *sm.* traitor.

fedina *sf.* criminal record.

fégato *sm.* 1. liver 2. (*fig.*) courage.

fegatoso *agg.* 1. bilious 2. (*fig.*) irritable.

felce *sf.* fern.

feldspato *sm.* felspar.

felice *agg.* **1.** happy **2.** (*fortunato*) lucky **3.** (*piacevole*) pleasant.

felicità *sf.* happiness.

felicitarsi *vr.* to congratulate (so. on sthg.).

felicitazioni *sf. pl.* congratulation (*sing.*).

felino *agg.* e *sm.* feline.

fellone *sm.* villain, traitor.

fellonìa *sf.* felony, treason.

felpato *agg.* **1.** plushy **2.** (*fig.*) soft || *a passi felpati*, stealthily.

feltro *sm.* felt.

feluca *sf.* **1.** (*mar.*) felucca **2.** (*cappello*) cocked hat.

fémmina *sf.* female || *mala* —, bad woman.

femminile *agg.* **1.** female **2.** (*da donna*) feminine.

femminilità *sf.* womanliness.

femminismo *sm.* feminism.

femminuccia *sf.* **1.** simple woman **2.** (*uomo senza coraggio*) coward.

fèmore *sm.* thigh-bone.

fendente *sm.* cutting blow.

fèndere *vt.* to rend (*v. irr.*).

fenditura *sf.* cleft, fissure.

fenice *sf.* phoenix.

fènico *agg.* phenic.

fenolo *sm.* phenol.

fenomenale *agg.* phenomenal.

fenomenismo *sm.* phenomenalism.

fenòmeno *sm.* phenomenon (*pl.* -na).

fenomenologìa *sf.* phenomenology.

ferace *agg.* fruitful, rich (*anche fig.*).

ferale *agg.* feral, deadly.

fèretro *sm.* coffin.

ferie *sf. pl.* holidays.

feriale *agg.* working: *giorno* —, working-day.

ferimento *sm.* wounding.

ferino *agg.* ferine, wild.

ferire *vt.* to wound, to hurt (*v. irr.*).

ferita *sf.* wound (*anche fig.*).

ferito *agg.* wounded, injured.

feritoia *sf.* loophole.

ferma *sf.* **1.** (*mil.*) service **2.** (*caccia*) pointing.

fermacarte *sm.* paper-weight.

fermaglio *sm.* **1.** clasp **2.** (*per gioielli*) brooch **3.** (*per carte*) clip.

fermare *vt.* **1.** to stop, to arrest **2.** (*fissare*) to fix (*anche fig.*) **3.** (*giur.*) to hold (*v. irr.*). ◆ **fermarsi** *vr.* **1.** to stop **2.** (*soggiornare*) to stay **3.** (*fare una pausa*) to pause.

fermata *sf.* **1.** stop **2.** (*pausa*) pause.

fermentare *vi.* to ferment (*anche fig.*).

fermentazione *sf.* fermentation.

fermento *sm.* **1.** ferment **2.** (*fig.*) turmoil, ferment.

fermezza *sf.* firmness, strength.

fermo *agg.* **1.** still **2.** (*irremovibile*) steady, firm || *mano ferma*, firm hand; *volontà ferma*, unfaltering will. ◆ **fermo** *sm.* **1.** (*mecc.*) lock, catch, stop **2.** (*giur.*) provisional arrest.

fermoposta *sm.* poste-restante.

feroce *agg.* fierce, cruel.

ferocia *sf.* fierceness.

ferraglia *sf.* scrap-iron.

ferragosto *sm.* **1.** August holiday **2.** (*in Inghilterra*) August Bank holiday.

ferraio *sm.* blacksmith.

ferramenta *sf. pl.* hardware (*sing.*).

ferramento *sm.* iron tool.

ferrare *vt.* **1.** to fit with iron **2.** (*di cavalli*) to shoe.

ferrato *agg.* **1.** ironshod **2.** (*di scarpe*) hobnailed **3.** (*strada ferrata*) railway **4.** (*fig.*) well read.

ferratura *sf.* shoeing.

fèrreo *agg.* iron (*attr.*).

ferriera *sf.* iron-foundry.

ferro *sm.* iron: — *battuto*, wrought iron; — *da stiro*, flat-iron; — *da calza*, knitting needle || *i ferri del mestiere*, the tools of the trade; *tocca* —!, touch wood!

ferroso *agg.* ferrous.

ferrovìa *sf.* railway.

ferroviario *agg.* railway (*attr.*).

ferroviere *sm.* railwayman (*pl.* -men).

ferruginoso *agg.* ferruginous.

fèrtile *agg.* fertile (*anche fig.*).

fertilità *sf.* fertility.

fertilizzante *agg.* fertilizing. ◆ **fertilizzante** *sm.* fertilizer.

fertilizzare *vt.* to fertilize.

fèrula *sf.* rod.

fervente *agg.* burning, ardent (*anche fig.*).

fèrvido *agg.* fervid, ardent || *fervidi auguri*, best wishes.

fervore *sm.* fervour, heat.

fessura *sf.* **1.** crack **2.** (*per liquidi*) leak.

festa *sf.* **1.** (*giorno di riposo*) holiday **2.** (*religiosa*) feast **3.** (*anniversario*) birthday **4.** (*onomasti-

co) Saint's day **5.** (*banchetto, ballo*) feast, ball || *giorno di —,* festal day.

festaiolo *sm.* reveller.

festante *agg.* rejoicing.

festeggiamento *sm.* celebration.

festeggiare *vt.* **1.** to celebrate **2.** (*accogliere festosamente*) to give (*v. irr.*) a hearty welcome.

festévole *agg.* festive.

festino *sm.* feast.

fèstival *sm.* festival.

festività *sf.* festivity.

festivo *agg.* **1.** festive **2.** (*domenicale*) Sunday (*attr.*).

festone *sm.* festoon.

festoso *agg.* joyous.

festuca *sf.* straw.

feticcio *sm.* fetish.

feticismo *sm.* fetishism.

feticista *s.* fetishist.

fètido *agg.* foetid, foul.

feto *sm.* foetus.

fetore *sm.* stink.

fetta *sf.* **1.** slice **2.** (*piccolo pezzo*) piece.

fettuccia *sf.* tape.

feudale *agg.* feudal.

feudalésimo *sm.* feudalism.

feudatario *sm.* feudatory.

fèudo *sm.* feud.

fiaba *sf.* **1.** fable **2.** (*falsità*) falsehood.

fiabesco *agg.* fairy-like.

fiacca *sf.* weariness || *battere la —* (*fam.*), to be sluggish.

fiaccare *vt.* to exhaust. ♦ **fiaccarsi** *vr.* to break (*v. irr.*) down.

fiacchezza *sf.* weakness, weariness.

fiacco *agg.* weak, exhausted.

fiàccola *sf.* torch.

fiaccolata *sf.* torchlight procession.

fiala *sf.* phial.

fiamma *sf.* **1.** flame **2.** (*molto viva*) blaze.

fiammante *agg.* **1.** flaming **2.** (*fig.*) bright || *nuovo —,* brand-new.

fiammata *sf.* blaze.

fiammeggiante *agg.* blazing, burning.

fiammeggiare *vi.* to blaze, to flame, to burn.

fiammifero *sm.* match: *accendere un —,* to strike (*v. irr.*) a match.

fiammingo *agg.* Flemish. ♦ **fiammingo** *sm.* Fleming.

fiancata *sf.* **1.** side **2.** (*mar.*) broadside.

fiancheggiare *vt.* **1.** to flank **2.** (*fig.*) to support.

fiancheggiatore *sm.* flanker, supporter.

fianco *sm.* **1.** hip, side (*anche fig.*) **2.** (*di animali; mil.*) flank.

fiasca *sf.* flask.

fiasco *sm.* flask || *fare —,* to fail utterly.

fiatare *vi.* to breathe: *senza —,* without speaking.

fiato *sm.* breath.

fibbia *sf.* buckle.

fibra *sf.* **1.** fibre **2.** (*costituzione*) constitution.

fibroma *sm.* fibroma (*pl.* -ata).

fibroso *agg.* fibrous.

fibula *sf.* **1.** fibula **2.** (*med.*) splint-bone.

ficcanaso *sm.* meddler.

ficcare *vt.* to thrust (*v. irr.*); to drive (*v. irr.*) (in). ♦ **ficcarsi** *vr.* to interfere || *— in testa qc.,* to get (*v. irr.*) sthg. into one's head.

fico *sm.* fig.

fidanzamento *sm.* engagement.

fidanzare *vt.* to engage. ♦ **fidanzarsi** *vr.* to become (*v. irr.*) engaged (to so.).

fidanzata *sf.* fiancée.

fidanzato *sm.* fiancé.

fidare *vi.* to trust. ♦ **fidarsi** *vr.* to trust (upon so., sthg.).

fidato *agg.* reliable.

fideiussione *sf.* suretyship.

fidente *agg.* confiding.

fido *agg.* faithful. ♦ **fido** *sm.* **1.** devoted follower **2.** (*comm.*) credit.

fiducia *sf.* trust, confidence: *— in se stessi,* self-confidence.

fiduciario *agg.* fiduciary. ♦ **fiduciario** *sm.* fiduciary, trustee.

fiducioso *agg.* trusting, hopeful.

fiele *sm.* **1.** gall **2.** (*fig.*) hatred.

fienagione *sf.* haymaking.

fienile *sm.* hay-loft.

fieno *sm.* hay: *asma da —,* hay-asthma.

fiera *sf.* **1.** fair **2.** (*esposizione*) exhibition || *— campionaria,* samples fair.

fierezza *sf.* fierceness.

fiero *agg.* proud.

fièvole *agg.* **1.** feeble **2.** (*di luce, suono*) dim.

figgere *vt.* to fix.

figlia *sf.* daughter.

figliare *vt.* to bring (*v. irr.*) forth.

figliastra *sf.* step-daughter.

figliastro *sm.* step-son.

figlio *sm.* son.

figlioccia *sf.* goddaughter.

figlioccio *sm.* godson.

figliolanza *sf.* children (*pl.*), family.

figliolo *sm.* son.

figura *sf.* 1. figure 2. (*illustrazione*) illustration, picture 3. (*personaggio di romanzi, opere teatrali ecc.*) character ‖ *fare una bella, brutta —*, to cut (*v. irr.*) a fine, poor figure.

figurare *vt.* 1. to represent 2. (*far figura*) to look smart 3. (*apparire*) to appear.

figurativo *agg.* figurative.

figurato *agg.* 1. (*illustrato*) illustrated 2. (*di linguaggio, senso*) figurative.

figurazione *sf.* figuration.

figurinista *s.* dress-designer.

figurino *sm.* fashion-plate.

figuro *sm.* scoundrel.

fila *sf.* 1. row, file 2. (*coda*) queue: *fare la —*, to queue (up).

filaccia *sf.* lint.

filamento *sm.* filament.

filamentoso *agg.* filamentous.

filanda *sf.* spinning-mill.

filandaia *sf.* spinner.

filante *agg.: stella —* 1. (*astr.*) falling-star 2. (*di carta*) (paper) streamer.

filantropìa *sf.* philanthropy.

filàntropo *sm.* philanthrope.

filare[1] *vt.* 1. to spin (*v. irr.*) 2. (*correre*) to run (*v. irr.*) 3. (*amoreggiare*) to flirt.

filare[2] *sm.* row, line.

filarmònico *agg. e sm.* philharmonic.

filastrocca *sf.* nursery rhyme.

filatelìa *sf.* stamp-collecting.

filatèlico *agg.* philatelic. ♦ **filatèlico** *sm.* philatelist.

filato *agg.* 1. spun 2. (*di seguito*) running.

filatura *sf.* spinning.

filettare *vt.* (*mecc.*) to thread.

filettatura *sf.* (*mecc.*) threading.

filetto *sm.* 1. (*filo sottile*) thin thread 2. (*mecc.*) thread ‖ *— della lingua*, fraenum.

filiale *agg.* filial. ♦ **filiale** *sf.* branch house.

filiazione *sf.* filiation.

filibustiere *sm.* 1. filibuster 2. (*fig.*) adventurer, rascal.

filiera *sf.* 1. (*mecc.*) screw cutting die 2. (*ind. tess.*) spinneret.

filiforme *agg.* threadlike.

filigrana *sf.* 1. filigree 2. (*di carta*) watermark.

filìppica *sf.* philippic.

fillòssera *sf.* phylloxera.

film *sm.* picture ‖ *girare un —*, to shoot (*v. irr.*) a picture.

filmare *vt.* to film.

filo *sm.* 1. thread 2. (*ind. tessile*) yarn 3. (*tec.*) wire ‖ *un — d'acqua*, a fine stream of water; *un — d'aria*, a breath of air.

filobus *sm.* trolley-bus.

filologìa *sf.* philology.

filòlogo *sm.* philologist.

filone *sm.* 1. (*di pane*) long loaf 2. (*min.*) vein.

filosofare *vi.* to philosophize.

filosofìa *sf.* philosophy.

filòsofo *sm.* philosopher.

filovìa *sf.* trolley-bus line.

filtrare *vt.* to filter, to strain.

filtro *sm.* 1. filter 2. (*colino*) strainer.

filza *sf.* 1. string 2. (*fig.*) series (*pl.*) 3. (*cucito*) running stitch.

finale *agg.* last, final.

finalità *sf.* aim, end.

finalmente *avv.* 1. at last 2. (*in conclusione*) finally.

finanche *avv.* even.

finanza *sf.* finance.

finanziamento *sm.* financing.

finanziare *vt.* to finance.

finanziario *agg.* financial.

finanziatore *sm.* financing capitalist.

finanziere *sm.* financier.

finché *cong.* 1. till, until 2. (*per tutto il tempo che*) as long as.

fine[1] *sf.* end ‖ *alla fin —*, after all. ♦ **fine** *sm.* (*scopo*) purpose.

fine[2] *agg.* fine, thin.

finestra *sf.* window.

finestrino *sm.* window.

finezza *sf.* 1. thinness 2. (*acume*) subtlety 3. (*raffinatezza*) refinement 4. (*gentilezza*) kindness.

fingere *vi.* to pretend. ♦ **fingersi** *vr.* to feign oneself.

finimenti *sm. pl.* harness (*sing.*).

finimondo *sm.* 1. end of the world 2. (*fig.*) catastrophe.

finire *vt.* 1. to finish, to end 2. (*interrompersi*) to stop ‖ *— con*, to end by: *finii con l'andare*, I ended by going.

finitezza *sf.* perfection.

finìtimo *agg.* bordering.

finito *agg.* 1. finished, ended 2. (*rovinato*) done for.

finitura *sf.* finishing.

fino *prep.* 1. (*di tempo*) till, until, up to: — *a dicembre*, till December 2. (*di spazio*) as far as: *andammo fino a Roma*, we went as far as Rome 3. (*fino da*) from 4. (*a partire da*) since.

finocchio *sm.* fennel.

finora *avv.* till now, so far.

finta *sf.* 1. sham 2. (*scherma*) feint.

fintantoché *avv.* V. *finché*.

finto *agg.* false.

finzione *sf.* pretence, duplicity.

fio *sm.* penalty: *pagare il —*, to pay (*v. irr.*) the penalty (of).

fioccare *vi.* 1. to snow 2. (*fig.*) to shower.

fiocco *sm.* 1. ribbon 2. (*di lana*) staple 3. (*falda*) flake 4. (*di neve*) snowflake.

fiòcina *sf.* harpoon.

fioco *agg.* 1. (*rauco*) hoarse 2. (*debole*) weak 3. (*di luce*) dim 4. (*di voce*) faint.

fionda *sf.* sling.

fioraio *sm.* florist.

fiorame *sm.* floral design.

fiordaliso *sm.* bluebottle.

fiordo *sm.* fjord.

fiore *sm.* 1. flower 2. (*fioritura*) bloom: *essere in — (anche fig.)*, to be in bloom 3. (*parte scelta*) the best part 4. (*nelle carte*) clubs (*pl.*).

fiorente *agg.* 1. blooming 2. (*fig.*) flourishing.

fioretto *sm.* 1. little flower 2. (*relig.*) act of mortification 3. (*scherma*) foil.

fioricultore *sm.* floriculturist.

fiorino *sm.* florin.

fiorire *vi.* 1. to flower, to bloom, to blossom 2. (*fig.*) to flourish.

fiorista *s.* florist.

fiorito *agg.* 1. flowery 2. (*in fiore*) in bloom.

fioritura *sf.* 1. flowering 2. (*fig.*) flourishing.

fiotto *sm.* wave, stream: *a fiotti*, in streams.

firma *sf.* signature.

firmamento *sm.* firmament.

firmare *vt.* to sign.

firmatario *sm.* 1. signatory 2. (*comm.*) signer.

fisarmònica *sf.* accordion.

fisarmonicista *s.* accordionist.

fiscale *agg.* 1. fiscal 2. (*inquisitorio*) strict.

fiscalismo *sm.* rigorism.

fischiare *vi.* 1. to whistle 2. (*di segnale acustico*) to hoot 3. (*di serpente; per disapprovare*) to hiss 4. (*nelle orecchie*) to buzz 5. (*di proiettili*) to whiz.

fischiata *sf.* 1. whistling 2. (*di disapprovazione*) hissing.

fischiettare *vt.* to whistle softly.

fischietto *sm.* whistle.

fischio *sm.* 1. whistle 2. (*di serpente; di disapprovazione*) hiss 3. (*segnali acustici*) hoot 4. (*nelle orecchie*) buzzing.

fisco *sm.* public treasury.

fisica *sf.* physics.

fisico *agg.* physical, bodily. ♦ fisico *sm.* 1. (*scienziato*) physicist 2. (*costituzione*) physique.

fisima *sf.* caprice, whim.

fisiologia *sf.* physiology.

fisiològico *agg.* physiologic(al).

fisiòlogo *sm.* physiologist.

fisionomia *sf.* 1. features (*pl.*) 2. (*carattere*) character.

fisionomista *sm.* physiognomist.

fisioterapia *sf.* physiotherapy.

fissaggio *sm.* fixing.

fissare *vt.* 1. to fix 2. (*guardare fisso*) to gaze 3. (*prenotare*) to book. ♦ fissarsi *vr.* 1. to be fixed 2. (*stabilirsi*) to settle down.

fissato *agg.* 1. fixed 2. (*fam.*) obsessed.

fissatore *sm.* 1. fixer 2. (*foto*) fixing bath.

fissazione *sf.* fixed idea.

fissione *sf.* fission.

fissità *sf.* fixity.

fisso *agg.* fixed.

fistola *sf.* 1. Pan-pipe 2. (*patol.*) fistula.

fitologia *sf.* phytology.

fitta *sf.* stitch.

fittàvolo *sm.* tenant farmer.

fittizio *agg.* fictitious.

fitto[1] *agg.* 1. (*conficcato*) driven in 2. (*denso*) thick.

fitto[2] *sm.* rent.

fiumana *sf.* 1. broad stream 2. (*fig.*) crowd, stream.

fiume *sm.* 1. river 2. (*fig.*) flood.

fiutare *vt.* 1. to smell (*v. irr.*) 2. (*fig.*) to guess.

fiuto *sm.* 1. scent, smell 2. (*fig.*) intuition.

flàccido agg. flabby.

flacone sm. vial.

flagellare vt. 1. to flagellate 2. (fig.) to scourge.

flagellazione sf. flagellation.

flagello sm. 1. scourge, whip 2. (fig.) scourge, plague.

flagrante agg. flagrant || cogliere qu. in —, to catch (v. irr.) so. in the open act.

flagranza sf. flagrancy.

flanella sf. flannel.

flato sm. flatus.

flatulenza sf. flatulence.

flautato agg. fluted.

flautista sm. flute-player.

flàuto sm. flute.

flèbile agg. plaintive, feeble.

flebite sf. phlebitis.

fleboclisi sf. phleboclysis.

flebòtomo sm. phlebotomist.

flemma sf. coolness, phlegm.

flemmàtico agg. phlegmatic.

flèmmone sm. phlegmon.

flessìbile agg. flexible, pliant (anche fig.).

flessibilità sf. flexibility.

flessione sf. flexion, bending.

flessuosità sf. 1. flexuosity 2. (di corpo) suppleness.

flessuoso agg. 1. flexuous 2. (di corpo) supple.

flèttere vt. to bend (v. irr.).

flirtare vi. to flirt.

flogìstico agg. (med.) phlogistic.

flora sf. flora.

floreale agg. floral.

floricoltore sm. floriculturist.

floricoltura sf. floriculture.

floridezza sf. prosperity.

flòrido agg. 1. prosperous 2. (fig.) buxom 3. (di colorito) ruddy.

florilegio sm. florilegium (pl. -ia).

floscio agg. flabby.

flotta sf. fleet: — metropolitana (in Gran Bretagna), the Home Fleet.

flottante agg. floating.

flottiglia sf. flotilla.

fluente agg. fluent (anche fig.).

fluidità sf. fluency.

fluido agg. e sm. fluid.

fluire vi. to flow.

fluorescente agg. fluorescent.

fluorescenza sf. 1. (fig.) fluorescence 2. (elettr.) glow.

fluorìdrico agg. hydrofluoric.

fluorite sf. fluorite.

fluoro sm. fluorine.

fluoruro sm. fluoride.

flussione sf. fluxion.

flusso sm. 1. (di marea) flood(-tide) 2. (fig.) flux.

flutto sm. wave.

fluttuante agg. 1. fluctuating, floating 2. (incerto) irresolute.

fluttuare vi. to fluctuate, to waver.

fluttuazione sf. fluctuation.

fluviale agg. river (attr.).

fobìa sf. phobia, aversion.

foca sf. seal.

focaccia sf. cake || rendere pan per —, to give (v. irr.) tit for tat.

focaia sf. pietra —, flint.

focale agg. focal.

foce sf. mouth.

focolaio sm. centre of infection.

focolare sm. 1. hearth 2. (caminetto) fireplace 3. (fig.) home.

focoso agg. hot, fiery.

fòdera sf. lining.

foderare vt. to line.

fòdero sm. scabbard, sheath.

foga sf. impetuosity.

foggia sf. 1. (moda) fashion 2. (maniera) way 3. (forma) shape.

foggiare vt. to shape.

foglia sf. leaf (pl. leaves) || mangiare la —, to take (v. irr.) the hint.

fogliame sm. foliage, leafage.

foglio sm. sheet.

fogna sf. sewer.

fognatura sf. sewage.

foia sf. lust.

fola sf. 1. fable 2. (fandonia) fib.

folata sf. (di vento) gust.

folclore sm. folklore.

folclorìstico agg. folkloristic.

folgorante agg. flashing, dazzling.

folgorare vt. to strike (v. irr.) with lightning.

folgorazione sf. 1. (elettr.) electrocution 2. (fig.) fulmination.

fòlgore sf. thunderbolt.

folla sf. crowd.

folle agg. 1. mad 2. (mecc.) idle 3. (auto) neutral.

folleggiare vi. 1. to behave foolishly 2. (divertirsi) to make (v. irr.) merry.

folletto sm. 1. imp 2. (ragazzo) restless child.

follìa sf. madness || amare qu. alla —, to be madly in love with so.

folto agg. thick. ♦ **folto** sm. thick.

fomentare vt. to foster.

fomentatore sm. fomenter.

fomento sm. fomentation.

fonda *sf.* anchorage || *nave alla —*, ship at anchor.

fòndaco *sm.* draper's shop.

fondale *sm.* **1.** (*teat.*) background **2.** (*mar.*) depth.

fondamentale *agg.* fundamental.

fondamento *sm.* **1.** foundation: *gettare le fondamenta*, to lay (*v. irr.*) the foundation **2.** (*fig.*) basis, ground.

fondare *vt.* to found. ◆ **fondarsi** *vr.* to base oneself on.

fondatezza *sf.* foundation, ground.

fondato *agg.* well-grounded.

fondatore *sm.* founder.

fondazione *sf.* **1.** foundation **2.** (*istituzione*) institution.

fòndere *vt.* **1.** to melt **2.** (*fondere in forma*) to cast (*v. irr.*) **3.** (*unire*) to blend.

fonderìa *sf.* foundry.

fondiario *agg.* land (*attr.*).

fondista *sm.* long-distance runner.

fonditore *sm.* melter, caster.

fonditura *sf.* **1.** melting **2.** (*colata*) casting.

fondo *agg.* deep. ◆ **fondo** *sm.* **1.** (*parte inferiore*) bottom **2.** (*estremità*) end **3.** (*indole*) nature **4.** (*possedimento*) estate **5.** (*capitale*) fund || *articolo di —*, leading article.

fonema *sm.* phoneme.

fonètica *sf.* phonetics.

fonogramma *sm.* phonogram.

fonologìa *sf.* phonology.

fontana *sf.* fountain.

fontanella *sf.* (*anat.*) fontanel.

fonte *sf.* spring, source (*anche fig.*).

foraggio *sm.* forage.

foràneo *agg.* **1.** rural **2.** (*mar.*) outer.

forare *vt.* **1.** to pierce **2.** (*di pneumatico*) to puncture **3.** (*di biglietti*) to punch.

foratura *sf.* **1.** piercing **2.** (*di pneumatico*) puncture.

fòrbici *sf. pl.* scissors.

forbire *vt.* **1.** to clean **2.** (*di stile*) to polish.

forbito *agg.* **1.** elegant **2.** (*di stile*) polished.

forca *sf.* **1.** fork **2.** (*patibolo*) gallows.

forcella *sf.* **1.** forked stick **2.** (*mecc.*) fork **3.** (*per capelli*) hairpin.

forchetta *sf.* fork.

forcina *sf.* hairpin.

fòrcipe *sm.* forceps (*pl.*).

forcuto *agg.* forked.

forense *agg.* forensic.

foresta *sf.* forest (*anche fig.*), wood.

forestale *agg.* forestal: *guardia —*, forester.

foresterìa *sf.* guest-rooms (*pl.*).

forestiero *agg.* foreign. ◆ **forestiero** *sm.* foreigner.

fòrfora *sf.* dandruff, scurf.

forgiare *vt.* **1.** to forge **2.** (*modellare*) to shape.

forma *sf.* **1.** form, shape **2.** (*tec.*) mould.

formaggio *sm.* cheese.

formale *agg.* **1.** formal **2.** (*solenne*) solemn.

formalismo *sm.* formalism.

formalista *agg. e s.* formalist.

formalità *sf.* formality.

formalizzarsi *vr.* to be shocked (at, by).

formare *vt.* **1.** to form **2.** (*fare*) to make (*v. irr.*), to create **3.** (*modellare*) to shape **4.** (*addestrare*) train. ◆ **formarsi** *vr.* **1.** to form **2.** (*crescere, affinarsi*) to grow (*v. irr.*), to develop.

formativo *agg.* formative.

formato *sm.* **1.** form **2.** (*misura*) size **3.** (*di libro*) format.

formazione *sf.* formation.

formica *sf.* ant.

formichiere *sm.* ant-eater.

formicolare *vi.* **1.** to swarm **2.** (*sentire un formicolio*) to tingle.

formicolìo *sm.* **1.** swarming **2.** (*intorpidimento*) tingling.

formidàbile *agg.* formidable.

fòrmula *sf.* formula (*pl.* -ae).

formulare *vt.* to formulate.

fornace *sf.* furnace.

fornaio *sm.* **1.** baker **2.** (*negozio*) baker's shop.

fornello *sm.* stove.

fornire *vt.* **1.** to supply (with), to provide (with) **2.** (*equipaggiare*) to equip (with).

fornito *agg.* **1.** furnished (with), supplied (with) **2.** (*equipaggiato*) equipped (with).

fornitore *sm.* furnisher, supplier.

fornitura *sf.* **1.** (*il fornire*) supplying **2.** (*attrezzatura*) furniture, fitting.

forno *sm.* **1.** (*da cucina*) oven **2.** (*metal.*) furnace.

foro[1] *sm.* hole.

foro[2] *sm.* **1.** court of justice **2.** (*gli avvocati*) the Bar **3.** (*stor.*) forum.

forse *avv.* 1. perhaps, maybe 2. (*circa*) about.

forsennato *agg.* mad, frantic.

forte *agg.* 1. strong (*anche fig.*) 2. (*di mali*) severe 3. (*violento*) heavy 4. (*di suono*) loud. ♦ **forte** *sm.* 1. strong man 2. (*punto di forza*) strong point 3. (*fortezza*) fortress. ♦ **forte** *avv.* strongly.

fortezza *sf.* stronghold, fortress.

fortificare *vt.* to strengthen, to fortify (*anche fig.*).

fortificazione *sf.* fortification.

fortino *sm.* block-house.

fortùito *agg.* fortuitous, accidental.

fortuna *sf.* 1. luck 2. (*ricchezza*) fortune, wealth 3. (*riuscita*) success 4. (*emergenza*) emergency.

fortunale *sm.* storm.

fortunato *agg.* lucky.

fortunoso *agg.* 1. stormy 2. (*fig.*) eventful.

forùncolo *sm.* boil.

foruncolosi *sf.* furunculosis.

forviare *vt.* to lead (*v. irr.*) astray.

forza *sf.* 1. strength 2. (*fig.*) power || — *di volontà*, will-power; *a — di*, by dint of 3. (*mil.*) force.

forzare *vt.* 1. to force, to compel 2. (*scassinare*) to pick the lock of.

forzato *agg.* forced. ♦ **forzato** *sm.* convict.

forziere *sm.* coffer.

forzoso *agg.* forced.

foschìa *sf.* haze, mist.

fosco *agg.* 1. dark, hazy 2. (*di aspetto*) gloomy.

fosfato *sm.* phosphate.

fosforescente *agg.* phosphorescent.

fosforescenza *sf.* phosphorescence.

fòsforo *sm.* 1. phosphorus 2. (*fig.*) intelligence.

fossa *sf.* 1. ditch 2. (*cavità*) hollow 3. (*tomba*) grave.

fossato *sm.* ditch.

fòssile *agg.* e *sm.* fossil || *carbon —*, pit-coal.

fosso *sm.* ditch.

foto *sf.* photo.

fotocèllula *sf.* photoelectric cell.

fotocopia *sf.* photocopy.

fotogènico *agg.* photogenic.

fotografare *vt.* to photograph.

fotografia *sf.* 1. (*arte fotografica*) photography 2. (*immagine fotografica*) photograph || — *istantanea*, snapshot; *fare una —*, to take (*v. irr.*) a photograph.

fotògrafo *sm.* photographer.

fotomontaggio *sm.* photomontage.

fra *prep.* V. *tra.*

fra' *sm.* (*relig.*) Brother.

frac *sm.* tail-coat.

fracassare *vt.* to smash, to shatter.

fracasso *sm.* 1. noise, hubbub 2. (*di cose rotte*) crash.

fracco *sm.* 1. a great deal 2. (*di botte*) a good thrashing.

fràdicio *agg.* 1. rotten 2. (*bagnato*) wet through.

fràgile *agg.* 1. fragile 2. (*fig.*) frail.

fragilità *sf.* fragility (*anche fig.*).

fràgola *sf.* strawberry.

fragore *sm.* loud noise.

fragoroso *agg.* noisy.

fragrante *agg.* fragrant.

fragranza *sf.* fragrance.

fraintèndere *vt.* · to misunderstand (*v. irr.*).

frammassone *sm.* freemason.

frammassonerìa *sf.* freemasonry.

frammentario *agg.* fragmentary.

frammento *sm.* fragment.

framméttere *vt.* to interpose. ♦ **framméttersi** *vr.* to interpose, to intrude.

frammezzare *vt.* to intersperse.

frammezzo *prep.* V. *tra.*

frammischiare *vt.* to intermingle. ♦ **frammischiarsi** *vr.* to intermingle.

frana *sf.* landslide.

franare *vi.* 1. (*di terreno*) to slide (*v. irr.*) down 2. (*di casa*) to fall (*v. irr.*) in.

francescano *agg.* e *sm.* Franciscan.

francese *agg.* French. ♦ **francese** *sm.* Frenchman (*pl.* -men).

francesismo *sm.* Gallicism.

franchezza *sf.* frankness, outspokenness.

franchigia *sf.* 1. immunity 2. (*postale*) post-free 3. (*mar.*) furlough.

franco[1] *agg.* 1. frank, outspoken 2. (*libero; comm.*) free: *un porto —*, a free port; *— a bordo*, free on board; *— di spese*, free of charge.

franco[2] *sm.* franc.

francobollo *sm.* stamp.

francotiratore *sm.* sharp-shooter.

frangente *sm.* 1. (*mar.*) breaker 2. (*situazione difficile*) emergency.

fràngere *vt.* 1. to break (*v. irr.*) 2. (*schiacciare*) to crush.

frangetta *sf.* fringe.

frangia *sf.* 1. fringe 2. (*fig.*) embellishment.

frangiare *vt.* to fringe.
frangibile *agg.* frangible.
frangibilità *sf.* frangibility.
frangiflutti *agg. e sm.* breakwater.
frangizolle *sm.* (*agr.*) clod-smasher.
franoso *agg.* crumbling.
frantoio *sm.* oil-mill.
frantumare *vt.* to shatter.
frantume *sm.* fragment ‖ *andare in frantumi*, to break (*v. irr.*) into fragments.
frappé *sm.* shake.
frapporre *vt.* to interpose. ♦
frapporsi *vr.* to interpose.
frasario *sm.* jargon.
frasca *sf.* 1. leafy branch 2. (*donna leggera*) coquette.
frascheggiare *vi.* 1. to rustle 2. (*civettare*) to flirt.
fraschetta *sf.* 1. twig 2. (*fig.*) frivolous girl.
frase *sf.* sentence.
fraseggiare *vi.* to phrase.
fraseologìa *sf.* phraseology.
fràssino *sm.* ash-tree.
frastagliare *vt.* to indent.
frastagliato *agg.* indented.
frastaglio *sm.* indentation.
frastornare *vt.* to disturb.
frastuono *sm.* noise, uproar, hub-bub.
frate *sm.* 1. friar 2. (*come appellativo*) Brother.
fratellanza *sf.* brotherhood, fraternity.
fratellastro *sm.* half-brother.
fratello *sm.* brother ‖ *fratelli siamesi*, Siamese twins.
fraternità *sf.* brotherhood, fraternity.
fraternizzare *vi.* to fraternize.
fraternizzazione *sf.* fraternization.
fraterno *agg.* brotherly.
fratricida *agg.* fratricidal. ♦ **fratricida** *s.* fratricide.
fratricidio *sm.* fratricide.
fratta *sf.* thicket.
frattaglie *sf. pl.* chitterlings.
frattanto *avv.* meantime, meanwhile.
frattempo (*nella loc. avv.*) *nel* —, in the meanwhile.
fratto *agg.* broken, crushed.
frattura *sf.* fracture.
fratturare *vt.* to fracture, to break (*v. irr.*). ♦ **fratturarsi** *vr.* to fracture, to break.
fraudolento *agg.* fraudulent.
fraudolenza *sf.* fraudulence.

frazionamento *sm.* division.
frazionare *vt.* to divide.
frazionario *agg.* fractional.
frazione *sf.* fraction.
freccia *sf.* arrow.
frecciata *sf.* (*fig.*) gibe.
freddare *vt.* 1. to cool 2. (*ammazzare*) to kill.
freddezza *sf.* coldness, coldheartedness.
freddo *agg.* cold. ♦ **freddo** *sm.* cold: *avere* —, to be cold; *tremare di* —, to shiver with cold.
freddoloso *agg.* sensitive to cold.
freddura *sf.* pun.
fregagione *sf.* massage.
fregare *vt.* 1. to rub 2. (*imbrogliare; volg.*) to swindle.
fregata¹ *sf.* rubbing.
fregata² *sf.* (*nave*) frigate.
fregatura *sf.* swindle.
fregiare *vt.* to decorate, to adorn.
fregio *sm.* 1. ornament 2. (*arch.*) frieze.
frego *sm.* stroke: *tirare un* — *su qc.*, to cross sthg. out.
frégola *sf.* heat.
fremente *agg.* quivering: — *d'ira*, fuming.
frèmere *vi.* to quiver, to tremble.
frèmito *sm.* quiver, thrill.
frenare *vt.* 1. to brake 2. (*trattenere*) to restrain.
frenata *sf.* braking.
frenesìa *sf.* 1. frenzy 2. (*desiderio sfrenato*) immoderate desire.
frenètico *agg.* 1. frantic 2. (*entusiastico*) enthusiastic.
freno *sm.* 1. brake ‖ *bloccare i freni*, to jam the brakes; *togliere il* —, to release the brake 2. (*ritegno*) check restraint ‖ *mordere il* —, to fret under restraint; *stringere i freni*, to shorten the reins 3. (*di cavallo*) bit.
frenologìa *sf.* phrenology.
frequentare *vt.* 1. to frequent 2. (*di scuola*) to attend 3. (*di luogo pubblico*) to patronize.
frequentato *agg.* 1. frequented 2. (*di scuola*) attended 3. (*di luogo pubblico*) patronized.
frequentatore *sm.* 1. frequenter 2. (*cliente assiduo*) regular customer.
frequente *agg.* frequent.
frequenza *sf.* 1. frequency 2. (*affluenza*) concourse 3. (*assiduità*) attendance.

fresa *sf.* milling machine.

fresatrice *sf.* milling machine.

freschezza *sf.* freshness (*anche fig.*), coolness.

fresco *agg.* 1. fresh 2. (*di temperatura*) cool.

frescura *sf.* coolness.

fretta *sf.* haste, hurry: *avere —*, to be in a hurry.

frettoloso *agg.* hurried.

freudiano *agg.* Freudian.

friàbile *agg.* crumbly.

friabilità *sf.* friability.

fricassea *sf.* fricassee.

friggere *vt.* to fry || *andare a farsi —*, to go (*v. irr.*) to the devil.

friggitorìa *sf.* fried food shop.

frigidezza, frigidità *sf.* frigidity.

frìgido *agg.* frigid (*anche fig.*).

frignare *vi.* to whimper.

frigorìfero *agg.* refrigerant. ♦ **frigorìfero** *sm.* 1. refrigerator 2. (*fam.*) fridge.

fringuello *sm.* finch.

frittata *sf.* omelette.

frittella *sf.* pancake.

fritto *agg.* fried.

frittura *sf.* fry.

frivolezza *sf.* 1. frivolity 2. (*cosa frivola*) trifle.

frìvolo *agg.* frivolous.

frizionare *vt.* to rub, to massage.

frizione *sf.* 1. rub, rubbing, massage 2. (*auto*) clutch.

frizzante *agg.* 1. biting 2. (*di bevanda*) sparkling.

frizzare *vi.* 1. to tingle 2. (*di bevanda*) to sparkle.

frizzo *sm.* 1. witticism 2. (*scherno*) gibe.

frodare *vt.* to defraud.

frodatore *sm.* defrauder.

frode *sf.* fraud, swindle.

frodo *sm.* smuggling || *cacciare di —*, to poach; *cacciatore di —*, poacher.

frollare *vt.* to hang. ♦ **frollare** *vi.* to become (*v. irr.*) tender.

frollatura *sf.* hanging.

frollo *agg.* tender, high || *pasta frolla*, pastry.

fronda[1] *sf.* leafy branch.

fronda[2] *sf.* (*rivolta*) rebellion: *vento di —*, trouble brewing.

frondoso *agg.* leafy.

frontale *agg.* frontal.

fronte *sf.* 1. forehead: *— ampia, sfuggente*, broad, receding forehead 2. (*arch.*) front || *di — a*, in front of; *far — a*, to face. ♦ **fronte** *sm.* 1. (*mil.*) front 2. (*pol.*) union.

fronteggiare *vt.* to face.

frontespizio *sm.* 1. (*arch.*) frontispiece 2. (*di libro*) title page.

frontiera *sf.* frontier, border.

frontone *sm.* 1. pediment 2. (*di porta, finestra*) gable.

frònzolo *sm.* frill || *senza fronzoli*, plain.

frotta *sf.* 1. crowd 2. (*di animali*) flock.

fròttola *sf.* fib.

frugacchiare *vi.* to rummage.

frugale *agg.* frugal.

frugalità *sf.* frugality.

frugare *vi.* to search, to rummage.

frùgolo *sm.* lively child.

fruire *vi.* to enjoy, to avail oneself of.

fruizione *sf.* fruition.

frullare *vi.* 1. to whip, to beat (*v. irr.*) up 2. (*di ali*) to whir.

xrullato *sm.* *— di frutta*, fruit-shake.

frullatore *sm.* mill.

frullino *sm.* whisk.

frullìo *sm.* whirring.

frullo *sm.* whir.

frumento *sm.* wheat.

frusciare *vi.* to rustle.

fruscìo *sm.* rustle.

frusta *sf.* 1. whip 2. (*cuc.*) whisk.

frustare *vt.* to whip, to lash.

frustata *sf.* lash.

frustino *sm.* riding-whip.

frusto *agg.* worn-out, thread-bare.

frustrare *vt.* to frustrate.

frutta *sf.* fruit: *— candita*, candied fruit; *— sciroppata*, fruit in syrup; *— cotta*, compote.

fruttare *vi.* 1. to bear (*v. irr.*) fruit, to pay (*v. irr.*) 2. (*comm.*) to yield.

frutteto *sm.* orchard.

frutticultura *sf.* fruit-growing.

fruttiera *sf.* fruit-dish.

fruttìfero *agg.* 1. fruitful 2. (*econ.* interest-bearing: *buono —*, interest-bearing security.

fruttificare *vi.* to bear (*v. irr.* fruit.

fruttivéndolo *sm.* greengrocer.

frutto *sm.* fruit || *frutti di mare*, edible mussels.

fruttuoso *agg.* fruitful, profitable.

fu *agg.* late.

fucilare *vt.* to shoot (*v. irr.*).

fucilata *sf.* shot.

fucilazione *sf.* shooting.

fucile *sm.* rifle, gun: — *ad aria compressa*, air-gun; — *da caccia*, shotgun; *calcio del* —, butt; *canna del* —, gun-barrel; *caricare un* —, to load a gun.

fucilerìa *sf.* 1. rifle fire 2. (*insieme di fucili*) musketry.

fuciliere *sm.* rifleman (*pl.* -men).

fucina *sf.* forge.

fucinare *vt.* to forge.

fuco *sm.* 1. drone 2. (*bot.*) fucus.

fucsia *sf.* fuchsia.

fuga *sf.* 1. flight, escape 2. (*di innamorati*) elopement 3. (*falla, apertura*) escape, leak 4. (*mus.*) fugue.

fugace *agg.* short-lived, transient.

fugacità *sf.* fugacity.

fugare *vt.* 1. to put (*v. irr.*) to flight, to disperse 2. (*scacciare*) to dispel.

fuggévole *agg.* flying, ephemeral.

fuggiasco *agg.* e *sm.* runaway.

fuggire *vi.* 1. to run (*v. irr.*) away, to flee (*v. irr.*) 2. (*di innamorati*) to elope. ♦ **fuggire** *vt.* to shun.

fuggitivo *agg.* e *sm.* fugitive.

fulcro *sm.* fulcrum (*pl.* -ra).

fùlgido *agg.* shining.

fulgore *sm.* brightness.

fulìggine *sf.* soot.

fuligginoso *agg.* sooty.

fulminante *agg.* fulminant. ♦ **fulminante** *sm.* 1. (*chim.*) fulminate 2. (*di arma*) primer.

fulminare *vt.* 1. to strike (*v. irr.*) by lightning 2. (*colpire*) to strike.

fulminato *agg.* 1. struck by lightning 2. (*fig.*) thunder-struck.

fùlmine *sm.* lightning.

fulmìneo *agg.* flashing.

fulvo *agg.* tawny.

fumaiolo *sm.* smoke-stack.

fumante *agg.* smóking, steaming.

fumare *vt.* e *vi.* to smoke.

fumarola *sf.* fumarole.

fumata *sf.* 1. smoke 2. (*segnale*) smoke signal.

fumatore *sm.* smoker.

fumetto *sm.* strip cartoon || *giornali a fumetti*, comics.

fumista *s.* stove-repairer.

fumo *sm.* 1. smoke || *venditore di* —, windbag; *andare in* —, to end in smoke 2. (*vapore*) fume (*anche fig.*) 3. (*di pentole*) steam.

fumògeno *agg.* smoke-producing.

fumoso *agg.* smoky.

funàmbolo *sm.* rope-dancer.

fune *sf.* 1. rope 2. (*cavo*) cáble.

fùnebre *agg.* 1. funeral: *canto* —, *dirge*; *carro* —, hearse 2. (*cupo*) gloomy.

funerale *sm.* funeral || *i funerali*, the obsequies.

funerario *agg.* funerary.

funèreo *agg.* funereal.

funestare *vt.* to afflict.

funesto *agg.* baneful, woeful.

fungaia *sf.* mushroom-bed.

fùngere *vi.* to act (as).

fungo *sm.* mushroom.

funicolare *sf.* funicular.

funivìa *sf.* telpherage.

funzionale *agg.* functional.

funzionamento *sm.* working.

funzionare *vi.* 1. to act (as) 2. (*andar bene*) to work.

funzionario *sm.* official.

funzione *sf.* 1. function 2. (*carica*) office 3. (*relig.*) service.

fuochista *sm.* stoker.

fuoco *sm.* 1. fire 2. (*cine; foto; mat.*) focus: *mettere a* —, to focus.

fuorché *cong.* except, but.

fuori *avv.* 1. out, outdoors 2. (*all'estero*) abroad. ♦ **fuori (di)** *prep.* out of, outside.

fuoribordo *sm.* outboard motor.

fuoriclasse *sm.* first-rater.

fuorigioco *sm.*, *agg.* e *avv.* off-side.

fuorilegge *sm.* outlaw.

fuoriserie *agg.* e *sm.* special body car.

fuoruscito *sm.* exile, refugee.

fuorviare *vt.* to lead (*v. irr.*) astray.

furberìa *sf.* cunning.

furbo *agg.* cunning, shrewd.

furente *agg.* furious, mad.

furerìa *sf.* orderly room.

furetto *sm.* ferret.

furfante *sm.* rascal, scamp.

furgoncino *sm.* small van.

furgone *sm.* van.

furia *sf.* fury: *montare su tutte le furie*, to fly (*v. irr.*) into a fury.

furibondo *agg.* furious.

furioso *agg.* 1. furious 2. (*violento*) violent.

furore *sm.* fury: *far* —, to be a hit.

furoreggiare *vi.* to be all the rage.

furtivo *agg.* stealthy.

furto *sm.* theft.

fuscello *sm.* 1. twig, straw 2. (*fig.*) thin person.

fusìbile *sm.* fuse.

fusione *sf.* 1. fusion 2. (*di società comm.*) merging.

fuso *sm.* spindle || — *orario,* time zone.
fusoliera *sf.* fuselage.
fustigare *vt.* to flog.
fusto *sm.* **1.** (*bot.*) stalk **2.** (*tronco umano*) trunk **3.** (*per benzina*) drum **4.** (*di legno per liquori*) barrel **5.** (*giovane prestante*) muscle--man (*pl.* -men) **6.** (*di colonna*) shaft.
fùtile *agg.* trifling.
futilità *sf.* trifle.
futurismo *sm.* futurism.
futurista *agg.* e *sm.* futurist.
futuro *agg.* e *sm.* future.

G

gabbamondo *sm.* swindler.
gabbare *vt.* to swindle.
gabbia *sf.* **1.** cage **2.** (*per imballaggio*) crate.
gabbiano *sm.* sea-gull.
gabellare *vt.* (*far credere*) to pass off as.
gabinetto *sm.* **1.** (*studio*) study **2.** (*pol.*) cabinet **3.** (*latrina*) water-closet, toilet.
gagà *sm.* dandy.
gagliardamente *avv.* vigorously.
gagliardetto *sm.* pennon.
gagliardo *agg.* vigorous.
gaglioffo *sm.* rascal.
gaiezza *sf.* **1.** cheerfulness **2.** (*di colore*) brightness.
gaio *agg.* **1.** cheerful **2.** (*di colore*) bright.
gala *sf.* **1.** (*trina*) frill **2.** (*festa*) gala: *abito di* —, gala dress.
galante *agg.* e *sm.* gallant || *lettera* —, love letter; *fare il* —, to flirt.
galanterìa *sf.* **1.** gallantry **2.** (*complimento*) compliment.
galantina *sf.* galantine.
galantuomo *sm.* honest man.
galassia *sf.* galaxy.
galateo *sm.* **1.** good manners (*pl.*) **2.** (*libro*) book of manners.
galena *sf.* galena.
galeone *sm.* galleon.
galeotto *sm.* **1.** convict **2.** (*mezzano*) pander **3.** (*mar.*) galley-slave.
galera *sf.* **1.** jail **2.** (*mar.*) galley.
galileo *agg.* e *sm.* Galilean.

galla¹ (*nella loc. avv.*) *a* —, afloat || *stare a* —, to float; *venire a* —, to come (*v. irr.*) to the surface; (*fig.*) to come to light.
galla² *sf.* (*bot.*) gall.
galleggiamento *sm.* floating: *linea di* —, water-line.
galleggiante *agg.* floating, afloat (*pred.*). ♦ **galleggiante** *sm.* **1.** float **2.** (*boa*) buoy.
galleggiare *vi.* to float.
gallerìa *sf.* **1.** tunnel **2.** (*d'arte, in teatro*) gallery.
gallese *agg.* Welsh. ♦ **gallese** *sm.* Welshman (*pl.* -men).
galletta *sf.* biscuit.
gallina *sf.* **1.** hen **2.** (*cibo*) chicken.
gallinàceo *agg.* e *sm.* gallinacean.
gallio *sm.* gallium.
gallismo *sm.* cocksure behaviour (towards women).
gallo *sm.* **1.** cock **2.** (*stor.*) Gaul.
gallonato *agg.* gallooned.
gallone *sm.* **1.** braid, galloon **2.** (*mil.*) chevron stripes (*pl.*) **3.** (*misura*) gallon.
galoppante *agg.* galloping.
galoppare *vi.* to gallop.
galoppata *sf.* gallop.
galoppatoio *sm.* riding-track.
galoppino *sm.* **1.** errand-boy **2.** (*tirapiedi*) drudge.
galoppo *sm.* gallop: *al* —, at a gallop, (*fig.*) at full speed; *andare al gran* —, to ride (*v. irr.*) full gallop.
galoscia *sf.* galosh.
galvànico *agg.* galvanic.
galvanizzare *vt.* **1.** to galvanize **2.** (*rivestire di metallo*) to electroplate.
galvanizzazione *sf.* **1.** galvanization **2.** (*rivestitura di metallo*) electroplating.
galvanoplàstica *sf.* galvanoplastics.
gamba *sf.* leg || *avere le gambe lunghe,* to be long-legged; *male in* —, down at heel; *in* — (*fig.*), smart.
gambale *sm.* **1.** legging **2.** (*di armatura*) jamb.
gamberetto *sm.* shrimp.
gàmbero *sm.* **1.** (*di mare*) lobster **2.** (*d'acqua dolce*) crayfish || *andare come un* —, to go (*v. irr.*) backwards.
gambo *sm.* stem.
gamma *sf.* range: — *di lunghezza d'onda,* waveband.

ganascia *sf.* jaw || *mangiare a quattro ganasce,* to eat (*v. irr.*) voraciously.

gancio *sm.* hook.

ganga *sf.* gang.

gànghero *sm.* hinge || *andare fuori dai gangheri,* to lose (*v. irr.*) one's temper.

ganglio *sm.* ganglion (*pl.* -ia).

gangsterismo *sm.* gangsterism.

ganimede *sm.* dandy.

gara *sf.* competition.

garagista *sm.* garage keeper.

garante *sm.* **1.** warranter **2.** (*per un imputato*) bail || *essere* —, to answer for.

garantire *vt.* **1.** to warrant **2.** (*farsi garante per*) to answer for **3.** (*un imputato*) to go (*v. irr.*) bail for.

garanzìa *sf.* **1.** warranty, guarantee **2.** (*somma di* —) security **3.** (*cauzione*) bail || *dare, non dare* —, to be reliable, unreliable; *a* — *di,* as a guarantee for.

garbare *vi.* to like.

garbatamente *avv.* politely.

garbatezza *sf.* politeness.

garbato *agg.* polite.

garbo *sm.* politeness || *con bel* —, with a good grace.

garbuglio *sm.* entanglement.

gardenia *sf.* gardenia.

gareggiare *vi.* to compete.

garganella (*nella loc. avv.*) *bere a* —, to gulp down.

gargarismo *sm.* gargle.

gargarizzare *vi.* to gargle.

garibaldino *agg.* e *sm.* Garibaldian.

garitta *sf.* **1.** sentry-box **2.** (*torretta*) look-out turret **3.** (*di guardiano*) cabin.

garòfano *sm.* carnation || *chiodo di* —, clove.

garrese *sm.* withers (*pl.*).

garretto *sm.* **1.** back of heel **2.** (*di animale*) hock.

garrire *vi.* **1.** (*di bandiere*) to flutter, to flap **2.** (*di uccelli*) to chirp.

gàrrulo *agg.* talkative.

garza *sf.* gauze.

garzone *sm.* shop-boy, apprentice.

gas *sm.* gas.

gasolio *sm.* gas oil.

gasometro *sm.* gasholder.

gassare *vt.* to gas.

gassato *agg.* aerated || *acqua gassata,* soda-water.

gassista *sm.* gas-fitter.

gassògeno *sm.* gas producer.

gassoso *agg.* **1.** gaseous **2.** (*gassato*) aerated.

gàstrico *agg.* gastric.

gastrite *sf.* gastritis.

gastroenterite *sf.* gastroenteritis.

gastronomìa *sf.* gastronomy.

gastronòmico *agg.* gastronomic(al).

gatta *sf.* she-cat.

gattabuia *sf.* jail.

gatto *sm.* cat.

gattopardo *sm.* leopard.

gaudente *agg.* **1.** jolly **2.** (*dissipato*) fast. ♦ **gaudente** *sm.* fast person.

gàudio *sm.* joy.

gavetta *sf.* mess-tin.

gavitello *sm.* buoy.

gazza *sf.* magpie.

gazzarra *sf.* din.

gazzella *sf.* gazelle.

gazzetta *sf.* gazette.

gelare *vt.* e *vi.* to freeze (*v. irr.*).

gelata *sf.* frost.

gelataio *sm.* ice-cream vendor.

gelaterìa *sf.* ice-cream shop.

gelatina *sf.* **1.** (*cuc.*) jelly **2.** (*chim.*) gelatine.

gelatinoso *agg.* gelatinous.

gelato *agg.* frozen, icy. ♦ **gelato** *sm.* ice-cream.

gèlido *agg.* icy (*anche fig.*).

gelo *sm.* **1.** intense cold **2.** (*fig.*) chill **3.** (*ghiaccio*) ice **4.** (*brina*) frost.

gelone *sm.* chilblain.

gelosìa *sf.* **1.** jealousy **2.** (*cura*) care **3.** (*persiana*) shutter.

geloso *agg.* jealous.

gelso *sm.* mulberry(-tree).

gelsomino *sm.* jasmine.

gemebondo *agg.* groaning.

gemelli *sm. pl.* (*di polsino*) cuff-links.

gemello *agg.* e *sm.* twin.

gèmere *vi.* to groan.

gèmito *sm.* groan.

gemma *sf.* **1.** gem **2.** (*bot.*) bud.

gemmare *vi.* (*bot.*) to bud.

gendarme *sm.* policeman (*pl.* -men).

gendarmerìa *sf.* **1.** police-force **2.** (*caserma*) police-station.

genealogìa *sf.* genealogy.

genealògico *agg.* genealogical.

generàbile *agg.* generable.

generale[1] *agg.* general || *quartier* —, headquarters (*pl.*).

generale² sm. general.
generalità sf. generality || *dare le proprie —*, to give (v. irr.) one's particulars.
generalizzare vt. to generalize.
generalizzazione sf. generalization.
generare vt. 1. to beget (v. irr.) 2. (*produrre, anche tec.*) to produce. ♦ **generarsi** vr. to be born.
generatore agg. generative. ♦ **generatore** sm. generator.
generazione sf. generation.
genere sm. 1. kind 2. (*gramm.*) gender 3. (*letterario*) genre 4. (*prodotto*) product || *generi alimentari*, foodstuffs; *generi di prima necessità*, commodities.
genèrico agg. generic, vague.
gènero sm. son-in-law.
generosità sf. generosity.
generoso agg. generous.
gènesi sf. genesis (pl. -ses).
genètica sf. genetics.
genètico agg. genetic.
genetlìaco sm. birthday.
gengiva sf. gum.
genìa sf. 1. race 2. (*spreg.*) tribe.
geniale agg. clever.
genialità sf. 1. cleverness 2. (*genio*) genius.
genio sm. genius || *andare a —*, to please.
genitale agg. e sm. genital.
genitivo sm. genitive.
genitore sm. 1. parent 2. (*padre*) father.
genitrice sf. mother.
gennaio sm. January.
genocidio sm. genocide.
gentaglia sf. rabble.
gente sf. people: *c'è molta —*, there are a lot of people; *le genti dell'Asia*, the peoples of Asia.
gentildonna sf. lady.
gentile agg. 1. kind 2. (*cortese*) polite || *è — da parte sua*, it is kind of him.
gentilezza sf. 1. kindness 2. (*cortesia*) politeness 3. (*favore*) favour.
gentilizio agg. noble: *stemma —*, coat of arms.
gentiluomo sm. gentleman (pl. -men).
genuflessione sf. genuflection.
genuflèttersi vr. to kneel down.
genuinità sf. genuineness.
genuino agg. genuine.
genziana sf. gentian.
geodesìa sf. geodesy.

geofìsica sf. geophysics.
geografìa sf. geography.
geogràfico agg. geographic(al) || *carta geografica*, map.
geògrafo sm. geographer.
geologìa sf. geology.
geològico agg. geologic(al).
geòlogo sm. geologist.
geòmetra sm. 1. geometer 2. (*agrimensore*) land-surveyor.
geometrìa sf. geometry.
geomètrico agg. geometric(al).
geopolìtica sf. geopolitics.
geòrgico agg. georgic.
geranio sm. geranium.
gerarca sm. leader.
gerarchìa sf. hierarchy.
gerente sm. manager.
gerenza sf. management.
gergo sm. 1. slang 2. (*di una classe professionale*) jargon.
germànico agg. Germanic.
germanio sm. germanium.
germanismo sm. Germanism.
germanista s. Germanist.
germanìstica sf. Germanic studies.
germano¹ agg. e sm. German.
germano² agg. german: *fratello —*, brother-german.
germe sm. germ.
germicida agg. germicidal. ♦ **germicida** sm. germicide.
germinare vi. V. *germogliare*.
germinazione sf. germination.
germogliare vi. 1. to sprout 2. (*fig.*) to spring (v. irr.) (up).
germoglio sm. sprout.
geroglìfico sm. hieroglyphic.
gerontologìa sf. gerontology.
gerundio sm. gerund.
gessetto sm. chalk.
gesso sm. 1. chalk 2. (*med.; scult.; edil.*) plaster.
gesta sf. pl. deeds.
gestante sf. pregnant woman.
gestazione sf. gestation.
gesticolare vi. to gesticulate.
gestione sf. management.
gestire¹ vt. to manage.
gestire² vi. to gesture.
gesto sm. gesture || *un bel —*, a noble deed.
gestore sm. manager.
gesuita sm. Jesuit.
gesuìtico agg. Jesuitic(al).
gettare vt. 1. to throw (v. irr.), (*anche metal.; edil.*) to cast (v. irr.) 2. (*bot.*) to sprout 3. (*fruttare*) to yield || *— le fondamenta*,

to lay (*v. irr.*) the foundations; — *un grido*, to utter a cry. ♦ **gettarsi** *vr.* (*di fiume*) to flow.

gettata *sf.* 1. throw 2. (*edil.; metal.*) cast 3. (*di arma*) range 4. (*molo*) jetty.

gèttito *sm.* (*delle imposte*) yield.

getto *sm.* 1. throw 2. (*mecc.; di liquidi*) jet 3. (*bot.*) sprout 4. (*metal.; edil.*) casting || *di* —, effortlessly; *a* — *continuo*, continuously.

gettone *sm.* 1. counter: — *telefonico*, telephone counter 2. (*contromarca*) check || *macchina a* —, slot-machine.

geyser *sm.* geyser.

gheriglio *sm.* kernel.

gherminella *sf.* trick: *fare una* —, to play a trick (on).

ghermire *vt.* to clutch.

ghette *sf. pl.* spats.

ghetto *sm.* 1. ghetto 2. (*insieme degli ebrei*) Jewry.

ghiacciaia *sf.* 1. ice-box 2. (*stanza*) ice-house.

ghiacciaio *sm.* glacier.

ghiacciare *vi. e vt.* to freeze (*v. irr.*).

ghiacciato *agg.* 1. frozen 2. (*molto freddo*) icy.

ghiaccio *sm.* ice.

ghiacciolo *sm.* icicle.

ghiaia *sf.* gravel.

ghiaioso *agg.* gravelly.

ghianda *sf.* acorn.

ghiàndola *sf.* gland.

ghibellino *agg. e sm.* Ghibelline.

ghigliottina *sf.* guillotine.

ghigliottinare *vt.* to guillotine.

ghignare *vi.* to grin.

ghigno *sm.* grin.

ghìngheri (*nella loc. avv.*) *mettersi in* —, to dress up.

ghiotto *agg.* 1. greedy 2. (*appetitoso*) dainty.

ghiottone *sm.* glutton.

ghiottonerìa *sf.* 1. gluttony 2. (*cibo prelibato*) dainty.

ghiribizzo *sm.* whim.

ghirigoro *sm.* doodle.

ghirlanda *sf.* wreath.

ghiro *sm.* dormouse (*pl.* dormice) || *dormire come un* —, to sleep (*v. irr.*) like a log.

ghisa *sf.* cast iron.

già *avv.* 1. already 2. (*un tempo*) once 3. (*certamente*) of course.

giacca *sf.* coat, jacket.

giacché *cong.* as, since.

giacente *agg.* 1. lying 2. (*di capitale*) uninvested 3. (*di posta*) unclaimed.

giacenza *sf.* lying || *capitale in* —, uninvested capital; *lettera in* —, unclaimed letter; *merci in* —, goods in stock.

giacere *vi.* to lie (*v. irr.*).

giaciglio *sm.* couch.

giacimento *sm.* (*min.*) deposit: — *di petrolio*, oil-field.

giacinto *sm.* hyacinth.

giacobino *sm. e agg.* Jacobin.

giada *sf.* jade.

giaggiolo *sm.* iris.

giaguaro *sm.* jaguar.

giallastro *agg.* yellowish.

giallo *agg.* yellow || *romanzo, film, dramma* —, thriller.

giammai *avv.* never.

giansenismo *sm.* Jansenism.

giansenista *s.* Jansenist.

giapponese *agg. e sm.* Japanese (*invariato al pl.*).

giara *sf.* jar.

giardinaggio *sm.* gardening.

giardinetta *sf.* station wagon.

giardiniere *sm.* gardener.

giardino *sm.* garden || — *d'infanzia*, nursery-school.

giarrettiera *sf.* garter.

giavellotto *sm.* javelin: *lancio del* —, javelin throwing.

gibbosità *sf.* hump.

giberna *sf.* cartridge-pouch.

gigante *sm.* giant || *fare passi da* —, to make (*v. irr.*) rapid progress.

giganteggiare *vi.* to tower.

gigantesco *agg.* gigantic.

gigantismo *sm.* giantism.

gigione *sm.* ham.

giglio *sm.* lily.

gilè *sm.* waistcoat.

gincana *sf.* gymkhana.

gineceo *sm.* gynaeceum (*pl.* -ea).

ginecologìa *sf.* gynaecology.

ginecològico *agg.* gynaecological.

ginecòlogo *sm.* gynaecologist.

ginepraio *sm.* 1. juniper thicket 2. (*fig.*) fix: *ficcarsi in un* —, to get (*v. irr.*) into a scrape.

ginepro *sm.* juniper.

ginestra *sf.* broom.

gingillarsi *vr.* to dawdle.

gingillo *sm.* 1. knick-knack 2. (*balocco*) plaything.

ginnasio *sm.* 1. grammar school 2.

(*in Italia e stor.*) gymnasium (*pl.* -ia).

ginnasta *sm.* athlete.

ginnàstica *sf.* gymnastics.

gìnnico *agg.* gymnastic, athletic.

ginocchiata *sf.* blow with the knee.

ginocchiera *sf.* **1.** knee-guard **2.** (*mecc.*) toggle.

ginocchio *sm.* **1.** knee: *in* —, on one's knees **2.** (*mecc.*) bend.

ginocchioni *avv.* on one's knees.

giocare *vi.* **1.** to play **2.** (*d'azzardo*) to gamble **3.** (*scommettere*) to bet (*v. irr.*) **4.** (*in borsa*) to speculate. ◆ **giocare** *vt.* **1.** to play **2.** (*ingannare*) to deceive. ◆ **giocarsi** *vr.* (*beffarsi*) to trifle (with).

giocata *sf.* **1.** game **2.** (*puntata*) stake.

giocatore *sm.* **1.** player **2.** (*d'azzardo*) gambler **3.** (*in borsa*) stock- -jobber.

giocàttolo *sm.* toy.

giocherellare *vi.* to toy.

gioco *sm.* **1.** play **2.** (*regolato da norme*) game **3.** (*d'azzardo*) gambling **4.** (*scherzo*) joke || *per* —, for fun; — *di pazienza*, puzzle; — *di parole*, pun; *essere in* —, to be involved.

giocoforza *sm.* necessary: *è* —, it is absolutely necessary.

giocoliere *sm.* juggler.

giocondità *sf.* gaiety.

giocondo *agg.* gay.

giocosità *sf.* playfulness.

giocoso *agg.* playful.

giogaia *sf.* mountain range.

giogo *sm.* **1.** yoke **2.** (*di monte*) summit.

gioia *sf.* **1.** joy **2.** (*gioiello*) jewel.

gioiellerìa *sf.* **1.** jewelry **2.** (*negozio*) jeweller's shop.

gioielliere *sm.* jeweller.

gioiello *sm.* jewel.

gioioso *agg.* joyful.

gioire *vi.* to rejoice (at).

giornalaio *sm.* newsman (*pl.* -men).

giornale *sm.* **1.** newspaper **2.** (*comm.*) journal || — *radio*, news bulletin; *cine* —, news-reel.

giornaliero *agg.* daily.

giornalismo *sm.* **1.** journalism **2.** (*la stampa*) press.

giornalista *s.* journalist, reporter.

giornalìstico *agg.* journalistic || *ambiente* —, press.

giornalmente *avv.* daily.

giornata *sf.* day: *lavorare a* —, to work by the day || *donna a* —, charwoman (*pl.* -women).

giorno *sm.* day: *di* —, by day; *a giorni*, in a few days' time; *due volte al* —, twice a day; *un* — (*avv.*), one day || — *festivo*, holiday.

giovamento *sm.* benefit || *trarre* — *da*, to benefit by.

giòvane *agg.* young. ◆ **giòvane** *sm.* young man (*pl.* -men). ◆ **giòvane** *sf.* young woman (*pl.* women).

giovanetta *sf.* girl.

giovanetto *sm.* boy.

giovanile *agg.* **1.** juvenile **2.** (*da giovane*) youthful.

giovanotto *sm.* young man (*pl.* men).

giovare *vi.* to be of use. ◆ **giovare** *vt.* to be good (for). ◆ **giovarsi** *vr.* to benefit (by).

giovedì *sm.* Thursday.

giovenca *sf.* heifer.

gioventù *sf.* youth.

gioviale *agg.* jolly.

giovialità *sf.* jollity.

giovinastro *sm.* hooligan.

giovincello *sm.* lad.

giovinezza *sf.* youth.

giràbile *agg.* endorsable.

giradischi *sm.* record player.

giradito *sm.* whitlow.

giraffa *sf.* giraffe.

giramento *sm.* turning: — *di capo*, giddiness; *avere un* —, to feel (*v. irr.*) giddy.

giramondo *sm.* **1.** wanderer **2.** (*turista*) globe-trotter.

giràndola *sf.* **1.** (*fuoco d'artificio*) Catherine-wheel **2.** (*fig.*) fickle person.

girandolare *vi.* to saunter.

girandolone *sm.* saunterer.

girante *sm.* **1.** (*comm.*) endorser **2.** (*mecc.*) impeller (*di pompa*), wheel (*di turbina*).

girare *vi.* e *vt.* **1.** to turn **2.** (*evitare*) to avoid **3.** (*viaggiare*) to tour **4.** (*vagare*) to stroll **5.** (*comm.*) to endorse **6.** (*riprendere un film*) to shoot (*v. irr.*). ◆ **girarsi** *vr.* to turn.

girarrosto *sm.* spit.

girasole *sm.* sunflower.

girata *sf.* **1.** turn **2.** (*comm.*) endorsement.

giratario *sm.* (*comm.*) endorsee.

giravolta sf. 1. turning 2. (fig.) shift || fare una —, to turn round.

girello sm. 1. (per bambini) go-cart 2. (parte di bue) rump.

giretto sm. stroll: fare un —, to take (v. irr.) a short walk.

girévole agg. revolving.

girino sm. tadpole.

giro sm. 1. turn 2. (viaggio) tour 3. (passeggiata) stroll 4. (percorso) round || a — di posta, by return of post; — d'affari, turnover; nel — di pochi giorni, in a few days' time; fare un — in auto, to go (v. irr.) for a drive in a car; fare un — in bicicletta, to take (v. irr.) a ride on a bicycle.

girondino agg. e sm. Girondist

gironzolare vi. to stroll.

giroscopio sm. gyroscope.

girotondo sm. round dance.

girovagare vi. to wander.

giròvago agg. wandering. ♦ giròvago sm. tramp || venditore —, pedlar.

gita sf. trip: fare una —, to take (v. irr.) a trip.

gitano sm. Spanish gipsy.

gitante s. tripper.

giù avv. 1. down 2. (dabbasso) downstairs || — per, down; su per —, approximately.

giubba sf. coat.

giubbetto sm. 1. jacket 2. (da donna) bodice.

giubbotto sm. (heavy) coat.

giubilare vi. to exult.

giubileo sm. jubilee.

giùbilo sm. rejoicing.

giudàico agg. Judaic.

giudaismo sm. Judaism.

giudeo agg. Jewish. ♦ giudeo sm. Jew. ♦ giudea sf. Jewess.

giudicare vt. 1. to judge 2. (pensare) to think (v. irr.).

giùdice sm. judge || i giudici, the Bench.

giudiziario agg. judicial.

giudizio sm. 1. judgement 2. (causa) trial 3. (sentenza) sentence 4. (buon senso) common sense || far —, to behave oneself; rinviare a —, to commit for trial.

giudizioso agg. sensible.

giùggiola sf. jujube || andare in brodo di giuggiole, to be extremely pleased.

giuggiolone sm. simpleton.

giugno sm. June.

giugulare agg. jugular.

giuliano agg. Julian.

giulivo agg. cheerful.

giullare sm. jester.

giumenta sf. (cavalla) mare.

giunca sf. junk.

giunco sm. reed.

giùngere vi. 1. to arrive (at), to reach (sthg.) 2. (riuscire) to succeed (in). ♦ giùngere vt. (congiungere) to join.

giungla sf. jungle.

giunta¹ sf. 1. addition: per —, in addition 2. (di peso) make-weight.

giunta² sf. — comunale, town council.

giunto sm. (mecc.) joint.

giuntura sf. juncture.

giunzione sf. 1. connection 2. (giunto) joint || fare una —, to joint.

giuramento sm. oath: sotto —, on oath.

giurare vt. to swear (v. irr.).

giurato sm. juryman (pl. -men) || i giurati, the jury (sing.).

giurìa sf. jury.

giurìdico agg. juridical: stato —, legal status.

giurisdizione sf. jurisdiction.

giurisprudenza sf. law.

giurista sm. jurist.

giustezza sf. 1. exactness 2. (tip.) measure.

giustificàbile agg. justifiable.

giustificare vt. to justify.

giustificazione sf. justification.

giustizia sf. justice.

giustiziare vt. to execute.

giustiziato sm. executed man.

giustiziere sm. 1. executioner 2. (vendicatore) avenger.

giusto agg. 1. just 2. (esatto) right 3. (legittimo) legitimate.

glabro agg. hairless.

glaciale agg. icy: regione —, ice region.

glaciazione sf. glaciation.

gladiatore sm. gladiator.

gladìolo sm. gladiolus.

glande sm. glans (pl. -ndes).

glàndola sf. V. ghiandola.

glandolare agg. glandular.

glassare vt. 1. (con zucchero) to ice 2. (con gelatina) to glaze.

glàuco agg. glaucous.

glaucoma sm. glaucoma.

gleba sf. clod || servo della —, serf.

gli[1] *art.* **1.** the **2.** (*in senso generico non si traduce*): — *stranieri amano l'Italia*, foreigners love Italy **3.** (*si traduce col possessivo coi capi di vestiario ecc.*): *si tolse — occhiali*, he took off his glasses.

gli[2] *pron.* **1.** (*per persona*) him, to him **2.** (*per cosa*) it, to it || — *mandai un libro*, I sent him a book, I sent a book to him.

glicerina *sf.* glycerine.

glicine *sm.* wistaria.

glicògeno *sm.* glycogen.

glielo *pron.* it (to) him; it (to) her; him to him; him to her; it to it.

globale *agg.* total.

globo *sm.* globe.

globulare *agg.* globular.

glòbulo *sm.* (*biol.*) corpuscle.

gloria *sf.* glory.

gloriarsi *vr.* to glory (in).

glorificare *vt.* to glorify.

glorificazione *sf.* glorification.

glorioso *agg.* glorious.

glossa *sf.* gloss.

glossario *sm.* glossary.

glòttide *sf.* glottis.

glottologìa *sf.* glottology.

glottològico *agg.* glottological.

glottòlogo *sm.* glottologist.

glucosio *sm.* glucose.

glùteo *sm.* gluteus (*pl.* -ei).

glutinato *agg.* gluten (*attr.*).

glutine *sm.* gluten.

gnomo *sm.* gnome.

gnosticismo *sm.* gnosticism.

gnòstico *agg.* e *sm.* gnostic.

gobba *sf.* **1.** hump (*anche fig.*) **2.** (*donna —*) humpbacked woman.

gobbo *agg.* **1.** humpbacked **2.** (*curvo*) bent. ♦ **gobbo** *sm.* humpback.

goccia *sf.* **goccio** *sm.* drop.

gocciolare *vi.* e *vt.* to drip.

gocciolìo *sm.* dripping.

godere *vi.* e *vt.* to enjoy || *godersela*, to have a good time.

godereccio *agg.* **1.** (*amante dei godimenti*) pleasure-loving **2.** (*che dà godimento*) pleasant.

godimento *sm.* enjoyment.

goffàggine *sf.* **1.** clumsiness **2.** (*atto goffo*) clumsy action.

goffo *agg.* clumsy.

gogna *sf.* pillory: *mettere alla —*, to pillory.

?ola *sf.* **1.** throat: *aver mal di —*, to have a sorethroat **2.** (*golosità*) gluttony: *far —*, to tempt **3.** (*geogr.*) gorge.

goletta *sf.* (*mar.*) schooner.

golf *sm.* **1.** jersey **2.** (*gioco*) golf.

golfo *sm.* gulf.

goliàrdico *agg.* of students.

goliardo *sm.* university student.

golosità *sf.* **1.** greediness **2.** (*cibo prelibato*) dainty.

goloso *agg.* greedy. ♦ **goloso** *sm.* glutton.

gòmena *sf.* rope.

gomitata *sf.* nudge || *farsi avanti a gomitate*, to elbow one's way.

gòmito *sm.* **1.** elbow **2.** (*di strada*) sharp bend || — *a —*, side by side.

gomìtolo *sm.* clew.

gomma *sf.* **1.** rubber **2.** (*sostanza resinosa*) gum **3.** (*pneumatico*) tyre.

gommapiuma *sf.* foam rubber.

gòndola *sf.* gondola.

gonfalone *sm.* standard.

gonfiare *vt.* **1.** to swell (*v. irr.*) **2.** (*esagerare*) to exaggerate. ♦ **gonfiarsi** *vr.* to swell (*anche fig.*).

gonfiatura *sf.* **1.** swelling **2.** (*esagerazione*) exaggeration.

gonfio *agg.* **1.** swollen **2.** (*di stile*) bombastic.

gonfiore *sm.* swelling.

gong *sm.* gong.

gongolante *agg.* rejoicing (at).

gongolare *vi.* to rejoice (at).

goniòmetro *sm.* goniometer.

gonna *sf.* **1.** skirt **2.** (*di costume storico anche maschile*) gown.

gonnellino *sm.* — *scozzese*, kilt.

gonzo *sm.* blockhead.

gorgheggiare *vi.* to trill.

gorgheggio *sm.* trill.

gorgo *sm.* whirlpool.

gorgogliare *vi.* to gurgle.

gorgoglio *sm.* gurgling.

gorilla *sm.* gorilla.

gota *sf.* cheek.

gòtico *agg.* Gothic.

gotta *sf.* gout.

governàbile *agg.* governable.

governante *sm.* **1.** ruler **2.** (*statista*) statesman (*pl.* -men). ♦ **governante** *sf.* **1.** housekeeper **2.** (*bambinaia*) nurse.

governare *vt.* **1.** to govern, to rule **2.** (*badare a*) to look after **3.** (*mar.*) to steer.

governativo *agg.* government (*attributivo*).

governatore *sm.* governor.

governo *sm.* **1.** government **2.** (*dominio*) rule **3.** (*comm.*) management **4.** (*mar.*) steerage || — *della* *casa,* housekeeping.

gozzo *sm.* 1. goitre 2. *(di uccello)* crop.

gozzoviglia *sf.* revelry.

gozzovigliare *vi.* to revel.

gozzuto *agg.* goitrous.

gracchiare *vi.* to croak.

gracidare *vi.* to croak.

gracidìo *sm.* croaking.

gràcile *agg.* frail.

gracilità *sf.* frailty.

gradassata *sf.* boastfulness, brag.

gradasso *sm.* boaster, braggart.

gradatamente *avv.* gradually.

gradazione *sf.* 1. gradation 2. *(sfumatura)* shade.

gradévole *agg.* agreeable.

gradimento *sm.* 1. pleasure 2. satisfaction 3. *(approvazione)* approval.

gradinata *sf.* 1. flight of steps 2. *(negli stadi)* tiers of seats.

gradino *sm.* 1. step 2. *(di stadio)* stage.

gradire *vt.* 1. to like 2. *(accettare)* to accept.

gradito *agg.* 1. *(piacevole)* pleasant 2. *(ben accetto)* welcome.

grado *sm.* 1. degree 2. *(mil.)* rank || *essere in* —, to be able; *di buon* —, willingly.

graduale *agg.* gradual.

gradualità *sf.* graduality.

graduare *vt.* to graduate.

graduato *agg.* 1. graded 2. *(di strumento)* graduated. ♦ **graduato** *sm.* non-commissioned officer.

graduatoria *sf.* 1. classification 2. *(sport)* position.

graduazione *sf.* graduation.

graffa *sf.* clip.

graffiare *vt.* to scratch.

graffiatura *sf.* scratch.

graffio *sm.* scratch.

graffito *sm.* graffito *(pl.* -ti).

grafìa *sf.* 1. writing 2. *(ortografia)* spelling.

gràfico *agg.* graphic. ♦ **gràfico** *sm.* graph.

grafite *sf.* graphite.

grafologìa *sf.* graphology.

grafòlogo *sm.* graphologist.

grafòmane *s.* graphomaniac.

grafomanìa *sf.* graphomania.

gragnuola *sf.* 1. hail 2. *(fig.)* shower.

gramaglie *sf. pl.* mourning *(sing.):* *mettersi in* —, to go *(v. irr.)* into mourning.

gramigna *sf.* couch-grass.

graminàcee *sf. pl.* Gramineae.

grammàtica *sf.* grammar.

grammaticale *agg.* grammatical.

grammàtico *sm.* grammarian.

grammo *sm.* gram.

grammòfono *smi.* gramophone.

gramo *agg.* 1. miserable 2. *(scarso)* scanty.

grana *sf.* 1. grain 2. *(noia)* trouble 3. *(denaro)* dough.

granaglie *sf. pl.* corn *(sing.).*

granaio *sm.* barn.

granata[1] *sf.* *(scopa)* broom.

granata[2] *sf.* *(mil.)* grenade.

granatiere *sm.* grenadier.

granatina *sf.* grenadine.

granato *agg.* 1. garnet red 2. *(fatto a grani)* grainy.

grancassa *sf.* big drum.

granchio *sm.* crab || *prendere un* —, to make *(v. irr.)* a blunder.

grande *agg.* 1. great 2. *(esteso)* large 3. *(grosso)* big 4. *(alto)* high; *(di statura)* tall 5. *(adulto)* grownup.

grandeggiare *vi.* 1. to tower 2. *(ostentare)* to show *(v. irr.)* off.

grandezza *sf.* 1. greatness 2. *(dimensione)* size 3. *(estensione)* largeness 4. *(grandiosità)* grandeur 5. *(liberalità)* liberality 6. *(mat.)* quantity.

grandiloquenza *sf.* magniloquence.

grandinare *vi.* to hail *(anche fig.).*

grandinata *sf.* hail-storm.

gràndine *sf.* hail.

grandiosità *sf.* grandeur.

grandioso *agg.* grand.

granduca *sm.* Grand Duke.

granducato *sm.* Grand Duchy.

granduchessa *sf.* Grand Duchess.

granello *sm.* grain.

granita *sf.* grated-ice drink.

granìtico *agg.* granitic.

granito *sm.* granite.

granìvoro *agg.* granivorous.

grano *sm.* 1. grain 2. *(frumento)* wheat 3. *(ogni cereale)* corn.

granturco *sm.* maize.

granulare *agg.* granular.

granuloma *sm.* granuloma.

granuloso *agg.* granulose.

grappa[1] *sf.* *(per unire blocchi di legno ecc.)* cramp.

grappa[2] *sf.* *(liquore)* "grappa".

gràppolo *sm.* cluster.

grassaggio *sm.* greasing.

grassatore *sm.* robber.

grassazione *sf.* robbery.

grassetto *sm.* (*tip.*) heavytype.

grassezza *sf.* fatness.

grasso *agg.* fat. ♦ **grasso** *sm.* **1.** fat **2.** (*lubrificante*) grease.

grassoccio *agg.* plump.

grata *sf.* grating.

graticciata *sf.* trellis-work.

graticola *sf.* **1.** grill **2.** (*di forno*) grate.

graticolato *sm.* **1.** trellis **2.** (*inferriata*) grating.

gratifica *sf.* bonus.

gratificare *vt.* to gratify.

gratificazione *sf.* gratuity.

gratis *avv.* free.

gratitùdine *sf.* gratitude.

grato *agg.* **1.** grateful **2.** (*gradito*) welcome **3.** (*piacevole*) pleasant.

grattacapo *sm.* trouble.

grattacielo *sm.* skyscraper.

grattare *vt.* **1.** to scratch **2.** (*grattugiare*) to grate.

grattugia *sf.* grater.

grattugiare *vt.* to grate.

gratùito *agg.* **1.** free **2.** (*ingiustificato*) gratuitous.

gravame *sm.* **1.** burden **2.** (*ipoteca*) mortgage.

gravare *vi.* to weigh. ♦ **gravare** *vt.* to burden.

grave *agg.* **1.** grave **2.** (*pesante*) heavy **3.** (*importante, pericoloso*) serious.

gravezza *sf.* **1.** (*pesantezza*) heaviness **2.** (*serietà*) gravity **3.** (*stanchezza*) weariness.

gravidanza *sf.* pregnancy.

gràvido *agg.* **1.** (*di femmina*) pregnant **2.** (*fig.*) fraught (with).

gravità *sf.* **1.** gravity **2.** (*severità*) severity.

gravitare *vi.* to gravitate.

gravitazionale *agg.* gravitational.

gravitazione *sf.* gravitation.

gravosità *sf.* heaviness.

gravoso *agg.* heavy.

grazia *sf.* **1.** grace **2.** (*favore*) favour **3.** (*clemenza*) mercy **4.** (*teol.*) grace **5.** *Sua, Vostra Grazia,* His, Her, Your Grace || *in — di,* owing to.

graziare *vt.* to pardon.

grazie *inter.* thank you!, thanks! *— tante,* many thanks!

grazioso *agg.* pretty, graceful.

greca *sf.* **1.** (*disegno*) Greek fret **2.** (*mil.*) zig-zag braid.

grecale *sm.* north-east wind.

grecismo *sm.* Hellenism.

grecista *s.* Hellenist.

greco *agg.* e *sm.* Greek.

greco-romano *agg.* Graeco-Roman.

gregario *sm.* **1.** follower **2.** (*aiutante*) helper.

gregge *sm.* flock.

greggio *agg.* **1.** raw **2.** (*di tessuto*) unbleached **3.** (*di metallo e fig.*) unrefined.

gregoriano *agg.* Gregorian.

grembiale, grembiule *sm.* apron.

grembo *sm.* **1.** lap **2.** (*ventre materno*) womb **3.** (*fig.*) bosom.

gremire *vt.* to fill.

gremito *agg.* filled (with).

greppia *sf.* crib.

gres *sm.* stoneware.

greto *sm.* **1.** (*di fiume*) gravel bank **2.** (*di mare*) shingly shore.

grettezza *sf.* meanness.

gretto *agg.* mean, narrow-minded.

greve *agg.* heavy.

grezzo *agg.* V. greggio.

gridare *vt.* e *vi.* **1.** to cry **2.** (*gridare forte, protestare*) to cry out: *gridò per il dolore,* he cried out with pain.

grido *sm.* cry || *di —,* famous.

grifagno *agg.* **1.** rapacious **2.** (*fig.*) fierce.

grifo *sm.* snout.

grifone *sm.* griffin.

grigiastro *agg.* greyish.

grigio *agg.* grey: *— perla,* pearl grey.

grigiore *sm.* greyness.

griglia *sf.* **1.** (*di finestra*) shutter **2.** (*di forno*) grate **3.** (*grata, graticola*) grill || *cuocere alla —,* to grill.

grilletto *sm.* trigger.

grillo *sm.* **1.** cricket **2.** (*fig.*) fancy.

grillotalpa *sm.* mole-cricket.

grimaldello *sm.* picklock.

grinfia *sf.* clutch.

grinta *sf.* grim face.

grinza *sf.* **1.** (*di pelle*) wrinkle **2.** (*di stoffa*) crease || (*fig.*) *non fa una —,* it is quite correct.

grinzoso *agg.* **1.** (*di pelle*) wrinkly **2.** (*di stoffa*) creasy.

grisù *sm.* fire-damp.

gronda *sf.* eaves (*pl.*).

grondaia *sf.* **1.** gutter **2.** (*tubo di discesa*) gutter pipe.

grondante *agg.* dripping.

grondare *vi.* to drip || *— sangue,* to bleed (*v. irr.*).

groppa *sf.* back.

groppo *sm.* knot: *avere un — in gola,* to have a lump in one's throat.

groppone *sm.* back: *piegare il —,* to submit.

grossa *sf. dormire della —,* tó sleep (*v. irr.*) soundly.

grossezza *sf.* 1. bigness 2. (*dimensione*) size 3. (*spessore*) thickness.

grossista *s.* wholesaler.

grosso *agg.* 1. (*anche fig.*) big 2. (*denso*) thick.

grossolanità *sf.* coarseness.

grossolano *agg.* coarse: *errore —,* blunder.

grotta *sf.* cave.

grottesco *agg.* grotesque.

groviera *sf.* gruyère.

groviglio *sm.* tangle.

gru *sf.* (*zool.; mecc.*) crane.

gruccia *sf.* 1. crutch 2. (*per abiti*) dress-hanger 3. (*per uccelli*) perch.

grufolare *vi.* to root.

grugnire *vi.* to grunt.

grugnito *sm.* grunt.

grugno *sm.* snout.

grumo *sm.* clot.

grumoso *agg.* clotted.

gruppo *sm.* group.

grùzzolo *sm.* hoard; (*risparmi*) savings (*pl.*).

guadàbile *agg.* fordable.

guadagnare *vt.* 1. to gain 2. (*col lavoro*) to earn.

guadagno *sm.* 1. earnings (*pl.*) 2. (*comm.*) profits (*pl.*) 3. (*fig.*) gain.

guadare *vt.* to ford.

guado *sm.* ford.

guai *inter.* woe!

guaina *sf.* 1. (*bot.; fodero per armi*) sheath 2. (*custodia, astuccio*) case 3. (*anat.*) theca (*pl.* -ae).

guaio *sm.* trouble.

guaire *vi.* to yelp.

guaito *sm.* yelp.

gualcire *vt.* to rumple.

gualdrappa *sf.* saddle-cloth.

guancia *sf.* cheek.

guanciale *sm.* pillow || *dormire fra due guanciali,* to have no worries.

guantaio *sm.* glover.

guantiera *sf.* 1. (*scatola per guanti*) glove-box 2. (*vassoio*) tray.

guantificio *sm.* glove-factory.

guanto *sm.* glove.

guantone *sm.* boxing-glove.

guardabarriere *sm.* gate-keeper.

guardaboschi *sm.* forester.

guardacaccia *sm.* gamekeeper.

guardacoste *sm.* coastguard.

guardalìnee *sm.* (*sport*) linesman (*pl.* -men).

guardamano *sm.* (*di scala*) hand--rail.

guardapesca *sm.* fishing warden.

guardaportone *sm.* doorkeeper.

guardare *vt.* 1. to look (at) 2. (*proteggere*) to protect. ♦ **guardare** *vi.* 1. (*tentare*) to try 2. (*essere orientato*) to face. ♦ **guardarsi** *vr.* (*da*), to beware (of).

guardaroba *sm.* 1. wardrobe 2. (*in teatro ecc.*) cloak-room.

guardarobiera *sf.* 1. (*nei locali pubblici*) cloak-room attendant 2. (*in alberghi e case private*) linen maid.

guardarobiere *sm.* (*nei locali pubblici*) cloak-room attendant.

guardasala *sm.* ticket-collector.

guardasigilli *sm.* keeper of the seals.

guardavìa *sm.* guard-rail.

guardia *sf.* guard || *— medica,* first-aid station; *fare la — a,* to guard; *mettere in —,* to warn.

guardiamarina *sm.* midshipman (*pl.* -men).

guardiano *sm.* 1. keeper 2. (*di armenti*) herdsman (*pl.* -men) || *— notturno,* night watchman (*pl.* -men).

guardina *sf.* guard-room.

guardingo *agg.* wary.

guardiola *sf.* guard-room.

guarìbile *agg.* 1. curable 2. (*di ferita*) healable.

guarigione *sf.* recovery.

guarire *vt.* 1. to cure 2. (*una ferita*) to heal. ♦ **guarire** *vi.* 1. to recover 2. (*di ferita*) to heal.

guaritore *sm.* healer.

guarnigione *sf.* garrison.

guarnire *vt.* 1. to trim 2. (*cuc.*) to garnish 3. (*fornire*) to furnish 4. (*mecc.*) to pack.

guarnitu.a, guarnizione *sf.* 1. trimming 2. (*cuc.*) garniture 3. (*mecc.*) packing.

guasconata *sf.* gasconade.

guascone *agg. e sm.* (*anche fig.*) Gascon.

guastafeste *s.* kill-joy.

guastamestieri *sm.* bungler.

guastare *vt.* 1. to spoil (*v. irr.*) 2. (*danneggiare*) to damage.

guastatore *sm.* 1. destroyer 2. (*mil.*) sapper.

guasto *agg.* 1. damaged 2. (*marcio*) rotten 3. (*corrotto*) tainted 4. (*mecc.*) out of order.

guasto *sm.* 1. damage 2. (*mecc.*) breakdown || *ci deve essere un —*, there must be something wrong.

guatare *vt.* to gaze (at).

guazzabuglio *sm.* mess.

guazzare *vi.* 1. to paddle 2. (*rotolarsi*) to wallow 3. (*di liquidi in recipienti*) to splash about.

guazzo *sm.* (*pitt.*) gouache.

guelfo *agg.* e *sm.* Guelph.

guercio *agg.* squinting. ♦ **guercio** *sm.* squinter.

guerra *sf.* war.

guerrafondaio *sm.* warmonger.

guerreggiante *agg.* e *sm.* belligerent.

guerreggiare *vi.* to fight (*v. irr.*), to war.

guerresco *agg.* 1. war (*attr.*) 2. (*bellicoso*) warlike.

guerriero *agg.* warlike. ♦ **guerriero** *sm.* warrior.

guerriglia *sf.* guerrilla.

guerrigliero *sm.* 1. guerrilla 2. partisan.

gufo *sm.* owl.

guglia *sf.* spire.

gugliata *sf.* needleful.

guida *sf.* 1. guide 2. (*auto*) drive || *patente di —*, driving licence; *— telefonica*, telephone book.

guidare *vt.* 1. to guide 2. (*auto*) to drive (*v. irr.*).

guidatore *sm.* driver.

guidoslitta *sf.* bobsleigh.

guinzaglio *sm.* leash: *mettere al —*, to leash.

guisa *sf.* manner || *a — di*, like.

guitto *sm.* strolling player.

guizzante *agg.* 1. darting 2. (*di luce*) flashing 3. (*di pesci*) wriggling.

guizzare *vi.* 1. to dart 2. (*di luce*) to flash 3. (*di pesci*) to wriggle.

guizzo *sm.* 1. dart 2. (*di luce*) flash 3. (*di pesci*) wriggle.

guscio *sm.* shell.

gustare *vt.* 1. to enjoy 2. (*assaggiare*) to taste.

gustativo *agg.* gustative.

gustatore *sm.* taster.

gusto *sm.* 1. taste 2. (*gradimento*) liking || *di, con —*, with relish.

gustoso *agg.* 1. (*saporito*) tasty 2. (*piacevole*) pleasant.

guttaperca *sf.* gutta-percha.

gutturale *agg.* guttural.

H

harem *sm.* harem.

hascisc *sm.* hashish.

hawaiano *agg.* e *sm.* Hawaiian.

hurrà *inter.* hurrah.

i *art.* the.

iarda *sf.* yard.

iato *sm.* hiatus.

iattanza *sf.* boastfulness.

iattura *sf.* misfortune.

ibèrico *agg.* e *sm.* Iberian.

ibernazione *sf.* hibernation.

ibisco *sm.* hibiscus.

ibridazione *sf.* hybridization.

ibridismo *sm.* hybridism.

ìbrido *agg.* e *sm.* hybrid.

icona *sf.* icon.

iconoclasta *sm.* iconoclast.

idea *sf.* idea.

ideàbile *agg.* imaginable.

ideale *agg.* e *sm.* ideal.

idealismo *sm.* idealism.

idealista *s.* idealist.

idealìstico *agg.* idealistic.

idealizzare *vt.* to idealize.

idealizzazione *sf.* idealization.

ideare *vt.* to conceive, to devise.

ideatore *sm.* inventor, deviser.

ideazione *sf.* ideation.

idèntico *agg.* identic.

identificàbile *agg.* identifiable.

identificare *vt.* to identify.

identificazione *sf.* identification.

identità *sf.* identity.

ideografia *sf.* ideography.

ideogramma *sm.* ideogram.

ideologìa *sf.* ideology.

ideològico *agg.* ideologic(al).

ideologismo *sm.* ideology.

ideòlogo *sm.* ideologist.

idìlliaco *agg.* idyllic.

idillio *sm.* idyl.

idioma *sm.* language.

idiomàtico *agg.* idiomatic.

idiosincrasìa *sf.* idiosyncrasy.

idiota *sm.* idiot. ♦ **idiota** *agg.* idiotic.

idiotismo *sm.* idiom.

idiozìa *sf.* idiocy.

idolatra *sm.* idolater.

idolatrare vt. to worship.
idolatrìa sf. idolatry.
ìdolo sm. idol.
idoneità sf. fitness.
idòneo agg. fit.
idrante sm. hydrant.
idratare vt. to hydrate.
idrato sm. hydrate.
idràulica sf. hydraulics.
idràulico agg. hydraulic. ♦ **idràulico** sm. plumber.
ìdrico agg. water.
idrocarburo sm. hydrocarbon.
idrocefalìa sf. hydrocephalus.
idrocèfalo sm. hydrocephalus.
idroelèttrico agg. hydroelectric.
idròfilo agg. absorbent: *cotone* —, cotton wool.
idrofobìa sf. rabies.
idròfobo agg. 1. rabid 2. (*fig.*) furious.
idrògeno sm. hydrogen.
idrografìa sf. hydrography.
idròlisi sf. hydrolysis (*pl.* -ses).
idrologìa sf. hydrology.
idròpico agg. dropsical.
idropisìa sf. dropsy.
idroscalo sm. seaplane station.
idrostàtica sf. hydrostatics.
idrovolante sm. seaplane.
idròvora sf. water-scooping machine.
iella sf. bad luck.
iena sf. 1. hyaena 2. (*fig.*) vixen.
ieràtico agg. hieratic(al).
ieri avv. yesterday.
iettatore sm. evil-eyed man.
iettatura sf. evil-eye.
igiene sf. 1. hygiene 2. (*sistema sanitario*) sanitation.
igiènico agg. sanitary.
igienista s. hygienist.
ignaro agg. ignorant.
ignavia sf. laziness.
ignavo agg. lazy.
igneo agg. igneous.
ignòbile agg. mean.
ignominia sf. ignominy.
ignominioso agg. ignominious.
ignorante agg. e sm. ignorant.
ignoranza sf. ignorance.
ignorare vt. to ignore.
ignoto agg. unknown.
ignudo agg. naked.
igrometrìa sf. hygrometry.
iguana sf. iguana.
il art. the.
ilare agg. cheerful.
ilarità sf. hilarity.

ilìaco agg. iliac.
illanguidire vt. to weaken.
illazione sf. illation.
illécito agg. illicit.
illegale agg. illegal.
illegalità sf. illegality.
illeggìbile agg. illegible.
illegittimità sf. illegitimacy.
illegìttimo agg. illegitimate.
illeso agg. unhurt.
illibatezza sf. purity.
illibato agg. pure.
illiberale agg. illiberal.
illimitato agg. unlimited.
illividire vt. to make (*v. irr.*) livid. ♦ **illividire** vi. to turn livid.
illogicità sf. illogicality.
illogico agg. illogical.
illùdere vt. to delude. ♦ **illùdersi** vr. to delude oneself.
illuminante agg. illuminating.
illuminare vt. to light up.
illuminazione sf. lighting.
illuminismo sm. Illuminism.
illusione sf. illusion.
illusionismo sm. illusionism.
illusionista s. conjurer.
illuso agg. deluded. ♦ **illuso** sm. day-dreamer.
illusorio agg. illusory.
illustrare vt. to illustrate.
illustrativo agg. illustrative.
illustrato agg. illustrated || *cartolina illustrata*, picture post-card.
illustrazione sf. illustration.
illustre agg. renowned.
imbacuccare vt. to muffle up.
imbaldanzire vt. to embolden. ♦ **imbaldanzirsi** vr. to grow (*v. irr.*) bold.
'mballaggio sm. packing.
imballare vt. to pack (up). ♦ **imballarsi** vr. (*di motori*) to race.
imbalsamare vt. 1. to embalm 2. (*di animali*) to stuff.
imbalsamatore sm. 1. embalmer 2. (*di animali*) stuffer.
imbalsamazione sf. 1. embalming 2. (*di animali*) stuffing.
imbambolato agg. dull.
imbandierare vt. to deck with flags.
imbandire vt. 1. (*la tavola*) to lay (*v. irr.*) 2. to prepare.
imbarazzante agg. embarrassing.
imbarazzare vt. to embarrass. ♦ **imbarazzarsi** vr. to meddle.
imbarazzato agg. embarrassed.
imbarazzo sm. embarrassment.

imbarcadero *sm.* landing-stage.
imbarcare *vt.* to take (*v. irr.*) on board. ♦ **imbarcarsi** *vr.* to embark.
imbarcazione *sf.* boat.
imbarco *sm.* embarkation.
imbastardire *vt.* to debase.
imbastardito *agg.* debased.
imbastire *vt.* 1. to tack 2. (*fig.*) to put (*v. irr.*) together.
imbastitura *sf.* tacking.
imbàttersi *vr.* to meet (*v. irr.*) (with).
imbattìbile *agg.* invincible.
imbattibilità *sf.* invincibility.
imbavagliare *vt.* to gag.
imbeccare *vt.* 1. to feed (*v. irr.*) 2. (*fig.*) to prompt.
imbeccata *sf.* 1. beakful 2. (*fig.*) prompting.
imbecille *agg.* e *sm.* imbecile.
imbecillità *sf.* imbecility.
imbelle *agg.* weak.
imbellettare *vt.* to make (*v. irr.*) up.
imbellire *vt.* to embellish.
imberbe *agg.* beardless.
imbestialire *vi.* to get (*v. irr.*) furious. ♦ **imbestialirsi** *vr.* to get furious.
imbévere *vt.* to imbue with.
imbiancamento *sm.* whitening.
imbiancare *vt.* 1. to whiten 2. (*i muri*) to whitewash.
imbiancatura *sf.* 1. (*di muri*) whitewashing 2. (*di tessuti*) bleaching.
imbianchino *sm.* house painter.
imbiondire *vt.* to make (*v. irr.*) fair. ♦ **imbiondire** *vi.* to become (*v. irr.*) fair.
imbizzarrirsi *vr.* 1. to become (*v. irr.*) restive 2. (*adirarsi*) to fire up.
imboccare *vt.* 1. to feed (*v. irr.*) 2. (*di strada*) to enter.
imboccatura *sf.* 1. mouth 2. (*di strumento*) mouthpiece.
imbonimento *sm.* sales talk.
imbonire *vt.* to allure.
imbonitore *sm.* charlatan.
imborghesimento *sm.* getting into middle-class habits.
imborghesire *vt.* to give (*v. irr.*) middle-class habits. ♦ **imborghesirsi** *vr.* to acquire middle-class habits.
imboscare *vt.* 1. to put (*v. irr.*) into safe keeping 2. (*mil.*) to help to evade military service. ♦ **im-**

boscarsi *vr.* 1. to lie (*v. irr.*) in ambush 2. (*mil.*) to evade military service.
imboscata *sf.* ambush.
imboscato *sm.* shirker.
imboschimento *sm.* afforestation.
imboschire *vt.* to afforest.
imbottigliamento *sm.* bottling ‖ — *stradale*, traffic jam.
imbottigliare *vt.* 1. to bottle 2. (*fig.*) to block.
imbottire *vt.* 1. to stuff 2. (*di vestiti*) to wad 3. (*fig.*) — *la testa*, to cram. ♦ **imbottirsi** *vr.* 1. to fill oneself (with), to stuff oneself (with) 2. (*coprirsi*) to wrap oneself (into).
imbottita *sf.* quilt.
imbottito *agg.* stuffed, filled ‖ *panino* —, sandwich.
imbottitura *sf.* 1. stuffing 2. (*di vestiti*) wadding.
imbracciare *vt.* 1. to put (*v. irr.*) sthg. on one's hands 2. (*di fucile*) to bring (*v. irr.*) to firing position.
imbrancare *vt.* to herd.
imbrattacarte *sm.* scribbler.
imbrattamento *sm.* soiling.
imbrattare *vt.* to soil.
imbrattatele *sm.* dauber.
imbrigliamento *sm.* bridling.
imbrigliare *vt.* to bridle.
imbrigliatura *sf.* bridling.
imbroccare *vt.* 1. to hit (*v. irr.*) 2. (*fig.*) to guess.
imbrogliare *vt.* 1. to cheat 2. (*confondere*) to confuse.
imbroglio *sm.* cheat, swindle.
imbroglione *sm.* cheat, swindler.
imbronciarsi *vr.* to pout.
imbronciato *agg.* sulky.
imbrunire *vi.* 1. to brown 2. (*farsi sera*) to get (*v. irr.*) dark.
imbrunire *sm.* nightfall.
imbruttire *vt.* to make (*v. irr.*) ugly. ♦ **imbruttirsi** *vr.* to become (*v. irr.*) ugly.
imbucare *vt.* to post.
imburrare *vt.* to butter.
imbuto *sm.* funnel.
imene *sm.* hymen.
imeneo *sm.* wedding.
imenòttero *sm.* hymenopteron (*pl.* -ra).
imitare *vt.* to imitate.
imitativo *agg.* imitative.
imitatore *sm.* imitator.
imitazione *sf.* imitation.

immacolato *agg.* spotless.
immagazzinare *vt.* to store (up).
immaginàbile *agg.* imaginable.
immaginare *vt.* to imagine.
immaginario *agg.* imaginary.
immaginativa *sf.* imagination.
immaginativo *agg.* imaginative.
immaginazione *sf.* imagination.
immàgine *sf.* image.
immalinconire *vt.* to make (*v. irr.*) melancholy. ◆ **immalinconire** *vi.* to grow (*v. irr.*) sad.
immancàbile *agg.* unfailing.
immane *agg.* 1. huge 2. (*fig.*) frightful.
immanente *agg.* immanent.
immanenza *sf.* immanence.
immangiàbile *agg.* uneatable.
immarcescìbile *agg.* incorruptible.
immateriale *agg.* immaterial.
immaterialità *sf.* immateriality.
immatricolare *vt.* to matriculate. ◆ **immatricolarsi** *vr.* to matriculate.
immatricolazione *sf.* matriculation.
immaturità *sf.* immaturity.
immaturo *agg.* 1. (*di frutto*) unripe 2. (*di persona*) immature.
immedesimare *vt.* 1. to unify. ◆ **immedesimarsi** *vr.* to identify oneself (with).
immedesimazione *sf.* unifying.
immediatamente *avv.* at once.
immediatezza *sf.* immediateness.
immediato *agg.* immediate.
immemoràbile *agg.* immemorial.
immèmore *agg.* forgetful.
immensità *sf.* immensity.
immenso *agg.* immense.
immèrgere *vt.* to immerse. ◆ **immèrgersi** *vr.* to immerse oneself.
immeritato *agg.* undeserved.
immeritévole *agg.* undeserving.
immersione *sf.* immersion.
immèttere *vt.* to let (*v. irr.*) in. ◆ **immèttersi** *vr.* to penetrate.
immigrante *agg. e sm.* immigrant.
immigrare *vi.* to immigrate.
immigrato *agg.* immigrated. ◆ **immigrato** *sm.* immigrant.
immigrazione *sf.* immigration.
imminente *agg.* impending.
imminenza *sf.* imminence.
immischiare *vt.* to involve. ◆ **immischiarsi** *vr.* to meddle (with).
immiserimento *sm.* impoverishing.
immiserire *vt.* to impoverish. ◆

immiserirsi *vr.* 1. to become (*v. irr.*) poor 2. (*fig.*) to weaken.
immissario *sm.* affluent.
immissione *sf.* letting in.
immòbile *agg.* immobile ‖ *beni immobili*, immovables.
immobiliare *agg.* immovable.
immobilismo *sm.* ultra-conservatism.
immobilità *sf.* immobility.
immobilizzare *vt.* 1. to immobilize 2. (*comm.*) to lock up.
immobilizzazione *sf.* 1. immobilization 2. (*comm.*) locking up.
immoderato *agg.* immoderate.
immodestia *sf.* immodesty.
immodesto *agg.* immodest.
immolare *vt.* to immolate.
immondezza *sf.* dirtiness.
immondezzaio *sm.* garbage heap.
immondizia *sf.* 1. filth 2. (*spazzatura*) garbage.
immondo *agg.* dirty.
immorale *agg.* immoral.
immoralità *sf.* immorality.
immortalare *vt.* to immortalize.
immortale *agg.* immortal.
immortalità *sf.* immortality.
immoto *agg.* motionless.
immune *agg.* immune.
immunità *sf.* immunity.
immunizzare *vt.* to immunize.
immunizzazione *sf.* immunization.
immusonirsi *vr.* to sulk.
immusonito *agg.* sulky.
immutàbile *agg.* immutable.
immutabilità *sf.* immutability.
impacchettare *vt.* to package.
impacciare *vt.* to hamper.
impacciato *agg.* 1. embarrassed 2. (*goffo*) awkward.
impaccio *sm.* hindrance.
impacco *sm.* compress.
impadronirsi *vr.* to take (*v. irr.*) possession (of).
impagàbile *agg.* priceless.
impaginare *vt.* to make-up.
impaginatore *sm.* maker-up.
impaginazione *sf.* making-up.
impagliare *vt.* 1. to cover with straw 2. (*di animali*) to stuff with straw.
impagliatore *sm.* 1. chair-mender 2. (*di animali*) stuffer.
impagliatura *sf.* 1. chair-mending 2. (*di animali*) stuffing.
impalare *vt.* to impale.
impalato *agg.* stiff.
impalcatura *sf.* 1. scaffolding 2.

(*di corna di cervo*) antlers (*pl.*).

impallidire *vi.* to turn pale.

impallinare *vt.* to shot.

impalmare *vt.* to marry.

impalpàbile *agg.* impalpable.

impalpabilità *sf.* impalpability.

impanare *vt.* **1.** (*cuc.*) to bread **2.** (*mecc.*) to thread.

impantanare *vt.* to swamp. ♦ **impantanarsi** *vr.* to swamp (*anche fig.*).

impaperarsi *vr.* to slip up.

impappinarsi *vr.* to stammer.

imparagonàbile *agg.* incomparable.

imparare *vt.* to learn (*v. irr.*).

impareggiàbile *agg.* unparalleled.

imparentare *vt.* to relate. ♦ **imparentarsi** *vr.* to become (*v. irr.*) related (to).

impari *agg.* unequal.

imparisillabo *agg. e sm.* imparisyllabic.

imparruccato *agg.* bewigged.

impartire *vt.* to impart.

imparziale *agg.* impartial.

imparzialità *sf.* impartiality.

impassìbile *agg.* impassive, unmoved.

impassibilità *sf.* impassibility.

impastare *vt.* to knead || — *i colori*, to impaste.

impastato *agg.* **1.** kneaded **2.** (*fig.*) full.

impastatore *sm.* kneader.

impastatrice *sf.* kneading-machine.

impasto *sm.* **1.** dough **2.** (*miscuglio*) mixture.

impastoiare *vt.* (*fig.*) to impede.

impatto *sm.* impact.

impaurire *vt.* to frighten. ♦ **impaurirsi** *vr.* to get (*v. irr.*) scared.

impaurito *agg.* afraid: *sguardo* —, fearful look.

impàvido *agg.* fearless.

impaziente *agg.* impatient.

impazientirsi *vr.* to lose (*v. irr.*) one's patience.

impazienza *sf.* impatience.

impazzare *vi.* to be at one's height.

impazzata (*nella loc. avv.*) all'—, madly.

impazzire *vi.* to go (*v. irr.*) mad.

impeccàbile *agg.* faultless.

impeciare *vt.* to pitch.

impedimento *sm.* obstacle.

impedire *vt.* to prevent (from).

impegnare *vt.* **1.** (*dare in pegno*) to pawn **2.** (*prenotare*) to reserve,

to book. ♦ **impegnarsi** *vr.* to engage (oneself).

impegnativo *agg.* binding || *lavoro* —, exacting job.

impegno *sm.* engagement.

impegolarsi *vr.* (*fig.*) to get (*v. irr.*) involved.

impelagarsi *vr.* to get (*v. irr.*) in trouble.

impellente *agg.* urgent.

impellicciare *vt.* to fur.

impellicciatura *sf.* veneering.

impenetràbile *agg.* impenetrable.

impenetrabilità *sf.* impenetrableness.

impenitente *agg.* impenitent.

impennacchiare *vt.* to plume.

impennarsi *vr.* **1.** (*di cavallo*) to rear **2.** (*fig.*) to rear up.

impennata *sf.* (*di cavallo*) rearing **2.** (*fig.*) bristling.

impensàbile *agg.* unthinkable.

impensato *agg.* unexpected.

impensierire *vt.* to worry.

imperante *agg.* ruling.

imperare *vi.* to rule (over).

imperativo *agg.* imperative.

imperatore *sm.* emperor.

imperatrice *sf.* empress.

impercettìbile *agg.* imperceptible.

impercettibilità *sf.* imperceptibility.

imperdonàbile *agg.* unpardonable.

imperfetto *agg.* **1.** (*gramm.*) imperfect **2.** (*fig.*) faulty.

imperfezione *sf.* imperfection.

imperiale[1] *agg.* imperial.

imperiale[2] *sm.* imperial.

imperialismo *sm.* imperialism.

imperialista *s.* imperialist.

imperialìstico *agg.* imperialistic

imperio *sm.* command, authority.

imperioso *agg.* imperious.

imperito *agg.* unskilful.

imperituro *agg.* everlasting.

imperizia *sf.* unskilfulness.

imperlare *vt.* to bead. ♦ **imperlarsi** *vr.* to bead.

impermalirsi *vr.* to resent (sthg.).

impermeàbile *agg.* impermeable. ♦ **impermeàbile** *sm.* raincoat.

impermeabilità *sf.* impermeability.

impermeabilizzare *vt.* to waterproof.

impermeabilizzazione *sf.* waterproofing.

imperniare *vt.* to pivot (upon).

impero *sm.* empire.

imperscrutàbile *agg.* inscrutable.

imperscrutabilità *sf.* inscrutableness.
impersonale *agg.* impersonal.
impersonalità *sf.* impersonality.
impersonare *vt.* to impersonate. ♦ impersonarsi *vr.* to materialize.
impertèrrito *agg.* undaunted.
impertinente *agg.* impertinent.
impertinenza *sf.* impertinence.
imperturbàbile *agg.* impassive.
imperturbabilità *sf.* imperturbability.
imperturbato *agg.* imperturbed.
imperversare *vi.* to rage.
impervio *agg.* inaccessible.
impeto *sm.* 1. rush, impetus 2. (*impulso*) impulse.
impetrare *vt.* to impetrate.
impettito *agg.* stiff.
impetuosità *sf.* impetuosity.
impetuoso *agg.* impetuous.
impiantare *vt.* to found.
impiantito *sm.* 1. (*di legno*) parquet floor 2. (*di piastrelle*) tiled floor.
impianto *sm.* plant, installation.
impiastricciare *vt.* to daub.
impiastro *sm.* 1. plaster 2. (*fig.*) bore.
impiccagione *sf.* hanging.
impiccare *vt.* to hang.
impiccato *agg.* hanged. ♦ impiccato *sm.* hanged man.
impicciare *vt.* to hinder. ♦ impicciarsi *vr.* to meddle (in).
impiccio *sm.* hindrance.
impiccolire *vt.* to make (*v. irr.*) smaller.
impiegare *vt.* 1. to employ 2. (*spendere*) to spend (*v. irr.*) 3. (*comm.*) to invest.
impiegatizio *agg.* white-collar (*attributivo*).
impiegato *agg.* employed. ♦ impiegato *sm.* employee, clerk.
impiego *sm.* 1. employment 2. (*uso*) use.
impietosire *vt.* to move to pity. ♦ impietosirsi *vr.* to feel (*v. irr.*) sorry (for).
impietrire *vt.* to petrify.
impigliare *vt.* to entangle.
impigrire *vt.* to make (*v. irr.*) lazy.
impinguare *vt.* 1. to fatten 2. (*fig.*) to enrich.
impiombare *vt.* 1. to plumb 2. (*otturare*) to fill 3. (*coprire di piombo*) to lead.
impiombatura *sf.* 1. plumbing 2.

(*otturazione*) filling 3. (*copertura di piombo*) leading.
implacàbile *agg.* implacable.
implacabilità *sf.* implacability.
implicare *vt.* to involve.
implìcito *agg.* implicit.
implorare *vt.* to implore.
implorazione *sf.* entreaty.
implume *agg.* featherless.
impolìtico *agg.* impolitic.
impollinare *vt.* to pollinate.
impollinazione *sf.* pollination.
impoltronire *vt.* to make (*v. irr.*) lazy. ♦ impoltronirsi *vr.* to grow (*v. irr.*) lazy.
impolverare *vt.* to cover with dust.
impolverato *agg.* dusty.
impomatare *vt.* to pomade. ♦ impomatarsi *vr.* to pomade oneself.
imponderàbile *agg.* imponderable.
imponderabilità *sf.* imponderability.
imponente *agg.* imposing.
imponenza *sf.* grandeur, majesty.
imponìbile *agg.* taxable.
imponibilità *sf.* taxability.
impopolare *agg.* unpopular.
impopolarità *sf.* unpopularity.
imporporarsi *vr.* to purple.
imporre *vt.* to impose: — *un nome*, to give (*v. irr.*) a name. ♦ imporsi *vr.* 1. to impose oneself 2. (*avere successo*) to become (*v. irr.*) popular.
importante *agg.* important.
importanza *sf.* importance.
importare *vi. imp.* to matter, to care. ♦ importare *vt.* (*comm.*) to import.
importatore *sm.* importer.
importazione *sf.* import.
importo *sm.* amount.
importunare *vt.* to importune, to bother.
importunità *sf.* importunity.
importuno *agg.* boring. ♦ importuno *sm.* bore.
imposizione *sf.* imposition.
impossessarsi *vr.* to take (*v. irr.*) possession (of).
impossìbile *agg.* impossible.
impossibilità *sf.* impossibility.
impossibilitato *agg.* unable.
imposta *sf.* 1. tax 2. (*edil.*) shutter.
impostare *vt.* 1. to start 2. (*di lettera*) to post.
impostazione *sf.* general lines (*pl.*).
impostore *sm.* impostor.

impostura *sf.* 1. imposture 2. (*frode*) fraud.
impotente *agg.* powerless. ♦ **impotente** *agg. e sm.* (*med.*) impotent.
impotenza *sf.* impotence.
impoverimento *sm.* impoverishment.
impoverire *vt.* to impoverish. ♦ **impoverirsi** *vr.* to become (*v. irr.*) poor.
impraticàbile *agg.* impracticable: *strada* —, impassable road.
impraticabilità *sf.* impracticability.
impratichire *vt.* to train. ♦ **impratichirsi** *vr.* to get (*v. irr.*) trained.
imprecare *vi.* to curse.
imprecazione *sf.* curse.
imprecisàbile *agg.* indeterminable.
imprecisato *agg.* undetermined.
imprecisione *sf.* 1. vagueness 2. (*inesattezza*) inaccuracy.
impreciso *agg.* inaccurate.
impregnare *vt.* to impregnate (with). ♦ **impregnarsi** *vr.* to become (*v. irr.*) imbued (with).
imprèndere *vt.* to undertake (*v. irr.*).
imprendìbile *agg.* elusive, invincible.
imprenditore *sm.* 1. entrepreneur 2. (*edil.*) contractor.
impreparato *agg.* unprepared.
impreparazione *sf.* unpreparedness.
impresa *sf.* 1. (*iniziativa*) undertaking 2. (*gesta*) deed 3. (*azienda*) firm, company.
impresario *sm.* 1. contractor 2. (*teat.*) manager.
imprescindìbile *agg.* unavoidable.
imprescrittìbile *agg.* indefeasible.
impressionàbile *agg.* impressionable.
impressionabilità *sf.* impressionability.
impressionante *agg.* frightening.
impressionare *vt.* 1. to impress 2. (*foto*) to expose.
impressione *sf.* impression.
impressionismo *sm.* impressionism.
impressionista *s.* impressionist.
impresso *agg.* printed.
imprestare *vt.* to lend (*v. irr.*).
imprevedìbile *agg.* unforeseeable.
impreveduto *agg.* unforeseen.
imprevidente *agg.* improvident.

imprevidenza *sf.* improvidence.
imprevisto *agg.* unexpected. ♦ **imprevisto** *sm.* unforeseen event.
impreziosire *vt.* to make (*v. irr.*) precious. ♦ **impreziosirsi** *vr.* to become (*v. irr.*) precious.
imprigionamento *sm.* imprisonment.
imprigionare *vt.* to imprison.
imprìmere *vt.* to impress.
improbàbile *agg.* improbable.
improbabilità *sf.* improbability.
ìmprobo *agg.* 1. dishonest 2. (*faticoso*) hard.
improduttività *sf.* unproductiveness.
improduttivo *agg.* unproductive.
impronta *sf.* 1. impression: — *del piede*, *digitale*, footprint, fingerprint 2. (*fig.*) mark.
improntare *vt.* 1. to prepare 2. (*fig.*) to mark.
improntitùdine *sf.* impudence.
impronunciàbile *agg.* unpronounceable.
improperio *sm.* insult.
improprietà *sf.* impropriety.
improprio *agg.* improper.
improrogàbile *agg.* undelayable.
immprovvido *agg.* improvident.
improvvisamente *avv.* suddenly.
improvvisare *vt.* e *vi.* to improvise. ♦ **improvvisarsi** *vr.* to act.
improvvisata *sf.* surprise.
improvvisatore *sm.* improviser.
improvvisazione *sf.* improvisation.
improvviso *agg.* sudden.
imprudente *agg.* imprudent.
imprudenza *sf.* imprudence.
impudente *agg.* impudent.
impudenza *sf.* impudence.
impudicizia *sf.* immodesty.
impudico *agg.* shameless, immodest.
impugnàbile *agg.* (*giur.*) impugnable.
impugnabilità *sf.* (*giur.*) impugnment.
impugnare *vt.* 1. to grasp, to hold 2. (*giur.*) to impugn.
impugnatura *sf.* hilt.
impulsività *sf.* impulsiveness.
impulsivo *agg.* impulsive.
impulso *sm.* impulse.
impunemente *avv.* safely.
impunità *sf.* impunity.
impunito *agg.* unpunished.
impuntare *vi.* to stumble (over).

◆ **impuntarsi** *vr.* 1. to jib 2. (*ostinarsi*) to stick (*v. irr.*) (to).

impuntura *sf.* stitching.

impurità *sf.* impurity.

impuro *agg.* impure.

imputàbile *agg.* 1. imputable 2. (*giur.*) chargeable (with).

imputare *vt.* 1. to impute 2. (*giur.*) to charge (with).

imputato *sm.* defendant.

imputazione *sf.* imputation.

imputridimento *sm.* putrefaction.

imputridire *vi.* to rot.

in *prep.* (*stato in luogo*) in, at: *essere — campagna, — città*, to be in the country, in town; *essere — casa, — chiesa*, to be at home, at church 2. (*moto a luogo*) to: *andò — America*, he went to America 3. (*moto dentro luogo*) into: *va' nello studio*, go into the study 4. (*coi mezzi di trasporto*) by: *sono venuto — treno*, I came by train.

inàbile *agg.* 1. unable 2. (*non idoneo*) unfit.

inabilità *sf.* 1. inability 2. (*inidoneità*) unfitness.

inabilitare *vt.* to disable.

inabilitazione *sf.* disability.

inabissamento *sm.* sinking.

inabissarsi *vr.* to sink (*v. irr.*).

inabitàbile *agg.* uninhabitable.

inabitabilità *sf.* uninhabitableness.

inabitato *agg.* 1. uninhabited 2. (*deserto*) deserted.

inaccessìbile *agg.* inaccessible.

inaccessibilità *sf.* inaccessibility.

inaccettàbile *agg.* unacceptable.

inaccettabilità *sf.* unacceptableness.

inacerbire *vt.* to exacerbate. ◆ **inacerbirsi** *vr.* to grow (*v. irr.*) bitter.

inacidire *vt.* to sour. ◆ **inacidirsi** *vr.* to turn sour.

inacidito *agg.* sour.

inadattàbile *agg.* unadaptable.

inadattabilità *sf.* inadaptability.

inadatto *agg.* 1. unfit (for) 2. (*sconveniente*) unbecoming.

inadeguato *agg.* inadequate.

inadempìbile *agg.* unfulfillable.

inadempiente *agg.* defaulting.

inadempienza *sf.* non-execution.

inafferràbile *agg.* unseizable.

inalare *vt.* to inhale.

inalatore *sm.* inhaler.

inalazione *sf.* inhalation.

inalberare *vt.* to hoist. ◆ **inalberarsi** *vr.* 1. to rear up 2. (*fig.*) to lose (*v. irr.*) one's temper.

inalienàbile *agg.* inalienable.

inalienabilità *sf.* inalienability.

inalteràbile *agg.* inalterable.

inalterabilità *sf.* inalterability.

inalterato *agg.* unaltered.

inalveare *vt.* to canalize.

inamidare *vt.* to starch.

inammissìbile *agg.* inadmissible.

inammissibilità *sf.* inadmissibility.

inamovìbile *agg.* irremovable.

inamovibilità *sf.* irremovability.

inane *agg.* inane.

inanellare *vt.* to curl.

inanimato *agg.* lifeless.

inanità *sf.* inanity.

inappagàbile *agg.* unsatisfiable.

inappagato *agg.* unsatisfied.

inappellàbile *agg.* inappellable.

inappetenza *sf.* inappetence.

inapplicàbile *agg.* inapplicable.

inapprezzàbile *agg.* priceless.

inappuntàbile *agg.* 1. irreproachable 2. (*nel vestire*) faultlessly dressed.

inarcamento *sm.* bending, arching.

inarcare *vt.* to bend (*v. irr.*) || *— le sopracciglia*, to raise one's brows. ◆ **inarcarsi** *vr.* to arch.

inargentare *vt.* to silver.

inaridire *vt.* to dry. ◆ **inaridirsi** *vr.* to dry up.

inarticolato *agg.* inarticulate.

inascoltato *agg.* unheard.

inaspettato *agg.* unexpected.

inasprimento *sm.* embitterment.

inasprire *vt.* to embitter. ◆ **inasprirsi** *vr.* to become (*v. irr.*) embittered.

inattaccàbile *agg.* unassailable.

inattendìbile *agg.* unreliable.

inatteso *agg.* unexpected.

inattività *sf.* inactivity.

inattivo *agg.* inactive.

inattuàbile *agg.* impracticable.

inattuale *agg.* outdated.

inaudito *agg.* unheard of.

inaugurale *agg.* inaugural.

inaugurare *vt.* to inaugurate.

inaugurazione *sf.* inauguration.

inavvedutezza *sf.* carelessness.

inavveduto *agg.* careless.

inavvertenza *sf.* inadvertence.

inavvertito *agg.* unperceived.

inazione *sf.* inaction.

incagliare *vt.* to hinder. ◆ **incagliarsi** *vr.* to strand.

incaglio *sm.* 1. stranding 2. (*fig.*) obstacle.

incalcolàbile *agg.* incalculable.

incallire *vi.* to harden. ♦ **incallirsi** *vr.* to harden.

incallito *agg.* hardened.

incalzante *agg.* 1. pursuing 2. (*fig.*) pressing.

incalzare *vt.* 1. to pursue 2. (*fig.*) to urge.

incameramento *sm.* confiscation.

incamerare *vt.* to confiscate.

incamminare *vt.* to set (*v. irr.*) going. ♦ **incamminarsi** *vr.* to set out (for).

incanalamento *sm.* canalization.

incanalare *vt.* to canalize.

incancellàbile *agg.* indelible.

incancrenire *vi.* to become (*v. irr.*) gangrenous.

incandescente *agg.* white-hot.

incandescenza *sf.* incandescence.

incantamento *sm.* charm.

incantare *vt.* to charm. ♦ **incantarsi** *vr.* to be charmed.

incantato *agg.* enchanted.

incantatore *agg.* enchanting. ♦ **incantatore** *sm.* enchanter.

incantésimo *sm.* spell.

incantévole *agg.* charming.

incanto[1] *sm.* enchantment.

incanto[2] *sm.* (*comm.*) auction: *vendere all'—,* to sell (*v. irr.*) by auction.

incanutire *vi.* to grow (*v. irr.*) hoary.

incapace *agg.* unable.

incapacità *sf.* incapacity.

incaparbirsi *vr.* to become (*v. irr.*) obstinate.

incappare *vi.* to get (*v. irr.*) into, to stumble.

incappucciare *vt.* to hood. ♦ **incappucciarsi** *vr.* to put (*v. irr.*) on one's hood.

incapricciarsi *vr.* to take (*v. irr.*) a fancy (to).

incapsulare *vt.* to capsule.

incarcerare *vt.* to imprison.

incarcerazione *sf.* imprisonment.

incaricare *vt.* to charge (so. with). ♦ **incaricarsi** *vr.* to charge oneself (with).

incaricato *agg.* charged (with). ♦ **incaricato** *sm.* appointee.

incàrico *sm.* task, duty.

incarnare *vt.* to embody. ♦ **incarnarsi** *vr.* to take (*v. irr.*) body.

incarnato *sm.* complexion.

incarnazione *sf.* incarnation.

incarnire *vi.* to grow (*v. irr.*) into to flesh.

incartamento *sm.* dossier.

incartapecorire *vi.* to wrinkle.

incartapecorito *agg.* ʼwrinkled with age.

incartare *vt.* to wrap in paper.

incarto *sm.* set of papers.

incartocciare *vt.* to wrap up in a cornet.

incasellare *vt.* to put (*v. irr.*) in squares.

incassamento *sm.* 1. boxing 2. (*mecc.; arch.*) embedding.

incassare *vt.* 1. to box 2. (*riscuotere*) to cash.

incassatura *sf.* hollow.

incasso *sm.* 1. collection 2. (*di spettacoli*) receipts (*pl.*).

incastellamento *sm.* 1. fortifications (*pl.*) 2. (*arch.*) scaffolding.

incastellare *vt.* to fortify with battlements.

incastellatura *sf.* 1. frame 2. (*arch.*) scaffolding.

incastonare *vt.* to set (*v. irr.*).

incastonatura *sf.* setting.

incastrare *vt.* 1. to embed 2. (*adattare*) to fit in. ♦ **incastrarsi** *vr.* 1. to fit 2. (*impigliarsi*) to get (*v. irr.*) stuck.

incastro *sm.* joint.

incatenamento *sm.* chaining.

incatenare *vt.* to chain. ♦ **incatenarsi** *vr.* to be linked (with).

incatramare *vt.* to tar.

incattivire *vt.* to exasperate. ♦ **incattivirsi** *vr.* to get (*v. irr.*) crossed.

incàuto *agg.* rash.

incavare *vt.* to hollow out.

incavatura *sf.* hollowness.

incavo *sm.* hollow.

incèdere *vi.* to advance.

incendiare *vt.* to set (*v. irr.*) on fire.

incendiario *agg.* e *sm.* incendiary.

incendio *sm.* fire.

incenerire *vt.* to reduce to ashes.

incensamento *sm.* 1. incensation 2. (*fig.*) flattery.

incensare *vt.* 1. to incense 2. (*fig.*) to flatter.

incenso *sm.* incense.

incensuràbile *agg.* irreproachable.

incensurato *agg.* blameless: *essere —,* to be a first-offender.

incentivo *sm.* incentive.

inceppamento *sm.* 1. obstacle 2. (*mecc.*) jam.

inceppare *vt.* 1. to clog 2. (*ostacolare*) to encumber. ♦ **incepparsi** *vr.* to jam.

incerare *vt.* to wax.

incertezza *sf.* uncertainty, doubt.

incerto *agg.* uncertain. ♦ **incerto** *sm.* uncertainty.

incespicare *vi.* to stumble.

incessante *agg.* unceasing.

incesto *sm.* incest.

incestuoso *agg.* incestuous.

incetta *sf.* cornering: *fare — di*, to make (*v. irr.*) a corner in.

incettare *vt.* to corner.

incettatore *sm.* cornerer.

inchiesta *sf.* inquiry, investigation.

inchinare *vt.* to bow. ♦ **inchinarsi** *vr.* to bow (down).

inchino *sm.* bow.

inchiodare *vt.* to nail.

inchiodatura *sf.* nailing.

inchiostro *sm.* ink.

inciampare *vi.* to stumble.

inciampo *sm.* obstacle.

incidentale *agg.* 1. incidental 2. (*gramm.*) parenthetic.

incidente *agg.* incident. ♦ **incidente** *sm.* accident.

incidenza *sf.* incidence.

incidere[1] *vt.* 1. to cut (*v. irr.*) 2. (*intagliare*) to engrave 3. (*su disco, nastro ecc.*) to record.

incidere[2] *vi.* to weigh heavily: — *sul bilancio*, to weigh heavily on one's budget.

incinta *agg. f.* pregnant.

incipiente *agg.* incipient.

incipriare *vt.* to powder. ♦ **incipriarsi** *vr.* to powder (oneself).

incirca (*nella loc. avv.*) *all'—*, about.

incisione *sf.* 1. cut 2. (*arte*) engraving 3. (*su disco, nastro ecc.*) recording.

incisività *sf.* sharpness.

incisivo *agg.* incisive. ♦ **incisivo** *sm.* (*anat.*) incisor.

inciso *sm.* parenthetic clause: *per —*, incidentally.

incisore *sm.* engraver.

incitamento *sm.* urge.

incitare *vt.* to urge, to stimulate.

incitrullire *vi.* to become (*v. irr.*) silly.

incivile *agg.* 1. uncivilized 2. (*scortese*) rude.

incivilimento *sm.* civilization.

incivilire *vt.* to civilize. ♦ **incivilirsi** *vr.* to become (*v. irr.*) civilized.

inciviltà *sf.* 1. barbarism 2. (*fig.*) rudeness.

inclassificàbile *agg.* unclassifiable.

inclemente *agg.* 1. inclement: *tempo —*, inclement weather 2. (*spietato*) merciless.

inclemenza *sf.* 1. (*di tempo*) inclemency 2. (*crudeltà*) mercilessness.

inclinare *vt.* to incline, to bend (*v. irr.*).

inclinato *agg.* inclined (*anche fig.*).

inclinazione *sf.* 1. inclination 2. (*attitudine*) bent.

incline *agg.* disposed.

inclito *agg.* famous.

inclùdere *vt.* to include.

inclusione *sf.* inclusion.

inclusivo *agg.* inclusive.

incluso *agg.* 1. included 2. (*accluso*) enclosed.

incoccare *vt.* to nock.

incoercìbile *agg.* irrepressible.

incoercibilità *sf.* irrepressibleness.

incoerente *agg.* incoherent.

incoerenza *sf.* incoherence.

incògnita *sf.* 1. (*mat.*) unknown quantity 2. (*fig.*) uncertainty.

incògnito *agg.* unknown. ♦ **incògnito** *sm.* incognito (*pl.* -tos).

incollamento *sm.* pasting.

incollare *vt.* to stick (*v. irr.*). ♦ **incollarsi** *vr.* to stick.

incollatrice *sf.* sizing-machine.

incollatura[1] *sf.* sticking.

incollatura[2] *sf.* (*ippica*) neck.

incollerire *vi.* to get (*v. irr.*) angry. ♦ **incollerirsi** *vr.* to get angry.

incollerito *agg.* angry.

incolonnamento *sm.* column formation.

incolonnare *vt.* to form into columns. ♦ **incolonnarsi** *vr.* to rank.

incolore *agg.* colourless.

incolpàbile *agg.* accusable.

incolpare *vt.* to charge (with), to accuse (of). ♦ **incolparsi** *vr.* to accuse oneself.

incolpévole *agg.* blameless.

incolto *agg.* uncultivated.

incòlume *agg.* unhurt.

incolumità *sf.* safety.

incombente *agg.* impending.

incombenza *sf.* errand, task.

incòmbere *vi.* 1. (*spettare*) to be

one's job **2.** (*sovrastare*) to impend (over).

incombustìbile *agg.* incombustible.

incominciare *vt.* e *vi.* V. *cominciare.*

incommensuràbile *agg.* incommensurable.

incommensurabilità *sf.* incommensurability.

incommerciàbile *agg.* not negotiable.

incommutàbile *agg.* incommutable.

incomodare *vt.* to annoy. ♦ **incomodarsi** *vr.* to trouble.

incomodità *sf.* uncomfortableness.

incomodo *agg.* uncomfortable || *essere d' —*, to be in the way.

incomparàbile *agg.* incomparable.

incompatìbile *agg.* incompatible.

incompatibilità *sf.* incompatibility.

incompetente *agg.* incompetent.

incompetenza *sf.* incompetence.

incompiuto *agg.* unfinished.

incompletezza *sf.* incompleteness.

incompleto *agg.* incomplete.

incompostezza *sf.* disorder.

incomposto *agg.* disorderly.

incomprensìbile *agg.* incomprehensible.

incomprensibilità *sf.* incomprehensibility.

incomprensione *sf.* incomprehension.

incompreso *agg.* **1.** not understood **2.** (*non apprezzato*) unappreciated.

incomputàbile *agg.* incalculable.

incomunicàbile *agg.* incommunicable.

incomunicabilità *sf.* incommunicability.

inconcepìbile *agg.* inconceivable.

inconciliàbile *agg.* irreconcilable.

inconciliabilità *sf.* irreconcilability.

inconcludente *agg.* **1.** inconclusive **2.** (*di persona*) good-for-nothing.

inconcusso *agg.* unshaken.

incondizionato *agg.* unconditional.

inconfessàbile *agg.* unavowable.

inconfessato *agg.* unconfessed.

inconfondìbile *agg.* unmistakable.

inconfutàbile *agg.* irrefutable.

incongruente *agg.* incongruous.

incongruenza *sf.* incongruity.

incòngruo *agg.* incongruous.

inconsapévole *agg.* unconscious, unaware.

inconsapevolezza *sf.* unconsciousness, unawareness.

inconscio *agg.* e *sm.* unconscious.

inconseguente *agg.* inconsequent.

inconseguenza *sf.* inconsequence.

inconsideratezza *sf.* rashness.

inconsiderato *agg.* rash.

inconsistente *agg.* insubstantial.

inconsistenza *sf.* insubstantiality.

inconsolàbile *agg.* inconsolable.

inconsueto *agg.* unusual.

inconsulto *agg.* unadvised, rash.

incontaminato *agg.* unpolluted.

incontentàbile *agg.* insatiable.

incontentabilità *sf.* insatiability.

incontestàbile *agg.* incontestable.

incontinente *agg.* incontinent.

incontinenza *sf.* incontinence.

incontrare *vt.* to meet (*v. irr.*). ♦ **incontrarsi** *vr.* to meet || *i nostri gusti non si incontrano*, our tastes do not agree.

incontrastàbile *agg.* incontestable.

incontrastato *agg.* uncontested.

incontro[1] *sm.* **1.** meeting **2.** (*sport*) match.

incontro[2] *prep.* — *a*, towards, to.

incontrollàbile *agg.* uncontrollable.

incontrollato *agg.* uncontrolled.

incontrovertìbile *agg.* indisputable.

inconveniente *sm.* inconvenience, drawback.

inconvertìbile *agg.* inconvertible.

inconvertibilità *sf.* inconvertibility.

incoraggiamento *sm.* encouragement.

incoraggiante *agg.* encouraging.

incoraggiare *vt.* to encourage.

incorniciare *vt.* to frame.

incorniciatura *sf.* framing.

incoronamento *sm.* V. *coronamento.*

incoronare *vt.* V. *coronare.*

incoronazione *sf.* coronation.

incorporare *vt.* to incorporate.

incorporazione *sf.* incorporation.

incorpòreo *agg.* incorporeal.

incorreggìbile *agg.* incorrigible.

incòrrere *vi.* to incur, to suffer (sthg.).

incorretto *agg.* incorrect.

incorrotto *agg.* incorrupt.

incorruttìbile *agg.* incorruptible.

incorruttibilità *sf.* incorruptibility.

incosciente *agg.* **1.** unconscious **2.** (*irresponsabile*) reckless. ♦ **incosciente** *sm.* irresponsible.

incoscienza *sf.* **1.** unconsciousness **2.** (*spericolatezza*) rashness.

incostante

138

incostante agg. inconstant: *tempo* —, changeable weather.
incostituzionale agg. unconstitutional.
incostituzionalità sf. unconstitutionality.
incredìbile agg. incredible.
incredibilità sf. incredibility.
incredulità sf. incredulity.
incrèdulo agg. incredulous.
incrementare vt. to increase.
incremento sm. increase.
increscioso agg. unpleasant.
increspamento sm. 1. (*di acque*) rippling 2. (*di capelli*) ruffling.
increspare vt., **incresparsi** vr. 1. (*di acque*) to ripple 2. (*di capelli*) to ruffle.
incretinire vt. to make (v. irr.) stupid. ♦ **incretinirsi** vr. to dull.
incrimìnàbile agg. impeachable.
incriminare vt. to impeach.
incriminazione sf. 1. (*l'accusare*) crimination 2. (*atto d'accusa*) indictment.
incrinare vt. to crack. ♦ **incrinarsi** vr. to crack.
incrinatura sf. crack.
incriticàbile agg. uncensurable.
incrociare vt. to cross. ♦ **incrociarsi** vr. to cross.
incrociatore sm. cruiser.
incrocio sm. 1. crossing || — *stradale*, cross-road 2. (*di razze*) crossbreed.
incrollàbile agg. unshakable.
incrostare vt. to incrust. ♦ **incrostarsi** vr. to become (v. irr.) incrusted.
incrostazione sf. incrustation.
incrudelimento sm. toughening.
incrudelire vi. to become (v. irr.) cruel || — *contro qu.*, to be pitiless towards so.
incrudire vi. to grow (v. irr.) worse.
incruento agg. bloodless.
incubatrice sf. incubator.
incubazione sf. incubation.
incubo sm. nightmare.
incùdine sf. anvil.
inculcare vt. to inculcate.
incunàbolo sm. incunabulum.
incuneare vt. to wedge. ♦ **incunearsi** vr. to wedge oneself.
incupire vt. e vi. to darken. ♦ **incupirsi** vr. to become (v. irr.) gloomy.
incuràbile agg. e sm. incurable.

incurabilità sf. incurability.
incurante agg. careless, heedless.
incuria sf. heedlessness.
incuriosire vt. to make (v. irr.) curious. ♦ **incuriosirsi** vr. to become (v. irr.) curious.
incuriosito agg. made curious.
incursione sf. raid.
incurvare vt. e **incurvarsi** vr. to bend (v. irr.), to curve.
incurvatura sf. bend.
incustodito agg. unguarded.
incùtere vt. to rouse.
ìndaco sm. indigo.
indaffarato agg. busy.
indagare vt. to investigate.
indagatore agg. investigating.
indàgine sf. 1. research, investigation 2. (*giur.*) inquiry.
indebitare vt. to involve in debt. ♦ **indebitarsi** vr. to run (v. irr.) into debt.
indébito agg. undue.
indebolimento sm. weakening.
indebolire vt. to weaken. ♦ **indebolirsi** vr. to weaken.
indecente agg. indecent.
indecenza sf. indecency.
indecifràbile agg. 1. indecipherable 2. (*di calligrafia*) illegible.
indecisione sf. indecision.
indeciso agg. 1. irresolute 2. (*di cose*) undecided.
indeclinàbile agg. 1. indeclinable 2. (*che non si può eludere*) unavoidable.
indecoroso agg. unseemly.
indefesso agg. indefatigable.
indefinìbile agg. indefinable.
indefinito agg. indefinite.
indeformàbile agg. indeformable.
indegno agg. 1. unworthy 2. (*spregevole*) disgraceful.
indelèbile agg. indelible.
indelicatezza sf. indelicacy.
indelicato agg. tactless.
indemoniato agg. 1. possessed 2. (*fig.*) frantic. ♦ **indemoniato** sm. demoniac.
indenne agg. undamaged.
indennità sf. allowance.
indennizzare vt. to indemnify.
indennizzo sm. indemnity.
inderogàbile agg. intransgressible.
indescrivìbile agg. indescribable.
indesideràbile agg. undesirable.
indeterminàbile agg. indeterminable.
indeterminatezza sf. vagueness.

indeterminativo *agg.* (*gramm.*) indefinite.

indeterminato *agg.* indeterminate.

indeterminazione *sf.* indetermination.

indi *avv.* **1.** (*di tempo*) then **2.** (*di luogo*) (from) thence.

indiano *agg.* Indian: — *d'America*, Red Indian; *in fila indiana*, in Indian file.

indiavolato *agg.* frenzied, furious.

indicare *vt.* **1.** to show (*v. irr.*) **2.** (*col dito*) to point at.

indicativo *agg.* indicative.

indicato *agg.* **1.** (*adatto*) suitable **2.** (*consigliabile*) advisable.

indicatore *agg.* indicatory. ♦ **indicatore** *sm.* indicator.

indicazione *sf.* indication.

indice *sm.* **1.** (*dito della mano*) forefinger **2.** (*di libro, statistica ecc.*) index.

indicibile *agg.* inexpressible.

indietreggiare *vi.* to withdraw (*v. irr.*).

indietro *avv.* (*di spazio, tempo*) back, behind.

indifendibile *agg.* indefensible.

indifeso *agg.* undefended.

indifferente *agg.* indifferent.

indifferenza *sf.* indifference.

indifferibile *agg.* undelayable.

indigeno *agg. e sm.* native.

indigente *agg.* indigent, poor.

indigenza *sf.* indigence.

indigestione *sf.* indigestion.

indigesto *agg.* **1.** indigestible **2.** (*fig.*) heavy.

indignare *vt.* to make (*v. irr.*) indignant. ♦ **indignarsi** *vr.* to get (*v. irr.*) angry.

indignazione *sf.* indignation.

indimenticàbile *agg.* unforgettable.

indimostràbile *agg.* indemonstrable.

indipendente *agg.* independent (of). ♦ **indipendente** *sm.* (*pol.*) independent.

indipendenza *sf.* independence.

indire *vt.* to call, to announce.

indiretto *agg.* indirect.

indirizzare *vt.* to address. ♦ **indirizzarsi** *vr.* **1.** (*dirigersi*) to set (*v. irr.*) out (for) **2.** (*rivolgersi*) to address oneself (to).

indirizzo *sm.* **1.** address **2.** (*linea di condotta*) trend.

indisciplina *sf.* indiscipline.

indisciplinato *agg.* undisciplined.

indiscretezza *sf.* indiscretion.

indiscreto *agg.* indiscreet.

indiscrezione *sf.* indiscretion.

indiscriminato *agg.* indiscriminate.

indiscusso *agg.* undiscussed.

indiscutìbile *agg.* unquestionable.

indispensàbile *agg.* indispensable.

indispettire *vt.* to vex. ♦ **indispettirsi** *vr.* to become (*v. irr.*) vexed.

indispettito *agg.* vexed.

indisponente *agg.* irritating.

indisporre *vt.* to irritate.

indisposizione *sf.* indisposition.

indisposto *agg.* unwell (*pred.*).

indissolùbile *agg.* indissoluble.

indissolubilità *sf.* indissolubility.

indistinto *agg.* indistinct.

indistruttìbile *agg.* indestructible.

indisturbato *agg.* undisturbed.

individuale *agg.* individual.

individualismo *sm.* individualism

individualista *s.* individualist.

individualìstico *agg.* individualistic.

individuare *vt.* to single out.

individuo *sm.* individual.

indivisìbile *agg.* indivisible.

indivisibilità *sf.* indivisibility.

indiviso *agg.* undivided.

indiziare *vt.* to make (*v. irr.*) suspect.

indiziario *agg.* presumptive.

indiziato *agg. e sm.* suspect.

indizio *sm.* **1.** indication **2.** (*giur.*) circumstantial proof.

indòcile *agg.* indocile.

indocilità *sf.* indocility.

indoeuropeo *agg. e sm.* Indo-European.

indole *sf.* nature, disposition || *un ragazzo di buona* —, a good-natured boy.

indolente *agg.* indolent.

indolenza *sf.* indolence.

idolenzimento *sm.* numbness.

indolenzire *vt.* to numb. ♦ **indolenzirsi** *vr.* to become (*v. irr.*) numb.

indolenzito *agg.* numb.

indolore *agg.* painless.

indomàbile *agg.* untamable.

indomani *sm.* next day || *all'* —, on the day after.

indòmito *agg.* indomitable.

indorare *vt.* V. *dorare*.

indossare *vt.* **1.** (*avere indosso*) to wear (*v. irr.*) **2.** (*mettere indosso*) to put (*v. irr.*) on.

indossatrice sf. mannequin.
indosso avv. on.
indotto agg. (spinto) driven.
indovinare vt. to guess.
indovinello sm. riddle.
indovino sm. soothsayer.
indubbio agg. undoubted.
indubitàbile agg. indubitable.
indugiare vi. to delay, to hesitate.
indugio sm. delay.
indulgente agg. indulgent.
indulgenza sf. indulgence.
indùlgere vi. to indulge (in).
indulto sm. 1. (eccl.) indult 2. (giur.) free pardon.
indumento sm. garment.
indurimento sm. hardening.
indurire vt. e vi. to harden. ♦ **indurirsi** vr. to harden.
indurre vt. to induce, to get (v. irr.) || — in errore, to mislead (v. irr.). ♦ **indursi** vr. to bring (v. irr.) oneself (to).
industria sf. industry.
industriale agg. industrial. ♦ **industriale** sm. industrialist, manufacturer.
industrialismo sm. industrialism.
industrializzare vt. to industrialize.
industrializzazione sf. industrialization.
industriarsi vr. to do (v. irr.) one's best.
industrioso agg. industrious.
induttivo agg. inductive.
induttore sm. inductor.
induzione sf. induction.
inebetire vt. e vi. to dull.
inebetito agg. dull.
inebriante agg. inebriating.
inebriare vt. 1. to make (v. irr.) drunk 2. (fig.) to inebriate. ♦ **inebriarsi** vr. 1. to get (v. irr.) drunk 2. (fig.) to go (v. irr.) into raptures.
ineccepìbile agg. unexceptionable.
inedia sf. starvation.
inèdito agg. unpublished.
ineducato agg. ill-bred.
ineffàbile agg. ineffable.
inefficace agg. ineffective.
inefficacia sf. inefficacy.
inefficiente agg. inefficient.
inefficienza sf. ineffectiveness.
ineguaglianza sf. inequality.
ineguale agg. 1. unlike 2. (irregolare) irregular 3. (di superficie) uneven.

ineleggìbile agg. ineligible.
ineleggibilità sf. ineligibility.
ineluttàbile agg. ineluctable.
ineluttabilità sf. inevitableness.
inenarràbile agg. unutterable.
inequivocàbile agg. unmistakable
'nerente agg. concerning.
inerme agg. unarmed.
inerpicarsi vr. to climb (up).
inerte agg. inert.
inerzia sf. inertness.
inesattezza sf. inaccuracy.
inesatto agg. incorrect.
inesaudito agg. ungranted.
inesaurìbile agg. inexhaustible.
inesàusto agg. unexhausted.
ineseguìbile agg. inexecutable.
inesigìbile agg. 1. uncollectable 2. (di assegno) worthless.
inesistente agg. inexistent.
in·sistenza sf. inexistence.
in·soràbile agg. inexorable.
inesorabilità sf. inexorability.
inesperienza sf. inexperience.
inesperto agg. unskilled.
inespiàbile agg. inexpiable.
inesplicàbile agg. inexplicable.
inesploràbile agg. inexplorable.
inesplorato agg. unexplored.
inespressivo agg. inexpressive.
inespresso agg. implied.
inesprimìbile agg. inexpressible.
inespugnàbile agg. inexpugnable.
inespugnabilità sf. inexpugnability.
inestimàbile agg. inestimable.
inestinguìbile agg. unquenchable.
inestirpàbile agg. ineradicable.
inestricàbile agg. inextricable.
inettitùdine sf. unfitness.
inetto agg. 1. unapt 2. (dappoco) good-for-nothing.
inevaso agg. outstanding, unanswered.
inevitàbile agg. inevitable.
inezia sf. trifle.
infagottare vt. to muffle up. ♦ **infagottarsi** vr. to muffle oneself up.
infallìbile agg. infallible.
infallibilità sf. infallibility.
infamante agg. shameful.
infamare vt. to defame, to disgrace.
infame agg. wicked.
infamia sf. infamy.
infangare vt. to muddy. ♦ **infangarsi** vr. to become (v. irr.) muddy.
infanticida s. child-murderer.

infanticidio *sm.* child-murder.

infantile *agg.* childlike, childish.

infantilismo *sm.* infantilism.

infanzia *sf.* 1. infancy 2. *(coll.)* children *(pl.)*.

infarcire *vt.* V. *farcire*.

infarinare *vt.* to flour. ♦ **infarinarsi** *vr.* to get *(v. irr.)* covered with flour.

infarinatura *sf.* 1. flouring 2. *(fig.)* smattering.

infarto *sm.* infarct.

infastidire *vt.* to annoy. ♦ **infastidirsi** *vr.* to get *(v. irr.)* bored.

infaticàbile *agg.* tireless.

infatti *cong.* in fact.

infatuare *vt.* to infatuate. ♦ **infatuarsi** *vr.* to get *(v. irr.)* crazy (about).

infatuato *agg.* crazy (about).

infatuazione *sf.* infatuation.

infàusto *agg.* unlucky.

infecondità *sf.* sterility.

infecondo *agg.* steril.

infedele *agg.* unfaithful. ♦ **infedele** *sm.* infidel.

infedeltà *sf.* unfaithfulness.

infelice *agg.* 1. unhappy 2. *(non appropriato)* ill-timed. ♦ **infelice** *s.* wretch.

infelicità *sf.* unhappiness.

inferiore *agg.* 1. inferior 2. *(più basso)* lower 3. *(al di sotto)* below. ♦ **inferiore** *sm.* inferior.

inferiorità *sf.* inferiority.

inferire *vt.* 1. *(dedurre)* to infer 2. *(dare)* to inflict.

infermeria *sf.* infirmary.

infermiera *sf.* nurse.

infermiere *sm.* hospital attendant.

infermità *sf.* infirmity.

infermo *agg. e sm.* invalid.

infernale *agg.* 1. infernal 2. *(fig.)* awful.

inferno *sm.* hell.

inferocire *vt.* to enrage. ♦ **inferocire** *vi.* to get *(v. irr.)* fierce.

inferriata *sf.* grating.

infervorare *vt.* to excite. ♦ **infervorarsi** *vr.* to get *(v. irr.)* excited.

infervorato *agg.* fervent.

infestare *vt.* to infest.

infestazione *sf.* infestation.

infettare *vt.* to infect. ♦ **infettarsi** *vr.* to become *(v. irr.)* infected.

infettivo *agg.* contagious.

infetto *agg.* infected.

infezione *sf.* infection.

infiacchimento *sm.* weakening.

infiacchire *vt. e vi.* to weaken. ♦ **infiacchirsi** *vr.* to become *(v. irr.)* weak.

infiammàbile *agg.* inflammable.

infiammabilità *sf.* inflammability.

infiammare *vt.* 1. to set *(v. irr.)* on fire 2. *(fig.)* to inflame. ♦ **infiammarsi** *vr.* 1. to take *(v. irr.)* fire 2. *(fig.)* to get *(v. irr.)* excited.

infiammato *agg.* inflamed (with).

infiammatorio *agg.* inflammatory.

infiammazione *sf.* inflammation.

infiascare *vt.* to put *(v. irr.)* into flasks.

inficiare *vt.* 1. to invalidate 2. *(giur.)* to impugn.

infido *agg.* false.

infierire *vi.* to be pitiless.

infìggere *vt.* 1. to infix 2. *(conficcare)* to drive *(v. irr.)* (into).

infilare *vt.* 1. to thread 2. *(introdurre)* to insert 3. *(passare per)* to enter. ♦ **infilarsi** *vr.* to slip into.

infilata *sf.* row.

infiltrarsi *vr.* to penetrate.

infiltrazione *sf.* infiltration.

infilzare *vt.* 1. to transfix 2. *(conficcare)* to stick *(v. irr.)*. ♦ **infilzarsi** *vr.* 1. to run *(v. irr.)* oneself through 2. *(conficcarsi)* to get *(v. irr.)* stuck.

infilzata *sf.* string.

infimo *agg.* lowest.

infine *avv.* at last.

infingardàggine *sf.* laziness.

infingardo *agg.* lazy.

infinità *sf.* infinity.

infinitamente *avv.* infinitely.

infinitesimale *agg.* infinitesimal.

infinito *agg.* boundless. ♦ **infinito** *sm.* 1. infinite 2. *(gramm.)* infinitive.

infioccare *vt.* to tassel.

infiorare *vt.* to flower.

infirmare *vt.* to invalidate.

infischiarsi *vr.* not to care (about).

infittire *vi.* to thicken. ♦ **infittirsi** *vr.* to thicken.

inflazione *sf.* inflation.

inflazionìstico *agg.* inflationary.

inflessìbile *agg.* inflexible.

inflessibilità *sf.* inflexibility.

inflessione *sf.* inflexion.

inflìggere *vt.* to inflict.

influente *agg.* influential.

influenza *sf.* 1. influence 2. *(med.)* *(fam.)* 'flu.

influenzare *vt.* to influence.

influire *vi.* to exert influence (on, upon, over).

influsso *sm.* influence.

infocare *vt.* **1.** to heat up **2.** to inflame.

infocato *agg.* **1.** red hot **2.** (*fig.*) inflamed.

infoltire *vi.* to thicken.

infondatezza *sf.* groundlessness.

infondato *agg.* groundless.

infòndere *vt.* to infuse.

inforcare *vt.* **1.** to pitchfork **2.** (*montare a cavalcioni*) to get (*v. irr.*) on || — *gli occhiali*, to put (*v. irr.*) on one's glasses.

informale *agg.* informal.

informare *vt.* **1.** to inform **2.** (*dare forma*) to shape. ♦ **informarsi** *vr.* to inquire (about).

informativo *agg.* informative.

informato *agg.* informed.

informatore *sm.* informer.

informazione *sf.* information (*solo sing.*), news (*pl.*).

informe *agg.* shapeless.

infornare *vt.* to put (*v. irr.*) into an oven.

infornata *sf.* batch.

infortunarsi *vr.* to get (*v. irr.*) injured.

infortunato *agg.* injured.

infortunio *sm.* accident.

infortunìstica *sf.* industrial accident research.

infossamento *sm.* hollow.

infossare *vt.* to hollow. ♦ **infossarsi** *vr.* to become (*v. irr.*) hollow.

infradiciare *vt.* **1.** to drench **2.** (*marcire*) to rot (*v. irr.*).

inframmettenza *sf.* interference.

inframméttere *vt.* to interpose. ♦ **inframméttersi** *vr.* to meddle (with).

infràngere *vt.* **1.** to shatter **2.** (*trasgredire*) to infringe. ♦ **infràngersi** *vr.* to break (*v. irr.*) (up).

infrangìbile *agg.* unbreakable: *vetro* —, shatter-proof glass.

infranto *agg.* **1.** shattered, broken **2.** (*di legge*) infringed.

infrarosso *agg.* infrared.

infrasettimanale *agg.* midweek.

infrastruttura *sf.* infrastructure.

infrazione *sf.* infraction.

infreddolirsi *vr.* to feel (*v. irr.*) cold.

infreddolito *agg.* chilly.

infrequente *agg.* infrequent.

infrollirsi *vr.* **1.** to become (*v. irr.*) tender **2.** (*di selvaggina*) to become (*v. irr.*) high.

infruttìfero *agg.* unfruitful.

infruttuoso *agg.* **1.** unfruitful **2.** (*fig.*) useless.

infuori (*loc. prep.*) *all'*—, except.

infuriare *vi.* to enrage. ♦ **infuriarsi** *vr.* to flare up.

infusione *sf.* infusion.

infuso *agg.* infused. ♦ **infuso** *sm.* infusion.

infusorio *sm.* infusorial.

ingabbiare *vt.* **1.** to cage **2.** (*fig.*) to lock up.

ingaggiare *vt.* to engage.

ingaggio *sm.* engagement.

ingagliardire *vt.* to strengthen. ♦ **ingagliardirsi** *vr.* to strengthen.

ingannare *vt.* to deceive || — *il tempo*, to while away the time. ♦ **ingannarsi** *vr.* to be mistaken.

ingannatore *agg.* deceiving. ♦ **ingannatore** *sm.* deceiver.

ingannévole *agg.* deceitful.

inganno *sm.* deception, fraud.

ingarbugliare *vt.* to entangle. ♦ **ingarbugliarsi** *vr.* to get (*v. irr.*) mixed up.

ingegnarsi *vr.* to contrive (to).

ingegnere *sm.* engineer.

ingegnerìa *sf.* engineering.

ingegno *sm.* talent.

ingegnosità *sf.* ingeniousness.

ingegnoso *agg.* ingenious.

ingelosire *vt.* to make (*v. irr.*) jealous. ♦ **ingelosirsi** *vr.* to become (*v. irr.*) jealous.

ingenerare *vt.* to engender.

ingeneroso *agg.* selfish.

ingente *agg.* huge.

ingentilire *vt.* to refine.

ingenuità *sf.* naïveness.

ingenuo *agg.* naïve.

ingerenza *sf.* interference.

ingerimento *sm.* swallowing.

ingerire *vt.* to swallow.

ingessare *vt.* to plaster.

ingessatura *sf.* **1.** plastering **2.** (*med.*) plaster cast.

inghiaiare *vt.* to gravel.

inghiottire *vt.* **1.** to swallow **2.** (*di acque ecc.*) to engulf **3.** (*sopportare*) to lump.

inghirlandare *vt.* to wreathe.

ingiallire *vt.* e *vi.* to yellow.

ingigantire *vt.* to magnify. ♦ **ingigantire** *vi.* to become (*v. irr.*) gigantic.

inginocchiarsi *vr.* to kneel (*v. irr.*) (down).

inginocchiatoio *sm.* kneeler.

ingioiellare *vt.* to bejewel.

ingiú *avv.* down, downwards.

ingiùngere *vt.* to order.

ingiuntivo *agg.* injunctive.

ingiunzione *sf.* injunction.

ingiuria *sf.* insult.

ingiuriare *vt.* to insult.

ingiurioso *agg.* insulting.

ingiustamente *avv.* unjustly.

ingiustificàbile *agg.* unjustifiable.

ingiustificato *agg.* unjustified.

ingiustizia *sf.* unjustice.

ingiusto *agg.* unjust.

inglese *agg.* English. ♦ **inglese** *sm.* Englishman (*pl.* -men) || *gli Inglesi*, the English (people).

inglobare *vt.* to inglobe.

inglorioso *agg.* inglorious.

ingobbire *vi.* to become (*v. irr.*) humpbacked. ♦ **ingobbirsi** *vr.* to become humpbacked.

ingoiare *vt.* to swallow.

ingolfarsi *vr.* (*fig.*) to throw (*v. irr.*) oneself (into).

ingoiare *vt.* to gulp down.

ingolosire *vt.* to make (*v. irr.*) greedy.

ingombrante *agg.* cumbersome.

ingombrare *vt.* to encumber.

ingombro *agg.* encumbered (with). ♦ **ingombro** *sm.* encumbrance.

ingommare *vt.* 1. to gum 2. (*incollare*) to stick (*v. irr.*).

ingordigia *sf.* greed.

ingordo *agg.* greedy.

ingorgare *vt.* to choke. ♦ **ingorgarsi** *vr.* to become (*v. irr.*) choked.

ingorgo *sm.* 1. obstruction 2. (*del traffico*) traffic jam.

ingozzare *vt.* to gulp.

ingranaggio *sm.* 1. gear 2. (*fig.*) mechanism.

ingranare *vt.* 1. to put (*v. irr.*) into gear 2. (*auto*) — *una marcia*, to engage a gear. ♦ **ingranare** *vi.* (*fam.*) to get (*v. irr.*) along (with).

ingrandimento *sm.* 1. enlargement 2. (*ott.*) magnification.

ingrandire *vt.* 1. to enlarge 2. (*ott.*) to magnify. ♦ **ingrandirsi** *vr.* to become (*v. irr.*) larger.

ingrassare *vt.* 1. to fatten 2. (*lubrificare*) to grease. ♦ **ingrassare** *vi.* to grow (*v. irr.*) fat.

ingrasso *sm.* fattening.

ingratitùdine *sf.* ingratitude.

ingrato *agg.* ungrateful. ♦ **ingrato** *sm.* ingrate.

ingravidare *vt.* to make (*v. irr.*) pregnant. ♦ **ingravidare** *vi.* to become (*v. irr.*) pregnant.

ingraziarsi *vr.* to get (*v. irr.*) into so.'s good graces.

ingrediente *sm.* ingredient.

ingresso *sm.* 1. entry 2. (*entrata*) entrance 3. (*accesso*) admittance.

ingrossamento *sm.* enlargement.

ingrossare *vt.* e *vi.* to enlarge. ♦ **ingrossarsi** *vr.* to become (*v. irr.*) bigger.

ingrosso (*nella loc. avv.*) all'—, wholesale.

ingualcìbile *agg.* crease-resistant.

inguaribile *agg.* incurable.

inguinale *agg.* inguinal.

inguine *sm.* inguen.

ingurgitare *vt.* to swallow.

inibire *vt.* to inhibit.

inibito *agg.* inhibited.

inibizione *sf.* inhibition.

iniettare *vt.* to inject.

iniezione *sf.* injection.

inimicare *vt.* to alienate. ♦ **inimicarsi** *vr.* to estrange from oneself.

inimicizia *sf.* enmity.

inimitàbile *agg.* incomparable, inimitable.

inimmaginàbile *agg.* unimaginable.

inintelligìbile *agg.* unintelligible.

ininterrotto *agg.* continuous, unceasing.

iniquità *sf.* iniquity.

iniquo *agg.* 1. unfair 2. (*malvagio*) wicked.

iniziale *agg.* initial, starting. ♦ **iniziale** *sf.* initial.

iniziare *vt.* 1. to begin (*v. irr.*), to start 2. (*introdurre*) to initiate.

iniziativa *sf.* initiative.

iniziato *agg.* e *sm.* initiate.

iniziazione *sf.* initiation.

inizio *sm.* beginning.

innaffiare *vt.* to water.

innaffiatoio *sm.* watering-pot.

innalzamento *sm.* elevation.

innalzare *vt.* 1. to raise 2. (*rendere più alto*) to heighten. ♦ **innalzarsi** *vr.* to rise (*v. irr.*).

innamoramento *sm.* falling in love.

innamorare *vt.* to charm. ♦ **innamorarsi** *vr.* to fall (*v. irr.*) in love (with)

innamorato *agg.* in love (with).
♦ **innamorato** *sm.* lover.

innanzi *avv.* 1. forward, on 2. (*di fronte*) in front of 3. (*più avanti*) further || *d'ora —*, from now on. ♦ **innanzi** *prep.* before.

innato *agg.* inborn.

innaturale *agg.* unnatural.

innegàbile *agg.* undeniable.

inneggiare *vi.* 1. to exalt 2. (*acclamare*) to cheer.

innervare *vt.* to innervate.

innervosire *vt.* to get (*v. irr.*) on so.'s nerves. ♦ **innervosirsi** *vr.* to get nervous.

innescamento *sm.* priming.

innescare *vt.* to prime.

innesco *sm.* primer.

innestare *vt.* 1. (*agr.; med.*) to graft 2. (*mecc.*) to engage.

innesto *sm.* 1. (*agr.; med.*) graft 2. (*mecc.*) clutch.

inno *sm.* hymn || *— nazionale*, national anthem.

innocente *agg. e sm.* innocent.

innocenza *sf.* innocence.

innocuità *sf.* innocuousness.

innocuo *agg.* harmless.

innominàbile *agg.* unmentionable.

innovare *vt.* to innovate.

innovatore *agg.* innovating. ♦ **innovatore** *sm.* innovator.

innovazione *sf.* innovation.

innumerévole *agg.* numberless.

inoculare *vt.* to inoculate.

inoculazione *sf.* inoculation.

inodoro *agg.* odourless.

inoffensivo *agg.* harmless.

inoltrare *vt.* to forward. ♦ **inoltrarsi** *vr.* to advance.

inoltrato *agg.* advanced, late.

inoltre *avv.* moreover, besides.

inoltro *sm.* 1. (*di merci*) forwarding 2. (*di documenti*) sending on.

inondare *vt.* to flood.

inondazione *sf.* flood.

inoperosità *sf.* inactivity.

inoperoso *agg.* inactive.

inopinàbile *agg.* inconceivable.

inopinato *agg.* unexpected.

inopportunità *sf.* inopportunity.

inopportuno *agg.* inopportune.

inoppugnàbile *agg.* incontestable.

inoppugnabilità *sf.* incontestability.

inorgànico *agg.* inorganic.

inorgoglire *vt.* to make (*v. irr.*) proud. ♦ **inorgoglirsi** *vr.* to become (*v. irr.*) proud.

inorridire *vt.* to horrify. ♦ **inorridire** *vi.* to be horrified.

inospitale *agg.* inhospitable.

inosservanza *sf.* inobservance.

inosservato *agg.* unobserved.

inossidàbile *agg.* rust-proof || *acciaio —*, stainless steel.

inquadramento *sm.* framing.

inquadrare *vt.* 1. to frame 2. (*fig.*) to set (*v. irr.*) 3. (*mil.*) to rank 4. (*foto, cine*) to frame.

inquadratura *sf.* (*cine*) shot.

inqualificàbile *agg.* despicable.

inquietante *agg.* worrying.

inquietare *vt.* to worry. ♦ **inquietarsi** *vr.* to get (*v. irr.*) angry.

inquieto *agg.* 1. restless 2. (*preoccupato*) worried 3. (*arrabbiato*) angry.

inquietùdine *sf.* 1. restlessness 2. (*preoccupazione*) anxiety.

inquilino *sm.* tenant.

inquinamento *sm.* defilement.

inquinare *vt.* to defile.

inquirente *agg.* investigating.

inquisire *vt.* to investigate. ♦ **inquisire** *vi.* to inquire.

inquisitore *agg.* inquiring. ♦ **inquisitore** *sm.* inquisitor.

inquisizione *sf.* inquisition.

insabbiamento *sm.* (*fig.*) hindering.

insabbiare *vt.* 1. to sand 2. (*fig.*) to hinder.

insaccare *vt.* to sack.

insalata *sf.* salad.

insalatiera *sf.* salad-bowl.

insalubre *agg.* unhealthy.

insalubrità *sf.* insalubrity.

insanàbile *agg.* incurable.

insanguinare *vt.* to cover (with blood). ♦ **insanguinarsi** *vr.* to become (*v. irr.*) bloodstained.

insano *agg.* insane.

insaponare *vt.* to soap.

insaponatura *sf.* soaping.

insaporire *vt.* to flavour.

insaporo *agg.* flavourless.

insaputa *sf.* (*nella loc. avv.*) *all'— di*, unknown (to).

insaziàbile *agg.* insatiable.

insaziabilità *sf.* insatiability.

insaziato *agg.* unappeased.

inscatolare *vt.* to tin.

inscenare *vt.* to stage.

inscindìbile *agg.* inseparable.

inscrìvere *vt.* 1. (*a una scuola, esame ecc.*) to enrol 2. (*scrivere, scolpire; geom.*) to inscribe.

insediamento *sm.* installation.

insediare *vt.* to install. ♦ **insediarsi** *vr.* to install oneself.

insegna *sf.* **1.** insignia (*pl.*) **2.** (*bandiera*) flag **3.** (*di negozio*) sign-board.

insegnamento *sm.* **1.** teaching **2.** (*precetto, lezione*) precept, lesson.

insegnante *agg.* teaching. ♦ **insegnante** *s.* teacher.

insegnare *vt.* to teach (*v. irr.*).

inseguimento *sm.* pursuit.

inseguire *vt.* to pursue.

inseguitore *sm.* pursuer.

insellare *vt.* to saddle.

inselvatichire *vi.* to grow (*v. irr.*) wild.

insenatura *sf.* inlet, creek.

insensatezza *sf.* **1.** craziness **2.** (*atto insensato*) foolish action.

insensato *agg.* foolish, crazy.

insensìbile *agg.* **1.** insensible **2.** (*indifferente*) indifferent **3.** (*frigido*) unfeeling.

insensibilità *sf.* **1.** insensibility **2.** (*indifferenza*) indifference.

insensibilmente *avv.* **1.** (*impercettibilmente*) imperceptibly, slightly **2.** (*senza sentimento*) insensibly.

inseparàbile *agg.* inseparable.

insepolto *agg.* unburied.

inserimento *sm.* insertion.

inserire *vt.* **1.** to insert **2.** (*elettr.*) to connect.

inserto *sm.* **1.** file, dossier **2.** (*cine, stampa*) insert.

inservìbile *agg.* useless.

inserviente *sm.* attendant.

inserzione *sf.* **1.** insertion **2.** (*pubblicitaria*) advertisement.

inserzionista *sm.* advertiser.

insetticida *agg. e sm.* insecticide.

insettìvoro *agg.* insectivorous. ♦ **insettìvoro** *sm.* insectivore.

insetto *sm.* insect.

insicurezza *sf.* insecurity.

insidia *sf.* **1.** snare **2.** (*pericolo*) danger.

insidiare *vt.* to endanger ‖ — *la vita di una persona*, to attempt a person's life.

insidioso *agg.* insidious.

insieme *avv.* **1.** together **2.** (*allo stesso tempo*) at the same time. ♦ **insieme** *prep.* together (with). ♦ **insieme** *sm.* whole: *nell'*—, as a whole ‖ *sguardo d'*—, comprehensive view.

insigne *agg.* famous.

insignificante *agg.* insignificant.

insignire *vt.* to confer (sthg. upon).

insincerità *sf.* insincerity.

insincero *agg.* insincere.

insindacàbile *agg.* undisputable.

insinuante *agg.* insinuating.

insinuare *vt.* to hint. ♦ **insinuarsi** *vr.* to insinuate oneself.

insinuazione *sf.* hint, insinuation.

insipidezza *sf.* insipidness.

insìpido *agg.* **1.** tasteless **2.** (*fig.*) insipid.

insistente *agg.* **1.** insistent, steady **2.** (*molesto*) irritating.

insistenza *sf.* insistence.

insìstere *vi.* to insist (on).

ìnsito *agg.* inborn, inherent.

insoddisfatto *agg.* dissatisfied (with).

insoddisfazione *sf.* dissatisfaction (with).

insofferente *agg.* intolerant.

insofferenza *sf.* intolerance.

insoffrìbile *agg.* unbearable.

insolazione *sf.* sunstroke.

insolente *agg. e sm.* insolent.

insolentire *vt.* to insult.

insolenza *sf.* insolence.

insòlito *agg.* unusual.

insolùbile *agg.* insoluble.

insolubilità *sf.* insolubility.

insoluto *agg.* **1.** unsolved **2.** (*non pagato*) unpaid.

insolvente *agg.* insolvent.

insolvenza *sf.* insolvency.

insolvìbile *agg.* **1.** (*di debito*) unpayable **2.** (*di persona*) insolvent.

insolvibilità *sf.* insolvency.

insomma *avv.* finally, in short.

insondàbile *agg.* unfathomable.

insonne *agg.* sleepless.

insonnia *sf.* insomnia.

insonnolito *agg.* drowsy, sleepy.

insopportàbile *agg.* unbearable.

insopprimìbile *agg.* insuppressible.

insòrgere *vi.* **1.** to rise (*v. irr.*) **2.** (*protestare*) to protest, to rebel **3.** (*manifestarsi*) to arise (*v. irr.*).

insormontàbile *agg.* insurmountable.

insorto *sm.* rebel.

insospettàbile *agg.* beyond suspicion.

insospettato *agg.* unsuspected.

insospettire *vt.* to make (*v. irr.*) suspicious. ♦ **insospettirsi** *vr.* to grow (*v. irr.*) suspicious.

insostenìbile *agg.* unsustainable.

insostituìbile *agg.* irreplaceable.

insozzare vt. 1. to soil 2. (fig.) to disgrace.

insperàbile agg. beyond hope.

insperato agg. unhoped for.

inspiegàbile agg. inexplicable.

inspirare vt. to breathe in.

inspirazione sf. breathing in, inhalation.

instàbile agg. unstable || tempo —, unsettled weather.

instabilità sf. 1. instability 2. (fig.) fickleness.

installare vt. to install. ♦ **installarsi** vr. to settle.

installazione sf. installation.

instancàbile agg. untiring.

instaurare vt. to set (v. irr.) up.

instaurazione sf. establishment.

instradare vt. to direct, to coach.

insù avv. up, upwards.

insubordinatezza sf. insubordination.

insubordinato agg. insubordinate.

insubordinazione sf. insubordination.

insuccesso sm. failure.

insudiciare vt. to soil.

insufficiente agg. insufficient.

insufficienza sf. 1. insufficiency 2. (scol.) low mark.

insulare agg. insular.

insulina sf. insulin.

insulsàggine sf. 1. silliness 2. (cosa insulsa) nonsense.

insulso agg. silly.

insultare vt. to insult.

insulto sm. insult.

insuperàbile agg. insuperable.

insuperato agg. unsurpassed.

insuperbire vt. to elate. ♦ **insuperbirsi** vr. to pride oneself (on).

insurrezionale agg. insurrectional.

insurrezione sf. insurrection.

insussistente agg. unfounded.

intaccare vt. 1. to notch 2. (chim.) to etch 3. (fig.) to injure.

intacco sm. notch.

intagliare vt. 1. to carve 2. (incidere) to engrave.

intaglio sm. 1. carving 2. (incisione) engraving.

intangìbile agg. intangible.

intanto avv. meanwhile.

intarsiare vt. to inlay.

intarsio sm. inlay.

intasamento sm. obstruction.

intasare vt. to obstruct.

intascare vt. to pocket.

intatto agg. intact.

intavolare vt. 1. to plank 2. (iniziare) to begin (v. irr.), to start.

integèrrimo agg. strictly honest.

integràbile agg. integrable.

integrale agg. integral: (mat.) calcolo —, integral calculus.

integrante agg. integrant.

integrare vt. to integrate.

integrazione sf. integration.

integrità sf. integrity.

ìntegro agg. 1. integral 2. (onesto) honest.

intelaiatura sf. 1. framework 2. (di finestre) sash.

intellettivo agg. intellective.

intelletto sm. intellect.

intellettuale agg. e sm. intellectual.

intellettualismo sm. intellectualism.

intelligente agg. intelligent.

intelligenza sf. intelligence.

intelligìbile agg. intelligible.

intelligibilità sf. intelligibility.

intemerata sf. reprimand.

intemerato agg. faultless.

intemperante agg. intemperate.

intemperanza sf. intemperance.

intemperie sf. pl. inclemency of the weather (sing.).

intempestività sf. untimeliness.

intempestivo agg. untimely.

intendente agg. expert. ♦ **intendente** sm. superintendent.

intendenza sf. superintendence.

intèndere vt. 1. (capire) to understand (v. irr.) 2. (significare) to mean (v. irr.) 3. (avere intenzione di) to intend to. ♦ **intèndersi** vr. 1. (avere cognizione) to be a good judge 2. (mettersi d'accordo) to come (v. irr.) to an agreement.

intendimento sm. 1. understanding 2. (intenzione) intention.

intenditore sm. 1. good judge 2. (d'arte) connoisseur.

intenerimento sm. 1. softening 2. (fig.) tenderness.

intenerire vt. 1. to soften 2. (fig.) to move to pity. ♦ **intenerirsi** vr. to be moved to pity.

intensificare vt. to intensify.

intensificazione sf. intensification.

intensità sf. intensity.

intensivo agg. intensive.

intenso agg. intense.

intentàbile agg. 1. unattemptable 2. (giur.) suable.

intentare *vt.* to bring (*v. irr.*).
intento *agg.* intent. ♦ **intento** *sm.* aim, purpose.
intenzionale *agg.* deliberate.
intenzionato *agg.* disposed.
intenzione *sf.* intention.
intepidire *vt.* to warm, to make (*v. irr.*) tepid. ♦ **intepidirsi** *vr.* to get (*v. irr.*) tepid.
interamente *avv.* wholly, entirely.
intercalare *agg.* intercalary. ♦ **intercalare** *sm.* pet phrase.
intercalare *vt.* to intercalate.
intercambiàbile *agg.* interchangeable.
intercèdere *vi.* to intercede, to plead.
intercessione *sf.* intercession.
intercessore *sm.* intercessor.
intercettare *vt.* to intercept.
intercettatore *sm.* interceptor.
intercettazione *sf.* interception.
intercomunale *sf.* (*tel.*) long-distance call.
intercontinentale *agg.* intercontinental.
intercòrrere *vi.* 1. to pass 2. (*accadere*) to happen.
intercostale *agg.* intercostal.
interdetto *agg.* 1. prohibited 2. (*giur.*) interdicted. ♦ **interdetto** *sm.* interdict.
interdipendente *agg.* interdependent.
interdipendenza *sf.* interdependence.
interdire *vt.* to interdict.
interdizione *sf.* interdiction.
interessamento *sm.* concern.
interessante *agg.* interesting.
interessare *vt.* 1. to interest 2. (*riguardare*) to concern. ♦ **interessarsi** *vr.* 1. to be interested (in) 2. (*provvedere*) to take (*v. irr.*) care (of).
interessato *agg.* interested.
interesse *sm.* interest.
interessenza *sf.* share, profit.
interezza *sf.* wholeness.
interferenza *sf.* interference.
interferire *vi.* to interfere.
interiezione *sf.* interjection.
interinale *agg.* temporary.
interiora *sf. pl.* entrails.
interiore *agg.* inner. ♦ **interiore** *sm.* interior, inside.
interiorità *sf.* inwardness.
interiormente *avv.* 1. (*intimamente*) innerly 2. (*nell'interno*) inside.

interlìnea *sf.* 1. interline 2. (*tip.*) lead.
interlineare *vt.* 1. to interline 2. (*tip.*) to lead (*v. irr.*).
interlineare *vt.* to interline.
interlocutore *sm.* interlocutor.
interlocutorio *agg.* interlocutory.
interloquire *vi.* to join in the conversation.
interludio *sm.* interlude.
intermediario *agg.* intermediary. ♦ **intermediario** *sm.* 1. go-between 2. (*comm.*) middleman (*pl.* -men).
intermedio *agg.* intermediate, middle.
intermezzo *sm.* 1. intermission 2. (*mus.*) intermezzo.
interminàbile *agg.* endless.
intermittente *agg.* intermittent.
intermittenza *sf.* intermittence.
internamento *sm.* internment.
internare *vt.* to intern.
internato *agg.* interned. ♦ **internato** *sm.* (*scol.*) boarding-school.
internazionale *agg.* international.
internazionalismo *sm.* internationalism.
internazionalizzare *vt.* to internationalize.
interno *agg.* 1. internal, interior 2. (*interiore*) inner. ♦ **interno** *sm.* interior.
intero *agg.* 1. whole 2. (*intatto*) intact.
interpellanza *sf.* interrogation.
interpellare *vt.* 1. (*pol.*) to interpellate 2. (*giur.*) to summon 3. (*chiedere*) to ask.
interplanetario *agg.* interplanetary.
interpolare *vt.* to interpolate.
interpolazione *sf.* interpolation.
interporre *vt.* to interpose.
interpretare *vt.* 1. to interpret, to render 2. (*teat.*) to play.
interpretativo *agg.* interpretative.
interpretazione *sf.* 1. interpretation 2. (*cine*) starring 3. (*mus.*) performance 4. (*teat.*) acting.
intèrprete *s.* 1. interpreter 2. (*teat.; cine*) actor, player.
interpunzione *sf.* punctuation.
interramento *sm.* burial.
interrare *vt.* 1. to bury 2. (*riempire di terra*) to fill up with earth.
interrogare *vt.* to question.
interrogativo *agg.* interrogative ‖ *punto —*, question mark. ♦ **interrogativo** *sm.* interrogative.

interrogatore *agg.* interrogating. ♦
interrogatore *sm.* examiner.
interrogatorio *sm.* examination.
interrogazione *sf.* **1.** interrogation
2. (*scol.*) oral test.
interròmpere *vt.* to interrupt. ♦
interròmpersi *vr.* to stop.
interrotto *agg.* interrupted || *strada interrotta*, blocked road.
interruttore *sm.* (*elettr.*) switch.
interruzione *sf.* interruption.
intersecare *vt.* to intersect.
intersezione *sf.* intersection.
interstizio *sm.* interstice.
intervallare *vt.* to space.
intervallo *sm.* **1.** interval **2.** (*spazio*) space.
intervenire *vi.* **1.** to intervene **2.**
(*essere presenti*) to be present.
interventismo *sm.* interventionism.
interventista *s.* interventionist.
intervento *sm.* **1.** intervention **2.**
(*presenza*) presence **3.** (*chir.*) operation.
intervenuto *agg.* present. ♦ **intervenuto** *sm.* person present.
intervista *sf.* interview.
intervistare *vt.* to interview.
intesa *sf.* agreement.
inteso *agg.* **1.** agreed (upon) **2.** (*mirante*) aiming (at).
intèssere *vt.* to interweave (*v. irr.*).
intestare *vt.* to head, to register. ♦
intestarsi *vr.* to be determinated.
intestatario *sm.* holder.
intestato *agg.* **1.** headed **2.** (*giur.*) registered **3.** (*senza testamento*) intestate **4.** (*ostinato*) stubborn.
intestazione *sf.* **1.** title **2.** (*di lettera ecc.*) heading.
intestinale *agg.* intestinal.
intestino *sm.* intestine.
intimare *vt.* **1.** (*ordinare*) to order **2.** (*ingiungere*) to summon.
intimazione *sf.* **1.** order **2.** (*ingiunzione*) summons.
intimidatorio *agg.* intimidatory.
intimidazione *sf.* intimidation.
intimidire *vt.* **1.** to make (*v. irr.*) shy **2.** (*impaurire*) to intimidate.
intimità *sf.* **1.** privacy **2.** (*familiarità*) familiarity.
intimo *agg.* **1.** intimate **2.** (*profondo*) deep. ♦ **intimo** *sm.* **1.** (*amico*) intimate **2.** (*animo*) soul || *nell'*~, at heart.
intimorire *vt.* to frighten. ♦ **intimorirsi** *vr.* to get (*v. irr.*)

frightened.
intingere *vt.* to dip.
intingolo *sm.* **1.** gravy **2.** (*salsa*) sauce.
intirizzire *vt.* to benumb.
intitolare *vt.* **1.** to entitle **2.** (*dedicare*) to dedicate.
intoccàbile *agg. e sm.* untouchable.
intolleràbile *agg.* intolerable.
intollerante *agg.* intolerant.
intolleranza *sf.* intolerance.
intonacare *vt.* to plaster.
intonacatura *sf.* plastering.
intònaco *sm.* plaster.
intonare *vt.* **1.** to tune **2.** (*cantilenare*) to intone. ♦ **intonarsi** *vr.* **1.** to harmonize (with) **2.** (*di colori*) to match.
intonato *agg.* **1.** in tune **2.** (*di colori*) matching.
intonazione *sf.* **1.** intonation **2.** (*di strumenti*) tuning **3.** (*di colori, voce*) tone.
intonso *agg.* (*di libri*) uncut.
intontimento *sm.* stunning.
intontire *vt.* to stun.
intoppare *vt.* to stumble (on).
intoppo *sm.* **1.** obstacle **2.** (*fig.*) hitch.
intorbidare *vt.* to make (*v. irr.*) muddy. ♦ **intorbidarsi** *vr.* to become (*v. irr.*) muddy.
intorno *avv.* round, around. ♦ **intorno a** *prep.* **1.** round, around **2.** (*circa, su di*) about.
intorpidimento *sm.* numbness.
intorpidire *vt.* to benumb. ♦ **intorpidirsi** *vr.* to grow (*v. irr.*) numb.
intossicare *vt.* to poison.
intossicazione *sf.* poisoning.
intraducìbile *agg.* untranslatable.
intralciare *vt.* to hinder, to interfere.
intralcio *sm.* hindrance.
intrallazzo *sm.* **1.** plotting **2.** (*imbroglio*) swindle.
intramezzare *vt.* to interpose, to alternate.
intramontàbile *agg.* everlasting.
intramuscolare *agg.* intermuscular.
intransigente *agg.* strict, intransigent.
intransigenza *sf.* intransigence.
intransitivo *agg. e sm.* intransitive.
intrappolare *vt.* to entrap.
intraprendente *agg.* enterprising.
intraprendenza *sf.* enterprise.

intraprèndere *vt.* **1.** to undertake (*v. irr.*), to start **2.** (*una professione*) to go (*v. irr.*) in for.

intrattàbile *agg.* intractable.

intrattenere *vt.* to entertain. ♦ **intrattenersi** *vr.* **1.** to linger **2.** (*dilungarsi*) to dwell (*v. irr.*).

intravedere *vt.* **1.** (*vedere di sfuggita*) to catch (*v. irr.*) a glimpse of **2.** (*vedere indistintamente*) to see (*v. irr.*) indistinctly.

intrecciare *vt.* **1.** to interlace || — *danze*, to dance **2.** (*capelli, nastri*) to plait.

intreccio *sm.* **1.** interlacement **2.** (*di romanzi*) plot.

intrèpido *agg.* brave, fearless.

intricare *vt.* to tangle. ♦ **intricarsi** *vr.* to get (*v. irr.*) entangled.

intrico *sm.* tangle.

intrìdere *vt.* to soak.

intrigante *agg.* crafty. ♦ **intrigante** *sm.* intriguer.

intrigare *vi.* to intrigue. ♦ **intrigarsi** *vr.* to meddle (with).

intrigo *sm.* intrigue, plot.

intrìnseco *agg.* intrinsic.

intristire *vi.* **1.** to pine away **2.** (*incattivire*) to grow (*v. irr.*) wicked.

introdotto *agg.* **1.** (*importato*) imported **2.** (*conosciuto*) well-known.

intriso *agg.* soaked (with), imbrued.

introdurre *vt.* **1.** to introduce **2.** (*far entrare*) to show (*v. irr.*) in. ♦ **introdursi** *vr.* to get (*v. irr.*) into, to slip into.

introduttivo *agg.* introductory.

introduzione *sf.* introduction.

introitare *vt.* to cash.

intròito *sm.* profit.

introméttere *vt.* to introduce. ♦ **introméttersi** *vr.* to interfere.

intromissione *sf.* intrusion.

intronare *vt.* to stun.

introspettivo *agg.* introspective.

introspezione *sf.* introspection.

introvàbile *agg.* not to be found.

introversione *sf.* introversion.

introverso *agg.* introverted. ♦ **introverso** *sm.* introvert.

intrufolarsi *vr.* to intrude (in).

intruglio *sm.* bad mixture.

intruppamento *sm.* trooping.

intrupparsi *vr.* to troop.

intrusione *sf.* intrusion.

intruso *sm.* intruder.

intuìbile *agg.* guessable.

intuire *vt.* to guess, to perceive.

intuitivo *agg.* intuitive.

intùito *sm.* intuition, insight.

intuizione *sf.* intuition.

inturgidimento *sm.* swelling.

inturgidire *vi.* to swell (up). **inturgidirsi** *vr.* to swell (up).

inuguale *agg.* unlike.

inumanità *sf.* inhumanity.

inumano *agg.* inhuman.

inumare *vt.* to inter.

inumazione *sf.* interment.

inumidire *vt.* to moisten. ♦ **inumidirsi** *vr.* to moisten.

inurbanità *sf.* incivility.

inurbano *agg.* uncivil.

inurbarsi *vr.* to inurbate.

inusitato *agg.* unusual.

inùtile *agg.* useless.

inutilità *sf.* uselessness.

inutilizzàbile *agg.* unusable.

invadente *agg.* intrusive.

invadenza *sf.* intrusiveness.

invàdere *vt.* to invade.

invaghimento *sm.* fancy (for).

invaghirsi *vr.* to take (*v. irr.*) a fancy (for), to fall (*v. irr.*) in love (with).

invaghito *agg.* fond (of), infatuated.

invalere *vi.* to prevail.

invalicàbile *agg.* impassable.

invalidare *vt.* to invalidate.

invalidazione *sf.* invalidation.

invalidità *sf.* invalidity.

invàlido *agg.* e *sm.* invalid.

invalso *agg.* prevailed.

invano *avv.* in vain.

invariàbile *agg.* **1.** invariable **2.** (*di tempo*) unchangeable.

invariabilità *sf.* invariability.

invariato *agg.* unchanged.

invasamento *sm.* obsession.

invasare *vt.* to possess.

invasato *agg.* possessed. ♦ **invasato** *sm.* possessed person.

invasione *sf.* invasion.

invasore *sm.* invader.

invecchiamento *sm.* ageing.

invecchiare *vt.* to make (*v. irr.*) old. ♦ **invecchiare** *vi.* to grow (*v. irr.*) old.

invece *avv.* on the contrary || — *di*, instead of.

inveire *vi.* to rail (at).

invelenire *vt.* to embitter.

invendìbile *agg.* unsaleable.

invendicato *agg.* unavenged.

invenduto *agg.* unsold.

inventare vt. to invent.

inventariare vt. to inventory.

inventario sm. inventory ‖ con beneficio d'—, with reservation.

inventiva sf. inventiveness.

inventivo agg. inventive.

inventore sm. inventor.

invenzione sf. invention.

inverdire vi. to turn green.

inverecondia sf. immodesty.

inverecondo agg. immodest.

inverificàbile agg. unverifiable.

invernale agg. 1. winter (attr.) 2. (da inverno) wintry.

invernata sf. wintertime.

inverno sm. winter.

invero avv. indeed.

inverosimiglianza sf. unlikelihood.

inverosimile agg. unlikely.

inversione sf. inversion.

inverso agg. 1. (mat.) inverse 2. opposite, contrary. ♦ **inverso** sm. opposite, contrary.

invertebrato agg. e sm. invertebrate.

invertibile agg. invertible.

invertire vt. to invert ‖ — la marcia, to reverse.

invertito sm. invert.

invertitore sm. reverse gear.

investigare vt. to inquire.

investigativo agg. investigative.

investigatore sm. detective.

investigazione sf. investigation.

investimento sm. 1. investment 2. collision 3. (stradale) running down.

investire vt. 1. to invest (with) 2. (comm.) to invest 3. (assalire) to assail 4. (auto) to run (v. irr.) down.

investitore sm. (comm.) investor.

investitura sf. investiture.

inveterato agg. inveterate.

invetriata sf. glass window.

invettiva sf. invective.

inviare vt. to send (v. irr.).

inviato sm. 1. messenger 2. (in diplomazia) envoy 3. (in giornalismo) correspondent.

invidia sf. envy: per —, out of envy.

invidiàbile agg. enviable.

invidiare vt. to envy.

invidioso agg. envious.

invigorire vt. to strengthen. ♦ **invigorirsi** vr. to strengthen.

inviluppare vt. to envelop, to wrap up.

invincìbile agg. invincible.

invincibilità sf. invincibility.

invìo sm. 1. (per posta) mailing 2. (di merci) forwarding 3. (per nave) shipment 4. (di danaro) remittance.

inviolàbile agg. inviolable.

inviolabilità sf. inviolability.

inviperirsi vr. to become (v. irr.) furious.

inviperito agg. furious.

invischiare vt. 1. to lime 2. (fig.) to entangle. ♦ **invischiarsi** vr. to get (v. irr.) entangled.

invisibile agg. invisible.

invisibilità sf. invisibility.

inviso agg. disliked.

invitante agg. inviting.

invitare vt. 1. to invite 2. (domandare) to request.

invitato agg. invited. ♦ **invitato** sm. guest.

invito sm. invitation.

invitto agg. unconquered.

invocare vt. to invoke.

invocazione sf. invocation.

invogliare vt. to tempt.

involare vt. to abduct. ♦ **involarsi** vr. to flee, to run (v. irr.) away.

involontario agg. unintentional.

involto sm. bundle, parcel.

invòlucro sm. 1. envelope 2. (bot.) involucre.

involutivo agg. involutionary.

involuto agg. involved.

involuzione sf. 1. involution 2. (decadenza) decline.

invulneràbile agg. invulnerable.

invulnerabilità sf. invulnerability.

inzaccherare vt. to muddy. ♦ **inzaccherarsi** vr. to get (v. irr.) muddy.

inzuppare vt. 1. to soak 2. (intingere) to dip.

io pron. I: — stesso, I myself.

iodato agg. iodized. ♦ **iodato** sm. iodate.

iodio sm. iodine.

iole sf. gig.

ione sm. ion.

iònico agg. Ionic.

ionizzazione sf. ionization.

ionosfera sf. ionosphere.

iosa (nella loc. avv.) a —, in plenty.

iperalimentazione sf. hypernutrition.

ipèrbole sf. hyperbole.

iperbòlico agg. hyperbolic(al).

iperbòreo agg. hyperborean.

ipercrìtico *agg.* hypercritical.
ipermetropìa *sf.* hypermetropia.
ipermètrope *agg.* hypermetropic.
ipernutrizione *sf.* hypernutrition.
ipersensibile *agg.* hypersensitive.
ipersensibilità *sf.* hypersensitivity.
ipertensione *sf.* hypertension.
iperteso *agg. e sm.* hypertensive.
ipertrofìa *sf.* hypertrophy.
ipnosi *sf.* hypnosis.
ipnòtico *agg.* hypnotic.
ipnotismo *sm.* hypnotism.
ipnotizzare *vt.* to hypnotize.
ipnotizzatore *sm.* hypnotizer.
ipocondrìa *sf.* hypochondria.
ipocondrìaco *agg. e sm.* hypochondriac.
ipocrisìa *sf.* hypocrisy.
ipòcrita *agg.* hypocritical. ♦ **ipòcrita** *sm.* hypocrite.
ipodèrmico *agg.* hypodermic.
ipodermoclisi *sf.* hypodermoclysis.
ipòfisi *sf.* hypophysis.
ipoteca *sf.* mortgage.
ipotecare *vt.* to mortgage.
ipotenusa *sf.* hypotenuse.
ipòtesi *sf.* **1.** hypothesis (*pl.* -ses) **2.** (*supposizione*) supposition.
ipotètico *agg.* hypothetical.
ìppica *sf.* horse-racing.
ìppico *agg.* horse (*attr.*).
ippocampo *sm.* hippocampus (*pl.* -pi).
ippocastano *sm.* horse-chestnut.
ippòdromo *sm.* race-course.
ippopòtamo *sm.* hippopotamus.
ira *sf.* anger, rage.
iracondo *agg.* irascible.
irascìbile *agg.* irritable.
irascibilità *sf.* irritability.
irato *agg.* angry.
iridato *agg.* iridescent.
ìride *sf.* iris.
iridescente *agg.* iridescent.
iridescenza *sf.* iridescence.
irlandese *agg.* Irish.
ironìa *sf.* irony.
irònico *agg.* ironic(al).
ironizzare *vi.* to make (*v. irr.*) ironical remarks.
iroso *agg.* wrathful.
irradiamento *sm.* irradiation.
irradiare *vt.* to irradiate.
irradiazione *sf.* V. *irradiamento.*
irraggiare *vt.* V. *irradiare.*
irraggiungìbile *agg.* unreachable.
irragionévole *agg.* unreasonable.
irrancidire *vi.* to grow (*v. irr.*) rank.

irrazionale *agg.* irrational.
irrazionalità *sf.* irrationality.
irreale *agg.* unreal.
irrealizzàbile *agg.* unrealizable.
irrealtà *sf.* unreality.
irreconciliàbile *agg.* irreconcilable.
irrecuperàbile *agg.* irrecoverable.
irrefrenàbile *agg.* unrestrainable.
irrefutàbile *agg.* irrefutable.
irregolare *agg.* irregular.
irregolarità *sf.* irregularity.
irremovìbile *agg.* **1.** immovable **2.** (*inflessibile*) inflexible.
irreparàbile *agg.* irreparable.
irreperìbile *agg.* elusive: *rendersi —,* to hide (*v. irr.*) oneself.
irreprensìbile *agg.* irreproachable.
irrequietezza *sf.* restlessness.
irrequieto *agg.* restless.
irresistìbile *agg.* irresistible.
irresolutezza *sf.* irresolution.
irresoluto *agg.* hesitating.
irrespiràbile *agg.* unbreathable.
irresponsàbile *agg.* irresponsible.
irresponsabilità *sf.* irresponsibility.
irrestringìbile *agg.* unshrinkable.
irretire *vt.* to snare.
irreversìbile *agg.* irreversible.
irreversibilità *sf.* irreversibility.
irrevocàbile *agg.* irrevocable.
irriconoscìbile *agg.* unrecognizable.
irrìdere *vt.* to laugh at.
irriducìbile *agg.* irreducible.
irriflessione *sf.* thoughtlessness.
irriflessivo *agg.* thoughtless.
irrigàbile *agg.* irrigable.
irrigare *vt.* to irrigate.
irrigazione *sf.* irrigation.
irrigidimento *sm.* stiffening.
irrigidire *vt.* to stiffen. ♦ **irrigidirsi** *vr.* to stiffen.
irriguo *agg.* well-watered.
irrilevante *agg.* insignificant.
irrimediàbile *agg.* irremediable.
irrisione *sf.* mockery.
irrisorio *agg.* derisory, paltry.
irrispettoso *agg.* disrespectful.
irritàbile *agg.* **1.** (*di persona*) irritable **2.** (*di pelle*) sensitive.
irritabilità *sf.* **1.** (*di persona*) irritability **2.** (*di pelle*) sensitiveness.
irritante *agg.* irritating.
irritare *vt.* to irritate. ♦ **irritarsi** *vr.* **1.** to grow (*v. irr.*) angry **2.** (*di pelle*) to become (*v. irr.*) irritated.
irritazione *sf.* **1.** irritation **2.** (*di pelle*) inflammation.

irriverente *agg.* disrespectful.
irriverenza *sf.* irreverence.
irrobustire *vt.* to strengthen. ♦
  irrobustirsi *vr.* to strengthen.
irròmpere *vi.* 1. to break (*v. irr.*)
  into 2. (*di acque*) to overflow.
irrorare *vt.* to sprinkle.
irroratrice *sf.* sprayer.
irruente *agg.* impetuous.
irruenza *sf.* impetuosity.
irruvidire *vt.* to roughen.
irruzione *sf.* irruption: *fare —,*
  to rush into.
irsuto *agg.* shaggy.
irto *agg.* bristling (with).
iscritto *sm.* member.
iscrivere *vt.* 1. (*a scuola, esami
  ecc.*) to enrol 2. (*registrare*) to record 3. (*scolpire*) to engrave. ♦
  iscriversi *vr.* to enter, to join.
iscrizione *sf.* 1. inscription 2. (*a
  scuola, esami ecc.*) entry || *do-
  manda d'—,* application.
islàmico *agg.* Islamic.
islamismo *sm.* Islamism.
isocronismo *sm.* isochronism.
ìsola *sf.* island.
isolamento *sm.* 1. isolation 2.
  (*elettr.*) insulation || *— acustico,*
  sound-proofing.
isolano *agg.* insular. ♦ **isolano** *sm.*
  islander.
isolante *agg.* insulating. ♦ **isolante** *sm.* insulator.
isolare *vt.* 1. to isolate 2. (*elettr.*)
  to insulate || *— acusticamente,* to
  soundproof. ♦ **isolarsi** *vr.* to
  seclude oneself.
isolato *agg.* 1. isolated 2. (*elettr.*)
  insulated. ♦ **isolato** *sm.* (*edil.*)
  block.
isolatore *sm.* insulator.
isolazionismo *sm.* isolationism.
isolazionista *s.* isolationist.
isolotto *sm.* islet.
isomorfismo *sm.* isomorphism.
isomorfo *agg.* isomorphous.
isòscele *agg.* isosceles.
isotèrmico *agg.* isothermal.
isòtopo *sm.* isotope.
isòtropo *sm.* isotrope.
ispànico *agg.* Hispanic.
ispanismo *sm.* Hispanicism.
ispanista *s.* Hispanist.
ispettorato *sm.* inspectorate.
ispettore *sm.* inspector.
ispezionare *vt.* to inspect.
ispezione *sf.* inspection.
ispido *agg.* hispid.

ispirare *vt.* to inspire (with). ♦
  ispirarsi *vr.* to draw (*v. irr.*) one's
  inspiration (from).
ispirato *agg.* 1. inspired 2. (*basato*)
  imbued (with).
ispiratore *agg.* inspiring. ♦ **ispiratore** *sm.* inspirer.
ispirazione *sf.* inspiration.
israeliano *agg. e sm.* Israeli.
israelita *agg. e s.* Israelite.
issare *vt.* to hoist.
istantànea *sf.* snapshot: *fare un'—,*
  to snapshot.
istantaneità *sf.* instantaneousness.
istantàneo *agg.* instantaneous.
istante *sm.* instant || *all'—, sull'—,*
  instantly.
istanza *sf.* 1. request, instance 2.
  (*supplica*) entreaty 3. (*domanda
  scritta*) application.
istèrico *agg.* hysteric(al). ♦ **istèrico** *sm.* hysterical man (*pl.* -men).
isterilire *vt.* to sterilize. ♦ **isteri-
  lirsi** *vr.* to become (*v. irr.*) barren.
isterismo *sm.* hysteria.
istigare *vt.* to instigate.
istigatore *sm.* instigator.
istigazione *sf.* instigation.
istintivo *agg.* instinctive.
istinto *sm.* instinct.
istituire *vt.* 1. to institute 2. (*fondare*) to found 3. (*giur.*) to appoint.
istituto *sm.* 1. institute 2. (*istituzione*) institution 3. (*scuola*)
  school.
istitutore *sm.* tutor.
istitutrice *sf.* governess.
istituzionale *agg.* institutional.
istituzione *sf.* institution.
istmo *sm.* isthmus (*pl.* -mi).
istologìa *sf.* histology.
ìstrice *sm.* hedgehog.
istrione *sm.* 1. (*teat.*) histrion 2.
  (*ciarlatano*) quack.
istriònico *agg.* histrionic.
istruire *vt.* 1. to teach (*v. irr.*) 2.
  (*dare istruzioni*) to instruct, to direct 3. (*giur.*) to institute. ♦
  istruirsi *vr.* to educate oneself.
istruito *agg.* learned.
istruttivo *agg.* instructive.
istruttore *sm.* instructor: *giudice
  —,* examining magistrate.
istruttorìa *sf.* examination || *apri-
  re l'—,* to open proceedings.
istruzione *sf.* 1. education 2. (*cultura*) learning 3. (*insegnamento*)
  teaching 4. (*ordine*) instruction.

istupidire *vt.* to make (*v. irr.*) stupid. ♦ **istupidirsi** *v.r.* to become (*v. irr.*) stupid.
italiano *agg.* e *sm.* Italian.
itinerario *sm.* itinerary.
itterizia *sf.* jaundice.
ittiologia *sf.* ichthyology.
ittiòlogo *sm.* ichthyologist.
iugoslavo *agg.* e *sm.* Yugoslav.
iugulare *agg.* jugular.
iuta *sf.* jute.
ivi *avv.* there.

L

la¹ *art.* the. ♦ **la** *pron.* **1.** (*per donna*) her **2.** (*per animale e cosa*) it **3.** (*forma di cortesia*) you.
la² *sm.* (*mus.*) A.
là *avv.* there ‖ *l'al di —*, the hereafter; *— per —*, on the spot; *al di — di*, beyond; *più in —*, (*spazio*) further on, (*tempo*) later on.
labbro *sm.* lip.
labiale *agg.* labial.
làbile *agg.* fleeting: *memoria —*, weak memory.
labirinto *sm.* labyrinth.
laboratorio *sm.* **1.** laboratory **2.** (*artigianale*) workshop.
laboriosità *sf.* laboriousness.
laborioso *agg.* laborious.
laburismo *sm.* labourism.
laburista *agg.* labour ‖ *partito —*, Labour Party. ♦ **laburista** *s.* Labourite.
lacca *sf.* lacquer.
laccare *vt.* to lacquer.
laccatura *sf.* lacquering.
laccio *sm.* **1.** string ‖ *lacci da scarpe*, shoe-laces **2.** (*trappola*) snare ‖ *prendere al — (fig.)*, to ensnare.
laceramento *sm.* tearing.
lacerante *agg.* rending.
lacerare *vt.* to tear (*v. irr.*) (up), to rend (*v. irr.*) (*anche fig.*). ♦ **lacerarsi** *vr.* to tear.
lacerazione *sf.* laceration.
làcero *agg.* **1.** torn **2.** (*med.*) lacerated.
laconicità *sf.* laconicism.
lacònico *agg.* laconic(al).
làcrima *sf.* tear.
lacrimale *agg.* lachrymal.

lacrimare *vi.* to weep (*v. irr.*).
lacrimazione *sf.* lachrymation.
lacrimévole *agg.* tearful.
lacrimògeno *agg.* lachrymatory: *gas —*, tear-gas.
lacrimoso *agg.* tearful.
lacuna *sf.* gap.
lacunoso *agg.* lacunous.
lacustre *agg.* lacustrine.
laddove *cong.* whereas. ♦ **laddove** *avv.* (there) where.
ladra *sf.* woman thief.
ladro *agg.* thieving. ♦ **ladro** *sm.* thief: *al —!*, stop thief!
ladrocinio *sm.* theft.
ladrone *sm.* robber.
ladroneria *sf.* robbery.
laggiù *avv.* down there.
lagna *sf.* lament.
lagnanza *sf.* complaint.
lagnarsi *vr.* to complain (of).
lago *sm.* lake.
laguna *sf.* lagoon.
lagunare *agg.* lagoon (*attr.*).
laicato *sm.* laity.
laicismo *sm.* laicism.
laicizzare *vt.* to laicize.
làico *agg.* laic. ♦ **làico** *sm.* layman (*pl.* -men).
laidezza *sf.* ugliness, foulness.
làido *agg.* **1.** dirty **2.** (*brutto*) ugly.
lama¹ *sf.* blade.
lama² *sm.* (*zool.*) llama.
lama³ *sm.* (*monaco buddista*) lama.
lambiccare *vt.* to distil ‖ *lambiccarsi il cervello*, to rack one's brains.
lambiccato *agg.* **1.** distilled **2.** (*ricercato*) over-elaborate.
lambicco *sm.* alembic.
lambire *vt.* to lick.
lamella *sf.* lamella (*pl.* -lae).
lamentare *vt.* to lament. ♦ **lamentarsi** *vr.* to moan.
lamentazione *sf.* lamentation.
lamentela *sf.* complaint.
lamentévole *agg.* mournful.
lamento *sm.* moan.
lamentoso *agg.* mournful.
lametta *sf.* razor-blade.
lamiera *sf.* sheet.
làmina *sf.* lamina (*pl.* -nae).
laminare *vt.* to laminate.
laminato *sm.* **1.** (*tessuto*) lamé **2.** (*metallo*) rolled section.
laminatoio *sm.* rolling-mill.
làmpada *sf.* lamp.
lampadario *sm.* chandelier, lamp holder.

lampadina *sf.* bulb.
lampante *agg.* glaring, evident.
lampeggiamento *sm.* 1. flashing, lightning 2. (*di fari, semafori ecc.*) winking 3. (*di auto*) to blink.
lampeggiare *vi.* 1. to flash, to lighten 2. (*di fari, semafori ecc.*) to wink.
lampeggiatore *sm.* 1. winking light 2. (*di auto*) blinker.
lampione *sm.* street-lamp.
lampo *sm.* 1. lightning 2. (*luce istantanea, anche fig.*) flash || *chiusura* —, zip-fastener.
lampone *sm.* raspberry.
lampreda *sf.* lamprey.
lana *sf.* wool.
lancetta *sf.* 1. (*di quadrante*) hand 2. (*di chirurgo*) lancet.
lancia¹ *sf.* lance.
lancia² *sf.* (*mar.*) launch || — *di salvataggio*, lifeboat.
lanciafiamme *sm.* flame-thrower.
lanciare *vt.* 1. to throw (*v. irr.*) 2. (*fig.*) to launch || — *un'occhiata*, to cast (*v. irr.*) a glance. ♦ **lanciarsi** *vr.* to dash.
lanciatore *sm.* thrower.
lanciere *sm.* lancer.
lancinante *agg.* piercing.
lancio *sm.* 1. throwing 2. (*pubblicitario*) launching.
landa *sf.* moor.
languido *agg.* languid.
languire *vi.* to languish.
languore *sm.* languor.
laniero *agg.* woollen.
lanificio *sm.* wool factory.
lanolina *sf.* lanolin.
lanoso *agg.* woolly.
lanterna *sf.* lantern.
lanùgine *sf.* down.
laparatomìa *sf.* laparotomy.
lapidare *vt.* to stone.
lapidario *agg.* lapidary.
lapidazione *sf.* lapidation.
làpide *sf.* 1. tablet 2. (*sepolcrale*) tombstone.
lapis *sm.* pencil.
lardellare *vt.* to .lard.
lardo *sm.* lard, bacon.
larga (*nella loc. avv.*) *alla* —, away (from).
largheggiare *vi.* to abound (with).
larghezza *sf.* 1. breadth 2. (*liberalità*) liberality 3. (*abbondanza*) plenty.
largire *vt.* to bestow (upon).
largitore *sm.* bestower.

largizione *sf.* bestowal.
largo *agg.* broad, wide. ♦ **largo** *sm.* 1. (*mar.*) open sea 2. (*piazza*) square || *prendere il* —, to set (*v. irr.*) · sail; (*fig.*) to run (*v. irr.*) away; *andare al* —, to take (*v. irr.*) to the open sea; *fare* —, to make (*v. irr.*) room.
làrice *sm.* larch.
laringe *sf.* larynx.
laringite *sf.* laryngitis.
larva *sf.* larva (*pl.* -ae).
lasciapassare *sm.* pass.
lasciare *vt.* 1. to leave (*v. irr.*) 2. (*permettere*) to let (*v. irr.*), to allow. ♦ **lasciarsi** *vr. rec.* (*separarsi*) to part.
làscito *sm.* legacy.
lascivia *sf.* lust.
lascivo *agg.* lustful.
lassativo *agg. e sm.* laxative.
lasso *sm.* lapse: *dopo un certo* — *di tempo*, after a lapse of time.
lassù *avv.* up there.
lastra *sf.* 1. (*vetro*) glass′ sheet 2. (*di pietra*) slab 3. (*di metallo, foto*) plate.
lastricare *vt.* to pave.
lastricatura *sf.* paving.
làstrico *sm.* pavement || *essere sul* — (*fig.*), to be destitute.
latente *agg.* latent.
laterale *agg.* side: *via* —, by-street.
lateralmente *avv.* sideways.
laterizi *sm. pl.* bricks.
làtice *sm.* latex.
latifondista *sm.* landowner.
latifondo *sm.* large landed estate.
latinismo *sm.* Latinism.
latinista · *s.* Latinist.
latinità *sf.* Latinity.
latino *agg. e sm.* Latin.
latitante *agg.* absconding: *essere* —, to be in hiding. ♦ **latitante** *s.* absconder.
latitanza *sf.* hiding: *darsi alla* —, to evade arrest.
latitùdine *sf.* latitude.
lato¹ *sm.* 1. side 2. (*fig.*) point of view || *d'altro* —, on the other hand; *da un* —, on the one hand.
lato² *agg.* wide || *in senso* —, in a broad sense.
latore *sm.* bearer.
latrare *vi.* to bark.
latrato *sm.* barking.
latrina *sf.* lavatory.
latta *sf.* tin.

lattaio sm. milkman (pl. -men).
lattante agg. unweaned. ♦ **lattante** s. suckling (baby).
latte sm. milk.
làtteo agg. milky.
latterìa sf. dairy.
latticini sm. pl. dairy products.
lattiera sf. milk-jug.
lattiginoso agg. 1. milky 2. (bot.) lactescent.
lattoniere sm. tinker.
lattosio sm. lactose.
lattuga sf. lettuce.
laudativo agg. laudatory.
làurea sf. degree.
laureare vt. to confer a degree (on). ♦ **laurearsi** vr. to graduate.
laureato agg. graduated. ♦ **laureato** sm. graduate || — in lettere, Doctor of Literature Degree.
làuro sm. laurel.
làuto agg. sumptuous || lauti guadagni, large profits.
lava sf. lava.
lavàbile agg. washable.
lavabo sm. washbowl.
lavaggio sm. washing: — a secco, dry cleaning.
lavagna sf. 1. blackboard 2. (ardesia) slate.
lavanda[1] sf. 1. washing 2. (med.) lavage.
lavanda[2] sf. (bot.) lavender.
lavandaia sf. laundress.
lavanderìa sf. laundry.
lavandino sm. sink.
lavapiatti s. dish-washer.
lavare vt. to wash: — a secco, to dry-clean. ♦ **lavarsi** vr. to wash (oneself).
lavata sf. wash || dare una — di capo (fig.), to scold.
lavativo sm. 1. (med.) enema 2. (fig.) lazy-bones.
lavatoio sm. 1. wash-house 2. (asse per lavare) wash-board.
lavatrice sf. 1. washer 2. (lavabiancheria) washing machine.
lavatura sf. washing.
lavina sf. landslip.
lavorante sm. worker.
lavorare vi. e vt. to work.
lavorativo agg. working || ora lavorativa, man-hour.
lavoratore agg. working. ♦ **lavoratore** sm. worker || — a giornata, day-labourer.
lavorazione sf. 1. processing 2. (fattura) work 3. (agr.) tilling || —

a mano, handwork.
lavorìo sm. intense activity.
lavoro sm. 1. work 2. (occupazione) job || — a ore, work by the hour; lavori di casa, housework; — su ordinazione, work to order; eccesso di —, overwork; — in proprio, self-employment.
lazzaretto sm. lazaretto.
lazzarone sm. slacker.
lazzo sm. joke.
le art. the. ♦ **le** pron. 1. (sing.) her, to her 2. (pl.) them 3. (forma di cortesia) you, to you.
leale agg. 1. loyal 2. (corretto) fair.
lealtà sf. 1. loyalty 2. (correttezza) fairness.
lebbra sf. leprosy.
lebbrosario sm. leper hospital.
lebbroso agg. leprous. ♦ **lebbroso** sm. leper.
leccapiedi sm. bootlicker.
leccare vt. to lick. ♦ **leccarsi** vr. to lick (oneself).
leccata sf. licking.
leccornìa sf. dainty.
lécito agg. 1. lawful 2. (giusto) right 3. (permesso) allowed. ♦ **lécito** sm. right.
lèdere vt. 1. to injure 2. (danneggiare) to damage.
lega sf. 1. league 2. (di metalli) alloy || di buona —, genuine; di cattiva —, low.
legaccio sm. string.
legale agg. legal, lawful || procedere per vie legali, to have recourse to the law. ♦ **legale** sm. lawyer.
legalità sf. legality.
legalizzare vt. 1. to legalize 2. (autenticare) to authenticate.
legalizzazione sf. 1. legalization 2. (autenticazione) authentication.
legame sm. 1. string 2. (vincolo) tie 3. (connessione) link.
legamento sm. 1. string 2. (anat.) ligament.
legare[1] vt. 1. to tie 2. (di metalli) to alloy (with) 3. (aver connessione) to be connected. ♦ **legarsi** vr. to bind (v. irr.) oneself.
legare[2] vt. (giur.) to bequeath.
legatario sm. legatee.
legato[1] sm. 1. ambassador 2. (eccl.) legate.
legato[2] sm. (giur.) legacy.
legatore sm. binder.
legatorìa sf. bookbinder's establishment.

legatura *sf.* **1.** binding **2.** (*mus.; med.*) ligature.

legazione *sf.* legation.

legge *sf.* **1.** law **2.** (*singola*) act **3.** (*regola*) rule || *progetto di —*, bill; *a norma di —*, according to the law; *a termini di —*, as by law enacted.

leggenda *sf.* legend.

leggendario *agg.* legendary.

lèggere *vt.* to read (*v. irr.*).

leggerezza *sf.* lightness.

leggero *agg.* light.

leggiadrìa *sf.* loveliness.

leggiadro *agg.* lovely.

leggìbile *agg.* readable.

leggìo *sm.* **1.** reading-desk **2.** (*mus.*) music-stand.

legiferare *vi.* to legislate.

legionario *agg.* e *sm.* legionary.

legione *sf.* legion.

legislativo *agg.* legislative.

legislatore *sm.* legislator.

legislatura *sf.* legislature.

legislazione *sf.* legislation.

legittimare *vt.* to legitimate.

legittimazione *sf.* legitimation.

legittimità *sf.* legitimacy.

legìttimo *agg.* legitimate.

legna *sf.* wood || *— da ardere*, firewood.

legnaia *sf.* wood-store.

legname *sm.* **1.** wood **2.** (*da costruzione*) timber.

legnata *sf.* blow with a cudgel.

legno *sm.* wood || *di —*, wooden.

legnosità *sf.* woodiness.

legnoso *agg.* **1.** woody **2.** (*duro*) tough.

legume *sm.* legume.

leguminoso *agg.* leguminous.

lei *pron.* **1.** (*sogg.*) she, (*compl.*) her **2.** (*forma di cortesia*) you.

lembo *sm.* **1.** edge **2.** (*pezzo*) strip.

lemma *sm.* lemma.

lèmure *sm.* lemur. ♦ **lèmuri** *sm. pl.* (*mit.*) lemures.

lena *sf.* **1.** energy **2.** (*respiro*) breath.

lenire *vt.* to soothe.

lenone *sm.* pander.

lente *sf.* lens: *— d'ingrandimento*, magnifying lens || *lenti*, glasses.

lentezza *sf.* slowness.

lenticchia *sf.* lentil.

lentìggine *sf.* freckle.

lentigginoso *agg.* freckly.

lento *agg.* **1.** slow **2.** (*non teso*) loose.

lenza *sf.* fishing-line.

lenzuolo *sm.* sheet.

leone *sm.* lion.

leonessa *sf.* lioness.

leonino *agg.* leonine.

leopardo *sm.* leopard.

lèpido *agg.* witty.

lepidòttero *sm.* lepidopteron (*pl.* -era).

leporino *agg.* leporine || *labbro —*, hare-lip.

lepre *sf.* hare.

lercio *agg.* filthy.

lèsbica *agg.* e *sf.* Lesbian.

lésina *sf.* awl.

lesinare *vi.* to be stingy. ♦ **lesinare** *vt.* to grudge.

lesionare *vt.* to damage, to injure.

lesione *sf.* **1.** lesion, injury **2.** (*danno*) damage.

lesivo *agg.* harmful.

leso *agg.* **1.** injured **2.** (*danneggiato*) damaged.

lessare *vt.* to boil.

lessicale *agg.* lexical.

lèssico *sm.* lexicon.

lessicografìa *sf.* lexicography.

lessicologìa *sf.* lexicology.

lesso *agg.* boiled. ♦ **lesso** *sm.* boiled meat.

lestezza *sf.* quickness.

lesto *agg.* quick.

lestofante *sm.* swindler.

letale *agg.* lethal.

letamaio *sm.* dunghill.

letame *sm.* dung.

letàrgico *agg.* **1.** lethargic **2.** (*di animali, in inverno*) hibernating; (*id., in estate*) estivating.

letargo *sm.* **1.** lethargy **2.** (*di animali, in inverno*) hibernation; (*id., in estate*) estivation.

letizia *sf.* joy.

lèttera *sf.* letter || *alla —*, literally.

letterale *agg.* literal.

letterario *agg.* literary.

letterato *agg.* lettered. ♦ **letterato** *sm.* literary man.

letteratura *sf.* literature.

lettiga *sf.* stretcher.

letto *sm.* bed || *camera da —*, bedroom; *vagone —*, sleeping-car.

lettore *sm.* reader.

lettura *sf.* reading.

leucemìa *sf.* leukaemia.

leucociti *sm. pl.* leucocytes.

leucoma *sm.* leucoma.

leva[1] *sf.* **1.** lever **2.** (*fig.*) stimulus || *far — sui sentimenti di qu.*, to play on so.'s feelings.

leva² sf. (mil.) draft: essere di —, to be due for draft.

levante sm. 1. east 2. (vento) levanter.

levare vt. 1. (sollevare) to raise 2. (togliere) to take (v. irr.) off. ♦ **levarsi** vr. 1. to rise (v. irr.) 2. (togliersi) to take off.

levata sf. 1. (di sole) rising 2. (di posta) collection || — di scudi rebellion.

levataccia sf. early rising.

levatoio agg. ponte —, drawbridge.

levatrice sf. midwife (pl. -wives).

levatura sf. intelligence.

levigare vt. to smooth.

levigatezza sf. 'smoothness.

levigato agg. smooth.

levitazione sf. levitation.

levriere sm. greyhound.

lezione sf. 1. lesson 2. (universitaria) lecture 3. (lett.) reading.

leziosàggine sf. affectation.

lezioso agg. affected.

lezzo sm. stench.

li pron. them.

lì avv. there: — vicino, near there; — dentro, in there || — per —, at first; di — a poco, soon after; giù di — (press'a poco), thereabouts; essere — per, to be on the point of.

liana sf. liana.

libagione sf. libation.

libbra sf. pound.

libeccio sm. Southwest wind.

libello sm. libel.

libèllula sf. dragonfly.

liberale agg. e sm. liberal.

liberalismo sm. liberalism.

liberalità sf. generosity.

liberalizzare vt. to liberalize.

liberare vt. 1. to free 2. (da pericoli) to rescue 3. (sbarazzare) to rid (v. irr.) (of). ♦ **liberarsi** vr. (sbarazzarsi) to get (v. irr.) rid (of).

liberatore agg. liberating. ♦ **liberatore** sm. deliverer.

liberazione sf. liberation.

libero agg. free.

liberoscambista agg. e sm. free-trader.

libertà sf. liberty, freedom.

libertario agg. e sm. libertarian.

liberticida agg. e s. liberticide.

libertinaggio sm. libertinage.

libertino agg. e sm. libertine.

libìdine sf. lust.

libidinoso agg. lustful.

libido sf. lustfulness.

libraio sm. bookseller.

librarsi vr. to hover.

librerìa sf. 1. bookshop 2. (mobile) bookcase.

libresco agg. bookish.

libretto sm. 1. booklet 2. (d'opera) libretto || — di assegni, cheque-book; — di risparmio, savings-book; — personale, record-book.

libro sm. book.

licenza sf. 1. (abuso) licence 2. (permesso) permission, leave 3. (documento) licence.

licenziamento sm. dismissal.

licenziare vt. to dismiss. ♦ **licenziarsi** vr. to give (v. irr.) up one's job.

licenziosità sf. licentiousness.

licenzioso agg. licentious.

lichene sm. lichen.

licitazione sf. sale by auction.

lido sm. shore.

lieto agg. glad.

lieve agg. slight.

lievitare vi. to rise (v. irr.). ♦ **lievitare** vt. to leaven.

lievitazione sf. leavening.

lièvito sm. 1. yeast 2. (fermento) ferment.

ligio agg. faithful, observant (of).

lignaggio sm. lineage.

ligneo agg. wooden.

lignite sf. lignite.

lillà sm. lilac.

lillipuziano agg. e sm. Lilliputian.

lima sf. file.

limaccioso agg. slimy.

limare vt. 1. to file 2. (fig.) to polish.

limatrice sf. (mecc.) shaping-machine.

limatura sf. filing.

limbo sm. limbo.

limitare vt. to limit. ♦ **limitarsi** vr. (controllarsi) to check oneself.

limitatezza sf. limitation.

limitativo agg. limitative.

limitato agg. limited.

limitazione sf. limitation: — delle nascite, birth-control.

limite sm. limit: — di velocità, speed-limit || — di rottura, breaking-point.

limìtrofo agg. neighbouring.

limo sm. slime.

limonata sf. lemonade.

limone *sm.* lemon.

limpidezza *sf.* clearness.

limpido *agg.* limpid, clear.

lince *sf.* lynx.

linciaggio *sm.* lynching

linciare *vt.* to lynch.

lindo *agg.* neat.

linea *sf.* line || *aereo di —*, air-liner; *mantenere la —*, to keep (*v. irr.*) one's figure.

lineamenti *sm. pl.* 1. features 2. (*linee essenziali*) outlines.

lineare *agg.* 1. linear 2. (*fig.*) unswerving.

lineetta *sf.* 1. dash 2. (*trattino d'unione*) hyphen.

linfa *sf.* (*biol.*) lymph.

linfatico *agg.* lymphatic.

linfatismo *sm.* lymphatism.

lingotto *sm.* ingot.

lingua *sf.* 1. tongue 2. (*linguaggio*) language.

linguacciuto *agg.* talkative.

linguaggio *sm.* language.

linguetta *sf.* 1. flap 2. (*mecc.; di scarpe*) tongue.

linguista *s.* linguist.

linguistica *sf.* linguistics.

linguistico *agg.* linguistic.

linimento *sm.* liniment.

lino *sm.* flax.

linòleum *sm.* linoleum.

linone *sm.* lawn.

linotipìa *sf.* linotyping.

linotipista *s.* linotypist.

liquefare *vt.* to liquefy. ♦ **liquefarsi** *vr.* to liquefy.

liquefazione *sf.* liquefaction.

liquidare *vt.* 1. to liquidate 2. (*comm.*) to sell (*v. irr.*) off, to settle || *— una questione,* to settle a question.

liquidatore *sm.* liquidator.

liquidazione *sf.* liquidation, sale.

liquido *agg. e sm.* liquid || *dena ro —,* cash.

liquirizia *sf.* liquorice.

liquore *sm.* liqueur || *i liquori,* spirits.

liquoroso *agg.* liqueur-like.

lira *sf.* 1. (*moneta*) lira 2. (*mus.*) lyre.

lirica *sf.* 1. lyric poetry 2. (*teatro lirico*) opera.

lirico *agg.* lyric(al). ♦ **lirico** *sm.* lyrist.

lirismo *sm.* lyrism.

lisciare *vt.* 1. to smooth 2. (*adulare*) to flatter. ♦ **lisciarsi** *vr.* to sleek oneself.

liscio *agg.* 1. smooth 2. (*di bevanda*) undiluted 3. (*semplice*) plain 4. (*di capelli*) sleek.

lisciva *sf.* lye.

liso *agg.* threadbare.

lista *sf.* 1. (*elenco*) list, note 2. (*striscia*) stripe.

listare *vt.* 1. to stripe 2. (*bordare*) to border.

listino *sm.* list.

litania *sf.* litany.

lite *sf.* 1. quarrel, wrangle 2. (*giur.*) lawsuit.

litigante *sm.* 1. wrangler 2. (*giur.*) litigant.

litigare *vi.* 1. to quarrel 2. (*giur.*) to litigate.

litigio *sm.* quarrel.

litigioso *agg.* quarrelsome.

litografia *sf.* 1. lithography 2. (*pezzo singolo*) lithograph.

litografico *agg.* lithographic.

litorale *agg.* littoral. ♦ **litorale** *sm.* coast.

litro *sm.* litre.

liturgia *sf.* liturgy.

liturgico *agg.* liturgic(al).

liuto *sm.* lute.

livellamento *sm.* levelling.

livellare *vt.* to level.

livellatrice *sf.* bulldozer.

livello *sm.* level: *a — del mare,* at sea-level; *passaggio a —,* level-crossing; *essere allo stesso — di,* to be on a level with.

livido *agg.* livid. ♦ **livido** *sm.* bruise.

livore *sm.* 1. (*invidia*) envy 2. (*odio*) hatred.

livrea *sf.* livery.

lizza *sf.* competition, lists (*pl.*) || *essere in — (fig.),* to be competing.

lo *art.* the. ♦ **lo** *pron.* 1. (*per uomo*) him 2. (*per animale, cosa*) it || *— credo,* I think so.

lobo *sm.* lobe.

locale *agg.* local. ♦ **locale** *sm.* 1. room 2. (*ritrovo*) place.

località *sf.* locality, spot.

localizzare *vt.* to localize.

localizzazione *sf.* localization.

locanda *sf.* inn.

locandiere *sm.* innkeeper.

locandina *sf.* play-bill.

locare *vt.* to rent.

locatario *sm.* tenant.

locativo *agg.* locative || *valore —,* rental value.

locatore sm. lessor.
locazione sf. lease.
locomotiva sf. locomotive.
locomotore agg. e sm. locomotive.
locomozione sf. locomotion.
locusta sf. locust.
locuzione sf. locution.
lodàbile agg. laudable.
lodare vt. to praise
lodatore sm. praiser.
lode sf. praise.
lodévole agg. praiseworthy.
logaritmo sm. logarithm.
loggia sf. 1. (arch.) loggia 2. (massonica) lodge.
loggione sm. gallery.
lògica sf. logic.
logicità sf. logicality.
lògico agg. logical. ♦ **lògico** sm. logician.
logistica sf. logistics.
logìstico agg. logistic(al).
loglio sm. darnel.
logomachìa sf. logomachy.
logoramento sm. 1. wear 2. (fig.) wasting away.
logorante agg. wearing.
logorare vt. to wear (v. irr.) (out, down). ♦ **logorarsi** vr. to wear (out, down).
logorìo sm. wear and tear.
lògoro agg. worn (out, down).
lombàggine sf. lumbago.
lombardo agg. e sm. Lombard.
lombare agg. lumbar.
lombi sm. pl. loins.
lombrico sm. earth-worm.
longànime agg. forbearing.
longanimità sf. forbearance.
longevità sf. longevity.
longevo agg. longevous.
longitudinale agg. longitudinal.
longitùdine sf. longitude.
lontananza sf. distance: in —, in the distance.
lontano agg. 1. far 2. (nel tempo) far off, distant 3. (vago) vague. ♦ **lontano** avv. far ‖ da —, from afar.
lontra sf. otter.
loquace agg. talkative.
loquacità sf. talkativeness.
loquela sf. glibness.
lordare vt. to soil. ♦ **lordarsi** vr. to get (v. irr.) dirty.
lordo agg. 1. (sporco) filthy 2. (di peso) gross.
loro agg. poss. their. ♦ **loro** pron. poss. theirs. ♦ **loro** pron. pers.

1. (sogg.) they, (compl.) them 2. (forma di cortesia) you.
losanga sf. lozenge.
losco agg. 1. (bieco) sinister 2. (sospetto) suspicious.
loto sm. 1. (fango) mud 2. (bot.) lotus.
lotta sf. 1. struggle 2. (sport) wrestling.
lottare vi. 1. to struggle 2. (sport) to wrestle.
lottatore sm. 1. struggler 2. (sport) wrestler.
lotterìa sf. lottery.
lottizzare vt. to lot.
lottizzazione sf. division into lots.
lotto sm. 1. lot 2. (gioco) state lottery.
lozione sf. lotion.
lubricità sf. lubricity.
lùbrico agg. 1. lubricous 2. (fig.) lascivious.
lubrificante agg. lubricating. ♦ **lubrificante** sm. lubricant.
lubrificare vt. to lubricate.
lubrificazione sf. lubrication.
lucchetto sm. padlock.
luccicante agg. glittering.
luccicare vi. to glitter.
luccichìo sm. glitter.
lùcciola sf. 1. firefly 2. (senz'ali) glow-worm.
luce sf. light ‖ alla — del sole (fig.), openly; dare alla — un bambino, to give (v. irr.) birth to a child; mettere in —, to show (v. irr.); venire alla — (nascere), to be born.
lucente agg.. bright.
lucentezza sf. brightness.
lucerna sf. oil-lamp.
lucernario sm. skylight.
lucèrtola sf. lizard.
lucidare vt. to polish.
lucidatrice sf. 1. floor-polisher 2. (mecc.) polishing machine.
lucidatura sf. polishing.
lucidezza sf. 1. brightness 2. (di mente) lucidness.
lucidità sf. lucidity.
lùcido agg. 1. lucid 2. (lucidato) glossy. ♦ **lùcido** sm. 1. (per scarpe) shoe-polish 2. (lucidezza) shine.
lucìgnolo sm. wick.
lucrare vt. to profit.
lucrativo agg. profitable.
lucro sm. profit: a scopo di —, for the sake of gain.
ludibrio sm. mockery

luglio *sm.* July.
lùgubre *agg.* lugubrious.
lui *pron.* **1.** (*sogg.*) he **2.** (*compl.*) him.
lumaca *sf.* snail.
lume *sm.* light || *al — di candela*, by candle-light; *perdere il — della ragione*, to be blinded by anger.
lumeggiare *vt.* (*fig.*) to put (*v. irr.*) in evidence.
luminare *sm.* luminary.
luminescenza *sf.* luminescence.
luminosità *sf.* brightness.
luminoso *agg.* bright.
luna *sf.* moon: — *calante*, waning moon; — *crescente*, waxing moon || *chiaro di —*, moonlight; — *di miele*, honeymoon; *avere la —* (*fig.*), to be in the sulks.
lunare *agg.* lunar.
lunario *sm.* almanac || *sbarcare il —*, to make (*v. irr.*) both ends meet.
lunàtico *agg.* moody.
lunazione *sf.* lunation.
lunedì *sm.* Monday.
lunetta *sf.* lunette.
lungàggine *sf.* slowness, delay.
lunghezza *sf.* length.
lungimirante *agg.* far-sighted.
lungo *agg.* **1.** long: *a —*, long; *a — andare*, in the long run **2.** (*lento*) slow || *in — e in largo*, far and wide; *di gran lunga*, by far. ◆ **lungo** *prep.* **1.** along **2.** (*durante*) during.
lungofiume *sm.* embankment.
lungolago *sm.* lake-front.
lungomare *sm.* sea-front.
lungometraggio *sm.* feature film.
luogo *sm.* place: — *di nascita*, birthplace; *sul —*, on the spot; *aver —*, to take (*v. irr.*) place; *dar —*, to cause.
luogotenente *sm.* lieutenant.
lupa *sf.* she-wolf.
lupanare *sm.* brothel.
lupara *sf.* shotgun.
lupino *sm.* (*bot.*) lupine.
lupo *sm.* wolf || — *di mare*, sea-dog; *in bocca al —!*, good luck!
lùppolo *sm.* hop.
lùrido *agg.* dirty.
luridume *sm.* dirt.
lusinga *sf.* allurement, flattery.
lusingare *vt.* to allure, to flatter.
lusinghiero *agg.* alluring, flattering.
lussare *vt.* to dislocate.
lussazione *sf.* dislocation.

lusso *sm.* luxury.
lussuoso *agg.* luxurious, rich.
lussureggiante *agg.* luxuriant.
lussureggiare *vi.* to thrive (*v. irr.*).
lussuria *sf.* lust.
lussurioso *agg.* lustful.
lustrale *agg.* lustral.
lustrare *vt.* to polish.
lustrascarpe *sm.* shoeblack.
lustratura *sf.* polish.
lustrino *sm.* spangle.
lustro *agg.* shining, shiny. ◆ **lustro** *sm.* lustre.
luteranésimo *sm.* Lutheranism.
luterano *agg. e sm.* Lutheran.
lutto *sm.* mourning: *mettere il —*, to go (*v. irr.*) into mourning.
luttuoso *agg.* mournful.

M

ma *cong.* **1.** but **2.** (*tuttavia*) however, still.
màcabro *agg.* macabre.
macaco *sm.* **1.** macaque **2.** (*fig.*) runt.
macché *inter.* you don't say it!
maccheroni *sm. pl.* macaroni (*sing.*).
macchia[1] *sf.* spot, stain.
macchia[2] *sf.* (*boscaglia*) bush: *darsi alla —*, to take (*v. irr.*) to the bush.
macchiare *vt.* to stain. ◆ **macchiarsi** *vr.* **1.** to get (*v. irr.*) stained **2.** (*fig.*) to soil oneself.
macchiato *agg.* spotted.
macchietta *sf.* **1.** caricature **2.** (*di persona*) character.
màcchina *sf.* **1.** engine, machine: — *calcolatrice*, calculating machine; — *per cucire*, sewing-machine; — *da presa*, cine-camera; — *per scrivere*, typewriter; — *fotografica*, camera; *fatto a —*, machine-made; *andare in —* (*di giornali*), to go (*v. irr.*) to press **2.** (*automobile*) car.
macchinale *agg.* mechanical.
macchinare *vt.* to plot.
macchinario *sm.* machinery.
macchinazione *sf.* machination.
macchinista *sm.* **1.** (*ferr.*) engine-driver **2.** (*teat.*) scene-shifter.
macchinoso *agg.* complicated.

macedonia sf. (cuc.) fruit-salad.
macellaio sm. butcher.
macellare vt. to slaughter.
macelleria sf. butcher's shop.
macello sm. 1. (luogo dove si macella) slaughter-house 2. (massacro) slaughter.
macerare vt. 1. to soak 2. (di lino, canapa) to ret. ♦ **macerarsi** vr. (fig.) to waste (away).
maceratoio sm. rettery.
macerazione sf. 1. soaking 2. (industria tessile) retting.
macerie sf. pl. rubble (sing.), ruins.
màcero sm. (per canapa e lino) retting-ground: carta da —, waste-paper.
machiavèllico agg. Machiavellian.
machiavellismo sm. Machiavellism.
macigno sm. boulder.
macilento agg. emaciated.
macilenza sf. emaciation.
màcina sf. grindstone.
macinacaffè sm. coffee-mill.
macinapepe sm. pepper-mill.
macinare vt. 1. to grind (v. irr.), to mince.
macinino sm. grinder.
maciullare vt. to crush.
macrocèfalo agg. macrocephalous.
macrocosmo sm. macrocosm.
macromolècola sf. macromolecule.
macroscòpico agg. macroscopic.
maculato agg. spotted.
madia sf. 1. kitchen cupboard 2. (per pane) kneading trough.
màdido agg. wet: — di sudore, bathed in sweat.
madonna sf. 1. (titolo) Lady, My Lady 2. (relig.) The Virgin Mary, Our Lady 3. (pitt.) Madonna.
madornale agg. huge.
madre sf. mother.
madrepatria sf. mother-country.
madreperla sf. mother-of-pearl.
madreperlàceo agg. pearly:
madrèpora sf. madrepore.
madrepòrico agg. madreporic.
madrevite sf. 1. nut screw 2. (utensile) die.
madrigale sm. madrigal.
madrina sf. godmother.
maestà sf. majesty.
maestosità sf. majesty.
maestoso agg. majestic.
maestra sf. (scol.) teacher.
maestrale sm. mistral.
maestranza sf. skilled workers (pl.).

maestria sf. skill, ability.
maestro sm. 1. (scol.) teacher 2. (uomo dotto) master 3. (mus.) conductor, "maestro" || albero —, mainmast.
mafia sf. "Mafia".
maga sf. sorceress.
magagna sf. flaw, imperfection.
magari inter. if only! ♦ **magari** avv. (forse) perhaps, maybe. ♦ **magari** cong. even if.
magazzinaggio sm. storage.
magazziniere sm. store-keeper.
magazzino sm. warehouse || fondi di —, unsold stock.
maggese sm. fallow land.
maggio sm. May.
maggiolino sm. May-bug.
maggiorana sf. marjoram.
maggioranza sf. majority, most (of).
maggiorare vt. to increase.
maggiorazione sf. increase, charge.
maggiordomo sm. butler.
maggiore agg. 1. (più grande, ampio) greater, larger 2. (più vecchio) older: il —, the oldest 3. (di fratelli) elder (fra due), eldest (fra molti). ♦ **maggiore** sm. 1. (mil.) major 2. (superiore) superior.
maggiorenne agg. of age: diventare —, to come (v. irr.) of age. ♦ **maggiorenne** sm. major.
maggiorente sm. notable.
maggioritario agg. majority (attr.).
maggiormente avv. more, much more.
magia sf. magic.
màgiaro agg. e sm. Magyar.
magicamente avv. magically.
màgico agg. magical.
magistrale agg. 1. magisteral || scuola —, teachers' institute 2. (eccellente) masterly.
magistralmente avv. skilfully.
magistrato sm. Magistrate.
magistratura sf. magistracy.
maglia sf. 1. (di lavoro a maglia) stitch || lavorare a —, to knit (v. irr.) 2. (indumento) vest 3. (di catena) link.
magliaia sf. knitter.
maglieria sf. hosiery.
maglificio sm. hosiery.
maglio sm. 1. mallet 2. (mecc.) hammer.
maglione sm. sweater.
magma sm. magma.
magnanimità sf. magnanimity.

magnànimo agg. magnanimous.

magnate sm. magnate.

magnesia sf. magnesia.

magnesio sm. magnesium. *lampo al* —, flash.

magnete sm. magnet.

magnètico agg. magnetic.

magnetismo sm. magnetism.

magnetite sf. magnetite.

magnetizzare vt. to magnetize.

magnetizzatore sm. magnetizer.

magnetizzazione sf. magnetization.

magnetòfono sm. tape-recorder.

magnetòmetro sm. magnetometer.

magnificamente avv. magnificently.

magnificare vt. to extol, to glorify.

magnificenza sf. magnificence.

magnìfico agg. magnificent.

magniloquente agg. magniloquent.

magniloquenza sf. magniloquence.

magnolia sf. magnolia.

mago sm. wizard.

magra sf. (di fiumi) low water.

magrezza sf. thinness.

magro agg. 1. thin 2. (di carni) lean.

mah inter. who knows!

mai avv. 1. ever 2. (non mai) never: — e poi —, never never; — più, never more; caso —, if; non si sa —, you never can tell; meglio tardi che —, better late than never.

maiale sm. 1. pig 2. (carne) pork.

maièutica sf. maieutics.

maiòlica sf. majolica.

maionese sf. mayonnaise.

mais sm. maize.

maiùscola sf. capital letter.

maiuscoletto sm. small capitals.

maiùscolo agg. capital.

malaccorto agg. ill-advised.

malachite sf. malachite.

malacreanza sf. rudeness.

malafede sf. bad faith.

malaffare sm. 1. donna di —, whore 2. gente di —, crooks (pl.).

malagévole agg. difficult, hard.

malagrazia sf. bad grace.

malalingua sf. backbiter.

malamente avv. badly.

malandato agg. in bad condition.

malandrino sm. 1. brigand 2. (fam.) rogue.

malànimo sm. malevolence.

malanno sm. 1. calamity 2. (malattia) illness.

malapena (nella loc. avv.) a —, hardly.

malaria sf. malaria.

malaticcio agg. sickly.

malato agg. sick, ill. ♦ **malato** sm. patient.

malattia sf. sickness, disease.

malauguratamente avv. unluckily.

malaugurato agg. ill-fated.

malaugurio sm. ill-omen.

malavita sf. underworld.

malavoglia sf. unwillingness || di —, reluctantly.

malcapitato agg. unlucky. ♦ **malcapitato** sm. victim.

malconcio agg. 1. battered 2. (contuso) bruised.

malcontento agg. dissatisfied (with). ♦ **malcontento** sm. discontent.

malcostume sm. immorality, corruption.

maldestro agg. awkward.

maldicente agg. disparaging. ♦ **maldicente** sm. slanderer.

maldicenza sf. backbiting.

maldisposto agg. ill-disposed, hostile.

male sm. 1. evil 2. (malattia) illness, disease 3. (dolore fisico) pain || — di testa, headache. ♦ **male** avv. badly, ill.

maledettamente avv. awfully.

maledetto agg. cursed.

malèdico agg. slanderous.

maledire vt. to curse.

maledizione sf. curse, malediction || —! (inter.), damn!

maleducato agg. rude, impolite.

maleducazione sf. rudeness.

malefatta sf. mischief.

maleficio sm. sorcery.

malèfico agg. harmful.

malerba sf. weed.

malese agg. e sm. Malay.

malèssere sm. 1. malaise 2. (disagio) uneasiness.

malestro sm. mischief.

malevolenza sf. malevolence,

malèvolo agg. malevolent.

malfamato agg. ill-famed.

malfatto agg. 1. ill-shaped 2. (di abito) ill-fitting.

malfattore sm. evil-doer.

malfermo agg. shaky || salute malferma, poor health.

malfido agg. unreliable.

malfondato agg. ill-grounded.

malformato *agg.* malformed.
malformazione *sf.* malformation.
malgarbo *sm.* bad grace.
malgoverno *sm.* misgovernment, misrule.
malgrado *prep.* e *avv.* in spite of. ♦ **malgrado (che)** *cong.* though, although.
malìa *sf.* (*fascino*) fascination.
maliarda *sf.* 1. (*donna affascinante*) fascinating woman 2. (*maga*) witch.
malignamente *avv.* maliciously.
malignare *vi.* to speak (*v. irr.*) ill (of).
malignità *sf.* malice.
maligno *agg.* malicious: *tumore* —, malignant tumor.
malinconìa *sf.* melancholy.
malinconicamente *avv.* sadly.
malincònico *agg.* melancholy.
malincuore (*nella loc. avv.*) a —, unwillingly.
malintenzionato *agg.* ill-disposed.
malinteso *agg.* misplaced. ♦ **malinteso** *sm.* misunderstanding.
malizia *sf.* 1. malice 2. (*astuzia*) cunning.
maliziosamente *avv.* artfully.
malizioso *agg.* malicious, mischievous.
malleàbile *agg.* malleable.
malleabilità *sf.* malleability.
malleverìa *sf.* bail.
malloppo *sm.* swag.
malmenare *vt.* to manhandle.
malmesso *agg.* poorly dressed.
malnato *agg.* ill-bred.
malocchio *sm.* evil eye.
malora *sf.* ruin || *va alla* —!, go to the devil!
malore *sm.* illness.
malpensante *agg.* wrong-thinking.
malsano *agg.* unhealthy.
malsicuro *agg.* unsafe.
malta *sf.* mortar.
maltempo *sm.* bad weather.
maltenuto *agg.* untidy.
maltese *agg.* e *sm.* Maltese.
malto *sm.* malt.
maltolto *agg.* ill-gotten. ♦ **maltolto** *sm.* ill-gotten property.
maltosio *sm.* maltose.
maltrattamento *sm.* maltreatment.
maltrattare *vt.* to maltreat.
maltusianismo *sm.* Malthusianism.
maltusiano *agg.* e *sm.* Malthusian.
malumore *sm.* ill-humour.
malva *sf.* mallow.

malvagio *agg.* wicked.
malvagità *sf.* wickedness.
malversatore *sm.* embezzler.
malversazione *sf.* embezzlement.
malvisto *agg.* unpopular (with).
malvivente *sm.* gangster.
malvivenza *sf.* delinquency.
malvolentieri *avv.* unwillingly.
malvolere *sm.* ill-will.
malvolere *vi.* to dislike.
mamma *sf.* mama, mummy.
mammalucco *sm.* (*fam.*) simpleton.
mammella *sf.* 1. mamma (*pl.* -ae) 2. (*di animali da latte*) udder.
mammìfero *agg.* mammiferous. ♦ **mammìfero** *sm.* mammal.
màmmola *sf.* sweet-smelling violet.
mammùt *sm.* mammoth.
manata *sf.* slap.
manca *sf.* 1. left hand 2. (*parte sinistra*) left || *a dritta e a* —, on all sides.
mancante *agg.* incomplete.
mancanza *sf.* 1. lack, shortage 2. (*fallo*) fault || *sentire la* — *di qu.*, to miss so.
mancare *vi.* 1. to be lacking (in) 2. (*non esserci*) to be missing 3. (*venir meno*) to fail 4. (*agire scorrettamente*) to wrong (so.).
mancato *agg.* unsuccessful.
manchévole *agg.* defective.
manchevolezza *sf.* defect, fault.
mancia *sf.* tip || *dare la* — *a qu.*, to tip so.
manciata *sf.* handful.
mancina *sf.* left-hand.
mancino *agg.* left-handed. ♦ **mancino** *sm.* left-hander.
manco *avv.* not even.
mandamento *sm.* district.
mandante *sm.* 1. instigator 2. (*giur.*) principal.
mandare *vt.* 1. to send (*v. irr.*) 2. (*spedire*) to forward 3. (*emettere*) to give (*v. irr.*) out.
mandarino *sm.* mandarin.
mandata *sf.* batch || — *di chiave*, turn.
mandatario *sm.* mandatary.
mandato *sm.* 1. mandate 2. (*comm.* agency 3. (*giur.*) warrant.
mandìbola *sf.* mandible.
mandola *sf.* mandola.
mandolinista *s.* mandolinist.
mandolino *sm.* mandolin.
màndorla *sf.* almond.
màndorlo *sm.* almond-tree.

mandràgora *sf.* mandrake.

mandria *sf.* herd.

mandriano *sm.* herdsman (*pl.* -men).

maneggévole *agg.* handy.

maneggiare *vt.* to handle.

maneggio *sm.* **1.** (*equitazione*) riding-ground **2.** (*uso*) use **3.** (*intrigo*) plot.

manesco *agg.* rough, aggressive.

manette *sf. pl.* handcuff (*sing.*).

manforte *sf.* help.

manganellare *vt.* to cudgel.

manganello *sm.* cudgel.

manganese *sm.* manganese.

mangereccio *agg.* eatable.

mangiàbile *agg.* eatable.

mangiare *vt.* to eat (*v. irr.*).

mangiata *sf.* square meal.

mangiatoia *sf.* manger.

mangime *sm.* fodder.

mangiucchiare *vt.* to nibble (at).

manìa *sf.* mania.

manìaco *agg.* **1.** maniac **2.** (*fig.*) crazy. ♦ **manìaco** *sm.* maniac.

mànica *sf.* sleeve || *essere di — larga, stretta,* to be indulgent, strict.

manicheismo *sm.* Manicheism.

manicheo *agg. e sm.* Manichean.

manichino *sm.* manikin.

mànico *sm.* handle.

manicomio *sm.* mental hospital.

manicotto *sm.* **1.** muff **2.** (*mecc.*) sleeve.

maniera *sf.* manner, way.

manierato *agg.* affected.

manierismo *sm.* mannerism.

maniero *sm.* castle.

manifattura *sf.* manufacture.

manifatturiero *agg.* manufacturing.

manifestante *s.* demonstrator.

manifestare *vt.* **1.** to manifest, to show (*v. irr.*) **2.** (*pol.*) to demonstrate.

manifestazione *sf.* **1.** manifestation **2.** (*pol.*) demonstration.

manifesto *agg.* manifest, clear, obvious. ♦ **manifesto** *sm.* **1.** (*affisso*) poster **2.** (*volantino*) leaflet **3.** (*dichiarazione*) manifesto.

maniglia *sf.* handle.

manigoldo *sm.* scoundrel.

manioca *sf.* manioc.

manipolare *vt.* to manipulate.

manipolatore *sm.* manipulator.

manipolazione *sf.* manipulation.

manìpolo *sm.* (*eccl.; stor.*) maniple.

maniscalco *sm.* blacksmith.

manna *sf.* **1.** manna **2.** (*fig.*) blessing.

mannaia *sf.* **1.** axe **2.** (*della ghigliottina*) knife.

mannaro *agg. lupo —,* werewolf.

mano *sf.* hand: *fatto a —,* hand-made; *stringere la —,* to shake (*v. irr.*) hands with || *a — armata,* by force of arms; *sotto —,* underhand.

manodòpera *sf.* labour.

manòmetro *sm.* manometer.

manométtere *vt.* to tamper with.

manomissione *sf.* tampering.

manòpola *sf.* **1.** knob **2.** (*impugnatura*) handle.

manoscritto *agg.* handwritten. ♦ **manoscritto** *sm.* manuscript.

manovale *sm.* hodman (*pl.* -men).

manovella *sf.* crank.

manovra *sf.* manoeuvre, operation.

manovràbile *agg.* manoeuvrable.

manovrare *vt.* **1.** to manoeuvre **2.** (*mecc.*) to operate.

manovratore *sm.* operator, driver.

manrovescio *sm.* back-handed slap.

mansarda *sf.* mansard.

mansione *sf.* function.

mansuefare *vt.* to tame.

mansueto *agg.* meek, mild.

mansuetùdine *sf.* meekness.

mantella *sf.* cape.

mantello *sm.* cloak.

mantenere *vt.* to keep (*v. irr.*), to maintain: *— la parola,* to keep one's word.

mantenimento *sm.* maintenance.

màntice *sm.* bellows (*pl.*).

manto *sm.* cloak.

manuale *agg.* manual. ♦ **manuale** *sm.* handbook.

manubrio *sm.* **1.** handle **2.** (*di bicicletta ecc.*) handle-bar.

manufatto *agg.* hand-made. ♦ **manufatto** *sm.* hand-manufactured article.

manutèngolo *sm.* abettor.

manutenzione *sf.* maintenance, servicing.

manzo *sm.* **1.** (*zool.*) steer **2.** (*carne*) beef.

maomettano *agg. e sm.* Mohammedan.

mappa *sf.* map.

mappamondo *sm.* globe.

marachella *sf.* trick.

marasma *sm.* **1.** (*med.*) marasmus **2.** (*fig.*) decadence.

maratona *sf.* marathon race.

marca sf. brand: — di fabbrica, trade mark.

marcare vt. 1. to mark 2. (sport) to score.

marcato agg. marked, branded.

marcatore sm. 1. marker 2. (sport) scorer.

marcatura sf. 1. marking 2. (sport) scoring.

marchesa sf. 1. marchioness 2. (se non è inglese) marquise.

marchesato sm. marquisate.

marchese sm. marquis.

marchiano agg. enormous, glaring.

marchiare vt. to brand.

marchiatura sf. branding.

marchio sm. 1. stamp 2. (a fuoco) brand 3. (fig.; comm.) mark.

marcia sf. 1. (auto) gear 2. (mil.; mus.) march.

marciapiede sm. 1. pavement 2. (ferr.) platform.

marciare vi. to march.

marciatore sm. (sport) road-walker.

marcio agg. 1. rotten 2. (fig.) corrupted. ♦ **marcio** sm. (fig.) corruption.

marcire vi. 1. (guastarsi) to go (v. irr.) bad 2. (decomporsi) to rot (v. irr.).

marciume sm. rottenness.

marco sm. mark.

marconigrafia sf. marconigraphy.

mare sm. sea.

marea sf. tide.

mareggiata sf. sea-storm.

maremma sf. maremma (pl. -me).

maremoto sm. seaquake.

mareògrafo sm. tide-gauge.

maresciallo sm. marshal.

margarina sf. margarine.

margherita sf. daisy.

marginale agg. marginal.

marginare vt. 1. to border 2. (tip.) to margin.

marginatura sf. 1. edging 2. (tip.) furniture.

màrgine sm. 1. border, edge 2. (fig.) margin.

marina sf. 1. navy 2. (costa) sea-shore 3. (pitt.) sea-scape.

marinaio sm. sailor.

marinara sf. 1. (cappotto) duffle coat 2. (cappello) sailor hat.

marinare vt. (cuc.) to pickle || — la scuola, to play truant.

marinaresco agg. sailor-like.

marinaro agg. 1. maritime 2. sail-or-like. ♦ **marinaro** sm. sailor.

marineria sf. 1. seamanship 2. (marina) navy.

marino agg. sea (attr.).

mariolo sm. rogue.

marionetta sf. puppet.

maritale agg. marital.

maritare vt. to marry. ♦ **maritarsi** vr. to get (v. irr.) married.

marito sm. husband.

marìttimo agg. maritime || città marittima, sea-town; commercio —, shipping business. ♦ **marìttimo** sm. seafarer || i marittimi, seafolk (sing.).

marmaglia sf. rabble.

marmellata sf. 1. jam 2. (d'arance) marmalade.

marmista sm. marble-cutter.

marmitta sf. 1. (cuc.) stock-pot 2. (auto) silencer's muffler.

marmo sm. marble.

marmocchio sm. kid.

marmòreo agg. marble.

marmotta sf. 1. marmot 2. (di persona) lazy-bones.

marna sf. marl.

marocchino agg. Moroccan. ♦ **marocchino** sm. 1. (persona) Moroccan 2. (cuoio) Morocco leather.

maroso sm. billow.

marra sf. 1. (agr.) hoe 2. (mar.) fluke.

marrone agg. brown. ♦ **marrone** sm. chestnut.

martedì sm. Tuesday.

martellamento sm. hammering.

martellare vt. 1. to hammer 2. (mil.) to pound 3. (pulsare) to throb.

martellata sf. hammer-blow.

martello sm. hammer.

martinetto sm. jack.

martingala sf. half-belt.

màrtire sm. martyr.

martirio sm. martyrdom.

martirizzare vt. to martyrize.

martirologio sm. martyrology.

màrtora sf. marten.

martoriare vt. to torture.

marxismo sm. Marxism.

marxista agg. e s. Marxist.

marzapane sm. marzipan.

marziale agg. martial.

marziano sm. Martian.

marzo sm. March.

mascalzonata sf. knavery.

mascalzone sm. rascal.

mascella sf. jaw.

mascellare *agg.* jaw (*attr.*).

màschera *sf.* 1. mask 2. (*figura mascherata*) masker 3. (*cosmesi*) face-pack 4. (*inserviente di cinema, teatro*) usher.

mascheramento *sm.* masking.

mascherare *vt.* to mask.

mascherata *sf.* masquerade.

maschietto *sm.* male.

maschile *agg.* male.

maschio[1] *agg.* 1. male 2. (*virile*) manly. ♦ **maschio** *sm.* 1. (*di animale*) (*uccelli*) cock, (*mammiferi*) bull (*attributivi*) 2. (*di uomo*) male 3. (*bambino*) boy.

maschio[2] *sm.* (*torre*) donjon.

mascolinità *sf.* masculinity.

masnada *sf.* gang.

masnadiere *sm.* highwayman (*pl.* -men).

masochismo *sm.* masochism.

masonite *sf.* masonite.

massa *sf.* mass, heap.

massacrante *agg.* exhausting.

massacrare *vt.* to massacre.

massacratore *sm.* slaughterer.

massacro *sm.* massacre.

massaggiare *vt.* to massage.

massaggiatore *sm.* masseur.

massaggiatrice *sf.* masseuse.

massaggio *sm.* massage.

massaia *sf.* housewife (*pl.* -wives).

massello *sm.* ingot.

masseria *sf.* farm.

masserizie *sf. pl.* household goods.

massicciata *sf.* road-bed.

massiccio *agg.* solid. ♦ **massiccio** *sm.* massif.

massima *sf.* maxim, rule || *in linea di* —, on the whole; *accordo di* —, general agreement.

massimalismo *sm.* Maximalism.

massimalista *s.* Maximalist.

màssimo *agg.* 1. greatest, highest 2. (*l'estremo*) utmost 3. (*il più lungo*) longest. ♦ **màssimo** *sm.* 1. most 2. (*il meglio*) best 3. (*mat.; fis.*) maximum.

masso *sm.* boulder.

massone *sm.* freemason.

massoneria *sf.* freemasonry.

mastello *sm.* tub.

masticare *vt.* to chew.

masticazione *sf.* mastication.

màstice *sm.* rubber.

mastino *sm.* mastiff.

mastite *sf.* mastitis.

mastodonte *sm.* 1. (*zool.*) mastodon 2. (*fig.*) giant.

mastodòntico *agg.* colossal.

mastòide *sf.* mastoid.

mastoidite *sf.* mastoiditis.

mastro *sm.* 1. (*libro*) ledger 2. (*appellativo*) Master.

masturbazione *sf.* masturbation.

matassa *sf.* 1. hank 2. (*fig.*) tangle.

matemàtica *sf.* mathematics.

matemàtico *agg.* mathematical. ♦ **matemàtico** *sm.* mathematician.

materasso *sm.* mattress.

materia *sf.* matter, subject.

materiale *agg.* 1. material 2. (*rozzo*) rough. ♦ **materiale** *sm.* material.

materialismo *sm.* materialism.

materialista *s.* materialist.

materialistico *agg.* materialistic.

materializzare *vt.* to materialize.

maternità *sf.* maternity.

materno *agg.* motherly, maternal || *scuola materna*, nursery-school.

matita *sf.* pencil.

matriarcato *sm.* matriarchy.

matrice *sf.* 1. matrix (*pl.* matrices) 2. (*comm.*) counterfoil.

matricida *s.* matricide.

matricidio *sm.* matricide.

matricola *sf.* 1. matricula, register || *numero di* —, matriculation number 2. (*scol.*) freshman (*pl.* -men).

matricolato *agg.* matriculated || *briccone* —, arrant knave.

matrigna *sf.* stepmother.

matrimoniale *agg.* matrimonial.

matrimonio *sm.* 1. marriage 2. (*cerimonia nuziale*) wedding.

matrona *sf.* matron.

matta *sf.* 1. mad woman (*pl.* women) 2. (*al gioco*) jolly joker.

mattacchione *sm.* joker.

mattatoio *sm.* slaughter-house.

matterello *sm.* rolling-pin.

mattina *sf.* morning.

mattinata *sf.* 1. morning 2. (*teat.*) matinée.

mattiniero *agg.* early-rising.

mattino *sm.* morning.

matto[1] *agg.* mad, crazy. ♦ **matto** *sm.* madman (*pl.* -men).

matto[2] *agg.* 1. (*non lucido*) mat 2. (*di gioielli*) false.

mattone *sm.* 1. brick 2. (*fig.*) bore.

mattonella *sf.* tile.

mattutino *agg.* morning (*attr.*). ♦ **mattutino** *sm.* (*eccl.*) matins (*pl.*).

maturare *vi. e vt.* to ripen, to mature (*anche fig.*).

maturazione *sf.* maturation, ripening (*anche fig.*).

maturità *sf.* ripening, maturity (*anche fig.*).

maturo *agg.* ripe, mature (*anche fig.*).

mausoleo *sm.* mausoleum.

mazurca *sf.* mazurka.

mazza *sf.* 1. (*clava*) club 2. (*martello di legno*) mallet.

mazzata *sf.* heavy blow (*anche fig.*).

mazziere *sm.* 1. mace-bearer 2. (*di carte*) dealer.

mazzo *sm.* 1. bunch 2. (*di carte*) pack || *fare il* —, to shuffle 3. (*di fiori*) bouquet.

mazzolino *sm.* (*di fiori*) posy.

mazzuolo *sm.* mallet.

me *pron.* 1. me 2. (*me stesso*) myself.

meandro *sm.* 1. meander 2. (*labirinto*) maze.

meato *sm.* meatus.

meccànica *sf.* mechanics.

meccànico *agg.* mechanical. ♦ **meccànico** *sm.* mechanic.

meccanismo *sm.* 1. gear 2. (*movimento*) motion.

meccanizzare *vt.* to mechanize.

meccanizzazione *sf.* mechanization.

meccanografìa *sf.* mechanography.

meccanogràfico *agg.* mechanographic.

mecenate *sm.* Maecenas.

mecenatismo *sm.* patronage.

medaglia *sf.* medal.

medaglione *sm.* 1. locket 2. (*arch.*) medallion.

medaglista *sm.* 1. (*incisore*) medallist 2. (*collezionista*) collector of medals.

medésimo *agg. e pron.* V. *stesso.*

media *sf.* 1. average: *alla* — *di*, at an average of 2. (*mat.*) mean.

mediana *sf.* median line.

mediànico *agg.* mediumistic.

mediano *agg.* 1. medial, middle (*attr.*) 2. (*geom.; anat; bot.*) median. ♦ **mediano** *sm.* (*sport*) half-back.

mediante *prep.* by, by means of, through.

mediato *agg.* indirect.

mediatore *sm.* 1. mediator 2. (*comm.*) broker.

mediazione *sf.* 1. mediation 2. (*comm.*) brokerage.

medicamento *sm.* medicament.

medicare *vt.* to dress.

medicastro *sm.* quack (doctor).

medicazione *sf.* 1. medication 2. (*di ferita*) dressing.

medicina *sf.* medicine.

medicinale *sm.* medicinal.

mèdico *agg.* medical. ♦ **mèdico** *sm.* physician, doctor.

medievale *agg.* medieval.

medio *sm.* 1. (*dito*) middle finger 2. (*mat.*) mean. ♦ **medio** *agg.* 1. middle 2. (*normale, che risulta da una media*) average.

mediocre *agg.* second-rate.

mediocrità *sf.* mediocrity.

medioevo *sm.* Middle Ages (*pl.*).

meditabondo *agg.* thoughtful.

meditare *vt.* 1. to ponder 2. (*avere un'intenzione*) to meditate.

meditativo *agg.* meditative.

meditazione *sf.* meditation.

mediterràneo *agg.* 1. inland 2. Mediterranean.

medium *sm.* medium.

medusa *sf.* medusa (*pl.* -ae).

mefistofèlico *agg.* satanic.

mefitico *agg.* poisonous.

megaciclo *sm.* megacycle.

megàfono *sm.* megaphone.

megalòmane *sm.* megalomaniac.

megalomanìa *sf.* megalomania.

megatone *sm.* megaton.

meglio *avv.* 1. (*comp.*) better 2. (*superl. rel.*) best. ♦ **meglio** *agg.* 1. (*comp.*) better: *questo vestito è* — *di quello*, this dress is better than that 2. (*superl. rel.*) best. ♦ **meglio** *sm.* best, best thing || *in mancanza di* —, for lack of anything better. ♦ **meglio** *sf.* *avere la* —, to have the better || *alla* —, as well as possible.

mela *sf.* apple.

melacotogna *sf.* quince.

melagrana *sf.* pomegranate.

melanismo *sm.* melanism.

melanzana *sf.* aubergine.

melassa *sf.* molasses (*pl.*).

melato *agg.* 1. sweetened with honey 2. (*fig.*) honeyed.

melenso *agg.* dull, silly.

mellifluo *agg.* honeyed.

melma *sf.* slime.

melmoso *agg.* slimy.

melo *sm.* apple-tree.

melodìa *sf.* melody.

melòdico *agg.* melodic.

melodioso *agg.* melodious.

melodramma *sm.* 1. opera 2. (*fig.*) melodrama.

melodrammàtico agg. 1. operatic 2. (fig.) melodramatic.

melograno sm. pomegranate-tree.

melòmane s. melomaniac.

melomanìa sf. melomania.

melone sm. melon.

membra sf. pl. limbs.

membrana sf. membrane.

membratura sf structure.

membro sm. 1. member 2. (anat.) limb.

memoràbile agg. memorable.

memorandum sm. memorandum (pl. -da).

mèmore agg. mindful.

memoria sf. 1. memory: — di ferro, cast-iron memory || a —, by heart 2. (ricordo) memory, recollection.

memoriale sm. 1. (petizione) memorial 2. (libro di memorie) memoirs (pl.).

memorialista s. memorialist.

menabò sm. dummy.

menadito (nella loc. avv.) a —, perfectly || sapere qc. a —, to have sthg. at one's finger-tips.

menagramo sm. bearer of ill-luck.

menare vt. (condurre) to lead (v. irr.) || — vanto, to boast; — il can per l'aia, to beat (v. irr.) about the bush; — buono, gramo, to bring (v. irr.) good, bad luck.

mendace agg. mendacious, false.

mendacia sf. mendacity.

mendicante sm. beggar.

mendicare vi. to beg.

mendicità sf. mendicity.

mendico agg. e sm. mendicant.

menestrello sm. minstrel.

meninge sf. meninx (pl. meninges).

menisco sm. meniscus.

meno avv. 1. (comp.) less 2. (superl. rel.) least || fare a —, to do (v. irr.) without; non poter fare a —, cannot help: non posso fare a — di andare, I cannot help going 3. (mat.) minus. ♦ **meno** prep. but for || a — che (non), unless. ♦ **meno** agg. 1. (comp. sing.) less: è — bella di sua sorella, she is less beautiful than her sister 2. (comp. con s. pl.) fewer: ho — libri di te, I have fewer books than you 3. (superl. rel. sing.) the least: è il — intelligente dei miei amici, he is the least intelligent of my friends 4. (superl. rel. con s. pl.) the fewest (raro).

♦ **meno** sm. 1. (comp.) less 2. (superl. rel.) the least.

menomare vt. to lessen.

menomato agg. 1. lessened 2. (di vista, udito) impaired.

menomazione sf. 1. lessening 2. (di arti, sensi) impairment 3. (di persona) disablement.

menopàusa sf. menopause.

mensa sf. table.

mensile agg. monthly. ♦ **mensile** sm. 1. (salario) month's salary 2. (pubblicazione mensile) monthly.

mensilità sf. monthly instalment || tredicesima —, Christmas bonus.

mensilmente avv. monthly, once a month.

mènsola sf. 1. bracket 2. (scaffale) shelf (pl. -lves).

menta sf. mint.

mentale agg. mental.

mentalità sf. mentality.

mente sf. mind: persona dalla — ristretta, narrow-minded person; aguzzare la —, to sharpen one's wits.

mentecatto agg. insane. ♦ **mentecatto** sm. madman (pl. -men).

mentina sf. peppermint-drop.

mentire vi. to lie.

mentito agg. false: sotto mentite spoglie, under false pretences.

mentitore sm. liar.

mento sm. chin.

mentolo sm. menthol.

mèntore sm. mentor.

mentre cong. 1. (temporale) while, as, when 2. (avversativo) whereas, while 3. (finché) as long as, while. ♦ **mentre** sm. moment: in quel —, at that moment.

menzionare vt. to mention.

menzione sf. mention.

menzogna sf. falsehood.

menzognero agg. 1. (di persona) mendacious 2. (di cosa) false.

meraviglia sf. wonder: sopraffatto dalla —, wonder-struck; non fa — che, nessuna — che, no wonder.

meravigliare vt. to astonish. ♦ **meravigliarsi** vr. to be astonished (at).

meravigliato agg. astonished.

meraviglioso agg. wonderful.

mercante sm. merchant.

mercanteggiare vi. (tirare sul prezzo) to bargain, to haggle.

mercantile agg. mercantile. ♦ **mercantile** sm. cargo boat.

mercantilismo *sm.* mercantilism.
mercanzia *sf.* merchandise.
mercato *sm.* market || *a buon —,* cheap.
merce *sf.* goods (*pl.*).
mercé *sf.* mercy.
mercede *sf.* pay, reward.
mercenario *agg. e sm.* mercenary.
merceologìa *sf.* technology of marketable goods.
mercerìa *sf.* 1. haberdashery 2. (*negozio*) haberdasher's shop.
mercerizzato *agg.* mercerized.
merciaio *sm.* haberdasher.
mercoledì *sm.* Wednesday: *— delle Ceneri,* Ash Wednesday.
mercurio *sm.* mercury, quicksilver.
merenda *sf.* afternoon snack.
meretrice *sf.* prostitute.
meretricio *sm.* prostitution.
meridiana *sf.* sun-dial.
meridiano *agg. e sm.* meridian.
meridionale *agg.* Southern. ♦ **meridionale** *sm.* Southerner.
meridione *sm.* south.
meringa *sf.* meringue.
merino *sm.* merino.
meritare *vt.* to deserve.
meritévole *agg.* deserving.
mèrito *sm.* merit || *in — a,* as to.
meritorio *agg.* meritorious, deserving.
merletto *sm.* lace.
merlo *sm.* 1. blackbird 2. (*sciocco*) simpleton.
merluzzo *sm.* codfish.
mero *agg.* 1. pure 2. (*fig.*) mere.
mesata *sf.* 1. month 2. (*paga di un mese*) month's pay.
méscere *vt.* to pour (out).
meschinità *sf.* meanness.
meschino *agg.* mean. ♦ **meschino** *sm.* wretch.
méscita *sf.* pouring (out).
mescolanza *sf.* 1. mixing 2. (*miscuglio*) mixture.
mescolare *vt.* 1. to mix 2. (*tè, caffè, liquori, tabacco*) to blend. ♦ **mescolarsi** *vr.* to mingle.
mescolatrice *sf.* mixer.
mese *sm.* month.
messa *sf.* 1. (*eccl.*) Mass 2. (*azione del mettere*) putting, setting: *— a punto,* setting up || *— a fuoco,* focusing.
messaggero *sm.* messenger.
messaggio *sm.* 1. message 2. (*allocuzione*) address.
messale *sm.* missal.

messe *sf.* crop, harvest.
messìa *sm.* Messiah.
messiànico *agg.* Messianic.
messianismo *sm.* Messianism.
messicano *agg. e sm.* Mexican.
messinscena *sf.* staging.
mestare *vt.* to stir.
mestiere *sm.* 1. trade 2. (*perizia*) skill 3. (*lavoro*) work.
mestizia *sf.* sadness.
méstola *sf.* ladle.
méstolo *sm.* ladle.
mestruazione *sf.* menstruation.
meta *sf.* 1. destination 2. (*scopo*) aim, purpose: *senza —,* aimless.
metà *sf.* 1. half (*pl.* halves) 2. (*parte mediana*) middle 3. (*coniuge*) *la mia —,* my better half.
metabolismo *sm.* metabolism.
metafisica *sf.* metaphysics.
metàfora *sf.* metaphor.
metafòrico *agg.* metaphoric(al).
metàllico *agg.* metallic.
metallo *sm.* metal.
metallurgìa *sf.* metallurgy.
metallùrgico *agg.* metallurgic(al). ♦ **metallùrgico** *sm.* metallurgist.
metalmeccànico *sm.* metallurgist and mechanic.
metamòrfico *agg.* metamorphic.
metamorfismo *sm.* metamorphism.
metamòrfosi *sf.* metamorphosis (*pl.* -ses).
metano *sm.* methane.
metapsìchica *sf.* metapsychics.
metapsìchico *agg.* metapsychic(al).
metàstasi *sf.* metastasis (*pl.* -asi).
metempsicosi *sf.* metempsychosis (*pl.* -ses).
metèora *sf.* meteor.
metèorico *agg.* meteoric.
meteorite *sm.* meteorite.
meteorologìa *sf.* meteorology.
meteorològico *agg.* meteorological || *previsioni meteorologiche,* weather-forecast (*sing.*).
meteoròlogo *sm.* meteorologist.
meticcio *agg. e sm.* mestizo (*pl.* -za).
meticoloso *agg.* meticulous.
metodicità *sf.* methodicalness.
metòdico *agg.* methodical.
metodista *agg. e s.* Methodist.
mètodo *sm.* method.
metodologìa *sf.* methodology.
metodològico *agg.* methodological.
mètopa *sf.* metope.
metraggio *sm.* 1. length (in metres) 2. (*cine*) *corto, lungo —,* short, full-length film.

mètrica sf. prosody.
mètrico agg. metric.
metrite sf. metritis.
metro sm. 1. metre 2. (strumento per misurare) rule.
metrònomo sm. metronome.
metronotte sm. night-watch.
metròpoli sf. metropolis (pl. -ses).
metropolitana sf. underground.
metropolitano agg. metropolitan.
méttere vt. 1. to put (v. irr.) || — in chiaro qc., to make (v. irr.) sthg. clear; — in dubbio qc., to doubt sthg.; — in serbo, to lay (v. irr.) aside; — in moto, to start; — in luce, to emphasize; — in guardia qu., to put so. on his guard; — le mani su qc., to take (v. irr.) possession of; — le mani sul fuoco per qu., to speak (v. irr.) for so. 2. (impiegare, di tempo) to take 3. (indossare) to put on 4. (paragonare) to compare. ◆ **mettersi** vr. 1. to put oneself || — in contatto còn qu., to get (v. irr.) in touch with so.; — in testa di fare qc., to take into one's head to do sthg.; — sotto, to get down to it 2. (incominciare) to begin (v. irr.) 3. (indossare) to put (v. irr.) on.
mettifoglio sm. (tip.) feeder.
mezzadrìa sf. métayage.
mezzadro sm. métayer.
mezzaluna sf. 1. half-moon 2. (emblema islamico) crescent 3. (cuc.) mincing-knife.
mezzana¹ sf. (mar.) mizzen sail.
mezzana² sf. procuress.
mezzano agg. middle. ◆ **mezzano** sm. go-between.
mezzanotte sf. midnight.
mezzatìnta sf. half-tone.
mezzo¹ agg. 1. half 2. (medio) middle. ◆ **mezzo** avv. half. ◆ **in mezzo a** prep. 1. in the middle of 2. (fra molti) among 3. (fra due) between.
mezzo² sm. 1. means 2. (fis.) medium.
mezzo³ agg. (marcio) rotten.
mezzobusto sm. bust.
mezzocerchio sm. semicircle.
mezzodì sm. midday, noon.
mezzofondo sm. middle-distance race.
mezzogiorno sm. 1. midday 2. (Sud) South.
mezzosoprano sm. mezzo-soprano.

mi¹ pron. 1. me 2. (me stesso) myself 3. (a me) to me.
mi² sm. (mus.) E, mi.
miagolare vi. to mew
miagolìo sm. mewing
miasma sm. miasma.
mica sf. mica.
miccia sf. fuse.
michetta sf. roll.
micidiale agg. lethal,. deadly.
micino sm. kitten, pussy.
micosì sf. mycosis (pl. -ses).
microbio sm. microbe.
microbiologìa sf. microbiology.
microcosmo sm. microcosm.
microfilm sm. microfilm.
micròfono sm. microphone.
microfotografìa sf. microphotography.
micrometrìa sf. micrometry.
micròmetro sm. micrometer.
micron sm. micron.
microrganismo sm. microorganism.
microscopìa sf. microscopy.
microscòpico agg. microscopic(al).
microscopio sm. microscope.
microsolco sm. long-playing record.
microtelèfono sm. microtelephone.
midolla sf. crumb.
midollare agg. medullar.
midollo sm. marrow: — spinale, spinal cord.
miele sm. honey.
miètere vt. to reap.
mietitrice sf. reaper.
mietitura sf. reaping.
migliaio sm. thousand.
miglio¹ sm. (bot.) millet.
miglio² sm. (misura di lunghezza) mile.
miglioramento sm. improvement.
migliorare vt. to better, to improve.
migliore agg. 1. (comp.) better: questo libro è — di quello, this book is better than that 2. (superl.) the best: è il — alunno della classe, he is the best pupil in his class.
miglioria sf. improvement.
mignatta sf. leech.
mignolo sm. little finger.
migrare vi. to migrate.
migratore agg. migratory. ◆ **migratore** sm. migrant.
migratorio agg. migratory.
migrazione sf. migration.
miliardario sm. multi-millionaire.

miliardo *sm.* a thousand millions.
miliare *a.g. pietra —*, milestone.
milionario *sm.* millionaire.
milione *sm.* million.
milionèsimo *agg.* millionth.
militante *agg.* militant.
militare[1] *agg.* military. ♦ **militare** *sm.* soldier.
militare[2] *vi.* 1. to be a soldier 2. (*lavorare a favore di*) to support.
militaresco *agg.* soldierlike.
militarismo *sm.* militarism.
militarista *sm.* militarist.
militarizzare *vt.* to militarize.
militarizzazione *sf.* militarization.
militarmente *avv.* militarily.
mìlite *sm.* militiaman (*pl.* -men).
milizia *sf.* Army.
miliziano *sm.* militiaman (*pl.* -men).
millantare *vt.* to boast of. ♦ **millantarsi** *vr.* to boast.
millantatore *sm.* boaster.
millanterìa *sf.* boasting.
mille *agg.* one thousand.
millenario *agg.* e *sm.* millenary.
millennio *sm.* millennium.
millepiedi *sm.* millepede.
millèsimo *agg.* thousandth.
milligrammo *sm.* milligram.
millìmetro *sm.* millimetre.
milza *sf.* spleen.
mimare *vt.* e *vi.* to mime.
mimètico *agg.* mimetic.
mimetismo *sm.* 1. (*di animali*) mimicry 2. (*mil.*) camouflage.
mimetizzare *vt.* to camouflage.
mimetizzazione *sf.* camouflage.
mìmica *sf.* 1. (*teat.*) mimic art 2. (*di gesti*) gesticulation.
mìmico *agg.* miming, mimic.
mimo *sm.* mime.
mimosa *sf.* mimosa.
mina *sf.* mine.
minaccia *sf.* threat.
minacciare *vt.* to threaten.
minaccioso *agg.* threatening.
minare *vt.* 1. to mine 2. (*fig.*) undermine.
minareto *sm.* minaret.
minatore *sm.* miner.
minatorio *agg.* threatening.
minchione *sm.* simpleton.
minerale *agg.* mineral. ♦ **minerale** *sm.* mineral.
mineralizzare *vt.* to mineralize.
mineralogìa *sf.* mineralogy.
minerario *agg.* mining (*attr.*).
minestra *sf.* soup.
mingherlino *agg.* slim.

miniare *vt.* 1. to paint in miniature 2. (*di manoscritti*) to illuminate.
miniato *agg.* illuminated.
miniatura *sf.* miniature.
miniaturista *sm.* miniaturist.
miniera *sf.* mine.
minigonna *sf.* miniskirt.
minimamente *avv.* not in the least.
minimizzare *vt.* to minimize.
mìnimo *agg.* least, slightest, smallest. ♦ **mìnimo** *sm.* minimum..
minio *sm.* red lead.
ministeriale *agg.* ministerial.
ministero *sm.* ministry: — *dell'Istruzione*, ministry of Education || — *degli Esteri, dell'Interno* Foreign, Home Office; — *del Tesoro*, Treasury.
ministro *sm.* minister.
minoranza *sf.* minority.
minorare *vt.* to diminish.
minorato *agg.* disabled.
minorazione *sf.* 1. (*diminuzione*) reduction 2. (*invalidità*) disablement.
minore *agg.* 1. (*comp.*) (*più piccolo*) smaller, less; (*più basso*) lower; (*più corto*) shorter; (*più giovane*) younger 2. (*superl.*) the smallest, least, lowest, shortest, youngest.
minorile *agg.* juvenile.
minorenne *agg.* under age. ♦ **minorenne** *s.* minor.
minorile *agg.* juvenile.
minorità *sf.* minority.
minoritario *agg.* minority (*attr.*)
minuetto *sm.* minuet.
minugia *sf.* gut.
minùscolo *agg.* small letter.
minuta *sf.* rough copy.
minutaglia *sf.* bits and pieces (*pl.*).
minuto[1] *agg.* 1. minute 2. (*dettagliato*) detailed.
minuto[2] *sm.* minute.
minuto[3] *sm.* (*comm.*) retail.
minuzia *sf.* trifle.
minuziosamente *avv.* minutely.
minuziosità *sf.* minuteness.
minuzioso *agg.* minute, detailed.
minùzzolo *sm.* crumb.
mio *agg.* my. ♦ **mio** *pron.* mine.
miocardìa *sf.* myocardia.
miocardio *sm.* myocardium.
miocardite *sf.* myocarditis.
miocene *sm.* miocene.
mìope *agg.* short-sighted.
miopìa *sf.* myopia.

mira *sf.* 1. aim: *prendere la* —, to take (*v. irr.*) aim 2. (*fig.*) aim, design.
miràbile *agg.* admirable.
mirabìlia *sf. pl.* wonders.
mirabolante *agg.* astonishing.
miràcolo *sm.* miracle: *fare miràcoli*, to do (*v. irr.*) miracles, (*fig.*) to work wonders.
miracoloso *agg.* miraculous.
miràggio *sm.* mirage.
mirare *vt.* to look at. ♦ **mirare** *vi.* to aim (at).
mirìade *sf.* myriad.
miriagrammo *sm.* myriagram.
miriàmetro *sm.* myriametre.
miriàpodi *sm. pl.* Myriapoda.
mirìfico *agg.* wondrous.
mirino *sm.* 1. sight 2. (*foto*) view- -finder.
mirra *sf.* myrrh.
mirtillo *sm.* bilberry.
mirto *sm.* myrtle.
misantropìa *sf.* misanthropy.
misàntropo *sm.* misanthrope.
miscela *sf.* 1. mixture 2. (*di caffè, tè, liquori, tabacco*) blend.
miscelare *vt.* 1. to mix 2. (*di caffè, tabacco, liquori ecc.*) to blend.
miscellànea *sf.* miscellany.
mischia *sf.* fray.
mischiare *vt.* to mix, to mingle.
mischiatura *sf.* 1. (*il mischiare*) mixing 2. (*miscuglio*) mixture.
misconòscere *vt.* not to acknowledge.
miscredente *agg.* misbelieving. ♦ **miscredente** *sm.* misbeliever.
miscredenza *sf.* misbelief.
miscùglio *sm.* 1. mixture 2. (*amalgama*) blend.
miseràbile *agg.* 1. miserable 2. (*scarso*) poor 3. (*vile*) despicable, mean. ♦ **miseràbile** *sm.* wretch.
miserando *agg.* miserable.
miserévole *agg.* miserable, pitiable.
miseria *sf.* 1. misery, poverty 2. (*scarsità*) lack 3. (*inezia*) trifle.
misericòrdia *sf.* mercy.
misericordioso *agg.* merciful.
mìsero *agg.* 1. poor, scanty 2. (*meschino*) wretched.
misfatto *sm.* misdeed.
misoginìa *sf.* misogyny.
misògino *agg.* misogynous. ♦ **misògino** *sm.* misogynist.
misoneismo *sm.* misoneism.
missàggio *sm.* mixing.
mìssile *sm.* missile.

missionario *sm.* missionary.
missione *sf.* mission.
missiva *sf.* letter.
misteriosamente *avv.* mysteriously.
misterioso *agg.* mysterious.
mistero *sm.* mystery.
mìstica *sf.* mysticism.
misticismo *sm.* mysticism.
mìstico *agg.* mystic.
mistificare *vt.* to mystify.
mistificatore *sm.* mystifier.
mistificazione *sf.* mystification.
misto *agg.* mixed.
mistura *sf.* mixture.
misura *sf.* 1. (*misurazione, precauzione*) measure 2. (*taglia*) size 3. (*limite*) limit.
misuràbile *agg.* measurable.
misurare *vt.* 1. to measure 2. (*tec.*) to gauge 3. (*limitare*) to limit. ♦ **misurarsi** *vr.* to compete.
misurato *agg.* measured.
misuratore *sm.* 1. (*persona che misura*) measurer 2. (*strumento*) gauge.
misurazione *sf.* measurement.
misurino *sm.* small measure.
mite *agg.* gentle, meek.
mitezza *sf.* gentleness, meekness.
mìtico *agg.* mythical.
mitigare *vt.* 1. to mitigate 2. (*passioni*) to appease 3. (*dolori*) to relieve. ♦ **mitigarsi** *vr.* to be appeased.
mitigazione *sf.* 1. mitigation 2. (*di passioni*) appeasement 3. (*di dolore*) relief.
mìtilo *sm.* mussel.
mito *sm.* myth.
mitologìa *sf.* mythology.
mitològico *agg.* mythological.
mitòmane *s.* mythomaniac.
mitomanìa *sf.* mythomania.
mitra[1] *sf.* (*eccl.*) mitre.
mitra[2] *sm.* (*mil.*) tommy-gun.
mitràglia *sf.* grape-shot.
mitragliare *vt.* to machine-gun.
mitragliatore *sm.* machine-gunner.
mitragliatrice *sf.* machine-gun.
mitragliere *sm.* machine-gunner.
mitrale *agg.* mitral.
mitrato *agg.* mitred.
mitridàtico *agg.* mithridatic.
mitridatismo *sm.* mithridatism.
mittente *sm.* sender.
mnemònica *sf.* mnemonics.
mnemònico *agg.* mnemonic.
mo' (*nella loc. prep.*) *a* — *di*, like.

mòbile *agg.* **1.** movable || *scala —,* escalator; *beni mobili,* personal property **2.** (*mutevole*) inconstant. ◆ **mòbile** *sm.* piece of furniture.

mobilia *sf.* furniture.

mobiliare[1] *agg.* movable, personal.

mobiliare[2] *vt.* to furnish.

mobilità *sf.* **1.** mobility **2.** (*fig.*) inconstancy.

mobilitare *vt.* to mobilize.

mobilitazione *sf.* mobilization.

mocassino *sm.* moccasin.

moccioso *agg.* snivelling. ◆ **moccioso** *sm.* young scoundrel, brat.

mòccolo *sm.* **1.** candle-end **2.** (*bestemmia*) curse.

moda *sf.* **1.** fashion: *di —,* in fashion; *fuori —,* out of fashion || *alla —,* fashionable **2.** (*abitudine, modo*) manner, way: *alla — di,* after the manner of.

modale *agg.* modal.

modalità *sf.* modality.

modanatura *sf.* moulding.

mòdano *sm.* model.

modella *sf.* model.

modellare *vt.* to model, to shape.

modellatore *sm.* modeller.

modellazione *sf.* modelling.

modello *sm.* **1.** model, pattern **2.** (*stampo*) mould.

moderare *vt.* to moderate, to check.

moderato *agg.* moderate.

moderatore *agg.* moderating. ◆ **moderatore** *sm.* moderator.

moderazione *sf.* moderation.

modernismo *sm.* modernism.

modernità *sf.* modernity.

modernizzare *vt.* to modernize.

moderno *agg.* modern, up-to-date (*attr.*).

modestia *sf.* modesty: *— a parte,* modesty apart.

modesto *agg.* modest.

modicità *sf.* **1.** moderateness **2.** (*di prezzi*) cheapness.

mòdico *agg.* moderate: *a prezzo —,* cheap.

modìfica *sf.* alteration, change.

modificare *vt.* to modify.

modificazione *sf.* V. *modifica.*

modista *sf.* milliner.

modisteria *sf.* milliner's shop.

modo *sm.* **1.** way, manner **2.** (*gramm.*) mood **3.** (*mezzo*) means: *in nessun —,* by no means || *di — che,* so (that); *in — da,* so as to; *in che —,* how; *in qualche —,* anyhow; *oltre —,* beyond measure.

modulare *vt.* to modulate.

modulato *agg.* modulated.

modulazione *sf.* modulation

mòdulo *sm.* form.

moffetta *sf.* skunk.

mògano *sm.* mahogany.

moggio *sm.* bushel.

mogio *agg.* depressed.

moglie *sf.* wife (*pl.* wives).

moina *sf.* simpering.

mola[1] *sf.* **1.** (*di mulino*) millstone **2.** (*per arrotare*) grindstone.

mola[2] *sf.* (*itt.*) sun-fish.

molare[1] *vt.* to grind (*v. irr.*).

molare[2] *agg.* molar. ◆ **molare** *sm.* (*dente*) molar (tooth).

molatura *sf.* grinding.

molazza *sf.* muller.

mole *sf.* **1.** mass, bulk **2.** (*dimensione*) size.

molècola *sf.* molecule.

molecolare *agg.* molecular.

molestare *vt.* to molest, to tease.

molestatore *agg.* molesting. ◆ **molestatore** *sm.* molester.

molestia *sf.* nuisance, trouble.

molesto *agg.* troublesome.

molibdeno *sm.* molybdenum.

molitorio *agg.* molinary.

molla *sf.* **1.** spring **2.** (*incentivo*) spur.

mollare *vt.* **1.** (*allentare*) to slacken **2.** (*mar.*) to let (*v. irr.*) go. ◆ **mollare** *vi.* to give (*v. irr.*) in.

molle *agg.* **1.** soft **2.** (*floscio*) flabby **3.** (*debole*) weak **4.** (*inzuppato*) soaking wet. ◆ **molle** *sf. pl.* tongs.

molleggiamento *sm.* **1.** (*elasticità*) springiness **2.** (*di veicoli*) springing system.

molleggiare *vi.* to be springy.

molleggiato *agg.* sprung.

molleggio *sm.* (*di veicoli*) suspension.

molletta *sf.* **1.** (*per il bucato*) clothes-peg **2.** (*per i capelli*) hair-pin.

mollettiere *sf. pl.* puttees.

mollettone *sm.* thick flannel.

mollezza *sf.* **1.** (*morbidezza*) softness **2.** (*debolezza*) weakness.

mollica *sf.* crumb.

mollo *agg.* damp: *mettere a —,* to steep.

mollusco *sm.* mollusc.

molo *sm.* pier, wharf.

moltéplice *agg.* manifold.

molteplicità *sf.* multiplicity.

moltìplica *sf.* (*mecc.*) chain gearing.

moltiplicando *sm.* multiplicand.

moltiplicare *vt.* to multiply.

moltiplicatore *sm.* multiplier.

moltiplicazione *sf.* multiplication.

moltìssimo *agg. indef.* 1. very much (*pl.* very many) 2. (*di tempo*) very long. ♦ **moltìssimo** *avv.* a great deal, very much.

moltitùdine *sf.* multitude.

molto *agg. indef.* 1. (*sing.*) much, a great deal of, a lot of, plenty of 2. (*pl.*) many, a good many, a lot of, plenty of 3. (*di tempo*) long. ♦ **molto** *avv.* 1. very 2. (*con comp.*) much, far 3. (*di tempo*) long, a long time.

momentaneamente *avv.* at the moment.

momentàneo *agg.* momentary.

momento *sm.* 1. moment || *dal — che*, since 2. (*tempo, circostanza*) time 3. (*opportunità*) chance.

mònaca *sf.* nun.

monacale *agg.* monastic.

mònaco *sm.* monk.

mònade *sf.* monad.

monarca *sm.* monarch.

monarchìa *sf.* monarchy.

monàrchico *agg.* monarchic.

monastero *sm.* monastery.

monàstico *agg.* monastic.

moncherino *sm.* stump.

monco *agg.* 1. maimed 2. (*fig.*) incomplete.

moncone *sm.* stump.

mondanità *sf.* 1. society life 2. worldliness.

mondano *agg.* worldly.

mondare *vt.* 1. to clean || *— il grano*, to winnow the corn 2. (*fig.*) to cleanse.

mondiale *agg.* world-wide, world (*attr.*).

mondina *sf.* rice-weeder.

mondo[1] *sm.* world: *fare il giro del —*, to go (*v. irr.*) round the world; *da che — è —*, since the world began.

mondo[2] *agg.* clean.

monellerìa *sf.* prank.

monello *sm.* little rascal, urchin.

moneta *sf.* 1. money (*solo sing.*) 2. (*ogni singolo pezzo*) coin 3. (*spiccioli*) change.

monetàrio *agg.* monetary.

monetizzare *vt.* to monetize.

mongolfièra *sf.* montgolfier.

mongolismo *sm.* mongolism.

mòngolo *agg.* Mongolian. ♦ **mòngolo** *sm.* Mongol.

mongolòide *agg. e sm.* mongoloid.

monile *sm.* jewel.

monismo *sm.* monism.

mònito *sm.* warning.

monoblocco *sm.* monobloc.

monòcolo *sm.* monocle.

monocromàtico *agg.* monochromatic.

monòcromo *agg.* monochrome.

monodìa *sf.* monody.

monogamìa *sf.* monogamy.

monògamo *agg.* monogamous. ♦ **monògamo** *sm.* monogamist.

monografìa *sf.* monograph.

monogràfico *agg.* monographic.

monogramma *sm.* monogram.

monolìtico *agg.* monolithic.

monòlogo *sm.* monologue, soliloquy.

monometallismo *sm.* monometallism.

monomìo *sm.* monomial.

monopàttino *sm.* scooter.

monoplano *sm.* monoplane.

monopolio *sm.* monopoly.

monopolista *sm.* monopolist.

monopolizzare *vt.* to monopolize.

monoposto *agg. e sm.* single-seater.

monorotaia *sf.* monorail.

monosillàbico *agg.* monosyllabic.

monosìllabo *sm.* monosyllable.

monoteismo *sm.* monotheism.

monoteista *s.* monotheist.

monoteìstico *agg.* monotheistic.

monotipo *sm.* monotype.

monotonìa *sf.* monotony.

monòtono *agg.* monotonous.

monovalente *agg.* monovalent.

monsignore *sm.* monsignor (*pl.* -ri).

monsone *sm.* monsoon.

montacàrichi *sm.* goods-lift.

montaggio *sm.* 1. assembly: *linea di —*, assembly line 2. (*cine*) editing 3. (*foto*) montage.

montagna *sf.* mountain.

montagnoso *agg.* mountainous.

montanaro *agg.* mountain (*attr.*). ♦ **montanaro** *sm.* mountaineer.

montante *sm.* 1. (*boxe*) uppercut 2. (*mecc.; edil.*) vertical rod.

montare *vt.* 1. (*mettere insieme*) to assemble 2. (*cavalcare*) to ride (*v. irr.*) 3. (*di panna*) to whip. ♦ **montare** *vi.* 1. to climb 2. (*alzarsi, aumentare*) to rise (*v. irr.*). ♦ **montarsi** *vr.* to get (*v. irr.*) excited.

montatore *sm.* assembler.

montatura *sf.* 1. fitting 2. (*fig.*) hot hair.

montavivande *sm.* dumb-waiter.

monte *sm.* 1. mount (*seguito dal nome*) 2. mountain || *andare a* —, to come (*v. irr.*) to nothing; *mandare a* —, to cause to fail.

montone *sm.* 1. ram 2. (*carne*) mutton.

montuosità *sf.* hilliness.

montuoso *agg.* hilly.

monumentale *agg.* monumental.

monumento *sm.* monument.

mora[1] *sf.* (*bot.*) mulberry.

mora[2] *sf.* (*giur.*) delay.

morale *agg.* moral. ♦ **morale** *sm.* morale. ♦ **morale** *sf.* 1. morals (*pl.*) 2. (*fil.*) ethics 3. (*conclusione*) moral.

moralismo *sm.* moralism.

moralista *s.* moralist.

moralistico *agg.* moralistic.

moralità *sf.* morality.

moralizzare *vt.* to moralize.

moralizzazione *sf.* moralization.

moratorio *agg.* moratory.

morbidezza *sf.* softness.

mòrbido *agg.* soft.

morbillo *sm.* measles (*pl.*).

morbo *sm.* disease, plague.

morbosità *sf.* morbidity.

morboso *agg.* morbid.

mordace *agg.* biting, pungent.

mordacità *sf.* mordacity.

mordente *sm.* 1. (*mus.*) mordent 2. (*spirito aggressivo*) bite.

mòrdere *vt.* 1. to bite (*v. irr.*) 2. (*tormentare*) to torment || — *il freno*, to strain at the leash; — *la polvere*, to bite the dust.

morena *sf.* moraine.

morènico *agg.* morainic.

morente *agg.* dying. ♦ **morente** *sm.* dying man.

moresco *agg.* Moorish.

morfina *sf.* morphine.

morfinòmane *s.* morphinomaniac.

morfologìa *sf.* morphology.

morfològico *agg.* morphologic(al).

morganàtico *agg.* morganatic.

moribondo *agg.* dying. ♦ **moribondo** *sm.* dying man.

morigeratezza *sf.* moderation.

morigerato *agg.* moderate, sober.

morire *vi.* 1. to die 2. (*di luci e colori*) to fade 3. (*di suoni*) to die out 4. (*tramontare*) to set (*v. irr.*). ♦ **morire** *sm.* death.

mormone *agg. e sm.* Mormon.

mormorare *vt.* to murmur. ♦ **mormorare** *vi.* (*parlar male*) to gossip.

mormorìo *sm.* 1. murmur 2. (*lamento*) complaining 3. (*malignità*) evil gossip.

moro *agg.* dark. ♦ **moro** *sm.* 1. moor 2. (*bot.*) mulberry-tree.

morra *sf.* "morra".

morsa *sf.* vice.

morsetto *sm.* (*mecc.*) clamp.

morsicare *vt.* to bite (*v. irr.*).

morsicatura *sf.* bite.

morsicchiare *vt.* to nibble.

morso *sm.* 1. bite 2. (*puntura, stimolo*) sting, pang 3. (*del cavallo*) bit 4. (*boccone*) morsel, bit.

mortaio *sm.* mortar.

mortale *agg.* mortal, deadly.

mortalità *sf.* mortality.

mortalmente *avv.* mortally.

mortaretto *sm.* cracker.

morte *sf.* death || *pena di* —, capital punishment; *dar la* — *a qu.*, to kill so.; *odiare a* — *qu.*, to hate so. like poison.

mortella *sf.* myrtle.

mortìfero *agg.* lethal.

mortificare *vt.* 1. to humiliate 2. (*reprimere*) to mortify.

mortificato *agg.* humiliated.

mortificazione *sf.* mortification.

morto *agg.* 1. dead || *natura morta* (*pitt.*), still life; *stanco* —, dead tired 2. (*senza vivacità*) dull. ♦ **morto** *sm.* dead man.

mortorio *sm.* funeral.

mortuario *agg.* mortuary.

mosaicista *s.* mosaicist.

mosàico *sm.* mosaic.

mosca *sf.* fly.

moscatello *sm.* muscatel.

moscato *sm.* (*vino*) muscatel. ♦ **moscato** *agg. noce moscata*, nutmeg.

moscerino *sm.* gnat.

moschea *sf.* mosque.

moschettiere *sm.* musketeer.

moschetto *sm.* musket.

moscio *agg.* flabby.

moscone *sm.* blue-bottle.

mossa *sf.* 1. movement 2. (*spostamento al gioco; fig.*) move 3. (*sport*) starting post.

mossiere *sm.* (*sport*) starter.

mosso *agg.* 1. (*di mare*) rough 2. (*di capelli*) wavy.

mosto *sm.* must.

mostra *sf.* 1. (*esposizione*) show, exhibition 2. (*vetrina*) shop-window 3. (*ostentazione*) display.

mostrare *vt.* 1. to show (*v. irr.*) 2. (*ostentare*) to show (*v. irr.*) off 3. (*dimostrare*). to prove 4. (*fingere*) to pretend.

mostrina *sf.* collar badge.

mostro *sm.* monster.

mostruosamente *avv.* monstrously.

mostruosità *sf.* monstrosity.

mostruoso *agg.* monstrous. for 2. (*giur.*) to allege.

mota *sf.* mud, mire.

motivare *vt.* 1. to state the reason

motivazione *sf.* 1. motivation 2. (*giur.*) opinion.

motivo *sm.* 1. reason || *a — di*, owing to; *senza —*, groundless 2. (*mus.*) theme.

moto *sm.* 1. motion, movement 2. (*esercizio fisico*) exercise 3. (*impulso*) impulse. ♦ **moto** *sf.* motor-cycle.

motobarca *sf.* motor-boat.

motocarrozzetta *sf.* side-car.

motocicletta *sf.* motor-cycle.

motociclismo *sm.* motor-cycling.

motociclista *s.* motor-cyclist.

motofurgone *sm.* van.

motore *agg.* motor, driving. ♦ **motore** *sm.* engine, motor.

motorista *sm.* engineer.

motorizzare *vt.* to motorize. ♦ **motorizzarsi** *vr.* to buy (*v. irr.*) a car, a motor-cycle.

motorizzazione *sf.* motorization.

motoscafo *sm.* motor-boat.

motoveicolo *sm.* motòr vehicle.

motrice *sf.* 1. tractor 2. (*ferr.*) engine.

motteggiare *vt.* to make (*v. irr.*) fun of. ♦ **motteggiare** *vi.* to joke.

motteggiatore *agg.* joking. ♦ **motteggiatore** *sm.* joker.

motteggio *sm.* 1. (*il motteggiare*) raillery 2. (*detto arguto*) joke.

mottetto *sm.* motet.

motto *sm.* 1. word 2. (*proverbio*) saying 3. (*facezia*) witticism.

movente *sm.* motive, cause.

movenza *sf.* movements (*pl.*).

movìbile *agg.* movable.

movimentare *vt.* to enliven.

movimentato *agg.* 1. lively 2. (*pieno di movimento*) eventful.

movimento *sm.* 1. movement 2.

(*traffico, trambusto*) traffic, bustle.

moviola *sf.* film-editing machine.

mozione *sf.* motion.

mozzare *vt.* to cut (*v. irr.*) off.

mozzicone *sm.* 1. stump 2. (*di sigaretta*) butt.

mozzo[1] *agg.* cut (off).

mozzo[2] *sm.* 1. (*di ruota*) hub 2. (*mar.*) ship-boy.

mucca *sf.* cow.

mucchio *sm.* heap, mass.

mùcido *agg.* mouldy. ♦ **mùcido** *sm.* mould.

muco *sm.* mucus.

mucosa *sf.* mucous membrane.

mucoso *agg.* mucous.

muffa *sf.* mould.

muffire *vi.* to mildew.

muflone *sm.* moufflon.

mugghiare *vi.* 1. to bellow 2. (*fig.*) to roar 3. (*del vento*) to howl.

mugghio *sm.* 1. bellow 2. (*fig.*) roar 3. (*del vento*) howl.

muggire *vi.* V. *mugghiare*.

muggito *sm.* V. *mugghio*.

mughetto *sm.* lily of the valley.

mugnaio *sm.* miller.

mugolare *vi.* 1. to howl 2. (*piagnucolare*) to whimper.

mugolìo *sm.* 1. howling 2. (*piagnucolìo*) whimpering.

mugugnare *vi.* to mumble.

mulattiera *sf.* mule-track.

mulattiere *sm.* mule-driver.

mulatto *sm.* mulatto.

muliebre *agg.* feminine, womanly.

mulinare *vt.* 1. to whirl 2. (*fig.*) to brood (over).

mulinello *sm.* 1. (*d'acqua*) whirlpool 2. (*d'aria*) whirlwind 3. (*rapido movimento*) twirl.

mulino *sm.* mill.

mulo *sm.* mule.

multa *sf.* fine.

multare *vt.* to fine.

multicolore *agg.* many-coloured.

multiforme *agg.* multiform.

mùltiplo *agg.* e *sm.* multiple.

mummia *sf.* mummy.

mummificare *vt.* to mummify.

mummificazione *sf.* mummification.

mùngere *vt.* to milk.

mungitore *sm.* milker.

mungitura *sf.* milking.

municipale *agg.* municipal.

municipalità *sf.* municipality.

municipalizzare *vt.* to municipalize.

municipalizzazione sf. municipalization.

municipio sm. 1. municipality 2. (*palazzo*) townhall 3. (*stor.*) municipium (*pl.* -ia).

munificenza sf. munificence.

munifico agg. munificent.

munire vt. 1. (*fortificare*) to fortify 2. (*provvedere*) to supply (with).

munizione sf. munition.

muòvere vt. to move. ♦ **muòversi** vr. to move, to stir ‖ *muoviti!* hurry up!

mura¹ sf. (*mar.*) tack.

mura² sf. pl. walls.

muraglia sf. wall.

muraglione sm. massive wall.

murale agg. mural.

murare vt. 1. to wall up 2. (*cingere di mura*) to wall.

murario agg. building (*attr.*).

murata sf. ship's side.

muratore sm. bricklayer.

muratura sf. masonry ‖ *lavoro in* —, brickwork.

murena sf. moray.

muriàtico agg. muriatic.

muricciolo sm. low wall.

murice sm. murex.

muro sm. wall ‖ *armadio a* —, built-in cupboard; — *del suono*, sound barrier.

musa sf. muse.

muschiato agg. musky.

muschio¹ sm. (*sostanza odorosa*) musk.

muschio² sm. (*bot.*) moss.

muscolare agg. muscular.

muscolatura sf. musculature.

mùscolo sm. muscle.

muscoloso agg. muscular.

muscoso agg. mossy.

museo sm. museum.

museruola sf. muzzle.

mùsica sf. music.

musicale agg. musical.

musicalità sf. musicality.

musicante sm. musician.

musicare vt. to set (*v. irr.*) to music.

musicista sm. musician.

mùsico sm. musician.

musicologia sf. musicology.

musicòlogo sm. musicologist.

musivo agg. mosaic (*attr.*).

muso sm. 1. muzzle 2. (*broncio*) long face: *fare il* —, to pull a long face.

musone sm. 1. large muzzle 2. (*per-* *sona che tiene il broncio*) sulky person.

musonerìa sf. sulkiness.

mussare vi. to froth.

mussolina sf. muslin.

mustèlidi sm. pl. mustelidae.

musulmano agg. e sm. Muslim.

muta sf. 1. (*di cani*) pack of hounds 2. (*della guardia*) change 3. (*biol.*) moult.

mutàbile agg. changeable.

mutabilità sf. 1. (*di cosa*) changeability 2. (*di persona*) fickleness.

mutamento sm. change.

mutande sf. pl. drawers.

mutandine sf. pl. trunks.

mutare vt. 1. to change 2. (*di animali*) to shed (*v. irr.*), to moult. ♦ **mutarsi** vr. to change.

mutazione sf. change.

mutévole agg. changeable.

mutilare vt. 1. to maim 2. (*fig.*) to mutilate.

mutilato agg. 1. maimed 2. (*fig.*) mutilated. ♦ **mutilato** sm. cripple.

mutilazione sf. 1. maiming 2. (*fig.*) mutilation.

mùtilo agg. mutilated.

mutismo sm. dumbness.

muto agg. 1. dumb ‖ *carta geografica muta*, blank map 2. (*fonetica*) mute.

mutria sf. stand-offishness.

mutua sf. national insurance ‖ *medico della* —, panel doctor.

mutualistico agg. insurance (*attr.*).

mutualità sf. mutual help.

mutuare vt. 1. (*dare in mutuo*) to lend (*v. irr.*) 2. (*prendere a mutuo*) to borrow.

mutuatario sm. borrower.

mutuato agg. insured.

mutuo agg. mutual. ♦ **mutuo** sm. loan.

N

nababbo sm. nabob.

nàcchera sf. castanet.

nafta sf. 1. oil 2. (*chim.*) naphtha.

naftalina sf. moth-balls (*pl.*).

naia¹ sf. (*zool.*) cobra.

naia² sf. (*mil.*) *fare la* —, to do (*v. irr.*) one's bit.

nàiade sf. naiad.

nàilon sm. nylon.

nandù sm. nandu.

nanismo sm. nanism.

nano sm. dwarf.

nappa sf. tassel.

narcisismo sm. narcissism.

narcisista sm. narcissist.

narciso sm. narcissus.

narcosi sf. narcosis (pl. -ses).

narcòtico agg. e sm. narcotic.

narcotizzare vt. to narcotize.

narice sf. nostril.

narrare vt. to tell (v. irr.).

narrativa sf. fiction.

narrativo agg. narrative.

narratore sm. 1. story-teller 2. (scrittore) writer.

narrazione sf. narration.

narvalo sm. narwhal.

nasale agg. nasal.

nascente agg. rising.

nàscere vi. 1. to be born 2. (di piante) to spring (v. irr.) up 3. (di fiume; sorgere) to rise (v. irr.) 4. (avere origine) to originate || far —, to give (v. irr.) rise to.

nàscita sf. 1. birth 2. (origine) origin.

nascituro sm. unborn child.

nascòndere vt. to hide (v. irr.). ◆ **nascòndersi** vr. to hide (oneself).

nascondiglio sm. hiding-place.

nascosto agg. hidden || di —, secretly.

nasello sm. (itt.) whiting.

naso sm. nose || a lume di —, by guesswork; ficcare il — in qc., to poke one's nose into sthg.; avere buon —, to be shrewd.

nassa sf. bow-net.

nastro sm. 1. ribbon 2. (tec.) tape.

natale agg. native. ◆ **Natale** sm. Christmas.

natalità sf. birth-rate.

natalizio agg. Christmas (attr.).

natante agg. floating. ◆ **natante** sm. watercraft.

natatoia sf. fin.

natatorio agg. swimming (attr.).

nàtica sf. buttock.

natività sf. nativity.

nativo agg. 1. native 2. (innato) inborn.

nato agg. born.

natura sf. nature.

naturale agg. natural.

naturalezza sf. naturalness, simplicity.

naturalismo sm. naturalism.

naturalista s. naturalist.

naturalizzare vt. to naturalize.

naturalizzazione sf. naturalization.

naturalmente avv. naturally, of course.

naturismo sm. naturism.

naturista s. naturist.

naufragare vi. 1. to be shipwrecked 2. (fig.) to be wrecked.

naufragio sm. 1. shipwreck 2. (fig.) wreck.

nàufrago sm. shipwrecked person.

nàusea sf. disgust, nausea || avere la —, to feel (v. irr.) sick.

nauseabondo agg. nauseating.

nauseare vt. to make (v. irr.) sick.

nàutica sf. navigation.

nàutico agg. nautical.

navale agg. naval.

navata sf. 1. (centrale) nave 2. (laterale) aisle.

nave sf. ship.

navetta sf. shuttle.

navicella sf. (aer.) nacelle.

navigàbile agg. navigable.

navigabilità sf. navigability.

navigare vi. to sail.

navigato agg. (fig.) cunning.

navigatore sm. navigator.

navigazione sf. navigation.

naviglio sm. 1. fleet 2. (nave) craft.

nazionale agg. national.

nazionalismo sm. nationalism.

nazionalista s. nationalist.

nazionalità sf. nationality.

nazionalizzare vt. to nationalize.

nazionalizzazione sf. nationalization.

nazionalsocialismo sm. National Socialism.

nazione sf. nation.

nazismo sm. Nazism.

nazista agg. e sm. Nazi.

nazzareno agg. e sm. Nazarene.

ne pron. 1. of him, about him; of her, about her; of it, about it; of them, about them; of this, about this; of that, about that 2. (partitivo) some: — ho, I have some; any: non — ho, I haven't any. ◆ **ne** (particella avv. di moto da luogo) from there.

né cong. 1. neither, nor 2. (né... né...) neither... nor; (in presenza di altra negazione) either... or.

neanche avv. not even. ◆ **neanche** cong. neither; nor: essi non anda-

rono e — to, they did not go and neither did I.

nebbia *sf.* fog.

nebbioso *agg.* foggy.

nebulizzare *vt.* to nebulize.

nebulizzatore *sm.* nebulizer.

nebulosa *sf.* nebula (*pl.* -ae).

nebulosità *sf.* 1. nebulosity 2. (*fig.*) haziness.

nebuloso *agg.* 1. nebulous 2. (*fig.*) vague.

necessario *agg.* necessary. ♦ **necessario** *sm.* 1. necessary 2. (*l'indispensabile*) necessities (*pl.*).

necessità *sf.* 1. necessity 2. (*bisogno*) need.

necessitare *vi.* to need.

necrologìa *sf.* obituary-notice.

necrologio *sm.* 1. necrology 2. (*annuncio*) obituary.

necròpoli *sf.* necropolis.

necrosi *sf.* necrosis (*pl.* -ses).

necrotizzare *vt.* to necrotize.

nefandezza *sf.* wickedness.

nefando *agg.* wicked.

nefasto *agg.* ill-omened.

nefrite *sf.* nephritis.

nefrìtico *agg.* nephritic. ♦ **nefrìtico** *sm.* nephritic subject.

negare *vt.* 1. to deny 2. (*rifiutare*) to refuse.

negativa *sf.* (*anche foto*) negative.

negativo *agg.* negative.

negato *agg.* 1. refused, denied 2. (*inadatto*) unfit (for).

negatore *agg.* negatory. ♦ **negatore** *sm.* denier.

negazione *sf.* 1. denial 2. (*gramm.*) negative 3. (*cosa diametralmente opposta all'altra*) negation.

neghittoso *agg.* slothful.

negletto *agg.* 1. neglected 2. (*di aspetto*) slovenly.

negligente *agg.* negligent, careless.

negligenza *sf.* negligence, carelessness.

negozìàbile *agg.* negotiable.

negoziante *sm.* 1. merchant, trader 2. (*chi ha negozio*) shopkeeper.

negoziare *vt.* to negotiate.

negoziato *agg.* negotiated. ♦ **negoziato** *sm.* negotiation.

negozio *sm.* 1. shop 2. (*commercio*) trade 3. (*faccenda*) affair.

negriero *agg.* slave (*attr.*). ♦ **negriero** *sm.* slave-trader.

negro *agg. e sm.* 1. negro 2. (*spreg.*) nigger.

negròide *agg. e s.* negroid.

negromante *sm.* necromancer.

negromanzìa *sf.* necromancy.

nembo *sm.* 1. raincloud 2. (*fig.*) multitude.

nèmesi *sf.* nemesis (*pl.* -ses).

nemico *agg.* 1. adverse 2. (*del nemico*) enemy (*attr.*). ♦ **nemico** *sm.* enemy.

neo[1] *sm.* 1. mole 2. (*fig.*) flaw.

neo[2] *agg.* neo.

neocapitalismo *sm.* neo-capitalism.

neocapitalista *agg. e sm.* neo-capitalist.

neocapitalìstico *agg.* neo-capitalistic.

neoclassicismo *sm.* neo-classicism.

neoclàssico *agg.* neo-classic.

neofascismo *sm.* neofascism.

neofascista *agg. e s.* neofascist.

neòfita *sm.* 1. neophyte 2. (*fig.*) beginner.

neolìtico *agg.* .Neolithic.

neologismo *sm.* neologism.

neon *sm.* neon: *insegna al —*, neon sign.

neonato *agg.* new-born. ♦ **neonato** *sm.* (new-born) baby.

neorealismo *sm.* Neorealism.

neorealista *agg. e sm.* neorealist.

neozelandese *agg.* New Zealand (*attr.*). ♦ **neozelandese** *s.* New Zealander.

nepotismo *sm.* 'nepotism.

nerastro *agg.* blackish.

nerbo *sm.* 1. sinew 2. (*fig.*) strength, vigour.

nerboruto *agg.* brawny.

neretto *sm.* (*tip.*) boldface.

nerezza *sf.* blackness.

nero *agg.* black.

nerofumo *sm.* lamp-black.

nerògnolo *agg.* blackish.

nerume *sm.* mass of black.

nervatura *sf.* ribbing.

nervo *sm.* nerve.

nervosamente *agg.* nervously.

nervosismo *sm.* nervousness.

nervoso *agg.* nervous, irritable.

nèspola *sf.* medlar.

nèspolo *sm.* medlar(-tree).

nesso *sm.* connection.

nessuno *agg.* 1. no 2. (*in presenza di altra neg.*) any. ♦ **nessuno** *pron.* 1. (*per persone*) nobody, no one; (*per cose*) none 2. (*in presenza di altra neg.*) anybody (*solo per persone*), anyone, any ‖ *— di*, none of, (*in presenza di altra neg.*) any of.

nèttare sm. nectar.

nettare vt. to clean.

nettezza sf. cleanness: — urbana, municipal street cleansing.

netto agg. 1. clean, spotless (anche fig.) 2. (comm.) net.

nettunio sm. neptunium.

neurite sf. neuritis.

neurochirurgìa sf. neurosurgery.

neurologìa sf. neurology.

neuròlogo sm. neurologist.

neuropàtico agg. neuropathic. ♦ neuropàtico sm. neuropath.

neuropatologìa sf. neuropathology.

nèurosi sf. neurosis (pl. -ses).

neurovegetativo agg. vegetative nervous.

neutrale agg. neutral.

neutralismo sm. neutralism.

neutralista s. neutralist.

neutralità sf. neutrality.

neutralizzare vt. to neutralize.

neutralizzazione sf. neutralization.

nèutro agg. 1. neutral 2. (gramm.; bot.; zool.) neuter.

neutrone sm. neutron.

neve sf. snow.

nevicare vi. to snow: nevica, it is snowing.

nevicata sf. snowfall.

nevischio sm. sleet.

nevoso agg. snowy.

nevralgìa sf. neuralgia.

nevràlgico agg. neuralgic.

nevrastenìa sf. neurasthenia.

nevrastènico agg. neurasthenic.

nevròtico agg. e sm. neurotic.

nibbio sm. kite.

nicchia sf. niche.

nicchiare vi. to shilly-shally.

nichel sm. nickel.

nichelare vt. to nickel.

nichelatura sf. nickel-plating.

nichelino sm. nickel coin.

nichilismo sm. nihilism.

nichilista s. nihilist.

nicotina sf. nicotine.

nidiata sf. 1. nest 2. (covata) brood || una — di bambini, a swarm of children.

nidificare vi. to nest.

nido sm. nest.

niente pron. 1. nothing 2. (in presenza di altre negazioni) anything.

nimbo sm. halo.

ninfa sf. nymph.

ninfea sf. water-lily.

ninfòmane sf. nymphomaniac.

ninnananna sf. lullaby.

nìnnolo sm. 1. knick-knack 2. (balocco) plaything.

nipote sm. 1. (di nonno) grand-son 2. (di zio) nephew. ♦ nipote sf. 1. (di nonno) grand-daughter 2. (di zio) niece.

nippònico agg. e sm. Japanese.

nirvana sm. nirvana.

nitidezza sf. neatness.

nìtido agg. neat, clear.

nitrato sm. nitrate.

nìtrico agg. nitric.

nitrire vi. to whinny.

nitrito[1] sm. (di cavallo) whinny.

nitrito[2] sm. (chim.) nitrite.

nitroglicerina sf. nitroglycerin.

nìveo agg. snowy.

no avv. no.

nòbile agg. e sm. noble.

nobiliare agg. nobiliary.

nobilitare vt. to ennoble.

nobilitazione sf. ennobling.

nobilmente avv. nobly.

nobiltà sf. nobility.

nocca sf. knuckle.

nocchiere sm. helmsman (pl. -men).

nocciola sf. hazel-nut.

nòcciolo sm. 1. stone 2. (ciò che è essenziale) heart.

nocciolo sm. (bot.) hazel-tree.

noce sm. walnut-tree. ♦ noce sf. walnut || guscio di — (barchetta), cockle-shell; — moscata, nutmeg.

nocivo agg. noxious, harmful.

nodo sm. knot.

nodoso agg. knotty.

noi pron. 1. (sogg.) we 2. (compl.) us.

noia sf. 1. boredom 2. (fastidio) worry, nuisance.

noioso agg. 1. boring 2. (molesto) annoying.

noleggiante sm. (mar.) charterer.

noleggiare vt. 1. to hire 2. (di navi) to charter.

noleggiatore sm. hirer.

noleggio sm. 1. hire 2. (mar.) freight.

nolente agg. unwilling || volente o —, willy-nilly.

nolo sm. 1. hire 2. (mar.) freight.

nòmade agg. e s. nomad.

nomadismo sm. nomadism.

nome sm. 1. name 2. (di battesimo) Christian name || senza —, nameless; a — di, on behalf of; per —, by name 3. (gramm.) noun.

nomea sf. notoriety.

nomenclatura *sf.* nomenclature.

nomìgnolo *sm.* nickname.

nòmina *sf.* appointment.

nominale *agg.* nominal.

nominalismo *sm.* nominalism.

nominalista *s.* nominalist.

nominalmente *avv.* nominally.

nominare *vt.* 1. to name 2. (*eleggere*) to appoint.

nominativo *agg.* 1. nominative 2. (*comm.*) registered. ♦ **nominativo** *sm.* name.

non *avv.* not.

nona *sf.* 1. (*eccl.*) Nones (*pl.*) 2. (*mus.*) ninth.

nonagenario *agg.* ninety years old (*pred.*); ninety-year-old (*attr.*). ♦ **nonagenario** *sm.* nonagenarian.

nonconformista *s.* non-conformist.

noncurante *agg.* careless.

noncuranza *sf.* carelessness.

nondimeno *avv.* nevertheless.

nonna *sf.* grandmother.

nonno *sm.* grandfather: *i miei nonni*, my grandparents.

nonnulla *sm.* trifle.

nono *agg.* ninth.

nonostante *prep.* notwithstanding || — *che*, though, although.

nonsenso *sm.* nonsense.

non-ti-scordar-di-me *sm.* forget--me-not.

nord *sm.* north.

nordamericano *agg.* e *sm.* North American.

nòrdico *agg.* 1. northern 2. (*dell'Europa settentrionale*) Nordic. ♦ **nòrdico** *sm.* 1. Northerner 2. (*dell'Europa settentrionale*) Nordic.

nordista *sm.* (*stor. amer.*) Federal.

norma *sf.* 1. rule, norm 2. (*istruzioni*) instruction, direction || *a* — *di legge*, according to law.

normale *agg.* e *sm.* 1. normal 2. (*che dà una norma*) standard.

normalità *sf.* normality.

normalizzare *vt.* to normalize.

normalizzazione *sf.* normalization.

normalmente *avv.* usually.

normanno *agg.* e *sm.* Norman: *anglo*-—, (*stor.*) Anglo-Norman.

normativo *agg.* normative.

normògrafo *sm.* stencil.

norvegese *agg.* e *sm.* Norwegian.

nosocòmio *sm.* hospital.

nostalgìa *sf.* home-sickness.

nostàlgico *agg.* homesick.

nostràno *agg.* home (*attr.*), national.

nostro *agg.* our: *i nostri amici*, our friends. ♦ **nostro** *pron.* ours: *questa casa è nostra*, this house is ours. ♦ **nostro** *sm.* 1. *viviamo del* —, we live on our own income 2. *il Nostro* (*di autore*), the Author 3. *i nostri*, our family.

nostromo *sm.* boatswain.

nota *sf.* 1. note 2. (*lista*) list.

notàbile *agg.* notable.

notaio *sm.* notary.

notare *vt.* to note.

notariato *sm.* profession of notary.

notarile *agg.* notarial.

notazione *sf.* notation.

notévole *agg.* remarkable, notable.

notevolmente *avv.* remarkably.

notìfica *sf.* 1. notification 2. (*giur.*) service.

notificare *vt.* 1. to notify 2. (*informare*) to inform 3. (*giur.*) to serve.

notizia *sf.* 1. news (*pl. con costruzione sing.*), piece of news (*solo sing.*) 2. (*informazione*) information (*solo sing.*) 3. (*dato*) note: *notizie biografiche*, biographical notes.

notiziario *sm.* news (*pl., con costruzione sing.*).

noto *agg.* well-known. ♦ **noto** *sm.* the known.

notoriamente *avv.* notoriously.

notorietà *sf.* notoriety.

notorio *agg.* 1. (*in senso sfavorevole*) notorious 2. well-known.

nottàmbulo *agg.* noctambulous. ♦ **nottàmbulo** *sm.* night-bird.

nottata *sf.* night.

notte *sf.* night.

nottetempo *avv.* by night.

notturno *agg.* night (*attr.*). ♦ **notturno** *sm.* (*mus.*) nocturne.

novanta *agg.* ninety.

novantenne *agg.* 1. ninety years old (*pred.*) 2. ninety-year-old (*attr.*).

novantèsimo *agg.* ninetieth.

novatore *sm.* innovator.

nove *agg.* nine.

novecento *agg.* nine hundred.

novella *sf.* short story, tale.

novellino *agg.* inexperienced. ♦ **novellino** *sm.* beginner.

novellista *s.* short-story writer.

novellìstica *sf.* story-telling.

novello *agg.* 1. new, spring (*attr.*) 2. (*nuovo*) second: *un — Raffaello*, a second Raffaello.

novembre sm. November.
novena sf. novena (pl. -ae).
nòvero sm. number 2. (categoria) class.
novilunio sm. new moon.
novità sf. 1. novelty 2. (notizia) news (pl. con costruzione sing.), piece of news (solo sing.).
noviziato sm. novitiate.
novizio sm. novice.
nozione sf. notion.
nozze sf. pl. wedding (sing.).
nube sf. cloud.
nubifragio sm. downpour.
nùbile agg. unmarried, single. ♦ **nùbile** sf. single woman.
nuca sf. nape.
nucleare agg. nuclear.
nucleina sf. nuclein.
nùcleo sm. nucleus (pl. -ei).
nudismo sm. nudism.
nudista s. nudist.
nudità sf. nakedness.
nudo agg. naked, bare.
nùgolo sm. cloud.
nulla pron. V. niente.
nullaosta sm. permit.
nullatenente agg. without property. ♦ **nullatenente** s. person without property.
nullità sf. 1. (di cose) nullity 2. (di persone) nonentity.
nullo agg. (giur.) null, void.
nume sm. numen, deity.
numeràbile agg. numerable.
numerabilità sf. numerability.
numerale agg. numeral.
numerare vt. 1. to count 2. (segnare con numero) to number.
numerato agg. 1. counted 2. (segnato con un numero) numbered.
numerario agg. numerary. ♦ **numerario** sm. (comm.) ready cash.
numeratore sm. (mat.) numerator.
numerazione sf. 1. numbering 2. (mat.) numeration.
numericamente avv. numerically.
numèrico agg. numerical.
nùmero sm. number.
numeroso agg. numerous.
numismàtica sf. numismatics.
numismàtico agg. numismatic. ♦ **numismàtico** sm. numismatist.
nunziatura sf. (eccl.) nunciature.
nunzio sm. nuncio.
nuòcere vi. to damage, to harm.
nuora sf. daughter-in-law.
nuotare vi. to swim (v. irr.).
nuotata sf. swim.

nuotatore sm. swimmer.
nuoto sm. swimming: gara di —, swimming-race.
nuova sf. news (pl. con costruzione sing.), piece of news (solo sing.).
nuovamente avv. again.
nuovo agg. new: — di zecca, fiammante, brand-new.
nutazione sf. nutation.
nutrice sf. wet-nurse.
nutriente agg. nourishing.
nutrimento sm. 1. feeding 2. (fig.) nourishment.
nutrire vt. 1. to feed (v. irr.) 2. (mantenere) to maintain 3. (di sentimenti, passioni) to foster. ♦ **nutrirsi** vr. to feed (on).
nutritivo agg. nourishing.
nutrito agg. fed, nourished.
nutrizione sf. 1. feeding 2. (fig.) nourishment.
nùvola sf. cloud.
nuvoloso agg. overcast, cloudy.
nuziale agg. wedding (attr.).

O

o cong. or || o ... o, either ... or: — tu — tua madre dovete venire, either you or your mother must come; — l'uno — l'altro, either: prendi — l'uno — l'altro, take either.
òasi sf. oasis (pl. -ses).
obbligare vt. to compel. ♦ **obbligarsi** vr. to bind (v. irr.) oneself.
obbligatorietà sf. compulsoriness.
obbligatorio agg. compulsory.
obbligazione sf. 1. obligation 2. (comm.) bond.
obbligazionista sm. bond-holder.
òbbligo sm. obligation: assumersi l'—, to undertake (v. irr.).
obbrobrio sm. disgrace.
obbrobrioso agg. disgraceful.
obelisco sm. obelisk.
oberare vt. to burden.
obesità sf. obesity.
obeso agg. obese.
òbice sm. howitzer.
obiettare vt. to object.
obiettivamente avv. objectively.
obiettivismo sm. objectivism.
obiettività sf. objectivity.

obiettivo *agg.* objective. ♦ obiettivo *sm.* 1. (*mil.*) objective 2. (*scopo*) aim 3. (*foto*) lens.

obiettore *sm.* objector: — *di coscienza*, conscentious objector.

obiezione *sf.* objection.

obitorio *sm.* morgue.

oblatore *sm.* donor.

oblazione *sf.* donation.

obliare *vt.* to forget (*v. irr.*).

oblìo *sm.* oblivion.

obliquamente *avv.* obliquely.

obliquità *sf.* obliquity.

obliquo *agg.* oblique.

obliterare *vt.* to obliterate.

obliterazione *sf.* obliteration.

oblò *sm.* porthole.

oblungo *agg.* oblong.

òboe *sm.* oboe.

òbolo *sm.* offering.

obsoleto *agg.* obsolete.

oca *sf.* goose (*pl.* geese): *pelle d'—*, goose flesh; *penna d'—*, goose-quill.

occasionale *agg.* occasional.

occasionalismo *sm.* occasionalism.

occasionalmente *avv.* occasionally.

occasione *sf.* occasion.

occhiaia *sf.* eye-socket || *avere le occhiaie*, to have rings under one's eyes.

occhiali *sm. pl.* spectacles, glasses.

occhialuto *agg.* spectacled, wearing spectacles (*pred.*).

occhiata *sf.* look, glance.

occhiataccia *sf.* glare.

occhieggiare *vt.* to cast (*v. irr.*) glances (at). ♦ occhieggiare *vi.* to peep (at).

occhiello *sm.* 1. button-hole 2. (*mecc.*) eye.

occhietto *sm. fare l'— a qu.*, to wink at so.

occhio *sm.* eye || *costare un —*, to be terribly expensive; *chiudere un — su*, to turn a blind eye to; *dare nell'—*, to strike (*v. irr.*) the eye; *tenere d'—*, to keep (*v. irr.*) an eye on; *in un batter d'—*, in the twinkling of an eye.

occidentale *agg.* west, western. ♦ occidentale *s.* westerner.

occidentalizzare *vt.* to occidentalize.

occidente *sm.* west.

occipitale *agg.* occipital.

occìpite *sm.* occiput (*pl.* occipita).

occlusione *sf.* occlusion.

occlusivo *agg.* occlusive.

oecorrente *agg.* necessary. ♦ occorrente *sm.* the necessary.

occorrenza *sf. all'—*, in case of need.

occòrrere *vi.* 1. (*imp.*) to be necessary 2. (*abbisognare*) to need.

occultamento *sm.* concealment.

occultare *vt.* to hide (*v. irr.*), to conceal. ♦ occultarsi *vr.* to hide.

occultatore *sm.* hider.

occultismo *sm.* occultism.

occulto *agg.* 1. occult 2. (*nascosto*) hidden.

occupante *agg.* occupying. ♦ occupante *s.* occupant.

occupare *vt.* 1. to occupy 2. (*ingaggiare*) to employ. ♦ occuparsi *vr.* 1. (*impiegarsi*) to find (*v. irr.*) a job 2. (*badare*) to attend (to).

occupato *agg.* engaged || *essere —* (*fare un lavoro*), to work.

occupazione *sf.* 1. occupation 2. (*lavoro*) job.

oceànico *agg.* oceanic.

ocèano *sm.* ocean.

oceanografia *sf.* oceanography.

ocello *sm.* ocellus (*pl.* -li).

ocra *sf.* ochre.

oculare *agg.* ocular, eye (*attr.*). ♦ oculare *sm.* (*fis.*) eyepiece.

oculatezza *sf.* shrewdness.

oculato *agg.* prudent.

oculista *sm.* oculist.

oculìstica *sf.* ophthalmology.

odalisca *sf.* odalisque.

ode *sf.* ode.

odiare *vt.* to hate.

odierno *agg.* of today, today's.

odio *sm.* hatred.

odioso *agg.* hateful.

odontàlgico *agg.* odontalgic.

odontoiatra *s.* odontologist, dentist.

odontoiatrìa *sf.* odontology.

odontoiàtrico *agg.* odontological.

odorare *vt. e vi.* to smell (*v. irr.*).

odorato *sm.* smell.

odore *sm.* smell.

odorìfero *agg.* odoriferous.

odoroso *agg.* fragrant.

offèndere *vt.* to offend. ♦ offendersi *vr.* to be offended (at, by); to feel (*v. irr.*) hurt (by).

offensiva *sf.* offensive.

offensivo *agg.* offensive.

offensore *sm.* offender.

offerente *s.* 1. offerer 2. (*a un'asta*) bidder.

offerta *sf.* offer, donation.
offesa *sf.* offence.
offeso *agg.* offended, injured.
officiare *vi.* to officiate.
officina *sf.* workshop.
officinale *agg.* officinal.
offrire *vt.* to offer. ♦ **offrirsi** *vr.* to offer (oneself).
offuscamento *sm.* 1. dimming 2. (*oscurità*) dimness.
offuscare *vt.* to dim. ♦ **offuscarsi** *vr.* to grow (*v. irr.*) dim.
oftalmìa *sf.* ophthalmia.
oftàlmico *agg.* ophthalmic.
oftalmologìa *sf.* ophthalmology.
oftalmoscopìa *sf.* ophthalmoscopy.
oftalmoscopio *sm.* ophthalmoscope.
oggettivamente *avv.* objectively.
oggettivare *vt.* to objectify.
oggettivazione *sf.* objectification.
oggettivismo *sm.* objectivism.
oggettività *sf.* objectivity.
oggettivo *agg.* objective.
oggetto *sm.* object.
oggi *avv.* today.
ogiva *sf.* ogive.
ogivale *agg.* ogival.
ogni *agg.* every, each || *in — modo*, anyhow; *in — luogo*, everywhere.
ogniqualvolta *cong.* whenever.
ognuno *pron.* everybody, everyone || *— di*, each of.
oleandro *sm.* oleander.
oleario *agg.* oil (*attr.*).
oleato *agg.* oiled || *carta oleata*, grease-proof paper.
oleificio *sm.* oil mill.
oleografìa *sf.* 1. oleography 2. (*pezzo singolo*) oleograph.
oleoso *agg.* oily.
olezzare *vi.* to smell (*v. irr.*) sweetly.
olezzo *sm.* fragrance.
olfattivo *agg.* olfactory.
olfatto *sm.* smell.
oliare *vt.* to oil.
oliatore *sm.* oil-can.
oliera *sf.* cruet.
oligarca *sm.* oligarch.
oligarchìa *sf.* oligarchy.
oligàrchico *agg.* oligarchic(al).
oligocene *sm.* Oligocene.
olimpìaco *agg.* V. *olimpico*.
olimpìade *sf.* Olympiad || *le Olimpiadi*, Olympic games.
olìmpico *agg.* Olympic.
olimpiònico *agg.* Olympic games (*attr.*). ♦ **olimpiònico** *sm.*

Olympic champion.
olio *sm.* oil.
oliva *sf.* olive.
olivastro *agg.* olive.
oliveto *sm.* olive-grove.
olivo *sm.* olive.
olmo *sm.* elm.
olocàusto *sm.* holocaust.
ològrafo *agg.* holograph.
oltraggiare *vt.* to outrage.
oltraggio *sm.* outrage.
oltraggioso *agg.* outrageous.
oltramontano *agg.* e *sm.* ultramontane.
oltranza *sf.* (*nella loc. avv.*) *a —*, to the bitter end.
oltranzista *sm.* extremist.
oltre *avv.* 1. (*di luogo*) further, farther 2. (*di tempo*) longer. ♦ **oltre** *prep.* 1. (*di luogo*) beyond 2. (*più di*) over 3. (*in aggiunta*) in addition to. ♦ **oltre a, che** *cong.* besides.
oltrecortina *avv.* beyond the Iron Curtain.
oltremare *avv.* overseas: *d'—*, overseas (*attr.*).
oltremodo *avv.* extremely.
oltrepassare *vt.* to go (*v. irr.*) beyond || *— i limiti* (*fig.*), to go (*v. irr.*) too far.
oltretomba *sm.* hereafter.
omaccione *sm.* burly man (*pl.* men).
omaggio *sm.* 1. homage 2. (*offerta*) gift.
ombelicale *agg.* umbilical.
ombelico *sm.* navel.
ombra *sf.* 1. shade (*anche spettro*) 2. (*immagine proiettata, parvenza*) shadow || *dar — a qu.*, to overshadow so.
ombreggiare *vt.* to shade.
ombreggiatura *sf.* shading.
ombrella *sf.* (*bot.*) umbel.
ombrellìfero *agg.* umbelliferous.
ombrellino *sm.* parasol.
ombrello *sm.* umbrella.
ombrellone *sm.* sunshade.
ombretto *sm.* eye shadow.
ombrina *sf.* umbrina.
ombrosità *sf.* 1. shadiness 2. (*di persona*) touchiness 3. (*di cavallo*) skittishness.
ombroso *agg.* 1. shady 2. (*di persona*) touchy 3. (*di cavallo*) skittish.
omega *sm.* omega.
omelìa *sf.* homily.
omeopatìa *sf.* homeopathy.

omeopàtico agg. homeopathic. ♦
   omeopàtico sm. homeopath
omèrico agg. Homeric.
òmero sm. humerus (pl. -ri).
omertà sf. silence.
omesso agg. omitted.
ométtere vt. to omit, to leave out.
omicida agg. homicidal. ♦ omi-
   cida s. homicide.
omicidio sm. homicide.
omissione sf. omission.
òmnibus sm. bus.
omogeneità sf. homogeneity.
omogeneizzare vt. to homogenize.
omogèneo agg. homogeneous.
omologare vt. 1. to homologate 2.
   (sport) to ratify.
omologazione sf. 1. homologation
   2. (sport) ratification.
omòlogo agg. homologous.
omonimia sf. homonymy.
omònimo agg. homonymous. ♦
   omònimo sm. homonym.
omosessuale agg. e s. homosexual.
omosessualità sf. homosexuality.
oncia sf. ounce.
onda sf. wave || mettere in — (ra-
   dio), to broadcast (v. irr.).
ondata sf. wave: a ondate, in
   waves.
onde avv. 1. whence 2. (affinché) so
   that 3. (cosicché) therefore 4. (da,
   con cui) from, by, with which.
ondeggiamento sm. 1. waving 2.
   (di barca) rolling 3. (esitazione)
   wavering.
ondeggiante agg. 1. waving 2. (di
   barca) rolling 3. (esitante) wavering.
ondeggiare vi. 1. to wave 2. (di
   barca) to roll 3. (esitare) to waver.
ondina sf. undine.
ondoso agg. undulatory.
ondulare vt. to wave.
ondulato agg. 1. wavy 2. (tec.) cor-
   rugated.
ondulatorio agg. undulatory.
ondulazione sf. 1. undulation 2.
   (di capelli) wave.
onerare vt. to burden.
ònere sm. burden || — fiscale, tax.
oneroso agg. burdensome.
onestà sf. 1. honesty 2. (castità)
   chastity.
onesto agg. 1. honest 2. (casto)
   chaste.
ònice sf. onyx.
onìrico agg. oneiric.

onnipotente agg. omnipotent. ♦
   Onnipotente (l') sm. the Almighty.
onnipotenza sf. omnipotence.
onnipresente agg. omnipresent.
onnisciente agg. omniscient.
onniscienza sf. omniscience.
onniveggente agg. omnipercipient.
onnìvoro agg. omnivorous. ♦ on-
   nìvoro sm. omnivore.
onomàstico agg. onomastic. ♦
   onomàstico sm. name-day.
onomatopea sf. onomatopoeia.
onomatopèico agg. onomatopoeic.
onoràbile agg. honourable.
onorabilità sf. honourableness.
onoranza sf. honour.
onorare vt. to honour. ♦ onorar-
   si vr. to be proud (of).
onorario agg. honorary. ♦ onora-
   rio sm. fee.
onorato agg. 1. honoured 2. (onesto) honourable.
onore sm. honour || farsi —, to ex-
   cel; a onor del vero, to tell (v.
   irr.) the truth; serata d'—, gala
   night.
onorévole agg. honourable.
onorificenza sf. 1. honour 2. (decorazione) decoration.
onorifico agg. honorific(al).
onta sf. 1. shame 2. (offesa) insult
   || ad — di, in spite of.
ontano sm. alder.
ontologìa sf. ontology.
ontològico agg. ontological.
opacità sf. opacity.
opaco agg. 1. opaque 2. (di suoni,
   colori) dull.
opale sm. opal.
opalescente agg. opalescent.
opalino agg. opaline.
òpera sf. 1. work 2. (melodramma)
   opera 3. (istituto) institution.
operàbile agg. 1. workable.
   2. (chir.) operable.
operaio agg. working. ♦ operaio
   sm. worker: — specializzato,
   skilled worker.
operante agg. operating.
operare vi. to work, to operate (anche med.).
operativo agg. operative.
operato agg. (di tessuto) diapered.
   ♦ **operato** sm. 1. (condotta)
   behaviour 2. (chi ha subìto un'operazione) operated patient.
operatore sm. 1. operator 2. (cine)
   cameraman (pl. -men).

operatorio *agg.* operating.

operazione *sf.* operation: *fare un'— a qu.*, to perform an operation on so.; *subire un'—*, to undergo (*v. irr.*) an operation.

operetta *sf.* operetta.

operistico *agg.* opera (*attr.*).

operosità *sf.* industry.

operoso *agg.* industrious.

opificio *sm.* factory.

opimo *agg.* fertile.

opinàbile *agg.* thinkable.

opinare *vi.* to think (*v. irr.*).

opinione *sf.* opinion: *secondo l'— di qu.*, in so.'s opinion.

opossum *sm.* opossum.

oppiare *vt.* to opiate.

oppiato *agg. e sm.* opiate.

oppio *sm.* opium.

oppiòmane *s.* opium-addict.

opponente *agg. e sm.* opponent.

opponìbile *agg.* opposable.

opporre *vt.* 1. to oppose 2. (*obiettare*) to object. ♦ **opporsi** *vr.* to object (to), to be opposed.

opportunismo *sm.* opportunism.

opportunista *s.* opportunist.

opportunìstico *agg.* opportunistic.

opportunità *sf.* 1. (*occasione*) opportunity 2. (*l'essere opportuno*) timeliness.

opportuno *agg.* 1. opportune 2. (*giusto*) right.

oppositore *sm.* opponent.

opposizione *sf.* opposition || *fare — (a qu., qc.)*, to oppose (so., sthg.).

opposto *agg. e sm.* opposite.

oppressione *sf.* oppression.

oppressivo *agg.* oppressive.

oppresso *agg.* oppressed.

oppressore *sm.* oppressor.

opprimente *agg.* oppressive.

opprìmere *vt.* to oppress.

oppugnare *vt.* to assail.

oppure *cong.* 1. or 2. (*altrimenti*) or else.

optare *vi.* to opt.

opulento *agg.* opulent.

opulenza *sf.* opulence.

opùscolo *sm.* pamphlet.

opzione *sf.* option.

ora[1] *sf.* 1. hour 2. (*tempo*) time: *che — è?*, what time is it?; *— di punta*, rush hour; *all'—*, by the hour; *di — in —*, hourly; *di buon'—*, early; *— legale*, summer time; *non veder l'— di*, to look forward to.

ora[2] *avv.* now || *— come —*, at the moment; *d'— in poi*, from now on; *fino ad —*, so far; *sin d'—*, now; *prima d'—*, before; *or —*, just. ♦ **ora che** *cong.* now (that).

oràcolo *sm.* oracle.

òrafo *sm.* goldsmith.

orale *agg. e sm.* oral.

oralmente *avv.* orally.

oramai *avv.* V. *ormai*.

orango *sm.* orang-outang.

orario *agg.* 1. time (*attr.*) 2. (*all'ora*) per hour. ♦ **orario** *sm.* 1. hours (*pl.*) 2. (*tabella*) time-table || *in —*, on time.

orata *sf.* dory.

oratore *sm.* orator.

oratoria *sf.* oratory.

oratorio *sm.* oratory.

orazione *sf.* 1. oration 2. (*preghiera*) prayer.

orbare *vt.* to bereave (*v. irr.*).

orbene *avv.* well.

òrbita *sf.* orbit.

orbitale *agg.* orbital.

orbo *agg.* (*di un occhio*) one-eyed.

orchestra *sf.* orchestra.

orchestrale *agg.* orchestral. ♦ **orchestrale** *s.* member of an orchestra.

orchestrare *vt.* to orchestrate.

orchestrazione *sf.* orchestration.

orchestrina *sf.* band.

orchidea *sf.* orchid.

orcio *sm.* pitcher.

orco *sm.* ogre.

orda *sf.* horde.

ordigno *sm.* device.

ordinale *agg. e sm.* ordinal.

ordinamento *sm.* 1. arrangement 2. (*regolamento*) code, system.

ordinanza *sf.* 1. order 2. (*attendente mil.*) batman (*pl.* -men).

ordinare *vt.* 1. to order 2. (*mettere in ordine*) to put (*v. irr.*) in order 3. (*eccl.*) to ordain 4. (*med.*) to prescribe. ♦ **ordinarsi** *vr.* 1. to straighten up 2. (*mil.*) to draw (*v. irr.*) up.

ordinario *agg. e sm.* ordinary.

ordinata *sf.* 1. (*mat.*) ordinate 2. (*aer.; mar.*) frame.

ordinatamente *avv.* tidily.

ordinato *agg.* tidy, orderly.

ordinazione *sf.* 1. order 2. (*med.*) prescription 3. (*eccl.*) ordination.

òrdine *sm.* order || *— d'idee*, scheme of things; *all'— del giorno,* on the agenda; *per — di*, by order of; *parola d'—*, password; *di primi'—*, firstclass (*attr.*).

ordire *vt.* **1.** to warp **2.** (*fig.*) to plot.

ordito *sm.* warp.

orecchiàbile *agg.* catchy.

erecchino *sm.* earring.

orecchio *sm.* ear.

orecchioni *sm. pl.* mumps.

oréfice *sm.* jeweller.

oreficerìa *sf.* **1.** jeweller's art **2.** (*negozio*) jeweller's shop.

òrfano *agg. e sm.* orphan.

orfanotrofio *sm.* orphanage.

organetto *sm.* barrel-organ || *suonatore di —*, organ-grinder.

organicità *sf.* organic unity.

organico[1] *agg.* organic.

organico[2] *sm.* staff.

organismo *sm.* **1.** organism **2.** (*ente*) body.

organista *s.* organist.

organizzàbile *agg.* organizable.

organizzare *vt.* to organize.

organizzatore *sm.* organizer.

organizzazione *sf.* organization.

òrgano *sm.* organ.

organza *sf.* organza.

organzino *sm.* organzine.

orgasmo *sm.* orgasm.

orgia *sf.* orgy.

orgiàstico *agg.* orgiastic.

orgoglio *sm.* pride.

orgoglioso *agg.* proud.

orientale *agg.* eastern.

orientalista *s.* orientalist.

orientamento *sm.* orientation || *perdere l'—*, to lose (*v. irr.*) one's bearings.

orientare *vt.* to orient. ♦ **orientarsi** *vr.* **1.** to find (*v. irr.*) one's bearings **2.** (*tendere*) to tend.

oriente *sm.* east.

orifiamma *sf.* oriflamme.

orifizio *sm.* orifice.

orìgano *sm.* origan.

originale *agg.* **1.** original **2.** (*strano*) odd. ♦ **originale** *sm.* **1.** original **2.** (*persona eccentrica*) eccentric.

originalità *sf.* **1.** originality **2.** (*stranezza*) oddity.

originare *vt. e vi.* to originate.

originariamente *avv.* originally.

originario *agg.* original.

orìgine *sf.* origin || *avere —*, to originate; *dare —*, to cause.

origliare *vi.* to eavesdrop.

orina *sf.* urine.

orinale *sm.* chamber pot.

orinare *vi.* to urinate.

orinatoio *sm.* public lavatory.

orizzontale *agg.* horizontal.

orizzontalmente *avv.* horizontally.

orizzontare *vt.*, **orizzontarsi** *vr.* V. *orientare, orientarsi*.

orizzonte *sm.* horizon.

orlare *vt.* **1.** (*bordare*) to edge **2.** (*fare l'orlo*) to hem.

orlatura *sf.* hemming.

orlo *sm.* **1.** (*di abito ecc.*) hem **2.** (*bordatura*) border **3.** (*estremità*) edge **4.** (*di oggetto rotondo*) rim || *— a giorno*, hem-stitch; *sull'— della rovina*, on the verge of ruin.

orma *sf.* **1.** mark **2.** (*traccia*) trace **3.** (*di piede*) footprint || *seguire le orme di qu.*, to follow in so.'s footsteps; *tornare sulle proprie orme*, to go (*v. irr.*) back on one's tracks.

ormai *avv.* **1.** (by) now **2.** (*al passato*) (by) then.

ormeggiare *vt.* to moor. ♦ **ormeggiarsi** *vr.* to moor.

ormeggio *sm.* mooring.

ormone *sm.* hormone.

ormònico *agg.* hormonic.

ornamentale *agg.* ornamental.

ornamentazione *sf.* ornamentation.

ornamento *sm.* ornament.

ornare *vt.* to adorn.

ornato *agg.* **1.** adorned (with) **2.** (*di stile*) ornate.

ornitologìa *sf.* ornithology.

ornitològico *agg.* ornithological.

ornitòlogo *sm.* ornithologist.

oro *sm.* gold || *d'—*, golden.

orografia *sf.* orography.

orogràfico *agg.* orographic(al).

orologerìa *sf.* **1.** (*arte*) horology **2.** (*negozio*) watchmaker's shop || *movimento d'—*, clock movement.

orologiaio *sm.* watchmaker.

orologio *sm.* **1.** watch **2.** (*a muro, da tavolo*) clock.

oròscopo *sm.* horoscope.

orpello *sm.* tinsel.

orrendamente *avv.* dreadfully.

orrendo *agg.* dreadful.

orrìbile *agg.* horrible.

orribilmente *avv.* horribly.

òrrido *agg.* frightful.

orripilante *agg.* terrifying.

orrore *sm.* horror.

orsa *sf.* she-bear: *— Maggiore*,

Great Bear; — *Minore*, Little Bear.

orsacchiotto *sm.* 1. young bear 2. (*giocattolo*) Teddy bear.

orso *sm.* bear.

ortaggio *sm.* vegetable.

ortensia *sf.* hydrangea.

ortica *sf.* nettle.

orticaria *sf.* nettle-rash.

orticultore *sm.* horticulturist.

orticultura *sf.* horticulture.

orto *sm.* 1. kitchen garden 2. (*di orticoltore*) market garden.

ortodossìa *sf.* orthodoxy.

ortodosso *agg.* orthodox.

ortofruttìcolo *agg.* horticultural.

ortogonale *agg.* orthogonal.

ortografìa *sf.* orthography, spelling.

ortogràfico *agg.* orthographic(al).

ortolano *sm.* 1. market-gardener 2. (*negoziante*) greengrocer.

ortopedìa *sf.* orthopedics.

ortopèdico *agg.* orthopedic. ♦ **ortopèdico** *sm.* orthopedist.

orzaiolo *sm.* sty.

orzata *sf.* (*bibita*) orgeat.

orzo *sm.* barley.

osanna *sf.* hosanna.

osare *vi.* to dare (*v. semidif.*). ♦ **osare** *vt.* (*tentare*) to attempt.

oscenità *sf.* obscenity.

osceno *agg.* obscene.

oscillare *vi.* 1. to swing (*v. irr.*) 2. (*di fiamma; opinioni*) to waver 3. (*elettr.*) to oscillate 4. (*di prezzi*) to fluctuate.

oscillatore *sm.* oscillator.

oscillatorio *agg.* oscillatory.

oscillazione *sf.* 1. swing 2. (*di fiamma; opinioni*) wavering 3. (*elettr.*) oscillation 4. (*di prezzi*) fluctuation.

oscillògrafo *sm.* oscillograph.

oscurantismo *sm.* obscurantism.

oscurantista *agg. e s.* obscurantist.

oscurare *vt.* 1. to darken 2. (*fig.*) to overshadow. ♦ **oscurarsi** *vr.* to darken.

oscurità *sf.* 1. darkness 2. (*fig.*) obscurity.

oscuro *agg.* 1. dark 2. (*sconosciuto, umile*) obscure 3. (*difficile*) hard, difficult 4. (*sconosciuto*) unknown.

osmosi *sf.* osmosis (*pl.* -ses).

ospedale *sm.* hospital.

ospedaliero *agg.* hospital (*attr.*).

ospitale *agg.* hospitable.

ospitalità *sf.* hospitality.

ospitare *vt.* to entertain.

òspite *s.* 1. (*chi ospita, uomo*) host; (*id., donna*) hostess 2. (*chi è ospitato*) guest.

ospìzio *sm.* 1. (*per poveri*) alms-house 2. (*per trovatelli*) foundling hospital 3. (*per vecchi ecc.*) home (for the old etc.).

ossario *sm.* charnel-house, ossuary.

ossatura *sf.* 1. skeleton 2. (*di edificio, discorso*) framework.

òsseo *agg.* bony.

ossequente *agg.* respectful.

ossequio *sm.* 1. homage 2. (*obbedienza*) obedience 3. (*saluti*) regards (*pl.*).

ossequiosità *sf.* deference.

ossequioso *agg.* deferential.

osservàbile *agg.* observable.

osservante *agg.* observant.

osservanza *sf.* 1. observance 2. (*ossequio*) regards (*pl.*).

osservare *vt.* 1. to observe 2. (*esaminare*) to examine.

osservatore *agg.* observing. ♦ **osservatore** *sm.* observer.

osservatorio *sm.* observatory.

osservazione *sf.* 1. observation: *in* —, under observation 2. (*rimprovero*) reproach.

ossessionante *agg.* haunting.

ossessionare *vt.* to haunt.

ossessione *sf.* obsession.

ossessivo *agg.* haunting.

ossesso *sm.* person possessed.

ossìa *cong.* (*cioè*) that is.

ossidàbile *agg.* oxidizable.

ossidare *vt.* to oxidize. ♦ **ossidarsi** *vr.* to oxidize.

ossidazione *sf.* oxidation.

òssido *sm.* oxide.

ossìdrico *agg.* oxyhydrogen.

ossificare *vt.* to ossify. ♦ **ossificarsi** *vr.* to ossify.

ossificazione *sf.* ossification.

ossigenare *vt.* 1. to oxygenate 2. (*di capelli*) to peroxide.

ossigenato *agg.* 1. oxygenated 2. (*di capelli*) peroxided || *acqua ossigenata*, hydrogen peroxide.

ossìgeno *sm.* oxygen.

osso *sm.* bone || *in carne e ossa*, in flesh and blood; *avere le ossa rotte*, to be aching all over.

ossuto *agg.* bony.

ostacolare *vt.* to hamper.

ostàcolo *sm.* 1. obstacle 2. (*sport*) hurdle || *corsa ippica ad ostacoli*, steeple-chase.

ostaggio *sm.* hostage.

oste *sm.* innkeeper.
osteggiare *vt.* to oppose.
ostello *sm.* — *della gioventù,* (youth) hostel.
ostensorio *sm.* monstrance.
ostentare *vt.* 1. to show (*v. irr.*) off 2. (*fingere*) to feign.
ostentatamente *avv.* ostentatiously.
ostentazione *sf.* ostentation.
osteologia *sf.* osteology.
osteria *sf.* pub.
ostètrica *sf.* midwife (*pl.* -wives).
ostetricia *sf.* obstetrics.
ostètrico *sm.* obstetrician.
ostia *sf.* 1. wafer 2. (*eccl.*) host.
òstico *agg.* 1. irksome 2. (*di sapore*) unpalatable 3. (*fig.*) difficult.
ostile *agg.* hostile.
ostilità *sf.* hostility.
ostinarsi *vr.* to persist (in).
ostinato *agg.* stubborn.
ostinazione *sf.* obstinacy.
ostracismo *sm.* ostracism.
òstrica *sf.* oyster.
ostricaio *sm.* oyster-seller.
ostricultura *sf.* oyster-breeding.
ostruire *vt.* to obstruct.
ostruzione *sf.* obstruction.
ostruzionismo *sm.* obstructionism.
ostruzionista *s.* obstructionist.
otaria *sf.* otary.
otite *sf.* otitis.
otorinolaringoiatra *s.* otorhino-laryngologist.
otorinolaringoiatrìa *sf.* otorhino-laryngology.
ottaedro *sm.* octahedron.
ottagonale *agg.* octagonal.
ottàgono *sm.* octagon.
ottanta *agg.* eighty.
ottantenne *agg.* eighty years old, eighty-year-old (*attr.*).
ottantèsimo *agg.* eightieth.
ottava *sf.* octave.
ottavo *agg. e sm.* eighth.
ottemperanza *sf.* compliance.
ottemperare *vi.* to comply (with).
ottenebrare *vt.* to cloud.
ottenere *vt.* to obtain, to get (*v. irr.*).
ottetto *sm.* octet.
òttica *sf.* optics.
òttico *agg.* optic(al). ♦ **òttico** *sm.* optician.
ottimismo *sm.* optimism.
ottimista *s.* optimist.
ottimìstico *agg.* optimistic.
òttimo *agg.* best, very good. ♦ **òttimo** *sm.* optimum (*pl.* -ma).

otto *agg.* eight.
ottobre *sm.* October.
ottocento *agg.* eight hundred. ♦ ottocento *sm.* l'—, the nineteenth century.
ottomana *sf.* ottoman.
ottomano *agg. e sm.* Ottoman.
ottone *sm.* brass.
ottuagenario *agg. e sm.* octogenarian.
otturare *vt.* to stop. ♦ **otturarsi** *vr.* to stop.
otturatore *sm.* (*foto*) shutter.
otturazione *sf.* stopping.
ottusità *sf.* obtuseness.
ottuso *agg.* obtuse.
ovaia *sf.* ovary.
ovale *agg. e sm.* oval.
ovatta *sf.* 1. wadding 2. (*cotone idrofilo*) cotton-wool.
ovattare *vt.* to stuff with wadding.
ovazione *sf.* ovation.
ove *avv.* where.
ovest *sm.* west.
ovile *sm.* fold.
ovino *agg.* ovine. ♦ **ovino** *sm.* sheep (*invariato al pl.*).
ovìparo *agg.* oviparous.
ovòide *agg.* egg-shaped.
òvolo *sm.* (*fungo*) agaric.
ovulazione *sf.* ovulation.
òvulo *sm.* ovule.
ovunque *avv.* 1. everywhere 2. (*in qualsiasi posto*) anywhere. ♦ ovunque *cong.* wherever.
ovvero *cong.* or.
ovviare *vi.* to obviate (sthg.).
ovvio *agg.* obvious.
oziare *vi.* to loaf, to idle.
ozio *sm.* idleness.
oziosamente *avv.* idly.
ozono *sm.* ozone.

P

pacare *vt.* to calm.
pacatezza *sf.* calmness.
pacato *agg.* calm.
pacca *sf.* slap.
pacchetto *sm.* packet.
pacchia *sf.* godsend.
pacchianata *sf.* coarse action.
pacchiano *agg.* coarse.
pacco *sm.* 1. (*postale*) parcel 2. (*collo*) package.

paccottiglia sf. cheap stuff.

pace sf. peace || darsi —, to set (v. irr.) one's mind at rest.

pachiderma sm. pachyderm.

pachistano agg. e sm. Pakistani.

pacificare vt. 1. to pacify 2. (riconciliare) to reconcile. ♦ **pacificarsi** vr. to become (v. irr.) reconciled.

pacificazione sf. 1. pacification 2. (riconciliazione) reconciliation.

pacifico agg. 1. pacific 2. (evidente) self-evident.

pacifismo sm. pacifism.

pacifista s. pacifist.

pacioccone sm. easy-going person.

padella sf. frying-pan.

padiglione sm. pavilion.

padre sm. father.

padrino sm. godfather.

padronale agg. (privato) private || casa —, manor-house.

padronanza sf. mastery: — di sé, self-control.

padrone sm. 1. master 2. (proprietario) owner 3. (di casa, albergo) landlord || essere — di sé, to have self-control; padronissimo!, do as you like!

paesaggio sm. landscape.

paesano agg. rural. ♦ **paesano** sm. peasant.

paese sm. 1. (nazione, territorio) country 2. (villaggio) village.

paesista s. landscape painter.

paffuto agg. chubby.

paga sf. pay, wages (pl.): libro —, wages book; giorno di —, pay day.

pagàbile agg. payable.

pagaia sf. paddle.

pagamento sm. payment.

paganésimo sm. paganism.

pagano agg. e sm. pagan.

pagare vt. to pay (v. irr.).

pagella sf. schoolreport.

pàggio sm. page.

pagherò sm. promissory note.

pàgina sf. page.

paglia sf. straw.

pagliacciata sf. buffoonery.

pagliaccio sm. clown.

pagliaio sm. strawstack.

pagliericcio sm. paillasse.

paglierino agg. straw-coloured.

paglietta sf. 1. (cappello) straw-hat 2. (paglia di ferro) steel-wool 3. (trucioli per imballaggio) wood-shavings (pl.) 4. (trucioli, di carta) paper-wool.

pagnotta sf. round loaf (pl. -aves).

pagoda sf. pagoda.

paio sm. 1. (di cose necessariamente unite) pair 2. (due) couple.

pala sf. 1. shovel 2. (di remo, elica) blade 3. (di ruota) paddle || — d'altare, altar-piece.

paladino sm. 1. paladin 2. (fig.) champion.

palafitta sf. 1. pile 2. (abitazione) pile-dwelling.

palafreniere sm. groom.

palafreno sm. palfrey.

palanchino sm. palanquin.

palata sf. 1. shovelful 2. (colpo) blow with a shovel || a palate (fig.), in plenty.

palatale agg. palatal.

palatino agg. palatine.

palato sm. palate.

palazzo sm. palace.

palco sm. 1. (di teatro) box 2. (pedana) stand.

palcoscènico sm. stage.

paleocristiano agg. paleo-christian.

paleografia sf. paleography.

paleògrafo sm. paleographer.

paleontologìa sf. paleontology.

paleontològico agg. paleontologic(al).

paleontòlogo sm. paleontologist.

palesare vt. to reveal.

palese agg. evident.

palestra sf. gymnasium.

paletta sf. (di capostazione) signal stick.

palinodìa sf. palinode.

palissandro sm. rosewood.

palizzata sf. palisade.

palla sf. 1. ball 2. (pallottola) bullet.

pallacanestro sf. basket-ball.

pallanuoto sf. water-polo.

pallavolo sf. volley-ball.

palleggiare vi. (calcio) to dribble. ♦ **palleggiare** vt. to toss. ♦ **palleggiarsi** vr. rec. to shift on one another.

palleggio sm. 1. (calcio) dribbling 2. (tennis) tossing.

palliativo agg. e sm. palliative.

pallidezza sf. paleness.

pàllido agg. pale.

pallino sm. 1. (di fucile) shot 2. (mania) craze.

palloncino sm. 1. balloon 2. (lampioncino) Chinese lantern.

pallone sm. ball || gioco del —, football.

pallore sm. pallor.

pallòttola sf. 1. pellet 2. (mil.) bullet.

pallottoliere sm. abacus (pl. -ci).

palma[1] sf. (della mano) palm.

palma[2] sf. (albero) palm(-tree).

palmare agg. 1. (anat.) palmar 2. (evidente) clear.

palmato agg. 1. (bot.) palmate 2. (zool.) webbed.

palmeto sm. palm-grove.

palmìpede agg. e sm. palmìped.

palmo sm. palm.

palo sm. 1. pole 2. (per fondamenta, ormeggio) pile || — indicatore, signpost; fare il —, to be on the lookout.

palombaro sm. diver.

palpàbile agg. tangible.

palpare vt. 1. to finger 2. (med.) to palpate.

pàlpebra sf. eyelid || battere le palpebre, to blink.

palpitante agg. 1. throbbing 2. (fig.) fascinating.

palpitare vi. to throb (with sthg.).

palpitazione sf. 1. throbbing 2. (med.) palpitation.

pàlpito sm. throb.

paltò sm. overcoat.

palude sf. marsh.

paludoso agg. marshy.

pàmpino sm. vine-leaf (pl. -leaves).

panacea sf. panacea.

panare vt. to bread

panca sf. bench.

pancetta sf. 1. (cu persona) pot-belly.

panchina sf. bench.

pancia sf. belly.

panciera sf. body-belt.

panciotto sm. waistcoat.

panciuto agg. pot-bellied.

pancotto sm. panada.

pàncreas sm. pancreas.

pancreàtico agg. pancreatic

pandemonio sm. pandemonium.

pane sm. bread.

panegìrico sm. panegyric.

panetterìa sf. bakery.

panettiere sm. baker.

pànfilo sm. yacht.

pangermanismo sm. Pan-Germanism.

pànico agg. e sm. panic.

panico sm. (bot.) millet.

paniere sm. basket.

panificare vi. to make (v. irr.) bread.

panificazione sf. bread-making.

panificio sm. bakery.

panino sm. roll: — imbottito, sandwich.

panna[1] sf. cream: — montata, whipped cream.

panna[2] sf. restare in —, to have a breakdown.

pannello sm. 1. (edil.) panel 2. (di stoffa) light cloth.

panno sm. 1. cloth (pl. cloths) 2. pl. (vestiti) clothes.

pannocchia sf. cob.

pannolino sm. 1. (per bambini) napkin 2. (assorbente igienico) sanitary towel.

panorama sm. view.

panslavismo sm. Pan-slavism.

pantagruèlico agg. Pantagruelian.

pantaloni sm. pl. trousers || — corti, shorts.

pantano sm. 1. mire 2. (luogo pantanoso; fig.) quagmire.

panteismo sm. pantheism.

panteista s. pantheist.

panteìstico agg. pantheistic(al).

pantera sf. panther.

pantòfola sf. slipper.

pantògrafo sm. pantograph.

pantomima sf. pantomime.

panzana sf. fib.

paonazzo agg. purple.

papa sm. pope.

papà sm. daddy.

papale agg. papal.

papalina sf. skull-cap.

papato sm. papacy.

papàvero sm. poppy || alto —, (fig.) bigwig.

pàpera sf. 1. (zool.) duckling 2. (errore) slip 3. (teat.) fluff.

papilla sf. papilla (pl. -ae).

papillare agg. papillary.

papiro sm. papyrus (pl. -ri).

papirologìa sf. papyrology.

papismo sm. popery.

papista s. papist.

pappa sf. pap.

pappagallo sm. parrot || ripetere a —, to parrot.

pappagorgia sf. double chin.

pappare vt. to gorge. ♦ **papparsi** vr. to eat up.

pàprica sf. paprika.

paràbola sf. 1. parable 2. (geom.; mil.) parabola.

parabòlico agg. parabolic.

parabrezza sm. windscreen.

paracadutare vt. to parachute. ♦

paracadutarsi vr. to bail out.
paracadute sm. parachute.
paracadutismo sm. parachutism.
paracadutista sm. 1. parachutist 2. (mil.) paratrooper.
paracarro sm. wayside post.
paradigma sm. paradigm.
paradisìaco agg. paradisiac(al).
paradiso sm. paradise.
paradossale agg. paradoxical.
paradosso sm. paradox.
parafango sm. mudguard.
paraffina sf. paraffin.
parafrasare vt. to paraphrase.
paràfrasi sf. paraphrase.
parafùlmine sm. lightning-rod.
paragonàbile agg. comparable.
paragonare vt. to compare.
paragone sm. comparison: a — di, in comparison with.
paràgrafo sm. paragraph.
paràlisi sf. palsy.
paralìtico agg. e sm. paralytic.
paralizzare vt. to paralyze.
parallela sf. parallel: le parallele (sport), parallel bars.
parallelepìpedo sm. parallelepiped (pl. -da).
parallelismo sm. parallelism.
parallelo agg. e sm. parallel.
parallelogrammo sm. parallelogram.
paralume sm. lamp-shade.
paramento sm. 1. hanging 2. (eccl.) vestment.
paràmetro sm. parameter.
paraninfo sm. paranymph.
paranoia sf. paranoia.
paranòico agg. e sm. paranoiac.
paraocchi sm. pl. blinkers.
parapetto sm. 1. parapet 2. (davanzale) sill.
parapiglia sm. turmoil.
parapioggia sm. umbrella.
parare vt. 1. (riparare) to shield 2. (evitare) to parry 3. (ornare) to decorate || andare a —, to drive (v. irr.) at. ♦ **pararsi** vr. 1. (comparire) to appear 2. (adornarsi) to deck oneself.
parasole sm. parasol.
parassita agg. parasitic. ♦ **parassita** s. parasite.
parassitismo sm. parasitism.
parastatale agg. State controlled || ente —, semi-governmental body.
parata sf. 1. parade 2. (sport) parry || fare una — (sport), to parry.
paratìa sf. bulkhead.

paratifo sm. paratyphoid.
parato sm. hanging || carta da parati, wallpaper.
paratoia sf. cataract.
paraurti sm. bumper.
paravento sm. screen.
parcella sf. fee.
parcheggiare vt. to park.
parcheggio sm. 1. parking 2. (luogo) car park.
parco¹ sm. park: — di divertimenti, fun-fair.
parco² agg. sparing.
parecchio agg. quite a lot of. ♦ **parecchio** avv. quite a lot, quite (+ agg.). ♦ **parecchio** pron. a good deal of it, several (pl.).
pareggiare vt. 1. (livellare) to level 2. (comm.) to balance 3. (parificare una scuola) to recognize officially. ♦ **pareggiare** vi. (sport) to draw (v. irr.).
pareggio sm. 1. (comm.) balance 2. (sport) draw, tie.
parentado sm. V. parentela.
parente sm. relative.
parentela sf. 1. relationship 2. (i parenti) relatives.
parèntesi sf. 1. parenthesis (pl. -ses) 2. (segno grafico) bracket.
parere¹ vi. 1. to seem 2. (essere simile a) to look like 3. (pensare) to think (v. irr.) (of).
parere² sm. opinion.
paresi sf. paresis.
parete sf. wall: — divisoria, partition.
pàrgolo sm. little child (pl. children).
pari agg. 1. equal, same 2. (simile) like 3. (divisibile per due) even. ♦ **pari** sm. equal, peer.
paria sm. pariah.
parietale agg. parietal.
parificazione sf. 1. (comm.) balance 2. (scuola) official recognition 3. (livellamento) levelling.
parigino agg. e sm. Parisian
pariglia sf. pair.
parimenti avv. likewise.
parità sf. equality.
paritario agg. equalitarian.
parlamentare¹ agg. parliamentary. ♦ **parlamentare** sm. Member of Parliament.
parlamentare² vi. to parley.
parlamentarismo sm. parliamentarianism.

parlamento *sm.* parliament.

parlantina *sf.* talkativeness ‖ *aver buona* —, to be a glib talker.

parlare *vi.* to speak (*v. irr.*), to talk.

parlare *sm.* 1. (*discorso*) speech 2. (*chiacchiere*) talk 3. (*idioma*) language.

parlato *agg. cinema* —, talkies (*pl.*).

parlatore *sm.* speaker.

parlatorio *sm.* parlour.

parlottare *vi.* to mutter.

parodìa *sf.* parody.

parodiare *vt.* to parody.

parodista *s.* parodist.

parola *sf.* 1. word 2. (*facoltà di parlare; discorso*) speech ‖ *parole incrociate*, crosswords; *gioco di parole*, pun; *far* —, to mention; *restare senza* —, to be left speechless; *venire a parole con*, to have words with; *rivolgere la* — *a qu.*, to address so.; *avere la* — *facile*, to be a glib talker.

parolaccia *sf.* nasty word: *dire parolacce*, to swear (*v. irr.*).

parolaio *sm.* 1. chatterbox 2. (*di scrittore*) word-monger.

paroliere *sm.* « lyrics » writer.

parossismo *sm.* paroxysm.

paròtide *sf.* parotid.

parricida *s.* parricide.

parricidio *sm.* parricide.

parrocchia *sf.* parish.

parrocchiale *agg.* parish (*attr.*).

parrocchiano *sm.* parishioner.

pàrroco *sm.* 1. (*cattolico*) parish priest 2. (*protestante*) parson.

parrucca *sf.* wig.

parrucchiere *sm.* hairdresser.

parsimonia *sf.* thriftiness.

parsimonioso *agg.* thrifty.

parte *sf.* 1. part 2. (*lato*) side 3. (*porzione*) share 4. (*pol.; comm.; giur.*) party ‖ *da* —, aside: *da* — *di*, from; *da* — *a* —, right through; *da una* — *... dall'altra*, on one hand ... on the other; *la maggior di*, most (of); *a* — *ciò*, apart from that; *farsi da* —, to get (*v. irr.*) out of the way; *fare la* — *di*, to play.

partecipante *s.* 1. sharer 2. (*chi annuncia*) spokesman (*pl.* -men) 3. (*chi presenzia*) the bystander.

partecipare *vi.* 1. to share (in) 2. (*esser presente*) to be present. ♦ **partecipare** *vt.* to announce.

partecipazione *sf.* 1. sharing 2.

(*esser presente*) presence 3. (*annuncio*) announcement 4. (*biglietto*) card.

partécipe *agg.* 1. sharing 2. (*informato*) acquainted ‖ *rendere* — *qu. di qc.*, to acquaint so. with sthg.

parteggiare *vi.* to take (*v. irr.*) sides (with).

partenogènesi *sf.* parthenogenesis.

partenza *sf.* 1. departure, leaving 2. (*sport*) start ‖ *punto di* —, starting-point; *essere in* —, to be leaving.

particella *sf.* particle.

participiale *agg.* participial.

participio *sm.* participle.

particolare *agg.* particular. ♦ **particolare** *sm.* detail.

particolareggiato *agg.* detailed.

particolarismo *sm.* particularism.

particolarità *sf.* 1. particularity 2. (*dettaglio*) detail.

partigiano *agg.* e *sm.* partisan.

partire[1] *vi.* 1. to leave (*v. irr.*) 2. (*muoversi, iniziare, anche fig.*) to start ‖ *a* — *da*, (*beginning*) from.

partire[2] *vt.* to separate.

partita *sf.* 1. (*giocata*) game, match 2. (*di merce*) lot 3. (*in contabilità*) entry ‖ *dar* — *vinta* (*fig.*), to give (*v. irr.*) in.

partitivo *agg.* e *sm.* partitive.

partito *sm.* party.

partitura *sf.* (*mus.*) score.

partizione *sf.* division.

parto *sm.* 1. delivery 2. (*fig.*) product.

partoriente *agg.* parturient. ♦ **partoriente** *sf.* lying-in woman.

partorire *vt.* to bring (*v. irr.*) forth, to beget (*v. irr.*) (*anche fig.*).

parvenza *sf.* 1. appearance 2. (*ombra*) shadow.

parziale *agg.* partial.

parzialità *sf.* partiality.

parzialmente *avv.* partially.

pàscere *vt.* e *vi.* 1. to feed (*v. irr.*) 2. (*al pascolo*) to graze. ♦ **pàscersi** *vr.* to feed (on).

pascià *sm.* pasha.

pasciuto *agg.* fed.

pascolare *vt.* e *vi.* to pasture.

pàscolo *sm.* pasture ‖ *essere al* —, to be grazing.

Pasqua *sf.* Easter.

pasquale *agg.* Easter (*attr.*).

passàbile *agg.* passabl-

passabilmente *avv.* passably.
passaggio *sm.* 1. passage 2. (*traversata*) crossing ‖ *dare un — in macchina*, to give (*v. irr.*) a lift; *vietato il —*, no thoroughfare; *di —*, of transition; (*incidentalmente*) incidentally.
passamaneria *sf.* passementerie.
passamano *sm.* (*fettuccia*) braid.
passamontagna *sm.* snow-cap.
passante *sm.* 1. (*di cinghia ecc.*) loop 2. (*persona*) passer-by.
passaporto *sm.* passport.
passare *vi.* 1. to pass 2. (*andare*) to call (on so., at sthg.). ♦ **passare** *vt.* 1. to pass 2. (*di tempo*) to spend (*v. irr.*) 3. (*sopportare, trafiggere*) to pass through.
passatempo *sm.* pastime.
passatista *s.* traditionalist.
passato *agg.* 1. past 2. (*scorso*) last. ♦ **passato** *sm.* 1. past 2. (*cuc.*) mash.
passaverdura *sm.* vegetable masher.
passeggero *agg.* passing. ♦ **passeggero** *sm.* passenger.
passeggiare *vi.* to walk, to take (*v. irr.*) a walk.
passeggiata *sf.* 1. walk 2. (*in auto*) drive 3. (*in bicicletta, a cavallo*) ride 4. (*lungomare*) promenade.
passeggino *sm.* perambulator.
passeggio *sm.* 1. walk 2. (*gente che passeggia*) promenaders (*pl.*) ‖ *andare a —*, to go (*v. irr.*) for a walk.
passeraceo *sm.* e *agg.* passerine.
passerella *sf.* 1. (*ponte pedonale*) footbridge 2. (*provvisoria*) trestle--bridge 3. (*mar.; edil.*) gangway 4. (*teat.*) parade.
passero *sm.* sparrow.
passibile *agg.* liable (to).
passiflora *sf.* passion-flower.
passino *sm.* strainer.
passionale *agg.* 1. passional 2. (*appassionato*) passionate.
passione *sf.* passion.
passivamente *avv.* passively.
passività *sf.* 1. passivity 2. (*comm.*) liabilities (*pl.*).
passivo *agg.* passive. ♦ **passivo** *sm.* 1. passive 2. (*comm.*) liabilities (*pl.*).
passo *sm.* 1. step 2. (*andatura*) pace 3. (*di montagna*) pass 4. (*brano, passaggio*) passage 5. (*cine*)

gauge 6. (*tec.*) pitch ‖ *passo passo*, very slowly; *segnare il —*, to mark time; *camminare a grandi passi*, to stride (*v. irr.*).
pasta *sf.* 1. paste 2. (*pasticcino*) cake 3. (*per minestre*) "pasta".
pasteggiare *vi.* to feed (*v. irr.*) (on).
pastella *sf.* (*cuc.*) batter.
pastello *sm.* pastel: *matita, disegno a —*, pastel.
pasticca *sf.* tablet.
pasticceria *sf.* confectionery.
pasticciare *vt.* e *vi.* to make (*v. irr.*) a mess (of).
pasticciere *sm.* confectioner.
pasticcino *sm.* cake.
pasticcio *sm.* 1. (*cuc.*) pie 2. (*fig.*) mess ‖ *essere nei pasticci*, to be in trouble.
pasticcione *sm.* bungler.
pastificio *sm.* « pasta » factory.
pastiglia *sf.* tablet.
pasto *sm.* meal.
pastola *sf.* hobble.
pastone *sm.* mash.
pastorale *agg.* pastoral.
pastore *sm.* 1. shepherd 2. (*relig.*) parson.
pastorizia *sf.* stock-raising.
pastorizzare *vt.* to pasteurize.
pastorizzazione *sf.* pasteurization.
pastosità *sf.* 1. mellowness 2. (*morbidezza*) doughiness.
pastoso *agg.* 1. mellow 2. (*morbido*) doughy.
pastrano *sm.* overcoat.
pastura *sf.* pasture.
patacca *sf.* 1. (*macchia*) spot 2. (*cosa senza valore*) worthless object.
patata *sf.* potato: — *americana*, sweet potato ‖ —*fritta*, chip; (*id., croccante*) crisp.
patema *sm.* worry.
patentato *agg.* licenced.
patente *agg.* patent. ♦ **patente** *sf.* licence.
patereccio *sm.* whitlow.
paternale *sf.* scolding ‖ *fare una — a qu.*, to lecture so.
paternalismo *sm.* paternalism.
paternalistico *agg.* paternalistic.
paternità *sf.* paternity.
paterno *agg.* paternal.
pateticamente *avv.* pathetically.
patetico *agg.* e *sm.* pathetic.
patibolare *agg.* sinister.
patibolo *sm.* scaffold.
patimento *sm.* pain.
patina *sf.* 1. patina 2. (*di vernice*)

coat of varnish 3. (*sulla lingua*) coat 4. (*su carta, terracotta*) glaze.

patinare *vt.* 1. to varnish 2. (*carta, terracotta*) to glaze.

patire *vt.* e *vi.* to suffer: — *il freddo*, to suffer from the cold || — *la fame*, to starve.

patito *agg.* sickly. ♦ **patito** *sm.* (*fig.*) fan.

patògeno *agg.* pathogenic.

patologìa *sf.* pathology.

patològico *agg.* pathologic(al).

patòlogo *sm.* pathologist.

patria *sf.* 1. country, fatherland 2. (*luogo natale*) birthplace.

patriarca *sm.* patriarch.

patriarcale *agg.* patriarchal.

patriarcato *sm.* patriarchate.

patricida *s.* V. *parricida.*

patrigno *sm.* stepfather.

patrimoniale *agg.* patrimonial.

patrimonio *sm.* patrimony.

patrio *agg.* 1. native 2. (*paterno*) paternal.

patriota *s.* patriot.

patriottardo *sm.* e *agg.* jingoist.

patriòttico *agg.* patriotic.

patriottismo *sm.* patriotism.

patriziato *sm.* patriciate.

patrizio *sm.* e *agg.* patrician.

patrocinante *sm.* pleader.

patrocinare *vt.* 1. (*sostenere*) to support 2. (*giur.*) to plead.

patrocinio *sm.* 1. support 2. (*giur.*) pleading.

patronato *sm.* 1. patronage 2. (*istituto benefico*) charitable institution.

patronessa *sf.* patroness.

patrono *sm.* 1. patron 2. (*giur.*) counsel for the defence.

patteggiare *vi.* to come (*v. irr.*) to terms.

pattinaggio *sm.* skating.

pattinare *vi.* to skate.

pattinatore *sm.* skater.

pàttino *sm.* 1. (*a rotelle*) roller-skate 2. (*da ghiaccio*) ice-skate 3. (*di slitta*) shoe 4. (*aer.*) skid 5. (*mecc.*) sliding-block.

patto *sm.* 1. agreement, pact 2. (*condizione*) term || *a* — *che*, provided that; *a nessun* —, by no means.

pattuglia *sf.* patrol.

pattugliare *vi.* to patrol.

pattuire *vi.* to reach an agreement (upon). ♦ **pattuire** *vt.* to agree (on).

pattume *sm.* rubbish.

pattumiera *sf.* dust-bin.

pauperismo *sm.* pauperism.

paura *sf.* 1. fear, dread 2. (*spavento*) fright, scare.

pauroso *agg.* fearful.

pàusa *sf.* pause.

pavesare *vt.* to dress (with flags).

pavese *sm.* (*mar.*) hoist.

pavimentare *vt.* 1. to pave 2. (*una stanza*) to floor.

pavimento *sm.* floor.

pavone *sm.* peacock.

pavoneggiarsi *vr.* to show (*v. irr.*) off.

pazientare *vi.* to have patience.

paziente *agg.* e *sm.* patient.

pazienza *sf.* patience || —*!*, never mind!

pazzesco *agg.* foolish.

pazzìa *sf.* 1. madness 2. (*azione, idea pazza*) folly || *fare pazzie*, to act like a fool.

pazzo *agg.* mad. ♦ **pazzo** *sm.* madman (*pl.* -men).

pecca *sf.* fault || *senza* —, faultless.

peccaminoso *agg.* sinful.

peccare *vi.* 1. to sin 2. (*errare*) to err 3. (*esser manchevole*) to lack (sthg.).

peccato *sm.* sin || *che* —*!*, what a pity!; *è un* — *che*, it is a pity that.

peccatore *sm.* sinner.

pece *sf.* pitch.

pècora *sf.* 1. sheep (*pl. invariato*) 2. (*femmina*) ewe.

pecoraio *sm.* shepherd.

peculiare *agg.* peculiar.

peculiarità *sf.* peculiarity.

peculio *sm.* money.

pecuniario *agg.* pecuniary.

pedaggio *sm.* toll.

pedagogìa *sf.* pedagogy.

pedagògico *agg.* pedagogic(al).

pedagogista *s.* pedagogist.

pedagogo *sm.* pedagogue.

pedalare *vi.* to pedal.

pedale *sm.* pedal.

pedaliera *sf.* 1. (*aer.*) rudder-bar 2. (*mus.*) pedal keyboard.

pedana *sf.* 1. (*sport*) spring-board 2. (*piedistallo*) stand.

pedante *agg.* pedantic. ♦ **pedante** *s.* pedant.

pedanterìa *sf.* pedantry.

pedantesco *agg.* pedantic.

pedata *sf.* 1. kick 2. (*impronta*) footprint.

pedemontano *agg.* piedmont.
pederasta *sm.* homosexual.
pederastìa *sf.* homosexuality.
pedestre *agg.* pedestrian.
pediatra *s.* pediatrist.
pediatrìa *sf.* pediatrics.
pedicure *s.* chiropodist.
pediluvio *sm.* foot-bath.
pedina *sf.* **1.** (*alla dama*) piece **2.** (*agli scacchi*) pawn ‖ *muovere una — (anche fig.)*, to make (*v. irr.*) a move.
pedinare *vt.* to shadow.
pedonale *agg.* pedestrian (*attr.*): *passaggio —*, pedestrian crossing.
pedone *sm.* pedestrian ‖ *strada riservata ai pedoni*, footpath.
pedùncolo *sm.* stalk.
peggio *agg.* (*comp.*) worse. ♦ **peggio** *sm.* the worst. ♦ **peggio** *avv.* **1.** (*comp.*) worse **2.** (*superl. rel.*) the worst ‖ *— per lui*, so much the worse for him; *alla —*, at worst; *avere la —*, to get (*v. irr.*) the worst of it.
peggioramento *sm.* aggravation.
peggiorare *vt.* to make (*v. irr.*) worse. ♦ **peggiorare** *vi.* to get (*v. irr.*) worse.
peggiorativo *agg.* e *sm.* pejorative.
peggiore *agg.* **1.** (*comp.*) worse: *questo libro è — di quello*, this book is worse than that **2.** (*superl. rel.*) the worst: *era il suo — nemico*, he was his worst enemy.
pegno *sm.* pledge ‖ *dare qc. in —*, to pledge sthg.; *polizza di —*, pawn-ticket; *agenzia di pegni*, pawnshop.
pelàgico *agg.* pelagic.
pelame *sm.* hair.
pelapatate *sm.* potato peeler.
pelare *vt.* **1.** to unhair **2.** (*sbucciare*) to peel **3.** (*spellare*) to skin **4.** (*far pagare caro*) to fleece. ♦ **pelarsi** *vr.* to lose (*v. irr.*) one's hair.
pelato *agg.* bald.
pelatura *sf.* **1.** unhairing **2.** (*sbucciatura*) peeling.
pellaio *sm.* furrier.
pellame *sm.* hides (*pl.*).
pelle *sf.* skin; (*di animale grosso*) hide ‖ *articoli in —*, leather articles; *amici per la —*, bosom friends.
pellegrina *sf.* (*mantella*) tippet.
pellegrinaggio *sm.* pilgrimage: *in —*, on a pilgrimage.

pellegrinare *vi.* to wander, to roam.
pellegrino *sm.* pilgrim.
pellerossa *agg.* e *sm.* redskin.
pelletterìa *sf.* **1.** leather goods **2.** (*negozio*) leather goods shop.
pellicano *sm.* pelican.
pelliccerìa *sf.* **1.** furriery **2.** (*negozio*) furrier's shop
pelliccia *sf.* fur.
pellicciaio *sm.* furrier.
pellìcola *sf.* film: *— a passo ridotto*, substandard film.
pelo *sm.* hair: *per un —*, by a hair's breadth; *cercare il — nell'uovo*, to split (*v. irr.*) hairs ‖ *non avere peli sulla lingua*, to be outspoken.
peloso *agg.* hairy.
pelota *sf.* pelota.
peltro *sm.* pewter.
peluria *sf.* down ‖ *coperto di —*, downy.
pelvi *sf.* pelvis.
pèlvico *agg.* pelvic.
pena *sf.* **1.** (*punizione*) punishment **2.** (*dolore*) pain **3.** (*disturbo*) trouble ‖ *essere in —*, to worry; *aver — di*, to pity; *a mala —*, hardly; *non ne vale la —*, it is not worth while.
penale *agg.* **1.** criminal **2.** (*relativo alla pena*) penal.
penalista *sm.* criminal lawyer.
penalità *sf.* penalty.
penalizzare *vt.* to penalize.
penare *vi.* **1.** to suffer **2.** (*far fatica*) to be hardly able.
pendaglio *sm.* pendant.
pendente *agg.* **1.** pendent **2.** (*inclinato*) leaning. ♦ **pendente** *sm.* pendant.
pendenza *sf.* **1.** slope **2.** (*grado d'inclinazione*) gradient **3.** (*giur.*) pending suit **4.** (*comm.*) outstanding account.
pèndere *vi.* **1.** to hang (*v. irr.*) **2.** (*inclinare*) to lean (*v. irr.*) **3.** (*essere in declino*) to slope **4.** (*incombere*) to overhang (*v. irr.*) **5.** (*essere incerto*) to waver.
pendìo *sm.* slope.
pèndola *sf.* pendulum-clock.
pendolare *agg.* pendular.
pèndolo *sm.* pendulum.
pèndulo *agg.* pendulous.
pene *sm.* penis.
penetràbile *agg.* penetrable.
penetrabilità *sf.* penetrability.

penetrante agg. piercing.
penetrare vi. e vt. 1. to penetrate 2. (con fatica; di freddo, suono) to pierce 3. (furtivamente) to steal (v. irr.) (into).
penetrazione sf. penetration.
penicillina sf. penicillin.
peninsulare agg. peninsular.
penìsola sf. peninsula.
penitente agg. e s. penitent.
penitenza sf. 1. (teol.) penance 2. (pentimento) repentance 3. (nei giochi) forfeit.
penitenziale agg. penitential.
penitenziario agg. penitentiary. ◆ **penitenziario** sm. jail.
penna sf. 1. pen 2. (di uccello) feather.
pennacchio sm. 1. plume 2. (mil.) panache.
pennecchio sm. wool on the distaff.
pennellare vi. 1. to brush 2. (med.) to paint.
pennellata sf. touch (of the brush).
pennellessa sf. flat brush.
pennello sm. brush.
pennino sm. nib.
pennone sm. (mar.) yard.
pennuto agg. feathered. ◆ **pennuto** sm. bird.
penombra sf. half-light
penoso agg. painful.
pensare vi. e vt. 1. to think (v. irr.) (of) 2. (badare) to look after || pensa ai fatti tuoi, mind your own business.
pensata sf. thought, idea.
pensatore sm. thinker.
pensiero sm. 1. thought 2. (opinione) mind, opinion 3. (ansia) worry.
pensieroso agg. thoughtful.
pènsile agg. hanging || giardino —, roof garden.
pensilina sf. 1. penthouse 2. (di attesa) shelter.
pensionàbile agg. pensionable.
pensionante s. boarder.
pensionato[1] agg. retired. ◆ **pensionato** sm. pensioner, retired person.
pensionato[2] sm. (istituto) hostel.
pensione sf. 1. (assegno vitalizio) pension || essere in —, to be retired; mettere in —, to pension off 2. (albergo) boarding-house || essere a —, to be boarding (at); — completa, full board.

pensoso agg. pensive.
pentaedro sm. pentahedron.
pentàgono sm. pentagon.
pentagramma sm. (mus.) pentagram.
pentàmetro sm. pentameter.
pentano sm. pentane.
Pentecoste sf. Pentecost, Whitsunday.
pentimento sm. repentance.
pentirsi vr. 1. to repent 2. (rimpiangere) to regret.
pèntodo sm. pentode.
péntola sf. pot.
penùltimo agg. e sm. last but one.
penuria sf. shortage, penury.
penzolare vi. to dangle.
penzoloni agg. 1. (dondolante) dangling 2. (pèndente) hanging.
peocio sm. mussel.
peonia sf. peony.
pepaiola sf. pepper-box.
pepare vt. to pepper.
pepato agg. peppery (anche fig.).
pepe sm. pepper.
peperone sm. pepper: peperoni sott'aceto, pickled peppers.
pepita sf. nugget.
peplo sm. peplum.
pepsina sf. pepsin.
peptone sm. peptone.
per prep. 1. for: fallo — me, do it for me 2. (moto per luogo) through: passai per Roma, I passed through Rome 3. (entro, per mezzo di) by: devo farlo — la fine dell'anno, I have to do it by the end of the year; — telegramma, by telegram 4. (causa) owing to, because of: non potemmo andare — la nebbia, we couldn't go owing to (because of) fog || — l'addietro, in the past; — caso, by chance; — nulla, not at all; — sempre, for ever; — tempo, early. ◆ **per** cong. 1. (finale) to, in order to 2. (causale) for.
pera sf. pear.
peràcido sm. peracid.
perbacco inter. by Jove.
perbene agg. respectable.
percalle sm. percale.
percentuale agg. per cent. ◆ **percentuale** sf. percentage.
percepìbile agg. 1. perceptible 2. (di somme) receivable.
percepire vt. 1. to perceive 2. (di stipendio) to receive.

percettìbile agg. perceptible.

percettivo agg. perceptive.

percezione sf. perception.

perché cong. 1. (int.) why 2. (nelle risposte) because 3. (affinché) so that. ♦ **perché** sm. reason, why: chiedersi il —, to wonder why.

perciò cong. therefore, so.

perclorato sm. perchlorate.

percòrrere vt. 1. to cover 2. (attraversare) to run (v. irr.) through.

percorso sm. 1. (distanza) distance 2. (tragitto) way 3. (tracciato) course.

percossa sf. blow.

percuòtere vt. to strike (v. irr.).

percussione sf. percussion.

percussore sm. percussion-pin.

perdente agg. losing. ♦ **perdente** s. loser.

pèrdere vt. 1. to lose (v. irr.) 2. (di treno, occasione) to miss 3. (far acqua) to leak. ♦ **pèrdersi** vr. 1. to get (v. irr.) lost 2. (svanire) to fade 3. (rovinarsi) to be ruined || — d'animo, to lose heart.

perdifiato (nella loc. avv.) a —, with all one's strength.

perdigiorno sm. idler.

pèrdita sf. 1. loss 2. (falla, fuga) leak.

perditempo sm. waste of time.

perdizione sf. perdition.

perdonàbile agg. pardonable.

perdonare vt. 1. to forgive (v. irr.) 2. (risparmiare) to spare. ♦ **perdonarsi** vr. to forgive oneself. ♦ **perdonarsi** v. rec. to forgive each other (one another).

perdono sm. forgiveness || chiedere —, to beg one's pardon.

perdurare vi. to continue.

perdutamente avv. desperately.

perduto agg. lost.

peregrinare vi. to wander, to roam.

peregrinazione sf. wandering, roaming.

peregrino agg. rare.

perenne agg. 1. perennial 2. (eterno) everlasting.

perennemente avv. 1. perennially 2. (per sempre) for ever.

perentorio agg. peremptory.

perequazione sf. equalization.

perfettamente avv. perfectly.

perfettìbile agg. perfectible.

perfettibilità sf. perfectibility.

perfetto agg. perfect. ◄ **perfetto** sm. (gramm.) perfect.

perfezionamento sm. perfecting.

perfezionare vt. 1. to perfect 2. (migliorare) to improve. ♦ **perfezionarsi** vr. to improve.

perfezione sf. perfection: alla —, to perfection.

perfidamente avv. wickedly.

perfidia sf. wickedness.

pèrfido agg. wicked.

perfino avv. even.

perforare vt. 1. to pierce 2. (d biglietti, schede) to punch 3. (mecc.) to drill, to bore.

perforatore agg. perforating. ♦ **perforatore** sm. perforator.

perforatrice sf. (macchina) drill, punch.

perforazione sf. 1. perforation 2. (mecc.) drilling 3. (di biglietti, schede) punching.

pergamena sf. parchment.

pèrgola sf. bower.

pergolato sm. arbour.

pericardio sm. pericardium (pl. -ia).

pericolante agg. tottering.

perìcolo sm. danger || mettere in —, to endanger; correre un —, to be in danger.

pericolosamente avv. dangerously.

pericoloso agg. dangerous.

periferìa sf. 1. periphery 2. (di città) suburbs (pl.).

perifèrico agg. 1. peripheral 2. (suburbano) suburban.

perìfrasi sf. periphrasis (pl. -ses).

perifràstico agg. periphrastic.

perigeo sm. perigee.

perìmetro sm. perimeter.

periodicità sf. periodicity.

perìodico agg. e sm. periodical.

perìodo sm. period.

peripezìa sf. vicissitude.

pèriplo sm. circumnavigation.

perire vi. to perish.

periscopio sm. periscope.

peristilio sm. peristyle.

perito sm. 1. expert 2. (comm.) estimator.

peritonite sf. peritonitis.

perituro agg. perishable.

perizia sf. 1. (abilità) skill 2. (valutazione) survey.

perla sf. pearl.

perlàceo agg. pearly.

perlìfero agg. pearl (attr.).

perlomeno avv. at least.

perlustrare vt. 1. to reconnoitre 2. (di polizia) to patrol.

perlustratore *sm.* scout.
perlustrazione *sf.* 1. reconnaissance 2. (*di polizia*) patrol || *essere in* —, to be on a reconnaissance.
permalosità *sf.* touchiness.
permaloso *agg.* touchy.
permanente *agg.* permanent. ♦ **permanente** *sf.* permanent wave.
permanentemente *avv.* permanently.
permanenza *sf.* 1. permanence 2. (*soggiorno*) stay.
permanere *vi.* 1. to remain 2. (*durare*) to last.
permanganato *sm.* permanganate.
permeàbile *agg.* permeable.
permeabilità *sf.* permeability.
permeare *vt.* to permeate.
permésso *agg.* allowed. ♦ **permésso** *sm.* 1. leave: *in* —, on leave 2. (*autorizzazione*) licence || *documento di* —, permit.
perméttere *vt.* to allow || *permettete?*, may I? ♦ **perméttersi** *vr.* (*prendersi la libertà*) to take (*v. irr.*) the liberty (of) || — *il lusso*, to afford.
pèrmuta *sf.* exchange.
permutàbile *agg.* exchangeable.
permutare *vt.* to exchange.
permutazione *sf.* permutation.
pernice *sf.* partridge.
pernicioso *agg.* pernicious.
perno *sm.* pivot.
pernottamento *sm.* overnight stay.
pernottare *vi.* to stay overnight.
pero *sm.* pear-tree.
però *cong.* but.
peronòspora *sf.* mildew.
perorare *vt.* to plead.
perorazione *sf.* pleading.
peròssido *sm.* peroxide.
perpendicolare *agg.* e *sf.* perpendicular.
perpetrare *vt.* to perpetrate.
perpetuamente *avv.* perpetually.
perpetuare *vt.* to perpetuate. ♦ **perpetuarsi** *vr.* to last.
perpetuità *sf.* perpetuity.
perpetuo *agg.* perpetual: *in* —, perpetually.
perplessità *sf.* perplexity.
perplesso *agg.* perplexed: *rendere* —, to perplex.
perquisire *vt.* to search.
perquisizione *sf.* search.
persecutore *sm.* persecutor.
persecuzione *sf.* persecution.
perseguìbile *agg.* (*giur.*) prosecu-

table.
perseguire *vt.* 1. to pursue 2. (*giur.*) to prosecute.
perseguitare *vt.* to persecute.
perseguitato *sm.* persecuted person.
perseverante *agg.* persevering.
perseveranza *sf.* perseverance.
perseverare *vi.* to persevere.
persiana *sf.* shutter.
persiano *agg.* e *sm.* Persian.
persistente *agg.* persistent.
persistenza *sf.* persistence.
persìstere *vi.* to persist.
persona *sf.* person: *di* —, personally; — *giuridica*, artificial person.
personaggio *sm.* 1. personage 2. (*di romanzo ecc.*) character.
personale *agg.* personal. ♦ **personale** *sm.* 1. staff 2. (*corporatura*) figure.
personalità *sf.* personality: — *giuridica*, legal status.
personalmente *avv.* personally.
personificare *vt.* 1. to personify 2. (*teat.*) to play.
personificazione *sf.* personification.
perspicace *agg.* shrewd.
perspicacia *sf.* shrewdness
perspicuo *agg.* perspicuous.
persuadere *vt.* to persuade. ♦ **persuadersi** *vr.* to convince oneself.
persuasione *sf.* persuasion.
persuasivo *agg.* persuasive.
pertanto *cong.* therefore.
pèrtica *sf.* perch.
pertinace *agg.* pertinacious.
pertinacia *sf.* pertinacity.
pertinente *agg.* pertinent.
pertinenza *sf.* pertinence.
pertosse *sf.* whooping cough.
pertugio *sm.* hole.
perturbare *vt.* to disturb.
perturbatore *agg.* disturbing. ♦ **perturbatore** *sm.* disturber.
perturbazione *sf.* disturbance.
pervàdere *vt.* to pervade.
pervenire *vi.* to arrive (at).
perversione *sf.* perversion.
perversità *sf.* perversity.
perverso *agg.* perverse.
pervertire *vt.* to pervert. ♦ **pervertirsi** *vr.* to go (*v. irr.*) astray.
pervicace *agg.* obstinate.
pervicacia *sf.* obstinacy.
pervinca *sf.* periwinkle.
pesa *sf.* 1. (*luogo*) weigh-house 2. (*apparecchio*) weighing-machine.
pesante *agg.* heavy.

pesantezza *sf.* heaviness.

pesare *vt.* to weigh. ♦ **pesare** *vi.*
1. to weigh 2. (*fig.*) to lie (*v. irr.*)
heavy.

pesata *sf.* weighing.

pesca[1] *sf.* (*bot.*) peach.

pesca[2] *sf.* 1. (*il pescare*) fishing 2.
(*industria*) fishery 3. (*il pescato*)
catch.

pescaggio *sm.* (*mar.*) draught.

pescare *vt.* 1. to fish 2. (*fig.*) to
fish out 3. (*cogliere sul fatto*) to
catch (*v. irr.*) red-handed 4. (*carte*)
to draw (*v. irr.*). ♦ **pescare** *vi.*
to draw.

pescatore *sm.* 1. fisher 2. (*con lenza*) angler.

pesce *sm.* fish: — *rosso*, goldfish;
— *persico*, perch.

pescecane *sm.* shark.

peschereccio *agg.* fishing. ♦ peschereccio *sm.* fishing-boat.

pescherìa *sf.* 1. fish-shop 2. (*mercato*) fish-market.

peschiera *sf.* fish-pond.

pesciaiola *sf.* (*cuc.*) fish-kettle.

pesco *sm.* peach-tree.

pescoso *agg.* fishy.

pesista *sm.* weight thrower.

peso *sm.* weight: *a* —, by weight.

pessimismo *sm.* pessimism.

pessimista *agg.* pessimistic. ♦ pessimista *s.* pessimist.

pessimistico *agg.* pessimistic.

pessimo *agg.* worst, very bad.

pesta *sf.* 1. track 2. (*difficoltà*) difficulty.

pestaggio *sm.* scuffle.

pestare *vt.* 1. to pound 2. (*picchiare*) to beat (*v. irr.*) 3. (*calpestare*) to tread (*v. irr.*) on.

pestata *sf.* 1. (*lo schiacciare*) pounding 2. (*il calpestare*) treading.

peste *sf.* plague.

pestello *sm.* pestle.

pestifero *agg.* pestiferous.

pestilenza *sf.* plague.

pestilenziale *agg.* pestilential.

pesto *agg.* pounded: *buio* —, pitch
dark; *avere gli occhi pesti*, to have
rings under one's eyes.

pètalo *sm.* petal.

petardo *sm.* petard.

petizione *sf.* petition.

petraia *sf.* 1. (*cava*) quarry 2. (*mucchio di pietre*) heap of stones.

petrografia *sf.* petrography.

petroliera *sf.* tanker.

petrolifero *agg.* oil (*attr.*).

petrolio *sm.* oil.

pettégola *sf.* gossiper.

pettegolare *vi.* to gossip.

pettegolezzo *sm.* gossip.

pettégolo *agg.* gossipy. ♦ pettégolo *sm.* gossiper.

pettinare *vt.* to comb. ♦ pettinar-
si *vr.* to comb one's hair.

pettinato *sm.* worsted.

pettinatrice *sf.* 1. hairdresser 2.
(*industria tessile*) comber.

pettinatura *sf.* 1. hairdo 2. (*industria tessile*) combing.

pèttine *sm.* comb.

pettirosso *sm.* robin.

petto *sm.* 1. breast 2. (*torace*) chest
|| — *a* —, face to face; *prendere
di* —, to face.

pettorale *agg.* e *sm.* pectoral.

pettorina *sf.* stomacher.

pettoruto *agg.* 1. full-breasted 2.
(*fig.*) haughty.

petulante *agg.* pert.

petulanza *sf.* pertness.

petunia *sf.* petunia.

pezza *sf.* 1. patch 2. (*macchia*) spot
|| — *di stoffa*, roll.

pezzato *agg.* spotted.

pezzente *agg.* beggarly. ♦ pezzente *s.* ragamuffin.

pezzo *sm.* piece: *fare a pezzi*, to
tear (*v. irr.*) to pieces; *a pezzi e
bocconi*, piecemeal; — *grosso* (*fig.*),
bigwig; — *di ricambio*, spare part.

pezzuola *sf.* handkerchief.

piacente *agg.* pleasant.

piacere[1] *sm.* 1. pleasure 2. (*favore*)
favour || *per* —, please; —! (*nelle
presentazioni*), how do you do!

piacere[2] *vi.* to like: *gli piace leggere*, he likes reading, he likes to
read; *come pare e piace*, as one
pleases.

piacévole *agg.* pleasant.

piacimento *sm.* pleasure, liking: *a
—*, as much as one likes.

piaga *sf.* 1. sore 2. (*calamità*)
plague 3. (*fig.*) nuisance.

piagnisteo *sm.* moaning.

piagnucolare *vi.* to whimper.

piagnucolio *sm.* whimper.

piagnucoloso *agg.* whimpering.

pialla *sf.* plane.

piallare *vt.* to plane.

piallatrice *sf.* planer.

piallatura *sf.* 1. planing 2. (*trucioli*) shavings (*pl.*).

piana *sf.* plane.

pianeggiante *agg.* level.

pianella *sf.* **1.** (*pantofola*) slipper **2.** (*mattonella*) flat tile.

pianeròttolo *sm.* landing.

pianeta *sm.* planet.

piangente *agg.* weeping, crying.

piàngere *vi.* to cry, to weep (*v. irr.*). ♦ **piàngere** *vt.* to weep **2.** (*un lutto*) to mourn ‖ — *a calde lacrime,* to weep one's heart out.

planificare *vt.* to plan.

pianificazione *sf.* planning.

pianista *s.* pianist.

piano¹ *agg.* **1.** flat **2.** (*chiaro*) clear **3.** (*semplice*) simple.

piano² *sm.* **1.** plain **2.** (*di casa*) floor, storey **3.** (*strato*) layer **4.** (*superficie piana, livello*) plane **5.** (*progetto*) plan **6.** (*cine*) primo —, close up ‖ — *stradale,* roadway; *in primo* —, in the foreground.

piano³ *avv.* **1.** (*lentamente*) slowly **2.** (*sommessamente*) softly **3.** (*con cautela*) gently.

pianoforte *sm.* piano.

pianola *sf.* barrel-organ.

pianta *sf.* **1.** plant **2.** (*carta topografica*) map **3.** (*del piede*) sole ‖ *di sana* — (*completamente*), completely; (*di nuovo*) anew.

piantagione *sf.* plantation.

piantare *vt.* **1.** to plant **2.** (*conficcare*) to drive (*v. irr.*) **3.** (*lasciare*) to leave (*v. irr.*) ‖ *piantarla,* to stop.

piantatore *sm.* planter.

pianterreno *sm.* ground-floor.

pianto *sm.* **1.** tears (*pl.*): *scoppiare in* —, to burst (*v. irr.*) into tears **2.** (*dolore*) grief.

piantonamento *sm.* guarding.

piantonare *vt.* to guard.

piantone¹ *sm.* soldier on guard.

piantone² *sm.* (*agr.*) shoot.

pianura *sf.* plain.

piastra *sf.* **1.** plate **2.** (*di marmo*) slab **3.** (*moneta*) piastre.

piastrella *sf.* tile.

piastrellare *vt.* to tile.

piastrellatura *sf.* tiling.

piastrina *sf.* plaque.

piattaforma *sf.* platform.

piattello *sm.* pan ‖ *tiro al* —, trap-shooting.

piattino *sm.* saucer.

piatto¹ *agg.* flat.

piatto² *sm.* **1.** dish **2.** (*portata*) course **3.** (*di lama*) flat **4.** (*di grammofono*) turn-table.

piazza *sf.* **1.** square **2.** (*comm.*) market ‖ *mettere qc. in* —, to make (*v. irr.*) sthg. public.

piazzaforte *sf.* stronghold.

piazzale *sm.* large square.

piazzamento *sm.* place.

piazzare *vt.* to place. ♦ **piazzarsi** *vr.* (*sport*) to be placed.

piazzista *sm.* salesman (*pl.* -men).

picaresco *agg.* picaresque.

picca *sf.* pike ‖ *picche* (*alle carte*), spades (*pl.*).

piccante *agg.* **1.** piquant **2.** (*salace*) spicy.

piccarsi *vr.* to plume oneself (on).

piccato *agg.* resentful.

picchettare *vt.* **1.** to peg out **2.** (*mil.*) to picket.

picchetto *sm.* **1.** peg **2.** (*mil.*) picket: *essere di* —, to be on picket.

picchiare *vt. e vi.* **1.** (*percuotere*) to beat (*v. irr.*) **2.** (*battere*) to strike (*v. irr.*) **3.** (*bussare*) to knock **4.** (*aer.*) to pitch ‖ — *in testa* (*di motore*), to ping. ♦ **picchiarsi** *vr. rec.* to fight (*v. irr.*).

picchiata *sf.* **1.** beating **2.** (*aer.*) dive ‖ *scendere in* —, to dive.

picchiatello *agg.* slightly crazy.

picchiettare *vt.* **1.** (*battere*) to tap **2.** (*chiazzare*) to spot.

picchiettato *agg.* spotted.

picchiettìo *sm.* tapping.

picchio¹ *sm.* **1.** (*colpo*) blow **2.** (*alla porta*) knock.

picchio² *sm.* (*zool.*) woodpecker.

picchiotto *sm.* door-knocker.

piccineria *sf.* meanness.

piccino *agg.* **1.** little **2.** (*fig.*) mean.

piccionaia *sf.* **1.** pigeon-house **2.** (*teat.*) gallery.

piccione *sm.* pigeon.

picco *sm.* peak ‖ *a* —, vertically; *colare a* —, *mandare a* —, to sink (*v. irr.*).

piccolezza *sf.* **1.** smallness **2.** (*meschinità*) meanness **3.** (*inezia*) trifle.

piccolo *agg.* **1.** small, little **2.** (*di statura, breve*) short **3.** (*giovane*) young **4.** (*meschino*) mean **5.** (*leggero*) light.

piccone *sm.* pick(axe).

piccozza *sf.* axe.

pidocchieria *sf.* meanness.

pidocchio *sm.* **1.** louse (*pl.* lice) **2.** (*fig.*) miser.

pidocchioso *agg.* **1.** lousy **2.** (*fig.*) stingy.

piede *sm.* foot (*pl.* feet): *a piedi*, on foot || *a — libero*, on bail; *prender —*, to get (*v. irr.*) a footing.

piedistallo *sm.* pedestal.

piega *sf.* 1. fold 2. (*fatta ad arte*) pleat 3. (*segno*) crease || *messa in — (di capelli)*, set.

piegàbile *agg.* folding.

piegamento *sm.* 1. folding 2. (*flessione*) flexing.

piegare *vt.* 1. to fold 2. (*flettere, anche fig.*) to bend (*v. irr.*). ◆ **piegare** *vi.* 1. (*voltare*) to turn 2. (*curvarsi*) to bend. ◆ **piegarsi** *vr.* to bend.

piegatrice *sf.* (*mecc.*) bending-machine.

pieghettare *vt.* to pleat.

pieghévole *agg.* 1. pliable 2. (*atto a essere piegato*) folding. ◆ **pieghévole** *sm.* folder.

pieghevolezza *sf.* pliability.

piena *sf.* 1. flood, spate 2. (*folla*) crowd.

pienamente *avv.* fully.

pienezza *sf.* 1. fullness 2. (*massimo grado*) height.

pieno *agg.* full: *— zeppo*, full up; *in — (completamente)*, fully, (*esattamente*) exactly, (*nel mezzo*) in the middle; *in — giorno*, in broad daylight. ◆ **pieno** *sm.* (*il colmo*) middle || *fare il — (auto)*, to fill up.

pietà *sf.* 1. pity 2. (*relig.*) piety || *aver — di*, to have mercy on; *far —*, to arouse pity; *per —!*, for pity's sake!

pietanza *sf.* 1. main course 2. (*piatto*) dish.

pietismo *sm.* pietism.

pietosamente *avv.* pitifully.

pietoso *agg.* pitiful.

pietra *sf.* stone: *posare la prima —*, to lay the foundation stone.

pietraia *sf.* V. *petraia*.

pietrificare *vt.* to petrify. ◆ **pietrificarsi** *vr.* to petrify.

pietrina *sf.* flint.

pietrisco *sm.* rubble.

pietroso *agg.* stony.

piffero *sm.* pipe.

pigiama *sm.* pyjamas (*pl.*).

pigia pigia *sm.* awful crush.

pigiare *vt.* to press. ◆ **pigiarsi** *vr.* to crowd.

pigione *sf.* rent: *stare a — presso*, to lodge with.

pigmentato *agg.* pigmented.

pigmentazione *sf.* pigmentation.

pigmento *sm.* pigment.

pigmeo *sm.* pigmy.

pigna *sf.* pinecone.

pignatta *sf.* pot.

pignoleria *sf.* faultfinding.

pignolo *sm.* 1. (*bot.*) pine-seed 2. (*fig.*) faultfinder.

pignoramento *sm.* attachment.

pignorare *vt.* to distrain.

pigolare *vi.* to peep.

pigolìo *sm.* peep.

pigramente *avv.* 1. lazily 2. (*lentamente*) sluggishly.

pigrizia *sf.* 1. laziness 2. (*lentezza*) sluggishness.

pigro *agg.* 1. lazy 2. (*lento*) sluggish.

pila *sf.* pile: *— a secco*, dry battery.

pilastro *sm.* pillar.

pillola *sf.* pill: *— anticoncezionale*, contraceptive (pill), the "pill".

pilone *sm.* 1. pylon 2. (*di ponte*) pier || *— d'ormeggio*, mooring-mast.

piloro *sm.* pylorus (*pl.* -ri).

pilota *sm.* 1. pilot 2. (*di auto*) driver.

pilotaggio *sm.* pilotage: *scuola di —*, flying-school.

pilotare *vt.* 1. to pilot 2. (*un'auto*) to drive (*v. irr.*).

piluccare *vt.* to nibble.

piluccone *sm.* nibbler.

pinacoteca *sf.* picture-gallery.

pinastro *sm.* pinaster.

pindàrico *agg.* Pindaric.

pineta *sf.* pinewood.

pingue *agg.* 1. fat 2. (*ricco*) rich.

pinguèdine *sf.* fatness.

pinguino *sm.* penguin.

pinna *sf.* 1. fin 2. (*sport*) flipper.

pinnàcolo[1] *sm.* pinnacle.

pinnàcolo[2] *sm.* (*gioco*) pinochle.

pino *sm.* pine (-tree).

pinolo *sm.* pine-seed.

pinta *sf.* pint.

pinza *sf.* pliers (*pl.*), pincers (*pl.*).

pinzetta *sf.* tweezers (*pl.*).

pio *agg.* pious || *opera pia*, charitable organization.

pioggia *sf.* rain: *sotto la —*, in the rain.

piolo *sm.* V. *piuolo*.

piombare *vt.* 1. to plumb 2. (*tip.*) to lead || *— un dente*, to stop a tooth. ◆ **piombare** *vi.* 1. (*cade-*

re) to fall (*v. irr.*) heavily 2. (*assalire*) to assail 3. (*precipitarsi*) to rush.

piombatura *sf.* sealing, leading.

piombino *sm.* 1. plummet 2. (*sigillo*) leaden seal.

piombo *sm.* 1 lead 2. (*sigillo*) leaden seal 3. (*pallottola*) bullet || *filo a* —, plumb line; *a* —, perpendicularly; *di* —, leaden; *andare coi piedi di* —, to proceed very cautiously.

pioniere *sm.* pioneer.

pioppeto *sm.* poplargrove.

pioppo *sm.* poplar.

piorrea *sf.* pyorrhoea.

piovano *agg.* rain (*attr.*).

piovasco *sm.* shower.

piòvere *vi.* to rain, to pour (*anche fig.*).

piovigginare *vi.* to drizzle.

piovigginoso *agg.* drizzly, rainy.

piovoso *agg.* rainy.

piovra *sf.* octopus.

pipa *sf.* pipe.

pipetta *sf.* (*chim.*) pipette.

pipistrello *sm.* bat.

pipita *sf.* agnail.

pira *sf.* pyre.

piramidale *ag.* pyramidal.

piràmide *sf.* pyramid.

pirata *sm.* pirate || — *della strada*, hit-and-run driver.

pirateria *sf.* piracy.

pirico *agg. polvere pirica*, gunpowder.

pirite *sf.* pyrite(s).

piroetta *sf.* pirouette.

piroettare *vi.* to pirouette.

piroga *sf.* pirogue.

pirografia *sf.* pyrography.

piròscafo *sm.* steamer.

pirotècnica *sf.* pyrotechnics.

pirotècnico *agg.* pyrotechnic(al): *spettacolo* —, fireworks. ♦ **pirotècnico** *sm.* pyrotechnist.

piscia *sf.* piss.

pisciare *vi.* to piss.

pisciata *sf.* piss.

pisciatoio *sm.* urinal.

piscicoltura *sf.* pisciculture.

piscina *sf.* swimming-pool.

pisello *sm.* pea.

pisolino *sm.* nap.

pista *sf.* 1. (*traccia*) track 2. (*di animale*) trail 3. (*aer.*) strip.

pistacchio *sm.* pistachio.

pistillo *sm.* pistil.

pistola *sf.* pistol

pistone *sm.* piston.

pitagòrico *agg. e sm.* Pythagorean: *tavola pitagorica*, multiplication table.

pitale *sm.* chamber pot.

pitocco *agg.* 1. mean 2. (*fig.*) stingy. ♦ **pitocco** *sm.* 1. beggar 2. (*fig.*) mean person.

pitone *sm.* python.

pitonessa *sf.* pythoness.

pittore *sm.* painter.

pittoresco *agg.* picturesque.

pittòrico *agg.* pictorial.

pittrice *sf.* paintress.

pittura *sf.* 1. painting 2. (*dipinto, descrizione*) picture 3. (*vernice*) paint.

pitturare *vt.* to paint.

più *avv.* 1. (*comp. di maggioranza con agg. polisillabi, con s., v. e avv.*) more: *questo libro è* — *costoso di quello*, this book is more expensive than that; *ho* — *libri di te*, I have more books than you; *lavoro* — *di te*, I work more than you 2. (*comp. di maggioranza con agg. e avv. monosillabi e bisillabi terminanti in y, er, ow*) ...er: *è* — *gentile di lui*, he is kinder than he is 3. (*superl. rel., corrispondente a "more"*) the most, the more (*fra due*): *è il libro* — *costoso di tutti*, it is the most expensive book of all; *la* — *bella delle due sorelle*, the more beautiful of the two sisters 4. (*superl. rel., corrispondente a "...est"*) the ...est, the ...er (*fra due*): *è la persona* — *felice che conosca*, she is the happiest person I know; *è la* — *graziosa delle due sorelle*, she is the prettier of the sisters 4. (*di tempo*) no longer, no more, not again || *mai* —, never again. ♦ **più** *agg.* 1. more 2. (*diversi*) several. ♦ **più** *sm.* most: *il* — *è fatto*, most of it is done || *i* —, most people (*al sing.*).

piuma *sf.* 1. feather, down 2. (*ornamento*) plume.

piumaggio *sm.* plumage.

piumino *sm.* 1. down 2. (*copriletto*) eiderdown 3. (*per la cipria*) powder-puff 4. (*per spolverare*) duster.

piuttosto *avv.* rather. ♦ **piuttosto che**, *di cong.* rather than.

piuolo *sm.* 1. peg: *scala a piuoli*, ladder 2. (*paletto*) post.

piva *sf.* bagpipe.

pivello *sm.* greenhorn.

piviere *sm.* plover.

pizzicàgnolo *sm.* delicatessen seller.

pizzicare *vt.* **1.** to pinch, to nip **2.** (*di insetti*) to bite (*v. irr.*) **3.** (*di sostanza acre*) to burn (*v. irr.*) **4.** (*con parole*) to tease **5.** (*sorprendere*) to catch (*v. irr.*). ◆ **pizzicare** *vi.* (*prudere*) to itch, to tingle.

pizzicherìa *sf.* **1.** delicatessen shop **2.** (*merci*) delicatessen.

pìzzico *sm.* **1.** pinch **2.** (*pizzicore*) itch **3.** (*fig.*) bit.

pizzicore *sm.* itch.

pizzicotto *sm.* pinch.

pizzo *sm.* **1.** lace (*solo sing.*) **2.** (*di montagna*) peak **3.** (*barba*) pointed beard.

placare *vt.* to appease: — *la fame di qu.*, to satisfy so.'s hunger; — *la sete di qu.*, to quench so.'s thirst. ◆ **placarsi** *vr.* to calm down.

placca *sf.* plaque.

placcare *vt.* to plate (sthg. with).

placcatura *sf.* plating.

placenta *sf.* placenta.

placidità *sf.* placidity.

plàcido *agg.* placid.

plaga *sf.* region.

plagiare *vt.* e *vi.* to plagiarize.

plagiario *agg.* plagiaristic. ◆ **plagiario** *sm.* plagiarist.

plagio *sm.* plagiarism.

planare *vi.* to glide down.

planata *sf.* glide.

plancia *sf.* (*mar.*) 'deck.

plancton *sm.* plankton.

planetario *agg.* planetary. ◆ **planetario** *sm.* planetarium (*pl.* -ia).

planimetrìa *sf.* planimetry, plan.

planimètrico *agg.* planimetric(al).

planisfero *sm.* planisphere.

plantìgrado *agg.* e *sm.* plantigrade.

plasma *sm.* plasma.

plasmare *vt.* to mould.

plàstica *sf.* **1.** (*operazione*) plastic operation **2.** (*materiale*) plastic.

plasticare *vt.* to plasticize.

plasticità *sf.* plasticity.

plàstico *agg.* plastic. ◆ **plàstico** *sm.* **1.** plastic model **2.** (*carta topografica*) relief map.

plastilina *sf.* plasticine.

plàtano *sm.* plane (-tree).

platea *sf.* pit: *poltrona di* —, stall.

plateale *agg.* coarse.

platinare *vt.* **1.** to platinize **2.** (*di capelli*) to bleach.

plàtino *sm.* platinum.

platònico *agg.* Platonic.

plaudente *agg.* applauding.

plausìbile *agg.* plausible.

plàuso *sm.* **1.** applause **2.** (*lode*) praise.

plebaglia *sf.* mob.

plebe *sf.* populace.

plebeo *agg.* e *sm.* plebeian.

plebiscitario *agg.* plebiscitary.

plebiscito *sm.* plebiscite.

plenario *agg.* plenary.

plenilunio *sm.* plenilune.

plenipotenziario *agg.* e *sm.* plenipotentiary.

pleonasmo *sm.* pleonasm.

pleonàstico *agg.* pleonastic.

plesso *sm.* plexus.

plètora *sf.* plethora.

plettòrico *agg.* plethoric.

plettro *sm.* plectrum (*pl.* -ra).

plèura *sf.* pleura (*pl.* -rae).

pleurite *sf.* pleurisy.

plico *sm.* **1.** packet **2.** (*busta*) cover: *in* — *separato*, under separate cover.

plotone *sm.* platoon.

plùmbeo *agg.* leaden.

plurale *agg.* e *sm.* plural.

pluralismo *sm.* pluralism.

pluralità *sf.* plurality.

pluricellulare *agg.* multicellular.

plusvalore *sm.* plus value.

plutòcrate *sm.* plutocrat.

plutocrazìa *sf.* plutocracy.

pneumàtico *agg.* pneumatic, inflatable. ◆ **pneumàtico** *sm.* (*di auto*) tyre.

pneumatorace *sm.* pneumothorax.

pochezza *sf.* (*scarsità, ristrettezza*) scantiness, insufficiency.

pochìssimo *agg.* e *avv.* **1.** very little **2.** (*rarissimamente*) very seldom. ◆ **pochìssimi** *sm. pl.* very few.

poco *avv.* **1.** not very (*con agg. e avv.*), little (*con comp., p. passati, verbi*): *a* — *a* —, little by little; — *per volta*, a little at a time **2.** (*di tempo*) a short time || *fra* —, soon. ◆ **poco** *agg.* **1.** little (*pl.* few) **2.** (*di tempo*) short. ◆ **poco** *pron.* e *sm.* little (*pl.* few): *un* — *di*, a little.

podere *sm.* farm.

poderoso *agg.* powerful.

podio *sm.* platform.

podismo *sm.* **1.** walking **2.** (*sport*) foot-racing.

podista *sm.* (*sport*) foot-racer.

podìstico *agg.* foot (*attr.*).

poema *sm.* poem.

poesìa *sf.* **1.** poetry **2.** (*composizione poetica*) poem.

poeta *sm.* poet.

poetare *vi.* e *vt.* to write (*v. irr.*) poetry.

poètico *agg.* poetic(al).

poggiapiedi *sm.* footstool.

poggiare *vi.* e *vt.* to rest. ♦ **poggiarsi** *vr.* to lean (*v. irr.*) against.

poggio *sm.* hillock.

poi *avv.* **1.** then **2.** (*più tardi*) later || *d'ora in* —, from now on.

poiché *cong.* since, as.

polacca *sf.* (*mus.*) polonaise.

polacco *agg.* Polish. ♦ **polacco** *sm.* Pole.

polare *agg.* polar || *stella* —, pole-star.

polarità *sf.* polarity.

polarizzare *vt.* to polarize.

polarizzatore *agg.* polarizing. ♦ **polarizzatore** *sm.* polarizer.

polarizzazione *sf.* polarization.

polca *sf.* polka.

polèmica *sf.* polemic.

polèmico *agg.* e *sm.* polemic.

polemista *s.* polemist.

polemizzare *vi.* to polemize.

poliandrìa *sf.* polyandry.

policlìnico *sm.* polyclinic.

policromìa *sf.* polychromy.

policromo *agg.* polychrome.

polièdrico *agg.* **1.** polyhedral **2.** (*fig.*) versatile.

poliedro *sm.* polyhedron.

polifonìa *sf.* polyphony.

polifònico *agg.* polyphonic.

poligamìa *sf.* polygamy.

polìgamo *agg.* polygamous. ♦ **polìgamo** *sm.* polygamist.

poliglotta *s.* polyglot.

polìgono *sm.* polygon || — *di tiro*, shooting-range.

polimerizzazione *sf.* polymerization.

polìmero *agg.* polymeric. ♦ **polìmero** *sm.* polymer.

polimorfismo *sm.* polymorphism.

poliomielite *sf.* poliomyelitis.

poliomielìtico *agg.* polio (*attr.*). ♦ **poliomielìtico** *sm.* person who has had polio.

pòlipo *sm.* polyp.

polisìllabo *agg.* polysyllabic(al). ♦ **polisillabo** *sm.* polysyllable.

politècnico *agg.* e *sm.* polytechnic.

politeismo *sm.* polytheism.

politeista *agg.* polytheistic. ♦ **politeista** *s.* polytheist.

polìtica *sf.* **1.** politics **2.** (*linea di condotta*) policy.

politicante *sm.* petty politician.

polìtico *agg.* **1.** political **2.** (*sagace*) politic || *uomo* —, politician.

polivalente *agg.* polyvalent.

polizìa *sf.* police (*us. al pl.*).

poliziesco *agg.* **1.** police (*attr.*) **2.** (*di film ecc.*) detective (*attr.*).

poliziotto *sm.* policeman (*pl.* -men).

pòlizza *sf.* **1.** policy **2.** (*ricevuta*) bill.

polla *sf.* spring.

pollaio *sm.* hen-house.

pollame *sm.* poultry.

pollastra *sf.* pullet.

pollastro *sm.* cockerel.

pòllice *sm.* **1.** thumb **2.** (*del piede*) big toe **3.** (*misura*) inch.

pollicoltore *sm.* poultryman (*pl.* -men).

pollicoltura *sf.* poultry-farming.

pòlline *sm.* pollen.

pollivéndolo *sm.* poulterer.

pollo *sm.* **1.** chicken **2.** (*fig.*) dupe.

polmonare *agg.* pulmonary.

polmone *sm.* lung: — *d'acciaio*, iron lung.

polmonite *sf.* pneumonia.

polo[1] *sm.* pole.

polo[2] *sm.* (*sport*) polo.

polpa *sf.* **1.** (*di frutta*) pulp **2.** (*carne*) lean meat.

polpaccio *sm.* calf (*pl.* calves).

polpastrello *sm.* finger-tip.

polpetta *sf.* meat-ball, croquette.

polposo *agg.* pulpy.

polsino *sm.* cuff.

polso *sm.* **1.** wrist **2.** (*fig.*) energy **3.** (*pulsazione*) pulse **4.** (*polsino*) cuff || *tastare il* — *a qu.*, to feel (*v. irr.*) so.'s pulse; *uomo di* —, energetic man.

poltiglia *sf.* **1.** pulp **2.** (*fanghiglia*) mud.

poltrire *vi.* to idle.

poltrona *sf.* **1.** armchair **2.** (*teat.*) stall.

poltrone *agg.* idle. ♦ **poltrone** *sm.* idler.

poltronerìa *sf.* idleness.

pòlvere *sf.* **1.** dust **2.** (*sostanza polverizzata*) powder || *togliere.la* —, to dust.

polveriera *sf.* powder-magazine.

polverizzare vt. to pulverize. ♦
 polverizzarsi vr. to pulverize.
polverone sm. cloud of dust.
polveroso agg. dusty.
pomata sf. salve.
pomello sm. **1.** (di porta ecc.) knob
 2. (di guancia) cheek-bone.
pomeridiano agg. **1.** afternoon
 (attr.) **2.** (con le ore) p. m. (post
 meridiem): alle 5 pomeridiane,
 at five o'clock.
pomeriggio sm. afternoon.
pòmice sf. pumice.
pomo sm. **1.** (mela) apple **2.** (di
 porta ecc.) knob.
pomodoro sm. tomato.
pompa sf. **1.** pump **2.** (fasto) pomp
 3. (ostentazione) display || impresa
 di pompe funebri, undertaker's
 business; far — di sé, to show (v.
 irr.) off.
pompare vt. **1.** to pump **2.** (fig.)
 to puff up.
pompelmo sm. grapefruit.
pompiere sm. fireman (pl. -men).
pomposità sf. pomposity.
pomposo agg. pompous.
ponderàbile agg. ponderable.
ponderabilità sf. ponderability.
ponderare vt. to ponder.
ponderatamente avv. after reflection.
ponderatezza sf. circumspection.
ponderato agg. pondered.
ponderazione sf. consideration.
ponderoso agg. ponderous.
ponente sm. west.
ponte sm. **1.** bridge: — girevole,
 swing bridge **2.** (mar.) deck **3.**
 (impalcatura) scaffold || rompere i
 ponti con (fig.), to break (v. irr.)
 with.
pontéfice sm. pope.
pontificale agg. pontifical.
pontificare vi. to pontificate.
pontificato sm. pontificate.
pontificio agg. papal.
pontile sm. landing-stage.
pontone sm. pontoon.
ponzare vi. to rack one's brains.
popolamento sm. peopling.
popolano agg. common. ♦ **popola-**
 no sm. man of the people || i
 popolani, the common people.
popolare[1] vt. to people. ♦ **popo-**
 larsi vr. to become (v. irr.) pop-
 ulated.
popolare[2] agg. **1.** popular **2.** (tradizionale) folk (attr.).

popolaresco agg. popular-like.
popolarità sf. popularity.
popolarizzare vt. to popularize.
popolazione sf. population.
pòpolo sm. **1.** (gente) people (pl.)
 2. (nazione) people.
popoloso agg. populous.
popone sm. melon.
poppa[1] sf. **1.** (mar.) stern || avere il
 vento in —, to sail before the
 wind; a —, astern.
poppa[2] sf. breast.
poppante s. suckling.
poppare vt. to suck.
poppata sf. suck: ora della —,
 feeding-time.
poppatoio sm. feeding-bottle.
populismo sm. populism.
populista agg. populistic. ♦ **popu-**
 lista s. populist.
porcaro sm. swineherd.
porcellana sf. china (solo sing.).
porcherìa sf. **1.** dirt **2.** (azione di-
 sonesta) dirty trick **3.** (detto indecente) obscene word **4.** (atto indecente) obscene act **5.** (cibo cattivo) revolting stuff **6.** (cose senza
 valore) rubbish.
porcile sm. pigsty.
porcino agg. pig (attr.). ♦ **por-**
 cino sm. (fungo) boletus.
porco sm. **1.** pig **2.** (cuc.) pork.
porcospino sm. porcupine.
pòrfido sm. porphyry.
pòrgere vt. **1.** to hand **2.** (offrire)
 to offer.
pornografìa sf. pornography.
pornogràfico agg. pornographic
poro sm. pore.
porosità sf. porosity.
poroso agg. porous.
pòrpora sf. purple.
porporato sm. Cardinal.
porre vt. **1.** to put (v. irr.) **2.** (sup-
 porre) to suppose || — le fonda-
 menta, to lay (v. irr.) the foundations; — mano, to begin (v. irr.).
porro sm. **1.** leek **2.** (med.) wart.
porta sf. **1.** door **2.** (di mura ecc.)
 gate **3.** (sport) goal.
portabagagli sm. **1.** luggage-rack
 2. (facchino) porter.
portabandiera sm. ensign.
portacarte sm. portfolio.
portacénere sm. ash-tray.
portachiavi sm. key-holder.
portacipria sm. compact.
portaèrei sf. aircraft carrier.
portaferiti sm. stretcher-bearer.

portafiori *sm.* flower-holder.

portafoglio *sm.* 1. wallet 2. (*pol.*) portfolio.

portafortuna *sm.* mascot.

portagioielli *sm.* jewel-case.

portalèttere *sm.* ·postman (*pl.* -men).

portamento *sm.* 1. gait 2. (*condotta*) behaviour.

portamonete *sm.* purse.

portantina *sf.* sedan-chair.

portaombrelli *sm.* umbrella-stand.

portaòrdini *sm.* messenger.

portapacchi *sm.* carrier.

portapenne *sm.* penholder.

portare *vt.* 1. (*verso chi parla o ascolta*) to bring (*v. irr.*) 2. (*lontano da chi parla, accompagnare*) to take (*v. irr.*) 3. (*trasportare*) to carry 4. (*condurre*) to lead (*v. irr.*) 5. (*indossare*) to wear (*v. irr.*) 6. (*avere*) to have.

portasapone *sm.* soap-dish.

portasigarette *sm.* cigarette-case.

portaspilli *sm.* pincushion.

portata *sf.* 1. (*di pranzo*) course 2. (*di arma, strumento ottico*) range 3. (*di fiume*) flow 4. (*di ponte, auto ecc.*) capacity 5. (*stazza*) tonnage 6. (*fig.*) importance.

portàtile *agg.* portable.

portatore *sm.* bearer.

portauovo *sm.* egg-cup.

portavoce *sm.* spokesman (*pl.* -men).

portello *sm.* hatch.

portento *sm.* prodigy.

portentosamente *avv.* prodigiously.

portentoso *agg.* prodigious.

porticato *sm.* arcade.

pòrtico *sm.* 1. (*loggia*) porch 2. (*porticato*) arcade.

portiera[1] *sf.* (*porta*) door.

portiera[2] *sf.* doorkeeper.

portiere *sm.* 1. (*sport*) goal-keeper 2. porter.

portinaio *sm.* door keeper.

portineria *sf.* porter's lodge.

porto[1] *sm.* 1. port (*anche fig.*) 2. (*bacino*) harbour (*anche fig.*).

porto[2] *sm.* (*trasporto*) carriage: *franco di* —, carriage paid 2 — *d'armi*, shooting licence; *condurre in* — (*fig.*), to carry out.

portoghese *agg.* e *sm.* Portuguese.

portone *sm.* main door.

portuale *agg.* harbour (*attr.*): *città* —, port. ◆ **portuale** *sm.* docker.

porzione *sf.* portion.

posa *sf.* 1. (*il porre*) laying 2. (*posizione*) posture 3. (*affettazione*) pose 4. (*pausa*) pause 5. (*foto*) exposure || *mettersi in* —, to pose; *senza* —, incessantly.

posare *vt.* to lay (*v. irr.*). ◆ **posare** *vi.* 1. (*aver fondamento*) to rest 2. (*assumere un atteggiamento non spontaneo*) to pose 3. (*di liquido*) to stand (*v. irr.*). ◆ **posarsi** *vr.* 1. to settle 2. (*aer.; di uccello*) to alight.

posata *sf.* 1. (*coltello*) knife (*pl.* knives) 2. (*forchetta*) fork 3. (*cucchiaio*) spoon.

posato *agg.* staid.

poscritto *sm.* postscript.

positiva *sf.* (*foto*) positive.

positivamente *avv.* positively.

positivismo *sm.* positivism.

positivista *s.* positivist.

positivo *agg.* positive.

posizione *sf.* position.

posologìa *sf.* posology.

posporre *vt.* 1. to place after 2. (*posticipare*) to postpone.

possedere *vt.* to possess.

possedimento *sm.* V. *possesso*.

possente *agg.* powerful.

possessivo *agg.* possessive.

possesso *sm.* 1. possession 2. (*proprietà*) property.

possessore *sm.* possessor, owner.

possìbile *agg.* possible: *il più presto* —, as soon as possible; *fare il* —, to do (*v. irr.*) one's best.

possibilità *sf.* 1. possibility 2. (*potere*) power || — *finanziarie*, means.

possidente *sm.* 1. man (*pl.* -men) of property 2. (*terriero*) landowner.

posta *sf.* 1. post, mail 2. (*ufficio postale*) post-office || *fermo* —, poste restante; *a giro di* —, by return of post; *per* —, by mail 3. (*al gioco*) stake.

postale *agg.* postal, post (*attr.*), mail (*attr.*): *per pacco* —, by parcel post; *spese postali*, postage.

postazione *sf.* stationing.

postbèllico *agg.* post-war (*attr.*).

postdatare *vt.* to postdate.

posteggiare *vt.* to park.

posteggiatore *sm.* 1. car-park attendant 2. (*venditore*) stall-keeper.

posteggio *sm.* car-park || — *di taxi*, taxi rank.

postelegrafònico *agg.* postal telegraph and telephone (*attr.*). ◆

postelegrafònico *sm.* post-office clerk.

postema *sf.* aposteme.

pòsteri *sm. pl.* descendants.

posteriore *agg.* **1.** (*nel tempo*) following **2.** (*nello spazio*) back, rear.

posterità *sf.* posterity.

posticcio *agg.* false. ♦ **posticcio** *sm.* toupee.

posticipare *vt.* to postpone.

posticipazione *sf.* deferment.

postiglione *sm.* postilion.

postilla *sf.* (marginal) note.

postillare *vt.* to annotate.

postino *sm.* postman (*pl.* -men).

posto *sm.* **1.** place **2.** (*spazio*) room **3.** (*lavoro*) job **4.** (*posto a sedere*) seat **5.** (*stazione*) station || *al — di*, instead of.

postoperatorio *agg.* postoperative.

postribolo *sm.* brothel.

postulante *sm.* **1.** petitioner **2.** (*eccl.*) postulant.

postulare *vt.* to petition (for sthg.).

postulato *sm.* postulate.

pòstumo *agg.* posthumous.

potàbile *agg.* drinkable.

potare *vt.* to prune.

potassa *sf.* potash.

potàssico *agg.* potassic.

potassio *sm.* potassium.

potatore *sm.* pruner.

potatura *sf.* pruning.

potente *agg.* powerful.

potenza *sf.* power || *in — (a:v.)*, potentially, (*agg.*) potential.

potenziale *agg. e sm.* potential.

potenzialità *sf.* potentiality.

potenziamento *sm.* **1.** (*rafforzamento*) strengthening **2.** (*sviluppo*) development.

potenziare *vt.* **1.** (*rafforzare*) to strengthen **2.** (*sviluppare*) to develop.

potere[1] *vi.* **1.** can (*pres.*), could (*pass., condiz.*), to be able: *non può venire*, he cannot come **2.** (*eventualità, augurio, permesso*) may (*pres.*), might (*pass., condiz.*), to be allowed to: *può darsi*, maybe; *può darsi che venga*, he may come.

potere[2] *sm.* power.

potestà *sf.* power, authority.

poveraccio *sm.* poor devil.

pòvero *agg.* poor.

povertà *sf.* poverty.

pozione *sf.* potion.

pozza *sf.* pool.

pozzànghera *sf.* puddle.

pozzetto *sm.* **1.** (*di motore*) sump **2.** (*di fognatura*) drain well.

pozzo *sm.* well: *— nero*, cesspool; *— carbonifero*, coal-pit.

pragmatismo *sm.* pragmatism.

pragmatista *s.* pragmatist.

pragmatìstico *agg.* pragmatist.

prammàtica *sf.* custom: *di —*, customary.

prammàtico *agg.* pragmatic.

pranzare *vi.* to dine.

pranzo *sm.* **1.** dinner **2.** (*di mezzogiorno*) lunch.

prassi *sf.* praxis.

prataiolo *agg.* field (*attr.*).

prateria *sf.* prairie.

pràtica *sf.* **1.** practice **2.** (*affare*) matter **3.** (*esperienza*) experience **4.** (*incartamento*) file **5.** (*trattativa*) dealing **6.** (*passo presso un'autorità*) step || *far —*, to practise; *aver — di*, to be familiar with.

praticàbile *agg.* practicable.

praticabilità *sf.* practicability.

praticaccia *sf.* practical knowledge.

praticante *agg.* practising.

praticare *vt.* **1.** to practise **2.** (*frequentare*) to frequent **3.** (*fare*) to make (*v. irr.*).

praticità *sf.* practicality.

pràtico *agg.* **1.** practical **2.** (*esperto*) skilled || *esser — di*, to be familiar with.

prativo *agg.* grass (*attr.*).

prato *sm.* **1.** meadow **2.** (*artificiale*) lawn.

pratolina *sf.* daisy.

pravo *agg.* perverse.

preallarme *sm.* prewarning.

preàmbolo *sm.* preface.

preannunziare *vt.* to portend.

preavvertire *vt.* to forewarn.

preavvisare *vt.* to forewarn.

preavviso *sm.* **1.** forewarning **2.** (*disdetta*) notice.

prebèllico *agg.* pre-war (*attr.*).

prebenda *sf.* **1.** (*eccl.*) prebend **2.** (*salario*) salary.

precarietà *sf.* precariousness.

precario *agg.* precarious.

precauzionale *agg.* precautionary.

precauzione *sf.* **1.** precaution **2.** (*cautela*) caution.

precedente *agg.* previous. ♦ **precedente** *sm.* precedent || *i precedenti* (*condotta*), record.

precedenza *sf.* precedence || *in —*, previously.

precèdere vt. to precede. ♦ **precèdere** vi. to come (v. irr.) first

precessione sf. precession.

precettare vt. 1. (giur.) to summon 2. (mil.) to call to arms.

precetto sm. 1. precept 2. (mil.) call-up notice.

precettore sm. tutor.

precipitare vt. to precipitate. ♦ **precipitare** vi. 1. to fall (v. irr.) 2. (chim.) to precipitate. ♦ **precipitarsi** vr. to dash.

precipitato agg. e sm. precipitate.

precipitazione sf. 1. (atmosferica) precipitation 2. (furia) haste.

precipitoso agg. 1. (impetuoso) headlong 2. (frettoloso) hasty 3. (scosceso) precipitous.

precipizio sm. precipice: a — (precipitosamente), headlong; (a picco) perpendicularly.

precipuo agg. principal.

precisare vt. to specify.

precisazione sf. specification.

precisione sf. 1. precision 2. (chiarezza) clarity.

preciso agg. 1. precise 2. (accurato) careful 3. (definito) definite 4. (identico) identical 5. (di ore) sharp.

preclaro agg. prominent.

preclùdere vt. to preclude.

precoce agg. 1. precocious 2. (di frutto, stagione) early 3. (prematuro) premature.

precocità sf. precociousness.

preconcetto agg. preconceived. ♦ **preconcetto** sm. prejudice.

preconizzare vt. to foretell (v. irr.).

precordi sm. pl. praecordia.

precòrrere vt. to anticipate.

precursore agg. precursory. ♦ **precursore** sm. forerunner.

preda sf. 1. prey 2. (bottino) booty || cadere in — a, to fall (v. irr.) a prey to; far — di, to plunder.

predace agg. predacious.

predare vt. to plunder.

predatore agg. predatory. ♦ **predatore** sm. plunderer.

predatorio agg. predatory.

predecessore sm. forerunner.

predella sf. 1. platform 2. (sgabello) stool.

predellino sm. 1. (di vettura) footboard 2. (poggiapiedi) footstool.

predestinare vt. to predestine.

predestinazione sf. 1. predestination 2. (destino) destiny.

predeterminare vt. to predetermine.

predeterminazione sf. predetermination.

predetto agg. 1. (suddetto) above mentioned 2. (presagito) foretold (pred.).

prediale agg. praedial.

prèdica sf. sermon: fare la — a qu., to lecture so.

predicàbile agg. predicable.

predicare vt. e vi. to preach.

predicativo agg. predicate.

predicato sm. predicate: essere in — per, to be considered for.

predicatore sm. preacher.

predicatorio agg. preachifying.

predicazione sf. preaching.

predicozzo sm. lecture.

predigestione sf. preliminary digestion.

prediletto agg. favourite. ♦ **prediletto** sm. pet.

predilezione sf. predilection.

predilìgere vt. to prefer.

predire vt. to foretell (v. irr.).

predisporre vt. 1. to predispose 2. (provvedere) to arrange. ♦ **predisporsi** vr. to prepare oneself.

predisposizione sf. 1. (med.) predisposition 2. (inclinazione) bent.

predizione sf. prediction.

predominante agg. prevailing.

predominanza sf. prevalence.

predominare vi. to prevail.

predominio sm. predominance.

predone sm. plunderer.

preesistente agg. pre-existing.

preesistenza sf. pre-existence.

preesìstere vi. to pre-exist.

prefabbricare vt. to prefabricate.

prefazio sm. preface.

prefazione sf. preface.

preferenza sf. preference: di —, generally.

preferenziale agg. preferential.

preferìbile agg. preferable.

preferire vt. to prefer.

preferito agg. e sm. V. prediletto.

prefettizio agg. prefectorial.

prefetto sm. prefect.

prefettura sf. prefecture.

prefìggere vt. to (pre-)establish. ♦ **prefìggersi** vr. to be resolved: — uno scopo, to propose an aim to oneself.

prefigurare vt. to prefigure.

prefigurazione sf. prefiguration.

prefisso *sm.* prefix.
preformare *vt.* to preform.
pregare *vt.* **1.** to pray **2.** (*chiedere*) to beg.
pregévole *agg.* valuable.
preghiera *sf.* **1.** prayer **2.** (*domanda*) request.
pregiare *vt.* to esteem. ♦ **pregiarsi** *vr.* to beg (to).
pregiato *agg.* valuable: *vino* —, vintage wine.
pregio *sm.* **1.** (*valore*) value **2.** (*merito*) merit ‖ *di* —, valuable.
pregiudicare *vt.* to prejudice.
pregiudicato *sm.* previous offender.
pregiudiziale *agg.* prejudicial
pregiudizio *sm.* prejudice.
pregnante *agg.* pregnant.
pregno *agg.* **1.** pregnant (with) **2.** (*pieno*) full (of).
pregustare *vt.* to foretaste.
preistoria *sf.* prehistory.
preistòrico *agg.* prehistoric.
prelatizio *agg.* prelatic.
prelato *sm.* prelate.
prelazione *sf.* pre-emption.
prelevamento *sm.* drawing: *fare un —* (*comm.*), to draw (*v. irr.*).
prelevare *vt.* to draw (*v. irr.*).
prelibare *vt.* to foretaste.
prelibato *agg.* excellent.
prelievo *sm.* V. *prelevamento*.
preliminare *agg.* preliminary.
prelùdere *vi.* to prelude (sthg.), to foreshadow (sthg.).
preludiare *vi.* to prelude.
preludio *sm.* prelude.
prematuro *agg.* premature.
premeditare *vt.* to premeditate.
premeditato *agg.* premeditated.
premeditazione *sf.* premeditation.
prèmere *vi.* **1.** to press **2.** (*importare*) to interest **3.** (*essere urgente*) to be urgent. ♦ **prèmere** *vt.* to press.
premessa *sf.* introduction.
premesso *agg.* previous.
premèttere *vt.* **1.** to premise **2.** (*mettere prima*) to put (*v. irr.*) before.
premiare *vt.* **1.** to give (*v. irr.*) a prize **2.** (*ricompensare*) to reward.
premiazione *sf.* awarding of prizes.
preminente *agg.* pre-eminent.
preminenza *sf.* pre-eminence.
premio *sm.* **1.** prize **2.** (*ricompensa*) reward **3.** (*comm.*) premium.
prènaito *sm.* tenesmus.

premolare *agg.* e *sm.* premolar.
premonitore *agg.* premonitory.
premorire *vi.* to predecease.
premunire *vt.* to forearm. ♦ **premunirsi** *vr.* to secure.
premura *sf.* **1.** (*cura*) care **2.** (*fretta*) hurry **3.** (*gentilezza*) kindness ‖ *aver* —, to be in a hurry.
premuroso *agg.* **1.** (*servizievole*) helpful **2.** (*gentile*) obliging.
prèndere *vt.* **1.** to take (*v. irr.*) **2.** (*sorprendere, afferrare*) to catch (*v. irr.*) **3.** (*comprare, ottenere*) to get (*v. irr.*). ♦ **prèndersi** *vr.* to take ‖ *che ti prende?*, what's the matter with you?
prendisole *sm.* sun-suit.
prenome *sm.* praenomen (*pl.* -mina).
prenotare *vt.* to book. ♦ **prenotarsi** *vr.* to engage oneself.
prenotazione *sf.* booking.
prènsile *agg.* prehensile.
prensione *sf.* prehension.
preoccupante *agg.* worrying.
preoccupare *vt.* to worry. ♦ **preoccuparsi** *vr.* to be worried (about).
preoccupazione *sf.* worry.
preordinare *vt.* to prearrange.
preparare *vt.* to prepare. ♦ **prepararsi** *vr.* to get (*v. irr.*) ready.
preparativo *sm.* preparation.
preparato *agg.* ready. ♦ **preparato** *sm.* (*med.*) preparation.
preparatore *sm.* preparer.
preparatorio *agg.* preparatory.
preparazione *sf.* preparation.
preponderante *agg.* preponderant.
preponderanza *sf.* preponderance.
preporre *vt.* **1.** to put (*v. irr.*) before **2.** (*preferire*) to prefer **3.** (*mettere a capo*) to put at the head.
prepositivo *agg.* prepositional.
preposizione *sf.* preposition.
preposto *sm.* **1.** provost **2.** (*relig., prevosto*) parish priest.
prepotente *agg.* overbearing.
prepotentemente *avv.* overbearingly.
prepotenza *sf.* **1.** arrogance **2.** (*azione*) overbearing action.
preraffaellismo *sm.* Pre-Raphaelitism.
preraffaellita *agg.* e *s.* Pre-Raphaelite.
prerogativa *sf.* **1.** prerogative **2.** (*di persona*) faculty **3.** (*di cosa*) property.
presa *sf.* **1.** taking **2.** (*stretta*) grip

3. (*cattura*) capture **4.** (*elettr.*) plug **5.** (*pizzico*) pinch || *macchina da* —, camera; *far* — (*di cemento*), to set (*v. irr.*).

presagio *sm.* presage, omen.

presagire *vt.* **1.** to foresee (*v. irr.*) **2.** (*essere presago di*) to forebode.

presago *agg.* essere — *di* (*prevedere*), to have a presentiment of.

presbiopia *sf.* long-sightedness.

prèsbite *agg.* long-sighted.

presbiterianismo *sm.* Presbyterianism.

presbiteriano *agg.* e *sm.* Presbyterian.

presbiterio *sm.* presbytery.

prescégliere *vt.* to choose (*v. irr.*).

prescelto *agg.* chosen.

prescienza *sf.* prescience.

prescìndere *vi.* to leave (*v. irr.*) out of consideration: *a — da*, apart from.

prescritto *sm.* prescript.

prescrìvere *vt.* to prescribe.

prescrizione *sf.* **1.** regulation **2.** (*med.; giur.*) prescription: *caduto in —*, invalidated by prescription.

presentàbile *agg.* presentable.

presentare *vt.* **1.** to present **2.** (*mostrare*) to show (*v. irr.*) **3.** (*far conoscere*) to introduce. ♦ **presentarsi** *vr.* **1.** to present oneself **2.** (*capitare*) to occur.

presentatore *sm.* **1.** announcer **2.** (*teat.*) showman (*pl.* -men).

presentazione *sf.* **1.** presentation **2.** (*di una persona*) introduction.

presente *agg.* e *s.* present || *i presenti*, the people present; *la —* (*lettera*), this letter.

presentemente *avv.* now.

presentimento *sm.* presentiment.

presentire *vt.* to foresee (*v. irr.*).

presenza *sf.* **1.** presence **2.** (*frequenza*) attendance.

presenziare *vt.* e *vi.* to be present (at).

presepio *sm.* crib.

preservare *vt.* to preserve.

preservativo *agg.* e *sm.* preservative.

preservazione *sf.* preservation.

prèside *sm.* headmaster. ♦ **prèside** *sf.* headmistress.

presidente *sm.* **1.** president **2.** (*di assemblea*) chairman (*pl.* -men).

presidenza *sf.* **1.** presidency **2.** (*di assemblea*) chairmanship **3.** (*di società*) management **4.** (*insieme di* *direttori*) board of directors **5.** (*di scuola*) headmastership.

presidenziale *agg.* presidential.

presidiare *vt.* to garrison.

presidio *sm.* garrison.

presièdere *vt.* e *vi.* to preside (over, at).

pressa *sf.* press.

pressacarte *sm.* paper-weight.

pressante *agg.* pressing.

pressantemente *avv.* pressingly.

pressappoco *avv.* approximately.

pressare *vt.* to press.

pressi *sm. pl.* **1.** neighbourhood (*sing.*) **2.** (*sobborghi*) outskirts.

pressione *sf.* pressure: *fare — su qu.* (*fig.*), to put (*v. irr.*) pressure on so.

presso *avv.* nearly: *a un dì —*, *press'a poco*, approximately; *da —*, closely. ♦ **presso** *prep.* **1.** near **2.** (*a casa di*) at **3.** (*nell'ufficio di*) with **4.** (*fra*) among **5.** (*negli indirizzi*) c/o (care of).

pressoché *avv.* almost.

pressurizzare *vt.* to pressurize.

pressurizzazione *sf.* pressurization.

prestabilire *vt.* to pre-arrange.

prestamente *avv.* quickly.

prestanome *sm.* man of straw.

prestante *agg.* good-looking.

prestanza *sf.* fine appearance.

prestare *vt.* V. *imprestare.* ♦ **prestarsi** *vr.* to volunteer.

prestatore *sm.* lender: — *d'opera*, workman (*pl.* -men).

prestazione *sf.* **1.** (*prestito*) loan **2.** (*servizio*) service **3.** (*sport*) performance.

prestezza *sf.* quickness.

prestidigitatore *sm.* conjurer.

prestigio *sm.* prestige || *gioco di —*, conjuring trick.

prestigioso *agg.* **1.** (*affascinante*) glamorous **2.** (*favoloso*) fabulous.

prèstito *sm.* loan: *prendere in —*, to borrow; *dare in —*, to lend (*v. irr.*).

presto¹ *agg.* — *di mano*, dexterous.

presto² *avv.* **1.** soon **2.** (*di buon'ora*) early **3.** (*in fretta*) quickly || — *o tardi*, sooner or later; *al più —*, as soon as possible. ♦ **presto!** *inter.* quick!

presùmere *vt.* to presume.

presumìbile *agg.* presumable.

presumibilmente *avv.* presumably.

presuntivo *agg.* presumptive.

presunto *agg.* supposed.

presuntuosamente *avv.* presumptuously.

presuntuosità *sf.* conceit.

presuntuoso *agg.* presumptuous.

presunzione *sf.* presumption.

presupporre *vt.* 1. to presuppose 2. (*supporre*) to suppose.

presupposizione *sf.* 1. presupposition 2. (*supposizione*) supposition.

presupposto *sm.* V. *presupposizione.*

prete *sm.* priest.

pretendente *sm.* 1. pretender 2. (*corteggiatore*) suitor.

pretèndere *vt.* 1. to pretend 2. (*esigere*) to want. ♦ **pretèndere** *vi.* to claim.

pretensione *sf.* pretension.

pretenzioso *agg.* 1. pretentious 2. (*presuntuoso*) conceited.

preterintenzionale *agg.* unintentional.

pretèrito *agg. e sm.* past.

pretesa *sf.* 1. pretence 2. (*richiesta*) claim || *avere molte pretese*, to be hard to please; *avanzare pretese su*, to claim rights over.

pretesto *sm.* 1. pretext 2. (*occasione*) occasion.

pretore *sm.* magistrate.

prettamente *avv.* purely.

pretto *agg.* pure.

pretura *sf.* magistrate's court.

prevalente *agg.* prevailing.

prevalenza *sf.* prevalence.

prevalere *vi.* to prevail.

prevaricare *vi.* 1. to prevaricate 2. (*abusare del potere*) to abuse one's office.

prevaricatore *sm.* prevaricator.

prevaricazione *sf.* 1. prevarication 2. (*abuso di potere*) abuse of office.

prevedere *vt.* 1. to foresee (*v. irr.*) 2. (*di legge, contratto*) to provide (for).

prevedìbile *agg.* foreseeable.

preveggente *agg.* foreseeing.

preveggenza *sf.* foresight.

prevenire *vt.* 1. (*precedere*) to forestall 2. (*evitare*) to prevent 3. (*avvertire*) to warn.

preventivamente *avv.* 1. beforehand 2. (*in modo preventivo*) preventively.

preventivare *vt.* to estimate.

preventivo *agg.* 1. preventive 2. (*comm.*) estimated || *bilancio —*, budget. ♦ **preventivo** *sm.* estimate

preventorio *sm.* preventive sanatorium.

prevenuto *agg. essere — contro*, to have a prejudice against.

prevenzione *sf.* 1. prejudice 2. (*il prevenire*) prevention.

previdente *agg.* provident.

previdenza *sf.* providence: — *sociale*, social security.

previdenziale *agg.* social security (*attr.*).

previo *agg.* 1. previous 2. (*soggetto a*) subject to.

previsione *sf.* 1. forecast 2. (*comm.*) estimate.

previsto *agg.* 1. foreseen 2. (*comm.*) estimated 3. (*giur.*) provided.

prevosto *sm.* V. *preposto.*

preziosismo *sm.* preciosity.

preziosità *sf.* preciousness.

prezioso *agg.* precious. ♦ **prezioso** *sm.* jewel.

prezzémolo *sm.* parsley.

prezzo *sm.* 1. price, cost 2. (*valore*) value || *a — di*, at the cost of.

prezzolare *vt.* to hire.

prezzolato *agg.* (*mercenario*) mercenary.

prigione *sf.* 1. prison 2. (*pena*) imprisonment.

prigionìa *sf.* imprisonment.

prigioniero *agg.* imprisoned. ♦ **prigioniero** *sm.* prisoner.

prillare *vi.* to twirl.

prima¹ *avv.* 1. before 2. (*in anticipo*) in advance 3. (*un tempo*) once 4. (*più presto*) earlier, sooner 5. (*per prima cosa*) first || *— o poi*, sooner or later; *quanto —*, soon. ♦ **prima** *prep.* before. ♦ **prima che, di** *cong.* before.

prima² *sf.* 1. (*ferr.; scuola*) first class 2. (*teat.*) première.

primario *agg.* primary. ♦ **primario** *sm.* head physician.

primate *sm.* (*eccl.*) primate.

primati *sm. pl.* (*zool.*) Primates.

primaticcio *agg.* early.

primatista *s.* record-holder.

primato *sm.* 1. supremacy 2. (*sport*) record.

primavera *sf.* spring.

primaverile *agg.* spring (*attributivo*), springlike.

primeggiare *vi.* to excel.

primigenio *agg.* primigenial.

primìpara *sf.* primipara (*pl.* -ae).

primitivo *agg. e sm.* primitive.

primizia *sf.* 1. (*frutta*) early fruit

2. (*verdura*) early vegetable 3. (*novità*) novelty.

primo *agg.* **1.** first **2.** (*principale*) chief **3.** (*iniziale*) early **4.** (*prossimo*) next ‖ *in un — tempo*, at first.

primogènito *agg. e sm.* first-born.

primogenitura *sf.* primogeniture.

primordiale *agg.* primeval.

primordi *sm. pl.* beginnings.

prìmula *sf.* primrose.

principale *agg.* principal. ♦ **principale** *sm.* master, boss.

principato *sm.* principality.

prìncipe *sm.* prince.

principesco *agg.* princely.

principessa *sf.* princess.

principiante *sm.* beginner.

principiare *vt. e vi.* to begin (*v. irr.*).

principio *sm.* **1.** (*inizio*) beginning **2.** (*norma*) principle: *per —*, on principle.

priora *sf.* prioress.

priorato *sm.* priorate.

priore *sm.* prior.

priorità *sf.* priority.

prisma *sm.* prism.

prismàtico *agg.* prismatic(al).

prìstino *agg.* former.

privare *vt.* to deprive.

privatista *s.* external student.

privativa *sf.* **1.** (*esclusiva*) sole right **2.** (*monopolio*) monopoly **3.** (*tabaccheria*) tobacconist's shop.

privativo *agg.* privative.

privato *agg.* **1.** private **2.** (*privo*) deprived. ♦ **privato** *sm.* private citizen.

privazione *sf.* **1.** (*disagio*) privation **2.** (*perdita*) loss.

privilegiare *vt.* to privilege.

privilegiato *agg.* **1.** privileged **2.** (*comm.*) preferred.

privilegio *sm.* privilege.

privo *agg.* devoid: *— di padre*, fatherless; *— di madre*, motherless.

pro¹ *prep.* for.

pro² *sm. a che —?*, what is the use of?

proavo *sm.* great grandfather.

probàbile *agg.* probable.

probabilismo *sm.* probabilism.

probabilità *sf.* probability.

probante *agg.* probatory.

probativo *agg.* probative.

probità *sf.* uprightness.

probiviri *sm. pl.* arbiters.

problema *sm.* problem.

problematicità *sf.* problematic nature.

problemàtico *agg.* problematic(al).

probo *agg.* upright.

proboscidati *sm. pl.* Proboscidea.

probòscide *sf.* trunk.

procaccia *sm.* postman (*pl.* -men).

procacciare *vt.* to get (*v. irr.*). ♦ **procacciarsi** *vr.* to get.

procacciatore *sm.* procurer.

procace *agg.* **1.** (*provocante*) provoking **2.** (*inverecondo*) immodest.

procacità *sf.* **1.** provocativeness **2.** (*inverecondia*) immodesty.

pro capite *loc. avv.* each.

procèdere *vi.* **1.** to proceed, to go (*v. irr.*) on **2.** (*agire*) to act.

procedimento *sm.* **1.** (*progressione*) course **2.** (*condotta*) behaviour **3.** (*giur.*) proceedings (*pl.*) **4.** (*tec.*) process.

procedura *sf.* **1.** procedure **2.** (*giur.*) practice.

procedurale *agg.* procedural.

procella *sf.* storm.

procellaria *sf.* stormy-petrel.

procelloso *agg.* stormy.

processare *vt.* to try: *far —*, to prosecute.

processionaria *sf.* processioner.

processione *sf.* procession.

processo *sm.* **1.** (*giur.*) trial **2.** (*med.; chim.; tec.*) process ‖ *andare sotto —*, to be tried; *intentare un —*, to bring (*v. irr.*) an action.

processuale *agg.* trial (*attr.*).

procinto (*nella loc. avv.*) *in — di*, on the point of.

proclama *sm.* proclamation.

proclamare *vt.* to proclaim.

proclamatore *sm.* proclaimer.

proclamazione *sf.* proclamation.

proclive *agg.* inclined.

proclività *sf.* inclination.

procònsole *sm.* proconsul.

procrastinare *vt.* to postpone. ♦ **procrastinare** *vi.* to procrastinate.

procrastinazione *sf.* procrastination.

procreare *vt.* to procreate.

procreatore *sm.* procreator.

procreazione *sf.* procreation.

procura *sf.* **1.** proxy: *per —*, by proxy **2.** (*documento*) letter of attorney.

procurare *vt.* **1.** to get (*v. irr.*) **2.** (*causare*) to cause **3.** (*cercare*) to try. ◆ **procurarsi** *vr.* to get (*v. irr.*).

procuratore *sm.* attorney.

prode *agg.* brave.

prodezza *sf.* 1. bravery 2. (*azione*) brave deed.

prodiere *sm.* bowman (*pl.* -men).

prodierò *agg.* forward.

prodigalità *sf.* lavishness.

prodigare *vt.* to lavish. ◆ **prodigarsi** *vr.* to do (*v. irr.*) all one can.

prodigio *sm.* prodigy.

prodigiosità *sf.* prodigiousness.

prodigioso *agg.* prodigious.

pròdigo *agg.* lavish.

proditoriamente *avv.* treacherously.

proditorio *agg.* treacherous.

prodotto *sm.* 1. product 2. (*risultato*) result 3. (*agr.*) produce.

pròdromo *sm.* 1. warning sign 2. (*med.*) symptom.

produrre *vt.* to produce. ◆ **prodursi** *vr.* 1. (*causarsi*) to cause oneself 2. (*accadere*) to happen 3. (*esibirsi*) to perform (before).

produttività *sf.* productivity.

produttivo *agg.* productive.

produttore *agg.* productive. ◆ **produttore** *sm.* producer.

produzione *sf.* production.

proemio *sm.* proem.

profanamente *avv.* profanely.

profanare *vt.* to profane.

profanatore *agg.* profaning. ◆ **profanatore** *sm.* profaner.

profanazione *sf.* profanation.

profanità *sf.* profanity.

profano *agg.* profane. ◆ **profano** *sm.* (*persona inesperta*) layman (*pl.* -men) ‖ *i profani*, the laity.

proferire *vt.* 1. to pronounce 2. (*dire*) to utter.

professare *vt.* to profess.

professionale *agg.* professional: *scuola* —, vocational school.

professione *sf.* profession.

professionismo *sm.* professionalism.

professionista *sm.* 1. professional man 2. (*sport*) professional.

professorale *agg.* professorial.

professore *sm.* 1. teacher 2. (*ordinario di università*) professor.

profeta *sm.* prophet.

profetare *vt.* to prophesy.

profètico *agg.* prophetic(al).

profetizzare *vt.* V. *profetare*.

profezìa *sf.* prophecy.

profferire *vt.* 1. (*offrire*) to offer 2. (*pronunciare*) to utter.

profferta *sf.* offer.

proficuo *agg.* profitable.

profilare *vt.* 1. to profile 2. (*orlare*) to edge. ◆ **profilarsi** *vr.* 1. to be outlined 2. (*apparire*) to loom.

profilassi *sf.* prophylaxis.

profilato *agg.* 1. (*delineato*) outlined 2. (*affilato*) sharp 3. (*orlato*) edged. ◆ **profilato** *sm.* section.

profilàttico *agg.* e *sm.* prophylactic.

profilo *sm.* 1. (*contorno*) outline 2. (*di viso*) profile 3. (*studio letterario*) monograph.

profittare *vi.* 1. (*trar profitto*) to avail oneself (of) 2. (*progredire*) to make (*v. irr.*) progress 3. (*guadagnare*) to make profits.

profittatore *sm.* profiteer.

profittévole *agg.* profitable.

profitto *sm.* profit: *trar* —, to profit (by); *mettere qc. a* —, to make (*v. irr.*) good use of sthg.

profluvio *sm.* flood.

profondamente *avv.* deeply: *dormire* —, to sleep (*v. irr.*) soundly.

profòndere *vt.* to lavish. ◆ **profòndersi** *vr.* to be profuse (in, of).

profondità *sf.* depth.

profondo *agg.* deep. ◆ **profondo** *sm.* depth.

pròfugo *sm.* refugee.

profumare *vt.* to scent. ◆ **profumarsi** *vr.* to spray oneself with scent.

profumatamente *avv.* (*fig.*) dearly.

profumerìa *sf.* perfumery.

profumiere *sm.* perfumer.

profumo *sm.* perfume, scent.

profusamente *avv.* 1. profusely 2. (*lungamente*) at length.

profusione *sf.* profusion.

progenerare *vt.* to procreate.

progenie *sf.* progeny.

progenitore *sm.* ancestor.

progettare *vt.* to plan.

progettazione *sf.* planning.

progettista *s.* planner.

progetto *sm.* plan.

prognatismo *sm.* prognathism.

prognato *agg.* prognathous.

prògnosi *sf.* prognosis (*pl.* -ses).

programma *sm.* program(me).

programmare *vt.* to program(me).

programmatore *sm.* programmist.

programmazione *sf.* programming.

programmista *sm.* programmer.

progredire *vi.* 1. to advance 2. (*fig.*) to get (*v. irr.*) on 3. (*far progressi*) to make (*v. irr.*) progress.

progressione *sf.* progression.

progressista *agg.* e *s.* progressive.

progressivamente *avv.* progressively.

progressivo *agg.* progressive.

progresso *sm.* progress.

proibire *vt.* 1. to forbid (*v. irr.*) 2. (*impedire*) to prevent.

proibitivo *agg.* prohibitive.

proibizione *sf.* prohibition.

proibizionismo *sm.* prohibitionism.

proibizionista *agg.* e *s.* prohibitionist.

proiettare *vt.* 1. to project 2. (*cine*) to show (*v. irr.*) ◆ **proiettare** *vi.* to project. ◆ **proiettarsi** *vr.* to be projected.

proiettile *sm.* shell.

proiettore *sm.* 1. (*riflettore*) searchlight 2. (*cine*) projector.

proiezione *sf.* 1. projection 2. (*cine*) movie show || *macchina da* —, projector; *sala di* —, projection room.

prole *sf.* issue.

proletariato *sm.* proletariat.

proletario *agg.* e *sm.* proletarian.

proliferare *vi.* to proliferate.

proliferazione *sf.* proliferation.

prolifico *agg.* prolific.

prolissità *sf.* prolixity.

prolisso *agg.* prolix.

prologo *sm.* prologue.

prolungàbile *agg.* extendable.

prolungamento *sm.* extension.

prolungare *vt.* 1. to extend 2. (*differire*) to postpone. ◆ **prolungarsi** *vr.* 1. to extend 2. (*dilungarsi*) to dwell (*v. irr.*) (on).

prolusione *sf.* opening lecture.

promemoria *sm.* memorandum (*pl.* -da).

promessa *sf.* promise.

promettente *agg.* promising.

promettere *vt.* to promise: — *bene*, to be full of promise.

prominente *agg.* prominent.

prominenza *sf.* prominence.

promiscuità *sf.* promiscuity.

promiscuo *agg.* mixed, promiscuous.

promontorio *sm.* promontory.

promosso *agg.* 1. (*a scuola*) successful 2. (*sostenuto*) promoted.

promotore *sm.* promoter.

promozione *sf.* promotion.

promulgare *vt.* to promulgate.

promulgatore *sm.* promulgator.

promulgazione *sf.* promulgation.

promuòvere *vt.* 1. to promote 2. (*a scuola*) to pass.

prònao *sm.* pronaos (*pl.* -aoi).

pronipote *sm.* 1. (*di bisnonno*) great-grandson, great-grandchild (*pl.* -children) 2. (*di prozio*) grandnephew || *i pronipoti* (*discendenti*), descendants. ◆ **pronipote** *sf.* 1. (*di bisnonno*) great-granddaughter, great-grandchild 2. (*di prozio*) grandniece.

prono *agg.*· prone.

pronome *sm.* pronoun.

pronominale *agg.* pronominal.

pronosticare *vt.* 1. to forecast (*v. irr.*) 2. (*predire*) to foretell (*v. irr.*) 3. (*far prevedere*) to portend.

pronòstico *sm.* forecast.

prontezza *sf.* readiness.

pronto *agg.* 1. (*preparato*) ready 2. (*veloce*) prompt 3. (*al telefono*) hallo || — *soccorso*, first aid.

prontuario *sm.* handbook.

pronuncia *sf.* pronunciation.

pronunciamento *sm.* pronouncement.

pronunciare *vt.* 1. to pronounce 2. (*proferire*) to utter || — *un discorso*, to deliver a speech. ◆ **pronunciarsi** *vr.* to give (*v. irr.*) one's opinion.

pronunciato *agg.* pronounced.

propaganda *sf.* 1. propaganda 2. (*comm.*) advertising: *far* — (*comm.*), to advertise 3. (*pol.*) canvass.

propagandare *vt.* 1. to propagandize 2. (*comm.*) to advertise.

propagandista *s.* 1. propagandist 2. (*comm.*) advertiser.

propagandìstico *agg.* 1. propagandist 2. (*comm.*) advertising.

propagare *vt.* to propagate. ◆ **propagarsi** *vr.* to propagate.

propagatore *sm.* propagator.

propagazione *sf.* propagation.

propagginare *vt.* (*agr.*) to layer.

propàggine *sf.* 1. (*agr.*) layer 2. (*geogr.*) ramification 3. (*discendenza*) offspring.

propalare *vt.* to spread (*v. irr.*).

propano *sm.* propane.

propedèutica *sf.* propaedeutics.

propedèutico *agg.* propaedeutic(al).

propellente *agg.* propellent. ♦
propellente *sm.* propellant.
propèndere *vi.* to be inclined. ,
propensione *sf.* propensity.
propenso *agg.* inclined.
propilene *sm.* propylene.
propìleo *sm.* propylaeum (*pl.* -laea).
propina *sf.* examiner's fee.
propinare *vt.* to give (*v. irr.*).
propiziare *vt.* to propitiate. ♦
propiziarsi *vr.* to gain so.'s favour.
propiziatore *sm.* propitiator.
propiziatorio *agg.* propitiatory.
propiziazione *sf.* propitiation.
propizio *agg.* favourable.
proponimento *sm.* resolution: *far
—,* to resolve.
proporre *vt.* 1. to propose 2. (*suggerire*) to suggest. ♦ **proporsi** *vr.*
to intend, to mean (*v. irr.*).
proporzionale *agg.* proportional.
proporzionalità *sf.* proportionality.
proporzionare *vt.* to proportion.
proporzionato *agg.* (*adeguato*) proportionate: *ben —,* well-propor-
tioned.
proporzione *sf.* 1. proportion 2.
(*rapporto*) ratio.
propòsito *sm.* 1. purpose 2. (*intenzione*) intention ‖ *di —,* on
purpose; *a — di,* with regard to;
a — (*inter.*), by the way; *a —*
(*al momento giusto*), at the right
moment.
proposizione *sf.* sentence.
proposta *sf.* proposal.
proprietà *sf.* 1. property 2. (*l'essere
proprietario*) ownership 3. (*correttezza*) propriety ‖ *— letteraria,*
copyright.
proprietario *agg.* proprietary. ♦
proprietario *sm.* 1. owner 2.
(*di locanda*) landlord 3. (*possidente*) man of property ‖ *— terriero,*
landowner.
proprio *agg.* 1. (*rafforzativo del
poss.*) own 2. (*adatto*) suitable 3.
(*mat.; gramm.*) proper ‖ *vero e
—,* real. ♦ **proprio** *avv.* 1. (*esattamente*) exactly 2. (*veramente*)
really ‖ *— ora,* just now; *— così,*
just like that.
propugnare *vt.* to support.
propugnatore *sm.* supporter.
propulsione *sf.* propulsion.
propulsivo *agg.* propulsive.
propulsore *sm.* propeller.
prora *sf.* bow.

proravìa (*nella loc. avv.*) *a —,* at
the bow.
pròroga *sf.* 1. (*giur.*) adjournment
2. (*dilazione*) extension.
prorogàbile *agg.* 1. (*giur.*) adjour-
nable 2. extensible.
prorogare *vt.* 1. to delay, to extend
2. (*giur.*) to postpone.
prorompente *agg.* bursting (out).
prorómpere *vi.* 1. to burst-(*v. irr.*)
(out) 2. (*di liquidi*) to gush out.
prosa *sf.* prose ‖ *teatro di —,* drama; *compagnia di —,* dramatic
company.
prosaicità *sf.* prosaism.
prosàico *agg.* prosaic.
prosapia *sf.* race.
prosàstico *agg.* prose (*attr.*).
prosatore *sm.* prose-writer.
proscenio *sm.* proscenium.
proscìmmie *sf. pl.* lemurs.
prosciògliere *vt.* 1. (*da un obbligo*) to release 2. (*giur.*) to acquit.
proscioglimento *sm.* 1. release 2.
(*giur.*) acquittal.
prosciugamento *sm.* 1. drying up
2. (*artificiale*) draining.
prosciugare *vt.* 1. to dry up 2. (*ar-
tificialmente*) to drain. ♦ **prosciugarsi** *vr.* to dry up.
prosciutto *sm.* ham.
proscritto *sm.* exile.
proscrìvere *vt.* to banish.
proscrizione *sf.* banishment.
prosecuzione *sf.* prosecution.
proseguimento *sm.* continuation.
proseguire *vt.* to continue. ♦ **proseguire** *vi.* to go (*v. irr.*) on.
proselitismo *sm.* proselytism.
prosèlito *sm.* proselyte.
prosieguo *sm.* course.
prosodìa *sf.* prosody.
prosopopea *sf.* (*fig.*) haughtiness.
prosperare *vi.* to prosper.
prosperità *sf.* prosperity.
pròspero *agg.* prosperous.
prosperoso *agg.* 1. prosperous 2.
(*in salute*) healthy.
prospettare *vt.* 1. (*indicare*) to
point out 2. (*guardare*) to look
on to.
prospèttico *agg.* perspective (*attr.*).
prospettiva *sf.* 1. perspective 2.
(*possibilità*) prospect.
prospetto *sm.* 1. view 2. (*fronte*)
front 3. (*specchietto, programma*)
prospectus.
prospezione *sf.* prospecting.
prospiciente *agg.* facing.

prossimità sf. closeness: in — di, near.

pròssimo agg. 1. (vicino) near 2. (seguente) next. ♦ **pròssimo** sm. fellow creatures (pl.), neighbour.

pròstata sf. prostate.

prosternare vt. to prostrate.

prostituire vt. to prostitute.

prostituta sf. prostitute.

prostituzione sf. prostitution.

prostrare vt. to prostrate. ♦ **prostrarsi** vr. to bow down.

prostrazione sf. prostration.

protagonista s. protagonist.

protèggere vt. to protect.

protèico agg. protein (attr.).

proteina sf. protein.

protèndere vt. to stretch (out): — lo sguardo, to gaze. ♦ **protèndersi** vr. to stretch oneself.

protervia sf. insolence.

protervo agg. insolent.

pròtesi sf. prosthesis.

protesta sf. protest.

protestante agg. e s. protestant.

protestantésimo sm. Protestantism.

protestare vt. e vi. to protest.

protesto sm. protest: in —, under protest; lasciar andare una cambiale in —, to dishonour a bill.

protettivo agg. protective.

protetto agg. protected. ♦ **protetto** sm. favourite.

protettorato sm. protectorate.

protettore sm. 1. protector 2. (patrono) patron.

protezione sf. 1. protection 2. (patronato) patronage.

protezionismo sm. protectionism.

protezionista s. protectionist.

proto sm. overseer.

protocollare agg. protocol (attr.).

protocollo sm. 1. protocol 2. (registro) record || mettere a —, to record; carta —, foolscap.

protone sm. proton.

protoplasma sm. protoplasm.

protòtipo sm. prototype.

protozoi sm. pl. Protozoa.

protrarre vt. 1. to protract 2. (differire) to defer. ♦ **protrarsi** vr. to go (v. irr.) on.

protrazione sf. 1. protraction 2. (differimento) deferment.

protuberanza sf. bulge.

prova sf. 1. proof 2. (giur.) evidence (solo sing.) 3. (esperimento, esame) test 4. (tentativo) try 5. (sventura) trial 6. (teat.) rehearsal 7. (di abito) fitting || in —, on trial; dar — di essere, to prove to be; superare una —, to pass a test.

provare vt. 1. to prove 2. (tentare, mettere alla prova) to try 3. (sentire) to feel (v. irr.) 4. (di abiti) to try on 5. (teat.) to rehearse 6. (collaudare) to test. ♦ **provarsi** vr. 1. (tentare) to try 2. (cimentarsi) to engage (in).

provenienza sf. origin.

provenire vi. to come (v. irr.).

provento sm. 1. proceeds (pl.) 2. (reddito) income.

proverbiale agg. proverbial.

proverbio sm. proverb.

provetta sf. test-tube.

provetto agg. skilled.

provincia sf. province.

provinciale agg. e s. provincial: strada —, main road.

provincialismo sm. provincialism.

provino sm. 1. (teat.) tryout 2. (cine) test film.

provocante agg. 1. provocative 2. (procace) immodest.

provocare vt. 1. to provoke 2. (causare) to cause.

provocatore sm. provoker.

provocazione sf. provocation.

provvedere vi. 1. to provide (for) 2. (badare a) to see (v. irr.) (to) 3. (aver cura di) to take (v. irr.) care of. ♦ **provvedere** vt. 1. to provide 2. (preparare) to prepare.

provvedimento sm. measure.

provveduto agg. 1. provided (with) 2. (accorto) wary.

provvidenza sf. providence: essere una —, to be providential.

provvidenziale agg. providential.

pròvvido agg. provident.

provvigione sf. 1. (comm.) commission 2. (provvista) supply.

provvisorietà sf. temporariness.

provvisorio agg. temporary: in via provvisoria, temporarily.

provvista sf. supply, provision (specialmente di cibo).

provvisto agg. 1. supplied (with) 2. (fig.) well-off.

prua sf. bow.

prudente agg. 1. prudent 2. (cauto) careful.

prudenza sf. 1. prudence 2. (cautela) care 3. (precauzione) precaution.

prùdere *vi.* to itch.

prugna *sf.* plum.

prugno *sm.* plum-tree.

pruno *sm.* 1. thorn-bush 2. (*spina*) thorn.

pruriginoso *agg.* itching

prurito *sm.* itch.

prùssico *agg.* prussic.

pseudònimo *sm.* pseudonym.

psicanàlisi *sf.* psychoanalysis.

psicanalista *s.* psychoanalyst.

psicanalìtico *agg.* psychoanalytic(al).

psicanalizzare *vt.* to psychoanalyze.

psiche *sf.* psyche.

psichiatra *s.* psychiatrist.

psichiatrìa *sf.* psychiatry.

psichiàtrico *agg.* psychiatric(al).

psìchico *agg.* psychic(al).

psicologìa *sf.* psychology.

psicològico *agg.* psychologic(al).

psicòlogo *sm.* psychologist.

psicometrìa *sf.* psychometry.

psicopatìa *sf.* psychopathy.

psicopàtico *agg.* e *sm.* psychopathic.

psicopatologìa *sf.* psychopathology.

psicòsi *sf.* psychosis (*pl.* -ses).

psicoterapìa *sf.* psychotherapy.

psittacòsi *sf.* psittacosis.

pubblicàbile *agg.* publishable.

pubblicano *sm.* publican.

pubblicare *vt.* 1. to publish 2. (*di leggi ecc.*) to issue.

pubblicazione *sf.* publication: *fare le pubblicazioni di matrimonio*, to put up the banns.

pubblicista *s.* journalist.

pubblicità *sf.* 1. publicity 2. (*propaganda*) advertising || *fare —*, to advertise.

pubblicitario *agg.* advertising.

pùbblico *agg.* public. ♦ pùbblico *sm.* 1. public 2. (*in teatro ecc.*) audience 3. (*cine*) moviegoers (*pl.*).

pube *sm.* pubis (*pl.* -bes).

pubertà *sf.* puberty.

pudibondo *agg.* demure.

pudicizia *sf.* demureness.

pudico *agg.* demure.

pudore *sm.* decency.

puericoltura *sf.* puericulture.

puerile *agg.* childish.

puerilità *sf.* childishness.

puèrpera *sf.* childwife (*pl.* -wives).

pugilato *sm.* boxing: *fare del —*, to box

pùgile *sm.* boxer.

pugnalare *vt.* to stab.

pugnalata *sf.* 1. stab 2. (*fig.*) blow.

pugnale *sm.* dagger.

pugno *sm.* 1. fist 2. (*colpo*) punch 3. (*manciata*) handful || *colpire col —*, to punch; *in —*, in one's hand; *di proprio —*, in one's own handwriting; *fare a pugni*, to fight (*v. irr.*), (*fig.*) to clash.

pula *sf.* chaff.

pulce *sf.* flea: *— in un orecchio*, suspicion.

pulcino *sm.* chick.

puledro *sm.* colt.

puleggia *sf.* pulley.

pulire *vt.* to clean: *pulirsi la bocca*, to wipe one's mouth.

pulito *agg.* clean.

pulitore *sm.* cleaner.

pulizìa *sf.* 1. (*il pulire*) cleaning 2. (*l'essere pulito*) cleanliness.

pullulare *vi.* to swarm (with).

pùlpito *sm.* pulpit.

pulsante *sm.* push button.

pulsare *vi.* to beat (*v. irr.*)

pulsazione *sf.* beat.

pulverulento *agg.* dusty.

pulvìscolo *sm.* dust: *— atmosferico*, motes (*pl.*).

puma *sm.* puma.

pungente *agg.* 1. prickly 2. (*fig.*) biting.

pùngere *vt.* 1. to sting (*v. irr.*) 2. (*di ago*) to prick 3. (*fig.*) to tease. ♦ pùngersi *vr.* to prick oneself.

pungiglione *sm.* sting.

pungitopo *sm.* (*bot.*) butcher's broom.

pungolare *vt.* to goad.

pùngolo *sm.* goad.

punìbile *agg.* punishable.

punire *vt.* to punish: *— una offesa*, to revenge an insult.

punitivo *agg.* punitive.

punitore *agg.* punitory. ♦ punitore *sm.* punisher.

punizione *sf.* punishment.

punta *sf.* 1. point 2. (*estremità*) tip 3. (*cima*) top 4. (*un po'*) bit 5. (*dolore, fitta*) twinge || *sulla — dei piedi*, on tiptoe; *avere qc. sulla — delle dita*, to have sthg. at one's finger-tips.

puntale *sm.* (*di bastone ecc.*) ferrule.

puntamento *sm.* aim.

puntare *vt.* 1. to point (at) 2. (*mirare*) to aim (at) 3. (*spingere*) to push 4. (*scommettere*) to bet (*v. irr.*) || — *i piedi* (*fig.*), to put (*v. irr.*) one's foot down. ♦ **puntare** *vi.* to head.

puntata *sf.* 1. (*al gioco*) stake 2. (*di romanzo*) instalment.

puntatore *sm.* 1. (*mil.*) marksman (*pl.* -men) 2. (*al gioco*) better.

punteggiare *vt.* 1. to punctuate 2. (*nel disegno*) to dot.

punteggiatura *sf.* 1. punctuation 2. (*nel disegno*) dotting.

punteggio *sm.* (*sport*) score.

puntellare *vt.* to prop.

puntellatura *sf.* propping.

puntello *sm.* prop.

punteruolo *sm.* punch.

puntiglio *sm.* 1. punctilio 2. (*ostinazione*) obstinacy || *per* —, out of pique.

puntigliosamente *avv.* 1. punctiliously 2. (*ostinatamente*) obstinately.

puntiglioso *agg.* 1. punctilious 2. (*ostinato*) obstinate.

puntina *sf.* 1. (*da fonografo*) needle 2. (*da disegno*) drawing-pin.

puntino *sm.* dot: *puntini di sospensione*, dots || *a* —, properly.

punto¹ *sm.* 1. point 2. (*di cucito*) stitch 3. (*voto*) mark 4. (*gramm.*) full stop 5. (*macchiolina*) dot || *due punti*, colon; — *e virgola*, semicolon; *mettere a* —, to set (*v. irr.*) up.

punto² *avv.* not at all.

punto³ *agg. e pron.* not ... any.

puntone *sm.* (*edil.*) strut.

puntuale *agg.* punctual.

puntualità *sf.* punctuality.

puntualizzare *vt.* to stress.

puntualmente *avv.* punctually.

puntura *sf.* 1. (*di insetto*) sting 2. (*di ago*) prick 3. (*iniezione*) injection 4. (*dolore, fitta*) pain.

puntuto *agg.* pointed.

punzecchiamento *sm.* 1. (*d'insetto*) stinging 2. (*d'ago*) pricking 3. (*fig.*) teasing.

punzecchiare *vt.* 1. (*di insetti*) to sting (*v. irr.*) 2. (*fig.*) to tease.

punzonare *vt.* to punch.

punzonatrice *sf.* (*mecc.*) punch.

punzonatura *sf.* punching.

punzone *sm.* punch.

pupàttola *sf.* doll.

pupazzetto *sm.* (*disegno*) sketch.

pupazzo *sm.* puppet.

pupilla *sf.* pupil.

pupillo *sm.* pupil.

pupo *sm.* baby.

purché *cong.* provided (that).

pure *avv.* 1. (*anche*) also, too 2. (*eppure*) yet 3. (*di concessione*) as you like, of course. ♦ **pure** *cong.* 1. (*con frasi concessive*) even though 2. (*tuttavia*) but, yet. ♦ **pure di** *cong.* if only.

purè *sm.* purée: — *di patate*, mashed potatoes; *fare un* — *di verdura*, to mash vegetables.

purezza *sf.* purity.

purga *sf.* purgative, purge.

purgante *sm.* purgative, purge.

purgare *vt.* 1. to purge 2. (*di scritti*) to expurgate.

purgativo *agg.* purgative.

purgatorio *sm.* purgatory.

purificare *vt.* to purify.

purificatore *agg.* purificatory.

purificazione *sf.* purification.

purismo *sm.* purism.

purista *s.* purist.

puritanésimo *sm.* Puritanism.

puritano *agg. e sm.* Puritan.

puro *agg.* 1. pure 2. (*mero*) mere.

purosangue *sm.* thoroughbred.

purpùreo *agg.* purple.

purpurina *sf.* purpurin.

purtroppo *avv.* unfortunately.

purulento *agg.* purulent.

pus *sm.* pus.

pusillànime *agg.* pusillanimous. ♦ **pusillànime** *s.* coward.

pusillanimità *sf.* pusillanimity.

pùstola *sf.* pustule.

putacaso *loc. avv.* supposing.

putativo *agg.* putative.

putiferio *sm.* uproar: *sollevare un* —, to make (*v. irr.*) an uproar.

putrèdine *sf.* 1. putridness 2. (*cosa putrefatta*) rot.

putrefare *vi.* to rot. ♦ **putrefarsi** *vr.* to rot.

putrefatto *agg.* rotten.

putrefazione *sf.* putrefaction.

putrella *sf.* iron beam.

putrescenza *sf.* putrescence.

putrescìbile *agg.* putrescible.

putridità *sf.* rottenness.

pùtrido *agg.* rotten.

putridume *sm.* rot.

putto *sm.* putto (*pl.* -ti).

puzza *sf.* V. *puzzo*.

puzzare *vi.* to stink (*v. irr.*).

puzzo *smi.* stench.

pùzzola *sf.* polecat.

puzzolente *agg.* stinking.

Q

qua *avv.* here: *di — di*, on this side of; *per di —*, this way; *da quando in —?*, since when?

quàcchero *agg.* e *sm.* Quaker.

quaderno *sm.* exercise-book.

quadrangolare *agg.* quadrangular.

quadràngolo *sm.* quadrangle.

quadrante *sm.* 1. quadrant 2. (*di orologio*) dial.

quadrare *vt.* 1. (*geom.*) to square 2. (*formare*) to shape. ♦ **quadrare** *vi.* (*corrispondere*) to suit.

quadrato *agg.* 1. square 2. (*fig.*) strong. ♦ **quadrato** *sm.* 1. square 2. (*sport*) ring.

quadratura *sf.* 1. squaring 2. (*mat.*) quadrature.

quadrettato *agg.* 1. squared 2. (*di tessuto*) chequered.

quadriennale *agg.* quadrennial.

quadriennio *sm.* quadrennium (*pl.* -ia).

quadrifoglio *sm.* four-leaved clover.

quadriglia *sf.* quadrille.

quadrilàtero *sm.* quadrilateral.

quadrimotore *sm.* four-engined aircraft.

quadrivio *sm.* cross-roads.

quadro *agg.* V. *quadrato*. ♦ **quadro** *sm.* 1. picture 2. (*tabella*) table 3. (*teat.*) scene 4. (*elettr.*) board 5. (*mil.*) cadre || *galleria di quadri*, picture-gallery; — *riassuntivo*, summary; — *degli interruttori*, switch board.

quadrùmane *agg.* quadrumanous. ♦ **quadrùmane** *sm.* quadrumane.

quadrùpede *agg.* e *sm.* quadruped.

quadruplicare *vt.* to quadruple. ♦ **quadruplicarsi** *vr.* to quadruple.

quàdruplo *agg.* e *sm.* 1. quadruple 2. (*quattro volte tanto*) four times as much.

quaggiù *avv.* down here.

quaglia *sf.* quail.

qualche *agg.* (*in frasi affermative e interrogative che aspettano risposta affermativa*) some; (*in frasi interrogative, dubitative, condizionali*) any || — *volta*, sometimes; in — *luogo*, somewhere; in — *modo*, somehow.

qualcosa *pron.* something, anything (*per l'uso* V. *qualche*).

qualcuno *pron.* 1. somebody, someone 2. (*alcuni*) some, any: — *di*, some, any of (*per l'uso* V. *qualche*).

quale *pron. rel.* 1. (*per persone*) who (*sogg.*), whom (*altri casi*) 2. (*per animali, cose*) which 3. (*per tutti, solo sogg. e ogg.*) that || *del* — (*poss.*), whose: *l'uomo la casa del* —, the man whose house. ♦ **quale** *agg.* e *pron. int.* 1. (*di che tipo*) what 2. (*scelta tra numero limitato*) which. ♦ **quale** *agg. escl.* what. ♦ **quale** *pron.* (*correlativo di "tale"*) as || *è tale e* — *suo fratello*, he is just like his brother.

qualifica *sf.* 1. qualification 2. (*titolo*) title.

qualificare *vt.* to qualify.

qualificativo *agg.* qualifying.

qualificato *agg.* qualified: *operaio* —, skilled worker.

qualificazione *sf.* qualification.

qualità *sf.* 1. quality 2. (*specie*) kind 3. (*ufficio*) capacity.

qualitativo *agg.* qualitative.

qualora *cong.* in case.

qualsìasi *agg.* V. *qualunque*.

qualunque *agg.* 1. any 2. (*quale che sia*) whatever; (*riferito a numero limitato*) whichever 3. (*comune*) ordinary || *uno* —, anybody; — *cosa*, anything; in — *posto*, anywhere; in — *modo*, anyhow.

quando *avv.* e *cong.* when || *da* —, since; *da* —?, since when?; *quand'anche*, even though; *di* — *in* —, now and then.

quantità *sf.* quantity: *una gran* — *di*, a great deal of.

quantitativo *agg.* quantitative. ♦ **quantitativo** *sm.* V. *quantità*.

quanto *agg.* how much (*pl.* how many) || *tanto...* —, as much... as; *tanti... quanti*, as many... as; — *tempo?* how long? ♦ **quanto** *avv.* how, how much || *tanto* —, as much as; *tanto...* —, as... as; *tanto...* — (*sia... sia*), both ...and; — *più... tanto più*, the more... the more; — *più... tanto meno*, the more... the less; — *a*, as for; — *prima*, soon; *per* —, however; *fa?*, how much is it?

quantunque *cong.* though, although.

quaranta *agg.* forty.

quarantena *sf.* quarantine.

quarantenne *agg.* forty years old, forty-year-old (*attr.*).

quarantèsimo *agg.* fortieth.

quarantina *sf.* about forty: *aver*

passato la —, to be over forty.
quarésima *sf.* Lent.
quartetto *sm.* quartet.
quartiere *sm.* 1. (*di una città*) quarter 2. (*rione amministrativo*) district || — *generale*, headquarters (*pl.*).
quartina *sf.* quatrain.
quarto *agg.* fourth. ♦ **quarto** *sm.* quarter.
quarzo *sm.* quartz.
quasi *avv.* almost: — *mai*, hardly ever.
quassù *avv.* up here.
quaterna *sf.* set of four numbers.
quaternario *agg.* quaternary. ♦ **quaternario** *sm.* (*verso di una poesia*) line of four syllables.
quatto *agg.* 1. squatting 2. (*silenzioso*) silent || — —, very quietly.
quattordicèsimo *agg.* fourteenth.
quattòrdici *agg.* fourteen.
quattrini *sm. pl.* money (*us. al sing.*): *star male a* —, to be hard up.
quattro *agg.* four || *in* — *e* — *otto*, in no time; *fare il diavolo a* —, to make (*v. irr.*) a hullabaloo; *farsi in* —, to do (*v. irr.*) one's utmost.
quattrocchi (*nella loc. avv.*) *a* —, privately.
quattrocento *agg.* four hundred. ♦ **quattrocento** *sm. il* —, the fifteenth century.
quattromila *agg.* four thousand.
quegli *agg.* V. *quelli*. ♦ **quegli** *pron.* V. *egli*.
quei *agg.* e *pron.* V. *quelli*.
quella *agg.* e *pron.* V. *quello*.
quelle *agg.* e *pron.* V. *quelli*.
quelli *agg.* those. ♦ **quelli** *pron.* those, the ones.
quello *agg.* that. ♦ **quello** *pron.* that, the one || — *che* (*ciò che*), what; *tutto* — *che*, all that.
quercia *sf.* oak.
querela *sf.* 1. complaint 2. (*giur.*) action; *sporger* —, to bring (*v. irr.*) an action.
querelante *s.* plaintiff.
querelare *vt.* to proceed (against).
querelato *sm.* defendant.
quèrulo *agg.* querulous.
quesito *sm.* question.
questa *agg.* e *pron.* V. *questo*.
queste *agg.* e *pron.* V. *questi*.
questi *agg.* these. ♦ **questi** *pron.* 1. these 2. (*sing.*) this (man).

questionare *vi.* to quarrel.
questionario *sm.* questionnaire.
questione *sf.* 1. question 2. (*lite*) quarrel.
questo *agg.* this. ♦ **questo** *pron.* this, that || — ...*quello* (*il primo*... *il secondo*) the former... the latter.
questore *sm.* questor.
questua *sf.* 1. begging 2. (*in chiesa*) collection.
questuante *agg.* begging. ♦ **questuante** *s.* beggar.
questuare *vi.* to beg.
questura *sf.* police-headquarters (*pl.*).
questurino *sm.* cop.
qui *avv.* here: *per di* —, this way; — *vicino*, close by; *da* — *innanzi*, from now on; *di* — *a un anno*, a year from now; *di* — *a otto giorni*, a week today; *fin* — (*di tempo*), so far.
quiescenza *sf.* quiescence.
quietanza *sf.* receipt.
quietare *vt.* to quiet. ♦ **quietarsi** *vr.* to quiet down.
quiete *sf.* quiet.
quietismo *sm.* quietism.
quieto *agg.* quiet || *star* — (*zitto*), to keep (*v. irr.*) quiet; *star* — (*fermo*), to keep (*v. irr.*) still; — —, very quietly.
quindi *avv.* 1. therefore 2. (*poi*) then.
quindicenne *agg.* fifteen years old, fifteen-year-old (*attr.*).
quindicèsimo *agg.* fifteenth.
quìndici *agg.* fifteen.
quindicina *sf.* 1. about fifteen 2. (*salario*) a fortnight's wages || *una* — *di giorni*, about a fortnight.
quindicinale *agg.* fortnightly.
quinquennale *agg.* quinquennial.
quinta *sf.* (*teat.*) wing || *dietro le quinte*, behind the scenes.
quintale *sm.* quintal.
quinterno *sm.* five sheets (*pl.*).
quintessenza *sf.* quintessence.
quintetto *sm.* quintet(te).
quinto *agg.* fifth.
quintuplicare *vt.* to quintuple.
quìntuplo *agg.* e *sm.* quintuple.
quisquilia *sf.* trifle.
quivi *avv.* here.
quota *sf.* 1. share 2. (*aer.*) altitude 3. (*mar.*) depth || *perdere* —, to lose (*v. irr.*) height; *prender* —, to climb.

quotare vt. to quote. ♦ **quotarsi** vr. to subscribe.

quotato agg. 1. quoted 2. (fig.) esteemed.

quotazione sf. quotation.

quotidianamente avv. daily.

quotidiano agg. e sm. daily: vita quotidiana, everyday life.

quoziente sm. quotient.

R

rabàrbaro sm. rhubarb.

rabberciamento sm. patching (up).

rabberciare vt. to patch (up).

rabbia sf. 1. rage 2. (idrofobia) rabies || far — a qu., to make (v. irr.) so. angry.

rabbino sm. rabbi.

rabbioso agg. 1. (med.) rabid 2. (fig.) angry.

rabbonire vt. to calm down.

rabbrividire vi. 1. (di freddo) to shiver 2. (di paura ecc.) to shudder.

rabbuffare vt. 1. to ruffle 2. (rimproverare) to reprimand.

rabbuffo sm. rebuke.

rabbuiarsi vr. to darken.

rabdomante s. dowser.

rabdomanzia sf. dowsing.

rabesco sm. V. arabesco.

raccapezzare vt. 1. (raccogliere) to gather 2. (capire) to understand (v. irr.) ♦ **raccapezzarsi** vr. to see (v. irr.) one's way.

raccapricciante agg. horrifying.

raccapricciare vt. to horrify. ♦ **raccapricciarsi** vr. to be horrified.

raccapriccio sm. horror.

raccattare vt. to pick up.

racchetta sf. racket.

racchio agg. ugly.

racchiudere vt. to contain.

raccògliere vt. 1. to pick (up) 2. (radunare) to gather 3. (far collezione) to collect 4. (accogliere) to shelter 5. (agr.) to reap. ♦ **raccògliersi** vr. 1. to gather 2. (concentrarsi) to collect one's thoughts.

raccoglimento sm. 1. concentration 2. (meditazione) meditation.

raccogliticcio agg. picked up at random.

raccoglitore sm. 1. picker 2. (collezionista) collector 3. (cartella) folder.

raccolta sf. 1. (agr.) harvest; (di frutta, cotone) picking 2. (collezione) collection 3. (adunanza) gathering || fare la —, to harvest; chiamare a —, to collect.

raccoltamente avv. intently

raccolto sm. harvest.

raccomandàbile agg. recommendable.

raccomandare vt. 1. to recommend 2. (esortare) to urge 3. (di lettere, pacchi) to register. ♦ **raccomandarsi** vr. to beg (so.).

raccomandata sf. registered letter: fare una —, to register a letter.

raccomandazione sf. 1. recommendation 2. (consiglio) advice 3. (di lettere, pacchi) registration.

raccomodare vt. to mend.

raccontare vt. to tell (v. irr.) || si racconta, it is said.

racconto sm. 1. tale 2. (resoconto) relation.

raccorciare vt. to shorten. ♦ **raccorciarsi** vr. to grow (v. irr.) shorter.

raccordare vt. to connect.

raccordo sm. 1. connection 2. (mecc.) union 3. (ferr.) siding.

ràchide sf. rachis (pl. -ides).

rachitico agg. rickety.

rachitismo sm. rickets.

racimolare vt. to glean.

rada sf. roadstead.

radar sm. radar.

raddobbare vt. 1. (mar.) to repair 2. (riparare) to refit.

raddobbo sm. (mar.) repair.

raddolcimento sm. 1. sweetening 2. (fig.) softening.

raddolcire vt. 1. to sweeten 2. (fig.) to soften 3. (alleviare) to soothe. ♦ **raddolcirsi** vr. 1. to soften 2. (alleviarsi) to be soothed 3. (mitigarsi) to grow (v. irr.) milder.

raddoppiamento sm. doubling.

raddoppiare vt. to double. ♦ **raddoppiarsi** vr. to double.

raddoppio sm. doubling.

raddrizzamento sm. 1. straightening 2. (correzione) redressing.

raddrizzare vt. 1. to straighten 2. (correggere) to redress.

radente agg. 1. shaving 2. (rasente) grazing.

ràdere *vt*. 1. to shave 2. (*sfiorare*) to graze 3. (*distruggere*) to raze.

radezza *sf*. 1. thinness 2. (*rarità*) infrequency.

radiale *agg*. radial.

radiante *agg*. radiant.

radiare *vt*. 1. to radiate 2. (*espellere*) to expel 3. (*un nome*) to strike (*v. irr.*) off.

radiatore *sm*. radiator.

radiazione *sf*. 1. radiation 2. (*espulsione*) expulsion.

radicale *agg*. radical,

radicalismo *sm*. radicalism.

radicare *vi*. to root. ♦ **radicarsi** *vr*. to root.

radicato *agg*. deep-rooted.

radice *sf*. root.

radio[1] *sm*. (*anat.*) radius (*pl.* -dii).

radio[2] *sm*. (*chim.*) radium.

radio[3] *sf*. radio, wireless: *ponte* —, radiolink; *alla* —, on the radio; — *portatile ricevente e trasmittente*, walkie-talkie.

radioattività *sf*. radioactivity.

radioattivo *agg*. radioactive.

radioaudizione *sf*. 1. broadcasting 2. (*ascolto*) listening.

radiocomunicazione *sf*. wireless communication.

radiocrònaca *sf*. running commentary, radio account.

radiocronista *s*. radio commentator, wireless commentator.

radiodiffusione *sf*. broadcast.

radioestesìa *sf*. sensitivity to radiation.

radiofaro *sm*. radio beacon.

radiogoniòmetro *sm*. radio compass.

radiografare *vt*. to radiograph.

radiografìa *sf*. 1. radiograph 2. (*scienza*) radiography.

radiogramma *sm*. radiogram.

radiogrammòfono *sm*. radio-gramophone.

radiologìa *sf*. radiology.

radiòlogo *sm*. radiologist.

radioscopìa *sf*. radioscopy.

radioscòpico *agg*. radioscopic.

radiosità *sf*. radiance.

radioso *agg*. bright.

radiotècnica *sf*. radioengineering.

radiotècnico *sm*. radioengineer.

radiotelefonìa *sf*. radiotelephony.

radiotelèfono *sm*. radiotelephone.

radiotelegrafìa *sf*. radiotelegraphy.

radiotelegràfico *agg*. radiotele-graphic, wireless (*attr.*).

radiotelegrafista *s*. telegraphist.

radiotelevisione *sf*. radio and television.

radioterapìa *sf*. radiotherapy.

radiotrasméttere *vt*. to broadcast (*v. irr.*).

rado *agg*. 1. thin 2. (*non frequente*) infrequent || *di* —, seldom.

radunare *vt*. to gather. ♦ **radunarsi** *vr*. to gather.

raduno *sm*. gathering.

radura *sf*. glade.

raffazzonare *vt*. to patch up.

raffermo *agg*. stale.

ràffica *sf*. 1. gust 2. (*di arma*) burst 3. (*fig.*) hail.

raffigurare *vt*. to represent. ♦ **raffigurarsi** *vr*. (*immaginare*) to imagine.

raffinamento *sm*. 1. refining 2. (*fig.*) refinement.

raffinare *vt*. to refine. ♦ **raffinarsi** *vr*. to become (*v. irr.*) refined, to refine.

raffinatamente *avv*. refinedly.

raffinatezza *sf*. refinement.

raffinato *agg*. refined (*anche fig.*).

raffinazione *sf*. refining.

raffinerìa *sf*. refinery.

raffio *sm*. grapnel.

rafforzamento *sm*. strengthening.

rafforzare *vt*. to strengthen. ♦ **rafforzarsi** *vr*. to grow (*v. irr.*) stronger.

raffreddamento *sm*. 1. cooling 2. (*fig.*) coolness.

raffreddare *vt*. 1. to cool 2. (*fig.*) to lessen. ♦ **raffreddarsi** *vr*. 1. to cool 2. (*fig.*) to wane 3. (*prendere un raffreddore*) to catch (*v. irr.*) a cold.

raffreddato *agg*. essere —, to have a cold.

raffreddatore *sm*. cooler.

raffreddore *sm*. cold.

raffrenare *vt*. to restrain.

raffrontare *vt*. to compare.

raffronto *sm*. comparison.

rafia *sf*. raffia.

ràgadi *sf. pl.* rhagades.

raganella *sf*. 1. tree-frog 2. (*strumento*) rattle.

ragazza *sf*. girl.

ragazzaglia *sf*. crowd of youngsters.

ragazzata *sf*. escapade.

ragazzo *sm*. boy: *da* —, as a boy.

raggelare *vt*. to freeze (*v. irr.*). ♦ **raggelarsi** *vr*. to freeze.

raggiante *agg*. radiant (with).

raggiare *vi.* **1.** to shine (*v. irr.*) (with sthg.) **2.** (*fig.*) to beam (with sthg.). ♦ **raggiare** *vt.* to radiate.

raggiera *sf.* halo of rays: *a* —, radially.

raggio *sm.* **1.** ray **2.** (*geom.*) radius **3.** (*d'azione*) range **4.** (*di ruota*) spoke || — *di sole*, sunbeam.

raggirare *vt.* to cheat.

raggiro *sm.* cheat.

raggiùngere *vt.* to reach.

raggiungimento *sm.* reaching.

raggiustare *vt.* **1.** to repair **2.** (*riordinare*) to rearrange.

raggomitolare *vt.* to roll up. ♦ **raggomitolarsi** *vr.* to roll oneself up.

raggranellare *vt.* to scrape together.

raggrinzire *vt.* to wrinkle. ♦ **raggrinzirsi** *vr.* to wrinkle, to become (*v. irr.*) wrinkled.

raggrumare *vt.* to clot. ♦ **raggrumarsi** *vr.* to clot.

raggruppamento *sm.* **1.** grouping **2.** (*gruppo*) group.

raggruppare *vt.* to group. ♦ **raggrupparsi** *vr.* to gather.

ragguagliare *vt.* **1.** (*livellare*) to level **2.** (*informare*) to inform **3.** (*paragonare*) to compare **4.** (*comm.*) to balance.

ragguaglio *sm.* **1.** (*informazione*) information (*solo sing.*) **2.** (*paragone*) comparison **3.** (*comm.*) balance.

ragguardévole *agg.* considerable.

ragia *sf.* resin: *acqua* —, turpentine.

ragionamento *sm.* reasoning.

ragionare *vi.* **1.** to reason (about) **2.** (*discutere*) to discuss (sthg.).

ragionatore *sm.* reasoner.

ragione *sf.* **1.** reason **2.** (*diritto*) right **2.** (*rapporto*) rate || *la — per cui*, the reason why; *a — veduta*, after due consideration; *aver* —, to be right; *a maggior* —, all the more reason; *aver — di qu.*, to get (*v. irr.*) the better of so.; — *sociale* (*comm.*), style.

ragionerìa *sf.* bookkeeping.

ragionévole *agg.* **1.** reasonable **2.** (*di buon senso*) sensible.

ragionevolezza *sf.* reasonableness.

ragioniere *sm.* bookkeeper.

ragliare *vi.* to bray.

raglio *sm.* bray.

ragnatela *sf.* cobweb.

ragno *sm.* spider.

ragù *sm.* ragout.

raion *sm.* rayon.

rallegramenti *sm. pl.* congratulations.

rallegrare *vt.* to cheer (up). ♦ **rallegrarsi** *vr.* **1.** to rejoice (at) **2.** (*congratularsi*) to congratulate (so. on sthg.).

rallentamento *sm.* slowing down.

rallentare *vt.* to slacken. ♦ **rallentare** *vi.* **1.** to slacken **2.** (*di velocità*) to slow down. ♦ **rallentarsi** *vr.* to get (*v. irr.*) slack.

rallentatore *sm.* (*cine*) slow motion.

ramaiolo *sm.* ladle.

ramanzina *sf.* scolding.

ramare *vt.* to copper.

ramarro *sm.* green lizard.

ramazza *sf.* broom.

rame *sm.* copper.

ramìfero *agg.* copper-bearing (*attr.*).

ramificare *vi.* to ramify. ♦ **ramificarsi** *vr.* to ramify.

ramificazione *sf.* ramification.

ramingo *agg.* roving.

rammagliare *vt.* to mend a run.

rammaricare *vt.* to afflict. ♦ **rammaricarsi** *vr.* **1.** to be sorry **2.** (*lamentarsi*) to complain (of).

rammàrico *sm.* sorrow.

rammendare *vt.* to darn.

rammendatrice *sf.* darner.

rammendo *sm.* **1.** darning **2.** (*parte rammendata*) darn.

rammentare *vt.* to remember: — *qc. a qu.*, to remind so. of sthg. ♦ **rammentarsi** *vr.* to remember.

rammollimento *sm.* softening.

rammollire *vt.* to soften. ♦ **rammollirsi** *vr.* to soften, to go (*v. irr.*) soft.

rammollito *agg.* soft: *un vecchio* —, a dotard. ♦ **rammollito** *sm.* imbecile.

ramo *sm.* branch.

ramoscello *sm.* twig.

ramoso *agg.* branched.

rampa *sf.* **1.** ramp **2.** (*di scale*) flight.

rampante *agg.* rampant.

rampicante *agg.* climbing: *pianta* —, creeper.

rampino *sm.* hook.

rampogna *sf.* reproach.

rampollare *vi.* to spring (*v. irr.*).

rampollo *sm.* **1.** (*d'acqua*) spring **2.** (*di albero*) shoot **3.** (*discendente*) offspring.

rampone *sm.* **1.** (*mar.*) harpoon **2.** (*da montagna*) crampon.

rana *sf.* frog: *uomo* —, frogman (*pl.* -men); *nuotare a* —, to swim (*v. irr.*) the breast stroke.

ràncido *agg.* **1.** rancid **2.** (*fig.*) trite ‖ *sapere di* —, to have a rancid taste.

rancio *sm.* (*mil.*) mess.

rancore *sm.* grudge.

randagio *agg.* stray.

randellare *vt.* to cudgel.

randellata *sf.* blow with a cudgel.

randello *sm.* cudgel.

ranetta *sf.* rennet.

rango *sm.* rank.

rannicchiarsi *vr.* to crouch.

rannuvolamento *sm.* clouding over.

rannuvolare *vi.* to become (*v. irr.*) cloudy, to cloud over. ♦ **rannuvolarsi** *vr.* to get (*v. irr.*) cloudy.

ranocchio *sm.* frog.

rantolare *vi.* **1.** to wheeze **2.** (*in punto di morte*) to have the death-rattle.

ràntolo *sm.* **1.** wheeze **2.** (*di morte*) death-rattle.

ranùncolo *sm.* buttercup.

rapa *sf.* turnip.

rapace *agg.* greedy. ♦ **rapace** *sm.* bird of prey.

rapacità *sf.* greed.

rapare *vt.* to crop (so.'s hair).

rapato *agg.* shorn.

ràpida *sf.* rapid.

rapidità *sf.* swiftness.

ràpido *agg.* swift. ♦ **ràpido** *sm.* express (train).

rapimento *sm.* **1.** kidnapping **2.** (*di donna*) abduction **3.** (*fig.*) rapture.

rapina *sf.* robbery.

rapinare *vt.* to rob.

rapinatore *sm.* robber.

rapire *vt.* **1.** to kidnap **2.** (*una donna*) to abduct **3.** (*fig.*) to ravish.

rapitore *sm.* **1.** kidnapper **2.** (*di donna*) abductor.

rappacificare *vt.* to reconcile. ♦ **rappacificarsi** *vr.* to become (*v. irr.*) reconciled.

rappacificazione *sf.* reconciliation.

rappezzare *vt.* to patch.

rappezzatura *sf.* **1.** patching **2.** (*parte rappezzata*) patch.

rapporto *sm.* **1.** relation **2.** (*relazione*) report **3.** (*mat.*) ratio ‖ *chiamare a* —, to summon; *andare a*

— *da*, to report to; *essere in buoni rapporti*, to be on good terms; *sotto tutti i rapporti*, in every respect.

rapprèndere *vi.* to coagulate. ♦ **rapprèndersi** *vr.* to coagulate.

rappresaglia *sf.* retaliation: *far* —, to retaliate.

rappresentàbile *agg.* performable.

rappresentante *s.* **1.** representative **2.** (*comm.*) agent.

rappresentanza *sf.* **1.** representation **2.** (*comm.*) agency ‖ *in* — *di*, on behalf of.

rappresentare *vt.* **1.** to represent **2.** (*comm.*) to be agent (for) **3.** (*ana parte*) to play **4.** (*un'opera teatrale*) to stage. ♦ **rappresentarsi** *vr.* to imagine.

rappresentativo *agg.* representative.

rappresentazione *sf.* **1.** representation **2.** (*teat.*) performance **3.** (*cine*) exhibition.

rapsodìa *sf.* rhapsody.

rarefare *vt.* to rarefy. ♦ **rarefarsi** *vr.* to rarefy.

rarefatto *agg.* rarefied.

rarefazione *sf.* rarefaction.

rarità *sf.* rarity.

raro *agg.* rare: *rare volte*, seldom; *una bestia rara* (*fig.*), a queer fish.

rasare *vt.* **1.** to shave **2.** (*un prato*) to mow (*v. irr.*) **3.** (*lisciare*) to smooth. ♦ **rasarsi** *vr.* to shave.

rasato *agg.* **1.** shaven **2.** (*liscio*) smooth **3.** (*simile a raso*) satin (*attributivo*).

rasatura *sf.* **1.** shave **2.** (*di prato*) mowing.

raschiamento *sm.* **1.** scraping **2.** (*med.*) curettage.

raschiare *vt.* **1.** to scrape **2.** (*med.*) to curette ‖ *raschiarsi la gola*, to clear one's throat.

raschiata *sf.* scraping.

raschiatoio *sm.* **1.** scraper **2.** (*med.*) curette.

raschiatura *sf.* scraping.

raschietto *sm.* **1.** scraper **2.** (*per cancellare*) eraser.

rasciugare *vt.* to dry.

rasentare *vt.* **1.** to graze **2.** (*confinare*) to border (on).

rasente *prep.* close to: *passare* —, to skim.

raso *agg.* V. *rasato*. ♦ **raso** *sm.* satin.

rasoio *sm.* razor.

raspa *sf.* rasp.

raspamento *sm.* rasping.

raspare *vt.* 1. to rasp 2. (*con le unghie*) to scratch 3. (*frugare*) to rummage.

rassegna *sf.* 1. (*rivista, recensione*) review 2. (*esame*) survey || *passare in* —, to inspect.

rassegnare *vt.* to hand in: — *le dimissioni*, to resign. ♦ **rassegnarsi** *vr.* to resign oneself.

rassegnato *agg.* resigned.

rassegnazione *sf.* resignation.

rasserenare *vt.* 1. to clear 2. (*fig.*) to cheer up. ♦ **rasserenarsi** *vr.* to clear up.

rassettare *vt.* 1. to tidy 2. (*riparare*) to mend.

rassicurante *agg.* reassuring.

rassicurare *vt.* to reassure. ♦ **rassicurarsi** *vr.* to be reassured.

rassicurazione *sf.* reassurance.

rassodamento *sm.* consolidation.

rassodare *vt.* 1. to consolidate 2. (*indurire*) to harden. ♦ **rassodarsi** *vr.* to harden.

rassomigliante *agg.* like, alike (*pred.*).

rassomiglianza *sf.* likeness.

rassomigliare *vi.* to be like. ♦ **rassomigliarsi** *vr. rec.* to be alike.

rassottigliare *vt.* V. *assottigliare*.

rastrellamento *sm.* 1. raking 2. (*mil.*) mopping up 3. (*di polizia*) combing 4. (*dragaggio*) dragging.

rastrellare *vt.* 1. to rake 2. (*mil.*) to mop up 3. (*di polizia*) to comb 4. (*dragare*) to drag.

rastrelliera *sf.* rack.

rastrello *sm.* rake.

rastremare *vt.* to taper. ♦ **rastremarsi** *vr.* to taper.

rata *sf.* instalment: *a rate*, by instalments.

rateale *agg.* by instalments.

rateare *vt.* to divide into instalments.

ratifica *sf.* ratification.

ratificare *vt.* to ratify.

ratificatore *sm.* ratifier.

ratificazione *sf.* V. *ratifica*.

ratto[1] *sm.* 1. kidnapping 2. (*di donna*) rape.

ratto[2] *sm.* (*topo*) rat.

rattoppare *vt.* to patch (up).

rattoppo *sm.* 1. patching up 2. (*toppa*) patch.

rattrappimento *sm.* 1. (*intorpidi-*

mento) benumbing 2. (*contrazione*) contraction.

rattrappire *vt.* 1. (*contrarre*) to contract 2. (*intorpidire*) to benumb.

rattristare *vt.* to grieve. ♦ **rattristarsi** *vr.* 1. (*divenir triste*) to become (*v. irr.*) sad 2. (*essere triste*) to be sad.

raucedine *sf.* hoarseness: *avere la* —, to have a hoarse voice.

rauco *agg.* hoarse.

ravanello *sm.* radish.

ravvedersi *vr.* to mend one's way.

ravvedimento *sm.* reformation.

ravviamento *sm.* tidying (up).

ravviare *vt.* to tidy (up).

ravvicinamento *sm.* 1. approach 2. (*conciliazione*) reconciliation.

ravvicinare *vt.* 1. to bring (*v. irr.*) closer 2. (*riconciliare*) to reconcile 3. (*confrontare*) to compare. ♦ **ravvicinarsi** *vr.* 1. to draw (*v. irr.*) closer 2. (*riconciliarsi*) to become (*v. irr.*) reconciled.

ravvisàbile *agg.* recognizable.

ravvisare *vt.* to recognize.

ravvivamento *sm.* revival.

ravvivare *vt.* 1. to revive 2. (*rallegrare*) to brighten up || — *il fuoco*, to poke the fire. ♦ **ravvivarsi** *vr.* 1. to revive 2. (*rallegrarsi*) to brighten up.

raziocinante *agg.* reasoning.

raziocinio *sm.* 1. reason 2. (*buon senso*) common sense.

razionale *agg.* rational.

razionalismo *sm.* rationalism.

razionalista *s.* rationalist.

razionalità *sf.* rationality.

razionamento *sm.* rationing.

razionare *vt.* to ration.

razione *sf.* ration.

razza[1] *sf.* 1. race 2. (*di animali*) breed 3. (*genere*) kind.

razza[2] *sf.* (*itt.*) ray.

razzia *sf.* 1. raid 2. (*insetticida*) insecticide || *far* —, to plunder.

razziale *agg.* racial.

razziare *vt.* to plunder.

razziatore *sm.* plunderer.

razzismo *sm.* racialism.

razzista *s.* racialist.

razzo *sm.* rocket.

razzolare *vi.* to scratch about.

re[1] *sm.* king.

re[2] *sm.* (*mus.*) D, re.

reagente *sm.* reagent.

reagire *vi.* to react.

reale¹ *agg.* real.
reale² *agg.* (*del re*) royal.
realismo *sm.* realism.
realista¹ *agg. e s.* realist.
realista² *agg. e s.* (*del re*) royalist.
realìstico *agg.* realistic.
realizzàbile *agg.* realizable.
realizzare *vt.* to realize. ♦ **realizzarsi** *vr.* 1. to be realized 2. (*avverarsi*) to come (*v. irr.*) true.
realizzatore *sm.* realizer.
realizzazione *sf.* 1. realization 2. (*teat.*) staging 3. (*cine*) production.
realtà *sf.* reality.
reame *sm.* kingdom.
reato *sm.* 1. offence 2. (*crimine*) crime.
reattivo *agg.* reactive. ♦ **reattivo** *sm.* reagent.
reattore *sm.* 1. reactor 2. (*aereo*) jet.
reazionario *agg. e sm.* reactionary.
reazione *sf.* reaction: *motore a* —, jet engine; *aereo a* —, jet.
reboante *agg.* 1. thundering 2. (*fig.*) bombastic.
rebus *sm.* rebus.
recalcitrare *vi.* V. *ricalcitrare.*
recapitare *vt.* to deliver.
recàpito *sm.* 1. (*consegna*) delivery 2. (*indirizzo*) address.
recare *vt.* 1. to bring (*v. irr.*) 2. (*fig.*) to bear (*v. irr.*) 3. (*causare*) to cause. ♦ **recarsi** *vr.* to go (*v. irr.*).
recèdere *vi.* to withdraw (*v. irr.*).
recensione *sf.* review.
recensire *vt.* to review.
recensore *sm.* reviewer.
recente *agg.* recent.
recentemente *avv.* recently.
recentìssime *sf. pl.* latest news.
recessione *sf.* recession.
recessivo *agg.* receding.
recesso *sm.* 1. recess 2. (*recessione*) recession 3. (*giur.*) withdrawal.
recettivo *agg.* V. *ricettivo.*
recezione *sf.* reception.
recìdere *vt.* to cut (*v. irr.*) off.
recidiva *sf.* relapse.
recidività *sf.* 1. (*giur.*) recidivism 2. (*med.*) relapse.
recidivo *agg.* 1. (*giur.*) recidivous 2. (*med.*) relapsing. ♦ **recidivo** *sm.* 1. (*giur.*) recidivist 2. (*med.*) relapser.
recintare *vt.* to fence.
recinto *sm.* enclosure.
recipiente *sm.* vessel.

reciprocamente *avv.* reciprocally.
reciprocità *sf.* reciprocity.
recìproco *agg.* reciprocal.
recisamente *avv.* resolutely.
recisione *sf.* excision.
reciso *agg.* 1. cut 2. (*fig.*) resolute.
rècita *sf.* performance.
recitare *vt.* 1. to recite 2. (*teat.*) to act || — *una parte*, to play a part.
recitativo *sm.* recitative.
recitazione *sf.* 1. recitation 2. (*teat.*) acting.
reclamante *sm.* claimant.
reclamare *vt.* to claim. ♦ **reclamare** *vi.* to complain.
reclamìstico *agg.* advertising.
reclamizzare *vt.* to advertise.
reclamo *sm.* complaint.
reclinare *vt.* to bow.
reclusione *sf.* 1. seclusion 2. (*prigionia*) imprisonment.
recluso *agg.* 1. secluded 2. (*imprigionato*) imprisoned. ♦ **recluso** *sm.* prisoner.
rècluta *sf.* 1. recruit 2. (*fig.*) novice.
reclutamento *sm.* enlistment.
reclutare *vt.* to enlist, to recruit.
recòndito *agg.* hidden.
recriminare *vi.* 1. to recriminate 2. (*lamentarsi*) to complain.
recriminazione *sf.* 1. recrimination 2. (*lamentela*) complaint.
recrudescente *agg.* recrudescent.
recrudescenza *sf.* recrudescence.
redarguire *vt.* to reproach.
redattore *sm.* 1. drawer 2. (*di giornale*) member of the editorial staff || — *capo*, editor.
redazionale *agg.* editorial.
redazione *sf.* 1. drawing up 2. (*di giornale*) editing 2. (*i redattori*) editorial staff 3. (*ufficio*) editorial office.
redditività *sf.* profitableness.
redditizio *agg.* profitable.
rèddito *sm.* 1. income 2. (*dello Stato*) revenue.
redento *agg.* redeemed.
redentore *sm.* redeemer.
redenzione *sf.* redemption.
redìgere *vt.* to draw (*v. irr.*) up.
redìmere *vt.* to redeem.
redimìbile *agg.* redeemable.
rèdini *sf. pl.* reins.
redivìvo *agg.* 1. restored to life 2. (*nuovo*) new.
rèduce *agg.* back from. ♦ **rèduce** *sm.* veteran.

referendum *sm*. referendum.

referenza *sf*. reference.

referenziare *vt*. to give (*v. irr.*) references.

referto *sm*. report.

refettorio *sm*. refectory.

refezione *sf*. meal.

refrattario *agg*. refractory: *terra refrattaria*, fireclay.

refrigerante *agg*. e *sm*. refrigerant.

refrigerare *vt*. to refrigerate.

refrigeratore *sm*. refrigerator.

refrigerazione *sf*. refrigeration.

refrigerio *sm*. 1. cool 2. (*sollievo*) relief.

refurtiva *sf*. stolen goods (*pl.*).

refuso *sm*. misprint, wrong fount.

regalare *vt*. 1. to present (so. with sthg.) 2. (*vendere a poco prezzo*) to sell (*v. irr.*) cheap.

regalato *agg*. (*venduto a buon prezzo*) cheap.

regale *agg*. regal.

regalìa *sf*. (*mancia*) gratuity.

regalo *sm*. present: *in —*, as a present.

regata *sf*. regatta.

reggente *agg*. e *sm*. regent.

reggenza *sf*. regency.

règgere *vt*. 1. (*sorreggere*) to hold (*v. irr.*) 2. (*dirigere*) to run (*v. irr.*) 3. (*gramm.*) to govern ‖ *— una prova*, to stand (*v. irr.*) a test. ♦ **règgere** *vi*. 1. (*resistere*) to hold (out) 2. (*stare in piedi, anche fig.*) to stand. ♦ **règgersi** *vr*. 1. (*sostenersi*) to stand 2. (*appoggiarsi a*) to hold (on, to).

reggia *sf*. royal palace.

reggicalze *sm*. girdle.

reggimento *sm*. (*mil.*) regiment.

reggipetto *sm*. bra.

reggiseno *sm*. V. *reggipetto*.

reggitore *sm*. ruler.

regia *sf*. 1. (*teat.*) production 2. (*cine*) direction ‖ *— di*, produced, directed by.

regicida *sm*. regicide.

regicidio *sm*. regicide.

regime *sm*. 1. regime 2. (*mecc.*) speed 3. (*dieta*) diet ‖ *essere a —*, to be on a diet.

regina *sf*. queen.

regio *agg*. royal.

regionale *agg*. regional.

regionalismo *sm*. regionalism.

regionalista *s*. regionalist.

regione *sf*. 1. region 2. (*divisione amministrativa; fig.*) province.

regista *sm*. 1. (*teat.*) producer 2. (*cine*) director.

registràbile *agg*. registrable, recordable.

registrare *vt*. 1. to register 2. (*comm.*) to book 3. (*segnare; cine*) to record 4. (*su nastro*) to tape-record 5. (*mecc.*) to adjust.

registratore *sm*. 1. (*persona*) registrar 2. (*strumento*) register: *— di cassa*, cash-register 3. (*magnetofono*) taperecorder.

registrazione *sf*. 1. registration 2. (*comm.*) entry 3. (*di suoni*) recording.

registro *sm*. 1. register 2. (*comm.*) book 3. (*ufficio governativo*) registry.

regnante *agg*. reigning. ♦ **regnante** *s*. sovereign.

regnare *vi*. to reign.

regno *sm*. 1. reign 2. (*territorio; fig.*) kingdom.

règola *sf*. 1. rule 2. (*esempio*) example 3. (*misura*) moderation ‖ *in —*, in order; *è di —*, it is the custom.

regolamentare *agg*. prescribed: *non essere —*, to be against the rules.

regolamentarmente *avv*. according to the rules.

regolamentazione *sf*. regulations (*pl.*).

regolamento *sm*. regulation: *— dei conti*, settlement.

regolare¹ *vt*. 1. to regulate 2. (*sistemare*) to settle 3. (*sintonizzare*) to tune (in). ♦ **regolarsi** *vr*. 1. to act 2. (*controllarsi*) to control oneself.

regolare² *agg*. regular.

regolarità *sf*. regularity.

regolarizzare *vt*. to regularize.

regolarizzazione *sf*. regularization.

regolatamente *avv*. 1. regularly 2. (*con moderazione*) moderately.

regolatezza *sf*. sobriety.

regolato *agg*. regular.

regolatore *agg*. regulating: *piano —*, townplan. ♦ **regolatore** *sm*. regulator.

regolazione *sf*. regulation.

règolo *sm*. rule: *— calcolatore*, slide rule.

regredire *vi*. to regress.

regressione *sf*. regression.

regressivo *agg*. regressive.

regresso *sm*. regress.

reietto agg. rejected. ♦ **reietto** sm. outcast.

reiezione sf. rejection.

reincarnare vt. to reincarnate. ♦ **reincarnarsi** vr. to be reincarnated.

reincarnazione sf. reincarnation.

reintegrare vt. 1. to restore 2. (risarcire) to indemnify.

reintegrazione sf. 1. restoration 2. (risarcimento) indemnification.

reità sf. 1. (colpevolezza) guiltiness 2. (malvagità) wickedness.

reiterare vt. to reiterate.

reiterazione sf. reiteration.

relativamente avv. comparatively: — a, as regards.

relativismo sm. relativism.

relativìstico agg. relativistic.

relatività sf. relativity.

relativo agg. 1. relative 2. (rispettivo) respective 3. (attinente) pertinent.

relatore sm. 1. relator 2. (di leggi) proposer.

relazionare vt. to relate.

relazione sf. 1. report 2. (legame) relation 3. (contatto) touch 4. (conoscenza) acquaintance || aver — con, to be connected with; essere in buone relazioni, to be on good terms; mettersi in — con, to get (v. irr.) into touch with; — amorosa, love affair.

relegare vt. to relegate.

relegazione sf. relegation.

religione sf. 1. religion 2. (culto) worship.

religiosità sf. piety.

religioso agg. e sm. religious.

reliquia sf. relic.

reliquario sm. reliquary.

relitto sm. 1. wreckage 2. (di persona) outcast.

remare vi. 1. to row 2. (con pagaia) to paddle.

remata sf. 1. row 2. (colpo di remo) stroke.

rematore sm. oarsman (pl. -men).

remiganti sf. pl. remiges.

remigare vi. 1. to row 2. (di ali) to flap.

reminiscenza sf. reminiscence.

remissione sf. (giur.) remission.

remissività sf. submissiveness.

remissivo agg. submissive.

remo sm. oar.

rèmora sf. 1. (ostacolo) obstacle 2. (indugio) delay 3. (zool.) remora.

remoto agg. remote: passato — (gramm.) past simple tense.

remunerare vt. to remunerate.

remunerativo agg. remunerative.

remunerazione sf. remuneration.

rena sf. sand.

renale agg. renal.

rèndere vt. 1. to render 2. (fruttare) to yield || — conto di, to account for; — giustizia a qu., to do (v. irr.) so. justice. ♦ **rèndersi** vr. to become (v. irr.) || — conto di, to realize.

rendiconto sm. 1. statement 2. (resoconto) report.

rendimento sm. 1. rendering 2. (resa) output 3. (efficienza) efficiency.

rèndita sf. 1. revenue 2. (privata) income.

rene sm. kidne .

renella sf. grave .

reni sf. pl. back (sing.).

renitente agg. reluctant || essere — alla leva, to fail to appear at the draft.

renitenza sf. reluctance || — alla leva, failure to register for national service.

renna sf. reindeer (pl. invariato).

renoso agg. sandy.

reo agg. guilty. ♦ **reo** sm. culprit.

reòmetro sm. rheometer.

reòstato sm. rheostat.

reparto sm. 1. department 2. (mil.) detachment.

repellente agg. repulsive.

repentaglio sm. danger: a —, in danger.

repentino agg. sudden.

reperìbile agg. to be found (pred.).

reperire vt. to find (v. irr.).

reperto sm. 1. (giur.) evidence 2. (med.) report.

repertorio sm. (teat.) repertoire.

rèplica sf. 1. reply 2. (obiezione) objection 3. (copia) copy 4. (teat.) performance || avere molte repliche (teat.), to have a long run.

replicare vt. 1. to reply 2. (obiettare) to object 3. (ripetere) to repeat.

reprensìbile agg. reprehensible.

reprensione sf. reprehension.

repressione sf. repression.

repressivo agg. repressive.

represso agg. repressed.

reprimenda sf. reprimand.

reprìmere vt. to repress.

rèprobo *agg. e sm.* reprobate.
repùbblica *sf.* republic.
repubblicano *agg. e sm.* republican.
reputare *vt.* **1.** to consider **2.** (*pensare*) to think (*v. irr.*).
reputazione *sf.* reputation.
requie *sf.* rest.
requisire *vt.* to requisition.
requisito *sm.* qualification.
requisitoria *sf.* **1.** indictment **2.** (*giur.*) summing up.
requisizione *sf.* requisition.
resa *sf.* (*rendimento*) yield **2.** (*capitolazione*) surrender || — *dei conti*, rendering of accounts.
rescìndere *vt.* to rescind.
rescindìbile *agg.* rescindable.
rescissione *sf.* rescission.
reseda *sf.* reseda.
resezione *sf.* resection.
residente *agg. e sm.* resident.
residenza *sf.* residence.
residenziale *agg.* residential.
residuare *vi.* to be left.
residuato *agg.* residual. ♦ **residuato** *sm.* — *di guerra*, war surplus.
residuo *agg.* remaining. ♦ **residuo** *sm.* residue: *residui radioattivi*, radioactive waste.
rèsina *sf.* resin.
resinoso *agg.* resinous.
resipiscenza *sf.* resipiscence.
resistente *agg.* **1.** resistant **2.** (*forte*) strong.
resistenza *sf.* resistance.
resìstere *vi.* **1.** to resist **2.** (*sopportare*) to endure.
resoconto *sm.* report.
respingente *sm.* buffer.
respìngere *vt.* **1.** to repel **2.** (*rimandare*) to return **3.** (*rifiutare*) to reject **4.** (*scol.*) to pluck.
respinta *sf.* V. *parata*.
respiràbile *agg.* breathable.
respirare *vt. e vi.* to breathe.
respiratore *sm.* respirator.
respiratorio *agg.* respiratory.
respirazione *sf.* respiration, breathing.
respiro *sm.* **1.** breath **2.** (*riposo*) respite.
responsàbile *agg.* responsible (for).
responsabilità *sf.* responsibility.
responso *sm.* **1.** response **2.** (*opinione*) opinion.
responsorio *sm.* responsory.
ressa *sf.* crowd: *far — intorno a*

qu., to crowd round so.
resta *sf.* **1.** (*di cipolla, aglio ecc.*) string **2.** (*di lancia*) rest.
restante *agg. e sm.* V. *rimanente*.
restare *vi.* V. *rimanere*.
restaurare *vt.* to restore.
restauratore *sm.* restorer.
restaurazione *sf.* restoration.
restàuro *sm.* restoration: *in —*, under repair.
restìo *agg.* loath, reluctant.
restituire *vt.* **1.** to return **2.** (*reintegrare*) to restore.
restituzione *sf.* **1.** return **2.** (*reintegrazione*) restoration.
resto *sm.* **1.** rest **2.** (*mat.*) remainder **3.** (*di denaro*) change || *resti*, remains; *del —*, on the other hand.
restringente *sm.* astringent.
restrìngere *vt.* **1.** (*contrarre*) to contract **2.** (*limitare*) to limit **3.** (*un vestito*) to tighten. ♦ **restrìngersi** *vr.* **1.** to get (*v. irr.*) narrower **2.** (*contrarsi*) to contract **3.** (*affollarsi*) to close up **4.** (*di tessuti*) to shrink (*v. irr.*).
restringimento *sm.* **1.** narrowing **2.** (*contrazione*) contraction **3.** (*limitazione*) limitation **4.** (*di tessuto*) shrinking **5.** (*di vestito*) tightening.
restrittivo *agg.* restrictive.
restrizione *sf.* restriction.
retaggio *sm.* heritage.
retata *sf.* **1.** haul **2.** (*di polizia*) roundup.
rete *sf.* **1.** net **2.** (*di letto*) wire netting **3.** (*intreccio*) network.
reticella *sf.* **1.** (*per capelli*) hair-net **2.** (*per bagagli*) luggage-rack.
reticente *agg.* reticent.
reticenza *sf.* reticence.
reticolato *sm.* **1.** (*mil.*) barbed-wire entanglement **2.** (*tracciato di linee*) network.
retìcolo *sm.* **1.** (*anat.*) reticulum (*pl.* -la) **2.** (*ott.*) reticle.
rètina *sf.* retina.
retina *sf.* V. *reticella*.
rètore *sm.* rhetorician.
retòrica *sf.* rhetoric.
retòrico *agg.* rhetorical.
retrarre *vt.* to retract.
retràttile *agg.* retractile.
retrattilità *sf.* retractility.
retribuire *vt.* to pay (*v. irr.*).
retribuzione *sf.* payment.
retrivo *agg.* reactionary.
retro *sm.* back.

retroattività *sf.* retroactivity.

retroattivo *agg.* retroactive.

retrobottega *sm.* back of the shop.

retrocèdere *vi.* to withdraw (*v. irr.*). ◆ **retrocèdere** *vt.* 1. (*mil.*) to degrade 2. to retrocede.

retrocessione *sf.* 1. retrocession 2. (*mil.*) degradation.

retrodatare *vt.* to date back.

retrògrado *agg.* 1. out-of-date 2. (*reazionario*) reactionary.

retroguardia *sf.* rear-guard.

retromarcia *sf.* reverse-gear.

retroscena *sf.* 1. back of the stage 2. (*fig.*) intrigue.

retrospettivo *agg.* retrospective.

retrostante *agg.* at the back.

retroterra *sm.* hinterland.

retroversione *sf.* 1. retroversion 2. (*di traduzione*) back version.

retrovìe *sf. pl.* zone behind the front (*sing*).

retrovisore *sm. specchietto* —, driving mirror.

retta[1] *sf.* (*geom.*) straight line.

retta[2] *sf.* (*di pensione*) terms (*pl.*).

retta[3] *sf. dar* — *a qu.*, to listen to so.

rettale *agg.* rectal.

rettamente *avv.* 1. (*giustamente*) rightly 2. (*onestamente*) honestly.

rettangolare *agg.* rectangular.

rettàngolo *sm.* rectangle.

rettìfica *sf.* 1. rectification 2. (*mecc.*) grinding.

rettificare *vt.* 1. to rectify 2. (*mecc.*) to grind (*v. irr.*).

rettificatrice *sf.* grinder.

rettificazione *sf.* V. *rettìfica.*

rettifilo *sm.* straight, stretch.

rèttile *sm.* reptile.

rettilìneo *agg.* rectilinear. ◆ **rettilìneo** *sm.* straight, stretch.

rettitùdine *sf.* righteousness, honesty.

retto *agg.* 1. straight 2. (*geom.; giusto*) right. ◆ **retto** *sm.* (*anat.*) rectum (*pl.* -ta).

rettorato *sm.* rectorship.

rettore *sm.* 1. rector 2. (*di università*) chancellor.

rèuma *sm.* rheumatism.

reumàtico *agg.* e *sm.* rheumatic.

reumatismo *sm.* V. *reuma.*

reverendo *agg.* reverend. ◆ **reverendo** *sm.* clergyman (*pl.* -men).

reversìbile *agg.* reversible.

reversibilità *sf.* reversibility.

reversione *sf.* reversion.

revisionare *vt.* 1. (*mecc.*) to overhaul 2. (*comm.*) to audit.

revisione *sf.* 1. revision 2. (*mecc.*) overhaul 3. (*comm.*) audit.

revisionismo *sm.* revisionism.

revisore *sm.* 1. reviser 2. (*comm.*) auditor.

reviviscenza *sf.* reviviscence.

rèvoca *sf.* revocation.

revocàbile *agg.* revocable.

revocare *vt.* 1. (*richiamare*) to recall 2. (*giur.*) to revoke.

revocazione *sf.* revocation.

revolverata *sf.* revolver shot.

revulsione *sf.* revulsion.

revulsivo *agg.* revulsive.

riabbottonare *vt.* to button again.

riabilitare *vt.* to rehabilitate.

riabilitazione *sf.* rehabilitation.

riaccèndere *vt.* 1. to relight 2. (*radio, luce ecc.*) to turn on again. ◆ **riaccèndersi** *vr.* 1. to brighten again 2. (*riprender fuoco*) to catch (*v. irr.*) fire again.

riaccompagnare *vt.* to take (*v. irr.*) home.

riacquistare *vt.* 1. to buy (*v. irr.*) again 2. (*riprendere*) to recover.

riadattare *vt.* to adapt again. ◆ **riadattarsi** *vr.* (*rassegnarsi*) to resign oneself again.

riaddormentare *vt.* to send (*v. irr.*) to sleep again. ◆ **riaddormentarsi** *vr.* to fall (*v. irr.*) asleep again.

riaffacciare *vt.* to present again. ◆ **riaffacciarsi** *vr.* to reappear, to appear again.

riaffermare *vt.* to affirm again. ◆ **riaffermarsi** *vr.* to reaffirm oneself.

riafferrare *vt.* to grasp again. ◆ **riafferrarsi** *vr.* to catch (*v. irr.*) hold of (so., sthg.) again.

riallacciare *vt.* 1. to fasten again 2. (*riprendere*) to resume.

riallargare *vt.* to widen again. ◆ **riallargarsi** *vr.* to widen again.

rialto *sm.* rise, height.

rialzamento *sm.* 1. raising 2. (*rialzo*) rise, height.

rialzare *vt.* 1. to raise 2. (*rendere più alto*) to make (*v. irr.*) higher. ◆ **rialzarsi** *vr.* to rise (*v. irr.*) again.

rialzato *agg. piano* —, ground floor.

rialzo *sm.* 1. rise 2. (*di sostegno*) support.

riamare *vt.* to love again.

riamméttere *vt.* to readmit.

rianimare *vt.* to revive. ♦ **rianimarsi** *vr.* 1. (*riprendere allegria*) to cheer up 2. (*riprendere coraggio*) to take (*v. irr.*) courage again.

riapertura *sf.* reopening.

riapparire *vi.* to reappear.

riaprire *vt.* to open again. ♦ **riaprirsi** *vr.* to open again.

riarmare *vt.* to rearm. ♦ **riarmarsi** *vr.* to rearm.

riarmo *sm.* rearmament.

riarso *agg.* parched.

riassestare *vt.* to readjust. ♦ **riassestarsi** *vr.* to readjust.

riassettare *vt.* to put (*v. irr.*) in order again.

riassetto *sm.* rearrangement.

riassorbire *sf.* to reabsorb.

riassùmere *vt.* 1. (*assumere di nuovo*) to take (*v. irr.*) on again 2. (*riepilogare*) to sum up 3. (*riprendere*) to resume.

riassuntivo *agg.* summarizing.

riassunto *sm.* summary.

riattaccare *vt.* 1. (*con colla*) to stick (*v. irr.*) again 2. (*ricucire*) to sew (*v. irr.*) 3. (*riprendere*) to begin (*v. irr.*) again 4. (*mil.*) to attack again 5. (*tel.*) to hang (*v. irr.*) up. ♦ **riattaccarsi** *vr.* to stick again.

riattamento *sm.* repair.

riattare *vt.* to repair.

riattivare *vt.* to restore.

riavere *vt.* 1. to have again 2. (*ricuperare*) to get (*v. irr.*) back. ♦ **riaversi** *vr.* to recover.

riavvicinare *vt.* 1. to approach again 2. (*riconciliare*) to reconcile. ♦ **riavvicinarsi** *vr.* to approach again 2. (*riconciliarsi*) to be reconciled.

ribadire *vt.* to rivet.

ribalderìa *sf.* rascality.

ribaldo *sm.* rascal.

ribalta *sf.* 1. (*teat.*) footlights (*pl.*) 2. (*fig.*) limelight.

ribaltàbile *agg.* overturnable.

ribaltare *vt.* to overturn. ♦ **ribaltarsi** *vr.* to capsize.

ribassare *vt.* to reduce. ♦ **ribassare** *vi.* to fall (*v. irr.*).

ribasso *sm.* 1. fall 2. (*sconto*) discount.

ribàttere *vt.* 1. to beat (*v. irr.*) again 2. (*ribadire*) to rivet 3. (*confutare*) to confute. ♦ **ribàttere** *vi.* to insist.

ribattezzare *vt.* to rename.

ribellarsi *vr.* to rebel.

ribelle *agg.* rebellious. ♦ **ribelle** *s.* rebel.

ribellione *sf.* rebellion.

ribes *sm.* gooseberry.

riboccante *agg.* overflowing (with).

riboccare *vi.* to overflow (with).

ribollimento *sm.* ebullition.

ribollire *vi.* to boil.

ribollitura *sf.* reboiling.

ribrezzo *sm.* disgust: *fare* —, to disgust.

ributtante *agg.* disgusting.

ributtare *vt.* 1. to throw (*v. irr.*) again 2. (*respingere*) to repel 3. (*disgustare*) to disgust.

ricacciare *vt.* 1. (*respingere*) to push (out, back) 2. (*ficcare di nuovo*) to thrust (*v. irr.*) again. ♦ **ricacciarsi** *vr.* to plunge again.

ricadere *vi.* 1. to fall (*v. irr.*) again 2. (*avere una ricaduta*) to relapse 3. (*pendere*) to hang (*v. irr.*).

ricaduta *sf.* relapse.

ricalcare *vt.* 1. to pull down 2. (*un disegno*) to transfer ‖ — *le orme di qu.*, to tread (*v. irr.*) in so.'s steps.

ricalcitrante *agg.* recalcitrant.

ricalcitrare *vi.* to recalcitrate.

ricamare *vt.* e *vi.* to embroider.

ricamatore *sm.* embroiderer.

ricamatrice *sf.* embroideress.

ricambiare *vt.* 1. to change again 2. (*contraccambiare*) to return.

ricambio *sm.* 1. replacement 2. (*med.*) metabolism ‖ *di* —, spare (*agg. attr.*).

ricamo *sm.* embroidery: *un* —, a piece of embroidery.

ricapitolare *vt.* to summarize ‖ *ricapitolando*, in short.

ricapitolazione *sf.* summary.

ricaricare *vt.* 1. to reload 2. (*di batteria*) to recharge 3. (*di orologio*) to wind (*v. irr.*) up again.

ricascare *vi.* V. *ricadere*.

ricattare *vt.* to blackmail.

ricattatore *sm.* blackmailer.

ricattatorio *agg.* blackmailing.

ricatto *sm.* blackmail.

ricavare *vt.* 1. to draw (*v. irr.*) 2. (*ottenere*) to get (*v. irr.*).

ricavato *sm.* proceeds (*pl.*).

ricavo *sm.* V. *ricavato*.

riccamente *avv.* richly.

ricchezza *sf.* wealth (*solo sing.*).

riccio[1] *agg.* curly.

riccio² *sm.* **1.** curl **2.** (*bot.*) chestnut husk **3.** (*zool.*) hedgehog **4.** (*di mare*) sea-urchin.

ricciuto *agg.* curly.

ricco *agg.* rich: — *di*, rich in.

ricerca *sf.* **1.** search **2.** (*scientifica*) research **3.** (*indagine*) investigation.

ricercare *vt.* **1.** (*cercare*) to seek (*v. irr.*) for **2.** (*investigare*) to investigate **3.** (*cercare di nuovo*) to look for (so., sthg.) again.

ricercatezza *sf.* refinement.

ricercato *agg.* **1.** (*richiesto*) sought--after **2.** (*raffinato*) refined **3.** (*insolito*) far-fetched **4.** (*dalla polizia*) wanted.

ricercatore *sm.* **1.** searcher **2.** (*scientifico*) researcher.

ricetta *sf.* **1.** (*med.*) prescription **2.** (*cuc.*) recipe.

ricettàcolo *sm.* receptacle.

ricettare *vt.* (*custodire cose rubate*) to receive.

ricettario *sm.* **1.** (*med.*) book of prescriptions **2.** (*cuc.*) book of recipes.

ricettatore *sm.* receiver.

ricettazione *sf.* receiving of stolen goods.

ricettività *sf.* receptivity.

ricettivo *agg.* receptive.

ricevente *agg.* receiving. ♦ **ricevente** *s.* receiver.

ricévere *vt.* to receive.

ricevimento *sm.* **1.** receipt **2.** (*festa*) party.

ricevitore *sm.* receiver.

ricevitorìa *sf.* receiving-office.

ricevuta *sf.* receipt: *accusare —*, to acknowledge receipt.

ricezione *vt.* reception.

richiamare *vt.* **1.** to call again **2.** (*far tornare*) to recall **3.** (*attirare*) to attract **4.** (*rimproverare*) to rebuke || — *all'ordine*, to call to order. ♦ **richiamarsi** *vr.* (*riferirsi*) to refer.

richiamata *sf.* recall.

richiamato *sm.* (*mil.*) re-drafted soldier.

richiamo *sm.* **1.** recall **2.** (*allettamento*) call.

richiedente *s.* applicant.

richièdere *vt.* **1.** to ask (for sthg., so.) again **2.** (*chiedere*) to ask for **3.** (*in restituzione*) to ask (for sthg.) back **4.** (*necessitare di*) to require.

richiesta *sf.* **1.** request: *dietro —*, at request **2.** (*comm.*) demand.

richiùdere *vt.* to close again. ♦ **richiùdersi** *vr.* to close again.

rìcino *sm.* castor-oil plant: *olio di —*, castor-oil.

ricognitore *sm.* (*mil.*) scout.

ricognizione *sf.* reconnaissance.

ricollegare *vt.* to connect. ♦ **ricollegarsi** *vr.* to be connected.

ricollocamento *sm.* replacement.

ricolmare *vt.* **1.** to fill up **2.** (*fig.*) to load.

ricolmo *agg.* **1.** full **2.** (*fig.*) loaded (with).

ricominciare *vt.* to begin (*v. irr.*) again.

ricomparire *vi.* to reappear.

ricompensa *sf.* reward: *in —*, as a reward.

ricompensare *vt.* to reward.

ricomperare *vt.* to buy (*v. irr.*) again.

ricomporre *vt.* to recompose.

ricomposizione *sf.* recomposition.

riconciliare *vt.* to reconcile. ♦ **riconciliarsi** *vr.* to be reconciled.

riconciliatore *sm.* reconciler.

riconciliazione *sf.* reconciliation.

ricondurre *vt.* to take (*v. irr.*) back, to bring (*v. irr.*) back.

riconferma *sf.* reconfirmation.

riconfermare *vt.* to reconfirm.

riconfortare *vt.* to cheer up. ♦ **riconfortarsi** *vr.* to cheer up.

ricongiùngere *vt.* to join again. ♦ **ricongiùngersi** *vr.* to join again.

ricongiungimento *sm.* reunion.

riconnèttere *vt.* to connect again.

riconoscente *agg.* grateful.

riconoscenza *sf.* gratitude.

riconòscere *vt.* to recognize.

riconoscìbile *agg.* recognizable.

riconoscimento *sm.* **1.** recognition **2.** (*ammissione*) admission.

riconquista *sf.* recapture.

riconquistare *vt.* to conquer again.

riconsegna *sf.* return.

riconsegnare *vt.* to redeliver.

riconsiderare *vt.* to reconsider.

riconversione *sf.* reconversion.

riconvocare *vt.* to resummon.

riconvocazione *sf.* resummons.

ricopiare *vt.* to copy.

ricopiatura *sf.* (re)copying.

ricoprire *vt.* **1.** to cover **2.** (*coprire di nuovo*) to cover again **3.** (*fig.*) to load.

ricordare *vt.* 1. to remember 2. (*chiamare alla memoria altrui*) to remind (so. of sthg.) 3. (*nominare*) to mention. ♦ **ricordarsi** *vr.* to remember.

ricordo *sm.* 1. memory 2. (*oggetto ricordo*) souvenir 3. (*memorie*) (*lett.*) memoirs (*pl.*).

ricorrente *agg.* recurrent.

ricorrenza *sf.* 1. recurrence 2. (*anniversario*) anniversary 3. (*occasione*) occasion.

ricòrrere *vi.* 1. (*ripetersi*) to recur 2. (*rivolgersi*) to apply 3. (*fare appello*) to appeal 4. (*valersi*) to resort.

ricorso *sm.* 1. (*ritorno*) return 2. (*appello*) appeal || *su — di*, on a petition by.

ricostituente *agg. e sm.* tonic.

ricostituire *vt.* to form again. ♦ **ricostituirsi** *vr.* to form again.

ricostituzione *sf.* reconstitution.

ricostruire *vt.* to reconstruct.

ricostruttore *agg.* reconstructive. ♦ **ricostruttore** *sm.* reconstructor.

ricostruzione *sf.* reconstruction.

ricoverare *vt.* to shelter: *— in ospedale*, to hospitalize. ♦ **ricoverarsi** *vr.* to take (*v. irr.*) shelter.

ricòvero *sm.* 1. sheltering 2. (*in ospedale*) hospitalization 3. (*ospizio*) home.

ricreare[1] *vt.* to re-create.

ricreare[2] *vt.* (*divertire*) to recreate. ♦ **ricrearsi** *vr.* to recreate.

ricreativo *agg.* recreative.

ricreazione *sf.* recreation: *ora della —*, playtime.

ricrédersi *vr.* to change one's mind.

ricréscere *vi.* to grow (*v. irr.*) again.

ricréscita *sf.* fresh growth.

ricucire *vt.* 1. to sew (*v. irr.*) up 2. (*cucire di nuovo*) to sew (*v. irr.*) again.

ricucitura *sf.* sewing up.

ricuòcere *vt. e vi.* 1. to cook again 2. (*al forno*) to bake again.

ricuperàbile *agg.* recoverable.

ricuperare *vt.* 1. to recover 2. (*di tempo*) to make (*v. irr.*) up for.

ricùpero *sm.* recovery.

ricurvare *vt.* 1. to bend (*v. irr.*) 2. (*curvare di nuovo*) to bend again.

ricurvo *agg.* bent.

ricusàbile *agg.* refusable.

ricusare *vt.* to refuse.

ridacchiare *vi.* to giggle.

ridanciano *agg.* jolly.

ridare *vt.* 1. to give (*v. irr.*) again 2. (*restituire*) to return.

ridda *sf.* turmoil.

ridente *agg.* 1. smiling 2. (*di luogo*) charming.

rìdere *vi.* to laugh (at): *per —*, for fun. ♦ **rìdersi** *vr.* to make (*v. irr.*) fun (of).

ridestare *vt.* 1. to wake (*v. irr.*) (up) again 2. (*destare*) to awaken. ♦ **ridestarsi** *vr.* 1. to wake (up) again 2. (*destarsi*) to awake.

ridicolàggine *sf.* nonsense (*solo sing.*).

ridìcolo *agg.* ridiculous. ♦ **ridìcolo** *sm.* ridicule.

ridimensionare *vt.* to reorganize.

ridire *vt.* 1. to say (*v. irr.*) again, to tell (*v. irr.*) again 2. (*riferire*) to repeat 3. (*obiettare*) to object.

ridiscéndere *vi.* to come (*v. irr.*) down again, to go (*v. irr.*) down again.

ridiscòrrere *vi.* to talk again.

ridiventare *vi.* to become (*v. irr.*) again.

ridomandare *vt.* to ask again.

ridonare *vt.* 1. to give (*v. irr.*) again 2. (*restituire*) to give back.

ridondante *agg.* redundant.

ridondanza *sf.* redundancy.

ridondare *vi.* 1. to be redundant 2. (*risultare*) to redound.

ridosso (*nella loc. avv.*) *a — di*, close to.

ridotta *sf.* redoubt.

ridotto *agg.* 1. reduced 2. (*di libro*) abridged || *mal —*, in a sorry plight. ♦ **ridotto** *sm.* (*teat.*) foyer.

riducente *agg.* reducing. ♦ **riducente** *sm.* reducer.

riducìbile *agg.* reducible.

ridurre *vt.* 1. to reduce 2. (*adattare*) to. adapt 3. (*un libro*) to abridge. ♦ **ridursi** *vr.* 1. to be reduced 2. (*restringersi*) to shrink (*v. irr.*).

riduttore *agg. e sm.* V. *riducente*.

riduzione *sf.* 1. reduction 2. (*sconto*) discount 3. (*cine; tv*) adaptation 4. (*di libro*) abridgement.

riecheggiare *vt. e vi.* to re-echo.

riedificare *vt.* to rebuild (*v. irr.*).

riedificazione *sf.* rebuilding.

rieducare *vt.* to re-educate.

rieducazione *sf.* re-education.

rielaborare *vt.* to re-elaborate.

rieleggere vt. to re-elect.
rieleggibile agg. re-elegible.
rielezione sf. re-election.
riemergere vi. to re-emerge.
riemersione sf. re-emergence.
riempire vt. to fill. ◆ **riempirsi** vr. to fill.
riempitivo sm. filling.
rientrante agg. receding.
rientranza sf. recess.
rientrare vi. 1. to re-enter 2. (tornare) to return 3. (far parte) to be part (of) 4. (piegare in dentro) to recede.
rientro sm. 1. recess 2. (astronautica) retro-firing 3. (ritorno) return.
riepilogare vt. to recapitulate.
riepilogo sm. recapitulation.
riesame sm. re-examination.
riesaminare vt. to re-examine.
riessere vi. to be again.
riesumare vt. 1. to exhume 2. (fig.) to bring (v. irr.) to light.
rievocare vt. to recall.
rievocazione sf. recalling.
rifacimento sm. 1. reconstruction 2. (adattamento) adaptation.
rifare vt. 1. to do (v. irr.) again, to make (v. irr.) again 2. (ripercorrere) to retrace 3. (riparare) to repair 4. (imitare) to imitate 5. (indennizzare) to indemnify. ◆ **rifarsi** vr. 1. to make up 2. (vendicarsi) to revenge oneself 3. (risalire) to go (v. irr.) back.
rifasciare vt. 1. to bandage again 2. (un bambino) to swaddle again.
riferibile agg. 1. referable 2. (raccontabile) fit to be told.
riferimento sm. reference: linea, punto di —, datum-line, datum-point.
riferire vt. 1. to report 2. (attribuire) to ascribe. ◆ **riferirsi** vr. to refer.
rificcare vt. to thrust (v. irr.) again.
rifilare vt. 1. to spin again 2. (tagliare a filo) to trim 3. (appioppare) to palm off.
rifilatura sf. 1. trimming 2. (bordo) border.
rifinimento sm. finishing touch.
rifinire vt. to finish.
rifinitura sf. V. rifinimento.
rifiorire vi. 1. to blossom again 2. (fig.) to flourish again.
rifioritura sf. reflorescence.
rifiutàbile agg. refusable.

rifiutare vt. to refuse.
rifiuto sm. refusal || rifiuti, waste (solo sing.); i rifiuti della società, the dregs of society.
riflessione sf. reflection.
riflessivo agg. 1. reflective 2. (gramm.) reflexive.
riflesso agg. reflected, reflex (anche fig.). ◆ **riflesso** sm. 1. reflection 2. (di colore) tint 3. (med.) reflex || di —, as a consequence; per —, indirectly.
riflèttere vt. e vi. to reflect. ◆ **riflèttersi** vr. to be reflected.
riflettore sm. 1. reflector 2. (lampada) searchlight.
rifluire vi. 1. to flow again 2. (fluire indietro) to flow back.
riflusso sm. ebb.
rifocillare vt. to give (v. irr.) refreshment. ◆ **rifocillarsi** vr. to take (v. irr.) refreshment.
rifóndere vt. 1. to melt again 2. (rimborsare) to refund.
riforma sf. reformation.
riformare vt. 1. to reform 2. (mil.) to declare unfit for military service.
riformatore sm. reformer.
riformatorio sm. reformatory.
riformismo sm. reformism.
riformista s. reformist.
rifornimento sm. 1. supplying 2. (aer.; auto) refuelling 3. (scorta) supply || stazione di —, filling-station; far — di benzina, to fill up the tank.
rifornire vt. to supply (so. with).
rifornitore sm. supplier.
rifràngere vt. to refract. ◆ **rifràngersi** vr. to be refracted.
rifrangibilità sf. refrangibility.
rifrattore sm. refractor.
rifrazione sf. refraction.
rifritto agg. 1. fried again 2. (fig.) stale.
rifuggire vi. 1. to escape again 2. (essere alieno) to shrink (v. irr.).
rifugiarsi vr. to take (v. irr.) shelter.
rifugiato agg. e sm. refugee.
rifugio sm. 1. shelter 2. (di montagna) mountain hut.
rifùlgere vi. to shine (v. irr.) brightly (with sthg.).
rifusione sf. 1. re-melting 2. (rimborso) repayment.
riga sf. 1. line 2. (fila) row 3. (regolo) rule 4. (striscia) stripe 5. (scriminatura) parting 6. (mus.

stave || *mettersi in* —, to line up.

rigaglie *sf. pl.* giblets.

rigàgnolo *sm.* 1. rivulet 2. (*scolo*) gutter.

rigare *vt.* 1. to rule 2. (*solcare*) to furrow || — *diritto*, to behave well.

rigato *agg.* 1. ruled 2. (*a strisce*) striped 3. (*solcato*) furrowed.

rigattiere *sm.* second-hand dealer.

rigatura *sf.* 1. ruling 2. (*di arma*) rifling.

rigenerare *vt.* 1. to regenerate 2. (*mecc.*) to repair.

rigeneratore *agg.* regenerative. ◆ **rigeneratore** *sm.* regenerator.

rigenerazione *sf.* regeneration.

rigettare *vt.* 1. to throw (*v. irr.*) again 2. (*gettare indietro*) to throw back 3. (*vomitare*) to vomit 4. (*respingere*) to reject..

rigetto *sm.* rejection.

righello *sm.* ruler.

rigidezza *sf.* 1. stiffness 2. (*di clima*) rigour.

rigidità *sf.* V. *rigidezza.*

rìgido *agg.* 1. stiff 2. (*di clima*) rigorous.

rigirare *vt.* 1. to turn again 2. (*cambiare*) to change. ◆ **rigirare** *vi.* to walk about. ◆ **rigirarsi** *vr.* to turn about.

rigiro *sm.* 1. turning round 2. (*di parole*) involved expression.

rigo *sm.* V. *riga.*

rigoglio *sm.* bloom.

rigogliosità *sf.* luxuriancy.

rigoglioso *agg.* flourishing.

rigonfiamento *sm.* swelling.

rigonfiare *vt.* to swell (*v. irr.*). ◆ **rigonfiarsi** *vr.* to swell.

rigonfio *agg.* swollen (with). ◆ **rigonfio** *sm.* swelling.

rigore *sm.* 1. rigour 2. (*esattezza*) exactness || *di* —, compulsory; *a* —, according to the rules; *a* — *di termini*, in the strict sense, *area di* — (*sport*), penalty-area.

rigorismo *sm.* rigorism.

rigorista *s.* rigorist.

rigorosità *sf.* 1. rigour 2. (*esattezza*) preciseness.

rigoroso *agg.* 1. rigorous 2. (*esatto*) exact.

rigovernare *vt.* 1. to govern again 2. (*di piatti*) to wash up.

rigovernatura *sf.* washing-up.

riguadagnare *vt.* 1. to earn again

2. (*ricuperare, raggiungere*) to regain.

riguardare *vt.* 1. to look at (so., sthg.) again 2. (*esaminare*) to examine 3. (*considerare*) to regard. ◆ **riguardarsi** *vr.* to take (*v. irr.*) care of oneself.

riguardata *sf.* look.

riguardévole *agg.* 1. considerable 2. (*importante*) important.

riguardo *sm.* 1. regard 2. (*cura*) care || *persona di* —, person of consequence; — *a*, as regards; *a questo* —, in this connection.

riguardoso *agg.* respectful.

rigurgitare *vi.* 1. to overflow 2. (*di stomaco*) to regurgitate 3. (*brulicare*) to swarm (with).

rigùrgito *sm.* 1. overflow 2. (*di stomaco*) regurgitation 3. (*travaso*) extravasation 4. (*gorgo*) eddy.

rilanciare *vt.* 1. to throw (*v. irr.*) again 2. (*lanciare indietro*) to throw back 3. (*un'offerta*) to raise.

rilancio *sm.* 1. new throw 2. (*di offerta*) raising.

rilasciare *vt.* 1. to release 2. (*concedere*) to grant 3. (*emettere*) to issue. ◆ **rilasciarsi** *vr.* 1. to slacken 2. (*med.*) to prolapse 3. (*rilassarsi*) to relax.

rilascio *sm.* 1. release 2. (*concessione*) granting 3. (*emissione*) issue.

rilassamento *sm.* 1. slackening 2. (*med.*) prolapse 3. (*riposo*) relaxation.

rilassare *vt.* 1. to slacken 2. (*distendere*) to relax. ◆ **rilassarsi** *vr.* 1. to slacken 2. (*distendersi*) to relax.

rilassatezza *sf.* laxity.

rilegare *vt.* 1. to tie again 2. (*libri*) to bind (*v. irr.*).

rilegatura *sf.* binding.

rilèggere *vt.* to reread (*v. irr.*), to read (*v. irr.*) again.

rilento (*nella loc. avv.*) *a* —, slowly.

rilevamento *sm.* 1. (*topografico*) survey 2. (*mar.*) bearing 3. (*cambio*) relieving.

rilevante *agg.* prominent.

rilevare *vt.* 1. to take (*v. irr.*) off again 2. (*notare*) to notice 3. (*far notare*) to point out 4. (*prendere*) to take 5. (*topografia*) to survey 6. (*sostituire*) to relieve 7. (*comm.*) to take over.

rilevazione *sf.* V. *rilievo.*

rilievo *sm.* 1. relief 2. (*importanza*) importance 3. (*osservazione*) remark 4. (*topografico*) survey 5. (*comm.*) taking over || *mettere in* —, to stress.

rilucente *agg.* glittering.

rilùcere *vi.* to glitter.

riluttante *agg.* reluctant.

riluttanza *sf.* reluctance.

riluttare *vi.* to reluct (at).

rima *sf.* rhyme || *rispondere per le rime,* to give (*v. irr.*) tit for tat.

rimandare *vt.* 1. to send (*v. irr.*) again 2. (*restituire*) to send back 3. (*posporre*) to postpone 4. (*far riferimento*) to refer 5. (*agli esami*) to make (*v. irr.*) (so.) repeat (an exam).

rimando *sm.* 1. returning 2. (*differimento*) postponement 3. (*segno di richiamo*) reference-mark.

rimaneggiamento *sm.* 1. rearrangement 2. (*di opera letteraria*) adaptation 3. (*pol.*) shuffle.

rimaneggiare *vt.* 1. to rearrange 2. (*modificare*) to change 3. (*pol.*) to shuffle.

rimanente *agg.* remaining. ♦ **rimanente** *sm.* rest.

rimanenza *sf.* remainder.

rimanere *vi.* 1. to remain 2. (*avanzare*) to be left 3. (*essere sorpreso*) to be astonished.

rimangiare *vt.* to eat (*v. irr.*) again. ♦ **rimangiarsi** *vr.* to take (*v. irr.*) back.

rimarchévole *agg.* remarkable.

rimare *vt.* e *vi.* to rhyme.

rimarginare *vt.* to heal. ♦ **rimarginarsi** *vr.* to heal.

rimaritare *vt.* to marry again. ♦ **rimaritarsi** *vr.* to marry again.

rimasticare *vt.* 1. to chew again 2. (*fig.*) to muse.

rimasuglio *sm.* remains (*pl.*).

rimatore *sm.* rhymer.

rimbalzare *vi.* to rebound.

rimbalzello *sm.* ducks and drakes.

rimbalzo *sm.* rebound: *di* —, on the rebound.

rimbambimento *sm.* dotage.

rimbambire *vi.* to reach one's dotage.

rimbambito *agg.* in one's dotage (*pred.*): *un vecchio* —, a dotard.

rimbeccare *vt.* to retort.

rimbecco *sm.* retort.

rimbecillire *vi.* 1. to grow (*v. irr.*) stupid 2. (*per età*) to reach one's dotage.

rimbecillito *agg.* doting.

rimboccare *vt.* to tuck up. ♦ **rimboccarsi** *vr.* to tuck up.

rimbombante *agg.* thundering.

rimbombare *vi.* 1. to thunder 2. (*risuonare*) to resound.

rimbombo *sm.* roar.

rimborsàbile *agg.* repayable.

rimborsare *vt.* to reimburse.

rimborso *sm.* reimbursement.

rimboscare *vt.* V. *rimboschire.*

rimboschimento *sm.* reafforestation.

irr.) wooded again.

rimboschire *vt.* to reafforest. ♦ **rimboschirsi** *vr.* to become (*v. irr.*) wooded again.

rimbrottare *vt.* to reproach.

rimbrotto *sm.* reproach.

rimediàbile *agg.* remediable.

rimediare *vi.* to find (*v. irr.*) a remedy (for).

rimedio *sm.* remedy.

rimembranza *sf.* memory.

rimembrare *vt.* to remember.

rimeritare *vt.* to reward.

rimescolamento *sm.* 1. stir 2. (*turbamento*) shock.

rimescolare *vt.* 1. to stir again 2. (*mescolare*) to stir. ♦ **rimescolarsi** *vr.* to be upset || *gli si rimescolò il sangue* (*per rabbia*), his blood boiled, (*per paura*), his blood ran cold.

rimescolìo *sm.* confusion.

rimessa *sf.* 1. replacing 2. (*per auto*) garage 3. (*di denaro*) remittance 4. (*di merci*) consignment || — *in gioco,* throw-in.

rimesso *agg.* 1. (*falso*) false 2. (*ristabilito*) well again 3. (*perdonato*) forgiven.

rimestare *vt.* V. *rimescolare.*

riméttere *vt.* 1. to put (*v. irr.*) again, to put back 2. (*consegnare*) to hand 3. (*mandare, perdonare*) to remit 4. (*affidare*) to leave (*v. irr.*) 5. (*vomitare*) to vomit || — *in gioco,* to throw (*v. irr.*) in; *rimetterci,* to lose (*v. irr.*). ♦ **riméttersi** *vr.* 1. (*affidarsi*) to rely on 2. (*ristabilirsi*) to recover 3. (*rasserenarsi*) to clear up.

rimirare *vt.* to gaze (at). ♦ **rimirarsi** *vr.* to admire oneself.

rimisurare *vt.* to measure again.

rimodellare *vt.* to remodel.

rimodernamento *sm.* modernization.

rimodernare *vt.* to modernize. ♦ **rimodernarsi** *vr.* to become up--to-date.

rimondare *vt.* to clean again.

rimonta *sf.* 1. (*mil.*) remount 2. (*sport*) catching up.

rimontare *vt.* 1. to go (*v. irr.*) up 2. (*ricomporre*) to reassemble. ♦ **rimontare** *vi.* 1. to remount 2. (*fig.*) to go back 3. (*sport*) to catch (*v. irr.*) up ‖ — *in auto,* to get (*v. irr.*) into a car again.

rimorchiare *vt.* to tow.

rimorchiatore *sm.* tug.

rimorchio *sm.* 1. tow 2. (*veicolo*) trailer.

rimòrdere *vt.* 1. to bite (*v. irr.*) again 2. (*fig.*) to prick.

rimorso *sm.* remorse.

rimosso *agg.* removed.

rimostranza *sf.* remonstrance: *fare le proprie rimostranze,* to remonstrate.

rimostrare *vi.* to remonstrate.

rimovibile *agg.* removable.

rimozione *sf.* removal.

rimpacchettare *vt.* to package again.

rimpadronirsi *vr.* to seize again.

rimpagliare *vt.* 1. to re-cover with straw 2. (*imbottire*) to re-stuff with straw.

rimpallo *sm.* counterblow.

rimpannucciarsi *vr.* (*fig.*) to improve one's financial position.

rimpastare *vt.* 1. to knead again 2. (*fig.*) to rearrange.

rimpasto *sm.* 1. kneading again 2. (*fig.*) rearrangement 3. (*pol.*) reshuffle.

rimpatriare *vt.* to repatriate. ♦ **rimpatriare** *vi.* to return to one's country.

rimpatrio *sm.* repatriation.

rimpetto *avv.* opposite.

rimpiàngere *vt.* 1. to regret 2. (*una perdita*) to mourn.

rimpianto *sm.* regret.

rimpiattarsi *vr.* to hide (*v. irr.*) oneself.

rimpiattino *sm.* hide-and-seek.

rimpiazzare *vt.* to replace.

rimpiazzo *sm.* replacement.

rimpicciolire *vt.* to lessen. ♦ **rimpicciolirsi** *vr.* to lessen.

rimpiegare *vt.* to re-employ.

rimpiego *sm.* re-employment.

rimpinguare *vt.* 1. to fatten 2. (*arricchire*) to enrich. ♦ **rimpinguarsi** *vr.* 1. to fatten 2. (*arricchirsi*) to grow (*v. irr.*) rich.

rimpinzare *vt.* to stuff (with).

rimpolpare *vt.* V. *rimpinguare.*

rimproverare *vt.* to reproach.

rimpròvero *sm.* reproach: *muovere un* —, to reproach.

rimuginare *vt.* to brood over.

rimunerare *vt.* to remunerate.

rimuòvere *vt.* 1. to remove 2. (*dissuadere*) to dissuade 3. (*da una carica*) to dismiss.

rimutare *vt.* to change again.

rinascenza *sf.* Renaissance.

rinàscere *vi.* to revive.

rinascimentale *agg.* Renaissance (*attr.*).

rinascimento *sm.* Renaissance.

rinàscita *sf.* 1. rebirth 2. (*fig.*) revival.

rincagnarsi *vr.* to frown.

rincagnato *agg.* pug (*attr.*).

rincalzare *vt.* 1. (*rimboccare*) to tuck in 2. (*sostenere*) to prop up.

rincalzo *sm.* support: *a — di,* in support of.

rincantucciare *vt.* to put (*v. irr.*) in a corner. ♦ **rincantucciarsi** *vr.* to hide (*v. irr.*) in a corner.

rincarare *vt.* 1. to raise the price of 2. (*esagerare*) to exaggerate. ♦ **rincarare** *vi.* to become (*v. irr.*) more expensive.

rincaro *sm.* rise in prices.

rincasare *vi.* to return home.

rinchiùdere *vt.* to shut (*v. irr.*) up.

rincitrullire *vt.* to make (*v. irr.*) silly. ♦ **rincitrullirsi** *vr.* to grow (*v. irr.*) silly.

rincivilire *vt.* to civilize. ♦ **rincivilirsi** *vr.* 1. to become (*v. irr.*) civilized 2. (*raffinarsi*) to become refined.

rincollare *vt.* to paste again.

rincominciare *vt.* to begin (*v. irr.*) again.

rincontrare *vt.* to meet (*v. irr.*) again. ♦ **rincontrarsi** *vr.* to meet again.

rincontro *sm.* meeting.

rincoramento *sm.* encouragement.

rincorare *vt.* to encourage. ♦ **rincorarsi** *vr.* to pluck up courage.

rincòrrere *vt.* to run (*v. irr.*) after.

rincorsa *sf.* run-up.

rincréscere *vi.* 1. to be sorry: *mi*

rincresce, I am sorry 2. (*dar noia*) to mind: *ti rincresce aprire la finestra?*, do you mind opening the window?

rincrescimento *sm.* regret: *con mio —*, to my regret.

rincrudimento *sm.* aggravation.

rincrudire *vi.* 1. to aggravate 2. (*esacerbare*) to embitter 3. (*del tempo*) to get (*v. irr.*) worse.

rinculare *vi.* to recoil.

rinculo *sm.* recoil.

rinfacciare *vt.* to throw (*v. irr.*) (sthg.) in so.'s face.

rinfiancare *vt.* to support.

rinfilare *vt.* 1. to thread again 2. (*rinserire*) to insert again. ♦ **rinfilarsi** *vr.* 1. (*introdursi*) to slip again 2. (*rindossare*) to slip on again.

rinfiorare *vt.* to adorn with flowers again.

rinfittire *vt.* 1. to thicken 2. (*rendere più frequenti*) to make (*v. irr.*) more frequent. ♦ **rinfittirsi** *vr.* (*di lana*) to shrink (*v. irr.*).

rinfocolare *vt.* 1. to poke 2. (*fig.*) to stir up (again).

rinfoderare *vt.* to sheathe (again).

rinforzamento *sm.* strengthening.

rinforzare *vt.* 1. to strengthen 2. (*mecc.*) to stiffen. ♦ **rinforzarsi** *vr.* to become (*v. irr.*) stronger.

rinforzo *sm.* 1. strengthening 2. (*mil.*) reinforcements (*pl.*) 3. (*fig.*) support 4. (*mecc.*) stiffener.

rinfrancare *vt.* to encourage. ♦ **rinfrancarsi** *vr.* 1. (*migliorare*) to improve 2. (*riprendere coraggio*) to pluck up courage.

rinfrescamento *sm.* cooling.

rinfrescante *agg.* refreshing.

rinfrescare *vt.* 1. to cool 2. (*ristorare*) to refresh 3. (*rinnovare*) to renovate. ♦ **rinfrescare** *vi.* to cool.

rinfresco *sm.* 1. refreshments (*pl.*) 2. (*ricevimento*) cocktail party.

rinfusa (*nella loc. avv.*) *alla —*, in confusion.

ringalluzzire *vt.* to make (*v. irr.*) cocky. ♦ **ringalluzzirsi** *vr.* to become (*v. irr.*) cocky.

ringentilire *vt.* to refine.

ringhiare *vi.* to snarl.

ringhiera *sf.* 1. railing 2. (*di scale*) banisters (*pl.*).

ringhio *sm.* snarl.

ringhioso *agg.* snarling.

ringiovanimento *sm.* rejuvenation.

ringiovanire *vt.* 1. to make (*v. irr.*) young again 2. (*far sembrare più giovane*) to make (so.) look younger. ♦ **ringiovanire** *vi.* 1. to grow (*v. irr.*) young again 2. (*sembrare più giovane*) to look younger.

ringiovanito *agg.* young again.

ringolare *vt.* to swallow up again.

ringranare *vt.* to re-engage.

ringraziamento *sm.* thanks (*pl.*).

ringraziare *vt.* to thank.

ringuainare *vt.* V. *rinfoderare*.

rinite *sf.* rhinitis.

rinnegàbile *agg.* deniable.

rinnegamento *sm.* disowning.

rinnegare *vt.* to disown.

rinnegato *agg.* e *sm.* renegade.

rinnegatore *sm.* disowner.

rinnestare *vt.* 1. (*agr.*) to graft again 2. (*mecc.*) to re-engage.

rinnesto *sm.* 1. (*agr.*) new grafting 2. (*mecc.*) re-engagement.

rinnovàbile *agg.* renewable.

rinnovamento *sm.* renewal.

rinnovare *vt.* to renew. ♦ **rinnovarsi** *vr.* (*riaccadere*) to happen again.

rinnovatore *sm.* renewer.

rinnovazione *sf.* renewal.

rinnovellare *vt.* to renew. ♦ **rinnovellarsi** *vr.* to be renewed.

rinnovo *sm.* renewal.

rinoceronte *sm.* rhinoceros.

rinolaringite *sf.* rhinolaryngitis.

rinologìa *sf.* rhinology.

rinomanza *sf.* renown.

rinomato *agg.* renowned.

rinominare *vt.* 1. to name again 2. (*designare di nuovo*) to reappoint.

rinoplàstica *sf.* rhinoplasty.

rinoscopìa *sf.* rhinoscopy.

rinoscopio *sm.* rhinoscope.

rinsaccare *vt.* to pack again. ♦ **rinsaccarsi** *vr.* to shrug one's shoulders.

rinsaldamento *sm.* consolidation.

rinsaldare *vt.* to consolidate.

rinsanguare *vt.* 1. to supply with new blood 2. (*fig.*) to reinvigorate. ♦ **rinsanguarsi** *vr.* 1. to recover 2. (*finanziariamente*) to re-establish one's financial condition.

rinsanire *vi.* 1. to recover 2. (*rinsavire*) to return to reason.

rinsavimento *sm.* return to reason.

rinsavire *vi.* to recover one's wits.

rinsecchire *vi.* 1. to dry up 2. (*di persone*) to get (*v. irr.*) thin 3.

(*avvizzire*) to wither.

rinserrare *vt.* to shut (*v. irr.*) up (again).

rintanarsi *vr.* to shut (*v. irr.*) oneself up.

rintascare *vt.* to pocket again.

rintavolare *vt.* to start again.

rintoccare *vi.* 1. (*di orologio*) to strike (*v. irr.*) 2. (*di campana*) to toll.

rintocco *sm.* 1. (*di orologio*) stroke 2. (*di campana*) toll.

rintontire *vt.* to stun. ♦ **rintontirsi** *vr.* to be stunned.

rintracciare *vt.* 1. to trace 2. (*trovare*) to find (*v. irr.*) out.

rintronamento *sm.* booming.

rintronare *vt.* 1. to deafen 2. (*stordire*) to stun. ♦ **rintronare** *vi.* to boom.

rintuzzare *vt.* 1. to blunt 2. (*ribattere*) to retort.

rinuncia *sf.* renouncement.

rinunciare *vi.* to renounce (sthg.).

rinunciatario *agg.* releasee.

rinvenimento *sm.* recovery.

rinvenire *vt.* to find (*v. irr.*). ♦ **rinvenire** *vi.* 1. to recover one's senses 2. (*riprendere freschezza*) to revive 3. (*riprendere morbidezza*) to soften.

rinverdire *vt.* (*ravvivare*) to reawaken. ♦ **rinverdire** *vi.* 1. to turn green again 2. (*ravvivarsi*) to revive.

rinvestimento *sm.* reinvestment.

rinvestire *vt.* 1. to restore to the possession of 2. (*comm.*) to reinvest.

rinviare *vt.* 1. to put (*v. irr.*) off 2. (*mandare indietro*) to return.

rinvigorimento *sm.* reinvigoration.

rinvigorire *vt.* to reinvigorate. ♦ **rinvigorirsi** *vr.* to regain strength.

rinvilire *vt.* to lower. ♦ **rinvilire** *vi.* to become (*v. irr.*) cheaper.

rinvìo *sm.* 1. postponement 2. (*il rimandare indietro*) returning.

rinvoltare *vt.* to wrap up again.

rinzaffare *vt.* 1. to bung again 2. (*arch.*) to rough in.

rinzaffatura *sf.* (*arch.*) roughing-in coat.

rio¹ *sm.* rivulet.

rio² *agg.* evil.

rioccupare *vt.* to reoccupy.

rioccupazione *sf.* reoccupation.

rionale *agg.* local, ward (*attr.*).

rione *sm.* ward, district.

riordinare *vt.* 1. to tidy up 2. (*riorganizzare*) to reorganize 3. (*comandare di nuovo*) to order again.

riordinatore *sm.* 1. rearranger 2. (*riorganizzatore*) reorganizer.

riordinazione *sf.* 1. rearrangement 2. (*riorganizzazione*) reorganization 3. (*nuova ordinazione*) new order.

riòrdino *sm.* V. *riordinazione.*

riorganizzare *vt.* to reorganize.

riorganizzatore *sm.* reorganizer.

riorganizzazione *sf.* reorganization.

riottosità *sf.* 1. turbulence 2. (*indocilità*) indocility.

riottoso *agg.* 1. turbulent 2. (*indocile*) indocile.

ripa *sf.* 1. bank 2. (*scarpata*) scarp.

ripagare *vt.* 1. to repay (*v. irr.*) 2. (*pagare di nuovo*) to pay (*v. irr.*) again.

riparare *vt.* 1. (*proteggere*) to shelter 2. (*aggiustare*) to repair 3. (*risarcire*) to redress || — un esame, to repeat an exam. ♦ **riparare** *vi.* 1. (*porre rimedio*) to remedy 2. (*rifugiarsi*) to take (*v. irr.*) shelter. ♦ **ripararsi** *vr.* to take shelter.

riparatore *agg.* repairing. ♦ **riparatore** *sm.* repairer.

riparazione *sf.* 1. repair: in —, under repair 2. (*fig.*) reparation.

riparlare *vi.* to speak (*v. irr.*) again.

riparo *sm.* 1. shelter 2. (*rimedio*) remedy 3. (*mecc.*) guard.

ripartire¹ *vi.* to start again.

ripartire² *vt.* to divide.

ripartizione *sf.* division.

ripassare *vi.* 1. to pass again 2. (*far visita*) to call again. ♦ **ripassare** *vt.* 1. (*riattraversare*) to cross again 2. (*dare di nuovo*) to pass again 3. (*rileggere, rivedere*) to go (*v. irr.*) through 4. (*mecc.*) to overhaul.

ripassata *sf.* 1. (*revisione*) revision 2. (*mecc.*) overhauling 3. (*pulita*) cleaning 4. (*mano di vernice*) new coat.

ripasso *sf.* 1. (*ritorno*) return 2. (*revisione*) revision 3. (*di lezioni*) review.

ripensamento *sm.* reflection: avere un —, to change one's mind.

ripensare *vi.* 1. to think (*v. irr.*) (of sthg., so.) again 2. (*riconside-*

rare) to think over **3.** (*cambiar pa-rere*) to change one's mind: *ci ho ripensato*, I have changed my mind.

ripercòrrere *vt.* to travel over (sthg.) again.

ripercuòtere *vt.* to strike (*v. irr.*) again. ♦ **ripercuòtersi** *vr.* **1.** to reverberate **2.** (*fig.*) to influence (so., sthg.).

ripercussione *sf.* repercussion.

ripescare *vt.* **1.** to catch (*v. irr.*) again **2.** (*ritrovare*) to find (*v. irr.*) again.

ripetente *s.* repeater.

ripètere *vt.* to repeat.

ripetitore *sm.* **1.** repeater **2.** (*scol.*) private tutor.

ripetizione *sf.* **1.** (*rifacimento*) repetition **2.** (*ripasso*) revision **3.** (*lezione privata*) private lesson || *arma a* —, repeater.

ripetuto *agg.* repeated.

ripiano *sm.* **1.** (*terreno*) terrace **2.** (*pianerottolo*) landing **3.** (*scaffale*) shelf (*pl.* -lves).

ripicco *sm.* spite: *per* —, out of spite.

ripidezza *sf.* steepness.

rìpido *agg.* steep.

ripiegamento *sm.* **1.** folding **2.** (*il curvare*) bending **3.** (*mil.*) withdrawal.

ripiegare *vt.* **1.** to bend (*v. irr.*) again **2.** (*piegare*) to fold. ♦ **ri-piegare** *vi.* **1.** to bend **2.** (*ritirar-si*) to withdraw (*v. irr.*). ♦ **ripie-garsi** *vr.* to bend.

ripiegatura *sf.* **1.** folding **2.** (*piega*) fold **2.** (*curva*) bend.

ripiego *sm.* **1.** expedient **2.** (*rimedio*) remedy.

ripienezza *sf.* fullness.

ripieno *agg.* **1.** full **2.** (*cuc.*) stuffed (with). ♦ **ripieno** *sm.* **1.** filling **2.** (*cuc.*) stuffing.

ripigliare *vt.* V. *riprendere.*

ripiombare *vt.* to plunge back. ♦ **ripiombare** *vi.* to fall (*v. irr.*) again.

ripopolamento *sm.* **1.** repeopling **2.** (*di animali*) restocking.

ripopolare *vt.* **1.** to repeople **2.** (*di animali*) to restock.

riporre *vt.* **1.** to replace **2.** (*metter via*) to put (*v. irr.*) away **3.** (*porre*) to place. ♦ **riporsi** *vr.* (*riprender-re*) to resume.

riportare *vt.* **1.** to bring (*v. irr.*)

again, to take (*v. irr.*) again **2.** (*portare indietro*) to bring back, to take back **3.** (*riferire*) to report **4.** (*citare*) to quote **5.** (*ricevere*) to get (*v. irr.*) **6.** (*mat.*) to carry. ♦ **riportarsi** *vr.* (*tornare*) to go (*v. irr.*) back.

riporto *sm.* **1.** (*mat.*) carry over **2.** (*in borsa*) contango **3.** (*ornamento*) appliqué.

riposante *agg.* restful.

riposare *vt.* **1.** to rest **2.** (*posare di nuovo*) to place back. ♦ **riposare** *vi.* to rest. ♦ **riposarsi** *vr.* to rest.

riposato *agg.* **1.** (*fresco*) fresh **2.** (*tranquillo*) quiet.

riposo *sm.* rest: *andare a* —, to retire.

ripostiglio *sm.* cupboard.

riprèndere *vt.* **1.** to take (*v. irr.*) again **2.** (*riavere*) to take back **3.** (*riassumere, ricominciare*) to re-sume **4.** (*ricuperare*) to recover **5.** (*rimproverare*) to reprove **6.** (*teat.*) to revive **7.** (*cine*) to shoot (*v. irr.*). ♦ **riprèndersi** *vr.* **1.** to recover **2.** (*da turbamento*) to collect oneself **3.** (*correggersi*) to correct oneself.

riprensione *sf.* reprehension.

riprensivo *agg.* reprehensive.

ripresa *sf.* **1.** renewal **2.** (*teat.; ri-nascita*) revival **3.** (*riconquista*) recapture **4.** (*da malattia*) recovery **5.** (*cine*) shot **6.** (*auto*) accelera-tion **7.** (*registrazione*) recording **8.** (*di pugilato*) round **9.** (*sport*) second half.

ripresentare *vt.* to present again.

ripristinare *vt.* **1.** to restore **2.** (*ri-mettere in vigore*) to re-establish.

ciprìstino *sm.* **1.** restoration **2.** (*il rimettere in vigore*) re-establish-ment.

riproducìbile *agg.* reproducible.

riprodurre *vt.* to reproduce. ♦ **ri-prodursi** *vr.* to reproduce.

riproduttivo *agg.* reproductive.

riproduttore *agg.* reproducing. ♦ **riproduttore** *sm.* reproducer.

riproduzione *sf.* reproduction.

ripromèttere *vt.* to promise again. ♦ **ripromèttersi** *vr.* **1.** to intend **2.** (*aspettarsi*) to expect.

riproporre *vt.* to re-propose. ♦ **ri-proporsi** *vr.* to re-propose.

riprova *sf.* (new) proof.

riprovare *vt.* **1.** to try again **2.** (*sentire di nuovo*) to feel (*v. irr.*)

again 3. (*disapprovare*) to criticize 4. (*scol.*) to fail.

riprovazione *sf.* reprobation.

riprovévole *agg.* 1. blamable 2. (*spregévole*) despicable.

ripubblicare *vt.* to republish.

ripudiare *vt.* to repudiate.

ripudio *sm.* repudiation.

ripugnante *agg.* repugnant.

ripugnanza *sf.* repugnance.

ripugnare *vi.* 1. (*disgustare*) to disgust 2. (*essere contrario*) to be repugnant.

ripulire *vt.* 1. to clean again 2. (*pulire*) to clean 3. (*fig.*) to polish 4. (*saccheggiare*) to ransack.

ripulita *sf.* clean: *darsi una —*, to tidy oneself up.

ripulsa *sf.* repulse.

ripulsione *sf.* repulsion.

ripulsivo *agg.* repulsive.

riquadrare *vt.* 1. to square 2. (*una stanza*) to decorate.

riquadratura *sf.* 1. square 2. (*decorazione*) decoration.

riquadro *sm.* 1. square 2. (*su parete*) panel.

risacca *sf.* surf.

risaia *sf.* rice-field.

risalire *vt.* 1. to go up (*v. irr.*) up again 2. (*contro corrente*) to go up: *— la corrente*, to go upstream. ♦ **risalire** *vi.* 1. to go up again 2. (*nel tempo*) to go back.

risaltare[1] *vi.* 1. to show (*v. irr.*) up 2. (*di persona*) to stand (*v. irr.*) out.

risaltare[2] *vt.* to jump again.

risalto *sm.* 1. prominence 2. (*rilievo*) relief.

risanàbile *agg.* 1. curable 2. (*bonificabile*) reclaimable.

risanamento *sm.* 1. curing 2. (*guarigione*) recovery 3. (*bonifica*) reclamation 4. (*fig.*) reformation ‖ *— di quartiere*, slum-clearance.

risanare *vt.* 1. to cure 2. (*bonificare*) to reclaim 3. (*un quartiere*) to clear (a slum). ♦ **risanare** *vi.* to recover.

risanatore *agg.* healing. ♦ **risanatore** *sm.* healer.

risapere *vt.* to come (*v. irr.*) to know.

risaputo *agg.* well-known.

risarcìbile *agg.* that can be indemnified.

risarcimento *sm.* indemnity.

risarcire *vt.* to indemnify.

risata *sf.* laugh: *scoppiare in una —*, to burst (*v. irr.*) out laughing.

riscaldamento *sm.* heating.

riscaldare *vt.* 1. to warm (up) 2. (*di casa*) to heat 3. (*fig.*) to excite. ♦ **riscaldarsi** *vr.* to warm up.

riscaldo *sm.* inflammation.

riscattàbile *agg.* redeemable.

riscattare *vt.* to redeem.

riscatto *sm.* 1. ransom 2. (*redenzione*) redemption.

rischiaramento *sm.* brightening.

rischiarare *vt.* to light (*v. irr.*) (up). ♦ **rischiararsi** *vr.* 1. to light up 2. (*diventare più chiaro*) to get (*v. irr.*) clearer 3. (*di cielo*) to clear up.

rischiare *vt.* to risk. ♦ **rischiare** *vi.* to run (*v. irr.*) the risk (of).

rischio *sm.* risk.

rischioso *agg.* risky.

risciacquare *vt.* to rinse. ♦ **risciacquarsi** *vr.* to rinse.

risciacquata *sf.* rinse.

risciacquatura *sf.* 1. rinsing 2. (*acqua*) dish-water.

riscontare *vt.* to rediscount.

risconto *sm.* rediscount.

riscontrare *vt.* 1. (*controllare*) to check 2. (*trovare*) to find (*v. irr.*) 3. (*confrontare*) to compare.

riscontro *sm.* 1. (*controllo*) checking 2. (*confronto*) comparison 3. (*risposta*) reply 4. (*corrispondenza simmetrica*) pendant.

riscoprire *vt.* to discover again.

riscossa *sf.* 1. (*rivolta*) revolt 2. (*riscatto*) redemption ‖ *andare alla —*, to counterattack.

riscossione *sf.* collection.

riscotìbile *agg.* collectable.

riscotimento *sm.* collection.

riscrìvere *vt.* 1. to rewrite (*v. irr.*) 2. (*in risposta*) to write (*v. irr.*) back.

riscuòtere *vt.* 1. (*denaro*) to collect 2. (*conseguire*) to win (*v. irr.*) 3. (*scuotere*) to shake (*v. irr.*). ♦ **riscuòtersi** *vr.* (*trasalire*) to start.

riseccare *vt.* to dry up. ♦ **riseccarsi** *vr.* to dry up.

risedersi *vr.* to sit (*v. irr.*) down again.

risega *sf.* 1. (*arch.*) offset 2. (*della pelle*) fold.

riseminare *vt.* to sow (*v. irr.*) again.

risentimento *sm.* resentment: *con —*, resentfully.

risentire *vt.* **1.** (*sentire di nuovo*) to feel (*v. irr.*) again **2.** (*riudire*) to hear (*v. irr.*) again **3.** (*sentire*) to feel || — *di qc.*, to show (*v. irr.*) traces of sthg.; (*di persona*) to feel the effect of sthg. ♦ **risentirsi** *vr.* to take (*v. irr.*) offence (at).

risentito *agg.* (*sdegnato*) resentful.

riserbare *vt.* V. *riservare.*

riserbo *sm.* **1.** reserve **2.** (*discrezione*) discretion.

riserva *sf.* **1.** reserve **2.** (*di caccia, pesca*) preserve.

riservare *vt.* to reserve. ♦ **riservarsi** *vr.* (*ripromettersi*) to intend: — *la diagnosi*, to refuse to formulate a definite diagnosis.

riservatezza *sf.* reservedness.

riservato *agg.* **1.** reserved **2.** (*segreto*) private.

risibile *agg.* laughable.

risicoltore *sm.* rice-grower.

risicoltura *sf.* rice-growing.

risièdere *vi.* to reside.

risma *sf.* **1.** ream **2.** (*fig.*) kind.

riso[1] *sm.* (*bot.*) rice.

riso[2] *sm.* laugh.

risolare *vt.* to resole.

risolatura *sf.* resoling.

risollevare *vt.* **1.** to raise again **2.** (*confortare*) to cheer up. ♦ **risollevarsi** *vr.* **1.** to rise again **2.** (*confortarsi*) to cheer up.

risolutezza *sf.* resolution.

risolutivo *agg.* resolutive.

risoluto *agg.* resolute.

risoluzione *sf.* **1.** resolution **2.** (*giur.*) cancellation.

risòlvere *vt.* **1.** to resolve **2.** (*rescindere*) to rescind. ♦ **risòlversi** *vr.* **1.** (*decidersi*) to make (*v. irr.*) up one's mind **2.** (*mutarsi*) to turn (into) **3.** (*di malattia*) to clear up.

risolvìbile *agg.* **1.** resolvable **2.** (*rescindibile*) rescindable.

risonante *agg.* resonant.

risonanza *sf.* resonance.

risonare *vt.* **1.** to play again **2.** (*un campanello*) to ring (*v. irr.*) again. ♦ **risonare** *vi.* to resound.

risòrgere *vi.* **1.** to rise (*v. irr.*) again **2.** (*rifiorire*) to revive || *far* —, to revive.

risorgimento *sm.* revival.

risorsa *sf.* resource.

risparmiare *vt.* **1.** to save **2.** (*evitare, salvare*) to spare.

risparmiatore *agg.* thrifty. ♦ **risparmiatore** *sm.* saver.

risparmio *sm.* saving: *senza* —, lavishly.

rispecchiare *vt.* to reflect. ♦ **rispecchiarsi** *vr.* to be reflected.

rispedire *vt.* **1.** to send (*v. irr.*) again **2.** (*spedire indietro*) to send back.

rispettàbile *agg.* respectable.

rispettabilità *sf.* respectability.

rispettare *vt.* **1.** to respect **2.** (*onorare*) to honour.

rispettivo *agg.* respective.

rispetto *sm.* respect: — *a*, as regards; *a* — *di*, in comparison to; *mancare di* — *a*, to be disrespectful to.

rispettoso *agg.* respectful.

risplendente *agg.* shining.

risplèndere *vi.* to shine (*v. irr.*).

rispolverare *vt.* **1.** to dust again **2.** (*fig.*) to brush up.

rispondente *agg.* answering (to).

rispondenza *sf.* correspondence.

rispòndere *vt.* e *vi.* **1.** to answer (so., sthg.) **2.** (*obbedire*) to respond || — *di qu., qc.*, to answer for so., sthg.

risposare *vt.* V. *rimaritare.*

risposta *sf.* answer, reply.

rispuntare *vi.* **1.** to reappear **2.** (*risorgere*) to rise (*v. irr.*) again **3.** (*di germogli*) to sprout again.

rissa *sf.* brawl.

rissare *vi.* to brawl.

rissoso *agg.* quarrelsome.

ristabilimento *sm.* **1.** restoration **2.** (*di salute*) recovery.

ristabilire *vt.* to restore. ♦ **ristabilirsi** *vr.* **1.** to settle again **2.** (*rimettersi*) to recover.

ristagnamento *sm.* **1.** stagnation **2.** (*di sangue*) staunching.

ristagnare *vi.* to stagnate. ♦ **ristagnare** *vt.* to staunch.

ristagno *sm.* (*econ.*) slackness.

ristampa *sf.* reprint: *essere in* —, to be reprinting.

ristampare *vt.* to reprint.

ristare *vi.* **1.** (*cessare*) to stop **2.** (*rimanere*) to remain.

ristoràbile *agg.* restorable.

ristorante *sm.* restaurant.

ristorare *vt.* to refresh, to restore (*anche fig.*).

ristoratore *agg.* refreshing. ♦ **ristoratore** *sm.* restorer.

ristoro *sm.* **1.** relief **2.** (*cibo, be-*

vanda) refreshment || *luogo di —*, refreshment-room.

ristrettezza *sf.* **1.** narrowness **2.** (*insufficienza*) lack || *— di idee*, narrow-mindedness.

ristretto *agg.* **1.** narrow **2.** (*condensato*) condensed.

ristringere *vt.* **1.** to tighten again **2.** (*premere di nuovo*) to press again || *— la mano a qu.*, to shake (*v. irr.*) hands with so. again.

ristuccare *vt.* **1.** (*edil.*) to replaster **2.** (*nauseare*) to surfeit.

ristuccatura *sf.* (*edil.*) replastering.

ristudiare *vt.* to study again.

risucchiare *vt.* to suck (again).

risucchio *sm.* whirlpool.

risultante *agg.* e *sf.* resultant.

risultanza *sf.* result.

risultare *vi.* **1.** to result **2.** (*venire a sapere*) to turn out || *mi risulta*, I know.

risultato *sm.* result.

risurrezione *sf.* resurrection.

risuscitamento *sm.* resuscitation.

risuscitare *vt.* e *vi.* to resuscitate.

risvegliare *vt.* to wake (*v. irr.*) (up). ♦ **risvegliarsi** *vr.* to wake up.

risveglio *sm.* **1.** awakening **2.** (*fig.*) revival.

risvoltare *vt.* to turn up.

risvolto *sm.* **1.** (*di giacca*) lapel **2.** (*di calzoni*) turn-up.

ritagliare *vt.* **1.** to cut (*v. irr.*) out **2.** (*tagliare di nuovo*) to cut again.

ritaglio *sm.* **1.** (*di stoffa*) remnant **2.** (*di giornale*) clipping || *ritagli di tempo*, odd moments.

ritardare *vt.* to delay. ♦ **ritardare** *vi.* **1.** to be late **2.** (*di orologio*) to be slow.

ritardatario *sm.* late-comer.

ritardo *sm.* delay: *in —*, late.

ritegno *sm.* **1.** reserve **2.** (*freno*) restraint **3.** (*riluttanza*) reluctance.

ritemprare *vt.* **1.** to strengthen **2.** (*metalli*) to harden again. ♦ **ritemprarsi** *vr.* to get (*v. irr.*) stronger.

ritenere *vt.* **1.** to hold (*v. irr.*) **2.** (*giudicare*) to consider **3.** (*pensare*) to think (*v. irr.*).

ritentare *vt.* **1.** to tempt again **2.** (*riprovare*) to try again.

ritenuta *sf.* deduction.

ritenzione *sf.* retention.

ritingere *vt.* to dye again.

ritirare *vt.* **1.** to withdraw (*v. irr.*)

2. (*farsi consegnare*) to collect. ♦ **ritirarsi** *vr.* **1.** to retire **2.** (*di stoffa*) to shrink (*v. irr.*).

ritirata *sf.* **1.** retreat **2.** (*latrina*) lavatory.

ritiro *sm.* **1.** withdrawal **2.** (*il ritirarsi*) retirement **3.** (*luogo appartato*) retreat **4.** (*il farsi consegnare*) collection.

ritmare *vt.* to mark.

ritmica *sf.* rhythmic(s).

ritmico *agg.* rhythmic(al).

ritmo *sm.* rhythm.

rito *sm.* rite: *essere di —*, to be customary.

ritoccare *vt.* to retouch.

ritoccatore *sm.* retoucher.

ritocco *sm.* retouch.

ritògliere *vt.* **1.** to take (*v. irr.*) off again **2.** (*riappropriarsi*) to take back. ♦ **ritògliersi** *vr.* to take off again.

ritòrcere *vt.* **1.** to twist again **2.** (*torcere*) to twist **3.** (*rivolgere*) to retort. ♦ **ritòrcersi** *vr.* **1.** to get (*v. irr.*) twisted **2.** (*fig.*) to recoil (on, upon).

ritorcitura *sf.* twisting.

ritornare *vi.* to return.

ritornello *sm.* refrain.

ritorno *sm.* return: *— di fiamma*, backfire; *essere di —*, to be back.

ritorsione *sf.* retortion.

ritorto *agg.* twisted.

ritrarre *vt.* **1.** to withdraw (*v. irr.*) **2.** (*distogliere*) to turn away **3.** (*rappresentare*) to represent **4.** (*dedurre*) to understand (*v. irr.*). ♦ **ritrarsi** *vr.* to withdraw.

ritrattare *vt.* **1.** to retract **2.** (*trattare di nuovo*) to treat again.

ritrattazione *sf.* **1.** retraction **2.** (*nuova trattazione*) new treatment.

ritrattista *s.* portraitist.

ritrattìstica *sf.* portraiture.

ritratto *sm.* portrait.

ritrazione *sf.* retraction.

ritrito *agg.* stale.

ritrosìa *sf.* **1.** (*riluttanza*) reluctance **2.** (*timidezza*) shyness.

ritroso *agg.* **1.** (*riluttante*) reluctant **2.** (*timido*) shy || *a —*, backwards.

ritrovamento *sm.* finding.

ritrovare *vt.* **1.** to find (*v. irr.*) again **2.** (*ricuperare*) to recover **3.** (*scoprire*) to discover. ♦ **ritrovarsi** *vr.* **1.** to find oneself **2.** (*rincontrarsi*) to meet (*v. irr.*) again.

ritrovato *sm.* 1. invention 2. (*scoperta*) discovery.
ritrovo *sm.* meeting-place, haunt.
ritto *agg.* upright.
rituale *agg.* e *sm.* ritual.
rituffare *vt.* to plunge again. ♦ **rituffarsi** *vr.* to plunge again.
riudire *vt.* to hear (*v. irr.*) again.
riunione *sf.* meeting.
riunire *vt.* 1. to re-unite 2. (*raccogliere*) to gather 3. (*unire*) to join. ♦ **riunirsi** *vr.* 1. to come (*v. irr.*) together again 2. (*unirsi*) to unite 3. (*incontrarsi*) to meet (*v. irr.*).
riuscire *vi.* 1. to succeed (in), to be good (at) 2. (*risultare*) to be 3. (*uscire di nuovo*) to go (*v. irr.*) out again.
riuscita *sf.* 1. issue 2. (*successo*) success.
riutilizzare *vt.* to utilize again.
riva *sf.* 1. (*di mare, lago*) shore 2. (*di fiume*) bank.
rivale *agg.* e *sm.* rival.
rivaleggiare *vi.* to rival (so., sthg.).
rivalersi *vr.* 1. to make (*v. irr.*) up for one's losses 2. (*valersi di nuovo*) to make use again.
rivalicare *vt.* to recross.
rivalità *sf.* rivalry.
rivalsa *sf.* 1. (*rivincita*) revenge 2. (*risarcimento*) compensation 3. (*comm.*) recourse.
rivalutare *vt.* 1. to revalue 2. (*elevare*) to raise.
rivalutazione *sf.* 1. revaluation 2. (*aumento*) rise.
rivangare *vt.* e *vi.* to dig (*v. irr.*) up again.
rivedere *vt.* 1. to see (*v. irr.*) again 2. (*revisionare*) to revise.
riveduta *sf.* look, revision.
rivelare *vt.* to reveal. ♦ **rivelarsi** *vr.* 1. to reveal oneself 2. (*dimostrarsi*) to prove.
rivelatore *agg.* revealing. ♦ **rivelatore** *sm.* 1. revealer 2. (*radio*) detector.
rivelazione *sf.* 1. revelation 2. (*fis.; radio*) detection.
rivéndere *vt.* 1. to resell (*v. irr.*) 2. (*al dettaglio*) to retail.
rivendicare *vt.* 1. to claim 2. (*vendicare*) to revenge.
rivendicare *agg.* 1. claiming 2. (*vendicatore*) revenging. ♦ **rivendicatore** *sm.* 1. claimant 2. (*vendicatore*) revenger.
rivendicazione *sf.* claim.

rivéndita *sf.* 1. resale 2. (*spaccio*) shop.
rivenditore *sm.* retailer.
rivendùgliolo *sm.* V. *rigattiere*.
riverberare *vt.* to reverberate. ♦ **riverberarsi** *vr.* to reverberate.
rivèrbero *sm.* reverberation: *di —*, indirectly.
riverente *agg.* reverent.
riverenza *sf.* 1. reverence 2. (*inchino*) bow.
riverenziale *agg.* reverential.
riverire *vt.* 1. to revere 2. (*salutare*) to pay (*v. irr.*) one's respects (to).
riversare *vt.* 1. to pour again 2. (*versare*) to pour 3. (*di fiume*) to flow. ♦ **riversarsi** *vr.* to flow.
riverso *avv.* on one's back.
rivestimento *sm.* 1. covering 2. (*interno*) lining.
rivestire *vt.* 1. to dress again 2. (*foderare*) to line (with sthg.) 3. (*coprire*) to cover (with sthg.) 4. (*fig.*) to hold (*v. irr.*).
riviera *sf.* coast ‖ *la Riviera*, the Riviera.
rivierasco *agg.* coast (*attr.*).
rivìncere *vt.* 1. to win (*v. irr.*) again 2. (*recuperare*) to win back.
rivìncita *sf.* 1. (*vendetta*) revenge 2. (*sport*) return match 3. (*al gioco*) return game.
rivista *sf.* 1. review 2. (*teat.*) revue 3. (*mil.*) parade ‖ *passare in —*, to review.
rivivere *vi.* e *vt.* to live again.
rivo *sm.* stream.
rivolere *vt.* 1. to want again 2. (*volere indietro*) to want back.
rivòlgere *vt.* 1. to turn 2. (*indirizzare*) to address. ♦ **rivòlgersi** *vr.* 1. to turn 2. (*parlando*) to address (so.) 3. (*ricorrere, riferirsi*) to apply (to).
rivolgimento *sm.* 1. upheaval 2. (*cambio*) change.
rivolo *sm.* streamlet.
rivolta *sf.* revolt.
rivoltante *agg.* revolting.
rivoltare *vt.* 1. to turn (over) again 2. (*rovesciare*) to turn 3. (*capovolgere*) to turn upside-down 4. (*con l'interno all'esterno*) to turn inside out 5. (*fig.*) to upset (*v. irr.*). ♦ **rivoltarsi** *vr.* 1. to turn round 2. (*rigirarsi*) to turn over 3. (*ribellarsi*) to revolt 4. (*fig.*) to turn.
rivoltella *sf.* revolver.

rivoltoso *agg. e sm.* rebel.

rivoluzionare *vt.* to revolutionize.

rivoluzionario *agg. e sm.* revolutionary.

rivoluzione *sf.* revolution.

rizoma *sm.* rhizome.

rizzare *vt.* to raise: — *le orecchie,* to prick one's ears. ◆ **rizzarsi** *vr.* **1.** to stand (*v. irr.*) up **2.** (*di capelli*) to stand on end.

roba *sf.* stuff, things (*pl.*).

robaccia *sf.* rubbish.

robinia *sf.* locust-tree.

robustezza *sf.* robustness.

robusto *agg.* robust.

rocambolesco *agg.* daring.

rocca¹ *sf.* **1.** stronghold **2.** (*roccia*) rock.

rocca² *sf.* (*conocchia*) distaff.

roccaforte *sf.* stronghold.

rocchetto *sm.* **1.** spool **2.** (*elettr.*) coil.

rocchio *sm.* **1.** (*di tronco*) log **2.** (*di colonna*) drum.

roccia *sf.* rock.

rocciatore *sm.* rock-climber.

roccioso *agg.* rocky.

roco *agg.* hoarse.

rodaggio *sm.* (*auto*) running in.

rodare *vt.* to run (*v. irr.*) in.

ròdere *vt.* **1.** to gnaw **2.** (*corrodere*) to corrode. ◆ **ròdersi** *vr.* **1.** to worry **2.** (*di rabbia ecc.*) to be consumed (with).

rodimento *sm.* **1.** gnawing **2.** (*fig.*) anxiety.

roditore *agg. e sm.* rodent.

rododendro *sm.* rhododendron.

rogare *vt.* to draw (*v. irr.*) up.

rogatoria *sf.* request.

rogazioni *sf. pl.* rogations.

roggia *sf.* irrigation ditch.

rògito *sm.* deed.

rogna *sf.* **1.** scabies **2.** (*fig.*) trouble.

rognone *sm.* kidney.

rognoso *agg.* scabby.

rogo *sm.* **1.** fire **2.** (*pira*) pyre **3.** (*supplizio*) stake.

rollare *vi.* to roll.

rollìo *sm.* roll.

romancio *agg.* Romansh.

romànico *agg.* **1.** (*arch.*) Romanesque **2.** Romanic.

romano *agg. e sm.* Roman.

romanticherìa *sf.* **1.** (*atteggiamento*) romantic attitude **2.** (*azione*) romantic deed.

romanticismo *sm.* Romanticism.

romàntico *agg. e sm.* romantic.

romanza *sf.* romance.

romanzare *vt.* to romanticize.

romanzesco *agg.* romantic.

romanziere *sm.* novelist.

romanzo¹ *agg.* Romance.

romanzo² *sm.* **1.** novel **2.** (*storia incredibile*) romance || — *a puntate,* serial; — *a fumetti,* comics.

romba *sf.* roar.

rombare *vi.* to rumble.

ròmbico *agg.* rhombic(al).

rombo¹ *sm.* (*rumore*) rumble.

rombo² *sm.* (*geom.*) rhomb.

rombo³ *sm.* (*itt.*) brill.

romboèdrico *agg.* rhombohedral.

romboedro *sm.* rhombohedron (*pl.* -ra).

romboidale *agg.* rhomboid(al).

rombòide *agg. e sm.* rhomboid.

romeno *agg. e sm.* Rumanian.

romeo *sm.* pilgrim.

romitaggio *sm.* hermitage.

ròmito *agg.* solitary. ◆ **romito** *sm.* hermit.

romitorio *sm.* hermitage.

ròmpere *vt.* to break (*v. irr.*): — *i ponti con qu.,* to break with so. ◆ **ròmpersi** *vr.* to break (up).

rompicapo *sm.* puzzle.

rompicollo *sm.* madcap: *a —,* headlong.

rompighiaccio *sm.* ice-breaker.

rompiscàtole *s.* nuisance.

rompitore *sm.* breaker.

ronca *sf.* pruning-knife (*pl.* -ives).

ronciglio *sm.* hook.

ròncola *sf.* pruning-hook.

ronda *sf.* **1.** rounds (*pl.*) **2.** (*pattuglia*) patrol.

rondella *sf.* washer.

ròndine *sf.* swallow: *a coda di —,* swallow-tailed.

rondinotto *sm.* young swallow.

rondò *sm.* **1.** (*mus.*) rondo **2.** (*poet.*) rondel **3.** (*piazza circolare*) circus.

rondone *sm.* swift.

ronfare *vi.* to snore.

ronzare *vi.* **1.** to buzz **2.** (*fig.*) to hang (*v. irr.*) around.

ronzino *sm.* jade.

ronzìo *sm.* buzz.

ròrido *agg.* **1.** (*bagnato*) wet **2.** (*rugiadoso*) dewy.

rosa *sf.* rose || *all'acqua di rose* (*fig.*), moderate. ◆ **rosa** *agg. e sm.* pink.

rosàceo *agg.* rosy.

rosaio *sm.* rose-bush.

rosario *sm.* rosary.

rosato *agg.* rosy.

ròseo *agg.* rosy.

rosèola *sf.* roseola.

roseto *sm.* rose-garden.

rosetta *sf.* 1. rosette 2. (*diamante*) rose 3. (*mecc.*) washer.

rosicchiare *vt.* to gnaw.

rosmarino *sm.* rosemary.

rosolare *vt.* to brown. ♦ **rosolarsi** *vr.* 1. to get (*v. irr.*) brown 2. (*prendere il sole*) to bask.

rosolìa *sf.* German measles (*pl.*).

rosolio *sm.* rosolio.

rosone *sm.* rose-window.

rospo *sm.* toad.

rossastro *agg.* reddish.

rosseggiare *vi.* to be reddish.

rossetto *sm.* 1. (*per labbra*) lipstick 2. (*per guance*) rouge.

rossiccio *agg.* ruddy.

rosso *agg.* e *sm.* red: — *d'uovo*, yolk; *diventar* —, to flush.

rossore *sm.* flush.

rosticcerìa *sf.* rotisserie.

rosticciere *sm.* owner of a rotisserie.

rostro *sm.* 1. rostrum (*pl.* -ra) 2. (*becco*) beak.

rotàbile *agg.* carriage (*attr.*).

rotaia *sf.* 1. rail 2. (*solco*) rut.

rotare *vi.* e *vt.* to rotate, to revolve.

rotativa *sf.* rotary press.

rotativo *agg.* rotary.

rotatorio *agg.* rotating.

rotazione *sf.* rotation.

roteare *vt.* 1. to swing (*v. irr.*) 2. (*gli occhi*) to roll. ♦ **roteare** *vi.* to wheel.

rotella *sf.* small wheel.

rotocalco *sm.* 1. rotogravure 2. (*rivista*) illustrated magazine.

rotolamento *sm.* rolling.

rotolare *vt.* e *vi.* to roll. ♦ **rotolarsi** *vr.* to roll.

ròtolo *sm.* roll || *andare a rotoli*, to go (*v. irr.*) to rack and ruin; *mandare a rotoli*, to ruin.

rotolone *sm.* V. *ruzzolone*.

rotonda *sf.* rotunda.

rotondità *sf.* roundness.

rotondo *agg.* 1. round 2. (*grassoccio*) plump.

rotore *sm.* rotor.

rotta *sf.* 1. course 2. (*rottura*) breach 3. (*sconfitta*) rout || *a — di collo*, headlong; *essere in — con*, to be on bad terms with; *mettere in* —, to rout.

rottame *sm.* 1. wreck 2. (*di scarto*) scraps (*pl.*).

rotto *agg.* 1. broken 2. (*stracciato*) torn 3. (*avvezzo*) accustomed.

rottura *sf.* break(ing).

ròtula *sf.* knee-cap.

rovente *agg.* red-hot.

ròvere *sm.* oak.

rovesciamento *sm.* 1. overthrowing 2. (*cambiamento*) reversal.

rovesciare *vt.* 1. to overturn 2. (*capovolgere*) to turn upside down 3. (*gettare*) to throw (*v. irr.*) 4. (*rivoltare*) to turn inside out 5. (*versare intenzionalmente*) to pour 6. (*versare accidentalmente*) to spill 7. (*abbattere*) to overthrow (*v. irr.*). ♦ **rovesciarsi** *vr.* 1. to overturn 2. (*riversarsi*) to pour.

rovescio *sm.* 1. reverse 2. (*opposto*) opposite 3. (*di pioggia*) heavy shower 4. (*di critiche ecc.*) hail || *a —* (*capovolto*), upside down.

roveto *sm.* bramble-bush.

rovina *sf.* ruin.

rovinare *vt.* 1. to ruin 2. (*sciupare*) to spoil (*v. irr.*). ♦ **rovinare** *vi.* to crash.

rovinìo *sm.* 1. downfall 2. (*rumore*) crash.

rovinoso *agg.* ruinous.

rovistare *vt.* e *vi.* to rummage.

rovo *sm.* blackberry bush.

rozza *sf.* jade.

rozzezza *sf.* roughness.

rozzo *agg.* rough.

ruba *sf.* *andare a* —, to sell (*v. irr.*) like wildfire.

rubacchiare *vt.* to pilfer.

rubacuori *agg.* bewitching. ♦ **rubacuori** *sm.* lady-killer.

rubare *vt.* to steal (*v. irr.*).

ruberìa *sf.* theft.

rubicondo *agg.* ruddy.

rubinetterìa *sf.* plumbing fixtures (*pl.*).

rubinetto *sm.* tap.

rubino *sm.* ruby.

rubizzo *agg.* hale.

rublo *sm.* rouble.

rubrica *sf.* 1. (*di giornale*) column 2. (*per indirizzi*) addressbook.

rude *agg.* rough.

rùdere *sm.* ruin.

rudezza *sf.* roughness.

rudimentale *agg.* rudimentary.

rudimento *sm.* rudiment.

ruffiano *sm.* pander.

ruga *sf.* wrinkle.

ruggente *agg.* roaring.

rùggine sf. 1. rust 2. (fig.) grudge.
rugginoso agg. rusty.
ruggire vi. to roar.
ruggito sm. roar.
rugiada sf. dew: goccia di —, dew-drop.
rugiadoso agg. dewy.
rugosità sf. 1. wrinkledness 2. (scabrosità) ruggedness.
rugoso agg. 1. wrinkled 2. (scabro) rugged.
rullaggio sm. pista di —, taxi-track.
rullare vi. 1. to roll 2. (di aereo) to taxi.
rullino sm. roll.
rullìo sm. roll.
rullo sm. 1. roll 2. (mecc.) roller.
rum sm. rum.
ruminante agg. e sm. ruminant.
ruminare vt. to ruminate.
ruminazione sf. rumination.
rùmine sm. rumen.
rumore sm. 1. noise 2. (diceria) rumour || far — (fig.), to arouse great interest.
rumoreggiare vi. 1. to rumble 2. (fig.) to rumour.
rumorìo sm. noise.
rumorista sm. noise-maker.
rumoroso agg. noisy.
ruolino sm. (di marcia) time schedule.
ruolo sm. 1. roll, list 2. (teat.) role 3. (amm.) roster.
ruota sf. wheel.
rupe sf. cliff.
rupestre agg. rocky.
rurale agg. rural || i rurali, country people.
ruscello sm. brook.
ruspa sf. scraper.
ruspare vi. (razzolare) to scratch about.
russare vi. to snore.
russo agg. e sm. Russian.
rusticità sf. rusticity.
rùstico agg. 1. rustic 2. (ritroso) unsociable.
ruta sf. rue.
rutilante agg. glowing.
ruttare vi. to belch.
rutto sm. belch.
rùvido agg. rough.
ruzzare vi. to romp.
ruzzolare vt. to roll. ♦ **ruzzolare** vi. 1. to roll 2. (cadere) to tumble down.
ruzzolone sm. tumble: fare un —, to tumble down.

S

sàbato sm. Saturday.
sabba sm. witches' Sabbath.
sabbia sf. sand.
sabbiare vt. to sand.
sabbiatura sf. sand-bath.
sabbioso agg. sandy.
sabotaggio sm. sabotage.
sabotare vt. to sabotage.
sabotatore sm. saboteur.
sacca sf. bag.
saccarina sf. saccharine.
saccarosio sm. saccharose.
saccente agg. pedantic. ♦ **saccente** s. ped.int.
saccheggiare vt. to sack.
saccheggio sm. sack.
sacchetto sm. small bag.
sacco sm. 1. sack, bag || colazione al —, picnic; mettere qu. nel —, to take (v. irr.) so. in 2. (grande quantità) a lot of.
saccoccia sf. pocket.
saccone sm. palliasse.
sacerdotale agg. sacerdotal.
sacerdote sm. priest.
sacerdozio sm. priesthood.
sacrale agg. sacral.
sacramentale agg. sacramental.
sacramentare vi. (fig.) to swear (v. irr.).
sacramento sm. sacrament.
sacrario sm. shrine.
sacrificare vt. to sacrifice.
sacrificio sm. sacrifice.
sacrilegio sm. sacrilege.
sacrìlego agg. sacrilegious.
sacrista sm. sacristan.
sacro agg. sacred, holy.
sacrosanto agg. 1. sacrosanct 2. (indiscutibile) absolute.
sàdico agg. sadistic. ♦ **sàdico** sm. sadist.
sadismo sm. sadism.
saetta sf. 1. arrow 2. (fulmine) thunderbolt.
saettare vt. 1. to shoot (v. irr.) arrows at 2. (fig.) to dart. ♦ **saettare** vi. to dart.
sàffico agg. Sapphic.
sagace agg. sagacious.
sagacia sf. sagacity.
saggezza sf. wisdom.
saggiare vt. to assay, to test.
saggiatore sm. 1. assayer 2. (bilancia) assay balance.
saggina sf. sorghum.

saggio[1] *agg.* wise. ◆ **saggio** *sm.* wise man (*pl.* men).

saggio[2] *sm.* 1. essay 2. (*campione*) sample 3. (*saggio ginnico*) display.

saggista *s.* essayist.

sagittario *sm.* 1. archer 2. (*astr.*) Sagittarius.

sàgoma *sf.* shape || **è** *una* —! (*fam.*), he is a character!

sagomare *vt.* to shape.

sagra *sf.* festival.

sagrato *sm.* church-square.

sagrestano *sm.* sacristan.

sagrestìa *sf.* sacristy.

saia *sf.* serge.

saio *sm.* habit.

sala *sf.* hall, room: — *da pranzo*, dining-room.

salace *agg.* salacious.

salacità *sf.* salacity.

salamandra *sf.* salamander.

salame *sm.* salami (*pl.*).

salamelecco *sm.* salaam.

salamoia *sf.* pickle.

salare *vt.* to salt.

salariale *agg.* salary (*attr.*).

salariato *agg.* wage-earning. ◆ **salariato** *sm.* wage-earner.

salario *sm.* wages (*pl.*).

salassare *vt.* to bleed (*v. irr.*).

salasso *sm.* 1. bleeding 2. (*fig.*) extortion.

salato *agg.* 1. salty 2. (*costoso*) dear 3. (*salace*) keen.

salatura *sf.* salting.

salda *sf.* starch-water.

saldamente *avv.* firmly.

saldare *vt.* 1. to solder, to weld 2. (*un conto*) to settle.

saldatore *sm.* solderer, welder.

saldatrice *sf.* welding machine.

saldatura *sf.* soldering, welding.

saldezza *sf.* firmness.

saldo[1] *agg.* firm.

saldo[2] *sm.* balance: — *attivo*, *passivo*, credit, debit balance.

sale *sm.* salt.

salesiano *agg.* e *sm.* Salesian.

salgemma *sm.* rock-salt.

sàlice *sm.* willow.

salicilato *sm.* salicylate.

saliente *agg.* important.

saliera *sf.* salt-cellar.

salina *sf.* salt-pit.

salino *agg.* saline, salt (*attr.*).

salire *vi.* 1. to rise (*v. irr.*), to go (*v. irr.*) up 2. (*di prezzi*) to increase.

saliscendi *sm.* 1. latch 2. (*alter-*

narsi di salite e discese) ups and downs (*pl.*).

salita *sf.* 1. slope, ascent 2. (*aumento*) rise.

saliva *sf.* saliva, spittle.

salivare *agg.* salivary.

salivare *vi.* to salivate.

salivazione *sf.* salivation.

salma *sf.* corpse.

salmastro *agg.* saltish.

salmo *sm.* psalm.

salmodìa *sf.* psalmody.

salmodiare *vi.* to sing (*v. irr.*) psalms.

salmone *sm.* salmon.

salnitro *sm.* saltpetre.

salone *sm.* large hall, reception-room.

salottiero *agg.* drawing-room (*attr.*).

salotto *sm.* sitting-room.

salpare *vi.* to set (*v. irr.*) sails.

salsa *sf.* sauce.

salsèdine *sf.* saltness.

salsiccia *sf.* sausage.

salsiera *sf.* sauce-boat.

salso *agg.* salt (*attr.*).

saltare *vt.* e *vi.* to jump, to leap (*v. irr.*): — *di palo in frasca*, to jump from one subject to another; *far* — *una serratura*, to break (*v. irr.*) a lock.

saltatore *agg.* jumping. ◆ **saltatore** *sm.* jumper.

saltellare *vi.* to hop.

saltimbanco *sm.* tumbler.

salto *sm.* jump, leap.

saltuario *agg.* desultory.

salubre *agg.* healthy.

salubrità *sf.* healthiness.

salume *sm.* salted meat.

salumiere *sm.* delicatessen seller.

salumerìa *sf.* delicatessen.

salutare[1] *agg.* healthy.

salutare[2] *vt.* to greet, to hail.

salute *sf.* health.

saluto *sm.* greeting, salute.

salva *sf.* volley (*anche fig.*): *colpo a* —, blank shot.

salvacondotto *sm.* safe-conduct.

salvadanaio *sm.* money-box.

salvagente *sm.* 1. life-belt 2. (*marciapiede*) traffic island.

salvaguardare *vt.* to safeguard.

salvaguardia *sf.* safeguard.

salvare *vt.* 1. to save (*anche fig.*) 2. (*trarre in salvo*) to rescue. ◆ **salvarsi** *vr.* to save oneself.

salvataggio *sm.* rescue.

salvatore *sm.* saviour, saver.

salve *inter.* hail.

salvezza *sf.* salvation.

salvia *sf.* sage.

salvietta *sf.* towel.

salvo *agg.* safe. ♦ **salvo** *prep.* except, save. ♦ **salvo che** *cong.* except that, unless.

sanàbile *agg.* curable, remediable.

sanare *vt.* to heal.

sanatorio *sm.* sanatorium (*pl.* -ia).

sancire *vt.* to sanction.

sanculotto *sm.* sansculotte.

sàndalo[1] *sm.* (*calzatura*) sandal.

sàndalo[2] *sm.* (*mar.*) punt.

sandolino *sm.* small canoe.

sangue *sm.* blood: *spargimento di* —, bloodshed; *perdita di* —, bleeding; — *freddo*, coolness; *a* — *freddo*, in cold blood; *farsi cattivo* —, to worry over; *buon* — *non mente*, blood will tell.

sanguigno *agg.* sanguineous, blood (*attr.*).

sanguinaccio *sm.* blood-sausage.

sanguinante *agg.* bleeding.

sanguinare *vi.* to bleed (*v. irr.*).

sanguinario *agg. e sm.* sanguinary: *uomo* —, bloodthirsty man.

sanguinoso *agg.* bloody.

sanguisuga *sf.* leech.

sanità *sf.* soundness, sanity.

sanitario *agg.* sanitary.

sano *agg.* 1. healthy 2. (*fig.*) sound 3. (*intero, intatto*) intact.

sansa *sf.* husk.

sànscrito *sm.* Sanskrit.

santarellina *sf.* goody-goody.

santificante *agg.* sanctifying.

santificare *vt.* to canonize: — *le feste*, to observe holy days.

santificazione *sf.* sanctification.

santino *sm.* small holy picture.

santìssimo *agg.* most holy: *il* — *Sacramento*, the Blessed Sacrament.

santità *sf.* holiness.

santo *agg.* 1. holy 2. (*seguito da nome proprio*) saint. ♦ **santo** *sm.* saint.

santone *sm.* santon.

santuario *sm.* sanctuary.

sanzionare *vt.* to ratify.

sanzione *sf.* sanction.

sapere[1] *vt.* 1. to know (*v. irr.*): *non* — *che fare*, to be at a loss what to do; *chi sa!*, who knows!; *non si sa mai*, you never know; *venire a* —, to hear (*v. irr.*) 2. (*essere capace*) can, to be able: *sai parlare inglese?*, can you speak English?; *non so farlo*, I am not able to do it. ♦ **sapere** *vi.* (*aver sapore*) to taste.

sapere[2] *sm.* 1. knowledge 2. (*cultura*) learning.

sàpido *agg.* sapid.

sapiente *agg.* wise. ♦ **sapiente** *sm.* sage.

sapienza *sf.* wisdom.

saponaria *sf.* soapwort.

saponata *sf.* lather (*solo sing.*).

sapone *sm.* soap: — *da barba*, shaving-soap; — *da bagno*, bath soap.

saponetta *sf.* cake of soap.

saponificare *vt.* to saponify.

saponificazione *sf.* saponification.

saponificio *sm.* soap-works (*pl. con costruzione sing.*).

sapore *sm.* taste, flavour (*anche fig.*).

saporire *vt.* to flavour.

saporitamente *avv.* savourily || *dormire* —, to sleep (*v. irr.*) soundly.

saporito *agg.* savoury, tasty.

saputello *sm.* wiseacre.

saputo *agg.* 1. learned 2. (*noto*) well-known.

sarabanda *sf.* saraband.

saraceno *sm.* saracen.

saracinesca *sf.* rolling-shutter.

sarcasmo *sm.* sarcasm.

sarcàstico *agg.* sarcastic.

sarchiare *vt.* to weed.

sarchiatore *agg.* weeding. ♦ **sarchiatore** *sm.* weeder.

sarchiatura *sf.* weeding.

sarchio *sm.* hoe.

sarcòfago *sm.* sarcophagus (*pl.* -gi).

sardina *sf.* sardine.

sardònico *agg.* sardonic.

sarmento *sm.* runner.

sarta *sf.* dressmaker.

sartie *sf. pl.* shrouds.

sartina *sf.* grisette.

sarto *sm.* tailor.

sartorìa *sf.* 1. (*da uomo*) tailor's 2. (*da donna*) dressmaker's.

sassaia *sf.* stony place.

sassaiuola *sf.* 1. shower of stones 2. (*battaglia di sassi*) stone-fight.

sassata *sf.* blow with a stone.

sasso *sm.* stone: *a un tiro di* — *da*, within a stone's throw of.

sassofonista *sm.* saxophonist

sassòfono *sm.* saxophone.

sassolino *sm.* pebble.

sàssone *agg. e sm.* Saxon.

sassoso *agg.* stony.
satànico *agg.* Satanic.
satèllite *sm.* satellite.
sàtira *sf.* satire.
satìrico *agg.* satirical.
sàtiro *sm.* satyr.
satollare *vt.* to satiate.
satollo *agg.* satiated.
sàtrapo *sm.* satrap.
saturare *vt.* to saturate.
saturazione *sf.* saturation.
saturnali *sm. pl.* saturnalia.
sàturo *agg.* saturated.
sàuro *agg.* sorrel.
savana *sf.* savannah.
savio *agg.* wise. ◆ **savio** *sm.* sage.
saziàbile *agg.* satiable.
saziare *vt.* to satisfy, to glut. ◆
   saziarsi *vr.* to get (*v. irr.*) full.
sazietà *sf.* satiety: *mangiare, bere
   a* —, to eat (*v. irr.*), to drink (*v.
   irr.*) one's fill.
sazio *agg.* replete, full.
sbaciucchiare *vt.* to smother with
   kisses.
sbadatàggine *sf.* carelessness.
sbadato *agg.* careless.
sbadigliare *vi.* to yawn.
sbadiglio *sm.* yawn.
sbafare *vi.* to scrounge.
sbafatore *sm.* scrounger.
sbafo (*nella loc. avv.*) *prendere qc.
   a* —, to scrounge sthg.
sbagliare *vi.* to mistake (*v. irr.*).
   ◆ **sbagliarsi** *vr.* to make (*v. irr.*)
   a mistake.
sbagliato *agg.* wrong.
sbaglio *sm.* mistake.
sbalestrare *vt.* 1. to send (*v. irr.*)
   2. (*fig.*) to flounder.
sballare *vt.* to unpack.
sballato *agg.* (*fig.*) foolhardy.
sballottamento *sm.* jolting.
sballottare *vt.* to jolt (about), to
   toss (about).
sbalordimento *sm.* amazement.
sbalordire *vt.* to amaze.
sbalorditivo *agg.* amazing.
sbalordito *agg.* amazed.
sbalzamento *sm.* 1. overthrow 2.
   (*fig.*) dismissal.
sbalzare[1] *vt.* to throw (*v. irr.*), to
   toss.
sbalzare[2] *vt.* (*arte*) to emboss.
sbalzato *agg.* (*arte*) embossed.
sbalzo *sm.* 1. bound, jump 2. (*cambio*) change.
sbancare *vt.* to leave (*v. irr.*)
   broke.

sbandamento *sm.* 1. dispersal 2.
   (*auto*) skid 3. (*mar.*) list.
sbandare *vt.* 1. to disperse 2. (*auto*) to cause a skid.
sbandata *sf.* V. *sbandamento.*
sbandato *sm.* straggler.
sbandierare *vt.* (*fig.*) to display.
sbaragliare *vt.* to rout.
sbaraglio *sm.* jeopardy: *mettere
   allo* —, to jeopardize.
sbarazzare *vt.* to clear up. ◆ **sbarazzarsi** *vr.* to get (*v. irr.*) rid
   (of).
sbarazzino *agg.* free and easy. ◆
   sbarazzino *sm.* little scamp.
sbarbare *vt.* to shave.
sbarbatello *sm.* young colt.
sbarcare *vt. e vi.* to land, to disembark.
sbarco *sm.* 1. (*di passeggeri*) landing 2. (*di merci*) unloading.
sbarra *sf.* 1. bar 2. (*del timone*)
   tiller.
sbarramento *sm.* 1. barricade 2.
   (*di acque*) dam 3. (*mil.*) barrage.
sbarrare *vt.* 1. to bar: — *un assegno*, to cross a cheque 2. (*spalancare*) to open wide.
sbarrato *agg.* blocked ‖ *occhi
   sbarrati*, wide open eyes.
sbatacchiamento *sm.* banging,
   slamming.
sbatacchiare *vt.* to bang, to slam.
sbàttere *vt.* 1. (*urtare contro*) to
   knock 2. (*scaraventare*) to throw
   (*v. irr.*) 3. (*chiudere violentemente*) to slam 4. (*di panna, uova*) to
   whip, to beat (*v. irr.*).
sbattezzare *vt.* to force to abjure
   Christianity.
sbattimento *sm.* banging.
sbattiuova *sm.* egg-whisk.
sbattuto *agg.* 1. depressed: *viso*
   —, tired face 2. (*di uova*) beaten.
sbavare *vi.* 1. to dribble 2. (*tip.*)
   to smudge.
sbavatura *sf.* 1. dribble 2. (*tip.*)
   smudge.
sbellicarsi *vr.* — *dalle risa*, to split
   (*v. irr.*) one's sides with laughter.
sbendare *vt.* to unbandage.
sberla *sf.* slap.
sberleffo *sm.* grimace.
sbertucciare *vt.* 1. to mock 2.
   (*sgualcire*) to crumple.
sbiadire *vi.* to fade.
sbiancare *vt.* to bleach. ◆ **sbiancare** *vi.* to turn white. ◆ **sbian-
   carsi** *vr.* to turn white.

sbieco agg. slanting: *guardare qu. di —*, to look askance at so.; *tagliare una stoffa di —*, to cut (v. irr.) a cloth on the bias.

sbigottimento sm. dismay.

sbigottire vt. to dismay. ♦ **sbigottirsi** vr. to be dismayed.

sbigottito agg. dismayed.

sbilanciare vt. to unbalance. ♦ **sbilanciarsi** vr. 1. to lose (v. irr.) one's balance 2. (fig.) to commit oneself.

sbilancio sm. lack of balance; disproportion.

sbilenco agg. crooked.

sbirciare vt. to cast (v. irr.) a sidelong glance.

sbirraglia sf. police (us. al pl.).

sbirro sm. policeman (pl. -men).

sbizzarrirsi vr. to satisfy one's whims.

sbloccare vt. to raise the blockade: *— gli affitti*, to decontrol rents.

sblocco sm. 1. raising the blockade 2. (mecc.) releasing the brake 3. (econ.) decontrol.

sboccare vi. 1. (di corso d'acqua) to flow 2. (di strada) to lead (v. irr.).

sboccato agg. (fig.) coarse.

sbocciare vi. to open, to blossom.

sboccio sm. blooming.

sbocco sm. outlet, exit.

sbocconcellare vt. to nibble.

sbollire vi. (fig.) to cool down.

sbolognare vt. to palm off.

sbornia sf. drunkenness: *prendere la —*, to get (v. irr.) drunk.

sborsamento sm. paying out.

sborsare vt. to pay (v. irr.) out.

sborso sm. 1. payment 2. (denaro sborsato) outlay.

sbottare vi. to burst (v. irr.) out.

sbotto sm. outburst.

sbottonare vt. to unbutton. ♦ **sbottonarsi** vr. 1. to undo (v. irr.) one's buttons 2. (fig.) to disclose one's feelings.

sbozzare vt. to sketch out.

sbracare vt. to unbreech.

sbracato agg. (fig.) unseemly.

sbracciare vi. to gesticulate. ♦ **sbracciarsi** vr. 1. to roll up one's sleeves 2. (agitarsi) to strive (v. irr.).

sbracciato agg. (di persona) with bare arms.

sbraitare vi. to shout.

sbranamento sm. tearing to pieces.

sbranare vt. to tear (v. irr.) to pieces.

sbrancare vt. to separate. ♦ **sbrancarsi** vr. to scatter.

sbrattare vt. to clean.

sbriciolamento sm. crumbling.

sbriciolare vt. to crumble.

sbrigare vt. to finish off, to get (v. irr.) through. ♦ **sbrigarsi** vr. to hurry up.

sbrigativo agg. quick, hasty.

sbrigliare vt. to unbridle.

sbrinamento sm. defrosting.

sbrinare vt. to defrost.

sbrindellare vt. to tear (v. irr.) to ribbons.

sbrodolare vt. to spill (v. irr.).

sbrodolone sm. 1. slovenly eater 2. (chi parla a lungo) babbler.

sbrogliare vt. to disentangle. ♦ **sbrogliarsi** vr. to extricate oneself.

sbronza sf. V. *sbornia*.

sbronzarsi vr. to get (v. irr.) drunk.

sbronzo agg. drunk.

sbruffare vt. to besprinkle. ♦ **sbruffare** vi. (fig.) to brag.

sbruffo sm. sprinkle.

sbruffone sm. braggart.

sbucare vi. 1. to come (v. irr.) out 2. (fig.) to spring (v. irr.).

sbucciare vt. 1. to peel 2. (sgranare) to shell.

sbucciatura sf. 1. peeling 2. (scalfittura) scratch.

sbudellamento sm. stabbing.

sbudellare vt. to stab.

sbuffare vi. 1. to pant, to puff 2. (per noia, ira) to snort.

sbuffo sm. 1. puff 2. (per noia, ira) snort.

sbugiardare vt. to give (v. irr.) the lie to.

sbullonare vt. to unbolt.

scabbia sf. scabies.

scabbioso agg. scabby.

scabro agg. rough.

scabrosità sf. 1. roughness 2. (fig.) difficulty.

scabroso agg. 1. rough 2. (fig.) scabrous.

scacchiera sf. chess-board.

scacchiere sm. (stor.) Exchequer.

scacchista sm. chess-player.

scacciacani sf. dummy pistol.

scacciare vt. 1. to drive (v. irr.) away 2. (da scuola) to expel.

scacciata sf. expulsion.

scaccino *sm.* church cleaner.

scacco *sm.* 1. (*quadratino*) square 2. (*disegno su tessuti*) check 3. (*giuoco*) chess || — *matto*, checkmate.

scadente *agg.* 1. poor 2. (*comm.*) falling due.

scadenza *sf.* (*comm.*) maturity: *a breve, lunga scadenza* (*comm.*), at short, long maturity || *a breve* —, in a short time.

scadenzario *sm.* discount bill-book.

scadere *vi.* 1. to expire 2. (*di pagamenti ecc.*) to become (*v. irr.*) due 3. (*peggiorare*) to fall (*v. irr.*) off.

scadimento *sm.* decay.

scafandro *sm.* diving-suit.

scaffalare *vt.* to shelve.

scaffalatura *sf.* shelving.

scaffale *sm.* shelf (*pl.* shelves).

scafo *sm.* hull, body.

scagionare *vt.* to acquit. ♦ **scagionarsi** *vr.* to exculpate oneself.

scaglia *sf.* 1. scale 2. (*di legno, pietra*) chip.

scagliare *vt.* to fling (*v. irr.*), to throw (*v. irr.*).

scaglionare *vt.* to divide into groups.

scaglione *sm.* 1. group 2. (*mil.*) echelon.

scaglioso *agg.* scaly.

scala *sf.* 1. stairs (*pl.*) 2. (*trasportabile*) ladder 3. (*scala graduata*) scale || *salire, scendere le scale*, to go (*v. irr.*) upstairs, downstairs.

scalare[1] *agg.* gradual.

scalare[2] *vt.* 1. to climb (up) 2. (*diminuire*) to scale down.

scalata *sf.* climbing.

scalatore *sm.* climber.

scalcagnato *agg.* down-at-heel, shabby.

scalciare *vi.* to kick.

scalcinato *agg.* 1. unplastered 2. (*sciatto*) shabby.

scaldabagno *sm.* water-heater.

scaldaletto *sm.* bed-warmer.

scaldapiedi *sm.* foot-warmer.

scaldare *vt.* to heat, to warm. ♦ **scaldarsi** *vr.* to warm oneself, to get (*v. irr.*) warm.

scaldavivande *sm.* dish-warmer.

scaldino *sm.* hand-warmer.

scalea *sf.* flight of stairs.

scaleno *agg.* scalene.

scalfire *vt.* to scratch.

scalfittura *sf.* scratch.

scalinata *sf.* flight of steps.

scalino *sm.* step.

scalmanarsi *vr.* (*fig.*) to get (*v. irr.*) excited.

scalmanato *agg.* out of breath, excited.

scalmo *sm.* rowlock.

scalo *sm.* 1. (*mar.; aer.*) port of call: *volo senza* —, non-stop flight 2. (*ferr.*) goods station || *fare* — *a*, to touch at.

scalogna *sf.* bad luck.

scalognato *agg.* unlucky.

scalone *sm.* great staircase.

scaloppina *sf.* veal cutlet.

scalpellare *vt.* to chisel.

scalpellino *sm.* stone-cutter.

scalpello *sm.* chisel.

scalpicciare *vi.* to shuffle.

scalpiccìo *sm.* shuffling.

scalpitare *vi.* 1. to paw 2. (*di persona*) to stamp.

scalpitìo *sm.* 1. pawing 2. (*di persona*) stamping.

scalpore *sm.* fuss, noise.

scaltrezza *sf.* shrewdness.

scaltrire *vt.* to sharpen so.'s wits. ♦ **scaltrirsi** *vr.* to become (*v. irr.*) sharp.

scaltro *agg.* shrewd.

scalzacane *sm.* 1. (*incompetente*) botcher 2. (*malridotto*) down-and- -out.

scalzare *vt.* 1. to take (*v. irr.*) so.'s shoes and socks off 2. (*fig.*) to undermine.

scalzo *agg.* barefoot.

scambiare *vt.* 1. to exchange 2. (*sbagliarsi*) to mistake (*v. irr.*).

scambiévole *agg.* reciprocal.

scambio *sm.* 1. exchange 2. (*ferr.*) points (*pl.*).

scambista *sm.* (*ferr.*) pointsman (*pl.* -men).

scamiciato *agg.* shirt-sleeved (*attr.*).

scamosciare *vt.* to chamois.

scamosciato *agg.* shammy.

scampagnata *sf.* trip into the country.

scampanare *vt.* to chime.

scampanellare *vi.* to ring (*v. irr.*) long and loudly.

scampanellata *sf.* loud long ring.

scampare *vi.* to escape || *l'hai scampata bella!*, you have had a narrow escape.

scampato *sm.* survivor.

scampo[1] *sm.* escape: *via di* —, escape.

scampo² *sm.* (*itt.*) shrimp.
scàmpolo *sm.* remnant.
scanalare *vt.* to channel.
scanalatura *sf.* groove.
scandagliare *vt.* to sound.
scandaglio *sm.* sounding-lead.
scandalizzare *vt.* to shock.
scandalizzato *agg.* shocked.
scàndalo *sm.* scandal: *fare uno —,* to stir up a scandal.
scandaloso *agg.* scandalous, shocking.
scandire *vt.* **1.** to scan **2.** (*parole*) to syllabize **3.** (*mus.*) to stress.
scannare *vt.* **1.** to cut (*v. irr.*) so.'s throat **2.** (*uccidere crudelmente*) to slaughter.
scannatoio *sm.* slaughter-house.
scanno *sm.* seat.
scansafatiche *sm.* lazy-bones.
scansare *vt.* to avoid, to shun. ◆ **scansarsi** *vr.* to step aside.
scansìa *sf.* shelves (*pl.*).
scantinato *sm.* basement.
scantonamento *sm.* (*l'evitare*) avoiding.
scantonare *vt.* (*evitare*) to avoid. ◆ **scantonare** *vi.* to turn the corner.
scanzonato *agg.* unconventional.
scapaccione *sm.* slap.
scapatàggine *sf.* recklessness.
scapestrato *agg.* e *sm.* madcap.
scapigliare *vt.* to dishevel.
scapigliato *agg.* **1.** dishevelled **2.** (*fig.*) unruly.
scàpito *sm.* damage, detriment: *a — di,* to the detriment of.
scàpola *sf.* shoulder-blade.
scapolare *agg.* e *sm.* scapular.
scàpolo *agg.* single. ◆ **scàpolo** *sm.* bachelor.
scappamento *sm.* **1.** escape **2.** (*di motori*) exhaust.
scappare *vi.* to escape, to run (*v. irr.*) away ‖ *lasciarsi —,* to miss.
scappata *sf.* **1.** escape **2.** (*breve visita*) call.
scappatella *sf.* prank.
scappatoia *sf.* loop-hole.
scappellarsi *vr.* to take (*v. irr.*) off one's hat.
scappellata *sf.* raising one's hat.
scappellotto *sm.* slap.
scarabeo *sm.* scarab.
scarabocchiare *vt.* e *vi.* to scribble.
scarabocchio *sm.* scribble.
scarafaggio *sm.* black-beetle.
scaramanzìa *sf.* per —, for luck.

scaramuccia *sf.* skirmish.
scaraventare *vt.* to hurl.
scarcerare *vt.* to release (from prison).
scarcerazione *sf.* release (from prison).
scardinare *vt.* to unhinge.
scàrica *sf.* **1.** (*di armi da fuoco; elettr.*) discharge **2.** (*di proiettili, frecce; fig.*) shower.
scaricabarili *sm. fare a —,* to lay (*v. irr.*) the blame on so. else.
scaricamento *sm.* unloading.
scaricare *vt.* to discharge.
scaricatoio *sm.* **1.** wharf **2.** (*tubo*) waste-pipe.
scaricatore *sm.* unloader: *— di porto,* docker.
scàrico *sm.* **1.** (*scolo*) drain **2.** (*di merci*) discharge. ◆ **scàrico** *agg.* **1.** (*di arma*) unloaded **2.** discharged.
scarlattina *sf.* scarlet fever.
scarlatto *agg.* scarlet.
scarmigliare *vt.* to dishevel.
scarnire *vt.* to take (*v. irr.*) flesh off.
scarno *agg.* thin, lean.
scarpa *sf.* shoe: *— col tacco alto,* high-heeled shoe; *lucido per scarpe,* shoe polish.
scarpata *sf.* scarp.
scarpone *sm.* boot.
scarroccio *sm.* (*mar.*) leeway.
scarrozzare *vt.* e *vi.* to drive (*v. irr.*) about.
scarsamente *avv.* scarcely.
scarseggiare *vi.* to be lacking (in).
scarsità *vt.* shortage, lack.
scarso *agg.* scanty, lacking in.
scartabellare *vt.* to look through.
scartafaccio *sm.* note-book.
scartamento *sm.* (*ferr.*) gauge: *— ridotto,* narrow gauge.
scartare¹ *vt.* (*mettere da parte*) to reject.
scartare² *vi.* to unwrap.
scartare³ *vt.* (*sport*) to swerve.
scarto¹ *sm.* **1.** (*cosa scartata*) discard **2.** (*lo scartare*) discarding.
scarto² *sm.* (*deviazione*) swerve.
scartocciare *vt.* to unwrap.
scartoffie *sf. pl.* heap of papers.
scassare *vt.* (*rompere*) to force open.
scassinare *vt.* to break (*v. irr.*) open.
scassinatore *sm.* **1.** house-breaker **2.** (*di notte*) burglar.

scasso *sm.* lock-picking, house--breaking: *furto con —* (*di giorno*), house-breaking; (*di notte*) burglary.

scatenamento *sm.* (*fig.*) outburst.

scatenare *vt.* **1.** (*aizzare*) to stir up **2.** (*suscitare*) to rouse. ♦ **scatenarsi** *vr.* **1.** to break (*v. irr.*) loose **2.** (*fig.*) to break out.

scàtola *sf.* **1.** box **2.** (*di latta*) tin.

scatolame *sm.* **1.** tins (*pl.*) **2.** (*cibo in scatola*) tinned food.

scattare *vi.* **1.** (*adirarsi*) to lose (*v. irr.*) one's temper **2.** to go (*v. irr.*) off; to spring (*v. irr.*). ♦ **scattare** *vt.* (*foto*) to shoot (*v. irr.*).

scatto *sm.* **1.** (*d'ira*) outburst ‖ *di —,* suddenly; *a scatti,* in jerks **2.** (*rumore*) click **3.** (*di stipendio*) increase.

scaturire *vi.* **1.** to spring (*v. irr.*) **2.** (*derivare*) to originate.

scavalcare *vt.* **1.** (*gettare da cavallo*) to unhorse **2.** (*fig.*) to supplant **3.** (*passare sopra*) to step, to jump over.

scavare *vt.* **1.** to dig (*v. irr.*) **2.** (*archeologia*) to excavate.

scavatrice *sf.* excavator.

scavezzacollo *sm.* reckless fellow.

scavo *sm.* **1.** digging **2.** (*archeologia*) excavation.

scégliere *vt.* to choose (*v. irr.*), to pick out.

sceicco *sm.* sheik.

scelleratezza *sf.* **1.** wickedness **2.** (*atto scellerato*) misdeed. ♦ **scellerato** *agg.* wicked. ♦ **scellerato** *sm.* wicked person.

scellino *sm.* shilling: *mezzo —,* sixpence.

scelta *sf.* choice.

scelto *agg.* choice, selected.

scemare *vi.* to diminish.

scemenza *sf.* stupidity.

scemo *agg. e sm.* stupid.

scempiare *vt.* to halve.

scempio¹ *agg.* stupid, foolish.

scempio² *sm.* havoc.

scena *sf.* **1.** scene **2.** (*palcoscenico*) stage: *colpo di —,* stage effect.

scenario *sm.* scenery.

scenata *sf.* row.

scéndere *vi.* **1.** to go (*v. irr.*) down, to come (*v. irr.*) down **2.** (*da un veicolo*) to get (*v. irr.*) off; (*da cavallo*), to dismount (from a horse) **3.** (*declinare*) to slope down **4.** (*di astri*) to sink (*v. irr.*) **5.** (*avere origini*) to descend.

scendiletto *sm.* bedside-carpet.

sceneggiare *vt.* to arrange into scenes.

sceneggiatore *sm.* scenarist.

sceneggiatura *sf.* screenplay.

scenicamente *avv.* scenically.

scenografia *sf.* scenography.

scèrnere *vt.* to choose (*v. irr.*).

scervellarsi *vr.* to rack one's brains.

scervellato *agg.* brainless. ♦ **scervellato** *sm.* brainless person.

scetticismo *sm.* scepticism.

scèttico *agg.* sceptical. ♦ **scèttico** *sm.* sceptic.

scettro *sm.* sceptre.

sceverare *vt.* to discern.

scevro *agg.* exempt.

scheda *sf.* card: *— elettorale,* voting-paper.

schedario *sm.* card-index.

scheggia *sf.* splinter, chip.

scheggiare *vt.* to chip, to splinter.

schelètrico *agg.* skeletal.

schèletro *sm.* skeleton.

schema *sm.* **1.** scheme **2.** (*tec.*) diagram.

schemàtico *agg.* schematic.

schematismo *sm.* schematism.

scherma *sf.* fencing.

schermaglia *sf.* skirmish.

schermare *vt.* **1.** to screen **2.** (*elettr.*) to shield.

schermirsi *vr.* to act coy.

schermitore *sm.* fencer.

schermo *sm.* **1.** protection **2.** (*cine*) screen **3.** (*fis.*) shield **4.** (*foto*) filter.

schernire *vt.* to laugh at.

scherno *sm.* mockery, derision.

scherzare *vi.* **1.** to joke **2.** (*considerare con leggerezza*) to trifle with.

scherzo *sm.* **1.** joke: *per —,* for fun **2.** (*effetto*) effects (*pl.*).

scherzosamente *avv.* playfully.

scherzoso *agg.* playful.

schettinare *vi.* to roller-skate.

schettini *sm. pl.* roller-skates.

schiaccianoci *sm.* nut-cracker.

schiacciante *agg.* (*decisivo*) overwhelming.

schiacciare *vt.* to crush, to squash.

schiacciasassi *sm.* steam-roller.

schiaffare *vt.* to hurl.

schiaffeggiare *vt.* to slap.

schiaffo *sm.* **1.** slap **2.** (*affronto*) slap in the face.

schiamazzare *vi.* to make (*v. irr.*) a din.

schiamazzo *sm.* din, uproar.

schiantare *vt.* to break (*v. irr.*). ♦
schiantarsi *vr.* to break, to crash.
schiarimento *sm.* (*spiegazione*) explanation.
schiarire *vt.* to clear, to make (*v. irr.*) clear: — *i capelli*, to bleach one's hair. ♦ **schiarirsi** *vr.* (*fig.*) to brighten.
schiarita *sf.* 1. clearing 2. (*miglioramento*) improvement.
schiattare *vi.* to burst: — *di rabbia*, to burst with rage.
schiavista *sm.* 1. anti-abolitionist 2. (*mercante di schiavi*) slave-trader.
schiavitù *sf.* slavery.
schiavo *agg. e sm.* slave.
schidionata *sf.* spitful.
schidione *sm.* spit.
schiena *sf.* 1. back 2. (*di monte*) ridge.
schienale *sm.* back.
schiera *sf.* 1. formation 2. (*gruppo di persone*) group.
schieramento *sm.* array.
schierare *vt.* to array. ♦ **schierarsi** *vr.* 1. to draw (*v. irr.*) up 2. (*parteggiare*) to side with.
schiettezza *sf.* openness, purity.
schietto *agg.* pure, open.
schifare *vt.* to loathe. ♦ **schifarsi** *vr.* to feel (*v. irr.*) disgusted (at).
schifezza *sf.* disgusting thing.
schifiltoso *agg.* squeamish.
schifo[1] *sm.* disgust.
schifo[2] *sm.* (*mar.*) skiff.
schifoso *agg.* disgusting.
schioccare *vi.* 1. to crack 2. (*le dita*) to snap 3. (*le labbra*) to smack.
schiocco *sm.* 1. crack 2. (*di labbra*) smack.
schiodare *vt.* to unnail.
schiodatura *sf.* unnailing.
schioppettata *sf.* shot.
schioppo *sm.* gun.
schiùdere *vt.* to open. ♦ **schiùdersi** *vr.* to open.
schiuma *sf.* 1. foam 2. (*di vino, birra*) froth 3. (*di sapone*) lather.
schiumare *vt.* to skim. ♦ **schiumare** *vi.* 1. to foam 2. (*di bevande*) to froth.
schiumarola *sf.* skimmer.
schiumoso *agg.* 1. (*di mare*) foamy 2. (*di bevande*) frothy 3. (*di sapone*) lathery.
schiuso *agg.* open.

schivare *vt.* to avoid.
schivata *sf.* dodge.
schivo *agg.* shy, bashful.
schizofrenia *sf.* schizophrenia.
schizofrènico *agg.* schizophrenic. ♦ **schizofrènico** *sm.* schizophrene.
schizzare *vt.* 1. to splash, to spatter 2. (*abbozzare*) to sketch. ♦ **schizzare** *vi.* to spurt.
schizzata *sf.* splashing.
schizzatoio *sm.* spray.
schizzetto *sm.* spray.
schizzinoso *agg.* squeamish, fussy.
schizzo *sm.* 1. splash, squirt 2. (*pitt.*) sketch.
sci *sm.* ski.
scia *sf.* 1. (*mar.*) wake 2. (*traccia*) trail.
scià *sm.* shah.
sciàbica *sf.* trawl.
sciàbola *sf.* sabre.
sciabolata *sf.* sabre-cut.
sciabolatore *sm.* sabreur.
sciabordare *vi.* to wash.
sciabordìo *sm.* washing, lapping.
sciacallo *sm.* 1. jackal 2. (*fig.*) profiteer.
sciacquare *vt.* to rinse (out).
sciacquatura *sf.* 1. rinsing 2. (*acqua*) rinsing-water.
sciacquìo *sm.* rinsing.
sciacquone *sm.* flush.
sciagura *sf.* misfortune.
sciagurato *agg.* 1. unlucky 2. (*malvagio*) wicked. ♦ **sciagurato** *sm.* wretch.
scialacquare *vt.* to squander.
scialacquatore *sm.* squanderer.
scialacquìo *sm.* squandering.
scialare *vt.* to squander money.
scialbare *vt.* to plaster.
scialbo *agg.* pale, wan.
scialle *sm.* shawl.
scialo *sm.* waste.
scialuppa *sf.* boat.
sciamannato *agg.* slovenly.
sciamano *sm.* shaman.
sciamare *vi.* to swarm.
sciame *sm.* swarm.
sciancarsi *vr.* to become (*v. irr.*) lame.
sciancato *agg.* lame.
sciarada *sf.* charade.
sciare[1] *vi.* to ski.
sciare[2] *vi.* (*mar.*) to back water.
sciarpa *sf.* scarf.
sciàtica *sf.* sciatica.
sciàtico *agg.* sciatic.
sciatore *sm.* skier.

sciatterìa *sf.* slovenliness.

sciatto *agg.* 1. slovenly, untidy 2. (*di stile ecc.*) careless.

scìbile *sm.* knowledge.

sciccherìa *sf.* smartness.

scientifico *agg.* scientific.

scienza *sf.* science.

scienziato *sm.* scientist.

scilinguàgnolo *sm.* glib tongue.

scimitarra *sf.* scimitar.

scimmia *sf.* monkey, ape (*anche fig.*).

scimmiesco *agg.* monkeyish.

scimmiottare *vt.* to ape.

scimmiotto *sm.* young monkey.

scimpanzé *sm.* chimpanzee.

scimunito *agg.* silly. ♦ **scimunito** *sm.* blockhead.

scìndere *vt.* to divide: — le questioni, to deal (*v. irr.*) with each matter separately.

scintilla *sf.* spark.

scintillamento *sf.* sparkling.

scintillante *agg.* sparkling.

scintillare *vi.* to sparkle.

scintillìo *sm.* sparkling.

scintoismo *sm.* Shintoism.

scintoista *sm.* Shintoist.

scioccamente *avv.* foolishly.

sciocchezza *sf.* 1. foolishness 2. foolish thing 3. trifle.

sciocco *agg.* silly.

sciògliere *vt.* 1. to melt 2. (*slegare, disfare*) to untie 3. (*liberare*) to release 4. (*risolvere*) to solve. ♦ **sciògliersi** *vr.* to dissolve, to get (*v. irr.*) loose.

scioglilingua *sm.* tongue-twister.

scioglimento *sm.* 1. dissolution, breaking up 2. (*epilogo*) unravelling.

sciolina *sf.* ski wax.

scioltezza *sf.* 1. agility 2. (*spigliatezza*) ease 3. (*nel parlare*) fluency.

sciolto *agg.* 1. melted 2. (*slegato*) untied 3. (*agile*) agile 4. (*disinvolto*) easy || *capelli sciolti*, loose hair; *avere la lingua sciolta*, to have a ready tongue; — *da obblighi*, free from obligations.

scioperante *sm.* striker.

scioperare *vi.* to strike (*v. irr.*).

scioperatàggine *sf.* laziness.

scioperato *agg.* lazy. ♦ **scioperato** *sm.* lazy fellow.

sciòpero *sm.* strike.

sciorinare *vt.* to air, to display (*anche fig.*).

sciovìa *sf.* ski-lift.

sciovinismo *sm.* chauvinism.

sciovinista *sm.* chauvinist.

scipitàggine *sf.* insipidity (*anche fig.*).

scipito *agg.* insipid.

scirocco *sm.* sirocco.

sciroppare *vt.* to syrup.

sciroppato *agg.* in syrup.

sciropposo *agg.* syrupy.

scisma *sm.* schism.

scismàtico *agg. e sm.* schismatic.

scissione *sf.* 1. scission, split (*anche fig.*) 2. (*fis.; biol.*) fission.

scisso *agg.* divided.

scissura *sf.* 1. cleft, split 2. (*fig.*) dissension.

sciupare *vt.* 1. to spoil (*v. irr.*), to damage 2. (*sprecare*) to waste.

sciupato *agg.* 1. spoilt 2. (*sprecato*) wasted.

sciupìo *sm.* waste.

sciupone *agg.* wasteful. ♦ **sciupone** *sm.* waster.

scivolamento *sm.* sliding.

scivolare *vi.* 1. to slide (*v. irr.*) 2. (*involontariamente*) to slip.

scivolata *sf.* 1. slide 2. (*involontaria*) slip.

scivolo *sm.* 1. (*aer.; mar.*) slipway 2. skid.

scivolone *sm.* slip.

scivoloso *agg.* slippery.

sclerosi *sf.* sclerosis.

scleròtica *sf.* sclerotic.

scleròtico *agg.* sclerotic.

scoccare *vt. e vi.* 1. to shoot (*v. irr.*) 2. (*l'ora*) to strike (*v. irr.*).

scocciare *vt.* to bother.

scocciatore *sm.* bore.

scocciatura *sf.* bother.

scodella *sf.* bowl.

scodellare *vt.* to dish up.

scodinzolare *vi.* to wag the tail.

scodinzolìo *sm.* tail-wagging.

scogliera *sf.* cliff.

scoglio *sm.* 1. rock 2. (*fig.*) difficulty.

scoiare *vt.* V. *scuoiare*.

scoiàttolo *sm.* squirrel.

scolapasta *sm.* colander.

scolara *sf.* pupil, schoolgirl.

scolare *vt.* 1. to drain 2. (*in un colabrodo*) to strain.

scolaresca *sf.* student-body.

scolaro *sm.* pupil, schoolboy.

scolàstica *sf.* scholasticism.

scolàstico *agg.* 1. school (*attr.*) 2. (*dispregiativo*) bookish.

scolatoio *sm.* drain.

scolatura *sf.* draining.
scoliosi *sf.* scoliosis.
scollacciato *agg.* 1. (*di abito*) low--necked 2. (*fig.*) coarse.
scollare¹ *vt.* to cut (*v. irr.*) away the neck of.
scollare² *vt.* (*staccare*) to unglue.
scollato¹ *agg.* (*di abito*) low-necked.
scollato² *agg.* unglued.
scollatura *sf.* neckline.
scollo *sm.* neck-opening.
scolo *sm.* draining.
scolorare *vt.* to discolour. ♦ **scolorarsi** *vr.* to grow (*v. irr.*) pale.
scolorimento *sm.* discolouration.
scolorire *vt.* to bleach.
scolorito *agg.* faded, pale.
scolpare *vt.* to exculpate.
scolpire *vt.* to sculpture.
scombinare *vt.* to upset (*v. irr.*).
scombinato *agg.* screwy.
scombussolamento *sm.* upsetting.
scombussolare *vt.* to upset (*v. irr.*).
scommessa *sf.* bet.
scomméttere *vt.* to bet (*v. irr.*).
scommettitore *sm.* bettor.
scomodamente *avv.* uncomfortably.
scomodare *vt.* to trouble, to bother.
scomodità *sf.* lack of comfort.
scòmodo *agg.* uncomfortable.
scompaginamento *sm.* upsetting, upset.
scompaginare *vt.* to upset (*v. irr.*).
scompagnare *vt.* to break (*v. irr.*) up (a pair).
scompagnato *agg.* odd.
scomparire *vi.* 1. to disappear 2. (*non spiccare*) not to stand (*v. irr.*) out.
scomparsa *sf.* 1. disappearance 2. (*morte*) death.
scomparso *agg.* 1. disappeared 2. (*morto*) dead.
scompartimento *sm.* 1. partition 2. (*ferr.*) compartment.
scompartire *vt.* to divide, to share out.
scomparto *sm.* V. *scompartimento.*
scompenso *sm.* lack of balance: — *cardiaco*, cardiac decompensation.
scompiacenza *sf.* unkindness.
scompigliare · *vt.* 1. to upset (*v. irr.*) 2. (*arruffare*) to ruffle.
scompigliatamente *avv.* confusedly.

scompiglio *sm.* confusion, disorder.
scomponìbile *agg.* decomposable.
scomponimento *sm.* decomposition.
scomporre *vt.* 1. to decompose 2. (*i lineamenti*) to distort.
scompostamente *avv.* in an unseemly manner.
scompostezza *sf.* unseemliness.
scomposto *agg.* 1. (*sguaiato*) unseemly 2. decomposed.
scomùnica *sf.* excommunication.
scomunicare *vt.* to excommunicate.
scomunicato *agg. e sm.* excommunicate.
sconcertante *agg.* disconcerting.
sconcertare *vt.* to disconcert, to baffle.
sconcertato *agg.* disconcerted.
sconcerto *sm.* perturbation.
sconcezza *sf.* indecency.
sconciamente *avv.* indecently.
sconcio *agg.* indecent.
sconclusionatamente *avv.* inconclusively.
sconclusionato *agg.* inconclusive.
scondito *agg.* 1. unseasoned 2. (*di insalata*) undressed.
sconfessare *vt.* to disown.
sconfessione *sf.* disowning.
sconfìggere *vt.* to defeat.
sconfinamento *sm.* 1. (*in paese straniero*) crossing the frontier 2. (*in proprietà privata*) trespass.
sconfinare *vi.* 1. (*in paese straniero*) to cross the frontier 2. (*in proprietà privata*) to trespass.
sconfinato *agg.* boundless.
sconfitta *sf.* defeat.
sconfitto *agg.* defeated.
sconfortante *agg.* discouraging.
sconfortare *vt.* to discourage.
sconfortato *agg.* discouraged.
sconforto *sm.* 1. discouragement 2. (*dolore*) sorrow.
scongiurare *vt.* 1. to beseech (*v. irr.*) 2. (*evitare*) to avoid.
scongiuro *sm.* exorcism.
sconnessione *sf.* disconnectedness.
sconnesso *agg.* 1. disconnected 2. (*fig.*) rambling.
sconnèttere *vt.* to disconnect. ♦ **sconnèttere** *vi.* to wander.
sconoscente *agg.* ungrateful.
sconoscenza *sf.* ingratitude.
sconòscere *vt.* to disown.
sconosciuto *agg.* unknown. ♦ **sconosciuto** *sm.* stranger.

sconquassare *vt.* to shatter.

sconquassato *agg.* ramshackle.

sconquasso *sm.* mess, disorder.

sconsacrare *vt.* to deconsecrate.

sconsideratezza *sf.* rashness.

sconsiderato *agg.* thoughtless.

sconsigliare *vt.* to advise against.

sconsigliato *agg.* rash.

sconsolante *agg.* discouraging.

sconsolare *vt.* to dishearten.

sconsolato *agg.* disconsolate.

scontàbile *agg.* discountable.

scontare *vt.* **1.** (*comm.*) to discount **2.** (*detrarre*) to deduct **3.** (*espiare*) to expiate.

scontato *agg.* (*previsto*) expected.

scontentare *vt.* to displease.

scontentezza *sf.* discontent.

scontento *agg.* displeased.

sconto *sm.* discount.

scontrarsi *vr.* to clash.

scontrino *sm.* ticket, check.

scontro *sm.* **1.** encounter **2.** (*di veicoli*) crash **3.** (*fig.*) clash.

scontrosamente *avv.* peevishly.

scontrosità *sf.* bad temper.

scontroso *agg.* bad-tempered.

sconveniente *agg.* **1.** unprofitable **2.** (*indecente*) unseemly.

sconvenientemente *avv.* unbecomingly.

sconvenienza *sf.* **1.** unprofitableness **2.** (*mancanza di correttezza*) unseemliness.

sconvolgente *agg.* upsetting.

sconvòlgere *vt.* to upset (*v. irr.*).

sconvolgimento *sm.* upsetting, confusion.

sconvolto *agg.* upset.

scopa *sf.* broom.

scopare *vt.* to sweep (*v. irr.*).

scoperchiare *vt.* to take (*v. irr.*) off the lid.

scoperta *sf.* discovery.

scopertamente *avv.* openly.

scoperto *agg.* uncovered ‖ *automobile scoperta*, open car; *a capo —*, bare-headed; *giocare a carte scoperte*, to act openly.

scopino *sm.* street-sweeper.

scopo *sm.* aim, purpose: *senza —*, aimless.

scopolamina *sf.* scopolamine.

scoppiare *vi.* **1.** to burst (*v. irr.*) **2.** (*di guerre, epidemie ecc.*) to break (*v. irr.*) out.

scoppiettante *agg.* crackling.

scoppiettare *vi.* to crackle.

scoppiettìo *sm.* crackling.

scoppio *sm.* **1.** burst, explosion: *motore a —*, piston-engine **2.** (*di guerre, rivoluzioni ecc.*) outbreak.

scoprimento *sm.* **1.** discovering **2.** (*di monumento*) unveiling.

scoprire *vt.* **1.** to discover **2.** (*avvistare*) to sight **3.** (*togliere ciò che copre*) to uncover **4.** (*palesare*) to show (*v. irr.*). ◆ **scoprirsi** *vr.* (*rivelarsi*) to reveal oneself.

scopritore *sm.* discoverer.

scoraggiamento *sm.* discouragement.

scoraggiante *agg.* discouraging.

scoraggiare *vt.* to discourage. ◆ **scoraggiarsi** *vr.* to get (*v. irr.*) discouraged.

scoraggiato *agg.* discouraged.

scoramento *sm.* discouragement.

scorato *agg.* disheartened.

scorbùtico *agg.* **1.** (*med.*) scorbutic **2.** (*fig.*) ill-tempered.

scorbuto *sm.* scurvy.

scorciare *vt.* to shorten.

scorciatoia *sf.* short cut.

scorcio *sm.* **1.** foreshortening **2.** (*spazio di tempo*) end, close.

scordare[1] *vt.* to forget (*v. irr.*).

scordare[2] *vt.* (*mus.*) to untune.

scordato[1] *agg.* forgotten.

scordato[2] *agg.* (*mus.*) untuned.

scòrfano *sm.* **1.** sea-scorpion **2.** (*di persona*) fright: *che —!*, what a fright!

scòrgere *vt.* to perceive, to discern.

scoria *sf.* **1.** (*metal.*) dross **2.** (*fig.*) scum.

scornare *vt.* **1.** to horn **2.** (*fig.*) to humiliate.

scornato *agg.* humiliated.

scorno *sm.* shame.

scorpacciata *sf.* blow out: *fare una — di*, to stuff oneself with.

scorpione *sm.* scorpion.

scorporare *vt.* to disembody.

scòrporo *sm.* breaking up.

scorrazzare *vi.* to run (*v. irr.*) about.

scòrrere *vi.* **1.** to run (*v. irr.*) **2.** (*scivolare*) to glide **3.** (*fluire*) to flow **4.** (*di tempo*) to fly (*v. irr.*).

scorrerìa *sf.* raid.

scorrettezza *sf.* incorrectness.

scorretto *agg.* **1.** incorrect **2.** (*di costumi*) dissolute **3.** (*maleducato*) rude.

scorrévole *agg.* **1.** sliding **2.** (*fig.*) fluent.

scorrevolezza *sf.* fluency.

scorribanda *sf.* incursion, raid.

scorrimento *sm.* sliding.

scorsa *sf.* glance.

scorso *agg.* last, past.

scorsoio *agg.* running.

scorta *sf.* 1. escort 2. (*provvista*) supply || *ruota di* —, spare wheel.

scortare *vt.* to escort.

scortecciare *vt.* 1. to peel 2. (*un albero*) to bark.

scortese *agg.* rude, impolite.

scortesìa *sf.* rudeness.

scorticare *vt.* to skin.

scorticatura *sf.* scratch.

scortichino *sm.* flaying-knife.

scorza *sf.* 1. (*corteccia*) bark 2. (*buccia*) skin, rind.

scoscéndere *vt.* to split (*v. irr.*).

scoscendimento *sm.* 1. collapse 2. (*di terreno*) break.

scosceso *agg.* steep, sloping.

scossa *sf.* shock, shake.

scosso *agg.* 1. shaken 2. (*fig.*) upset.

scossone *sm.* 1. shake 2. (*strattone*) jerk.

scostare *vt.* to shift, to move away. ♦ **scostarsi** *vr.* 1. to move away 2. (*staccarsi*) to turn off.

scostumatezza *sf.* dissoluteness.

scostumato *agg.* dissolute. ♦ **scostumato** *sm.* dissolute person.

scotennare *vt.* to scalp.

scottante *agg.* burning.

scottare *vt.* 1. to burn (*v. irr.*) 2. (*cuc.*) to half-cook 3. (*fig.*) to hurt (*v. irr.*).

scottatura *sf.* burn.

scotto[1] *sm.* score: *pagare lo* —, to pay (*v. irr.*) one's piper.

scotto[2] *agg.* overdone.

scovare *vt.* 1. to put (*v. irr.*) up 2. (*scoprire*) to discover.

scozzare *vt.* to shuffle.

scozzese *agg.* Scotch, Scottish. ♦ **scozzese** *sm.* Scotchman (*pl.* -men).

scozzonare *vt.* 1. to break (*v. irr.*) in 2. (*fig.*) to teach (*v. irr.*) the first elements.

screanzatamente *avv.* rudely.

screanzato *agg.* rude, impolite. ♦ **screanzato** *sm.* rude person.

screditare *vt.* to discredit.

screditato *agg.* discredited.

scrédito *sm.* discredit.

scremare *vt.* to skim.

scremato *agg.* skimmed: *latte* —, skim-milk.

scrematura *sf.* skimming.

screpolare *vi.* 1. to crack 2. (*della pelle*) to get (*v. irr.*) chapped.

screpolatura *sf.* 1. crack 2. (*della pelle*) chap.

screziare *vt.* to variegate.

screziato *agg.* variegated.

screziatura *sf.* variegation.

screzio *sm.* disagreement.

scribacchiare *vt. e vi.* to scribble.

scribacchino *sm.* scribbler.

scricchiolare *vi.* 1. to creak 2. (*di denti*) to grind (*v. irr.*).

scricchiolìo *sm.* 1. creaking 2. (*di denti*) grinding.

scrigno *sm.* casket: — *di gioielli*, jewel-case.

scriminatura *sf.* (hair-)parting.

scriteriato *agg.* senseless.

scritta *sf.* 1. inscription 2. (*cartello*) notice 3. (*dicitura*) caption.

scritto *sm.* writing.

scrittoio *sm.* writing-desk.

scrittore *sm.* writer.

scrittrice *sf.* woman writer.

scrittura *sf.* 1. writing: — *a macchina*, typewriting; — *a mano*, handwriting 2. (*teat.*) engagement 3. (*giur.*) deed.

scritturare *vt.* to engage.

scrivanìa *sf.* writing-desk.

scrivano *sm.* clerk, copyist.

scrìvere *vt.* to write (*v. irr.*): — *a mano*, to write by hand; — *a penna, a matita*, to write in pen, in pencil; — *sotto dettatura*, to write from dictation; — *a macchina*, to typewrite (*v. irr.*) 2. (*registrare*) to enter, to record.

scroccare *vt.* to scrounge.

scrocco *sm. vivere a* —, to sponge one's living.

scroccone *sm.* sponger.

scrofa *sf.* sow.

scrofoloso *agg.* scrofulous.

scrollamento *sm.* 1. shaking 2. (*di spalle*) shrugging.

scrollare *vt.* 1. to shake (*v. irr.*) 2. (*le spalle*) to shrug.

scrollata *sf.* 1. (*di testa*) shake 2. (*di spalle*) shrug.

scrosciante *agg.* (*di risa ecc.*) roaring: *pioggia* —, pelting rain.

scrosciare *vi.* 1. (*di pioggia*) to pelt down 2. (*fig.*) to roar.

scroscio *sm.* 1. (*di cascata, torrente ecc.*) roar 2. (*fig.*) roar, burst || — *di pioggia*, shower.

scrostamento *sm.* peeling.

scrostare vt. 1. to take (v. irr.) the crust off, to peel off 2. (dei muri) to remove the plaster from a wall. ♦ **scrostarsi** vr. to fall (v. irr.) off, to peel off.

scrùpolo sm. scruple.

scrupolosamente avv. scrupulously.

scrupolosità sf. scrupulosity.

scrupoloso agg. scrupulous.

scrutare vt. to search, to scan.

scrutatore agg. searching, inquisitive. ♦ **scrutatore** sm. 1. searcher 2. (di elezioni) scrutineer.

scrutinare vt. to scrutinize.

scrutìnio sm. 1. (di elezioni) poll 2. (scolastico) assignment of a term's marks 3. (attento esame) scrutiny.

scucire vt. to unsew (v. irr.), to unstitch. ♦ **scucirsi** vr. to rip.

scucito agg. 1. unsewn 2. (fig.) incoherent.

scucitura sf. unsewing.

scuderìa sf. stable.

scudetto sm. 1. small shield 2. (sport) (championship) shield.

scudiero sm. squire.

scudisciare vt. to lash.

scudisciata sf. lash.

scudiscio sm. switch, lash.

scudo sm. shield.

scuffia sf. (sbornia) drunkenness.

sculacciare vt. to spank.

sculacciata sf. spank.

sculettare vi. to waddle.

scultore sm. sculptor.

scultòreo agg. sculptural.

scultura sf. sculpture.

scuoiare vt. to skin.

scuola sf. school: — diurna, day-classes; — elementare, primary school; — media inferiore, superiore, secondary school; — pubblica, State school; maestro di —, schoolmaster.

scuòtere vt. 1. to shake (v. irr.) (anche fig.) 2. (agitare) to stir.

scuotimento sm. shaking.

scure sf. axe.

scurire vt. 1. to darken 2. (pitt.) to tone down. ♦ **scurirsi** vr. to grow (v. irr.) dark.

scuro agg. dark || faccia scura, grim face.

scurrìle agg. scurrilous.

scurrilità sf. scurrility.

scusa sf. 1. excuse, apology 2. (pretesto) pretext.

scusàbile agg. excusable.

scusare vt. to excuse, to forgive (v. irr.) || scusi!, scusate!, sorry!, excuse me! ♦ **scusarsi** vr. to apologize.

sdebitarsi vr. 1. to pay (v. irr.) off one's debts 2. (disobbligarsi) to return a kindness.

sdegnare vt. 1. to disdain 2. (provocare lo sdegno) to enrage.

sdegnato agg. indignant.

sdegno sm. disdain, indignation.

sdegnosamente avv. disdainfully.

sdegnoso agg. 1. (di atti e parole) disdainful 2. (di persona) haughty.

sdentare vt. to break (v. irr.) the teeth.

sdentato agg. toothless.

sdilinquimento sm. mawkishness.

sdilinquirsi vr. to melt away.

sdoganamento sm. clearing (through the customs).

sdolcinato agg. sugary, affected.

sdolcinatura sf. mawkishness.

sdoppiamento sm. splitting.

sdoppiare vt. to split.

sdraia sf. deck-chair.

sdraiarsi vr. to lie (v. irr.) down.

sdrucciolare vi. to slip, to slide.

sdrucciolévole agg. slippery.

sdrucciolone sm. slip.

sdrucire vt. to tear (v. irr.).

sdrucito agg. torn.

se cong. 1. if 2. (dubitativo) whether || — mai, in case; — non altro, at least; — non che, except that; anche —, even if.

sé pron. pers. 1. one, him, her, it, them 2. (riflessivi) oneself, himself, herself, itself, themselves || una donna piena di —, a conceited woman; essere fuori di —, to be beside oneself; tornare in —, to recover consciousness; amore di —, selfishness; padronanza di —, self-control; un uomo sicuro di —, a self-confident man; un uomo che si è fatto da —, a self-made man; rispetto di —, self-respect.

sebàceo agg. sebaceous.

sebbene cong. though, although.

sebo sm. sebum.

secante sf. secant.

secca sf. 1. shoal 2. (siccità) drought.

seccamente avv. coldly.

seccante agg. (fig.) annoying, irritating || una cosa, persona —, a nuisance.

seccare vt. 1. to dry up 2. (annoiare) to annoy, to irritate. ◆ seccarsi vr. (infastidirsi) to be annoyed (with).

seccatore sm. bother.

seccatura sf. 1. (essicamento) drying 2. (noia) bother, nuisance.

secchia sf. pail, bucket.

secchiello sm. bucket.

secchio sm. V. secchia.

secco agg. 1. dry 2. (appassito) withered 3. (magro) thin 4. (brusco) sharp 5. (freddo) cold.

secentesco agg. of the seventeenth century.

secèrnere vt. to secrete.

secessione sf. secession.

secessionista agg. e sm. secessionist.

seco pron. with him, with her, with them.

secolare agg. 1. secular 2. (in opposizione a ecclesiastico) lay.

secolarizzare vt. to secularize.

secolarizzazione sf. secularization.

sècolo sm. 1. century 2. (epoca) epoch, age || Padre Carlo, al — John Smith, Father Charles, in the world John Smith.

seconda sf. (auto) second gear || a — di (loc. prep.), according to.

secondare vt. to favour.

secondario agg. secondary.

secondino sm. warder.

secondo[1] agg. 1. second 2. (favorevole) favourable. ◆ secondo sm. 1. (minuto) second 2. (ufficiale in seconda) executive officer.

secondo[2] prep. according to. ◆ secondo avv. second.

secrezione sf. secretion.

sèdano sm. celery.

sedare vt. to soothe.

sedativo agg. e sm. sedative.

sede sf. 1. seat, centre 2. (residenza) residence 3. (eccl.) see 4. (edificio per pubblici uffici) office.

sedentario agg. sedentary.

sedere[1] vi. 1. (stare seduto) to sit (v. irr.), to be sitting 2. (mettersi a sedere) to sit (down).

sedere[2] sm. bottom.

sedia sf. chair: — a dondolo, rocking-chair.

sedicenne agg. 1. (attr.) sixteen-year-old 2. (pred.) sixteen years old.

sedicente agg. would-be.

sedicèsimo agg. sixteenth.

sédici agg. sixteen.

sedile sm. seat, chair.

sedimentario agg. sedimentary.

sedimentazione sf. sedimentation.

sedimento sm. sediment.

sedizione sf. sedition.

sedizioso agg. seditious.

seducente agg. 1. alluring 2. (affascinante) charming.

sedurre vt. to seduce, to tempt.

seduta sf. sitting, session.

seduttore agg. seducing. ◆ seduttore sm. seducer.

seduzione sf. 1. seduction 2. (attrazione) attraction.

sega sf. saw.

ségala sf. rye.

segaligno agg. 1. rye (attr.) 2. (di persona) wiry.

segare vt. to saw (v. irr.).

segatura sf. sawdust.

seggio sm. chair, seat: — elettorale, poll.

sèggiola sf. chair.

seggiovìa sf. chair-lift.

segherìa sf. saw-mill.

seghettare vt. to jag.

segmentazione sf. segmentation.

segmento sm. segment.

segnalare vt. 1. to signal 2. (far notare) to point out. ◆ segnalarsi vr. to distinguish oneself.

segnalatore sm. 1. signaller 2. (segnalatore di direzione) direction indicator.

segnalazione sf. signal: — stradale, traffic signal.

segnale sm. signal: — di pericolo, allarme, danger, alarm signal; — di linea libera, occupata (tel.), ringing, engaged tone; — di passaggio a livello, level-crossing signal.

segnalètica sf. signals (pl.).

segnalètico agg. descriptive.

segnalibro sm. book-mark.

segnare vt. 1. to mark 2. (indicare) to show (v. irr.) 3. (sport) to score. ◆ segnarsi vr. to cross oneself.

segnatura sf. 1. marking 2. (sport) scoring.

segno sm. 1. sign, mark: passare il —, to overstep the mark 2. (limite) limit 3. (simbolo) symbol.

sego sm. tallow.

segregare vt. to segregate.

segregazione sf. segregation.

segreta sf. dungeon.

segretamente *avv.* in secret.

segretariato *sm.* secretariate.

segretario *sm.* secretary.

segreteria *sf.* 1. secretariat 2. (*di ministero*) secretariat of State.

segretezza *sf.* secrecy.

segreto *agg.* secret. ◆ **segreto** *sm.* 1. secret: *nel — del cuore*, in the depths of one's heart 2. (*parte interna, intimità*) secrecy.

seguace *sm.* follower, supporter.

seguente *agg.* following, next.

segugio *sm.* bloodhound.

seguire *vt.* e *vi.* 1. to follow 2. (*sorvegliare*) to supervise 3. (*frequentare regolarmente*) to attend.

séguito *sm.* 1. (*corteo*) retinue 2. (*successione, sequela*) series 3. (*continuazione*) continuation || *il — alla prossima puntata*, to be continued 4. (*comm.*): *a — di*, following up.

sei *agg.* six.

seicento *agg.* six hundred. ◆ **seicento** *sm.* the seventeenth century.

selce *sf.* flint.

selciare *vt.* to pave.

selciato *sm.* pavement.

selenio *sm.* selenium.

selenite *agg.* lunar. ◆ **selenite** *sf.* selenite.

selettività *sf.* selectivity.

selettivo *agg.* selective.

selettore *sm.* selector.

selezionare *vt.* to select.

selezione *sf.* selection.

sella *sf.* saddle.

sellaio *sm.* saddler.

sellare *vt.* to saddle.

sellino *sm.* saddle.

selva *sf.* 1. wood 2. (*fig.*) mass.

selvaggina *sf.* game.

selvaggio *agg.* wild, primitive. ◆ **selvaggio** *sm.* savage.

selvàtico *agg.* 1. wild 2. (*non socievole*) unsociable.

selvoso *agg.* woody.

semàforo *sm.* traffic-lights (*pl.*).

semàntica *sf.* semantics.

semàntico *agg.* semantic.

sembianza *sf.* features (*pl.*).

sembrare *vi.* 1. to seem 2. (*somigliare*) to look like.

seme *sm.* 1. seed 2. (*carte da giuoco*) suit.

sementa *sf.* 1. seeds (*pl.*) 2. (*epoca della semina*) seed-time.

semente *sf.* seeds (*pl.*).

semenza *sf.* seeds (*pl.*).

semenzaio *sm.* seed-bed.

semestrale *agg.* six-monthly (*attr.*).

semestralmente *avv.* twice a year.

semestre *sm.* half-year.

semiaperto *agg.* half-open.

semicerchio *sm.* semicircle.

semichiuso *agg.* half-closed.

semicircolare *agg.* semicircular.

semiconduttore *sm.* semiconductor.

semidiàmetro *sm.* semi-diameter.

semidìo *sm.* demigod.

semifinale *sf.* semifinal.

semilavorato *agg.* e *sm.* semi--manufactured.

sémina *sf.* sowing.

seminàbile *agg.* fit to be sown.

seminagione *sf.* sowing.

seminare *vt.* to sow (*v. irr.*).

seminario *sm.* seminary.

seminarista *sm.* seminarist.

seminato *agg.* 1. sown 2. (*fig.*) strewn.

seminatore *sm.* sower.

seminfermità *sf.* partial infirmity: *— mentale*, partial insanity.

seminudo *agg.* half-naked.

semiserio *agg.* half-serious.

semisfera *sf.* hemisphere.

semita *s.* Semite.

semìtico *agg.* Semitic.

semitono *sm.* semitone.

semivivo *agg.* half-alive.

sémola *sf.* bran.

semolino *sm.* semolina.

semovente *agg.* self-moving.

sempiterno *agg.* everlasting.

sémplice *agg.* simple.

semplicione *sm.* simpleton.

semplicismo *sm.* superficiality.

semplicìstico *agg.* superficial.

semplicità *sf.* simplicity.

semplificare *vt.* to simplify.

semplificazione *sf.* simplification

sempre *avv.* 1. always: *— avanti!* always onward!; *— meglio, peggio*, better and better, worse and worse; *per —*, for ever; *una volta per —*, once for all 2. (*tuttora*) still: *vivi — qui?*, do you still live here?

sempreverde *sm.* evergreen.

sènape *sf.* mustard.

senato *sm.* senate.

senatore *sm.* senator.

senatoriale *agg.* senatorial.

senescenza *sf.* senescence.

senile *agg.* senile.

senilità *sf.* senility.

senno *sm.* sense, wisdom.

seno *sm.* **1.** breast, bosom **2.** (*grembo*) womb.

sensale *sm.* broker.

sensatezza *sf.* good sense.

sensato *agg.* sensible.

sensazionale *agg.* sensational.

sensazione *sf.* sensation, feeling.

sensibile *agg.* sensitive.

sensibilità *sf.* sensitiveness.

sensibilizzare *vt.* to sensitize.

sensibilmente *avv.* **1.** sensitively **2.** (*notevolmente*) sensibly.

sensitività *sf.* sensitivity.

sensitivo *agg.* **1.** sensory **2.** (*sensibile*) sensitive.

senso *sm.* **1.** sense **2.** (*sensazione*) sensation **3.** (*direzione*) direction, way **4.** (*modo*) way, manner.

sensorio *agg.* sensorial.

sensuale *agg.* sensual.

sensualità *sf.* sensuality.

sensualmente *avv.* sensually.

sentenza *sf.* **1.** sentence **2.** (*massima*) saying.

sentenziare *vi.* to judge, to hold (*v. irr.*).

sentenziosamente *avv.* sententiously.

sentenzioso *agg.* sententious.

sentiero *sm.* path.

sentimentale *agg.* sentimental.

sentimentalismo *sm.* sentimentalism.

sentimentalità *sf.* sentimentality.

sentimento *sm.* **1.** sentiment **2.** (*disposizione spirituale*) feeling.

sentinella *sf.* sentry.

sentire *vt.* **1.** to feel (*v. irr.*) **2.** (*udire*) to hear (*v. irr.*) **3.** (*gustare*) to taste **4.** (*odorare*) to smell (*v. irr.*) **5.** (*ascoltare*) to listen to. ♦ **sentirsi** *vr.* to feel.

sentitamente *avv.* heartily.

sentito *agg.* **1.** heart-felt **2.** (*udito*) heard ‖ *per — dire*, by hearsay.

sentore *sm.* inkling: *aver — di*, to suspect.

senza *prep.* — without: — *scarpe*, barefoot; — *fine*, endless; — *confronto*, unrivalled; — *numero*, countless; — *testa*, thoughtless.

senzatetto *s.* homeless person.

separare *vt.* to separate. ♦ **separarsi** *vr.* to separate.

separatamente *avv.* separately.

separatismo *sm.* separatism.

separatista *s.* separatist.

separativo *agg.* separative.

separato *agg.* separated.

separazione *sf.* separation.

sepolcrale *agg.* sepulchral.

sepolcro *sm.* sepulchre, tomb.

sepolto *agg.* buried.

sepoltura *sf.* burial.

seppellimento *sm.* burial.

seppellire *vt.* to bury.

seppia *sf.* cuttle-fish.

seppure *cong.* even if.

sequela *sf.* series (*invariato al pl.*).

sequenza *sf.* **1.** series **2.** (*cine*) sequence.

sequestràbile *agg.* seizable.

sequestrare *vt.* to seize.

sequestro *sm.* **1.** seizure **2.** (*per debiti*) distress.

sequoia *sf.* sequoia.

sera *sf.* evening.

seràfico *agg.* seraphic.

serafino *sm.* seraph.

serale *agg.* evening (*attr.*).

serata *sf.* **1.** evening **2.** (*ricevimento serale*) party.

serbare *vt.* **1.** (*mettere in serbo*) to put (*v. irr.*) aside **2.** (*conservare*) to keep (*v. irr.*) ‖ — *odio, rancore*, to nourish hatred, rancour. ♦ **serbarsi** *vr.* to keep, to remain.

serbatoio *sm.* reservoir, tank.

serbo (*nella loc.*) *tenere in* —, to keep (*v. irr.*) aside.

serenamente *avv.* serenely.

serenata *sf.* serenade.

serenìssimo *agg.* Serene Highness.

serenità *sf.* serenity.

sereno *agg.* serene, clear ‖ *giudizio* —, objective judgement.

sergente *sm.* sergeant.

sèrico *agg.* silk (*attr.*), silky.

sericoltore *sm.* silkgrower.

sericoltura *sf.* sericulture.

serie *sf.* **1.** series (*invariato al pl.*): *in* —, mass-produced **2.** (*assieme*) set **3.** (*fila*) row.

serietà *sf.* seriousness.

serio *agg.* serious, earnest.

sermone *sm.* **1.** sermon **2.** (*rimprovero*) lecture.

seròtino *agg.* evening (*attr.*).

serpe *sf.* snake.

serpeggiante *agg.* winding.

serpeggiare *vi.* to wind (*v. irr.*).

serpente *sm.* snake, serpent.

serpentina *sf.* **1.** coil **2.** (*di strada*) winding road.

serpentino *agg.* snakelike. ♦ **serpentino** *sm.* serpentine.

serra *sf.* greenhouse.

serraglio sm. 1. menagerie 2. (del sultano) seraglio.
serramànico (nella loc. avv.) coltello a —, flick-knife.
serramento sm. lock.
serrare vt. 1. to shut (v. irr.), to close 2. (a chiave) to lock 3. (stringere) to tighten 4. (concludere) to conclude.
serrata sf. (econ.) lockout.
serratura sf. lock: buco della —, keyhole.
serva sf. maid-servant.
servibile agg. usable.
servigio sm. service, favour.
servile agg. servile.
servilismo sm. servility.
servire vt. 1. to serve 2. (di persona di servizio) to wait on 3. (le carte) to deal (v. irr.). ♦ **servire** vi. (occorrere) to need: vi serve qualcosa?, can I help you? ♦ **servirsi** vr. 1. to use 2. (a tavola) to help oneself (to).
servitore sm. servant.
servitù sf. 1. servitude, slavery 2. (personale di servizio) servants (pl.).
serviziévole agg. obliging.
servizio sm. 1. service 2. (lavoro) work: fuori —, off duty 3. (favore) favour.
servo sm. 1. servant 2. (schiavo) slave.
servofreno sm. brake booster.
sèsamo sm. sesame.
sessanta agg. sixty.
sessantenne agg. 1. (attr.) sixty-year-old 2. (pred.) sixty years old. ♦ **sessantenne** s. sixty-year-old person.
sessantèsimo agg. sixtieth.
sessantina sf. about sixty: un uomo sulla —, a man in his sixties.
sessione sf. session.
sesso sm. sex.
sessuale agg. sexual.
sessualità sf. sexuality.
sestante sm. sextant.
sesterzio sm. sesterce.
sestetto sm. sextet.
sesto¹ agg. sixth.
sesto² sm. 1. order 2. (arch.) curve.
sèstuplo agg. e sm. sextuple.
seta sf. silk.
setacciare vt. to sieve.
setaccio sm. sieve.
sete sf. thirst: avere —, to be thirsty.

seterìa sf. 1. silk factory 2. (negozio di seta) silk shop.
setificio sm. silk factory.
sétola sf. 1. bristle 2. (crine) hair.
setta sf. sect.
settanta agg. seventy.
settantenne agg. 1. (attr.) seventy-year-old 2. (pred.) seventy years old. ♦ **settantenne** s. seventy-year-old person.
settantèsimo agg. seventieth.
settario agg. sectarian.
settarismo sm. sectarianism.
sette agg. seven.
settecentesco agg. of eighteenth century.
settecento agg. seven hundred. ♦ **settecento** sm. the eighteenth century.
settembre sm. September.
settentrionale agg. northern.
settentrione sm. north.
setticemìa sf. septicaemia.
sèttico agg. septic.
settimana sf. week.
settimanale agg. weekly. ♦ **settimanale** sm. weekly magazine.
settimino sm. seven months' child.
setto sm. septum (pl. -ta).
settore sm. 1. (geom.) sector 2. (campo) field.
settoriale agg. sectorial.
severità sf. severity.
severo agg. severe, strict.
sevizia sf. torture.
seviziare vt. to torture.
sezionamento sm. dissection.
sezionare vt. (anat.) to dissect.
sezione sf. 1. section 2. (reparto) department 3. (di scuola) side.
sfaccendato agg. idle. ♦ **sfaccendato** sm. idler.
sfaccettare vt. to facet.
sfacchinare vi. to drudge.
sfacciatàggine sf. impudence.
sfacciato agg. 1. impudent, cheeky 2. (di colori) gaudy.
sfacelo sm. break-up.
sfaldamento sm. flaking.
sfaldarsi vr. to flake away.
sfamare vt. to appease so.'s hunger.
sfarfallare vi. to flutter about.
sfarzo sm. pomp.
sfarzoso agg. sumptuous.
sfasamento sm. 1. (mecc.; elettr.) phase-displacement, phase-difference 2. (fig.) inconsequence.
sfasato agg. 1. out of phase 2. (fig.) inconsequent.

sfasciare[1] vt. (togliere le fasce) to unbandage.

sfasciare[2] vt. to smash. ♦ sfasciarsi vr. to collapse.

sfasciato agg. (rotto) in pieces.

sfatare vt. to discredit.

sfaticato agg. lazy. ♦ sfaticato sm. lazy-bones.

sfatto agg. undone.

sfavillante agg. shining.

sfavillare vi. to shine (v. irr.), to sparkle.

sfavore sm. disfavour, discredit.

sfavorévole agg. unfavourable.

sfebbrato agg. without a temperature.

sfegatarsi vr. to wear (v. irr.) oneself out.

sfegatato agg. fanatic.

sfenòide sm. sphenoid.

sfera sf. 1. sphere 2. (lancetta) hand 3. (mecc.) ball.

sfericità sf. sphericity.

sfèrico agg. spherical.

sferragliare vi. to clang.

sferrare vt. 1. (un attacco) to launch 2. (un colpo) to land a blow. ♦ sferrarsi vr. to hurl oneself (at).

sferruzzare vi. to knit (v. irr.).

sferza sf. whip, lash (anche fig.).

sferzare vt. 1. to whip, to lash 2. (fig.) to reprimand.

sferzata sf. 1. lash 2. (fig.) sharp rebuke.

sfiancare vt. to wear (v. irr.) out.

sfiatare vi. to leak. ♦ sfiatarsi vr. to talk oneself hoarse.

sfiatato agg. out of breath.

sfiatatoio sm. vent.

sfibbiare vt. to unbuckle.

sfibramento sm. enfeeblement.

sfibrante agg. exhausting.

sfibrare vt. to weaken, to wear (v. irr.) out.

sfibratura sf. breaking.

sfida sf. challenge: in tono di —, defiantly.

sfidante sm. challenger.

sfidare vt. 1. to challenge 2. (affrontare) to face, to dare: — la morte, to face death.

sfiducia sf. mistrust: avere —, to mistrust.

sfiduciare vt. to discourage. ♦ sfiduciarsi vr. to become (v. irr.) discouraged.

sfiduciato agg. discouraged.

sfigurare vt. to spoil (v. irr.). ♦

sfigurare vi. to cut (v. irr.) a poor figure.

sfigurato agg. disfigured.

sfilacciare vt. to fray.

sfilacciato agg. frayed.

sfilare[1] vt. to unthread, to unstring (v. irr.).

sfilare[2] vi. to parade.

sfilata sf. 1. march, parade 2. (fila) line, string.

sfinge sf. sphinx.

sfinimento sm. exhaustion.

sfinire vt. to exhaust.

sfinitezza sf. extreme weakness.

sfinito agg. worn out.

sfintere sm. sphincter.

sfiorare vt. to graze, to touch on.

sfiorire vi. to wither, to fade.

sfiorito agg. faded, withered (anche fig.).

sfittare vt. to vacate.

sfitto agg. vacant.

sfocato agg. out of focus.

sfociare vi. to flow.

sfoderare vt. 1. to unline 2. (sguainare) to unsheathe 3. (ostentare) to display.

sfoderato agg. 1. unlined 2. (sguainato) unsheathed.

sfogare vt. to give (v. irr.) vent to. ♦ sfogarsi vr. to relieve one's feelings.

sfoggiare vi. to show (v. irr.) off.

sfoggio sm. show, ostentation.

sfoglia sf. 1. (lamina) foil 2. (cuc.) pastry.

sfogliare[1] vt. to pluck the petals off.

sfogliare[2] vt. 1. (voltare le pagine) to turn over the pages 2. (dare un'occhiata) to glance through.

sfogliata sf. 1. (cuc.) puff-pastry 2. (di libro) thumbing.

sfogo sm. vent, outlet.

sfolgoramento sm. blazing.

sfolgorante agg. flaming.

sfolgorare vi. to blaze.

sfolgorìo sm. blaze.

sfollagente sm. truncheon.

sfollamento sm. 1. dispersal 2. (mil.) evacuation.

sfollare vt. e vi. to disperse 2. (mil.) to evacuate.

sfollato agg. 1. evacuated. ♦ sfollato sm. evacuee.

sfoltire vt. to thin.

sfondamento sm. breaking.

sfondare vt. 1. (rompere il fondo) to break (v. irr.) the bottom 2.

(*mil.*) to break through. ♦ **sfondare** *vi.* to have success.

sfondato *agg.* **1.** without a bottom
|| *scarpe sfondate*, worn-out shoes
2. (*insaziabile*) voracious.

sfondo *sm.* background.

sforbiciare *vt.* to cut (*v. irr.*) with
scissors.

sformare *vt.* **1.** to pull out of
shape **2.** (*togliere dalla forma*) to
remove from the mould. ♦ **sfor-
marsi** *vr.* to get (*v. irr.*) out of
shape.

sformato *agg.* shapeless.

sfornare *vt.* **1.** to take (*v. irr.*) out
of the oven **2.** (*produrre*) to bring
(*v. irr.*) out.

sfornito *agg.* destitute, lacking (in).

sfortuna *sf.* bad luck.

sfortunato *agg.* unlucky.

sforzare *vt.* to strain, to force. ♦
sforzarsi *vr.* to try hard.

sforzatamente *avv.* **1.** with much
effort **2.** (*in modo forzato*) for-
cedly.

sforzato *agg.* **1.** forced **2.** (*fig.*)
false.

sforzatura *sf.* (*cosa sforzata*) far-
-fetched thing.

sforzo *sm.* **1.** effort **2.** (*mecc.*) stress.

sfòttere *vt.* to pull so.'s legs.

sfracellare *vt.* to smash. ♦ **sfra-
cellarsi** *vr.* to smash.

sfrangiare *vt.* to undo (*v. irr.*), to
form a fringe. ♦ **sfrangiarsi** *vr.*
to fray.

sfrangiatura *sf.* fraying.

sfrattare *vt.* to evict.

sfratto *sm.* eviction.

sfrecciare *vi.* to dart.

sfregamento *sm.* rubbing.

sfregare *vt.* to rub.

sfregiare *vt.* to disfigure.

sfregiato *agg.* disfigured.

sfregio *sm.* slash, scar.

sfrenare *vt.* to unbridle.

sfrenatezza *sf.* unrestraint.

sfrenato *agg.* wild, unbridled.

sfrigolare *vi.* to sizzle.

sfrigolìo *sm.* sizzle.

sfringuellare *vi.* to twitter.

sfrondare *vt.* **1.** to strip off leaves
2. (*fig.*) to curtail.

sfrontatezza *sf.* effrontery.

sfrontato *agg.* brazen, impudent. ♦
sfrontato *sm.* impudent fellow.

sfrusciare *vi.* to rustle.

sfruscìo *sm.* rustling.

sfruttamento *sm.* exploitation.

sfruttare *vt.* to exploit.

sfruttatore *sm.* profiteer.

sfuggente *agg.* receding: *sguardo*
—, elusive look.

sfuggévole *agg.* transitory.

sfuggire *vi.* to escape, to slip. ♦
sfuggire *vt.* to avoid.

sfuggita *sf. di* —, quickly: *vedere
qu. di* —, to have a glimpse of so.

sfumare *vt.* to shade. ♦ **sfumare**
vi. **1.** to evaporate **2.** (*fig.*) to
come (*v. irr.*) to nothing.

sfumatamente *avv.* softly.

sfumato *agg.* **1.** vanished **2.** (*di colori*) soft.

sfumatura *sf.* **1.** (*lo sfumare*)
shading **2.** (*gradazione*) shade.

sfuriata *sf.* outburst.

sgabello *sm.* stool.

sgabuzzino *sm.* closet.

sgambettare *vi.* to kick (one's
legs) about.

sgambetto *sm.* trip: *fare lo* —, to
trip (so.); (*fig.*) to supplant.

sganasciamento *sm.* dislocation
(of so.'s jaw).

sganasciarsi *vr.* — *dalle risa*, to
laugh oneself silly.

sganascione *sm.* slap.

sganciare *vt.* **1.** to unhook **2.** (*ferr.*)
to uncouple **3.** (*di bombe*) to re-
lease. ♦ **sganciarsi** *vr.* (*liberarsi di qu.*) to get (*v. irr.*) away (so.).

sgangherare *vt.* to unhinge.

sgangherato *agg.* **1.** unhinged **2.**
(*sguaiato*) wild.

sgarbatamente *avv.* impolitely.

sgarbato *agg.* rude, impolite.

sgarberìa *sf.* rudeness.

sgarbo *sm.* offence.

sgargiante *agg.* gaudy.

sgarrare *vi.* **1.** to be wrong **2.** (*di
orologio*) (*se è avanti*) to gain; (*se
è indietro*) to lose (*v. irr.*).

sgattaiolare *vi.* to slip away.

sgelare *vi.* to thaw. ♦ **sgelarsi** *vr.*
to thaw.

sgelo *sm.* thawing.

sghembo *agg.* oblique: *di* —, obliquely.

sgherro *sm.* hired assassin.

sghignazzare *vi.* to guffaw.

sghignazzata *sf.* guffaw.

sghimbescio (*nella loc. avv.*) *di*
—, awry.

sghiribizzo *sm.* whim.

sgobbare *vi.* to work hard.

sgobbone *sm.* **1.** hard worker **2.**
(*studentesco*) swot.

sgocciolare vi. to drip.
sgocciolio sm. dripping.
sgolarsi vr. to shout oneself hoarse.
sgombrare vt. to clear.
sgombro agg. 1. clear (of) 2. (fig.) free (from).
sgomentare vt. to dismay.
sgomento agg. dismayed. ♦ sgomento sm. dismay.
sgominare vt. to rout.
sgonfiamento sm. deflation.
sgonfiare vt. to deflate.
sgonfio agg. deflated.
sgorbia sf. gouge.
sgorbiare vt. to scrawl.
sgorbio sm. 1. scrawl 2. (pittura mal fatta) daub 3. (fig.) deformed man (pl. men).
sgorgare vi. to gush, to flow.
sgozzare vt. to cut (v. irr.) so.'s throat.
sgradévole agg. unpleasant.
sgradito agg. 1. disagreeable 2. (mal accetto) unwelcome.
sgrammaticato agg. ungrammatical.
sgranare vt. 1. to shell: — gli occhi, to open one's eyes wide 2. (mangiare) to devour.
sgranatrice sf. husker.
sgranchire vt. to stretch.
sgranocchiare vt. to munch.
sgrassare vt. to take (v. irr.) the grease off: — il brodo, to skim the grease from the broth.
sgravare vt. 1. to lighten 2. (fig.) to relieve.
sgravio sm. 1. lightening 2. (fig.) relief.
sgraziato agg. awkward.
sgretolamento sm. pounding.
sgretolare vt. to pound. ♦ sgretolarsi vr. to crumble.
sgridare vt. to scold.
sgroppare[1] vt. (sciogliere) to untie.
sgroppare[2] vi. (di cavallo) to buck.
sgroppata sf. bucking.
sgrossamento sm. rough-shaping.
sgrossare vt. 1. to rough 2. (dirozzare) to refine.
sgrovigliare vt. to unravel.
sguaiato agg. 1. unbecoming 2. (volgare) coarse.
sguainare vt. to unsheathe.
sgualcire vt. to crease.
sgualdrina sf. harlot, whore.
sguardo sm. look, glance: dare uno —, to have a look.

sguarnire vt. 1. to untrim 2. (mil.) to dismantle.
sguàttero sm. scullery-boy.
sguazzare vi. to wallow.
sguinzagliare vt. to unleash.
sgusciare vt. to shell. ♦ sgusciare vi. to slip away.
sì[1] pron. 1. (riflessivo) oneself, himself, herself, itself, themselves 2. (rec.) (fra due) each other; (fra molti) one another 3. (pron. indef.) one, people, we, they: — dice, people say.
sì[2] sm. (mus.) si, B.
sì avv. yes: penso di —, I think so; — certo, certainly; e — che, yet; uno —, uno no, every other one; forse che —, forse che no, maybe yes, maybe no.
sia cong. 1. (o l'uno o l'altro) whether... or, either... or 2. (entrambi) both... and.
siamese agg. e s. Siamese.
sibarita s. sybarite.
siberiano agg. Siberian.
sibilante agg. 1. hissing 2. (fonetica) sibilant.
sibilare vi. to whistle, to hiss.
sibilla sf. sibyl.
sibillino agg. sibylline.
sìbilo sm. hiss, whistle.
sicario sm. cut-throat.
sicché cong. 1. so... that 2. (dunque) therefore.
siccità sf. drought.
siccome cong. as, since.
siciliano agg. e sm. Sicilian.
sicomoro sm. sycamore.
sicumera sf. presumption.
sicura sf. safety belt.
sicurezza sf. 1. (certezza) certainty 2. (immunità da pericoli) safety || dispositivo di —, safety device; misura di —, precautionary measure; uscita di —, emergency door; rasoio, spilla di —, safety-razor, pin.
sicuro agg. 1. (certo) sure: — di sé, self-confident 2. (immune da pericoli) safe 3. (che non sbaglia) unfailing 4. (calmo, saldo) calm, steady 5. (esperto) skilful.
siderale agg. sidereal.
siderurgìa sf. metallurgy of iron.
siderùrgico agg. iron (attr.): stabilimento —, iron-works (pl.). ♦ siderùrgico sm. iron worker.
sidro sm. cider.
siepe sf. hedge.

siero *sm.* serum.

sieroso *agg.* serous.

sieroterapìa *sf.* serotherapy.

siesta *sf.* nap.

siffatto *agg.* such.

sifìlide *sf.* syphilis.

sifone *sm.* siphon.

sigaraia *sf.* cigar-seller.

sigaretta *sf.* cigarette.

sìgaro *sm.* cigar.

sigillare *vt.* to seal.

sigillatura *sf.* sealing.

sigillo *sm.* seal.

sigla *sf.* monogram.

siglare *vt.* to initial.

significare *vt.* 1. to mean (*v. irr.*) 2. (*comunicare*) to signify 3. (*simboleggiare*) to represent.

significativo *agg.* meaningful.

significato *sm.* 1. meaning 2. (*valore*) import.

signora *sf.* 1. lady, woman (*pl.* women) 2. (*seguito da cognome*) Mrs: *la — Smith*, Mrs. Smith 3. (*vocativo*) Madam: *buon giorno —*, good morning Madam 4. (*padrona*) mistress 5. (*donna ricca*) rich lady 6. (*moglie*) wife (*pl.* wives).

signore *sm.* 1. gentleman, man (*pl.* -men) 2. (*seguito da cognome*) Mr.: *il — Smith*, Mr. Smith 3. (*padrone*) master 4. (*vocativo*) Sir: *sì —!* yes, Sir! 5. (*uomo ricco*) lord 6. (*Dio*) God, Lord.

signoreggiare *vt.* to rule.

signorìa *sf.* 1. (*di uomo*) Lordship; (*di donna*) Ladyship 2. (*dominio*) dominion.

signorile *agg.* 1. (*riferito a uomo*) gentlemanlike; (*riferito a donna*) ladylike 2. (*elegante*) luxury.

signorilità *sf.* distinction, high class.

signorina *sf.* 1. young lady 2. (*seguito da cognome*) Miss: *la — Smith*, Miss Smith 3. (*vocativo*) Madam: *Buon giorno —*, good morning Madam 4. (*padroncina*) young mistress 5. (*donna non sposata*) unmarried woman.

signorotto *sm.* squire.

silenziatore *sm.* silencer.

silenzio *sm.* silence.

silenzioso *agg.* silent ‖ *una strada silenziosa*, a noiseless street.

sìlfide *sf.* sylph.

silfo *sm.* sylph.

sìlice *sf.* silica.

silicio *sm.* silicon.

silicone *sm.* silicone.

silicosi *sf.* silicosis.

sìllaba *sf.* syllable.

sillabare *vt.* to syllabize.

sillabo *sm.* summary.

sillogismo *sm.* syllogism.

sillogìstico *agg.* syllogistic.

silo *sm.* silo (*pl.* silos).

siluramento *sm.* 1. torpedoing 2. (*fig.*) firing.

silurante *sf.* torpedo-boat.

silurare *vt.* 1. to torpedo 2. (*fig.*) to dismiss.

siluriano *agg.* e *sm.* Silurian.

siluro *sm.* (*mil.; zool.*) torpedo.

silvestre *agg.* sylvan.

silvicoltore *sm.* forester.

silvicoltura *sf.* forestry.

simbiosi *sf.* symbiosis.

simboleggiare *vt.* to symbolize.

simbòlico *agg.* 1. symbolic 2. (*nominale*) nominal.

simbolismo *sm.* symbolism.

simbolista *agg.* e *sm.* symbolist.

simbolo *sm.* symbol.

similare *agg.* similar.

sìmile *agg.* 1. like, similar 2. (*pred.*) alike 3. (*tale*) such. ♦ **sìmile** *sm.* fellow-creature.

similitùdine *sf.* 1. likeness 2. (*lett.*) simile.

simmetrìa *sf.* symmetry.

simmètrico *agg.* symmetric(al).

simonìa *sf.* simony.

simonìaco *agg.* e *sm.* simoniac.

simpatìa *sf.* liking.

simpàtico *agg.* nice, pleasant.

simpatizzante *agg.* sympathizing. ♦ **simpatizzante** *s.* sympathizer.

simpatizzare *vi.* 1. to sympathize 2. (*rec.*) to take (*v. irr.*) a liking to each other.

simposio *sm.* symposium (*pl.* -ia).

simulacro *sm.* 1. simulacre 2. (*finzione*) sham.

simulare *vt.* to feign.

simulato *agg.* simulated.

simulatore *sm.* simulator.

simulazione *sf.* simulation.

simultaneità *sf.* simultaneity.

simultàneo *agg.* simultaneous (with).

sinagoga *sf.* synagogue.

sincerarsi *vr.* to make (*v. irr.*) sure.

sincerità *sf.* sincerity.

sincero *agg.* sincere, true.

sincopare *vt.* to syncopate.

sincopato *agg.* syncopated.

sincope *sf.* 1. (*med.*) syncope 2. (*mus.; gramm.*) syncopation.

sincronismo *sm.* synchronism.

sincronizzare *vt.* to synchronize.

sincronizzazione *sf.* synchronization.

sindacale *agg.* trade-union (*attr.*).

sindacalismo *sm.* trade-unionism.

sindacalista *s.* trade-unionist.

sindacare *vt.* 1. to control 2. (*criticare*) to criticize.

sindacato *sm.* trade-union.

sindaco *sm.* 1. mayor 2. (*di società*) auditor.

sindrome *sf.* syndrome.

sinecura *sf.* sinecure.

sinfonìa *sf.* symphony.

sinfònico *agg.* symphonic.

singhiozzare *vi.* to sob.

singhiozzo *sm.* 1. hiccup 2. (*di pianto*) sob.

singolare *agg.* 1. singular 2. (*singolo*) single.

singolarità *sf.* singularity.

singolarmente *avv.* 1. (*ad uno ad uno*) singly 2. (*segnatamente*) particularly.

singolo *agg.* single, individual.

singulto *sm.* 1. hiccup 2. (*di pianto*) sob.

sinistra *sf.* 1. left: *alla mia* —, on my left 2. (*mano*) left hand 3. (*parte*) left-hand side || *uomo di* — (*pol.*), left-winger.

sinistramente *avv.* sinisterly.

sinistrato *agg.* 1. (*di edificio*) bomb-damaged 2. (*di persona*) injured. ♦ **sinistrato** *sm.* (damage) sufferer.

sinistro *agg.* 1. left 2. (*truce*) sinister, grim. ♦ **sinistro** *sm.* 1. accident, mishap 2. (*boxe*) left.

sinòlogo *sm.* Sinologist.

sinonimìa *sf.* synonymy.

sinònimo *agg.* synonymous. ♦ **sinònimo** *sm.* synonym.

sinora *avv.* till now, so far.

sinovite *sf.* synovitis.

sintassi *sf.* syntax.

sintàttico *agg.* syntactic(al).

sìntesi *sf.* synthesis (*pl.* -ses).

sintètico *agg.* synthetic.

sintetizzare *vt.* to synthetize.

sintomàtico *agg.* symptomatic.

sìntomo *sm.* symptom.

sintonìa *sf.* syntony.

sintonizzare *vt.* to tune in.

sinuosità *sf.* winding.

sinuoso *agg.* winding.

sinusite *sf.* sinusitis.

sionismo *sm.* Zionism.

sionista *s.* Zionist.

sipario *sm.* curtain.

sirena *sf.* 1. (*mit.*) siren, mermaid 2. (*acustica*) hooter.

siringa *sf.* syringe.

siringare *vt.* to syringe.

sìsmico *agg.* seismic.

sismògrafo *sm.* seismograph.

sismologìa *sf.* seismology.

sismòlogo *sm.* seismologist.

sistema *sm.* system: — *di vita*, way of life.

sistemare *vt.* 1. (*mettere in ordine*) to arrange 2. (*definire*) to settle.

sistemàtico *agg.* systematic(al).

sistemazione *sf.* 1. (*ordine*) arrangement 2. (*collocazione di macchinari*) layout 3. (*il sistemarsi*) settling 4. (*lavoro*) job.

sito *sm.* place.

situare *vt.* to place.

situazione *sf.* situation.

slabbrare *vt.* to chip the rim of.

slabbratura *sf.* chipping.

slacciare *vt.* 1. to untie 2. (*sbottonare*) to unbutton.

slanciarsi *vr.* to rush.

slanciato *agg.* slim.

slancio *sm.* 1. rush 2. (*energia*) energy.

slargare *vt.* to widen.

slattamento *sm.* weaning.

slattare *vt.* to wean.

slavato *agg.* pale.

slavina *sf.* landslide; (*di neve*) snowslide.

slavo *agg. e sm.* Slav.

sleale *agg.* unfair.

slealtà *sf.* disloyalty.

slegare *vt.* to untie.

slegato *agg.* 1. untied 2. (*di discorso ecc.*) disconnected.

slitta *sf.* sleigh.

slittamento *sm.* skidding.

slittare *vi.* 1. to slide (*v. irr.*) 2. (*di ruote*) to skid.

slogamento *sm.* dislocation.

slogare *vt.* to dislocate.

slogatura *sf.* dislocation.

sloggiare *vi.* to clear out. ♦ **sloggiare** *vt.* to drive (*v. irr.*) out.

smaccato *agg.* sickly-sweet.

smacchiare *vt.* to clean.

smacchiatore *sm.* stain-remover.

smacchiatura *sf.* cleaning.

smacco *sm.* mortification.

smagliante agg. dazzling.

smagliare vt. to unravel. ♦ **smagliarsi** vr. (di calze) to ladder.

smagliato agg. unravelled.

smagliatura sf. 1. (di calze) ladder.

smagnetizzare vt. to demagnetize.

smagnetizzazione sf. demagnetization.

smagrire vt. e vi. to thin.

smagrito agg. thin, grown thin.

smaliziare vt. to smarten up. ♦ **smaliziarsi** vr. to wisen.

smaliziato agg. cunning.

smaltare vt. to enamel: — le unghie, to paint one's nails.

smaltato agg. 1. enamelled 2. (di unghie) painted.

smaltire vt. to digest: — la sbornia, to get (v. irr.) over one's drunkenness.

smalto sm. enamel: — per unghie, nail-polish.

smancerìa sf. mawkishness.

smangiare vt. to corrode.

smania sf. 1. great desire 2. (agitazione) frenzy.

smaniare vi. 1. to yearn (for) 2. (essere agitati) to be restless.

smanioso agg. 1. eager 2. (agitato) restless.

smantellamento sm. dismantling.

smantellare vt. to dismantle.

smarcare vt. to unmark.

smargiassata sf. swagger.

smargiasserìa sf. bragging.

smargiasso sm. braggart.

smarginare vt. to trim the edge.

smarrimento sm. 1. loss 2. (turbamento) bewilderment.

smarrire vt. to lose (v. irr.). ♦ **smarrirsi** vr. 1. to lose one's way 2. (di lettera, pacco) to miscarry 3. (turbarsi) to be bewildered.

smascellarsi vr. to dislocate one's jaws.

smascherare vt. to unmask.

smembramento sm. dismemberment.

smembrare vt. to dismember.

smemorataggine sf. 1. lack of memory 2. (dimenticanza) lapse of memory.

smemorato agg. absent-minded.

smentire vt. to deny. ♦ **smentirsi** vr. 1. to contradict oneself 2. (venir meno) to be untrue to oneself.

smentita sf. denial.

smeraldo sm. emerald.

smerciare vt. to sell (v. irr.) off.

smercio sm. sale.

smerigliare vt. 1. to polish with emery 2. (di vetri) to frost glass.

smerigliato agg. emery: carta smerigliata, emery paper; vetro —, frosted glass.

smeriglio sm. emery.

smerlo sm. scallop.

smesso agg. cast off.

sméttere vt. to stop, to leave (v. irr.) off: — un vestito, to cast (v. irr.) off a dress.

smezzare vt. to halve.

smidollato agg. (di persona) spineless.

smilitarizzare vt. to demilitarize.

smilitarizzazione sf. demilitarization.

smilzo agg. thin.

sminuire vt. to diminish. ♦ **sminuirsi** vr. to belittle oneself.

sminuzzare vt. 1. (tritare) to mince 2. (tagliuzzare) to chop up 3. (sbriciolare) to crumble.

smistamento sm. 1. clearing 2. (ferr.) shunting 3. (di corrispondenza) sorting.

smistare vt. 1. (di corrispondenza) to sort out 2. (ferr.) to shunt.

smisuratamente avv. beyond measure.

smisurato agg. enormous, huge.

smobilitare vt. to demobilize.

smobilitazione sf. demobilization.

smoccolare vt. to snuff.

smoccolatoio sm. snuffers (pl.).

smoccolatura sf. snuffing.

smodato agg. immoderate.

smoderatezza sf. immoderateness.

smoderato agg. immoderate.

smontàbile agg. demountable.

smontaggio sm. disassembling.

smontare vt. 1. (far scendere) (da cavallo) to unhorse; (da un'automobile) to drop 2. (scomporre in parti) to take (v. irr.) to pieces 3. (mecc.) to disassemble 4. (fig.) to dishearten, to cool. ♦ **smontare** vi. 1. (da un treno, tram ecc.) to get (v. irr.) off 2. (da un'automobile) to get (v. irr.) out 3. (da cavallo) to dismount 4. (dal lavoro) to go (v. irr.) off duty 5. (sbiadire) to fade.

smorfia sf. grimace.

smorfioso agg. affected.

smorto agg. pale.

smorzamento sm. 1. (di luci) shading 2. (*di colori*) toning down 3. (*di suoni*) lowering 4. (*di sete; fig.*) quenching.

smorzare *vt.* 1. (*di luci*) to shade 2. (*di colori*) to tone down 3. (*di suoni*) to lower 4. (*di sete; fig.*) to quench 5. (*spegnere*) to put (*v. irr.*) down.

smottamento *sm.* landslip.

smottare *vi.* to slip.

smozzicare *vt.* 1. to hack to pieces 2. (*di parole*) to clip.

smunto *agg.* pale.

smuòvere *vt.* 1. to shift 2. (*fig.*) to move.

smussare *vt.* 1. to round off 2. (*fig.*) to soften.

smussato *agg.* 1. blunted 2. (*fig.*) softened.

snaturare *vt.* to pervert.

snaturato *agg.* unnatural.

snazionalizzare *vt.* to denationalize.

snebbiare *vt.* 1. to dispel the fog 2. (*fig.*) to clear.

snellezza *sf.* slenderness.

snellire *vt.* 1. to make (*v. irr.*) slender 2. (*fig.*) to simplify. ♦ **snellirsi** *vr.* to grow (*v. irr.*) slender.

snello *agg.* slender.

snervante *agg.* enervating.

snervare *vt.* to enervate.

snidare *vt.* 1. to flush 2. (*fig.*) to dislodge.

snobbare *vt.* to snob.

snobismo *sm.* snobbery.

snocciolare *vt.* 1. to stone 2. (*fig.*) to tell (*v. irr.*).

snodare *vt.* 1. to untie 2. (*rendere agile*) to make (*v. irr.*) supple. ♦ **snodarsi** *vr.* (*di strade*) to wind (*v. irr.*).

snodato *agg.* 1. supple 2. (*di cosa*) jointed.

snodo *sm.* joint.

soave *agg.* sweet.

soavità *sf.* sweetness.

sobbalzare *vi.* 1. to jerk 2. (*trasalire*) to start.

sobbalzo *sm.* 1. jerk 2. (*sussulto*) start.

sobbarcarsi *vr.* to take (*v. irr.*) upon oneself.

sobborgo *sm.* suburb.

sobillare *vt.* to stir up.

sobillatore *sm.* instigator.

sobrietà *sf.* sobriety.

sobrio *agg.* sober.

socchiùdere *vt.* 1. to half-close 2. (*aprire un po'*) to half-open.

socchiuso *agg.* half-closed, half-open.

sòccida *sf.* agistment.

soccòmbere *vi.* to succumb.

soccòrrere *vt.* to help, to assist.

soccorritore *agg.* helpful. ♦ **soccorritore** *sm.* helper.

soccorso *sm.* help || *pronto* —, first aid.

socialdemocràtico *agg.* socialdemocratic.

socialdemocrazìa *sf.* socialdemocracy.

sociale *agg.* social.

socialismo *sm.* Socialism.

socialista *agg.* e *sm.* Socialist.

socialità *sf.* sociality.

socializzare *vt.* to socialize.

socializzazione *sf.* socialization.

società *sf.* 1. society 2. (*comm.*) company: — *anonima*, joint-stock company; — *a responsabilità limitata*, limited company || *entrare in* —, to enter into partnership.

sociévole *agg.* sociable.

socievolezza *sf.* sociability.

socio *sm.* 1. member 2. (*comm.*) partner.

sociologìa *sf.* sociology.

sociològico *agg.* sociological.

sociòlogo *sm.* sociologist.

socràtico *agg.* Socratic.

soda *sf.* soda.

sodalizio *sm.* 1. society 2. (*confraternita*) brotherhood.

sodare *vt.* to consolidate.

sodatura *sf.* (*tessile*) fulling.

soddisfacente *agg.* satisfactory.

soddisfare *vt.* 1. to satisfy 2. (*adempiere*) to fulfil 3. (*far fronte a*) to discharge 4. (*riparare*) to make (*v. irr.*) amends.

soddisfazione *sf.* satisfaction.

sodio *sm.* sodium.

sodo *agg.* solid, firm: *uovo* —, hard-boiled egg; *darle sode a qu.*, to strike (*v. irr.*) so. hard.

sofferente *agg.* 1. suffering 2. (*malaticcio*) poorly.

sofferenza *sf.* pain.

soffermare *vt.* to stop. ♦ **soffermarsi** *vr.* to stop.

soffiare *vt.* e *vi.* to blow (*v. irr.*): *soffiarsi il naso*, to blow one's nose.

soffiata *sf.* puff.

soffiato *agg.* puffed.

soffiatore *sm.* blower.

soffiatura *sf.* blowing.

sòffice *agg.* soft.

soffietto *sm.* 1. bellows (*pl.*) 2. (*edit.*) blurb.

soffio *sm.* puff, whiff.

soffione *sm.* 1. blow-pipe 2. (*geol.*) fumarole.

soffitta *sf.* garret.

soffitto *sm.* ceiling.

soffocamento *sm.* choking.

soffocante *agg.* choking: *caldo —*, sultry heat.

soffocare *vt.* 1. to choke 2. (*reprimere*) to repress.

soffocato *agg.* choked.

sòffoco *sm.* sultriness.

soffòndere *vt.* to suffuse.

soffrìggere *vt.* to fry slightly.

soffrire *vt.* 1. to suffer 2. (*sopportare*) to stand (*v. irr.*).

soffuso *agg.* suffused.

sofisma *sm.* sophism.

sofista *sm.* sophist.

sofistica *sf.* sophistry.

sofisticare *vi.* to quibble. ♦ sofisticare *vt.* to adulterate.

sofisticato *agg.* 1. sophisticated 2. (*adulterato*) adulterated.

sofisticazione *sf.* adulteration.

sofisticherìa *sf.* quibbling.

sofìstico *agg.* sophistical.

soggettista *sm.* scenario writer.

soggettivismo *sm.* subjectivism.

soggettività *sf.* subjectivity.

soggettivo *agg.* subjective.

soggetto *agg. e sm.* subject.

soggezione *sf.* 1. subjection 2. (*timidezza*) shyness.

sogghignare *vi.* to sneer.

sogghigno *sm.* sneer.

soggiacere *vi.* to be subjected.

soggiogare *vt.* to subdue.

soggiornare *vi.* to stay.

soggiorno *sm.* stay: *stanza di —*, living-room.

soggiùngere *vt.* to add.

soglia *sf.* threshold.

sògliola *sf.* sole.

sognante *agg.* dreaming: *occhi sognanti*, dreamy eyes.

sognare *vt.* to dream (*v. irr.*): *— ad occhi aperti*, to have daydreams.

sognatore *agg.* dreaming. ♦ sognatore *sm.* dreamer.

sogno *sm.* dream.

soia *sf.* soya.

solaio *sm.* attic.

solamente *avv.* only.

solare *agg.* 1. solar 2. (*radioso*) radiant.

solatìo *agg.* sunny.

solcare *vt.* 1. to plough 2. (*fig.*) to furrow.

solcato *agg.* 1. ploughed 2. (*fig.*) furrowed.

solcatura *sf.* ploughing, furrowing.

solco *sm.* 1. (*agr.*) furrow 2. (*ruga*) wrinkle 3. (*mar.*) wake 4. (*di ruota sul terreno*) track.

solcòmetro *sm.* log.

soldataglia *sf.* soldiery.

soldatesco *agg.* soldierly.

soldato *sm.* soldier.

soldo *sm.* 1. penny 2. (*denaro*) money 3. (*salario*) pay: *essere al — di qu.*, to be in so.'s pay.

sole *sm.* sun: *bagno di —*, sun-bathing; *colpo di —*, sunstroke; *un giorno di —*, *senza —*, a sunny day, a sunless day; *tramonto del —*, sunset.

soleggiare *vt.* to sun-dry.

soleggiato *agg.* sunny.

solenne *agg.* solemn.

solennità *sf.* 1. solemnity 2. (*cerimonia*) ceremony.

solennizzare *vt.* to solemnize.

solenòide *sm.* solenoid.

solere *vi.* to use (*usato solo al passato*).

solerte *agg.* diligent.

solerzia *sf.* diligence.

soletta *sf.* sole.

solfa *sf.* 1. scale 2. (*fig.*) old story.

solfara *sf.* sulphur mine.

solfare *vt.* to sulphur.

solfatara *sf.* solfatara.

solfato *sm.* sulphate.

solfeggiare *vt.* to sol-fa.

solfeggio *sm.* solfeggio.

solfito *sm.* sulphite.

solfuro *sm.* sulphide.

solidale *agg.* solid (for).

solidamente *avv.* solidly.

solidarietà *sf.* solidarity.

solidarizzare *vi.* to be solid (for).

solidificare *vt.* to solidify.

solidificazione *sf.* solidification.

solidità *sf.* 1. solidity 2. (*di colori*) fastness.

sòlido *agg.* 1. solid 2. (*di colori*) fast 3. (*fig.*) sound. ♦ sòlido *sm.* solid.

soliloquio *sm.* soliloquy.

solipsismo *sm.* solipsism.

solista *s.* soloist.

solitamente *avv.* usually.
solitario¹ *agg.* solitary. ♦ **solitario**
sm. 1. hermit 2..(*brillante*) solitaire.
solitario² *sm.* (*a carte*) solitaire.
sòlito *agg.* usual, customary: *essere*
—, to be used to (doing); *di —*,
usually.
solitùdine *sf.* loneliness.
sollazzare *vt.* to amuse.
sollazzo *sm.* amusement.
sollecitante *agg.* urging.
sollecitare *vt.* 1. (*far premura*) to
urge 2. (*brigare*) to solicit 3. (*affrettare*) to hurry up.
sollecitazione *sf.* 1. solicitation 2.
(*preghiera*) entreaty.
sollécito *agg.* 1. (*rapido*) prompt
2. (*preoccupato*) solicitous 3. (*premuroso*) obliging.
sollecitùdine *sf.'* 1. (*rapidità*)
promptness 2. (*interessamento*) concern 3. (*gentilezza*) kindness.
solleone *sm.* dog-days (*pl.*).
solleticante *agg.* alluring.
solleticare *vt.* to tickle.
sollético *sm.* 1. tickle: *soffrire il*
—, to be ticklish 2. (*fig.*) itch.
sollevamento *sm.* lifting.
sollevare *vt.* 1. to lift 2. (*issare*) to
hoist 3. (*fig.*) to raise 4. (*dar sollievo*) to relieve. ♦ **sollevarsi**
vr. 1. to rise (*v. irr.*) 2. (*riaversi*)
to recover 3. (*insorgere*) to rebel.
sollevato *agg.* (*rasserenato*) cheered
up.
sollevazione *sf.* (*rivolta*) rising.
sollievo *sm.* relief.
sollùchero *sm.* andare in —, to go
(*v. irr.*) into raptures.
solo *agg.* 1. alone (*pred.*): *da —*,
by oneself 2. (*unico*) only. ♦
solo *avv.* only.
solstizio *sm.* solstice.
soltanto *avv.* only.
solùbile *agg.* soluble.
solubilità *sf.* solubility.
soluzione *sf.* solution.
solvente *agg.* e *sm.* solvent.
solvenza *sf.* (*comm.*) solvency.
solvibile *agg.* solvent.
solvibilità *sf.* solvency.
soma *sf.* load, burden.
somaràggine *sf.* stupidity.
somaro *sm.* ass.
somàtico *agg.* somatic.
somigliante *agg.* alike, similar.
somiglianza *sf.* likeness.
somigliare *vi.* to look like.

somma *sf.* 1. (*mat.*) addition 2.
(*di denaro*) sum.
sommamente *avv.* extremely.
sommare *vt.* to add.
sommariamente *avv.* summarily.
sommario *agg.* e *sm.* summary.
sommèrgere *vt.* to submerge.
sommergibile *agg.* submersible. ♦
sommergibile *sm.* submarine.
sommergibilista *sm.* submariner.
sommersione *sf.* submersion.
sommerso *agg.* submerged.
sommessamente *avv.* 1. submissively 2. (*a bassa voce*) in a low
voice.
sommesso *agg.* 1. submissive 2. (*di
voce*) low.
somministrare *vt.* to administer.
somministratore *sm.* giver.
somministrazione *sf.* giving.
sommissione *sf.* V. *sottomissione.*
sommità *sf.* summit, top.
sommo¹ *agg.* 1. highest 2. (*fig.*) supreme.
sommo² *sm.* summit, top.
sommossa *sf.* rising.
sommovimento *sm.* movement,
agitation.
sommozzatore *sm.* frogman (*pl.*
-men).
sommuòvere *vt.* to stir up.
sonagliera *sf.* collar with bells.
sonaglio *sm.* 1. harness-bell 2.
(*giocattolo*) rattle || *serpente a so-
nagli*, rattlesnake.
sonante *agg.* resounding || *denaro*
—, ready money.
sonare *vt.* 1. to sound 2. (*musica*)
to play 3. (*di orologio*) to strike
(*v. irr.*). ♦ **sonare** *vi.* (*di campanello*) to ring (*v. irr.*).
sonata *sf.* (*mus.*) sonata.
sonatore *sm.* player.
sonda *sf.* 1. (*mar.*) sounding line
2. (*med.*) probe 3. (*min.*) drill.
sondaggio *sm.* 1. sounding 2. (*med.*)
probing 3. (*min.*) drilling.
sondare *vt.* 1. to sound 2. (*fig.*) to
throw (*v. irr.*) out.
soneria *sf.* 1. (*di orologio*) striking-
-mechanism 2. alarm.
sonetto *sm.* sonnet.
sonnacchiosamente *avv.* drowsily.
sonnacchioso *agg.* 1. sleepy 2.
(*fig.*) torpid.
sonnambulismo *sm.* sleep-walking.
sonnàmbulo *sm.* sleep-walker.
sonnecchiare *vi.* to doze.
sonnellino *sm.* nap.

275   **sopravvivenza**

sonnìfero sm. sleeping pills (pl.).
sonno sm. sleep: — profondo, sound sleep.
sonnolento agg. drowsy.
sonnolenza sf. drowsiness.
sonoramente avv. sonorously.
sonorità sf. sonority.
sonorizzare vt. to post-score.
sonorizzazione sf. post-scoring.
sonoro agg. 1. sonorous 2. (rumoroso) loud 3. (cine) sound.
sontuosamente avv. sumptuously.
sontuosità sf. sumptuousness.
sontuoso agg. sumptuous.
soperchierìa sf. V. soverchierìa.
sopire vt. 1. to make (v. irr.) drowsy 2. (calmare) to soothe.
sopore sm. doze.
soporìfero agg. soporific.
sopperire vi. 1. to provide (for) 2. (supplire) to make (v. irr.) up (for).
soppesare vt. 1. to weigh in one's hand 2. (considerare) to weigh.
soppiantare vt. to supplant.
soppiatto (nella loc. avv.) di —, stealthily.
sopportàbile agg. bearable.
sopportabilità sf. bearableness.
sopportabilmente avv. bearably.
sopportare vt. to bear (v. irr.).
sopportazione sf. endurance.
soppressare vt. to press.
soppressione sf. 1. suppression 2. (abolizione) abolition.
soppresso agg. 1. suppressed 2. (abolito) abolished.
sopprimere vt. 1. to suppress 2. (abolire) to abolish.
sopra prep. 1. (con contatto) on, upon 2. (senza contatto) over 3. (al di sopra) above. ♦ **sopra** avv. 1. above 2. (al piano superiore) upstairs.
soprabbondanza sf. V. sovrabbondanza.
soprabbondare vi. V. sovrabbondare.
sopràbito sm. overcoat.
sopraccaricare vt. V. sovraccaricare.
sopraccàrico sm. V. sovraccàrico.
sopraccennato agg. above-mentioned.
sopracciglio sm. eyebrow.
sopraccitato agg. V. sopraddetto.
sopraccoperta sf. 1. (di libro) jacket 2. (di letto) counterpane. ♦ **sopraccoperta** avv. (mar.) on deck.

sopraddetto agg. above-mentioned.
sopraelevare vt. 1. (edil.) to increase the height of 2. (di strade, rotaie ecc.) to bank.
sopraelevazione sf. 1. (edil.) heightening 2. (di strade, rotaie ecc.) superelevation.
sopraffare vt. to overwhelm.
sopraffazione sf. 1. overwhelming 2. (abuso) abuse.
sopraffino agg. first-rate.
sopraggiùngere vi. 1. to arrive 2. (accadere) to happen.
sopraggiunta sf. addition.
sopraindicato agg. V. sopraddetto.
sopralluogo sm. investigation on the spot.
soprammercato (nella loc. avv.) per —, moreover.
soprammèttere vt. to place on.
soprammòbile sm. knick-knack.
soprannaturale agg. supernatural.
soprannome sm. nickname.
soprannominare vt. to nickname.
soprannùmero sm. excess.
soprano sm. soprano.
soprappassaggio sm. overbridge.
soprappensiero avv. lost in thought.
soprappiù sm. extra, addition.
soprapprezzo sm. extra charge.
soprascarpa sf. galosh.
soprascritta sf. inscription.
soprascritto agg. above-written.
soprasensìbile agg. supersensible.
soprassalto sm. jerk: di —, all of a sudden.
soprassedere vi. 1. to wait 2. (rimandare) to postpone.
soprassoldo sm. extra pay.
soprastruttura sf. superstructure.
soprattassa sf. extra tax.
soprattutto avv. above all.
sopravanzare vt. 1. (superare) to surpass 2. (avanzare) to be left over.
sopravanzo sm. surplus.
sopravvalutare vt. to overrate.
sopravvenire vi. 1. (di persone) to turn up 2. (di cose) to come (v. irr.) about.
sopravvento sm. 1. (mar.) windward 2. (fig.) upper hand: prendere il —, to get (v. irr.) the upper hand.
sopravvissuto agg. e sm. surviving. ♦ **sopravvissuto** sm. survivor.
sopravvivenza sf. survival.

sopravvìvere *vi.* to survive.

sopruso *sm.* abuse of power.

soqquadro *sm.* confusion: *a —,* topsy-turvy.

sorbettare *vt.* to freeze (*v. irr.*).

sorbetto *sm.* sherbet.

sorbire *vt.* to sip. ♦ **sorbirsi** *vr.* to put (*v. irr.*) up with.

sorcio *sm.* mouse (*pl.* mice).

sordamente *avv.* dully.

sordidamente *avv.* filthily.

sordidezza *sf.* filthiness.

sòrdido *agg.* filthy.

sordina *sf.* (*mus.*) mute: *in —* (*fig.*), on the sly.

sordità *sf.* deafness.

sordo *agg.* deaf.

sordomuto *sm.* deaf-mute.

sorella *sf.* sister.

sorellastra *sf.* half-sister.

sorgente *sf.* spring, source.

sòrgere *vi.* to rise (*v. irr.*).

sorgiva *sf.* spring-water.

sorgivo *agg.* spring (*attr.*).

soriano *agg.* syrian: *gatto —,* tabby cat.

sormontare *vt.* 1. to surmount 2. (*superare*) to overcome (*v. irr.*).

sornione *agg.* sly. ♦ **sornione** *sm.* sly person.

sorpassare *vt.* 1. to overtake (*v. irr.*) 2. (*sport*) to outrun (*v. irr.*).

sorpassato *agg.* old-fashioned.

sorpasso *sm.* overtaking.

sorprendente *agg.* surprising.

sorprèndere *vt.* 1. (*cogliere inaspettatamente*) to catch (*v. irr.*) 2. (*meravigliare*) to surprise.

sorpresa *sf.* surprise: *di —,* by surprise.

sorrèggere *vt.* to support.

sorridente *agg.* smiling.

sorrìdere *vi.* 1. to smile 2. (*attrarre*) to appeal.

sorriso *sm.* smile.

sorsata *sf.* sip.

sorseggiare *vt.* to sip.

sorso *sm.* gulp, sip.

sorta *sf.* kind, sort.

sorte *sf.* 1. destiny, lot 2. (*avvenire*) future.

sorteggiare *vt.* to draw (*v. irr.*) lots (for).

sorteggio *sm.* draw.

sortilegio *sm.* witchcraft.

sortire[1] *vt.* to get (*v. irr.*).

sortire[2] *vi.* to come (*v. irr.*) out.

sortita *sf.* sally.

sorvegliante *sm.* overseer.

sorveglianza *sf.* overseeing.

sorvegliare *vt.* to oversee (*v. irr.*).

sorvolare *vt.* 1. to fly (*v. irr.*) over 2. (*passar sopra*) to pass over.

sorvolo *sm.* flying over.

sosia *sm.* double.

sospèndere *vt.* 1. (*attaccare*) to suspend 2. (*interrompere*) to defer.

sospensione *sf.* 1. (*incertezza; chim.*) suspension 2. (*interruzione*) interruption.

sospensiva *sf.* suspension.

sospensivo *agg.* suspensive.

sospeso *agg.* 1. hanging 2. (*interrotto*) suspended.

sospettàbile *agg.* liable to suspicion.

sospettare *vt.* to suspect.

sospetto *sm.* suspicion.

sospettosamente *avv.* suspiciously.

sospettoso *agg.* suspicious.

sospìngere *vt.* to drive (*v. irr.*) ‖ *ad ogni piè sospinto,* at every moment.

sospirare *vi.* 1. to sigh 2. (*fig.*) to pine. ♦ **sospirare** *vt.* to long (for).

sospirato *agg.* (*desiderato*) longed for.

sospiro *sm.* sigh.

sosta *sf.* 1. (*fermata*) stop 2. (*pausa*) pause.

sostantivamente *avv.* substantively.

sostantivare *vt.* to substantivize.

sostantivo *sm.* substantive, noun.

sostanza *sf.* substance ‖ *in — (in breve*), in short.

sostanziale *agg.* substantial.

sostanzialmente *avv.* substantially.

sostanzioso *agg.* substantial.

sostare *vi.* to stop.

sostegno *sm.* support.

sostenere *vt.* 1. to support 2. (*affermare*) to maintain 3. (*tener alto*) to keep (*v. irr.*) up.

sostenìbile *agg.* 1. supportable 2. (*di opinioni*) maintainable.

sostenimento *sm.* 1. support 2. (*sostentamento*) sustenance.

sostenitore *sm.* supporter.

sostentamento *sm.* sustenance.

sostenuto *agg.* 1. stiff, distant 2. (*comm.*) steady.

sostituìbile *agg.* replaceable.

sostituire *vt.* to replace.

sostituto *sm.* substitute.

sostituzione *sf.* replacement.

sostrato *sm.* substratum (*pl.* -ta).

sottacere *vt.* to keep (*v. irr.*) (sthg.) from.

sottaceti *sm. pl.* pickles.

sottana *sf.* 1. skirt 2. (*di prete*) cassock.

sottecchi (*nella loc. avv.*) *di* —, stealthily.

sotterfugio *sm.* subterfuge.

sotterramento *sm.* burial.

sotterrànea *sf.* underground.

sotterràneo *agg.* underground. ◆ **sotterràneo** *sm.* 1. (*di basilica*) vault 2. (*di castello*) dungeon.

sotterrare *vt.* to bury.

sottigliezza *sf.* 1. thinness 2. (*acutezza*) subtlety.

sottile *agg.* 1. thin 2. (*fig.*) subtle.

sottilizzare *vi.* to split (*v. irr.*) hairs.

sottilmente *avv.* 1. finely 2. (*con acutezza*) subtly.

sottintèndere *vt.* to imply.

sottinteso *agg.* implied. ◆ **sottinteso** *sm.* allusion.

sotto *prep.* 1. under 2. (*al di sotto, più in basso*) below, beneath 3. (*in espressioni di tempo*) — *Natale*, at Christmas; *essere* — *gli esami*, to be close to the exams. ◆ **sotto** *avv.* 1. underneath, below 2. (*al piano di sotto*) downstairs.

sottobanco *loc. avv.* underthecounter.

sottobosco *sm.* underbrush.

sottocchio *avv.* in front of: *tenere qc.* —, to keep (*v. irr.*) an eye on sthg.

sottochiave *avv.* under lock and key.

sottocoperta *sf.* (*mar.*) below deck.

sottocoppa *sf.* saucer.

sottocutàneo *agg.* subcutaneous.

sottofondo *sm.* 1. (*edil.*) foundation 2. (*sfondo*) background.

sottogamba (*nella loc. avv.*) *prendere qc.* —, to make (*v. irr.*) light of sthg.

sottolineare *vt.* 1. to underline 2. (*fig.*) to lay (*v. irr.*) stress (on).

sottolineatura *sf.* underlining.

sottomano *avv.* 1. (*di nascosto*) underhand 2. (*a portata di mano*) at hand.

sottomarino *agg. e sm.* submarine.

sottomesso *agg.* 1. subdued 2. (*obbediente*) submissive.

sottométtere *vt.* to subject. ◆ **sottométtersi** *vr.* to submit (oneself).

sottomissione *sf.* 1. subdual 2. (*obbedienza*) submission.

sottopassaggio *sm.* subway.

sottoporre *vt.* 1. (*al giudizio di qu.*) to submit 2. (*subire, far subire*) to subject 3. (*esporre*) to expose.

sottoposto *sm.* subordinate.

sottoprodotto *sm.* by-product.

sottoscritto *agg.* subscribed. ◆ **sottoscritto** *sm.* undersigned.

sottoscrivere *vt.* 1. to sign 2. (*comm.*) to underwrite. ◆ **sottoscrivere** *vi.* to subscribe.

sottoscrizione *sf.* subscription.

sottosegretario *sm.* under-secretary.

sottosopra *avv.* 1. upside down 2. (*in disordine*) topsy-turvy.

sottospecie *sf.* subspecies (*invariato al pl.*).

sottostante *agg.* below.

sottostare *vi.* 1. (*essere sotto*) to be below 2. (*essere soggetto*) to be subjected 3. (*sottomettersi*) to submit.

sottosuolo *sm.* subsoil.

sottotenente *sm.* second lieutenant.

sottotìtolo *sm.* subtitle.

sottovalutare *vt.* to undervalue.

sottovento *avv.* (*mar.*) leeward.

sottoveste *sf.* petticoat.

sottovoce *avv.* in a low voice.

sottrarre *vt.* 1. (*mat.*) to subtract 2. (*portar via*) to take (*v. irr.*) away 3. (*rubare*) to steal (*v. irr.*) 4. (*salvare da*) to deliver. ◆ **sottrarsi** *vr.* to avoid (sthg.).

sottrazione *sf.* subtraction.

sottufficiale *sm.* non-commissioned officer.

sovente *avv.* often, frequently.

soverchiare *vi.* to overcome (*v. irr.*).

soverchierìa *sf.* oppression.

soviètico *agg. e sm.* Soviet.

sovrabbondante *agg.* superabundant.

sovrabbondanza *sf.* superabundance.

sovrabbondare *vi.* to superabound.

sovraccaricare *vt.* to overload.

sovraccàrico *sm.* overload.

sovraccoperta *sf. e avv.* V. *sopraccoperta.*

sovranità *sf.* 1. sovereignty 2. (*supremazia*) supremacy.

sovrannaturale *agg.* V. *soprannaturale.*

sovrano *agg.* sovereign.

sovrappopolare *vt.* to overpopulate.

sovrappopolato *agg.* overpopulated.

sovrappopolazione *sf.* overpopulation.

sovrapporre *vt.* to superimpose.

sovrapposizione *sf.* superimposition.

sovrastampa *sf.* overprint.

sovrastante *agg.* impending, overhanging.

sovrastare *vi.* 1. to overhang (*v. irr.*) over 2. (*fig.*) to impend 3. (*essere superiore*) to be superior.

sovreccedente *agg.* superabundant.

sovreccedenza *sf.* surplus.

sovreccitabile *agg.* overexcitable.

sovreccitabilità *sf.* overexcitability.

sovreccitare *vt.* to overexcite.

sovreccitazione *sf.* overexcitement.

sovrimposta *sf.* additional tax.

sovrimpressione *sf.* (*foto; cine*) superimposure.

sovrintendente *sm.* superintendent.

sovrintendenza *sf.* superintendence.

sovrumano *agg.* superhuman.

sovvenzionare *vt.* to subsidize.

sovvenzione *sf.* subsidy.

sovversione *sf.* overthrow.

sovversivo *agg.* subversive. ♦ **sovversivo** *sm.* subverter.

sovvertimento *sm.* subversion.

sovvertire *vt.* to overthrow (*v. irr.*).

sozzo *agg.* filthy.

sozzume *sm.* filth.

spaccalegna *sm.* wood-cutter.

spaccamontagne *sm.* braggart.

spaccapietre *sm.* stone-breaker.

spaccare *vt.* 1. to split (*v. irr.*) 2. (*rompere*) to break (*v. irr.*) || *il mio orologio spacca il minuto*, my watch is dead right; *il sole spacca le pietre*, the sun is blazing down.

spaccatura *sf.* split, cleft.

spacchettare *vt.* to unpack.

spacciare *vt.* 1. (*vendere*) to sell (*v. irr.*) 2. (*mettere in circolazione*) to circulate 3. (*far credere*) to make (*v. irr.*) (so.) believe 4. (*uccidere*) to kill. ♦ **spacciarsi** *vr.* to pretend to be || *lo danno per spacciato* (*di malato*), they give him up.

spacciato *agg.* done for.

spacciatore *sm.* 1. seller 2. (*di monete false*) forger.

spaccio *sm.* 1. shop 2. (*vendita*) sale.

spacco *sm.* 1. split 2. (*di abiti*) vent.

spacconata *sf.* bluff.

spaccone *sm.* boaster.

spada *sf.* sword.

spadaccino *sm.* fencer.

spadino *sm.* court-sword.

spadroneggiare *vi.* to lord it.

spaesato *agg.* (*fig.*) lost.

spaghetto *sm.* 1. (*piccolo spago*) string 2. (*fam.*) (*paura*) fright.

spagliare *vt.* to take (*v. irr.*) the straw off.

spagnoletta *sf.* 1. (*di filo*) spool 2. (*arachide*) peanut.

spagnolismo *sm.* Hispanicism.

spagnolo *agg.* Spanish. ♦ **spagnolo** *sm.* Spaniard.

spago *sm.* string.

spaiare *vt.* to uncouple.

spaiato *agg.* odd.

spalancare *vt.* to open wide.

spalancato *agg.* wide open.

spalare *vt.* to shovel away.

spalatore *sm.* shoveller.

spalatura *sf.* shovelling.

spalla *sf.* 1. shoulder 2. (*pl.*) back (*sing.*) 3. (*teat.*) stooge man || *alle spalle*, behind; *vivere alle spalle di qu.*, to live on so.

spallata *sf.* 1. push with the shoulders 2. (*alzata di spalle*) shrug.

spalleggiare *vt.* to back.

spalletta *sf.* parapet.

spalliera *sf.* 1. back 2. (*di piante*) espalier.

spallina *sf.* 1. shoulder-strap 2. (*mil.*) epaulette.

spalluccia *sf.* far *spallucce*, to shrug one's shoulders.

spalmare *vt.* to smear.

spalto *sm.* glacis.

spampanare *vt.* to strip a vine of its leaves.

spàndere *vt.* 1. to spread (*v. irr.*) 2. (*versare*) to shed (*v. irr.*) 3. (*scialacquare*) to squander.

spanna *sf.* span.

spannare *vt.* to skim.

spannocchiare *vt.* to husk.

spappolare *vt.* to pulp. ♦ **spappolarsi** *vr.* to become (*v. irr.*) mushy.

sparare[1] *vt.* to shoot (*v. irr.*), to fire.

sparare[2] *vt.* (*squartare*) to split (*v. irr.*).

sparata *sf.* **1.** discharge **2.** (*spacconata*) brag.

sparato *sm.* (*di camicia*) shirt-front.

sparatore *sm.* shooter.

sparatoria *sf.* shooting.

sparecchiare *vt.* to clear.

spareggio *sm.* **1.** disparity **2.** (*sport*) deciding game.

spàrgere *vt.* **1.** to scatter **2.** (*divulgare*) to spread (*v. irr.*) **3.** (*versare; di luce*) to shed (*v. irr.*).

spargimento *sm.* **1.** spreading **2.** (*versamento*) shedding || — *di sangue*, bloodshed.

sparigliare *vt.* to unmatch.

sparire *vi.* to disappear.

sparizione *sf.* disappearance.

sparlare *vi.* to speak (*v. irr.*) badly.

sparo *sm.* shot.

sparpagliare *vt.* to scatter. ♦ **sparpagliarsi** *vr.* to scatter.

sparso *agg.* **1.** (*versato*) shed **2.** (*sciolto*) loose.

spartano *agg.* Spartan.

spartiacque *sm.* watershed.

spartineve *sm.* snow-plough.

spartire *vt.* to share out.

spartito *sm.* score.

spartizióne *sf.* sharing.

sparuto *agg.* lean, spare.

spàrviero *sm.* sparrow-hawk.

spasimante *sm.* wooer.

spasimare *vi.* **1.** to suffer agonies **2.** (*fig.*) to yearn.

spàsimo *sm.* pang.

spasmo *sm.* spasm.

spasmodicamente *avv.* spasmodically.

spasmòdico *agg.* spasmodic.

spassare *vt.* to amuse || *spassarsela*, to have a very good time.

spassionato *agg.* impartial.

spasso *sm.* **1.** amusement: *che —!*, what fun! **2.** (*passeggiata*) *andare a —*, to go (*v. irr.*) for a walk; *essere a —*, to be out of work.

spassoso *agg.* funny, amusing.

spàstico *agg.* spastic.

spato *sm.* spar.

spàtola *sf.* broad knife.

spatriare *vt.* V. *espatriare*.

spauracchio *sm.* **1.** scarecrow **2.** (*fig.*) bugbear.

spaurire *vt.* to frighten. ♦ **spaurirsi** *vr.* to get (*v. irr.*) frightened.

spaurito *agg.* frightened.

spavalderìa *sf.* boldness.

spavaldo *agg.* bold, arrogant.

spaventapàsseri *sm.* scarecrow.

spaventare *vt.* to frighten, to scare. ♦ **spaventarsi** *vr.* to be frightened.

spaventato *agg.* frightened, scared.

spavento *sm.* fright.

spaventoso *agg.* dreadful, frightful.

spaziale *agg.* space (*attr.*).

spaziare *vt.* to space. ♦ **spaziare** *vi.* to range.

spaziatura *sf.* spacing.

spazieggiare *vt.* to space.

spazientirsi *vr.* to lose (*v. irr.*) one's patience.

spazio *sm.* **1.** space **2.** (*posto*) room.

spazioso *agg.* wide.

spazzacamino *sm.* chimney-sweep.

spazzamine *sm.* mine-sweeper.

spazzaneve *sm.* snow-plough.

spazzare *vt.* to sweep (*v. irr.*).

spazzata *sf.* sweep.

spazzatura *sf.* (*rifiuti*) sweepings (*pl.*): *bidone della —*, dust-bin; *carro della —*, dust-cart.

spazzino *sm.* **1.** road-sweeper **2.** (*spazzaturaio*) dustman (*pl.* -men).

spàzzola *sf.* brush || *capelli a —*, crew-cut.

spazzolare *vt.* to brush.

spazzolata *sf.* brush.

spazzolino *sm.* (small) brush: — *da denti*, tooth-brush.

spazzolone *sm.* scrubbing-brush.

specchiarsi *vr.* **1.** to look at oneself in a mirror **2.** (*riflettersi*) to be mirrored.

specchiera *sf.* looking-glass.

specchietto *sm.* **1.** hand-mirror **2.** (*tabella*) table || — *retrovisore*, driving-mirror.

specchio *sm.* **1.** mirror **2.** (*prospetto*) register **3.** (*modello*) model || — *d'acqua*, sheet of water.

speciale *agg.* special.

specialista *s.* specialist.

specialità *sf.* speciality.

specializzare *vt.* to specialize. ♦ **specializzarsi** *vr.* to specialize.

specializzazione *sf.* specializaèíon.

specie *sf.* **1.** kind **2.** (*scientifico; teol.*) species (*pl. invariato*) || *far —*, to surprise.

specificamente *avv.* specifically.

specificare *vt.* to specify.

specificazione *sf.* specification.

specìfico *agg.* e *sm.* specific.

specioso *agg.* specious.

speculare[1] *vi.* to speculate (on): — *al rialzo, al ribasso,* to speculate for the advance, for the fall.

speculare[2] *agg.* mirror-like.

speculativo *agg.* speculative.

speculatore *agg.* speculative. ♦ **speculatore** *sm.* speculator.

speculazione *sf.* speculation.

spedire *vt.* 1. to send (*v. irr.*) 2. (*via mare*) to ship 3. (*via terra*) to forward.

speditamente *avv.* 1. quickly 2. (*correntemente*) fluently.

speditezza *sf.* 1. quickness 2. (*nel parlare*) fluency.

spedito *agg.* 1. (*svelto*) quick 2. (*nel parlare*) fluent.

speditore *sm.* sender.

spedizione *sf.* 1. forwarding 2. (*per mare*) shipment 3. (*di lettere, pacchi*) dispatch 4. (*scientifico; mil.*) expedition || — *per via aerea,* air-freight.

spedizioniere *sm.* forwarding agent.

spègnere *vt.* 1. (*un fuoco*) to put (*v. irr.*) out 2. (*gas, luce ecc.*) to turn off 3. (*fig.*) to stifle || — *la sete,* to quench one's thirst. ♦ **spègnersi** *vr.* 1. to go (*v. irr.*) out 2. (*fig.*) to fade 3. (*morire*) to pass away.

spegnimento *sm.* extinction.

spegnitoio *sm.* snuffer.

spelacchiare *vt.* to tear (*v. irr.*) out the hair of. ♦ **spelacchiarsi** *vr.* to lose (*v. irr.*) one's hair.

spelacchiato *agg.* 1. scanty-haired 2. (*di stoffe, pellicce*) worn-out.

spelare *vt.* to balden. ♦ **spelarsi** *vr.* V. *spelacchiarsi.*

spelato *agg.* 1. hairless 2. (*di indumento*) worn.

spelatura *sf.* 1. hairless patch 2. (*di indumento*) worn patch.

speleologìa *sf.* speleology.

speleològico *agg.* speleological.

speleòlogo *sm.* speleologist.

spellare *vt.* to skin. ♦ **spellarsi** *vr.* to peel.

spellatura *sf.* 1. skinning 2. (*parte spellata*) graze.

spelonca *sf.* den.

spendaccione *sm.* spendthrift.

spèndere *vt.* to spend (*v. irr.*) (*anche fig.*).

spennacchiare *vt.* to pluck. ♦ **spennacchiarsi** *vr.* to lose (*v. irr.*) one's feathers.

spennare *vt.* to pluck.

spennellare *vt.* 1. to brush 2. (*med.*) to paint.

spennellata *sf.* touch of the brush.

spennellatura *sf.* (*med.*) painting.

spensieratamente *avv.* thoughtlessly.

spensieratezza *sf.* thoughtlessness.

spensierato *agg.* thoughtless.

spento *agg.* 1. extinguished, out (*pred.*) 2. (*estinto*) extinct 3. (*smorto*) duli.

speràbile *agg.* to be hoped (for).

speranza *sf.* hope.

speranzoso *agg.* hopeful.

sperare *vt.* e *vi.* to hope (for sthg., in so.).

spèrdersi *vr.* 1. to get (*v. irr.*) lost 2. (*dileguare*) to vanish.

sperduto *agg.* 1. scattered 2. (*isolato*) secluded 3. (*smarrito*) lost.

sperequazione *sf.* inequality.

spergiurare *vi.* to swear (*v. irr.*) falsely: *giurare e* —, to swear again and again.

spergiuro *sm.* 1. perjury 2. (*di persona*) perjurer.

spericolato *agg.* reckless. ♦ **spericolato** *sm.* daredevil.

sperimentale *agg.* experimental.

sperimentalismo *sm.* experimentalism.

sperimentalmente *avv.* experimentally.

sperimentare *vt.* 1. to experiment (with) 2. (*mettere alla prova*) to test.

sperimentato *agg.* 1. (*provato*) tried 2. (*esperto*) experienced.

sperimentatore *sm.* experimenter.

sperimentazione *sf.* experimentation.

sperma *sm.* sperm.

spermatozoo *sm.* spermatozoon (*pl.* -zoa).

speronare *vt.* 1. (*mar.*) to ram 2. (*un cavallo*) to spur.

speronata *sf.* 1. (*mar.*) ramming 2. (*colpo di sperone*) spur.

sperone *sm.* V. *sprone.*

sperperamento *sm.* squandering.

sperperare *vt.* to squander.

sperperatore *sm.* squanderer.

spèrpero *sm.* dissipation.

sperticato *agg.* excessive.

spesa *sf.* 1. expense: *far fronte a una* —, to meet (*v. irr.*) an expense 2. (*compera*) shopping: *andare a far spese,* to go (*v. irr.*) shopping.

spesare *vt.* to maintain.

spesato *agg. essere —,* to have all expenses paid.

spessire *vt.* to thicken. ◆ **spessirsi** *vr.* to thicken.

spesso¹ *agg.* 1. thick 2. *(frequente)* frequent.

spesso² *avv.* often.

spessore *sm.* thickness.

spettàbile *agg.* respectable.

spettàcolo *sm.* 1. spectacle 2. *(teat.)* performance.

spettacoloso *agg.* spectacular.

spettante *agg.* due.

spettanze *sf. pl.* dues.

spettare *vi.* 1. to be (for so.) 2. *(essere dovuto)* to be due.

spettatore *sm.* 1. spectator 2. *(testimone)* witness ‖ *gli spettatori,* the audience.

spettegolare *vi.* to gossip.

spettinare *vt.* to ruffle so.'s hair. ◆ **spettinarsi** *vr.* to ruffle one's hair.

spettinato *agg.* uncombed.

spettrale *agg.* spectral.

spettro *sm.* 1. ghost 2. *(fis.)* spectrum *(pl.* -ra).

spettroscopìa *sf.* spectroscopy.

spettroscòpico *agg.* spectroscopic(al).

spettroscopio *sm.* spectroscope.

speziale *sm. (farmacista)* chemist.

spezie *sf. pl.* spices.

spezzàbile *agg.* breakable.

spezzare *vt.* to break (*v. irr.*). ◆ **spezzarsi** *vr.* to break.

spezzatino *sm.* stew.

spezzato *agg.* broken.

spezzettamento *sm.* chopping.

spezzettare *vt.* to chop.

spezzone *sm.* 1. *(mil.)* incendiary bomb 2. *(metal.)* cut-down size.

spia *sf.* 1. spy 2. *(indizio)* evidence 3. *(di porta)* peep-hole ‖ *— luminosa,* warning light; *fare la —,* to play the spy.

spiaccicare *vt.* to squash. ◆ **spiaccicarsi** *vr.* to get (*v. irr.*) squashed.

spiacente *agg.* sorry.

spiacere *vi.* V. *dispiacere.*

spiacévole *agg.* unpleasant.

spiacevolmente *avv.* unpleasantly.

spiaggia *sf.* 1. beach 2. *(riva)* (sea)shore.

spianamento *sm.* 1. levelling 2. *(il radere al suolo)* razing.

spianare *vt.* 1. to level 2. *(radere al suolo)* to raze 3. *(appianare, lisciare)* to smooth. ◆ **spianarsi** *vr.* to become (*v. irr.*) smooth.

spianata *sf.* 1. levelling 2. *(luogo spianato)* open space 3. *(arch.)* esplanade 4. *(in un bosco)* clearing.

spianato *agg.* 1. levelled 2. *(liscio)* smooth.

spiano *(nella loc. avv.) a tutto —,* profusely; *(sodo)* hard.

spiantare *vt.* 1. to pull out 2. *(rovinare)* to ruin. ◆ **spiantarsi** *vr.* *(rovinarsi)* to go (*v. irr.*) to ruin.

spiantato *agg. (fig.)* penniless. ◆ **spiantato** *sm. (fig.)* pauper.

spiare *vt.* 1. to spy (upon) 2. *(aspettare)* to watch (for).

spiattellare *vt.* to blab (out).

spiazzo *sm.* 1. open space 2. *(nel bosco)* clearing.

spiccare *vt.* 1. to pick 2. *(tagliare)* to cut (*v. irr.*) off 3. *(pronunciare)* to enunciate distinctly 4. *(emettere)* to issue ‖ *— un salto,* to take (*v. irr.*) a leap; *— il volo,* to fly (*v. irr.*) up; *— una tratta,* to draw (*v. irr.*) a bill. ◆ **spiccare** *vi.* to stand (*v. irr.*) out.

spiccatamente *avv.* distinctly.

spiccato *agg.* 1. *(marcato)* marked 2. *(nitido)* clear.

spicchio *sm.* 1. slice 2. *(di agrumi)* segment 3. *(di aglio)* clove 4. *(geom.)* sector ‖ *a spicchi,* sliced.

spicciare *vt.* to dispatch. ◆ **spicciarsi** *vr.* to hurry up.

spicciativo *agg.* V. *spiccio.*

spiccicare *vt.* 1. to detach 2. *(pronunciare)* to utter.

spiccio *agg.* 1. quick 2. *(franco)* straightforward ‖ *andar per le spicce,* to go (*v. irr.*) straight to the point; *moneta spiccia,* small change.

spicciolata *(nella loc. avv.) alla —,* few at a time.

spìccioli *sm. pl.* change (solo sing.).

spicco *sm. far —,* to stand (*v. irr.*) out.

spidocchiare *vt.* to delouse.

spiedo *sm.* spit.

spiegàbile *agg.* explainable.

spiegamento *sm.* 1. spreading out 2. *(mil.)* deployment.

spiegare *vt.* 1. to explain 2. *(stendere)* to spread (*v. irr.*) out 3. *(di vele)* to unfurl 4. *(mil.)* to deploy. ◆ **spiegarsi** *vr.* 1. *(farsi* *capire*) to make (*v. irr.*) oneself understood 2. (*stendersi*) to spread out.

spiegazione *sf.* explanation.

spiegazzare *vt.* to crumple.

spietatamente *avv.* ruthlessly.

spietatezza *sf.* ruthlessness.

spietato *agg.* ruthless.

spifferare *vt.* to blurt out.

spiffero *sm.* draught.

spiga *sf.* 1. spike 2. (*di cereali*) ear.

spigare *vi.* to ear.

spighetta *sf.* braid.

spigliatamente *avv.* easily.

spigliatezza *sf.* ease.

spigliato *agg.* easy.

spigo *sm.* lavender.

spigolare *vt.* to glean (*anche fig.*).

spigolatore *sm.* gleaner.

spigolatrice *sf.* gleaner.

spigolatura *sf.* gleaning.

spigolo *sm.* edge.

spigoloso *agg.* edgy.

spilla *sf.* 1. pin 2. (*gioiello*) brooch.

spillare *vt.* 1. to draw (*v. irr.*) 2. (*fig.*) to worm.

spillo *sm.* pin: — *da balia*, safety-pin.

spillone *sm.* (*per cappello*) hat-pin.

spilorceria *sf.* stinginess.

spilorcio *agg.* stingy. ♦ **spilorcio** *sm.* miser.

spilungona *sf.* lanky woman.

spilungone *sm.* lanky man.

spina *sf.* 1. thorn 2. (*lisca*) fishbone 3. (*elettr.*) plug 4. (*mecc.*) pin 5. (*di botte*) bung 6. (*fig.*) sorrow, grief || — *dorsale*, backbone; *a* — *di pesce*, herring-bone.

spinacio *sm.* spinach (*solo sing.*).

spinale *agg.* spinal.

spinare *vt.* (*pesce*) to bone.

spinato *agg.* (*a spina di pesce*) herring-bone || *filo* —, barbed wire.

spinetta *sf.* spinet.

spingere *vt.* 1. to push 2. (*condurre*) to drive (*v. irr.*) 3. (*stimolare*) to urge 4. (*portare*) to carry. ♦ **spingersi** *vr.* to push.

spino *sm.* thorn.

spinone *sm.* (*cane*) griffon.

spinosità *sf.* thorniness.

spinoso *agg.* thorny.

spinta *sf.* 1. push 2. (*stimolo*) incentive 3. (*mecc.; edil.*) thrust.

spinterogeno *sm.* (battery) coil ignition.

spinto *agg.* 1. (*eccessivo*) excessive 2. (*audace*) risky.

spintone *sm.* shove || *farsi avanti a spintoni*, to elbow one's way forward.

spiombare *vt.* to unseal.

spionaggio *sm.* espionage.

spioncino *sm.* peep-hole.

spione *sm.* spy.

spiovente *agg.* 1. drooping 2. (*inclinato*) sloping. ♦ **spiovente** *sm.* 1. slope 2. (*sport*) high kick.

spiovere *vi.* 1. to stop raining 2. (*ricadere*) to come (*v. irr.*) down.

spira *sf.* coil.

spiraglio *sm.* 1. small hole 2. (*barlume*) gleam.

spirale *sf.* 1. spiral 2. (*molla*) spring.

spirante *agg.* 1. (*soffiante*) blowing 2. (*morente*) passing away 3. (*esalante*) exhaling.

spirare *vi.* 1. (*soffiare*) to blow (*v. irr.*) 2. (*morire*) to pass away 3. (*scadere*) to expire 4. (*emanare*) to emanate. ♦ **spirare** *vt.* to exhale.

spiritato *agg.* 1. possessed 2. (*spaventato*) frightened.

spiritico *agg.* spiritualistic.

spiritismo *sm.* spiritualism.

spiritista *s.* spiritualist.

spiritistico *agg.* V. *spiritico.*

spirito *sm.* 1. spirit 2. (*fantasma*) ghost 3. (*arguzia*) wit 4. (*alcool*) alcohol || *far dello* —, to be witty.

spiritosaggine *sf.* witticism.

spiritosamente *avv.* wittily.

spiritoso *agg.* 1. witty 2. (*alcoolico*) alcoholic.

spirituale *agg.* spiritual.

spiritualismo *sm.* spiritualism.

spiritualista *agg.* spiritualistic. ♦ **spiritualista** *s.* spiritualist.

spiritualità *sf.* spirituality.

spiritualizzare *vt.* to spiritualize.

spiritualmente *avv.* spiritually.

spizzicare *vt.* to nibble.

spizzico (*nella loc. avv.*) *a* —, little by little.

splendente *agg.* bright.

splendere *vi.* to shine (*v. irr.*).

splendido *agg.* splendid.

splendore *sm.* splendour.

spocchia *sf.* haughtiness.

spocchioso *agg.* haughty.

spodestamento *sm.* 1. dispossession 2. (*da posizione autorevole*) dethronement.

spodestare *vt.* 1. to dispossess 2. (*detronizzare*) to dethrone.

spoetizzare *vt.* to disenchant.

spoglia sf. **1.** (di animale) skin **2.** (veste) dress **3.** (bottino) spoils (pl.) ‖ spoglie mortali, mortal remains.

spogliare vt. **1.** to strip **2.** (derubare) to rob **3.** (saccheggiare) to plunder. ♦ **spogliarsi** vr. **1.** to strip **2.** (di alberi) to shed (v. irr.) **3.** (privarsi) to strip oneself (of).

spogliarello sm. strip-tease.

spogliatoio sm. **1.** dressing-room **2.** (teat. ecc.) cloak-room.

spoglio agg. bare. ♦ **spoglio** sm. **1.** (computo) counting **2.** (esame) examination **3.** (vestito smesso) cast-off ‖ fare lo —, to go (v. irr.) through.

spola sf. shuttle.

spoletta sf. **1.** spool **2.** (di arma) fuse.

spoliazione sf. spoliation.

spolmonarsi vr. to talk oneself hoarse.

spolpare vt. **1.** to take (v. irr.) the flesh off **2.** (fig.) to skin.

spolpato agg. **1.** stripped of the flesh **2.** (fig.) skinned.

spolverare vt. to dust.

spolveratura sf. **1.** dusting **2.** (fig.) smattering.

spolverino sm. dust-coat.

spolverizzare vt. to dust.

spolvero sm. **1.** dusting **2.** (disegno) perforated pattern.

sponda sf. **1.** edge **2.** (di fiume) bank **3.** (di mare) shore **4.** (parapetto) parapet.

sponsali sm. pl. nuptials.

spontaneamente avv. spontaneously.

spontaneità sf. spontaneity.

spontàneo agg. spontaneous.

spopolamento sm. depopulation.

spopolare vt. to depopulate. ♦ **spopolarsi** vr. to become (v. irr.) depopulated.

spopolato agg. (deserto) deserted.

spora sf. spore.

sporàdico agg. sporadic.

sporcaccione sm. dirty man

sporcare vt. to dirty.

sporcizia sf. dirt.

sporco agg. dirty.

sporgente agg. protruding.

sporgenza sf. protrusion.

spòrgere vi. to put (v. irr.) out. ♦ **spòrgere** vt. to put (v. irr.) out. ♦ **spòrgersi** vr. to lean (v. irr.) out.

sport sm. sport.

sporta sf. basket.

sportello sm. **1.** door **2.** (di biglietteria) ticket-window **3.** (di ufficio postale ecc.) counter.

sportivamente avv. sportingly.

sportivo agg. sporting. ♦ **sportivo** sm. sportsman (pl. -men).

sporto agg. **1.** leaning out **2.** (proteso) outstretched.

sposa sf. bride.

sposalizio sm. wedding.

sposare vt. to marry. ♦ **sposarsi** vr. to get (v. irr.) married.

sposo sm. bridegroom.

spossamento sm. exhaustion.

spossante agg. exhausting.

spossare vt. to exhaust.

spossatezza sf. V. spossamento.

spossato agg. weary.

spossessare vt. to dispossess.

spostàbile agg. shiftable.

spostamento sm. **1.** shifting **2.** (cambiamento) change.

spostare vt. **1.** to shift, to move **2.** (cambiare) to change. ♦ **spostarsi** vr. to shift.

spostato agg. out of one's place (pred.). ♦ **spostato** sm. misfit.

spranga sf. bar.

sprangare vt. to bar.

sprazzo sm. flash: — d'ingegno, brain-wave.

sprecare vt. to waste.

spreco sm. waste.

sprecone sm. waster.

spregévole agg. despicable.

spregiare vt. to scorn.

spregiativo agg. **1.** scornful **2.** (gramm.) pejorative. ♦ **spregiativo** sm. (gramm.) pejorative.

spregio sm. contempt.

spregiudicatamente avv. open-mindedly.

spregiudicatezzá sf. open-mindedness.

spregiudicato agg. open-minded.

sprèmere vt. **1.** to squeeze **2.** (torcere) to wring (v. irr.) out. ♦ **spremersi** vr. to rack oneself.

spremilimoni sm. lemon-squeezer.

spremitura sf. **1.** squeezing **2.** (di panni bagnati) wringing.

spremuta sf. squash.

spremuto agg. **1.** squeezed **2.** (di panni) wrung.

spretare vt. to unfrock. ♦ **spretarsi** vr. to renounce one's priesthood.

spretato *agg.* unfrocked. ♦ **spretato** *sm.* unfrocked priest.

sprezzante *agg.* scornful.

sprezzare *vt.* V. *disprezzare.*

sprezzo *sm.* scorn.

sprigionamento *sm.* **1.** exhalation **2.** (*violento*) bursting out.

sprigionare *vt.* to emit. ♦ **sprigionarsi** *vr.* **1.** to be emitted **2.** (*con violenza*) to burst (*v. irr.*) out.

sprimacciare *vt.* to shake (*v. irr.*) up.

sprizzare *vt.* e *vi.* to spurt: — *scintille,* to spit (*v. irr.*) sparks; — *gioia,* to burst (*v. irr.*) with joy.

sprizzo *sm.* spurt.

sprofondamento *sm.* **1.** sinking **2.** (*crollo*) collapse.

sprofondare *vt.* (*far cadere*) to cause to collapse. ♦ **sprofondare** *vi.* **1.** to sink (*v. irr.*) **2.** (*crollare*) to collapse **3.** (*fig.*) to be absorbed. ♦ **sprofondarsi** *vr.* **1.** to sink **2.** (*crollare*) to collapse **3.** (*fig.*) to be absorbed.

sproloquio *sm.* long rigmarole.

spronare *vt.* to spur.

spronata *sf.* spurring.

sprone *sm.* **1.** spur **2.** (*mar.*) ram || *a spron battuto,* at full speed.

sproporzionato *agg.* disproportionate, out of proportion (*pred.*).

sproporzione *sf.* disproportion.

spropositato *agg.* **1.** full of blunders **2.** (*fig.*) enormous.

spropòsito *sm.* **1.** blunder **2.** (*eccesso*) excess || *a —,* off the point.

sprovveduto *agg.* **1.** (*incauto*) unwary **2.** (*sprovvisto*) devoid **3.** (*impreparato*) unprepared.

sprovvisto *agg.* devoid || *alla sprovvista,* unawares.

spruzzare *vt.* **1.** to spray **2.** (*inzaccherare*) to splash.

spruzzata *sf.* spray.

spruzzatore *sm.* sprayer.

spruzzatura *sf.* spraying.

spruzzo *sm.* **1.** spray **2.** (*di liquido sporco*) splash.

spudoratezza *sf.* shamelessness.

spudorato *agg.* shameless.

spugna *sf.* **1.** sponge **2.** (*tessuto*) sponge-cloth || *cancellare con la —,* to sponge; *bere come una —,* to drink (*v. irr.*) like a fish.

spugnatura *sf.* sponge down.

spugnosità *sf.* sponginess.

spugnoso *agg.* spongy.

spulciare *vt.* **1.** to look for fleas (on) **2.** (*esaminare; fig.*) to peruse **3.** (*raccogliere; fig.*) to gather here and there.

spuma *sf.* foam.

spumante *agg.* foaming. ♦ **spumante** *sm.* sparkling wine.

spumare *vi.* to foam.

spumeggiante *agg.* foaming.

spumeggiare *vi.* to foam.

spumoso *agg.* foamy.

spuntare[1] *vt.* **1.** (*smussare*) to blunt **2.** (*tagliare*) to trim **3.** (*staccare*) to unpin || *spuntarla,* to succeed. ♦ **spuntarsi** *vr.* **1.** (*smussarsi*) to get (*v. irr.*) blunt **2.** (*staccarsi*) to become (*v. irr.*) unpinned.

spuntare[2] *vi.* **1.** (*sorgere*) to rise (*v. irr.*) **2.** (*germogliare*) to sprout **3.** (*di capelli*) to begin (*v. irr.*) to grow **4.** (*apparire*) to appear.

spuntato *agg.* pointless.

spuntatura *sf.* **1.** (*lo smussare*) blunting **2.** (*il tagliare*) trimming.

spuntino *sm.* snack.

spunto *sm.* **1.** cue **2.** (*punto di partenza*) starting point.

spuntone *sm.* spike.

spurgare *vt.* **1.** to clean **2.** (*med.*) to discharge. ♦ **spurgarsi** *vr.* (*espettorare*) to expectorate.

spurgo *sm.* **1.** (*lo spurgare*) discharging **2.** (*l'espettorare*) expectorating **3.** (*ciò che viene espulso*) discharge.

spurio *agg.* spurious.

sputacchiare *vi.* V. *sputare.*

sputacchiera *sf.* spittoon.

sputacchio *sm.* spittle.

sputare *vt.* to spit (*v. irr.*).

sputasentenze *sm.* wiseacre.

sputo *sm.* spit.

squadra *sf.* **1.** (*da disegno*) square **2.** (*gruppo; sport*) team **3.** (*di operai*) gang **4.** (*mil.*) squad **5.** (*mar.*) squadron || *— mobile,* flying squad.

squadrare *vt.* **1.** to square **2.** (*guardare*) to look (so.) up and down.

squadratura *sf.* squaring.

squadriglia *sf.* squadron.

squadro *sm.* squaring.

squadrone *sm.* squadron.

squagliamento *sm.* melting.

squagliare *vt.* to melt. ♦ **squagliarsi** *vr.* **1.** to melt **2.** (*andar via*) to steal (*v. irr.*) away.

squalifica *sf.* disqualification.

squalificare *vt.* to disqualify.

squàllido *agg.* dreary.

squallore *sm.* dreariness.

squalo *sm.* shark.

squama *sf.* scale.

squamare *vt.* to scale. ♦ **squamarsi** *vr.* to scale.

squamoso *agg.* scaly.

squarciagola (*nella loc. avv.*) *a —,* at the top of one's voice.

squarciamento *sm.* tearing.

squarciare *vt.* 1. to tear (*v. irr.*) 2. (*fig.*) to dispel. ♦ **squarciarsi** *vr.* to be torn.

squarcio *sm.* gash.

squartare *vt.* to mangle.

squartatore *sm.* mangler.

squassare *vt.* to jolt.

squasso *sm.* jolt.

squattrinato *agg.* penniless.

squilibrare *vt.* to unbalance. ♦ **squilibrarsi** *vr.* to lose (*v. irr.*) one's balance.

squilibrato *agg.* unbalanced. ♦ **squilibrato** *sm.* lunatic.

squilibrio *sm.* 1. lack of balance 2. (*mentale*) derangement.

squillante *agg.* 1. shrill 2. (*di trombe*) blaring 3. (*di campane*) pealing.

squillare *vi.* 1. to ring (*v. irr.*) 2. (*di trombe*) to blare.

squillo *sm.* 1. ring 2. (*di tromba*) blare.

squinternare *vt.* 1. to ruin 2. (*fig.*) to upset (*v. irr.*).

squisitezza *sf.* exquisiteness.

squisito *agg.* exquisite.

squittio *sm.* squeak.

squittire *vi.* to squeak.

sradicare *vt.* to uproot.

sragionare *vi.* to talk nonsense.

sregolatezza *sf.* disorderliness.

sregolato *agg.* disorderly.

stabbio *sm.* 1. sty 2. (*letame*) manure.

stàbile , *sm.* building. ♦ **stàbile** *agg.* 1. stable 2. (*permanente*) permanent: *in pianta —,* on the permanent staff.

stabilimento *sm.* 1. (*fabbrica*) factory 2. (*edificio, lo stabilire*) establishment.

stabilire *vt.* 1. to establish 2. (*decidere*) to decide. ♦ **stabilirsi** *vr.* to settle.

stabilità *sf.* stability.

stabilizzare *vt.* to stabilize.

stabilizzatore *sm.* stabilizer.

stabilizzazione *sf.* stabilization.

stabilmente *avv.* firmly.

stacanovismo *sm.* Stakhanovism.

staccàbile *agg.* detachable.

staccare *vt.* 1. to take (*v. irr.*) off 2. (*tagliare*) to cut (*v. irr.*) off 3. (*separare*) to separate 4. (*slegare*) to unfasten || *— un assegno,* to issue a cheque. ♦ **staccarsi** *vr.* 1. to come (*v. irr.*) off 2. (*sciogliersi*) to break (*v. irr.*) loose 3. (*scostarsi*) to move away 4. (*separarsi*) to part 5. (*distaccarsi*) to pull ahead (of) 6. (*esser diverso*) to differ.

stacciare *vt.* to sieve.

staccio *sm.* sieve.

staccionata *sf.* fence.

stacco *sm.* detachment.

stadera *sf.* steelyard.

stadio *sm.* 1. stadium (*pl.* -ia), sports ground 2. (*fase*) stage.

staffa *sf.* stirrup || *perder le staffe* (*fig.*), to lose (*v. irr.*) one's self--control.

staffetta *sf.* 1. courier 2. (*sport*) relay race.

staffilare *vt.* to lash.

staffilata *sf.* lash.

staffile *sm.* whip.

stafilococco *sm.* staphylococcus (*pl.* -ci).

staggio *sm.* 1. (*di scala*) shaft 2. (*di sedia*) back leg.

stagionale *agg.* seasonal.

stagionare *vt.* to season.

stagionato *agg.* 1. seasoned 2. (*fig.*) oldish.

stagionatura *sf.* seasoning.

stagione *sf.* season.

stagnaio *sm.* tinsmith.

stagnante *agg.* stagnant.

stagnare[1] *vi.* to stagnate.

stagnare[2] *vt.* 1. to tin 2. (*saldare*) to solder 3. (*impermeabilizzare*) to waterproof 4. (*fermare*) to staunch.

stagnatura *sf.* tinning.

stagnino *sm.* tinker.

stagno[1] *sm.* tin.

stagno[2] *sm.* (*bacino d'acqua*) pond.

stagno[3] *agg.* water-tight.

stagnola *sf.* tin-foil.

staio *sm.* bushel.

stalagmite *sf.* stalagmite.

stalattite *sf.* stalactite.

stalla *sf.* stable.

stalliere *sm.* stable-boy.

stallo *sm.* stall.

stallone *sm.* stallion.

stamattina *avv.* this morning.

stambecco *sm.* ibex.

stamberga *sf.* hovel.

stambugio *sm.* hole.

stame *sm.* (*bot.*) stamen.

stamigna *sf.* bunting.

stampa *sf.* 1. print 2. (*atto di stampare*) printing 3. (*periodici, giornali*) press 4. (*genere*) stamp || *agenzia di —*, news-agency; *errore di —*, misprint.

stampare *vt.* 1. to print 2. (*mecc.*) to press 3. (*coniare*) to coin. ◆ **stamparsi** *vr.* — *in mente*, to impress (sthg.) firmly on one's mind.

stampatello *sm.* block letters (*pl.*).

stampato *sm.* 1. printed matter 2. (*modulo*) form.

stampatore *sm.* printer.

stampatrice *sf.* printing-press.

stampella *sf.* crutch.

stamperìa *sf.* printing-office.

stampigliare *vt.* to stamp.

stampo *sm.* 1. die, mould 2. (*genere*) stamp.

stanare *vt.* to drive (*v. irr.*) out.

stancare *vt.* 1. to tire 2. (*infastidire*) to annoy. ◆ **stancarsi** *vr.* 1. to get (*v. irr.*) tired 2. (*annoiarsi*) to get bored.

stanchezza *sf.* tiredness.

stanco *agg.* tired.

standardizzare *vt.* to standardize.

stanga *sf.* 1. bar 2. (*di carro*) shaft 3. (*di passaggio a livello*) barrier.

stangare *vt.* 1. to bar 2. (*percuotere*) to thrash.

stanghetta *sf.* 1. (*degli occhiali*) bar 2. (*di serratura*) bolt.

stanotte *avv.* tonight.

stantìo *agg.* stale.

stantuffo *sm.* 1. piston 2. (*di pompa ecc.*) plunger.

stanza *sf.* 1. room 2. (*strofa*) stanza || *prendere, avere —*, to settle.

stanziamento *sm.* appropriation.

stanziare *vt.* to appropriate. ◆ **stanziarsi** *vr.* to settle.

stappare *vt.* to uncork.

stare *vi.* 1. to stay 2. (*abitare*) to live 3. (*di salute, essere*) to be 4. (*in piedi*) to stand (*v. irr.*) 5. (*dipendere*) to depend (on) 6. (*spettare*) to be up 7. (*andare*) to go (*v. irr.*) 8. (*di abito*) to suit || *— per*, to be going (to); *lasciar —*, to leave (*v. irr.*) alone; *sta' a sentire!*, listen!; *ben ti sta!*, it

serves you right!

starnazzare *vi.* to flutter.

starnutire *vi.* to sneeze.

starnuto *sm.* sneeze.

stasare *vt.* to unclog.

stasera *avv.* this evening.

stasi *sf.* 1. standstill 2. (*med.*) stasis (*pl. -ses*).

statale *agg.* State (*attr.*), of the State. ◆ **statale** *s.* State employee.

stàtica *sf.* statics.

stàtico *agg.* static.

statista *sm.* statesman (*pl. -men*).

statìstica *sf.* statistics.

statizzare *vt.* to nationalize.

statizzazione *sf.* nationalization.

stato *sm.* 1. state, condition (*anche posizione sociale*) 2. (*giur.*) status 3. (*pol.*) State || *ufficio di — civile*, registry office; *ufficiale di — civile*, registrar.

statua *sf.* statue.

statuaria *sf.* statuary.

statuario *agg.* statuesque.

statuire *vt.* to decree.

statunitense *agg.* United States (*attr.*). ◆ **statunitense** *sm.* United States citizen.

statura *sf.* stature.

statuto *sm.* statute.

stazionamento *sm.* standing.

stazionare *vi.* 1. to stay 2. (*di vetture*) to be parked.

stazionario *agg.* stationary.

stazione *sf.* station.

stazza *sf.* tonnage.

stazzare *vt.* to have the tonnage of.

stecca *sf.* 1. (*di ombrello, ventaglio*) rib 2. (*da biliardo*) cue 3. (*di persiana*) slat 4. (*di busto*) whalebone 5. (*stonatura*) false note.

steccare *vt.* 1. (*chiudere con steccato*) to fence in 2. (*mus.*) to fluff. ◆ **steccare** *vi.* 1. (*cantando*) to sing (*v. irr.*) a false note 2. (*suonando*) to play a false note.

steccato *sm.* fence.

stecchito *agg.* 1. (*secco*) dried up 2. (*magro*) skinny 3. (*morto*) stone dead.

stecco *sm.* 1. stick 2. (*persona magra*) bag of bones.

stecconata *sf.* paling.

stele *sf.* stele (*pl. -lae*).

stella *sf.* star: *— marina*, starfish; *a forma di —*, starlike.

stellare *agg.* 1. stellar 2. (*a forma di stella*) star-shaped.

stellato *agg.* starry.

stelletta *sf.* **1.** (*tip.*) asterisk **2.** (*mil.*) star.

stelloncino *sm.* short paragraph.

stelo *sm.* stem.

stemma *sm.* coat-of-arms.

stemperare *vt.* **1.** to mix **2.** (*diluire*) to spin out. ◆ **stemperarsi** *vr.* to dissolve.

stempiarsi *vr.* to go (*v. irr.*) bald.

stendardo *sm.* standard.

stèndere *vt.* **1.** to spread (*v. irr.*) **2.** (*allungare*) to stretch **3.** (*scrivere*) to draw (*v. irr.*) up **4.** (*rilassare*) to relax || — *il bucato*, to hang (*v. irr.*) out the washing. ◆ **stèndersi** *vr.* **1.** to stretch **2.** (*adagiarsi*) to lie (*v. irr.*) down.

stenodattilografia *sf.* shorthand and typewriting.

stenografare *vt.* to write (*v. irr.*) down in shorthand.

stenografia *sf.* shorthand.

stenògrafo *sm.* shorthand-writer.

stentare *vi.* **1.** to have difficulty (in) **2.** (*mancare del necessario*) to be in need.

stentato *agg.* **1.** hard **2.** (*cresciuto a stento*) stunted.

stento *sm.* privation: *a* —, hardly, with difficulty.

stentòreo *agg.* stentorian.

steppa *sf.* steppe.

sterco *sm.* dung.

stereofonìa *sf.* stereophony.

stereofònico *agg.* stereophonic.

stereografia *sf.* stereography.

stereogràfico *agg.* stereographic(al).

stereoscopìa *sf.* stereoscopy.

stereoscopio *sm.* stereoscope.

stereotipato *agg.* stereotyped.

stereotipìa *sf.* stereotyping.

stèrile *agg.* barren.

sterilità *sf.* barrenness.

sterilizzare *vt.* to sterilize.

sterilizzatore *agg.* sterilizing. ◆ **sterilizzatore** *sm.* sterilizer.

sterilizzazione *sf.* sterilization.

sterlina *sf.* pound.

sterminare *vt.* to exterminate.

sterminatezza *sf.* immensity.

sterminato *agg.* (*smisurato*) immense.

sterminatore *sm.* exterminator.

sterminio *sm.* extermination.

sterno *sm.* breast-bone.

sterpaglia *sf.* brushwood.

sterpo *sm.* dry twig.

sterrare *vt.* to dig (*v. irr.*) up.

sterratore *sm.* navvy.

sterzare *vt.* to steer.

sterzata *sf.* sudden turn.

sterzo *sm.* (*auto*) steering-gear.

stesso *agg.* **1.** (*medesimo*) same **2.** (*intensivo*) *se* —, oneself; *io*, *me* —, myself; *tu*, *te* —, yourself; *egli*, *lui* —, himself; *ella*, *lei stessa*, herself; *esso* —, itself; *noi stessi*, ourselves; *voi stessi*, yourselves; *loro stessi*, themselves **3.** (*proprio*) very. ◆ **stesso** *sm.* same. ◆ **stesso** *avv.* all the same

stesura *sf.* **1.** (*redazione*) draft **2.** (*di contratto*) drawing up.

stetoscopio *sm.* stethoscope.

stìgmate *sf. pl.* **1.** stigmata (*pl.*) **2.** (*marchio*) brand (*sing.*).

stigmatizzare *vt.* to stigmatize.

stilare *vt.* to draw (*v. irr.*) up.

stile *sm.* style: *aver* —, to be stylish; *con* —, stylishly.

stilettata *sf.* stab.

stilista *s.* stylist.

stilìstica *sf.* stylistics.

stilizzare *vt.* to stylize.

stilizzazione *sf.* stylization.

stilla *sf.* drop.

stillare *vi.* e *vt.* to ooze. ◆ **stillarsi** *vr.* — *il cervello*, to rack one's brain.

stilliicidio *sm.* dripping.

stilo *sm.* stylus.

stilogràfica *sf.* fountainpen.

stilogràfico *agg.* stylographic(al).

stima *sf.* **1.** (*valutazione*) estimate **2.** (*buona opinione*) esteem.

stimàbile *agg.* estimable.

stimare *vt.* **1.** (*valutare*) to estimate **2.** (*tenere in considerazione*) to esteem **3.** (*ritenere*) to consider.

stimatore *sm.* estimator.

stimolante *agg.* stimulating. ◆ **stimolante** *sm.* stimulant.

stimolare *vt.* to stimulate.

stìmolo *sm.* **1.** stimulus (*pl.* -li) **2.** (*pungolo*) goad.

stinco *sm.* shin.

stìngere *vt.* to fade. ◆ **stìngersi** *vr.* to fade.

stinto *agg.* faded.

stipare *vt.* to cram.

stipato *agg.* crammed (with).

stipendiare *vt.* to pay (*v. irr.*) a salary (to so.).

stipendio *sm.* salary.

stipite *sm.* jamb.

stipulante *agg.* stipulating. ◆ **stipulante** *s.* stipulator.

stipulare *vt.* to stipulate.

stipulazione *sf.* stipulation.

stiracchiare *vt.* 1. to stretch 2. (*distorcere*) to twist.

stiracchiato *agg.* (*fig.*) forced.

stiramento *sm.* 1. stretching 2. (*muscolare*) strain.

stirare *vt.* 1. to stretch 2. (*col ferro da stiro*) to iron.

stiratura *sf.* ironing.

stirerìa *sf.* (*e tintoria*) laundry shop.

stirpe *sf.* 1. stock 2. (*progenie*) issue.

stitichezza *sf.* constipation.

stìtico *agg.* constipated.

stiva *sf.* hold.

stivale *sm.* boot.

stivaletto *sm.* ankle-boot.

stizza *sf.* anger.

stizzire *vt.* to vex. ♦ **stizzirsi** *vr.* to get (*v. irr.*) cross.

stizzito *agg.* cross.

stizzoso *agg.* peevish.

stoccata *sf.* thrust: *lanciare una —* (*fig.*), to gibe (at).

stoffa *sf.* 1. cloth 2. (*fig.*) stuff.

stoicismo *sm.* stoicism.

stòico *agg.* e *sm.* stoic.

stoino *sm.* door-mat.

stola *sf.* stole.

stolidità *sf.* stolidity.

stòlido *agg.* stolid.

stoltezza *sf.* foolishness.

stolto *agg.* foolish. ♦ **stolto** *sm.* fool.

stomacare *vt.* to sicken. ♦ **stomacarsi** *vr.* to sicken.

stomachévole *agg.* sickening.

stòmaco *sm.* stomach: *dare di —,* to vomit; *restare sullo —,* to lie (*v. irr.*) on one's stomach.

stomatite *sf.* stomatitis.

stomatologìa *sf.* stomatology.

stonare *vi.* 1. to be out of tune 2. (*fig.*) to be out of place 3. (*di colori*) to clash. ♦ **stonare** *vt.* to upset (*v. irr.*).

stonato *agg.* 1. out of tune 2. (*fig.*) out of place 3. (*turbato*) upset 4. (*di nota*) false.

stonatura *sf.* false note.

stoppa *sf.* tow.

stoppaccio *sm.* wad.

stoppare *vt.* 1. to plug 2. (*sport*) to stop.

stoppia *sf.* stubble.

stoppino *sm.* wick.

stopposo *agg.* 1. towy 2. (*di carne*) stringy.

stòrcere *vt.* 1. to twist 2. (*un'articolazione*) to sprain || *— gli occhi,* to roll one's eyes. ♦ **stòrcersi** *vr.* 1. to twist 2. (*lussarsi, slogarsi*) to wrench.

stordimento *sm.* 1. dizziness 2. (*meraviglia*) bewilderment.

stordire *vt.* 1. to stun 2. (*di alcoolici*) to dull 3. (*assordare*) to deafen 4. (*innervosire*) to drive (*v. irr.*) crazy. ♦ **stordirsi** *vr.* to dull one's senses.

stordito *agg.* 1. (*sbalordito*) bewildered 2. (*sbadato*) heedless 3. (*sciocco*) foolish.

storia *sf.* 1. history 2. (*racconto*) story.

storicismo *sm.* historical method.

storicità *sf.* historicity.

stòrico *agg.* historical. ♦ **stòrico** *sm.* historian.

storiografìa *sf.* historiography.

storiògrafo *sm.* historiographer.

stormire *vi.* to rustle.

stormo *sm.* 1. flight 2. (*folla*) crowd || *suonare a —,* to ring (*v. irr.*) the tocsin.

stornare *vt.* to divert.

stornello[1] *sm.* ditty.

stornello[2] *sm.* (*zool.*) starling.

storno[1] *agg.* dapple-grey.

storno[2] *sm.* (*zool.*) starling.

storno[3] *sm.* (*comm.*) transfer.

storpiare *vt.* 1. to cripple 2. (*rovinare*) to mangle.

storpiatura *sf.* 1. crippling 2. (*fig.*) mangling 3. (*cosa malfatta*) botch.

storpio *sm.* cripple.

storta *sf.* 1. twist 2. (*in una articolazione*) sprain 3. (*chim.*) retort.

storto *agg.* 1. twisted 2. (*piegato*) crooked 3. (*di occhi*) squinting 4. (*sbagliato*) wrong.

stortura *sf.* 1. deformity 2. (*errore*) mistake.

stoviglie *sf. pl.* kitchenware (*sing.*).

stràbico *agg.* squinting. ♦ **stràbico** *sm.* squinter.

strabiliante *agg.* amazing.

strabiliare *vt.* to amaze (*anche far strabiliare*). ♦ **strabiliare** *vi.* to be amazed. ♦ **strabiliarsi** *vr.* to be amazed.

strabismo *sm.* squint.

straboccare *vi.* 1. to overflow 2. (*fig.*) to abound (in).

strabocchévole *agg.* overflowing.

strabuzzare *vt.* *— gli occhi,* to roll one's eyes.

stracàrico agg. overloaded (with).
stracciare vt. to tear (v. irr.). ♦ **stracciarsi** vr. to tear.
stracciato agg. 1. torn 2. (di persona) in rags.
straccio agg. torn, in rags || carta straccia, waste paper. ♦ **straccio** sm. rag: — per la polvere, duster.
straccione sm. ragamuffin.
straccivéndolo sm. rag-and-bone--man (pl. -men).
stracotto agg. overdone. ♦ **stracotto** sm. stew.
strada sf. 1. road 2. (di città) street 3. (percorso; fig.) way || — a senso unico, one-way street; — ferrata, railway; — maestra, main road.
stradale agg. road (attr.), of the road: fondo —, road-bed.
stradino sm. roadman (pl. -men).
strafalcione sm. blunder.
strafare vi. to overdo (v. irr.).
strafottente agg. 1. (noncurante) unconcerned 2. (arrogante) arrogant.
strage sf. 1. slaughter 2. (distruzione) destruction || fare una —, to slaughter.
stragrande agg. enormous.
stralciare vt. 1. (comm.) to remove 2. (fig.) to take (v. irr.) off.
stralcio sm. 1. removal 2. (estratto) extract.
strale sm. dart.
stralunare vt. — gli occhi, to roll one's eyes, to open one's eyes wide.
stralunato agg. 1. (di occhi) rolling, wild-eyed 2. (di persona) upset.
stramazzare vi. to fall (v. irr.) heavily.
stramberìa sf. oddity.
strambo agg. odd.
strame sm. litter.
strampalato agg. queer.
stranezza sf. oddity.
strangolamento sm. strangling.
strangolare vt. to strangle.
strangolatore sm. strangler.
straniero agg. foreign. ♦ **straniero** sm. foreigner.
strano agg. strange.
straordinario agg. extraordinary.
strapazzare vt. 1. to ill-use 2. (sgridare) to scold 3. (far lavorare troppo) to overwork 4. (di uova) to scramble. ♦ **strapazzarsi** vr. to overwork oneself.

strapazzata sf. 1. scolding 2. (fatica) overwork.
strapazzo sm. overwork: abiti da —, working-clothes; scrittore da —, hack.
strapieno agg. full up.
strapiombare vi. 1. to lean (v. irr.) 2. (scendere a precipizio) to fall (v. irr.) perpendicularly.
strapiombo sm. precipice: a —, sheer.
strapotente agg. very powerful.
strappare vt. 1. (lacerare) to tear (v. irr.) 2. (togliere) to snatch 3. (estirpare) to pull up 4. (un dente) to pull out 5. (estorcere) to wring (v. irr.). ♦ **strapparsi** vr. (lacerarsi) to tear.
strappo sm. 1. tear 2. (strappata) pull 3. (infrazione) breach || — muscolare, sprain.
strapuntino sm. folding seat.
straricco agg. immensely rich.
straripamento sm. overflowing.
straripare vi. to overflow.
strascicare vt. 1. to drag 2. (i piedi) to shuffle 3. (le parole) to drawl.
stràscico sm. 1. train 2. (residuo) after-effect 3. (rete) trawl.
strascinare vt. V. trascinare.
stratagemma sm. stratagem.
stratega sm. strategist.
strategìa sf. strategy.
stratègico agg. strategic(al).
stratificare vt. to stratify.
stratificazione sf. stratification.
strato sm. 1. layer 2. (di rivestimento) coat 3. (della società) class.
stratosfera sf. stratosphere.
stratosfèrico agg. stratospheric(al).
strattone sm. 1. pull 2. (sobbalzo) jerk || a strattoni, jerkily; (a intervalli) by fits and starts.
stravagante agg. odd, queer.
stravaganza sf. oddity.
stravecchio agg. very old.
stravedere vi. to see (v. irr.) badly: — per qu., to be crazy about so.
stravìncere vi. to crush. ♦ **stravìncere** vi. to win (v. irr.) all along the line.
stravizio sm. excess.
stravòlgere vt. 1. to twist 2. (gli occhi) to roll.
stravolto agg. 1. (turbato) upset 2. (di occhi) rolling.
straziante agg. tormenting, heartrending (solo fig.).

straziare *vt.* to tear (*v. irr.*).

strazio *sm.* torment: *far — di*, to play havoc with.

strega *sf.* witch.

stregare *vt.* to bewitch.

stregone *sm.* wizard.

stregonerìa *sf.* witchcraft.

stremare *vt.* to exhaust.

stremo *sm.* extreme.

strenna *sf.* gift.

strenuo *agg.* brave.

strepitare *vi.* to shout.

strèpito *sm.* din, uproar.

strepitoso *agg.* uproarious: *successo —*, striking success.

streptococco *sm.* streptococcus (*pl. -ci*).

streptomicina *sf.* streptomycin.

stretta *sf.* 1. grasp 2. (*calca*) press 3. (*gola*) gorge || *— di mano*, handshake; *essere alle strette*, to be in dire straits; *mettere alle strette qu.*, to put (*v. irr.*) so. with his back against the wall.

strettezza *sf.* 1. narrowness 2. (*povertà*) financial difficulty.

stretto *agg.* 1. narrow 2. (*serrato, piccolo*) tight 3. (*rigoroso*) strict 4. (*pigiato*) packed. ◆ **stretto** *sm.* strait.

strettoia *sf.* narrow passage.

stria *sf.* streak.

striare *vt.* to streak.

stricnina *sf.* strychnine.

stridente *agg.* 1. shrill 2. (*discordante*) jarring.

stridere *vi.* 1. to creak 2. (*di insetti*) to chirp 3. (*contrastare*) to jar.

stridìo *sm.* 1. creaking 2. (*di insetti*) chirping.

strido *sm.* 1. scream 2. (*di animale*) screech.

strìdulo *agg.* shrill.

striglia *sf.* curry-comb.

strigliare *vt.* 1. to curry 2. (*fig.*) to rebuke.

strillare *vi.* to scream.

strillo *sm.* scream.

strillone *sm.* newsboy.

striminzito *agg.* 1. stunted 2. (*di persona*) thin.

strimpellare *vt.* 1. (*di violino*) to scrape 2. (*di pianoforte*) to strum.

strinare *vt.* to singe.

stringa *sf.* lace.

stringare *vt.* 1. to lace tightly 2. (*fig.*) to condense.

stringato *agg.* 1. laced 2. (*fig.*) concise.

stringente *agg.* 1. (*urgente*) urgent 2. (*convincente*) persuasive.

stringere *vt.* 1. to press 2. (*restringere, avvitare*) to tighten 3. (*abbracciare*) to clasp 4. (*impugnare*) to grasp 5. (*fare*) to make (*v. irr.*) || *— la mano a*, to shake (*v. irr.*) hands with; *— i pugni*, to clench one's fists; *stringi stringi*, in conclusion. ◆ **stringere** *vi.* to be tight. ◆ **stringersi** *vr.* 1. to press (against) 2. (*far spazio*) to squeeze up || *— nelle spalle*, to shrug one's shoulders.

stringimento *sm.* 1. pressing 2. (*restringimento, legamento, avvitamento*) tightening 3. (*l'impugnare*) clasp 4. (*fitta*) pang.

striscia *sf.* 1. strip 2. (*riga*) stripe 3. (*scia*) trail || *a strisce*, striped.

strisciante *agg.* 1. creeping 2. (*servile*) fawning.

strisciare *vi.* 1. to creep (*v. irr.*) 2. (*fig.*) to grovel. ◆ **strisciare** *vt.* 1. to drag 2. (*i piedi*) to shuffle 3. (*radere*) to graze 4. (*fig.*) to fawn (on).

stritolamento *sm.* crushing.

stritolare *vt.* to crush.

strizzare *vt.* 1. to squeeze 2. (*torcere*) to wring (*v. irr.*) || *— l'occhio*, to wink (at so.).

strizzata *sf.* 1. squeeze 2. (*il torcere*) wring.

strofa *sf.* stanza.

strofinaccio *sm.* 1. duster 2. (*per asciugare*) towel.

strofinamento *sm.* rubbing.

strofinare *vt.* to rub.

strombatura *sf.* splay.

strombazzare *vt.* e *vi.* to trumpet.

strombettare *vi.* 1. to blow (*v. irr.*) a trumpet 2. (*auto*) to honk.

stroncare *vt.* 1. to break (*v. irr.*) off 2. (*fig.*) to demolish.

stroncatura *sf.* harsh criticism.

stronzio *sm.* strontium.

stropicciare *vt.* 1. to rub 2. (*i piedi*) to shuffle 3. (*sgualcire*) to crease. ◆ **stropicciarsi** *vr.* 1. (*gli occhi*) to rub oneself 2. (*sgualcirsi*) to crease.

stropiccìo *sm.* — *di piedi*, shuffling.

strozzare *vt.* 1. to strangle 2. (*ostruire*) to obstruct 3. (*fig.*) to choke.

strozzato *agg.* 1. strangled 2. (*soffocato*) choked 3. (*con strozzature*) with narrow passages 4. (*med.*)

strangulated 5. (*ostruito*) obstructed.

strozzatura *sf.* 1. strangling 2. (*il soffocare*) choking 3. (*ostruzione*) obstruction 4. (*restringimento*) narrow passage 5. (*med.*) strangulation.

strozzinaggio *sm.* usury.

strozzino *sm.* usurer.

struggente *agg.* pining.

strùggere *vt.* 1. to melt 2. (*fig.*) to wear (*v. irr.*) out. ♦ **strùggersi** *vr.* 1. to melt 2. (*affliggersi*) to be distressed 3. (*languire*) to be consumed (with), to pine (for).

struggimento *sm.* longing.

strumentale *agg.* instrumental.

strumentalismo *sm.* instrumentalism.

strumentare *vt.* to instrument.

strumentazione *sf.* instrumentation.

strumento *sm.* instrument.

strusciare *vt.* 1. to rub 2. (*adulare*) to fawn (on). ♦ **strusciarsi** *vr.* to rub (oneself).

strutto *sm.* lard.

struttura *sf.* structure.

strutturale *agg.* structural.

strutturare *vt.* to structure.

strutturazione *sf.* structure.

struzzo *sm.* ostrich.

stuccare[1] *vt.* 1. to stucco 2. (*turare*) to fill.

stuccare[2] *vt.* 1. (*nauseare*) to sicken 2. (*annoiare*) to bore. ♦ **stuccarsi** *vr.* 1. to get (*v. irr.*) sick 2. (*annoiarsi*) to get bored.

stuccatura *sf.* 1. plastering 2. (*di dente*) filling.

stucchévole *agg.* 1. filling 2. (*nauseante*) sickening 3. (*noioso*) boring.

stucco *sm.* 1. stucco 2. (*per vetri*) putty || *restare di —*, to be nonplussed.

studente *sm.* student.

studentesco *agg.* student (*attr.*).

studiacchiare *vt.* to study fitfully.

studiare *vt.* to study. ♦ **studiarsi** *vr.* to try.

studiato *agg.* (*affettato*) affected.

studio *sm.* 1. study 2. (*progetto*) plan 3. (*cine*) studio || *programma di studi*, curriculum; *essere allo —*, to be under consideration.

studioso *agg.* studious. ♦ **studioso** *sm.* scholar.

stufa *sf.* stove.

stufare *vt.* 1. to stew 2. (*fig.*) to bore. ♦ **stufarsi** *vr.* to get (*v. irr.*) bored.

stufato *sm.* stew.

stufo *agg.* fed up (with).

stuoia *sf.* mat.

stuolo *sm.* crowd.

stupefacente *agg.* stupefying. ♦ **stupefacente** *sm.* drug.

stupefare *vt.* to stupefy. ♦ **stupefarsi** *vr.* to be stupefied.

stupefazione *sf.* stupefaction.

stupendamente *avv.* wonderfully.

stupendo *agg.* wonderful.

stupidàggine *sf.* stupidity.

stupidità *sf.* stupidity.

stùpido *agg. e sm.* stupid.

stupire *vt.* to astonish. ♦ **stupirsi** *vr.* to be astonished.

stupito *agg.* astonished.

stupore *sm.* astonishment.

stupro *sm.* rape.

sturare *vt.* 1. to uncork 2. (*botti*) to unbung.

stuzzicadenti *sm.* tooth-pick.

stuzzicare *vt.* 1. to prod 2. (*frugare*) to pick 3. (*molestare*) to tease 4. (*stimolare*) to whet.

su *prep.* on 2. (*senza contatto; rivestimento*) over 3. (*al di sopra di*) above 4. (*circa*) about || *nove volte — dieci*, nine times out of ten. ♦ **su** *avv.* 1. up 2. (*al piano superiore*) upstairs 3. (*indosso*) on || *— per giù*, more or less; *in — (in avanti)*, onwards; *più —*, further up; *—, andiamo!*, come on!

sua *agg. e pron.* V. *suo.*

suadente *agg.* persuasive.

subàcqueo *agg.* underwater (*attr.*). ♦ **subàcqueo** *sm.* frogman (*pl.* -men).

subaffittare *vt.* to sublease.

subaffitto *sm.* sublease.

subalpino *agg.* subalpine.

subalterno *agg. e sm.* subaltern.

subbuglio *sm.* 1. turmoil 2. (*disordine*) mess.

subconscio *sm.* subconscious.

subcosciente *agg. e sm.* subconscious.

subdolamente *avv.* underhand.

sùbdolo *agg.* sly.

subentrare *vi.* to take (*v. irr.*) the place (of).

subire *vt.* to undergo (*v. irr.*).

subissare *vt.* 1. (*sprofondare*) to sink (*v. irr.*) 2. (*fig.*) to overwhelm.

subisso *sm.* (*gran quantità*) shower.
subitaneità *sf.* suddenness.
subitàneo *agg.* sudden.
sùbito *avv.* 1. at once 2. (*presto*) soon || — *prima,* just before; — *dopo,* just after.
sublimare *vt.* to sublimate.
sublimato *sm.* sublimate.
sublimazione *sf.* sublimation.
sublime *agg.* e *sm.* sublime.
sublimità *sf.* sublimity.
sublocazione *sf.* subletting.
sublunare *agg.* sublunar.
subodorare *vt.* to suspect.
subordinare *vt.* to subordinate.
subordinata *sf.* subordinate clause.
subordinato *agg.* e *sm.* subordinate.
subordinazione *sf.* subordination.
subornare *vt.* to suborn.
subornazione *sf.* subornation.
substrato *sm.* substratum (*pl.* -ta).
suburbano *agg.* suburban.
suburbio *sm.* suburb.
succèdere *vi.* 1. to succeed 2. (*capitare*) to happen. ♦ **succèdersi** *vr.* to follow one another.
successione *sf.* succession.
successivamente *avv.* afterwards.
successo *sm.* 1. success 2. (*esito*) outcome || *aver* —, to be successful.
successore *sm.* successor.
succhiare *vt.* to suck.
succhiata *sf.* suck.
succhiello *sm.* gimlet.
succinto *agg.* 1. (*di abiti*) scanty 2. (*conciso*) concise.
succo *sm.* 1. juice 2. (*fig.*) pith.
succosità *sf.* 1. juiciness 2. (*fig.*) pithiness.
succoso *agg.* 1. juicy 2. (*fig.*) pithy.
sùccubo *agg.* entirely dominated (by).
succulento *agg.* 1. juicy 2. (*gustoso*) rich.
succursale *sf.* branch.
sud *sm.* south: *del* —, southern, south (*attr.*); *verso* —, southwards.
sudare *vi.* to sweat: — *sette camicie,* to toil hard; — *freddo,* to be in a cold sweat.
sudario *sm.* shroud.
sudata *sf.* sweat.
sudaticcio *agg.* clammy.
sudato *agg.* 1. sweaty 2. (*fig.*) hard-earned.
suddetto *agg.* above-mentioned.

suddiàcono *sm.* subdeacon.
sudditanza *sf.* subjection.
sùddito *sm.* subject.
suddivìdere *vt.* to subdivide.
suddivisione *sf.* subdivision.
sùdicio *agg.* dirty.
sudicione *sm.* dirty fellow.
sudiciume *sm.* dirt.
sudore *sm.* 1. sweat 2. (*fig.*) toil.
sudorìfero *agg.* 1. (*che secerne sudore*) sudoriferous 2. (*che produce sudore*) sudorific.
sue *agg.* e *pron.* V. *suo.*
sufficiente *agg.* 1. sufficient 2. (*altezzoso*) conceited 2. (*voto sufficiente*) pass mark.
sufficienza *sf.* 1. sufficiency 2. (*alterigia*) conceit 3. (*voto sufficiente*) pass mark || *aria di* —, superior air; *a* —, enough.
suffisso *sm.* suffix.
suffragare *vt.* 1. to support 2. (*eccl.*) to pray for.
suffragio *sm.* 1. suffrage 2. (*approvazione*) approval.
suggellare *vt.* to seal.
suggello *sm.* seal.
suggerimento *sm.* 1. suggestion 2. (*teat.*) prompting.
suggerire *vt.* 1. to suggest 2. (*dar l'imbeccata; teat.*) to prompt.
suggeritore *sm.* prompter.
suggestionàbile *agg.* impressionable.
suggestionabilità *sf.* impressionability.
suggestionare *vt.* to influence. ♦ **suggestionarsi** *vr.* to will oneself (to do sthg.), to be influenced.
suggestione *sf.* suggestion.
suggestività *sf.* suggestiveness.
suggestivamente *avv.* evocatively.
suggestivo *agg.* evocative.
sùghero *sm.* 1. cork 2. (*albero*) cork-tree.
sugna *sf.* pork fat.
sugo *sm.* 1. juice 2. (*di carne*) gravy 3. (*di pomodoro*) sauce 4. (*fig.*) gist.
sugosità *sf.* V. *succosità.*
sugoso *agg.* V. *succoso.*
suicida *agg.* suicidal. ♦ **suicida** *s.* suicide.
suicidarsi *vr.* to commit suicide.
suicidio *sm.* suicide.
suino *agg.* swine (*attr.*) || *carne suina,* pork. ♦ **suino** *sm.* swine (*pl. invariato*).
sulfamìdico *sm.* sulphonamide.

sulfùreo *agg.* sulphureous.

sultanato *sm.* sultanate.

sultanina *sf.* sultana.

sultano *sm.* sultan.

summenzionato *agg.* aforesaid.

sunto *sm.* summary.

suo *agg.* **1.** (*di lui*) his **2.** (*di lei*) her **3.** (*di esso*) its **4.** (*formula di cortesia*) your. ♦ **suo** *pron.* **1.** (*di lui*) his **2.** (*di lei*) hers **3.** (*di esso*) its **4.** (*formula di cortesia*) yours || *i suoi* (*famigliari*), his, her family.

suòcera *sf.* mother-in-law.

suòcero *sm.* father-in-law.

suoi *agg. e pron.* V. *suo*.

suola *sf.* sole.

suolo *sm.* soil, ground.

suonare *vt.* V. *sonare*.

suono *sm.* sound.

suora *sf.* nun, sister.

superàbile *agg.* surmountable.

superaffollato *agg.* overcrowded.

superalimentare *vt.* **1.** to overrish **2.** (*mecc.*) to overcharge.

superalimentazione *sf.* **1.** overfeeding **2.** (*mecc.*) overcharging.

superamento *sm.* **1.** overcoming **2.** (*auto*) overtaking.

superare *vt.* **1.** (*oltrepassare*) to exceed **2.** (*auto*) to overtake (*v. irr.*) **3.** (*attraversare*) to cross **4.** (*vincere*) to overcome (*v. irr.*) **5.** (*una persona*) to surpass **6.** (*un esame, una prova*) to pass.

superbia *sf.* pride.

superbo *agg.* **1.** proud **2.** (*magnifico*) superb.

superdotato *agg.* highly gifted.

superficiale *agg.* superficial.

superficialità *sf.* superficiality.

superficie *sf.* **1.** surface **2.** (*area*) area.

superfluo *agg.* superfluous. ♦ **superfluo** *sm.* surplus.

superiora *sf.* Mother Superior.

superiore *agg.* **1.** superior **2.** (*sovrastante*) upper **3.** (*più avanzato*) advanced. ♦ **superiore** *sm.* superior.

superiorità *sf.* superiority.

superlativo *agg. e sm.* superlative.

supermercato *sm.* supermarket.

supernutrizione *sf.* overfeeding.

supersònico *agg.* supersonic.

supèrstite *agg.* surviving. ♦ **supèrstite** *s.* survivor.

superstizione *sf.* superstition.

superstizioso *agg.* superstitious.

superuomo *sm.* superman (*pl.* -men).

supervisione *sf.* supervision.

supervisore *sm.* supervisor.

supinamente *avv.* supinely.

supino *agg.* supine.

suppellèttile *sf.* furnishings (*pl.*).

supplementare *agg.* supplementary.

supplemento *sm.* **1.** supplement **2.** (*spesa supplementare*) additional charge **3.** (*di biglietto ferroviario*) excess fare.

supplente *agg.* temporary. ♦ **supplente** *s.* temporary teacher.

supplenza *sf.* temporary post.

suppletivo *agg.* supplementary.

sùpplica *sf.* **1.** entreaty **2.** (*petizione*) petition.

supplicante *agg. e s.* suppliant.

supplicare *vt.* to entreat.

supplichévole *agg.* entreating.

supplire *vi.* **1.** (*compensare*) to make (*v. irr.*) up (for) **2.** (*sostituire*) to substitute (for). ♦ **supplire** *vt.* to take (*v. irr.*) the place of.

supplizio *sm.* torment: *andare al —*, to go (*v. irr.*) to the scaffold.

supporre *vt.* to suppose.

supporto *sm.* support.

supposizione *sf.* supposition.

supposta *sf.* suppository.

supposto che *cong.* suppose (that).

suppurare *vi.* to suppurate.

suppurazione *sf.* suppuration.

supremazìa *sf.* supremacy.

supremo *agg.* supreme: *Comando — (mil.*), headquarters (*pl.*).

surclassare *vt.* to outclass.

surgelare *vt.* to deep-freeze (*v. irr.*).

surrealismo *sm.* surrealism.

surrealista *agg. e s.* surrealist.

surrealìstico *agg.* surrealistic.

surrenale *agg.* suprarenal.

surrettizio *agg.* surreptitious.

surriscaldamento *sm.* overheating.

surriscaldare *vt.* to overheat. ♦ **surriscaldarsi** *vr.* to get (*v. irr.*) overheated.

surrogàbile *agg.* replaceable.

surrogare *vt.* to replace.

surrogato *sm.* substitute.

surrogazione *sf.* (*giur.*) surrogation.

suscettìbile *agg.* **1.** susceptible **2.** (*permaloso*) touchy.

suscettibilità *sf.* **1.** susceptibility **2.** (*permalosità*) touchiness || *urtare la — di qu.*, to hurt (*v. irr.*) so.'s feelings.

suscitare *vt.* 1. to provoke 2. (*eccitare*) to stir up.

suscitatore *sm.* provoker.

susina *sf.* plum.

susino *sm.* plum-tree.

susseguente *agg.* following.

susseguire *vi.* to follow.

sussidiare *vt.* 1. to support 2. (*di governo*) to subsidize.

sussidiario *agg.* subsidiary.

sussidio *sm.* subsidy.

sussiego *sm.* haughtiness.

sussistenza *sf.* 1. existence 2. (*sostentamento*) subsistence 3. (*mil.*) Catering Corps.

sussistere *vi.* 1. to subsist 2. (*reggere*) to hold (*v. irr.*) water.

sussultare *vi.* 1. to start 2. (*di cose*) to shake (*v. irr.*).

sussulto *sm.* start.

sussurrare *vt. e vi.* 1. to whisper 2. (*criticare*) to murmur.

sussurro *sm.* whisper.

sutura *sf.* suture.

suturare *vt.* to suture.

svagare *vt.* 1. to divert 2. (*divertire*) to amuse. ♦ svagarsi *vr.* 1. to divert one's mind 2. (*divertirsi*) to amuse oneself.

svagatezza *sf.* absent-mindedness.

svagato *agg.* absent-minded.

svago *sm.* amusement.

svaligiamento *sm.* 1. robbery 2. (*di una casa*) burglary.

svaligiare *vt.* 1. to rob 2. (*una casa*) to burgle.

svaligiatore *sm.* 1. robber 2. (*di case*) burglar.

svalutare *vt.* 1. to devaluate 2. (*sottovalutare*) to undervalue.

svalutazione *sf.* devaluation.

svanire *vi.* 1. to disappear 2. (*dileguarsi, di luce ecc.*) to fade.

svanito *agg.* 1. (*dileguato*) vanished 2. (*di mente*) feeble-minded.

svantaggio *sm.* disadvantage.

svantaggioso *agg.* disadvantageous.

svaporamento *sm.* evaporation.

svaporare *vi.* to evaporate.

svariare *vt.* to vary.

svariato *agg.* various.

svarione *sm.* blunder.

svasare *vt.* (*mecc.*) to flare.

svasato *agg.* (*di abito*) bell-shaped.

svasatura *sf.* 1. (*di abito*) bell-shaping 2. (*mecc.; lo svasare*) flaring 3. (*apertura*) countersink.

svàstica *sf.* swastika.

svecchiamento *sm.* renewal.

svecchiare *vt.* to renew.

svedese *agg.* Swedish. ♦ svedese *sm.* Swede.

sveglia *sf.* 1. early call 2. (*orologio*) alarm clock 3. (*mil.*) reveille.

svegliare *vt.* to wake (*v. irr.*) (up). ♦ svegliarsi *vr.* to wake (up).

sveglio *agg.* 1. awake (*pred.*) 2. (*fig.*) quick-witted.

svelare *vt.* 1. to reveal, to disclose 2. (*togliere il velo*) to unveil.

svelenire *vt.* (*fig.*) to remove the sting from.

svèllere *vt.* to extirpate.

sveltezza *sf.* quickness.

sveltire *vt.* 1. to quicken 2. (*scaltrire*) to wake (*v. irr.*) up || — *la figura*, to slim. ♦ sveltirsi *vr.* 1. to become (*v. irr.*) quick(er) 2. (*scaltrirsi*) to wake up.

svelto *agg.* 1. quick 2. (*slanciato*) slender 3. (*intelligente*) smart. ♦ svelto *avv.* fast || —!, hurry up!

svenare *vt.* to open so.'s veins. ♦ svenarsi *vr.* to cut (*v. irr.*) one's veins.

svéndere *vt.* to undersell (*v. irr.*).

svéndita *sf.* (clearance) sale.

svenévole *agg.* maudlin.

svenimento *sm.* faint.

svenire *vi.* to faint.

sventagliare *vt.* to fan.

sventare *vt.* to baffle.

sventatezza *sf.* 1. thoughtlessness 2. (*atto sventato*) thoughtless action.

sventato *agg.* (*sbadato*) thoughtless. ♦ sventato *sm.* scatter-brain.

svèntola *sf.* (*schiaffo*) slap.

sventolare *vt. e vi.* to wave. ♦ sventolarsi *vr.* to fan oneself.

sventolìo *sm.* waving.

sventramento *sm.* 1. disembowelment 2. (*demolizione*) demolition.

sventrare *vt.* 1. to disembowel 2. (*demolire*) to demolish.

sventura *sf.* misfortune: *per* —, unluckily; *per colmo di* —, to crown it all.

sventuratamente *avv.* unfortunately.

sventurato *agg.* unfortunate.

svenuto *agg.* unconscious.

svergognare *vt.* to shame.

svergognatamente *avv.* shamelessly.

svergognato *agg.* shameless.

svernamento *sm.* wintering.

svernare *vi.* to winter.

svestire *vt.* to undress. ♦ **svestirsi** *vr.* to undress.

svettare *vt.* to lop. ♦ **svettare** *vi.* to stand (*v. irr.*) out.

svezzamento *sm.* weaning.

svezzare *vt.* to wean.

sviamento *sm.* 1. diversion 2. (*il traviare*) leading astray 3. (*il traviarsi*) going astray.

sviare *vt.* 1. to divert 2. (*traviare*) to lead (*v. irr.*) astray. ♦ **sviarsi** *vr.* 1. to be diverted 2. (*traviarsi*) to go (*v. irr.*) astray.

sviato *agg.* led astray (*pred.*).

svignàrsela *vr.* to slink (*v. irr.*) away.

svigorire *vt.* to weaken. ♦ **svigorirsi** *vr.* to grow (*v. irr.*) weak.

svilimento *sm.* depreciation.

svilire *vt.* to depreciate.

sviluppare *vt.* 1. to develop 2. (*sciogliere*) to loosen 3. (*sprigionare*) to generate. ♦ **svilupparsi** *vr.* to develop.

sviluppatore *sm.* (*foto*) developer.

sviluppo *sm.* 1. development 2. (*sprigionamento*) generation.

svincolamento *sm.* 1. release 2. (*doganale*) clearance 3. (*riscatto*) redemption.

svincolare *vt.* 1. to release 2. (*sdoganare*) to clear 3. (*riscattare*) to redeem. ♦ **svincolarsi** *vr.* to get (*v. irr.*) free.

svisare *vt.* (*travisare*) to twist.

sviscerare *vt.* 1. to disembowel 2. (*fig.*) to dissect.

sviscerato *agg.* passionate.

svista *sf.* oversight.

svitare *vt.* to unscrew.

svìzzero *agg. e sm.* Swiss.

svogliatezza *sf.* 1. unwillingness 2. (*pigrizia*) laziness.

svogliato *agg.* 1. unwilling 2. (*pigro*) lazy. ♦ **svogliato** *sm.* lazy--bones.

svolazzare *vi.* to flutter.

svolazzo *sm.* 1. fluttering 2. (*tratto di penna*) flourish.

svòlgere *vt.* 1. to unwind (*v. irr.*) 2. (*trattare*) to develop 3. (*mettere in opera*) to carry out. ♦ **svòlgersi** *vr.* 1. to unwind 2. (*svilupparsi*) to develop 3. (*accadere*) to take (*v. irr.*) place.

svolgimento *sm.* 1. unwinding 2. (*trattazione*) treatment 3. (*corso*) course 4. (*sviluppo*) development.

svolta *sf.* 1. turn 2. (*fig.*) turning

point ‖ *fare una* —, to turn.

svoltare *vi.* to turn.

svuotamento *sm.* emptying.

svuotare *vt.* 1. to empty 2. (*fig.*) to deprive.

T

tabaccaio *sm.* tobacconist.

tabaccare *vt.* to snuff.

tabaccherìa *sf.* tobacconist's.

tabacchiera *sf.* snuff-box.

tabacco *sm.* tobacco.

tabella *sf.* 1. (*lista*) list 2. (*quadro*) board.

tabellone *sm.* notice board.

tabernàcolo *sm.* tabernacle.

tabù *sm.* taboo.

tabulatore *sm.* tabulator.

tacca *sf.* 1. notch 2. (*fig.*) condition.

taccagnerìa *sf.* stinginess.

taccagno *agg.* stingy. ♦ **taccagno** *sm.* miser.

tacchino *sm.* turkey.

taccia *sf.* 1. reputation 2. (*accusa*) charge.

tacciare *vt.* to charge (with).

tacco *sm.* heel.

taccuino *sm.* note-book.

tacere *vi.* to be silent: *far* —, to silence.

tachicardìa *sf.* tachycardia.

tachìmetro *sm.* tachometer.

tacitare *vt.* 1. to hush up 2. (*un creditore*) to pay (*v. irr.*) off.

tàcito *agg.* 1. silent 2. (*non espresso*) tacit.

taciturno *agg.* silent.

tafano *sm.* gad-fly.

tafferuglio *sm.* brawl.

taglia *sf.* 1. (*riscatto*) ransom 2. (*ricompensa*) reward 3. (*misura*) size.

tagliacarte *sm.* paper-knife (*pl.* -knives).

taglialegna *sm.* wood-cutter.

tagliando *sm.* coupon.

tagliapietre *sm.* stone-cutter.

tagliare *vt.* 1. to cut (*v. irr.*) 2. (*attraversare*) to cut across: — *via*, to cut off ‖ — *a pezzi*, to cut into pieces; — *la corda* (*fig.*), to run (*v. irr.*) away; — *la strada a qu.*, to bar so.'s way. ♦ **tagliarsi** *vr.* to cut.

tagliatelle *sf. pl.* noodles.

tagliato *agg.* 1. cut 2. (*inclinato, disposto*) cut out, fit: *essere —
fuori*, to be cut off.

tagliatore *sm.* cutter.

taglieggiare *vt.* to ransom.

tagliente *agg.* sharp.

tagliere *sm.* trencher.

taglio *sm.* 1. cut 2. (*il tagliare*) cutting 3. (*parte tagliente, orlo*) edge 4. (*dimensione*) size 5. (*raccolto*) harvest.

tagliola *sf.* snare.

taglione *sm.* retaliation.

tagliuzzare *vt.* to mince.

talare *agg.* talaric: *veste —*, cassock.

talco *sm.* talc: *— borato*, talcum powder.

tale *agg.* 1. such 2. (*per tralasciare i dati determinati*) such and such: *il — giorno*, on such and such day 3. (*suddetto*) above-mentioned || *— e quale*, exactly like, exactly as. ♦ **tale** *pron. indef.* someone.

talea *sf.* scion.

talento *sm.* talent.

talismano *sm.* talisman.

tallonare *vi.* to follow.

talloncino *sm.* slip.

tallone *sm.* heel.

talora *avv.* sometimes.

talpa *sf.* mole.

taluno *agg.* some. ♦ **taluno** *pron.* someone (*pl.* some people).

talvolta *avv.* V. *talora.*

tamarindo *sm.* tamarind.

tambureggiare *vi.* to drum.

tamburellare *vi.* to drum one's fingers on.

tamburino *sm.* drummer.

tamburo *sm.* 1. drum 2. (*mecc.*) cylinder.

tamponamento *sm.* 1. plugging 2. (*med.*) tamponage 3. (*auto*) bumping.

tamponare *vt.* 1. to plug 2. (*med.*) to tampon 3. (*auto*) to bump (against).

tampone *sm.* 1. plug 2. (*med.*) tampon 3. (*di carta asciugante*) blotter.

tana *sf.* den.

tanfo *sm.* stench.

tangente *agg. e sf.* tangent.

tangenza *sf.* tangency: *punto di —*, tangential point.

tangenziale *agg.* tangential.

tànghero *sm.* boor.

tangibile *agg.* tangible.

tangibilità *sf.* tangibility.

tànnico *agg.* (*chim.*) tannic.

tannino *sm.* tannin.

tanto *avv.* 1. so 2. (*coi verbi*) so much 3. (*di tempo*) so long 4. (*ad ogni modo*) anyhow || *— quanto*, as much as; *— ... quanto*, as... as (*sia... sia*) both ... and; *— meglio*, so much the better; *— per cambiare*, just for a change. ♦ **tanto** *agg.* so much (*pl.* so many): *—
... quanto*, as much... as (*pl.* as many... as). ♦ **tanto che** *cong.* so (that).

tapiro *sm.* tapir.

tappa *sf.* 1. (*luogo*) halting-place 2. (*parte di viaggio*) stage 3. (*sport*) lap.

tappare *vt.* 1. to stop 2. (*con tappo*) to cork.

tapparella *sf.* rolling shutter.

tappeto *sm.* carpet.

tappezzare *vt.* 1. (*con carta*) to paper 2. (*coprire*) to cover 3. (*foderare*) to upholster.

tappezzerìa *sf.* 1. (*di carta*) paper 2. (*di stoffa*) tapestry.

tappezziere *sm.* 1. (*per pareti*) paper hanger 2. (*per divani ecc.*) upholsterer.

tappo *sm.* 1. plug 2. (*per bottiglia*) cap.

tara *sf.* 1. tare 2. (*med.; difetto*) taint.

taràntola *sf.* tarantula.

tarare *vt.* 1. (*mecc.*) to set (*v. irr.*) 2. (*calibrare*) to calibrate 3. (*comm.*) to tare.

tarato *agg.* 1. (*comm.*) tared 2. (*mecc.*) set 3. (*med.*) with a taint 4. (*fig.*) corrupted.

tarchiato *agg.* sturdy.

tardare *vi.* to be late. ♦ **tardare** *vt.* to delay.

tardi *avv.* late: *far —*, to be late.

tardivo *agg.* 1. (*arretrato*) backward 2. (*che viene tardi*) tardy.

tardo *agg.* 1. tardy 2. (*ottuso*) dull 3. (*di tempo*) late || *a tarda notte*, late in the night; *tarda età*, old age.

targa *sf.* 1. (*di metallo*) plate 2. (*di marmo*) slab 3. (*auto*) number-plate.

targare *vt.* (*auto*) to give (*v. irr.*) a number-plate (to a car).

tariffa *sf.* tariff.

tarlarsi *vr.* to get (*v. irr.*) worm-eaten.

tarlatura *sf.* worm-hole.

tarlo *sm.* **1.** woodworm **2.** (*fig.*) gnawings (*pl.*).

tarma *sf.* moth.

tarmarsi *vr.* to get (*v. irr.*) moth--eaten.

tarpare *vt.* to clip.

tartagliare *vi.* to stammer.

tartàrico *agg.* tartaric.

tàrtaro *sm.* tartar.

tartaruga *sf.* tortoise.

tartassare *vt.* to harass.

tartina *sf.* canapé.

tartufo *sm.* truffle.

tasca *sf.* pocket.

tascàbile *agg.* pocket (*attributivo*).

tassa *sf.* **1.** tax **2.** (*d'iscrizione*) fee.

tassàbile *agg.* taxable.

tassàmetro *sm.* taximeter: — *di parcheggio*, parking meter.

tassare *vt.* to tax.

tassativo *agg.* peremptory.

tassazione *sf.* taxation.

tassello *sm.* dowel.

tassì *sm.* taxi.

tassista *sm.* taxi-driver.

tasso¹ *sm.* (*comm.*) rate.

tasso² *sm.* (*bot.*) yew.

tasso³ *sm.* (*zool.*) badger.

tastare *vt.* to feel (*v. irr.*): — *il terreno* (*fig.*), to feel one's way.

tastiera *sf.* keyboard.

tasto *sm.* **1.** key **2.** (*tatto*) feel **3.** (*argomento*) subject.

tastoni *avv. a* —, gropingly; *andare a* —, to grope.

tàttica *sf.* tactics.

tàttico *agg.* tactical. ♦ **tàttico** *sm.* tactician.

tàttile *agg.* tactile.

tatto *sm.* **1.** touch **2.** (*fig.*) tact ‖ *con* —, tactfully.

tatuaggio *sm.* tattoo.

tatuare *vt.* to tattoo.

taumatùrgico *agg.* thaumaturgic(al).

taumaturgo *sm.* thaumaturge.

taurino *agg.* bull-like (*attr.*): *dal collo* —, bull-necked.

tauromachìa *sf.* bullfight.

tautologìa *sf.* tautology.

taverna *sf.* tavern.

taverniere *sm.* tavern-keeper.

tàvola *sf.* **1.** table **2.** (*asse*) board **3.** (*di marmo*) slab **4.** (*illustrazione*) plate.

tavolaccio *sm.* plank-bed.

tavolata *sf.* table.

tavolato *sm.* **1.** (*di pavimento*) plank floor **2.** (*mar.*) planking **3.**

(*geogr.*) plateau.

tavolozza *sf.* palette.

tazza *sf.* cup: — *da tè*, tea-cup.

te *pron.* you.

tè *sm.* tea.

teatrale *agg.* theatrical.

teatro *sm.* theatre: — *di posa*, studio.

tècnica *sf.* technique.

tecnicismo *sm.* technicality.

tècnico *agg.* technical. ♦ **tècnico** *sm.* technician.

tecnologìa *sf.* technology.

tecnològico *agg.* technological.

tedesco *agg.* e *sm.* German.

tediare *vt.* to bore.

tedio *sm.* boredom.

tedioso *agg.* boring.

tegame *sm.* saucepan.

teglia *sf.* bakepan.

tégola *sf.* tile: *coprire di tegole*, to tile.

teiera *sf.* tea-pot.

teismo *sm.* theism.

tela *sf.* **1.** cloth **2.** (*teat.*) curtain **3.** (*dipinto*) painting **4.** (*per dipingere*) canvas ‖ — *cerata*, oilcloth; — *di sacco*, sackcloth; — *di lino*, linen; — *di ragno*, cobweb.

telaio *sm.* **1.** loom **2.** (*ossatura, cornice*) frame.

telecàmera *sf.* camera.

telecomandare *vt.* to radiocontrol.

telecomunicazione *sf.* telecommunication.

telefèrica *sf.* cableway.

telefonare *vt.* to (tele)phone.

telefonata *sf.* (telephone) call.

telefonìa *sf.* telephony.

telefònico *agg.* telephone (*attr.*): *cabina telefonica*, telephone booth.

telefonista *sm.* (telephone) operator. ♦ **telefonista** *sf.* switchboard girl.

telèfono *sm.* (tele)phone: *dare un colpo di* —, to ring (*v. irr.*) up.

telefoto *sf.* telephotograph.

telegiornale *sm.* (television) news (-reel).

telegrafare *vt.* to telegraph.

telegrafìa *sf.* telegraphy.

telegràfico *agg.* telegraphic(al).

telegrafista *sm.* telegraphist.

telègrafo *sm.* **1.** telegraph **2.** (*ufficio*) telegraph-office.

telegramma *sm.* telegram, wire: *fare un* — *a qu.*, to wire so.

telèmetro *sm.* **1.** telemeter **2.** (*in arma da fuoco; foto*) rangefinder.

teleobbiettivo *sm.* telephoto lens.
teleologìa *sf.* teleology.
telepatìa *sf.* telepathy.
telerìe *sf. pl.* linen (*sing.*): *commerciante in* —, linen-draper.
teleschermo *sm.* television screen.
telescopio *sm.* telescope.
telescrivente *sf.* teletypewriter.
teleselezione *sf.* long distance dialing.
telespettatore *sm.* televiewer.
teletipìa *sf.* teletype.
teletrasméttere *vt.* to telecast (*v. irr.*).
televisione *sf.* television: *guardare la* —, to watch television; *alla* —, on television; *trasmettere per* —, to telecast.
televisivo *agg.* televisional, television (*attr.*): *trasmissione televisiva*, telecast.
televisore *sm.* television set.
tellùrico *agg.* telluric.
telo *sm.* sheet.
telone *sm.* 1. (*teat.*) curtain 2. (*cine*) screen.
tema[1] *sf.* (*paura*) fear: *per* — *che*, lest.
tema[2] *sm.* 1. theme 2. (*scolastico*) composition.
temàtica *sf.* themes (*pl.*).
temàtico *agg.* thematic(al).
temerarietà *sf.* rashness.
temerario *agg.* rash.
temere *vt.* e *vi.* 1. to fear 2. (*patire*) not to stand (*v. irr.*) || ·*temo di sì*, I fear so; *temo di no*, I fear not.
temìbile *agg.* dreadful.
tèmpera *sf.* 1. (*metal.*) hardening 2. (*pitt.*) distemper || *dipingere a* —, to distemper.
temperamatite *sm.·* pencil-sharpener.
temperamento *sm.* 1. temperament 2. (*alleviamento*) mitigation.
temperante *agg.* temperate.
temperanza *sf.* temperance.
temperare *vt.* 1. to temper 2. (*matite*) to sharpen.
temperato *agg.* 1. temperate 2. (*di matita*) sharpened.
temperatura *sf.* temperature.
temperino *sm.* penknife (*pl.* -knives).
tempesta *sf.* tempest, storm.
tempestare *vt.* 1. (*assalire*) to assail 2. (*importunare*) to harass 3. (*cospargere*) to strew (*v. irr.*) (sthg.

with). ◆ **tempestare** *vi.* 1. to storm 2. (*grandinare*) to hail.
tempestività *sf.* timeliness.
tempestivo *agg.* timely.
tempestoso *agg.* stormy.
tempia *sf.* temple.
tempio *sm.* temple.
tempo *sm.* 1. time 2. (*atmosferico*) weather 3. (*gramm.*) tense 4. (*fase*) stage 5. (*cine*) part || *un* —, once; *col passare del* —, in the long run; *molto* — *prima, dopo*, long before, after; *a* — *perso*, in one's spare time; *per* —, early.
temporale[1] *agg.* temporal.
temporale[2] *agg.* (*anat.*) temporal.
temporale[3] *sm.* storm.
temporalesco *agg.* stormy.
temporaneità *sf.* temporariness.
temporàneo *agg.* temporary.
temporeggiare *vi.* to temporize.
tempra *sf.* 1. temper 2. (*metal.*) hardening 3. (*fig.*) character.
temprare *vt.* 1. to temper 2. (*fig.*) to strengthen 3. (*plasmare*) to form.
temprato *agg.* (*abituato*) inured.
tenace *agg.* tenacious.
tenacia *sf.* tenacity.
tenaglia *sf.* pincers (*pl.*).
tenda *sf.* 1. curtain 2. (*da campo*) tent.
tendaggio *sm.* curtain.
tendente *agg.* tending.
tendenza *sf.* 1. tendency 2. inclination.
tendenziale *agg.* tendential.
tendenziosità *sf.·* tendentiousness.
tendenzioso *agg.* tendentious.
tèndere *vt.* 1. (*protendere*) to stretch (out) 2. (*mettere in tensione*) to tighten. ◆ **tèndere** *vi.* 1. to tend 2. (*mirare*) to aim (at).
tendina *sf.* curtain.
tèndine *sm.* tendon.
tenditore *sm.* turnbuckle.
tènebra *sf.* darkness.
tenebroso *agg.* 1. dark 2. (*sinistro*) sinister.
tenente *sm.* lieutenant.
tenere *vt.* 1. to keep (*v. irr.*) 2. (*sostenere, considerare, contenere*) to hold (*v. irr.*) || — *una lezione*, to give (*v. irr.*) a lesson. ◆ **tenersi** *vr.* (*seguire*) to follow: — *al corrente*, to keep tabs on.
tenerezza *sf.* tenderness.
tènero *agg.* tender. ◆ **tènero** *sm.* 1. (*parte tenera*) tender part 2. (*affetto*) sympathy.

tenia *sf.* tapeworm.
tennis *sm.* tennis.
tennista *s.* tennis-player.
tenore *sm.* tenor.
tenorile *agg.* tenor (*attr.*).
tensione *sf.* tension.
tentacolare *agg.* tentacular.
tentàcolo *sm.* tentacle.
tentare *vt.* 1. to tempt 2. (*provare*) to try.
tentativo *sm.* attempt.
tentatore *agg.* tempting. ♦ **tentatore** *sm.* tempter.
tentazione *sf.* temptation.
tentennamento *sm.* 1. shaking 2. (*traballamento*) tottering 3. (*esitazione*) hesitation.
tentennare *vt.* to shake (*v. irr.*). ♦ **tentennare** *vi.* 1. to totter 2. (*esitare*) to waver.
tentoni *agg.* gropingly.
tenue *agg.* 1. small 2. (*leggero*) soft.
tenuità *sf.* 1. smallness 2. (*levità*) slightness.
tenuta *sf.* 1. (*proprietà*) estate 2. (*capacità*) capacity 3. (*abiti*) clothes (*pl.*) 4. (*tec.*) seal || — *di strada*, roadability; *a — d'acqua*, watertight.
teocràtico *agg.* theocratic(al).
teocrazìa *sf.* theocracy.
teologale *agg.* theological.
teologìa *sf.* theology.
teològico *agg.* theologic(al).
teòlogo *sm.* theologian.
teorema *sm.* theorem.
teorìa *sf.* 1. theory 2. (*fila*) string.
teòrico *agg.* theoretic(al).
teorizzare *vi.* to theorize.
tepore *sm.* lukewarmness.
teppa *sf.* rabble.
teppista *sm.* teddy-boy.
terapèutico *agg.* therapeutic(al).
terapìa *sf.* therapy.
terebìnto *sm.* terebinth.
tèrgere *vt.* to wipe (off).
tergicristallo *sm.* windscreen wiper.
tergiversare *vi.* to hesitate.
tergiversazione *sf.* hesitation.
tergo *sm.* back: *segue a —*, please turn over.
termale *agg.* thermal: *stazione —*, spa.
terme *sf. pl.* thermal springs.
tèrmico *agg.* thermic.
terminale *agg.* terminal.
terminare *vt.* e *vi.* to end.

tèrmine *sm.* 1. term 2. (*limite*) limit 3. (*fine*) end || *contratto a —*, time-contract; *portare a —*, to carry out.
terminologìa *sf.* terminology.
tèrmite *sf.* termite.
termocoperta *sf.* thermal blanket.
termodinàmica *sf.* thermodynamics.
termoelèttrico *agg.* thermoelectric(al).
termòforo *sm.* warming pad.
termògeno *agg.* thermogenetic.
termoiònico *agg.* thermionic.
termòmetro *sm.* thermometer: *il — segna...*, the thermometer stands at...
termonucleare *agg.* thermonuclear.
termos *sm.* vacuum bottle.
termosifone *sm.* (*radiatore*) radiator.
termòstato *sm.* thermostat.
ternario *agg.* ternary.
terno *sm.* tern. ♦ **terno** *agg.* triple.
terra *sf.* 1. (*globo terracqueo*) earth 2. (*paese; l'opposto del mare*) land 3. (*terreno*) ground || — —, earth bound; *raso —*, to the ground.
terracotta *sf.* terracotta: *vasellame di —*, earthenware.
terraferma *sf.* dry land.
terraglia *sf.* pottery.
terranova *sm.* (*cane*) Newfoundland dog.
terrapieno *sm.* 1. bank 2. (*di fiume*) embankment. '
terràqueo *agg.* terraqueous.
terrazza *sf.* 1. terrace 2. (*balcone*) balcony.
terrazziere *sm.* digger.
terrazzo *sm.* V. *terrazza.*
terremoto *sm.* earthquake.
terreno[1] *agg.* earthly.
terreno[2] *sm.* ground.
tèrreo *agg.* 1. earthy 2. (*di colorito*) wan, sallow.
terrestre *agg.* terrestrial, earthly.
terrìbile *agg.* terrible.
terriccio *sm.* mould.
terriero *agg.* land (*attr.*).
terrificante *agg.* terrifying.
terrificare *vt.* to terrify.
terrina *sf.* tureen.
territoriale *agg.* territorial.
territorio *sm.* territory.
terrore *sm.* terror: *incutere — a qu.*, to strike (*v. irr.*) so. with terror.
terrorismo *sm.* terrorism.

terrorista s. terrorist.
terrorìstico agg. terroristic.
terrorizzare vt. to terrorize.
terroso agg. earthy.
terso agg. clear.
terza sf. 1. (di scuola, treno) third class 2. (di auto) third gear.
terzetto sm. trio.
terziario agg. e sm. tertiary.
terzina sf. tercet.
terzino sm. (sport) full back.
terzo agg. third. ◆ **terzo** sm. 1. third 2. (terza persona) third person || terzi, third party.
terzùltimo agg. e sm. last but two.
tesa sf. brim.
tesaurizzare vt. to treasure.
teschio sm. skull.
tesi sf. thesis (pl. -ses).
teso agg. taut.
tesorerìa sf. treasury.
tesoriere sm. treasurer.
tesoro sm. 1. treasure 2. (pol.) treasury.
tèssera sf. 1. card 2. (di mosaico) tessera (pl. -rae).
tesseramento sm. 1. rationing 2. (reclutamento) enrolment.
tesserare vt. 1. to ration 2. (arruolare) to enrol.
tèssere vt. to weave (v. irr.).
tèssile agg. textile. ◆ **tèssile** sm. weaver.
tessitore sm. weaver.
tessitura sf. 1. weaving 2. (disposizione dei fili) texture.
tessuto sm. 1. fabric 2. (med.; fig.) tissue || negozio di tessuti, draper's shop.
testa sf. head: colpo di —, rash act; essere in — a tutti, to be ahead of everybody.
testamentario agg. testamentary.
testamento sm. will.
testardàggine sf. stubbornness.
testardo agg. stubborn.
testata sf. 1. head 2. (colpo) butt 3. (di giornale) heading.
teste s. witness: — d'accusa, di difesa, witness for the prosecution, the defence.
testìcolo sm. testicle.
testimonianza sf. 1. witness 2. (prova) evidence || far —, to bear (v. irr.) witness.
testimoniare vt. e vi. 1. to witness 2. (attestare) to testify.
testimonio sm. witness.
testo sm. text.

testuale agg. 1. textual 2. (esatto) exact.
tetànico agg. tetanic.
tètano sm. tetanus.
tetraedro sm. tetrahedron.
tetràggine sf. gloom.
tetràgono agg. (fig.) steadfast.
tetralogìa sf. tetralogy.
tetro agg. gloomy.
tettarella sf. dummy.
tetto sm. roof: — a capanna, saddle roof.
tettoia sf. shed.
tettònica sf. tectonics.
teutònico agg. Teutonic. ◆ **teutònico** sm. Teuton.
ti pron. 1. you, to you 2. (r.) yourself.
tiara sf. tiara.
tibia sf. tibia.
tic sm. tic.
ticchettare vi. to tick.
ticchettìo sm. ticking.
ticchio sm. fancy.
tièpido agg. tepid.
tifo sm. 1. typhus 2. (fig.) fanaticism.
tifone sm. typhoon.
tifoso sm. 1. typhus patient 2. (fig.) fan.
tiglio sm. lime.
tigna sf. ringworm.
tignola sf. moth.
tigrato agg. striped.
tigre sf. tiger.
timbrare vt. 1. to stamp 2. (lettere) to postmark || — a secco, to emboss.
timbratura sf. 1. stamping 2. (postale) postmarking.
timbro sm. 1. stamp 2. (di suono) timbre 3. (postale) postmark || — a secco, embossed stamp.
timidezza sf. shyness.
tìmido agg. shy.
timo sm. thyme.
timone sm. helm.
timoniere sm. helmsman (pl. -men).
timorato agg. 1. respectful 2. (scrupoloso) scrupulous.
timore sm. fear: aver —, to fear, to be afraid.
timoroso agg. fearful.
tìmpano sm. 1. eardrum 2. (mus.) kettle-drum 3. (arch.) gable.
tinca sf. tench.
tinello sm. living-room.
tìngere vt. to dye (v. irr.). ◆ **tìngersi** vr. to dye oneself.

tino sm. vat.

tinozza sf. tub.

tinta sf. 1. (colore) hue 2. (materia colorante) dye 3. (tingitura) dyeing.

tinteggiare vt. to paint.

tintinnare vi. to tinkle.

tintinnìo sm. tinkling.

tintore sm. 1. dyer 2. (anche per lavature a secco) cleaner.

tintorìa sf. 1. dyeworks (pl.) 2. (negozio anche per lavature a secco) dry cleaners' shop.

tintura sf. V. tinta.

tìpico agg. typical.

tipo sm. 1. type 2. (modello) pattern 3. (individuo) fellow.

tipografìa sf. 1. typography 2. (mecc.) letterpress printing.

tipogràfico agg. typographic(al).

tipògrafo sm. typographer.

tiraggio sm. draught.

tiralìnee sm. drawing-pen.

tiranneggiare vt. to tyrannize.

tirannìa sf. tyranny.

tirànnico agg. tyrannical.

tirànnide sf. tyranny.

tiranno sm. tyrant.

tirante sm. 1. (mecc.) connecting rod 2. (arch.) tie-beam.

tirapiedi sm. drudge.

tirare vt. 1. to draw (v. irr.), to pull 2. (scagliare) to throw (v. irr.). ♦ **tirare** vi. 1. (sparare) to shoot (v. irr.) 2. (di tiraggio) to draw 3. (di vestito) to be tight. ♦ **tirarsi** vr. to draw.

tirata sf. 1. pull 2. (invettiva) tirade.

tiratore sm. shooter.

tiratura sf. 1. (tip.) printing 2. (numero di copie stampate) circulation.

tirchierìa sf. niggardliness.

tirchio agg. niggardly.

tiritera sf. rigmarole.

tiro sm. 1. (trazione) draught 2. (lancio) throw 3. (sparo) shot 4. (scherzo) trick.

tirocinio sm. apprenticeship.

tiròide sf. thyroid.

tisana sf. ptisan.

tisi sf. consumption.

tìsico agg. e sm. consumptive.

tisiologìa sf. phthisiology.

tisiòlogo sm. phthisiologist.

titànico agg. titanic.

titillare vt. to tickle.

titolare agg. 1. regular 2. (nominale) titular. ♦ **titolare** s. 1. regular holder 2. (proprietario) owner 3. (capo) principal.

titolato agg. titled.

tìtolo sm. 1. title 2. (qualifica) qualification 3. (documento) document 4. (comm.) security.

titubante agg. hesitating.

titubanza sf. hesitation.

titubare vi. to hesitate.

tizianesco agg. 1. Titianesque 2. (di capelli) titian.

tizio sm. fellow.

tizzone sm. brand.

toccare vt. to touch || — un porto, to call at. ♦ **toccare** vi. 1. (capitare) to happen 2. (spettare) to fall (v. irr.).

toccasana sm. cure-all.

tocco[1] agg. (pazzoide) touched.

tocco[2] sm. 1. touch 2. (battito) knock 3. (rintocco) toll || al —, at one o'clock.

tocco[3] sm. (berretto) toque.

toga sf. gown.

togato agg. gowned.

tògliere vt. 1. to take (v. irr.) 2. (liberare) to relieve. ♦ **tògliersi** vr. 1. to get (v. irr.) off 2. (un indumento) to take off || — la vita, to commit suicide.

toletta sf. toilet.

tolleràbile agg. tolerable.

tollerante agg. tolerant.

tolleranza sf. tolerance.

tollerare vt. 1. to tolerate 2. (sopportare) to bear (v. irr.).

tomaia sf. vamp.

tomba sf. grave.

tombale agg. grave (attr.).

tombino sm. manhole.

tòmbola sf. 1. (gioco) "tombola" 2. (caduta) tumble.

tombolare vi. to tumble down.

tomismo sm. Thomism.

tomista agg. e sm. Thomist.

tomo sm. 1. tome 2. (persona) chap.

tònaca sf. frock: gettare la —, to give (v. irr.) up the frock.

tonalità sf. tonality.

tonante agg. thundering.

tondeggiante agg. roundish.

tondeggiare vi. to be roundish.

tondello sm. round.

tondo agg. e sm. round || chiaro e —, clearly.

tonfo sm. splash.

tònico agg. e sm. tonic.

tonificare vt. to brace.

tonnellaggio sm. tonnage.

tonnellata sf. ton.

tonno sm. tunny.

tono *sm.* **1.** tone **2.** (*accordo*) tune **3.** (*mus.*) strain.

tonsilla *sf.* tonsil.

tonsillectomìa *sf.* tonsillectomy.

tonsillite *sf.* tonsillitis.

tonsura *sf.* tonsure.

tonsurare *vt.* to tonsure.

tonto *agg.* dull. ♦ **tonto** *sm.* dunce.

topaia *sf.* (*fig.*) hovel.

topazio *sm.* topaz.

tòpica *sf.* **1.** topic **2.** (*errore*) blunder.

tòpico *agg.* topical.

topo *sm.* mouse (*pl.* mice), rat || — *di biblioteca* (*fig.*), bookworm; — *di albergo* (*fig.*), hotel thief.

topografia *sf.* topography.

topogràfico *agg.* topographic(al).

topologìa *sf.* topology.

toponomàstica *sf.* toponymy.

toppa *sf.* **1.** (*pezza*) patch **2.** (*di serratura*) keyhole || *mettere una* —, to patch up.

torace *sm.* thorax, chest.

torba *sf.* peat.

torbidezza *sf.* **1.** turbidity **2.** (*esser fosco*) gloominess.

tòrbido *agg.* **1.** turbid **2.** (*fosco*) gloomy **3.** (*inquieto*) troubled. ♦ **tòrbido** *sm.* (*disordine*) disorder: *pescare nel* —, to fish in troubled water.

torbiera *sf.* peat-bog.

tòrcere *vt.* **1.** to wring (*v. irr.*) **2.** (*attorcigliare*) to twist || *dare del filo da* —, to give (*v. irr.*) a lot of trouble; — *il naso* (*fig.*), to turn up one's nose (at). ♦ **tòrcersi** *vr.* to twist.

torchiare *vt.* to press.

torchiatura *sf.* pressing.

torchio *sm.* press.

torcia *sf.* torch.

torcicollo *sm.* stiff- neck.

torcitore *sm.* twister.

torcitura *sf.* twist.

tordo *sm.* thrush.

torero *sm.* bullfighter.

torma *sf.* swarm.

tormalina *sf.* tourmaline.

tormenta *sf.* blizzard.

tormentare *vt.* to torment. ♦ **tormentarsi** *vr.* to worry.

tormentato *agg.* (*inquieto*) restless.

tormento *sm.* torment.

tormentoso *agg.* tormenting.

tornaconto *sm.* profit.

tornado *sm.* tornado.

tornante *sm.* bend.

tornare *vi.* **1.** to return **2.** (*di conti*) to be correct.

tornasole *sm.* litmus.

torneo *sm.* tournàment.

tornio *sm.* lathe.

tornire *vt.* **1.** (*mecc.*) to turn **2.** (*fig.*) to polish.

tornito *agg.* **1.** (*rotondo*) round **2.** (*ben fatto*) well-shaped.

tornitore *sm.* turner.

toro *sm.* bull.

torpediniera *sf.* torpedo-boat.

torpedo *sf.* torpedo.

torpedone *sm.* (motor-)coach.

tòrpido *agg.* torpid.

torpore *sm.* torpor.

torre *sf.* tower.

torrefare *vt.* **1.** to torrefy **2.** (*caffè*) to roast.

torrefazione *sf.* **1.** torrefaction **2.** (*di caffè*) roasting **3.** (*negozio*) coffee store.

torreggiare *vi.* to tower.

torrente *sm.* torrent.

torrentizio *agg.* torrent-like.

torrenziale *agg.* torrential.

torretta *sf.* (*mil.; mar.*) turret.

tòrrido *agg.* torrid.

torrione *sm.* donjon.

torrone *sm.* noùgat.

torsione *sf.* torsion.

torso *sm.* **1.** trunk **2.** (*di statua*) torso.

tòrsolo *sm.* **1.** (*di verdura*) stump **2.** (*di frutta*) core.

torta *sf.* cake.

tortiera *sf.* bakepan.

torto *agg.* **1.** (*piegato*) bent **2.** (*contorto*) twisted.

torto *sm.* **1.** wrong **2.** (*colpa*) fault || *aver* —, to be wrong; *far* — *a qu.*, to wrong so.; *a* —, wrongly.

tòrtora *sf.* turtle-dove.

tortuosità *sf.* tortuosity.

tortuoso *agg.* tortuous.

tortura *sf.* torture.

torturare *vt.* to torture. ♦ **torturarsi** *vr.* to worry.

torvo *agg.* grim.

tosare *vt.* to shear (*v. irr.*).

tosatrice *sf.* clippers (*pl.*).

tosatura *sf.* shearing.

toscano *agg. e sm.* Tuscan.

tosse *sf.* cough.

tossicchiare *vi.* to keep (*v. irr.*) on coughing.

tossicità *sf.* toxicity.

tòssico *agg.* toxic. ♦ **tòssico** *sm.* toxicant.

tossicologìa sf. toxicology.
tossicòlogo sm. toxicologist.
tossicomanìa sf. toxicomania.
tossina sf. toxin.
tossire vi. to cough.
tostapane sm. toaster.
tostare vt. 1. to toast 2. (caffè) to roast.
tosto¹ avv. at once.
tosto² agg. hard || faccia tosta, cheek.
tosto³ sm. toast.
totale agg. e sm. total: in —, in all.
totalità sf. 1. totality 2. (numero complessivo) mass.
totalitario agg. totalitarian.
totalitarismo sm. totalitarianism.
totalizzare vt. 1. to totalize 2. (sport) to score.
totalizzatore sm. totalizer.
tovaglia sf. (table-)cloth.
tovagliolo sm. napkin.
tozzo¹ agg. squat, stocky.
tozzo² sm. piece: un — di pane, a crust of bread.
tra prep. 1. (fra due persone, cose, gruppi) between 2. (fra più di due) among 3. (nel mezzo di) amid 4. (di tempo) (with)in.
traballare vi. 1. to·stagger 2. (di vettura) to jolt || entrare, uscire traballando, to stagger in, out.
trabeazione sf. trabeation.
trabìccolo sm. ramshackle vehicle.
traboccare vi. to overflow.
trabocchetto sm. trap.
tracagnotto agg. squat.
tracannare vt. to gulp down.
traccia sf. 1. trace 2. (segno) mark 3. (orme) footsteps (pl.) 4. (schema) outline.
tracciare vt. to trace (out): — a grandi linee, to outline.
tracciato sm. layout.
tracciatore sm. tracer.
trachea sf. windpipe.
tracheale agg. tracheal.
tracheite sf. tracheitis.
tracolla sf. baldric: portare qc. a —, to carry sthg. across one's back.
tracollare vi. 1. to lose (v. irr.) one's balance 2. (cadere) to collapse.
tracollo sm. collapse: portare al —, to bring (v. irr.) to ruin.
tracoma sm. trachoma.
tracotante agg. haughty.
tracotanza sf. haughtiness.

tradimento sm. 1. treason 2. (infedeltà) betrayal || a — (agg.), treacherous, (avv.) treacherously.
tradire vt. 1. to betray 2. (di coniuge) to be unfaithful (to).
traditore agg. treacherous. ♦ **traditore** sm. traitor.
tradizionale agg. traditional.
tradizionalismo sm. traditionalism.
tradizionalista s. traditionalist.
tradizione sf. tradition: per —, traditionally.
tradotta sf. troop-train.
traducìbile agg. translatable.
tradurre vt. to translate: — in atto, to carry out; — in carcere, to take (v. irr.) to prison.
traduttore sm. translator.
traduzione sf. translation.
traente s. (comm.) drawer.
trafelato agg. breathless.
trafficante sm. dealer.
trafficare vi. 1. to deal (v. irr.) 2. (affaccendarsi) to bustle about.
tràffico sm. 1. traffic 2. (comm.) trade.
trafìggere vt. to pierce (through).
trafila sf. 1. procedure 2. (mecc.) draw-plate.
trafilare vt. to draw (v. irr.).
trafiletto sm. paragraph.
traforare vt. 1. to perforate 2. (ricamare) to embroider with open-work.
traforato agg. 1. perforated 2. (ricamato a traforo) open-work (attr.).
traforatrice sf. fret-sawing machine.
traforo sm. 1. perforation 2. (galleria) tunnel 3. (falegnameria) fretwork 4. (ricamo) open-work.
trafugamento sm. stealing.
trafugare vt. to steal (v. irr.).
tragedia sf. tragedy.
tragediògrafo sm. tragedian.
traghettare vt. to ferry.
traghetto sm. ferry-boat.
tragicità sf. tragicalness.
tràgico agg. tragical. ♦ **tràgico** sm. tragedian.
tragicòmico agg. tragicomic(al).
tragicommedia sf. tragicomedy.
tragitto sm. 1. way 2. (viaggio) journey.
traguardo sm. goal.
traiettoria sf. trajectory.
trainare vt. to haul.
tràino sm. 1. haulage 2. (carro) truck.

tralasciare *vt.* to leave (*v. irr.*) out, to omit.

tralcio *sm.* shoot.

traliccio *sm.* **1.** (*tela*) ticking **2.** (*per costruzioni*) trellis || — *di ferro*, iron framework.

tralice (*nella loc. avv.*) in —, askance.

tralignamento *sm.* degeneration.

tralignare *vi.* to degenerate.

tralùcere *vi.* to shine (*v. irr.*) (through).

tram *sm.* tramcar.

trama *sf.* **1.** weft **2.** (*fig.*) plot.

tramaglio *sm.* trammel.

tramandare *vt.* to hand down.

tramare *vt.* **1.** to weave (*v. irr.*) **2.** (*fig.*) to plot.

trambusto *sm.* bustle.

tramenare *vt.* e *vi.* to move about.

tramenìo *sm.* bustle.

tramestare *vt.* to rummage.

tramestìo *sm.* **1.** rummaging **2.** (*trepestio*) stamping.

tramezzare *vt.* to partition.

tramezzino *sm.* sandwich.

tramezzo *sm.* partition.

tràmite *sm.* path: — *qu.*, through so.

tramoggia *sf.* hopper.

tramontana *sf.* **1.** north **2.** (*vento*) north wind || *perder la* —, to lose (*v. irr.*) one's head.

tramontare *vi.* **1.** to set (*v. irr.*) **2.** (*svanire*) to fade.

tramonto *sm.* **1.** setting **2.** (*del sole*) sunset **3.** (*declino*) decline.

tramortimento *sm.* swoon.

tramortire *vt.* to stun.

trampoliere *sm.* wader.

trampolino *sm.* spring-board.

tràmpolo *sm.* stilt.

tramutare *vt.* to change. ♦ **tramutarsi** *vr.* to change.

trancia *sf.* **1.** shears (*pl.*) **2.** (*fetta*) slice.

tranciare *vt.* to shear.

tranello *sm.* snare.

trangugiare *vt.* to swallow.

tranne *prep.* but.

tranquillante *agg.* tranquillizing. ♦ **tranquillante** *sm.* tranquillizer.

tranquillità *sf.* calmness.

tranquillizzare *vt.* **1.** to calm **2.** (*rassicurare*) to reassure.

tranquillo *agg.* calm: *star* —, to keep (*v. irr.*) quiet; *sta' —!*, do not worry!

transalpino *agg.* transalpine.

transatlàntico *agg.* transatlantic. ♦ **transatlàntico** *sm.* liner.

transazione *sf.* **1.** transaction **2.** (*accomodamento*) arrangement **3.** (*compromesso*) compromise.

transcontinentale *agg.* transcontinental.

transetto *sm.* transept.

trànsfuga *s.* runaway.

transìgere *vt.* e *vi.* to compromise.

transistore *sm.* transistor.

transitàbile *agg.* practicable.

transitabilità *sf.* practicability.

transitare *vi.* to pass through.

transitivo *agg.* e *sm.* transitive.

trànsito *sm.* transit.

transitorio *agg.* transitory.

transizione *sf.* transition.

transoceànico *agg.* transoceanic.

transustanziazione *sf.* transubstantiation.

tranvìa *sf.* tramway.

tranviario *agg.* tramcar (*attr.*).

tranviere *sm.* **1.** tram-driver **2.** (*biglittario*) tram-conductor.

trapanare *vt.* **1.** to drill **2.** (*med.*) to trepan.

trapanazione *sf.* **1.** drilling **2.** (*med.*) trepanation.

tràpano *sm.* **1.** drill **2.** (*med.*) trepan.

trapassare *vt.* to pierce through. ♦ **trapassare** *vi.* (*morire*) to die.

trapasso *sm.* **1.** (*morte*) death **2.** (*giur.; comm.*) transfer.

trapelare *vi.* to leak out.

trapezio *sm.* **1.** trapezium **2.** (*da ginnastica*) trapeze.

trapiantare *vt.* to transplant. ♦ **trapiantarsi** *vr.* (*stabilirsi*) to settle.

trapianto *sm.* **1.** transplantation **2.** (*tessuto trapiantato*) graft.

trappista *sm.* Trappist.

tràppola *sf.* trap: *prendere in* —, to trap.

trapunta *sf.* quilt.

trapuntare *vt.* **1.** to quilt **2.** (*ricamare*) to embroider.

trapunto *agg.* **1.** quilted **2.** (*ricamato*) embroidered || — *di stelle*, starry.

trarre *vt.* **1.** to draw (*v. irr.*) **2.** (*ottenere*) to get (*v. irr.*). ♦ **trarsi** *vr.* to draw.

trasalire *vi.* to startle: *far* —, to startle.

trasandato *agg.* shabby.

trasbordare vt. 1. to transfer 2. (traghettare) to ferry.

trasbordo sm. 1. transfer 2. (traghetto) ferrying across.

trascendentale agg. transcendental.

trascendentalismo sm. transcendentalism.

trascendente agg. transcendent.

trascendenza sf. transcendence.

trascéndere vt. to transcend. ♦ **trascéndere** vi. to let (v. irr.) oneself go.

trascinare vt. 1. to drag 2. (affascinare) to fascinate.

trascórrere vt. (il tempo) to spend (v. irr.). ♦ **trascórrere** vi. 1. (di tempo) to pass 2. (lasciar correre) to pass over.

trascorso agg. past. ♦ **trascorso** sm. (errore) slip.

trascrittore sm. transcriber.

trascrìvere vt. 1. to transcribe 2. (giur.) to register.

trascrizione sf. 1. transcription 2. (giur.) registration 3. (trapasso) transfer.

trascuràbile agg. negligible.

trascurare vt. to neglect. ♦ **trascurarsi** vr. not to care of oneself.

trascuratezza sf. 1. negligence 2. (sciatteria) slovenliness.

trascurato agg. 1. (negligente) careless 2. (sciatto) sloven.

trasecolare vi. to be amazed.

trasecolato agg. amazed.

trasferìbile agg. transferable.

trasferimento sm. transfer.

trasferire vt. to transfer. ♦ **trasferirsi** vr. to (re)move.

trasferta sf. 1. transfer 2. (indennità) travelling allowance || in —, on transfer; partita in — (sport), out match.

trasfigurare vt. to transfigure. ♦ **trasfigurarsi** vr. to become (v. irr.) transfigured.

trasfigurazione sf. transfiguration.

trasfòndere vt. 1. to transfuse 2. (fig.) to instil.

trasformàbile agg. convertible.

trasformare vt. to change, to turn. ♦ **trasformarsi** vr. to change.

trasformatore sm. transformer.

trasformazione sf. transformation.

trasformismo sm. transformism.

trasfusione sf. transfusion.

trasgredire vt. e vi. to infringe.

trasgressione sf. infringement.

trasgressore sm. infringer.

traslazione sf. 1. transfer 2. (fis.; eccl.) translation.

traslocare vt. e vi. to move.

trasloco sm. removal.

traslùcido agg. translucent.

trasméttere vt. to transmit.

trasmettitore sm. transmitter.

trasmigrare vi. to transmigrate.

trasmigrazione sf. transmigration.

trasmissìbile agg. transmissible.

trasmissione sf. 1. transmission 2. (giur.) transfer 3. (mecc.) drive || — radio, broadcast; — televisiva, telecast.

trasmittente agg. transmitting.

trasognato agg. dreamy.

trasparente agg. transparent.

trasparenza sf. transparence.

trasparire vi. 1. to shine (v. irr.) through 2. (esser trasparente) to be transparent || lasciar —, to betray.

traspirare vi. to transpire.

traspirazione sf. transpiration.

trasporre vt. to transpose.

trasportàbile agg. transportable.

trasportare vt. 1. to carry 2. (fig.) to carry away. ♦ **trasportarsi** vr. to go (v. irr.).

trasportatore sm. conveyer: — a nastro, belt-conveyer.

trasporto sm. transport: nave da —, cargo; spese di —, carriage.

trasposizione sf. transposition.

trastullare vt. to amuse. ♦ **trastullarsi** vr. 1. (giocare) to play 2. (scherzare) to trifle.

trastullo sm. 1. plaything 2. (divertimento) amusement.

trasudamento sm. sweating.

trasudare vt. e vi. to sweat.

trasversale agg. transversal, cross (attr.). ♦ **trasversale** sf. 1. transversal 2. (strada) cross-road.

trasvolare vt. to fly (v. irr.) across.

trasvolata sf. flight (across).

tratta sf. 1. (traffico) trade 2. (comm.) draft || — a vista, sight draft; spiccare una — su qu., to draw (v. irr.) upon so.

trattàbile agg. 1. tractable 2. (di argomento) that can be dealt with.

trattabilità sf. tractability.

trattamento sm. 1. treatment 2. (paga) salary.

trattare vt. 1. to treat 2. (maneggiare) to handle 3. (commerciare) to deal (v. irr.) (in) 4. (negoziare) to negotiate 5. (un argomento) to deal (with). ♦ **trattarsi** v. imp. to be a question of, to be involved.

trattativa *sf.* negotiation.

trattato *sm.* 1. (*patto*) treaty 2. (*libro*) treatise.

trattazione *sf.* treatment.

tratteggiare *vt.* 1. to outline 2. (*ombreggiare*) to hatch.

tratteggio *sm.* 1. (*abbozzo*) outline 2. (*ombreggiatura*) hatching.

trattenere *vt.* 1. to keep (*v. irr.*) 2. (*dedurre*) to deduct 3. (*frenare*) to refrain || — *il respiro*, to hold (*v. irr.*) one's breath. ◆ **trattenersi** *vr.* (*fermarsi*) to stay || *non posso trattenermi dal fare*, I cannot help doing.

trattenimento *sm.* (*festa*) party.

trattenuta *sf.* deduction.

trattino *sm.* 1. dash 2. (*di unione*) hyphen.

tratto *sm.* 1. (*tirata*) pull 2. (*colpo*) stroke 3. (*linea*) line 4. (*brano*) passage 5. (*estensione di spazio*) way 6. (*lineamento*) feature 7. (*comportamento*) manners (*pl.*) || *d'un* —, suddenly; *di* — *in* —, now and then.

trattore[1] *sm.* (*mecc.*) tractor.

trattore[2] *sm.* (*oste*) inn-keeper.

trattorìa *sf.* inn.

tratturo *sm.* cattle-track.

tràuma *sm.* trauma.

traumàtico *agg.* traumatic.

traumatologìa *sf.* traumatology.

travagliare *vt.* V. *tormentare.*

travaglio *sm.* 1. (*fatica*) labour 2. (*cruccio*) trouble.

travasare *vt.* to pour off.

travaso *sm.* 1. pouring off 2. (*med.*) effusion.

travatura *sf.* truss.

trave *sf.* beam.

travéggole *sf. pl. avere le* —, to mistake (*v. irr.*) one thing for another.

traversa *sf.* 1. (*sbarra*) cross-bar 2. (*via*) side-road.

traversata *sf.* crossing.

traversìa *sf.* misfortune.

traversina *sf.* sleeper.

traverso *agg.* 1. transverse, cross (*attr.*) 2. (*obliquo*) slanting || *di* —, askance; *andare per* — (*fig.*), to go (*v. irr.*) wrong with.

travestimento *sm.* disguise.

travestire *vt.* to disguise (as).

traviamento *sm.* corruption.

traviare *vt.* to mislead (*v. irr.*). ◆ **traviarsi** *vr.* to go (*v. irr.*) astray.

travisamento *sm.* alteration.

travisare *vt.* to alter.

travolgente *agg.* sweeping.

travòlgere *vt.* 1. to sweep (*v. irr.*) away 2. (*investire*) to run (*v. irr.*) over.

trazione *sf.* traction.

tre *agg.* three.

trebbiare *vt.* to thrash.

trebbiatrice *sf.* thrasher.

trebbiatura *sf.* thrashing.

treccia *sf.* plait: *farsi le trecce*, to plait one's hair.

trecento *agg.* three hundred || *il* — (*secolo*), the fourteenth century.

tredicenne *agg.* thirteen years old, thirteen-year-old (*attr.*).

tredicèsimo *agg.* thirteenth.

trédici *agg.* thirteen.

tregua *sf.* 1. truce 2. (*riposo*) rest.

tremante *agg.* 1. trembling 2. (*di freddo*) shivering.

tremare *vi.* 1. to tremble 2. (*di freddo*) to shiver.

tremendo *agg.* awful.

trementina *sf.* turpentine.

tremila *agg.* three thousand.

trèmito *sm.* 1. tremble 2. (*di freddo*) shiver.

tremolante *agg.* 1. trembling 2. (*di luce*) flickering 3. (*di stelle*) twinkling.

tremolare *vi.* 1. to tremble 2. (*di luce*) to flicker 3. (*di stelle*) to twinkle.

tremolìo *sm.* 1. tremble 2. (*di luce*) flickering 3. (*di stelle*) twinkle.

tremore *sm.* V. *trèmito.*

treno *sm.* 1. train: — *accelerato*, slow train; — *direttissimo*, fast train; — *rapido*, express train 2. (*tenore*) way of living, routine.

trenta *agg.* thirty.

trentenne *agg.* thirty years old, thirty-year-old (*attr.*).

trentennio *sm.* period of thirty years.

trentèsimo *agg.* thirtieth.

trentina *sf.* about thirty.

trepestìo *sm.* stamping.

trepidante *agg.* anxious.

trepidare *vi.* to be anxious.

trepidazione *sf.* anxiety.

treppiede *sm.* tripod.

tresca *sf.* intrigue.

tréspolo *sm.* trestle.

trìade *sf.* triad.

triangolare *agg.* triangular.

triangolazione *sf.* triangulation.

triàngolo *sm.* triangle.
tribale *agg.* tribal.
tribolare *vi.* 1. to toil 2. (*soffrire*) to suffer. ♦ **tribolare** *vt.* to vex.
tribolazione *sf.* suffering.
tribordo *sm.* starboard.
tribù *sf.* tribe.
tribuna *sf.* 1. (*per oratori*) platform 2. (*sport*) stand.
tribunale *sm.* court.
tribuno *sm.* tribune.
tributare *vt.* to bestow.
tributario *agg.* 1. tributary 2. (*fiscale*) fiscal. ♦ **tributario** *sm.* tributary.
tributo *sm.* tribute.
tricheco *sm.* walrus.
triciclo *sm.* tricycle.
triclinio *sm.* triclinium (*pl.* -nia).
tricolore *agg.* e *sm.* tricolour.
tricorno *sm.* tricorn.
tricromìa *sf.* 1. trichromatism 2. (*pezzo singolo*) trichromatic print.
tridente *sm.* 1. trident 2. (*per fieno*) hayfork.
tridimensionale *agg.* tridimensional.
triedro *sm.* trihedron.
triennale *agg.* e *sm.* triennial.
triennio *sm.* period of three years.
trifase *agg.* three-phase (*attr.*).
trifoglio *sm.* clover.
trigèmino *agg.* e *sm.* trigeminal: parto —, birth of triplets.
trigèsimo *agg.* thirtieth: *nel — della sua morte*, on the thirtieth day after his death.
trigonometrìa *sf.* trigonometry.
trilione *sm.* 1. (*in sistema italiano, francese e americano* = 1000⁴) billion; (*amer.*) trillion 2. (*in sistema inglese e tedesco* = 1000⁶) trillion; (*amer.*) quintillion.
trillare *vi.* 1. to trill 2. (*squillare*) to ring (*v. irr.*).
trillo *sm.* 1. trill 2. (*di sveglia, telefono*) ring.
trilogìa *sf.* trilogy.
trimestrale *agg.* quarterly.
trimestre *sm.* 1. quarter 2. (*scol.*) term 3. (*paga trimestrale*) quarterage.
trimotore *agg.* three-engined aeroplane.
trina *sf.*. lace.
trincare *vt.* to gulp. ♦ **trincare** *vi.* to drink (*v. irr.*).
trincea *sf.* trench.
trincerare *vt.* to entrench.

trincetto *sm.* shoemaker's knife (*pl.* knives).
trinchetto *sm.* albero di —, foremast; *vela di* —, foresail.
trinciante *agg.* sharp. ♦ **trinciante** *sm.* carver.
trinciare *vt.* 1. to cut (*v. irr.*) (up) 2. (*carne*) to carve || — *giudizi*, to judge rashly.
trinciato *sm.* cut-tobacco.
trinità *sf.* trinity.
trinomio *sm.* trinomial.
trionfante *agg.* triumphant.
trionfare *vt.* to triumph.
trionfatore *sm.* triumpher.
trionfo *sm.* triumph.
tripartito *agg.* tripartite.
tripartizione *sf.* tripartition.
triplicare *vt.* to treble.
triplo *agg.* triple. ♦ **triplo** *sm.* 1. triple 2. (*tre volte tanto*) three times as much.
trippa *sf.* (*cuc.*) tripe.
tripudiare *vi.* to exult.
tripudio *sm.* exultation.
trisàvolo *sm.* great-great-grand-father.
trisillabo *agg.* trisyllabic. ♦ **trisìllabo** *sm.* trisyllable.
triste *agg.* sad.
tristezza *sf.* 1. sadness 2. (*dolore*) grief.
tristo *agg.* wicked.
tritacarne *sm.* mincer.
tritare *vt.* to mince.
tritatutto *sm.* mincer.
trito *agg.* (*fig.*) trite.
tritolo *sm.* trinitrotoluene.
trìttico *sm.* triptych.
trittongo *sm.* triphthong.
tritume *sm.* crumbs (*pl.*).
triturare *vt.* to triturate.
triumvirato *sm.* triumvirate.
triùmviro *sm.* triumvir.
trivalente *agg.* trivalent.
trivella *sf.* 1. (*min.*) drill 2. (*falegnameria*) auger.
trivellare *vt.* to drill.
trivellazione *sf.* drilling: *torre di* —, derrick.
triviale *agg.* coarse.
trivialità *sf.* 1. coarseness 2. (*detto triviale*) coarse expression.
trofeo *sm.* trophy.
troglodita *sm.* troglodyte.
troglodìtico *agg.* troglodytic(al).
trògolo *sm.* trough.
troia *sf.* (*zool.*) sow.
tromba *sf.* 1. trumpet 2. (*di scale*)

well ‖ — *d'aria,* tornado; — *d'acqua,* water-spout.

trombettiere *sm.* trumpeter.

trombone *sm.* 1. (*mus.*) trombone 2. (*schioppo*) blunderbuss ‖ *suonatore di* —, trombonist.

trombosi *sf.* thrombosis.

troncare *vt.* 1. to cut (*v. irr.*) off 2. (*fig.*) to break (*v. irr.*) off.

tronco¹ *agg.* 1. cut off 2. (*fig.*) broken.

tronco² *sm.* 1. trunk 2. (*d'albero abbattuto*) log 3. (*geom.*) frustum ‖ — *ferroviario,* railway section; *licenziare in* —, to sack on the spot.

troncone *sm.* stump.

troneggiare *vi.* to dominate (sthg.).

tronfio *agg.* 1. conceited 2. (*di stile*) bombastic.

trono *sm.* throne.

tropicale *agg.* tropical.

tròpico *sm.* tropic.

tropismo *sm.* tropism.

troposfera *sf.* troposphere.

troppo *avv.* 1. (*con agg. e avv.*) too 2. (*con v.*) too much 3. (*di tempo*) too long. ♦ **troppo** *agg. e pron.* too much (*pl.* too many): *anche* —, only too; *essere di* —, to be unwelcome.

trota *sf.* trout (*pl. invariato*).

trottare *vi.* to trot: *far* — *qu.* (*fig.*) to make (*v. irr.*) so. run.

trottata *sf.* trot.

trottatore *sm.* trotter.

trotterellare *vi.* 1. to trot along 2. (*di bambini*) to toddle.

trotto *sm.* trot: *mettere un cavallo al* —, to trot a horse.

tròttola *sf.* top.

trovare *vt.* 1. to find (*v. irr.*) 2. (*far visita*) to see (*v. irr.*) 3. (*pensare*) to think (*v. irr.*). ♦ **trovarsi** *vr.* 1. (*essere*) to be 2. (*sentirsi*) to feel (*v. irr.*).

trovata *sf.* trick.

trovatello *sm.* foundling.

trovatore *sm.* troubadour.

truccare *vi.* 1. to make (*v. irr.*) up 2. (*sport*) to fix.

truccatore *sm.* maker-up.

truccatura *sf.* make-up.

trucco *sm.* 1. trick 2. (*cosmetici*) make-up 3. (*inganno*) deceit.

truce *agg.* grim.

trucidare *vt.* to slay (*v. irr.*).

trùciolo *sm.* shaving.

truculento *agg.* truculent.

truffa *sf.* cheat.

truffaldino *agg.* cheating.

truffare *vt.* to cheat.

truffatore *sm.* cheat.

truismo *sm.* truism.

truppa *sf.* troop.

tu *pron.* you.

tua *agg. e pron.* V. *tuo.*

tuba *sf.* 1. tuba 2. (*cappello*) top-hat.

tubare *vi.* to coo.

tubatura *sf.* piping.

tubercolare *agg.* tubercular.

tubercolina *sf.* tuberculin.

tubercolosario *sm.* sanatorium.

tubercolosi *sf.* tuberculosis: — *polmonare,* consumption.

tubercoloso *agg.* tuberculous. ♦ **tubercoloso** *sm.* consumptive.

tùbero *sm.* tuber.

tuberosa *sf.* tuberose.

tubino *sm.* bowler-hat.

tubo *sm.* 1. tube 2. (*di conduttura*) pipe 3. (*anat.*) canal.

tubolare *agg.* tubular.

tue *agg. e pron.* V. *tuo.*

tuffare *vt.* to plunge, to dip. ♦ **tuffarsi** *vr.* to plunge, to dive.

tuffatore *sm.* diver.

tuffo *sm.* plunge, dive.

tufo *sm.* tuff.

tugurio *sm.* hovel.

tulipano *sm.* tulip.

tumefare *vt.* to swell (*v. irr.*). ♦ **tumefarsi** *vr.* to swell.

tumefatto *agg.* swollen.

tumefazione *sf.* swelling.

tùmido *agg.* tumid: *labbra tumide,* thick lips.

tumore *sm.* tumour.

tumulare *vt.* to bury.

tumulazione *sf.* burial.

tùmulo *sm.* 1. tumulus (*pl.* -li) 2. (*tomba*) grave.

tumulto *sm.* tumult.

tumultuante *agg.* riotous.

tumultuare *vi.* to riot.

tumultuoso *agg.* tumultuous.

tundra *sf.* tundra.

tungsteno *sm.* tungsten.

tùnica *sf.* tunic.

tunnel *sm.* tunnel.

tuo *agg.* your. ♦ **tuo** *pron.* yours.

tuoi *agg. e pron.* V. *tuo* ‖ *i* —, your family.

tuonare *vi.* to thunder.

tuono *sm.* thunder.

tuorlo *sm.* yolk.

turàcciolo *sm.* 1. stopper 2. (*di su-*

ghero) cork || *mettere il — a una bottiglia*, to cork a bottle.

turare vt. to stop, to fill up. ◆ **turarsi** vr. 1. to stop 2. (*chiudersi*) to shut oneself up.

turba[1] sf. crowd.

turba[2] sf. (*med.*) trouble.

turbamento sm. 1. perturbation 2. (*eccitazione*) excitement 3. (*sconvolgimento*) upsetting.

turbante sm. turban.

turbare vt. 1. to upset (*v. irr.*) 2. (*agitare intorbidando*) to muddy. ◆ **turbarsi** vr. to get (*v. irr.*) upset.

turbina sf. turbine.

turbinare vi. to whirl.

turbine sm. 1. whirl 2. (*uragano*) hurricane.

turbinio sm. whirling.

turbinoso agg. 1. whirling 2. (*tumultuoso*) tumultuous.

turbolento agg. boisterous.

turbolenza sf. boisterousness.

turbomotore sm. turbojet engine.

turbonave sf. turboship.

turboreattore sm. (*aer.*) turbojet.

turcasso sm. quiver.

turchese sm. turquoise.

turchino agg. deep blue.

turco agg. Turkish. ◆ **turco** sm. Turk.

turgidezza sf. turgidity.

turgido agg. turgid.

turibolo sm. censer.

turismo sm. tourism.

turista s. tourist.

turistico agg. tourist (*attr.*).

turlupinare vt. to swindle.

turlupinatura sf. swindle.

turno sm. 1. turn 2. (*servizio*) duty || *di —*, on duty; *a —*, on turn.

turpe agg. filthy.

turpiloquio sm. coarse language.

turpitudine sf. baseness.

turrito agg. turreted.

tuta s. overalls (*pl.*): *— spaziale*, spacesuit.

tutela sf. 1. guardianship 2. (*protezione*) protection.

tutelare vt. to guard.

tutelare agg. tutelary.

tutore sm. guardian.

tuttavia cong. yet.

tutto agg. all, whole (*pl.* all); (*ogni*) every || *tutt'e due*, both; *tutt'al più*, at the most; *tutt'altro che*, anything but; *tutt'altro!*, on the contrary! ◆ **tutto** pron. all,

everything (*pl.* all); (*ognuno*) everybody. ◆ **tutto** s.s. whole: *del —*, quite.

tuttofare agg. *cameriera —*, maid-of-all-work.

tuttora avv. still.

U

ubbia sf. whim.

ubbidiente agg. obedient.

ubbidienza sf. obedience.

ubbidire vi. to obey (so., sthg.).

ubicare vt. to locate.

ubicato agg. situated.

ubicazione sf. location.

ubiquità sf. ubiquity.

ubriacare vt. to make (*v. irr.*) drunk. ◆ **ubriacarsi** vr. to get (*v. irr.*) drunk.

ubriacatura sf. intoxication.

ubriachezza sf. drunkenness.

ubriaco agg. drunk. ◆ **ubriaco** sm. drunken man (*pl.* men).

ubriacone sm. drunkard.

uccellagione sf. feathered game.

uccellare vi. to fowl.

uccelliera sf. aviary.

uccello sm. bird.

uccidere vt. 1. to kill 2. (*assassinare*) to murder 3. (*con pugnale*) to stab to death 4. (*con arma da fuoco*) to shoot (*v. irr.*) ◆ **uccidersi** vr. 1. to get (*v. irr.*) killed 2. (*suicidarsi*) to commit suicide, to kill oneself.

uccisione sf. killing.

uccisore sm. killer.

udibile agg. audible.

udienza sf. hearing.

udire vt. to hear (*v. irr.*).

uditivo agg. auditory.

udito sm. hearing.

uditore sm. 1. listener 2. (*nella scuola*) auditor.

uditorio sm. audience.

ufficiale agg. official. ◆ **ufficiale** sm. 1. officer 2. (*governativo, postale*) official.

ufficialità sf. official character.

ufficialmente avv. officially.

ufficiare vi. to officiate.

ufficio sm. office: *capo —*, head clerk; *d'—*, officially; *— informazioni*, information bureau.

ufficiosamente *avv.* unofficially.
ufficioso *agg.* unofficial.
ufo (*nella loc. avv.*) **a —**, without paying.
ugello *sm.* nozzle.
uggia *sf.* boredom: *questo libro mi è venuto in —*, I have grown tired of this book.
uggiolare *vi.* to whine.
uggioso *agg.* dull.
ùgola *sf.* 1. uvula 2. (*voce*) voice.
uguaglianza *sf.* equality.
uguagliare *vt.* 1. to be equal (to) 2. (*rendere uguale*) to make (*v. irr.*) equal.
uguale *agg.* 1. equal 2. (*simile*) like, alike (*pred.*) 3. (*stesso*) same.
ugualitario *agg.* equalitarian.
ugualmente *avv.* 1. equally 2. (*lo stesso*) all the same.
ùlcera *sf.* ulcer.
ulcerare *vt.* to ulcerate. ♦ **ulcerarsi** *vr.* to ulcerate.
ulcerato *agg.* ulcerated.
ulcerazione *sf.* ulceration.
ulceroso *agg.* ulcerous.
ulteriore *agg.* further.
ulteriormente *avv.* further on.
ultimamente *avv.* 1. recently 2. (*da ultimo*) finally.
ultimare *vt.* to finish.
ultimazione *sf.* conclusion.
ùltimo *agg.* 1. last 2. (*il più recente*) latest 3. (*estremo*) utmost.
ultramicroscòpico *agg.* ultramicroscopic(al).
ultramoderno *agg.* ultramodern.
ultrasensìbile *agg.* ultrasensitive.
ultrasònico *agg.* ultrasonic.
ultrasuono *sm.* ultrasound.
ultraterreno *agg.* supernatural.
ultravioletto *agg.* ultraviolet.
ululare *vi.* 1. to howl 2. (*di sirena*) to hoot.
ululato *sm.* 1. howl 2. (*di sirena*) hoot.
umanésimo *sm.* Humanism.
umanista *sm.* humanist.
umanìstico *agg.* humanistic.
umanità *sf.* humanity.
umanitario *agg.* humanitarian.
umanitarismo *sm.* humanitarianism.
umanizzare *vt.* to humanize.
umano *agg.* 1. human 2. (*comprensivo*) humane.
umerale *agg.* humeral.
umettare *vt.* to moisten.
umidità *sf.* humidity, dampness.

ùmido *agg.* damp.
ùmile *agg.* humble.
umiliante *agg.* humiliating.
umiliare *vt.* to humble.
umiliazione *sf.* humiliation.
umiltà *sf.* 1. humbleness 2. (*virtù dell'umile*) humility.
umore *sm.* humour: *essere di buon —*, to be in a good humour.
umorismo *sm.* humour.
umorista *s.* humorist.
umorìstico *agg.* humorous.
una *art. e agg.* V. *uno.*
unànime *agg.* unanimous.
unanimità *sf.* unanimity: *all'—*, unanimously.
uncinare *vt.* to hook.
uncinato *agg.* hooked || *croce uncinata,* swastika.
uncinetto *sm.* crochet-hook: *lavorare all'—*, to crochet.
uncino *sm.* hook.
undicèsimo *agg.* eleventh.
ùndici *agg.* eleven.
ùngere *vt.* to grease.
unghia *sf.* 1. nail 2. (*di equino*) hoof 3. (*fig.*) clutch.
unghiata *sf.* scratch: *dare un'—*, to scratch.
unguento *sm.* ointment.
ungulato *agg.* hoofed.
unicamente *avv.* only.
unicellulare *agg.* unicellular.
unicità *sf.* uniqueness.
ùnico *agg.* 1. only 2. (*senza uguale*) unique.
unificare *vt.* 1. to unify 2. (*uniformare*) to standardize.
unificatore *agg.* unifying. ♦ **unificatore** *sm.* unifier.
unificazione *sf.* 1. unification 2. (*uniformazione*) standardization.
uniformare *vt.* 1. to conform 2. (*rendere conforme*) to standardize. ♦ **uniformarsi** *vr.* to conform (to).
uniforme[1] *agg.* uniform.
uniforme[2] *sf.* uniform.
uniformemente *avv.* uniformly.
uniformità *sf.* uniformity.
unigènito *agg.* only child.
unilaterale *agg.* unilateral.
unilateralmente *avv.* unilaterally.
uninominale *agg.* uninominal.
unione *sf.* union.
unionista *sm.* unionist.
unipolare *agg.* unipolar.
unire *vt.* to unite, to join. ♦ **unirsi** *vr.* to unite, to join.

unìsono *sm.* unison.

unità *sf.* 1. unity 2. *(fis.; mat.; mil.)* unit.

unitamente *avv.* unitedly: **— a**, together with.

unitario *agg.* unitary.

unito *agg.* 1. united 2. *(accluso)* enclosed.

universale *agg.* universal.

universalità *sf.* universality.

universalizzare *vt.* to universalize.

università *sf.* university.

universitario *agg.* university *(attr.).* ♦ **universitario** *sm.* university student.

universo *agg.* whole. ♦ **universo** *sm.* universe.

unìvoco *agg.* univocal.

uno, un, una *art.* a, an *(davanti a vocale e h muta).* ♦ **uno, un, una** *agg.* one. ♦ **uno, una** *pron.* 1. one 2. *(un tale)* a man; *(una tale)* a woman || **— a —**, one by one; *l' — e l'altro*, both; *l' — o l'altro*, either; *né l'— né l'altro*, neither; *l' — l'altro*, each other; *un po' per —*, a part each; *costano 5 sterline l'—*, they cost 5 pounds each.

unto *agg.* greasy.

untume *sm.* grease.

untuosamente *avv.* *(fig.)* unctuously.

untuosità *sf.* 1. greasiness 2. *(fig.)* unctuousness.

untuoso *agg.* 1. greasy 2. *(fig.)* unctuous.

unzione *sf.* unction.

uomo *sm.* man *(pl.* men): *un — da nulla*, a nobody.

uopo *sm.* *esser d'—*, to be necessary; *all'—*, if necessary.

uovo *sm.* egg: *rosso d'—*, yolk; *cercare il pelo nell'—*, to split *(v. irr.)* hairs.

uragano *sm.* hurricane.

uranìfero *agg.* uranic.

uranio *sm.* uranium.

uranite *sf.* uranite.

uranografìa *sf.* uranography.

urbanésimo *sm.* urbanization.

urbanista *s.* town planner.

urbanìstica *sf.* town-planning.

urbanìstico *agg.* town-planning.

urbanità *sf.* urbanity.

urbanizzare *vt.* to urbanize.

urbanizzazione *sf.* urbanization.

urbano *agg.* 1. urban 2. *(cortese)* urbane.

ùrea *sf.* urea.

uremìa *sf.* uraemia.

urèmico *agg.* uraemic.

uretra *sf.* urethra.

urgente *agg.* urgent.

urgentemente *avv.* urgently.

urgenza *sf.* urgency.

ùrgere *vt.* to urge. ♦ **ùrgere** *vi.* to be urgent.

uricemìa *sf.* uricaemia.

ùrico *agg.* uric.

urina *sf.* V. *orina*.

urinare *vi.* V. *orinare*.

urlare *vt.* e *vi.* 1. to shout, to scream 2. *(di vento, animale; per il dolore)* to howl.

urlatore *agg.* shouting. ♦ **urlatore** *sm.* shouter.

urlo *sm.* 1. shout 2. *(di vento, animale; per il dolore)* howl.

urna *sf.* 1. urn 2. *(per i voti)* ballot-box || *andare alle urne*, to go *(v. irr.)* to the polls.

urogallo *sm.* grouse.

urologìa *sf.* urology.

uròlogo *sm.* urologist.

urtante *agg.* irritating.

urtare *vt.* 1. to knock 2. *(infastidire)* to irritate 3. *(offendere)* to hurt *(v. irr.).* ♦ **urtarsi** *vr.* to get *(v. irr.)* cross. ♦ **urtarsi** *vr. rec.* to collide.

urticante *agg.* urticating.

urticaria *sf.* nettle rash.

urto *sm.* 1. push 2. *(scontro, contrasto)* collision || *essere in —*, to be at variance.

urtone *sm.* shove.

usanza *sf.* 1. custom 2. *(abitudine personale)* habit.

usare *vt.* to use: *— una cortesia*, to do *(v. irr.)* a favour. ♦ **usare** *vi.* 1. to be accustomed; *(solo al passato)* to use 2. *(essere di moda)* to be fashionable.

usato *agg.* 1. used 2. *(in uso)* in use 3. *(abituale)* usual 4. *(non nuovo)* second-hand.

uscente *agg.* 1. retiring 2. *(con espressioni di tempo)* closing.

usciere *sm.* 1. usher 2. *(ufficiale giudiziario)* bailiff.

uscio *sm.* door: *abitare — a — (con)*, to live next door (to).

uscire *vi.* 1. to go *(v. irr.)* out, to come *(v. irr.)* out 2. *(sboccare)* to lead *(v. irr.)* 3. *(uscire di strada)* to go off || *uscirne bene, male*, to come off well, badly.

uscita *sf.* **1.** way out **2.** (*atto di uscire*) going out, coming out **3.** (*spese*) expense ‖ *strada senza* —, blind-alley.

usignolo *sm.* nightingale.

uso[1] *agg.* accustomed.

uso[2] *sm.* use: *d'* —, usual; *all'* — *di*, after the fashion of.

ùssaro *sm.* hussar.

ustionare *vt.* to scald.

ustionato *agg.* scalded.

ustione *sf.* scald.

usuale *agg.* usual.

usufruire *vi.* to benefit (by).

usufrutto *sm.* usufruct.

usufruttuario *agg.* e *sm.* usufructuary.

usura *sf.* **1.** usury **2.** (*logorio*) wear and tear.

usuraio *sm.* usurer.

usurpare *vt.* to usurp.

usurpatore *agg.* usurping. ♦ **usurpatore** *sm.* usurper.

usurpazione *sf.* usurpation.

utènsile *sm.* utensil.

utente *s.* user.

uterino *agg.* uterine.

ùtero *sm.* uterus (*pl.* -ri).

ùtile *agg.* useful. ♦ **ùtile** *sm.* profit.

utilità *sf.* **1.** usefulness **2.** (*vantaggio*) profit ‖ *non ne vedo l'* —, I do not see the use of it.

utilitaria *sf.* (*auto*) utility car.

utilitario *agg.* e *sm.* utilitarian.

utilitarismo *sm.* utilitarianism.

utilitarìstico *agg.* V. *utilitario.*

utilizzàbile *agg.* utilizable.

utilizzare *vt.* to utilize.

utilizzatore *agg.* utilizing. ♦ **utilizzatore** *sm.* utilizer.

utilizzazione *sf.* utilization.

utopìa *sf.* utopia.

utopista *s.* utopian.

utopìstico *agg.* utopian.

uva *sf.* grapes (*pl.*): — *passa*, raisin.

uxoricida *sm.* uxoricide.

uxoricidio *sm.* uxoricide.

V

vacante *agg.* vacant.

vacanza *sf.* **1.** holiday **2.** (*posto vacante*) vacancy.

vacca *sf.* cow.

vaccaro *sm.* cowherd.

vaccherìa *sf.* cowhouse.

vacchetta *sf.* cowhide.

vaccinàbile *agg.* that can be vaccinated.

vaccinare *vt.* to vaccinate.

vaccinazione *sf.* vaccination.

vaccino *sm.* vaccine.

vaccinògeno *agg.* vaccinogenous.

vaccinoterapìa *sf.* vaccinotherapy.

vacillamento *sm.* **1.** unsteadiness **2.** (*di luce*) flickering **3.** (*fig.*) wavering.

vacillante *agg.* **1.** unsteady **2.** (*di luce*) flickering **3.** (*fig.*) uncertain.

vacillare *vi.* **1.** to be unsteady **2.** (*di luce*) to flicker **3.** (*fig.*) to waver.

vacuità *sf.* vacuity.

vacuo *agg.* vacuous.

vademecum *sm.* vade-mecum.

vagabondaggio *sm.* vagrancy.

vagabondare *vi.* to wander.

vagabondo *agg.* vagabond. ♦ **vagabondo** *sm.* vagrant.

vagamente *avv.* vaguely.

vagante *agg.* wandering.

vagare *vi.* to wander.

vagheggiamento *sm.* longing (for).

vagheggiare *vt.* to long (for).

vagheggino *sm.* gallant.

vaghezza *sf.* **1.** charm **2.** (*indeterminatezza*) vagueness.

vagina *sf.* vagina (*pl.* -nae).

vagire *vi.* to wail.

vagito *sm.* wail.

vaglia[1] *sf.* (*valore*) worth.

vaglia[2] *sm.* money order: — *postale*, postal order.

vagliare *vt.* to sieve **2.** (*fig.*) to weigh.

vagliatura *sf.* screening.

vaglio *sm.* **1.** sieve **2.** (*fig.*) sifting.

vago *agg.* **1.** vague **2.** (*leggiadro*) pretty.

vagoncino *sm.* wag(g)on.

vagolare *vi.* to rove.

vagone *sm.* carriage, coach.

vaio[1] *agg.* dark grey.

vaio[2] *sm.* vair.

vaiolo *sm.* smallpox.

valanga *sf.* avalanche.

valchirìa *sf.* Walkyrie.

valente *agg.* **1.** skilful **2.** (*valoroso*) brave.

valentemente *avv.* **1.** skilfully **2.** (*valorosamente*) bravely.

valentìa *sf.* **1.** skill **2.** (*valore*) worth.

valentuomo *sm.* worthy man.

valenza *sf.* valence.

valere *vi.* 1. to be worth: — *la pena,* to be worth while; *far —̀ i propri diritti,* to assert one's rights; *farsi —,* to make (*v. irr.*) oneself appreciated 2. (*contare*) to count 3. (*servire*) to be of use 4. (*essere valido*) to be valid. ♦ **valersi** *vr.* to avail oneself (of).

valeriana *sf.* valerian.

valévole *agg.* valid.

valicàbile *agg.* that can be crossed.

valicare *vt.* to cross.

vàlico *sm.* pass.

validamente *avv.* validly.

validità *sf.* validity.

vàlido *agg.* 1. valid 2. (*fondato*) well-grounded 3. (*forte*) strong.

valigerìa *sf.* leatherware shop.

valigia *sf.* suit-case; *fare le valigie,* to pack up.

vallata *sf.* valley.

valle *sf.* valley.

valletto *sm.* valet.

vallo *sm.* rampart.

vallone *agg. e sm.* Walloon.

valore *sm.* 1. value 2. (*coraggio*) bravery.

valorizzare *vt.* 1. to turn to account 2. (*accentuare*) to emphasize.

valorizzazione *sf.* 1. turning to account 2. (*comm.*) valorization.

valorosamente *avv.* bravely.

valoroso *agg.* brave.

valsente *sm.* commercial value.

valuta *sf.* 1. value 2. (*moneta*) currency: — *estera,* foreign currency.

valutàbile *agg.* valuable.

valutare *vt.* 1. to value 2. (*considerare*) to consider.

valutazione *sf.* 1. evaluation 2. (*considerazione*) careful consideration.

valva *sf.* valve.

vàlvola *sf.* 1. valve 2. (*elettr.*) fuse 3. (*radio*) valve, tube.

valvolare *agg.* valvular.

valzer *sm.* waltz: *ballare il —,* to waltz.

vampa *sf.* 1. blaze 2. (*al viso*) flush.

vampata *sf.* 1. blaze 2. (*folata*) blast 3. (*al viso*) flush.

vampeggiante *agg.* blazing.

vampeggiare *vi.* to blaze.

vampiro *sm.* vampire.

vanagloria *sf.* vainglory.

vanagloriarsi *vr.* to boast.

vanaglorioso *agg.* boastful.

vanamente *avv.* vainly.

vandàlico *agg.* vandalic.

vandalismo *sm.* vandalism.

vàndalo *agg. e sm.* vandal.

vaneggiamento *sm.* raving.

vaneggiare *vi.* to rave.

vanesio *agg.* foppish. ♦ **vanesio** *sm.* fop.

vanga *sf.* spade.

vangare *vt.* to spade.

vangata *sf.* blow with a spade.

vangatore *sm.* spademan.

vangatura *sf.* spading.

vangelo *sm.* Gospel.

vaniglia *sf.* vanilla.

vanigliato *agg.* vanilla-flavoured.

vaniloquio *sm.* empty talk.

vanità *sf.* vanity.

vanitoso *agg.* conceited.

vano¹ *agg.* vain.

vano² *sm.* space, room.

vantaggio *sm.* 1. advantage 2. (*sport*) lead.

vantaggiosamente *avv.* advantageously.

vantaggioso *agg.* advantageous.

vantare *vt.* 1. to boast (of) 2. (*lodare*) to praise 3. (*millantare*) to brag. ♦ **vantarsi** *vr.* to boast (of).

vanterìa *sf.* boast.

vanto *sm.* boast.

vànvera (*nella loc. avv.*) *a —,* at random.

vapore *sm.* 1. steam 2. (*mar.*) steamer.

vaporetto *sm.* steamboat.

vaporiera *sf.* steam-engine.

vaporizzare *vt.* to vaporize.

vaporizzatore *sm.* vaporizer.

vaporizzazione *sf.* vaporization.

vaporosità *sf.* 1. haziness 2. (*di abito*) gauziness.

vaporoso *agg.* 1. hazy 2. (*di abito*) gauzy.

varare *vt.* to launch (*anche fig.*).

varcare *vt.* to cross, to pass.

varco *sm.* passage, opening: *aprirsi un — fra la folla,* to force one's way through the crowd.

variàbile *agg.* variable, unsteady.

variabilità *sf.* variability, unsteadiness.

variante *sf.* variant.

variare *vt.* 1. to vary 2. (*di mercato*) to fluctuate.

variato *agg.* V. *vario.*

variazione *sf.* variation, change.

varice *sf.* varix (*pl.* varices).

varicella *sf.* chicken-pox.

varicoso *agg.* varicose.

variegato *agg.* variegated.

varietà *sf.* variety.

vario *agg.* 1. varied 2. (*differente*) various 3. (*parecchi*) several.

variopinto *agg.* many-coloured.

varo *sm.* launch.

vasaio *sm.* potter.

vasca *sf.* basin: — *da bagno*, bath (tub).

vascello *sm.* vessel.

vascolare *agg.* vascular.

vaselina *sf.* vaseline.

vasellame *sm.* 1. (*di terracotta*) earthenware 2. (*di porcellana*) china 3. (*d'argento, d'oro*) silver, gold plate.

vaso *sm.* 1. vase 2. (*rotondo*) pot 3. (*recipiente; anat.*) vessel.

vasocostrittore *agg.* e *sm.* vasoconstrictor.

vasodilatatore *agg.* e *sm.* vasodilator.

vasomotore *agg.* vasomotor.

vasomotorio *agg.* vasomotor.

vassallaggio *sm.* 1. (*stor.*) vassallage 2. subjection.

vassallo *agg.* e *sm.* 1. (*stor.*) vassal 2. subject.

vassoio *sm.* tray.

vastità *sf.* 1. vastness 2. (*estensione*) expanse.

vasto *agg.* wide, large.

vate *sm.* 1. prophet 2. (*poeta*) poet.

Vaticano *agg.* Vatican.

vaticinare *vt.* to prophesy.

vaticinio *sm.* prophecy.

vattelappesca *inter.* who knows!

ve *pron:* you: — *lo scrissi*, I wrote it to you. ♦ **ve** *avv.* there: — *ne sono due*, there are two.

ve' *inter.* look, see.

vecchiaia *sf.* old age.

vecchiezza *sf.* great age.

vecchio *agg.* 1. old 2. (*antico*) ancient 3. (*stantio*) stale. ♦ **vecchio** *sm.* old man.

veccia *sf.* vetch.

vece *sf.* stead, place.

vedere *vt.* to see (*v. irr.*): — *la luce* (*nascere*), to be born; *far* —, to show (*v. irr.*); *farsi* —, to show oneself; *non* — *l'ora di*, to look forward to (*con gerundio*). ♦ **vedersi** *vr.* 1. to see oneself 2. (*vedersela*) to deal (*v. irr.*) with.

vedetta *sf.* 1. (*sentinella*) watchman (*pl.* -men) 2. (*posto di osservazione*) look-out.

védova *sf.* widow.

vedovanza *sf.* widowhood.

vedovile *agg.* 1. (*di vedova*) of a widow 2. (*di vedovo*) of a widower.

védovo *sm.* widower.

vedretta *sf.* small steep glacier.

veduta *sf.* 1. sight, view 2. (*opinione*) view, idea.

veemente *agg.* vehement.

veemenza *sf.* vehemence.

vegetale *agg.* e *sm.* vegetable.

vegetare *vi.* to vegetate.

vegetariano *agg.* e *sm.* vegetarian.

vegetativo *agg.* vegetative.

vegetazione *sf.* vegetation.

vègeto *agg.* 1. (*di pianta*) thriving 2. (*di persona*) vigorous, strong ‖ *vivo e* —, hale and hearty

veggente *sm.* seer.

veglia *sf.* 1. waking 2. (*il vegliare*) watch.

vegliardo *sm.* old man.

vegliare *vi.* 1. to be awake 2. (*far la veglia*) to watch.

veglione *sm.* masked ball.

veìcolo *sm.* vehicle.

vela *sf.* sail.

velame *sm.* 1. veil 2. (*mar.*) sails (*pl.*).

velare *vt.* to veil.

velario *sm.* curtain.

velatura *sf.* sails (*pl.*).

veleggiare *vi.* to sail.

veleno *sm.* poison.

velenoso *agg.* poisonous, venomous.

veletta *sf.* 1. (*mar.*) topsail 2. (*di cappello*) veil.

veliero *sm.* sailing-ship.

velina *sf.* tissue-paper.

velismo *sm.* sailing.

velìvolo *sm.* aeroplane.

velleità *sf.* foolish ambition, fancy.

vellicare *vt.* to tickle.

vello *sm.* fleece.

vellutato *agg.* velvety: *pelle vellutata*, downy skin.

velluto *sm.* velvet.

velo *sm.* veil.

veloce *agg.* fast, quick, swift.

velocìpede *sm.* velocipede.

velocità *sf.* speed, velocity: *a tutta* —, at full speed; *limite di* —, speed limit; *cambio di* — (*auto*), gearbox; *indicatore di* —, speedometer.

velòdromo *sm.* cycle-racing track.

veltro *sm.* greyhound.
vena *sf.* vein.
venale *agg.* venal.
venalità *sf.* venality.
venare *vt.* 1. to vein 2. (*di legno*) to grain.
venato *agg.* 1. veined 2. (*di legno*) grained.
venatorio *agg.* venatorial.
venatura *sf.* 1. vein 2. (*di legno*) grain.
vendemmia *sf.* vintage.
vendemmiare *vi.* to gather grapes.
vendemmiatore *sm.* vintager.
véndere *vt.* to sell (*v. irr.*): — *a buon mercato*, to sell cheaply; — *a credito*, to sell on credit; — *all'ingrosso*, *al minuto*, to sell wholesale, by retail; — *a rate*, to sell by instalments.
vendetta *sf.* revenge.
vendibile *agg.* salable.
vendicare *vt.* to revenge.
vendicativo *agg.* revengeful.
vendicatore *sm.* revenger.
véndita *sf.* sale: — *all'asta*, auction.
venditore *sm.* seller.
venduto *agg.* 1. sold 2. (*fig.*) corrupted.
veneficio *sm.* poisoning.
venèfico *agg.* poisonous.
veneràbile *agg.* venerable.
venerando *agg.* venerable.
venerare *vt.* to worship.
venerazione *sf.* worship.
venerdì *sm.* Friday: — *Santo*, Good Friday.
vènere *sf.* 1. Venus 2. (*fig.*) beauty.
venèreo *agg.* venereal.
veneziana *sf.* Venetian-blind.
veniale *agg.* venial.
venire *vi.* 1. to come (*v. irr.*): — *al sodo*, to come to the point; — *in mente*, to come into one's head; — *meno*, to faint; — *alla luce*, to come to light 2. (*riuscire*) to turn out 3. (*derivare*) to derive.
venoso *agg.* venous.
ventaglio *sm.* fan.
ventata *sf.* gust of wind.
ventèsimo *agg.* twentieth.
venti *agg.* twenty.
ventilare *vt.* to ventilate.
ventilato *agg.* airy, windy.
ventilatore *sm.* fan.
ventilazione *sf.* ventilation.
ventina *sf.* score: *essere sulla* — (*di anni*), to be about twenty.

vento *sm.* wind.
ventosa *sf.* sucker.
ventosità *sf.* flatulence.
ventoso *agg.* windy.
ventrale *agg.* ventral.
ventre *sm.* 1. abdomen 2. (*fam.*) tummy.
ventricolo *sm.* ventricle.
ventriera *sf.* body-belt.
ventriglio *sm.* gizzard.
ventriloquio *sm.* ventriloquism.
ventriloquo *sm.* ventriloquist.
ventura *sf.* chance, fortune.
venturo *agg.* next, coming.
venustà *sf.* beauty.
venusto *agg.* beautiful.
venuta *sf.* coming, arrival.
vera *sf.* wedding-ring.
verace *agg.* true.
veracità *sf.* veracity, truth.
veramente *avv.* really, truly, indeed.
veranda *sf.* verandah.
verbale *agg.* verbal. ♦ **verbale** *sm.* minutes (*pl.*).
verbalizzare *vt.* to record.
verbo *sm.* 1. verb 2. (*parola*) word.
verbosità *sf.* verbosity.
verboso *agg.* verbose.
verdastro *agg.* greenish.
verde *agg.* green.
verdeggiante *agg.* verdant.
verdeggiare *vi.* to be verdant.
verdemare *sm.* sea-green.
verderame *sm.* verdigris.
verdetto *sm.* verdict.
verdògnolo *agg.* greenish.
verdura *sf.* vegetables (*pl.*).
verecondia *sf.* modesty.
verecondo *agg.* modest.
verga *sf.* 1. twig 2. (*bacchetta*) rod.
vergare *vt.* (*scrivere*) to write (*v. irr.*).
vergata *sf.* blow with a rod.
vergato *agg.* 1. striped 2. (*scritto*) written ‖ *carta vergata*, laid paper.
verginale *agg.* virginal.
vérgine *agg.* e *sf.* virgin.
vergìneo *agg.* virginal.
verginità *sf.* virginity.
vergogna *sf.* shame: *aver* —, to be ashamed.
vergognarsi *vr.* to be, to feel (*v. irr.*) shamed.
vergognosamente *avv.* shamefully.
vergognoso *agg.* 1. shameful 2. (*timido*) shy.
veridicamente *avv.* veraciously.
veridicità *sf.* veracity.

verìdico *agg.* veracious.
verìfica *sf.* verification.
verificàbile *agg.* verifiable.
verificare *vt.* to verify, to check.
verificatore *sm.* verifier.
verificazione *sf.* V. *verifica.*
verismo *sm.* realism.
verista *sm.* realist.
verìstico *agg.* realistic.
verità *sf.* truth: *dire la* —, to tell (*v. irr.*) the truth.
veritiero *agg.* truthful.
verme *sm.* worm.
vermìfugo *agg.* e *sm.* vermifuge.
vermiglio *agg.* bright red.
verminoso *agg.* verminous.
vernàcolo *agg.* vernacular.
vernice *sf.* 1. paint 2. (*apparenza*) varnish.
verniciare *vt.* to paint, to varnish.
verniciatura *sf.* painting, varnishing.
vero *agg.* true, real.
verosimigliante *agg.* likely.
verosimiglianza *sf.* likelihood.
verosimile *agg.* likely, probable.
verricello *sm.* windlass.
verro *sm.* boar.
verruca *sf.* wart.
versamento *sm.* 1. pouring 2. (*comm.*) payment, deposit.
versante *sm.* side, slope.
versare *vt.* 1. to pour 2. (*rovesciare*) to spill (*v. irr.*) 3. (*comm.*) to pay (*v. irr.*).
versàtile *agg.* versatile.
versatilità *sf.* versatility.
versato *agg.* 1. poured out 2. (*esperto*) versed.
verseggiare *vt.* to versify.
verseggiatore *sm.* versifier.
versetto *sm.* 1. short line 2. (*della Bibbia*) verse.
versificare *vt.* to versify.
versificatore *sm.* versifier.
versificazione *sf.* versification.
versione *sf.* version, translation.
verso[1] *sm.* 1. verse, line 2. (*suono*) sound 3. (*direzione*) way.
verso[2] *prep.* 1. towards, to 2. (*contro*) against 3. (*circa*) about.
vèrtebra *sf.* vertebra (*pl.* -rae).
vertebrale *agg.* vertebral.
vertebrato *agg.* e *sm.* vertebrate.
vertenza *sf.* 1. dispute 2. (*giur.*) litigation.
vèrtere *vi.* to be about, to concern.
verticale *agg.* vertical.
verticalità *sf.* verticality.

vèrtice *sm.* 1. vertex (*pl.* vertices) 2. (*fig.*) height, top.
vertìgine *sf.* dizziness (*solo sing.*).
vertiginoso *agg.* dizzy.
verza *sf.* cabbage.
vescica *sf.* bladder.
vescovado *sm.* bishop's residence.
vescovile *agg.* episcopal.
véscovo *sm.* bishop.
vespa *sf.* wasp.
vespaio *sm.* 1. wasps' nest 2. (*fig.*) hornets' nest.
vespro *sm.* 1. evening 2. (*relig.*) evensong.
vessare *vt.* to vex.
vessatorio *agg.* vexatious.
vessazione *sf.* vexation.
vessillo *sm.* flag.
vestaglia *sf.* dressing-gown.
vestale *sf.* vestal.
veste *sf.* 1. dress 2. (*eccl.*) vestment 3. (*qualità*) capacity.
vestiario *sm.* clothes (*pl.*).
vestìbolo *sm.* hall.
vestigio *sm.* vestige.
vestimento *sm.* V. *veste.*
vestire *vt.* 1. to dress 2. (*fig.*) to clothe 3. (*indossare*) to wear (*v. irr.*). ◆ **vestirsi** *vr.* to dress oneself.
vestito *sm.* 1. (*da uomo*) suit 2. (*da donna*) frock, dress.
vestizione *sf.* 1. (*eccl.*) ceremony of taking the habit 2. (*di monaca*) ceremony of taking the veil.
veterano *sm.* veteran.
veterinaria *sf.* veterinary science.
veterinario *sm.* veterinary.
veto *sm.* veto.
vetraio *sm.* glazier.
vetrame *sm.* glassware.
vetrata *sf.* glass partition: — *a colori,* stained glass window.
vetrato *agg.* glazed: *carta vetrata,* glass-paper.
vetrerìa *sf.* glass-work.
vetrificàbile *agg.* vitrifiable.
vetrificare *vt.* to vitrify.
vetrificazione *sf.* vitrification.
vetrina *sf.* shop-window.
vetrioleggiare *vt.* to vitriolize.
vetriolo *sm.* vitriol.
vetro *sm.* 1. glass 2. (*di finestra*) window-pane.
vetrocromìa *sf.* glass-painting.
vetroso *agg.* glassy.
vetta *sf.* top, summit.
vettore *sm.* vector.
vettoriale *agg.* vectorial.

vettovagliamento *sm.* provisi-n-ing.

vettovagliare *vt.* to provision.

vettura *sf.* **1.** coach **2.** (*automobile*) car || — *di piazza*, taxi-cab.

vetturino *sm.* cabman (*pl.* -men).

vetustà *sf.* antiquity.

vetusto *agg.* ancient.

vezzeggiare *vt.* to fondle.

vezzeggiativo *sm.* petname.

vezzo *sm.* **1.** habit **2.** (*collana*) necklace.

vezzosamente *avv.* charmingly.

vezzoso *agg.* charming.

vi[1] *pron.* you, to you.

vi[2] *avv.* **1.** (*qui*) here **2.** (*là*) there.

via[1] *sf.* **1.** street **2.** (*strada di comunicazione*) road **3.** (*cammino*) way (*anche fig.*) **4.** (*linea di condotta*) course. ◆ **via** *sm. dare il* —, to give (*v. irr.*) the starting.

via[2] *avv.* away: *andar* —, to go (*v. irr.*) away.

viabilità *sf.* state of a road.

viadotto *sm.* viaduct.

viaggiante *agg.* travelling.

viaggiare *vi.* to travel: — *in treno, automobile, aereo*, to travel by train, by car, by air.

viaggiatore *sm.* traveller: — *di commercio*, commercial traveller.

viaggio *sm.* **1.** journey, trip **2.** (*per mare*) voyage **3.** (*in aereo*) flight.

viale *sm.* avenue; (*di giardino*) alley.

viandante *sm.* wayfarer.

viatico *sm.* viaticum (*pl.* -ca).

viavai *sm.* coming-and-going.

vibrante *agg.* vibrating (with).

vibrare *vi.* **1.** to vibrate **2.** (*colpi*) to strike (*v. irr.*).

vibràtile *agg.* vibratile.

vibrato *agg.* energetic.

vibratore *sm.* vibrator.

vibrazione *sf.* vibration.

vicariato *sm.* vicariate.

vicario *sm.* vicar.

vicecònsole *sm.* vice-consul.

vicedirettore *sm.* assistant-director.

vicegovernatore *sm.* vice-governor.

vicenda *sf.* vicissitude **2.** (*evento*) event **3.** (*successione*) succession.

vicendévole *agg.* mutual.

vicendevolmente *avv.* mutually.

vicepresidente *sm.* vice-president.

viceré *sm.* viceroy.

vicesegretario *sm.* vice-secretary.

viceversa *avv.* vice versa. ◆ **vice-versa** *cong.* whereas.

vicinale *sf.* local road.

vicinanza *sf.* **1.** vicinity: *in* — *di*, close to **2.** (*adiacenze*) neighbourhood: *nelle vicinanze*, in the neighbourhood.

vicinato *sm.* **1.** neighbourhood **2.** (*i vicini*) neighbours (*pl.*).

vicino[1] *agg.* near, close. ◆ **vicino** *sm.* neighbour.

vicino[2] *avv.* near, near by. ◆ **vicino** *prep.* near, close to.

vicissitùdine *sf.* vicissitude.

vìcolo *sm.* lane, alley.

vìdeo *sm.* video.

vidimare *vt.* **1.** (*firmare*) to sign **2.** (*autenticare*) to authenticate.

vidimazione *sf.* **1.** (*firma*) signature **2.** (*autenticazione*) authentication.

vietare *vt.* to forbid (*v. irr.*).

vietato *agg.* forbidden: — *fumare*, no smoking; — *entrare*, no admittance.

vieto *agg.* antiquated.

vigente *agg.* in force.

vigere *vi.* to be in force.

vigilante *agg.* watchful.

vigilanza *sf.* watch.

vigilare *vt.* to watch over.

vigilato *agg.* watched.

vigile *agg.* watchful. ◆ **vìgile** *sm.* policeman (*pl.* -men).

vigilia *sf.* **1.** eve **2.** (*relig.*) fast.

vigliaccamente *avv.* in a cowardly way.

vigliaccherìa *sf.* **1.** cowardice **2.** (*azione vigliacca*) cowardly action.

vigliacco *agg.* cowardly.

vigna *sf.* vineyard.

vigneto *sm.* vineyard.

vignetta *sf.* cartoon.

vigore *sm.* vigour: *in* —, in force.

vigoroso *agg.* vigorous.

vile *agg.* **1.** cowardly **2.** (*meschino*) mean **3.** (*basso*) low.

vilipèndere *vt.* to despise.

vilipendio *sm.* contempt.

villa *sf.* villa.

villaggio *sm.* village.

villanìa *sf.* **1.** rudeness **2.** (*azione villana*) rude action.

villano *agg.* rude. ◆ **villano** *sm.* peasant, countryman (*pl.* -men).

villeggiante *s.* holiday-maker.

villeggiatura *sf.* holiday: *luogo di* —, (holiday) resort.

villino *sm.* cottage.

villoso *agg.* hairy.

viltà *sf.* **1.** cowardice **2.** (*azione vile*) cowardly action.

vilucchio *sm.* bearbind.

viluppo *sm.* tangle.

vìmine *sm.* withe: *paniere di vimini*, wicker basket.

vinaccia *sf.* dregs of pressed grapes (*pl.*).

vinaio *sm.* wine-merchant.

vinario *agg.* wine (*attr.*).

vincente *agg.* winning. ♦ **vincente** *sm.* winner.

vìncere *vt.* 1. to win (*v. irr.*) 2. (*battere*) to beat (*v. irr.*) 3. (*sopraffare*) to overcome (*v. irr.*) 4. (*superare*) to outdo (*v. irr.*).

vincìbile *agg.* conquerable.

vìncita *sf.* 1. win 2. (*denaro vinto*) winnings (*pl.*).

vincitore *sm.* winning. ♦ **vincitore** *sm.* winner.

vinco *sm.* withe.

vincolare *vt.* 1. to bind (*v. irr.*) 2. (*comm.*) to lock up.

vincolato *agg.* 1. bound 2. (*comm.*) locked up.

vincolo *sm.* tie, bond.

vinello *sm.* light wine.

vinìcolo *agg.* wine (*attr.*).

vinificazione *sf.* wine-making.

vino *sm.* wine.

vinto *agg.* 1. that has been won 2. (*sconfitto*) beaten 3. (*sopraffatto*) overcome || *darsi —*, to give (*v. irr.*) in. ♦ **vinto** *sm.* 1. (*al giuoco o in qualsiasi contesa*) loser 2. (*in battaglia*) vanquished man.

viola¹ *sf.* 1. violet: *— del pensiero*, pansy. ♦ **viola** *agg.* e *sm.* violet.

viola² *sf.* (*mus.*) viola.

violàcee *sf. pl.* violaceae.

violàceo *agg.* violet.

violare *vt.* to violate.

violatore *sm.* violator.

violazione *sf.* violation: *— di domicilio*, house-breaking.

violentare *vt.* 1. to violate, to rape 2. (*fig.*) to do (*v. irr.*) violence to.

violento *agg.* violent.

violenza *sf.* violence, rape.

violetto *agg.* violet.

violinista *s.* violin-player.

violino *sm.* violin.

violoncellista *s.* violoncellist.

violoncello *sm.* violoncello.

viòttola *sf.* path, lane.

viòttolo *sm.* path, lane.

vìpera *sf.* 1. adder 2. (*fig.*) viper.

viperino *agg.* viperous.

viraggio *sm.* (*foto*) toning.

virago *sf.* virago.

virare *vt.* e *vi.* 1. to veer: *— di bordo*, to veer round 2. (*fig.*) to turn about.

virata *sf.* veer.

virginale *agg.* virginal.

virginia *sm.* Virginia.

vìrgola *sf.* 1. (*gramm.*) comma 2. (*mat.*) point.

virgolette *sf. pl.* inverted commas: *tra —*, in inverted commas.

virgulto *sm.* shoot.

virile *agg.* manly.

virilità *sf.* 1. manliness 2. (*età virile*) manhood.

virilmente *avv.* manfully.

virologia *sf.* virology.

virosi *sf.* virosis (*pl.* -ses).

virtù *sf.* virtue.

virtuale *agg.* virtual.

virtualità *sf.* virtuality.

virtuosismo *sm.* virtuosity.

virtuoso *agg.* virtuous.

virulento *agg.* virulent.

virulenza *sf.* virulence.

virus *sm.* virus.

viscerale *agg.* visceral.

vìscere *sm.* 1. vital organ 2. (*f. pl.*) le *viscere*, viscera.

vischio *sm.* 1. mistletoe 2. (*pania*) bird-lime.

vischiosità *sf.* stickiness.

vischioso *agg.* sticky.

viscidità *sf.* viscidity.

vìscido *agg.* 1. sticky 2. (*scivoloso*) slippery.

visciola *sf.* wild cherry.

visconte *sm.* viscount.

viscontessa *sf.* viscountess.

viscosità *sf.* viscosity.

viscoso *agg.* viscous.

visibile *agg.* visible, clear.

visibilio *sm.* great number: *andare in —*, to go (*v. irr.*) into raptures.

visibilità *sf.* visibility.

visiera *sf.* 1. (*di elmo*) visor 2. (*di berretto*) peak.

visionario *agg.* e *sm.* visionary.

visione *sf.* vision: *prendere — di*, to look over; *prima — (cine)*, first screening.

vìsita *sf.* 1. visit, call: *fare una —*, to pay (*v. irr.*) a visit 2. (*persona che visita*) visitor 3. (*med.*) examination.

visitare *vt.* to visit.

visitatore *sm.* visitor.

visivo *agg.* visual.

viso *sm.* face: *— a —*, face to face.

visone *sm.* mink.

vispo *agg.* lively, brisk.

vista *sf.* **1.** sight **2.** (*occhi*) eyes (*pl.*).

vistare *vt.* to visa.

visto[1] *sm.* visa.

visto[2] *agg.* seen || — *che,* since as.

vistoso *agg.* **1.** showy **2.** (*fig.*) considerable.

visuale *agg.* visual. ♦ **visuale** *sf.* sight.

vita[1] *sf.* **1.** life (*pl.* lives): *a* —, for life; *in* —, during one's life **2.** (*necessario per vivere*) living: *costo della* —, cost of living.

vita[2] *sf.* (*anat.*) waist.

vitaiolo *sm.* bon viveur.

vitalba *sf.* clematis.

vitale *agg.* vital.

vitalità *sf.* vitality.

vitalizio *agg.* for life. ♦ **vitalizio** *sm.* annuity.

vitamina *sf.* vitamin.

vitaminico *agg.* vitaminic.

vite[1] *sf.* vine.

vite[2] *sf.* (*mecc.*) screw.

vitello *sm.* calf (*pl.* calves).

viticcio *sm.* vine-tendril.

viticolo *agg.* viticultural.

viticoltore *sm.* viticulturist.

viticoltura *sf.* grape-growing.

vitreo *agg.* vitreous.

vittima *sf.* victim.

vittimismo *sm.* victimization.

vitto *sm.* **1.** food **2.** (*pasti in pensione o albergo*) board: — *e alloggio,* board and lodging.

vittoria *sf.* victory.

vittorioso *agg.* victorious.

vituperare *vt.* to vituperate.

vituperio *sm.* insult.

viuzza *sf.* lane.

viva *inter.* hurrah!

vivacchiare *vi.* to live poorly.

vivace *agg.* **1.** lively, sprightly **2.** (*pronto, sveglio*) quick **3.** (*di colori*) bright.

vivacemente *avv.* **1.** lively **2.** (*prontamente*) quickly **3.** (*vivamente*) brightly.

vivacità *sf.* **1.** liveliness **2.** (*di colori*) brightness.

vivaio *sm.* **1.** (*di pesci*) fish-pond **2.** (*di piante*) nursery.

vivamente *avv.* deeply, keenly.

vivanda *sf.* food.

vivandiere *sm.* sutler.

vivente *agg.* alive (*pred.*), living. ♦ **vivente** *sm.* living being.

vivere *vt.* e *vi.* to live: *cessare di*

—, to die; *insegnare a* — *a qu.,* to teach (*v. irr.*) so. good manners; — *alle spalle di qu.,* to sponge on so.

viveri *sm. pl.* victuals.

vivido *agg.* vivid.

vivificare *vt.* to enliven.

vivificatore *agg.* vivifying. ♦ **vivificatore** *sm.* vivifier.

viviparo *agg.* e *sm.* viviparous.

vivisezione *sf.* vivisection.

vivo *agg.* **1.** living, alive (*pred.*) || *a viva forza,* by main force; *argento* —, quicksilver; *calce viva,* quicklime; *farsi* —, to turn up **2.** (*vivace*) lively **3.** (*profondo, acuto*) deep, sharp **4.** (*vivido*) vivid **5.** (*di colori*) bright.

viziare *vt.* **1.** to spoil (*v. irr.*) **2.** (*guastare*) to vitiate.

viziato *agg.* **1.** spoilt **2.** (*guasto*) vitiated.

vizio *sm.* **1.** vice **2.** (*cattiva abitudine*) bad habit.

vizioso *agg.* vicious. ♦ **vizioso** *sm.* vicious man.

vocabolario *sm.* **1.** vocabulary **2.** (*dizionario*) dictionary.

vocabolo *sm.* word.

vocale[1] *agg.* vocal.

vocale[2] *sf.* vowel.

vocalizzare *vt.* e *vi.* to vocalize.

vocalizzo *sm.* vocalization.

vocativo *agg.* e *sm.* vocative.

vocazione *sf.* vocation, bent.

voce *sf.* **1.** voice: *a* — *alta, bassa,* in a loud, low voice; *parlare sotto* —, to whisper **2.** (*diceria*) rumour **3.** (*articolo di elenco*) item.

vociare *vi.* to shout.

vociferare *vi.* **1.** to shout **2.** (*spargere una voce*) to rumour.

vocìo *sm.* shouting.

voga[1] *sf.* (*mar.*) rowing.

voga[2] *sf.* **1.** (*moda*) fashion **2.** (*energia*) energy.

vogare *vi.* (*mar.*) to row.

vogata *sf.* row.

vogatore *sm.* rower.

voglia *sf.* **1.** wish: *aver* —, to feel (*v. irr.*) like **2.** (*volontà*) will.

voglioso *agg.* desirous, willing.

voi *pron.* you: — *stessi,* you yourselves.

volano *sm.* battledore and shuttlecock.

volante[1] *agg.* flying: *cervo* —, kite; *foglio* —, loose sheet. ♦ **volante** *sf.* (*di polizia*) flying squad.

volante² *sm.* steering-wheel.

volantino *sm.* leaflet.

volare *vi.* to fly (*v. irr.*): *far —*, to blow (*v. irr.*).

volata *sf.* 1. flight 2. (*corsa*) rush 3. (*sport*) final sprint.

volàtile¹ *agg.* (*chim.*) volatile.

volàtile² *sm.* bird.

volatilizzare *vt.* to volatilize. ◆ **volatilizzarsi** *vr.* to volatilize.

volente *agg. — o nolente*, willy-nilly.

volenterosamente *avv.* willingly.

volenteroso *agg.* V. *volontoroso*.

volentieri *avv.* willingly.

volere¹ *vt.* 1. (*forte volontà*) (*pres. indicativo e congiuntivo*) will; (*passato indicativo e congiuntivo, condizionale*) would 2. (*desiderio*) to want, to wish: *voglio che egli venga*, I want him to come 3. (*gradire*) to like (*costr. pers.*): *vorrei, avrei voluto*, I should like, I should have liked 4. (*desiderio intenso*) to wish: *vorrei essere ricco!*, I wish I were rich! 5. (*aver bisogno di*) to need, to require 6. (*con espressioni di tempo*) to take (*v. irr.*): *ci vogliono due ore per andare alla stazione*, it takes two hours to go to the station 7. (*cercare*) to ask for: *c'è qualcuno che ti cerca*, there is somebody asking for you 8. (*essere disposti*) to be willing || *che tu voglia o no*, whether you like it or not; *vuoi ... vuoi* (*sia ... sia*), both ... and; *Dio lo voglia, Dio non voglia!*, God grant it, God forbid!

volere² *sm.* will, wish.

volgare *agg.* vulgar, common.

volgarità *sf.* vulgarity.

volgarizzare *vt.* to divulge.

volgarizzatore *sm.* popularizer.

volgarizzazione *sf.* popularization.

volgarmente *avv.* vulgarly, commonly.

vòlgere *vt.* to turn.

vòlgere *sm.* course.

volgo *sm.* common people.

voliera *sf.* aviary.

volitivo *agg.* 1. strong-willed 2. (*gramm.*) volitive.

volo *sm.* flight: *prendere il —*, to run (*v. irr.*) away; *capire qc. al —*, to grasp sthg. immediately.

volontà *sf.* will: *di sua spontanea —*, of his own free-will.

volontariamente *avv.* voluntarily.

volontario *agg.* voluntary. ◆ **volontario** *sm.* volunteer.

volontarismo *sm.* voluntarism.

volonteroso *agg.* willing.

volontieri *avv.* V. *volentieri*.

volpe *sf.* fox.

volpino *agg.* foxy: *cane —*, Pomeranian.

volpone *sm.* old fox.

volta¹ *sf.* 1. time: *una —*, once; *due, tre volte*, twice, three times; *ancora una —*, once again; *una — e mezzo*, half as much; *una — o l'altra*, sooner or later; *rare volte*, seldom; *una — tanto*, once in a while; *c'era una —*, once upon a time there was 2. (*turno*) turn: *a mia —*, in my turn.

volta² *sf.* 1. (*curva*) bend 2. (*arch.*) vault.

voltafaccia *sm.* volte-face.

voltaggio *sm.* voltage.

voltàmetro *sm.* voltameter.

voltare *vt.* to turn.

voltastòmaco *sm.* sickness.

voltata *sf.* bend, turning, curve.

volteggiare *vi.* 1. to whirl 2. (*svolazzare*) to fly (*v. irr.*) about.

volteggio *sm.* vaulting.

volto¹ *sm.* 1. face 2. (*aspetto*) aspect.

volto² *agg.* 1. turned 2. (*rivolto*) directed.

volùbile *agg.* changeable.

volubilità *sf.* inconstancy.

volume *sm.* volume.

volumètrico *agg.* volumetric.

voluminoso *agg.* voluminous, bulky.

voluta *sf.* volute.

volutamente *avv.* intentionally.

voluttà *sf.* 1. delight 2. (*dei sensi*) voluptuousness.

voluttuario *agg.* voluptuary.

voluttuosamente *avv.* voluptuously.

voluttuoso *agg.* voluptuous.

vòmere *sm.* 1. ploughshare 2. (*anat.*) vomer.

vomitare *vt.* to vomit, to be sick.

vòmito *sm.* vomiting: *conato di —*, retch.

vòngola *sf.* mussel.

vorace *agg.* voracious, greedy.

voracità *sf.* voracity, greed.

voràgine *sf.* chasm.

vorticare *vi.* to whirl.

vòrtice *sm.* whirl: *— di vento*, whirlwind.

vorticosamente *avv.* in whirls.

vorticoso *agg.* whirling.

vostro *agg. poss.* your ‖ *in vece vostra*, instead of you. ♦ **vostro** *pron. poss.* yours ‖ *rispondiamo alla vostra del 3 giugno* (*comm.*), in reply to your letter of June 3rd; *sono dalla vostra*, I am on your side.

votante *agg.* voting. ♦ **votante** *sm.* voter.

votare *vt.* to vote. ♦ **votarsi** *vr.* to devote oneself.

votato *agg.* **1.** passed **2.** (*dedicato*) devoted.

votazione *sf.* voting.

votivo *agg.* votive.

voto *sm.* **1.** (*promessa solenne*) vow **2.** (*augurio*) wish **3.** (*per elezioni*) vote **4.** (*scolastico*) mark: *prendere un bel, brutto —*, to get (*v. irr.*) a good, bad mark.

vulcànico *agg.* volcanic.

vulcanismo *sm.* vulcanism.

vulcanizzare *vt.* to vulcanize.

vulcanizzato *agg.* vulcanized.

vulcanizzazione *sf.* vulcanization.

vulcano *sm.* volcano.

vulneràbile *agg.* vulnerable.

vulnerabilità *sf.* vulnerability.

vuotare *vt.* to empty: *— il sacco*, to speak (*v. irr.*) out one's mind.

vuoto *agg.* **1.** empty **2.** (*sprovvisto*) devoid. ♦ **vuoto** *sm.* **1.** empty space **2.** (*recipiente vuoto*) empty **3.** (*vacuità*) emptiness.

X

xenofobìa *sf.* xenophobia.

xenòfobo *sm.* xenophobe.

xilòfono *sm.* xylophone.

xilografìa *sf.* **1.** (*incisione*) xylograph **2.** (*arte*) xylography.

Z

zaffata *sf.* whiff.

zafferano *sm.* saffron.

zaffiro *sm.* sapphire.

zàino *sm.* knapsack.

zampa *sf.* **1.** paw **2.** (*con zoccolo*) hoof **3.** (*di uccello*) claw **4.** (*di insetto*) leg ‖ *zampe di gallina* (*scrittura*), scrawl; (*rughe*) crow's feet.

zampata *sf.* blow with a paw.

zampettare *vt.* to toddle.

zampillante *agg.* gushing.

zampillare *vi.* to gush.

zampillo *sm.* gush.

zampino *sm.* little paw ‖ *mettere lo — in una faccenda*, to have a hand in the matter.

zampogna *sf.* **1.** reed-pipe **2.** (*cornamusa*) bag-pipe.

zampognaro *sm.* piper.

zanna *sf.* **1.** fang **2.** (*di elefante*) tusk.

zanzara *sf.* mosquito.

zanzariera *sf.* mosquito-net.

zappa *sf.* hoe.

zappare *vt.* to hoe.

zappata *sf.* blow with a hoe.

zappatore *sm.* **1.** hoer **2.** (*mil.*) pioneer.

zappatura *sf.* hoeing.

zar *sm.* czar.

zarina *sf.* czarina.

zarista *s.* czarist.

zàttera *sf.* raft.

zavorra *sf.* **1.** ballast **2.** (*fig.*) rubbish.

zavorrare *vt.* to ballast.

zàzzera *sf.* mane.

zazzeruto *agg.* shockheaded.

zebra *sf.* zebra.

zebrato *agg.* striped.

zebratura *sf.* stripes (*pl.*).

zebù *sm.* zebu.

zecca[1] *sf.* mint: *nuovo di —*, brand-new.

zecca[2] *sf.* (*zool.*) tick.

zecchino *sm.* sequin: *oro —*, first-quality-gold.

zèfiro *sm.* zephyr.

zelante *agg.* zealous.

zelantemente *avv.* zealously.

zelo *sm.* zeal.

zenit *sm.* zenith.

zénzero *sm.* ginger.

zeppo *agg.* crammed (with).

zerbino *sm.* door-mat.

zerbinotto *sm.* dandy.

zero *sm.* **1.** nought **2.** (*in gradazioni*) zero **3.** (*tel.*) 0 ‖ *ridursi a —*, to come (*v. irr.*) to nought.

zia *sf.* aunt.

zibaldone *sm.* miscellany.

zibellino *sm.* sable.

zigano *agg. e sm.* tzigane.

zìgomo *sm.* cheek-bone.

zigrinare *vt.* to knurl.
zigrinato *agg.* knurled.
zig-zag (*nella loc. avv.*) *a* —, zigzag.
zigzagare *vi.* to zigzag.
zimbello *sm.* 1. decoy 2. (*fig.*) laughing-stock.
zincare *vt.* to zinc.
zincatura *sf.* zinc-plating.
zinco *sm.* zinc.
zincografia *sf.* zincography.
zingaresco *agg.* gipsy (*attr.*).
zingaro *sm.* gipsy.
zio *sm.* uncle.
zircone *sm.* zircon.
zirconio *sm.* zirconium.
zitella *sf.* spinster.
zittire *vt.* to hiss.
zitto *agg.* silent: *star* —, to be silent.
zizzania *sf.* 1. darnel 2. (*fig.*) discord.
zoccolaio *sm.* clog-maker.
zoccolare *vi.* to clatter about with one's clogs.
zoccolo *sm.* 1. clog 2. (*di animale*) hoof 3. (*piedistallo*) base.
zodiacale *agg.* zodiacal.
zodiaco *sm.* zodiac.
zolfanello *sm.* match.
zolfatara *sf.* V. *solfatara*.
zolfatura *sf.* sulfurization.
zolfo *sm.* sulphur
zolla *sf.* clod.
zolletta *sf.* lump.
zona *sf.* zone, area.
zonzo (*nella loc. avv.*) *andare a* —, to loaf.
zoo *sm.* zoo.
zoofilia *sf.* zoophilia.
zoòfilo *agg.* zoophilous. ♦ **zoòfilo** *sm.* animal-lover.

zoofobìa *sf.* zoophobia.
zoologìa *sf.* zoology.
zoològico *agg.* zoological.
zoòlogo *sm.* zoologist.
zootecnìa *sf.* zootechny.
zootècnico *agg.* zootechnic: *patrimonio* —, live-stock. ♦ **zootècnico** *sm.* animal expert.
zoppicamento *sm.* limping.
zoppicante *agg.* lame.
zoppicare *vi.* 1. to limp 2. (*di mobile*) to be shaky.
zoppo *agg.* 1. lame 2. (*di mobile*) shaky. ♦ **zoppo** *sm.* lame person.
zoticàggine *sf.* boorishness.
zòtico *agg.* boorish. ♦ **zòtico** *sm.* boor.
zuavo *sm.* zouave || *calzoni alla zuava*, knickerbockers.
zucca *sf.* 1. pumpkin 2. (*testa*) pate.
zuccherare *vt.* to sugar.
zuccherato *agg.* sugared.
zuccheriera *sf.* sugar-basin.
zuccherificio *sm.* sugar-refinery.
zuccherino *sm.* 1. sweet 2. (*fig.*) sugar-plum.
zùcchero *sm.* sugar.
zucchina *sf.* vegetable marrow.
zucconàggine *sf.* 1. (*ottusità*) dullness 2. (*ostinatezza*) stubbornness.
zuccone *sm.* 1. (*ottuso*) blockhead 2. (*testardo*) donkey.
zuffa *sf.* brawl.
zufolare *vt.* e *vi.* to whistle.
zufolìo *sm.* whistle.
zùfolo *sm.* 1. whistle 2. (*mus.*) pipe.
zuppa *sf.* soup.
zuppiera *sf.* tureen.
zuppo *agg.* soaked.
zuzzurellone *sm.* skittish boy.

Prefazione alla sezione inglese–italiano

1. Questa parte del presente dizionario comprende una serie di informazioni che valgono a completare l'opera, a facilitarne la consultazione o ad arricchire le conoscenze del lettore; tali si debbono considerare le regole di pronuncia e l'elenco dei verbi irregolari inglesi.

2. Nella parte italiano-inglese, i lemmi italiani non recano accento se si tratta di parole piane (es. *violino, rosa, determinazione*); recano l'accento se si tratta di parole tronche (es. *così, però, lassù*) o sdrucciole (es. *richiùdere, rimpròvero, nàutico*) o bisdrucciole o terminanti in *ia, io* con l'accento sulla *i* (es. *filosofìa, mormorìo*). Tali accenti sono tutti gravi, salvo nelle parole con accento su una *e*, nel qual caso ci si è attenuti a un criterio strettamente ortoepico (es. *règola, desèrtico, maneggévole, prègévole*): si è, cioè, distinto fra accento grave (pronuncia aperta) e accento acuto (pronuncia chiusa).

3. Nel corpo delle singole voci sono stati ampiamente adottati, secondo la consuetudine generale dei grandi dizionari, i seguenti segni grafici:

   a) la **doppia barra** (||) che sta a segnalare la peculiarità della fraseologia, o una certa differenza di significato nell'ambito del lemma, o il passaggio da un senso proprio a uno figurato, o il passaggio dal significato corrente a uno più specialistico, o, infine, l'inizio dell'elencazione di parole composte e di analoghe associazioni semantiche;

   b) i **numeri arabi in neretto** (1., 2., 3. ecc.) che valgono ad attirare l'attenzione sui diversi significati in cui è stato possibile articolare una determinata voce del dizionario;

   c) la **losanga nera** (♦) che sta a indicare il cambiamento di natura grammaticale che sopravviene internamente a due omonimi appartenenti a un medesimo gruppo etimologico (es. passaggio da sostantivo maschile a sostantivo femminile; da sostantivo ad aggettivo; da aggettivo ad avverbio; da verbo transitivo a verbo riflessivo ecc.);

   d) gli **esponenti in numeri arabi** ([1], [2], [3] ecc.) che servono a distinguere parole omonime appartenenti però a gruppi etimologici diversi.

4. In entrambe le parti, nel caso di sostantivi che abbiano **numero diverso** nelle due lingue, si è data l'indicazione del numero stesso sùbito dopo il lemma. Es. **fare** *sm.* manners (*pl.*); **postage** *s.* spese postali (*pl.*); **embers** *s. pl.* brace (*sing.*).

5. Per i **plurali irregolari inglesi** si sono usati i seguenti criteri:

   a) nella parte **italiano-inglese** si è fatta seguire al lemma, fra parentesi, la forma plurale irregolare, per esteso – es.: **child** *s.* (*pl.* children) – nei casi generali o abbreviata – es.: **diagnosis** *s.* (*pl.* -ses) – nei casi di parole derivanti da altre lingue antiche o moderne. Nel primo caso i plurali sono stati elencati anche come voce a sé e con rimando: es.: **children** *V. child*;

   b) nella parte **italiano-inglese** si è fatta seguire alla traduzione, fra parentesi, la forma plurale irregolare, per esteso – es.: **bambino** *sm.* child (*pl.* children) – nei casi generali o abbreviati – es.: **diàgnosi** *sf.* diagnosis (*pl.* -ses) – nei casi di parole derivanti da altre lingue antiche o moderne.

6. Per i **verbi irregolari inglesi** si sono usati i seguenti criteri:

    a) nella parte **inglese-italiano** si è fatto seguire al lemma, fra parentesi, il paradigma: es.: to **bring (brought, brought)**. Le due forme del passato remoto e del participio passato sono state elencate anche come voce a sé e con rimando: es.: **brought** *V. to bring*;

    b) nella parte **italiano-inglese** si è fatta seguire alla traduzione, fra parentesi, l'indicazione dell'irregolarità – es.: **costare** *vi*. to cost (*v. irr.*) – a meno che lo stesso verbo inglese ricorra più volte nell'ambito della stessa voce ed escludendo inoltre i due verbi ausiliari *to be* e *to have* (per i quali ultimi si suppone una costante attenzione del lettore circa l'irregolarità).

7. Per i **comparativi** e **superlativi irregolari inglesi** sono stati seguiti analoghi criteri.

Regole di pronuncia

Alfabeto

L'alfabeto inglese è composto di 26 lettere, 5 in più dell'alfabeto italiano e precisamente: *j, k, w, x, y*. L'elenco completo delle lettere è il seguente:

a (pron. *ei*)
b (pron. *bi*, con la *i* allungata)
c (pron. *si*, con la *i* allungata e la *s* aspra, come in *sordo*)
d (pron. *di*, con la *i* allungata)
e (pron. *i*, con la *i* allungata)
f (pron. *ef*)
g (pron. *gi*, con la *i* allungata)
h (pron. *eic*, con la *c* dolce)
i (pron. *ai*)
j (pron. *gei*)
k (pron. *kei*)
l (pron. *el*)
m (pron. *em)*

n (pron. *en*)
o (pron. *ou*)
p (pron. *pi*, con la *i* allungata)
q (pron. *chiù*)
r (pron. *ar*, con la *a* allungata)
s (pron. *es*, con la *s* aspra)
t (pron. *ti*, con la *i* allungata)
u (pron. *iù*)
v (pron. *vi*, con la *i* allungata)
w (pron. *dabliu*)
x (pron. *ecs*)
y (pron. *uai*)
z (pron. *sed*, con la *s* dolce, come in *rosa*)

La pronuncia inglese è particolarmente difficile da apprendere ed è altresì difficile dare norme precise per l'apprendimento della stessa. Diamo comunque, qui di seguito, un elenco delle vocali, dei gruppi vocalici, delle consonanti e di alcuni gruppi consonantici con indicazioni approssimative sulla pronuncia.

Vocali

La vocale A ha vari suoni:

1. *ei* in sillaba tonica aperta, come nella parola *tale* (racconto); nei gruppi **ange** e **aste**, come nelle parole *danger* (pericolo) e *haste* (fretta);
2. *e* aperta in sillaba tonica chiusa, come nella parola *cat* (gatto);
3. ha un suono incerto tra *e* aperta e *a* in sillabe iniziali o mediane, come nelle parole *about* (circa) e *final* (finale);
4. *a* allungata quando è seguita da *r* finale (*r* muta), come nelle parole *car* (automobile) e *far* (lontano);
5. *ea* se è seguita da *re* finale (*e* aperta e *a* appena accennata), come nelle parole *care* (cura) e *dare* (sfida);
6. *o* breve in molti vocaboli che cominciano con il gruppo **qua**, come in *quality* (qualità) e in *quantity* (quantità);
7. *o* aperta e prolungata se seguita da *l* o *ll*, come in *all* (tutto), *tall* (alto); nel gruppo **alk** (*l* muta), come in *talk* (chiacchiera); preceduta da *w* (ma non seguita da *k* o *g*), come in *war* (guerra);
8. *a* allungata nei gruppi **ance**, **and**, **ant**, **ask**, **alf** (*l* muta), **ast**, **alm** (*l* muta), **aff**, **aft**, **asp** e **ath** quando la *a* è tonica;
9. *i* breve e velata nelle desinenze **age** e **ate** non accentate.

Regole di pronuncia

La vocale E ha vari suoni:

1. i allungata in sillaba tonica aperta, come in *these* (questi) e nei mono-sillabi, come in *me* (me);
2. e aperta come nella parola italiana *bello*, in sillaba tonica chiusa, come in *let* (lasciare);
3. i come nella parola italiana *vita*, in sillaba atona, come in *repeat* (ripetere);
4. i brevissima quando è preceduta da s, z, c, ch, sh, g e seguita da s, come in *roses* (rose) e quando è tra due dentali come in *rested* (riposato);
5. è muta in fine di parola, come in *love* (amore) e nelle desinenze es, ed, come in *loves* (amori) e *loved* (amato);
6. eu francese quando è seguita da r in sillaba tonica, come in *term* (termine);
7. a gutturale quando è nel gruppo er in fine di parola, come in *letter* (lettera);
8. ia con la a appena accennata quando è seguita da re in fine di parola, come in *severe* (severo) e in *mere* (semplice).

La vocale I ha vari suoni:

1. ai in sillaba tonica aperta, come in *fine* (bello) e in sillaba chiusa quando è seguita dai gruppi gh (muto), come in *high* (alto); ght (gh muto), come in *night* (notte); gn (g muta), come in *sign* (segno); ld, come in *child* (bambino) e nd, come in *mind* (mente);
2. i breve in sillaba tonica chiusa, come in *tin* (stagno);
3. eu francese, se seguita da r, come in *fir* (abete);
4. aia, se seguita da re come in *fire* (fuoco).

La vocale O ha vari suoni:

1. ou (con la o chiusa) in sillaba tonica aperta, come in *home* (casa) e se seguita da ld, come in *cold* (freddo);
2. o aperta e breve in sillaba tonica chiusa, come in *not* (non);
3. o aperta e lunga se seguita da r, come in *morning* (mattino);
4. oa se seguita da re in fine di parola, come in *more* (più);
5. eu francese se preceduta da w e seguita da r, come in *work* (lavoro);
6. u allungata nei seguenti vocaboli: *to do* (fare); *to move* (muovere); *to prove* (provare); *to lose* (perdere); *who* (chi); *two* (due); *tomb* (tomba); *womb* (grembo); *shoe* (scarpa); *wolf* (lupo); *woman* (donna);
7. a se preceduta da w e seguita da n, come in *won* (vinto);
8. ua in *one* (uno).

La vocale U ha vari suoni:

1. iù in sillaba tonica aperta, come in *tune* (tono);
2. a in sillaba tonica chiusa, come in *but* (ma);
3. u allungata se preceduta da l o r, come in *Lucy* (Lucia) e *rule* (regola);
4. u breve, se preceduta da b, f, p e seguita da l, ll, sh, come in *bush* (cespuglio); *to push* (spingere); *bull* (toro); *full* (pieno); *to pull* (tirare);
5. eu francese se seguita da r in sillaba aperta, come in *fur* (pelliccia);
6. iua se seguita da re in fine di parola, come in *pure* (puro).

Regole di pronuncia

Gruppi vocalici

AI si pronuncia **ea** se seguito da **r**, come in *air* (aria).

AU, AW si pronunciano **o** allungata, come in *fraud* (frode) e *law* (legge).

EA si pronuncia **e** in circa 40 parole e loro composti; *bread* (pane); *dead* (morto); *death* (morte); *head* (testa); *heavy* (pesante) ecc.;
    i lunga in moltissime sillabe toniche: *heat* (calore); *meat* (carne);
    ei nelle seguenti parole: *great* (grande); *break* (rompere); *steak* (bistecca);
    eu francese se all'inizio di parola e seguito da **r**, come in *bear* (sopportare); in molte parole suona però **ia**, come in *tear* (lacrima), o **a** allungata, come in *heart* (cuore).

EE si pronuncia **i** allungata, come in *feeling* (sentimento).

EI si pronuncia **ei** in genere, come in *rein* (briglia);
    i se preceduto da sibilante, come in *ceiling* (soffitto).

EY si pronuncia **ei** in sillaba tonica, come in *prey* (preda);
    i in sillaba atona, come in **money** (denaro). L'eccezione più comune è *key* (chiave) che si pronuncia **ki**.

EU, EW si pronunciano **iù**, come in *Europe* (Europa) e in *new* (nuovo).

IE si pronuncia **i** allungata, come in *piece* (pezzo).

OI, OY si pronunciano **oi**, come in *soil* (suolo) e *royal* (reale).

OA si pronuncia **ou**, come in *boat* (barca).

OO si pronuncia **u** allungata, come in *moon* (luna);
    u breve se seguita da **k**, come in *book* (libro).
    Vi sono alcune eccezioni, come *door* (porta) e *floor* (pavimento) dove il gruppo **oo** viene pronunciato **oa** e *blood* (sangue), e *flood* (alluvione) dove il gruppo **oo** viene pronunciato **a**.

OU, OW si pronunciano **au**, come in *mouth* (bocca) e *now* (ora).

Consonanti

B è in generale pronunciata come in italiano; è però muta nei gruppi **bt** e **mb** in fine di parola, come in *debt* (debito) e *comb* (pettine).

C suono **s** aspra come nell'italiano *sordo* davanti a **e, i, y**, come in *cellar* (cantina), *city* (città) e *cyder* (cidro); suona **k** in fine di parola, come in *logic* (logico);
    cce, cci, suonano **kse** e **ksi**;
    ch suona **c** palatale, come nell'italiano *città*, se seguito da vocale o in fine di parola; suona **k** in parole di origine greca o orientale. Suona **sc**, come in italiano *sciare*, in parole di origine francese, come *machine* (macchina);
    ck suona **k**;
    ch suona **c** dolce.

G in fine di parola suona **g** gutturale, come nell'italiano *gomma*;
    ge, gi hanno suono palatale, come nell'italiano *gesto, gita* in parole di origine latina; hanno suono gutturale in parole di origine germanica;
    gh seguito da **t** o in fine di parola è muto;
    gn ha la **g** muta quando le due lettere fanno parte della stessa sillaba, come in *sign* (segno); si pronunciano separate e la **g** ha suono gutturale

Regole di pronuncia

quando le due lettere appartengono a due sillabe diverse, come in *signal* (segnale);

dge suona g palatale.

H è sempre aspirata tranne in *heir* (erede); *honest* (onesto); *honour* (onore) e *hour* (ora) e loro derivati.

J suona g palatale.

K è muta davanti a **n**, come in *knee* (ginocchio).

L come in italiano.

M come in italiano.

N è nasale nei gruppi **ng**, come in *ring* (anello) (la g è muta).

P suona **f** nei gruppi **ph**; è muta nel gruppo iniziale **psy**.

Q come in italiano.

R in genere, se mediana, non si pronuncia, ma allunga il suono della vocale che precede, come in *farm* (fattoria). Se è finale non si pronuncia.

S è in genere aspra all'inizio di parola o sillaba; è dolce se è posta tra due vocali;

sc suona s aspra se è seguita da e, i, y;

sh suona **sc**, come nell'italiano *sciare*.

• La s è muta in *aisle* (navata); *isle* e *island* (isola); *viscount* (visconte).

T ha due pronunce caratteristiche nel gruppo **th**:

a) un suono duro pronunciato con la lingua tra i denti, come in *thin* (sottile);

b) un suono dolce pronunciato con la lingua tra i denti, come in *this* (questo).

V come in italiano.

W in principio di parola suona **u**, come in *west* (occidentale); seguita da **r** è muta, come in *wrong* (sbagliato).

X finale ha il suono sordo **ks**; mediana può avere il suono sordo **ks** o il suono dolce **gs**; in principio di parola suona come la s dolce di *rosa*.

Y è semivocale; all'inizio di parola ha il suono consonantico **i**, come in *yes* (si); ha tale suono anche in fine di polisillabi, come in *dignity* (dignità), e nel corpo della parola, come in *graveyard* (cimitero); in fine di monosillabi, invece, si pronuncia **ai**, come in *fly* (mosca) e in *cry* (grido).

Z s dolce di *rosa*.

Osservazioni

1. I gruppi finali **ble**, **cle**, **kle**, **gle** hanno la **l** appena accennata e le due consonanti vengono pronunciate staccate.

2. Nei gruppi **gua**, **gue**, **gui**, **build** e **cuit** finale la u è muta, come in *building* (fabbricato).

3. **ough** seguito da t si pronuncia **o** allungato, come in *thought* (pensiero); **ough** suona **of** in: *cough* (tosse) e *trough* (trogolo); suona **af** in: *enough* (abbastanza), *rough* (ruvido) e *tough* (duro); suona **au** in: *plough* (arare) e *bough* (ramo); suona **ou** in *though* (sebbene) e *dough* (pasta); suona **u** allungato in *through* (attraverso).

4. I gruppi **ci**, **sci**, **si**, **ti**, **xi** seguiti da vocale suonano **sc**, come in *scelto*.

5. I gruppi finali **sten** i **stle** suonano rispettivamente **sn** e **sl**.

6. Il gruppo finale **sure** suona **ja** (j francese).

7. Il gruppo finale **ture** suona **cia** con la a allungata.

Verbi irregolari inglesi

Infinito	Passato	Participio passato	
to abide	abode, abided	abode, abided	dimorare
to arise	arose	arisen	sorgere
to awake*	awoke, awaked	awoken	svegliare, svegliarsi
to be	was	been	essere
to bear	bore	borne	generare, sopportare
to beat	beat	beaten	battere
to become	became	become	diventare
to befall	befell	befallen	accadere
to beget	begot	begotten	generare
to begin	began	begun	cominciare
to behold	beheld	beheld	mirare
to bend	bent	bent	piegare
to bereave*	bereaved, bereft	bereaved, bereft	orbare
to bet	bet, betted	bet, betted	scommettere
to bid	bade, bid	bidden, bid	ordinare
to bind	bound	bound	(ri)legare
to bite	bit	bitten	mordere
to bleed	bled	bled	sanguinare
to blow	blew	blown	soffiare
to break	broke	broken	rompere
to breed	bred	bred	allevare
to bring	brought	brought	portare
to build	built	built	costruire
to burn*	burnt, burned	burnt, burned	bruciare
to burst	burst	burst	scoppiare
to buy	bought	bought	comperare
to cast	cast	cast	gettare, fondere
to catch	caught	caught	prendere, acchiappare
to chide*	chid, chided	chid, chided	sgridare
to choose	chose	chosen	scegliere
to cleave	clove, cleft	cloven, cleft	fendere
to cling	clung	clung	attaccarsi
to come	came	come	venire
to cost	cost	cost	costare
to creep	crept	crept	strisciare
to cut	cut	cut	tagliare
to deal	dealt	dealt	trattare. commerciare
to dig*	dug	dug	scavare
to do	did	done	fare
to draw	drew	drawn	tirare, disegnare
to dream*	dreamt, dreamed	dreamt, dreamed	sognare
to drink	drank	drunk	bere
to drive	drove	driven	guidare
to dwell	dwelt, dwelled	dwelt, dwelled	dimorare

Verbi irregolari inglesi

Infinito	Passato	Participio passato	
to eat	ate	eaten	mangiare
to fall	fell	fallen	cadere
to feed	fed	fed	nutrire
to feel	felt	felt	sentire, tastare
to fight	fought	fought	combattere
to find	found	found	trovare
to flee	fled	fled	fuggire
to fling	flung	flung	scagliare
to fly	flew	flown	volare
to forbid	forbad(e)	forbidden	proibire
to forecast	forecast	forecast	predire
to forget	forgot	forgotten	dimenticare
to forgive	forgave	forgiven	perdonare
to forsake	forsook	forsaken	abbandonare
to freeze	froze	frozen	gelare
to get	got	got, gotten	ottenere, diventare
to gird	girt, girded	girt, girded	cingere
to give	gave	given	dare
to go	went	gone	andare
to grind	ground	ground	macinare
to grow	grew	grown	crescere, coltivare
to hang	hung	hung	appendere
to have	had	had	avere
to hear	heard	heard	udire
to hew*	hewed	hewn, hewed	recidere
to hide	hid	hidden, hid	nascondere
to hit	hit	hit	colpire
to hold	held	held	tenere, trattenere
to hurt	hurt	hurt	far male, ferire
to keep	kept	kept	tenere, conservare
to kneel*	knelt, kneeled	knelt, kneeled	inginocchiarsi
to knit*	knit, knitted	knit, knitted	lavorare a maglia
to know	knew	known	conoscere, sapere
to lay	laid	laid	deporre, posare
to lead	led	led	condurre, guidare
to lean	leant, leaned	leant, leaned	appoggiarsi, inclinarsi
to leap	leapt, leaped	leapt, leaped	saltare
to learn*	learnt, learned	learnt, learned	imparare
to leave	left	left	lasciare, partire
to lend	lent	lent	prestare
to let	let	let	lasciare
to lie	lay	lain	giacere, trovarsi
to light*	lit, lighted	lit, lighted	accendere
to lose	lost	lost	perdere
to make	made	made	fare
to mean	meant	meant	intendere, significare
to meet	met	met	incontrare

(viii)

Verbi irregolari inglesi

Infinito	Passato	Participio passato	
to mislay	mislaid	mislaid	smarrire
to mislead	misled	misled	sviare
to mistake	mistook	mistaken	sbagliare
to mow*	mowed	mown, mowed	falciare
to pay	paid	paid	pagare
to put	put	put	mettere
to read	read	read	leggere
to rend	rent	rent	strappare
to ride	rode	ridden	cavalcare
to ring	rang	rung	suonare
to rise	rose	risen	alzarsi, sorgere
to run	ran	run	correre
to saw	sawed	sawn	segare
to say	said	said	dire
to see	saw	seen	vedere
to seek	sought	sought	cercare
to sell	sold	sold	vendere
to send	sent	sent	mandare
to set	set	set	porre
to sew	sewed	sewn, sewed	cucire
to shake	shook	shaken	scuotere, tremare
to shear*	sheared	shorn, sheared	tosare
to shed	shed	shed	spargere
to shine	shone	shone	brillare, splendere
to shoe	shod, shoed	shod, shoed	calzare
to shoot	shot	shot	sparare
to show	showed	shown, showed	mostrare
to shred	shred, shredded	shred, shredded	tagliuzzare
to shrink	shrank, shrunk	shrunk, shrunken	restringersi
to shut	shut	shut	chiudere
to sing	sang	sung	cantare
to sink	sank, sunk	sunk, sunken	affondare
to sit	sat	sat	sedere
to slay	slew	slain	trucidare
to sleep	slept	slept	dormire
to slink	slunk	slunk	svignàrsela
to smell*	smelt, smelled	smelt, smelled	fiutare, odorare
to sow*	sowed	sown, sowed	seminare
to speak	spoke	spoken	parlare
to spell	spelt, spelled	spelt, spelled	compitare
to spend	spent	spent	spendere
to spill*	spilt, spilled	spilt, spilled	spandere, versare
to spin	spun	spun	filare
to spit	spat	spat	sputare
to split	split	split	spaccare
to spoil	spoilt, spoiled	spoilt, spoiled	guastare, viziare
to spread	spread	spread	diffondere, stendere
to spring	sprang	sprung	saltare

Verbi irregolari inglese

Infinito	Passato	Participio passato	
to stand	stood	stood	stare (in piedi)
to steal	stole	stolen	rubare
to stick	stuck	stuck	appiccicare
to sting	stung	stung	pungere
to stink	stank, stunk	stunk	puzzare
to strike	struck	struck	battere, colpire
to strive	strove	striven	sforzarsi
to swear	swore	sworn	giurare
to sweat*	sweated	sweated	sudare
to sweep	swept	swept	spazzare
to swell*	swelled	swollen, swelled	gonfiare
to swim	swam	swum	nuotare
to swing	swung	swung	dondolare
to take	took	taken	prendere
to teach	taught	taught	insegnare
to tear	tore	torn	lacerare
to tell	told	told	dire, raccontare
to think	thought	thought	pensare
to thrive	throve, thrived	thriven, thrived	prosperare
to throw	threw	thrown	gettare
to thrust	thrust	thrust	spingere, gettare
to tread	trod	trod, trodden	calpestare
to understand	understood	understood	capire
to upset	upset	upset	capovolgere
to wake	woke	woken	svegliare, svegliarsi
to wear	wore	worn	indossare, logorare
to weave	wove	woven	intrecciare, tessere
to weep	wept	wept	piangere
to win	won	won	vincere
to wind	wound	wound	serpeggiare
to withdraw	withdrew	withdrawn	ritirare, ritirarsi
to wring	wrung	wrung	torcere
to write	wrote	written	scrivere

INGLESE – ITALIANO
ENGLISH – ITALIAN

A

a *art.* **1.** un, uno, una **2.** un certo || *once a week*, una volta alla settimana.

A *s.* *(mus.)* la.

aback *avv.* alla sprovvista.

abacus *s.* **1.** abaco **2.** pallottoliere.

abandon *s.* abbandono.

to abandon *vt.* abbandonare.

to abase *vt.* abbassare, umiliare.

abasement *s.* umiliazione.

to abash *vt.* confondere.

abashment *s.* confusione.

to abate *vt.* diminuire. ♦ to abate *vi.* placarsi *(di tempo atmosferico).*

abatement *s.* diminuzione.

abbess *s.* badessa.

abbey *s.* abbazia.

abbot *s.* abate.

abbreviation *s.* abbreviazione.

to abdicate *vt.* e *vi.* **1.** abdicare a **2.** dimettersi.

abdication *s.* abdicazione.

abdomen *s.* addome.

abdominal *agg.* addominale.

to abduct *vt.* rapire.

abduction *s.* rapimento.

abductor *s.* **1.** rapitore **2.** *(anat.)* abduttore.

aberration *s.* aberrazione.

abetter *s.* fautore.

abeyance *s.* sospensione.

to abhor *vt.* aborrire.

abhorrence *s.* aborrimento.

to abide (abode, abode) *vi.* abitare || *to — by,* conformarsi a.

ability *s.* abilità, capacità.

abject *agg.* abietto.

abjection *s.* abiezione.

abjuration *s.* abiura.

to abjure *vt.* abiurare.

ablation *s.* ablazione.

ablative *agg.* e *s.* ablativo.

able *agg.* capace || *to be — to,* essere in grado di, potere.

ablution *s.* abluzione.

abnegation *s.* **1.** abnegazione **2.** rinuncia.

abnormal *agg.* anormale.

aboard *avv.* e *prep.* a bordo.

abode V. *to abide.* ♦ abode *s.* dimora.

to abolish *vt.* abolire.

abolishment, abolition *s.* abolizione.

abolitionism *s.* abolizionismo.

abolitionist *agg.* e *s.* abolizionista.

abominable *agg.* abominevole.

to abominate *vt.* detestare.

abomination *s.* abominazione.

aboriginal *agg.* e *s.* aborigeno.

to abort *vi.* abortire.

abortion *s.* aborto.

abortive *agg.* abortivo.

to abound *vi.* abbondare.

about *avv.* **1.** circa **2.** intorno || *to be —,* stare per. ♦ about *prep.* **1.** intorno a **2.** presso di **3.** riguardo a.

above *prep.* **1.** al di sopra di **2.** più di || *— mentioned,* suddetto. ♦ above *avv.* in alto, sopra.

abrasion *s.* abrasione.

to abridge *vt.* **1.** abbreviare **2.** privare di.

abridg(e)ment *s.* **1.** abbreviazione, sommario **2.** privazione.

abroad *avv.* **1.** all'estero **2.** fuori.

to abrogate *vt.* abrogare.

abrogation *s.* abrogazione.

abrupt *agg.* **1.** scosceso **2.** brusco **3.** inaspettato.

abruptness *s.* **1.** ripidezza **2.** rudezza **3.** precipitazione.

abscess *s.* ascesso.

abscissa *s.* ascissa.

absence *s.* assenza.

absent *agg.* assente || *— -minded,* distratto; *— -mindedness,* distrazione.

to absent *vt.* *to — oneself,* assentarsi.

absenteeism *s.* assenteismo.

absinth(e) *s.* assenzio.

absolute *agg.* e *s.* assoluto.

absolution *s.* assoluzione.

absolutism *s.* assolutismo.

absolutist *agg.* e *s.* assolutista.

to absolve *vt.* assolvere.

to absorb *vt.* assorbire.

absorbent *agg.* e *s.* assorbente.

absorption *s.* assorbimento.

to abstain *vi.* astenersi.

abstemious *agg.* sobrio.

abstention *s.* astensione.

abstentionist *s.* astensionista.

abstinence *s.* astinenza.

abstract *agg.* astratto. ♦ abstract *s.* **1.** astrazione **2.** estratto.

to abstract *vt.* **1.** astrarre **2.** estrarre **3.** sottrarre **4.** riassumere.

abstraction *s.* **1.** astrazione **2.** distrazione **3.** furto.

abstractly *avv.* astrattamente.

abstruse *agg.* astruso.

abstruseness *s.* astrusità.

absurd *agg.* assurdo.
absurdity *s.* assurdità.
absurdly *avv.* assurdamente.
abundance *s.* abbondanza.
abundant *agg.* abbondante.
abuse *s.* 1. abuso 2. ingiuria.
to **abuse** *vt.* 1. abusare 2. ingiuriare.
abusive *agg.* 1. abusivo 2. ingiurioso.
abysm, abyss *s.* abisso.
abysmal, abyssal *agg.* abissale.
academic *agg.* e *s.* accademico.
academician *s.* accademico.
academy *s.* accademia: — *of music*, conservatorio.
acanthus *s.* acanto.
acarus *s.* (*pl.* -ri) acaro.
to **accelerate** *vt.* accelerare.
acceleration *s.* accelerazione.
accelerative *agg.* accelerativo.
accelerator *s.* acceleratore.
accent *s.* accento.
to **accent** *vt.* 1. accentare 2. accentuare.
to **accentuate** V. *to accent.*
accentuation *s.* accentuazione.
to **accept** *vt.* accettare, approvare.
acceptable *agg.* accettabile.
acceptance *s.* 1. accettazione 2. consenso.
acceptation *s.* accezione, significato.
access *s.* accesso.
accessible *agg.* accessibile.
accession *s.* 1. assunzione (*al trono*) 2. adesione 3. aggiunta.
accessory *agg.* e *s.* 1. accessorio 2. complice.
accident *s.* 1. caso: *by* —, per caso 2. incidente 3. irregolarità.
accidental *agg.* accidentale.
to **acclaim** *vt.* acclamare.
acclamation *s.* acclamazione.
acclimation, acclimatization *s.* acclimazione, acclimatazione.
to **acclimate**, to **acclimatize** *vt.* acclimatare. ♦ to **acclimate**, to **acclimatize** *vi.* acclimatarsi.
to **accommodate** *vt.* 1. adattare 2. ospitare 3. fornire.
accommodating *agg.* accomodante.
accommodation *s.* 1. accomodamento 2. comodità 3. alloggio 4. (*comm.*) facilitazione.
accompaniment *s.* accompagnamento.
accompanist *s.* (*mus.*) accompagnatore.
to **accompany** *vt.* accompagnare

(*anche mus.*).
accomplice *s.* complice.
to **accomplish** *vt.* compiere, realizzare.
accomplishment *s.* 1. compimento 2. compitezza 3. dote.
accord *s.* accordo.
to **accord** *vt.* accordare. ♦ to **accord** *vi.* accordarsi.
accordance *s.* accordo.
accordant *agg.* concorde, conforme.
according *agg.* 1. concordante, conforme 2. armonioso. ♦ **according** *avv.* — *as*, secondo che; — *to*, secondo.
accordingly *avv.* 1. in conseguenza 2. conformemente.
accordion *s.* fisarmonica.
accordionist *s.* fisarmonicista.
account *s.* 1. (*comm.*) conto 2. (*comm.*) acconto 3. valore 4. resoconto ‖ *to take into* —, prendere in considerazione; *on* — *of*, a causa di.
to **account** *vt.* considerare ‖ *to* — *for*, essere responsabile di.
accountable *agg.* responsabile.
accountancy *s.* ragioneria.
accountant *s.* contabile ‖ *chartered* —, ragioniere.
to **accredit** *vt.* accreditare.
to **accrue** *vi.* 1. derivare 2. accumularsi.
to **accumulate** *vt.* accumulare. ♦ to **accumulate** *vi.* accumularsi.
accumulation *s.* accumulazione.
accumulative *agg.* accumulativo.
accumulator *s.* accumulatore.
accuracy *s.* esattezza.
accurate *agg.* esatto.
accusation *s.* accusa.
accusative *agg.* e *s.* accusativo.
to **accuse** *vt.* accusare.
accused *s.* accusato.
accuser *s.* accusatore.
to **accustom** *vt.* abituare.
accustomed *agg.* 1. abituale 2. abituato.
ace *s.* asso.
acetone *s.* acetone.
acetylene *s.* acetilene.
ache *s.* dolore.
to **ache** *vi.* far male: *my head aches*, mi fa male la testa.
to **achieve** *vt.* 1. compiere 2. ottenere.
achievement *s.* 1. compimento 2. conseguimento 3. gesta.
aching *agg.* 1. doloroso 2. afflitto.

♦ **aching** s. dolore.

acid agg. e s. acido.

acidity s. acidità.

acidulous agg. acidulo.

to **acknowledge** vt. riconoscere || to — receipt of, accusare ricevuta di.

acknowledg(e)ment s. riconoscimento.

acolyte s. accolito.

acorn s. ghianda.

acoustic(al) agg. acustico.

acoustics s. acustica.

to **acquaint** vt. informare || to become acquainted with, fare la conoscenza di.

acquaintance s. conoscenza.

acquiescence s. acquiescenza.

to **acquire** vt. acquisire, acquistare.

acquisition s. acquisto.

to **acquit** vt. 1. pagare 2. liberare 3. assolvere.

acquittal s. (giur.) assoluzione.

acquittance s. 1. saldo 2. quietanza.

acrid agg. acre.

acridity s. asprezza.

acrimony s. acrimonia.

acrobat s. acrobata.

acrobatic(al) agg. acrobatico.

acrobatics s. pl. acrobazia (sing.).

acropolis s. acropoli.

across avv. per traverso. ♦ **across** prep. attraverso || to come —. incontrare.

act s. atto, legge.

to **act** vt. e vi. 1. agire, fare 2. (teat.) recitare.

acting agg. facente funzione di. ♦ **acting** s. 1. azione 2. (teat.) rappresentazione.

action s. 1. azione 2. (giur.) processo 3. (mecc.) funzionamento.

active agg. attivo.

activism s. attivismo.

activist s. attivista.

activity s. attività.

actor s. attore.

actress s. attrice.

actual agg. reale.

actuality s. realtà.

actually avv. realmente.

to **actuate** vt. mettere in moto.

acuminate agg. acuminato.

acute agg. acuto.

ad s. V. advertisement.

adamantine agg. adamantino.

to **adapt** vt. adattare.

adaptable agg. adattabile.

adaptation s. adattamento.

to **add** vt. aggiungere || to — up, fare una somma.

addendum s. (pl. -da) aggiunta.

adder s. vipera.

addict s. tossicomane.

addition s. 1. (mat.) addizione 2. aggiunta.

additional agg. supplementare.

address s. 1. indirizzo 2. abilità. ♦ **addresses** s. pl. omaggi.

to **address** vt. e vi. indirizzare, arringare. ♦ to **address** vi. rivolgersi.

addressee s. destinatario.

addresser s. mittente.

to **adduce** vt. addurre.

adenoids s. pl. adenoidi.

adept agg. e s. perito, esperto.

adequate agg. adeguato.

to **adhere** vi. aderire.

adherence s. aderenza, adesione.

adherent agg. e s. aderente.

adhesion s. V. adherence.

adhesive agg. e s. adesivo.

adipose agg. adiposo.

adjacent agg. adiacente.

adjective agg. 1. aggettivale 2. addizionale. ♦ **adjective** s. aggettivo.

to **adjoin** vt. 1. aggiungere 2. essere contiguo.

adjoining agg. adiacente.

to **adjourn** vt. aggiornare.

adjournment s. aggiornamento.

adjunct s. 1. aggiunta 2. aggiunto 3. (gramm.) complemento.

adjuration s. implorazione.

to **adjust** vt. 1. aggiustare 2. adattare 3. regolare.

adjustment s. 1. adattamento, compromesso 2. (comm.) liquidazione.

adjutant s. aiutante.

to **administer** vt. 1. amministrare 2. fornire. ♦ to **administer** vi. contribuire.

administration s. 1. amministrazione 2. somministrazione.

administrative agg. amministrativo.

administrator s. amministratore.

admirable agg. ammirabile.

admiral s. ammiraglio.

admiralty s. ammiragliato.

admiration s. ammirazione.

to **admire** vt. ammirare.

admirer s. ammiratore.

admiringly avv. con ammirazione.

admissible agg. ammissibile.

admission s. 1. ammissione 2. confessione.

to **admit** vt. **1.** ammettere **2.** contenere.

admittance s. ammissione, ingresso.

to **admonish** vt. ammonire.

admonition s. ammonimento.

ado s. **1.** fatica **2.** confusione.

adolescence s. adolescenza.

adolescent agg. e s. adolescente.

to **adopt** vt. adottare.

adoption s. adozione.

adoptive agg. adottivo.

adorable agg. adorabile.

adoration s. adorazione.

to **adore** vt. adorare.

to **adorn** vt. adornare.

adornment s. ornamento.

adrenalin s. adrenalina.

adrift avv. alla deriva.

to **adulate** vt. adulare.

adulation s. adulazione.

adulator s. adulatore.

adult agg. e s. adulto.

to **adulterate** vt. adulterare.

adulteration s. adulterazione.

adulterer s. adultero.

adulteress s. adultera.

adulterine agg. adulterino.

adultery s. adulterio.

advance s. **1.** avanzamento **2.** anticipo **3.** approccio.

to **advance** vt. **1.** portar avanti **2.** anticipare (denaro) **3.** (comm.) aumentare. ♦ to **advance** vi. avanzare.

advancement s. **1.** avanzamento **2.** (comm.) rialzo.

advantage s. vantaggio || to take — of, approfittare di.

to **advantage** vt. avvantaggiare.

advantageous agg. vantaggioso.

advent s. avvento.

adventure s. avventura.

to **adventure** vt. rischiare. ♦ to **adventure** vi. avventurarsi.

adventurer s. avventuriero.

adventurous agg. avventuroso.

adverb s. avverbio.

adverbial agg. avverbiale.

adversary s. avversario.

adverse agg. avverso.

adversity s. avversità.

to **advert** vi. alludere, riferirsi.

to **advertise** vt. e vi. fare pubblicità a, divulgare.

advertisement s. **1.** avviso **2.** cartellone pubblicitario **3.** inserzione.

advertiser s. inserzionista.

advertising agg. pubblicitario. ♦ **advertising** s. pubblicità.

advice s. **1.** consiglio **2.** notizia.

advisability s. opportunità.

advisable agg. consigliabile.

to **advise** vt. **1.** consigliare **2.** avvisare || to — with so., consultarsi con qu.

advised agg. giudizioso.

adviser s. consigliere.

advocacy s. avvocatura.

advocate s. difensore.

aegis s. egida.

Aeolian agg. eolio.

to **aerate** vt. **1.** aerare **2.** gassare.

aeration s. **1.** aerazione **2.** (chim.) aggiunta di acido carbonico.

aerial agg. aereo. ♦ **aerial** s. (radio) antenna.

aerodrome s. aerodromo.

aerodynamics s. aerodinamica.

aeronaut s. aeronauta.

aeronautics s. aeronautica.

aeroplane s. aeroplano.

aerostat s. aerostato.

aerostatics s. aerostatica.

aesthete s. esteta.

aesthetic(al) agg. estetico.

aestheticism s. estetismo.

aesthetics s. estetica.

aestivation s. letargo estivo.

aether s. etere.

afar avv. lontano.

affability s. affabilità.

affable agg. affabile.

affair s. **1.** affare **2.** tresca.

to **affect**[1] vt. **1.** ostentare **2.** simulare.

to **affect**[2] vt. **1.** concernere **2.** commuovere **3.** (med.) intaccare.

affectation s. affettazione.

affected agg. **1.** affettato **2.** affetto **3.** commosso **4.** disposto.

affection s. **1.** affetto **2.** (med.) affezione.

affectionate agg. affezionato, affettuoso.

affective agg. affettivo.

to **affiliate** vt. affiliare. ♦ to **affiliate** vi. affiliarsi.

affiliation s. affiliazione.

affinity s. affinità, parentela.

to **affirm** vt. **1.** affermare **2.** ratificare.

affirmation s. **1.** affermazione **2.** ratificazione.

affirmative agg. affermativo || in the —, affermativamente.

to **affix** vt. aggiungere, apporre.

to **afflict** vt. affliggere.
affliction s. afflizione.
affluence s. 1. affluenza 2. abbondanza.
affluent agg. ricco. ◆ **affluent** s. (geogr.) affluente.
afflux s. afflusso.
to **afford** vt. offrire || can —, potersi permettere.
to **afforest** vt. imboschire.
afforestation s. imboschimento.
affront s. affronto || to take — at, offendersi per.
to **affront** vt. 1. affrontare 2. insultare.
afloat avv. a galla. ◆ **afloat** agg. 1. galleggiante 2. in circolazione.
afore avv. precedentemente. ◆ **afore** prep. prima di.
aforementioned, aforesaid agg. predetto.
afraid agg. spaventato || to be —, temere.
African agg. e s. africano.
after agg. seguente. ◆ **after** prep. 1. dopo, dietro 2. secondo 3. alla maniera di. ◆ **after** avv. dopo. ◆ **after** cong. dopo che.
afternoon s. pomeriggio.
afterthought s. riflessione.
afterward(s) avv. poi.
again avv. ancora, di nuovo.
against prep. 1. contro 2. in previsione di.
agape agg. e avv. a bocca aperta.
age s. 1. età 2. secolo || old —, vecchiaia; to be of —, essere maggiorenne; to be under —, essere minorenne; Middle Ages, Medioevo.
to **age** vt. e vi. invecchiare.
aged agg. 1. vecchio 2. dell'età di.
agency s. 1. causa, azione 2. (comm.) agenzia, rappresentanza.
agent s. agente.
agglomerate agg. e s. agglomerato.
to **agglomerate** vt. agglomerare. ◆ to **agglomerate** vi. agglomerarsi.
agglomeration s. agglomerazione.
to **agglutinate** vt. agglutinare. ◆ to **agglutinate** vi. agglutinarsi.
to **aggravate** vt. 1. aggravare 2. irritare.
aggravation s. 1. aggravamento 2. esasperazione.
aggregate agg. e s. aggregato.
to **aggregate** vt. 1. aggregare 2. ammontare a. ◆ to **aggregate** vi. aggregarsi.

aggregation s. aggregazione.
aggression s. aggressione.
aggressive agg. aggressivo.
aggressiveness s. aggressività.
aggressor s. aggressore.
aghast agg. 1. atterrito 2. stupefatto.
agile agg. agile.
agility s. agilità.
to **agitate** vt. agitare.
agitation s. agitazione.
agitator s. agitatore.
agnostic agg. e s. agnostico.
ago agg. e avv. fa.
agonistic(al) agg. agonistico.
to **agonize** vt. tormentare. ◆ to **agonize** vi. 1. tormentarsi 2. agonizzare.
agony s. 1. agonia 2. dolore.
agrarian agg. e s. agrario.
to **agree** vt. e vi. 1. accordarsi 2. accettare 3. essere adatto.
agreeable agg. 1. gradevole 2. conforme.
agreement s. 1. accordo 2. conformità 3. consenso.
agricultural agg. agricolo.
agriculture s. agricoltura.
agronomist s. agronomo.
agronomy s. agronomia.
ague s. febbre malarica.
ahead avv. avanti.
aid s. aiuto.
to **aid** vt. aiutare, soccorrere.
to **ail** vt. affliggere. ◆ to **ail** vi. sentirsi male.
aileron s. alettone.
aim s. 1. mira 2. scopo.
to **aim** vt. e vi. 1. mirare 2. aspirare a.
aimless agg. senza scopo.
air s. aria || — conditioning, condizionamento d'aria; — lift, ponte aereo; —line, aviolinea; —raid, incursione aerea; — -mail, posta aerea.
to **air** vt. aerare.
aircraft s. aereo, aerei || — -carrier, portaerei.
airfield s. campo d'aviazione.
airiness s. leggerezza, disinvoltura.
airing s. 1. ventilazione 2. passeggiata.
to **air-mail** vt. trasportare per via aerea.
airman s. aviatore.
airport s. aeroporto.
airship s. aeronave.
airsickness s. mal d'aria.

airstrip s. pista (d'areoporto).
airtight agg. a tenuta d'aria.
airway s. via aerea.
airy agg. 1. arioso 2. aereo 3. gaio.
aisle s. navata (laterale).
ajar avv. socchiuso.
akin agg. 1. consanguineo 2. simile.
alacrity s. alacrità.
alarm s. allarme || — -clock, sveglia; to take —, allarmarsi.
to alarm vt. allarmare.
alas inter. ahimè.
Albanian agg. e s. albanese.
albatross s. albatro.
albumen s. albume.
albumin s. albumina.
alchemist s. alchimista.
alchemy s. alchimia.
alcohol s. alcool: wood —, alcool metilico.
alcoholic agg. alcolico. ◆ **alcoholic** sm. alcolizzato.
alcoholism s. alcoolismo.
alcove s. alcova.
alder s. ontano.
alderman s. assessore.
ale s. birra || —house, birreria.
aleatory agg. aleatorio.
alembic s. alambicco.
alert agg. 1. all'erta 2. svelto. ◆ **alert** s. allarme.
algebraic(al) agg. algebrico.
alien agg. e s. 1. estraneo 2. straniero.
to alienate vt. alienare.
alienation s. alienazione.
alienist s. alienista.
alight agg. illuminato.
to alight vi. 1. scendere 2. posarsi, atterrare.
to align vt. allineare. ◆ **to align** vi. allinearsi.
alignment s. allineamento.
alike agg. simile. ◆ **alike** avv. similmente.
aliment s. alimento.
alimentary agg. alimentare.
alimentation s. alimentazione.
aliquot agg. e s. aliquota.
alive agg. 1. vivo 2. vivace 3. sensibile.
alkaline agg. alcalino.
all agg. tutto, tutti, ogni || — the way, lungo tutto il cammino. ◆ **all** pron. tutto, tutti || not at —, niente affatto; — the better, tanto meglio || — of us, noi tutti; it is — up, tutto è finito. ◆ **all** avv. completamente, interamente || —

right, va bene; — but, quasi. ◆ all s. tutto, totalità.
to allege vt. addurre.
allegiance s. fedeltà.
allegoric(al) agg. allegorico.
allegory s. allegoria.
allergic agg. allergico.
allergy s. allergia.
to alleviate vt. alleviare.
alleviation s. alleviamento.
alley s. vialetto, vicolo.
alliance s. 1. alleanza 2. unione.
allied agg. alleato.
alligator s. alligatore.
alliteration s. allitterazione.
alliterative agg. allitterativo.
to allocate vt. assegnare, distribuire.
allocution s. allocuzione.
to allot vt. assegnare.
allotment s. 1. distribuzione 2. lotto (di terreno).
to allow vt. 1. permettere 2. riconoscere 3. concedere.
allowance s. 1. permesso 2. assegno, indennità 3. razione 4. riconoscimento 5. sconto.
alloy s. (metal.) lega.
to allude vi. alludere.
to allure vt. attrarre.
allurement s. allettamento.
allusion s. allusione.
allusive agg. allusivo.
alluvion s. alluvione.
ally s. alleato.
to ally vt. 1. unire 2. alleare. ◆ **to ally** vi. allearsi.
almanac s. almanacco.
almighty agg. onnipotente: the Almighty, l'Onnipotente.
almond s. mandorla || — -tree, mandorlo.
almost avv. quasi.
alms s. elemosina || - -house, ospizio per i poveri; — -man, accattone.
alone agg. e avv. solo.
along avv. e prep. 1. lungo 2. avanti.
alongside avv. (mar.) accanto, accosto. ◆ **alongside** prep. a fianco di, lungo.
aloof avv. a distanza. ◆ **aloof** agg. riservato, scontroso.
aloofness s. freddezza.
aloud avv. ad alta voce.
alp s. alpe.
alpha s. alfa.
alphabet s. alfabeto.
alphabetic(al) agg. alfabetico.

alpine agg. alpino.
already avv. già.
also avv. anche, inoltre.
altar s. altare || — -boy, chierichet-to; — -piece, pala d'altare.
to **alter** vt. alterare. ♦ to **alter** vi. alterarsi, trasformarsi.
alteration s. alterazione.
altercation s. alterco.
alternacy s. alternanza.
alternate agg. alterno, alternato.
to **alternate** vt. alternare. ♦ to **alternate** vi. alternarsi.
alternation s. alternazione.
alternative agg. alternativo. ♦ **alternative** s. alternativa.
alternator s. (elettr.) alternatore.
although cong. benché.
altimeter s. altimetro.
altitude s. 1. altitudine 2. (aer.) quota.
altogether avv. interamente.
altruism s. altruismo.
altruist s. altruista.
altruistic agg. altruistico.
aluminium s. alluminio.
always avv. sempre.
amalgam s. amalgama.
to **amalgamate** vt. amalgamare. ♦ to **amalgamate** vi. amalgamarsi.
amalgamation s. amalgamazione.
amaranth s. amaranto.
to **amass** vt. ammucchiare.
amateur agg. e s. amatore, dilet-tante.
amateurism s. dilettantismo.
to **amaze** vt. stupire.
amazement s. sorpresa.
amazing agg. sorprendente.
Amazon s. amazzone.
ambages s. pl. ambagi.
ambassador s. ambasciatore.
amber s. ambra.
ambient agg. circostante. ♦ **ambient** s. ambiente.
ambiguity s. ambiguità.
ambiguous agg. ambiguo.
ambit s. ambito.
ambition s. ambizione.
ambitious agg. ambizioso.
ambivalence s. ambivalenza.
ambivalent agg. ambivalente.
amble s. ambio.
ambo s. ambone.
ambulance s. ambulanza.
ambush s. imboscata.
to **ambush** vt. e vi. tendere una im-boscata (a).
to **ameliorate** vt. e vi. migliorare.

to **amend** vt. emendare. ♦ to **amend** vi. emendarsi.
amendment s. emendamento.
amends s. ammenda.
amenity s. amenità.
American agg. e s. americano.
Americanism s. americanismo.
amethyst s. ametista.
amiability s. amabilità.
amiable agg. amabile.
amiably avv. amabilmente.
amianthus s. amianto.
amicable agg. amichevole.
amid prep. in mezzo a, tra, fra.
amiss avv. a male; to take sthg. —, aversene a male. ♦ **amiss** agg. inopportuno, errato.
amity s. amicizia.
ammonia s. ammoniaca.
ammunition s. munizioni.
amnesty s. amnistia.
to **amnesty** vt. amnistiare.
amoeba s. ameba.
among(st) prep. tra, fra (più di due); in mezzo a.
amoral agg. amorale.
amorality s. amoralità.
amorous agg. amoroso.
amorphous agg. amorfo.
to **amortize** vt. (comm.) ammortiz-zare.
amount s. 1. somma 2. totale 3. valore 4. quantità.
to **amount** vi. 1. ammontare 2. e-quivalere.
amperometer s. amperometro.
amphibian agg. e s. anfibio.
amphibious agg. anfibio.
amphitheatre s. anfiteatro.
amphitryon s. anfitrione.
amphora s. anfora.
ample agg. ampio.
amplification s. amplificazione.
amplifier s. amplificatore.
to **amplify** vt. amplificare. ♦ to **amplify** vi. dilungarsi.
to **amputate** vt. amputare.
amputation s. amputazione.
amulet s. amuleto.
to **amuse** vt. divertire.
amusement s. divertimento.
an art. V. a.
anachronic agg. anacronistico.
anachronism s. anacronismo.
anachronistic(al) agg. anacroni-stico.
anaemia s. anemia.
anaemic agg. anemico.
anaesthesia s. anestesia.

anaesthetic *agg.* e *s.* anestetico.
anaesthetist *s.* anestesista.
to **anaesthetize** *vt.* anestetizzare.
anagram *s.* anagramma.
anal *agg.* anale.
analgesic *agg.* e *s.* analgesico.
analogic(al) *agg.* analogico.
analogous *agg.* analogo.
analogy *s.* analogia.
to **analyse** *vt.* analizzare.
analysis *s.* (*pl.* -ses) analisi.
analyst *s.* analista.
analytic(al) *agg.* analitico.
anarchic(al) *agg.* anarchico.
anarchism *s.* anarchia.
anarchist *s.* anarchico.
anarchy *s.* anarchia.
anathema *s.* anatema.
anatomic(al) *agg.* anatomico.
anatomist *s.* anatomista.
to **anatomize** *vt.* anatomizzare.
anatomy *s.* anatomia.
ancestor *s.* antenato.
ancestral *agg.* ancestrale.
ancestry *s.* stirpe.
anchor *s.* (*mar.*) ancora.
to **anchor** *vt.* ancorare. ♦ to **anchor** *vi.* ancorarsi.
anchorage *s.* ancoraggio.
anchoret *s.* anacoreta.
anchovy *s.* acciuga.
ancient *agg.* e *s.* antico.
and *cong.* e.
androgynous *agg.* androgino.
anecdote *s.* aneddoto.
anecdotic(al) *agg.* aneddotico.
anew *avv.* di nuovo.
anfractuosity *s.* anfrattuosità.
anfractuous *agg.* anfrattuoso.
angel *s.* angelo: *guardian* —, angelo custode.
angelic(al) *agg.* angelico.
anger *s.* collera.
to **anger** *vt.* irritare.
angle *s.* (*geom.*) angolo ‖ *at right angles*, perpendicolarmente.
to **angle** *vi.* 1. pescare (*con l'amo*) 2. *to — for*, andare in cerca di.
angler *s.* pescatore (*con l'amo*).
Anglican *agg.* e *s.* anglicano.
Anglo-Saxon *agg.* e *s.* anglosassone.
angrily *avv.* irosamente.
angry *agg.* irato, arrabbiato ‖ *to get* —, adirarsi.
anguish *s.* angoscia.
to **anguish** *vt.* angosciare. ♦ to **anguish** *vi.* angosciarsi.
angular *agg.* angolare.
anhydride *s.* anidride.

aniline *s.* anilina.
animadversion *s.* biasimo.
to **animadvert** *vi.* criticare: *to — on so., sthg., criticare qu., qc.*
animal *agg.* e *s.* animale.
to **animate** *vt.* animare.
animatedly *avv.* animatamente.
animation *s.* animazione.
animator *s.* animatore.
animism *s.* animismo.
animosity *s.* animosità.
anise *s.* anice.
ankle *s.* caviglia.
ankylosis *s.* anchilosi.
annals *s. pl.* annali.
Annelida *s. pl.* anellidi.
to **annex** *vt.* annettere.
annexation *s.* annessione.
to **annihilate** *vt.* annichilire.
annihilation *s.* annichilimento.
anniversary *s.* anniversario.
to **annotate** *vt.* e *vi.* annotare.
annotation *s.* annotazione.
to **announce** *vt.* annunciare.
announcement *s.* annuncio.
announcer *s.* annunciatore.
to **annoy** *vt.* infastidire.
annoyance *s.* fastidio.
annoying *agg.* fastidioso.
annual *agg.* annuale. ♦ **annual** *s.* annuario.
annuity *s.* rendita annuale.
to **annul** *vt.* annullare.
annulment *s.* annullamento.
to **annunciate** *vt.* annunciare.
annunciation *s.* annuncio, annunciazione.
anode *s.* anodo.
anodyne *agg.* e *s.* anodino.
to **anoint** *vt.* ungere, consacrare.
anomalous *agg.* anomalo.
anomaly *s.* anomalia.
anonym *s.* anonimo.
anonymous *agg.* anonimo.
another *agg.* e *pron.* un altro ‖ *one* —, l'un l'altro.
answer *s.* risposta.
to **answer** *vt.* e *vi.* rispondere.
ant *s.* formica ‖ — *-bear*, formichiere.
antagonism *s.* antagonismo.
antagonist *s.* antagonista.
Antarctic *agg.* antartico.
antecedent *agg.* e *s.* antecedente. ♦ **antecedents** *s. pl.* antenati.
to **antedate** *vt.* 1. antidatare 2. anticipare.
antediluvian *agg.* e *s.* antidiluviano.

antelope *s.* antilope.

anteroom *s.* anticamera.

anthem *s.* inno.

anthological *agg.* antologico.

anthology *s.* antologia.

anthracite *s.* antracite.

anthropocentric *agg.* antropocentrico.

anthropologist *s.* antropologo.

anthropology *s.* antropologia.

anthropomorphic *agg.* antropomorfo.

anthropomorphism *s.* antropomorfismo.

anthropomorphous *agg.* antropomorfo.

anthropophagous *agg.* e *s.* (*pl.* -gi) antropofago.

anthropophagy *s.* antropofagia.

antiaesthetic *agg.* antiestetico.

anti-aircraft *agg.* antiaereo.

antibiotic *agg.* e *s.* antibiotico.

antibody *s.* anticorpo.

to anticipate *vt.* 1. anticipare 2. prevedere 3. pregustare.

anticipation *s.* 1. anticipo 2. previsione 3. pregustazione.

anticlerical *agg.* anticlericale.

anticlericalism *s.* anticlericalismo.

anticonceptive *s.* antifecondativo.

anticonstitutional *agg.* anticostituzionale.

anticyclone *s.* anticiclone.

anti-dazzle *agg.* antiabbagliante.

antidote *s.* antidoto.

anti-freeze *s.* anticongelante.

anti-gas *agg.* antigas.

antimilitarism *s.* antimilitarismo.

antimilitarist *s.* antimilitarista.

antimony *s.* antimonio.

antinomy *s.* antinomia.

antiparticle *s.* antiparticella.

antipathetic(al) *agg.* avverso.

antipathy *s.* antipatia.

antiphon(y) *s.* antifona.

antipodal *agg.* degli, agli antipodi.

antipode *s.* antipodo.

antiquarian *agg.* e *s.* antiquario.

antiquary *s.* antiquario.

antiquated *agg.* antiquato.

antique *agg.* antico. ♦ **antique** *s.* antichità ‖ — *dealer*, antiquario.

antiquity *s.* antichità.

antirheumatic *agg.* antireumatico.

anti-rust *agg.* e *s.* antiruggine.

anti-Semite *s.* antisemita.

anti-Semitism *s.* antisemitismo.

antiseptic *agg.* e *s.* antisettico.

antisocial *agg.* antisociale.

antispasmodic *agg.* e *s.* antispasmodico.

anti-tank *agg.* anticarro.

antitetanic *agg.* antitetanico.

anti-theft *agg.* e *s.* antifurto.

antithesis *s.* (*pl.* -ses) antitesi.

antithetic(al) *agg.* antitetico.

antitoxic *agg.* antitossico.

anus *s.* ano.

anvil *s.* incudine.

anxiety *s.* ansietà.

anxious *agg.* ansioso.

any *agg.* 1. qualunque 2. (*in frasi neg.; int.; dubitative*) qualche, nessuno, del ‖ *at — rate*, in ogni modo. ♦ **any** *pron.* 1. alcuno, nessuno 2. ne ‖ *have you — bread?*, hai del pane?; *I haven't* —, non ne ho.

anybody *pron.* 1. chiunque 2. (*in frasi neg.; int.; dubitative*) qualcuno, nessuno.

anyhow *avv.* e *cong.* comunque.

anyone *pron.* V. *anybody*.

anything *pron.* 1. qualunque cosa 2. (*in frasi neg.; int.; dubitative*) qualche cosa, niente.

anyway *avv.* in ogni modo, comunque.

anywhere *avv.* dovunque.

apace *avv.* presto.

apanage *s.* appannaggio.

apart *avv.* 1. a parte 2. lontano.

apartheid *s.* discriminazione razziale.

apartment *s.* alloggio (*in affitto*).

apathy *s.* apatia.

ape *s.* scimmia.

to ape *vt.* scimmiottare.

aperitif *s.* aperitivo.

apex *s.* apice.

aphaeresis *s.* aferesi.

aphonia *s.* afonia.

aphorism *s.* aforisma.

aphrodisiac *agg.* e *s.* afrodisiaco.

aphtha *s.* afta.

apiece *avv.* a testa.

apish *agg.* scimmiesco.

apocalypse *s.* apocalisse.

apocalyptic(al) *agg.* apocalittico.

apocrypha *s. pl.* libri apocrifi.

apocryphal *agg.* apocrifo.

apogee *s.* apogeo.

apologetic(al) *agg.* apologetico.

apologist *s.* apologista.

to apologize *vi.* scusarsi.

apologue *s.* apologo.

apology *s.* scusa.

apoplexy *s.* apoplessia.

apostasy s. apostasia.
apostate agg. e s. apostata.
apostle s. apostolo.
apostolate s. apostolato.
apostolic(al) agg. apostolico.
apostrophe s. apostrofo.
to **apostrophize** vt. apostrofare.
apothecary s. farmacista.
apotheosis s. (pl. -ses) apoteosi.
to **appal** vt. spaventare.
appalling agg. spaventoso.
apparatus s. apparato.
apparent agg. 1. visibile, evidente 2. (giur.) legittimo.
apparition s. apparizione.
appeal s. 1. appello 2. attrattiva.
to **appeal** vi. 1. appellarsi 2. attrarre.
appealing agg. 1. supplichevole 2. attraente.
to **appear** vi. 1. apparire 2. sembrare.
appearance s. 1. apparenza, aspetto 2. apparizione.
to **appease** vt. placare.
appeasement s. pacificazione, tregua.
appellative agg. e s. appellativo.
appendicitis s. appendicite.
appendix s. appendice.
appetite s. appetito.
appetizer s. aperitivo.
appetizing agg. appetitoso.
to **applaud** vt. e vi. applaudire.
applauding agg. plaudente.
applause s. applauso.
apple s. mela || — -tree, melo.
appliance s. 1. applicazione 2. apparecchio.
applicant s. richiedente.
application s. 1. applicazione 2. domanda.
to **apply** vt. applicare. ♦ to **apply** vi. 1. applicarsi 2. rivolgersi.
to **appoint** vt. 1. fissare 2. nominare, assegnare.
appointee s. persona designata.
appointment s. 1. appuntamento 2. nomina 3. impiego.
apposition s. apposizione.
appraisal s. stima.
to **appraise** vt. stimare.
appreciable agg. apprezzabile.
to **appreciate** vt. 1. apprezzare 2. rendersi conto di. ♦ to **appreciate** vi. aumentare di valore.
appreciation s. 1. apprezzamento 2. aumento di valore.
to **apprehend** vt. assodare.

apprehension s. 1. apprensione 2. percezione 3. arresto.
apprehensive agg. 1. apprensivo 2. perspicace.
apprentice s. apprendista.
apprenticeship s. apprendistato.
approach s. 1. avvicinamento 2. approccio 3. impostazione (di una pratica ecc.).
to **approach** vt. avvicinare. ♦ to **approach** vi. avvicinarsi.
approachable agg. accessibile.
appropriate agg. appropriato.
to **appropriate** vt. 1. appropriarsi di 2. stanziare.
appropriation s. 1. appropriazione 2. stanziamento.
approval s. 1. approvazione 2. , (comm.) prova: on —, in prova.
to **approve** vt. 1. approvare 2. mostrare.
approximate agg. approssimativo.
to **approximate** vt. approssimare. ♦ to **approximate** vi. approssimarsi.
approximation s. approssimazione.
approximative agg. approssimativo.
apricot s. albicocca || — -tree, albicocco.
April s. aprile.
apron s. 1. grembiale 2. riparo 3. (teat.) proscenio.
apse s. abside.
apt agg. 1. atto 2. intelligente 3. proclive.
aptitude, aptness s. 1. idoneità 2. intelligenza 3. proprietà (di vocabolo).
aqualung s. autorespiratore.
aquamarine s. acquamarina.
aquarium s. acquario.
aquatic(al) agg. acquatico.
aqueduct s. acquedotto.
aqueous agg. acqueo, acquoso.
Arab agg. e s. arabo.
arabesque s. arabesco.
Arabian agg. e s. arabo.
Arabic agg. arabico.
arable agg. arabile.
arbiter s. arbitro.
arbitrage s. arbitraggio.
arbitrary agg. arbitrario.
to **arbitrate** vt. e vi. arbitrare.
arbitrator s. (giur.) arbitro.
arboreal, arboreous agg. arboreo.
arboriculture s. arboricoltura.
arbour s. pergolato.
arc s. arco.
arcade s. galleria.

Arcadian *agg.* e *s.* arcadico.

arch *s.* arco.

to **arch** *vt.* 1. fabbricare ad arco 2. inarcare. ♦ to **arch** *vi.* inarcarsi.

archaeologic(al) *agg.* archeologico.

archaeologist *s.* archeologo.

archaeology *s.* archeologia

archaic(al) *agg.* arcaico.

archaism *s.* arcaismo.

archangel *s.* arcangelo.

archbishop *s.* arcivescovo

archduke *s.* arciduca.

archer *s.* arciere.

archetype *s.* archetipo.

archipelago *s.* arcipelago.

architect *s.* architetto.

architectonic, architectural *agg* architettonico.

architecture *s.* architettura.

archive *s.* archivio.

archivist *s.* archivista.

Arctic *agg.* e *s.* artico.

ardent *agg.* ardente.

ardour *s.* ardore.

arduous *agg.* arduo.

area *s.* area.

arena *s.* (*arch.*) arena.

Areopagus *s.* areopago.

argent *s.* argenteo.

Argentine *agg.* e *s.* argentino.

argil *s.* argilla.

to **argue** *vi.* 1. discutere 2. ragionare. ♦ to **argue** *vt.* dimostrare.

argument *s.* 1. discussione 2. argomentazione.

arid *agg.* arido.

aridity *s.* aridità.

to **arise (arose, arisen)** *vi.* 1. alzarsi 2. (*fig.*) nascere.

aristocracy *s.* aristocrazia.

aristocrat *s.* aristocratico.

aristocratic(al) *agg.* aristocratico.

Aristotelian *agg.* e *s.* aristotelico.

arithmetic *s.* aritmetica.

arithmetic(al) *agg.* aritmetico.

arm[1] *s.* braccio ‖ — -*in*- —, a braccetto.

arm[2] *s.* arma ‖ *coat of arms,* stemma.

to **arm** *vt.* armare. ♦ to **arm** *vi.* armarsi.

armament *s.* armamento.

armchair *s.* poltrona.

armful *s.* bracciata.

armistice *s.* armistizio.

armless *agg.* inerme.

armlet *s.* braccialetto.

armour *s.* corazza.

to **armour** *vt.* corazzare ‖ *armour-*

ed-car, autoblinda.

armoury *s.* 1. arsenale 2. armeria.

armpit *s.* ascella.

army *s.* esercito.

aromatic(al) *agg.* aromatico.

arose V. *to arise.*

around *avv.* intorno. ♦ **around** *prep.* 1. intorno a 2. circa.

to **arouse** *vt.* 1. destare 2. eccitare.

to **arrange** *vt.* 1. accomodare 2. predisporre 3. (*mus.*) arrangiare.

arrangement *s.* 1. accomodamento 2. (*mus.*) arrangiamento 3. dispositivo. ♦ **arrangements** *s. pl.* preparativi.

arras *s.* arazzo.

array *s.* 1. apparato 2. (*mil.*) spiegamento.

to **array** *vt.* 1. ornare 2. (*mil.*) schierare.

arrest *s.* arresto.

to **arrest** *vt.* arrestare.

arrival *s.* arrivo.

to **arrive** *vi.* arrivare.

arrogance *s.* arroganza.

arrogant *agg.* arrogante.

to **arrogate** *vt.* arrogarsi.

arrow *s.* freccia.

arsenal *s.* arsenale.

arsenic *s.* arsenico.

art *s.* arte.

arteriosclerosis *s.* arteriosclerosi.

artery *s.* arteria.

artesian *agg.* artesiano.

artful *agg.* 1. abile 2. artificioso 3. astuto.

arthritic(al) *agg.* artritico.

arthritis *s.* artrite.

artichoke *s.* carciofo.

article *s.* articolo.

articulate *agg.* 1. articolato 2. chiaro.

to **articulate** *vt.* articolare. ♦ to **articulate** *vi.* articolarsi.

articulation *s.* articolazione.

artifice *s.* 1. artificio 2. abilità.

artificial *agg.* artificiale.

artificiality *s.* artificiosità.

artillery *s.* artiglieria.

artilleryman *s.* artigliere.

artist *s.* artista.

artistic(al) *agg.* artistico.

artistry *s.* abilità artistica.

artless *agg.* ingenuo.

Aryan *agg.* e *s.* ariano.

as *avv.* come ‖ — ... —, tanto ... quanto; *so* — (*con infinito*), in modo da; — *for,* quanto a; — *far* —, sin dove, fino a; — *much,* al-

trettanto; — *well*, come pure. ◆
as *cong.* 1. poiché 2. mentre.
asbestos *s.* asbesto.
to ascend *vi.* ascendere. ◆ to
ascend *vt.* risalire, scalare.
ascendancy *s.* ascendente.
ascendant *agg.* e *s.* ascendente.
ascension *s.* ascensione.
ascent *s.* ascesa.
to ascertain *vt.* accertarsi di.
ascertainment *s.* accertamento.
ascetic *s.* asceta.
ascetic(al) *agg.* ascetico.
asceticism *s.* ascetismo.
to ascribe *vt.* ascrivere.
asepsis *s.* asepsi.
aseptic *agg.* e *s.* asettico.
asexual *agg.* asessuale.
ash *s.* cenere || — *-tray*, portacenere.
ash(-tree) *s.* frassino.
ashamed *agg.* vergognoso || *to be*
—, aver vergogna.
ashore *avv.* a terra.
ashy *agg.* cinereo.
Asiatic *agg.* e *s.* asiatico.
aside *avv.* a parte, da parte.
asininity *s.* asinità.
to ask *vt.* e *vi.* 1. chiedere 2. invi-
tare || *to — so. for sthg.*, chiedere
a qu. qc.; *to — for trouble*, cer-
car fastidi.
askance *avv.* di traverso.
asker *s.* interrogante.
asleep *agg.* addormentato.
asocial *agg.* asociale.
asp *s.* aspide.
asparagus *s. coll.* asparago, aspa-
ragi.
aspect *s.* aspetto.
aspen *s.* pioppo tremulo.
aspergillum *s.* aspersorio.
asperity *s.* 1. asperità 2. (*fig.*)
asprezza.
aspersion *s.* 1. aspersione 2. calunnia.
asphalt *s.* asfalto.
asphyxia *s.* asfissia.
to asphyxiate *vt.* asfissiare.
aspirant *agg.* e *s.* aspirante.
to aspirate *vt.* aspirare.
aspiration *s.* aspirazione.
aspirator *s.* aspiratore.
to aspire *vi.* aspirare.
aspirin *s.* aspirina.
aspiring *agg.* ambizioso.
asquint *avv.* di traverso.
ass *s.* asino || *to make an — of one-
self*, rendersi ridicolo.
to assail *vt.* assalire.

assailant, assailer *s.* assalitore.
assassin *s.* assassino.
to assassinate *vt.* assassinare.
assassination *s.* assassinio.
assault *s.* assalto, aggressione.
to assault *vt.* assalire.
assaulter *s.* assalitore.
to assay *vt.* saggiare.
assayer *s.* (as)saggiatore.
to assemble *vt.* riunire. ◆ to assemble *vi.* riunirsi.
assembly *s.* 1. assemblea 2. (*mil.*)
adunata 3. (*mecc.*) montaggio: —
line, catena di montaggio.
assent *s.* consenso.
to assent *vt.* approvare.
to assert *vt.* asserire || *to — one-
self*, farsi valere.
assertion *s.* asserzione.
assertor *s.* assertore.
to assess *vt.* 1. tassare 2. (*comm.*)
ripartire.
assessment *s.* 1. valutazione 2. tassazione.
assessor *s.* agente delle tasse.
asset *s.* 1. bene, vantaggio. ◆ assets *s. pl.* patrimonio, attività
(*sing.*).
assiduity *s.* assiduità.
assiduous *agg.* assiduo.
to assign *vt.* 1. assegnare 2. trasferire 3. designare.
assignation *s.* 1. assegnazione 2.
(*giur.*) cessione 3. appuntamento.
assignment *s.* 1. assegnazione 2.
(*giur.*) cessione.
assimilable *agg.* assimilabile.
to assimilate *vt.* 1. assimilare 2.
confrontare. ◆ to assimilate *vi.*
assimilarsi.
assimilation *s.* 1. assimilazione 2.
confronto.
to assist *vt.* e *vi.* assistere.
assistance *s.* assistenza.
assistant *agg.* e *s.* assistente || *shop*
—, commesso.
assize *s.* 1. (*giur.*) seduta. ◆ Assizes *s. pl.* Assise.
associate *agg.* e *s.* associato.
to associate *vt.* associare. ◆ to
associate *vi.* associarsi.
association *s.* associazione.
assonance *s.* assonanza.
to assort *vt.* 1. assortire 2. classificare. ◆ to assort *vi.* 1. armonizzarsi 2. frequentare: *to — with*
so., frequentare qu.
to assume *vt.* 1. assumere 2. fingere 3. presumere.

assuming *agg.* presuntuoso.

assumption *s.* **1.** assunzione **2.** finzione **3.** supposizione **4.** presunzione.

assurance *s.* **1.** assicurazione **2.** sicurezza **3.** fiducia.

to assure *vt.* **1.** assicurare **2.** rassicurare.

assurer *s.* assicuratore.

asterisk *s.* asterisco.

astern *avv.* a poppa.

asteroid *s.* asteroide.

asthenia *s.* astenia.

asthma *s.* asma.

asthmatic *agg.* e *s.* asmatico.

astigmatic *agg.* astigmatico.

astigmatism *s.* astigmatismo.

astir *agg.* e *avv.* in moto.

to astonish *vt.* stupire.

astonishing *agg.* sorprendente

astonishment *s.* sorpresa.

to astound *vt.* sbalordire.

astragal(us) *s.* astragalo.

astrakhan *s.* astracan.

astral *agg.* astrale.

astray *agg.* e *avv.* fuori strada.

astride *agg.* e *avv.* a cavalcioni. ♦ **astride** *prep.* a cavalcioni di.

astringent *agg.* e *s.* astringente

astrolabe *s.* astrolabio.

astrologer *s.* astrologo.

astrology *s.* astrologia.

astronaut *s.* astronauta.

astronautics *s.* astronautica.

astronomer *s.* astronomo.

astronomic(al) *agg.* astronomico.

astronomy *s.* astronomia.

astute *agg.* astuto.

asunder *avv.* **1.** separatamente **2.** in pezzi.

asylum *s.* **1.** asilo, ricovero **2.** manicomio.

asymmetric(al) *agg.* asimmetrico.

asymmetry *s.* asimmetria.

at *prep.* (*stato, tempo, modo*) a, da, in: *to arrive — a place*, arrivare in un luogo; *— that time*, in quel momento; *— will*, a volontà.

atavistic *agg.* atavico.

atavism *s.* atavismo.

ataxy *s.* atassia.

ate V. *to eat.*

atheism *s.* ateismo.

atheist *s.* ateo.

atheistic(al) *agg.* ateistico.

athlete *s.* atleta.

athletic *agg.* atletico.

athletics *s.* atletica.

atlas *s.* atlante.

atmosphere *s.* atmosfera.

atmospheric(al) *agg.* atmosferico.

atoll *s.* atollo.

atom *s.* atomo.

atomic(al) *agg.* atomico.

atomism *s.* atomismo.

to atomize *vt.* nebulizzare.

atomizer *s.* atomizzatore, nebulizzatore.

atomy *s.* atomo.

to atone *vt.* espiare.

atonement *s.* espiazione.

atonic *agg.* **1.** atono **2.** atonico.

atrocious *agg.* atroce.

atrocity *s.* atrocità.

atrophic *agg.* atrofico.

atrophy *s.* atrofia.

to atrophy *vt.* atrofizzare. ♦ **to atrophy** *vi.* atrofizzarsi.

atropin(e) *s.* atropina.

to attach *vt.* **1.** attaccare, unire **2.** attribuire **3.** attrarre. ♦ **to attach** *vi.* attaccarsi.

attaché *s.* addetto.

attachment *s.* **1.** attaccamento **2.** (*mecc.*) accessorio.

attack *s.* attacco.

to attack *vt.* attaccare.

attacker *s.* assalitore.

to attain *vt.* raggiungere. ♦ **to attain** *vi.* giungere.

attainable *agg.* raggiungibile.

attainment *s.* **1.** raggiungimento **2.** cultura.

attempt *s.* **1.** tentativo **2.** attentato.

to attempt *vt.* **1.** tentare **2.** attentare a.

to attend *vi.* **1.** badare a **2.** obbedire ‖ *to — on*, essere al servizio di. ♦ **to attend** *vt.* **1.** assistere **2.** accompagnare **3.** frequentare.

attendance *s.* **1.** servizio **2.** assistenza **3.** frequenza.

attendant *s.* **1.** servitore **2.** assistente **3.** assiduo frequentatore.

attention *s.* attenzione: *to pay —*, fare attenzione.

attentive *agg.* **1.** attento **2.** sollecito.

to attenuate *vt.* **1.** assottigliare **2.** attenuare. ♦ **to attenuate** *vi.* **1.** assottigliarsi **2.** attenuarsi.

attenuation *s.* **1.** assottigliamento **2.** attenuazione.

to attest *vt.* attestare.

attic *agg.* e *s.* attico.

to attire *vt.* vestire, agghindare. ♦ **to attire** *vi.* vestirsi.

attitude *s.* atteggiamento.

attorney s. 1. procura 2. procuratore || — (-at-law), procuratore legale.
to **attract** vt. attrarre.
attraction s. 1. attrazione 2. attrattiva.
attractive agg. attraente.
attribute s. attributo.
to **attribute** vt. attribuire.
attribution s. attribuzione.
attributive agg. attributivo. ♦ **attributive** s. attributo.
aubergine s. melanzana.
auction s. asta: — sale, vendita all'asta.
to **auction** vt. vendere all'asta.
auctioneer s. banditore.
audible agg. udibile.
audience s. 1. udienza 2. uditorio.
audiovisual agg. audiovisivo.
audit s. verifica, revisione.
audition s. audizione.
auditory agg. e s. uditorio.
auger s. trivella, succhiello.
to **augment** vt. aumentare. ♦ to **augment** vi. crescere.
augmentative agg. e s. accrescitivo.
to **augur** vt. e vi. predire.
august agg. augusto.
August s. agosto.
aunt s. zia || great- —, prozia.
auricle s. 1. padiglione auricolare 2. (med.) orecchietta.
auricular agg. auricolare.
auriferous agg. aurifero.
to **auscultate** vt. auscultare.
auscultation s. auscultazione.
auscultator s. stetoscopio.
auspice s. auspicio.
auspicious agg. propizio.
austere agg. austero.
austerity s. austerità.
austral agg. australe.
Australian agg. e s. australiano.
Austrian agg. e s. austriaco.
autarky s. autarchia.
authentic(al) agg. autentico.
to **authenticate** vt. autenticare.
authentication s. autenticazione.
authenticity s. autenticità.
author s. autore.
authoress s. autrice.
authoritative agg. 1. autoritario 2. autorevole.
authoritativeness s. autorevolezza.
authority s. autorità.
authorization s. autorizzazione.
to **authorize** vt. autorizzare.
authorless agg. anonimo.

authorship s. paternità (di un libro).
autobiographic(al) agg. autobiografico.
autobiography s. autobiografia.
autochthon s. autoctono.
autochthonous agg. autoctono.
autocracy s. autocrazia.
autocrat s. autocrate.
autocriticism s. autocritica.
autoeducation s. autoeducazione.
autofinancing s. autofinanziamento.
autograph s. autografo.
autography s. autografia.
autolesion s. autolesione.
automatic agg. automatico. ♦ **automatic** s. arma automatica.
automation s. automazione.
automatism s. automatismo.
automaton s. automa.
autonomist s. autonomista.
autonomous agg. autonomo.
autonomy s. autonomia.
autopsy s. autopsia.
auto-suggestion s. autosuggestione.
autumn s. autunno.
autumnal agg. autunnale.
auxiliary agg. e s. ausiliare.
avail s. utilità.
to **avail** vt. e vi. servire a || to — oneself of, approfittare di.
availability s. 1. disponibilità 2. validità.
available agg. 1. disponibile 2. valevole.
avalanche s. valanga.
avarice s. 1. avarizia 2. cupidigia.
avaricious agg. 1. avaro 2. cupido.
to **avenge** vt. vendicare.
avenger s. vendicatore.
avenue s. viale.
to **aver** vt. asserire, dichiarare.
average agg. medio. ♦ **average** s. 1. media 2. (comm.) avaria.
averse agg. avverso.
aversion s. avversione.
to **avert** vt. sviare.
aviary s. uccelliera.
aviation s. aviazione.
aviator s. aviatore.
avid agg. avido.
avidity s. avidità.
to **avoid** vt. 1. evitare 2. (giur.) annullare.
avoidable agg. 1. evitabile 2. (giur.) annullabile.
to **avow** vt. dichiarare, ammettere.
avowal s. dichiarazione, ammissione.

to **await** *vt.* attendere.

awake *agg.* **1.** sveglio **2.** conscio.

to **awake (awoke, awoke)** *vt.* svegliare. ♦ to **awake (awoke, awoke)** *vi.* svegliarsi.

to **awaken** *vt.* risvegliare, far aprire gli occhi. ♦ to **awaken** *vi.* risvegliarsi, aprire gli occhi.

awakening *s.* risveglio.

award *s.* **1.** sentenza **2.** ricompensa.

to **award** *vt.* aggiudicare.

aware *agg.* conscio.

away *avv.* via, lontano || *right* —, subito, seduta stante.

awe *s.* timore reverenziale.

awful *agg.* **1.** terribile **2.** imponente.

awkward *agg.* **1.** goffo, imbarazzato **2.** scomodo **3.** inopportuno **4.** delicato.

awkwardness *s.* **1.** goffaggine **2.** imbarazzo.

awl *s.* lesina.

awning *s.* tenda.

awoke V. *to awake.*

awry *agg.* **1.** storto **2.** bieco. ♦ **awry** *avv.* **1.** per traverso **2.** perversamente.

ax(e) *s.* scure.

axiom *s.* assioma.

axiomatic(al) *agg.* assiomatico.

axis *s.* (*pl.* axes) asse.

axle *s.* (*mecc.*) asse.

azimuth *s.* azimut.

azote *s.* azoto.

to **azotize** *vt.* azotare.

Aztec *agg.* e *s.* azteco.

azure *agg.* e *s.* azzurro.

B

b *s.* (*mus.*) si.

babble *s.* balbettio.

to **babble** *vi.* e *vt.* **1.** balbettare **2.** mormorare (*di acque*).

babe *s.* bambino.

babel *s.* babele.

baboon *s.* babbuino.

baby *s.* bimbo, neonato || — *sitter*, chi accudisce i bambini.

babyhood *s.* infanzia.

babyish *agg.* infantile.

baccarat *s.* baccarà.

Bacchanal *s.* **1.** baccante **2.** baccanale (*anche fig.*).

Bacchante *s.* baccante.

bacchic(al) *agg.* bacchico.

bachelor *s.* scapolo || *Bachelor of Arts,* titolo universitario in lettere.

bachelorhood *s.* celibato.

bacillus *s.* (*pl.* -li) bacillo.

back[1] *agg.* posteriore. ♦ **back** *avv.* dietro, indietro || *to be* —, essere di ritorno; *to go, to come* —, ritornare.

back[2] *s.* **1.** dorso, schiena **2.** spalle **3.** rovescio **4.** schienale **5.** fondo.

to **back** *vt.* **1.** sostenere **2.** fare indietreggiare || *to* — *a bill,* avallare una cambiale. ♦ to **back** *vi.* indietreggiare || — *down,* abbandonare la contesa.

to **backbite** *vt.* denigrare.

backbiter *s.* calunniatore.

backbiting *agg.* maldicente. ♦ **backbiting** *s.* maldicenza.

backbone *s.* **1.** spina dorsale **2.** (*fig.*) fermezza.

backer *s.* **1.** scommettitore **2.** sostenitore.

backfire *s.* ritorno di fiamma.

background *s.* **1.** sfondo **2.** curriculum **3.** ambiente.

backing *s.* **1.** sostegno **2.** marcia indietro.

backlash *s.* rimbalzo.

backslider *s.* apostata.

backward *agg.* **1.** lento **2.** tardo.

backward(s) *avv.* indietro.

backwash *s.* risacca.

bacon *s.* lardo affumicato, pancetta.

bacterial *agg.* batterico.

bacteriology *s.* batteriologia.

bacterium *s.* (*pl.* -ia) batterio.

bad (worse, worst) *agg.* **1.** cattivo **2.** brutto. ♦ **bad** *s.* **1.** male **2.** rovina.

bade V. *to bid.*

badge *s.* insegna.

badger *s.* tasso.

badly *avv.* male, malamente.

badness *s.* **1.** cattiveria **2.** cattiva qualità.

baffle *s.* (*-plate*) deflettore, diaframma.

to **baffle** *vt.* **1.** eludere **2.** confondere.

bag *s.* **1.** sacco **2.** borsa || *sleeping*—, sacco a pelo.

to **bag** *vt.* **1.** gonfiare **2.** rubare **3.** insaccare.

baggage *s.* bagaglio.

bagpipe *s.* cornamusa.

bail *s.* **1.** cauzione **2.** garante.

to **bail**[1] *vt.* **1.** dar garanzia per **2.**

affidare (*dietro cauzione*).
to **bail**[2] *vt.* e *vi.* (*mar.*) aggottare || *to — out*, lanciarsi col paracadute.
bailiff *s.* 1. magistrato inquirente 2. ufficiale fiscale.
bain-marie *s.* bagnomaria.
bait *s.* 1. esca 2. sosta (*per ristoro*).
to **bait** *vt.* 1. adescare 2. tormentare. ♦ to **bait** *vi.* fermarsi (*per prendere ristoro*).
to **bake** *vt.* e *vi.* cuocere al forno.
baker *s.* fornaio.
bakery *s.* forno.
baking *s.* cottura al forno.
balance *s.* 1. bilancia 2. bilanciere 3. equilibrio 4. bilancio.
to **balance** *vt.* 1. pesare 2. pareggiare. ♦ to **balance** *vi.* 1. bilanciarsi 2. oscillare.
balanced *agg.* equilibrato.
balancer *s.* acrobata.
balcony *s.* 1. balcone 2. (*teat.*).balconata.
bald *agg.* 1. calvo, pelato 2. povero, nudo.
baldness *s.* 1. calvizie 2. (*fig.*) nudità.
baldric *s.* bandoliera.
bale *s.* (*comm.*) balla.
Balkan *agg.* balcanico.
ball *s.* 1. palla 2. ballo || — *-bearing*, cuscinetto a sfere.
to **ball** *vt.* appallottolare. ♦ to **ball** *vi.* appallottolarsi.
ballad *s.* ballata.
ballast *s.* zavorra.
to **ballast** *vt.* zavorrare.
ballet *s.* balletto || — *-dancer*, ballerino classico.
ballistics *s.* balistica.
balloon *s.* 1. pallone 2. lambicco 3. fumetto.
ballot *s.* 1. pallina, scheda (*per votazione*) 2. voto 3. scrutinio || — *-box*, urna.
to **ballot** *vt.* mettere in ballottaggio.
balm *s.* balsamo.
balm-cricket *s.* (*zool.*) cicala.
balmy *agg.* balsamico.
Baltic *agg.* baltico.
balustrade *s.* balaustrata.
bamboo *s.* bambù.
ban *s.* bando.
to **ban** *vt.* proibire.
banal *agg.* banale.
banality *s.* banalità.
banana *s.* 1. banana 2. banano.
band *s.* 1. legame 2. benda 3. nastro 4. banda.

to **band** *vt.* 1. legare 2. bendare.
bandage *s.* bendaggio.
to **bandage** *vt.* bendare.
banderole *s.* banderuola.
bandit *s.* bandito.
bandmaster *s.* capobanda.
bandog *s.* cane da guardia.
bandsman *s.* bandista.
bane *s.* 1. calamità 2. veleno.
baneful *agg.* velenoso.
bang *s.* 1. botta 2. detonazione.
to **bang** *vt.* e *vi.* sbattere violentemente.
banging *s.* 1. colpi violenti 2. detonazioni.
to **banish** *vt.* bandire, esiliare.
banishment *s.* bando, esilio.
banister *s.* ringhiera (*di scala*).
bank *s.* 1. banca 2. banco 3. argine 4. terrapieno.
to **bank** *vt.* 1. arginare 2. depositare in banca || *to — upon*, contare su. ♦ to **bank** *vi.* gestire una banca.
bankbook *s.* libretto bancario.
banker *s.* banchiere.
banking *agg.* bancario. ♦ **banking** *s.* tecnica, professione bancaria.
bank note *s.* banconota.
bankrupt *agg.* e *s.* fallito || *to go —*, fallire.
bankruptcy *s.* fallimento.
banner *s.* vessillo.
banns *s. pl.* pubblicazioni matrimoniali.
banquet *s.* banchetto.
to **banquet** *vi.* banchettare.
banter *s.* scherzo, beffa.
to **banter** *vt.* canzonare.
baptism *s.* battesimo.
baptist(e)ry *s.* battistero.
to **baptize** *vt.* battezzare.
bar *s.* 1. sbarra 2. diga 3. striscia 4. ostacolo 5. (*fig.*) tribunale 6. bar 7. (*mus.*) battuta.
to **bar** *vt.* 1. sbarrare 2. ostacolare 3. proibire.
barbarian *agg.* e *s.* barbaro.
barbaric *agg.* barbarico.
barbarism *s.* 1. barbarie 2. (*gramm.*) barbarismo.
barbarous *agg.* barbaro.
barbarousness *s.* barbarie.
barbecue *s.* 1. animale arrostito intero 2. festa campestre.
to **barbecue** *vt.* arrostire un animale intero.
barbed *agg.* dentato.
barber *s.* barbiere.

barbiturate s. barbiturico.
bard s. bardo, trovatore.
bare agg. 1. nudo 2. logoro.
to **bare** vt. 1. denudare 2. snudare 3. smascherare.
barefoot agg. scalzo.
barehanded agg. e avv. 1. a mano nuda 2. senz'armi.
bareheaded agg. a capo scoperto.
barely avv. 1. apertamente 2. appena.
bargain s. affare.
to **bargain** vt. e vi. contrattare.
bargaining s. contrattazione.
barge s. chiatta.
baritone s. baritono.
bark[1] s. corteccia.
bark[2] s. latrato.
to **bark**[1] vt. scortecciare.
to **bark**[2] vi. latrare, abbaiare.
barking[1] s. scortecciamento.
barking[2] s. abbaiamento.
barley s. orzo.
barmaid s. barista (donna).
barman s. barista.
barn s. granaio.
barometer s. barometro.
barometric(al) agg. barometrico
baron s. barone.
baroness s. baronessa.
baroque agg. e s. barocco.
barracks s. pl. caserma (sing.).
barrage s. sbarramento.
barrel s. 1. barile 2. cilindro 3. canna (di arma da fuoco) || — -organ, organetto.
to **barrel** vt. mettere in barili.
barrelled agg. double- — gun, fucile a due canne.
barren agg. sterile.
barrenness s. sterilità.
barricade s. barricata.
to **barricade** vt. barricare.
barrier s. barriera || transonic —, muro del suono.
barrister s. avvocato (che può discutere cause nelle corti superiori).
barrow s. 1. barella 2. carriola.
bartender s. barista.
barter s. baratto.
to **barter** vt. e vi. barattare.
basal agg. basilare.
basalt s. basalto.
base[1] agg. basso, vile.
base[2] s. base.
to **base** vt. basare.
baseless agg. senza base.
basement s. 1. fondamento 2. seminterrato.

baseness s. bassezza.
to **bash** vt. colpire.
bashful agg. timido.
bashfulness s. timidezza.
basic agg. 1. fondamentale 2. (chim.) basico.
basil s. basilico.
basilar agg. basilare.
basilisk s. basilisco.
basin s. 1. bacino 2. catino, lavabo || sugar —, zuccheriera.
basis s. (pl. -ses) base.
to **bask** vi. crogiolarsi (al sole, al fuoco).
basket s. cesto || —ball, pallacanestro; — -chair, poltroncina di vimini.
Basque agg. e s. basco.
bas-relief s. bassorilievo.
bass agg. e s. (mus.) basso.
bass s. pesce persico.
bassoon s. (mus.) fagotto.
bastard agg. e s. bastardo.
to **baste** vt. imbastire.
basting s. imbastitura.
bastion s. bastione.
bat[1] s. pipistrello.
bat[2] s. (sport) mazza.
batch s. 1. infornata 2. gruppo.
to **bate** vt. ridurre.
bath s. bagno || — -robe, accappatoio; — -tub, vasca da bagno.
to **bath** vt. bagnare. ♦ to **bath** vi. bagnarsi, fare il bagno.
bathe s. bagno (in mare, lago ecc.).
to **bathe** vt. bagnare. ♦ to **bathe** vi. bagnarsi, fare il bagno (in mare, lago ecc.).
bather s. bagnante.
bathing s. il bagnarsi || — -suit, costume da bagno.
bathroom s. stanza da bagno.
bathysphere s. batisfera.
batiste s. batista.
batman s. attendente.
baton s. 1. bastone 2. bacchetta (di direttore d'orchestra).
batrachian s. batrace.
batsman s. (sport) battitore.
battalion s. battaglione.
to **batten** vt. (mar.) chiudere (i boccaporti).
batter s. (cuc.) pastella.
to **batter** vt. battere || to — down, abbattere; to — in, sfondare.
battering s. cannoneggiamento.
battery s. batteria || storage —, accumulatore.
battle s. battaglia.

to **battle** vt. e vi. combattere.

battledore s. racchetta di legno ||
— and shuttlecock, volano.

battlement s. (arch.) merlo.

battleship s. nave da guerra.

bauxite s. bauxite.

bawdiness s. oscenità.

bawdy agg. osceno || — house, bordello.

bawl s. grido.

to **bawl** vt. e vi. gridare, vociare.

bay[1] s. 1. baia 2. insenatura, recesso (nelle montagne).

bay[2] s. alloro || — -tree, lauro.

bay[3] s. 1. rientranza 2. campata || — -window, bovindo.

bay[4] s. latrato || at —, senza scampo.

bay[5] agg. e s. baio.

to **bay**[1] vt. arginare.

to **bay**[2] vi. latrare.

bayonet s. baionetta.

baza(a)r s. 1. bazar 2. vendita di beneficenza.

to **be** (was, been) vi. 1. essere 2. stare 3. andare 4. costare: how much is it?, quanto costa? 5. dovere || to — in, essere in casa; to — about, stare per; so be it, così sia.

beach s. spiaggia.

beacon s. faro.

to **beacon** vt. guidare con segnalazioni luminose.

bead s. 1. goccia 2. perlina. ♦ **beads** s. pl. rosario (sing.).

to **bead** vt. imperlare. ♦ to **bead** vi. imperlarsi.

beak s. 1. becco, rostro 2. beccuccio.

to **beak** vt. beccare.

beaker s. boccale.

beam s. 1. trave 2. raggio 3. asta (di bilancia) 4. fiancata (di nave).

to **beam** vi. brillare. ♦ to **beam** vt. irradiare.

beaming agg. raggiante.

bean s. fagiolo || French —, fagiolino; coffee —, grano di caffè.

bear s. orso.

to **bear**[1] vt. e vi. speculare al ribasso (in Borsa).

to **bear**[2] (bore, born(e)) vt. 1. portare 2. sopportare 3. generare. ♦ to **bear** (bore, borne) vi. 1. resistere 2. appoggiarsi 3. pazientare || to — with, aver pazienza con.

bearable agg. sopportabile.

beard s. 1. barba 2. chioma (di cometa).

to **beard** vt. affrontare, sfidare.

bearded agg. barbuto.

beardless agg. senza barba.

bearer s. portatore.

bearing s. 1. sopportazione 2. portamento 3. condotta 4. relazione 5. sostegno 6. raccolto || to lose one's bearings, perdere l'orientamento; to take the bearings of a coast (mar.), rilevare una costa.

beast s. bestia.

beastliness s. bestialità.

beastly agg. bestiale. ♦ **beastly** avv. bestialmente.

beat s. 1. battito 2. (mus.) battuta.

to **beat** (beat, beat(en)) vt. e vi. battere || to — down, abbattere; to — .back, respingere.

beaten agg. abbattuto, vinto.

beater s. battitore.

beatification s. beatificazione.

beating s. 1. battito 2. bastonatura 3. sconfitta.

beatitude s. beatitudine.

beautiful agg. bello.

beautifully avv. magnificamente.

to **beautify** vt. abbellire. ♦ to **beautify** vi. abbellirsi.

beauty s. bellezza.

beaver s. castoro.

became V. to become.

because cong. perché || — of, a causa di.

beck[1] s. ruscello.

beck[2] s. cenno, gesto.

to **become** (became, become) vi. 1. divenire 2. avvenire. ♦ to **become** (became, become) vt. addirsi a.

becoming agg. adatto.

bed s. 1. letto 2. fondo 3. (geol.) strato || double —, letto matrimoniale || flower- —, aiuola; — -cover, copriletto.

bedclothes s. pl. lenzuola.

bedlam s. manicomio.

bedouin agg. e s. beduino.

bedroom s. camera da letto.

bedside s. capezzale.

bedstead s. telaio del letto.

bedtime s. ora di andare a letto.

bee s. ape.

beech s. faggio || — -marten, faina.

beef s. manzo.

beefsteak s. bistecca.

beehive s. alveare.

beeline s. linea diretta, linea d'aria.

been V. to be.

beer s. birra.

341 — Berber

beet s. barbabietola.

beetle s. coleottero, scarafaggio.

beetroot s. V. beet.

to befall (befell, befallen) vt. e vi. accadere.

before avv. prima, già || — -mentioned, già citato. ♦ before prep. 1. prima (di) 2. davanti a. ♦ before cong. 1. prima che 2. piuttosto che.

beforehand avv. anticipatamente.

to beg vt. e vi. 1. chiedere, pregare 2. elemosinare.

began V. to begin.

to beget (begot, begot(ten)) vt. generare.

beggar s. mendicante.

beggarly agg. misero. ♦ beggarly avv. miseramente.

beggary s. mendicità.

begging agg. mendicante. ♦ begging s. accattonaggio.

to begin (began, begun) vt. e vi. cominciare || to — with, in primo luogo, per cominciare.

beginner s. 1. iniziatore 2. principiante.

beginning s. inizio.

begot V. to beget.

begotten V. to beget.

to begrime vt. insudiciare.

begun V. to begin.

behalf s. profitto, favore: on — of, da parte di, a nome di.

to behave vi. comportarsi: to — oneself, comportarsi bene || ill -behaved, maleducato.

behaviour s. comportamento, condotta.

to behead vt. decapitare.

beheld V. to behold.

behind avv. dietro, indietro. ♦ behind prep. dietro (a). ♦ behind s. parte posteriore.

to behold (beheld, beheld) vt. guardare.

beholder s. spettatore.

to behove vt. imp. convenire, essere doveroso.

being agg. presente. ♦ being s. 1. esistenza 2. essere vivente.

belch s. 1. rutto 2. eruzione.

to belch vi. ruttare. ♦ to belch vt. eruttare.

belfry s. campanile.

Belgian agg. e s. belga.

to belie vt. 1. smentire 2. deludere.

belief s. credenza, fede.

to believe vt. e vi. credere, aver

fede.

believer s. credente.

to belittle vt. sminuire.

bell s. 1. campana 2. campanello || — -boy, fattorino d'albergo; — -ringer, campanaro; — -tower, campanile.

belligerency s. belligeranza.

belligerent agg. e s. belligerante.

bellow s. muggito.

to bellow vi. muggire.

bellows s. pl. mantice, soffietto (sing.).

belly s. ventre.

to belong vi. 1. appartenere 2. concernere.

belongings s. pl. proprietà (sing.).

beloved agg. e s. amato.

below avv. giù, al di sotto. ♦ below prep. sotto: — zero, sotto zero.

belt s. 1. cintura 2. zona.

to belt vt. 1. cingere 2. staffilare.

to bemire vt. infangare. ♦ to bemire vi. impantanarsi.

bench s. 1. panca 2. banco 3. seggio 4. corte giudiziaria.

bend s. 1. curva 2. curvatura 3. (mar.) nodo.

to bend (bent, bent) vt. 1. piegare 2. tendere. ♦ to bend (bent, bent) vi. piegarsi.

bending s. V. bend.

beneath avv. e prep. V. below.

benediction s. benedizione.

benefactor s. benefattore.

benefactress s. benefattrice.

benefice s. beneficio.

beneficence s. beneficenza.

beneficent agg. benefico.

beneficiary agg. e s. beneficiario.

benefit s. 1. vantaggio 2. indennità 3. (giur.) beneficio.

to benefit vt. giovare, beneficare. ♦ to benefit vi. approfittare.

benevolence s. benevolenza.

benevolent agg. benevolo.

Bengal-light s. bengala.

benign agg. benigno.

benignity s. benignità.

bent V. to bend. ♦ bent agg. risoluto. ♦ bent s. inclinazione.

to benumb vt. intorpidire.

benumbing s. intorpidimento.

benzol s. benzolo.

to bequeath vt. lasciare per testamento.

bequest s. lascito.

Berber agg. e s. berbero.

to **bereave** (**bereaved, bereft**) *vt.* privare.
bergamot *s.* bergamotto.
berlin(e) *s.* berlina.
berry *s.* bacca.
berth *s.* 1. cuccetta 2. (*mar.*) ancoraggio 3. (*fig.*) posto.
to **berth** *vt.* ancorare.
beryllium *s.* berillio.
to **beseech** (**besought, besought**) *vt.* supplicare.
beseeching *s.* supplica.
to **beseem** *vt.* addirsi a.
beseeming *agg.* adatto.
beside *prep.* 1. vicino a 2. fuori di.
besides *avv.* inoltre. ◆ **besides** *prep.* oltre a.
to **besiege** *vt.* assediare.
besieger *s.* assediante.
besought V. *to beseech.*
to **besprinkle** *vt.* spruzzare.
best *agg.* (*superl. di* good) il migliore || — -*seller*, libro molto venduto. ◆ **best** *s.* il meglio. ◆ **best** *avv.* 1. nel modo migliore 2. maggiormente.
bestial *agg.* bestiale.
bestiality *s.* bestialità.
to **bestialize** *vt.* abbrutire.
to **bestir** *vt.* agitare.
to **bestow** *vt.* concedere.
bestowal *s.* conferimento.
to **bestrew** (**bestrewed, bestrewn**) *vt.* cospargere, disseminare.
bet *s.* scommessa.
to **bet** (**bet, bet**) *vt. e vi.* scommettere.
to **betake** (**betook, betaken**) *vr.* — *oneself*: dirigersi, recarsi.
to **betray** *vt.* tradire.
betrayal *s.* tradimento.
betrayer *s.* traditore.
betrothal *s.* fidanzamento.
betrothed *agg. e s.* fidanzato.
better[1] *s.* scommettitore.
better[2] *agg.* (*comp. di* good) migliore. ◆ **better** *avv.* meglio || *had* —, sarebbe meglio che; *all - the* —, *so much the* —, tanto meglio. ◆ **better** *s.* 1. il meglio 2. superiore.
to **better** *vt. e vi.* migliorare.
between *avv.* in mezzo. ◆ **between** *prep.* tra, fra (*due cose, due persone*).
beverage *s.* bevanda.
bevy *s.* stormo, frotta.
to **beware** *vi.* guardarsi, diffidare.

to **bewilder** *vt.* sconcertare.
bewildering *agg.* sbalorditivo.
bewilderment *s.* confusione.
to **bewitch** *vt.* incantare.
bewitcher *s.* incantatore.
bewitching *agg.* affascinante.
beyond *avv.* più in là. ◆ **beyond** *prep.* al di là di. ◆ **beyond** *s.* l'al di là.
bias *s.* 1. pregiudizio 2. predisposizione.
to **bias** *vt.* influenzare.
bib *s.* bavaglino.
Bible *s.* Bibbia.
biblical *agg.* biblico.
bibliographic(al) *agg.* bibliografico.
bibliography *s.* bibliografia.
bicameral *agg.* bicamerale.
bicarbonate *s.* bicarbonato.
bicentennial *agg. e s.* bicentenario.
bicephalous *agg.* bicipite.
biceps *s.* bicipite.
to **bicker** *vi.* litigare.
bicoloured *agg.* bicolore.
biconcave *agg.* biconcavo.
bicycle *s.* bicicletta.
bid *s.* 1. offerta (*a un'asta*) 2. appalto.
to **bid**[1] (**bid, bid**) *vt.* offrire (*a un'asta*). ◆ to **bid** (**bid, bid**) *vi.* fare offerta di appalto.
to **bid**[2] (**bade, bidden**) *vt. e vi.* 1. comandare 2. dire || *to* — *good-bye*, accomiatarsi.
biennial *agg.* biennale.
biennium *s.* (*pl.* -biennia) biennio.
bier *s.* bara.
big *agg.* 1. grosso 2. gravido 3. importante.
bigamous *agg.* bigamo.
bigamy *s.* bigamia.
bigness *s.* grossezza.
bigot *s.* bigotto.
bigoted *agg.* bigotto, fanatico.
bilateral *agg.* bilaterale.
bilberry *s.* mirtillo.
bile *s.* bile.
bilingual *agg.* bilingue.
bilious *agg.* 1. biliare 2. collerico.
bill[1] *s.* becco.
bill[2] *s.* 1. progetto di legge 2. certi- 5. lista 6. affisso || — *of lading*, polizza di carico; — *of rights*, dichiarazione dei diritti.
to **bill** *vt.* 1. fatturare 2. affiggere 3. (*teat.*) mettere in programma.
billhook *s.* falcetto.
billiard *agg.* di, da bigliardo: —

-cue, stecca da bigliardo.

billiards *s. pl.* bigliardo (*sing.*).

billion *s.* **1.** bilione **2.** (*amer.*) miliardo.

billow *s.* onda.

bimestrial *agg.* bimestrale.

bimonthly *agg.* e *s.* bimestrale. ♦ **bimonthly** *avv.* bimestralmente.

bin *s.* recipiente || *dust-* —, bidone della spazzatura.

bind *s.* **1.** legame **2.** fascia.

to bind (**bound**, **bound**) *vt.* **1.** legare **2.** fasciare **3.** rilegare **4.** obbligare.

binder *s.* **1.** rilegatore **2.** (*mecc.*) legatrice.

binding *agg.* impegnativo. ♦ **binding** *s.* **1.** legame **2.** fasciatura **3.** rilegatura.

binocular *s.* binocolo.

binomial *s.* binomio.

biochemistry *s.* biochimica.

biographer *s.* biografo.

biographic(al) *agg.* biografico.

biography *s.* biografia.

biological *agg.* biologico.

biologist *s.* biologo.

biology *s.* biologia.

biophysics *s.* biofisica.

biosphere *s.* biosfera.

bipartite *agg.* bipartito.

bipartition *s.* bipartizione.

biped *agg.* e *s.* bipede.

biplane *s.* biplano.

bipolar *agg.* bipolare.

birch *s.* **1.** betulla **2.** verga.

bird *s.* uccello.

birdcage *s.* gabbia (*per uccelli*).

birdseed *s.* miglio.

birth *s.* **1.** nascita **2.** stirpe.

birthday *s.* compleanno.

birthmark *s.* voglia, segno caratteristico (*di persona*).

birthplace *s.* luogo di nascita.

biscuit *s.* biscotto.

bisection *s.* bisezione.

bisector *s.* bisettrice.

bisexual *agg.* ermafrodito.

bishop *s.* vescovo.

bishopric *s.* vescovato.

bismuth *s.* bismuto.

bison *s.* bisonte.

bistoury *s.* bisturi.

bistre *s.* bistro.

bit *s.* **1.** pezzettino **2.** un poco **3.** (*mecc.*) parte tagliente di un utensile **4.** morso (*del cavallo*).

bit V. *to bite.*

bitch *s.* cagna.

bite *s.* **1.** morso **2.** presa.

to bite (**bit**, **bit(ten)**) *vt.* mordere. ♦ **to bite** (**bit**, **bit(ten)**) *vi.* abboccare || *to* — *in,* corrodere.

biting *agg.* **1.** mordente **2.** mordace.

bitten V. *to bite.*

bitter *agg.* **1.** amaro **2.** aspro **3.** (*di clima*) rigido || — *-sweet,* agrodolce. ♦ **bitter** *s.* amaro.

bitterish *agg.* amarognolo.

bitterness *s.* **1.** amarezza **2.** rancore **3.** rigidità (*di clima*).

bitumen *s.* bitume.

bivalent *agg.* bivalente.

bivouac *s.* bivacco.

bi-weekly *agg.* e *s.* bisettimanale. ♦ **bi-weekly** *avv.* due volte alla settimana.

to blab *vt.* e *vi.* **1.** chiacchierare **2.** spifferare.

black *agg.* **1.** nero **2.** negro **3.** (*fig.*) malvagio, minaccioso. ♦ **black** *s.* **1.** colore nero **2.** negro.

to black *vt.* annerire. ♦ **to black** *vi.* annerirsi.

to blackball *vt.* votare contro, bocciare.

blackberry *s.* mora selvatica.

blackbird *s.* merlo.

blackboard *s.* lavagna.

to blacken *vt.* **1.** annerire **2.** (*fig.*) diffamare. ♦ **to blacken** *vi.* diventare nero.

blackguard *s.* mascalzone.

blackish *agg.* nerastro.

blackleg *s.* **1.** truffatore **2.** crumiro.

blackmail *s.* ricatto.

to blackmail *vt.* ricattare.

blackmailer *s.* ricattatore.

blackness *s.* **1.** nerezza **2.** oscurità.

blackout *s.* oscuramento.

blacksmith *s.* fabbro ferraio.

bladder *s.* vescica.

blade *s.* **1.** stelo **2.** lama.

blamable *agg.* biasimevole.

blame *s.* **1.** biasimo **2.** colpa.

to blame *vt.* **1.** biasimare **2.** incolpare.

blameful *agg.* biasimevole.

blameless *agg.* irreprensibile.

bland *agg.* blando.

blandishment *s.* blandizie (*pl.*).

blandly *avv.* blandamente.

blank *agg.* **1.** vuoto **2.** in bianco || — *verse,* verso sciolto.. ♦ **blank** *s.* **1.** vuoto **2.** spazio in bianco **3.** mira || *point-* —, di punto in bianco.

blanket *s.* coperta.

blankly avv. 1. senza espressione
2. decisamente.

blare s. squillo (di tromba).

to **blaspheme** vt. e vi. bestemmiare.

blasphemous agg. blasfemo.

blasphemously avv. empiamente.

blasphemy s. bestemmia, empietà.

blast s. 1. raffica 2. squillo 3. scop-
pio 4. flagello || — -furnace, al-
toforno.

to **blast** vt. 1. far esplodere 2. rovinare.

blaze s. 1. fiamma 2. scoppio.

to **blaze** vi. ardere. ♦ to **blaze** vt.
1. bruciare 2. divulgare.

blazer s. giacca sportiva.

blazing s. 1. fiamma 2. splendore
3. vanteria.

blazon s. 1. blasone 2. ostentazione.

bleach s. imbianchimento, candeggio.

to **bleach** vt. imbiancare, candeggia-
re. ♦ to **bleach** vi. imbiancarsi.

bleacher s. recipiente per candeggio.

bleaching s. V. bleach.

bleak agg. 1. brullo 2. desolato 3.
incolore.

bleakness s. 1. freddezza 2. squallore.

blear agg. 1. cisposo 2. ottuso.

bleat s. belato.

to **bleat** vi. belare.

to **bleed** (bled, bled) vi. sanguinare. ♦ to **bleed** (bled, bled) vt.
salassare.

bleeding s. 1. emorragia 2. salasso
3. fuga.

blemish s. difetto.

blend s. miscela.

to **blend** vt. mescolare. ♦ to **blend**
vi. mescolarsi.

to **bless** vt. benedire.

blessed agg. beato, santo.

blessing s. benedizione.

blew V. to blow.

blind agg. cieco. ♦ **blind** s. 1. tenda 2. persiana 3. paraocchi 4. finzione.

to **blind** vt. 1. accecare 2. oscurare
3. nascondere.

blindness s. cecità.

to **blink** vi. 1. battere le palpebre
2. lampeggiare 3. (fig.) chiudere
gli occhi.

blinker s. 1. lampeggiatore 2. paraocchi.

blinking agg. 1. ammiccante 2. scintillante. ♦ **blinking** s. ammicco.

bliss s. beatitudine.

blissful agg. 1. beato 2. delizioso.

blister s. bolla.

blithe agg. gaio.

blizzard s. tormenta (di neve).

block s. 1. ceppo 2. masso 3. isolato (di case) 4. ostacolo 5. perso-
na stupida || — letters, stampa-
tello.

to **block** vt. bloccare.

blockade s. blocco.

blockhead s. stupido.

blonde s. donna bionda.

blood s. sangue.

bloodhound s. segugio.

bloodless agg. 1. esangue 2. incruento 3. (fig.) insensibile.

bloodshed s. spargimento di sangue.

bloodshot agg. iniettato di sangue.

bloody agg. 1. sanguinante 2. sanguinoso 3. sanguinario 4. maledetto.

bloom s. 1. fiore 2. rossore.

to **bloom** vi. 1. fiorire 2. arrossire.

blossom s. fiore.

to **blossom** vi. 1. fiorire 2. diventare.

blot s. macchia.

to **blot** vt. 1. macchiare 2. assorbire.

blotch s. 1. macchia 2. pustola.

blotting s. il macchiare 2. l'asciu-
gare || — -paper, carta assorbente;
— -pad, tampone di carta assorbente.

blouse s. camicetta.

blow s. 1. soffio 2. colpo 3. fioritura
|| to come to blows, venire alle
mani.

to **blow** (blew, blown) vt. 1. soffiare 2. suonare (strumenti a fiato)
|| to — up, (far) saltare in aria.
♦ to **blow** (blew, blown) vi.
sbocciare.

blower s. 1. soffiatore 2. sfiatatoio.

blown V. to blow.

blowpipe s. 1. cannello per soffiare
2. cerbottana.

blue agg. 1. azzurro, blu 2. livido
3. triste.

bluebell s. campanula.

bluebottle[1] s. fiordaliso.

bluebottle[2] s. tafano.

blueprint s. cianografia.

bluff s. ripida scogliera.

bluish agg. bluastro.

blunder s. errore.

blunt agg. 1. smussato 2. ottuso 3.
schietto.

blush s. rossore.

to **blush** *vi.* arrossire.

board *s.* **1.** asse, tavola **2.** vitto **3.** pensione **4.** consiglio, ministero **5.** (*mar.*) bordo || *on —*, a bordo; *full —*, pensione completa. ◆ **boards** *s. pl.* palcoscenico (*sing.*).

to **board** *vt.* **1.** fornire di assi **2.** prendere a pensione **3.** (*mar.*) abbordare. ◆ to **board** *vi.* **1.** essere a pensione **2.** imbarcarsi.

boarder *s.* pensionante.

boarding *s.* assito || *— -house*, pensione; *— -school*, collegio.

boast *s.* vanto.

to **boast** *vt.* vantare. ◆ to **boast** *vi.* vantarsi.

boaster *s.* spaccone.

boastful *agg.* vanaglorioso.

boastfulness *s.* millanteria.

boasting *s.* vanteria.

boat *s.* barca, battello || *flying- —*, idrovolante; *sauce- —*, salsiera; *ferry- —*, traghetto.

boating *s.* canottaggio.

boatman *s.* barcaiolo.

boatswain *s.* nostromo.

to **bob** *vi.* dondolarsi, oscillare || *to — up*, venire a galla.

bobbin *s.* bobina.

bobsled *s.* guidoslitta.

bodice *s.* busto.

bodkin *s.* punteruolo, stiletto.

body *s.* **1.** corpo **2.** corporazione, ente **3.** massa || *— belt*, panciera.

bodymaker *s.* carrozziere.

Boeotian *agg. e s.* beota.

bog *s.*

boggy *agg.* paludoso.

bogy *s.* spauracchio.

boil *s.* bollitura.

to **boil** *vt. e vi.* bollire, ribollire || *to — away*, consumarsi; *to — over*, traboccare bollendo.

boiler *s.* bollitore, caldaia.

boiling *agg.* bollente. ◆ **boiling** *s.* ebollizione.

boisterous *agg.* **1.** rumoroso **2.** violento.

boisterousness *s.* fracasso.

bold *agg.* **1.** audace **2.** sfacciato **3.** vigoroso || *— -face*, neretto.

boldness *s.* **1.** audacia **2.** sfacciataggine.

bolide *s.* bolide.

Bolshevism *s.* bolscevismo.

Bolshevist *agg. e s.* bolscevico.

bolster *s.* **1.** cuscino **2.** supporto.

bolt *s.* **1.** catenaccio **2.** bullone **3.** otturatore **4.** freccia **5.** fulmine.

to **bolt**[1] *vt.* **1.** sprangare **2.** imbullonare.

to **bolt**[2] *vt.* setacciare, vagliare.

bolter *s.* setaccio.

bomb *s.* bomba.

to **bomb** *vt.* bombardare.

to **bombard** *vt.* bombardare.

bombardier *s.* bombardiere.

bombardment *s.* bombardamento.

bombastic *agg.* ampolloso.

bomber *s.* bombardiere.

bond *s.* **1.** vincolo **2.** patto **3.** (*comm.*) titolo **4.** cauzione || *— -holder*, portatore di obbligazioni; *goods in —*, merci in attesa di sdoganamento.

bondage *s.* schiavitù.

bone *s.* **1.** osso **2.** lisca.

to **bone** *vt.* **1.** disossare **2.** spinare.

bonfire *s.* falò.

bonnet *s.* **1.** cuffia **2.** (*auto*) cofano.

bonus *s.* gratifica || *cost of living —*, carovita.

bony *agg.* **1.** osseo **2.** ossuto.

bonze *s.* bonzo.

booby *s.* sciocco.

book *s.* **1.** libro **2.** registro || *note- —*, taccuino; *copy- —*, quaderno.

to **book** *vt.* **1.** registrare **2.** prenotare.

bookbinding *s.* rilegatura.

bookcase *s.* libreria.

booking *s.* **1.** registrazione **2.** prenotazione || *— -office*, biglietteria.

bookish *agg.* **1.** studioso **2.** libresco.

bookkeeper *s.* contabile.

bookkeeping *s.* contabilità.

booklet *s.* libretto.

bookmaker *s.* allibratore.

bookseller *s.* libraio.

bookshelf *s.* (*pl.* -lves) scaffale.

bookshop *s.* libreria.

bookstall *s.* edicola, bancarella (*di libri*).

boom *s.* **1.** rombo **2.** periodo di prosperità.

to **boom** *vi.* **1.** rimbombare **2.** essere in periodo di prosperità.

boor *s.* persona zotica.

boorish *agg.* rustico.

boorishness *s.* rozzezza.

boot *s.* **1.** stivale, scarpa **2.** (*auto*) portabagagli.

bootblack *s.* lustrascarpe.

booth *s.* baracca || *telephone —*, cabina telefonica.

booty *s.* bottino.

border s. 1. orlo 2. frontiera.
to **border** vt. orlare || to — on, confinare con.
borderer s. abitante di confine.
bordering s. 1. il bordare 2. il confinare.
bore V. to bear.
bore[1] s. 1. buco 2. calibro (di arma).
bore[2] s. 1. seccatura 2. seccatore.
to **bore**[1] vt. forare.
to **bore**[2] vt. annoiare.
boreal agg. boreale.
boredom s. noia.
boric agg. borico.
boring[1] agg. noioso.
boring[2] s. perforazione || — test, sondaggio.
born V. to bear. ♦ **born** agg. nato, generato || to be —, nascere.
borne V. to bear.
borough s. 1. municipio 2. circoscrizione elettorale.
to **borrow** vt. prendere a prestito.
borrower s. chi prende a prestito.
bosom s. seno || — friend, amico intimo.
boss[1] s. 1. protuberanza 2. (arch.) bugna.
boss[2] s. capo, padrone.
bossy[1] agg. a bugnato.
bossy[2] agg. (gergo) prepotente.
botanist s. botanico.
botany s. botanica.
botch s. pasticcio.
to **botch** vt. 1. rattoppare 2. arruffare.
botcher s. pasticcione.
both agg. e pron. entrambi, tutti e due. ♦ **both** avv. nel medesimo tempo || — ... and, sia... sia, tanto... quanto.
bother s. seccatura.
to **bother** vt. infastidire. ♦ to **bother** vi. preoccuparsi.
bothersome agg. fastidioso.
bottle s. bottiglia || feeding- —, poppatoio; — -feeding, allattamento artificiale.
to **bottle** vt. imbottigliare.
bottling s. imbottigliamento.
bottom agg. 1. inferiore 2. basilare. ♦ **bottom** s. 1. fondo 2. fondamento 3. deretano 4. (mar.) chiglia.
to **bottom** vt. 1. mettere il fondo (a) 2. impagliare 3. capire. ♦ to **bottom** vi. posare, essere posato.
bottomless agg. 1. senza fondo 2.

senza fine.
bough s. ramo (d'albero).
bought V. to buy.
boulder s. macigno.
boulevard s. viale.
bounce s. 1. balzo 2. vanteria.
to **bounce** vt. far rimbalzare. ♦ to **bounce** vi. 1. rimbalzare 2. gloriarsi.
bouncer s. fanfarone.
bound[1] s. limite, confine.
bound[2] s. salto.
bound[3] V. to bind.
bound[4] agg. 1. destinato 2. diretto a 3. certo.
to **bound**[1] vt. confinare, limitare.
to **bound**[2] vi. balzare.
boundary s. limite, frontiera.
boundless agg. illimitato.
bounteous agg. generoso.
bounty s. generosità.
bourgeois agg. e s. borghese.
bourgeoisie s. borghesia.
bow[1] s. 1. arco 2. archetto 3. fiocco || — -window, bovindo.
bow[2] s. inchino.
bow[3] s. prua.
to **bow** vt. piegare. ♦ to **bow** vi. 1. piegarsi 2. inclinarsi.
bowels s. pl. viscere.
bower s. 1. pergolato 2. dimora.
bowl[1] s. ciotola.
bowl[2] s. boccia.
to **bowl** vt. far rotolare. ♦ to **bowl** vi. 1. rotolare 2. giocare a bocce.
bowler s. giocatore di bocce || — hat, bombetta.
bowling s. gioco delle bocce.
bowman s. arciere.
bowshot s. tiro d'arco.
box[1] s. 1. scatola 2. stanzetta 3. stalla 4. (teat.) palco 5. (giur.) banco || letter- —, buca per le lettere; money- —, salvadanaio; strong- —, cassaforte.
box[2] s. pugno, ceffone.
to **box**[1] vt. mettere in scatola.
to **box**[2] vt. schiaffeggiare. ♦ to **box** vi. fare del pugilato.
boxer s. pugile.
boxing s. pugilato.
boy s. ragazzo.
to **boycott** vt. boicottare.
boyhood s. fanciullezza.
boyish agg. fanciullesco.
bra s. reggipetto.
brace s. 1. sostegno 2. coppia, paio 3. (mar.) braccio. ♦ **braces** s. pl. bretelle.

to **brace** *vt*. 1. legare 2. fortificare.
bracelet *s*. braccialetto.
brachycardia *s*. brachicardia.
bracket *s*. 1. mensola, sostegno 2. parentesi.
brackish *agg*. salato, salso.
brag *s*. 1. millanteria 2. millantatore.
to **brag** *vt*. vantare. ♦ to **brag** *vi*. vantarsi.
braggart *agg*. e *s*. spaccone.
bragging *s*. millanteria.
braid *s*. 1. treccia 2. gallone.
to **braid** *vt*. 1. intrecciare 2. guarnire.
brain *s*. cervello.
brainless *agg*. scervellato.
brake[1] *s*. 1. felce 2. boschetto.
brake[2] *s*. freno.
to **brake** *vt*. frenare.
brakesman *s*. frenatore.
bramble *s*. rovo.
bran *s*. crusca.
branch *s*. 1. ramo 2. filiale.
to **branch** *vt*. ramificare. ♦ to **branch** *vi*. ramificarsi || *to — out*, estendersi (*di attività commerciale, affari*).
branching *s*. ramificazione.
brand *s*. 1. tizzone 2. marchio (*a fuoco*) 3. marca || *— -new*, nuovo fiammante.
to **brand** *vt*. 1. marchiare 2. stigmatizzare.
to **brandish** *vt*. brandire.
brass *agg*. 1. di ottone 2. (*fig.*) sfacciato. ♦ **brass** *s*. 1. ottone 2. (*mecc.*) bronzina 3. (*fig.*) sfacciataggine || *— band*, fanfara.
brassy *agg*. V. *brass*.
bravado *s*. bravata.
brave *agg*. e *s*. prode, coraggioso.
bravely *avv*. coraggiosamente.
bravery *s*. 1. coraggio 2. splendore.
brawl *s*. rissa.
to **brawl** *vi*. rissare.
brawn *s*. muscolo, forza muscolare.
brawny *agg*. muscoloso.
bray *s*. raglio.
to **bray**[1] *vi*. 1. ragliare 2. (*fig.*) stonare.
to **bray**[2] *vt*. frantumare, sminuzzare.
brazen *agg*. V. *brass*.
brazier[1] *s*. calderaio.
brazier[2] *s*. braciere.
Brazilian *agg*. e *s*. brasiliar..
breach *s*. 1. rottura 2. breccia 3. infrazione || *— of promise*, rottura di fidanzamento.

bread *s*. pane.
to **bread** *vt*. rimpanare.
breadth *s*. 1. larghezza 2. altezza (*di stoffe*).
breadthwise *avv*. in larghezza (*di stoffe*).
break *s*. 1. rottura 2. interruzione, intervallo 3. infrazione || *— -up*, collasso, smembramento, fine.
to **break** (**broke, broken**) *vt*. 1. rompere 2. interrompere 3. domare 4. rovinare. ♦ to **break** (**broke, broken**) *vi*. 1. rompersi 2. irrompere || *to — down*, demolire, (*auto*) restare in panne, esaurirsi; *to — off*, mandare a monte; *to — up*, fare a pezzi.
breakdown *s*. 1. collasso 2. rottura 3. dissesto || *nervous —*, esaurimento nervoso.
breaker *s*. 1. rompitore 2. violatore 3. domatore 4. (*mecc.*) macchina rompitrice 5. (*mar.*) frangente 6. (*elett.*) interruttore.
breakfast *s*. prima colazione.
to **breakfast** *vi*. fare la prima colazione.
breaking *s*. 1. rottura 2. (*comm.*) fallimento.
breakneck *agg*. a rotta di collo.
breakwater *s*. frangiflutti.
breast *s*. petto || *— -bone*, sterno.
breasted *agg*. dal petto || *double —*, a doppio petto.
breath *s*. 1. soffio 2. respiro.
breathable *agg*. respirabile.
to **breathe** *vi*. 1. respirare 2. spirare. ♦ to **breathe** *vt*. 1. infondere 2. sussurrare.
breathing *s*. V. *breath*.
breathless *agg*. 1. ansante 2. esanime.
breathlessness *s*. affanno.
bred V. to *breed*. ♦ **bred** *agg*. *ill- —*, maleducato.
breech *s*. 1. parte posteriore 2. culatta (*di arma*).
breeches *s*. *pl*. calzoni.
breed *s*. razza.
to **breed** (**bred, bred**) *vt*. 1. generare 2. allevare. ♦ to **breed** (**bred, bred**) *vi*. nascere.
breeder *s*. 1. chi genera 2. allevatore.
breeding *s*. 1. generazione 2. allevamento 3. educazione.
breeze *s*. brezza.
breezy *agg*. 1. ventilato 2. cordiale.
brethren *s*. *pl*. confratelli.

breviary s. breviario.
brevity s. brevità.
brew s. 1. mistura 2. fermentazione (di birra).
to **brew** vt. 1. mescolare 2. (fig.) macchinare. ♦ to **brew** vi. fare la birra.
brewer s. birraio.
brewery s. fabbrica di birra.
bribe s. dono (a scopo di corruzione), allettamento.
to **bribe** vt. corrompere.
briber s. corruttore.
bribery s. corruzione.
brick s. mattone.
bricklayer s. muratore.
brickwork s. muratura in mattoni.
brickyard s. mattonaia.
bride s. sposa.
bridegroom s. sposo.
bridge s. ponte || swing- —, ponte girevole; toll- —, ponte a pedaggio; — -head, testa di ponte.
bridle s. briglia, freno.
to **bridle** vt. imbrigliare.
bridling s. imbrigliamento.
brief agg. breve. ♦ **brief** s. riassunto.
to **brief** vt. 1. riassumere 2. (giur.) nominare (il proprio avvocato) 3. dare istruzioni.
briefness s. brevità, concisione.
brier s. 1. rovo 2. rosa selvatica.
brig s. brigantino.
brigade s. brigata.
bright agg. 1. chiaro, splendente 2. vivace.
to **brighten** vt. 1. far brillare 2. animare. ♦ to **brighten** vi. 1. brillare 2. animarsi.
brightness s. 1. splendore 2. gaiezza.
brill s. (itt.) rombo.
brilliance, brilliancy s. brillantezza.
brilliant agg. e s. brillante.
brilliantine s. brillantina.
brim s. 1. orlo 2. ala (di cappello).
brimful agg. colmo.
brindled agg. pezzato.
brine s. acqua salata.
to **bring (brought, brought)** vt. 1. portare 2. indurre || to — about, causare; to — back, richiamare alla memoria; to — forth, dare alla luce; to — up, educare, allevare.
brink s. orlo.
brisk agg. 1. vivace 2. frizzante.
briskness s. vivacità.

bristle s. setola.
to **bristle** vi. essere irto di.
bristly agg. 1. setoloso 2. ruvido.
British agg. britannico.
Briton agg. e s. britanno.
broad agg. 1. ampio 2. chiaro 3. marcato 4. volgare || — daylight, pieno giorno. ♦ **broad** s. larghezza. ♦ **broad** avv. ampiamente.
broadcast s. 1. radiodiffusione 2. radiocomunicazione.
to **broadcast (broadcast, broadcast)** (anche reg.) vt. e vi. radiotrasmettere.
broadcaster s. trasmettitore.
broadcasting s. radiodiffusione.
to **broaden** vt. allargare. ♦ to **broaden** vi. allargarsi, estendersi.
broadness s. 1. larghezza 2. grossolanità.
broadside s. (mar.) 1. bordo, fiancata 2. bordata.
brocade s. broccato.
bro(c)coli s. broccolo.
broil s. rissa.
to **broil** vt. cuocere alla griglia. ♦ to **broil** vi. abbrustolirsi (al sole).
broke V. to break.
broken V. to break. ♦ **broken** agg. 1. variabile (di tempo) 2. accidentato (di terreno) 3. indebolito 4. avvilito 5. scorretto.
broker s. 1. (comm.) agente 2. mediatore.
bromide s. bromuro.
bromine s. bromo.
bronchial agg. bronchiale.
bronchia s. pl. bronchi.
bronchitis s. bronchite.
broncho-pneumonia s. broncopolmonite.
bronze s. bronzo.
to **bronze** vt. abbronzare. ♦ to **bronze** vi. abbronzarsi.
brooch s. spilla.
brood s. covata.
to **brood** vt. 1. covare 2. (fig.) rimuginare, meditare.
brooding s. 1. cova 2. meditazione.
brook s. ruscello.
to **brook** vt. sopportare, tollerare.
brooklet s. ruscelletto.
broom s. 1. ginestra 2. scopa.
broth s. brodo.
brothel s. bordello.
brother s. 1. fratello 2. collega || — -in-law, cognato; half- —, fratellastro.

brotherhood s. 1. fratellanza 2. confraternita.
brotherlike agg. fraterno.
brotherly agg. fraterno. ♦ **brotherly** avv. fraternamente.
brought V. to bring.
brow s. fronte. ♦ **brows** s. pl. sopracciglia.
brown agg. 1. bruno 2. marrone. ♦ **brown** s. marrone.
to **brown** vt. 1. rendere bruno 2. rosolare. ♦ to **brown** vi. 1. diventare bruno 2. abbronzarsi
to **browse** vt. e vi. brucare.
bruise s. contusione.
to **bruise** vt. ammaccare. ♦ to **bruise** vi. ammaccarsi.
bruiser s. 1. pugilatore 2. (fig.) gradasso.
brush s. 1. spazzola, spazzolino 2. spazzolata 3. pennello 4. rissa || — -up, ripasso.
to **brush** vt. 1. spazzolare 2. sfiorare || to — aside (fig.), ignorare; to — up, ripassare.
brushwood s. sottobosco.
brushy agg. 1. ispido 2. folto (di bosco).
brusque agg. brusco.
brutal agg. brutale.
brutality s. brutalità.
to **brutalize** vt. 1. abbrutire 2. maltrattare. ♦ to **brutalize** vi. abbrutirsi.
brute agg. brutale. ♦ **brute** s. bruto.
brutish agg. brutale, rozzo.
bubble s. 1. bolla 2. gorgoglio.
to **bubble** vi. gorgogliare || to — over, traboccare.
bubo s. bubbone.
bubonic agg. bubbonico.
buccaneer s. bucaniere.
buck s. 1. daino 2. maschio (di molti animali).
to **buck** vi. sgroppare.
bucket s. secchio.
buckle s. fibbia.
to **buckle** vt. 1. affibbiare 2. piegare. ♦ to **buckle** vi. piegarsi.
bucolic agg. bucolico.
bud s. 1. gemma 2. germe.
to **bud** vi. germogliare.
Buddhism s. buddismo.
Buddhist agg. e s. buddista.
budget s. 1. raccolta (di documenti) 2. bilancio.
buffalo s. bufalo.
buffer s. respingente.

buffet¹ s. schiaffo.
buffet² s. credenza.
to **buffet** vt. schiaffeggiare.
buffoon s. buffone.
bug s. 1. coleottero 2. cimice || big —, (gergo) pezzo grosso.
bugbear s. spauracchio.
bugger s. sodomita.
build s. costruzione, struttura.
to **build (built, built)** vt. costruire || to — up, murare.
builder s. costruttore.
building agg. edilizio. ♦ **building** s. edificio.
built V. to build.
bulb s. 1. bulbo 2. lampadina || — socket, portalampada.
Bulgarian agg. e s. bulgaro.
bulge s. gonfiore.
to **bulge** vi. gonfiarsi. ♦ to **bulge** vt. 1. sporgere 2. gonfiare.
bulgy agg. rigonfio.
bulk s. 1. massa 2. carico.
bulkhead s. paratia.
bulky agg. massiccio.
bull s. 1. toro 2. maschio (di alcuni mammiferi) || —'s eye, oblò.
bulldog s. mastino.
bullet s. pallottola.
bulletin s. bollettino || news —, giornale radio.
bullfight s. corrida.
bullfighter s. torero.
bullock s. torello.
bully agg. borioso.
to **bully** vt. e vi. fare il prepotente (verso).
bulwark s. 1. bastione 2. (mar.) parapetto.
bumble-bee s. calabrone.
bump s. 1. urto 2. bernoccolo.
to **bump** vt. e vi. urtare, andare a sbattere contro.
bumper s. 1. paraurti 2. respingente.
bun s. 1. focaccia 2. crocchia.
bunch s. 1. mazzo 2. grappolo.
bundle s. 1. fagotto 2. fascio.
to **bundle** vt. riunire in fascio, fare un involto.
bung s. tappo.
bungler agg. e s. confusionario.
bunny s. coniglietto.
buoy s. boa.
buoyancy s. 1. galleggiabilità 2. ottimismo.
buoyant agg. 1. galleggiante 2. ottimista.
burden s. 1. peso 2. tonnellaggio.

to **burden** vt. caricare.
burdensome agg. gravoso.
bureau s. (pl. bureaux) ufficio.
bureaucracy s. burocrazia.
bureaucrat s. burocrate.
bureaucratic agg. burocratico.
burglar s. scassinatore (notturno).
burglary s. furto (notturno) con scasso.
to **burgle** vt. e vi. svaligiare con scasso.
burgomaster s. borgomastro.
burial s. sepoltura || — -ground, cimitero; — -service, ufficio funebre.
burin s. bulino.
burly agg. corpulento.
burn s. ustione.
to **burn** (**burnt, burnt**) (anche reg.) vt. e vi. bruciare, ardere.
burner s. bruciatore.
burning s. 1. incendio 2. (metal.) fusione.
to **burnish** vt. lustrare.
burnt V. to burn.
burrow s. tana, buca.
bursar s. economo.
bursary s. 1. ufficio dell'economato 2. borsa di studio.
burst s. 1. scoppio 2. squarcio.
to **burst** (**burst, burst**) vt. 1. far esplodere 2. sfondare. ♦ to **burst** (**burst, burst**) vi. 1. scoppiare 2. irrompere.
bursting s. scoppio.
to **bury** vt. seppellire.
bus s. autobus.
busby s. colbac.
bush s. cespuglio.
bushel s. staio.
bushy agg. folto.
busily avv. attivamente.
business s. 1. affare 2. mestiere 3. ditta 4. scopo || — -man, uomo d'affari; — -like, metodico, sistematico.
bust s. busto.
bustle s. trambusto.
to **bustle** vi. agitarsi.
busy agg. occupato.
to **busy** vt. occupare.
busybody s. ficcanaso.
but cong. ma. ♦ **but** avv. solo. ♦ **but** prep. tranne || — for, se non fosse per; — that, se non; cannot —, non poter far a meno di; all —, pressoché.
butane s. butano.
butcher s. macellaio.
butchery s. macello.

butler s. maggiordomo.
butt[1] s. 1. calcio (di arma) 2. impugnatura (di utensile) 3. mozzicone.
butt[2] s. urto.
to **butt** vt. e vi. cozzare.
butter s. burro.
to **butter** vt. imburrare.
buttercup s. ranuncolo.
butterfly s. farfalla.
buttery agg. burroso.
buttock s. natica.
button s. bottone.
to **button** vt. abbottonare.
button-hole s. occhiello.
to **button-hole** vt. 1. fare asole a 2. (fig.) attaccar bottone.
button-holer s. attaccabottoni.
buttress s. contrafforte.
buxom agg. formoso, avvenente (di donna).
to **buy** (**bought, bought**) vt. comprare || to — off, riscattare; to — up, accaparrare.
buyable agg. acquistabile.
buyer s. acquirente.
buzz s. ronzio.
buzzard s. poiana.
to **buzz** vi. e vt. ronzare, bisbigliare.
buzzer s. 1. insetto che ronza 2. cicala, segnale acustico.
by avv. 1. vicino 2. da parte, in disparte || — and —, fra poco; — and large, complessivamente. ♦ **by** prep. 1. (agente, causa, mezzo) per, da, con, di || a book (written) — Shakespeare, un libro di Shakespeare; to travel — train, viaggiare col treno 2. (tempo) entro, per, durante || day — day, di giorno in giorno; — night, di notte 3. (luogo) vicino a, a fianco di, attraverso || a house — the sea, una casa sul mare. ♦ **by** agg. secondario.
bye-bye inter. arrivederci.
bygone agg. e s. passato.
by-line s. (giorn.) firma.
byname s. soprannome.
by-pass s. 1. circonvallazione 2. deviazione.
by-product s. sottoprodotto.
byroad s. strada secondaria.
byssus s. bisso.
bystander s. spettatore.
bystreet s. viuzza.
byway s. via traversa.
byword s. proverbio, epiteto.
bywork s. lavoro supplementare (a tempo perso).
Byzantine agg. e s. bizantino.

C

C (*mus.*) do.
cab s. vettura di piazza.
cabal s. intrigo, cospirazione.
cabbage s. cavolo.
cab(b)ala s. cabala.
cab(b)alistic agg. cabalistico.
cabin s. **1.** capanna **2.** (*aer.; fer.; mar.*) cabina.
cabinet s. **1.** stanzino **2.** stipo, armadietto **3.** (*pol.*) gabinetto, consiglio dei ministri || — *-maker*, ebanista; — *-minister*, membro del gabinetto.
cable s. **1.** cavo **2.** cablogramma || — *-way*, teleferica.
to cable vt. e vi. **1.** fornire di cavo **2.** trasmettere un cablogramma.
cablegram s. cablogramma.
cabman s. tassista.
caboose (*mar.*) cambusa.
cabotage s. cabotaggio.
cacao s. cacao.
cacophony s. cacofonia.
cactus s. cactus.
cadaverous agg. **1.** cadaverico **2.** esangue.
cadence s. cadenza, ritmo.
cadet s. cadetto.
caducity s. caducità.
Caesarean agg. cesareo, imperiale || — *operation*, parto cesareo.
caesura s. cesura.
café s. caffè (*locale pubblico*).
caffeine s. caffeina.
cage s. **1.** gabbia **2.** impalcatura.
to cage vt. mettere in gabbia.
cake s. torta, focaccia.
calamary s. calamaro.
calamitous agg. calamitoso.
calamity s. calamità.
calcareous agg. calcareo.
calcification s. calcificazione.
to calcify vt. calcificare. ♦ **to calcify** vi. calcificarsi.
calcination s. calcinazione.
to calcine V. *to calcify*.
calcite s. calcite.
calcium s. calcio.
to calculate vt. **1.** calcolare **2.** contare. ♦ **to calculate** vi. fare affidamento.
calculated agg. **1.** calcolato **2.** premeditato **3.** (*fig.*) idoneo.
calculating agg. calcolatore || — *machine*, macchina calcolatrice.
calculation s. calcolo.

calculator s. calcolatore, calcolatrice.
calendar s. calendario, almanacco.
calf¹ s. (*pl.* calves) vitello.
calf² s. polpaccio.
to calibrate vt. **1.** calibrare **2.** (*mecc.*) tarare.
calibration s. calibratura, taratura.
calibre s. calibro.
calico s. calicò.
call s. **1.** richiamo, chiamata **2.** breve visita: *to pay* (*v. irr.*) *so. a* —, fare una breve visita a qu. **3.** (*giur.*) appello **4.** (*mil.*) adunata **5.** (*mar.*) scalo || — *bird*, uccello da richiamo; — *box*, cabina telefonica; — *up*, chiamata alle armi; *trunk* —, chiamata intercontinentale.
to call vt. e vi. **1.** chiamare, richiamare: *to* — *aside*, chiamare in disparte; *to* — *to arms*, chiamare alle armi; *to* — *to mind*, richiamare alla mente **2.** esortare, ordinare || *to* — *into being*, creare; *to* — *out*, chiamare ad alta voce, esclamare; *to* — *up*, telefonare; *to* — *at*, fare scalo a; *to* — *for*, passare a prendere; *to* — *on*, fare una breve visita a; *to* — *upon*, implorare, invocare.
caller s. visitatore, visitatrice.
calligrapher s. calligrafo.
calligraphic agg. calligrafico.
calling s. **1.** appello **2.** mestiere, professione **3.** vocazione.
callosity s. **1.** callosità **2.** (*fig.*) insensibilità.
callous agg. **1.** calloso **2.** (*fig.*) insensibile.
calm agg. calmo. ♦ **calm** s. calma.
to calm vt. calmare. ♦ **to calm** vi. *to* — *down*, calmarsi (*di tempesta ecc.*).
calming agg. calmante.
calmly avv. con calma.
calmness s. calma, tranquillità.
calorific agg. calorifico.
calorimeter s. calorimetro.
calory s. caloria.
to calumniate vt. calunniare.
Calvary s. Calvario.
calves V. *calf*.
Calvinism s. calvinismo.
Calvinist agg. e s. calvinista.
came V. *to come*.
camel s. cammello.
camellia s. camelia.
cameo s. cammeo.
camera s. **1.** (*foto*) macchina foto-

grafica **2.** (*giur.*) Camera di Consiglio.

camisole *s.* corpetto, farsetto.

camouflage *s.* **1.** mascheramento **2.** (*mil.*) mimetizzazione.

to **camouflage** *vt.* **1.** mascherare **2.** (*mil.*) mimetizzare.

camp *s.* **1.** (*mil.*) campo **2.** campeggio || — *-bed*, brandina.

to **camp** *vt.* (*mil.*) accampare. ♦ to **camp** *vi.* **1.** accamparsi **2.** attendarsi.

campaign *s.* (*mil.*) campagna.

camper *s.* campeggiatore.

camphor *s.* canfora.

camping *s.* **1.** (*mil.*) accampamento **2.** campeggio.

can[1] *s.* recipiente di latta, bidone.

can[2] *v. dif.* (*ind. cong. pres.*) **could** (*ind. cong. pass. e condiz.*) potere, essere in grado di.

Canadian *agg. e s.* canadese.

canal *s.* canale.

canalization *s.* canalizzazione.

to **canalize** *vt.* canalizzare.

canary *agg.* giallo canarino. ♦ **canary** *s.* canarino.

to **cancel** *vt.* annullare, cancellare.

cancellation *s.* annullamento, cancellatura.

cancer *s.* cancro.

candid *agg.* sincero, candido.

candidate *s.* candidato.

candidature *s.* candidatura.

candidly *avv.* sinceramente, candidamente.

candied *agg.* candito.

candle *s.* candela || — *-end*, moccolo; — *-holder*, candelabro; *by* — *-light*, a lume di candela.

candlestick *s.* candeliere.

candour *s.* candore, ingenuità.

candy *s.* candito.

to **candy** *vt.* candire. ♦ to **candy** *vi.* cristallizzarsi (*di zucchero*).

cane *s.* **1.** giunco, canna **2.** bastone da passeggio.

to **cane** *vt.* bastonare (*con una canna*).

canine *s.* dente canino.

caning *s.* bastonatura.

canned *agg.* conservato in scatola.

cannibal *s.* cannibale.

cannibalism *s.* cannibalismo.

cannon *s.* **1.** cannone **2.** carambola (*al biliardo*).

to **cannon** *vi.* **1.** cannoneggiare **2.** far carambola.

canoe *s.* canoa.

canon *s.* **1.** canone **2.** (*eccl.*) canonico: — *law*, diritto canonico.

canonical *agg.* canonico.

to **canonize** *vt.* canonizzare.

canopy *s.* **1.** baldacchino **2.** volta (*del cielo*).

cant *s.* **1.** (*arch.*) angolo esterno **2.** inclinazione **3.** gergo.

canteen *s.* **1.** (*mil.*) dispensa **2.** mensa aziendale.

canvas *s.* **1.** canovaccio **2.** (*mar.*) velatura **3.** tela **4.** tendone.

canyon *s.* burrone.

cap *s.* **1.** berretto **2.** (*arch.*) capitello **3.** (*mecc.; elettr.*) cappuccio, capsula.

capability *s.* capacità, abilità.

capable *agg.* abile, capace.

capacitor *s.* condensatore.

capacity *s.* **1.** capacità **2.** (*elettr.*) potenza (*di motore*).

cape[1] *s.* capo, promontorio.

cape[2] *s.* cappa.

caper[1] *s.* cappero.

caper[2] *s.* piroetta, capriola.

to **caper** *vi.* far capriole.

capercaillie *s.* gallo cedrone.

capillarity *s.* capillarità.

capillary *agg.* capillare. ♦ **capillary** *s.* (*anat.*) vaso capillare.

capital[1] *agg. e s.* capitale.

capital[2] *s.* (*arch.*) capitello.

capitalism *s.* capitalismo.

capitalist *s.* capitalista.

capitalistic *agg.* capitalistico.

to **capitalize** *vt.* capitalizzare.

capitular *agg.* capitolare.

capitulary *s.* capitolare.

to **capitulate** *vi.* capitolare.

capitulation *s.* capitolazione.

capon *s.* cappone.

caprice *s.* capriccio.

to **capsize** *vt.* capovolgere. ♦ to **capsize** *vi.* capovolgersi.

capstan *s.* argano.

capsule *s.* capsula.

to **capsule** *vt.* incapsulare.

captain *s.* **1.** capitano **2.** (*comm.*) magnate.

captious *agg.* capzioso.

to **captivate** *vt.* cattivare, ammaliare.

captivating *agg.* cattivante, ammaliante.

captive *s.* prigioniero: *to take* —, far prigioniero.

captivity *s.* prigionia, cattività.

capture *s.* cattura.

to **capture** *vt.* far prigioniero, prendere (*di città ecc.*).

Capuchin *s.* 1. (*eccl.*) Cappuccino 2. scimmia cappuccina.

car *s.* 1. carro 2. automobile 3. (*ferr.*) vagone || — *-licence*, permesso di circolazione; *dining-* —, vagone ristorante; *sleeping-* —, vagone letto.

carabin *s.* carabina.

carabineer *s.* carabiniere.

to caracole *vi.* caracollare.

carafe *s.* caraffa.

caramel *s.* caramello.

carat *s.* carato.

caravan *s.* 1. carovana 2. carro (*di zingari ecc.*).

caravel *s.* caravella.

carbon *s.* carbonio || — *paper*, carta carbone.

carbonate *s.* carbonato.

carboniferous *agg.* carbonifero.

to carbonize *vt.* carbonizzare.

carbuncle *s.* carbonchio.

carburation *s.* carburazione.

carburetter, carburettor *s.* carburatore.

carcase *s.* carcassa.

carcinogen *s.* sostanza cancerogena.

card *s.* 1. cartoncino, biglietto 2. carta da giuoco.

to card *vt.* schedare.

cardan *s.* cardano || — *joint*, giunto cardanico.

cardboard *s.* cartone.

cardiac *agg.* cardiaco.

cardigan *s.* giacca di lana.

cardinal *agg.* e *s.* cardinale.

cardiogram *s.* cardiogramma.

cardiologist *s.* cardiologo.

cardiopathy *s.* cardiopatia.

care *s.* 1. cura, attenzione, protezione: *take* —!, attenzione!; *to take* — *of*, aver cura 2. preoccupazione || — *-free*, senza pensieri; — *-worn*, pieno di pensieri.

to care *vi.* curarsi, interessarsi.

career *s.* 1. carriera 2. andatura veloce.

careful *agg.* 1. accurato 2. prudente.

carefully *avv.* 1. accuratamente 2. attentamente.

careless *agg.* noncurante.

carelessly *avv.* negligentemente.

carelessness *s.* trascuratezza.

caress *s.* carezza.

to caress *vt.* accarezzare.

caressing *agg.* carezzevole.

caretaker *s.* guardiano, custode.

caricature *s.* caricatura.

Carmelite *s.* carmelitano.

carmine *agg.* e *s.* carminio.

carnage *s.* carneficina, strage.

carnal *agg.* carnale, sensuale.

carnation *agg.* carnicino. ◆ **carnation** *s.* garofano.

carnival *s.* carnevale.

carnivore *s.* carnivoro.

carnivorous *agg.* carnivoro.

carol *s.* canto, inno.

carotid *s.* carotide.

carousel *s.* carosello.

carp *s.* carpa.

carpenter *s.* carpentiere, falegname.

carpet *s.* tappeto || *bedside* —, scendiletto.

carriage *s.* 1. carrozza, vettura 2. (*comm.*) trasporto.

carrier *s.* 1. portatore, spedizioniere 2. (*mecc.*) trasportatore 3. supporto.

carrion *s.* carogna.

carrot *s.* carota.

carry *s.* portata (*di arma da fuoco ecc.*).

to carry *vt.* e *vi.* 1. portare (*un peso*), trasportare 2. trasmettere (*suoni*) || *to* — *about*, portare addosso; *to* — *on*, continuare; *to* — *out*, eseguire, realizzare, compiere; *to* — *through*, portare a buon fine.

carrying *s.* trasporto.

cart *s.* carro.

cartel *s.* (*econ.; pol.*) cartello.

cartilage *s.* cartilagine.

cartography *s.* cartografia.

cartomancy *s.* cartomanzia.

carton *s.* scatola di cartone.

cartoon *s.* 1. vignetta 2. (*cine*) disegno animato.

cartridge *s.* 1. cartuccia 2. (*foto*) rotolo.

to carve *vt.* e *vi.* scolpire, incidere, cesellare.

carver *s.* intagliatore, scultore (*in legno e avorio*).

carving *s.* scultura, intaglio (*in legno e avorio*).

caryatid *s.* cariatide.

cascade *s.* piccola cascata (*d'acqua*).

case[1] *s.* 1. caso, avvenimento 2. (*giur.*) causa.

case[2] *s.* 1. astuccio 2. cassa, cassetta.

to case *vt.* imballare.

casement *s.* telaio di finestra (*a due battenti*), finestra.

cash s. cassa, contanti || — *on delivery*, pagamento alla consegna; *by ready* —, in contanti.

to **cash** *vt*. incassare, riscuotere.

cashier s. cassiere.

to **cashier** *vt*. destituire.

casing s. involucro, copertura.

cask s. barile, botte.

casket s. scrigno.

cassation s. cassazione.

cassock s. tunica (*del clero anglicano*).

cast s. 1. getto, lancio 2. (*metal.*) gettata, stampo 3. complesso (*di attori*) || — *-iron*, ghisa.

to **cast** (cast, cast) *vt. e vi.* 1. gettare, lanciare 2. (*metal.*) fondere (*in stampo*) || to — *aside*, gettare da parte; to — *down*, abbassare (*gli occhi*).

castanets s. *pl.* nacchere.

castaway agg. arenato, respinto. ♦ **castaway** s. naufrago, reprobo.

caste s. casta.

caster s. V. *castor*.

to **castigate** *vt.* castigare, punire.

casting s. 1. il gettare 2. (*metal.*) getto, colata 3. distribuzione (*delle parti agli attori*).

castle s. castello.

castor s. 1. pepaiuola, saliera 2. rotella da mobili.

castor-oil s. olio di ricino.

to **castrate** *vt.* castrare.

casual agg. casuale, fortuito.

casually *avv.* per caso.

casualness s. irregolarità, noncuranza.

casualty s. 1. infortunio 2. infortunato.

casuistry s. casistica.

cat s. gatto.

cataclysm s. cataclisma.

catacomb s. catacomba.

catalepsy s. catalessi.

cataleptic agg. e s. catalettico.

catalogue s. catalogo.

to **catalogue** *vt. e vi.* catalogare.

catalyst s. catalizzatore.

cataplasm s. cataplasma.

catapult s. catapulta.

cataract s. cateratta.

catarrh s. catarro.

catastrophe s. catastrofe, calamità.

catastrophic(al) agg. catastrofico.

catch s. 1. presa, cattura 2. trappola || — *-as-* —*-can*, lotta libera.

to **catch** (caught, caught) *vt.* 1. afferrare, acchiappare, prendere: to — *the train*, prendere il treno 2. pescare, sorprendere.

catching agg. 1. attraente 2. orecchiabile (*di melodia*) 3. (*med.*) contagioso.

catchy agg. 1. attraente 2. orecchiabile (*di melodia*) 3. insidioso.

catechism s. catechismo.

to **catechize** *vt.* catechizzare.

catechumen s. catecumeno.

categoric(al) agg. categorico.

category s. categoria.

to **cater** *vi.* 1. provvedere cibo 2. procurare svaghi.

caterpillar s. 1. bruco 2. (*mecc.*) cingolo 3. trattore a cingoli.

catharsis s. catarsi.

cathartic agg. catartico.

cathedral s. cattedrale.

Catherine-wheel s. girandola.

cathode s. catodo.

cathodic agg. catodico.

catholic agg. e s. cattolico.

Catholicism s. cattolicesimo.

cation s. catione.

cattish agg. felino.

cattle s. bestiame, armenti || — *-dealer*, negoziante di bestiame; — *-lifter*, ladro di bestiame.

caught V. to *catch*.

cauldron s. caldaia.

cauliflower s. cavolfiore.

causal agg. causale.

causality s. causalità.

causative agg. causativo.

cause s. 1. causa, ragione, motivo 2. (*giur.*) processo, causa.

to **cause** *vt.* causare, cagionare.

causeway s. strada rialzata.

caustic agg. caustico (*anche fig.*).

caustically *avv.* causticamente (*anche fig.*).

causticity s. causticità (*anche fig.*).

cauterization s. cauterizzazione.

to **cauterize** *vt.* cauterizzare.

caution s. 1. prudenza, cautela 2. cauzione, garanzia || — *-money*, cauzione, pegno.

to **caution** *vt.* mettere in guardia.

cautious agg. cauto, prudente.

cautiously *avv.* cautamente.

cavalier s. cavaliere.

cavalry s. cavalleria.

cave s. caverna, spelonca.

to **cave** *vt. e vi.* scavare || to — *in*, sprofondare.

cavernous agg. cavernoso (*anche fig.*).

caviar(e) s. caviale.

cavil *s.* cavillo.

to cavil *vi.* cavillare.

cavity *s.* cavità.

cavy *s.* cavia.

cayman *s.* caimano.

to cease *vt.* e *vi.* cessare, finire.

cedar *s.* cedro.

cedilla *s.* cediglia.

ceiling *s.* soffitto.

to celebrate *vt.* e *vi.* celebrare, solennizzare.

celebrated *agg.* famoso.

celebration *s.* celebrazione.

celebrity *s.* celebrità, persona famosa.

celerity *s.* celerità.

celery *s.* sedano.

celestial *agg.* celestiale, paradisiaco.

celibacy *s.* celibato.

cell *s.* **1.** cella **2.** cellula.

cellar *s.* cantina.

cellarman *s.* cantiniere.

cellular *agg.* cellulare, alveolare.

cellulitis *s.* cellulite.

celluloid *agg.* e *s.* celluloide.

cellulose *s.* cellulosa.

Celt *s.* celta.

Celtic *agg.* celtico.

cement *s.* **1.** cemento **2.** stucco, mastice.

to cement *vt.* cementare (*anche fig.*).

cemetery *s.* cimitero.

to cense *vt.* incensare.

censer *s.* turibolo.

censor *s.* censore.

to censor *vt.* censurare.

censorial *agg.* censorio.

censorship *s.* censura, censorato.

censure *s.* censura.

to censure *vt.* censurare.

census *s.* censo.

cent *s.* centesimo (*di dollaro*).

centaur *s.* centauro.

centenarian *agg.* e *s.* centenario.

centenary *agg.* e *s.* centenario.

centennial *agg.* centennale.

centesimal *agg.* centesimale.

centigrade *agg.* centigrado.

centigramme *s.* centigrammo.

centilitre *s.* centilitro.

centimetre *s.* centimetro.

central *agg.* **1.** centrale **2.** fondamentale.

centralism *s.* accentramento.

centralization *s.* concentrazione (*di poteri*).

to centralize *vt.* e *vi.* accentrare.

centre *s.* centro, parte centrale, interno.

centrifugal *agg.* centrifugo.

centripetal *agg.* centripeto.

centrism *s.* centrismo.

to centuplicate *vt.* centuplicare.

centurion *s.* centurione.

century *s.* **1.** secolo **2.** (*stor.*) centuria.

cephalalgia *s.* cefalea.

ceramics *s.* (*arte della*) ceramica.

cereal *agg.* e *s.* cereale.

cerebral *agg.* cerebrale.

cerebro-spinal *agg.* cerebro-spinale.

cerebrum *s.* cervello.

ceremonial *agg.* da cerimonia. ♦ **ceremonial** *s.* cerimoniale.

ceremonious *agg.* cerimonioso.

ceremony *s.* cerimonia || **to stand on** —, far complimenti.

certain *agg.* **1.** certo, sicuro **2.** indeterminato, certo.

certainly *avv.* certamente.

certainty *s.* certezza.

certificate *s.* certificato.

to certify *vt.* certificare, attestare.

certitude *s.* certezza.

cervical *agg.* cervicale. ♦ **cervical** *s.* vertebra cervicale. ♦ **cervicals** *s. pl.* nervi cervicali.

cessation *s.* cessazione.

cession *s.* cessione.

cess-pit, cess-pool *s.* pozzo nero.

cetacean *agg.* di cetaceo. ♦ **cetacean** *s.* cetaceo.

to chafe *vt.* **1.** riscaldare **2.** irritare.

to chafe *vi.* **1.** strofinarsi **2.** irritarsi.

chaff *s.* **1.** pula, paglia trinciata **2.** (*fig.*) oggetto di nessun valore.

chaffer *s.* contrattazione, baratto.

chain *s.* **1.** catena **2.** serie, concatenamento.

to chain *vt.* **1.** incatenare **2.** (*fig.*) mettere in ceppi.

chain-stores *s. pl.* catene (*di negozi o grandi magazzini*).

chair *s.* **1.** sedia: *deck-* —, sedia a sdraio; *easy-* —, poltrona **2.** cattedra (*universitaria*).

chairman *s.* presidente (*di consiglio, assemblea ecc.*).

chalice *s.* calice.

chalk *s.* **1.** gesso **2.** (*min.*) calcare || — *-drawing*, disegno a pastello; — *-stone* (*pat.*), calcolo.

chalky *agg.* gessoso.

challenge *s.* **1.** sfida **2.** (*mil.*) intimazione.

to challenge *vt.* **1.** sfidare **2.** (*mil.*) intimare.

challenger s. sfidatore, sfidante.

chamber s. 1. sala, aula 2. (*pol.; comm.*) camera || — *-music*, musica da camera; —*maid*, cameriera (*specialmente d'albergo*).

chamberlain s. 1. ciambellano 2. tesoriere.

chameleon s. camaleonte.

chamois s. camoscio.

champion s. 1. campione 2. difensore.

championship s. campionato.

chance s. 1. avvenimento fortuito, caso 2. occasione.

to **chance** vi. accadere.

chancellery s. cancelleria.

chancellor s. cancelliere.

chancery s. cancelleria.

chandelier s. candeliere, lampadario.

change s. 1. cambio, mutamento || — *for a* —, tanto per cambiare 2. moneta spicciola.

to **change** vt. e vi. cambiare.

changeability s. mutabilità.

changeable agg. 1. mutabile 2. incostante (*di tempo*).

changing agg. cangiante, mutevole.
♦ **changing** s. cambio.

channel s. 1. canale, stretto. ♦ **channels** s. pl. vie di comunicazione.

chant s. canto, cantilena.

to **channel** vt. 1. fare canali 2. incanalare.

chaos s. caos.

chap[1] s. (*fam.*) individuo, ragazzo.

chap[2] s. screpolatura.

chapel s. cappella.

chaplain s. cappellano.

chaplet s. ghirlanda, corona (*di fiori*).

chapter s. capitolo.

to **char** vt. carbonizzare. ♦ to **char** vi. carbonizzarsi.

character s. 1. carattere, indole 2. scrittura 3. (*lett.*) personaggio.

characteristic agg. caratteristico.
♦ **characteristic** s. caratteristica.

characterization s. caratterizzazione.

to **characterize** vt. caratterizzare.

charade s. sciarada.

charcoal s. carbone di legna.

charge s. 1. prezzo richiesto, spesa 2. incarico, sorveglianza 3. (*giur.*) accusa.

to **charge** vt. 1. far pagare, addebitare 2. incaricare 3. accusare: to

— *so. with a crime*, accusare qu. di un delitto.

chargeable agg. 1. a carico di, da addebitarsi a 2. accusabile.

chariot s. cocchio.

charitable agg. caritatevole.

charitably avv. caritatevolmente.

charity s. 1. carità, benevolenza 2. istituzione benefica.

charlatan s. ciarlatano.

charm s. 1. fascino 2. incantesimo, malia.

to **charm** vt. 1. affascinare 2. sottoporre a magia.

charming agg. affascinante.

charmingly avv. in modo affascinante.

charnel(-house) s. ossario.

chart s. 1. grafico 2. carta marina.

charter s. 1. licenza, brevetto 2. carta costituzionale.

chartography s. cartografia.

charwoman s. domestica ad ore.

charwork s. lavoro di domestica ad ore.

chase s. 1. inseguimento, caccia 2. riserva di caccia, cacciagione.

to **chase**[1] vt. inseguire, cacciare.

to **chase**[2] vt. cesellare.

chaser[1] s. cacciatore, inseguitore.

chaser[2] s. cesellatore.

chasing s. 1. cesellatura 2. filettatura (*di una vite*).

chasm s. baratro, abisso.

chaste agg. casto, puro.

chastely avv. castamente, virtuosamente.

chastity s. castità.

chat s. chiacchiera.

to **chat** vi. chiacchierare.

chatter s. 1. chiacchiera, chiacchierio 2. il battere dei denti.

to **chatter** vi. 1. chiacchierare 2. battere i denti.

chatterbox s. chiacchierone, chiacchierona.

chattering s. 1. chiacchierio 2. il battere dei denti.

chauvinism s. sciovinismo.

chauvinist s. sciovinista.

cheap agg. e avv. a buon mercato.

cheaply avv. economicamente, in modo poco costoso.

cheat s. 1. frode 2. imbroglione.

to **cheat** vt. e vi. imbrogliare.

cheater s. truffatore, baro.

cheating s. inganno.

check[1] s. 1. scacco 2. controllo, verifica 3. scontrino, contromarca.

check² *s.* disegno a scacchi.
to **check** *vi.* dare scacco. ♦ to
check *vt.* controllare, verificare.
checked *agg.* quadrettato.
checkmate *s.* scacco matto.
to **checkmate** *vt.* dare scacco matto.
cheek *s.* guancia.
cheekily *avv.* sfacciatamente.
cheeky *agg.* sfacciato.
to **cheer** *vt.* rallegrare, incoraggiare. ♦ to **cheer** *vi.* essere di buon
umore, rallegrarsi.
cheerful *agg.* di buon umore.
cheerfully *avv.* allegramente.
cheerfulness *s.* buon umore.
cheering *agg.* incoraggiante. ♦
cheering *s.* acclamazioni (*pl.*).
cheese *s.* formaggio.
cheetah *s.* ghepardo.
chemical *agg.* chimico.
chemically *avv.* chimicamente.
chemicals *s. pl.* prodotti chimici.
chemisette *s.* camicetta.
chemist *s.* 1. chimico 2. farmacista.
chemistry *s.* chimica.
cheque *s.* assegno: *to cash a* —,
cambiare un assegno; — -*book*,
libretto d'assegni; *blank* —, assegno in bianco; *crossed* —, assegno
sbarrato.
to **cherish** *vt.* 1. (*fig.*) nutrire 2.
curare teneramente, coccolare.
cherry *s.* ciliegia.
cherub *s.* cherubino.
chess *s.* giuoco degli scacchi || —
-*board*, scacchiera; — -*men*, pezzi degli scacchi.
chest *s.* 1. cassetta, cassone 2. torace.
chestnut *agg.* castano. ♦ **chestnut**
s. 1. castagno 2. castagna.
to **chew** *vt.* e *vi.* masticare.
chicanery *s.* cavillo (*legale*).
chick *s.* 1. pulcino 2. (*fig.*) bambino.
chicken *s.* gallinella, pollo.
chicory *s.* cicoria.
to **chide** (**chid, chid**) (*anche reg.*)
vt. e *vi.* redarguire, sgridare.
chief *agg.* principale. ♦ **chief** *s.*
capo, comandante.
chiefly *avv.* principalmente.
chieftain *s.* capo (*di tribù, clan
ecc.*).
chilblain *s.* gelone.
child *s.* (*pl.* children) 1. bambino,
bambina 2. figlio, figlia.
childhood *s.* infanzia.
childish *agg.* infantile.

childishness *s.* fanciullaggine, puerilità.
childless *agg.* senza figli.
childlike *agg.* infantile.
children V. *child.*
Chilean *agg.* e *s.* cileno.
chill *s.* 1. colpo di freddo 2. (*metal.*)
conchiglia.
to **chill** *vt.* 1. raffreddare, agghiacciare (*anche fig.*) 2. (*metal.*) fondere in conchiglia. ♦ to **chill** *vi.*
raffreddarsi.
chilled *agg.* 1. congelato 2. (*metal.*)
fuso in conchiglia.
chilliness *s.* 1. freddo 2. (*fig.*) freddezza.
chilly *agg.* 1. freddoloso (*di persona*)
2. fresco (*di tempo*).
chime *s.* scampanio.
to **chime** *vt.* e *vi.* scampanare, suonare a festa.
chiming *s.* lo scampanare.
chimney *s.* camino, comignolo || —
-*sweeper*, spazzacamino.
chimpanzee *s.* scimpanzè.
chin *s.* mento || — -*strap*, sottogola.
china *s.* 1. porcellana fine 2. (*fam.*)
stoviglie di porcellana.
chinchilla *s.* cincillà.
chine *s.* spina dorsale.
Chinese *agg.* e *s.* cinese.
chink *s.* fessura, crepa.
chip *s.* 1. scheggia 2. (*cuc.*) patatina fritta.
to **chip** *vt.* 1. scheggiare 2. rompere. ♦ to **chip** *vi.* scheggiarsi,
frantumarsi.
chiromancer *s.* chiromante.
chiromancy *s.* chiromanzia.
chiropodist *s.* pedicure.
chirp *s.* 1. cinguettio, pigolio 2.
stridio, il frinire (*di cicale ecc.*).
to **chirp** *vi.* 1. cinguettare, pigolare
2. frinire, stridere (*di cicale ecc.*).
chisel *s.* cesello.
to **chisel** *vt.* cesellare.
chiseller *s.* cesellatore.
chitterlings *s. pl.* trippa.
chivalrous *agg.* cavalleresco.
chivalry *s.* 1. cavalleria 2. condotta
cavalleresca.
chloride *s.* cloruro.
chlorine *s.* cloro.
chlorite *s.* clorito.
chloroform *s.* cloroformio.
chlorophyl(l) *s.* clorofilla.
chock *s.* 1. cuneo, bietta 2. (*mar*)
passacavi.
chocolate *agg.* 1. di cioccolato 2.

color cioccolata. ♦ **chocolate** s. cioccolato: *cake of* —, tavoletta di cioccolato.

choice agg. di prima qualità, scelto. ♦ **choice** s. 1. scelta 2. la cosa scelta 3. assortimento.

choir s. coro.

choke s. 1. soffocamento 2. strozzatura (*di tubo*).

to choke vt. 1. soffocare (*anche fig.*) 2. ingorgare. ♦ **to choke** v².: ostruirsi.

choker s. soffocatore.

cholera s. colera.

cholesterol s. colesterolo.

to choose (chose, chosen) vt. scegliere.

chooser s. chi sceglie.

chop s. 1. (*cuc.*) braciola 2. colpo (*di scure ecc.*).

to chop vt. e vi. 1. fendere, tagliare 2. (*cuc.*) tritare || *to — down*, abbattere (*alberi*); *to — off*, tagliar via.

chopper s. 1. ascia 2. chi taglia con l'ascia 3. tagliatrice.

choppy agg. 1. screpolato 2. increspato (*del mare*).

choral agg. corale.

chord s. 1. (*mus.; anat.; geom.*) corda 2. (*mus.*) accordo.

choreographer s. coreografo.

choreographic agg. coreografico.

choreography s. coreografia.

chorus s. coro || *— -singer*, corista.

chose V. *to choose*.

chosen V. *to choose*.

chrism s. crisma.

to christen vt. battezzare.

Christendom s. cristianità.

christening s. battesimo.

Christian agg. e s. cristiano || *— name*, nome di battesimo.

Christianity s. cristianesimo.

to christianize vt. convertire al cristianesimo.

Christmas s. Natale.

chromatic agg. cromatico.

chromatically avv. cromaticamente.

chromatism s. cromatismo.

chromatography s. cromatografia.

chrome s. cromo.

to chrome vt. cromare.

chromium s. cromo || *— -plated*, cromato; *— -plating*, cromatura.

chromolithograph s. cromolitografia.

chromosome s. cromosoma.

chromosphere s. cromosfera.

chronic agg. cronico (*anche fig.*).

chronicle s. cronaca.

chronicler s. cronista.

chronologic(al) agg. cronologico.

chronologically avv. cronologicamente.

chronology s. cronologia.

chronometer s. cronometro.

chrysalid s. crisalide.

chrysanthemum s. crisantemo.

chubby agg. paffuto.

church s. 1. chiesa 2. comunità religiosa || *— -going*, assiduità ai servizi religiosi; *— -living*, beneficio ecclesiastico; *— -service*, funzione religiosa.

churchman s. 1. ecclesiastico 2. membro della chiesa anglicana.

churchy agg. bigotto.

churchyard s. cimitero.

chyle s. (*fisiol.*) chilo.

ciborium s. ciborio.

cicada s. cicala.

to cicatrize vt. cicatrizzare. ♦ **to cicatrize** vi. cicatrizzarsi.

cider s. sidro.

cigar s. sigaro || *— -case*, portasigari, *— -end*, mozzicone; *— -holder*, bocchino per sigari.

cigarette s. sigaretta || *— -case*, portasigarette, *— -end*, mozzicone, *— -holder*, bocchino; *— paper*, cartina per sigaretta.

cilice s. cilicio.

cinder s. 1. brace 2. scoria.

cine-camera s. macchina da presa.

cinema s. cinematografo.

cinematograph s. 1. proiettore cinematografico 2. macchina da presa.

cinematographer s. 1. operatore cinematografico 2. cineasta.

cinematographic agg. cinematografico.

cinematography s. cinematografia.

cine-projector s. proiettore cinematografico.

cinerary agg. cinerario.

cinnabar s. cinabro.

cinnamon s. cannella.

cipher s. 1. cifrario 2. monogramma 3. (*mat.; anche fig.*) zero, nullità.

to cipher vt. e vi. cifrare.

circle s. 1. cerchio, circolo (*anche fig.*) 2. orbita (*dei pianeti*) 3. galleria (*di teatro*).

circlet s. cerchietto.

circuit *s.* **1.** cinta, circonvallazione **2.** rivoluzione, rotazione (*di astri*) **3.** (*elettr.; sport*) circuito.

circular *agg.* circolare. ◆ **circular** *s.* lettera circolare.

to **circulate** *vt.* mettere in circolazione, diffondere. ◆ to **circulate** *vi.* circolare.

circulating *agg.* circolante.

circulation *s.* **1.** circolazione **2.** diffusione **3.** (*giorn.*) tiratura.

circulatory *agg.* circolatorio.

to **circumcise** *vt.* circoncidere.

circumcision *s.* circoncisione.

circumference *s.* circonferenza.

circumflex *agg.* circonflesso.

circumlocution *s.* circonlocuzione.

to **circumnavigate** *vt.* circumnavigare.

circumnavigation *s.* circumnavigazione.

circumnavigator *s.* circumnavigatore.

to **circumscribe** *vt.* circoscrivere.

circumscription *s.* circoscrizione.

circumspect *agg.* circospetto.

circumspection *s.* circospezione.

circumstance *s.* circostanza.

circumstantial *agg.* **1.** circostanziale **2.** circostanziato.

circumstantiality *s.* abbondanza di particolari.

circumstantially *avv.* circostanziatamente.

to **circumvent** *vt.* circuire.

circumvention *s.* raggiro.

circumvolution *s.* circonvoluzione.

circus *s.* **1.** circo, arena **2.** piazza rotonda.

cirrhosis *s.* cirrosi.

cisalpine *agg.* cisalpino.

cistern *s.* cisterna.

citadel *s.* cittadella.

to **cite** *vt.* citare.

citizen *s.* cittadino.

citizenhood *s.* cittadinanza.

citizenship *s.* diritto di cittadinanza.

citrate *s.* citrato.

citric *agg.* citrico.

citron *s.* cedro.

city *s.* **1.** città (*grande*) **2.** centro di grande traffico di una città.

civic *agg.* civico.

civil *agg.* civile, cortese.

civilian *agg.* e *s.* civile, borghese.

civility *s.* civiltà, cortesia.

civilization *s.* civilizzazione, civiltà.

to **civilize** *vt.* civilizzare.

civilly *avv.* civilmente.

civism *s.* civismo.

claim *s.* **1.** richiesta **2.** (*giur.*) rivendicazione **3.** (*comm.*) reclamo.

to **claim** *vt.* **1.** esigere, chiedere **2.** (*giur.*) rivendicare **3.** (*comm.*) reclamare.

claimant *s.* **1.** rivendicatore **2.** richiedente.

clairvoyance *s.* chiaroveggenza.

clairvoyant *agg.* e *s.* chiaroveggente.

to **clamber** *vi.* arrampicarsi.

clammy *agg.* vischioso.

clamour *s.* clamore, vocio.

to **clamour** *vt.* e *vi.* vociferare.

clan *s.* gruppo familiare, tribù.

clandestine *agg.* clandestino.

to **clang** *vi.* emettere un suono, un grido. ◆ to **clang** *vt.* far risonare.

clangour *s.* fragore.

to **clank** *vi.* tintinnare. ◆ to **clank** *vt.* far tintinnare.

clap *s.* **1.** applauso **2.** rumore improvviso **3.** piccolo colpo (*con la mano*).

to **clap** *vt.* e *vi.* **1.** applaudire **2.** dare un colpo (*con la mano*) **3.** battere (*le ali*).

clapper *s.* **1.** battente (*di porta*) **2.** (*teat.*) membro della « claque ».

claret *s.* **1.** color rosso-violetto **2.** vino chiaretto.

clarification *s.* chiarificazione.

to **clarify** *vt.* chiarificare. ◆ to **clarify** *vi.* chiarificarsi.

clarinet *s.* clarinetto.

clarity *s.* chiarità.

clash *s.* **1.** cozzo, urto **2.** scontro (*d'opinioni*).

to **clash** *vt.* e *vi.* **1.** cozzare, far strepito **2.** scontrarsi (*d'opinioni*).

clasp *s.* fermaglio, fibbia.

to **clasp** *vt.* afferrare.

class *s.* **1.** classe, categoria **2.** (*scol.*) classe **3.** (*fig.*) distinzione.

classic *agg.* e *s.* classico.

classical *agg.* classico.

classically *avv.* classicamente.

classicism *s.* classicismo.

classification *s.* classificazione.

to **classify** *vt.* classificare.

classmate *s.* compagno di classe.

classroom *s.* aula.

classy *agg.* (*fam.*) di classe.

clatter *s.* fracasso.

to **clatter** *vi.* far fracasso.

clause *s.* clausola.

claustrophobia *s.* claustrofobia.

claw s. 1. artiglio, zampa con artigli 2. uncino 3. chela.
to claw vt. artigliare.
clawed agg. munito di artigli.
clay s. argilla: fire- —, argilla refrattaria || — pigeon, piattello.
clayey agg. argilloso.
clean agg. 1. pulito 2. netto, nitido 3. (fig.) puro, schietto.
to clean vt. pulire.
cleaner s. pulitore, pulitrice || dry- —, smacchiatore a secco.
cleaning s. pulitura.
cleanliness s. pulizia.
cleanly agg. pulito. ♦ **cleanly** avv. in modo pulito.
cleanness s. 1. pulizia (anche fig.) 2. nitidezza.
to cleanse vt. 1. pulire 2. purificare.
cleanser s. 1. pulitore 2. detersivo.
cleansing agg. purificante. ♦ **cleansing** s. 1. purificazione 2. depurazione.
clear agg. 1. chiaro, limpido 2. distinto, evidente || — -cut, nettamente stagliato; — -sighted, dalla vista buona.
to clear vt. 1. chiarire, schiarire 2. discolpare 3. (comm.) svincolare || to — away, sparecchiare, dissiparsi (di nebbia); to — up, rassettare (una stanza), chiarire (un malinteso). ♦ **to clear** vi. schiarirsi.
clearance s. 1. chiarificazione 2. sgombero 3. (comm.) sdoganamento.
clearing s. 1. chiarimento 2. rimozione.
clearly avv. chiaramente.
clearness s. 1. chiarezza 2. (fig.) limpidezza.
cleavage s. 1. spaccatura 2. (min.) clivaggio.
to cleave (cleft, cleft) vt. e vi. fendere, spaccare.
cleft s. fenditura.
clemency s. clemenza.
clement agg. 1. clemente 2. dolce, gentile (di carattere) 3. mite (di tempo).
to clench vt. 1. stringere (mani, denti ecc.) 2. ribadire.
clergy s. clero.
clergyman s. ecclesiastico.
clerical agg. 1. clericale 2. impiegatizio.
clericalism s. clericalismo.
clerk s. impiegato || chief —, ca-

poufficio.
to clerk vi. lavorare come impiegato.
clever agg. intelligente, abile, ingegnoso.
cleverly avv. intelligentemente.
cleverness s. intelligenza, abilità, ingegnosità.
clew s. gomitolo (di filo).
click s. scatto, rumore secco.
client s. cliente.
cliff s. scogliera.
climate s. clima.
climatic agg. climatico.
climax s. apice, culmine.
climb s. 1. rampa 2. ascesa.
to climb vt. e vi. 1. arrampicarsi 2. scalare (anche fig.).
climber s. 1. scalatore 2. (fig.) arrivista 3. pianta rampicante.
climbing s. 1. scalata 2. (fig.) arrivismo. ♦ **climbing** agg. rampicante.
to cling (clung, clung) vi. attaccarsi, aggrapparsi (anche fig.): to — to a hope, aggrapparsi ad una speranza.
clinical agg. clinico.
clinician s. clinico.
clinking s. tintinnio.
clip s. 1. fermaglio, molletta || hair —, forcina per capelli 2. graffa (per ferite) 3. tosatura (di pecore).
to clip vt. 1. tenere insieme (con un fermaglio) 2. tosare (pecore ecc.).
clipper s. 1. tosatore 2. (mar.) "clipper". ♦ **clippers** s. pl. 1. forbici 2. macchinetta per tosare (sing.).
cloak s. 1. mantello 2. (fig.) manto, velo.
clock s. orologio (da muro, da tavolo) || alarm- —, sveglia.
clockwise agg. in senso orario || counter- —, in senso antiorario.
clockwork s. meccanismo a orologeria.
clod s. zolla.
clog s. 1. impedimento, intoppo 2. zoccolo.
to clog vt. ostruire, impedire (anche fig.). ♦ **to clog** vi. incepparsi.
cloister s. chiostro.
close agg. 1. chiuso 2. serrato: — combat, combattimento corpo a corpo 3. afoso, viziato (di aria) 4. intimo: — friend, amico intimo 5. accurato, attento || — -fitting, aderente (di vestiti); —

-mouthed, riservato; — -shaven, rasato con cura.

close s. 1. spazio cintato 2. fine, termine 3. corpo a corpo.

close avv. vicino, presso.

to close vt. chiudere || to — up, turare, sbarrare (di strada). ♦ to close vi. chiudersi || to — in, avvicinarsi, accorciarsi (di giorni); to — with, venire a un accordo.

closed agg. chiuso.

closely avv. 1. da vicino 2. attentamente.

closeness s. 1. afa, mancanza d'aria 2. compattezza 3. intimità 4. vicinanza 5. accuratezza.

closet s. 1. studio, salotto privato 2. armadio a muro 3. gabinetto.

close-up s. (cine) primo piano.

closing s. chiusura (di negozi, teatri ecc.).

clot s. grumo.

to clot vt. raggrumare, coagulare. ♦ to clot vi. raggrumarsi, coagularsi.

cloth s. tessuto, stoffa, tela || (table-) —, tovaglia.

to clothe vt. vestire.

clothes s. pl. abiti, indumenti || —-book, attaccapanni; —-line, corda (per stendere il bucato); —-peg, molletta (fermabucato).

clothing s. 1. vestiario 2. copertura.

cloud s. 1. nuvola, nube 2. nugolo (di insetti).

to cloud vt. e vi. annuvolare, oscurare || to — (up, over), annuvolarsi.

clouded agg. 1. coperto (di nubi) 2. torbido (di liquidi).

cloudily avv. nebulosamente.

cloudy agg. 1. nuvoloso 2. torbido.

clover s. trifoglio.

clown s. pagliaccio.

clownish agg. pagliaccesco.

club s. 1. mazza, randello 2. circolo, associazione 3. (carte) fiori.

clue s. 1. indizio, traccia 2. filo di un racconto.

clumsily avv. goffamente.

clumsiness s. goffaggine.

clumsy agg. goffo, senza grazia.

clung V. to cling.

cluster s. 1. grappolo (d'uva), mazzo (di fiori), gruppo 2. folla, capannello (di gente) 3. sciame.

clutch s. 1. stretta, grinfia 2. (auto) frizione.

to clutch vt. e vi. afferrare, afferrarsi, agguantare.

coach s. 1. carrozza, cocchio 2. pullman 3. carrozza ferroviaria 4. (sport) allenatore, istruttore || -house, rimessa; mourning- —, carro funebre; stage- —, diligenza.

coachman s. cocchiere.

coachwork s. carrozzeria.

coadjutor s. coadiutore.

coagulant s. sostanza coagulante.

to coagulate vt. coagulare. ♦ to coagulate vi. coagularsi.

coagulation s. coagulazione.

coagulator s. coagulante.

coal s. carbone: — -bed, bacino carbonifero; — -black, nero come il carbone; — -fed, alimentato a carbone; — -mine, miniera di carbone.

to coalesce vi. 1. coalizzarsi, unirsi 2. fondersi.

coalition s. coalizione.

coarse agg. 1. grossolano, rozzo 2. ruvido, grosso (di materiale).

coarsely avv. grossolanamente.

coarseness s. 1. grossolanità 2. ruvidezza (di stoffe ecc.).

coast s. costa || — -guard, polizia costiera.

coastal agg. costiero.

coaster s. 1. nave cabotiera 2. sottobicchiere.

coat s. 1. giacca, soprabito 2. manto (anche fig.), pelliccia (di animale) 3. rivestimento, intonaco || — of arms, stemma.

to coat vt. rivestire, coprire.

coating s. rivestimento, mano di vernice.

to coax vt. blandire, circuire. ♦ to coax vi. far moine.

coaxial agg. coassiale.

cobalt s. cobalto.

cobble s. ciottolo.

to cobble vt. 1. pavimentare (con ciottoli) 2. rappezzare (scarpe).

cobbler s. ciabattino.

cobra s. cobra.

cobweb s. ragnatela.

cocaine s. cocaina.

coccyx s. (pl. -cyges) coccige.

cock s. 1. gallo 2. cane di fucile.

cockade s. coccarda.

cockatoo s. cacatoa.

cockboat s. (mar.) lancia.

cockerel s. galletto.

cock-eyed agg. strabico.

cockish agg. sfrontato.

cockney *agg.* e *s.* dialetto londinese.

cockpit *s.* **1.** arena (*per combattimento di galli*) **2.** (*mar.*) castello di poppa.

cockroach *s.* scarafaggio.

cockscomb *s.* **1.** cresta (*di gallo*) **2.** (*fig.*) zerbinotto.

cocktail *s.* **1.** cavallo con coda mozzata **2.** cocktail.

cocoa *s.* cacao.

coconut *s.* noce di cocco.

cocoon *s.* bozzolo.

cod *s.* merluzzo.

code *s.* codice.

to code *vt.* **1.** codificare **2.** cifrare (*un dispaccio*).

codeine *s.* codeina.

codex *s.* codice, manoscritto antico.

codfish *s.* merluzzo.

codicil *s.* codicillo.

codification *s.* codificazione.

to codify *vt.* codificare.

co-director *s.* condirettore.

co-education *s.* istruzione nella scuola mista.

co-educational *agg.* (*scol.*) misto.

coefficient *agg.* e *s.* coefficiente.

coenobium *s.* cenobio.

coercible *agg.* coercibile.

coercion *s.* coercizione.

coercive *agg.* coercitivo.

coeval *agg.* e *s.* coevo.

to coexist *vi.* coesistere.

coexistence *s.* coesistenza.

coffee *s.* caffè: — *-bean*, chicco di caffè; — *-grounds*, fondi di caffè || — *-house*, caffè, bar; — *-mill*, macinino; — *-pot*, caffettiera.

coffer *s.* cassa, cofano.

coffin *s.* bara.

cog *s.* dente (*di ruota*).

cognate *agg.* e *s.* consanguineo, congiunto.

cognition *s.* cognizione.

cognitive *agg.* avente conoscenza.

cognizable *agg.* **1.** conoscibile **2.** (*giur.*) entro la giurisdizione di una corte.

to cohabit *vi.* coabitare.

cohabitation *s.* coabitazione.

coheir *s.* coerede.

coheiress *s.* (*donna*) coerede.

coherence *s.* **1.** coerenza **2.** aderenza.

coherent *agg.* **1.** coerente **2.** aderente.

coherently *avv.* coerentemente.

cohesion *s.* coesione.

cohesive *agg.* coesivo.

cohort *s.* coorte.

coil *s.* **1.** rotolo, spira **2.** (*elettr.; mecc.*) bobina.

coin *s.* moneta (*di metallo*).

to coin *vt.* coniare (*anche fig.*).

coinage *s.* conio.

to coincide *vi.* coincidere.

coincidence *s.* coincidenza.

coiner *s.* falsario.

colander *s.* colino.

cold *agg.* **1.** freddo: *to be* —, aver freddo **2.** freddo (*di carattere*), apatico: *in* — *blood*, a sangue freddo. ◆ **cold** *s.* **1.** freddo **2.** raffreddore: *to catch a* —, prendere il raffreddore.

coldness *s.* freddezza (*anche fig.*).

Coleoptera *s. pl.* coleotteri.

colic *s.* colica.

colitis *s.* colite.

to collaborate *vi.* collaborare.

collaboration *s.* collaborazione.

collaborationist *s.* collaborazionista.

collaborator *s.* collaboratore.

collapse *s.* **1.** crollo (*anche fig.*) **2.** collasso.

to collapse *vi.* crollare (*anche fig.*).

collar *s.* **1.** colletto **2.** collare.

to collate *vt.* **1.** collezionare, confrontare **2.** riordinare (*pagine di un'opera*).

collateral *agg.* collaterale.

colleague *s.* collega.

to collect *vt.* **1.** riunire **2.** incassare, riscuotere **3.** fare una raccolta. ◆ **to collect** *vi.* **1.** riunirsi **2.** riscuotere.

collecting *s.* il raccogliere: *stamp* —, il raccogliere francobolli.

collection *s.* **1.** raccolta, collezione **2.** riunione di persone **3.** questua, colletta.

collective *agg.* collettivo || — *title* (*tip.*), titolo generale.

collectivism *s.* collettivismo.

collectivity *s.* collettività.

collectivization *s.* collettivizzazione.

to collectivize *vt.* collettivizzare.

collector *s.* **1.** collezionista **2.** esattore.

college *s.* **1.** collegio **2.** scuola secondaria (*con internato*).

collegial *agg.* collegiale.

collier *s.* minatore.

colliery *s.* miniera di carbone.

collimator *s.* collimatore.

collision s. **1.** collisione **2.** urto, conflitto (*d'interessi*).

collocation s. collocazione.

colloidal agg. colloidale.

colloquial agg. d'uso corrente, familiare.

colloquialism s. espressione familiare.

colloquially avv. nella lingua parlata.

colloquy s. colloquio.

collusion s. collusione.

colon s. (*gramm.*) due punti.

colonel s. colonnello.

colonial agg. coloniale.

colonialism s. sistema coloniale.

colonialist s. colonialista.

colonist s. **1.** colono **2.** colonizzatore.

colonization s. colonizzazione.

to **colonize** vt. colonizzare. ◆ to **colonize** vi. stabilirsi in colonia.

colonizer s. colonizzatore.

colonnade s. colonnato.

colony s. colonia.

colossal agg. colossale.

colossus s. colosso.

colour s. **1.** colore **2.** colorito || — -bearer, portabandiera; — -blind, daltonico; — -print, stampa a colori. ◆ **colours** s. pl. bandiera (*sing.*) || with the —, sotto le armi.

to **colour** vt. colorare, tingere. ◆ to **colour** vi. colorirsi, prender colore.

colourable agg. verosimile.

colouration s. colorazione.

coloured agg. colorato, colorito (*anche fig.*).

colourful agg. colorito, pittoresco.

colouring s. **1.** colorante **2.** coloramento.

colourless agg. incolore.

colt s. **1.** puledro **2.** (*fig.*) novellino.

columbarium s. (*pl.* -ria) colombario.

column s. colonna (*anche fig.*).

columnist s. giornalista (*che cura una rubrica*).

coma s. coma.

comatose agg. comatoso.

comb s. **1.** pettine **2.** cresta (*gallo, onde ecc.*).

to **comb** vt. pettinare. ◆ to **comb** vi. frangersi (*di onde*) || to — one's hair, pettinarsi.

combat s. combattimento, lotta.

combination s. **1.** combinazione **2.** associazione.

to **combine** vt. **1.** unire **2.** (*chim.*) combinare **3.** contribuire. ◆ to **combine** vi. **1.** unirsi **2.** combinarsi.

combing s. pettinata.

comb-out s. rastrellamento.

combustible agg. e s. combustibile.

combustion s. combustione.

to **come** (came, come) vi. venire, arrivare, giungere, provenire || to — about, accadere; to — across, incontrare per caso; to — along (*fam.*), capitare; to — back, ritornare; to — down, scendere; to — in, entrare, salire (*di marea*); to — on, avanzare, sopraggiungere (*di malattie, stagioni ecc.*), entrare in scena (*di attori*); to — through, superare; to — under, essere soggetti, essere catalogati; to — upon, trovare per caso.

comedian s. autore, attore di commedie.

comedy s. commedia.

comeliness s. avvenenza.

comely agg. avvenente.

comer s. chi viene.

comet s. cometa.

comfit s. confetto.

comfort s. **1.** conforto **2.** comodità.

to **comfort** vt. **1.** confortare **2.** ristorare.

comfortable agg. comodo, confortevole || to be —, sentirsi a proprio agio.

comfortably avv. comodamente.

comforting agg. confortante.

comic agg. comico, buffo. ◆ **comic** s. **1.** attore comico **2.** il ridicolo, il comico. ◆ **comics** s. pl. (*fam.*) fumetti.

comical agg. comico, buffo.

comicality s. comicità.

coming agg. prossimo, futuro. ◆ **coming** s. **1.** venuta, arrivo || — away, partenza; — back, ritorno; — down, discesa, calo (*dei prezzi*).

comity s. cortesia, gentilezza.

comma s. virgola || inverted commas, virgolette.

command s. **1.** comando, ordine **2.** padronanza.

to **command** vt. e vi. **1.** comandare **2.** dominare (*anche fig.*).

commandant s. comandante.

commander s. comandante.

commandership s. funzioni di comandante.

commandment s. comandamento.
to **commemorate** vt. commemorare.
commemoration s. commemorazione.
commemorative agg. commemorativo.
to **commend** vt. lodare, encomiare.
commendable agg. lodevole.
commendably avv. lodevolmente.
commendation s. elogio, lode.
commendatory agg. laudativo.
commensal s. commensale.
commensurability s. commensurabilità.
commensurable agg. commensurabile.
commensurate agg. proporzionato.
comment s. 1. commento 2. critica.
to **comment** vt. e vi. commentare: to — up (on) a test, commentare un testo.
commentary s. commentario.
commentation s. annotazione, commento.
commentator s. 1. commentatore 2. radiocronista.
commerce s. commercio.
commercial agg. commerciale.
commercialism s. mercantilismo.
commercialist s. commercialista.
to **commercialize** vt. rendere commerciabile.
commercially avv. commercialmente.
commination s. comminazione.
to **commiserate** vt. e vi. commiserare.
commissary s. commissario, delegato.
commissaryship s. commissariato.
commission s. 1. commissione, comitato 2. commissione, incarico || — agent (o merchant), commissionario.
to **commission** vt. 1. commissionare 2. delegare.
commissioned agg. munito di autorità || non- — officer, sottufficiale.
commissioner s. (pol.) delegato.
to **commit** vt. 1. affidare, rimettere: to — one's soul to God, rimettere la propria anima a Dio 2. commettere.
commitment, **committal** s. 1. consegna 2. incarico.
committed agg. (neol.) impegnato.
committee s. comitato.

commodity s. merce, oggetto di prima necessità || free commodities, merci esenti da dogana.
common agg. 1. comune 2. solito, abituale || — law, legge consacrata dalla consuetudine.
commoner s. 1. cittadino (non nobile) 2. membro della Camera dei Comuni.
commonness s. 1. banalità 2. frequenza (di un avvenimento).
commonplace s. luogo comune.
commons s. pl. il popolo (sing.) || the House of —, la Camera dei Comuni.
commonwealth s. 1. confederazione 2. repubblica (anche fig.).
commotion s. 1. agitazione, confusione 2. insurrezione, tumulto.
communal agg. della comunità.
commune s. comune.
communicability s. comunicabilità.
communicable agg. comunicabile.
to **communicate** vt. comunicare, trasmettere (malattie, calore ecc.).
   ♦ to **communicate** vi. mettersi in comunicazione.
communication s. 1. comunicazione, informazione 2. relazione, rapporto.
communicative agg. comunicativo.
communicativeness s. comunicativa.
communion s. comunione, comunanza || Holy Communion, Eucaristia.
communism s. comunismo.
communist s. comunista.
communistic agg. comunista.
community s. 1. comunanza (di beni ecc.) 2. collettività, società 3. (eccl.) comunità.
commutability s. permutabilità, commutabilità.
commutable agg. permutabile, commutabile.
commutative agg. commutativo.
commutator s. commutatore.
to **commute** vt. commutare.
compact[1] s. patto, contratto.
compact[2] agg. 1. compatto 2. ridotto.
compactness s. 1. compattezza 2. concisione (di stile).
companion[1] s. compagno.
companion[2] s. (mar.) boccaporto: — -way, scaletta (di boccaporto), scalandrone.
companionable agg. socievole.

companionship s. amicizia, cameratismo.

company s. **1.** compagnia **2.** comitiva **3.** (comm.) società.

comparable agg. paragonabile.

comparative agg. **1.** comparativo **2.** comparato. ♦ **comparative** s. (gramm.) comparativo.

comparatively avv. **1.** comparativamente **2.** relativamente.

to **compare** vt. paragonare, verificare. ♦ to **compare** vi. competere, rivaleggiare, reggere al confronto.

comparison s. **1.** paragone, confronto **2.** (gramm.) comparazione.

compartment s. compartimento, scompartimento.

compass s. **1.** circonferenza, spazio, estensione **2.** bussola. ♦ **compasses** s. pl. (a pair of —) compasso (sing.).

to **compass** vt. circondare.

compassion s. compassione: out of —, per compassione.

compassionate agg. compassionevole.

to **compassionate** vt. compassionare.

compassionately avv. con compassione.

compatibility s. compatibilità.

compatible agg. compatibile.

compatibly avv. compatibilmente.

to **compel** vt. costringere, obbligare.

compelling agg. irresistibile.

compendious agg. compendioso.

to **compensate** vt. ricompensare, risarcire. ♦ to **compensate** vi. supplire.

compensation s. **1.** compenso **2.** (mecc.) compensazione **3.** indennità, risarcimento.

compensator s. compensatore.

compensatory agg. compensativo.

to **compete** vi. competere, gareggiare.

competence s. **1.** competenza **2.** mezzi sufficienti per vivere (pl.).

competent agg. competente, abile.

competently avv. con competenza.

competition s. **1.** competizione, gara **2.** rivalità.

competitive agg. **1.** di competizione **2.** (comm.) di concorrenza.

competitively avv. per mezzo di concorso.

competitor s. concorrente, rivale.

compilation s. compilazione.

to **compile** vt. compilare.

compiler s. compilatore.

complacency s. **1.** soddisfazione **2.** compiacenza di sé.

complacent agg. **1.** compiacente **2.** soddisfatto di sé.

to **complain** vi. lagnarsi, dolersi.

complaint s. **1.** lamento **2.** reclamo.

complaisant agg. compiacente.

complement s. complemento.

complemental agg. complementare.

complementary agg. complementare.

complete agg. completo.

to **complete** vt. **1.** completare **2.** riempire (moduli ecc.).

completely avv. completamente.

completeness s. completezza.

completion s. compimento.

complex agg. **1.** complicato **2.** (gramm.) composto. ♦ **complex** s. complesso.

complexion s. carnagione, colorito.

complexity s. complessità.

compliance s. **1.** condiscendenza **2.** servilismo.

compliant agg. **1.** compiacente **2.** servile.

to **complicate** vt. complicare.

complicated agg. complicato.

complication s. complicazione.

complicity s. complicità.

compliment s. complimento: to pay so. a —, far un complimento a qu.

to **compliment** vt. complimentare, congratularsi con.

complimentary agg. **1.** complimentoso **2.** di favore: — tickets, biglietti di favore.

to **comply** vi. accondiscendere, conformarsi.

component agg. e s. componente.

to **comport** vi. comportarsi.

to **compose** vt. **1.** comporre, costituire **2.** (mus.) comporre ‖ to — a quarrel, comporre una vertenza.

composed agg. **1.** composto **2.** calmo.

composer s. compositore.

composing agg. calmante. ♦ **composing** s. **1.** il comporre **2.** (tip.) composizione.

composite agg. composto.

composition s. **1.** composizione **2.** compromesso (accordato, intesa).

compositor s. (tip.) compositore.

composure s. posatezza, sangue freddo.

compote s. conserva di frutta.
compound 1. miscela **2.** (*chim.*) composto **3.** (*gramm.*) parola composta.
to compound vt. e vi. **1.** comporre, mescolare **2.** combinare (*ingredienti, elementi ecc.*).
to comprehend vt. **1.** contenere **2.** capire.
comprehensibility s. comprensibilità.
comprehensible agg. **1.** comprensibile **2.** delimitato.
comprehension s. **1.** comprensione **2.** portata.
comprehensive agg. **1.** di vasta portata **2.** comprensivo.
comprehensively avv. comprensivamente.
compress s. compressa (*di garza*).
to compress vt. **1.** comprimere **2.** (*fig.*) condensare (*idee ecc.*).
compressibility s. compressibilità.
compression s. **1.** compressione **2.** (*fig.*) concentrazione.
to comprise vt. contenere, includere.
compromise s. compromesso.
to compromise vt. compromettere.
♦ **to compromise** vi. venire a un compromesso.
compromising agg. compromettente.
compulsion s. costrizione: *under* —, per costrizione.
compulsive agg. coercitivo.
compulsory agg. obbligatorio.
compunction s. compunzione.
computable agg. calcolabile.
computation s. calcolo.
to compute vt. computare, calcolare.
computer s. calcolatore.
comrade s. camerata, compagno.
comradeship s. cameratismo.
to concatenate vt. concatenare.
concatenation s. concatenazione.
concave agg. concavo.
to conceal vt. nascondere.
concealment s. **1.** occultamento **2.** nascondiglio.
conceit s. vanità, presunzione.
conceited agg. presuntuoso, vanitoso.
conceivability s. concepibilità.
conceivable agg. concepibile.
to conceive vt. **1.** concepire, generare **2.** immaginare, ideare.
to concentrate vt. **1.** concentrare

2. convergere. ♦ **to concentrate** vi. concentrarsi.
concentration s. **1.** concentrazione **2.** concentramento.
concentric agg. concentrico.
concept s. concetto.
conception s. **1.** concezione, concepimento **2.** concetto.
conceptional agg. concezionale.
conceptual agg. concettuale.
conceptualism s. concettualismo.
concern s. **1.** interesse, rapporto **2.** affare **3.** sollecitudine **4.** (*comm.*) ditta, azienda.
to concern vt. concernere, riguardare.
concerned agg. **1.** interessato **2.** ansioso, preoccupato || *as far as I am* —, per quanto mi riguarda.
concerning prep. riguardo a, circa.
concert s. **1.** concerto **2.** accordo.
concerted agg. **1.** (*mus.*) concertato **2.** convenuto.
concession s. concessione.
concessionary agg. e s. concessionario.
concettism s. concettismo.
conch s. conchiglia, mollusco.
conchoid s. concoide.
conchoidal agg. concoidale.
conciliar agg. conciliare.
to conciliate vt. conciliare.
conciliation s. conciliazione.
conciliator s. conciliatore, conciliatrice.
conciliatory agg. conciliante.
concise agg. conciso, succinto.
concision s. concisione.
conclave s. conclave.
to conclude vt. terminare, concludere. ♦ **to conclude** vi. terminare, concludersi.
conclusion s. conclusione.
conclusive agg. conclusivo.
to concoct vt. **1.** mescolare (*di ingredienti*) **2.** preparare, tramare.
concomitance s. concomitanza.
concomitant agg. concomitante.
concomitantly avv. simultaneamente.
concord s. **1.** concordia **2.** (*mus.*) accordo **3.** (*gramm.*) concordanza.
concordant agg. **1.** concorde **2.** (*mus.*) armonioso.
concordat s. concordato.
concourse s. concorso, affluenza (*di persone ecc.*).
concrete agg. concreto. ♦ **concrete** s. calcestruzzo.

concreteness s. concretezza.
concretion s. concrezione.
concubinage s. concubinato.
concubine s. concubina.
concupiscence s. concupiscenza.
to **concur** vi. concorrere, contribuire (di cause, avvenimenti).
concurrence s. 1. concorso (di circostanze) 2. cooperazione (di persone) 3. (geom.) convergenza.
concurrent agg. concorrente, simultaneo.
to **concuss** vt. 1. urtare 2. (med.) provocare un trauma 3. intimidire.
concussion s. 1. urto 2. (med.) commozione cerebrale, trauma.
to **condemn** vt. 1. condannare 2. biasimare, censurare.
condemnable agg. 1. condannabile 2. censurabile.
condemnation s. 1. condanna 2. biasimo, censura.
condensability s. condensabilità.
condensable agg. condensabile.
condensate s. (fis.; chim.) condensamento.
condensation s. condensazione.
to **condense** vt. condensare, abbreviare. ♦ to **condense** vi. condensarsi, concentrarsi.
condenser s. condensatore.
to **condescend** vi. accondiscendere.
condescending agg. condiscendente.
condescendingly avv. con condiscendenza.
condescension s. 1. condiscendenza 2. affabilità.
condition s. condizione, clausola: on — that, a condizione che.
to **condition** vt. condizionare.
conditional agg. e s. condizionale.
conditionally avv. condizionatamente.
conditioned agg. condizionato: — air, aria condizionata.
conditioning s. 1. condizionatura (di tessili) 2. condizionamento.
condolence s. condoglianza.
conduct s. 1. condotta, comportamento 2. metodo.
to **conduct** vi. 1. condurre, guidare, dirigere 2. (fis.) condurre, trasmettere. ♦ to **conduct** vi. 1. comportarsi 2. indicare la via.
conducibility s. conducibilità.
conductivity s. conducibilità.
conductor s. 1. guida (di persone) 2. (mus.) direttore 3. bigliettario.

conduit s. 1. conduttura 2. passaggio segreto.
cone s. 1. cono 2. pigna.
to **confabulate** vi. confabulare.
confectionary agg. di pasticceria.
confectioner s. pasticciere.
confectionery s. pasticceria.
confederate agg. confederato. ♦ **confederate** s. 1. confederato 2. complice.
to **confederate** vt. confederare. ♦ to **confederate** vi. confederarsi.
confederation s. confederazione.
to **confer** vt. conferire, dare. ♦ to **confer** vi. conferire, consultarsi.
conference s. 1. conferenza 2. congresso.
to **confess** vt. e vi. confessare, professare.
confessedly avv. apertamente, dichiaratamente.
confession s. confessione, professione: — of faith, professione di fede.
confessional agg. e s. confessionale.
confessionary agg. confessionale.
confessor s. 1. confessore 2. chi si confessa.
confetti s. pl. coriandoli.
confidant s. confidente.
to **confide** vt. confidare. ♦ to **confide** vi. confidarsi: to — in so., confidarsi con qu.
confidence s. 1. fiducia 2. confidenza 3. sicurezza in se stessi.
confident agg. fiducioso.
confidential agg. confidenziale, riservato.
confidently avv. con sicurezza, con fiducia.
confiding agg. senza sospetti.
configuration s. configurazione.
to **configure** vt. configurare.
to **confine** vt. relegare, limitare. ♦ to **confine** vi. confinare, essere contiguo.
confinement s. 1. reclusione 2. limitazione 3. puerperio.
to **confirm** vt. 1. confermare 2. cresimare.
confirmation s. 1. conferma 2. cresima 3. (pol.; giur.) ratifica.
confirmatory agg. confermativo.
confiscable agg. confiscabile.
to **confiscate** vt. confiscare.
confiscation s. confisca.
conflagration s. conflagrazione.
conflict s. conflitto, contrasto.

confluence s. 1. confluenza 2. incrocio (di strade ecc.).

confluent agg. confluente.

to **conform** vt. conformare. ◆ to **conform** vi. conformarsi, ottemperare.

conformation s. 1. conformazione 2. adattamento.

conformist s. conformista.

conformity s. 1. conformità 2. conformismo.

to **confound** vt. 1. confondere, disorientare 2. sconvolgere.

confounded agg. attonito, confuso.

confraternity s. confraternita.

to **confront** vt. 1. affrontare 2. trovarsi di fronte a.

confrontation s. confronto.

Confucianism s. confucianesimo.

to **confuse** vt. 1. disorientare, sconcertare 2. confondere.

confusedly avv. confusamente.

confusion s. 1. disordine, confusione 2. turbamento.

confutation s. confutazione.

to **confute** vt. confutare.

to **congeal** vt. ghiacciare. ◆ to **congeal** vi. gelarsi.

congenial agg. 1. congeniale, affine 2. amabile, simpatico.

congeniality s. 1. affinità 2. carattere simpatico.

congenially avv. amabilmente.

congenital agg. congenito.

conger s. anguilla marina.

congeries s. congerie.

to **congest** vt. congestionare. ◆ to **congest** vi. congestionarsi.

congested agg. congestionato.

congestion s. congestione.

to **conglobate** vt. conglobare. ◆ to **conglobate** vi. conglobarsi.

conglobation s. conglobazione.

conglomerate agg. e s. conglomerato.

to **conglomerate** vt. conglomerare. ◆ to **conglomerate** vi. conglomerarsi.

conglomeration s. conglomerazione.

to **congratulate** vt. congratulare, congratularsi con.

congratulation s. congratulazione.

congratulatory agg. congratulatorio.

to **congregate** vt. adunare. ◆ to **congregate** vi. adunarsi.

congregation s. 1. unione, adunata, assemblea 2. (relig.) congregazione.

congregational agg. della congregazione.

congress s. congresso, riunione.

congressional agg. di congresso.

congruence s. congruenza.

congruent agg. congruente, conforme.

congruity s. conformità.

congruous agg. congruente, conforme.

conic(al) agg. conico.

conifer s. conifera.

coniferous agg. conifero.

conjecture s. congettura.

to **conjecture** vt. e vi. congetturare, ipotizzare.

conjointly avv. congiuntamente.

conjugal agg. coniugale.

conjugate agg. congiunto. ◆ **conjugate** s. 1. (mat.) coniugato 2. (biol.) fusione.

to **conjugate** vt. coniugare. ◆ to **conjugate** vi. coniugarsi.

conjugation s. coniugazione.

conjunction s. congiunzione.

conjunctiva s. (anat.) congiuntiva.

conjunctive agg. 1. (biol.) connettivo 2. (gramm.) congiuntivo. ◆ **conjunctive** s. congiuntivo.

conjunctivitis s. congiuntivite.

conjuncture s. congiuntura, circostanza.

conjuration s. 1. incantesimo 2. evocazione solenne.

to **conjure** vt. 1. scongiurare 2. evocare. ◆ to **conjure** vi. fare giochi di prestigio.

conjurer s. prestigiatore.

conjuring s. prestidigitazione.

connatural agg. connaturale.

to **connect** vt. 1. connettere, collegare, unire 2. associare (mentalmente). ◆ to **connect** vi. 1. avere relazioni, collegarsi 2. (ferr.) far coincidenza.

connecting agg. che connette. ◆ **connecting** s. (elettr.) collegamento.

connection s. 1. collegamento, connessione 2. relazione, parentela 3. coincidenza 4. (comm.) clientela.

connective agg. connettivo.

conning-tower s. (mar.) torretta di comando.

connivance s. connivenza.

to **connive** vi. essere connivente.

connotation s. significato implicito.

to **connote** vt. implicare, significare.

to **conquer** vt. conquistare.

conqueror s. conquistatore.

conquest s. conquista.

consanguine agg. consanguineo.

consanguinity s. consanguineità.

conscience s. coscienza: for — ' sake, per scrupolo di coscienza; to be — -stricken, sentirsi rimordere la coscienza.

conscienceless agg. senza scrupoli.

conscientious agg. scrupoloso || — objector, obiettore di coscienza.

conscientiously avv. coscienziosamente.

conscious agg. consapevole, conscio.

consciousness s. coscienza, consapevolezza.

conscript agg. e s. coscritto.

conscription s. coscrizione.

to **consecrate** vt. consacrare, dedicare.

consecration s. consacrazione, dedizione.

consecutive agg. consecutivo.

consecutively avv. consecutivamente.

consensual agg. consensuale.

consensus s. consenso, accordo || — of opinion, unanimità.

consent s. consenso, accordo || by mutual —, amichevolmente.

to **consent** vi. acconsentire.

consequence s. 1. conseguenza, effetto 2. importanza.

consequent agg. conseguente, risultante.

consequential agg. consequenziale.

consequently avv. di conseguenza.

conservatism s. conservatorismo.

conservative agg. conservativo. ◆ **Conservative** s. conservatore.

conservator s. 1. conservatore 2. sovrintendente (di museo ecc.).

conserve s. conserva di frutta.

to **consider** vt. considerare, riflettere, stimare.

considerable agg. considerevole, importante.

considerate agg. rispettoso, pieno di riguardi.

consideration s. 1. considerazione 2. rimunerazione 3. (comm.) provvigione.

considering prep. tenuto conto di, considerando.

to **consign** vt. 1. (comm.) inviare, consegnare 2. depositare (soldi in banca).

consignation s. 1. (comm.) pagamento 2. consegna (di merce).

consignee s. consegnatario.

consigner s. mittente.

consignment s. 1. invio, spedizione 2. consegna, deposito.

to **consist** vi. consistere, essere composto.

consistence, consistency s. 1. consistenza, compattezza 2. costanza.

consistent agg. coerente, logico.

consistently avv. coerentemente.

consistory s. concistoro.

consolation s. consolazione.

consolatory agg. consolante.

to **console** vt. consolare.

to **consolidate** vt. consolidare. ◆ to **consolidate** vi. consolidarsi.

consolidation s. consolidazione.

consoling agg. consolante.

consonance s. consonanza, accordo.

consonant agg. consono. ◆ **consonant** s. consonante.

consort s. 1. consorte 2. compagno, collega.

to **consort** vi. associarsi, unirsi. ◆ to **consort** vt. associare, unire.

conspicuous agg. cospicuo, notevole.

conspicuousness s. cospicuità.

conspiracy s. congiura.

conspirator s. cospiratore.

to **conspire** vt. e vi. cospirare.

constable s. 1. agente di polizia 2. conestabile.

constabulary s. corpo della polizia.

constancy s. costanza.

constant agg. costante, fedele. ◆ **constant** s. (mat.) costante.

constantly agg. costantemente.

constellation s. costellazione.

consternation s. costernazione.

constipation s. stitichezza.

constituency s. 1. gli elettori (pl.) 2. circoscrizione elettorale.

constituent agg. costituente. ◆ **constituent** s. 1. elemento costitutivo 2. (pol.) elettore.

to **constitute** vt. 1. costituire 2. eleggere.

constitution s. 1. costituzione, statuto 2. costituzione, composizione (del corpo, dell'aria ecc.).

constitutional agg. costituzionale.

constitutionalism s. costituzionalismo.

constitutionality s. costituzionalità.

constitutive *agg.* costitutivo.
to constrain *vt.* costringere.
constrained *agg.* costretto, forzato.
constraint *s.* **1.** costrizione **2.** imbarazzo.
to constrict *vt.* costringere.
constriction *s.* costrizione.
to construct *vt.* costruire (*anche fig.*).
construction *s.* **1.** costruzione **2.** (*giur.*) interpretazione.
constructive *agg.* costruttivo.
to construe *vt.* **1.** costruire grammaticalmente **2.** interpretare. ♦ **to construe** *vi.* fare l'analisi grammaticale.
consuetudinary *agg.* consuetudinario: — *law*, diritto consuetudinario.
consul *s.* console.
consular *agg.* consolare.
consulate *s.* consolato.
to consult *vt.* consultare. ♦ **to consult** *vi.* consultarsi.
consultation *s.* **1.** consultazione **2.** consulto.
consultative *agg.* consultativo.
consulting *agg.* consulente || — -room, ambulatorio.
to consume *vt.* consumare. ♦ **to consume** *vi.* consumarsi.
consumer *s.* consumatore, utente.
consummate *agg.* consumato, perfetto.
consumption *s.* **1.** consumo **2.** sciupio **3.** distruzione **4.** tubercolosi.
consumptive *s.* tisico, tubercolotico.
contact *s.* contatto, relazione.
to contact *vt.* e *vi.* mettere, mettersi in contatto con, prender contatto.
contagion *s.* contagio.
contagious *agg.* contagioso.
to contain *vt.* **1.** contenere, comprendere **2.** reprimere, frenare (*i sentimenti*).
contained *agg.* frenato, contenuto (*di comportamento*).
container *s.* recipiente.
contamination *s.* contaminazione.
to contemplate *vt.* e *vi.* contemplare, meditare.
contemplation *s.* contemplazione.
contemplative *agg.* contemplativo.
contemplator *s.* contemplatore.
contemporaneousness *s.* contemporaneità.
contemporary *agg.* e *s.* contemporaneo.

contempt *s.* disprezzo || — *of Court* (*giur.*), vilipendio della Corte.
contemptibility *s.* spregevolezza.
contemptible *agg.* spregevole.
contemptuous *agg.* sprezzante.
contemptuously *avv.* sprezzantemente.
to contend *vi.* **1.** contendere. ♦ **to contend** *vt.* sostenere, affermare.
contending *agg.* contendente, rivale.
content *s.* **1.** volume, capacità **2.** contenuto. ♦ **contents** *s. pl.* indice (*di libro*) (*sing.*). ♦ **content** *agg.* contento, soddisfatto.
to content *vt.* contentare, soddisfare.
contented *agg.* contento, pago.
contention *s.* **1.** contesa **2.** emulazione **3.** controversia.
contentious *agg.* litigioso.
contest *s.* contestazione, contesa.
to contest *vt.* contestare, contendere. ♦ **to contest** *vi.* competere, rivaleggiare.
context *s.* contesto.
contiguity *s.* contiguità.
continence *s.* continenza.
continent *agg.* continente. ♦ **continent** *s.* (*geogr.*) continente.
continental *agg.* e *s.* continentale.
contingency *s.* contingenza, caso.
contingent *agg.* eventuale, imprevisto.
continual *agg.* continuo.
continuation *s.* continuazione, seguito.
to continue *vt.* e *vi.* continuare, far continuare.
continuity *s.* **1.** continuità **2.** (*cine*) sceneggiatura.
continuous *agg.* continuo.
to contort *vt.* contorcere.
contortion *s.* contorsione.
contortionist *s.* contorsionista.
contour *s.* contorno, profilo.
contraband *s.* contrabbando.
contraceptive *s.* anticoncezionale.
contract *s.* contratto, patto.
to contract *vt.* **1.** contrarre (*matrimonio, amicizia ecc.*) **2.** (*comm.*) contrattare **3.** contrarre, restringere. ♦ **to contract** *vi.* contrarsi, restringersi.
contractile *agg.* contrattile.
contraction *s.* accorciamento.
contractor *s.* **1.** contraente **2.** appaltatore **3.** imprenditore.

contractual *agg.* contrattuale.

to contradict *vt.* contraddire.

contradiction *s.* contraddizione.

contradictory *agg.* contraddittorio.

to contraindicate *vt.* controindicare.

contraindication *s.* controindicazione.

contraposition *s.* opposizione, antitesi.

contrarily *avv.* contrariamente.

contrary *agg.* contrario, opposto. ♦ **contrary** *s.* il contrario: on the —, al contrario. ♦ **contrary** *avv.* contrariamente, all'opposto.

contrast *s.* contrasto, opposizione.

to contrast *vt. e vi.* far contrasto, mettere in contrasto.

to contravene *vt.* contravvenire.

to contribute *vt.* contribuire. ♦ **to contribute** *vi.* collaborare (a un giornale).

contribution *s.* **1.** contributo **2.** (*comm.*) apporto di capitale **3.** collaborazione (a un giornale).

contributor *s.* **1.** contributore **2.** collaboratore (di giornale ecc.).

contrite *agg.* contrito.

contrition *s.* contrizione.

contrivance *s.* **1.** espediente **2.** apparato, congegno **3.** invenzione.

to contrive *vt.* escogitare. ♦ **to contrive** *vi.* adoperarsi, riuscire.

control *s.* autorità, influenza, dominio, controllo || — device (mecc.), dispositivo di controllo; — room, camera di manovra; birth- —, limitazione delle nascite; self- —, autocontrollo. ♦ **controls** *s. pl.* (mecc.) comandi.

to control *vt.* controllare, dirigere.

controller *s.* controllore, sovrintendente.

controversial *agg.* controverso.

controversy *s.* controversia, polemica.

controvertible *agg.* controvertibile.

contumacious *agg.* **1.** insubordinato **2.** contumace.

contumacy *s.* **1.** ribellione **2.** contumacia.

contumely *s.* onta, contumelia.

contusion *s.* contusione.

contusive *agg.* contundente.

convalescence *s.* convalescenza.

convalescent *agg. e s.* convalescente.

to convene *vt.* **1.** convocare, riunire **2.** (giur.) citare. ♦ to convene

vi. riunirsi, incontrarsi.

convenience *s.* **1.** comodo, vantaggio. ♦ **conveniences** *s. pl.* comodità.

convenient *agg.* conveniente, comodo, adatto.

convent *s.* convento.

conventicle *s.* conventicola.

convention *s.* **1.** patto, convenzione **2.** assemblea **3.** regola (di gioco). ♦ **conventions** *s. pl.* convenzioni (sociali).

conventional *agg.* convenzionale, comune.

conventionality *s.* convenzionalità.

conventual *agg. e s.* conventuale.

to converge *vi.* convergere. ♦ **to converge** *vt.* far convergere.

convergence *s.* convergenza.

convergent *agg.* convergente.

conversation *s.* conversazione.

converse *agg. e s.* inverso, contrario.

conversely *avv.* viceversa.

conversion *s.* conversione, trasformazione.

convert *s.* convertito.

to convert *vt.* **1.** convertire **2.** trasformare.

converter *s.* **1.** convertitore **2.** (elettr.; mecc.) convertitore, trasformatore.

convertible *agg.* convertibile || — car, automobile decappottabile.

convex *agg.* convesso.

convexity *s.* convessità.

to convey *vt.* **1.** trasportare, convogliare **2.** trasmettere (suoni, odori ecc.) **3.** dare l'idea, suggerire.

conveyable *agg.* trasportabile, trasmissibile.

conveyance *s.* **1.** trasporto **2.** trasmissione **3.** convogliamento.

conveyancer *s.* notaio.

conveyer *s.* **1.** trasportatore **2.** trasmettitore **3.** convogliatore.

convict *s.* condannato, forzato.

to convict *vt.* condannare, dichiarare colpevole.

conviction *s.* **1.** (giur.) verdetto di colpevolezza, condanna **2.** convinzione.

to convince *vt.* convincere.

convincing *agg.* convincente.

convincingly *avv.* in modo convincente.

convivial *agg.* allegro, conviviale, gioviale.

conviviality *s.* giovialità.

convivially *avv.* convivialmente.

to **convocate** *vt.* convocare.

convocation *s.* convocazione.

convolution *s.* circonvoluzione.

convoy *s.* 1. (*mar.; mil.*) convoglio 2. scorta.

to **convoy** *vt.* 1. (*mar.; mil.*) convogliare 2. scortare.

convulsion *s.* 1. convulsione 2. rivolgimento.

convulsive *agg.* convulso.

to **coo** *vi.* tubare.

cook *s.* cuoco, cuoca: *head* —, capocuoco.

to **cook** *vt.* e *vi.* cucinare, cuocere.

cookery *s.* arte culinaria, cucina.

cooking *s.* 1. cottura 2. arte culinaria, cucina.

cool *agg.* 1. fresco 2. leggero (*di abito*) 3. calmo 4. freddo, senza entusiasmo 5. sfacciato.

to **cool** *vt.* 1. rinfrescare 2. calmare. ◆ to **cool** *vi.* 1. rinfrescarsi 2. calmarsi.

cooling *agg.* rinfrescante. ◆ **cooling** *s.* abbassamento di temperatura.

coolness *s.* 1. frescura 2. freddezza, calma, sangue freddo.

coop *s.* stia.

to **coop** *vt.* mettere nella stia.

cooper *s.* bottaio.

to **co-operate** *vi.* cooperare.

co-operation *s.* cooperazione.

co-operative *agg.* cooperativo.

co-operator *s.* cooperatore.

to **co-opt** *vt.* eleggere membro (*di comitato*).

co-ordinate *agg.* 1. dello stesso rango 2. coordinato. ◆ **co-ordinate** *s.* (*mat.*) coordinata.

to **co-ordinate** *vt.* coordinare.

co-ordination *s.* coordinazione.

co-ordinative *agg.* coordinativo.

co-owner *s.* comproprietario.

co-ownership *s.* comproprietà.

cop[1] *s.* cima (*di collina ecc.*).

cop[2] *s.* (*gergo*) poliziotto.

copartnership *s.* società, associazione.

to **cope** *vi.* fronteggiare, tener testa.

co-pilot *s.* (*aer.*) secondo pilota.

copper *s.* 1. rame 2. moneta di rame.

to **copper** *vt.* rivestire di rame.

copperplate *s.* 1. lastra di rame (*per incisione*) 2. incisione in rame.

Coptic *agg.* copto.

copulation *s.* copulazione.

copulative *agg.* copulativo.

copy *s.* 1. copia, trascrizione 2. riproduzione 3. esemplare || — *-book*, quaderno; — *-reader*, revisore di stampa; *fair* —, bella copia; *rough* —, brutta copia.

to **copy** *vt.* 1. copiare 2. imitare.

copyist *s.* copista.

copyright *s.* diritto d'autore, proprietà letteraria.

coquetry *s.* civetteria.

coral *s.* corallo.

cord *s.* corda, spago || *spinal* —, midollo spinale.

cordage *s.* cordame.

cordial *agg.* cordiale. ◆ **cordial** *s.* (*bevanda*) cordiale.

cordiality *s.* cordialità.

cordially *avv.* cordialmente.

cordon *s.* cordone.

core *s.* 1. torsolo 2. centro, cuore.

co-respondent *s.* (*giur.*) correo (*in adulterio*).

coriaceous *agg.* coriaceo.

cork *s.* 1. sughero 2. tappo, turacciolo || — *jacket*, cintura di salvataggio.

corkscrew *s.* cavaturaccioli.

cormorant *s.* cormorano.

corn[1] *s.* 1. grano 2. cereale || *ear of* —, spiga di grano; — *-cob*, pannocchia.

corn[2] *s.* callo, durone.

cornea *s.* cornea.

corner *s.* 1. angolo 2. (*comm.*) accaparramento (*di merci*).

to **corner** *vt.* 1. mettere, spingere in un angolo 2. (*fig.*) mettere con le spalle al muro. ◆ to **corner** *vi.* formare un angolo.

cornet *s.* cornetta.

cornice *s.* cornicione.

corolla *s.* corolla.

corollary *s.* corollario.

coronary *agg.* coronario.

coronation *s.* incoronazione.

coroner *s.* magistrato inquirente.

corporal[1] *agg.* corporale.

corporal[2] *s.* caporale.

corporation *s.* 1. corporazione 2. azienda municipale.

corporative *agg.* corporativo: — *system*, sistema corporativo.

corporeal *agg.* corporeo.

corpse *s.* cadavere.

corpulent *agg.* corpulento.

corpuscle *s.* corpuscolo.

corral *s.* recinto (*per bestiame*).

correct *agg.* corretto.
to correct *vt.* correggere.
correction *s.* correzione, rettifica.
corrective *agg.* e *s.* correttivo.
correctness *s.* correttezza.
corrector *s.* correttore: — *of the press* (*tip.*), correttore di bozze.
to correlate *vt.* essere, mettere in correlazione. ✦ **to correlate** *vi.* essere in correlazione.
correlation *s.* correlazione.
correlative *agg.* correlativo.
to correspond *vi.* 1. corrispondere, essere in rapporti epistolari 2. rispondere a (*esigenze ecc.*) 3. equivalere.
correspondence 1. corrispondenza 2. accordo, rispondenza.
correspondent *s.* corrispondente.
corridor *s.* corridoio.
corroborant *agg.* corroborante.
corroboration *s.* conferma, convalida.
to corrode *vt.* corrodere. ✦ **to corrode** *vi.* corrodersi.
corrosion *s.* corrosione.
corrosive *agg.* e *s.* corrosivo.
to corrugate *vt.* corrugare.
corrugation *s.* corrugamento.
corrupt *agg.* corrotto, guasto, depravato.
to corrupt *vt.* corrompere, alterare. ✦ **to corrupt** *vi.* corrompersi, alterarsi.
corruption *s.* corruzione.
corsair *s.* corsaro.
corset *s.* corsetto.
cortisone *s.* cortisone.
corvette *s.* corvetta.
corvine *agg.* corvino.
coryphaeus *s.* (*pl.* -aei) corifeo.
cosecant *s.* cosecante.
cosily *avv.* comodamente.
cosine *s.* coseno.
cosmetic *agg.* e *s.* cosmetico.
cosmic(al) *agg.* cosmico.
cosmogony *s.* cosmogonia.
cosmographer *s.* cosmografo.
cosmography *s.* cosmografia.
cosmology *s.* cosmologia.
cosmopolitan *agg.* e *s.* cosmopolita.
cosmopolitanism *s.* cosmopolitismo.
cosmopolite *agg.* e *s.* cosmopolita.
cosmopolitism *s.* cosmopolitismo.
cosmos *s.* cosmo.
Cossack *s.* cosacco.
cost *s.* costo, prezzo ‖ — *of living*, carovita; *at all costs*, ad ogni costo;

extra —, spesa supplementare.
to cost (cost, cost) *vt.* e *vi.* costare.
costal *agg.* costale.
coster, costermonger *s.* venditore ambulante (*di frutta, verdura ecc.*).
costly *agg.* costoso.
costume *s.* 1. costume 2. abito.
cosy *agg.* comodo, intimo.
cot[1] *s.* capanna.
cot[2] 1. (*mar.*) cuccetta 2. culla.
cotangent *s.* cotangente.
cotenant *s.* coaffittuario.
cothurnus *s.* (*pl.*-ni) coturno.
cottage *s.* villino.
cotton *s.* cotone ‖ — *-mill*, cotonificio; — *-spinner*, operaio di filatura; — *-wool*, ovatta; — *-waste*, cascame.
couch *s.* divano.
cough *s.* tosse.
to cough *vt.* e *vi.* tossire.
could *v.* *can*.
council *s.* 1. consiglio (*adunanza di persone*) 2. (*eccl.*) concilio.
councillor *s.* consigliere.
counsel *s.* 1. consultazione 2. consiglio 3. legale.
to counsel *vt.* e *vi.* consigliare.
counsellor *s.* 1. consigliere 2. legale.
count[1] *s.* 1. conto, calcolo 2. (*pol.*) scrutinio 3. (*giur.*) capo d'accusa.
count[2] *s.* conte.
to count *vt.* e *vi.* 1. contare, calcolare 2. considerare, avere importanza.
countable *agg.* numerabile.
countenance *s.* espressione del volto, aria.
counter[1] *s.* calcolatore, contatore ‖ *revolution* —, contagiri.
counter[2] *s.* volta di poppa.
counter[3] *s.* 1. banco, cassa (*di negozio*) 2. sportello 3. gettone (*da gioco*).
counter[4] *agg.* contrario, opposto ‖ — *clockwise*, in senso antiorario; — *poison*, antidoto. ✦ **counter** *avv.* in senso contrario.
to counteract *vt.* agir contro, contrapporsi a.
counter-attack *s.* contrattacco.
to counter-attack *vt.* e *vi.* contrattaccare.
counterbalance *s.* contrappeso.
to counterbalance *vt.* controbilanciare.
counterblow *s.* contraccolpo.

countercharge s. controaccusa.

counterfeit agg. contraffatto, simulato. ♦ **counterfeit** s. contraffazione, simulazione.

counterfeiter s. 1. falsario 2. simulatore.

counterfoil s. matrice.

countermand s. revoca, contrordine.

counterpane s. copriletto.

counterpart s. 1. sostituto 2. duplicato, sosia 3. complemento.

counterpoint s. contrappunto.

countershaft s. contralbero.

countersign s. contrassegno.

counterweight s. contrappeso.

countess s. contessa.

countless agg. innumerevole.

countrified agg. campagnolo, rurale.

country s. 1. paese, regione 2. campagna 3. patria 4. nazione.

countryman s. 1. compaesano, compatriota 2. contadino.

countryside s. campagna.

countrywoman s. 1. compaesana, compatriota 2. contadina.

county s. contea, provincia.

coup s. 1. colpo 2. (fig.) impressione.

couple s. coppia, paio.

to **couple** vt. accoppiare. ♦ to **couple** vi. accoppiarsi.

coupling s. accoppiamento.

coupon s. cedola, tagliando.

courage s. coraggio, ardire.

courageous agg. coraggioso.

course s. 1. corso (del tempo), corso (di lezioni, conferenze) 2. serie 3. portata (dei pasti) 4. (sport) circuito || of —, naturalmente; in due — a tempo debito.

court s. 1. corte, cortile 2. (giur.) corte || — of justice, tribunale.

to **court** vt. corteggiare.

courtier s. cortigiano.

courting s. corteggiamento.

courtyard s. cortile.

courtship s. corteggiamento.

cousin s. cugino, cugina.

cove s. 1. insenatura 2. grotta.

covenant s. convenzione, patto.

cover s. 1. coperta, copertura 2. calotta 3. copertina (di libro) 4. riparo, ricovero 5. coperto (a tavola).

to **cover** vt. 1. coprire, ricoprire 2. proteggere 3. percorrere 4. nascondere 5. comprendere, includere.

covering s. copertura, rivestimento.

coverlet s. copriletto.

covert s. ricovero, rifugio.

covertly avv. nascostamente.

to **covet** vt. agognare.

covetousness s. cupidigia.

cow s. mucca, vacca || — bell, campanaccio; — -grass, trifoglio di campo; — -shed, stalla.

coward s. codardo, vile.

cowardice s. codardia, viltà.

cowardly agg. codardo. ♦ **cowardly** avv. vilmente.

cowboy s. bovaro.

cowherd s. vaccaro.

cowl s. 1. cappuccio, tonaca (di frate) 2. (auto; aer.) cofano del motore.

coxswain s. timoniere.

coy agg. timido, riservato.

crab s. granchio.

crabbed agg. sgarbato, bisbetico.

crack s. 1. schianto, detonazione, schiocco 2. incrinatura, rottura.

to **crack** 1. vt. schiantare, rompere, incrinare 2. schioccare. ♦ to **crack** vi. 1. screpolarsi, spezzarsi 2. scricchiolare.

cracked agg. 1. incrinato 2. fesso (di voce).

cracker s. petardo || nut-crackers, schiaccianoci; — of jokes, burlone.

crackle s. 1. crepitio 2. screpolatura, incrinatura.

to **crackle** vi. scoppiettare, scricchiolare. ♦ to **crackle** vt. screpolare.

crackling s. scoppiettio.

cradle s. culla (anche fig.).

craft s. 1. abilità, mestiere, professione 2. astuzia, inganno.

craftsman s. artigiano.

craftsmanship s. artigianato.

crafty agg. astuto, abile.

crag s. rupe, cresta.

to **cram** vt. riempire, stipare, rimpinzare. ♦ to **cram** vi. rimpinzarsi.

cramp s. crampo.

to **cramp** vt. (fig.) bloccare, paralizzare.

crane s. gru (anche mecc.).

to **crane** vt. e vi. 1. sollevare o abbassare (mediante una gru) 2. allungare (il collo).

cranium s. cranio.

crank[1] s. manovella, manubrio.

crank[2] agg. 1. piegato 2. disinnestato.

to **crank** vt. e vi. 1. piegare a gomito 2. mettere in moto (con manovella).

cranking s. avviamento (di motore).

crash s. 1. strepito, fracasso 2. caduta 3. scontro, collisione 4. rovina (anche morale).

to **crash** vt. e vi. 1. abbattere, precipitare, crollare con grande rumore 2. scontrare, scontrarsi.

crate s. cassa da imballaggio.

crater s. cratere.

to **crawl** vi. 1. strisciare, andar carponi 2. brulicare 3. avere la pelle d'oca.

crawl s. 1. strisciamento 2. (nuoto) « crawl ».

crayfish s. gambero (d'acqua dolce).

craze s. mania, smania.

craziness s. pazzia, follia.

crazy agg. 1. folle 2. maniaco, entusiasta.

to **creak** vi. cigolare, stridere.

cream s. 1. panna, crema 2. ogni sostanza densa e untuosa.

creamery s. caseificio.

creamy agg. cremoso.

crease s. piega, grinza.

to **crease** vt. fare pieghe, sgualcire. ♦ to **crease** vi. sgualcirsi.

to **create** vt. 1. creare, produrre, suscitare 2. nominare.

creation s. 1. creazione 2. universo, natura, il creato.

creative agg. creativo.

creator s. creatore.

creature s. 1. essere vivente 2. creatura (anche fig.), favorito.

credence s. credenza, fede.

credentials s. pl. credenziali.

credibility s. credibilità.

credible agg. credibile.

credit s. 1. fiducia 2. credito, reputazione, autorità 3. (comm.) fido, credito.

to **credit** vt. 1. prestar fede 2. attribuire 3. (comm.) accreditare

creditor s. creditore.

credulity s. credulità.

credulous agg. credulo.

creed s. credo, credenza religiosa.

creek s. 1. insenatura 2. (amer.) torrente.

to **creep** (**crept, crept**) vi. 1. strisciare, avanzare lentamente 2. arrampicarsi (di piante) || to — along, avanzare strisciando; to — away, allontanarsi strisciando.

creeper s. 1. rettile, verme 2. persona strisciante 3. pianta rampicante.

creepy agg. 1. strisciante 2. che dà i brividi.

to **cremate** vt. cremare.

cremation s. cremazione.

crematory s. crematoio.

creole agg. e s. creolo.

crept V. to creep.

crepuscular agg. crepuscolare.

crescent agg. 1. crescente 2. a mezzaluna. ♦ **crescent** s. 1. luna crescente 2. mezzaluna (emblema turco) 3. strada a semicerchio.

cress s. crescione.

crest s. 1. cresta 2. ciuffo, pennacchio 3. criniera.

to **crest** vt. ornare di pennacchio. ♦ to **crest** vi. incresparsi (di onde).

crevasse s. crepaccio.

crevice s. fessura.

crew[1] s. equipaggio, ciurma.

crew[2] V. to crow.

crib s. 1. greppia 2. presepio 3. stalla, capanna.

crick s. crampo || a — in the neck, torcicollo.

cricket s. grillo.

crime s. delitto, crimine.

criminal agg. e s. criminale.

criminalist s. penalista.

criminality s. criminalità.

criminology s. criminologia.

crimson s. cremisi.

to **cringe** vi. (fig.) farsi piccolo, umiliarsi.

cripple agg. e s. storpio, zoppo.

to **cripple** vt. storpiare. ♦ to **cripple** vi. essere zoppo.

crisis s. crisi.

crisp agg. 1. croccante 2. crespo 3. tonificante. ♦ **crisp** s. patatina fritta, croccante.

criss-cross agg. incrociato.

critic s. critico.

critical agg. critico.

criticism s. critica.

to **criticize** vt. criticare.

critique s. critica, recensione.

croak s. gracidamento.

to **croak** vt. e vi. 1. gracidare 2. (fig.) brontolare.

Croatian agg. e s. croato.

crochet s. lavoro all'uncinetto || — -hook (o — -pin), uncinetto.

crock[1] s. coccio, vaso di terracotta.

crock[2] s. 1. ronzino 2. persona vecchia e malandata.

crock³ s. fuliggine, sudiciume.
crockery s. terraglia.
crocodile s. coccodrillo.
croft s. piccolo podere, campicello.
crook s. 1. gancio, uncino 2. curva, flessione 3. (gergo) truffatore.
crookback s. gobba.
crooked agg. 1. curvo, storto, deforme 2. (fig.) perverso.
crookedly avv. 1. tortuosamente 2. indirettamente 3. perversamente.
crop s. 1. raccolto, messe 2. gozzo (di uccello) 3. (fig.) gruppo 4. rapata (di capelli).
to crop vt. 1. mietere 2. tosare.
cropper¹ s. mietitore.
cropper² s. (fam.) capitombolo.
cross agg. 1. obliquo, trasversale 2. adirato || — -bar, traversa; — -road, incrocio. ♦ **cross** s. 1. croce 2. tribolazione, pena.
to cross vt. e vi. 1. fare il segno della croce 2. attraversare 3. incrociare 4. cancellare || to — one's legs, accavallare le gambe.
crossbeam s. trave maestra.
crossbelt s. cartucciera a tracolla.
crossbow s. balestra.
crossbreed s. ibrido, incrocio.
cross-country agg. campestre.
cross-examination s. controinterrogatorio.
to cross-examine vt. controinterrogare.
cross-hatch s. tratteggio.
crossing s. 1. passaggio, traversata 2. incrocio || level —, passaggio a livello.
crossly avv. di malumore.
crosswise avv. 1. di traverso 2. a forma di croce.
crossword s. parole incrociate (pl.) || — puzzle, cruciverba.
crouch s. l'accovacciarsi.
to crouch vi. accovacciarsi, rannicchiarsi.
crow¹ s. corvo, cornacchia || a white —, una mosca bianca; to eat (v. irr.) a —, inghiottire un rospo.
crow² s. canto del gallo.
to crow (crew, crowed) vi. cantare (del gallo).
crowd s. folla, massa, moltitudine.
to crowd vt. affollare. ♦ **to crowd** vi. affollarsi, accalcarsi || to — together, stringere insieme.
crown s. 1. corona 2. cocuzzolo 3. coronamento, successo 4. (moneta) corona: half a —, mezza corona.

to crown vt. 1. incoronare 2. coronare, ricompensare.
crowning s. 1. incoronazione 2. coronamento.
crucial agg. cruciale.
crucible s. 1. crogiuolo 2. (fig.) dura prova.
crucifix s. crocifisso.
crucifixion s. crocifissione.
to crucify vt. crocifiggere.
crude agg. grezzo, rozzo, primitivo.
crudity s. asprezza.
cruel agg. crudele.
cruelty s. crudeltà.
cruet s. ampolla.
cruise s. crociera: to go on a —, fare una crociera.
cruiser s. incrociatore.
cruising s. crociera.
crumb s. 1. briciola 2. mollica.
to crumb vt. 1. sbriciolare 2. impanare.
to crumble vt. sbriciolare. ♦ **to crumble** vi. sbriciolarsi.
crumbly agg. friabile.
to crumple vt. spiegazzare. ♦ **to crumple** vi. spiegazzarsi.
to crunch vt. e vi. sgranocchiare rumorosamente.
crusade s. crociata.
crusader s. crociato.
crush s. 1. folla, calca 2. frantumazione 3. (gergo) cotta.
to crush vt. 1. frantumare, torchiare 2. (fig.) annientare, sconfiggere. ♦ **to crush** vi. accalcarsi, affollarsi.
crushing agg. schiacciante (anche fig.).
crust s. 1. crosta 2. incrostazione.
Crustacea s. pl. crostacei.
crutch s. 1. gruccia, stampella 2. forcella (di ramo).
cry s. grido, lamento, pianto || within —, a portata di voce.
to cry vt. e vi. 1. gridare 2. piangere || to — out, alzare la voce, protestare.
crypt s. cripta.
cryptogam s. crittogama.
cryptogram s. crittogramma.
cryptography s. crittografia.
crystal agg. cristallino. ♦ **crystal** s. cristallo || — work, cristalleria.
crystalline agg. cristallino (anche fig.).
crystallization s. cristallizzazione.
to crystallize vt. cristallizzare. ♦ **to crystallize** vi. cristallizzarsi.

crystallography *s.* cristallografia.
cub *s.* **1.** volpacchiotto **2.** (*fam.*) ragazzaccio.
cubage *s.* cubatura.
Cuban *agg.* e *s.* cubano.
cubature *s.* cubatura.
cube *s.* cubo || — *root*, radice cubica.
cubic *agg.* cubico.
cubism *s.* cubismo.
cubit *s.* cubito.
cuckold *s.* becco, cornuto.
to cuckold *vt.* tradire (*il marito*).
cuckoo *s.* cuculo.
cucumber *s.* cetriolo.
cudgel *s.* randello.
to cudgel *vt.* randellare.
cuff *s.* polsino (*di camicia*).
cuirass *s.* corazza.
cuirassier *s.* corazziere.
culinary *agg.* culinario.
to cull *vt.* scegliere.
culminant *agg.* culminante.
to culminate *vi.* culminare, giungere al culmine.
culottes *s. pl.* gonna pantaloni.
culprit *s.* **1.** colpevole **2.** imputato.
cult *s.* culto.
cultivable *agg.* coltivabile.
to cultivate *vt.* coltivare (*anche fig.*).
cultivation *s.* coltivazione.
cultural *agg.* culturale.
culture *s.* **1.** coltura, coltivazione **2.** cultura.
cultured *agg.* colto, educato.
cumbersome *agg.* ingombrante.
cumulative *agg.* cumulativo.
cumulus *s.* (*pl.* -li) cumulo.
cuneiform *agg.* cuneiforme.
cunette *s.* cunetta (*di trincea*).
cunning *agg.* astuto, furbo. ♦ **cunning** *s.* astuzia.
cup *s.* **1.** tazza **2.** (*sport*) coppa, trofeo || — *-bearer*, coppiere; *tea-* —, tazza da tè.
cupboard *s.* credenza, armadio.
cupel *s.* coppella.
cupidity *s.* cupidigia.
cupreous *agg.* cupreo.
cupric *agg.* ramico.
cur *s.* **1.** cane bastardo **2.** mascalzone.
curable *agg.* curabile.
curacy *s.* vicariato, cura.
curare *s.* curaro.
curate *s.* curato, vicario.
curative *agg.* curativo.
curator *s.* direttore (*di museo, istituto ecc.*).

curb *s.* **1.** cordone del marciapiede **2.** freno (*fig.*) || — *-bit*, morso della briglia.
curd *s.* giuncata.
to curdle *vt.* cagliare, coagulare. ♦ **to curdle** *vi.* cagliarsi, coagularsi.
curdy *agg.* cagliato, coagulato.
cure *s.* **1.** cura, rimedio: *to take a* —, fare una cura **2.** (*eccl.*) cura **3.** vulcanizzazione (*di gomma*).
to cure *vt.* **1.** curare, rimediare **2.** salare, affumicare (*di cibi*) **3.** vulcanizzare (*una gomma*). ♦ **to cure** *vi.* curarsi.
cureless *agg.* incurabile.
curette *s.* (*chir.*) raschiatoio.
curfew *s.* coprifuoco.
curio *s.* oggetto raro.
curiosity *s.* curiosità: *out of* —, per curiosità.
curious *agg.* **1.** curioso **2.** strano, singolare.
curl *s.* **1.** ricciolo **2.** curva, spirale.
to curl *vt.* **1.** arricciare **2.** torcere. ♦ **to curl** *vi.* **1.** arricciarsi **2.** torcersi **3.** sollevarsi in spire.
curler *s.* ferro per arricciare i capelli, bigodino.
curly *agg.* **1.** ricciuto **2.** a spirale.
currency *s.* **1.** (*comm.*) circolazione monetaria **2.** corso, credito, voga.
current *agg.* corrente. ♦ **current** *s.* corrente (*anche fig.*) || *alternating* —, corrente alternata; *direct* —, corrente continua.
currently *avv.* comunemente.
curriculum *s.* curriculum.
to curry *vt.* **1.** strigliare **2.** conciare (*di cuoio*).
curry-comb *s.* striglia.
curse *s.* maledizione, anatema: *a* — *upon him!*, sia maledetto!
to curse *vt.* **1.** maledire **2.** scomunicare. ♦ **to curse** *vi.* imprecare, pronunciare bestemmie.
cursed *agg.* maledetto.
cursive *agg.* e *s.* corsivo.
to curtail *vt.* accorciare, abbreviare.
curtain *s.* **1.** tenda, tendina **2.** cortina **3.** sipario || — *-call*, chiamata alla ribalta.
curtain-raiser *s.* avanspettacolo.
curtly *avv.* brevemente, bruscamente.
curtsey *s.* riverenza, inchino (*di donna*).
curve *s.* curva, svolta.
to curve *vt.* curvare. ♦ **to curve** *vi.*

curvarsi.
curvet s. falcata.
curvilinear agg. curvilineo.
cushion s. cuscino.
cusp s. 1. cuspide 2. (geom.) vertice.
custard s. crema (di uova e latte).
custody s. 1. custodia, vigilanza 2. arresto, detenzione.
custom s. costume, consuetudine. ◆ **customs** s. pl. dogana (sing.) ‖ — -house officer, doganiere.
customary agg. 1. abituale, d'uso comune 2. (giur.) consuetudinario.
customer s. cliente, avventore.
cut s. 1. taglio 2. decurtazione 3. (sport) colpo secco.
to cut (cut, cut) vt. e vi. 1. tagliare, tagliarsi ‖ to — a poor figure, fare una brutta figura 2. (comm.) ridurre 3. praticare un'apertura ‖ to — down, abbattere; to — out, ritagliare; to — up, trinciare (il pollo), sradicare (alberi).
cutlet s. costoletta.
cut-off s. 1. scorciatoia 2. ritaglio di giornale.
cutter[1] s. 1. tagliatore 2. (mecc.) fresa.
cutter[2] s. (mar.) "cutter".
cut-throat agg. spietato. ◆ **cutthroat** s. tagliagole.
cutting agg. tagliente, sferzante. ◆ **cutting** s. 1. taglio, incisione 2. ritaglio, truciolo 3. (comm.) riduzione.
cuttlefish s. seppia.
cyanide s. cianuro.
cybernetics s. cibernetica.
cycle s. ciclo.
cycling s. ciclismo.
cyclostyle s. ciclostile.
cyclotron s. ciclotrone.
cyclist s. ciclista.
cyclometer s. contachilometri.
cylinder s. 1. cilindro 2. rullo.
cylindrical agg. cilindrico.
cynic agg. e s. cinico.
cynicism s. cinismo.
cypress s. cipresso.
Cyprian agg. e s. cipriota.
Cyrillic agg. cirillico.
cyst s. cisti.
cystitis s. cistite.
cytology s. citologia.
Czar s. zar.
Czech agg. e s. ceco.
Czecho-Slovak agg. e s. cecoslovacco.

D

D s. (mus.) re.
dab s. 1. colpo 2. macchia.
to dab vt. 1. sfiorare 2. applicare.
to dabble vt. inumidire. ◆ **to dabble** vi. 1. inumidirsi 2. sguazzare ‖ to — in (at), dilettarsi di.
dachshund s. cane bassotto.
dad(dy) s. (fam.) papà, babbo.
daffodil s. narciso selvatico.
daft agg. sciocco, pazzoide.
dagger s. 1. pugnale 2. (tip.) croce ‖ at daggers drawn, ai ferri corti.
daguerreotype s. dagherrotipo.
daguerreotypy s. dagherrotipia.
dahlia s. dalia.
daily agg. quotidiano, giornaliero. ◆ **daily** s. (giornale) quotidiano. ◆ **daily** avv. ogni giorno.
daintily avv. delicatamente.
daintiness s. squisitezza.
dainty agg. 1. squisito 2. esigente 3. raffinato (di gusti). ◆ **dainty** s. leccornia.
dairy s. latteria.
dairymaid s. lattaia.
dairyman s. lattaio.
dais s. piattaforma.
daisy s. margherita.
dalliance s. amoreggiamento.
to dally vi. gingillarsi, oziare.
Dalmatian agg. e s. dalmata.
daltonism s. daltonismo.
dam[1] s. diga, sbarramento.
dam[2] s. madre (di animali).
to dam vt. arginare.
damage s. danno. ◆ **damages** s. pl. (giur.) indennizzo, risarcimento (sing.).
to damage vt. danneggiare.
damaging agg. dannoso.
damask s. damasco.
to damask vt. damascare.
dame s. dama, gentildonna.
damn s. maledizione.
to damn vt. 1. dannare 2. (spesso scritto d-) maledire, mandare all'inferno.
damnation s. dannazione.
damnatory agg. compromettente (di prove).
damp agg. umido. ◆ **damp** s. 1. umidità 2. (fig.) depressione ‖ fire-—, grisù.
to damp vt. 1. inumidire 2. (fig.) deprimere, smorzare.

damper s. **1.** regolatore (*di stufa, fornace ecc.*) **2.** (*mus.*) sordina.

dampness s. umidità.

dance s. danza.

to **dance** vt. e vi. danzare || to — *attendance on*, essere a disposizione di.

dancer s. ballerino.

dancing s. danza.

dandelion s. (*bot.*) soffione.

dandruff s. forfora.

dandy agg. elegante, raffinato. ♦ **dandy** s. zerbinotto.

Dane s. danese.

danger s. pericolo.

dangerous agg. pericoloso.

to **dangle** vi. ciondolare, penzolare ♦ to **dangle** vt. far penzolare.

dangling agg. penzolante.

Danish agg. danese.

dank agg. umido.

Dantean, Dantesque agg. dantesco.

dapple s. macchia || — *-grey*, leardo pomellato.

to **dapple** vt. chiazzare.

dare (**dared, durst**) v. dif. osare.

to **dare** vt. **1.** affrontare **2.** sfidare.

daredevil s. scavezzacollo.

daring agg. audace. ♦ **daring** s. audacia.

dark agg. **1.** scuro **2.** triste **3.** segreto. ♦ **dark** s. **1.** oscurità **2.** (*fig.*) ignoranza.

to **darken** vt. oscurare. ♦ to **darken** vi. oscurarsi.

darkling agg. oscuro. ♦ **darkling** avv. nell'oscurità.

darkness s. oscurità.

darling agg. e s. caro.

darn s. rammendo.

to **darn** vt. rammendare.

darnel s. loglio.

darner s. rammendatrice.

darning s. rammendo.

dart s. **1.** dardo **2.** slancio.

to **dart** vt. lanciare. ♦ to **dart** vi. lanciarsi (*in avanti*).

darting agg. dardeggiante.

Darwinism s. darwinismo.

dash s. **1.** slancio **2.** attacco **3.** tonfo **4.** spruzzo **5.** lineetta || — *-board*, cruscotto (*di automobili*).

to **dash** vt. **1.** frantumare **2.** macchiare. ♦ to **dash** vi. **1.** precipitarsi **2.** infrangersi.

dashing agg. impetuoso.

dastard s. vigliacco, furfante.

date[1] s. **1.** data **2.** appuntamento || *up to* —, aggiornato; *out of* —,

antiquato.

date[2] s. dattero.

to **date** vt. e vi. datare || to — *a girl*, dare un appuntamento a una ragazza.

dating s. datazione.

dative agg. e s. dativo.

datum s. (*pl.* data) dato, elemento.

to **daub** vt. **1.** intonacare **2.** impiastrare.

dauber s. imbrattatore.

daughter s. figlia || — *-in-law*, nuora; *grand-* — (*di nonni*), nipotina.

to **daunt** vt. spaventare, intimidire.

dauntless agg. intrepido.

to **dawdle** vi. oziare, bighellonare.

dawn s. alba.

to **dawn** vi. **1.** albeggiare **2.** apparire, balenare (*nella mente*).

day s. giorno || — *labourer*, lavoratore a giornata; *the* — *after tomorrow*, dopodomani; *the* — *before yesterday*, l'altro ieri; *this* — *week*, oggi a otto; — *off*, giorno di riposo; — *out*, giorno di libera uscita.

daybook s. (*comm.*) brogliaccio.

daybreak s. alba.

daydream s. fantasticheria.

to **daydream** vi. fantasticare.

daydreamer s. sognatore.

daylight s. luce del giorno.

daylong agg. che dura tutto il giorno. ♦ **daylong** avv. per tutto il giorno.

daytime s. giornata.

daze s. sbalordimento.

to **daze** vt. sbalordire.

dazzle s. abbagliamento || — *lamps* (*auto*), fari abbaglianti.

to **dazzle** vt. abbagliare.

deacon s. diacono.

dead agg. **1.** morto **2.** assoluto || — *drunk*, ubriaco fradicio. ♦ **dead** avv. assolutamente || — *sure*, arcisicuro.

to **deaden** vt. **1.** attutire **2.** isolare (*acusticamente*). ♦ to **deaden** vi. attutirsi.

deadening s. isolamento acustico.

deadline s. **1.** linea non superabile **2.** scadenza, termine massimo.

deadly agg. mortale. ♦ **deadly** avv. mortalmente.

deadness s. torpore.

deaf agg. sordo.

to **deafen** vt. assordare.

deaf-mute s. sordomuto.

deafness s. sordità.

deal s. 1. quantità 2. accordo 3. affare 4. mano (*del gioco delle carte*) || *a great* —, moltissimo.

to **deal** (**dealt, dealt**) vt. distribuire, dare. ♦ to **deal** (**dealt, dealt**) vi. trattare, comportarsi || *to* — *in*, commerciare in.

dealer s. 1. commerciante 2. mazziere (*delle carte*)

dealing s. 1. commercio 2. distribuzione 3. relazione || *double*-—, slealtà.

dealt V. *to deal*.

deambulatory agg. deambulatorio.

dean s. 1. decano 2. preside (*di facoltà universitaria*)

dear agg. caro || — *me!*, povero me!

dearly avv. 1. caramente 2. a caro prezzo.

dearness s. amorevolezza.

dearth s. penuria.

death s. morte || — *-rattles*, rantoli dell'agonia; — *-warrant*, ordine di esecuzione capitale.

deathly agg. e avv. V. *deadly*.

to **debase** vt. 1. avvilire 2. svalutare.

to **debar** vt. escludere, privare.

to **debark** vt. e vi. sbarcare.

debate s. dibattito.

to **debate** vt. e vi. 1. discutere 2. ponderare.

debauch s. intemperanza, corruzione.

debauched agg. corrotto.

debauchery s. 1. corruzione 2. dissolutezza.

debenture s. (*comm.*) obbligazione.

debit s. debito.

to **debit** vt. addebitare.

to **debouch** vi. sfociare.

debris s. detriti (*pl.*).

debt s. debito.

debtor s. debitore.

début s. debutto.

decadence s. decadenza.

decadent agg. e s. decadente.

decagram(m)e s. decagrammo.

decahedron s. decaedro.

to **decalcify** vt. decalcificare.

decalitre s. decalitro.

decalogue s. decalogo.

decametre s. decametro.

to **decamp** vi. levare le tende.

to **decant** vt. travasare.

decantation s. decantazione.

decanter s. caraffa.

to **decapitate** vt. decapitare.

decasyllabic agg. decasillabico.

decay s. 1. decadimento 2. rovina 3. carie (*dei denti*).

to **decay** vt. 1. far decadere 2. mandare in rovina. ♦ to **decay** vi. 1. decadere 2. andare in rovina 3. cariarsi.

decayable agg. deperibile.

decease s. decesso.

to **decease** vi. morire.

deceit s. 1. inganno 2. falsità.

deceitful agg. 1. ingannevole 2. falso.

to **deceive** vt. ingannare.

deceiving agg. ingannatore.

to **decelerate** vt. e vi. rallentare.

deceleration s. rallentamento.

decelerator s. rallentatore.

December s. dicembre.

decency s. decenza. ♦ **decencies** s. pl. convenienze.

decennary agg. decennale. ♦ **decennary** s. decennio.

decennial agg. e s. decennale.

decent agg. decente || *a* — *fellow*, un buon diavolo.

decentralization s. decentramento.

to **decentralize** vt. decentrare.

deception s. inganno.

deceptive agg. ingannevole.

to **decide** vt. decidere. ♦ to **decide** vi. decidersi, pronunciarsi.

decigram(me) s. decigrammo.

decimal agg. e s. decimale.

to **decimate** vt. decimare.

decimation s. decimazione.

decimetre s. decimetro.

to **decipher** vt. decifrare.

deciphering s. decifrazione.

decision s. decisione.

decisive agg. 1. decisivo 2. deciso.

deck s. (*mar.*) ponte, coperta || — *-chair*, sedia a sdraio; *quarter*-—, cassero.

to **deck** vt. ornare.

decker s. *double*-—, autobus a due piani.

to **declaim** vt. e vi. declamare.

declaimer s. declamatore.

declamation s. declamazione.

declamatory agg. declamatorio.

declaration s. dichiarazione.

to **declare** vt. e vi. dichiarare.

declension s. 1. declino 2. (*gramm.*) declinazione.

declinable agg. declinabile.

declination s. 1. inclinazione 2. declino.

decline s. declino, deperimento.

to **decline** *vt.* e *vi.* declinare.
declining *s.* 1. declinazione 2. deperimento 3. rifiuto.
declivity *s.* declivio.
to **decode** *vt.* decifrare, tradurre (*testi in codice*).
decolorization *s.* decolorazione.
decoloration *s.* decolorazione.
to **decolour(ize)** *vt.* decolorare.
decomposable *agg.* scomponibile.
to **decompose** *vt.* 1. decomporre 2. scomporre. ♦ to **decompose** *vi.* 1. decomporsi 2. scomporsi.
decomposition *s.* decomposizione.
to **deconsecrate** *vt.* sconsacrare.
to **decorate** *vt.* decorare.
decoration *s.* decorazione.
decorative *agg.* decorativo.
decorator *s.* decoratore.
decorous *agg.* decoroso.
decoy *s.* esca, richiamo.
decrease *s.* diminuzione.
to **decrease** *vt.* e *vi.* diminuire.
decree *s.* decreto.
to **decree** *vt.* decretare.
decrepit *agg.* decrepito.
decrepitude *s.* decrepitezza.
to **decry** *vt.* stigmatizzare, denigrare.
to **decuple** *vt.* decuplicare.
to **dedicate** *vt.* dedicare.
dedicatee *s.* persona a cui è dedicato qc.
dedication *s.* 1. dedica 2. consacrazione.
dedicative, dedicatory *agg.* dedicatorio.
to **deduce** *vt.* 1. dedurre 2. derivare.
to **deduct** *vt.* detrarre.
deduction *s.* 1. deduzione 2. detrazione.
deductive *agg.* deduttivo.
deed *s.* atto, azione.
to **deem** *vt.* giudicare.
deep *agg.* 1. profondo 2. cupo || —-freeze, surgelamento; — *mourning*, lutto stretto. ♦ **deep** *s.* abisso, profondità. ♦ **deep** *avv.* profondamente || — *into the night*, fino a notte tarda.
to **deepen** *vt.* 1. approfondire 2. incupire. ♦ to **deepen** *vi.* 1. approfondirsi 2. incupirsi.
deeply *avv.* profondamente.
deepness *s.* profondità.
deep-rooted *agg.* radicato.
deer *s.* cervo || (*fallow*) —, daino.
to **deface** *vt.* sfregiare.

defacement *s.* sfregio.
defamation *s.* diffamazione.
defamatory *agg.* diffamatorio.
to **defame** *vt.* diffamare.
defamer *s.* diffamatore.
default *s.* 1. mancanza 2. inadempienza 3. (*giur.*) contumacia: *judgement by* —, giudizio in contumacia.
defaulting *agg.* (*comm.*) insolvente.
defeat *s.* 1. sconfitta 2. fallimento.
to **defeat** *vt.* 1. sconfiggere 2. frustrare.
defeatism *s.* disfattismo.
defeatist *agg.* e *s.* disfattista.
to **defecate** *vt.* purificare. ♦ to **defecate** *vi.* defecare.
defect *s.* difetto.
defection *s.* defezione.
defective *agg.* 1. difettoso 2. (*gramm.*) difettivo. ♦ **defective** *s.* anormale.
defence *s.* difesa.
defenceless *agg.* indifeso.
to **defend** *vt.* difendere.
defendant *s.* imputato.
defender *s.* difensore.
defenestration *s.* defenestrazione.
defensible *agg.* difensibile.
defensive *agg.* difensivo. ♦ **defensive** *s.* difensiva.
to **defer**[1] *vt.* e *vi.* differire || *deferred payment*, pagamento a rate.
to **defer**[2] *vt.* rimettere. ♦ to **defer** *vi.* rimettersi.
deference *s.* deferenza.
deferential *agg.* deferente.
deferment *s.* differimento.
defiance *s.* sfida.
defiant *agg.* ardito.
deficiency *s.* 1. deficienza 2. disavanzo.
deficient *agg.* e *s.* deficiente.
deficit *s.* (*comm.*) disavanzo.
to **defile** *vi.* marciare in fila. ♦ to **defile** *vt.* 1. insozzare 2. profanare.
defilement *s.* 1. contaminazione 2. profanazione.
definable *agg.* definibile.
to **define** *vt.* definire.
definite *agg.* definito.
definitely *avv.* in modo preciso.
definiteness *s.* precisione.
definition *s.* 1. definizione 2. nitidezza.
definitive *agg.* definitivo.
to **deflagrate** *vt.* far deflagrare. ♦ to **deflagrate** *vi.* deflagrare.

deflagration s. deflagrazione.
to **deflate** vt. sgonfiare. ♦ to **deflate** vi. sgonfiarsi.
deflation s. 1. sgonfiamento 2. deflazione.
to **deflect** vt. e vi. deviare.
deflection s. deviazione.
defloration s. deflorazione.
to **deflower** vt. 1. deflorare 2. devastare 3. spogliare (dei fiori).
to **deforest** vt. diboscare.
deforestation s. diboscamento.
to **deform** vt. deformare. ♦ to **deform** vi. deformarsi.
deformation s. deformazione.
deformed agg. deforme.
deformity s. deformità.
to **defraud** vt. defraudare.
defrauder s. frodatore.
to **defray** vt. pagare, risarcire.
defrayal s. pagamento, risarcimento.
to **defrost** vt. sgelare.
defroster s. riscaldatore.
deft agg. abile, destro.
to **defy** vt. sfidare.
degenerate agg. e s. degenerato.
to **degenerate** vt. e vi. degenerare.
degeneration s. degenerazione.
degradation s. degradazione.
to **degrade** vt. degradare.
degree s. 1. grado 2. rango 3. laurea, diploma || by degrees, gradatamente.
to **dehydrate** vt. disidratare.
dehydration s. disidratazione.
to **deify** vt. deificare.
deism s. deismo.
deity s. divinità.
to **deject** vt. abbattere, scoraggiare.
dejected agg. triste, abbattuto.
dejectedly avv. con aria abbattuta.
dejection s. abbattimento.
delation s. delazione.
delator s. delatore.
delay s. 1. ritardo 2. proroga.
to **delay** vt. e vi. ritardare.
delegacy s. delegazione.
delegate s. delegato.
to **delegate** vt. delegare.
delegation s. delegazione.
to **delete** vt. cancellare (anche fig.).
deliberate agg. 1. deliberato 2. cauto.
to **deliberate** vt. e vi. deliberare.
deliberately avv. deliberatamente.
deliberation s. 1. deliberazione 2. ponderatezza.
delicacy s. 1. delicatezza 2. ghiottoneria.

delicate agg. 1. delicato 2. esigente.
delicatessen s. pl. 1. ghiottonerie 2. salumeria (sing.).
delicious agg. delizioso.
delict s. (giur.) delitto.
delight s. delizia, gioia.
to **delight** vt. deliziare. ♦ to **delight** vi. dilettarsi.
delighted agg. lietissimo, entusiasta.
delightful agg. delizioso.
to **delimit(ate)** vt. delimitare.
delimitation s. delimitazione.
to **delineate** vt. delineare.
delineation s. delineazione.
delinquency s. 1. delinquenza 2. colpevolezza.
delinquent agg. colpevole. ♦ **delinquent** s. delinquente.
delirious agg. delirante.
deliriously avv. in modo delirante.
delirium s. delirio, frenesia.
to **deliver** vt. 1. liberare 2. consegnare 3. partorire 4. pronunciare (un discorso).
deliverance s. liberazione.
delivery s. 1. liberazione 2. consegna 3. parto 4. resa 5. dizione, pronuncia || -man, fattorino.
deltoid agg. triangolare.
to **delude** vt. ingannare.
deluge s. diluvio.
delusion s. illusione.
delusive agg. illusorio.
to **delve** vt. scavare, esumare. ♦ to **delve** vi. compiere ricerche, frugare.
demagnetization s. demagnetizzazione.
to **demagnetize** vt. demagnetizzare.
demagogic(al) agg. demagogico.
demagogue s. demagogo.
demagogy s. demagogia.
demand s. 1. domanda 2. esigenza || on —, a richiesta.
to **demand** vt. 1. domandare 2. esigere.
demarcation s. demarcazione.
demeanour s. contegno.
demerit s. demerito.
demesne s. dominio, proprietà terriera.
demigod s. semidio.
demijohn s. damigiana.
demilitarization s. smilitarizzazione.
to **demilitarize** vt. smilitarizzare.
demise s. 1. trapasso (di proprietà)

2. decesso.
demiurge s. demiurgo.
demobilization s. smobilitazione.
to **demobilize** vt. smobilitare.
democracy s. democrazia.
democrat s. democratico.
democratic(al) agg. democratico.
democratization s. democratizza-
zione.
to **democratize** vt. democratizzare.
demographic(al) agg. demografico.
demography s. demografia.
to **demolish** vt. demolire.
demolisher s. demolitore.
demolition s. demolizione.
demon s. demonio.
demoniac(al) agg. demoniaco.
demonology s. demonologia.
demonstrability s. dimostrabilità.
demonstrable agg. dimostrabile.
demonstrant s. dimostrante.
to **demonstrate** vt. e vi. dimostrare.
demonstration s. dimostrazione.
demonstrative agg. **1.** dimostrativo
2. espansivo.
demonstrativeness s. **1.** dimostrazione **2.** espansività.
demonstrator s. **1.** dimostratore **2.**
dimostrante.
demoralization s. **1.** depravazione
2. demoralizzazione.
to **demoralize** vt. **1.** depravare **2.**
demoralizzare.
to **demur** vi. titubare, esitare.
demure agg. riservato, pudico.
demureness s. riservatezza, pudore.
den s. tana.
to **denationalize** vt. snazionalizzare.
to **denature** vt. denaturare.
deniable agg. negabile.
denial s. rifiuto || self- —, abnega-
zione.
to **denigrate** vt. denigrare.
denigration s. denigrazione.
denigrator s. denigratore.
to **denominate** vt. denominare.
denomination s. **1.** denominazione
2. setta **3.** valore (di monete).
denominational agg. confessionale.
denominative agg. denominativo.
denominator s. denominatore.
denotation s. **1.** indicazione **2.** significato.
to **denote** vt. denotare, indicare.
to **denounce** vt. denunciare.
dense agg. **1.** denso **2.** opaco **3.** stupido.
density s. **1.** densità **2.** opacità **3.**

stupidità.
dent s. incavo, tacca.
dental agg. e s. dentale.
dentary agg. dentario.
dentine s. dentina.
dentist s. dentista.
dentistry s. odontoiatria.
dentition s. dentizione.
denture s. dentiera.
denudation s. denudazione.
to **denude** vt. denudare.
denunciation s. denunzia.
to **deny** vt. negare, rifiutare.
deodorant agg. e s. deodorante.
to **deodorize** vt. deodorare.
deontology s. deontologia.
deoxidization s. disossidazione.
to **deoxidize** vt. disossidare.
to **depart** vi. partire, allontanarsi.
department s. **1.** reparto **2.** (amer.)
ministero || — store, grande ma-
gazzino.
departure s. **1.** partenza **2.** allontanamento.
to **depend** vi. **1.** dipendere: it all
depends on circumstances, tutto dipende dalle circostanze **2.** contare:
— on so., contare su qu.
dependable agg. fidato.
dependant agg. e s. dipendente.
dependence s. **1.** dipendenza **2.** fiducia.
dependency s. territorio dipendente.
dependent agg. dipendente.
to **depict** vt. dipingere.
to **depilate** vt. depilare.
depilatory agg. e s. depilatorio.
to **deplete** vt. **1.** vuotare **2.** esaurire.
depletion s. esaurimento.
deplorable agg. deplorevole.
to **deplore** vt. deplorare.
to **deploy** vt. schierare, spiegare. ♦
to **deploy** vi. schierarsi (di truppe ecc.).
to **depone** vt. deporre (in un processo).
deponent s. testimone.
to **depopulate** vt. spopolare.
to **deport** vt. deportare || to — one-
self, comportarsi.
deportation s. deportazione.
deportment s. atteggiamento.
deposal s. deposizione.
to **depose** vt. e vi. deporre.
deposit s. deposito.
to **deposit** vt. depositare.
deposition s. **1.** deposizione **2.** de-

posito.

depositor s. depositante.

depot s. deposito.

to **deprave** vt. depravare.

depravity s. depravazione.

deprecable agg. deprecabile.

to **deprecate** vt. disapprovare.

deprecation s. disapprovazione.

deprecative, deprecatory agg. disapprovante.

to **depreciate** vt. svalutare. ♦ to depreciate vi. svalutarsi.

depreciation s. 1. svalutazione 2. ammortamento: — charge, quota d'ammortamento.

depreciative, depreciatory agg. spregiativo.

depredation s. saccheggio.

depredatory agg. predatorio.

to **depress** vt. 1. deprimere 2. abbassare.

depression s. 1. depressione 2. (econ.) crisi.

depressor s. depressore.

deprivation s. privazione.

to **deprive** vt. privare.

depth s. 1. profondità 2. (mar.) fondale.

to **depurate** vt. depurare. ♦ to depurate vi. depurarsi.

depuration s. depurazione.

depurative agg. e s. depurativo.

depurator s. depuratore.

deputation s. delega.

to **depute** vt. deputare.

deputy s. 1. deputato 2. sostituto.

derailment s. deragliamento.

to **derange** vt. sconvolgere.

derangement s. sconvolgimento.

deratization s. derattizzazione.

to **deride** vt. deridere.

derision s. 1. derisione 2. zimbello.

derisive, derisory agg. derisorio.

derivable agg. derivabile.

derivation s. derivazione.

derivative agg. e s. derivato.

derivatively avv. per derivazione.

to **derive** vt. e vi. derivare.

derm s. derma.

dermatologist s. dermatologo.

dermatology s. dermatologia.

to **derogate** vi. derogare.

derogation s. deroga.

derogatory agg. derogatorio.

derrick s. 1. argano 2. torre di trivellazione.

descant s. 1. melodia 2. dissertazione.

to **descend** vt. e vi. (di)scendere ||

to — upon so., aggredire qu.

descendance s. discendenza.

descendant s. discendente.

descent s. 1. discesa 2. incursione 3. lignaggio 4. caduta.

describable agg. descrivibile.

to **describe** vt. descrivere.

description s. descrizione.

descriptive agg. descrittivo.

to **descry** vt. scoprire.

to **desecrate** vt. profanare.

desert[1] agg. deserto. ♦ **desert** s. deserto.

desert[2] s. 1. merito 2. compenso.

to **desert** vt. abbandonare. ♦ to desert vi. disertare.

deserted agg. deserto.

deserter s. disertore.

desertion s. 1. abbandono 2. diserzione.

to **deserve** vt. meritare.

deservedly avv. meritatamente.

deserving agg. meritevole.

design s. disegno.

to **design** vt. 1. destinare 2. progettare 3. disegnare.

designate agg. designato.

to **designate** vt. 1. designare 2. indicare.

designation s. designazione.

designer s. disegnatore.

designing agg. astuto. ♦ **designing** s. 1. disegno 2. complotto.

desirable agg. desiderabile.

desire s. desiderio.

to **desire** vt. 1. desiderare 2. domandare.

desirous agg. desideroso.

to **desist** vi. desistere.

desk s. 1. scrivania 2. cassa || school-master's —, cattedra (di insegnante).

desolate agg. desolato.

to **desolate** vt. 1. affliggere 2. devastare.

desolation s. desolazione.

despair s. disperazione.

to **despair** vi. disperare.

despairing agg. disperato.

desperate agg. disperato.

despicable agg. spregevole.

despicableness s. spregevolezza.

despisable agg. spregevole.

to **despise** vt. disprezzare.

despite prep. malgrado.

despiteful agg. maligno, dispettoso.

despondency s. scoraggiamento.

despondent agg. scoraggiato.

despot s. despota.

despotic(al) *agg.* dispotico.
despotism *s.* dispotismo.
destination *s.* destinazione.
to **destine** *vt.* destinare.
destiny *s.* destino.
destitute *agg.* 1. povero 2. privo.
destitution *s.* 1. povertà 2. privazione.
to **destroy** *vt.* distruggere.
destroyable *agg.* distruggibile.
destroyer *s.* 1. distruttore 2. cacciatorpediniere.
destroying *agg.* distruttore.
destruction *s.* distruzione, rovina.
destructive *agg.* distruttivo.
destructor *s.* distruttore.
desuetude *s.* disuso.
desultory *agg.* saltuario.
to **detach** *vt.* distaccare.
detachable *agg.* staccabile.
detached *agg.* 1. distaccato 2. isolato.
detachment *s.* 1. distacco 2. (*mil.*) distaccamento.
detail *s.* 1. dettaglio, particolare 2. pattuglia.
to **detail** *vt.* 1. dettagliare 2. (*mil.*) distaccare (*una pattuglia*).
to **detain** *vt.* 1. detenere 2. trattenere.
to **detect** *vt.* scoprire.
detectable *agg.* scopribile.
detection *s.* scoperta.
detective *s.* investigatore ‖ — *novel*, romanzo poliziesco.
detector *s.* (*radio*) rivelatore.
detent *s.* (*mecc.*) arpione.
detention *s.* 1. detenzione 2. ritardo forzato.
to **deter** *vt.* trattenere.
to **deterge** *vt.* detergere.
detergent *agg.* e *s.* detergente, detersivo.
to **deteriorate** *vt.* deteriorare. ◆ to **deteriorate** *vi.* deteriorarsi.
deterioration *s.* deterioramento.
determinable *agg.* determinabile.
determinant *s.* causa determinante.
determinate *agg.* determinato.
determination *s.* determinazione.
determinative *agg.* determinativo.
to **determine** *vt.* determinare, decidere. ◆ to **determine** *vi.* risolversi ‖ *to — on*, fissarsi su.
determined *agg.* deciso.
determinism *s.* determinismo.
determinist *agg.* e *s.* determinista.
deterrent *agg.* e *s.* (*neol.*) deterrente.

detersive *agg.* e *s.* detersivo.
to **detest** *vt.* detestare.
detestable *agg.* detestabile.
detestation *s.* 1. odio 2. esecrazione.
dethronement *s.* deposizione (*dal trono*).
to **detonate** *vt.* e *vi.* esplodere.
detonator *s.* detonatore.
detour *s.* deviazione, giravolta.
to **detract** *vt.* e *vi.* diminuire.
detraction *s.* detrazione.
detractor *s.* detrattore.
detriment *s.* detrimento.
detrimental *agg.* dannoso.
to **devaluate** *vt.* svalutare.
devaluation *s.* svalutazione.
to **devastate** *vt.* devastare.
devastation *s.* devastazione.
to **develop** *vt.* sviluppare. ◆ to **develop** *vi.* svilupparsi.
developer *s.* sviluppatore.
development *s.* sviluppo.
to **deviate** *vt.* e *vi.* deviare.
deviation *s.* deviazione.
deviationism *s.* deviazionismo.
device *s.* 1. trovata 2. dispositivo. ◆ **devices** *s. pl.* capriccio, inclinazione (*sing.*).
devil *s.* diavolo.
devilish *agg.* diabolico.
devious *agg.* 1. remoto 2. errante.
to **devise** *vt.* 1. escogitare 2. lasciare in eredità.
deviser *s.* inventore.
devising *s.* invenzione.
devoid *agg.* privo.
devolution *s.* 1. trasmissione (*di beni*) 2. degenerazione.
to **devolve** *vt.* trasmettere. ◆ to **devolve** *vi.* trasferirsi.
to **devote** *vt.* dedicare.
devoted *agg.* 1. devoto 2. votato.
devotion *s.* devozione.
devotional *agg.* devoto.
to **devour** *vt.* divorare.
devourer *s.* divoratore.
devout *agg.* devoto, pio, religioso.
dew *s.* rugiada.
dewy *agg.* rugiadoso.
dexterity *s.* destrezza.
dexterous *agg.* destro.
dextrin(e) *s.* destrina.
diabetes *s.* diabete.
diabetic *agg.* e *s.* diabetico.
diabolic(al) *agg.* diabolico.
diadem *s.* diadema.
to **diagnose** *vt.* diagnosticare.
diagnosis *s.* (*pl.* -ses) diagnosi.

diagnostic *agg.* diagnostico.
diagonal *agg.* e *s.* diagonale.
diagram *s.* diagramma.
dial *s.* quadrante.
to **dial** *vt.* comporre (*un numero telefonico*) ‖ *to — so.*, telefonare a qu.
dialect *s.* dialetto.
dialectal *agg.* dialettale.
dialectic(al) *agg.* dialettico.
dialectics *s.* dialettica.
dialogue *s.* dialogo.
to **dialogue** *vt.* e *vi.* dialogare.
diameter *s.* diametro.
diametrically *avv.* diametralmente.
diamond *s.* 1. diamante 2. losanga.
diaper *s.* 1. arabesco 2. pannolino.
diaphanous *agg.* diafano.
diaphragm *s.* diaframma.
diapositive *s.* diapositiva.
diarchy *s.* diarchia.
diarist *s.* diarista.
diarrhoea *s.* diarrea.
diary *s.* diario.
diatribe *s.* diatriba.
dice V. *die*.
to **dice** *vt.* 1. giocare ai dadi 2. tagliare a dadi 3. quadrettare.
dictaphone *s.* dittafono.
dictate *s.* dettame.
to **dictate** *vt.* e *vi.* dettare.
dictation *s.* 1. dettato 2. dettame.
dictator *s.* dittatore.
dictatorial *agg.* dittatoriale.
dictatorship *s.* dittatura.
diction *s.* 1. stile 2. dizione.
dictionary *s.* dizionario.
dictograph *s.* dittografo.
did V. *to do*.
didactic *agg.* didattico.
didactics *s.* didattica.
die *s.* (*pl.* dice) dado.
to **die** *vi.* morire ‖ *to — away*, svanire; *to — out*, estinguersi.
dielectric *agg.* e *s.* dielettrico.
diet *s.* dieta.
to **diet** *vt.* mettere a dieta. ♦ to **diet** *vi.* essere a dieta.
dietarian *s.* chi sta a dieta.
dietary *agg.* dietetico. ♦ **dietary** *s.* dieta.
dietetic(al) *agg.* dietetico.
to **differ** *vi.* differire.
difference *s.* 1. differenza 2. divergenza.
different *agg.* differente.
differential *agg.* e *s.* differenziale.
to **differentiate** *vt.* differenziare. ♦ to **differentiate** *vi.* differenziarsi.
differentiation *s.* differenziazione.
differently *avv.* differentemente.
differing *agg.* 1. differente, discordante.
difficult *agg.* difficile.
difficulty *s.* difficoltà.
diffidence *s.* timidezza.
diffident *agg.* esitante.
diffraction *s.* diffrazione.
diffuse *agg.* diffuso.
to **diffuse** *vt.* diffondere. ♦ to **diffuse** *vi.* diffondersi.
diffusedly, diffusely *avv.* 1. diffusamente 2. ovunque.
diffuser *s.* (*foto*) diffusore.
diffusion *s.* 1. diffusione 2. prolissità.
diffusive *agg.* 1. diffusivo 2. prolisso.
diffusor *s.* diffusore.
to **dig** (dug, dug) *vt.* vangare, scavare ‖ *to — in*, affondare; *to — out*, estrarre.
digest *s.* 1. sommario 2. condensato.
to **digest** *vt.* classificare, condensare, redigere. ♦ to **digest** *vt.* e *vi.* digerire.
digestibility *s.* digeribilità.
digestible *agg.* digeribile.
digestion *s.* digestione.
digestive *agg.* e *s.* digestivo.
digger *s.* 1. zappatore 2. scavatrice.
digging *s.* 1. scavo 2. miniera. ♦ **diggings** *s. pl.* (*gergo*) alloggio (*sing.*).
digital *agg.* digitale.
dignified *agg.* dignitoso.
to **dignify** *vt.* elevare, nobilitare.
dignitary *s.* dignitario.
dignity *s.* 1. dignità 2. dignitario.
digression *s.* digressione.
digressive *agg.* digressivo.
dike *s.* diga.
to **dike** *vt.* arginare.
to **dilapidate** *vt.* dilapidare. ♦ to **dilapidate** *vi.* andare in rovina.
dilatability *s.* dilatabilità.
dilatable *agg.* dilatabile.
dilatation *s.* dilatazione.
to **dilate** *vt.* dilatare. ♦ to **dilate** *vi.* dilatarsi.
dilatory *agg.* 1. dilatorio 2. lento.
diligence *s.* diligenza.
diligent *agg.* diligente.
diluent *agg.* e *s.* diluente.
to **dilute** *vt.* diluire.
dilution *s.* 1. diluzione 2. sostanza

diluita.

diluvial *agg.* diluviale.

dim *agg.* **1.** debole **2.** appannato **3.** oscuro.

to **dim** *vt.* **1.** indebolire **2.** oscurare. ◆ to **dim** *vi.* **1.** indebolirsi **2.** oscurarsi.

dime *s.* quarto di dollaro.

dimension *s.* dimensione.

dimeter *s.* dimetro.

to **diminish** *vt.* e *vi.* diminuire.

diminishable *agg.* diminuibile.

diminution *s.* diminuzione.

diminutive *agg.* minuscolo. ◆ **diminutive** *s.* diminutivo.

dimissory *agg.* dimissorio.

dimly *avv.* **1.** debolmente **2.** oscuramente.

dimness *s.* **1.** debolezza **2.** offuscamento (*di vista*).

dimple *s.* fossetta.

din *s.* baccano.

to **din** *vt.* e *vi.* rintronare.

to **dine** *vi.* pranzare.

diner *s.* commensale.

to **ding** *vt.* e *vi.* suonare, scampanellare.

dingy *agg.* scuro, sporco.

dining *s.* il pranzare || — -*room*, sala da pranzo.

dinner *s.* pranzo || — -*wagon*, carrello (*per i pasti*); — -*car*, vagone ristorante.

dinosaur *s.* dinosauro.

dint *s.* tacca || *by* — *of*, a forza di.

diocesan *agg.* e *s.* diocesano.

diocese *s.* diocesi.

diode *s.* diodo.

Dionysiac, Dionysian *agg.* dionisiaco.

diopter *s.* diottria.

dioptric *agg.* diottrico.

dioxid(e) *s.* biossido.

dip *s.* **1.** bagno **2.** inclinazione **3.** (*aer.*) picchiata **4.** tuffo.

to **dip** *vt.* **1.** imm~ ~ere **2.** abbassare. ◆ to **dip** *vi.* **1.** immergersi **2.** abbassarsi **3.** tuffarsi.

diphtheria *s.* difterite.

diphtheric *agg.* difterico.

diphthong *s.* dittongo.

diplomacy *s.* diplomazia.

diplomat *s.* diplomatico.

diplomatic *agg.* diplomatico.

diplomatically *avv.* diplomaticamente.

diplomatics *s.* diplomazia.

diplomatist *s.* diplomatico.

dipody *s.* dipodia.

dipper *s.* **1.** tuffatore **2.** mestolo || *the Big* —, l'Orsa Maggiore.

dipsomaniac *s.* dipsomane.

dipteral *agg.* dittero.

diptych *s.* dittico.

dire *agg.* terribile, orrendo.

direct *agg.* diretto.

to **direct** *vt.* **1.** dirigere **2.** ordinare.

direction *s.* **1.** direzione **2.** indicazione.

directional *agg.* direzionale.

directive *agg.* direttivo. ◆ **directive** *s.* direttiva.

directly *avv.* **1.** direttamente **2.** subito.

director *s.* **1.** direttore **2.** regista.

directorial *agg.* direttivo.

directory *agg.* direttivo. ◆ **directory** *s.* **1.** (*tel.*) guida **2.** (*amer.*) consiglio di amministrazione.

direful *agg.* orrendo.

dirge *s.* canto funebre.

diriment *agg.* dirimento.

dirt *s.* sporcizia.

dirtiness *s.* sozzura.

dirty *agg.* **1.** sporco **2.** brutto **3.** sboccato.

to **dirty** *vt.* sporcare. ◆ to **dirty** *vi.* sporcarsi.

disability *s.* **1.** incapacità **2.** invalidità.

to **disable** *vt.* rendere incapace, inabile.

to **disabuse** *vt.* disingannare.

to **disaccustom** *vt.* disabituare.

disadvantage *s.* svantaggio.

disadvantageous *agg.* svantaggioso.

to **disagree** *vi.* dissentire.

disagreeable *agg.* sgradevole.

disagreeableness *s.* sgradevolezza.

disagreement *s.* dissenso.

to **disappear** *vi.* scomparire.

disappearance *s.* sparizione.

to **disappoint** *vt.* deludere.

disappointingly *avv.* in modo deludente.

disappointment *s.* delusione.

disapprobation, disapproval *s.* disapprovazione.

to **disapprove** *vt.* e *vi.* disapprovare.

disapprovingly *avv.* con disapprovazione.

to' **disarm** *vt.* e *vi.* disarmare.

disarmament *s.* disarmo.

to **disarrange** *vt.* scompigliare.

disarrangement *s.* scompiglio.

disarray *s.* scompiglio, confusione.

to **disassemble** vt. smontare.
disassembling s. smontaggio.
disaster s. disastro.
disastrous agg. disastroso.
to **disavow** vt. ripudiare.
to **disband** vt. sciogliere. ♦ to **disband** vi. sbandarsi.
disbelief s. incredulità.
to **disbelieve** vt. e vi. non credere.
disbeliever s. incredulo.
disbursement s. pagamento.
to **discard** vt. scartare.
to **discern** vt. discernere.
discernible agg. visibile.
discernment s. discernimento.
discharge s. 1. scarico 2. scarica 3. congedo 4. assoluzione 5. liberazione 6. pagamento.
to **discharge** vt. 1. scaricare 2. congedare 3. assolvere 4. liberare. ♦ to **discharge** vi. scaricarsi.
disciple s. discepolo.
disciplinable agg. disciplinabile.
disciplinary agg. disciplinare.
discipline s. disciplina.
to **disclaim** vt. rifiutare, declinare (responsabilità).
disclaimer s. rinuncia, rifiuto.
to **disclose** vt. svelare.
disclosure s. rivelazione.
discoid agg. e s. discoide.
to **discolour** vt. scolorire. ♦ to **discolour** vi. scolorirsi.
discolouration s. scoloramento.
to **discomfit** vt. 1. sconfiggere 2. disorientare.
to **discomfort** vt. mettere a disagio.
to **discompose** vt. agitare.
to **disconcert** vt. turbare.
to **disconnect** vt. separare, disunire.
disconnected agg. 1. sconnesso 2. disinnestato.
disconnectedness s. sconnessione.
disconsolate agg. sconsolato.
discontent s. scontento.
to **discontinue** vt. e vi. cessare.
discontinuity s. discontinuità.
discontinuous agg. discontinuo.
discord s. 1. discordia, dissenso 2. (mus.) dissonanza.
discordance s. 1. disaccordo 2. discordanza (di suoni).
discordant agg. discorde.
discordantly avv. in disaccordo.
discount s. sconto ‖ at a —, sottocosto.
to **discount** vt. 1. scontare 2. tenere in poco conto.

discountable agg. 1. scontabile 2. poco attendibile.
to **discourage** vt. scoraggiare.
discouragement s. scoraggiamento.
to **discover** vt. scoprire.
discoverer s. scopritore.
discovery s. scoperta.
discredit s. 1. discredito 2. dubbio.
to **discredit** vt. 1. screditare 2. mettere in dubbio.
discreditable agg. vergognoso, infamante.
discreet agg. prudente, discreto.
discrepancy s. disaccordo.
discrete agg. separato, distinto.
discretion s. 1. discrezione 2. saggezza.
discretionary agg. discrezionale.
discriminate agg. discriminato.
to **discriminate** vt. e vi. discriminare.
discriminating agg. 1. sagace 2. discriminante.
discrimination s. 1. discriminazione 2. discernimento.
discursive agg. divagante.
discus s. disco ‖ — -thrower, discobolo.
to **discuss** vt. discutere.
discussion s. discussione.
disdain s. sdegno.
to **disdain** vt. disdegnare.
disdainful agg. sdegnoso.
disease s. malattia.
to **disembark** vt. e vi. sbarcare.
to **disembarrass** vt. sbarazzare.
to **disembody** vt. 1. disincarnare 2. congedare.
to **disembowel** vt. sventrare.
disembowelment s. sventramento.
to **disenchant** vt. disincantare.
disenchantment s. disincanto.
to **disengage** vt. 1. disimpegnare 2. disinnestare. ♦ to **disengage** vi. liberarsi.
disengagement s. 1. liberazione 2. disinnesto.
to **disentangle** vt. districare. ♦ to **disentangle** vi. districarsi.
disentanglement s. districamento.
disesteem s. disistima.
to **disesteem** vt. disprezzare.
disfavour s. 1. disgrazia 2. disapprovazione.
to **disfigure** vt. sfigurare.
disfigurement s. deturpamento.
to **disfranchise** vt. privare dei diritti (civili o di voto).
to **disgorge** vt. 1. emettere 2. vomi-

tare (*anche fig.*).

disgrace *s.* 1. vergogna 2. disgrazia.

to **disgrace** *vt.* disonorare.

disgraceful *agg.* vergognoso.

disgregation *s.* disgregazione.

disguise *s.* travestimento || *in* —, travestito, camuffato.

to **disguise** *vt.* mascherare.

disgust *s.* disgusto.

tò **disgust** *vt.* disgustare.

disgustedly *avv.* con disgusto.

disgustful, disgusting *agg.* disgustoso.

dish *s.* 1. piatto 2. vivanda || —-washer, lavapiatti.

to **dish** *vt.* servire || *to* — *up*, servire in tavola.

to **disharmonize** *vt.* disarmonizzare.

to **dishearten** *vt.* scoraggiare.

disheartenment *s.* scoraggiamento.

to **dishevel** *vt.* arruffare.

dishonest *agg.* disonesto.

dishonesty *s.* disonestà.

dishonour *s.* 1. disonore 2. mancato pagamento.

to **dishonour** · *vt.* 1. disonorare 2. rifiutare di pagare.

dishonourable *agg.* disonorevole.

dishonourableness *s.* disonorabilità.

disillusion(ment) *s.* disillusione.

to **disinfect** *vt.* disinfettare.

disinfectant *s.* disinfettante.

disinfection *s.* disinfezione.

to **disinfest** *vt.* disinfestare.

disinfestation *s.* disinfestazione.

to **disinherit** *vt.* diseredare.

to **disintegrate** *vt.* disintegrare. ♦ to **disintegrate** *vi.* disintegrarsi.

disintegration *s.* disintegrazione.

disintegrator *s.* disintegratore.

to **disinter** *vt.* dissotterrare.

disinterested *agg.* disinteressato.

disinterment *s.* dissotterramento.

to **disjoin** *vt.* disgiungere. ♦ to **disjoin** *vi.* disgiungersi.

to **disjoint** *vt.* 1. disgregare 2. disarticolare. ♦ to **disjoint** *vi.* disgregarsi.

disjunction *s.* separazione.

disjunctive *agg.* disgiuntivo.

disjunctively *avv.* disgiuntamente.

disk *s.* disco.

dislike *s.* avversione.

to **dislike** *vt.* detestare, provar avversione per.

to **dislocate** *vt.* 1. spostare 2. slogare 3. disorganizzare.

dislocation *s.* 1. dislocazione 2. slogatura 3. disorganizzazione.

to **dislodge** *vt.* sloggiare.

disloyal *agg.* sleale.

disloyalty *s.* slealtà.

dismal *agg.* tetro.

to **dismantle** *vt.* smantellare.

dismantlement *s.* smantellamento.

to **dismast** *vt.* (*mar.*) disalberare.

dismay *s.* costernazione.

to **dismay** *vt.* costernare.

to **dismember** *vt.* smembrare.

dismemberment *s.* smembramento.

to **dismiss** *vt.* 1. congedare 2. licenziare 3. bandire.

dismissal *s.* 1. congedo 2. licenziamento 3. destituzione 4. rigetto.

to **dismount** *vt.* e *vi.* smontare.

disobedience *s.* disubbidienza.

disobedient *agg.* disubbidiente.

to **disobey** *vt.* disubbidire.

to **disoblige** *vt.* essere scortese con.

disobliging *agg.* scortese.

disorder *s.* 1. disordine 2. disturbo.

to **disorder** *vt.* 1. scompigliare 2. disturbare.

disorderly *agg.* 1. disordinato 2. turbolento.

disorganization *s.* disorganizzazione.

to **disorganize** *vt.* disorganizzare.

to **disorient(ate)** *vt.* disorientare.

disorientation *s.* disorientamento.

to **disown** *vt.* rinnegare.

disowning *s.* rinnegamento.

to **disparage** *vt.* 1. deprezzare 2. screditare.

disparagement *s.* 1. deprezzamento 2. denigrazione.

disparaging *agg.* 1. sprezzante 2. denigratorio.

disparate *agg.* disparato.

disparity *s.* disparità.

dispassionate *agg.* spassionato.

dispatch *s.* 1. spedizione 2. dispaccio 3. disbrigo 4. celerità.

to **dispatch** *vt.* 1. spedire 2. sbrigare.

to **dispel** *vt.* dissipare.

dispensary *s.* dispensario.

dispensation *s.* 1. (*eccl.*) dispensa 2. distribuzione 3. beneficio.

to **dispense** *vt.* dispensare. ♦ to **dispense** *vi.* fare a meno di: *to* — *with so.*, fare a meno di qu.

dispersal *s.* dispersione.

to **disperse** *vt.* disperdere. ♦ to **disperse** *vi.* disperdersi.

dispersion *s.* dispersione.

dispersive *agg.* dispersivo.

dispirited *agg.* depresso.

to **displace** *vt.* **1.** spostare **2.** destituire.

displacement *s.* **1.** spostamento **2.** sostituzione **3.** (*mar.*) dislocamento.

display *s.* mostra, esibizione.

to **display** *vt.* mostrare, esporre.

to **displease** *vt.* dispiacere.

displeasing *agg.* spiacevole.

displeasure *s.* dispiacere.

disposal *s.* **1.** disposizione **2.** cessione.

to **dispose** *vt.* e *vi.* disporre || *to — of,* disfarsi di, smerciare.

disposition *s.* **1.** disposizione **2.** indole.

to **dispossess** *vt.* spogliare.

dispossession *s.* **1.** spoliazione **2.** (*giur.*) esproprio.

disproportion *s.* sproporzione.

disproportionate, disproportioned *agg.* sproporzionato.

to **disprove** *vt.* **1.** confutare **2.** dimostrare la falsità di.

disputable *agg.* discutibile.

dispute *s.* controversia, disputa.

to **dispute** *vt.* **1.** disputare **2.** contestare.

disqualification *s.* **1.** incapacità **2.** (*giur.*) interdizione **3.** squalifica.

to **disqualify** *vt.* **1.** rendere incapace **2.** (*giur.*) interdire **3.** squalificare.

disquieting *agg.* inquietante.

disquisition *s.* **1.** disquisizione **2.** inchiesta.

disregard *s.* noncuranza.

to **disregard** *vt.* ignorare.

disreputable *agg.* **1.** sconveniente **2.** screditato.

disreputably *avv.* disonorevolmente.

disrepute *s.* discredito.

disrespectful *agg.* irrispettoso.

to **disrobe** *vt.* svestire. ♦ to **disrobe** *vi.* svestirsi.

disruption *s.* rottura.

disruptive *agg.* **1.** che smembra **2.** dirompente.

dissatisfaction *s.* insoddisfazione.

dissatisfactory *agg.* insoddisfacente.

dissatisfied *agg.* scontento.

to **dissatisfy** *vt.* scontentare.

to **dissect** *vt.* sezionare.

dissection *s.* **1.** sezionamento **2.** parte sezionata.

to **dissemble** *vt.* e *vi.* dissimulare, ignorare.

dissembling *s.* dissimulazione. ♦ **dissembling** *agg.* ipocrita.

dissemblingly *avv.* ingannevolmente.

to **disseminate** *vt.* (dis)seminare.

dissemination *s.* disseminazione.

disseminator *s.* propagatore.

dissension *s.* divergenza.

dissent *s.* **1.** dissenso **2.** (*relig.*) separazione, scisma.

to **dissent** *vi.* dissentire.

dissenter *s.* dissidente.

dissenting *agg.* dissenziente.

to **dissertate** *vi.* dissertare.

dissertation *s.* dissertazione.

dissertator *s.* dissertatore.

disservice *s.* cattivo servizio.

to **dissever** *vt.* scindere. ♦ to **dissever** *vi.* scindersi.

dissidence *s.* dissidio.

dissident *agg.* e *s.* dissidente.

dissimilar *agg.* dissimile.

dissimilarity *s.* dissomiglianza.

dissimilation *s.* dissimilazione.

to **dissimulate** *vt.* e *vi.* dissimulare.

dissimulation *s.* dissimulazione.

dissimulator *s.* dissimulatore.

to **dissipate** *vt.* dissipare. ♦ to **dissipate** *vi.* dissiparsi.

dissipation *s.* dissipazione.

dissociable *agg.* **1.** dissociabile **2.** riservato.

to **dissociate** *vt.* dissociare. ♦ to **dissociate** *vi.* dissociarsi.

dissociation *s.* **1.** dissociazione **2.** sdoppiamento (*della personalità*).

dissolubility *s.* dissolubilità.

dissoluble *agg.* dissolubile.

dissolute *agg.* dissoluto.

dissoluteness *s.* dissolutezza.

dissolution *s.* dissoluzione.

to **dissolve** *vt.* dissolvere. ♦ to **dissolve** *vi.* dissolversi.

dissolvent *agg.* e *s.* dissolvente.

dissonance *s.* dissonanza.

dissonant *agg.* dissonante.

to **dissuade** *vt.* dissuadere.

dissuasion *s.* dissuasione.

dissyllabic *agg.* bisillabico.

dissyllable *s.* bisillabo.

dissymmetry *s.* asimmetria.

distaff *s.* conocchia.

distance *s.* distanza || *long- — call,* telefonata interurbana; *at a —,* da lontano.

distant *agg.* **1.** lontano **2.** riservato.

distantly *avv.* (da) lontano.

distaste *s.* ripugnanza.

distasteful *agg.* repellente.

distemper[1] *s.* **1.** turbamento fisico **2.** cimurro **3.** tumulto.

distemper[2] *s.* tempera.

to **distend** *vt.* distendere. ♦ to **distend** *vi.* distendersi.

to **distil(l)** *vt. e vi.* (di)stillare.

distillate *s.* distillato.

distillation *s.* distillazione.

distiller *s.* distillatore.

distillery *s.* distilleria.

distinct *agg.* distinto.

distinction *s.* distinzione.

distinctive *agg.* distintivo.

to **distinguish** *vt. e vi.* distinguere.

distinguished *agg.* **1.** distinto **2.** illustre.

to **distort** *vt.* distorcere.

distortion *s.* distorsione.

to **distract** *vt.* **1.** distrarre **2.** turbare, far impazzire.

distraction *s.* **1.** distrazione **2.** follia: *to love to —,* amare alla follia.

to **distrain** *vi.* sequestrare.

distrait *agg.* distratto, smarrito.

distraught *agg.* **1.** folle **2.** sconvolto.

distress *s.* **1.** angoscia **2.** pericolo **3.** sequestro.

to **distress** *vt.* **1.** affliggere **2.** sequestrare.

distressful *agg.* penoso.

distributable *agg.* distribuibile.

to **distribute** *vt.* distribuire.

distribution *s.* distribuzione.

distributive *agg.* distributivo.

distributor *s.* distributore.

district *s.* distretto.

distrust *s.* diffidenza.

to **distrust** *vt.* diffidare di.

distrustful *agg.* diffidente.

to **disturb** *vt.* **1.** disturbare **2.** turbare.

disturbance *s.* agitazione.

disturber *s.* disturbatore.

disunion *s.* separazione.

to **disunite** *vt.* disunire. ♦ to **disunite** *vi.* separarsi.

disunited *agg.* disunito.

disuse *s.* disuso.

disused *agg.* disusato.

ditch *s.* fosso || *to die in the last —,* resistere ad oltranza.

to **ditch** *vi.* scavare fossi.

dithyramb *s.* ditirambo.

dithyrambic *agg.* ditirambico.

ditty *s.* **1.** canzone **2.** poemetto.

diuretic *agg. e s.* diuretico.

diurnal *agg.* **1.** diurno **2.** quotidiano.

diuturnal *agg.* diuturno.

diuturnity *s.* diuturnità.

divan *s.* divano.

dive *s.* **1.** tuffo **2.** (*aer.*) picchiata.

to **dive** *vi.* **1.** tuffarsi **2.** (*aer.*) lanciarsi in picchiata.

diver *s.* **1.** tuffatore **2.** palombaro.

to **diverge** *vi.* divergere.

divergence *s.* divergenza.

divergent *agg.* divergente.

diverse *agg.* **1.** diverso **2.** mutevole.

to **diversify** *vt.* rendere diverso.

diversion *s.* **1.** diversione **2.** passatempo.

diversity *s.* diversità.

to **divert** *vt.* **1.** deviare **2.** divertire.

to **divest** *vt.* spogliare.

to **divide** *vt.* dividere. ♦ to **divide** *vi.* dividersi.

dividend *s.* dividendo.

dividing *s.* divisione.

divination *s.* divinazione.

divinatory *agg.* divinatorio.

divine *agg.* divino. ♦ **divine** *s.* (*eccl.*) teologo.

to **divine** *vt. e vi.* predire.

diviner *s.* indovino || *water —,* rabdomante.

diving *s.* tuffo || *— -bell,* campana subacquea; *-board,* trampolino.

divining *s.* divinazione.

divinity *s.* **1.** divinità **2.** teologia.

divisibility *s.* divisibilità.

divisible *agg.* divisibile.

division *s.* divisione.

divisional *agg.* di divisione.

divisor *s.* divisore.

divorce *s.* divorzio.

to **divorce** *vt.* divorziare.

divulgation *s.* divulgazione.

to **divulge** *vt.* divulgare.

divulger *s.* divulgatore.

dizzily *avv.* vertiginosamente.

dizziness *s.* vertigine.

dizzy *agg.* **1.** vertiginoso **2.** preso da vertigine **3.** stordito.

to **do** (did, done) *vt. e vi.* **1.** (*v. aus. in frasi int., neg., int.-neg.*) *— you understand English?,* capisci l'inglese?; *I do not* (*I don't*), non capisco; *he does not* (*he doesn't*) *speak English,* non parla l'inglese **2.** (*uso enfatico*) *I do study!,* studio veramente! **3.** (*sostitutivo*) *he said he would come and he did,* disse che sarebbe venuto e venne **4.** fare (*in senso generale, astratto*) *what are you doing?,* che cosa stai facendo?; *to*

— *one's duty*, fare il proprio dovere **5.** bastare: *that will do*, ciò basta **6.** addirsi, convenire: *this house will do me*, questa casa mi va bene || *to — without*, fare a meno.

docile *agg.* docile.

docility *s.* docilità.

dock[1] *s.* bacino: *dry- —*, bacino di carenaggio || *— -master*, capitano di porto; *wet- —*, darsena.

dock[2] *s.* banco degli imputati (*in tribunale*).

docker *s.* scaricatore.

docket *s.* **1.** (*giur.*) estratto verbale **2.** etichetta.

dockyard *s.* cantiere.

doctor *s.* dottore.

doctoral *agg.* dottorale.

doctorate *s.* dottorato.

doctrinaire *agg. e s.* dottrinario.

doctrinal *agg.* dottrinale.

doctrine *s.* dottrina.

document *s.* documento.

to document *vt.* documentare.

documentary *agg. e s.* documentario.

documentation *s.* documentazione.

to dodder *vi.* tremare, vacillare.

dodecagon *s.* dodecagono.

dodecahedron *s.* dodecaedro.

dodge *s.* **1.** schivata **2.** balzo.

to dodge *vt.* schivare. ♦ **to dodge** *vi.* scansarsi.

doe *s.* femmina (*di daino, cervo ecc.*).

doer *s.* chi agisce, chi fa.

dog *s.* **1.** cane **2.** (*mecc.*) gancio || *— -cart*, calesse; *— catcher*, accalappiacani; *— -days*, giorni di canicola; *— -ear*, orecchia (*a una pagina*); *— -tired*, stanco morto.

to dog *vt.* inseguire.

dogged *agg.* ostinato.

doggerel *s.* filastrocca.

dogmatic(al) *agg.* dogmatico.

dogmatism *s.* dogmatismo.

doily *s.* tovagliolino.

doings *s. pl.* azioni, imprese.

dole *s.* **1.** ripartizione **2.** sussidio.

doleful *agg.* triste.

dolichocephalic *agg.* dolicocefalo.

doll *s.* bambola.

dollar *s.* dollaro.

dolly *s.* **1.** bambola **2.** (*cine*) carrello.

dolomitic *agg.* dolomitico.

dolphin *s.* **1.** delfino **2.** boa.

dolt *s.* stupido.

domain *s.* dominio.

dome *s.* cupola.

domestic *agg.* **1.** domestico **2.** nazionale. ♦ **domestic** *s.* domestico.

domicile *s.* domicilio.

domiciliary *agg.* domiciliare.

dominant *agg.* dominante.

to dominate *vt. e vi.* dominare.

domination *s.* dominazione.

domineering *agg.* dispotico.

Dominican *agg. e s.* domenicano.

dominion *s.* dominio, possedimento (*di territori*).

donation *s.* donazione.

donative *s.* dono.

done V. *to do* || *over- —*, troppo cotto; *under- —*, poco cotto.

donjon *s.* torrione.

donkey *s.* asino.

donor *s.* donatore.

doodle *s.* ghirigoro.

doom *s.* **1.** destino **2.** giudizio.

to doom *vt.* condannare.

doomsday *s.* giudizio universale.

door *s.* porta, portiera || *— -keeper*, portinaio; *— -post*, stipite; *— -way*, soglia.

dope *s.* **1.** vernice **2.** stupefacente.

to dope *vt.* **1.** verniciare **2.** drogare.

doping *s.* drogaggio.

Doric *agg.* dorico.

dormer (window) *s.* abbaino.

dormitory *s.* dormitorio.

dormouse *s.* (*pl.* dormice) ghiro.

dorsal *agg.* dorsale.

dosage *s.* dosaggio.

to dose *vt.* **1.** dosare **2.** adulterare.

dosimeter *s.* dosatore.

dossal *s.* dossale.

dossier *s.* incartamento.

dot *s.* punto, puntino.

to dot *vt.* punteggiare.

dotage *s.* **1.** rimbambimento **2.** infatuazione.

dotal *agg.* dotale.

doting *agg.* **1.** senile **2.** infatuato. ♦ **doting** *s.* senilità.

double *agg.* doppio. ♦ **double** *s.* **1.** doppio **2.** (*cine*) controfigura. ♦ **double** *avv.* **1.** doppiamente **2.** in due.

to double *vt.* **1.** raddoppiare **2.** doppiare **3.** piegare. ♦ **to double** *vi.* **1.** raddoppiarsi **2.** piegarsi.

double-dealing *s.* imbroglio.

doubleness *s.* doppiezza.

doubling *s.* raddoppiamento.

doubly *avv.* doppiamente.

doubt *s.* dubbio || *no —*, indubbiamente.

to doubt *vt. e vi.* dubitare.

doubtful *agg.* incerto, dubbio.
doubtfulness *s.* dubbiosità.
doubtless *agg.* indubbio. ◆ **doubt-less** *avv.* indubbiamente.
dough *s.* pasta.
dove *s.* colomba || — -*cot(e)*, colombaia.
dowdy *agg.* sciatto.
dower *s.* dote.
down[1] *s.* 1. duna 2. collina.
down[2] *s.* 1. piumino 2. lanugine.
down[3] *agg.* 1. diretto verso il basso 2. depresso.
down[4] *avv.* (in) giù || — *with!*, abbasso: — *with the tyrant!*, abbasso il tiranno! ◆ **down** *prep.* giù per.
to down *vt.* abbattere, rovesciare.
downcast *agg.* abbattuto.
downfall *s.* rovescio.
downhearted *agg.* scoraggiato.
downhill *agg.* discendente, inclinato. ◆ **downhill** *avv.* in discesa.
downpour *s.* acquazzone.
downright *agg.* vero, sincero. ◆ **downright** *avv.* completamente.
downstairs *avv.* giù. ◆ **down-stairs** *agg.* dabbasso. ◆ **down-stairs** *s.* pianterreno.
downtrodden *agg.* calpestato, oppresso.
downward *agg.* in giù, discendente.
downward(s) *avv.* in giù.
downy[1] *agg.* ondulato.
downy[2] *agg.* 1. lanuginoso 2. morbido.
dowry *s.* dote.
dowser *s.* rabdomante.
doze *s.* sonnellino.
to doze *vi.* sonnecchiare.
dozen *s.* dozzina.
drab *s.* 1. sciattona 2. sgualdrina.
draff *s.* feccia.
draft *s.* 1. tiro 2. sorso 3. abbozzo 4. corrente d'aria 5. (*comm.*) tratta 6. (*mar.*) pescaggio.
to draft *vt.* 1. tirare 2. abbozzare.
drag *s.* 1. erpice 2. (*mar.*) draga 3. ostacolo.
to drag *vt.* 1. trascinare 2. dragare. ◆ **to drag** *vi.* trascinarsi || *to — on*, tirare in lungo.
to draggle *vt.* inzaccherare. ◆ **to draggle** *vi.* inzaccherarsi.
dragon *s.* drago || — -*fly*, libellula.
drain *s.* 1. canale, fogna 2. fuga.
to drain *vt.* prosciugare. ◆ **to drain** *vi.* 1. prosciugarsi 2. defluire.
drainage *s.* 1. fognatura 2. drenaggio.

draining *s.* 1. scolatura 2. drenaggio.
dram *s.* dramma (*unità di peso*).
drama *s.* dramma.
dramatic(al) *agg.* drammatico.
dramatics *s. pl.* produzioni drammatiche (*di dilettanti*).
dramatist *s.* drammaturgo.
to dramatize *vt.* e *vi.* drammatizzare.
dramaturgy *s.* drammaturgia.
drank V. *to drink*.
to drape *vt.* drappeggiare.
draper *s.* negoziante di tessuti.
drapery *s.* 1. tessuti 2. drappeggi.
drastic *agg.* drastico.
draught *s.* V. *draft*. ◆ **draughts** *s. pl.* gioco della dama (*sing.*).
draught-board *s.* scacchiera.
draw *s.* 1. tiro 2. estrazione 3. attrazione.
to draw (**drew, drawn**) *vt.* 1. tirare 2. attirare 3. disegnare 4. estrarre 5. (*comm.*) emettere || *to — up*, compilare. ◆ **to draw** (**drew, drawn**) *vi.* tirarsi || *to — on*, avvicinarsi; *to — in*, ritirarsi; *to — up*, fermarsi.
drawback *s.* ostacolo.
drawbridge *s.* ponte levatoio.
drawer *s.* 1. estrattore 2. disegnatore 3. cassetto.
drawers *s. pl.* mutande.
drawing *s.* 1. disegno 2. estrazione 3. attrazione || — -*pen*, tiralinee; — -*pin*, puntina da disegno.
drawing-room *s.* salotto.
to drawl *vt.* strascicare la voce.
drawn V. *to draw*.
dread *s.* spavento.
dreadful *agg.* terribile.
dreadnought *s.* 1. impavido 2. (*mar.*) corazzata.
dream *s.* sogno.
to dream (**dreamt, dreamt**) (*anche reg.*) *vt.* e *vi.* sognare.
dreamer *s.* sognatore.
dreamt V. *to dream*.
dreamless *agg.* senza sogni.
dreamy *agg.* 1. sognante 2. vago.
dreariness *s.* tristezza.
dreary *agg.* tetro, squallido.
dredge *s.* draga.
to dredge[1] *vt.* e *vi.* dragare.
to dredge[2] *vt.* cospargere, spolverizzare.
dredger[1] *s.* draga.
dredger[2] *s.* spolverizzatore.
dredging *s.* dragaggio.

dregs s. pl. 1. feccia (sing.) 2. sedimento (sing.).

to **drench** vt. inzuppare || to get drenched, inzupparsi.

dress s. abito, abbigliamento.

to **dress** vt. 1. vestire 2. bendare 3. condire, rifinire. ♦ to **dress** vi. vestirsi.

dressing s. 1. abbigliamento 2. medicazione 3. condimento || —-gown, vestaglia; — -table, toletta.

dressmaker s. sarta.

dressmaking s. sartoria.

drew V. to draw.

dribble s. 1. gocciolamento 2. (sport) palleggio.

to **dribble** vt. e vi. 1. stillare 2. (sport) palleggiare.

dribbling s. V. dribble.

drier s. essiccatore.

drift s. 1. spinta 2. deriva 3. raffica 4. (fig.) significato.

to **drift** vt. sospingere. ♦ to **drift** vi. andare alla deriva, essere trascinato.

drill s. 1. trapano, trivella 2. esercitazione.

to **drill** vt. 1. trapanare, trivellare 2. esercitare.

drilling s. 1. trapanazione, trivellazione 2. esercitazione || — machine, trapano.

drink s. 1. il bere 2. bevanda.

to **drink** (drank, drunk) vt. e vi. bere.

drinkable agg. bevibile.

drinker s. bevitore.

drinking s. il bere.

drip s. gocciolamento.

to **drip** vt. e vi. gocciolare.

dripping s. gocciolio.

drive s. 1. gita (in auto) 2. viale (carrozzabile) 3. spinta.

to **drive** (drove, driven) vt. 1. condurre 2. guidare 3. azionare || to — away, scacciare; to — in, conficcare. ♦ to **drive** (drove, driven) vi. andare (in veicolo) || to — off, partire (in veicolo); to — up, arrivare (in veicolo).

drive-in s. cinema, banca ecc. in cui si entra in auto.

driver s. conducente.

driving s 1. guida 2. comando.

drizzle s. pioggerella.

to **drizzle** vi. piovigginare.

drizzly agg. piovigginoso.

droll agg. buffo.

drollery s. 1. buffoneria 2. scherzo.

dromedary s. dromedario.

drone s. 1. fuco 2. ronzio.

to **drone** vt. e vi. ronzare.

to **droop** vt. abbassare. ♦ to **droop** vi. afflosciarsi, languire.

drooping agg. 1. pendente, abbassato 2. abbattuto.

drop s. 1. goccia 2. caduta 3. ribasso.

to **drop** vt. lasciar cadere. ♦ to **drop** vi. cadere || to — in, fare una visitina; to — away, scomparire.

dropper s. contagocce.

dropsical agg. idropico.

dropsy s. idropisia.

dross s. scoria.

drought s. siccità.

drove V. to drive.

to **drown** vt. 1. annegare 2. smorzare. ♦ to **drown** vi. annegare.

drowning s. annegamento.

to **drowse** vi. sonnecchiare, assopirsi.

drowsily avv. in modo sonnolento.

drowsiness s. sonnolenza.

drowsy agg. sonnolento.

to **drub** vt. percuotere, bastonare.

drudge s. sgobbone.

to **drudge** vi. sfacchinare.

drudgery s. lavoro faticoso.

drug s. 1. medicina 2. droga || —-store, farmacia (in cui si vendono articoli vari).

to **drug** vt. drogare.

druggist s. farmacista.

Druid s. druido.

drum s. 1. tamburo 2. timpano.

to **drum** vi. suonare il tamburo. ♦ to **drum** vt. (fig.) inculcare.

drummer s. tamburino.

drumming s. tambureggiamento.

drunk V. to drink. ♦ **drunk** agg. ubriaco.

drunkard s. ubriacone.

drunken agg. ubriaco.

drunkenness s. ubriachezza.

dry agg. asciutto, arido, secco || — cleaning, lavaggio a secco.

to **dry** vt. 1. seccare 2. asciugare. ♦ to **dry** vi. 1. seccarsi 2. asciugarsi || to — up, ammutolire.

dryad s. driade.

drying agg. essiccante. ♦ **drying** s. essiccamento.

dual agg. duplice.

dualism s. dualismo.

dualist s. dualista.

dualistic agg. dualistico.

duality s. dualità.
to dub[1] vt. creare cavaliere.
to dub[2] vt. (cine) doppiare.
dubbing s. doppiaggio.
dubious agg. 1. dubbio 2. dubbioso.
dubiousness s. dubbiosità.
dubitative agg. dubitativo.
ducal agg. ducale.
duchess s. duchessa.
duchy s. ducato.
duck[1] s. anitra.
duck[2] s. tela.
duck[3] s. tuffo.
to duck vt. 1. tuffare 2. piegare. ♦ **to duck** vi. 1. tuffarsi 2. piegarsi.
duckling s. anatroccolo.
duct s. condotto.
ductile agg. duttile.
ductility s. duttilità.
due agg. e s. dovuto || to be —, dover arrivare; to fall —, scadere.
duel s. duello.
to duel vi. duella.e.
duet s. duetto.
dug V. to dig.
duke s. duca.
dukedom s. ducato.
dull agg. 1. tardo, sciocco 2. sordo 3. triste 4. noioso 5. opaco.
to dull vt. 1. istupidire 2. intorpidire 3. smorzare. ♦ **to dull** vi. 1. istupidirsi 2. intorpidirsi 3. smorzarsi.
dullard s. imbecille.
dul(l)ness s. 1. lentezza 2. noia 3. opacità 4. ottusità.
dully avv. 1. ottusamente 2. lentamente 3. in modo noioso 4. debolmente.
duly avv. debitamente.
dumb agg. muto || — -show, pantomima.
to dumbfound vt. confondere.
dumbness s. mutismo.
dumb-waiter s. montavivande.
dummy agg. 1. muto 2. falso. ♦ **dummy** s. fantoccio.
dump s. 1. colpo sordo 2. ammasso.
dumping s. « dumping » (tipo di vendita concorrenziale sui mercati esteri).
dunce s. ignorante.
dune s. duna.
dung s. 1. sterco 2. letame.
dungarees s. pl. tuta (da lavoro) (sing.).
dungeon s. 1. torrione 2. prigione sotterranea.
dunghill s. letamaio.

to dunk vt. e vi. inzuppare.
duodenal agg. duodenale.
duodenum s. (pl. -na) duodeno.
dupe s. gonzo.
duplex agg. duplice.
duplicate agg. doppio. ♦ **duplicate** s. duplicato.
to duplicate vt. duplicare.
duplication s. 1. raddoppiamento 2. riproduzione.
duplicator s. copialettere.
duplicity s. doppiezza.
durability s. durata.
durable agg. durevole.
duralumin s. duralluminio.
duration s. durata.
duress s. 1. prigionia 2. coercizione.
during prep. durante.
durst V. dare.
dusk s. 1. oscurità 2. crepuscolo.
dusky agg. oscuro.
dust s. polvere || — -bin, pattumiera.
to dust vt. 1. impolverare 2. spolverare. ♦ **to dust** vi. impolverarsi.
duster s. 1. strofinaccio (per la polvere) 2. polverizzatore.
dustman s. spazzino.
dusty agg. polveroso.
Dutch agg. olandese.
Dutchman s. olandese.
dutiful agg. rispettoso.
duty s. 1. ubbidienza 2. dovere 3. tassa.
duumvirate s. duumvirato.
dwarf s. nano.
dwarfish agg. nano.
to dwell (dwelt, dwelt) vi. 1. abitare 2. fermarsi.
dweller s. abitatore.
dwelling s. abitazione.
dwelt V. to dwell.
dye s. tintura.
to dye vt. tingere. ♦ **to dye** vi. tingersi.
dyer s. tintore.
dyerworks s. pl. tintoria (sing.).
dying agg. morente.
dynamic(al) agg. dinamico.
dynamics s. dinamica.
dynamism s. dinamismo.
dynamite s. dinamite.
dynamiter s. dinamitardo.
dynamo s. dinamo.
dynamometer s. dinamometro.
dynast s. dinasta.
dynastic(al) agg. dinastico.
dynasty s. dinastia.
dyne s. dina.

dysenteric *agg.* dissenterico.
dysentery *s.* dissenteria.
dyspepsia *s.* dispepsia.
dyspeptic(al) *agg.* dispeptico.

E

E (*mus.*) mi.
each *agg.* ogni, ciascuno. ♦ **each** *pron.* ognuno, ciascuno || — *other*, l'un l'altro.
eager *agg.* **1.** ardente, appassionato **2.** avido, desideroso.
eagerly *avv.* **1.** ardentemente **2.** avidamente.
eagerness *s.* **1.** ardore **2.** impazienza, premura.
eagle *s.* aquila.
ear[1] orecchio || — *-ache* mal d'orecchi — *-drum;* timpano; — *-ring,* orecchino; — *-vax,* cerume; *within* — *-shot,* a portata di voce.
ear[2] *s.* spiga (*di grano*).
earl *s.* conte.
earldom *s.* **1.** titolo di conte **2.** contea.
early *agg.* **1.** primo, il principio, la prima parte (*di qualsiasi tempo*) **2.** mattiniero **3.** prematuro **4.** remoto || — *train,* treno del primo mattino.
early *avv.* **1.** presto, di buon'ora, per tempo **2.** al principio.
earmark *s.* **1.** marchio, caratteristica **2.** (*comm.*) contrassegno.
to earn *vt.* guadagnare, meritare.
earnest *agg.* **1.** serio, zelante **2.** ardente. ♦ **earnest** *s.* caparra, pegno.
earnestly *avv.* **1.** seriamente **2.** con ardore.
earnestness *s.* **1.** serietà **2.** ardore.
earnings *s. pl.* **1.** guadagni **2.** (*comm.*) utili.
earth *s.* **1.** terra, mondo **2.** terreno.
earth-bound *agg.* radicato, attaccato ai beni terreni.
earthen *agg.* di terra, di terracotta.
earthenware *s.* terraglia.
earthly *agg.* terrestre.
earthquake *s.* terremoto.
earthworm *s.* lombrico.
earthy *agg.* terroso, di terra.
ease *s.* **1.** tranquillità (*di spirito*),

benessere **2.** facilità, agevolezza **3.** sollievo.
to ease *vt.* e *vi.* **1.** alleviare, calmare **2.** liberare, alleggerire.
easeful *agg.* tranquillo.
easel *s.* cavalletto, telaio.
easily *avv.* **1.** facilmente **2.** comodamente.
easiness *s.* **1.** comodità, benessere **2.** facilità.
east *s.* est, oriente: *the Far East,* l'Estremo Oriente. ♦ **east** *avv.* ad est, verso est.
Easter *s.* Pasqua.
easterly *agg.* dell'est, dall'est, orientale.
eastern *agg.* dell'est, orientale.
eastward *agg.* verso est.
easy *agg.* **1.** facile **2.** agiato, modo **3.** piacevole.
easy *avv.* facilmente, comodamente.
easygoing *agg.* facilone, indolente.
to eat (ate, eaten) *vt.* e *vi.* **1.** mangiare **2.** rodere, corrodere.
eatable *agg.* mangiabile, commestibile.
eatables *s. pl.* vivande, viveri.
eaten V. *to eat.*
eater *s.* mangiatore.
eating *s.* il mangiare.
eaves *s. pl.* gronda, cornicione (*sing.*).
to eavesdrop *vi.* origliare.
ebb *s.* **1.** riflusso, l'abbassarsi della marea **2.** (*fig.*) decadenza || — *-tide,* bassa marea.
ebbing *agg.* **1.** defluente **2.** in declino.
ebonist *s.* ebanista.
ebonite *s.* ebanite.
ebony *s.* ebano.
ebullition *s.* ebollizione.
eccentric *agg.* e *s.* eccentrico (*anche fig.*).
eccentricity *s.* eccentricità.
ecclesiastic *agg.* e *s.* ecclesiastico.
ecclesiastical *agg.* ecclesiastico.
echelon *s.* scaglione.
echinoderm *s.* echinoderma.
echo *s.* eco.
to echo *vt.* e *vi.* **1.** far eco (a) **2.** echeggiare.
eclectic *agg.* e *s.* eclettico.
eclecticism *s.* eclettismo.
eclipse *s.* eclissi.
to eclipse *vt.* eclissare.
ecliptic *agg.* eclittico.
eclogue *s.* egloga.
ecology *s.* ecologia.

economic *agg.* economico.
economical *agg.* economico.
economics *s.* scienze economiche.
economist *s.* economista.
to economize *vt.* e *vi.* economizzare.
economy *s.* economia.
ecstasy *s.* estasi.
ecstatic *agg.* estatico.
ecstatically *avv.* estaticamente.
ecumenic(al) *agg.* ecumenico.
eczema *s.* eczema.
eddy *s.* **1.** turbine d'aria, vortice **2.** gorgo, risucchio.
edge *s.* **1.** orlo, margine **2.** ciglio, sponda **3.** taglio (*di lama*) **4.** spigolo.
to edge *vt.* e *vi.* **1.** bordare, fare un bordo **2.** affilare, arrotare, aguzzare (*anche fig.*).
edged *agg.* affilato, tagliente ‖ *double —*, a doppio taglio (*anche fig.*).
edgeless *agg.* **1.** senza bordo **2.** smussato, che non taglia.
edging *s.* orlatura, fettuccia.
edible *agg.* mangereccio.
edibles *s. pl.* commestibili.
edict *s.* editto.
edifice *s.* edificio (*anche fig.*).
edifying *agg.* edificante.
to edit *vt.* **1.** pubblicare, curare (*un libro*) **2.** redigere **3.** (*cine*) montare.
editing *s.* **1.** redazione, commento (*di un testo*) **2.** direzione (*di un giornale, ecc.*).
edition *s.* edizione.
editor *s.* **1.** commentatore, curatore (*di un testo*) **2.** direttore, redattore (*di un giornale*).
editorial *s.* editoriale, articolo di fondo. ♦ **editorial** *agg.* editoriale.
editorship *s.* direzione, redazione (*di giornali*).
to educate *vt.* **1.** istruire, educare **2.** affinare, esercitare.
educated *agg.* **1.** istruito, colto **2.** addestrato (*di animali*).
education *s.* **1.** cultura, educazione **2.** istruzione, insegnamento.
educational *agg.* educativo.
educative *agg.* istruttivo.
educator *s.* educatore.
to educe *vt.* estrarre, sviluppare.
educible *agg.* che si può estrarre.
to edulcorate *vt.* dolcificare.
eel *s.* anguilla.
eerie, eery *agg.* irreale, sovrannaturale.

to efface *vt.* cancellare, distruggere.
effect *s.* **1.** effetto, risultato **2.** impressione. ♦ **effects** *s. pl.* effetti personali.
to effect *vt.* effettuare, eseguire.
effective *agg.* **1.** efficace **2.** effettivo.
effectiveness *s.* efficacia.
effectual *agg.* efficace.
effectuality *s.* efficacia, validità.
effectuation *s.* effettuazione.
effeminacy *s.* effeminatezza.
effeminate *agg.* effeminato.
effervescence *s.* **1.** effervescenza **2.** (*fig.*) eccitamento.
effete *agg.* logoro, esaurito.
efficacious *agg.* efficace.
efficaciousness *s.* **1.** efficacia **2.** rendimento (*di una macchina*).
efficiency *s.* efficienza, rendimento.
efficient *agg.* **1.** efficiente, di alto rendimento **2.** abile, capace.
effigy *s.* effigie.
to effloresce *vi.* fiorire, germogliare.
effluent *agg.* defluente.
effort *s.* sforzo, fatica.
effortless *agg.* senza sforzo, facile.
effrontery *s.* sfrontatezza.
effulgence *s.* splendore.
effusion *s.* effusione, esuberanza.
effusive *agg.* espansivo, esuberante.
egg *s.* uovo ‖ *boiled —*, uovo alla coque; *hard-boiled —*, uovo sodo.
to egg *vt. to — on so.*, istigare, incitare qu.
egocentric *agg.* egocentrico.
egocentrism *s.* egocentrismo.
egoism *s.* egoismo.
egoist *s.* egoista.
egoistic(al) *agg.* egoistico.
egotism *s.* egotismo.
egotist *s.* egotista.
egregious *agg.* insigne, eminente.
egress *s.* uscita.
Egyptian *agg.* e *s.* egiziano.
eider-down *s.* piumino (*da letto*).
eight *agg.* otto.
eighteen *agg.* diciotto.
eighteenth *agg.* diciottesimo.
eighth *agg.* ottavo.
eightieth *agg.* ottantesimo.
eighty *agg.* ottanta.
either *agg.* **1.** l'uno o l'altro **2.** ciascuno dei due, tutti e due. ♦ **either** *avv.* anche, pure. ♦ **either** *avv.* (*in frasi neg.*) neanche, neppure. ♦ **either** *cong.* (*seguito da or*) o, oppure.
to ejaculate *vt.* **1.** eiaculare **2.** e-

sclamare.
ejaculation s. 1. eiaculazione 2. esclamazione.
to **eject** vt. gettar fuori.
ejection s. 1. espulsione 2. (fig.) destituzione.
ejector s. espulsore.
elaborate agg. elaborato, accurato.
to **elaborate** vt. e vi. elaborare.
elaboration s. elaborazione.
to **elapse** vi. trascorrere, passare (del tempo).
elastic agg. elastico (anche fig.).
elasticity s. elasticità.
to **elate** vt. inebriare, esaltare.
elbow s. gomito.
to **elbow** vt. e vi. spingere con il gomito, andare avanti a gomitate.
elder agg. (comp. di old) maggiore, più vecchio (tra due persone). ♦ **elder** s. maggiore, più vecchio (tra due).
elderly agg. attempato.
eldest agg. (superl. di old) maggiore (tra fratelli), primogenito.
elect agg. eletto, scelto.
to **elect** vt. eleggere.
election s. 1. elezione 2. scelta.
elective agg. 1. elettivo 2. elettorale.
elector s. elettore.
electoral agg. elettorale.
electorate s. elettorato.
electric(al) agg. elettrico.
electrician s. elettricista.
electricity s. elettricità.
to **electrify** vt. 1. elettrificare 2. elettrizzare.
electrization s. elettrizzazione.
electrocardiogram s. elettrocardiogramma.
to **electrocute** vt. fulminare mediante elettricità.
electrocution s. elettroesecuzione.
electrode s. elettrodo.
electrodynamics s. elettrodinamica.
electrolysis s. elettrolisi.
electro-magnet s. elettromagnete.
electromagnetic agg. elettromagnetico.
electron s. elettrone.
electronic agg. elettronico.
electronics s. elettronica.
electrostatics s. elettrostatica.
elegance s. eleganza.
elegant agg. elegante, raffinato.
elegiac agg. elegiaco.
elegy s. elegia.

element s. 1. elemento 2. principio costitutivo.
elemental agg. 1. dei quattro elementi 2. elementare 3. fondamentale.
elementary agg. elementare.
elephant s. elefante.
elephantiasis s. elefantiasi.
elephantine agg. elefantesco.
to **elevate** vt. innalzare, elevare (anche fig.).
elevated agg. 1. elevato 2. sopraelevato.
elevation s. 1. elevazione 2. collina, luogo alto.
elevator s. ascensore, montacarichi.
eleven agg. undici.
elevenses s. (fam.) spuntino a metà mattina.
eleventh agg. undicesimo.
elf s. (pl. elves) elfo, folletto.
elfish agg. 1. incantato 2. vivace.
to **elicit** vt. estrarre, strappare.
eligibility s. eleggibilità.
eligible agg. eleggibile.
to **eliminate** vt. eliminare.
elimination s. eliminazione.
elision s. elisione.
elixir s. elisir.
elk s. alce.
ellipse s. ellisse.
ellipsis s. ellissi.
elliptic(al) agg. ellittico.
elm s. olmo.
elocution s. 1. elocuzione 2. dizione.
to **elope** vi. fuggire (con un amante).
elopement s. fuga (con un amante).
eloquence s. eloquenza.
eloquent agg. eloquente (anche fig.).
else avv. (dopo avv. e pron. int., indef.) altro.
elsewhere avv. altrove.
to **elude** vt. eludere, schivare.
elusive agg. 1. elusivo, ambiguo 2. sfuggevole.
elytron s. (pl. elytra) elitra.
Elzevir agg. e s. elzeviro.
to **emaciate** vt. far deperire, far dimagrire.
emaciated agg. emaciato.
to **emanate** vi. emanare.
emanation s. emanazione.
to **emancipate** vt. emancipare.
emancipation s. emancipazione.
to **embalm** vt. 1. imbalsamare 2. profumare.
embalmer s. imbalsamatore.

embankment s. **1.** argine, diga **2.** alzaia.

embarcation s. imbarco.

embargo s. embargo, fermo.

to embark vt. imbarcare (truppe, merci). ♦ **to embark** vi. imbarcarsi.

embarkation s. imbarco.

to embarrass vt. mettere in imbarazzo.

embarrassing agg. imbarazzante.

embarrassment s. **1.** imbarazzo **2.** difficoltà.

embassy s. ambasciata.

to embattle vt. disporre in ordine di battaglia, fortificare.

to embed vt. incassare, conficcare.

to embellish vt. abbellire, ornare.

embellishment s. abbellimento, ornamento.

ember s. tizzone. ♦ **embers** s. pl. brace (sing.).

embezzler s. malversatore.

to embitter vt. **1.** rendere amaro **2.** (fig.) amareggiare.

embitterment s. amarezza, inasprimento.

to emblazon vt. **1.** decorare **2.** celebrare.

emblem s. emblema, simbolo (fig.).

emblematic(al) agg. emblematico.

embodiment s. **1.** incarnazione **2.** incorporamento.

to embody vt. **1.** incarnare **2.** personificare **3.** incorporare.

to embolden vt. incoraggiare.

embolism s. embolia.

embolus s. (pl. -li) embolo.

to emboss vt. **1.** scolpire **2.** stampare in rilievo.

embossed agg. **1.** sbalzato **2.** fatto in rilievo.

embrace s. abbraccio, amplesso.

to embrace vt. abbracciare (anche fig.). ♦ **to embrace** vi. abbracciarsi.

embrasure s. **1.** vano (di porta, finestra) **2.** feritoia.

to embroider vt. ricamare.

embroiderer s. ricamatore.

embroidery s. ricamo.

to embroil vt. coinvolgere in una disputa.

embryo s. embrione.

embryonic agg. embrionale (anche fig.).

to emend vt. emendare.

emendation s. emendamento.

emerald s. smeraldo.

to emerge vi. **1.** emergere, affiorare **2.** (fig.) risultare.

emergency s. emergenza, caso imprevisto || — -door, uscita di sicurezza; — means, mezzi di fortuna.

emersion s. emersione.

emery s. smeriglio || — -paper, carta smerigliata.

emetic agg. e s. emetico.

emigrant agg. e s. emigrante.

to emigrate vi. emigrare.

emigration s. emigrazione.

eminence s. **1.** luogo, parte eminente **2.** (anat.) protuberanza **3.** (fig.) eminenza, eccellenza.

eminent agg. eminente (anche fig.).

eminently avv. eminentemente.

emir s. emiro.

emissary s. emissario, agente segreto.

emission s. emissione.

to emit vt. **1.** emettere **2.** esalare.

emollient agg. e s. emolliente.

emolument s. remunerazione, salario.

emotion s. emozione, turbamento.

emotional agg. **1.** emotivo, impressionabile **2.** commovente.

emotionalism s. emotività.

emotionally avv. con emozione.

emotive agg. **1.** commovente **2.** emotivo.

emperor s. imperatore.

emphasis s. **1.** accentuazione, rilievo **2.** enfasi.

to emphasize vt. accentuare.

emphatic agg. **1.** accentuato **2.** enfatico.

emphysema s. enfisema.

emphyteusis s. enfiteusi.

empire s. impero.

empiric s. empirico.

empirical agg. empirico.

empiricism s. empirismo.

emplacement s. **1.** collocazione **2.** (mil.) piazzuola.

employ s. impiego: out of —, senza impiego.

to employ vt. **1.** impiegare, adoperare **2.** assumere.

employee s. impiegato.

employer s. datore di lavoro.

employment s. impiego, occupazione.

to empoison vt. avvelenare.

emporium s. **1.** centro commerciale **2.** emporio.

to empower vt. dare pieni poteri a.

emptiness s. **1.** vuoto **2.** vanità.
empty agg. **1.** vuoto **2.** vano **3.** vacante || — -handed, a mani vuote.
to **empty** vt. vuotare. ◆ to **empty** vi. vuotarsi.
to **emulate** vt. emulare.
emulation s. emulazione.
emulator s. emulatore.
emulous agg. emulo.
to **emulsify** vt. emulsionare.
emulsion s. emulsione.
emulsive agg. emulsivo.
to **enable** vt. mettere in grado.
to **enact** vt. decretare, emanare (una legge).
enactment s. **1.** promulgazione **2.** legge.
enamel s. smalto.
to **enamel** vt. smaltare.
to **encamp** vi. accamparsi.
encaustic agg. encaustico.
encephalic agg. encefalico.
encephalitis s. encefalite.
to **enchant** vt. incantare, affascinare.
enchanter s. incantatore, mago.
enchanting agg. incantevole.
enchantment s. incanto, incantesimo.
enchantress s. incantatrice.
to **encircle** vt. circondare, cingere.
enclitic agg. enclitico.
to **enclose** vt. **1.** racchiudere, cingere **2.** accludere.
enclosed agg. **1.** racchiuso, circondato **2.** accluso.
enclosure s. **1.** recinto, staccionata **2.** allegato.
encomiast s. encomiasta.
to **encompass** vt. circondare (anche fig.).
encore avv. (teat.) bis.
to **encore** vt. chiedere il bis.
encounter s. scontro.
to **encourage** vt. incoraggiare, animare.
encouragement s. incoraggiamento.
encouraging agg. incoraggiante.
to **encroach** vt. **1.** usurpare, invadere **2.** (giur.) ledere.
to **encrust** vt. incrostare.
to **encumber** vt. **1.** ingombrare, imbarazzare **2.** ostruire.
encumbrance s. ingombro, impedimento.
encyclic(al) agg. enciclico. ◆ **encyclic(al)** s. enciclica.
encyclop(a)edia s. enciclopedia.
encyclop(a)edic(al) agg. enciclo-

pedico.
end s. **1.** estremità, fine, termine **2.** scopo, mira **3.** morte.
to **end** vt. e vi. finire, concludere.
to **endanger** vt. mettere in pericolo, compromettere.
to **endear** vt. affezionare, rendere caro.
endearing agg. affettuoso, tenero.
endearment s. tenerezza. ◆ **endearments** s. pl. blandizie.
to **endeavo(u)r** vi. sforzarsi. ◆ to **endeavo(u)r** vt. tentare.
endemic agg. endemico.
ending agg. finale, ultimo. ◆ **ending** s. fine, conclusione.
endless agg. senza fine, eterno, continuo.
endocarditis s. endocardite.
endocardium s. endocardio.
endocarp s. endocarpo.
endocrine agg. endocrino.
endocrinology s. endocrinologia.
endogeny s. endogenesi.
to **endorse** vt. (comm.) girare, vistare.
endorsee s. (comm.) giratario.
endorsement s. (comm.) girata.
endorser s. (comm.) girante.
to **endow** vt. **1.** dotare **2.** fare una donazione.
endowment s. **1.** costituzione di dote, donazione **2.** (fig.) talento.
endurance s. **1.** resistenza, sopportazione **2.** durata.
to **endure** vt. tollerare, sopportare. ◆ to **endure** vi. resistere, durare.
enduring agg. **1.** tollerante, paziente **2.** durevole.
enema s. clistere.
enemy agg. e s. nemico.
energetic(al) agg. **1.** energico **2.** energetico.
to **energize** vt. infondere energia.
energumen s. energumeno.
energy s. energia, forza.
to **enervate** vt. snervare, indebolire.
enervation s. indebolimento.
to **enfeeble** vt. indebolire.
to **enfold** vt. **1.** avvolgere **2.** cingere.
to **enforce** vt. **1.** imporre, far rispettare **2.** mettere in vigore (una legge).
to **enframe** vt. incorniciare.
to **enfranchise** vt. affrancare, liberare.
enfranchisement s. affrancamento,

liberazione.

to **engage** *vt.* **1.** impegnare **2.** ingaggiare **3.** attrarre (*l'attenzione*). ♦ to **engage** *vi.* impegnarsi ‖ *to* — *in conversation*, prendere parte alla conversazione.

engaged *agg.* **1.** impegnato **2.** fidanzato **3.** occupato, riservato.

engagement *s.* **1.** impegno **2.** fidanzamento **3.** assunzione, impiego.

engaging *agg.* attraente, avvincente.

engagingly *avv.* in modo attraente.

to **engender** *vt.* produrre, causare.

engine *s.* **1.** macchina, motore **2.** (*ferr.*) locomotrice ‖ *fire- —*, autopompa.

engineer *s.* **1.** ingegnere **2.** tecnico.

engineering *s.* **1.** ingegneria **2.** costruzione meccanica.

English *agg.* inglese. ♦ **English** *s.* lingua inglese.

Englishman *s.* (*uomo*) inglese.

Englishwoman *s.* (*donna*) inglese.

to **engrave** *vt.* **1.** intagliare, incidere **2.** (*fig.*) imprimere.

engraver *s.* incisore.

engraving *s.* arte dell'incisione ‖ *wood- —*, xilografia.

to **engross** *vt.* **1.** copiare (*un atto legale*), redigere (*un documento*) **2.** assorbire (*l'attenzione*).

engrossing *s.* copiatura (*di documento*).

to **enhance** *vt.* accrescere.

enigma *s.* enigma.

enigmatic(al) *agg.* enigmatico.

to **enjoy** *vt.* **1.** godere, gioire **2.** gustare, provar piacere di ‖ *to* — *oneself*, divertirsi.

enjoyable *agg.* piacevole, gradevole.

enjoyably *avv.* piacevolmente.

enjoyment *s.* godimento, piacere.

to **enkindle** *vt.* infiammare, eccitare. ♦ to **enkindle** *vi.* infiammarsi, eccitarsi.

to **enlarge** *vt.* **1.** allargare, ampliare **2.** (*foto*) ingrandire. ♦ to **enlarge** *vi.* allargarsi, ampliarsi.

enlargement *s.* **1.** allargamento **2.** (*foto*) ingrandimento.

enlarger *s.* (*foto*) ingranditore.

to **enlighten** *vt.* rischiarare, illuminare (*anche fig.*).

enlightenment *s.* **1.** spiegazione, schiarimento **2.** (*lett.*) l'illuminismo.

to **enlist** *vt.* arruolare. ♦ to **enlist** *vi.* arruolarsi.

enlistment *s.* arruolamento, in-

gaggio.

to **enliven** *vt.* rianimare, ravvivare.

to **enmesh** *vt.* impegolare, irretire.

enmity *s.* ostilità, inimicizia.

to **ennoble** *vt.* nobilitare.

enormity *s.* mostruosità.

enormous *agg.* enorme, immenso.

enough *avv.* abbastanza, sufficientemente. ♦ **enough** *agg.* sufficiente. ♦ **enough** *s.* il necessario, quanto basta.

to **enrage** *vt.* far arrabbiare, esasperare.

to **enrapture** *vt.* rapire, estasiare.

to **enrich** *vt.* **1.** arricchire (*anche fig.*) **2.** abbellire.

enrichment *s.* **1.** arricchimento **2.** abbellimento.

to **enrol** *vt.* **1.** arruolare, ingaggiare **2.** iscrivere.

enrolment *s.* **1.** arruolamento, iscrizione **2.** (*giur.*) registrazione.

ensign *s.* **1.** bandiera, stendardo **2.** portabandiera.

to **enslave** *vt.* assoggettare, far schiavo (*anche fig.*).

enslavement *s.* asservimento, schiavitù (*anche fig.*).

to **ensnare** *vt.* adescare, intrappolare (*anche fig.*).

to **ensue** *vt.* e *vi.* seguire.

to **ensure** *vt.* assicurare, garantire.

entail *s.* eredità, ordine di successione (*vincolato*).

to **entangle** *vt.* impigliare, intralciare (*anche fig.*).

entanglement *s.* groviglio, impiccio.

to **enter** *vt.* e *vi.* **1.** entrare, penetrare **2.** iscrivere **3.** (*comm.*) registrare ‖ *to* — *upon*, intraprendere (*una carriera*).

enteric *agg.* enterico.

enteritis *s.* enterite.

enterocolitis *s.* enterocolite.

enterogastritis *s.* gastroenterite.

enterprise *s.* **1.** impresa **2.** iniziativa, intraprendenza.

enterprising *agg.* intraprendente.

to **entertain** *vt.* **1.** ricevere, ospitare **2.** intrattenere, divertire **3.** carezzare (*un'idea*), nutrire (*dubbi, speranze*).

entertainer *s.* **1.** anfitrione, ospite **2.** comico.

entertaining *agg.* divertente.

entertainment *s.* **1.** trattenimento, spettacolo **2.** ricevimento, festa **3.** divertimento.

to **enthral** vt. (fig.) affascinare, incantare.

enthralment s. incanto, malìa.

to **enthrone** vt. mettere sul trono.

enthronement s. investitura, intronizzazione.

enthusiasm s. entusiasmo.

enthusiast s. entusiasta.

enthusiastic(al) agg. entusiastico.

enthusiastically avv. entusiasticamente.

to **entice** vt. sedurre, allettare.

enticement s. 1. attrattiva 2. adescamento, istigazione.

enticing agg. seducente, attraente.

entire agg. intero, completo.

entirely avv. interamente, completamente.

to **entitle** vt. 1. intitolare (un libro) 2. dare un titolo.

entity s. entità, esistenza.

entomological agg. entomologico.

entomologist s. entomologo.

entomology s. entomologia.

entrails s. pl. intestino (sing.), visceri.

entrance s. 1. ingresso, entrata 2. ammissione || — hall, vestibolo.

to **entrap** vt. prendere in trappola, truffare.

to **entreat** vt. pregare, supplicare.

entreaty s. supplica, istanza.

to **entrench** vt. e vi. trincerare, fortificare (anche fig.) || to — upon, usurpare.

entrepreneur s. 1. (teat.) impresario 2. imprenditore.

to **entrust** vt. affidare, commettere.

entry s. 1. entrata 2. ingresso, passaggio 3. (comm.) registrazione.

to **entwine** vt. attorcigliare, intrecciare. ♦ to **entwine** vi. arrotolarsi.

to **enucleate** vt. spiegare, chiarire.

enucleation s. spiegazione, chiarimento.

to **enumerate** vt. enumerare.

enumeration s. enumerazione.

enumerator s. numeratore.

to **enunciate** vt. enunciare, proclamare.

enunciation s. enunciazione.

to **envelop** vt. avvolgere, avviluppare.

envelope s. busta, involucro.

envelopment s. avvolgimento.

enviable agg. invidiabile.

envious agg. invidioso.

to **environ** vt. circondare, accerchiare.

environment s. ambiente.

environs s. pl. dintorni.

envy s. invidia.

to **envy** vt. invidiare.

enzyme s. enzima.

epaulet(te) s. (mil.) spallina.

ephebe s. efebo.

ephemeral agg. effimero.

ephemeris s. (pl. -ides) effemeride.

epic agg. epico. ♦ **epic** s. poema epico.

epically avv. epicamente.

epicentre s. epicentro.

epicurean agg. e s. epicureo.

epidemic(al) agg. epidemico.

epidemically avv. epidemicamente.

epidermal agg. epidermico.

epidermis s. epidermide.

epigastric agg. epigastrico.

epigram s. epigramma.

epigrammatic agg. epigrammatico.

epigrammatist s. epigrammista.

epigraph s. epigrafe.

epigraphy s. epigrafia.

epilepsy s. epilessia.

epileptic agg. epilettico.

epilogue s. epilogo.

Epiphany s. Epifania.

episcopacy s. episcopato.

episcopal agg. episcopale.

episcopate s. episcopato.

episode s. episodio.

episodic(al) agg. episodico.

epistle s. epistola.

epistolary agg. epistolare.

epitaph s. epitaffio.

epithalamium s. epitalamio.

epithet s. epiteto.

epitome s. epitome, riassunto.

epoch s. epoca, età.

epopee s. epopea.

equability s. uguaglianza, uniformità.

equal agg. uguale, simile, stesso. ♦ **equal** s. pari (di rango).

equality s. uguaglianza, parità.

equalization s. eguagliamento.

to **equalize** vt. e vi. uguagliare.

equally avv. ugualmente, imparzialmente.

equanimity s. equanimità.

equanimous agg. equanime.

equation s. 1. equazione 2. pareggio.

equator s. equatore.

equatorial agg. equatoriale.

equestrian agg. equestre.

equidistant agg. equidistante.

equilateral agg. equilatero.

equine *agg.* equino.

equinoctial *agg.* equinoziale.

equinox *s.* equinozio.

to equip *vt.* **1.** equipaggiare **2.** fornire, arredare.

equipment *s.* **1.** equipaggiamento **2.** attrezzatura.

equipoise *s.* equilibrio.

equipollent *agg.* equipollente.

equitation *s.* equitazione.

equity *s.* giustizia, equità.

equivalence *s.* equivalenza.

equivalent *agg.* e *s.* equivalente.

equivocal *agg.* **1.** ambiguo, equivoco **2.** sospetto, losco.

equivocally *avv.* **1.** ambiguamente **2.** in modo losco.

to equivocate *vi.* equivocare, giocare sull'equivoco.

equivocation *s.* **1.** l'equivocare **2.** equivoco.

equivoke *s.* **1.** gioco di parole **2.** ambiguità (*d'espressione*).

era *s.* era, epoca.

eradicable *agg.* estirpabile.

to eradicate *vt.* sradicare, estirpare.

to erase *vt.* raschiare, cancellare.

eraser *s.* **1.** raschietto **2.** gomma per cancellare.

erasure *s.* raschiatura, cancellatura.

erect *agg.* diritto, ritto.

to erect *vt.* **1.** raddrizzare **2.** costruire.

erection *s.* **1.** raddrizzamento **2.** erezione.

eremite *s.* eremita.

ermine *s.* ermellino.

to erode *vt.* corrodere, logorare.

erosion *s.* erosione.

erosive *agg.* corrosivo.

erotic *agg.* erotico.

eroticism *s.* erotismo.

to err *vi.* **1.** sbagliare **2.** errare, vagabondare.

errand *s.* commissione || — *-boy*, fattorino.

errant *agg.* **1.** errante **2.** che sbaglia.

erratic *agg.* **1.** erratico **2.** irregolare.

erratically *avv.* **1.** irregolarmente **2.** eccentricamente.

erring *agg.* **1.** errante **2.** che sbaglia.

erroneous *agg.* erroneo.

error *s.* **1.** errore **2.** torto.

erudite *agg.* erudito.

erudition *s.* erudizione.

to erupt *vi.* eruttare.

eruption *s.* eruzione.

eruptive *agg.* eruttivo.

escalade *s.* scalata.

escalator *s.* scala mobile.

escape *s.* **1.** fuga, evasione **2.** scampo, salvezza.

to escape *vt.* e *vi.* **1.** fuggire, evadere **2.** scampare.

escapism *s.* evasione dalla realtà.

escapist *s.* chi cerca di evadere dalla realtà.

eschatology *s.* escatologia.

to eschew *vt.* evitare, astenersi da.

escort *s.* scorta.

to escort *vt.* scortare, accompagnare.

Eskimo *s.* esquimese.

esoteric *agg.* esoterico.

especial *agg.* speciale.

especially *avv.* specialmente.

espionage *s.* spionaggio.

esplanade *s.* spianata.

to espy *vt.* scorgere, avvistare.

esquire *s.* (*titolo di cortesia*) *John Smith Esq.*, egregio sig. John Smith.

essay *s.* **1.** esperimento, prova **2.** (*lett.*) saggio.

to essay *vt.* provare, mettere alla prova.

essayist *s.* saggista.

essence *s.* essenza.

essential *agg.* essenziale.

to establish *vt.* **1.** affermare (*un diritto ecc.*) **2.** instaurare **3.** (*comm.*) fondare, costituire.

established *agg.* **1.** stabilito, affermato **2.** fondato.

establishment *s.* **1.** affermazione, conferma **2.** instaurazione **3.** stabilimento, azienda.

estate *s.* **1.** terra, proprietà (*terriera*) **2.** stato, gruppo politico **3.** condizione, classe sociale || — *agent*, mediatore.

esteem *s.* stima, considerazione.

to esteem *vt.* **1.** stimare, tenere in gran conto **2.** considerare.

estimable *agg.* degno di stima.

estimate *s.* **1.** stima, giudizio **2.** (*comm.*) preventivo.

to estimate *vt.* **1.** stimare, valutare **2.** preventivare.

estimator *s.* perito, stimatore.

to estrange *vt.* alienare, alienarsi, allontanare.

estrangement *s.* alienazione, allontanamento.

estuary *s.* estuario.

etching *s.* acquaforte.

eternal *agg.* eterno.

eternity *s.* eternità.

ether *s.* etere.

ethereal *agg.* etereo.

ethic(al) *agg.* etico.

ethics *s.* etica.

Ethiopian *agg.* etiopico. ♦ **Ethiopian** *s.* etiope.

Ethiopic *agg.* etiopico.

ethnic(al) *agg.* etnico.

ethnography *s.* etnografia.

ethnologist *s.* etnologo.

ethnology *s.* etnologia.

ethylene *s.* etilene.

ethylic *agg.* etilico.

etiquette *s.* 1. etichetta 2. cerimoniale.

Etrurian, Etruscan *agg.* e *s.* etrusco.

etymologic(al) *agg.* etimologico.

etymology *s.* etimologia.

eucalyptus *s.* eucalipto.

Eucharist *s.* Eucaristia.

eucharistic(al) *agg.* eucaristico.

eugenics *s.* eugenetica.

eulogist *s.* elogiatore.

to eulogize *vt.* elogiare.

eulogy *s.* elogio, panegirico.

eunuch *s.* eunuco.

euphemism *s.* eufemismo.

euphonic *agg.* eufonico.

euphony *s.* eufonia.

euphoria *s.* euforia.

euphuism *s.* eufuismo.

euphuist *s.* affettato.

euphuistic *agg.* affettato, ricercato (*di stile*).

European *agg.* e *s.* europeo.

Eurovision *s.* eurovisione.

euthanasia *s.* eutanasia.

to evacuate *vt.* e *vi.* evacuare, sfollare.

evacuation *s.* evacuazione, sfollamento.

to evade *vt.* evitare, schivare, eludere.

to evaluate *vt.* valutare.

evaluation *s.* valutazione.

evanescent *agg.* evanescente.

evangelic(al) *agg.* evangelico.

evangelist *s.* evangelista.

evangelistic *agg.* di un evangelista, missionario.

evangelization *s.* evangelizzazione.

to evangelize *vt.* evangelizzare.

to evaporate *vi.* evaporare. ♦ **to evaporate** *vt.* far evaporare.

evaporation *s.* evaporazione.

evasion *s.* 1. evasione, scappatoia 2. scusa, pretesto.

evasive *agg.* evasivo.

evasively *avv.* evasivamente.

evasiveness *s.* ambiguità.

eve *s.* vigilia.

even *agg.* 1. uguale, uniforme, costante, regolare 2. pari, equo. ♦ **even** *avv.* 1. ancora (*con comp.*) 2. persino, anche || — *as*, nel momento in cui.

evening *s.* 1. sera, serata 2. (*fig.*) declino, fine.

evenly *avv.* in modo uguale, uniformemente.

evensong *s.* vespro.

event *s.* 1. caso, eventualità 2. avvenimento 3. (*sport*) prova.

eventful *agg.* ricco di avvenimenti, movimentato.

eventual *agg.* finale, definitivo.

eventuality *s.* eventualità.

eventually *avv.* alla fine.

ever *avv.* 1. mai 2. sempre.

evergreen *s.* sempreverde.

everlasting *agg.* eterno.

everliving *agg.* immortale.

evermore *avv.* perpetuamente.

every *agg.* ogni, ciascuno, tutti.

everybody *pron. indef.* ognuno, tutti.

everyday *agg.* di tutti i giorni, quotidiano.

everyone *pron. indef.* V. *everybody*.

everything *pron. indef.* ogni cosa, tutto.

everywhere *avv.* ovunque.

to evict *vt.* sfrattare, espellere.

eviction *s.* sfratto.

evidence *s.* 1. evidenza 2. prova.

to evidence *vt.* provare, dimostrare.

evident *agg.* evidente, chiaro.

evil *agg.* cattivo, malvagio || — *-eye*, malocchio. ♦ **evil** *s.* male, peccato.

to evirate *vt.* evirare.

to evocate *vt.* evocare.

evocation *s.* evocazione.

evocative *agg.* evocatore.

to evoke *vt.* evocare.

evolution *s.* evoluzione.

evolutional *agg.* evolutivo.

evolutionism *s.* evoluzionismo.

to evolve *vt.* evolvere. ♦ **to evolve** *vi.* evolversi.

evolvement *s.* evoluzione, sviluppo.

ewe *s.* pecora (*femmina*).

to exacerbate *vt.* esacerbare, inasprire.

exacerbation *s.* esacerbazione, inasprimento.

exact *agg.* 1. esatto, giusto 2. puntuale, rigoroso.

to **exact** *vt.* **1.** esigere **2.** rendere necessario.

exacting *agg.* **1.** esigente **2.** impegnativo.

exaction *s.* esazione, estorsione.

exactitude *s.* esattezza, precisione.

exactly *avv.* esattamente.

exactness *s.* esattezza, precisione.

to **exaggerate** *vt.* esagerare, ingrandire.

exaggeration *s.* esagerazione.

to **exalt** *vt.* **1.** innalzare, elevare **2.** esaltare, lodare.

exaltation *s.* **1.** innalzamento **2.** esaltazione.

exalted *agg.* **1.** elevato (*di grado ecc.*) **2.** esaltato, eccitato.

examination *s.* **1.** esame, ispezione **2.** esame scolastico **3.** (*giur.*) interrogatorio.

to **examine** *vt.* **1.** verificare, ispezionare **2.** esaminare **3.** (*giur.*) istruire un processo.

examiner *s.* esaminatore.

example *s.* esempio.

to **exasperate** *vt.* **1.** peggiorare, aggravare **2.** esasperare.

exasperatingly *avv.* in modo esasperante.

exasperation *s.* esasperazione.

to **excavate** *vt.* scavare, fare scavi (*archeologici*).

excavation *s.* **1.** scavo **2.** fossa, buca.

excavator *s.* **1.** operaio scavatore **2.** (*mecc.*) escavatore.

to **exceed** *vt.* e *vi.* **1.** eccedere, superare (*i limiti*) **2.** essere superiore.

exceeding *agg.* esagerato.

exceedingly *avv.* eccessivamente, troppo.

to **excel** *vt.* superare. ♦ to **excel** *vi.* primeggiare.

excellence *s.* **1.** eccellenza **2.** pregio, superiorità.

Excellency *s.* (*titolo*) Eccellenza.

excellent *agg.* eccellente.

except *prep.* eccetto, tranne.

to **except** *vt.* eccettuare, escludere. ♦ to **except** *vi.* obiettare, sollevare eccezioni.

excepting *prep.* eccetto, tranne.

exception *s.* eccezione.

exceptional *agg.* eccezionale, straordinario.

excerpt *s.* brano scelto.

excess *s.* **1.** eccesso, intemperanza **2.** supplemento.

exchange *s.* **1.** scambio **2.** (*finanza*)

excessive *agg.* eccessivo, smoderato, cambio **3.** borsa, mercato ‖ *bill of* —, cambiale; — -*broker*, agente di cambio.

to **exchange** *vt.* cambiare, scambiare. ♦ to **exchange** *vi.* fare un cambio.

exchangeable *agg.* scambiabile.

exchanger *s.* cambiavalute.

exchequer *s.* Tesoro, Scacchiere, fisco.

excise *s.* imposta indiretta ‖ — *duty*, dazio.

to **excise**[1] *vt.* tassare.

to **excise**[2] *vt.* estirpare, mutilare (*un testo*).

exciseman *s.* daziere, funzionario degli uffici delle imposte.

excision *s.* taglio, recisione.

excitability *s.* eccitabilità.

excitable *agg.* eccitabile.

excitant *agg.* e *s.* eccitante.

excitation *s.* eccitazione.

to **excite** *vt.* **1.** provocare, far nascere (*una rivolta, un sentimento ecc.*) **2.** eccitare, animare.

excited *agg.* eccitato.

excitement *s.* eccitazione.

to **exclaim** *vt.* e *vi.* esclamare.

exclamation *s.* esclamazione.

exclamatory *agg.* esclamativo.

to **exclude** *vt.* escludere.

exclusion *s.* esclusione.

exclusive *agg.* **1.** altezzoso **2.** chiuso, scelto (*di ambiente*) **3.** esclusivo.

exclusiveness *s.* esclusività.

to **excogitate** *vt.* escogitare.

excommunicable *agg.* scomunicabile.

excommunicate *agg.* e *s.* scomunicato.

to **excommunicate** *vt.* scomunicare.

excommunication *s.* scomunica.

excrement *s.* escremento.

excrescence *s.* escrescenza, protuberanza.

excruciating *agg.* tormentoso, straziante.

to **exculpate** *vt.* giustificare, scolpare.

excursion *s.* **1.** escursione, gita **2.** (*mil.*) sortita.

excursionist *s.* escursionista, gitante.

excusable *agg.* scusabile.

excuse *s.* **1.** scusa, giustificazione **2.**

pretesto.

to excuse *vt.* scusare, giustificare.

execrable *agg.* esecrabile.

to execrate *vt.* e *vi.* **1.** esecrare, detestare **2.** maledire.

execration *s.* **1.** esecrazione **2.** maledizione.

executant *s.* esecutore.

to execute *vt.* **1.** eseguire, mettere in esecuzione **2.** (*giur.*) convalidare **3.** giustiziare.

execution *s.* **1.** compimento, attuazione **2.** esecuzione.

executioner *s.* esecutore, boia.

executive *agg.* esecutivo.

executor *s.* esecutore.

exedra *s.* esedra.

exegesis *s.* (*pl.* -ses)· esegesi.

exegete *s.* esegeta.

exemplary *agg.* esemplare.

exemplification *s.* esemplificazione.

to exemplify *vt.* esemplificare.

exempt *agg.* esente, esonerato.

to exempt *vt.* esentare, esonerare.

exemption *s.* esenzione, esonero.

exequies *s. pl.* esequie.

exercise *s.* esercizio, esercitazione ‖ — -*book*, quaderno.

to exercise *vt.* esercitare, usare. ♦ **to exercise** *vi.* esercitarsi, allenarsi.

exercitation *s.* esercizio, uso (*di una facoltà*).

to exert *vt.* esercitare.

exertion *s.* **1.** esercizio (*di autorità*) **2.** sforzo.

exhalation *s.* esalazione.

to exhale *vt.* e *vi.* esalare, emettere.

exhaust *s.* **1.** (*mecc.*) scarico, scappamento **2.** apparato aspiratore.

to exhaust *vt.* e *vi.* **1.** aspirare (*aria, gas ecc.*) **2.** esaurire (*anche fig.*).

exhausted *agg.* **1.** aspirato **2.** esausto, spossato.

exhausting *agg.* che esaurisce.

exhaustion *s.* **1.** aspirazione **2.** esaurimento.

exhaustive *agg.* **1.** esauriente **2.** spossante.

exhibit *s.* **1.** insieme di oggetti in mostra **2.** (*giur.*) documento.

to exhibit *vt.* **1.** esibire, mostrare **2.** (*giur.*) produrre (*documenti ecc.*).

exhibition *s.* **1.** presentazione (*di documenti*) **2.** esposizione, mostra.

exhibitionism *s.* esibizionismo.

exhibitionist *s.* esibizionista.

exhibitor *s.* espositore.

to exhilarate *vt.* rallegrare, esilarare.

exhilarating *agg.* esilarante.

to exhort *vt.* esortare, ammonire.

exhortation *s.* esortazione.

exhortative *agg.* esortativo.

exhumation *s.* esumazione.

to exhume *vt.* esumare.

exigence *s.* **1.** esigenza, necessità **2.** situazione critica.

exigent *agg.* **1.** pressante, urgente **2.** esigente.

exigible *agg.* esigibile.

exiguity *s.* esiguità.

exiguous *agg.* esiguo.

exile *s.* **1.** esilio, bando **2.** esule.

to exile *vt.* esiliare.

to exist *vi.* esistere.

existence *s.* esistenza.

existent *agg.* esistente.

existential *agg.* esistenziale.

existentialism *s.* esistenzialismo.

existentialist *agg.* e *s.* esistenzialista.

existing *agg.* esistente, attuale.

exit *s.* uscita.

exode, exodus *s.* esodo.

exogenous *agg.* esogeno.

to exonerate *vt.* **1.** esonerare, dispensare **2.** giustificare.

exoneration *s.* **1.** dispensa, esonero **2.** giustificazione.

exorbitant *agg.* esorbitante.

to exorcise *vt.* esorcizzare.

exorciser *s.* esorcista.

exorcism *s.* esorcismo.

exorcist *s.* esorcista.

exothermic *agg.* esotermico.

exotic *agg.* esotico.

exoticism *s.* esotismo.

to expand *vt.* espandere, dilatare, allargare. ♦ **to expand** *vi.* espandersi, dilagare, dilatarsi, allargarsi, svilupparsi.

expanse *s.* distesa, estensione, spazio.

expansion *s.* espansione, dilatazione, allargamento.

expansionism *s.* espansionismo.

expansive *agg.* **1.** espansivo **2.** dilatabile.

to expatiate *vi.* **1.** errare, vagabondare **2.** parlare e scrivere diffusamente.

expatiation *s.* **1.** dissertazione **2.** prolissità.

expatriate *agg.* e *s.* espatriato.

to expatriate *vt.* esiliare. ♦ **to**

expatriate vi. espatriare.

expatriation s. espatrio.

to expect vt. **1.** aspettare, aspettarsi **2.** esigere, insistere **3.** pensare, credere || to — somebody to come, prevedere la venuta di qu.

expectance s. aspettativa, attesa.

expectant s. **1.** chi attende **2.** candidato.

expectation s. attesa, aspettativa. ♦ **expectations** s. pl. speranze.

expectorant agg. e s. espettorante.

expectoration s. espettorazione.

expediency s. **1.** convenienza **2.** opportunismo.

expedient s. espediente, ripiego.

to expedite vt. affrettare.

expedition s. **1.** spedizione **2.** prontezza, celerità.

expeditious s. svelto, sbrigativo.

to expel vt. espellere, cacciare.

expense s. **1.** spesa, sborso **2.** (fig.) sacrificio, prezzo.

expensive agg. costoso, caro.

experience s. esperienza.

to experience vt. sperimentare, provare.

experienced agg. pratico, esperto.

experiment s. esperimento, prova.

experimental agg. sperimentale.

experimentation s. sperimentasmo.

experimentalist s. sperimentalista.

experimentation s. sperimentazione.

expert agg. esperto. ♦ **expert** s. esperto, perito, competente.

expertly avv. abilmente.

to expiate vt. espiare.

expiation s. espiazione.

expiatory agg. espiatorio.

expiration s. **1.** fine, scadenza **2.** espirazione.

expiratory agg. espiratorio.

to expire vt. e vi. **1.** finire, scadere **2.** spirare, morire.

expiring agg. **1.** che scade **2.** spirante, morente.

expiry s. fine, cessazione.

to explain vt. e vi. spiegare, chiarire.

explanation s. spiegazione, delucidazione.

expletive agg. espletivo, pleonastico. ♦ **expletive** s. **1.** imprecazione **2.** pleonasmo.

explicable agg. spiegabile.

to explicate vt. sviluppare (un prin-

cipio, un'idea ecc.).

explication s. spiegazione, sviluppo.

explicit agg. esplicito, chiaro.

to explode vt. esplodere, far esplodere. ♦ **to explode** vi. scoppiare, esplodere.

to exploit vt. **1.** utilizzare, sfruttare **2.** approfittare di.

exploitation s. sfruttamento, utilizzazione.

exploiter s. **1.** chi valorizza (idea, invenzione ecc.) **2.** sfruttatore.

exploration s. esplorazione.

to explore vt. esplorare.

explorer s. esploratore, esploratrice.

explosion s. esplosione, scoppio.

explosive agg. e s. esplosivo.

exponent s. **1.** divulgatore **2.** esponente.

exponential agg. esponenziale.

export s. esportazione.

to export vt. esportare.

exportation s. esportazione.

exporter s. esportatore.

to expose vt. **1.** esporre **2.** (foto) impressionare.

exposé s. esposto, resoconto.

exposition s. **1.** spiegazione, commento **2.** mostra, esposizione.

expositive agg. espositivo.

expositor s. commentatore.

expository agg. esplicativo.

exposure s. **1.** esposizione (al freddo, al caldo ecc.) **2.** mostra **3.** (foto) (tempo di) esposizione.

to expound vt. spiegare (una teoria).

express agg. **1.** chiaro, preciso **2.** espresso, diretto. ♦ **express** s. espresso, corriere || — train, direttissimo.

to express vt. esprimere, manifestare.

expression s. espressione.

expressionism s. espressionismo.

expressionist s. espressionista.

expressive agg. espressivo, significativo.

expressly avv. espressamente.

to expropriate vt. espropriare.

expropriation s. espropriazione.

expulsion s. espulsione.

expulsive agg. espulsivo.

expunction s. cancellatura.

to expurgate vt. espurgare (uno scritto).

expurgation s. espurgazione (di uno scritto).

exquisite *agg.* 1. squisito 2. fine, sensibile. ♦ **exquisite** *s.* raffinato.

exquisiteness *s.* squisitezza, finezza.

extant *agg.* ancora esistente.

extemporaneous, extemporary *agg.* estemporaneo.

extempore *agg.* improvvisato.

extemporization *s.* improvvisazione.

to extemporize *vt.* e *vi.* improvvisare.

to extend *vt.* 1. estendere, allungare, prolungare. ♦ **to extend** *vi.* estendersi, allungarsi, prolungarsi.

extendible *agg.* estendibile.

extensible *agg.* estensibile.

extension *s.* 1. estensione, allungamento 2. (*comm.*) proroga.

extensive *agg.* 1. esteso, ampio 2. estensivo.

extent *s.* 1. estensione 2. volume 3. limite, grado.

to extenuate *vt.* attenuare.

extenuation *s.* attenuazione.

exterior *agg.* esterno, esteriore. ♦ **exterior** *s.* 1. l'esterno 2. esteriorità.

exteriority *s.* esteriorità.

exteriorization *s.* esteriorizzazione.

to exteriorize *vt.* esternare.

to exterminate *vt.* sterminare.

extermination *s.* sterminio.

external *agg.* esteriore, esterno.

externality *s.* superficialità.

to externalize *vt.* esternare.

externally *avv.* esternamente, esteriormente.

exterritorial *agg.* estraterritoriale.

extinct *agg.* 1. estinto 2. spento.

extinction *s.* estinzione.

to extinguish *vt.* 1. estinguere, spegnere 2. pagare, ammortizzare.

extinguisher *s.* spegnitore, estintore.

to extirpate *vt.* estirpare, sradicare.

extirpation *s.* estirpazione, sradicamento.

to extol *vt.* lodare, magnificare

to extort *vt.* estorcere, strappare.

extorter *s.* chi estorce.

extortion *s.* estorsione.

extortioner *s.* ricattatore.

extra *agg.* 1. straordinario 2. in più, extra. ♦ **extra** *s.* 1. supplemento 2. (*giorn.*) edizione straordinaria 3. (*cine*) comparsa. ♦ **extra** *avv.* extra, di più, in più, insolitamente.

extract *s.* 1. estratto 2. citazione.

to extract *vt.* estrarre, togliere.

extractable *agg.* estraibile.

extraction *s.* 1. estrazione 2. origine, stirpe.

extractive *agg.* estrattivo.

extractor *s.* estrattore.

to extradite *vt.* estradare.

extradition *s.* estradizione.

extraneous *agg.* estraneo.

extraordinary *agg.* straordinario, eccezionale.

extraterritorial *agg.* estraterritoriale.

extraterritoriality *s.* estraterritorialità.

extravagance *s.* 1. prodigalità, sperpero 2. stravaganza.

extravagant *agg.* 1. prodigo 2. stravagante.

extreme *agg.* 1. estremo, ultimo 2. grave. ♦ **extreme** *s.* estremo, estremità.

extremely *avv.* estremamente.

extremism *s.* estremismo.

extremist *s.* estremista.

extremity *s.* estremità.

extrinsic(al) *agg.* estrinseco.

extrovert *s.* estroverso.

to extrude *vt.* estromettere.

exuberance *s.* esuberanza.

exuberant *agg.* 1. copioso, abbondante 2. esuberante, pieno di vita.

exudation *s.* essudazione.

to exude *vt.* e *vi.* trasudare.

to exult *vi.* gioire, esultare.

exultant *agg.* esultante.

exultation *s.* esultanza.

eye *s.* occhio.

eyeball *s.* bulbo oculare.

eyebrow *s.* sopracciglio.

eyeglass *s.* lente, monocolo.

eyehole *s.* orbita, occhiaia.

eyelash *s.* ciglio.

eyelet *s.* occhiello, asola.

eyelid *s.* palpebra.

eyesight *s.* vista.

eyesore *s.* cosa brutta e spiacevole.

eyewitness *s.* testimone oculare.

F

F *s.* (*mus.*) fa.

fable *s.* favola.

fabled *agg.* 1. mitico 2. inventato.

fabric *s.* 1. tessuto 2. manufatto 3.

struttura 4. fabbricazione.

to **fabricate** vt. 1. fabbricare 2. inventare.

fabrication s. 1. fabbricazione 2. invenzione.

fabulist s. 1. favolista 2. bugiardo.

fabulosity s. favolosità.

fabulous agg. favoloso.

façade s. facciata.

face s. 1. faccia 2. aspetto 3. sfrontatezza 4. facciata 5. quadrante (di orologio) || to pull faces, fare boccacce || — -powder, cipria; — value, (comm.) valore nominale.

to **face** vt. 1. fronteggiare 2. affrontare 3. ricoprire || to — about, fare dietro-front.

facet s. sfaccettatura.

facetious agg. faceto.

facetiousness s. lepidezza.

facial agg. facciale.

facile agg. 1. facile 2. pronto 3. accomodante.

to **facilitate** vt. facilitare.

facilitation s. facilitazione.

facility s. facilità. ♦ **facilities** s. pl. facilitazioni.

facing agg. che sta di fronte. ♦ **facing** s. rivestimento. ♦ **facings** s. pl. mostrine.

fact s. 1. fatto 2. realtà || in —, infatti, di fatto; as a matter of —, effettivamente.

faction s. 1. fazione 2. faziosità.

factious agg. fazioso.

factiousness s. faziosità.

factitious agg. fittizio.

factitiousness s. artificiosità.

factor s. 1. fattore 2. agente.

factory s. fabbrica.

factual agg. effettivo.

facultative agg. 1. facoltativo 2. casuale.

faculty s. facoltà.

fad s. 1. mania 2. capriccio.

faddist s. maniaco.

faddy agg. capriccioso.

fade s. (radio) variazione graduale.

to **fade** vi. 1. appassire 2. sbiadire 3. svanire || to — in (cine) aprire in dissolvenza; to — out, (cine) chiudere in dissolvenza. ♦ to **fade** vt. 1. far sbiadire 2. far svanire.

fading s. 1. appassimento 2. scolorimento 3. affievolimento 4. dissolvenza.

to **fag** vt. affaticare. ♦ to **fag** vi. 1. affaticarsi 2. sfacchinare.

fag(g)ot s. fascina.

faience s. terracotta.

fail s. fallo.

to **fail** vi. 1. fallire 2. mancare, venir meno 3. indebolirsi 4. esser bocciato. ♦ to **fail** vt. 1. mancare di 2. bocciare 3. abbandonare.

failing[1] agg. debole. ♦ **failing** s. 1. debolezza 2. mancanza 3. fallimento.

failing[2] prep. in mancanza di.

failure s. 1. fallimento 2. incapacità 3. mancanza 4. indebolimento 5. guasto || to be a —, essere un fallito.

fain agg. contento, disposto. ♦ **fain** avv. volentieri || I would — stay, preferirei restare.

faint agg. 1. debole 2. timido 3. vago.

faint s. svenimento || — -hearted, codardo.

to **faint** vi. svenire.

faintness s. 1. debolezza 2. timidezza.

fair[1] agg. 1. onesto 2. biondo 3. gentile 4. bello 5. sereno (di tempo) 6. (comm.) libero || — -play, comportamento leale. ♦ **fair** avv. 1. con onestà 2. con precisione.

fair[2] s. fiera || fun —, Luna Park.

fairly avv. 1. onestamente 2. abbastanza.

fairness s. 1. bellezza 2. onestà 3. color biondo 4. bianchezza (di carnagione).

fairway s. canale navigabile.

fairy agg. 1. fatato 2. immaginario. ♦ **fairy** s. fata || — -tale, fiaba.

fairyland s. paese delle fate.

fairylike agg. simile a fata.

faith s. 1. fede 2. promessa || — -healer, guaritore.

faithful agg. 1. fedele 2. degno di fiducia.

faithfulness s. fedeltà.

faithless agg. 1. senza fede 2. sleale.

to **fake** vt. (gergo) falsificare.

fakir s. fachiro.

falcon s. falcone.

falconry s. falconeria.

fall s. 1. caduta, cascata 2. (amer.) autunno.

to **fall** (fell, fallen) vi. 1. cadere 2. abbassarsi 3. capitare in sorte 4. dividersi || to — back, ritirarsi; to — behind, restare indietro; to — in with, imbattersi; to — short, essere insufficiente; to — away, deperire; to — down, far fiasco; to — due, scadere.

fallacious agg. fallace.

fallaciousness s. fallacia.

fallacy s. 1. fallacia 2. errore 3. sofisma.

fallen V. to fall.

fallibility s. fallibilità.

fallible agg. fallibile.

falling agg. cadente. ♦ **falling** s. caduta || — back, ripiegamento; — off, diminuzione; — short, insufficienza.

fall-out s. pioggia radioattiva.

fallow agg. incolto.

false agg. 1. falso 2. stonato 3. ingannevole || — bottom, doppio fondo.

falsehood s. falsità.

falsely avv. falsamente.

falseness s. falsità.

falsifiable agg. falsificabile.

falsification s. falsificazione.

falsifier s. falsificatore.

to falsify vt. 1. falsificare 2. smentire.

falsity s. falsità.

to falter vi. vacillare. ♦ **to falter** vt. balbettare.

fame s. fama.

famed agg. celebre.

familiar agg. familiare. ♦ **familiar** s. amico intimo || to be — with, esser pratico di.

familiarity s. familiarità.

familiarization s. familiarità.

to familiarize vt. familiarizzare.

family s. famiglia.

famine s. carestia.

to famish vt. far morire di fame. ♦ **to famish** vi. morire di fame.

famous agg. famoso.

fan[1] s. 1. ventaglio 2. ventilatore 3. pala (d'elica).

fan[2] s. (gergo) tifoso, ammiratore.

to fan vt. 1. sventolare 2. (agr.) vagliare.

fanatic agg. e s. fanatico.

fanatical agg. fanatico.

fanaticism s. fanatismo.

to fanaticize vt. rendere fanatico. ♦ **to fanaticize** vi. agire da fanatico.

fanciful agg. 1. fantasioso 2. fantastico.

fancifulness s. 1. fantasia 2. capriccio.

fancy agg. 1. immaginario 2. stravagante 3. decorato. ♦ **fancy** s. 1. fantasia 2. capriccio 3. inclinazione || — ball, ballo in costume; — -dress, costume.

to fancy vt. 1. immaginare 2. ritenere.

fang s. 1. zanna 2. dente (velenoso).

fanning s. ventilazione.

fantastic(al) agg. 1. immaginario 2. bizzarro.

to fantasticate vt. e vi. fantasticare.

fantasy s. 1. fantasia 2. capriccio.

far agg. (farther, farthest) (further, furthest) lontano. ♦ **far** avv. 1. lontano 2. di gran lunga || — away, — off, lontano; as — as, fino a, per quanto; so —, finora; — -gone, a uno stadio avanzato (di malattie).

farce s. farsa.

farcical agg. farsesco.

farcicality s. qualità farsesca.

fare s. 1. tariffa 2. vitto 3. passeggero || bill of —, lista delle vivande.

to fare vi. 1. andare 2. riuscire 3. nutrirsi || to — badly, andar male.

farewell s. congedo. ♦ **farewell** inter. addio.

farfetched agg. remoto.

farinaceous agg. farinaceo.

farinose agg. farinoso.

farm s. fattoria || — -yard, aia.

to farm vt. coltivare. ♦ **to farm** vi. fare l'agricoltore.

farmer s. agricoltore.

farmhouse s. casa colonica.

farming s. agricoltura.

farmstead s. cascina.

farraginous agg. farraginoso.

farrier s. maniscalco.

farsighted agg. e s. presbite.

farther agg. (comp. di far) più lontano, ulteriore. ♦ **farther** avv. 1. (di) più 2. più lontano 3. inoltre.

farthermost agg. il più lontano.

farthest agg. (superl. di far) il più lontano, estremo. ♦ **farthest** avv. (il) più lontano.

farthing s. "farthing" (moneta inglese: un quarto di penny).

fascicle s. fascicolo.

to fascinate vt. affascinare.

fascinating agg. affascinante.

fascination s. fascino.

fascinator s. affascinatore.

fascism s. fascismo.

fascist agg. e s. fascista.

fashion s. 1. modo 2. abitudine 3. moda || — -*plate*, figurino; *a man of* —, un uomo di mondo.
to fashion vt. foggiare.
fashionable agg. 1. alla moda 2. elegante.
fast agg. 1. fermo 2. fedele 3. inalterabile 4. rapido 5. (*fig.*) dissoluto 6. in anticipo (*di orologio*). ♦ **fast** avv. 1. fermamente 2. fortemente 3. velocemente 4. in modo dissoluto.
fast s. digiuno.
to fast vi. digiunare.
to fasten vt. 1. attaccare 2. allacciare 3. chiudere 4. fissare. ♦ **to fasten** vi. 1. allacciarsi 2. chiudersi 3. fissarsi.
fastener s. 1. fermaglio 2. legaccio, chiusura || *snap* —, automatico.
fastening s. 1. legatura 2. gancio, chiavistello.
faster s. digiunatore.
fastidious agg. schizzinoso.
fastidiousness s. schizzinosità.
fastness s. 1. velocità 2. fermezza 3. solidità 4. dissolutezza.
fat agg. 1. grasso 2. (*fig.*) proficuo. ♦ **fat** s. grasso || — -*head*, zuccone.
to fat V. *to fatten*.
fatal agg. fatale.
fatalism s. fatalismo.
fatalist s. fatalista.
fatalistic agg. fatalistico.
fatality s. 1. fatalità 2. fatalismo.
fatally avv. 1. in modo fatale 2. fatalmente.
fate s. fato.
father s. padre || — -*in-law*, suocero.
fatherhood s. paternità.
fatherland s. madrepatria.
fatherless agg. senza padre.
fatherlike agg. paterno. ♦ **fatherlike** avv. paternamente.
fatherly agg. e avv. V. *fatherlike*.
fathom s. (*mar.*) braccio (*misura di profondità*).
to fathom vt. scandagliare.
fathomless agg. 1. incommensurabile 2. incomprensibile.
fatidic(al) agg. fatidico.
fatigue s. fatica.
to fatigue vt. affaticare. ♦ **to fatigue** vi. affaticarsi.
fatness s. grassezza.
to fatten vt. ingrassare. ♦ **to fatten** vi. ingrassarsi.

fattener s. ingrassatore.
fattening s. ingrassamento.
fattiness s. grassezza.
fatty agg. grasso.
fatuity s. fatuità.
fatuous agg. fatuo.
fault s. 1. fallo 2. colpa 3. difetto || — -*finder*, criticone.
faultiness s. imperfezione.
faultless agg. 1. perfetto 2. irreprensibile.
faulty agg. difettoso.
faun s. fauno.
favour s. favore.
to favour vt. 1. favorire 2. sostenere 3. (*fam.*) assomigliare a.
favourable agg. favorevole.
favourite agg. e s. favorito.
favouritism s. favoritismo.
fawn s. cerbiatto.
to fawn vt. fare le feste || *to* — *on*, adulare.
fawner s. adulatore.
fawning s. servilismo.
fear s. paura, timore.
to fear vt. e vi. temere, aver paura.
fearful agg. 1. terribile 2. timoroso.
fearfulness s. 1. aspetto terribile 2. timore.
fearless agg. intrepido.
feasibility s. fattibilità.
feasible agg. fattibile.
feast s. 1. festa 2. banchetto.
to feast vt. 1. rallegrare 2. festeggiare. ♦ **to feast** vi. banchettare.
feaster s. convitato.
feat s. impresa, prodezza.
feather s. penna, piuma.
to feather vt. 1. coprire di penne, piume 2. (*mar.*) spalare.
feathered agg. 1. pennuto 2. (*fig.*) alato.
feathering s. piumaggio.
featherless agg. implume.
feature s. 1. lineamento 2. (*cine*) attrazione 3. caratteristica || — *film*, parte principale di un film.
to feature vt. 1. caratterizzare 2. (*teat.*) dare una parte importante a.
featureless agg. senza caratteristiche.
febrifuge s. febbrifugo.
febrile agg. febbrile.
February s. febbraio.
fecal agg. fecale.
fecund agg. fecondo.
to fecundate vt. fecondare.
fecundation s. fecondazione.

fecundity s. fecondità.
fed V. to feed.
federacy s. federazione.
federal agg. federale.
federalism s. federalismo.
federate agg. confederato.
to **federate** vt. confederare. ◆ to **federate** vi. confederarsi.
federation s. (con)federazione.
federative agg. federativo.
fee s. 1. onorario 2. tassa 3. (giur.) proprietà ereditaria.
feeble agg. debole.
feebleness s. debolezza.
feed s. 1. alimentazione 2. pascolo.
to **feed** (fed, fed) vt. 1. nutrire 2. pascere 3. rifornire || to be fed up, essere stufo. ◆ to **feed** (fed, fed) vi. nutrirsi || to — up, ingrassare.
feeder s. 1. ciò che, chi nutre 2. cavo di alimentazione 3. affluente 4. serbatoio.
feeding s. alimentazione.
feel s. tatto.
to **feel** (felt, felt) vt. 1. sentire (col tatto o col sentimento) 2. tastare, sondare. ◆ to **feel** (felt, felt) vi. 1. sentirsi 2. andare a tastoni.
feeling agg. sensibile. ◆ **feeling** s. 1. sentimento 2. sensibilità 3. sensazione.
feet V. foot.
to **feign** vt. 1. inventare 2. falsificare. ◆ to **feign** vi. fingersi.
feignedly avv. simulatamente.
feigner s. simulatore.
feint s. 1. finta 2. simulazione.
to **feint** vi. fare una finta.
feldspar s. feldspato.
to **felicitate** vt. felicitarsi con || to — so. on sthg., felicitarsi con qu. di qc.
felicitation s. felicitazione.
felicitous agg. appropriato.
feline agg. e s. felino.
fell[1] V. to fall.
fell[2] agg. 1. crudele 2. funesto.
to **fell** vt. abbattere.
felling s. taglio (di un bosco).
fellow s. 1. individuo 2. compagno, collega || — -citizen, concittadino; — -creature, simile; a good —, un buon diavolo.
fellowship s. 1. amicizia 2. associazione.
felon agg. e s. criminale.
felony s. crimine, delitto.

felt[1] V. to feel.
felt[2] s. feltro.
to **felt** vt. feltrare.
felucca s. feluca.
female agg. 1. femminile 2. (mecc.) femmina. ◆ **female** s. femmina.
feminine agg. e s. femminile.
femininity s. femminilità.
feminism s. femminismo.
femur s. femore.
fen s. palude || — -berry, mirtillo; — -fire, fuoco fatuo.
fence s. 1. recinto 2. scherma 3. (fam.) ricettatore.
to **fence** vt. cintare. ◆ to **fence** vi. tirar di scherma.
fencer s. schermidore.
fencing s. 1. cinta 2. scherma.
fender s. 1. riparo 2. paraurti 3. (mar.) parabordo.
fennel s. finocchio.
feracity s. feracità.
feral[1] agg. ferale, funesto.
feral[2] agg. ferino.
ferial agg. feriale.
ferine agg. ferino.
ferment s. fermento.
to **ferment** vi. 1. fermentare 2. agitarsi. ◆ to **ferment** vt. 1. far fermentare 2. eccitare.
fermentation s. 1. fermentazione 2. fermento.
fermentative agg. fermentativo.
fern s. felce.
ferocious agg. feroce.
ferocity s. ferocia.
ferreous agg. 1. ferroso 2. ferreo.
ferret[1] s. furetto.
ferret[2] s. nastro, fettuccia.
ferro-concrete s. cemento armato.
ferrous agg. ferroso.
ferruginous agg. ferruginoso.
ferry s. traghetto.
to **ferry** vt. e vi. traghettare.
ferryman s. traghettatore.
fertile agg. fertile.
fertility s. fertilità.
fertilization s. fertilizzazione.
to **fertilize** vt. 1. fertilizzare 2. fecondare.
fertilizer s. fertilizzante.
fervency s. fervore.
fervent, fervid agg. ardente.
fervour s. ardore.
festal agg. festivo.
fester s. suppurazione, piaga.
to **fester** vi. suppurare (di ferita).
festival s. 1. festa 2. festival.
festive agg. 1. festivo 2. festoso.

festivity s. festività. ♦ **festivities**
s. pl. festeggiamenti.

festoon s. festone.

to **fetch** vt. 1. andare a prendere 2.
tirare 3. fruttare, rendere || to —
back, riportare.

fetid agg. fetido.

fetish s. feticcio.

fetishism s. feticismo.

fetishist s. feticista.

fetter s. ceppo, catena.

to **fetter** vt. incatenare.

fettle s. condizione || in fine —, in
forma.

feud[1] s. ostilità.

feud[2] s. feudo.

feudal agg. feudale.

feudalism s. feudalesimo.

feudality s. 1. feudalesimo 2. feudo.

feudatory agg. e s. feudatario.

fever s. febbre || to be in a —, avere
la febbre.

feverish agg. 1. febbricitante 2. febbrile.

few agg. e pron. pochi || a —, al-
cuni; quite a —, un numero considerevole; a good —, parecchi.

fewness s. scarsità, esiguità.

fiancé s. fidanzato.

fib s. fandonia.

to **fib** vi. dire fandonie.

fibre s. fibra.

fibroid, fibrous agg. fibroso.

fickle agg. incostante.

fickleness s. incostanza.

fictile agg. fittile.

fiction s. 1. narrativa 2. finzione.

fictional agg. immaginario.

fictitious agg. fittizio.

fiddle s. violino || fit as a —, in ot-
tima salute.

to **fiddle** vi. 1. suonare il violino 2.
gingillarsi.

fiddler s. violinista.

fiddlestick s. archetto. ♦ **fiddle-
sticks** s. pl. sciocchezze.

fidelity s. fedeltà.

to **fidget** vt. agitare. ♦ to **fidget** vi.
agitarsi.

fidgety agg. irrequieto.

fiduciary agg. e s. fiduciario.

field s. campo || — -glass, binoco-
lo; — -day, giorno di esercitazio-
ni; — -officer, ufficiale superiore.

fiend s. demonio.

fiendish agg. diabolico.

fierce agg. 1. fiero 2. selvaggio 3.
ardente.

fierceness s. 1. ferocia 2. ardore.

fiery agg. 1. di fuoco 2. focoso 3.
infiammabile.

fife s. piffero.

fifteen agg. e s. quindici.

fifteenth agg. e s. quindicesimo.

fifth agg. e s. quinto.

fiftieth agg. e s. cinquantesimo.

fifty agg. e s. cinquanta || — - —,
a metà.

fig[1] s. ficó.

fig[2] s. tenuta, vestiario.

fight s. 1. lotta 2. spirito combattivo.

to **fight** (**fought, fought**) vt. e vi.
combattere || to — down, vincere;
to — off, respingere; to — shy of,
tenersi alla larga da.

fighter s. 1. combattente 2. (aer.)
caccia.

fighting s. combattimento, rissa.

figuration s. figurazione.

figurative agg. 1. figurativo 2. figurato.

figure s. 1. figura, forma 2. cifra 3.
diagramma.

to **figure** vt. raffigurare. ♦ to **figure**
vi. 1. immaginarsi 2. passare per.

figurehead s. 1. prestanome 2.
(mar.) polena.

filament s. filamento.

filamentary, filamentous agg. filamentoso.

filcher s. ladruncolo.

file[1] s. lima.

file[2] s. 1. schedario, archivio 2. fila
3. raccolta.

to **file**[1] vt. limare.

to **file**[2] vt. 1. archiviare 2. ordinare.
♦ to **file** vi. marciare in fila.

filial agg. filiale.

filiation s. filiazione.

filibuster s. filibustiere.

filigree s. filigrana.

filing[1] s. limatura.

filing[2] s. 1. archiviazione 2. sfilata.

fill s. sazietà.

to **fill** vt. 1. riempire 2. occupare
3. otturare (di denti) || to — in,
to — up, riempire, compilare. ♦
to **fill** vi. riempirsi.

fillet s. 1. nastro 2. (cuc.) filetto.

filling s. 1. riempitura 2. otturazione
3. (cuc.) ripieno || — station, sta-
zione di rifornimento.

fillip s. 1. schiocco (delle dita) 2.
stimolo.

film s. 1. pellicola 2. velo 3. membrana.

to **film** vt. 1. coprire con una pelli-

cola 2. filmare. ♦ to **film** vi. 1.
coprirsi con una pellicola 2. girare
un film.

filmy agg. velato.

filter s. filtro.

to **filter** vt. e vi. filtrare.

filth s. sozzura.

filthily avv. in modo sudicio.

filthiness s. 1. sozzura 2. corruzione morale.

filthy agg. 1. sozzo 2. corrotto.

filtration s. filtrazione.

fin s. 1. pinna 2. (mecc.) aletta.

final agg. e s. finale.

finalist s. finalista.

finality s. 1. finalità 2. carattere definitivo.

finally avv. alla fine.

finance s. finanza.

to **finance** vt. finanziare.

financial agg. finanziario.

financier s. 1. finanziere 2. finanziatore.

financing s. finanziamento.

finch s. fringuello.

find s. scoperta, ritrovamento.

to **find** (found, found) vt. 1. tro-
vare 2. provvedere 3. ritenere ||
to — out, scoprire.

finding s. 1. scoperta 2. sentenza.

fine¹ agg. 1. bello 2. fine. ♦ **fine**
avv. bene.

fine² s. multa.

to **fine¹** vt. raffinare. ♦ to **fine** vi.
raffinarsi.

to **fine²** vt. multare.

finely avv. 1. bene 2. finemente.

finger s. dito || — -print, impronta
digitale; — -tip, punta delle dita;
— -post, cartello segnavia.

to **finger** vt. 1. toccare con le dita
2. rubare || to be light-fingered
(fig.), avere le mani lunghe.

finish s. 1. fine 2. finezza 3. finitura.

to **finish** vt. e vi. finire.

finished agg. (fig.) perfetto.

finishing agg. ultimo, conclusivo.
♦ **finishing** s. (ri)finitura.

finite agg. limitato.

Finn s. finlandese.

Finnic, Finnish agg. finlandese.

fir (-tree) s. abete || — -wood,
abetaia.

fire s. 1. fuoco 2. incendio || on —,
in fiamme; — -guard, parafuoco;
— -plug, bocca da incendio; —
station, caserma dei pompieri; —
-works, fuochi d'artificio.

to **fire** vt. 1. dar fuoco 2. far fuoco

3. (fig.) infiammare. ♦ to **fire** vi.
1. prender fuoco 2. (fig.) infiammarsi.

firedamp s. grisù.

fire escape s. 1. scala di sicurezza
2. scala dei pompieri.

firefly s. lucciola.

fireman s. pompiere.

fireplace s. caminetto.

fireproof agg. incombustibile.

fireside s. angolo del focolare.

firewood s. legna da ardere.

firing s. 1. accensione 2. sparo 3.
alimentazione (di un fuoco) ||
— squad, plotone d'esecuzione.

firm¹ agg. 1. fisso 2. solido 3. deciso.

firm² s. azienda, ditta.

firmament s. firmamento.

firmly avv. 1. fermamente 2. solidamente.

firmness s. 1. fermezza 2. stabilità.

first agg. primo || — -aid, pronto
soccorso; — -born, primogenito;
— -class, di prima qualità; —
-name, nome di battesimo. ♦ **first**
avv. 1. prima di tutto 2. per la
prima volta || at —, sulle prime.
♦ **first** s. 1. primo 2. principio.

firth s. fiordo.

fiscal agg. fiscale.

fish s. pesce || — -hook, amo.

to **fish** vi. 1. pescare 2. cercare. ♦
to **fish** vt. pescare.

fisher s. pescatore.

fisherman s. pescatore.

fishery s. pesca.

fishing s. pesca || — -boat, pesche-
reccio; — -line, lenza.

fishmonger s. pescivendolo.

fishy agg. 1. di pesce 2. pescoso 3.
(fig.) equivoco.

fission s. fissione.

fist s. pugno.

fit¹ agg. 1. adatto 2. pronto.

fit² s. 1. giusta misura 2. attacco, accesso (di febbre, ira ecc.).

to **fit** vt. 1. adattare 2. andar bene
a 3. provare || to — out, equipag-
giare.

fitful agg. 1. irregolare 2. spasmodico.

fitfulness s. irregolarità.

fitness s. convenienza.

fitter s. 1. aggiustatore 2. montatore.

fitting agg. adatto, conveniente. ♦
fitting s. 1. adattamento, prova
2. equipaggiamento. ♦ **fittings**

s. *pl.* **1.** accessori **2.** arredamento (*sing.*).

five *agg.* e *s.* cinque.

fix *s.* **1.** difficoltà **2.** (*mar.*) punto.

to fix *vt.* fissare || *to — up*, sistemare, riparare. ♦ **to fix** *vi.* stabilirsi.

fixation *s.* fissazione.

fixed *agg.* **1.** fisso **2.** stabilito.

fixer *s.* **1.** montatore **2.** fissatore.

fixing *s.* **1.** collocamento **2.** messa in opera **3.** fissaggio.

fixity *s.* **1.** stabilità **2.** fissità.

fizz *s.* **1.** effervescenza **2.** bevanda effervescente.

to fizz *vi.* frizzare.

fjord *s.* fiordo.

flabbiness *s.* **1.** mollezza **2.** fiacchezza (*di carattere ecc.*).

flabby *agg.* **1.** floscio **2.** fiacco.

flaccid *agg.* flaccido.

flaccidness *s.* flaccidezza.

flag[1] *s.* bandiera || *— -ship*, nave ammiraglia.

flag[2] *s.* lastra di pietra (*per pavimentazione*).

to flag[1] *vt.* **1.** imbandierare **2.** pavesare. ♦ **to flag** *vi.* **1.** pendere **2.** avvizzire.

to flag[2] *vt.* lastricare.

to flagellate *vt.* flagellare.

flagellation *s.* flagellazione.

flagellator *s.* flagellatore.

flagrancy *s.* flagranza.

flagrant *agg.* flagrante.

flagstaff *s.* asta di bandiera.

flair *s.* fiuto, intuizione.

flake *s.* **1.** fiocco (*di neve, lana ecc.*) **2.** favilla **3.** lamina **4.** scaglia.

to flake *vt.* **1.** sfaldare **2.** squamare **3.** coprire di fiocchi. ♦ **to flake** *vi.* **1.** sfaldarsi **2.** squamarsi **3.** cadere in fiocchi.

flaky *agg.* **1.** a falde **2.** a lamine, a scaglie.

flame *s.* fiamma || *— -thrower*, lanciafiamme.

to flame *vi.* fiammeggiare.

flaming *agg.* ardente.

flange *s.* orlo, frangia.

flank *s.* fianco.

to flank *vt.* **1.** fiancheggiare **2.** (*mil.*) attaccare il fianco di.

flannel *s.* flanella. ♦ **flannels** *s. pl.* calzoni di flanella.

flap *s.* **1.** lembo, falda **2.** colpo, agitazione **3.** linguetta **4.** (*aer.*) alettone.

flare *s.* **1.** fiammata improvvisa **2.** chiarore.

to flare *vi.* **1.** brillare (*di luce incerta*) **2.** agitarsi **3.** divampare.

flash *s.* **1.** lampo **2.** chiusa || *— -back*, scena retrospettiva; *— -light*, lampo al magnesio.

to flash *vt.* **1.** proiettare **2.** diffondere. ♦ **to flash** *vi.* **1.** lampeggiare **2.** muoversi rapidamente.

flashing *agg.* risplendente. ♦ **flashing** *s.* splendore, scintillio.

flask *s.* fiasca.

flat[1] *agg.* **1.** piatto, piano **2.** disteso **3.** deciso **4.** sgonfio (*di pneumatico*).

flat[2] *s.* **1.** superficie piana **2.** pianura **3.** bassofondo **4.** chiatta **5.** appartamento **6.** (*mus.*) bemolle || *— -iron*, ferro da stiro.

flatly *avv.* **1.** pianamente **2.** scialbamente **3.** recisamente.

flatness *s.* **1.** piattezza **2.** decisione.

to flatten *vt.* **1.** appiattire **2.** smorzare. ♦ **to flatten** *vi.* **1.** appiattirsi **2.** indebolirsi.

to flatter *vt.* **1.** adulare **2.** illudere.

flatterer *s.* adulatore.

flattery *s.* adulazione.

flatulence, flatulency *s.* **1.** flatulenza **2.** vanità.

flatus *s.* flatulenza.

to flaunt *vt.* **1.** sventolare **2.** ostentare.

flavour *s.* gusto, aroma.

to flavour *vt.* aromatizzare, dare gusto a.

flavoured *agg.* **1.** profumato **2.** saporito.

flavouring *s.* **1.** aroma **2.** condimento.

flavourless *agg.* insipido.

flaw *s.* **1.** screpolatura **2.** falla, pecca.

flawless *agg.* perfetto.

flax *s.* lino.

flaxen *agg.* **1.** di lino **2.** biondo.

to flay *vt.* **1.** scorticare **2.** criticare aspramente.

flea *s.* pulce || *— -bite* (*fig.*), inezia.

fleck *s.* **1.** macchia **2.** scaglia.

to flee (fled, fled) *vt.* **1.** abbandonare **2.** evitare, schivare. ♦ **to flee (fled, fled)** *vi.* **1.** fuggire **2.** svanire.

fleece *s.* vello.

fleecy *agg.* lanoso.

to fleer *vt.* e *vi.* far beffe (a).

fleet *s.* flotta.

fleeting *agg.* fugace.

Flemish *agg.* fiammingo.

flesh *s.* carne ‖ *to lose —*, dimagrire; *to put on —*, ingrassare.

fleshiness *s.* 1. carnosità 2. corpulenza.

fleshless *agg.* scarno.

fleshly *agg.* carnale, sensuale.

flew V. *to fly.*

to flex *vt.* flettere, piegare. ♦ **to flex** *vi.* flettersi.

flexibility *s.* 1. flessibilità 2. docilità.

flexible *agg.* 1. flessibile 2. docile.

flexion *s.* 1. flessione 2. curva.

flexuosity *s.* flessuosità.

flexuous *agg.* flessuoso.

flicker *s.* tremolio, bagliore.

to flicker *vi.* 1. tremolare 2. guizzare. ♦ **to flicker** *vt.* far tremolare.

flight[1] *s.* 1. volo 2. stormo 3. rampa *(di scale)*.

flight[2] *s.* fuga.

flimsiness *s.* leggerezza, frivolezza.

flimsy *agg.* leggero, sottile.

to flinch *vi.* indietreggiare, ritirarsi.

fling *s.* 1. getto 2. beffa 3. tentativo.

to fling (flung, flung) *vt.* gettare. ‖ *to — open*, spalancare. ♦ **to fling (flung, flung)** *vi.* gettarsi.

flint *s.* selce, pietra focaia.

to flip *vt.* 1. far schioccare 2. sbattere.

flippancy *s.* leggerezza.

flippant *agg.* leggero.

flipper *s.* pinna.

flirt *s.* 1. movimento rapido 2. amoreggiamento.

to flirt *vt.* muovere rapidamente. ♦ **to flirt** *vi.* amoreggiare.

flirtation *s.* amoreggiamento.

to flit *vi.* 1. volare 2. scorrere.

float *s.* galleggiante.

to float *vt.* 1. trasportare 2. inondare 3. *(comm.)* varare *(un progetto ecc.)*. ♦ **to float** *vi.* 1. galleggiare 2. spandersi.

floatage *s.* 1. galleggiamento 2. relitto.

floatation *s.* *(comm.)* varo.

floater *s.* galleggiante.

floating *agg.* 1. galleggiante 2. oscillante, fluttuante.

flock *s.* 1. bioccolo 2. gregge 3. cascame.

to flock *vi.* affollarsi.

floe *s.* banchisa.

to flog *vt.* fustigare ‖ *to — a dead horse*, fare una fatica inutile.

flogger *s.* fustigatore.

flood *s.* inondazione, diluvio.

to flood *vt.* inondare. ♦ **to flood** *vi.* straripare.

flooding *s.* 1. inondazione 2. emorragia.

floodlight *s.* illuminazione con riflettore.

flood tide *s.* flusso della marea.

floor *s.* 1. pavimento 2. piano ‖ *—-lamp*, lampada a stelo.

to floor *vt.* pavimentare.

flooring *s.* impiantito.

flop *s.* 1. tonfo 2. insuccesso.

floral *agg.* floreale.

floriculture *s.* floricultura.

floriculturist *s.* floricultore.

florid *agg.* 1. florido 2. fiorito *(di stile)*.

floridity *s.* floridezza.

florin *s.* fiorino.

florist *s.* fiorista.

flotilla *s.* flottiglia.

to flounce *vi.* agitarsi ‖ *to — out*, andarsene furibondo.

flour *s.* farina ‖ *potato- —*, fecola.

to flour *vt.* 1. infarinare 2. macinare.

flourish *s.* 1. ornamento 2. squillo di tromba.

to flourish *vi.* 1. prosperare 2. essere attivo.

flourishing *agg.* 1. fiorente 2. pomposo.

floury *agg.* 1. farinoso 2. infarinato.

flow *s.* corrente, flusso.

to flow *vi.* 1. scorrere 2. derivare da. ♦ **to flow** *vt.* inondare.

flower *s.* fiore ‖ *— -bed*, aiuola; *— -bud*, bocciuolo.

to flower *vi.* fiorire. ♦ **to flower** *vt.* infiorare.

flowering *agg.* in fiore. ♦ **flowering** *s.* fioritura.

flowerless *agg.* senza fiori.

flowery *agg.* fiorito.

flowing *agg.* 1. fluente 2. fluido.

flown V. *to fly.*

flu *s.* influenza.

to fluctuate *vi.* 1. fluttuare 2. ondeggiare.

fluctuation *s.* oscillazione.

flue *s.* condotto per l'aria.

fluency *s.* 1. fluidità 2. scioltezza.

fluent *agg.* 1. fluente 2. dalla parola facile.

fluently *avv.* 1. fluentemente 2. speditamente.

fluff *s.* peluria.

fluffy *agg.* **1.** soffice, vaporoso **2.** coperto di peluria.

fluid *agg.* e *s.* fluido.

fluidity *s.* fluidità.

flung V. *to* **fling**.

fluorescence *s.* fluorescenza.

fluorescent *agg.* fluorescente.

fluoride *s.* fluoruro.

fluorine *s.* fluoro.

flurry *s.* **1.** ventata **2.** agitazione.

to flurry *vt.* agitare.

flush *agg.* **1.** abbondante **2.** pieno di vita **3.** a pari livello **4.** ben fornito. ◆ **flush** *s.* **1.** flusso **2.** vampata **3.** vigore.

to flush *vt.* **1.** lavare **2.** far scorrere **3.** rianimare. ◆ **to flush** *vi.* **1.** scorrere **2.** arrossire.

flute *s.* **1.** flauto **2.** increspatura.

fluted *agg.* **1.** flautato **2.** increspato.

flutter *s.* **1.** battito, movimento rapido **2.** eccitazione.

to flutter *vt.* agitare. ◆ **to flutter** *vi.* **1.** agitarsi **2.** battere le ali.

fluttering *agg.* **1.** svolazzante **2.** palpitante. ◆ **fluttering** *s.* **1.** svolazzamento **2.** palpitazione.

fluxion *s.* flusso.

fly[1] *s.* **1.** volo **2.** calesse **3.** (*mecc.*) volano.

fly[2] *s.* mosca.

to fly (flew, flown) *vi.* volare. ◆ **to fly (flew, flown)** *vt.* **1.** far volare **2.** sventolare || *to* — *about*, svolazzare; *to* — *away*, fuggire; *to* — *off* (*aer.*), decollare.

flying *agg.* **1.** rapido **2.** sventolante || —*boat*, idrovolante.

flypaper *s.* carta moschicida.

foam *s.* schiuma || — *rubber* gommapiuma.

to foam *vi.* spumeggiare.

foamy *agg.* spumeggiante.

focal *agg.* focale.

focus *s.* **1.** fuoco **2.** focolaio.

to focus *vt.* mettere a fuoco.

fodder *s.* foraggio.

to fodder *vt.* foraggiare.

foe *s.* nemico.

foetus *s.* feto.

fog *s.* nebbia.

foggy *agg.* nebbioso (*anche fig.*).

foible *s.* debolezza.

foil[1] *s.* **1.** fioretto **2.** traccia.

foil[2] *s.* lamina.

fold[1] *s.* ovile.

fold[2] *s.* **1.** piega **2.** spira.

to fold[1] *vt.* **1.** piegare **2.** avvolgere **3.** abbracciare. ◆ **to fold** *vi.* piegarsi.

to fold[2] *vt.* chiudere nell'ovile.

folder *s.* **1.** volantino **2.** cartelletta.

folding *agg.* pieghevole. ◆ **folding** *s.* **1.** piega, piegatura **2.** avvolgimento **3.** abbraccio.

foliage *s.* fogliame.

folio *s.* (*tip.*) fo(g)lio.

folk *s.* gente, popolo.

folklore *s.* folclore.

folkloristic *agg.* folcloristico.

to follow *vt.* e *vi.* seguire.

follower *s.* seguace.

following *agg.* seguente. ◆ **following** *s.* seguito.

folly *s.* follia.

to foment *vt.* fomentare.

fomentation *s.* fomentazione.

fomenter *s.* fomentatore.

fond *agg.* **1.** amante **2.** affettuoso.

to fondle *vt.* vezzeggiare.

fondly *avv.* **1.** amorevolmente **2.** ingenuamente.

fondness *s.* tenerezza, amore.

font *s.* **1.** fonte battesimale **2.** acquasantiera.

food *s.* cibo.

foodstuff *s.* alimenti (*pl.*).

fool *s.* **1.** sciocco **2.** buffone || *to make a* — *of*, beffarsi di.

to fool *vt.* ingannare. ◆ **to fool** *vi.* fare lo sciocco || *to* — *away*, sperperare.

foolery *s.* follia.

foolhardiness *s.* folle temerarietà.

foolhardy *agg.* temerario.

foolish *agg.* sciocco.

foolishness *s.* sciocchezza.

foot *s.* (*pl.* feet) **1.** piede **2.** zampa || *on* —, a piedi.

football *s.* pallone.

footballer *s.* calciatore.

foot-bath *s.* pediluvio.

footboard *s.* predellino.

footbridge *s.* cavalcavia.

footfall *s.* passo.

footing *s.* punto d'appoggio.

footlights *s. pl.* luci della ribalta.

footman *s.* domestico.

footmark *s.* orma.

footnote *s.* poscritto.

footpath *s.* sentiero.

footprint, footstep *s.* orma.

footstool *s.* sgabello.

footway *s.* passaggio pedonale.

fop *s.* damerino.

foppery *s.* fatuità.

foppish *agg.* fatuo.

for[1] *prep.* per || — *all that*, ciò nonostante; *as* —, in quanto a.

for[2] *cong.* poiché.

forage *s.* foraggio.

foray *s.* incursione, saccheggio.

forbade V. *to forbid.*

to forbear (forbore, forborne) *vi.* **1.** astenersi **2.** essere paziente.

forbearance *s.* **1.** astensione **2.** pazienza.

forbearing *agg.* paziente.

to forbid (forbade, forbidden) *vt.* proibire, impedire.

forbidding *agg.* **1.** severo **2.** ripugnante.

forbore V. *to forbear.*

forborne V. *to forbear.*

force *s.* forza. ♦ **forces** *s. pl.* truppe || *the Armed Forces,* le Forze Armate.

to force *vt.* **1.** forzare **2.** costringere || *to — back,* respingere; *to — in,* sfondare; *to — on,* far avanzare.

forceful *agg.* forte.

forceps *s.* **1.** forcipe **2.** pinza.

forcible *agg.* **1.** violento **2.** potente.

ford *s.* guado.

to ford *vt.* guadare.

fordable *agg.* guadabile.

fore *agg.* anteriore. ♦ **fore** *s.* prua.

forearm *s.* avambraccio.

to forearm *vt.* premunire.

to forebode *vt.* presagire (*un male*).

foreboding *s.* presagio.

forecast *s.* previsione.

to forecast (forecast, forecast) *vt.* prevedere.

forecastle *s.* castello di prua.

forefather *s.* antenato.

forefinger *s.* indice.

foreground *s.* primo piano.

forehead *s.* fronte.

foreign *agg.* **1.** straniero **2.** estraneo || *— Office,* Ministero degli Esteri.

foreigner *s.* straniero.

forelock *s.* ciuffo.

foreman *s.* caposquadra, caporeparto.

foremast *s.* albero di trinchetto.

forename *s.* nome di battesimo.

forensic(al) *agg.* forense.

to forerun (foreran, forerun) *vt.* precorrere.

forerunner *s.* **1.** precursore **2.** messaggero.

foresail *s.* vela di trinchetto.

to foresee (foresaw, foreseen) *vt.* prevedere.

foreseeable *agg.* prevedibile.

foreseeing *s.* previsione.

foreseen V. *to foresee.*

to foreshadow *vt.* adombrare.

foreshortening *s.* scorcio.

foresight *s.* **1.** previsione **2.** previdenza.

forest *s.* foresta.

forestal *agg.* forestale.

to forestall *vt.* **1.** prevenire **2.** accaparrare.

forestalling *s.* **1.** anticipazione **2.** accaparramento.

forester *s.* **1.** guardia forestale **2.** abitante di foreste.

forestry *s.* **1.** foresta **2.** silvicultura.

foretaste *s.* pregustazione.

to foretaste *vt.* pregustare.

to foretell (foretold, foretold) *vt.* predire.

forethought *agg.* premeditato. ♦ **forethought** *s.* **1.** premeditazione **2.** previdenza.

foretold V. *to foretell.*

forever *avv.* per sempre.

to forewarn *vt.* avvertire.

foreword *s.* prefazione.

forfeit *s.* **1.** perdita **2.** ammenda **3.** penitenza.

forfeiture *s.* **1.** multa **2.** confisca.

to forgather *vi.* riunirsi, associarsi.

forgave V. *to forgive.*

forge *s.* fucina.

to forge *vt.* **1.** foggiare, fabbricare **2.** contraffare.

forger *s.* **1.** fabbro **2.** falsario.

forgery *s.* contraffazione.

to forget (forgot, forgotten) *vt.* e *vi.* dimenticare, dimenticarsi.

forgetful *agg.* **1.** immemore **2.** negligente.

forgetfulness *s.* **1.** oblio **2.** negligenza.

forget-me-not *s.* non-ti-scordar-di--me.

to forgive (forgave, forgiven) *vt.* perdonare.

forgiveness *s.* perdono.

forgot V. *to forget.*

forgotten V. *to forget.*

fork *s.* **1.** forchetta **2.** forca **3.** forcella **4.** biforcazione.

to fork *vi.* biforcarsi || *to — out,* (*gergo*) pagare. ♦ **to fork** *vt.* biforcare.

forked *agg.* biforcuto.

forlorn *agg.* abbandonato.

form *s.* **1.** forma **2.** modulo **3.** banco.

to **form** *vt.* formare. ◆ to **form** *vi.* formarsi.

formal *agg.* formale || — *dress*, abito da cerimonia.

formalism *s.* formalismo.

formalist *s.* formalista.

formality *s.* formalità.

to **formalize** *vt.* 1. formare 2. formalizzare.

format *s.* formato.

formation *s.* formazione.

formative *agg.* formativo.

forme *s.* (*tip.*) forma di stampa.

former[1] *agg.* e *pron.* precedente, il primo (*fra due*).

former[2] *s.* 1. artefice 2. stampo.

formerly *avv.* precedentemente.

formic *agg.* formico.

formidable *agg.* 1. formidabile 2. spaventoso.

formless *agg.* informe.

formulary *s.* formulario.

to **formulate** *vt.* formulare.

formulation *s.* formulazione.

to **forsake** (**forsook, forsaken**) *vt.* abbandonare.

forsaking *s.* abbandono.

forsook V. *to forsake.*

to **forswear** (**forswore, forsworn**) *vt.* 1. abiurare 2. spergiurare.

fort *s.* (*mil.*) fortezza.

forth *avv.* 1. avanti 2. fuori || *and so* —, e così via.

forthcoming *agg.* prossimo.

fortieth *agg.* e *s.* quarantesimo.

fortification *s.* fortificazione.

to **fortify** *vt.* fortificare.

fortitude *s.* forza d'animo.

fortnight *s.* due settimane.

fortnightly *agg.* quindicinale. ◆ **fortnightly** *avv.* ogni due settimane.

fortress *s.* (*mil.*) fortezza.

fortuitous *agg.* fortuito.

fortunate *agg.* 1. fortunato 2. propizio.

fortune *s.* 1. sorte: *to tell fortunes*, predire la sorte 2. fortuna.

fortune-teller *s.* indovino.

forty *agg.* e *s.* quaranta.

forward *agg.* 1. avanzato 2. precoce 3. pronto.

to **forward** *vt.* 1. promuovere 2. spedire.

forwarder *s.* spedizioniere.

forwarding *s.* spedizione.

forward(s) *avv.* avanti, in avanti.

fossil *agg.* e *s.* fossile.

fossilization *s.* fossilizzazione.

to **fossilize** *vt.* fossilizzare. ◆ to **fossilize** *vi.* fossilizzarsi.

to **foster** *vt.* 1. favorire 2. allevare, nutrire.

fought V. *to fight.*

foul *agg.* 1. sporco 2. tempestoso.

foulmouthed *agg.* sboccato.

to **foul** *vt.* 1. sporcare 2. urtare. ◆ to **foul** *vi.* 1. sporcarsi 2. urtarsi.

found V. *to find.*

to **found**[1] *vt.* fondare.

to **found**[2] *vt.* fondere.

foundation *s.* 1. fondazione 2. fondamenta 3. fondamento.

founder[1] *s.* fondatore.

founder[2] *s.* fonditore.

to **founder** *vi.* crollare. ◆ to **founder** *vt.* affondare.

foundling *s.* trovatello || — *-hospital*, brefotrofio.

foundry *s.* fonderia.

fountain *s.* 1. fontana 2. sorgente || — *-pen*, penna stilografica.

four *agg.* e *s.* quattro || — *-handed* quadrumane; — *-footed*, quadrupede.

fourscore *agg.* ottanta.

fourteen *agg.* e *s.* quattordici.

fourteenth *agg.* e *s.* quattordicesimo.

fourth *agg.* e *s.* quarto.

fowl *s.* pollo, pollame.

fox *s.* volpe: — *-hunt*, caccia alla volpe.

foxglove *s.* digitale.

foxy *agg.* 1. volpino 2. rossiccio 3. scolorito 4. aspro.

foyer *s.* ridotto.

fraction *s.* frazione.

fractional *agg.* frazionario.

to **fractionize** *vt.* frazionare.

fracture *s.* frattura.

to **fracture** *vt.* fratturare. ◆ to **fracture** *vi.* fratturarsi.

fragile *agg.* fragile.

fragility *s.* fragilità.

fragment *s.* frammento.

fragmentary *agg.* frammentario.

fragrance *s.* fragranza.

fragrant *agg.* fragrante.

frail *agg.* 1. debole 2. caduco.

frailness, frailty *s.* debolezza.

frame *s.* 1. cornice 2. struttura, intelaiatura.

to **frame** *vt.* 1. incorniciare 2. formare.

framework *s.* struttura.

framing *s.* incorniciatura.

franc s. franco.
franchise s. franchigia.
Franciscan agg. e s. francescano.
frank agg. franco.
frankness s. franchezza.
frantic agg. frenetico.
fraternal agg. fraterno.
fraternity s. 1. fraternità 2. confraternita.
fraternization s. affratellamento.
to **fraternize** vi. fraternizzare.
fratricidal agg. fratricida.
fratricide s. 1. fratricida 2. fratricidio.
fraud s. 1. frode 2. impostura 3. (fam.) impostore.
fraudulence s. frode.
fraudulent agg. fraudolento.
fray s. zuffa.
to **fray** vt. consumare. ♦ to **fray** vi. consumarsi.
freak s. 1. capriccio 2. macchiolina.
freakish, freaky agg. capriccioso.
freckle s. lentiggine.
freckled, freckly agg. lentigginoso.
free agg. 1. libero 2. (comm.) franco 3. abbondante 4. gratuito || — on board, franco porto. ♦ **free** avv. gratuitamente.
to **free** vt. liberare.
freedom s. libertà.
freely avv. 1. liberamente 2. gratuitamente.
freemason s. massone.
freemasonry s. massoneria.
freethinker s. libero pensatore.
freethinking s. libertà di pensiero.
freetrade s. libero scambio.
freetrader s. libero scambista.
freeze s. gelo, congelamento.
to **freeze (froze, frozen)** vt. e vi. 1. gelare 2. (imp.) far freddo.
freezer s. cella frigorifera.
freezing agg. glaciale, congelante. ♦ **freezing** s. congelamento.
freight s. 1. trasporto 2. nolo.
to **freight** vt. 1. trasportare 2. noleggiare 3. caricare.
French agg. francese. ♦ **French** s. lingua francese.
to **frenchify** vt. francesizzare. ♦ to **frenchify** vi. francesizzarsi.
Frenchman s. francese (uomo).
Frenchwoman s. francese (donna).
frenzied agg. frenetico.
frenzy s. frenesia, delirio.
frequency s. frequenza.
frequent agg. frequente.
to **frequent** vt. frequentare.

fresco s. affresco.
fresh agg. fresco, nuovo, puro || — water, acqua dolce. ♦ **fresh** s. sorgente.
fresh-water agg. d'acqua dolce.
to **freshen** vt. 1. rinfrescare 2. desalinizzare. ♦ to **freshen** vi. rinfrescarsi.
freshly avv. 1. in modo fresco 2. recentemente.
freshman s. matricola.
freshness s. 1. freschezza 2. inesperienza.
fret[1] s. agitazione.
fret[2] s. 1. fregio 2. traforo.
to **fret**[1] vt. rodere. ♦ to **fret** vi. 1. affliggersi 2. agitarsi.
to **fret**[2] vt. 1. ornare 2. traforare.
fretful agg. irritabile.
fretfully avv. con irritazione.
fretfulness s. irritabilità.
fretwork s. intaglio ornamentale.
friability s. friabilità.
friable agg. friabile.
friar s. frate || Black——, domenicano; Grey——, francescano; White——, carmelitano.
friction s. frizione, attrito.
Friday s. venerdì: Good —, Venerdì Santo.
fried agg. fritto.
friend s. amico || to make friends, fare amicizia; the Society of Friends, i quaccheri.
friendless agg. senza amici.
friendliness s. cordialità.
friendly agg. amichevole. ♦ **friendly** avv. amichevolmente.
friendship s. amicizia.
frigate s. fregata.
fright s. spavento.
to **frighten** vt. spaventare.
frightful agg. spaventevole.
frightfulness s. spavento.
frigid agg. 1. glaciale 2. frigido.
frigidity s. 1. freddezza 2. frigidità.
frill s. 1. fronzolo 2. gala increspata.
to **frill** vt. ornare di gale.
fringe s. 1. frangia 2. bordo.
to **fringe** vt. orlare.
frippery s. cianfrusaglie (pl.).
to **frisk** vi. fare capriole.
frisky agg. gaio.
frivolity s. frivolezza.
frivolous agg. frivolo.
frizzly, frizzy agg. crespo.
frock s. 1. abito 2. tonaca.
frog[1] s. rana.

frog² s. alamaro.
frogman s. sommozzatore.
frolic s. scherzo.
frolicsome agg. scherzoso.
from prep. da, di.
front agg. anteriore. ♦ **front** s. 1. fronte 2. sfrontatezza.
to **front** vt. fronteggiare.
frontal agg. frontale.
frontier s. frontiera.
frontispiece s. frontespizio.
frost s. 1. gelo 2. brina || —bite, congelamento; hoar— —, brinata.
to **frost** vt. 1. gelare 2. (cuc.) glassare 3. smerigliare.
frosty agg. 1. gelato 2. gelido 3. canuto.
froth s. 1. schiuma 2. frivolezza.
to **froth** vi. far schiuma.
frothy agg. 1. schiumoso 2. leggero.
frown s. 1. l'aggrottare le ciglia 2. cipiglio.
to **frown** vi. 1. aggrottare le ciglia 2. accigliarsi.
frowning agg. accigliato.
froze V. to freeze.
frozen V. to freeze.
fructiferous agg. fruttifero.
to **fructify** vi. fruttificare. ♦ to **fructify** vt. fertilizzare.
frugal agg. frugale.
frugalist s. persona frugale.
frugality s. frugalità.
fruit s. 1. frutta 2. frutto.
fruiterer s. fruttivendolo.
fruitful agg. 1. fruttifero 2. fertile 3. redditizio.
fruitfulness s. 1. fertilità 2. vantaggio.
fruition s. 1. godimento 2. realizzazione.
fruitless agg. infruttuoso.
to **frustrate** vt. frustrare.
frustration s. frustrazione.
frustum s. (pl. -ta) (geom.) tronco.
fry s. fritto, frittura.
to **fry** vt. e vi. friggere.
fudge s. fandonia, sciocchezza.
to **fudge** vt. rattoppare.
fuel s. combustibile || — oil, nafta.
to **fuel** vt. alimentare di combustibile.
fugacity s. fugacità.
fugitive agg. 1. fuggitivo 2. effimero. ♦ **fugitive** s. 1. fuggitivo 2. rifugiato.
fugitiveness s. fuggevolezza.
fugue s. (mus.) fuga.
fulcrum s. (pl. fulcra) fulcro.

to **fulfil** vt. 1. compiere 2. adempiere, esaurire.
fulfilment s. 1. compimento 2. adempimento, esaudimento.
fulgency s. fulgidezza.
fulgent agg. fulgente.
fulgid agg. fulgido.
fulguration s. folgorazione.
full agg. pieno || — up, completo; — -stop, punto. ♦ **full** avv. interamente. ♦ **full** s. 1. intero 2. massimo.
fullness s. pienezza.
fully avv. completamente.
fulminant agg. fulminante.
fulmination s. 1. fulminazione 2. imprecazione.
fumarole s. fumarola.
to **fumble** vi. annaspare. ♦ to **fumble** vt. maneggiare goffamente.
fume s. 1. fumo 2. eccitazione.
to **fume** vi. 1. fumare 2. irritarsi.
fun s. 1. divertimento 2. facezia || to make — of so., canzonare qu.; to have good —, divertirsi molto.
funambulism s. funambolismo.
funambulist s. funambolo.
function s. funzione.
to **function** vi. 1. funzionare 2. fungere da.
functional agg. funzionale.
functionary s. funzionario.
fund s. fondo, riserva.
to **fund** vt. 1. accumulare 2. investire in obbligazioni.
fundament s. base.
fundamental agg. fondamentale. ♦ **fundamental** s. fondamento.
funeral agg. funebre. ♦ **funeral** s. funerale.
funerary, funereal agg. funereo.
funicular agg. e s. funicolare.
funnel s. 1. imbuto 2. camino, ciminiera.
funny agg. 1. comico 2. strano.
fur s. 1. pelliccia 2. patina, rivestimento.
to **fur** vt. coprire con pelliccia.
furbelow s. falpalà.
furious agg. furioso.
to **furl** vt. 1. piegare, chiudere 2. ammainare (vele ecc.). ♦ to **furl** vi. piegarsi, chiudersi.
furnace s. fornace.
to **furnish** vt. 1. fornire 2. ammobiliare.
furnisher s. fornitore.
furnishings s. pl. arredamento (sing.).

furniture *s.* **1.** mobilio **2.** contenuto.
furrier *s.* pellicciaio.
furriery *s.* pellicceria.
furrow *s.* **1.** solco **2.** scia.
to furrow *vt.* **1.** solcare **2.** arare.
further *agg.* (*comp. di* far) **1.** più lontano **2.** ulteriore. ♦ **further** *avv.* **1.** più in là **2.** ancora.
to further *vt.* favorire.
furthermore *avv.* inoltre.
furthermost *agg.* il più lontano.
furthest *agg.* (*superl. di* far) estremo. ♦ **furthest** *avv.* all'estremo limite.
furtive *agg.* furtivo.
furunculosis *s.* furuncolosi.
fury *s.* furia.
fuse *s.* **1.** valvola, fusibile **2.** spoletta **3.** miccia.
to fuse *vt.* **1.** fondere **2.** liquefare. ♦ **to fuse** *vi.* **1.** fondersi **2.** saltare (*di valvola*).
fuselage *s.* fusoliera.
fusible *agg.* fusibile.
fusion *s.* fusione.
fuss *s.* **1.** trambusto **2.** smancerie.
to fuss *vi.* far confusione. ♦ **to fuss** *vt.* irritare.
fussily *avv.* **1.** con inutile scalpore **2.** con esagerata importanza.
fussy *agg.* **1.** che fa confusione **2.** meticoloso.
fusty *agg.* stantio.
futility *s.* futilità.
future *agg. e s.* futuro.
futurism *s.* futurismo.
fuzz *s.* lanuggine.
fuzzily *avv.* confusamente.
fuzziness *s.* **1.** increspatura (*di capelli*) **2.** (*foto*) sfocatura.
fuzzy *a'g.* **1.** lanuginoso **2.** confuso **3.** (*foto*) sfocato.

G

G *s.* (*mus.*) sol.
to gabble *vt. e vi.* parlare in modo confuso.
gabbler *s.* chiacchierone.
gable *s.* frontone.
gadfly *s.* **1.** tafano **2.** (*fig.*) persona irritante.
gadget *s.* aggeggio.
Gael *s.* gaelico.
Gaelic *agg. e s.* gaelico.

gaff *s.* uncino, rampone.
gag *s.* **1.** bavaglio **2.** improvvisazione **3.** trovata geniale.
to gag *vt.* imba·vagliare. ♦ **to gag** *vi.* improvvisare (*motti di spirito*).
gage *s.* garanzia.
to gage *vt.* dare in pegno.
gaiety *s.* gaiezza. ♦ **gaieties** *s. pl.* divertimenti.
gaily *avv.* gaiamente.
gain *s.* **1.** guadagno **2.** aumento, miglioramento.
to gain *vt. e vi.* **1.** guadagnare **2.** aumentare || *to — on,* guadagnar terreno su.
gainer *s.* chi guadagna.
gainful *agg.* lucroso.
gainings *s. pl.* guadagni.
to gainsay *vt.* contraddire.
gainsaying *s.* contraddizione.
gait *s.* andatura.
gaiter *s.* ghetta.
galalith *s.* galalite.
galaxy *s.* galassia.
gale *s.* tempesta.
galenic *agg.* galenico.
Galilean *agg. e s.* galileo.
gall[1] *s.* bile, fiele || *— -bladder,* cistifellea.
gall[2] *s.* **1.** scorticatura **2.** irritazione.
to gall *vt.* irritare. ♦ **to gall** *vi.* irritarsi.
gallant *agg.* **1.** prode **2.** galante. ♦ **gallant** *s.* uomo di mondo.
gallantry *s.* **1.** galanteria **2.** coraggio **3.** atto, discorso amoroso.
galleon *s.* galeone.
gallery *s.* galleria || *picture- —,* pinacoteca.
galley *s.* **1.** (*mar.*) galea **2.** (*mar.*) cambusa **3.** (*tip.*) vantaggio || *— proof* (*tip.*), bozza in colonna; *— slave,* galeotto.
Gallic *agg. e s.* gallico.
gallicism *s.* francesismo.
gallinacean *agg. e s.* gallinaceo.
gallium *s.* gallio.
gallon *s.* gallone (*misura*).
galloon *s.* gallone (*ornamento*).
gallooned *agg.* gallonato.
gallop *s.* **1.** galoppo: *at a —,* al galoppo **2.** galoppata.
to gallop *vt.* far galoppare. ♦ **to gallop** *vi.* galoppare.
gallows *s. pl.* patibolo (*sing.*).
galore *s.* abbondanza. ♦ **galore** *avv.* in abbondanza.
galosh(e) *s.* galoscia.

galvanic(al) *agg.* 1. galvanico 2. (*fig.*) galvanizzante.

galvanization *s.* galvanizzazione.

to **galvanize** *vt.* galvanizzare.

galvanometer *s.* galvanometro.

galvanoplastic *agg.* galvanoplastico.

gamble *s.* gioco d'azzardo.

to **gamble** *vt.* e *vi.* giocare (*d'azzardo*).

gambler *s.* giocatore d'azzardo.

gambling *s.* V. *gamble* ‖ — *-house*, casa da gioco.

gambol *s.* piroetta.

game *agg.* risoluto. ♦ **game** *s.* 1. gioco (*con regole*), mano (*in una partita*) 2. (*fig.*) progetto 3. selvaggina (*coll.*).

to **game** V. *to gamble.*

gamekeeper *s.* guardacaccia.

gamely *avv.* coraggiosamente.

gamesome *agg.* scherzoso.

gamester *s.* giocatore.

gammon *s.* (*mar.*) trinca di bompresso.

gang *s.* 1. squadra 2. banda.

to **gang** *vt.* e *vi.* formare una banda.

ganglion *s.* (*pl.* ganglia) ganglio.

gangrene *s.* cancrena.

to **gangrene** *vi.* andare in cancrena.

gangster *s.* bandito.

gangsterism *s.* banditismo.

gangway *s.* 1. passaggio (*tra file di sedie ecc.*) 2. (*mar.*) passerella.

gaol *s.* prigione.

to **gaol** *vt.* imprigionare.

gaoler *s.* carceriere.

gap *s.* 1. apertura, breccia 2. intervallo 3. divergenza 4. lacuna.

gape *s.* 1. sbadiglio 2. apertura 3. stupore.

to **gape** *vi.* 1. spalancare la bocca 2. sbadigliare 3. restare a bocca aperta.

gaping *agg.* 1. aperto 2. stupito.

garage *s.* autorimessa ‖ — *keeper*, garagista.

garb *s.* costume.

garbage *s.* rifiuto.

garden *s.* giardino.

to **garden** *vi.* fare del giardinaggio.

gardener *s.* giardiniere.

gardening *s.* giardinaggio.

gargarism *s.* gargarismo.

gargle *s.* liquido per gargarismi.

to **gargle** *vt.* e *vi.* gargarizzare.

gargoyle *s.* doccione.

garish *agg.* 1. abbagliante 2. appariscente.

garland *s.* ghirlanda.

garlic *s.* aglio.

garment *s.* abito, indumento.

garnet[1] *s.* granato.

garnet[2] *s.* (*mar.*) paranco.

to **garnish** *vt.* guarnire.

garnish(ment) *s.* ornamento.

garret *s.* soffitta.

garrison *s.* guarnigione.

to **garrison** *vt.* presidiare.

garrulity *s.* garrulità.

garrulous *agg.* garrulo.

garter *s.* giarrettiera ‖ *knight o, the Garter*, Cavaliere dell'Ordine della Giarrettiera.

gas *s.* gas ‖ — *-fitter*, gassista; — *-mask*, maschera antigas; — *-meter*, contatore del gas.

to **gas** *vt.* 1. fornire di gas 2. asfissiare col gas.

Gascon *agg.* e *s.* guascone.

gasconade *s.* guasconata.

gaseous *agg.* gassoso.

gash *s.* sfregio.

to **gash** *vt.* sfregiare.

gas oil *s.* gasolio.

gasoline (*amer.*) benzina.

gasp *s.* respiro affannoso.

to **gasp** *vi.* 1. ansare 2. restare senza fiato 3. parlare affannosamente.

gassy *agg.* gassoso.

gastric *agg.* gastrico.

gastritis *s.* gastrite.

gastroenteritis *s.* gastroenterite.

gastronome *s.* gastronomo.

gastronomic(al) *agg.* gastronomico.

gastronomy *s.* gastronomia.

gate *s.* 1. cancello 2. porta.

gatekeeper *s.* portiere, custode.

gateway *s.* portone, ingresso.

to **gather** *vt.* 1. raccogliere 2. acquistare 3. dedurre. ♦ to **gather** *vi.* raccogliersi.

gathering *s.* 1. raccolta 2. (*med.*) ascesso.

gaud *s.* fronzolo.

gaudiness *s.* sfarzo.

gaudy *agg.* sfarzoso. ♦ **gaudy** *s.* festa (*universitaria*).

gauge *s.* 1. misura 2. calibro 3. (*ferr.*) scartamento 4. pescaggio ‖ *narrow* —, scartamento ridotto.

to **gauge** *vt.* misurare.

gaunt *agg.* scarno.

gauze *s.* garza, velo, mussolina.

gauzy *agg.* trasparente.

gave V. *to give.*

gay *agg.* 1. gaio 2. licenzioso.

gaze s. sguardo fisso.

to **gaze** vi. fissare.

gazelle s. gazzella.

gazette s. gazzetta.

gazetteer s. **1.** giornalista **2.** dizionario geografico.

gear s. **1.** meccanismo **2.** (auto) marcia, cambio **3.** (mecc.) ingranaggio.

to **gear** vt. ingranare || to — up, down, aumentare, diminuire la velocità.

gearing s. ingranaggio, innesto.

geese V. goose.

gelatin(e) s. gelatina.

gelatinous agg. gelatinoso.

to **geld** vt. castrare.

gelid agg. gelido.

gem s. gemma.

gemmy agg. pieno di gemme.

gender s. genere.

genderless agg. di genere comune.

genealogical agg. genealogico.

genealogy s. genealogia.

generable agg. generabile.

general agg. e s. generale.

generality s. **1.** generalità **2.** maggioranza.

generalization s. generalizzazione.

to **generalize** vt. e vi. generalizzare.

generally avv. generalmente.

to **generate** vt. generare.

generation s. generazione.

generative agg. generativo.

generator s. generatore.

generic(al) agg. generico.

generosity s. generosità.

generous agg. **1.** generoso **2.** abbondante.

genesis s. (pl. -ses) genesi.

genetic(al) agg. genetico.

genetics s. genetica.

genial agg. **1.** gioviale **2.** geniale **3.** mite (di clima).

geniality s. **1.** giovialità **2.** mitezza (di clima).

genital agg. e s. genitale.

genitive agg. e s. genitivo.

genius s. genio.

genocide s. genocidio.

genre s. genere.

genteel agg. raffinato.

gentian s. genziana.

gentile agg. e s. pagano.

gentility s. signorilità.

gentle agg. **1.** nobile **2.** garbato **3.** moderato **4.** facile.

gentleman s. **1.** signore **2.** gentiluomo.

gentlemanlike, gentlemanly agg. da gentiluomo.

gentleness s. gentilezza.

gentlewoman s. gentildonna.

gently avv. **1.** gentilmente, con delicatezza **2.** gradualmente.

gentry s. classe gentilizia.

to **genuflect** vi. genuflettersi.

genuflection s. genuflessione.

genuine agg. **1.** autentico **2.** sincero **3.** puro.

genuineness s. **1.** autenticità **2.** sincerità.

genus s. (pl. -nera) genere.

geodesy s. geodesia.

geographer s. geografo.

geographic(al) agg. geografico.

geography s. geografia.

geologic(al) agg. geologico.

geologist s. geologo.

geology s. geologia.

geometer s. geometra.

geometric(al) agg. geometrico.

geometrician s. geometra.

geometry s. geometria.

geophysics s. geofisica.

geopolitics s. geopolitica.

georgic agg. georgico.

geranium s. geranio.

gerent s. gerente.

germ s. germe.

german agg. germano.

German agg. e s. tedesco.

Germanic agg. germanico.

Germanism s. germanesimo.

Germanist s. germanista.

germanium s. germanio.

germinal agg. germinale.

to **germinate** vt. far germinare. ◆ to **germinate** vi. germinare.

germination s. germinazione.

gerontology s. gerontologia.

gerund s. gerundio.

gerundial agg. gerundivo.

gerundive agg. e s. gerundivo.

gestation s. gestazione.

to **gesticulate** vi. gesticolare.

gesticulation s. gesticolazione.

gesture s. **1.** gesto **2.** il gestire.

to **gesture** vi. far gesti.

to **get** (got, got) vt. **1.** ottenere, procurare **2.** prendere **3.** portare **4.** fare. ◆ to **get** (got, got) vi. **1.** andare **2.** divenire || to — off, scendere; to — over, scavalcare; to — out, (far) uscire; to — up, alzarsi; to — married, sposarsi; to — hold of, impossessarsi di.

getaway s. **1.** fuga **2.** (sport) partenza.

gettable *agg.* ottenibile.

get-up *s.* **1.** equipaggiamento **2.** presentazione (*di libro, giornale ecc.*).

geyser *s.* **1.** geyser **2.** scaldabagno.

ghastliness *s.* **1.** aspetto spaventoso **2.** pallore spettrale.

ghastly *agg.* **1.** spaventoso **2.** spettrale.

gherkin *s.* cetriolo.

Ghibelline *agg. e s.* ghibellino.

ghost *s.* **1.** spirito **2.** spettro || *to give up the* —, spirare.

ghostliness *s.* **1.** l'essere spettrale **2.** spiritualità.

ghostly *agg.* **1.** spettrale **2.** spirituale.

giant *s.* gigante.

giantism *s.* gigantismo.

gibbet *s.* patibolo.

to gibbet *vt.* **1.** impiccare **2.** (*fig.*) mettere alla berlina.

gibbosity *s.* gibbosità.

gibbous *agg.* gibboso.

gibe *s.* scherno.

to gibe *vt. e vi.* schernire.

giblets *s. pl.* regaglie.

giddily *avv.* vertiginosamente.

giddiness *s.* **1.** capogiro **2.** (*fig.*) frivolezza.

giddy *agg.* **1.** stordito **2.** vertiginoso **3.** frivolo.

to giddy *vt.* stordire. ♦ **to giddy** *vi.* aver le vertigini.

gift *s.* **1.** dono **2.** dote.

to gift *vt.* dotare.

gig¹ *s.* **1.** calessino **2.** (*mar.*) iole.

gig² *s.* rampone, fiocina.

gigantean, gigantic *agg.* gigantesco.

giggle *s.* risatina.

to giggle *vi.* fare risatine.

to gild (gilt, gilt) (*anche reg.*) *vt.* (in)dorare.

gilder *s.* doratore.

gilding *s.* doratura.

gill *s.* **1.** branchia **2.** pappagorgia.

gilt V. *to gild.*

gilt *s.* doratura.

gimlet *s.* succhiello.

gin¹ *s.* "gin" (*liquore*).

gin² *s.* **1.** elevatore **2.** trappola (*per animali*).

ginger *s.* zenzero.

gingerly *agg.* cauto. ♦ **gingerly** *avv.* cautamente.

gipsy *s.* zingaro.

gipsydom *s.* gli zingari (*pl.*).

gipsyish *agg.* zingaresco.

giraffe *s.* giraffa.

to gird (girt, girt) (*anche reg.*) *vt.* cingere.

girder *s.* **1.** trave maestra **2.** sbarra

girdle *s.* **1.** cintura **2.** reggicalze.

to girdle *vt.* cingere.

girl *s.* ragazza || *flower* —, fioraia.

girlhood *s.* adolescenza (*di ragazza*).

Girondist *agg. e s.* girondino.

girt V. *to gird.*

girth *s.* **1.** circonferenza **2.** cinghia.

to give (gave, given) *vt.* dare || *to* — *in*, cedere; *to* — *out*, annunciare, venir meno; *to* — *up*, smettere, abbandonare; *to* — *birth to*, generare; *to* — *oneself up*, costituirsi (*alla polizia*); *to* — *oneself up to*, dedicarsi (a); *to* — *off*, emettere (*luce ecc.*).

giver *s.* datore.

glacial *agg.* glaciale.

glaciation *s.* glaciazione.

glacier *s.* ghiacciaio.

glacis *s.* spalto.

glad *agg.* lieto.

to gladden *vt.* rallegrare. ♦ **to gladden** *vi.* rallegrarsi.

glade *s.* radura.

gladiator *s.* gladiatore.

gladiolus *s.* (*pl.* -li) gladiolo.

gladly *avv.* con piacere.

gladness *s.* contentezza.

glair *s.* albume.

gladsome *agg.* gioioso.

glair *s.* albume.

glamorous *agg.* affascinante.

glamour *s.* **1.** fascino **2.** incantesimo

glance *s.* **1.** occhiata **2.** colpo obliquo.

to glance *vt. e vi.* **1.** gettare uno sguardo **2.** sfiorare **3.** balenare || *to* — *off*, sorvolare su.

gland *s.* **1.** ghiandola **2.** ghianda.

glandiferous *agg.* ghiandifero.

glandular *agg.* glandolare.

glare *s.* **1.** luce abbagliante **2.** sguardo truce **3.** abbagliamento.

to glare *vi.* **1.** splendere **2.** guardare torvamente.

glaring *agg.* **1.** abbagliante **2.** evidente.

glass *s.* **1.** vetro **2.** bicchiere **3.** specchio || — *-ware*, articoli in vetro; — *-work*, fabbrica di vetro; — *-paper*, carta vetrata. ♦ **glasses** *s. pl.* occhiali, cannocchiale (*sing.*).

to glass *vt.* **1.** specchiare **2.** imbottigliare.

glassy *agg.* **1.** vitreo **2.** cristallino.

glaucous *agg.* glauco.
glaze *s.* superficie vetrosa.
to **glaze** *vt.* 1. smaltare 2. mettere vetri a. ◆ to **glaze** *vi.* diventare vitreo.
glazier *s.* vetraio.
glazy *agg.* vitreo.
gleam *s.* barlume.
to **gleam** *vi.* scintillare.
gleamy *agg.* scintillante.
to **glean** *vt. e vi.* spigolare.
gleaner *s.* spigolatore.
gleaning *s.* spigolatura.
glee *s.* allegria.
gleeful *agg.* allegro.
glib *agg.* 1. liscio 2. facondo 3. sciolto.
glibness *s.* 1. disinvoltura 2. facondia.
glide *s.* scivolata.
to **glide** *vt.* 1. far scorrere 2. trascorrere. ◆ to **glide** *vi.* 1. scivolare 2. passare.
glider *s.* aliante.
gliding *agg.* scorrevole. ◆ **gliding** *s.* volo a vela.
glimmer *s.* barlume.
to **glimmer** *vi.* brillare.
glimpse *s.* 1. visione 2. occhiata 3. vaga idea.
to **glimpse** *vt. e vi.* intravedere.
glitter *s.* scintillio.
to **glitter** *vi.* scintillare.
gloaming *s.* crepuscolo.
to **gloat** *vi.* fissare avidamente.
global *agg.* globale.
globe *s.* 1. globo 2. pianeta.
globous, globular *agg.* sferico.
globule *s.* globulo.
gloom *s.* 1. oscurità 2. tristezza.
to **gloom** *vt.* 1. oscurare 2. rattristare. ◆ to **gloom** *vi.* 1. oscurarsi 2. rattristarsi.
gloomy *agg.* cupo.
glorification *s.* glorificazione.
to **glorify** *vt.* glorificare.
glorious *agg.* 1. glorioso 2. splendido.
gloriousness *s.* V. *glory.*
glory *s.* 1. gloria 2. splendore.
to **glory** *vi.* vantarsi.
gloss *s.* 1. glossa 2. lucentezza 3. apparenza.
glossarist *s.* glossatore.
glossary *s.* glossario.
glossy *agg.* lucido.
glottis *s.* glottide.
glottologist *s.* glottologo.
glottology *s.* glottologia.

glove *s.* guanto ‖ *to be hand in —— with*, essere molto intimo con.
gloved *agg.* inguantato.
glover *s.* guantaio.
glow *s.* 1. calore 2. splendore 3. colorito ‖ *—worm*, lucciola.
to **glow** *vi.* ardere.
glucose *s.* glucosio.
glue *s.* colla.
to **glue** *vt.* incollare.
glut *s.* 1. scorpacciata 2. saturazione.
to **glut** *vt.* 1. saziare 2. saturare. ◆ to **glut** *vi.* fare una scorpacciata.
gluten *s.* glutine.
gluteus *s.* (*pl.* glutei) gluteo.
glutton *s.* ghiottone.
gluttonous *agg.* ghiottone.
gluttony *s.* ghiottoneria.
glycerin(e) *s.* glicerina.
glycogen *s.* glicogeno.
gnarled *agg.* nodoso.
to **gnash** *vt. e vi.* digrignare.
gnat *s.* zanzara.
to **gnaw** *vt.* rodere.
gnawing *agg.* 1. rosicante 2. corrodente.
gnome[1] *s.* gnomo.
gnome[2] *s.* massima.
gnomic *agg.* gnomico.
gnosis *s.* gnosi.
gnostic *agg. e s.* gnostico.
gnosticism *s.* gnosticismo.
go *s.* 1. movimento 2. energia 3. colpo ‖ *— -between*, intermediario; *— -by*, evasione; *— -cart*, girello.
to **go** (went, gone) *vi.* 1. andare 2. divenire ‖ *to — by*, passare; *to — for*, andare a cercare; *to — on*, continuare.
goad *s.* pungolo.
to **goad** *vt.* stimolare.
goal *s.* 1. traguardo 2. (*sport*) rete ‖ *— -keeper*, portiere.
goat *s.* capra.
goatish *agg.* 1. caprino 2. lascivo.
to **gobble** *vt.* tranguggiare, inghiottire.
goblin *s.* folletto.
god *s.* 1. dio, divinità 2. Dio.
godchild *s.* (*pl.* -children) figlioccio.
goddaughter *s.* figlioccia.
goddess *s.* dea.
godfather *s.* padrino.
godless *agg.* 1. ateo 2. empio.
godlike *agg.* divino.
godliness *s.* devozione.
godly *agg.* religioso.
godmother *s.* madrina.

godown s. deposito.

godsend s. dono del cielo.

godship s. divinità.

godson s. figlioccio.

goggle agg. 1. stralunato 2. sporgente (di occhi).

to goggle vt. stralunare. ♦ **to goggle** vi. essere sporgenti (di occhi).

goggles s. pl. occhiali di protezione.

going s. 1. l'andare 2. partenza.

goitre s. gozzo.

goitrous agg. gozzuto.

gold agg. d'oro. ♦ **gold** s. oro || — -field, zona aurifera; — -dig »", cercatore d'oro.

golden agg. dorato, d'oro.

goldfinch s. cardellino.

goldsmith s. orefice.

gone V. to go.

gonfalon s. gonfalone.

goniometer s. goniometro.

goniometry s. goniometria.

good (better, best) agg. 1. buono 2. bravo 3. bello. ♦ **good** inter. bene!

good s. 1. bene 2. utilità || for —, per sempre.

good-bye inter. e s. addio, arrivederci.

good-for-nothing s. buono a nulla.

goodly agg. bello.

goodness s. 1. bontà 2. il meglio || my —!, Dio mio!

goods s. pl. merce (sing.).

goodwill s. 1. buona volontà 2. benevolenza.

goody agg. troppo buono. ♦ **goody** inter. bene!

goose s. (pl. geese) oca.

gooseberry s. uva spina.

goose-step s. passo dell'oca.

gore s. sangue rappreso.

gorge s. gola.

to gorge V. to glut.

gorgeous agg. magnifico.

gorgeousness s. magnificenza.

gospel s. vangelo.

gossamer s. ragnatela.

gossip s. 1. pettegolezzo 2. pettegolo.

to gossip vi. far pettegolezzi.

gossiper s. pettegolo.

gossipy agg. pettegolo.

got V. to get.

Gothic agg. e s. gotico.

gothicism s. 1. stile gotico 2. rozzezza.

gouache s. guazzo.

gouge s. sgorbia.

gourd s. zucca.

gourmand s. goloso.

gourmet s. buongustaio.

gout s. 1. gotta 2. goccia.

gouty agg. gottoso.

to govern vt. 1. governare 2. controllare 3. (gramm.) reggere.

governable agg. docile.

governess s. istitutrice.

government s. governo.

governmental agg. governativo.

governor s. 1. governatore 2. regolatore.

gown s. 1. veste 2. toga || dressing—, veste da camera; night- —, camicia da notte.

grab s. presa.

to grab vt. 1. afferrare 2. (mecc.) bloccare.

grace s. grazia.

to grace vt. adornare.

graceful agg. grazioso.

gracefulness s. grazia.

graceless agg. 1. sgraziato 2. depravato.

gracile agg. gracile.

gracility s. gracilità.

gracious agg. benigno || good —!, mio Dio!

gradation s. gradazione.

grade s. 1. grado 2. pendio.

to grade vt. 1. graduare 2. livellare.

gradient agg. che sale, scende gradatamente. ♦ **gradient** s. pendenza.

gradual agg. graduale.

graduality s. gradualità.

graduate s. laureato.

to graduate vt. 1. graduare 2. laureare. ♦ **to graduate** vi. laurearsi.

graduation s. 1. graduazione 2. laurea.

graft s. innesto.

to graft vt. innestare.

grain s. 1. granaglie (pl.) 2. chicco 3. grano.

grainy agg. 1. granuloso 2. granoso.

gram s. grammo.

Gramineae s. pl. graminacee.

grammar s. grammatica.

grammarian s. grammatico.

grammatic(al) agg. grammaticale.

gramophone s. grammofono.

granary s. granaio.

grand agg. 1. grande 2. nobile || — -aunt, prozia; — -uncle, prozio; — -nephew, pronipote (maschio); — -niece, pronipote (femmina).

grandchild s. (pl. -children) nipote (di nonni).

granddaughter s. nipote (femmina) (di nonni).

grandeur s. grandiosità.

grandfather s. nonno.

grandiloquence s. magniloquenza.

grandiloquent agg. magniloquente.

grandiose agg. grandioso.

grandiosity s. grandiosità.

grandmother s. nonna.

grandmotherly agg. protettivo.

grandparents s. pl. nonni.

grandson s. nipote (maschio) (di nonni).

grange s. fattoria, casa colonica.

granite s. granito.

granitic agg. granitico.

granivorous agg. granivoro.

grant s. concessione.

to **grant** vt. concedere || to take for granted, dare per scontato.

granular agg. granulare.

granularity s. granulosità.

to **granulate** vt. granulare. ♦ to granulate vi. granularsi.

granulation s. granulazione.

granulous agg. granuloso.

grape s. 1. acino || — -shot, mitraglia. ♦ grapes s. pl. uva.

grapefruit s. pompelmo.

grapevine s. 1. vigna 2. (fam.) notizia ufficiosa.

graph s. grafico.

graphic(al) agg. 1. grafico 2. pittoresco.

graphite s. grafite.

graphologist s. grafologo.

graphology s. grafologia.

graphomania s. grafomania.

graphomaniac s. grafomane.

grapnel s. (mar.) grappino.

to **grapple** vt. afferrare. ♦ to grapple vi. lottare.

grappling s. (mar.) aggancio || — irons, grappini d'abbordaggio.

grasp s. 1. stretta 2. manico 3. potere.

to **grasp** vt. e vi. afferrare.

grasping agg. avido.

grass s. erba.

grasshopper s. cavalletta.

grass-widow s. donna separata dal marito.

grassy agg. erboso.

grate s. 1. grata 2. graticola.

to **grate** vt. 1. fornire di grata 2. grattugiare. ♦ to grate vi. stridere.

grateful agg. grato.

gratefulness s. gratitudine.

grater s. grattugia.

to **gratify** vt. 1. ricompensare 2. appagare.

gratifying agg. soddisfacente.

grating[1] agg. 1. irritante 2. stridente. ♦ grating s. stridore.

grating[2] s. 1. grata 2. (ott.) reticolo.

gratitude s. gratitudine.

gratuitous agg. gratuito.

gratuity s. mancia.

grave[1] agg. grave.

grave[2] s. tomba.

gravel s. ghiaia.

to **gravel** vt. inghiaiare.

gravelly agg. ghiaioso.

graven agg. intagliato.

graver s. 1. incisore 2. bulino.

gravestone s. pietra tombale.

graveyard s. cimitero.

gravid agg. gravido.

to **gravitate** vi. gravitare.

gravitation s. gravitazione.

gravitational agg. gravitazionale.

gravity s. gravità.

gravy s. sugo.

gray agg. e s. grigio.

graze s. 1. colpo di striscio 2. escoriazione.

to **graze**[1] vt. e vi. 1. graffiare 2. sfiorare.

to **graze**[2] vt. e vi. pascolare, condurre al pascolo.

grazier s. allevatore (di bestiame).

grazing[1] s. abrasione.

grazing[2] s. pascolo.

grease s. grasso.

to **grease** vt. ungere, lubrificare.

greaser s. ingrassatore.

greasiness s. untuosità.

greasy agg. 1. grasso 2. unto, untuoso 3. scivoloso.

great agg. grande || — -grandchild, pronipote (di nonni); — -grandfather, bisnonno; — -grandmother, bisnonna.

greatness s. grandezza.

Grecian agg. e s. greco.

greed(iness) s. avidità.

greedy agg. avido.

Greek agg. e s. greco.

green agg. 1. verde 2. inesperto 3. vigoroso 4. recente. ♦ green s. prato. ♦ greens s. pl. frasche, verdura (sing.).

greenery s. 1. vegetazione 2. serra.

greengrocer s. erbivendolo.

greenhouse s. serra.

greenish *agg.* verdastro.

greenness *s.* **1.** color verde **2.** acerbezza **3.** ingenuità **4.** vigore.

greenroom *s.* (*teat.*) camerino.

to **greet** *vt.* e *vi.* salutare.

greeting *s.* saluto.

Gregorian *agg.* gregoriano.

grenadier *s.* granatiere.

grenadine *s.* granatina.

grew V. *to grow.*

grey *agg.* e *s.* grigio.

greyhound *s.* levriere.

greyness *s.* gigiore.

grid *s.* griglia.

gridiron *s.* graticola.

grief *s.* **1.** dolore **2.** fallimento || *to come to* —, fare fiasco.

grievance *s.* **1.** lagnanza **2.** torto.

to **grieve** *vt.* affliggere. ♦ to **grieve** *vi.* affliggersi.

grievous *agg.* **1.** doloroso **2.** grave.

griffon *s.* grifone.

grill *s.* **1.** graticola **2.** cibo ai ferri || — *-room,* rosticceria.

to **grill** *vt.* e *vi.* arrostire (*alla graticola*).

grille *s.* inferriata.

grim *agg.* cupo.

grimace *s.* smorfia.

grime *s.* sudiciume.

to **grime** *vt.* insudiciare.

grimly *avv.* cupamente.

grimy *agg.* sudicio.

grin *s.* **1.** largo sorriso **2.** sogghigno.

to **grin** *vi.* **1.** fare un largo sorriso **2.** sogghignare.

to **grind** (**ground, ground**) *vt.* **1.** macinare **2.** molare **3.** digrignare **4.** (*fig.*) opprimere.

grinder *s.* **1.** mola **2.** molare **3.** arrotino || *organ-* —, suonatore di organetto.

grinding *agg.* irritante. ♦ **grinding** *s.* **1.** macinatura **2.** stridore **3.** affilatura **4.** (*fig.*) oppressione.

grindstone *s.* mola.

grip *s.* **1.** stretta **2.** manico **3.** (*fig.*) padronanza || *to lose one's grips,* perdere le staffe.

to **grip** *vt.* e *vi.* afferrare.

gripe *s.* **1.** presa **2.** freno. ♦ **gripes** *s. pl.* colica (*sing.*).

gripper *s.* pinza.

grist *s.* grano da macinare || *to bring* — *to one's mill,* tirar l'acqua al proprio mulino.

grit *s.* sabbia, arenaria.

grizzly *agg.* grigio. ♦ **grizzly** *s.* orso grigio.

groan *s.* gemito.

to **groan** *vi.* gemere.

groaning *s.* gemito.

grocer *s.* droghiere.

grocery *s.* drogheria. ♦ **groceries** *s. pl.* droghe e coloniali.

groggy *agg.* vacillante.

groin *s.* inguine.

groom *s.* stalliere.

to **groom** *vt.* strigliare.

groove *s.* solco.

to **grope** *vi.* brancolare.

gropingly *avv.* a tastoni.

gross *agg.* **1.** grossolano **2.** pesante **3.** lussureggiante **4.** (*comm.*) lordo.

grotesque *agg.* grottesco.

grotto *s.* grotta.

ground[1] V. *to grind.*

ground[2] *s.* **1.** suolo, terreno **2.** distanza, territorio **3.** motivi, ragioni (*general. pl.*) || — *-floor,* pianterreno.

to **ground** *vt.* fondare. ♦ to **ground** *vi.* **1.** fondarsi **2.** arenarsi.

grounded *agg.* interrato.

groundless *agg.* infondato.

groundlessness *s.* infondatezza.

grounds *s. pl.* **1.** fondi, sedimenti **2.** parco (*sing.*).

group *s.* gruppo.

to **group** *vt.* raggruppare. ♦ to **group** *vi.* raggrupparsi.

grouping *s.* raggruppamento.

grove *s.* boschetto || *olive* —, oliveto.

to **grovel** *vi.* **1.** strisciare a terra **2.** (*fig.*) umiliarsi.

grovelling *s.* strisciamento. ♦ **grovelling** *agg.* **1.** strisciante **2.** (*fig.*) abbietto.

to **grow** (**grew, grown**) *vi.* **1.** crescere **2.** diventare || *to* — *better,* migliorare; *to* — *old,* invecchiare; *to* — *up,* crescere, diventare maturo (*di persone*). ♦ to **grow** (**grew, grown**) *vt.* coltivare.

grower *s.* coltivatore.

growing *s.* coltivazione.

growl *s.* brontolio.

to **growl** *vt.* e *vi.* brontolare.

growler *s.* brontolone.

grown V. *to grow.*

grown-up *agg.* e *s.* adulto.

growth *s.* **1.** crescita **2.** produzione.

grub *s.* **1.** verme **2.** larva.

to **grub** *vt.* e *vi.* scavare.

grubby *agg.* **1.** bacato **2.** sporco.

grudge *s.* malanimo || *to bear a* — *against so.,* nutrire rancore verso qu.

to **grudge** *vt.* **1.** dare a malincuore **2.** invidiare.

grudging *agg.* **1.** riluttante **2.** invidioso.

gruesome *agg.* raccapricciante.

gruff *agg.* burbero.

grumble *s.* brontolio.

to **grumble** *vt.* e *vi.* brontolare.

grumbler *s.* brontolone.

grumbling *s.* brontolio.

grumpy *agg.* burbero, tetro.

grunt *s.* grugnito.

to **grunt** *vt.* e *vi.* grugnire.

gruyère *s.* gruviera.

guarantee *s.* **1.** garanzia **2.** garante.

to **guarantee** *vt.* garantire.

guard *s.* **1.** guardia **2.** capotreno **3.** parapetto.

to **guard** *vt.* custodire.

guardian *s.* **1.** guardiano **2.** tutore.

guardianship *s.* **1.** protezione **2.** tutela.

guardless *agg.* indifeso.

guardrail *s.* **1.** spartitraffico **2.** corrimano (*di scala*).

Guelph *s.* guelfo.

guerrilla *s.* **1.** guerriglia **2.** guerrigliere.

guess *s.* supposizione.

to **guess** *vt.* e *vi.* **1.** supporre **2.** indovinare.

guess-work *s.* congettura.

guest *s.* ospite ‖ — *-house,* pensione.

guffaw *s.* riso sguaiato.

guide *s.* guida.

to **guide** *vt.* guidare.

guild *s.* corporazione.

guile *s.* insidia.

guileful *agg.* insidioso.

guileless *agg.* sincero.

guillotine *s.* ghigliottina.

guilt *s.* colpa.

guiltiness *s.* colpevolezza.

guiltless *agg.* innocente.

guilty *agg.* colpevole.

guinea *s.* ghinea.

Guinea-pig *s.* cavia.

guise *s.* **1.** aspetto, apparenza **2.** falso aspetto.

guitar *s.* chitarra.

guitarist *s.* chitarrista.

gulf *s.* golfo.

gull[1] *s.* gabbiano.

gull[2] *s.* sciocco.

to **gull** *vt.* truffare.

gully *s.* condotto (*di scolo*) ‖ —

-hole, tombino.

gulp *s.* **1.** boccone **2.** sorso.

to **gulp** *vt.* inghiottire.

gum[1] *s.* gengiva.

gum[2] *s.* gomma.

to **gum** *vt.* ingommare.

gummy *agg.* gommoso.

gun *s.* **1.** cannone **2.** fucile **3.** rivoltella, pistola ‖ — *-barrel,* canna da fucile; — *-carriage,* affusto di cannone.

gunfire *s.* sparatoria.

gunner *s.* artigliere.

gunpowder *s.* polvere da sparo.

gun-room *s.* armeria.

gunshot *s.* colpo di arma da fuoco.

gunsmith *s.* armaiolo.

gurgle *s.* gorgoglio.

to **gurgle** *vi.* gorgogliare.

gush *s.* **1.** getto **2.** effusione.

to **gush** *vi.* **1.** sgorgare **2.** essere espansivo.

gusher *s.* pozzo petrolifero.

gushing *agg.* **1.** sgorgante **2.** esuberante.

gust *s.* **1.** raffica **2.** (*fig.*) impeto.

gustative, gustatory *agg.* gustativo.

gusty *agg.* ventoso.

gut *s.* budello.

to **gut** *vt.* sventrare.

gutter *s.* **1.** grondaia **2.** rigagnolo.

to **gutter** *vt.* scanalare. ♦ to **gutter** *vi.* colare.

guttural *agg.* e *s.* gutturale.

to **guzzle** *vt.* tracannare.

gymkhana *s.* gincana.

gymnasium *s.* palestra.

gymnast *s.* ginnasta.

gymnastic(al) *agg.* ginnastico.

gymnastics *s.* ginnastica.

gynaeceum *s.* (*pl.* *-cea*) gineceo.

gynaecologic *agg.* ginecologico.

gynaecologist *s.* ginecologo.

gynaecology *s.* ginecologia.

gypsy *s.* V. *gipsy.*

to **gyrate** *vi.* girare.

gyroscope *s.* giroscopio.

gyves *s.* *pl.* ceppi, catene.

H

haberdasher *s.* merciaio.

haberdashery *s.* merceria.

habit *s.* **1.** abitudine **2.** temperamen-

to **3**. costume.
habitable *agg.* abitabile.
habitation *s.* abitazione.
habitual *agg.* abituale, consueto.
habitude *s.* abitudine.
hack[1] *s.* **1**. tacca, incisione **2**. piccone, mazza **3**. tosse secca.
hack[2] *s.* **1**. ronzino **2**. (*fig.*) scribacchino.
to **hack**[1] *vt.* sminuzzare. ♦ to **hack** *vi.* tossire a colpi secchi.
to **hack**[2] *vt.* e *vi.* **1**. adoperare cavalli da nolo **2**. adibire a un lavoro da scribacchino.
hackney *s.* **1**. cavallo da nolo **2**. vettura da nolo.
hacksaw *s.* seghetto.
had V. *to have.*
haematoma *s.* ematoma.
haemoglobin *s.* emoglobina.
haemophilia *s.* emofilia.
haemoptysis *s.* emottisi.
haemorrhage *s.* emorragia.
haemorrhoids *s. pl.* emorroidi.
haemostasia *s.* emostasi.
haemostatic *agg.* e *s.* emostatico.
haft *s.* manico, impugnatura.
hag *s.* **1**. strega, megera **2**. (*zool.*) lampreda.
haggard *agg.* sparuto, emaciato.
to **haggle** *vi.* mercanteggiare.
hagiographer *s.* agiografo.
hagiography *s.* agiografia.
hail[1] *s.* grandine || — -*stone*, chicco di grandine; — -*storm*, grandinata.
hail[2] *inter.* salve!, salute!
to **hail**[1] *vi.* grandinare.
to **hail**[2] *vt.* e *vi.* salutare, chiamare.
hair *s.* **1**. capelli, capigliatura **2**. pelo, crine, setola || — -*breadth*, spessore di un capello; — -*cut*, taglio dei capelli; — -*do*, acconciatura.
hairdresser *s.* parrucchiere.
hairiness *s.* pelosità.
hairless *agg.* senza capelli.
hairpin *s.* forcella (*per capelli*).
hairy *agg.* **1**. capelluto **2**. peloso.
halation *s.* alone.
halberd *s.* alabarda.
hale *agg.* robusto, gagliardo.
half *agg.* mezzo.
half *s.* (*pl.* halves) metà, mezzo. ♦ **half** *avv.* a mezzo, a metà || — -*brother*, fratellastro; — -*length*, di media lunghezza; — -*mast*, a mezz'asta; — -*pay*, stipendio ridotto; — -*processed*, semilavorato; — -*sister*, sorellastra; — -*year*, se-

mestre.
halfpenny *s.* mezzo penny.
halfway *agg.* e *avv.* a mezza strada.
hall *s.* **1**. sala, salone **2**. refettorio, sala di ritrovo.
hallo! *int.* pronto (*al telefono*).
to **hallow** *vt.* santificare.
to **hallucinate** *vt.* allucinare.
hallucination *s.* allucinazione.
halo *s.* alone, aureola.
to **halt**[1] *vt.* fermare. ♦ to **halt** *vi.* fermarsi.
to **halt**[2] *vi.* zoppicare.
halter *s.* **1**. capestro **2**. cavezza.
to **halve** *vt.* dividere a metà.
halyard *s.* (*mar.*) drizza.
ham *s.* **1**. prosciutto. ♦ **hams** *s. pl.* natiche.
hamlet *s.* piccolo villaggio.
hammer *s.* martello, martelletto: — -*blow*, colpo di martello, di maglio || *to bring under the* —, mettere all'asta.
to **hammer** *vt.* e *vi.* martellare.
hammering *s.* martellamento.
hammock *s.* amaca.
hamper[1] *s.* cesta.
hamper[2] *s.* impedimento.
to **hamper** *vt.* imbarazzare, ostacolare.
to **hamstring** *vt.* azzoppare.
hand *s.* **1**. mano: *hands off!*, via le mani!; *hands up!*, mani in alto! **2**. operaio, lavoratore **3**. calligrafia || *at* —, a portata di mano; *first*-—, di prima mano.
to **hand** *vt.* porgere, dare || *to* — *in*, consegnare; *to* — *out*, distribuire; *to* — *over*, rimettere.
handbag *s.* borsetta.
handbill *s.* volantino.
handbook *s.* manuale.
handcuffs *s. pl.* manette.
to **handcuff** *vt.* mettere le manette.
handful *s.* **1**. manciata **2**. piccolo numero (*di persone*).
handgrip *s.* stretta di mano, morsa della mano.
handicap *s.* svantaggio.
to **handicap** *vt.* svantaggiare, ostacolare.
handicraft *s.* **1**. lavoro manuale **2**. abilità manuale.
handicraftsman *s.* artigiano.
handily *avv.* **1**. abilmente **2**. a portata di mano.
handiwork *s.* lavoro fatto a mano.
handkerchief *s.* fazzoletto.
handle *s.* **1**. manico, impugnatura

2. (*fig.*) pretesto || — -*bar*, manubrio (*di bicicletta*).

to handle *vt.* **1.** maneggiare **2.** comportarsi verso.

handler *s.* manipolatore.

handling *s.* **1.** maneggiamento **2.** maniera di trattare.

handmade *agg.* fatto a mano.

handrail *s.* corrimano.

handshake *s.* stretta di mano.

handsome *agg.* bello, di bell'aspetto.

handwriting *s.* calligrafia.

handy *agg.* **1.** abile, destro **2.** a portata di mano || — -*man*, factotum.

hang *s.* inclinazione, pendio.

to hang (hung, hung) *vt.* appendere, attaccare.

to hang (hung, hung) *vi.* **1.** pendere **2.** appoggiarsi. ♦ **to hang** (*reg.*) *vt.* impiccare.

hanger *s.* gancio, uncino || — *on*, seguace, parassita; *dress*— , attaccapanni; *paper*— , tappezziere.

hanging *agg.* pendente, sospeso. ♦ **hanging** *s.* impiccagione.

hangman *s.* boia, carnefice.

hank *s.* matassa.

hapless *agg.* sfortunato.

to happen *vi.* avvenire, accadere.

happening *s.* avvenimento.

happily *avv.* felicemente.

happiness *s.* felicità.

happy *agg.* felice, contento.

harangue *s.* arringa.

to harangue *vt.* e *vi.* arringare, pronunciare un discorso solenne.

to harass *vt.* tormentare, molestare.

harbinger *s.* precursore.

harbour *s.* **1.** porto **2.** (*fig.*) rifugio.

to harbour *vt.* **1.** accogliere, dare asilo a **2.** nutrire (*pensieri ecc.*). ♦ **to harbour** *vi.* entrare in porto.

hard *agg.* **1.** duro **2.** severo, spietato **3.** difficile **4.** rigido (*di tempo*). ♦ **hard** *avv.* **1.** energicamente **2.** con difficoltà, duramente **3.** vicino, accanto || — -*boiled*, bollito fino a diventar duro; — -*headed*, ostinato; — -*set*, in bisogno.

to harden *vt.* indurire. ♦ **to harden** *vi.* indurirsi.

hardening *agg.* temprante. ♦ **hardening** *s.* tempra.

hardihood *s.* ardire, coraggio.

hardily *avv.* arditamente.

hardiness *s.* **1.** ardire **2.** robustezza.

hardly *avv.* **1.** a stento, a malapena **2.** quasi **3.** duramente, severamente.

hardness *s.* durezza (*anche fig.*).

hardship *s.* **1.** avversità **2.** stento.

hardware *s.* ferramenta.

hardy *agg.* ardito.

hare *s.* lepre || — -*brained*, scervellato; — -*lip*, labbro leporino.

to hark *vt.* e *vi.* ascoltare || — *back*, risalire a (*col pensiero*).

harlequin *s.* arlecchino.

harlequinade *s.* arlecchinata.

harlot *s.* prostituta.

harm *s.* danno (*morale e fisico*) || *out of* — 's *way*, in salvo.

to harm *vt.* far male, far torto.

harmful *agg.* nocivo, dannoso.

harmfulness *s.* l'essere nocivo.

harmless *agg.* innocuo.

harmonic *agg.* **1.** armonico, armonioso **2.** (*mat.*) in progressione.

harmonious *agg.* armonioso.

harmonium *s.* armonium.

to harmonize *vt.* armonizzare. ♦ **to harmonize** *vi.* armonizzarsi.

harmony *s.* armonia, accordo.

harness *s.* finimenti (*pl.*).

to harness *vt.* bardare, mettere i finimenti a.

harp *s.* arpa.

harpist *s.* arpista.

harpoon *s.* rampone, fiocina.

harpsichord *s.* clavicembalo.

harrow *s.* erpice.

harsh *agg.* **1.** duro, ruvido **2.** aspro **3.** discordante (*di suono*).

harshness *s.* asprezza, durezza.

harvest *s.* raccolto, messe.

harvester *s.* **1.** mietitore **2.** mietitrice meccanica.

haste *s.* fretta, rapidità || *to make* — , far presto.

to haste, to hasten *vt.* affrettare. ♦ **to haste, to hasten** *vi.* affrettarsi.

hastily *avv.* **1.** frettolosamente **2.** precipitosamente.

hasty *agg.* **1.** frettoloso, affrettato **2.** avventato, impetuoso.

hat *s.* cappello.

hatch *s.* **1.** portello, mezza porta **2.** (*mar.*) boccaporto.

hatchet *s.* accetta.

hate *s.* odio.

to hate *vt.* odiare, avere in odio.

hateful *agg.* **1.** odioso **2.** pieno di odio.

hatred *s.* odio.

hatstand *s.* attaccapanni.

hatter *s.* cappellaio.

haughtily *avv.* altezzosamente.

haughtiness s. alterigia, boria.

haughty agg. altezzoso, arrogante.

haul s. 1. trazione, tiro 2. raccolta, retata.

to **haul** vt. tirare, trainare. ♦ to **haul** vi. cambiare (di vento).

haulage s. 1. trasporto 2. costo del trasporto.

haunt s. 1. ricovero, ritiro 2. covo, tana.

to **haunt** vt. 1. frequentare assiduamente 2. perseguitare (di ricordi, pensieri ecc.).

haunted agg. 1. frequentato 2. perseguitato.

haunting agg. che perseguita.

to **have** (had, had) vt. 1. (ausiliare) avere: I — gone, sono andato; I — not (I haven't) read the book, non ho letto il libro 2. avere, possedere || to — breakfast, far colazione 3. dovere: I — to go there, devo andarci 4. ricevere, ottenere || had better, sarebbe meglio che; I had rather, preferirei.

haven s. (fig.) porto, rifugio.

havoc s. strage, rovina.

hawk s. 1. falco, sparviero 2. (fig.) avvoltoio.

hawker[1] s. falconiere.

hawker[2] venditore ambulante.

hawser s. gomena.

hawthorn s. biancospino.

hay s. fieno, paglia || — -loft, fienile; — -making, falciatura.

haycock s. mucchio di fieno.

hayseed s. seme di erba.

haystack s. mucchio di fieno.

hazard s. 1. azzardo, rischio 2. giuoco di dadi.

to **hazard** vt. azzardare, arrischiare.

haze s. foschia, nebbia.

hazel s. nocciuolo || — -nut, nocciuola.

hazily avv. indistintamente.

haziness s. 1. foschia 2. (fig.) confusione.

hazy agg. 1. nebbioso 2. indistinto (anche fig.).

he pron. sogg. m. egli, lui, colui.

head s. 1. testa 2. capo, direttore 3. individuo 4. parte alta di una cosa 5. capo, unità di bestiame || — -first, a capofitto; — -master, direttore di una scuola; — -money, taglia; — -work, lavoro mentale.

to **head** vt. 1. colpire con la testa 2. dirigere, comandare 3. intestare. ♦ to **head** vi. dirigersi.

headache s. mal di testa.

headed agg. munito di testa || hot- —, esaltato; pig- —, ostinato; swollen- —, tronfio; wrong- —, caparbio.

heading s. 1. intestazione, titolo (di un capitolo) 2. (aer.) rotta.

headland s. promontorio.

headless agg. senza testa (anche fig.).

headlight s. faro anteriore.

headline s. intestazione di capitolo, articolo.

headlong avv. a capofitto, precipitosamente.

headquarters s. pl. quartier generale (sing.).

headstone s. pietra tombale.

to **heal** vt. 1. guarire, curare 2. (fig.) sanare. ♦ to **heal** vi. 1. guarire 2. sanarsi.

healer s. guaritore.

healing agg. salutare.

health s. 1. salute 2. salvezza divina.

healthful agg. salubre.

healthily avv. salubremente.

healthiness s. 1. salute 2. salubrità.

healthy agg. 1. sano, robusto 2. salutare.

heap s. mucchio, cumulo.

to **heap** vt. ammucchiare, accumulare.

to **hear** (heard, heard) vt. e vi. 1. sentire, udire 2. sentir dire, venire a sapere.

hearing s. 1. udito 2. udienza.

hearsay s. diceria, voce.

hearse s. carro funebre.

heart s. 1. cuore (anche fig.) 2. affetto, coraggio 3. centro, parte principale || — -beat, pulsazione; — -break, crepacuore; — -breaking, straziante; — -failure, collasso cardiaco; — -felt, sincero, di cuore.

heartache s. angoscia, angustia.

heartburn s. bruciore di stomaco.

hearted agg. dal cuore, di cuore || broken- —, desolato; chicken- —, pauroso; down- —, depresso; lion- —, dal cuore di leone; whole- —, generoso.

to **hearten** vt. incoraggiare. ♦ to **hearten** vi. prendere coraggio.

hearth s. 1. focolare (anche fig.) 2. (metal.) crogiuolo, letto di fusione.

heartily avv. cordialmente.

heartiness s. 1. cordialità.

heartless agg. senza cuore.

hearty agg. 1. sincero, cordiale 2. sano, robusto.

heat s. 1. calore, caldo 2. animosità || — -stroke, colpo di calore; — -wave, ondata di calore.

to heat vt. 1. scaldare 2. animare. ♦ **to heat** vi. 1. scaldarsi 2. animarsi.

heater s. bollitore, riscaldatore.

heath s. brughiera.

heathen agg. e s. pagano.

heather s. erica.

heating s. riscaldamento.

heave s. 1. sforzo 2. rigonfiamento (di onde) 3. sollevamento.

heaven s. 1. cielo, paradiso (anche fig.) 2. stato di gioia.

heavenly agg. divino, celeste.

heavenward agg. rivolto al cielo.

heavily avv. pesantemente, gravemente.

heaviness s. pesantezza.

heavy agg. 1. pesante 2. violento, forte 3. fangoso, pesante (di terreno).

Hebrew agg. e s. ebreo.

hecatomb s. ecatombe.

hectare s. ettaro.

hectic agg. 1. tisico, etico 2. febbricitante.

hectogram(me) s. ettogrammo.

hectolitre s. ettolitro.

hectometre s. ettometro.

hedge s. 1. siepe 2. barriera.

to hedge vt. circondare con una siepe. ♦ **to hedge** vi. essere evasivo.

hedgehog s. riccio, porcospino.

hedonism s. edonismo.

hedonist s. edonista.

heed s. attenzione, cura.

heedful agg. attento, vigile.

heedless agg. sventato.

heedlessness s. sventatezza, trascuratezza.

heel s. 1. calcagno, tallone 2. sperone (di uccelli).

Hegelian agg. hegeliano.

hegemony s. egemonia.

heifer s. giovenca.

heigh inter. ehi!

height s. 1. altezza 2. altitudine 3. altura, collina 4. sommità, il più alto grado.

to heighten vt. 1. innalzare 2. accrescere, intensificare. ♦ **to heighten** vi. innalzarsi.

heinous agg. atroce.

heir s. erede.

heiress s. ereditiera.

held V. to hold.

helicoid agg. elicoidale.

helicopter s. elicottero.

heliocentric(al) agg. eliocentrico.

heliotherapy s. elioterapia.

heliport s. eliporto.

helium s. elio.

hell s. inferno (anche fig.).

Hellenic agg. ellenico.

Hellenism s. ellenismo.

Hellenist s. ellenista.

hellish agg. infernale.

hello inter. salve!

helm[1] s. elmo, casco.

helm[2] s. timone (anche fig.).

helmet s. elmetto, casco.

helmsman s. timoniere.

help s. aiuto, soccorso.

to help vt. 1. aiutare, soccorrere 2. servire (cibo) || cannot —, non poter fare a meno di; to — oneself to, servirsi di (cibo).

helper s. aiutante.

helpful agg. utile, servizievole.

helpless agg. senza aiuto, indifeso.

helpmate s. collaboratore.

Helvetic agg. elvetico.

hem[1] s. orlo, bordo.

hem[2] inter. ehm!.

to hem[1] vt. orlare || to — in, circondare, accerchiare.

to hem[2] vi. schiarirsi la gola.

hemicycle s. emiciclo.

hemiplegia s. emiplegia.

hemisphere s. emisfero.

hemispheric(al) agg. emisferico.

hemlock s. cicuta.

hemp s. canapa.

hen s. 1. gallina 2. femmina (di uccelli) || — -house, pollaio.

hence avv. 1. di qui, da questo momento 2. donde.

henceforth avv. d'ora innanzi.

hendecasyllabic agg. endecasillabico.

hendecasyllable s. endecasillabo.

henna s. alcanna.

hepatic agg. epatico.

hepatitis s. epatite.

heptagon s. ettagono.

heptagonal agg. ettagonale.

her agg. poss. f. suo, sua, suoi, sue. ♦ **her** pron. compl. f. la, lei, le, colei.

herald s. 1. araldo 2. nunzio 3. (fig.) precursore.

heraldic *agg.* araldico.
herb *s.* 1. erba 2. pianta medicinale.
herbaceous *agg.* erbaceo.
herbal *agg.* di erba.
herbarium *s.* erbario.
herbivorous *agg.* erbivoro.
herborist *s.* erborista.
Herculean *agg.* erculeo.
herd *s.* gregge, mandria.
herdsman *s.* mandriano.
here *avv.* qui, qua ‖ — *I am*, eccomi.
hereabouts *avv.* qui intorno.
hereafter *avv.* d'ora innanzi.
hereby *avv.* 1. con questo mezzo 2. qui vicino.
hereditary *agg.* ereditario.
heredity *s.* (*biol.*) ereditarietà.
herein *avv.* 1. in questo 2. (*comm.*) nella presente.
heresiarch *s.* eresiarca.
heresy *s.* eresia.
heretic(al) *agg. e s.* eretico.
herewith *avv.* qui accluso.
heritable *agg.* ereditabile.
heritage *s.* eredità.
hermaphrodite *agg. e s.* ermafrodito.
hermeneutics *s.* ermeneutica.
hermetic(al) *agg.* ermetico.
hermetically *avv.* ermeticamente.
hermit *s.* eremita.
hermitage *s.* eremo, eremitaggio.
hernia *s.* ernia.
hernial *agg.* erniario.
hero *s.* eroe.
heroic(al) *agg.* eroico.
heroin *s.* (*chim.*) eroina.
heroine *s.* eroina.
heroism *s.* eroismo.
heron *s.* airone.
herpes *s.* erpete.
herring *s.* aringa ‖ — *-bone*, spina di pesce (*nei tessuti ecc.*).
hers *pron. poss. f.* il suo, la sua, i suoi, le sue.
herself *pron. r. f.* 1. se stessa, sé, si 2. ella stessa.
hesitant *agg.* esitante.
to **hesitate** *vi.* esitare.
hesitatingly *avv.* con esitazione.
hesitation *s.* esitazione.
heteroclite *agg.* eteroclito.
heterodox *agg.* eterodosso.
heterodoxy *s.* eterodossia.
heterogeneity *s.* eterogeneità.
heterogeneous *agg.* eterogeneo.
to **hew** (**hewed**, **hewn**) *vt.* fendere, recidere ‖ *to — down*, abbat-

tere.
hexagon *s.* esagono.
hexagonal *agg.* esagonale.
hexahedron *s.* esaedro.
hexameter *s.*, esametro.
hiatus *s.* iato.
to **hibernate** *vi.* (*zool.*) cadere in letargo invernale.
hibernation *s.* 1. svernamento 2. ibernazione.
hiccough, hiccup *s.* singhiozzo, singulto.
hid V. *to hide*.
hidden V. *to hide*.
hide¹ *s.* pelle, cuoio.
hide² *s.* nascondiglio ‖ — *-and-seek*, rimpiattino.
to **hide¹** (**hid, hidden**) *vt.* nascondere, celare. ♦ to **hide** (**hid, hidden**) *vi.* nascondersi, celarsi.
to **hide²** *vt.* 1. spellare, scorticare 2. frustare.
hideous *agg.* orrendo, odioso.
hideousness *s.* odiosità, aspetto orribile.
hiding *s.* il nascondere.
hierarchy *s.* gerarchia.
hieratic *agg.* ieratico.
hieroglyph *s.* geroglifico.
hieroglyphic(al) *agg.* geroglifico.
high *agg.* 1. alto, elevato (*anche fig.*) 2. altezzoso 3. forte, intenso (*di luce, colori*) ‖ — *-born*, di alto lignaggio; — *-class*, di prim'ordine; — *-coloured*, dal colore acceso; — *-hearted*, pieno di coraggio; — *-life*, vita di alta società; — *school*, scuola media; — *sea*, mare aperto; — *-speed*, ad alta velocità. ♦ **high** *avv.* 1. alto, in alto 2. fortemente.
highbrow *agg. e s.* intellettuale.
highland *s.* regione montuosa.
highlander *s.* montanaro.
highly *avv.* 1. molto, assai 2. altamente, nobilmente.
highness *s.* 1. altezza, elevatezza 2. eccellenza, valore.
highway *s.* strada maestra.
highwayman *s.* bandito, rapinatore.
hilarious *agg.* ilare.
hill *s.* collina, altura.
hillock *s.* collinetta.
hillside *s.* pendio.
hilltop *s.* sommità della collina.
hilly *agg.* collinoso.
hilt *s.* elsa.
him *pron. pers. m.* lo, lui, gli, colui, sé.
himself *pron. r. m.* 1. si, sé, se

stesso **2.** egli stesso.

hind[1] *s.* cerva, daina.

hind[2] *s.* colono, fattore.

hind(er) *agg.* posteriore.

to hinder *vt.* e *vi.* **1.** impedire, ostruire **2.** imbarazzare.

hindrance *s.* ostacolo, impaccio.

Hindu *agg.* e *s.* indù.

hinge *s.* **1.** cardine **2.** (*fig.*) perno.

to hinge *vt.* munire di cardini. ♦ **to hinge** *vi.* **1.** girare sui cardini **2.** essere imperniato.

hint *s.* **1.** cenno, allusione **2.** consiglio.

to hint *vt.* e *vi.* alludere, accennare, suggerire.

hinterland *s.* retroterra.

hip *s.* anca, fianco.

hippocampus *s.* (*pl.* -pi.) ippocampo.

hippopotamus *s.* ippopotamo.

hire *s.* affitto, nolo.

to hire *vt.* prendere a servizio, noleggiare.

hireling *s.* mercenario.

his *agg. poss. m.* suo, sua, suoi, sue. ♦ **his** *pron. poss. m.* il suo, la sua, i suoi, le sue.

Hispanic *agg.* ispanico.

Hispanicism *s.* ispanismo.

Hispanist *s.* ispanista.

hispid *agg.* ispido.

hiss *s.* sibilo, fischio.

to hiss *vt.* e *vi.* **1.** sibilare **2.** fischiare.

histology *s.* istologia.

historian *s.* storico.

historic(al) *agg.* storico.

historicity *s.* storicità.

historiographer *s.* storiografo.

historiography *s.* storiografia.

history *s.* storia.

histrion *s.* istrione.

histrionic(al) *agg.* istrionico.

histrionism *s.* istrionismo.

hit *s.* **1.** colpo, botta **2.** osservazione sarcastica **3.** caso fortunato **4.** (*teat.*) successo.

to hit (hit, hit) *vt.* e *vi.* **1.** battere, picchiare **2.** urtare, venire a contatto **3.** (*fig.*) toccare, colpire ‖ *to — the mark,* colpire nel segno.

hitch *s.* **1.** colpo, strattone, balzo repentino **2.** nodo.

to hitch *vt.* **1.** muovere a sbalzi **2.** legare, attaccare. ♦ **to hitch** *vi.* muoversi a sbalzi.

to hitchhike *vi.* fare l'autostop.

hitchhiker *s.* autostoppista.

hitchhiking *s.* autostop.

hive *s.* **1.** alveare, arnia **2.** sciame (*anche fig.*).

hives *s. pl.* orticaria, eruzione cutanea.

hoar *s.* candore, vecchiaia ‖ — -*frost,* brina.

hoard *s.* gruzzolo.

to hoard *vt.* ammassare, ammucchiare. ♦ **to hoard** *vi.* ammucchiarsi.

hoarder *s.* incettatore.

hoarding *s.* recinto provvisorio.

hoarse *agg.* rauco, fioco.

hoarseness *s.* raucedine.

hoary *agg.* **1.** bianco, canuto **2.** venerando.

hobble *s.* **1.** zoppicamento **2.** imbarazzo.

to hobble *vi.* zoppicare. ♦ **to hobble** *vt.* azzoppare.

hobby *s.* svago preferito, passatempo.

hobnail *s.* chiodo (*per scarponi*).

hobnailed *agg.* chiodato.

hodman *s.* manovale.

hoe *s.* zappa.

to hoe *vt.* zappare, estirpare le erbacce.

hog *s.* maiale.

hogshead *s.* barilotto (*per tabacco, zucchero*).

hoist *s.* montacarichi.

to hoist *vt.* alzare, sollevare.

hold[1] *s.* **1.** presa **2.** (*fig.*) ascendente.

hold[2] *s.* (*mar.*) stiva.

to hold (held, held) *vt.* e *vi.* **1.** tenere, sostenere **2.** contenere **3.** ritenere, credere, pensare **4.** occupare una carica, possedere **5.** resistere, aggrapparsi ‖ *to — up,* sollevare; *to — back,* esitare.

holder *s.* **1.** possessore, detentore, proprietario **2.** sostegno, supporto **3.** dente canino.

holdings *s. pl.* beni, titoli.

hold-up *s.* intoppo nel traffico, panna di automobile.

hole *s.* **1.** foro, apertura, buco **2.** antro, tana.

holiday *s.* **1.** festa, giorno festivo **2.** vacanza.

holiness *s.* santità.

hollow *agg.* **1.** concavo, infossato **2.** cupo, caverноso **3.** (*fig.*) falso, irreale, vuoto.

to hollow *vt.* scavare, incavare.

hollow *avv.* (*fam.*) completamente.

hollowness *s.* **1.** cavità **2.** timbro

cavernoso (*di voce*).

holly *s.* agrifoglio.

holocaust *s.* olocausto.

holograph *agg. e s.* documento olografo.

holy *agg.* santo, sacro.

homage *s.* omaggio.

home[1] *s.* **1.** casa, focolare domestico **2.** patria **3.** rifugio, asilo, ospizio.

home[2] *agg.* domestico, casalingo.

home[3] *avv.* **1.** a casa, in patria **2.** direttamente, al segno || — -*born*, indigeno, locale; — -*bred*, allevato in casa; — -*made*, fatto in casa; — -*market*, mercato nazionale; — -*town*, città natia; — -*trade*, commercio interno

homeland *s.* patria.

homeless *agg.* senza casa.

homelike *agg.* domestico, familiare.

homely *agg.* **1.** semplice, modesto **2.** domestico.

homeopathic *agg.* omeopatico

homeopathy *s.* omeopatia.

Homeric *agg.* omerico.

homesick *agg.* nostalgico.

homesickness *s.* nostalgia.

homeward *agg. e avv.* verso casa, verso la patria.

homework *s. coll.* compiti per casa.

homicidal *agg.* omicida.

homicide *s.* omicidio.

homily *s.* omelia.

homogeneity *s.* omogeneità.

homogeneous *agg.* omogeneo.

to homogenize *vt.* omogeneizzare.

to homologate *vt.* omologare.

homologation *s.* omologazione.

homologous *agg.* omologo.

homology *s.* omologia.

homonymous *agg.* omonimo.

homonymy *s.* omonimia.

homosexual *agg. e s.* omosessuale.

homosexuality *s.* omosessualità.

homy *agg.* casalingo.

honest *agg.* **1.** onesto, integro **2.** leale.

honesty *s.* **1.** onestà, probità **2.** lealtà.

honey *s.* miele.

honeycomb *s.* favo.

honeyed *agg.* **1.** coperto di miele **2.** (*fig.*) sdolcinato, adulatorio.

honeymoon *s.* luna di miele.

honeysuckle *s.* caprifoglio.

honorary *agg.* onorario, onorifico.

honorific *agg.* onorifico.

honour *s.* **1.** onore, reputazione **2.** stima, reverenza **3.** Eccellenza.

to honour *vt.* onorare, fare onore a.

honourable *agg.* stimato, onorevole.

honourableness *s.* onorabilità.

hood *s.* cappuccio.

to hood *vt.* incappucciare, fornire di cappuccio.

hoof *s.* zoccolo (*di animale*).

hook *s.* **1.** uncino, gancio **2.** amo **3.** tagliola **4.** falce per grano || *by* — *or by crook*, di riffa o di raffa.

to hook *vt.* agganciare. ♦ **to hook** *vi.* agganciarsi.

hooked *agg.* **1.** fornito di uncini **2.** adunco, uncinato.

hoop *s.* collare, cerchio (*di botte, ruota ecc.*).

to hoop *vt.* cerchiare (*una botte*).

to hoot *vt. e vi.* **1.** urlare, gridare **2.** suonare il clacson.

hop[1] *s.* salto (*su una gamba sola*).

hop[2] *s.* luppolo.

to hop *vt. e vi.* saltare su una gamba sola.

hope *s.* speranza.

to hope *vt. e vi.* sperare, essere fiducioso.

hopeful *agg.* pieno di speranza, fiducioso.

hopefulness *s.* fiducia, buona speranza.

hopeless *agg.* senza speranza, irrimediabile.

hopelessness *s.* disperazione.

hopper *s.* persona od insetto che saltella.

horde *s.* orda.

horizon *s.* orizzonte.

horizontal *agg.* orizzontale.

horizontally *avv.* orizzontalmente.

hormone *s.* ormone.

horn *s.* **1.** corno, tentacolo, antenna **2.** (*mus.*) corno, tromba.

to horn *vt.* **1.** fornire di corna **2.** ferire con le corna.

hornet *s.* vespa, calabrone.

hornpipe *s.* cornamusa.

horology *s.* orologia.

horoscope *s.* oroscopo: *to cast a* —, fare un oroscopo.

horrible *agg.* **1.** orribile, orrendo **2.** (*fam.*) eccessivo.

horribly *avv.* orribilmente.

horrid *agg.* orrido, orrendo.

horrific *agg.* orribile, orripilante.

to horrify *vt.* **1.** atterrire, incutere timore **2.** scandalizzare.

horror *s.* **1.** orrore, spavento **2.** cosa orribile || — -*stricken*, atterrito.

hors-d'oeuvre s. antipasto.

horse s. cavallo || — -*bean*, fava; — -*boy*, mozzo di stalla; — -*chest-nut*, ippocastano; — -*doctor*, veterinario; — -*race*, corsa ippica; — -*shoe*, ferro di cavallo.

horseback s. dorso di cavallo || *on* —, a cavallo.

horseman s. cavaliere.

horticultural agg. attinente all'orticultura.

horticulture s. orticultura.

hosanna inter. osanna.

hose s. 1. idrante 2. calze (pl.).

hosier s. commerciante in calze.

hosiery s. maglieria.

hospice s. alloggio, ospizio.

hospitable agg. ospitale.

hospital s. ospedale.

hospitality s. ospitalità.

host[1] s. folla, moltitudine.

host[2] s. ospite, anfitrione.

hostage s. ostaggio.

hostel s. pensionato (*per giovani, studenti, militari ecc.*).

hostess s. 1. ospite, padrona di casa 2. assistente di volo.

hostile agg. ostile, nemico.

hostility s. inimicizia, ostilità.

hot agg. 1. caldo, ardente 2. forte, piccante 3. violento, impetuoso || — -*headed*, scalmanato.

hotel s. albergo || - -*keeper*, albergatore.

hothead s. testa calda.

hothouse s. serra.

hotly avv. caldamente.

hotspur s. persona impulsiva.

hound s. bracco, segugio.

to hound vt. cacciare (*con bracchi*).

hour s. 1. ora 2. periodo. ♦ **hours** s. pl. orario (*sing.*).

hourly agg. 1. continuo 2. all'ora 3. ad ogni ora. ♦ **hourly** avv. 1. continuamente 2. ad ogni ora 3. d'ora in ora.

house s. 1. casa, abitazione 2. albergo, pensione 3. clinica 4. convento 5. casato, dinastia 6. teatro 7. (*comm.*) ditta 8. (*mar.*) tuga.

to house vt. 1. alloggiare, ricevere in casa 2. (*fig.*) offrire un rifugio. ♦ **to house** vi. 1. prendere alloggio 2. rifugiarsi.

housebreaker s. scassinatore.

housebreaking s. demolizione edilizia.

household s. famiglia: *Royal Household*, la famiglia reale.

householder s. capofamiglia.

housekeeper s. governante, domestica.

housekeeping s. il governo della casa.

houseless agg. senza casa.

housemaid s. domestica, cameriera.

housewife s. (*pl.* -wives) massaia, casalinga.

housework s. lavoro domestico.

housing s. 1. il ricevere, l'accogliere 2. alloggio, rifugio, riparo.

hovel s. 1. tana 2. baracca.

to hover vi. 1. librarsi, svolazzare 2. gironzolare.

how avv. come, in che modo.

however avv. 1. comunque 2. però, tuttavia.

howitzer s. obice.

howl s. urlo, grido.

to howl vt. e vi. urlare, ululare.

howling agg. urlante, ululante.

hub s. mozzo di ruota.

hubbub s. tumulto, fracasso.

huddle s. calca, folla.

to huddle vt. ammucchiare. ♦ **to huddle** vi. affollarsi, accalcarsi.

hue s. tinta, colore.

hug s. abbraccio.

to hug vt. abbracciare (*anche fig.*) || *to* — *oneself*, compiacersi.

huge agg. enorme, vasto.

hugeness s. grandezza, enormità.

hull s. scafo.

hullabaloo s. tumulto, fracasso.

hullo inter. 1. (*fam.*) salve 2. (*tel.*) pronto.

hum s. ronzio, mormorio.

to hum vt. e vi. 1. ronzare, mormorare 2. cantare a bocca chiusa.

human agg. 1. umano 2. sensibile.

humane agg. umano, compassionevole.

humaneness s. benevolenza, umanità.

humanism s. umanesimo.

humanist s. umanista.

humanistic agg. umanistico.

humanitarian agg. filantropico, umanitario.

humanity s. 1. umanità, il genere umano 2. bontà, benevolenza.

to humanize vt. 1. rendere umano 2. adattare alla natura umana. ♦ **to humanize** vi. acquisire sentimenti migliori.

humankind s. il genere umano.

humble agg. umile, modesto.

to humble vt. umiliare.

humbleness s. umiltà.

humbly avv. umilmente.

humbug s. frode, impostura.

humdrum s. monotonia, tedio. ◆ **humdrum** agg. monotono.

humeral agg. omerale.

humerus s. (pl. -ri) omero.

humid agg. umido.

humidity s. umidità.

to humiliate vt. umiliare, mortificare.

humiliation s. umiliazione.

humility s. umiltà.

humming agg. ronzante. ◆ **humming** s. ronzio.

humorist s. umorista.

humorous agg. arguto, dotato di senso dell'umorismo.

humour s. 1. umorismo 2. umore.

hump s. 1. gobba, gibbosità 2. collinetta, cresta.

humpback s. 1. gobba 2. gobbo.

hunch s. gobba, gibbosità.

hunchback s. persona gobba.

hundred agg. cento. ◆ **hundred** s. centinaio.

hundredth agg. centesimo.

hung V. to hang.

Hungarian agg. e s. ungherese.

hunger s. 1. fame, appetito 2. (fig.) ingordigia.

hungrily avv. 1. con grande appetito 2. avidamente.

hungry agg. 1. affamato || to be —, aver fame 2. (fig.) avido, bramoso.

hunt s. 1. caccia 2. ricerca, inseguimento.

to hunt vt. e vi. 1. cacciare, andare a caccia 2. cercare affannosamente.

hunter s. cacciatore (anche fig.).

hunting s. 1. caccia 2. ricerca.

huntsman s. cacciatore.

hurdle s. ostacolo (anche fig.).

hurl s. lancio violento.

to hurl vt. lanciare, scagliare (anche fig.).

hurrah inter. urrah!

hurricane s. uragano, ciclone (anche fig.).

hurried agg. affrettato, precipitoso.

hurry s. fretta, precipitazione: to be in a —, aver fretta.

to hurry vt. affrettare. ◆ **to hurry** vi. affrettarsi || — up!, fa presto!

hurt s. lesione, ferita (anche fig.).

to hurt (hurt, hurt) vt. e vi. 1. dolere 2. recar dolore, offendere.

hurtful agg. 1. dannoso 2. offensivo.

husband s. marito.

husbandry s. 1. agricoltura 2. amministrazione domestica.

hush inter. silenzio.

to hush vt. 1. zittire, tacere 2. (fig.) calmare.

husk s. 1. guscio, baccello 2. involucro 3. (pl.) rifiuti.

to husk vt. sgusciare, sbucciare.

husky agg. rugoso, secco.

hussar s. ussaro.

hut s. 1. capanna, casupola 2. rifugio alpino.

hyacinth s. giacinto.

hybrid agg. e s. ibrido.

hybridism s. ibridismo.

hybridization s. ibridazione.

hydra s. idra.

hydrangea s. ortensia.

hydrant s. idrante.

hydrate s. idrato.

to hydrate vt. idratare.

hydraulic agg. idraulico.

hydraulics s. idraulica.

hydric agg. contenente idrogeno.

hydrocarbon s. idrocarburo.

hydrocephalus s. idrocefalo.

hydroelectric agg. idroelettrico.

hydrofluoric agg. fluoridrico.

hydrofoil boat s. aliscafo.

hydrogen s. idrogeno.

hydrology s. idrologia.

hydrolysis s. (pl. -ses) idrolisi.

hydrostatic(al) agg. idrostatico.

hyena s. iena.

hygiene s. igiene.

hygienics s. la scienza dell'igiene.

hygienist s. igienista.

hygrometry s. igrometria.

hymn s. inno.

hyperbole s. iperbole.

hyperbolic(al) agg. iperbolico.

hyperborean agg. e s. iperboreo.

hypercritical agg. ipercritico.

hypermetropy s. ipermetropia.

hypernutrition s. supernutrizione.

hypersensitive agg. ipersensibile.

hypersensitivity s. ipersensibilità.

hypertension s. ipertensione.

hypertrophy s. ipertrofia.

hyphen s. lineetta d'unione.

hypnosis s. (pl. -ses) ipnosi.

hypnotic agg. e s. ipnotico.

hypnotism s. ipnotismo.

to hypnotize vt. ipnotizzare.

hypochondria s. ipocondria.

hypochondriac agg. e s. ipocondriaco.

hypocrisy s. ipocrisia.

hypocrite s. ipocrita.
hypocritic(al) agg. ipocrita.
hypodermic agg. ipodermico.
hypodermoclysis s. ipodermoclisi.
hyposulphite s. iposolfito.
hypotenuse s. ipotenusa.
hypothecary agg. ipotecario.
to **hypothecate** vt. ipotecare.
hypothesis s. (pl. -ses) ipotesi.
to **hypothesize** vi. fare ipotesi.
hypothetic(al) agg. ipotetico.
hypothetically avv. ipoteticamente.
hysteria s. isterismo.
hysteric(al) agg. isterico.
hysterics s. attacco isterico.

I

I pron. pers. io.
iamb s. giambo.
iambic agg. giambico.
Iberian agg. e s. iberico.
ice s. ghiaccio || — -box, ghiacciaia;
— -breaker, rompighiaccio; —
-cream, gelato.
to **ice** vt. **1.** ghiacciare **2.** (cuc.) glassare.
iceboat s. nave rompighiaccio.
Icelander s. islandese.
Icelandic agg. islandese.
ichtyologist s. ittiologo.
ichthyology s. ittiologia.
icicle s. ghiacciuolo.
iciness s. gelo.
icing s. glassatura.
icon s. icona.
iconoclast s. iconoclasta.
iconoclastic agg. iconoclastico.
iconography s. iconografia.
icy agg. gelido, gelato.
idea s. idea.
ideal agg. e s. ideale.
idealism s. idealismo.
idealist s. idealista.
idealistic(al) agg. idealistico.
idealization s. idealizzazione.
to **idealize** vt. idealizzare.
ideally avv. idealmente.
to **ideate** vt. ideare.
ideation s. ideazione.
identic(al) agg. identico.
identifiable agg. identificabile.
identification s. identificazione.
to **identify** vt. identificare || to —
oneself with, immedesimarsi con.

identity s. identità.
ideogram s. ideogramma.
ideography s. ideografia.
ideologic(al) agg. ideologico.
ideologist s. ideologo.
ideology s. ideologia.
idiocy s. idiozia.
idiom s. **1.** idioma **2.** idiotismo.
idiomatic(al) agg. idiomatico.
idiosyncrasy s. idiosincrasia.
idiot s. idiota.
idiotic(al) agg. idiota.
idle agg. **1.** ozioso **2.** vano.
to **idle** vi. oziare.
idleness s. **1.** ozio **2.** futilità.
idler s. ozioso.
idly avv. oziosamente.
idol s. idolo.
idolater s. idolatra.
to **idolatrize** vt. idolatrare.
idolatrous agg. idolatrico.
idolatry, idolism s. idolatria.
idyl(l) s. idillio.
idyllic agg. idillico.
if cong. se || as —, come se.
igneous agg. igneo.
to **ignite** vt. accendere. ♦ to **ignite**
vi. accendersi.
ignition s. accensione || battery
coil —, spinterogeno.
ignobility s. ignobilità.
ignoble agg. ignobile.
ignominious agg. ignominioso.
ignominy, ignomy s. ignominia.
ignorance s. ignoranza.
ignorant agg. ignorante.
to **ignore** vt. ignorare.
ilex s. leccio.
iliac agg. iliaco.
ill (worse, worst) agg. **1.** ammalato **2.** cattivo. ♦ **ill** avv. male ||
— -advised, sconsiderato; — -disposed, malevolo; — -fated, sfortunato; — -mannered, maleducato.
♦ **ill** s. male.
illation s. illazione.
illegal agg. **1.** illegale **2.** illecito.
illegality s. illegalità.
illegible agg. illeggibile.
illegitimacy s. illegittimità.
illegitimate agg. illegittimo.
illiberal agg. **1.** illiberale **2.** meschino.
illiberality s. **1.** illiberalità **2.** meschinità.
illicit agg. illecito.
illimitable agg. illimitato.
illiteracy s. **1.** analfabetismo **2.** ignoranza.

illiterate *agg.* e *s.* 1. analfabeta 2. ignorante.

illness *s.* malattia.

illogical *agg.* illogico.

illogicality *s.* illogicità.

to ill-treat *vt.* maltrattare.

to illuminate *vt.* illuminare.

illumination *s.* illuminazione.

to illumine *vt.* illuminare.

illuminism *s.* illuminismo.

ill-usage *s.* maltrattamento.

to ill-use *vt.* maltrattare.

illusion *s.* illusione.

illusionism *s.* illusionismo.

illusionist *s.* illusionista.

illusive *agg.* illusorio.

illusiveness *s.* illusorietà.

illusory *agg.* illusorio.

to illustrate *vt.* illustrare.

illustration *s.* illustrazione.

illustrative *agg.* illustrativo.

illustrator *s.* illustratore.

illustrious *agg.* illustre.

ill-will *s.* malevolenza.

ill-wisher *s.* malevolo.

image *s.* immagine.

to image *vt.* 1. immaginare 2. descrivere 3. riflettere.

imagery *s.* raffigurazione.

imaginable *agg.* immaginabile.

imaginary *agg.* immaginario.

imagination *s.* immaginazione.

imaginative *agg.* immaginativo.

to imagine *vt.* e *vi.* immaginare.

imagining *s.* immaginazione.

imbecile *agg.* e *s.* 1. debole 2. imbecille.

imbecility *s.* 1. debolezza 2. imbecillità.

to imbibe *vt.* assorbire. ♦ to imbibe *vi.* imbeversi.

to imbue *vt.* impregnare.

imitable *agg.* imitabile.

to imitate *vt.* imitare.

imitation *s.* imitazione.

imitative *agg.* imitativo.

imitator *s.* imitatore.

immaculate *agg.* immacolato.

immanence *s.* immanenza.

immanent *agg.* immanente.

immanentism *s.* immanentismo.

immaterial *agg.* 1. immateriale 2. irrilevante.

immaterialism *s.* immaterialismo.

immaterialist *s.* immaterialista.

immateriality *s.* immaterialità.

immature *agg.* immaturo.

immaturity *s.* immaturità.

immeasurability *s.* incommensurabilità.

immeasurable *agg.* incommensurabile.

immediacy *s.* 1. immediatezza 2. rapporto diretto.

immediate *agg.* 1. immediato 2. diretto.

immediateness *s.* V. *immediacy.*

immemorial *agg.* immemorabile.

immense *agg.* immenso.

immenseness, immensity *s.* immensità.

immensurability *s.* immensurabilità.

immensurable *agg.* immensurabile.

to immerge, to immerse *vt.* immergere. ♦ to immerge *vi.* immergersi.

immersion *s.* 1. immersione 2. eclisse.

immigrant *agg.* e *s.* immigrante.

to immigrate *vi.* immigrare.

immigration *s.* immigrazione.

imminence *s.* 1. imminenza 2. pericolo.

imminent *agg.* 1. imminente 2. sovrastante.

immobile *agg.* immobile.

immobility *s.* immobilità.

immobilization *s.* immobilizzazione.

to immobilize *vt.* immobilizzare.

immoderate *agg.* smodato.

immoderateness *s.* smoderatezza.

immodest *agg.* 1. immodesto 2. indecente.

immodesty *s.* 1. immodestia 2. indecenza.

to immolate *vt.* immolare.

immolation *s.* immolazione.

immolator *s.* immolatore.

immoral *agg.* immorale.

immorality *s.* immoralità.

immortal *agg.* e *s.* immortale.

immortality *s.* immortalità.

immortalization *s.* l'immortalare.

to immortalize *vt.* immortalare.

immovability *s.* 1. immobilità 2. inamovibilità.

immovable *agg.* 1. immobile 2. inamovibile.

immovables *s.* *pl.* beni immobili.

immune *agg.* 1. immune 2. esente.

immunity *s.* 1. immunità 2. esenzione.

immunization *s.* immunizzazione.

to immunize *vt.* immunizzare.

to immure *vt.* 1. murare 2. impri-

gionare **3.** chiudere fra mura.
immutability *s.* immutabilità.
immutable *agg.* immutabile.
imp *s.* diavoletto.
impact *s.* urto, collisione.
to **impact** *vt.* conficcare.
to **impair** *vt.* menomare.
impairment *s.* menomazione.
to **impale** *vt.* impalare.
impalpability *s.* impalpabilità.
impalpable *agg.* impalpabile.
imparity *s.* imparità.
to **impart** *vt.* **1.** impartire **2.** rivelare.
impartial *agg.* imparziale.
impartiality *s.* imparzialità.
impassable *agg.* invalicabile, impraticabile.
impassibility *s.* impassibilità.
impassible *agg.* impassibile.
to **impassion** *vt.* appassionare.
impassionate, impassioned *agg.* eccitato, ardente.
impassive *agg.* impassibile.
impatience *s.* **1.** impazienza **2.** avversione.
impatient *agg.* **1.** impaziente **2.** intollerante.
impavid *agg.* impavido.
to **impeach** *vt.* **1.** imputare **2.** biasimare ‖ *to — so. for high treason,* accusare qu. di alto tradimento.
impeachable *agg.* accusabile.
impeacher *s.* accusatore.
impeachment *s.* accusa.
impeccability *s.* impeccabilità.
impeccable *agg.* impeccabile.
impecunious *agg.* povero.
to **impede** *vt.* **1.** impedire **2.** ostacolare.
impediment *s.* impedimento.
to **impel** *vt.* spingere, incitare.
impellent *agg.* impellente. ♦ **impellent** *s.* incentivo.
to **impend** *vi.* incombere.
impendence *s.* imminenza.
impendent *agg.* incombente.
impenetrability *s.* impenetrabilità.
impenetrable *agg.* impenetrabile.
impenitence *s.* impenitenza.
impenitent *agg.* impenitente.
imperative *agg.* e *s.* imperativo.
imperator *s.* imperatore.
imperceptibility *s.* impercettibilità.
imperceptible *agg.* impercettibile.
imperfect *agg.* **1.** imperfetto **2.** incompiuto.
imperfection *s.* **1.** imperfezione **2.**

incompiutezza.
imperial *agg.* imperiale.
imperialism *s.* imperialismo.
imperialist *s.* imperialista.
imperialistic *agg.* imperialistico.
to **imperil** *vt.* mettere in pericolo.
imperious *agg.* **1.** imperioso **2.** impellente.
imperiousness *s.* **1.** imperiosità **2.** urgenza.
imperishability *s.* indistruttibilità.
imperishable *agg.* indistruttibile, imperituro.
impermeability *s.* impermeabilità.
impermeable *agg.* impermeabile.
impersonal *agg.* impersonale.
impersonality *s.* l'essere impersonale.
to **impersonate** *vt.* impersonare.
impersonation *s.* personificazione.
impertinence *s.* **1.** impertinenza **2.** non pertinenza.
impertinent *agg.* **1.** impertinente **2.** non pertinente.
imperturbability *s.* imperturbabilità.
imperturbable *agg.* imperturbabile.
impervious *agg.* **1.** impervio **2.** impermeabile.
to **impetrate** *vt.* impetrare.
impetration *s.* impetrazione.
impetuosity *s.* impetuosità.
impetuous *agg.* impetuoso.
impetus *s.* impeto.
impiety *s.* empietà.
impious *agg.* empio.
impish *agg.* birichino.
implacability *s.* implacabilità.
implacable *agg.* implacabile.
to **implant** *vt.* **1.** impiantare **2.** inculcare.
implement *s.* utensile.
to **implement** *vt.* **1.** compiere **2.** attrezzare.
to **implicate** *vt.* implicare.
implication *s.* implicazione.
implicit, implied *agg.* implicito.
to **implore** *vt.* implorare.
imploring *agg.* supplichevole.
to **imply** *vt.* implicare.
impolite *agg.* scortese.
impoliteness *s.* scortesia.
impolitic *agg.* impolitico.
imponderability *s.* imponderabilità.
imponderable *agg.* imponderabile.
import *s.* **1.** importanza **2.** significato **3.** *(comm.)* importazione.
to **import** *vt.* **1.** importare **2.** si-

gnificare 3. (*comm.*) importare.
importance *s.* importanza.
important *agg.* importante.
importer *s.* importatore.
importunate, importune *agg.* urgente.
to **importune** *vt.* importunare.
importunity *s.* 1. insistenza 2. urgenza.
to **impose** *vt.* 1. imporre 2. (*tip.*) impaginare. ♦ to **impose** *vi.* imporsi || *to — on*, ingannare.
imposing *agg.* imponente.
imposition *s.* 1. imposizione 2. imposta 3. inganno 4. (*tip.*) messa in macchina.
impossibility *s.* impossibilità.
impossible *agg.* impossibile.
impostor *s.* impostore.
imposture *s.* impostura.
impotence *s.* impotenza.
impotent *agg.* impotente.
to **impoverish** *vt.* impoverire.
impoverishment *s.* impoverimento.
impracticability *s.* 1. inattuabilità 2. impraticabilità 3. intrattabilità.
impracticable *agg.* 1. inattuabile 2. impraticabile 3. intrattabile.
imprecation *s.* imprecazione.
imprecatory *agg.* imprecatorio.
impregnable *agg.* inespugnabile.
to **impregnate** *vt.* 1. impregnare 2. fecondare.
impregnation *s.* fecondazione.
to **impress** *vt.* 1. imprimere, stampare 2. impressionare.
impression *s.* 1. impressione 2. ristampa.
impressionability *s.* impressionabilità.
impressionable *agg.* impressionabile.
impressionism *s.* impressionismo.'
impressionist *agg. e s.* impressionista.
impressive *agg.* impressionante.
imprint *s.* 1. impronta 2. stampa.
to **imprint** *vt.* 1. imprimere 2. stampare.
to **imprison** *vt.* imprigionare.
imprisonment *s.* prigionia.
improbability *s.* improbabilità.
improbable *agg.* improbabile.
improbably *avv.* improbabilmente.
impromptu *agg.* improvvisato. ♦ **impromptu** *s.* improvvisazione.
improper *agg.* 1. erroneo 2. inadatto 3. sconveniente, irregolare.

impropriety *s.* 1. scorrettezza 2. sconvenienza.
to **improve** *vt.* 1. migliorare 2. valorizzare. ♦ to **improve** *vi.* migliorare, perfezionarsi.
improvement *s.* miglioramento.
improvidence *s.* imprevidenza.
improvident *agg.* imprevidente.
improvisation *s.* improvvisazione.
improvisator *s.* improvvisatore.
to **improvise** *vt. e vi.* improvvisare.
imprudence *s.* imprudenza.
imprudent *agg.* imprudente.
impudence *s.* impudenza.
impudent *agg.* impudente.
to **impugn** *vt.* (*giur.*) impugnare.
impugnable *agg.* (*giur.*) impugnabile.
impugner *s.* oppositore.
impulse, impulsion *s.* impulso.
impulsive *agg.* impulsivo.
impulsiveness, impulsivity *s.* impulsività.
impunity *s.* impunità.
impure *agg.* impuro.
impurity *s.* impurità.
imputable *agg.* imputabile.
imputation *s.* imputazione.
to **impute** *vt.* imputare.
in *avv. e prep.* a, in, dentro, entro, durante || *to be — Paris*, essere a Parigi; *the best — the world*, il migliore del mondo; *— my opinion*, secondo me; *— all*, in tutto; *— that*, in quanto che.
inability *s.* incapacità.
inaccessibility *s.* inaccessibilità.
inaccessible *agg.* inaccessibile.
inaccuracy *s.* inesattezza.
inaccurate *agg.* inesatto.
inaction *s.* inattività.
inactive *agg.* inattivo.
inactivity *s.* inattività.
inadaptability *s.* inadattabilità.
inadequacy *s.* inadeguatezza.
inadequate *agg.* inadeguato.
inadmissibility *s.* inammissibilità.
inadmissible *agg.* inammissibile.
inadvertence *s.* inavvertenza.
inadvertent *agg.* 1. disattento 2. involontario.
inalienability *s.* inalienabilità.
inalienable *agg.* inalienabile.
inalterability *s.* inalterabilità.
inalterable *agg.* inalterabile.
inane *agg. e s.* vuoto.
inanimate *agg.* 1. inanimato 2. fiacco.
inanity *s.* inanità.

inappeasable *agg.* implacabile.
inappellable *agg.* inappellabile.
inappetence *s.* inappetenza.
inapplicable *agg.* inapplicabile.
inappropriate *agg.* inadeguato.
inapt *agg.* **1.** inadatto **2.** inetto.
inarticulate *agg.* inarticolato.
inattention *s.* **1.** disattenzione **2.** negligenza.
inattentive *agg.* **1.** disattento **2.** negligente.
inaudible *agg.* impercettibile.
inaugural *agg.* inaugurale.
to inaugurate *vt.* inaugurare.
inauguration *s.* inaugurazione.
inboard *agg.* interno. ♦ **inboard** *avv.* internamente.
inborn, inbred *agg.* innato.
incalculable *agg.* **1.** incalcolabile **2.** incerto.
incandescence *s.* incandescenza.
incandescent *agg.* incandescente.
incantation *s.* incantesimo.
incapability *s.* incapacità.
incapable *agg.* incapace.
incapacity *s.* incapacità.
to incarnate *vt.* **1.** incarnare **2.** realizzare.
incarnation *s.* incarnazione.
incatenation *s.* incatenamento.
incautious *agg.* incauto.
incendiary *agg. e s.* **1.** incendiario **2.** sovversivo.
incensation *s.* incensamento.
incense *s.* incenso.
to incense[1] *vt.* incensare.
to incense[2] *vt.* provocare.
incensurable *agg.* incensurabile.
incentive *agg.* stimolante. ♦ **incentive** *s.* incentivo.
incertitude *s.* incertezza.
incessant *agg.* incessante.
incest *s.* incesto.
incestuous *agg.* incestuoso.
inch *s.* pollice (*misura*).
incidence *s.* incidenza.
incident *agg.* probabile. ♦ **incident** *s.* avvenimento.
incidental *agg.* fortuito. ♦ **incidental** *s.* caso.
incipient *agg.* incipiente.
to incise *vt.* incidere.
incisive *agg.* incisivo.
incisiveness *s.* incisività.
incisor *s.* incisivo.
incitation *s.* incitamento.
to incite *vt.* incitare.
incivility *s.* villania.
inclemency *s.* inclemenza.

inclement *agg.* inclemente.
inclinable *agg.* incline.
inclination *s.* inclinazione.
to incline *vt.* inclinare. ♦ **to incline** *vi.* propendere.
inclined *agg.* **1.** inclinato **2.** incline.
to include *vt.* includere.
included *agg.* incluso, compreso.
inclusion *s.* inclusione.
inclusive *agg.* compreso.
incoherence *s.* incoerenza.
incoherent *agg.* incoerente.
incombustible *agg.* incombustibile.
income *s.* rendita, reddito || — -*tax*, imposta sul reddito.
incoming *s.* entrata. ♦ **incoming** *agg.* entrante.
incommensurability *s.* incommensurabilità.
incommensurable *agg.* incommensurabile.
incommensurate *agg.* **1.** inadeguato **2.** smisurato.
incommunicability *s.* incomunicabilità.
incommunicable *agg.* incomunicabile.
incommutable *agg.* incommutabile.
incomparable *agg.* incomparabile.
incompatibility *s.* incompatibilità.
incompatible *agg.* incompatibile.
incompetence *s.* incompetenza.
incompetent *agg. e s.* incompetente.
incomplete *agg.* incompleto.
incompleteness, incompletion *s.* incompletezza.
incomprehensibility *s.* incomprensibilità.
incomprehensible *agg.* incomprensibile.
incomprehension *s.* incomprensione.
inconceivability *s.* inconcepibilità.
inconceivable *agg.* inconcepibile.
inconclusive *agg.* inconcludente.
inconclusiveness *s.* inconcludenza.
incongruity *s.* incongruenza.
incongruous *agg.* incongruo.
inconsequence *s.* incongruenza.
inconsequent *agg.* incongruente.
inconsequential *agg.* **1.** incoerente **2.** irrilevante.
inconsiderate *agg.* sconsiderato.
inconsistence *s.* incoerenza.
inconsistent *agg.* incoerente.
inconsolable *agg.* inconsolabile.
inconstancy *s.* incostanza.
inconstant *agg.* incostante.

incontestability s. incontestabilità.
incontestable agg. incontestabile.
incontinence s. incontinenza.
incontinent agg. incontinente.
incontinently avv. smoderatamente.
incontrollable agg. incontrollabile.
incontrovertible agg. incontrovertibile.
inconvenience s. 1. disturbo 2. scomodità.
to **inconvenience** vt. scomodare.
inconvenient agg. incomodo.
inconvertible agg. inconvertibile.
to **incorporate** vt. 1. incorporare 2. (comm.) costituire. ♦ to **incorporate** vi. incorporarsi.
incorporated agg. 1. (comm.) anonimo 2. incorporato.
incorporation s. 1. incorporazione 2. (comm.) costituzione.
incorporeal agg. incorporeo.
incorrect agg. scorretto.
incorrectness s. scorrettezza.
incorrigible agg. incorreggibile.
incorrupt agg. incorrotto.
incorruptibility s. incorruttibilità.
incorruptible agg. incorruttibile.
increase s. aumento.
to **increase** vt. e vi. aumentare.
increasing agg. crescente.
increasingly avv. sempre più.
incredibility s. incredibilità.
incredible agg. incredibile.
incredulity s. incredulità.
incredulous agg. incredulo.
increment s. incremento.
to **incriminate** vt. incriminare.
incrimination s. incriminazione.
incriminatory agg. incriminante.
incrustation s. incrostazione.
incubation s. incubazione.
incubator s. incubatrice.
to **inculcate** vt. inculcare.
inculcation s. inculcazione.
inculpable agg. innocente.
inculpation s. accusa.
incumbent agg. incombente.
to **incur** vt. incorrere in.
incurability s. incurabilità.
incurable agg. incurabile.
incursion s. incursione.
indebted agg. 1. indebitato 2. obbligato.
indecency s. indecenza.
indecent agg. indecente.
indecipherable agg. indecifrabile.

indecision s. indecisione.
indecisive agg 1. indeciso 2. non decisivo.
indeclinable agg. indeclinabile.
indecomposable agg. indecomponibile.
indecorous agg. indecoroso.
indeed avv. in verità, davvero.
indefatigable agg. infaticabile.
indefeasible agg. irrevocabile.
indefinable agg. indefinibile.
indefinite agg. indefinito.
indefiniteness s. indeterminatezza.
indelible agg. indelebile.
indelicacy s. 1. rozzezza 2. sconvenienza.
indelicate agg. 1. sgarbato 2. sconveniente.
to **indemnify** vt. 1. indennizzare 2. assicurare.
indemnity s. 1. indennità 2. assicurazione.
indemonstrable agg. indimostrabile.
indent s. 1. dentellatura 2. incavo 3. (comm.) ordinazione 4. (tip.) capoverso.
to **indent** vt. 1. dentellare, frastagliare 2. intagliare 3. (comm.) ordinare (merci).
indentation, **indention** s. 1. dentellatura 2. incisione.
indenture s. 1. dentellatura 2. contratto.
independence s. indipendenza.
independent agg. e s. indipendente.
indescribable agg. indescrivibile.
indestructibility s. indistruttibilità.
indestructible agg. indistruttibile.
indeterminable agg. indeterminabile.
indeterminate agg. indeterminato.
indetermination s. indeterminazione.
index s. indice.
Indian agg. e s. indiano.
to **indicate** vt. indicare.
indicating agg. indicatore.
indication s. 1. indicazione 2. segno.
indicative agg. e s. indicativo.
indicator s. indicatore.
to **indict** vt. accusare.
indictment s. (giur.) accusa.
indifference s. 1. indifferenza 2. imparzialità 3. mancanza di valore.
indifferent agg. 1. indifferente 2.

imparziale **3.** mediocre.
indifferentism s. indifferentismo.
indifferentist s. indifferentista.
indigence s. indigenza.
indigenous agg. indigeno.
indigent agg. indigente.
indigestible agg. indigesto.
indigestion s. dispepsia.
indignant agg. indignato.
indignation s. indignazione.
indignity s. **1.** indegnità **2.** offesa.
indigo s. indaco.
indirect agg. **1.** indiretto **2.** tortuoso.
indiscernible agg. indistinguibile.
indiscipline s. indisciplina.
indiscreet agg. **1.** sconsiderato **2.** indiscreto.
indiscrete agg. compatto.
indiscretion s. **1.** sconsideratezza **2.** indiscrezione.
indiscriminate agg. indiscriminato.
indispensable agg. indispensabile.
indisposed agg. indisposto.
indisposition s. **1.** avversione **2.** indisposizione.
indisputability s. indiscutibilità.
indisputable agg. indiscutibile.
indisputed agg. indiscusso.
indissolubility s. indissolubilità.
indissoluble agg. indissolubile.
indistinct agg. indistinto.
indistinguishable agg. indistinguibile.
individual agg. individuale. ♦ **individual** s. individuo.
individualism s. individualismo.
individualist agg. e s. individualista.
individualistic agg. individualistico.
individuality s. individualità.
individualization s. individualizzazione.
to **individualize** vt. individualizzare.
indivisibility s. indivisibilità.
indivisible agg. indivisibile.
indocility s. indocilità.
Indo-European agg. e s. indo-europeo.
indolence s. indolenza.
indolent agg. indolente.
indomitable agg. indomabile.
indoor agg. in casa.
indoors avv. in casa.
indraft, indraught s. risucchio, vortice.
indubitable agg. indubitabile.

to **induce** vt. indurre.
inducement s. **1.** allettamento **2.** movente.
induction s. **1.** induzione **2.** insediamento.
inductive agg. induttivo.
inductor s. induttore.
to **indulge** vt. essere indulgente verso. ♦ to **indulge** vi. indulgere.
indulgence s. **1.** indulgenza **2.** proroga.
indulgent agg. indulgente.
indult s. indulto.
industrial agg. industriale. ♦ **industrial** s. lavoratore dell'industria.
industrialism s. industrialismo.
industrialist s. industriale.
industrialization s. industrializzazione.
to **industrialize** vt. industrializzare.
industrious agg. industrioso.
industry s. **1.** industria **2.** operosità, diligenza.
inebriate agg. e s. ubriaco.
to **inebriate** vt. inebriare.
inedited agg. inedito.
ineffable agg. ineffabile.
ineffective agg. **1.** inefficace **2.** inefficiente.
ineffectiveness s. **1.** inefficacia **2.** inefficienza.
ineffectual agg. inutile.
inefficacy s. inefficacia.
inefficient agg. V. *ineffective*.
inelegance s. ineleganza.
inelegant agg. inelegante.
ineligibility s. ineleggibilità.
ineligible agg. ineleggibile.
ineluctable agg. ineluttabile.
inept agg. inadatto.
ineptitude, ineptness s. inettitudine.
inequality s. diseguaglianza.
inequity s. ingiustizia.
ineradicable agg. inestirpabile.
inerrability s. infallibilità.
inerrable agg. infallibile.
inert agg. inerte.
inertness s. inerzia.
inescapable agg. inevitabile.
inestimable agg. inestimabile.
inevitability s. inevitabilità.
inevitable agg. inevitabile.
inevitableness s. inevitabilità.
inexact agg. inesatto.
inexactitude s. inesattezza.
inexcusability s. inescusabilità.
inexcusable agg. imperdonabile.

inexecutable *agg.* ineseguibile.
inexhaustibility *s.* inesauribilità.
inexhaustible *agg.* inesauribile.
inexistence *s.* inesistenza.
inexistent *agg.* inesistente.
inexorability *s.* inesorabilità.
inexorable *agg.* inesorabile.
inexpedient *agg.* inopportuno.
inexpensive *agg.* poco costoso.
inexperience *s.* inesperienza.
inexperienced, inexpert *agg.* inesperto.
inexpiable *agg.* inespiabile.
inexplicable *agg.* inesplicabile.
inexplorable *agg.* inesplorabile.
inexpressible *agg.* inesprimibile.
inexpressive *agg.* inespressivo.
inexpressiveness *s.* inespressività.
inexpugnability *s.* inespugnabilità.
inexpugnable *agg.* inespugnabile.
inextinguishable *agg.* inestinguibile.
inextricable *agg.* inestricabile.
infallibility *s.* infallibilità.
infallible *agg.* infallibile.
infamous *agg.* infame.
infamy *s.* infamia.
infancy *s.* infanzia.
infant *agg.* infantile. ♦ **infant** *s.* 1. neonato 2. (*giur.*) minore.
infanticide *s.* 1. infanticida 2. infanticidio.
infantile *agg.* infantile.
infantilism *s.* infantilismo.
infantry *s.* fanteria || — *-man*, fante.
infarct *s.* infarto.
to infatuate *vt.* infatuare.
infatuation *s.* infatuazione.
to infect *vt.* contagiare.
infection *s.* contagio.
infectious *agg.* contagioso.
infective *agg.* infettivo.
infecund *agg.* infecondo.
infelicitous *agg.* infelice.
infelicity *s.* infelicità.
to infer *vt.* dedurre.
inferable *agg.* deducibile.
inference *s.* deduzione.
inferior *agg. e s.* inferiore.
inferiority *s.* inferiorità.
infernal *agg.* infernale.
to infest *vt.* infestare.
infestation *s.* infestamento.
infidel *agg. e s.* infedele.
infidelity *s.* 1. miscredenza 2. infedeltà.
to infiltrate *vt.* infiltrare. ♦ **to infiltrate** *vi.* infiltrarsi.
infiltration *s.* infiltrazione.

infinite *agg. e s.* infinito.
infinitesimal *agg.* infinitesimale.
infinitive *agg. e s.* infinito.
infinitude *s.* infinità.
infinity *s.* infinità, infinito.
infirm *agg.* 1. infermo 2. irresoluto.
infirmary *s.* infermeria.
infirmity *s.* 1. infermità 2. irresolutezza.
to inflame *vt.* infiammare. ♦ **to inflame** *vi.* infiammarsi.
inflammability *s.* infiammabilità.
inflammable *agg.* infiammabile.
inflammation *s.* 1. l'infiammare, l'infiammarsi 2. infiammazione.
inflammatory *agg.* infiammatorio.
to inflate *vt.* gonfiare.
inflation *s.* 1. gonfiore, gonfiatura 2. (*comm.*) inflazione.
inflationary *agg.* inflazionistico.
to inflect *vt.* 1. flettere 2. modulare.
inflection *s.* 1. flessione 2. inflessione.
inflexibility *s.* inflessibilità.
inflexible *agg.* inflessibile.
to inflict *vt.* infliggere.
infliction *s.* 1. inflizione 2. pena.
inflorescence *s.* infiorescenza.
influence *s.* 1. influenza 2. (*elettr.*) induzione.
to influence *vt.* influenzare.
influential *agg.* influente.
influenza *s.* (*med.*) influenza.
influx *s.* 1. affluenza 2. sbocco (*di fiume*).
inform *agg.* informe.
to inform *vt.* 1. informare 2. dar forma a.
informal *agg.* non ufficiale.
informality *s.* assenza di formalità.
information *s.* (*solo sing.*) 1. informazione 2. sapere 3. accusa.
informative, informatory *agg.* informativo.
informed *agg.* istruito.
informer *s.* 1. informatore 2. accusatore.
infraction *s.* 1. infrazione 2. violazione.
infrangibility *s.* infrangibilità.
infrangible *agg.* 1. infrangibile 2. inviolabile.
infrared *agg.* infrarosso.
infrequent *agg.* raro.
to infringe *vt.* violare.
infringement *s.* violazione.
infringer *s.* trasgressore.
infructuous *agg.* infruttuoso.

infuse 448

to **infuse** vt. 1. versare 2. infondere 3. mettere in infusione.
infusible agg. infusibile.
infusion s. 1. infusione 2. infuso.
ingenious agg. ingegnoso.
ingenuity s. ingegnosità.
ingenuous agg. 1. ingenuo 2. franco.
ingenuousness s. ingenuità.
to **ingest** vt. ingerire.
ingestion s. ingestione.
inglorious agg. inglorioso.
ingot s. lingotto.
ingratitude s. ingratitudine.
ingredient s. ingrediente.
inguen s. inguine.
inguinal agg. inguinale.
to **inhabit** vt. abitare.
inhabitable agg. abitabile.
inhabitancy s. domicilio.
inhabitant s. abitante.
inhalant s. 1. inalatore 2. sostanza da inalare.
inhalation s. inalazione.
to **inhale** vt. e vi. 1. aspirare 2. inalare.
inhaler s. inalatore.
inherent agg. inerente.
to **inherit** vt. e vi. ereditare.
inheritance s. eredità.
to **inhibit** vt. 1. inibire 2. interdire.
inhibition s. 1. inibizione 2. interdizione.
inhibitory agg. inibitorio.
inhospitable agg. inospitale.
inhospitality s. inospitalità.
inhuman agg. inumano.
inhumanity s. inumanità.
inhumation s. inumazione.
inimical agg. nemico.
inimitable agg. inimitabile.
iniquitous agg. iniquo.
iniquity s. iniquità.
initial agg. e s. iniziale.
to **initial** vt. siglare.
initiate agg. e s. iniziato.
to **initiate** vt. iniziare.
initiation s. 1. inizio 2. iniziazione.
initiative agg. introduttivo. ♦ **initiative** s. iniziativa.
initiator s. iniziatore.
to **inject** vt. iniettare.
injection s. iniezione.
injector s. iniettore.
injunction s. ingiunzione.
to **injure** vt. ledere, ferire.
injurer s. 1. danneggiatore 2. feritore.
injury s. 1. torto, danno 2. ferita.

injustice s. ingiustizia.
ink s. inchiostro || — -pot, calamaio.
inkholder s. calamaio.
inkling s. indizio.
inky agg. 1. di, simile a inchiostro 2. macchiato d'inchiostro.
inlaid V. to inlay.
inland agg. e s. interno. ♦ **inland** avv. all'interno.
inlay s. intarsio.
to **inlay (inlaid, inlaid)** vt. intarsiare.
inlet s. 1. piccola insenatura 2. apertura.
inmate s. 1. inquilino 2. ricoverato.
inmost agg. più interno.
inn s. locanda || — -keeper, locandiere; — of court, scuola di legge.
innate agg. innato.
innavigable agg. non navigabile.
inner agg. interno, intimo.
innermost agg. V. inmost.
innervation s. innervazione.
innocence s. innocenza.
innocent agg. e s. innocente.
innocuity s. innocuità.
innocuous agg. innocuo.
innominate agg. innominato.
to **innovate** vt. e vi. innovare.
innovation s. innovazione.
innovator s. innovatore.
innumerability s. innumerabilità.
innumerable agg. innumerevole.
inobservance s. 1. inosservanza 2. disattenzione.
inobservant agg. 1. inosservante 2. disattento.
to **inoculate** vt. 1. inoculare 2. inculcare.
inoculation s. inoculazione.
inodorous agg. inodoro.
inoffensive agg. inoffensivo.
inopportune agg. inopportuno.
inopportuneness s. inopportunità.
inordinate agg. smoderato.
inorganic agg. inorganico.
inoxidizable agg. inossidabile.
inpouring agg. affluente. ♦ **inpouring** s. afflusso.
input s. (mecc.; elettr.) alimentazione, entrata.
inquest s. 1. inchiesta 2. giuria.
inquietude s. inquietudine.
to **inquire** vt. e vi. chiedere || to — after, chiedere informazioni su; to — into, indagare su.
inquirer s. investigatore.
inquiring agg. 1. indagatore 2. cu-

rioso.
inquiry s. **1.** ricerca **2.** domanda **3.** inchiesta.
inquisition s. **1.** ricerca **2.** inchiesta.
inquisitive agg. V. inquiring.
inquisitiveness s. curiosità
inrush s. irruzione.
insalubrity s. insalubrità.
insane agg. insano.
insanitary agg. malsano.
insanity s. insania.
insatiability s. insaziabilità.
insatiable, insatiate agg. insaziabile.
to **inscribe** vt. **1.** iscrivere **2.** scolpire **3.** dedicare.
inscription s. **1.** iscrizione **2.** dedica.
inscrutability s. inscrutabilità.
inscrutable agg. inscrutabile.
inscrutableness s. inscrutabilità.
insect s. insetto.
insecticide s. insetticida.
insectivorous agg. insettivoro.
insecure agg. insicuro.
insecurity s. insicurezza.
insensate agg. **1.** insensibile **2.** insensato.
insensibility s. insensibilità.
insensible agg. **1.** insensibile **2.** inconscio.
insensitive agg. insensibile.
inseparable agg. inseparabile.
insert s. inserzione.
to **insert** vt. inserire.
insertion s. inserzione.
to **inset (inset, inset)** vt. inserire.
inside agg. e s. interno. ♦ **inside** avv. e prep. dentro.
insidious agg. insidioso.
insight s. **1.** intuito **2.** penetrazione.
insignificant agg. insignificante.
insincere agg. insincero.
insincerity s. falsità.
to **insinuate** vt. insinuare.
insinuation s. insinuazione.
insinuative agg. insinuante.
insipid agg. insipido.
insipidity, insipidness s. insipidezza.
insipience s. insipienza.
insipient agg. insipiente.
to **insist** vi. insistere.
insistence s. insistenza.
insistent agg. insistente.
insolation s. insolazione.
insolence s. insolenza.
insolent agg. e s. insolente.

insolubility s. insolubilità.
insoluble agg. insolubile.
insolvable agg. insolubile.
insolvency s. insolvenza.
insolvent agg. insolvente. ♦ **insolvent** s. debitore insolvente.
insomnia s. insonnia.
to **inspect** vt. ispezionare.
inspection s. ispezione.
inspector s. ispettore.
inspectoral agg. di ispettore, di ispezione.
inspectorate s. ispettorato.
inspiration s. **1.** inspirazione **2.** ispirazione.
to **inspire** vt. **1.** inspirare **2.** ispirare.
inspirer s. ispiratore.
inspiring agg. ispiratore.
instability s. instabilità.
to **install** vt. installare.
installation s. installazione.
instalment s. **1.** rata **2.** puntata.
instance s. **1.** esempio **2.** caso **3.** istanza.
instancy s. **1.** urgenza **2.** insistenza.
instant agg. **1.** urgente **2.** corrente.
♦ **instant** s. istante.
instantaneous agg. istantaneo.
instantly avv. all'istante. ♦ **instantly** cong. non appena che.
instead avv. invece.
instep s. **1.** collo del piede **2.** collo di scarpa.
to **instigate** vt. istigare.
instigation s. istigazione.
instigator s. istigatore.
to **instil(l)** vt. instillare.
instinct agg. imbevuto. ♦ **instinct** s. istinto.
instinctive agg. istintivo.
institute s. istituto. ♦ **institutes** s. pl. istituzioni.
to **institute** vt. istituire.
institution s. istituto.
institutional agg. istituzionale.
institutor s. istitutore.
to **instruct** vt. **1.** istruire **2.** informare **3.** ordinare.
instruction s. istruzione.
instructive agg. istruttivo.
instructor s. istruttore.
instrument s. **1.** strumento **2.** atto giuridico.
to **instrument** vt. **1.** strumentare **2.** redigere.
instrumental agg. **1.** strumentale **2.** utile.
instrumentation s. **1.** orchestrazio-

ne 2. uso di strumenti.
insubordinate *agg.* insubordinato.
insubordination *s.* insubordinazione.
insubstantial *agg.* incorporeo.
insufferable *agg.* insopportabile.
insufficiency *s.* insufficienza.
insufficient *agg.* insufficiente.
insular *agg.* 1. insulare 2. (*fig.*) di mentalità ristretta.
to **insulate** *vt.* isolare.
insulation *s.* isolamento.
insulator *s.* isolatore.
insulin *s.* insulina.
insult *s.* insulto.
to **insult** *vt.* insultare.
insuperable *agg.* insuperabile.
insuppressible *agg.* insopprimibile.
insurance *s.* assicurazione.
insurant *s.* assicurato.
to **insure** *vt.* assicurare.
insurer *s.* assicuratore.
insurgency *s.* insurrezione.
insurgent *agg.* e *s.* insorto.
insurmountable *agg.* insormontabile.
insurrection *s.* insurrezione.
insurrectional, insurrectionary *agg.* insurrezionale.
insurrectionist *s.* insorto.
intact *agg.* intatto.
intake *s.* 1. presa 2. energia assorbita.
intangible *agg.* intangibile.
integrable *agg.* integrabile.
integral *agg.* integrale.
integrant *agg.* integrante.
to **integrate** *vt.* integrare.
integration *s.* integrazione.
integrity *s.* integrità.
intellect *s.* intelletto.
intellective *agg.* intellettivo.
intellectual *agg.* e *s.* intellettuale.
intellectualism *s.* intellettualismo.
intelligence *s.* 1. intelligenza 2. informazioni (*pl.*).
intelligent *agg.* intelligente.
intelligibility *s.* intelligibilità.
intelligible *agg.* intelligibile.
intemperance *s.* intemperanza.
intemperate *agg.* 1. smoderato 2. rigido (*di clima*).
to **intend** *vt.* 1. intendere 2. destinare.
intendant *s.* intendente.
intended *agg.* progettato.
intense *agg.* intenso.
intensification *s.* intensificazione.
to **intensify** *vt.* intensificare. ♦ to

intensify *vi.* intensificarsi.
intensity *s.* 1. intensità 2. vigore.
intensive *agg.* intensivo, intenso.
intent *agg.* intento, dedito. ♦ **intent** *s.* intenzione, scopo.
intention *s.* intenzione.
intentional *agg.* intenzionale.
intently *avv.* intensamente.
to **inter** *vt.* seppellire.
to **intercalate** *vt.* intercalare.
to **intercede** *vi.* intercedere.
to **intercept** *vt.* intercettare.
interception *s.* intercettamento.
interceptor *s.* intercettatore.
intercession *s.* intercessione.
intercessor *s.* intercessore.
interchange *s.* scambio.
to **interchange** *vt.* scambiare. ♦
to **interchange** *vi.* scambiarsi.
interchangeable *agg.* scambievole.
intercom *s.* citofono.
intercommunication *s.* intercomunicazione.
intercontinental *agg.* intercontinentale.
intercostal *agg.* intercostale.
intercourse *s.* rapporto, relazione || *trade* —, scambi commerciali.
interdependence *s.* interdipendenza.
interdependent *agg.* interdipendente.
interdict *s.* 1. interdizione 2. interdetto 3. proibizione.
to **interdict** *vt.* 1. interdire 2. proibire.
interdiction *s.* V. *interdict*.
interest *s.* interesse.
to **interest** *vt.* interessare.
interested *agg.* interessato || *those* —, gli interessati.
interesting *agg.* interessante.
to **interfere** *vi.* 1. interferire 2. scontrarsi.
interference *s.* 1. interferenza 2. collisione.
interior *agg.* e *s.* interno.
to **interject** *vt.* intromettere.
interjection *s.* intromissione.
to **interlace** *vt.* intrecciare. ♦ to **interlace** *vi.* intrecciarsi.
interlacing *s.* intreccio.
to **interline** *vt.* interlineare.
interlinear *agg.* interlineare.
interlineation *s.* interlineazione.
to **interlink** *vt.* concatenare.
to **interlock** *vt.* sincronizzare.
interlocution *s.* interlocuzione.
interlocutor *s.* interlocutore.

to **interlope** vi. immischiarsi.

interlude s. 1. intervallo 2. intermezzo.

intermarriage s. matrimonio tra membri di famiglie, razze diverse.

to **intermarry** vt. e vi. imparentarsi per mezzo di matrimonio.

to **intermeddle** vi. intromettersi.

intermeddler s. intrigante.

intermediary agg. intermedio, frapposto. ♦ **intermediary** s. 1. intermediario, mediatore 2. cosa intermedia.

intermediate agg. V. *intermediary.*

intermediation s. mediazione.

interment s. sepoltura.

interminable agg. interminabile.

to **intermingle** vt. mescolare. ♦ **intermingle** vi. mescolarsi.

intermission s. sosta, pausa.

to **intermit** vt. interrompere. ♦ to **intermit** vi. interrompersi, essere intermittente.

intermittence s. intermittenza.

intermittent agg. intermittente.

to **intern** vt. internare.

internal agg. interno.

international agg. internazionale.

internationalism s. internazionalismo.

internationalist s. internazionalista.

to **internationalize** vt. internazionalizzare.

internment s. internamento.

to **interpellate** vt. interpellare.

interpellation s. interpellanza.

interphone s. citofono.

interplanetary agg. interplanetario.

interplay s. azione reciproca.

to **interpolate** vt. interpolare.

interpolation s. interpolazione.

to **interpose** vt. interporre. ♦ to **interpose** vi. interporsi.

interposition s. interposizione.

to **interpret** vt. interpretare. ♦ to **interpret** vi. fare l'interprete.

interpretation s. interpretazione.

interpretative agg. interpretativo.

interpreter s. interprete.

interpunction s. interpunzione.

interregnum s. 1. interregno 2. intervallo.

interrelation s. relazione.

interrelationship s. interdipendenza.

to **interrogate** vt. interrogare.

interrogation s. interrogazione || — -*mark*, punto interrogativo.

interrogative agg. e s. interrogativo.

interrogatory agg. interrogativo. ♦ **interrogatory** s. 1. interrogazione 2. interrogatorio.

to **interrupt** vt. e vi. interrompere.

interrupter s. interruttore.

interruption s. interruzione.

to **intersect** vt. intersecare. ♦ to **intersect** vi. intersecarsi.

intersection s. intersezione.

interspace s. intervallo, spazio.

to **intersperse** vt. cospargere.

interstice s. interstizio.

to **intertwine** vt. attorcigliare. ♦ to **intertwine** vi. attorcigliarsi.

interurban agg. interurbano.

interval s. intervallo.

to **intervene** vi. intervenire.

intervener s. chi interviene.

intervention s. intervento.

interventionist s. interventista.

interview s. intervista.

to **interview** vt. intervistare.

interviewer s. intervistatore.

to **interweave (interwove, interwoven)** vt. intessere, intrecciare.

intestinal agg. intestinale.

intestine agg. e s. intestino.

intimacy s. intimità.

intimate agg. intimo. ♦ **intimate** s. amico intimo.

to **intimate** vt. 1. intimare 2. accennare.

intimation s. 1. intimazione 2. preannunzio.

intimidation s. intimidazione.

intimidatory agg. intimidatorio.

into prep. in, dentro || *to go — the, park*, entrare nel parco; *far — the night*, fino a tarda notte.

intolerable agg. intollerabile.

intolerance s. intolleranza.

intolerant agg. e s. intollerante.

to **intonate** vt. intonare.

intonation s. intonazione.

to **intone** vt. intonare.

to **intoxicate** vt. inebriare.

intoxication s. ebbrezza.

intractable agg. intrattabile.

intramuscular agg. intramusculare.

intransgressible agg. che non può essere trasgredito.

intransigence s. intransigenza.

intransigent agg. e s. intransigente.

intransitive agg. intransitivo.

intravenous agg. endovenoso.

intrepid agg. intrepido.

intrepidity s. intrepidezza.
intricacy s. complicazione.
intricate agg. intricato.
intrigant s. intrigante.
intrigue s. intrigo.
to **intrigue** vt. 1. ingannare 2. rendere perplesso 3. affascinare. ◆ to **intrigue** vi. avere una tresca.
intriguer s. intrigante.
intrinsic agg. intrinseco.
to **introduce** vt. 1. introdurre 2. presentare.
introduction s. 1. introduzione 2. presentazione.
introductive, introductory agg. introduttivo.
intromission s. interferenza.
to **intromit** vt. introdurre.
to **introspect** vi. autoesaminarsi.
introspection s. introspezione.
introspective agg. introspettivo.
introversion s. introversione.
introvert agg. e s. introverso.
to **intrude** vt. imporre. ◆ to **intrude** vi. intromettersi.
intruder s. 1. intruso 2. importuno.
intrusion s. intrusione.
intrusive agg. 1. intruso 2. importuno.
intrusiveness s. indiscrezione.
intuition s. intuizione.
intuitional agg. intuitivo.
intuitionism s. intuizionismo.
intuitive agg. intuitivo.
to **inundate** vt. inondare.
inundation s. inondazione.
inurbane agg. inurbano.
inurbanity s. inurbanità.
to **inure** vt. abituare. ◆ to **inure** vi. venire in uso.
inurement s. abitudine.
inutility s. inutilità.
to **invade** vt. 1. invadere 2. violare.
invader s. invasore.
invalid agg. 1. invalido 2. nullo. ◆ **invalid** s. invalido.
to **invalid** vt. 1. rendere invalido 2. riformare.
to **invalidate** vt. invalidare.
invalidation s. invalidazione.
invalidity s. invalidità.
invaluable agg. inestimabile.
invariability s. invariabilità.
invariable agg. invariabile.
invasion s. invasione.
invective s. invettiva.
to **inveigh** vi. inveire.

to **invent** vt. inventare.
invention s. 1. invenzione 2. inventiva.
inventive agg. inventivo.
inventor s. inventore.
inventory s. inventario.
to **inventory** vt. fare l'inventario di.
inverse agg. e s. inverso.
inversion s. inversione.
invert agg. e s. invertito.
to **invert** vt. invertire.
invertebrate agg. e s. invertebrato.
invertible agg. invertibile.
to **invest** vt. 1. investire 2. rivestire.
to **investigate** vt. e vi. investigare.
investigation s. investigazione.
investigative agg. investigativo.
investigator s. investigatore.
investiture s. investitura.
investment s. investimento.
investor s. investitore.
inveterate agg. inveterato.
invidious agg. odioso.
invidiousness s. odiosità.
to **invigorate** vt. rinvigorire.
invigorative agg. rinforzante.
invincibility s. invincibilità.
invincible agg. invincibile.
inviolability s. inviolabilità.
inviolable agg. inviolabile.
inviolate agg. inviolato.
invisibility s. invisibilità.
invisible agg. invisibile.
invitation s. invito.
to **invite** vt. 1. invitare 2. provocare.
invocation s. invocazione.
invoice s. fattura.
to **invoice** vt. fatturare.
to **invoke** vt. 1. invocare 2. evocare.
involuntary s. involontario.
involute agg. 1. involuto 2. a spirale.
involution s. 1. involuzione 2. intrico 3. (mat.) elevazione a potenza.
to **involve** vt. 1. avvolgere 2. implicare 3. complicare.
invulnerability s. invulnerabilità.
invulnerable agg. invulnerabile.
inward agg. interiore.
inwardness s. interiorità.
inwards avv. internamente.
iodine s. iodio.
to **iodize** vt. iodare.
ion s. ione.
Ionic agg. ionico.

Ionization s. ionizzazione.
Ionosphere s. ionosfera.
Iranian agg. e s. iraniano.
Iraqi agg. e s. iracheno.
Irascibility s. irascibilità.
Irascible agg. irascibile.
Irate agg. adirato.
Ireful agg. irato.
Iridescence s. iridescenza.
Iridescent agg. iridescente.
Iris s. iride.
Irish agg. irlandese.
Irishman s. irlandese.
Irksome agg. noioso.
Iron agg. di ferro. ◆ **iron** s. ferro
‖ --*foundry*, ferriera. ◆ **irons**
s. pl. catene.
to **iron** vt. 1. rivestire di ferro 2.
stirare.
Ironclad agg. corazzato. ◆ **iron-
clad** s. corazzata.
Ironic(al) agg. ironico.
Ironing s. stiratura.
Ironmonger s. negoziante in ferra-
menta.
Ironsmith s. fabbro ferraio.
Ironware s. ferramenta.
Ironwork s. lavoro in ferro. ◆
ironworks s. pl. ferriera (sing.).
Irony s. ironia.
to **irradiate** vt. irradiare. ◆ to **ir-
radiate** vi. risplendere.
Irradiation s. 1. illuminazione 2.
irradiazione.
Irrational agg. irrazionale.
Irrationalism, irrationality s. ir-
᾽razionalità.
Irrealizable agg. irrealizzabile.
Irreconcilability s. inconciliabilità.
Irreconcilable agg. inconciliabile.
Irrecoverable agg. 1. irrecuperabi-
le 2. irrimediabile.
Irredentism s. irredentismo.
Irredentist s. irredentista.
Irreducible agg. irriducibile.
Irreflection s. irriflessione.
Irreflective agg. irriflessivo.
Irrefutable agg. irrefutabile.
Irregular agg. e s. irregolare.
Irregularity s. irregolarità.
Irrelevant agg. 1. non pertinente
2. insignificante.
Irreligious agg. irreligioso.
Irremediable agg. irrimediabile.
Irremissible agg. irremissibile.
Irremovability s. irremovibilità.
Irremovable agg. irremovibile.
Irreparable agg. irreparabile.
Irreplaceable agg. insostituibile.

Irreprehensible agg. irreprensibile.
Irrepressible agg. irrefrenabile.
Irrepressibleness s. irrefrenabilità.
Irreproachable agg. irreprensibile.
Irreprovable agg. irreprensibile.
Irresistible agg. irresistibile.
Irresolute agg. irresoluto.
Irresoluteness, irresolution s.
irresolutezza.
Irresolvable agg. insolubile.
Irrespective agg. noncurante.
Irresponsibility s. irresponsabilità.
Irresponsible agg. 1. irresponsabi-
le 2. insolvibile.
Irresponsive agg. che non risponde.
Irretrievable agg. irrecuperabile.
Irreverence s. irriverenza.
Irreverent agg. irriverente.
Irreversibility s. irreversibilità.
Irreversible agg. irreversibile.
Irrevocable agg. irrevocabile.
Irrigable agg. irrigabile.
to **irrigate** vt. irrigare.
Irrigation s. irrigazione.
Irritability s. irritabilità.
Irritable agg. irritabile.
Irritant agg. e s. irritante.
to **irritate** vt. irritare.
Irritation s. irritazione.
Irritative agg. irritante.
Irruption s. irruzione.
Islamic agg. islamico.
Islamism s. islamismo.
Island s. 1. isola 2. salvagente stra-
dale.
Islander s. isolano.
Isle s. piccola isola ‖ *the British
Isles*, le isole britanniche.
Islet s. isolotto.
Isochronism s. isocronismo.
to **isolate** vt. isolare.
Isolation s. isolamento.
Isolationism s. isolazionismo.
Isolationist s. isolazionista.
Isolator s. isolatore.
Isomorphism s. isomorfismo.
Isomorphous agg. isomorfo.
Isosceles agg. isoscele.
Isotherm s. isoterma.
Isothermal agg. isotermico.
Isotope s. isotopo.
Isotrope s. isotropo.
Israeli agg. e s. israeliano.
Israelite s. israelita.
Issue s. 1. uscita, sbocco, foce 2.
conclusione 3. prole, stirpe 4. pro-
blema 5. emissione, pubblicazione.
to **issue** vt. 1. emettere, pubblicare
2. rilasciare. ◆ to **issue** vi. 1.

uscire 2. risultare 3. discendere.

issueless *agg.* 1. senza sbocco 2. senza prole.

isthmus *s.* istmo.

it *pron. neutro* esso, essa, ciò, lo, gli, le, ne, sé || *I don't believe —,* non ci credo; *— is raining,* piove; *— is Sunday,* è domenica.

Italian *agg.* e *s.* italiano.

to italicize *vt.* e *vi.* 1. stampare in corsivo 2. sottolineare.

itch *s.* 1. prurito 2. scabbia.

to itch *vi.* 1. prudere 2. aver voglia di.

itching *s.* prurito.

item *s.* (*comm.*) voce.

to itemize *vt.* specificare, elencare.

to iterate *vt.* ripetere.

itinerant *agg.* ambulante.

itinerary *s.* itinerario.

its *agg.* e *pron. poss. neutro* suo, sua, suoi, sue.

itself *pron. r. neutro* esso stesso, essa stessa, sé, si || *by —,* da solo.

ivory *s.* avorio.

ivy *s.* edera.

J

jab *s.* 1. stoccata 2. colpo improvviso.

Jack *s.* 1. (*fam.*) marinaio 2. fante (*gioco delle carte*) 3. bandiera (*di nave*) 4. maschio (*di certi animali*) 5. uomo di fatica 6. (*mecc.*) cricco.

jackal *s.* sciacallo.

jackass *s.* somaro.

jackdaw *s.* cornacchia.

jacket *s.* 1. giacchetta 2. rivestimento protettivo, isolante.

Jacobin *s.* giacobino.

jade¹ *s.* giada.

jade² *s.* 1. cavallo, ronzino 2. megera.

to jag *vt.* frastagliare, dentellare.

jaguar *s.* giaguaro.

jail *s.* carcere.

to jail *vt.* incarcerare.

jailer *s.* carceriere.

to jam *vt.* premere, serrare, pigiare. ◆ **to jam** *vi.* bloccarsi, incepparsi.

jam¹ *s.* marmellata.

jam² *s.* 1. ammasso 2. compressione 3. ingorgo.

jamb *s.* stipite.

Jansenism *s.* giansenismo.

Jansenist *s.* giansenista.

January *s.* gennaio.

Japanese *agg.* e *s.* giapponese.

jar *s.* rumore aspro, stridio.

to jar *vi.* 1. discordare 2. stridere. ◆ **to jar** *vt.* 1. far discordare 2. far stridere.

jargon *s.* 1. gergo 2. linguaggio professionale.

jarring *agg.* discorde, stridente.

jasmin(e) *s.* gelsomino.

jasper *s.* diaspro.

jaundice *s.* itterizia.

javelin *s.* giavellotto.

jaw *s.* 1. mascella, mandibola 2. morsa, ganascia. ◆ **jaws** *s. pl.* stretta, gola.

jealous *agg.* geloso.

jealously *avv.* gelosamente.

jealousness, jealousy *s.* gelosia.

jeer *s.* beffa, scherno.

jelly *s.* gelatina (*anche di frutta*).

to jeopardize *vt.* mettere a repentaglio.

jeopardy *s.* rischio, pericolo.

jerk *s.* 1. scatto, strattone 2. spinta 3. sussulto, tic nervoso.

to jerk *vt.* dare uno strattone. ◆ **to jerk** *vi.* sobbalzare || *to — along,* avanzare a scatti.

jerky *agg.* 1. sussultante 2. convulso.

jersey *s.* camicetta a maglia con maniche.

jest *s.* facezia, scherzo.

to jest *vi.* scherzare, dire delle facezie.

jester *s.* burlone.

jestful *agg.* incline allo scherzo.

Jesuit *s.* gesuita.

Jesuitical *agg.* gesuitico.

jet¹ *agg.* nero lucido.

jet² *s.* 1. getto, spruzzo 2. spruzzatore || *— engine,* motore a reazione; *— plane,* aeroplano a reazione.

to jet *vt.* schizzare, sprizzare. ◆ **to jet** *vi.* slanciarsi.

jetty *s.* molo || *landing —,* imbarcadero.

Jew *s.* ebreo.

jewel *s.* gioiello.

jewelcase *s.* scrigno.

jeweller *s.* gioielliere.

jewellery *s.* 1. gioielli 2. commercio delle gemme.

Jewish *agg.* ebraico, ebreo.

to jib *vi.* recalcitrare, impuntarsi.

jig *s.* 1. giga 2. (*mecc.*) maschera.

jigsaw s. sega da traforo.
to **jingle** vt. far tintinnare. ♦ to **jingle** vi. tintinnare.
job s. 1. lavoro, impiego 2. (fam.) faccenda, situazione.
jobber s. 1. noleggiatore 2. lavoratore a cottimo 3. trafficante disonesto.
jockey s. fantino.
jocose agg. giocoso, allegro.
jocosity s. giocondità.
jocund agg. giocondo, gaio.
jocundity s. allegria, giocondità.
join s. giuntura.
to **join** vt. 1. unire 2. raggiungere. ♦ to **join** vi. 1. unirsi 2. essere contiguo.
joiner s. falegname.
joinery s. falegnameria.
joining s. congiunzione.
joint agg. unito, associato ‖ — account, conto di partecipazione; — -heir, coerede; — -stock, capitale sociale; — -tenant, comproprietario.
joint s. 1. giuntura, congiunzione 2. trancio di carne 3. articolazione.
jointer s. pialla.
jointly avv. unitamente.
joke s. scherzo, burla, facezia.
to **joke** vt. burlarsi di, canzonare. ♦ to **joke** vi. celiare.
joker s. tipo ameno, burlone.
jolly agg. gaio, vivace.
to **jolt** vt. far sobbalzare, scuotere. ♦ to **jolt** vi. traballare.
to **jostle** vt. spingere. ♦ to **jostle** vi. spingersi.
journal s. 1. giornale 2. diario.
journalism s. giornalismo.
journalist s. giornalista.
journalistic agg. giornalistico.
journey s. viaggio (general. per terra).
to **journey** vi. fare un viaggio.
journey-man s. operaio specializzato.
jovial agg. gioviale, allegro.
joviality s. giovialità.
jowl[1] s. 1. mascella 2. guancia.
jowl[2] s. gozzo.
joy s. gioia, contentezza.
joyful agg. giulivo, allegro.
joyfully avv. gaiamente, allegramente.
joyless agg. mesto, senza gioia.
joyous agg. gioioso, gaio.
joyously avv. gioiosamente.
jubilant agg. giubilante, trionfante.

to **jubilate** vi. esultare.
jubilation s. giubilo.
jubilee s. giubileo.
Judaic agg. giudaico.
Judaism s. giudaismo.
judge s. 1. giudice 2. intenditore.
to **judge** vt. e vi. 1. fare da giudice, giudicare 2. supporre, stimare.
judgement s. 1. giudizio 2. verdetto, sentenza 3. parere.
judicial agg. giudiziale, giudiziario.
judiciary agg. giudiziario. ♦ **judiciary** s. magistratura.
judicious agg. giudizioso.
jug s. 1. boccale 2. caraffa, bricco.
juggler s. 1. giocoliere 2. impostore.
jugular agg. e s. giugulare.
juice s. succo (di frutta ecc.).
juiciness s. succosità.
juicy agg. succoso.
jujube s. giuggiola.
Julian agg. giuliano.
July s. luglio.
jumble s. guazzabuglio.
jump s. salto, balzo: high — (sport), salto in alto.
to **jump** vt. 1. saltare, superare con un salto 2. mangiare (giuoco della dama). ♦ to **jump** vi. 1. saltare 2. trasalire.
jumper[1] s. saltatore.
jumper[2] s. maglione.
jumping agg. saltatore.
junction s. 1. congiunzione 2. nodo ferroviario.
juncture s. 1. articolazione 2. (fig.) congiuntura, momento critico.
June s. giugno.
jungle s. giungla.
junior agg. 1. minore, di secondaria importanza 2. il più giovane. ♦ **junior** s. 1. cadetto 2. minore.
juniper s. ginepro.
junk[1] s. 1. avanzo, rifiuto 2. gomena vecchia 3. carne salata.
junk[2] s. (mar.) giunca.
juridic(al) agg. giuridico.
jurisdiction s. giurisdizione.
jurisdictional agg. giurisdizionale.
jurisprudence s. giurisprudenza.
jurisprudent s. giurisprudente.
jurisprudential agg. legale.
jurist s. giurista.
jury s. giuria, giurì.
juryman s. giurato.
just agg. giusto, retto. ♦ **just** avv. appena, appunto, esattamente ‖ — now, proprio ora; — so-, proprio così; — then, proprio allora.

justice s. giustizia, imparzialità.
justiciable agg. processabile.
justiciary agg. giudiziario.
justifiability s. legittimità di difesa.
justifiable agg. giustificabile, legittimo || — *homicide*, omicidio per legittima difesa.
justification s. giustificazione.
justificative agg. giustificativo.
to justify vt. 1. giustificare 2. difendere 3. perdonare.
justly avv. giustamente, esattamente.
jut s. sporgenza.
to jut vt. e vi. sporgere.
jute s. iuta.
juvenile agg. giovanile.
juxtaposition s. accostamento.

K

kaleidoscope s. caleidoscopio.
kalends s. pl. calende.
kangaroo s. canguro.
kaolin(e) s. caolino.
karting s. andare in « go-kart ».
kathode s. catodo.
keel s. 1. chiglia 2. chiatta (da carbone).
to keel vt. 1. rovesciare 2. (mar.) carenare.
keen agg. 1. aguzzo, affilato 2. pungente 3. forte 4. appassionato 5. acuto.
keenly avv. 1. in modo penetrante 2. dolorosamente 3. avidamente 4. (comm.) al minimo.
keenness s. 1. sottigliezza 2. intensità 3. ardore 4. acume.
keep s. 1. sostentamento 2. torrione.
to keep (kept, kept) vi. 1. restare 2. conservarsi || *to — on*, continuare; *to — off*, tenersi in disparte. ♦ **to keep (kept, kept)** vt. 1. tenere 2. mantenere 3. custodire 4. rispettare || *to — back*, dissimulare; *to — up*, tener alto, sostenere.
keeper s. guardiano.
keeping s. 1. sorveglianza 2. mantenimento 3. armonia.
keepsake s. oggetto ricordo.
keg s. barilotto.
kennel s. 1. canile 2. muta di cani 3. rigagnolo.

to kennel vt. tenere in un canile. ♦ **to kennel** vi. rintanarsi.
kepi s. chepì.
kept V. to keep.
kerbstone s. cordonatura (del marciapiede).
kerchief s. fazzoletto.
kernel s. 1. gheriglio 2. seme 3. (fig.) essenza.
kettle s. bollitore, bricco.
key s. 1. chiave 2. tasto || — -money, buonuscita.
to key vt. 1. (mecc.) inchiavettare 2. (mus.) accordare 3. chiudere a chiave || *to — up* (fig.), eccitare.
keyboard s. tastiera.
keyed agg. 1. munito di chiavi 2. (mus.) a tasti.
keyhole s. buco della serratura.
keyless agg. senza chiave.
keystone s. chiave di volta.
kick s. 1. calcio 2. rinculo || — -off (sport), calcio d'inizio.
to kick vt. prendere a calci. ♦ **to kick** vi. 1. tirar calci 2. rinculare (di armi) 3. recalcitrare.
kicker s. chi scalcia.
kid[1] s. 1. capretto 2. bimbo.
kid[2] s. tinozza.
to kidnap vt. rapire.
kidnapper s. rapitore.
kidnapping s. ratto.
kidney s. 1. rene 2. temperamento || *stones in the kidneys*, calcoli renali.
kier s. caldaia.
to kill vt. 1. uccidere 2. respingere 3. smorzare 4. fermare.
killer s. uccisore || *lady-* —, dongiovanni.
killing agg. mortale. ♦ **killing** s. uccisione.
killjoy s. guastafeste.
kiln s. fornace.
kilo, kilogram(me) s. chilo(grammo).
kilometer s. chilometro.
kilt s. gonnellino degli scozzesi.
kin agg. consanguineo, affine. ♦ **kin** s. parentela.
kind[1] agg. gentile || *very — of you*, molto gentile da parte tua.
kind[2] s. specie, tipo.
to kindle vt. accendere. ♦ **to kindle** vi. accendersi.
kindliness s. gentilezza.
kindling s. 1. accensione 2. legna facilmente infiammabile.
kindly agg. gentile. ♦ **kindly** avv.

gentilmente.
kindness s. gentilezza.
kindred agg. 1. imparentato 2. affine. ◆ **kindred** s. parentela.
kinematics s. cinematica.
kinetic agg. cinetico.
kinetics s. cinetica.
king s. re || king's English, la lingua inglese ufficiale.
kingdom s. regno.
kinghood s. regalità.
kingly agg. regale, regio.
kingship s. regalità.
kinless agg. senza parenti.
kinsfolk s. pl. parenti.
kinship s. parentela.
kinsman s. parente.
kinswoman s. parente (donna).
kiosk s. chiosco || newspaper —, edicola.
kipper s. aringa, salmone affumicato.
to **kipper** vt. affumicare (pesce).
kiss s. bacio.
to **kiss** vt. baciare || to — the dust, mordere la polvere.
kit s. 1. cassetta 2. equipaggiamento.
kitchen s. cucina || — garden, orto.
kitchener s. cuciniere.
kitchenette s. cucinino.
kitchenware s. batteria da cucina.
kite s. 1. nibbio 2. aquilone 3. aliante.
kitten s. gattino.
kleptomania s. cleptomania.
kleptomaniac agg. e s. cleptomane.
knack s. 1. abilità 2. dispositivo ingegnoso.
knapsack s. zaino (per soldati).
knave s. furfante.
knavery s. disonestà.
knavish agg. disonesto.
to **knead** vt. impastare.
kneader s. 1. chi impasta 2. impastatrice.
kneading s. impasto || — trough, madia.
knee s. 1. ginocchio 2. tubo a gomito || — -cap, rotula, ginocchiera.
to **kneel** (knelt, knelt) vi. inginocchiarsi.
kneeler s. 1. chi s'inginocchia 2. inginocchiatoio.
knell s. rintocco funebre.
to **knell** vt. chiamare a raccolta. ◆ to **knell** vi. sonare a morto.
knelt V. to kneel.

knew V. to know.
knickerbockers s. pl. calzoni alla zuava.
knick-knack s. ninnolo.
knick-knackery s. cianfrusaglie.
knife s. (pl. knives) 1. coltello 2. bisturi || pen- —, temperino; pruning- —, falcetto || — -grinder, arrotino.
to **knife** vt. 1. tagliare 2. accoltellare.
knight s. cavaliere.
knighthood s. 1. rango di cavaliere 2. cavalleria.
knightliness s. cavalleria.
knightly agg. cavalleresco. ◆ **knightly** avv. cavallerescamente.
to **knit** (knit, knit) (anche reg.) vt. 1. lavorare a maglia 2. corrugare 3. unire. ◆ to **knit** (knit, knit) (anche reg.) vi. unirsi, saldarsi.
knitter s. 1. magliaia 2. telaio per maglieria.
knitting s. lavoro a maglia.
knitwear s. maglieria.
knob s. 1. protuberanza 2. pomo, manopola.
knobby agg. nodoso.
knock s. 1. colpo 2. (mecc.) battito in testa.
to **knock** vt. urtare. ◆ to **knock** vi. 1. bussare 2. detonare || to — down, abbattere; to — out, sopraffare.
knocker s. battente.
knot s. 1. nodo 2. coccarda 3. gruppo 4. difficoltà.
to **knot** vt. annodare. ◆ to **knot** vi. annodarsi.
knottiness s. 1. nodosità 2. (fig.) difficoltà.
knotty agg. 1. nodoso 2. (fig.) difficile.
to **know** (knew, known) vt. 1. conoscere 2. sapere 3. riconoscere || to — of, aver sentito parlare di; to — about, essere al corrente di.
knowable agg. 1. comprensibile 2. riconoscibile.
knowing agg. 1. intelligente 2. istruito.
knowledge s. conoscenza.
known V. to know.
knuckle s. articolazione, nocca || — -duster, pugno di ferro.
to **knuckle** vi. 1. (fig.) cedere 2. applicarsi || to — under, sottomettersi.

knurl s. zigrinatura.
to **knurl** vt. zigrinare.
Korean agg. e s. coreano.

L

la s. (mus.) la.
label s. etichetta.
to **label** vt. 1. mettere l'etichetta a 2. classificare.
labial agg. e s. labiale.
laboratory s. laboratorio.
laborious agg. laborioso.
laboriousness s. laboriosità.
labour s. 1. lavoro, fatica 2. mano d'opera 3. doglie (pl.) || hard —, lavori forzati; — party, partito laborista.
to **labour** vi. 1. lavorare, faticare 2. avere le doglie. ◆ to **labour** vt. elaborare, sviluppare.
laboured agg. 1. elaborato 2. penoso.
labourer s. lavoratore.
labouring agg. laborioso.
labourism s. laburismo.
labourist s. laburista.
labyrinth s. labirinto.
lace s. 1. laccio 2. pizzo 3. passamaneria.
to **lace** vt. 1. allacciare 2. guarnire con merletti, galloni.
to **lacerate** vt. lacerare.
lachrymal agg. lacrimale.
lachrymator s. gas lacrimogeno.
lack s. mancanza.
to **lack** vt. mancare di. ◆ to **lack** vi. mancare, scarseggiare.
lacker s. 1. lacca 2. oggetto laccato.
to **lacker** vt. laccare.
laconic(al) agg. laconico.
to **lacquer** V. to lacker.
lactation s. 1. lattazione 2. allattamento.
lacteal, lacteous agg. latteo.
lactose s. lattosio.
lacunar agg. lacunoso. ◆ **lacunar** s. soffitto a cassettoni.
lacustrine agg. lacustre.
lacy agg. simile a pizzo.
lad s. ragazzo.
ladder s. 1. scala a pioli 2. smagliatura.
to **ladder** vt. munire di scala. ◆ to

ladder vi. smagliarsi.
to **lade** (laded, laden) vt. caricare.
laden agg. (fig.) oppresso.
lading s. carico: bill of —, polizza di carico.
ladle s. mestolo.
to **ladle** vt. versare con un mestolo.
lady s. signora || Our Lady, la Madonna; — doctor, dottoressa.
ladybird s. coccinella.
ladykiller s. (fam.) dongiovanni.
ladylike agg. signorile, raffinato.
ladyship s. 1. rango di nobildonna 2. Signoria.
lag s. ritardo, rallentamento.
to **lag** vi. ritardare, restare indietro.
laggard agg. e s. pigro.
lagoon s. laguna.
to **laicize** vt. laicizzare.
laid V. to lay.
lain V. to lie.
lair s. tana.
laity s. 1. i laici 2. i profani.
lake s. lago.
laky agg. lacustre.
lamb s. agnello.
lambent agg. 1. lambente 2. scintillante.
lame agg. 1. zoppo 2. (fig.) debole (di argomenti).
to **lame** vt. storpiare.
lamellar agg. lamellare.
lameness s. 1. zoppaggine 2. imperfezione.
lament s. lamento.
to **lament** vt. lamentare. ◆ to **lament** vi. lamentarsi.
lamentable agg. lamentevole.
lamentation s. lamento.
lamented agg. 1. deplorato 2. compianto.
to **laminate** vt. laminare.
lamination s. 1. laminazione 2. lamina.
lamp s. lampada || — -black, nerofumo; — -shade, paralume.
lamplight s. luce artificiale.
lampoon s. libello.
lamprey s. lampreda.
lance s. 1. lancia 2. fiocina.
to **lance** vt. (med.) incidere.
lancer s. lanciere.
lancet s. bisturi.
land s. 1. terra 2. paese, contrada 3. campagna, terreno || — -surveying, agrimensura; — surveyor, agrimensore.
to **land** vi. 1. sbarcare 2. atterrare. ◆ to **land** vt. 1. sbarcare 2. de-

porre 3. prendere possesso di.

landed *agg.* fondiario.

landing *s.* 1. sbarco 2. atterraggio 3. pianerottolo || — *-stage*, pontile di sbarco; — *-strip*, pista d'atterraggio.

landlady *s.* 1. padrona di casa 2. albergatrice.

landless *agg.* senza terreni.

landlord *s.* 1. padrone di casa, di terra 2. albergatore.

landmark *s.* 1. punto di riferimento 2. pietra miliare.

landowner *s.* proprietario terriero.

landscape *s.* paesaggio || — *-painter*, paesaggista.

landslide, landslip *s.* frana.

lane *s.* 1. viottolo, vicolo 2. (*mar.*) rotta 3. corsia (*di strada*).

language *s.* linguaggio.

languid *agg.* languido.

languish *s.* languore.

to languish *vi.* languire.

languor *s.* languore.

languorous *agg.* languido.

lank *agg.* 1. allampanato 2. liscio (*di capelli*).

lanolin(e) *s.* lanolina.

lantern *s.* lanterna.

lap[1] *s.* 1. grembo 2. valletta 3. lembo.

lap[2] *s.* 1. sovrapposizione 2. (*sport*) giro di pista.

to lap *vt.* 1. piegare 2. avvolgere 3. lambire 4. bere avidamente. ♦ **to lap** *vi.* ripiegarsi.

laparotomy *s.* laparatomia.

lapel *s.* risvolto (*di giacca, soprabito*).

lapidary *agg.* lapidario. ♦ **lapidary** *s.* tagliatore di pietre.

lapidation *s.* lapidazione.

Lapp *agg.* e *s.* lappone.

lappet *s.* 1. falda 2. lobo dell'orecchio.

lapse *s.* 1. errore 2. intervallo.

to lapse *vi.* 1. errare 2. scivolare.

larboard *s.* fiancata sinistra (*di nave*).

larceny *s.* furto.

larch *s.* larice.

lard *s.* lardo.

to lard *vt.* 1. ungere con lardo 2. lardellare.

larder *s.* dispensa.

large *agg.* 1. largo 2. grande, ampio 3. generoso || *at* —, in genere; *to be at* —, essere in libertà.

largeness *s.* 1. ampiezza, grandezza 2. generosità.

lark *s.* allodola.

laryngitis *s.* laringite.

larynx *s.* laringe.

lascivious *agg.* lascivo.

lasciviousness *s.* lascivia.

lash *s.* 1. frusta 2. frustata 3. (*eye*)—, ciglio.

to lash *vt.* frustare || *to* — *at*, sferzare.

lashing *s.* 1. frustata 2. legatura.

lass, lassie *s.* ragazzina.

last *agg.* (*superl. di* late) 1. ultimo 2. scorso 3. massimo || *the* — *but one*, il penultimo. ♦ **last** *s.* 1. fine 2. ultimo. ♦ **last** *avv.* 1. ultimo 2. l'ultima volta || *at* —, alla fine.

to last *vi.* durare.

lasting *agg.* durevole. ♦ **lasting** *s.* durata.

latch *s.* chiavistello.

late (later, latter; latest, last) *agg.* 1. tardi 2. in ritardo 3. tardo 4. precedente 5. defunto. ♦ **late** *avv.* 1. tardi 2. in ritardo.

lately *avv.* recentemente.

latent *agg.* latente.

later *agg.* (*comp. di* late) posteriore. ♦ **later** *avv.* più tardi.

lateral *agg.* laterale.

latest *agg.* (*superl. di* late) ultimo, recentissimo || *at the* —, al più tardi.

latex *s.* lattice.

lathe *s.* tornio.

lather *s.* schiuma.

to lather *vt.* insaponare. ♦ **to lather** *vi.* schiumare.

Latin *agg.* e *s.* latino.

Latinism *s.* latinismo.

Latinist *s.* latinista.

Latinity *s.* latinità.

latitude *s.* 1. latitudine 2. ampiezza.

latter *agg.* (*comp. di* late) 1. posteriore 2. ultimo 3. secondo.

latterly *avv.* recentemente.

lattice *s.* grata, traliccio.

latticed *agg.* munito di grata.

laudable *agg.* lodevole.

laudanum *s.* laudano.

laudatory *agg.* laudatorio.

laugh *s.* risata.

to laugh *vi.* ridere || *to* — *at*, deridere.

laughable *agg.* comico.

laughing *s.* risata || — *-stock*, zimbello.

laughter *s.* riso || *to burst into* —, scoppiare a ridere.

launch¹ s. varo.
launch² s. (mar.) lancia.
to launch vt. 1. lanciare 2. varare.
to launder vt. e vi. 1. fare il bucato 2. lavare e stirare.
launderette s. lavanderia con macchine automatiche.
laundress s. lavandaia.
laundry s. 1. lavanderia 2. bucato.
laureate agg. coronato d'alloro.
laurel s. lauro, alloro.
to laurel vt. coronare d'alloro.
lavatory s. gabinetto.
lavender s. lavanda.
lavish agg. prodigo.
to lavish vt. prodigare.
lavishness s. prodigalità.
law s. 1. legge 2. professione legale 3. processo, causa || — -court, tribunale; to go to —, ricorrere in giudizio.
lawful agg. 1. legale 2. legittimo.
lawfulness s. 1. legalità 2. legittimità.
lawgiver s. legislatore.
lawless agg. 1. illegale 2. sregolato.
lawn s. prato (rasato).
lawsuit s. (giur.) processo.
lawyer s. avvocato.
lax agg. allentato.
laxative agg. e s. lassativo.
laxity s. 1. negligenza 2. rilassatezza.
lay V. to lie.
lay agg. 1. laico 2. profano || — -brother, converso; — -sister, conversa. ◆ **lay** s. configurazione.
to lay (laid, laid) vt. 1. porre 2. deporre 3. preparare 4. calmare || to — aside, mettere da parte; to — out, stendere, spendere.
lay-by s. piazzola di sosta.
layer s. 1. strato 2. gallina che fa uova 3. (mil.) puntatore.
laying s. 1. posa 2. covata.
layoff s. stagione morta (di lavoro).
layout s. 1. esposizione 2. schema.
lazaret s. lazzaretto.
laziness s. pigrizia.
lazy agg. pigro.
lead¹ s. 1. piombo 2. grafite || red—, minio; white—, biacca.
lead² s. 1. comando 2. guinzaglio 3. mano (di carte).
to lead¹ vt. impiombare.
to lead² (led, led) vt. 1. condurre, capeggiare 2. indurre.
leaden agg. di piombo, plumbeo.

leader s. 1. capo 2. articolo di fondo.
leadership s. direzione.
leading¹ agg. 1. dominante 2. primo. ◆ **leading** s. guida.
leading² s. impiombatura.
leaf s. (pl. leaves) 1. foglia 2. foglio.
to leaf vt. sfogliare. ◆ to leaf vi. mettere le foglie.
leafless agg. senza foglie.
leaflet s. 1. fogliolina 2. volantino.
league s. lega.
to league vi. allearsi.
leak s. 1. fessura 2. (mar.) falla 3. perdita.
to leak vi. perdere || to — out, trapelare.
leakage s. 1. colatura 2. dispersione.
leaky agg. che cola, perde.
lean¹ agg. magro, esile.
lean² s. inclinazione.
to lean (leant, leant) (anche reg.) vt. e vi. 1. pendere 2. appoggiarsi 3. sporgersi 4. inclinare.
leaning s. 1. inclinazione 2. l'appoggiarsi.
leanness s. magrezza.
leant V. to lean.
leap s. salto || — -year, anno bisestile.
to leap (leapt, leapt) (anche reg.) vt. e vi. saltare.
to learn (learnt, learnt) (anche reg.) vt. e vi. imparare, apprendere.
learned agg. colto.
learner s. allievo.
learning s. cultura.
learnt V. to learn.
lease s. 1. contratto d'affitto 2. durata (di contratto) || on —, in affitto.
to lease vt. affittare.
leash s. guinzaglio.
to leash vt. tenere al guinzaglio.
least agg. (superl. di little) il minimo. ◆ **least** s. (il) meno. ◆ **least** avv. (il) meno.
leather s. 1. cuoio 2. oggetto in cuoio || patent —, vernice.
leathern agg. di cuoio.
leave s. 1. permesso 2. congedo.
to leave (left, left) vt. lasciare. ◆ to leave (left, left) vi. partire || to — off, smettere.
leaven s. 1. lievito 2. (fig.) fermento.
to leaven vt. far lievitare.

leaves V. *leaf.*

leaving s. partenza.

lecherous agg. lascivo.

lechery s. lascivia.

lecture s. 1. conferenza 2. lezione 3. rimprovero.

to lecture vt. rimproverare. ◆ **to lecture** vi. fare una conferenza.

lecturer s. 1. conferenziere 2. lettore universitario.

led V. *to lead.*

ledger s. (*comm.*) libro mastro.

lee s. feccia.

leech s. sanguisuga (*anche fig.*).

to leer vt. e vi. guardare di sbieco.

leeward agg. e avv. sottovento.

leeway s. deriva.

left agg. sinistro. ◆ **left** s. sinistra || — -*handed,* mancino.

left V. *to leave.*

leftist s. (*pol.*) uomo di sinistra.

leg s. 1. gamba 2. (*cuc.*) cosciotto || *to pull so.'s* —, canzonare qu.

legacy s. legato.

legal agg. legale.

legality s. legalità.

legalization s. legalizzazione.

to legalize vt. legalizzare.

legatee s. legatario.

legation s. legazione.

legend s. leggenda.

legendary agg. leggendario.

leggins s. pl. gambali.

legible agg. leggibile.

legion s. legione.

legionary agg. e s. legionario.

to legislate vi. fare leggi. ◆ **to legislate** vt. trasformare per mezzo di leggi.

legislation s. legislazione.

legislative agg. legislativo.

legislator s. legislatore.

legislature s. 1. legislatura 2. corpo legislativo.

legitimacy s. legittimità.

legitimate agg. legittimo.

to legitimate vt. legittimare.

legitimation s. legittimazione.

legume s. legume.

leguminous agg. leguminoso.

leisure s. 1. agio 2. tempo libero.

leisurely agg. e avv. con comodo.

lemon s. limone.

lemonade s. limonata.

to lend (**lent, lent**) vt. prestare.

lender s. prestatore.

length s. 1. lunghezza 2. durata, spazio di tempo || *at* —, alla fine.

to lengthen vt. allungare. ◆ **to**

lengthen vi. allungarsi.

lengthy agg. lungo, prolisso.

lenient agg. 1. emolliente 2. mite.

lenitive agg. e s. calmante.

lens s. 1. (*ott.*) lente 2. (*foto*) obiettivo.

lent V. *to lend.*

Lent s. quaresima.

lentil s. lenticchia.

leonine agg. leonino.

leopard s. 1. leopardo 2. gattopardo.

leper s. lebbroso || — *hospital,* lebbrosario.

leporine agg. leporino.

leprosy s. lebbra.

leprous agg. lebbroso.

lesbian agg. e s. lesbica.

lesion s. lesione.

less agg. (*comp. di* little) minore, meno. ◆ **less** s. meno. ◆ **less** avv. meno. ◆ **less** prep. meno.

lessee s. affittuario.

to lessen vt. e vi. diminuire.

lesser agg. minore.

lesson s. lezione.

lest cong. per paura che.

to let (**let, let**) vt. 1. lasciare, permettere 2. affittare || *to* — *in,* far entrare; *to* — *off,* lasciar andare; *to* — *out,* lasciar uscire.

lethal agg. letale.

lethargy s. letargo.

letter s. lettera.

lettered agg. 1. letterato 2. intestato.

lettuce s. lattuga.

leucocyte s. leucocito.

leucocythaemia, leukemia s. leucemia.

levant s. levante.

level agg. 1. livellato 2. a livello 3. regolato. ◆ **level** s. 1. livello 2. superficie piana 3. livella || *on a* — *with,* sullo stesso piano di.

to level vt. 1. livellare 2. puntare (*un'arma*).

levelling s. 1. livellamento 2. puntamento (*di arma*).

lever s. 1. manubrio 2. leva.

to lever vi. far leva.

to levigate vt. 1. levigare 2. polverizzare.

levigation s. 1. levigazione 2. polverizzazione.

levity s. leggerezza.

levy s. 1. leva 2. imposta.

to levy vt. 1. arruolare 2. imporre (*di tasse*).

lewd 462

lewd *agg.* impudico.
lewdness *s.* impudicizia.
lexical *agg.* lessicale.
lexicographer *s.* lessicografo.
lexicography *s.* lessicografia.
lexicology *s.* lessicologia.
lexicon *s.* lessico.
liability *s.* 1. obbligo 2. tendenza 3. (*giur.*) responsabilità. ♦ **liabilities** *s. pl.* passività (*sing.*).
liable *agg.* 1. soggetto a 2. (*giur.*) responsabile.
liar *s.* bugiardo.
libation *s.* libagione.
libel *s.* 1. libello 2. (*giur.*) diffamazione.
to libel *vt.* 1. scrivere un libello contro 2. (*giur.*) sporgere querela.
liberal *agg.* 1. liberale 2. umanistico. ♦ **liberal** *s.* liberale.
liberalism *s.* liberalismo.
liberalist *s.* liberalista.
liberality *s.* liberalità.
to liberalize *vt.* rendere liberale.
to liberate *vt.* liberare.
liberation *s.* liberazione.
liberator *s.* liberatore.
liberticide *s.* 1. liberticida 2. liberticidio.
libertinage *s.* libertinaggio.
libertine *agg. e s.* libertino.
libertinism *s.* libertinaggio.
liberty *s.* libertà.
libidinous *agg.* libidinoso.
libido *s.* libidine.
librarian *s.* bibliotecario.
library *s.* biblioteca || *film* —, cineteca; *record* —, discoteca.
lice V. *louse*.
licence *s.* licenza || *driving* —, patente automobilistica.
to license *vt.* dare una licenza a.
licensed *agg.* autorizzato.
licentious *agg.* licenzioso.
licentiousness *s.* dissolutezza.
lichen *s.* lichene.
lick *s.* leccata.
to lick *vt.* 1. leccare 2. lambire.
lid *s.* coperchio.
lie[1] *s.* menzogna || *the* —, smentita.
lie[2] *s.* posizione.
to lie[1] *vi.* mentire.
to lie[2] (*lay, lain*) *vi.* giacere, trovarsi || *to* — *down*, coricarsi; *to* — *in*, partorire.
lieutenant *s.* tenente.
life *s.* (*pl.* lives) vita || — *-belt*, cintura di salvataggio; — *preserver*, salvagente.

lifeboat *s.* lancia di salvataggio.
lifeless *agg.* senza vita.
lifelike *agg.* vivido.
lift *s.* 1. ascensore 2. passaggio (*su un veicolo*) 3. sollevamento.
to lift *vt.* 1. alzare 2. rubare. ♦ **to lift** *vi.* alzarsi.
light[1] *agg.* 1. chiaro 2. biondo 3. leggero 4. agile 5. insignificante.
light[2] *s.* 1. luce 2. fuoco 3. lampada || *traffic lights*, semaforo.
to light (**lit, lit**) (*anche reg.*) *vt.* 1. accendere 2. illuminare. ♦ **to light** (**lit, lit**) (*anche reg.*) *vi.* 1. accendersi 2. illuminarsi 3. posarsi.
to lighten *vt.* 1. alleggerire, alleviare 2. illuminare. ♦ **to lighten** *vi.* 1. alleggerirsi 2. illuminarsi 3. (*imp.*) lampeggiare.
lighter *s.* 1. accenditore 2. (*mar.*) chiatta.
lighthouse *s.* faro.
lighting *s.* 1. accensione 2. luce (*di quadro*).
lightless *agg.* oscuro.
lightness *s.* 1. leggerezza 2. gaiezza 3. illuminazione.
lightning *s.* fulmine || — *-rod*, parafulmine.
Ligurian *agg. e s.* ligure.
like *agg.* 1. simile 2. caratteristico di. ♦ **like** *prep.* come || — *this*, — *that*, così; *to feel* —, aver voglia di; *to look* —, avere l'aria di.
like *s.* simile. ♦ **likes** *s. pl.* gusti.
to like *vt.* piacere. ♦ **to like** *vi.* volere.
likelihood *s.* probabilità.
likely *agg.* 1. probabile 2. adatto. ♦ **likely** *avv.* probabilmente.
likeness *s.* 1. somiglianza 2. immagine.
likewise *avv.* 1. allo stesso modo 2. anche.
liking *s.* 1. gusto 2. preferenza.
lilac *agg. e s.* lilla.
lily *agg.* bianco. ♦ **lily** *s.* giglio || *water* —, ninfea.
limb *s.* 1. membro 2. ramo.
lime[1] *s.* 1. calce 2. pania.
lime[2] *s.* cedro.
lime[3] *s.* tiglio.
to lime *vt.* 1. cementare 2. invischiare.
limelight *s.* luce della ribalta.
limestone *s.* calcare.
limit *s.* limite.
to limit *vt.* limitare.

limitary agg. **1.** limitato **2.** limitativo **3.** situato alla frontiera.
limitation s. limitazione.
limitative agg. limitativo.
limited agg. limitato || — *company*, società a responsabilità limitata; — *monarchy*, monarchia costituzionale.
limp agg. molle.
to **limp** vi. zoppicare.
limpid agg. limpido.
limpidity s. limpidezza.
limping s. zoppicamento.
line s. **1.** linea, riga **2.** ruga **3.** discendenza **4.** attività **5.** verso **6.** (comm.) articolo.
to **line** vt. **1.** rigare **2.** fiancheggiare **3.** foderare || *to — up*, allineare, allinearsi.
lineage s. lignaggio.
lineal agg. in linea diretta.
lineament s. lineamento.
linear agg. lineare.
linen agg. di lino. ♦ **linen** s. **1.** tela di lino **2.** biancheria.
liner s. **1.** transatlantico **2.** aereo di linea.
to **linger** vt. e vi. indugiare.
linguist s. linguista.
linguistic(al) agg. linguistico.
linguistics s. linguistica.
liniment s. linimento.
lining s. **1.** rigatura **2.** allineamento **3.** fodera **4.** rivestimento.
link s. **1.** anello **2.** (fig.) legame || *cuff-links*, gemelli da polso.
to **link** vt. collegare. ♦ to **link** vi. collegarsi.
linotyping s. linotipia.
linotypist s. linotipista.
lint s. garza.
lintel s. architrave.
lion s. leone.
lioness s. leonessa.
lip s. **1.** labbro **2.** margine || —-*stick*, rossetto per labbra.
to **lip** vt. **1.** toccare (*con le labbra*) **2.** sussurrare.
liquefaction s. liquefazione.
to **liquefy** vt. liquefare. ♦ to **liquefy** vi. liquefarsi.
liqueur s. rosolio.
liquid agg. **1.** liquido **2.** chiaro **3.** armonioso **4.** instabile. ♦ **liquid** s. liquido.
to **liquidate** vt. liquidare.
liquidation s. liquidazione.
liquidator s. liquidatore.
liquor s. **1.** liquido **2.** bevanda alcolica.

liquorice s. liquirizia.
to **lisp** vi. parlare bleso.
lisping agg. bleso. ♦ **lisping** s. pronuncia blesa.
list[1] s. **1.** lista **2.** striscia **3.** cimosa. ♦ **lists** s. pl. lizza (sing.).
list[2] s. (mar.) sbandamento.
to **list**[1] vt. elencare, catalogare.
to **list**[2] vi. (mar.) sbandare.
to **listen** vi. ascoltare: *to — to so.*, ascoltare qu.; *to — in*, ascoltare la radio.
listener s. ascoltatore.
listening s. ascolto.
listless agg. disattento.
lit V. *to light*.
litany s. litania.
literal agg. **1.** letterale **2.** prosaico **3.** di lettera alfabetica.
literalism s. interpretazione letterale.
literary agg. letterario.
literate agg. e s. letterato.
literature s. letteratura.
lithe agg. agile.
lithograph s. litografia.
to **lithograph** vt. litografare.
lithographic(al) agg. litografico.
lithography s. (arte della) litografia.
litigant s. (giur.) contendente.
litmus s. tornasole.
litre s. litro.
litter s. **1.** lettiga, barella **2.** strame **3.** rifiuti **4.** figliata.
little (less, least) agg. **1.** piccolo **2.** breve **3.** poco || *a —*, un po' di. ♦ **little** s. poco. ♦ **little** avv. poco || *a —*, piuttosto.
liturgic(al) agg. liturgico.
liturgy s. liturgia.
live agg. **1.** vivo **2.** ardente **3.** carico (di armi).
to **live** vi. e vt. vivere, abitare.
livelihood s. mezzi di sussistenza.
liveliness s. vivacità.
lively agg. vivace.
liver s. fegato.
livery[1] agg. bilioso.
livery[2] s. **1.** livrea **2.** (giur.) passaggio di proprietà.
lives V. *life*.
livestock s. bestiame.
livid agg. livido.
living agg. **1.** vivo **2.** perfetto (di somiglianza). ♦ **living** s. **1.** mezzo di mantenimento **2.** vita || —-*room*, soggiorno.

lizard *s.* lucertola.
llama *s.* (*zool.*) lama.
load *s.* **1.** carico, peso **2.** (*elettr.*) carica, tensione.
to load *vt.* **1.** caricare **2.** adulterare.
loader *s.* caricatore.
loading *s.* caricamento.
loadstar *s.* stella polare.
loaf *s.* (*pl.* loaves) pagnotta || *sugar-* —, pan di zucchero.
to loaf *vi.* oziare.
loafer *s.* fannullone.
loan *s.* prestito: *on* —, a prestito.
to loan *vt.* prestare.
loath *agg.* riluttante.
to loathe *vt.* detestare.
loathing *s.* disgusto.
loathsome *agg.* **1.** odioso **2.** disgustoso.
loaves V. *loaf.*
lobby *s.* anticamera.
lobe *s.* lobo.
lobster *s.* aragosta.
local *agg.* e *s.* locale.
locality *s.* località.
to localize *vt.* localizzare.
to locate *vt.* **1.** situare **2.** individuare **3.** indicare.
location *s.* **1.** posizione **2.** locazione.
lock[1] *s.* **1.** ricciolo **2.** fiocco.
lock[2] *s.* **1.** serratura **2.** diga **3.** otturatore (*di arma*).
to lock *vt.* serrare. ♦ **to lock** *vi.* (*mecc.*) incepparsi.
locker *s.* armadio, bauletto a chiave.
locket *s.* medaglione.
lockout *s.* (*econ.*) serrata.
locomotion *s.* locomozione.
locomotive *agg.* locomotorio. ♦ **locomotive** *s.* locomotiva.
locust *s.* locusta || — *-tree*, carrubo, robinia.
locution *s.* locuzione.
lodge *s.* **1.** loggia **2.** padiglione.
to lodge *vt.* **1.** alloggiare **2.** collocare. ♦ **to lodge** *vi.* **1.** alloggiare **2.** entrare.
lodging *s.* alloggio, dimora.
loftiness *s.* **1.** altezza **2.** nobiltà.
lofty *agg.* **1.** alto, elevato **2.** orgoglioso, altero.
log *s.* ceppo || — *-book*, giornale di bordo.
logarithm *s.* logaritmo.
logic *s.* logica.
logical *agg.* logico.
logistic(al) *agg.* logistico.

logistics *s. pl.* (*mil.*) logistica (*sing.*).
logomachy *s.* logomachia.
loin *s.* lombo. ♦ **loins** *s. pl.* reni.
to loiter *vt.* sprecare (*tempo ecc.*). ♦ **to loiter** *vi.* bighellonare, oziare.
loitering *s.* il bighellonare, l'andare a zonzo.
Lombard *agg.* e *s.* lombardo.
Londoner *s.* londinese.
Londonese *agg.* londinese.
loneliness *s.* solitudine.
lonely, lonesome *agg.* solo, solitario.
long *agg.* lungo || — *-distance call*, telefonata interurbana. ♦ **long** *s.* molto tempo. ♦ **long** *avv.* a lungo || *how* —?, quanto tempo?; *all day* —, tutto il giorno; *as* — *as*, fino a, purché; *so* —!, arrivederci!; *before* —, tra poco.
to long *vi.* desiderare ardentemente: *to* — *for sthg.*, desiderare ardentemente qc.
longanimity *s.* longanimità.
longboat *s.* lancia.
longevity *s.* longevità.
longevous *agg.* longevo.
longing *agg.* bramoso. ♦ **longing** *s.* brama.
longitude *s.* longitudine.
longitudinal *agg.* longitudinale.
long-sighted *agg.* **1.** presbite **2.** preveggente.
look *s.* sguardo. ♦ **looks** *s. pl.* aspetto (*sing.*).
to look *vi.* **1.** sembrare **2.** guardare || *to* — *after*, badare a; *to* — *at*, guardare; *to* — *for*, cercare; *to* — *forward to*, non veder l'ora di; *to* — *like*, somigliare; *to* — *up*, consultare (*orario, dizionario ecc.*); *to* — *through*, esaminare attentamente; *to* — *up to*, rispettare; *to* — *down on*, disprezzare.
looker-on *s.* spettatore.
looking-glass *s.* specchio.
lookout *s.* **1.** guardia **2.** vista panoramica **3.** prospettiva.
loom *s.* telaio.
to loom *vt.* tessere. ♦ **to loom** *vi.* apparire indistintamente.
loop *s.* **1.** cappio **2.** gancio.
loophole *s.* feritoia.
loose *agg.* **1.** sciolto **2.** ampio **3.** vago **4.** licenzioso **5.** allentato.
to loose *vt.* **1.** sciogliere **2.** liberare **3.** lanciare.

to **loosen** *vt.* **1.** sciogliere **2.** allentare.

looseness *s.* **1.** scioltezza **2.** ampiezza **3.** libertinaggio **4.** imprecisione.

to **lop** *vt.* potare, mozzare.

loquacious *agg.* loquace.

loquacity *s.* loquacità.

lord *s.* **1.** signore **2.** Pari || — *Mayor*, sindaco.

to **lord** *vt.* dominare.

lordly *agg.* **1.** fastoso, imponente **2.** altero.

lordship *s.* signoria, autorità.

lorry *s.* autocarro.

to **lose (lost, lost)** *vt.* e *vi.* perdere.

loser *s.* perdente.

losing, loss *s.* perdita.

lost V. *to lose.*

lot *s.* **1.** sorte **2.** parte **3.** lotto (*di terreno ecc.*) || *a — of*, una quantità di.

to **lot** *vt.* lottizzare.

lotion *s.* lozione.

lottery *s.* lotteria.

loud *agg.* forte, fragoroso, rumoroso || — *-speaker*, altoparlante. ◆ **loud(ly)** *avv.* ad alta voce.

lounge *s.* **1.** atrio (*di albergo, teat. ecc.*) **2.** lo stare in ozio.

to **lounge** *vi.* bighellonare.

lounger *s.* fannullone.

louse *s.* (*pl.* lice) pidocchio.

lousy *agg.* pidocchioso.

lovable *agg.* amabile.

love *s.* amore.

to **love** *vt.* amare.

loveless *agg.* senza amore.

loveliness *s.* bellezza.

lovely *agg.* bello.

lover *s.* amante, innamorato.

loving *agg.* amoroso.

lovingness *s.* affettuosità.

low[1] *agg.* **1.** basso **2.** debole || *-spirited*, depresso. ◆ **low** *avv.* **1.** in basso **2.** a voce bassa **3.** a basso prezzo.

low[2] *s.* muggito.

to **low** *vi.* muggire.

to **lower** *vt.* **1.** abbassare **2.** abbattere. ◆ to **lower** *vi.* abbattersi.

lowering *s.* abbassamento.

lowland *s.* pianura.

lowly *agg.* **1.** basso **2.** umile. ◆ **lowly** *avv.* umilmente.

loyal *agg.* leale.

loyalty *s.* lealtà.

lozenge *s.* **1.** (*geom.*) rombo **2.** pastiglia.

lubber *s.* zoticone.

lubricant *agg.* e *s.* lubrificante.

to **lubricate** *vt.* lubrificare.

lubricating, lubrication *s.* lubrificazione.

lubricator *s.* lubrificatore.

lubricity *s.* **1.** viscosità **2.** (*fig.*) lascivia.

lubricous *agg.* lubrico.

lucent *agg.* lucente.

lucid *agg.* lucido, chiaro.

lucidity *s.* lucidità, chiarezza.

luck *s.* **1.** sorte **2.** fortuna || *to be in* —, *out of* —, essere fortunato, sfortunato.

luckily *avv.* fortunatamente.

luckless *agg.* sfortunato.

lucky *agg.* fortunato.

lucrative *agg.* lucrativo.

to **lucubrate** *vi.* fare delle elucubrazioni.

lucubration *s.* elucubrazione.

ludicrous *agg.* ridicolo.

ludicrousness *s.* comicità.

luggage *s.* bagaglio.

lugubrious *agg.* lugubre.

lukewarm *agg.* tiepido, apatico.

to **lull** *vt.* **1.** cullare **2.** calmare.

lullaby *s.* ninna-nanna.

lumbago *s.* lombaggine.

lumbar *agg.* lombare.

lumber *s.* **1.** cianfrusaglie (*pl.*) **2.** legname || — *-room*, ripostiglio.

to **lumber** *vt.* **1.** ammucchiare **2.** ingombrare. ◆ to **lumber** *vi.* **1.** tagliare legname **2.** muoversi pesantemente e rumorosamente.

lumbering *s.* commercio di legname.

luminary *s.* **1.** corpo luminoso **2.** luminare.

luminous *agg.* luminoso.

luminousness *s.* luminosità.

lump *s.* **1.** mucchio **2.** gonfiore **3.** zolletta **4.** (*comm.*) blocco **5.** persona goffa.

to **lump** *vt.* ammassare. ◆ to **lump** *vi.* raggrumarsi.

lumpy *agg.* **1.** granuloso **2.** increspato (*di mare*) **3.** pesante.

lunacy *s.* pazzia.

lunar *agg.* lunare.

lunatic *agg.* e *s.* pazzo.

lunation *s.* lunazione.

lunch *s.* seconda colazione, pasto del mezzogiorno.

to **lunch** *vi.* fare la seconda colazione. ◆ to **lunch** *vt.* offrire la colazione a.

luncheon s. spuntino.
lunette s. (*arch.*) lunetta.
lung s. polmone: *iron* —, polmone d'acciaio.
lupine s. lupino.
lure s. esca.
to **lure** vt. adescare.
lurid agg. **1.** spettrale **2.** orribile.
lurk s. nascondiglio.
to **lurk** vi. nascondersi.
luscious agg. **1.** dolce **2.** sensuale.
lust s. **1.** lussuria **2.** brama.
to **lust** vi. bramare: *to — for so.*, *sthg.*, bramare qu., qc.
lustful agg. **1.** sensuale **2.** bramoso.
lustfulness s. **1.** sensualità **2.** brama.
lustral agg. lustrale.
lustre[1] s. lustro, splendore.
lustre[2] s. lustro, quinquennio.
lusty agg. vigoroso, gagliardo.
lute s. liuto.
Lutheran agg. e s. luterano.
Lutheranism s. luteranesimo.
to **luxate** vt. (*med.*) lussare.
luxation s. lussazione.
luxuriant agg. lussureggiante.
to **luxuriate** vi. lussureggiare || *to — in*, deliziarsi di.
luxurious agg. lussuoso, sontuoso.
luxury s. **1.** lusso **2.** oggetto di lusso.
lye s. lisciva.
lying[1] agg. bugiardo.
lying[2] agg. giacente, situato.
lymph s. linfa.
lymphatic agg. linfatico. ♦ **lymphatic** s. vaso linfatico.
to **lynch** vt. linciare.
lynch law s. linciaggio.
lynx s. lince.
lyre s. lira.
lyric(al) agg. lirico. ♦ **lyric** s. lirica.
lyricism, **lyrism** s. lirismo.
lyrist s. poeta lirico.

M

macabre agg. macabro.
macaroni s. maccheroni.
macaroon s. amaretto.
mace s. mazza || — -*bearer*, mazziere.
to **macerate** vt. macerare. ♦ to

macerate vi. macerarsi.
maceration s. macerazione.
Machiavellian agg. machiavellico.
Machiavellism s. machiavellismo.
to **machinate** vt. macchinare.
machination s. macchinazione.
machine s. macchina || *sewing-* —, macchina da cucire.
to **machine** vt. e vi. lavorare a macchina.
machine-gun s. mitragliatrice.
to **machine-gun** vt. mitragliare.
machine-gunner s. mitragliere.
machinery s. **1.** macchinario **2.** meccanismo.
machining s. lavorazione (*a macchina*).
machinist s. macchinista.
mackerel s. sgombro || — *sky*, cielo a pecorelle.
mackintosh s. impermeabile.
macrocephalic agg. macrocefalo.
macrocosm s. macrocosmo.
macrocosmic agg. macrocosmico.
macromolecule s. macromolecola.
macroscopic agg. macroscopico.
to **maculate** vt. maculare.
maculation s. maculamento.
mad agg. **1.** pazzo **2.** idrofobo || *to go* —, impazzire.
madam s. signora.
madcap s. scervellato.
to **madden** vt. far impazzire. ♦ to **madden** vi. diventare matto.
madding agg. folle.
made V. *to make.*
madhouse s. manicomio.
madly avv. pazzamente.
madman s. pazzo.
madness s. **1.** pazzia **2.** idrofobia.
madrepore s. madrepora.
madrigal s. madrigale.
Maecenas s. mecenate.
magazine s. **1.** magazzino **2.** rivista **3.** arsenale.
maggot s. **1.** bruco **2.** (*fig.*) capriccio.
maggoty agg. **1.** bacato **2.** (*fig.*) capriccioso.
magic s. magia.
magic(al) agg. magico.
magician s. mago.
magisterial agg. **1.** di magistrato **2.** autoritario.
magistracy s. magistratura.
magistrate s. magistrato.
magistrature s. magistratura.
magnanimity s. magnanimità.
magnanimous agg. magnanimo.

magnesium s. magnesio.
magnet s. magnete, calamita.
magnetic(al) agg. magnetico.
magnetism s. magnetismo.
magnetization s. **1.** magnetizzazione **2.** forza d'attrazione.
to **magnetize** vt. magnetizzare.
magnetizer s. magnetizzatore.
magneto s. magnete.
magnetometer s. magnetometro.
magnification s. **1.** esaltazione **2.** ingrandimento.
magnificence s. magnificenza.
magnificent agg. magnifico.
magnifier s. **1.** esaltatore **2.** lente d'ingrandimento.
to **magnify** vt. **1.** esaltare **2.** ingrandire.
magniloquence s. magniloquenza.
magniloquent agg. magniloquente.
magnitude s. grandezza.
magpie s. gazza.
Magyar agg. e s. magiaro.
mahogany s. mogano.
maid s. **1.** fanciulla **2.** cameriera ‖ old —, zitella.
maiden[1] agg. **1.** vergine, puro **2.** esordiente.
maiden[2] s. fanciulla ‖ — name, nome da ragazza.
maidenhead, maidenhood s. verginità.
maidenliness s. modestia, verecondia.
maidenly agg. verginale.
maidservant s. cameriera.
maieutics s. maieutica.
maigre agg. magro.
mail s. posta ‖ — -train, treno postale.
to **mail** vt. mandare per posta.
to **maim** vt. storpiare.
main[1] agg. **1.** principale **2.** vigoroso ‖ — road, strada maestra.
main[2] s. **1.** alto mare **2.** l'essenziale **3.** condotto principale.
mainland s. terraferma.
mainly avv. principalmente.
mainmast s. (mar.) albero maestro.
mainsail s. vela maestra.
mainspring s. molla principale.
to **maintain** vt. **1.** mantenere **2.** asserire.
maintenance s. **1.** mantenimento **2.** manutenzione **3.** difesa.
maize s. granoturco.
majestic(al) agg. maestoso.
majesty s. maestà.
major agg. maggiore, principale. ♦

major s. **1.** maggiorenne **2.** (mil.) maggiore.
majority s. **1.** maggioranza **2.** maggiore età.
make s. **1.** fattura **2.** costituzione **3.** marca.
to **make (made, made)** vt. e vi. **1.** fare **2.** rendere **3.** fabbricare ‖ to — for, dirigersi; to — up, preparare, truccare; to — up for, compensare per ‖ to — oneself understood, farsi capire; to — so. confess, obbligare qu. a confessare; to — so. do what one likes, far fare a qu. ciò che si vuole.
make-believe s. finzione.
maker s. **1.** creatore **2.** costruttore ‖ — -up, truccatore.
makeshift s. espediente.
make-up s. **1.** composizione **2.** trucco **3.** (tip.) impaginazione.
making s. **1.** fattura **2.** formazione.
♦ **makings** s. pl. il necessario (sing.).
maladjusted agg. **1.** disadatto **2.** disadattato.
maladjustment s. inadattabilità.
maladministration s. cattiva amministrazione.
maladroit agg. maldestro.
malady s. malattia.
malaise s. malessere.
Malayan agg. e s. malese.
malcontent agg. e s. malcontento. ♦
male agg. maschio, maschile. ♦
male s. maschio.
malediction s. maledizione.
malefactor s. malfattore.
malefic agg. malefico.
maleficence s. malvagità.
maleficent agg. malefico.
malevolence s. malevolenza.
malevolent agg. malevolo.
malformation s. malformazione.
malformed agg. malformato.
malice s. **1.** malignità **2.** astio: to bear — to so., nutrire rancore verso qu.
malicious agg. **1.** maligno **2.** premeditato.
malign agg. maligno.
malignancy s. malignità.
malignant agg. maligno.
malignity s. V. malignancy.
malleability s. malleabilità.
malleable agg. malleabile.
mallet s. mazzuolo.
mallow s. malva.
malnutrition s. malnutrizione.

malpractice s. pratica illecita.
malt s. malto.
Malthusian agg. e s. maltusiano.
Malthusianism s. maltusianesimo.
maltose s. maltosio.
to **maltreat** vt. maltrattare.
maltreatment s. maltrattamento.
malversation s. malversazione.
mama s. mamma.
mamma[1] s. mamma.
mamma[2] s. mammella.
mammal s. mammifero.
mammalian agg. e s. mammifero.
mammiferous agg. mammifero.
mammoth agg. enorme. ♦ **mammoth** s. mammut.
mammy s. mammina.
man s. (pl. **men**) 1. uomo 2. marito || — -hour, ora lavorativa; — -of-war, nave da guerra.
to **man** vt. munire, equipaggiare (di uomini).
manacle s. manetta.
to **manacle** vt. ammanettare.
to **manage** vt. 1. dirigere 2. maneggiare 3. riuscire. ♦ to **manage** vi. destreggiarsi, cavarsela.
manageable agg. 1. maneggevole 2. fattibile.
management s. 1. direzione, amministrazione 2. abilità.
manager s. 1. direttore 2. amministratore 3. impresario 4. organizzatore.
manageress s. 1. direttrice 2. amministratrice.
managerial agg. direttivo.
managership s. 1. direzione 2. amministrazione.
managing agg. dirigente || — director, consigliere delegato.
mandarin s. mandarino.
mandatary s. mandatario.
mandate s. mandato.
mandator s. mandante.
mandatory agg. e s. mandatario.
mandible s. mandibola.
mandolin s. mandolino.
mandrake s. mandragora.
mandrel s. anima metallica.
mandrill s. mandrillo.
mane s. criniera.
manful agg. valoroso.
manganate s. manganato.
mange s. rogna.
manger s. mangiatoia.
to **mangle** vt. 1. lacerare 2. storpiare.
mangy agg. 1. lacero 2. rognoso 3.

spregevole.
to **manhandle** vt. manovrare (a mano).
manhole s. botola.
manhood s. 1. virilità 2. vigore 3. genere umano.
maniac agg. e s. maniaco, pazzo.
Manich(a)eism s. manicheismo.
manicurist s. manicure.
manifest agg. manifesto.
to **manifest** vt. manifestare.
manifestant s. manifestante.
manifestation s. manifestazione.
manifold agg. molteplice.
manifoldness s. molteplicità.
manikin s. 1. omiciattolo 2. manichino.
maniple s. manipolo.
to **manipulate** vt. manipolare.
manipulation s. manipolazione.
manipulator s. manipolatore.
mankind s. umanità.
manlike agg. 1. civile 2. antropomorfo.
manliness s. virilità.
manly agg. maschio, virile.
manner s. 1. maniera 2. contegno. ♦ **manners** s. pl. 1. modi 2. usanze.
mannered agg. manierato || ill- —, maleducato.
mannerism s. manierismo.
mannerly agg. cortese.
manoeuvrable agg. manovrabile.
manoeuvre s. manovra.
to **manoeuvre** vt. manovrare. ♦ to **manoeuvre** vi. fare le manovre.
manoeuvrer s. stratega.
manometer s. manometro.
manor s. feudo || — -house, castello.
manorial agg. feudale.
mansard s. mansarda.
manservant s. domestico.
mansion s. palazzo.
manslaughter s. omicidio preterintenzionale.
mantelpiece, mantelshelf s. mensola di caminetto.
mantle s. manto, mantello.
to **mantle** vt. ammantare. ♦ to **mantle** vi. coprirsi.
manual agg. e s. manuale.
manufactory s. fabbrica.
manufacturable agg. fabbricabile.
manufacture s. 1. manifattura 2. manufatto.
to **manufacture** vt. fabbricare.
manufacturer s. fabbricante.

manufacturing *agg.* manifatturiero. ♦ **manufacturing** *s.* fabbricazione.

manure *s.* concime.

manuscript *agg.* e *s.* manoscritto.

many (more, most) *agg.* e *pron.* molti || — *a*, più di uno; — -sided, molteplice; *so* —, tanti; *too* —, troppi; *as* — *as*, tanti... quanti; *how* —?, quanti?

map *s.* carta geografica.

maple *s.* acero.

to **mar** *vt.* guastare.

marathon *s.* maratona.

to **maraud** *vt.* e *vi.* saccheggiare.

marauder *s.* predatore.

marble *s.* 1. marmo 2. biglia.

to **marble** *vt.* marmorizzare.

marble-cutter *s.* marmista.

March *s.* marzo.

march[1] *s.* confine.

march[2] *s.* marcia.

to **march** *vi.* 1. camminare 2. marciare || *to* — *in*, entrare marciando.

marching *agg.* in, di marcia.

marchioness *s.* marchesa.

mare *s.* cavalla.

margarine *s.* margarina.

margin *s.* margine.

marginal *agg.* marginale.

marine *agg.* marino, marittimo. ♦ **marine** *s.* 1. marina 2. fante di marina.

marital *agg.* maritale.

maritime *agg.* marittimo.

mark *s.* 1. segno 2. bersaglio 3. voto 4. marchio 5. importanza 6. marco || *question* —, punto interrogativo.

to **mark** *vt.* 1. segnare 2. dare i voti a 3. scegliere 4. osservare.

marked *agg.* notevole.

marker *s.* 1. chi segna 2. segnalibro.

market *s.* mercato.

to **market** *vt.* 1. vendere al mercato 2. introdurre sul mercato. ♦ to **market** *vi.* comprare, vendere sul mercato.

marketing *s.* 1. compra-vendita 2. « marketing » (*ricerche di mercato*).

marking *s.* segno.

marksman *s.* tiratore scelto.

marl *s.* marna.

marmalade *s.* marmellata (*d'arance*).

marmoreal *agg.* marmoreo.

marmot *s.* marmotta.

to **maroon** *vt.* abbandonare in un luogo deserto.

marquee *s.* tendone.

marquess, marquis *s.* marchese.

marquise *s.* marchesa.

marriage *s.* matrimonio, unione.

married *agg.* 1. sposato 2. coniugale.

marrow *s.* midollo || (*vegetable*) —, zucca.

to **marry** *vt.* sposare. ♦ to **marry** *vi.* sposarsi.

marsh *s.* palude || — -*fever*, malaria; — *gas*, metano.

marshal *s.* maresciallo.

to **marshal** *vt.* 1. schierare 2. introdurre.

marshy *agg.* paludoso.

marsupial *agg.* e *s.* marsupiale.

marten *s.* martora.

martial *agg.* 1. marziale 2. di Marte.

Martian *agg.* e *s.* marziano.

martyr *s.* martire.

martyrdom *s.* martirio.

to **martyrize** *vt.* martirizzare.

martyrology *s.* martirologio.

marvel *s.* meraviglia.

to **marvel** *vi.* meravigliarsi.

marvellous *agg.* meraviglioso.

Marxism *s.* marxismo.

Marxist *agg.* e *s.* marxista.

marzipan *s.* marzapane.

mascot(te) *s.* mascotte.

masculine *agg.* e *s.* maschile.

masculinity *s.* mascolinità.

mash *s.* 1. mistura 2. puré.

to **mash** *vt.* 1. mescolare 2. schiacciare.

mask *s.* maschera.

to **mask** *vt.* mascherare.

masking *s.* il mascherarsi.

masochism *s.* masochismo.

mason *s.* muratore || *Free Mason*, massone.

masonry *s.* 1. arte del muratore 2. costruzione in muratura 3. massoneria.

masquerade *s.* mascherata.

to **masquerade** *vi.* 1. mascherarsi 2. fingersi.

mass[1] *s.* messa.

mass[2] *s.* massa, ammasso.

to **mass** *vt.* ammassare. ♦ to **mass** *vi.* ammassarsi.

massacre *s.* massacro.

to **massacre** *vt.* massacrare.

massage *s.* massaggio.

to **massage** *vt.* massaggiare.

masseur *s.* massaggiatore.

masseuse *s.* massaggiatrice.

massif *s.* massiccio.

massive *agg.* 1. massiccio 2. potente.

massiveness *s.* compattezza.

to mass-produce *vt.* produrre in serie.

mass-producer *s.* produttore in serie.

mass-production *s.* produzione in serie.

massy *agg.* massiccio.

mast *s.* (*mar.*) albero.

to mast *vt.* (*mar.*) alberare.

master *s.* 1. padrone 2. maestro ‖ — *builder*, capomastro; *Master of Arts*, laureato in lettere.

to master *vt.* 1. conoscere a fondo 2. dominare.

masterful *agg.* 1. autoritario 2. abile.

masterhood *s.* padronanza.

masterly *agg.* magistrale.

masterpiece *s.* capolavoro.

mastership *s.* 1. autorità 2. abilità.

masterstroke *s.* colpo magistrale.

mastery *s.* 1. maestria 2. signoria.

mastication *s.* masticazione.

mastiff *s.* mastino.

mastitis *s.* mastite.

mastodon *s.* mastodonte.

mastoid *s.* mastoide.

mastoiditis *s.* mastoidite.

masturbation *s.* masturbazione.

mat *s.* stuoia ‖ *door-* —, zerbino.

to mat *vt.* 1. intrecciare 2. coprire con stuoie 3. smerigliare.

match¹ *s.* 1. gara, incontro 2. avversario 3. l'uguale 4. matrimonio.

match² *s.* fiammifero.

to match *vt.* 1. accoppiare, maritare 2. uguagliare. ♦ **to match** *vi.* 1. accoppiarsi 2. accordarsi 3. rivaleggiare.

matchless *agg.* impareggiabile.

mate *s.* 1. compagno 2. aiuto 3. (*mar.*) ufficiale in seconda.

to mate *vt.* accoppiare. ♦ **to mate** *vi.* accoppiarsi.

material *agg.* 1. materiale 2. essenziale. ♦ **material** *s.* 1. materia, materiale 2. stoffa. ♦ **materials** *s. pl.* articoli ‖ *raw* —, materie prime.

materialism *s.* materialismo.

materialist *agg. e s.* materialista.

materialistic *agg.* materialistico.

materialization *s.* materializzazione.

to materialize *vt.* materializzare. ♦ **to materialize** *vi.* 1. materializzarsi 2. avverarsi.

maternal *agg.* materno.

maternity *s.* maternità.

mathematic(al) *agg.* matematico.

mathematician *s.* matematico.

mathematics *s.* matematica.

matriarchy *s.* matriarcato.

matricidal *agg.* matricida.

matricide *s.* 1. matricida 2. matricidio.

to matriculate *vt.* immatricolare. ♦ **to matriculate** *vi.* immatricolarsi.

matriculation *s.* immatricolazione.

matrimonial *agg.* matrimoniale.

matrimony *s.* matrimonio.

matrix *s.* 1. matrice 2. (*anat.*) utero.

matron *s.* 1. matrona 2. direttrice 3. governante.

matronal, matronly *agg.* matronale.

matter *s.* 1. materia 2. faccenda ‖ *what is the* — *with you?*, che cosa vi succede?; *what is the* —?, che succede?

to matter *vi.* 1. importare: *it matters little*, poco importa 2. (*med.*) suppurare.

matter-of-fact *agg.* pratico.

matting *s.* stuoia.

mattock *s.* piccone.

mattress *s.* materasso.

to maturate *vi.* 1. maturare 2. suppurare.

maturation *s.* 1. maturazione 2. suppurazione.

mature *agg.* maturo.

to mature *vt. e vi.* maturare.

maturity *s.* 1. maturità 2. (*comm.*) scadenza.

matutine *agg.* mattutino.

maudlin *agg.* 1. sdolcinato 2. querulo.

to maunder *vi.* 1. parlare a vanvera 2. girovagare.

mausoleum *s.* mausoleo.

mawkish *agg.* 1. nauseante 2. sdolcinato.

mawkishness *s.* 1. sapore nauseante 2. sdolcinatezza.

maxim *s.* massima.

maximalist *s.* massimalista.

maximum *agg. e s.* massimo.

May *s.* maggio ‖ — *Day*, primo maggio.

may (might) *v. dif.* potere (*pres. ind. e congiuntivo*) || — *I go out?*, posso uscire?; *he — arrive to day*, può darsi che arrivi oggi; — *be live to repent it*, possa egli vivere tanto da pentirsene

maybe *avv.* forse.

maybug *s.* maggiolino.

mayflower *s.* biancospino.

mayonnaise *s.* maionese.

mayor *s.* sindaco.

maze *s.* labirinto.

to **maze** *vt.* disorientare, confondere.

mazily *avv.* confusamente.

mazy *agg.* intricato.

me *pron. pers.* me, mi.

meadow *s.* prato.

meagre *agg.* 1. magro 2. scarso.

meal[1] *s.* farina.

meal[2] *s.* pasto.

mealy *agg.* 1. farinoso 2. infarinato 3. pallido 4. chiazzato.

mean[1] *agg.* 1. meschino 2. mediocre.

mean[2] *s.* punto medio, mezzo. ♦ **means** *s. pl.* mezzi || *by no means*, ben lungi da.

to **mean (meant, meant)** *vt. e vi.* 1. intendere, significare 2. destinare.

meander *s.* meandro.

to **meander** *vi.* serpeggiare.

meaning *agg.* 1. disposto 2. significativo. ♦ **meaning** *s.* 1. significato 2. idea.

meaningful *agg.* significativo.

meaningless *agg.* senza senso.

meanly *avv.* 1. meschinamente 2. umilmente.

meanness *s.* meschinità.

meant V. *to mean.*

meantime *s.* frattempo. ♦ **meantime** *avv.* frattanto.

meanwhile *avv.* frattanto.

measles *s.* morbillo || *German —*, rosolia.

measurable *agg.* misurabile.

measure *s.* 1. misura 2. ritmo.

to **measure** *vt. e vi.* misurare.

measureless *agg.* smisurato.

measurement *s.* misurazione.

measurer *s.* misuratore.

meat *s.* carne.

meaty *agg.* 1. polposo 2. sostanzioso.

mechanic *s.* meccanico.

mechanical *agg.* meccanico.

mechanics *s.* meccanica.

mechanism *s.* 1. meccanismo 2. tecnica.

mechanization *s.* meccanizzazione.

to **mechanize** *vt.* meccanizzare.

medal *s.* medaglia.

to **meddle** *vi.* immischiarsi.

meddler *s.* intrigante.

meddlesome *agg.* importuno.

medi(a)eval *agg.* medievale.

medi(a)evalism *s.* medievalismo.

medi(a)evalist *s.* medievalista.

medial *agg.* medio.

median *agg.* mediano.

mediate *agg.* mediato.

to **mediate** *vt.* conseguire con mediazione. ♦ to **mediate** *vi.* fare da intermediario.

mediation *s.* mediazione.

mediator *s.* mediatore.

medical *agg.* medico.

medicament *s.* medicamento.

medication *s.* medicazione.

medicative *agg.* curativo.

medicinal *agg.* medicinale.

medicine *s.* medicina || — *-man*, stregone.

mediocrity *s.* mediocrità.

to **meditate** *vt. e vi.* meditare.

meditation *s.* meditazione.

meditative *agg.* meditativo.

Mediterranean *agg.* mediterraneo.

medium *agg.* medio. ♦ **medium** *s.* mezzo.

mediumistic *agg.* medianico.

medlar *s.* nespola || — *-tree*, nespolo.

medley *agg.* misto. ♦ **medley** *s.* miscuglio.

medulla *s.* midollo.

medullar(y) *agg.* midollare.

meek *agg.* mite.

meekness *s.* mansuetudine.

to **meet (met, met)** *vt.* 1. incontrare 2. far fronte a. ♦ to **meet (met, met)** *vi.* incontrarsi || *to — with*, imbattersi in.

meeting *s.* 1. incontro 2. riunione || *political —*, comizio.

megalomaniac *s.* megalomane.

megaphone *s.* megafono.

melancholic *agg.* malinconico.

melancholy *agg.* malinconico. ♦ **melancholy** *s.* malinconia.

mellifluous *agg.* mellifluo.

mellow *agg.* 1. maturo 2. pastoso 3. ubertoso.

to **mellow** *vt. e vi.* maturare.

mellowness *s.* 1. maturità 2. pastosità 3. ubertosità.

melodic *agg.* melodico.

melodious *agg.* melodioso.
melodiousness *s.* melodiosità.
melodrama *s.* melodramma.
melodramatic *agg.* melodrammatico.
melody *s.* melodia.
melomaniac *s.* melomane.
melon *s.* melone || *water- —,* anguria.
melt *s.* fusione.
to melt *vt.* 1. sciogliere 2. intenerire. ♦ **to melt** *vi.* 1. sciogliersi 2. intenerirsi || *to — away,* svanire.
melter *s.* fonditore.
melting *s.* fusione || *— -pot,* crogiuolo.
meltingly *avv.* teneramente.
member *s.* membro.
membership *s.* 1. qualifica di membro 2. i membri.
membrane *s.* membrana.
memoirs *s. pl.* memorie.
memorable *agg.* memorabile.
memorandum *s.* (*pl.* -da) promemoria.
memorial *agg.* commemorativo. ♦ **memorial** *s.* 1. monumento 2. memoriale.
memorialist *s.* memorialista.
to memorize *vt.* imparare a memoria.
memory *s.* memoria.
men V. *man.*
menace *s.* minaccia.
to menace *vt.* e *vi.* minacciare.
menacing *agg.* minaccioso.
menagerie *s.* serraglio.
mend *s.* rattoppo.
to mend *vt.* 1. riparare 2. correggere. ♦ **to mend** *vi.* 1. correggersi 2. migliorare.
mendacious *agg.* mendace.
mendacity *s.* 1. abitudine di mentire 2. bugia.
mender *s.* 1. riparatore 2. rammendatrice.
mendicant *agg.* e *s.* mendicante.
mendicity *s.* mendicità.
mending *s.* 1. riparazione 2. rammendo.
menial *agg.* servile. ♦ **menial** *s.* servo.
meninx *s.* (*pl.* meninges) meninge.
meniscus *s.* menisco.
menopause *s.* menopausa.
menses *s. pl.* mestruazioni.
menstruation *s.* mestruazione.
mental *agg.* mentale || *— -hospi-*
tal, manicomio.
mentality *s.* 1. mentalità 2. intelligenza.
menthol *s.* mentolo.
mention *s.* menzione || *don't — it,* non c'è di che (*risposta a* « *grazie* »).
to mention *vt.* nominare.
mentionable *agg.* menzionabile.
mentor *s.* mentore.
mephitic *agg.* mefitico.
mercantile *agg.* mercantile.
mercantilism *s.* mercantilismo.
mercenary *agg.* e *s.* mercenario.
merchandise *s.* merce.
to merchandise *vt.* e *vi.* commerciare.
merchant *s.* mercante || *— ship,* nave mercantile.
merciful *agg.* pietoso.
merciless *agg.* spietato.
mercury *s.* mercurio.
mercy *s.* pietà, misericordia.
mere[1] *agg.* 1. mero 2. solo.
mere[2] *s.* confine.
mere[3] *s.* laghetto, stagno.
to merge *vt.* assorbire. ♦ **to merge** *vi.* 1. essere assortito 2. immergersi.
merger *s.* (*comm.*) fusione (*di società*).
meridian *agg.* 1. meridiano 2. culminante. ♦ **meridian** *s.* 1. meridiano 2. culmine.
meridional *agg.* e *s.* meridionale.
merit *s.* merito.
to merit *vt.* meritare.
meritorious *agg.* meritorio.
mermaid *s.* sirena.
merman *s.* tritone.
merrily *avv.* allegramente.
merry *agg.* gaio.
merry-go-round *s.* giostra.
merrymaking *s.* festa.
mesh *s.* maglia. ♦ **meshes** *s. pl.* reti.
mesocarp *s.* mesocarpo.
mesozoic *agg.* e *s.* mesozoico.
mess *s.* 1. mensa 2. confusione 3. pasticcio.
to mess *vt.* mettere in disordine || *to — up,* mettere a soqquadro.
message *s.* 1. messaggio 2. commissione.
messenger *s.* messaggero || *— -boy,* fattorino.
Messiah *s.* Messia.
Messianic *agg.* messianico.
mestizo *s.* meticcio.

met V. *to meet.*
metabolism s. metabolismo.
metal s. 1. metallo 2. pietrisco.
metallic *agg.* metallico.
metallization s. metallizzazione.
to metallize *vt.* metallizzare.
metalloid s. metalloide.
metallurgic(al) *agg.* metallurgico.
metallurgist s. metallurgico.
metallurgy s. metallurgia.
metamorphic *agg.* metamorfico.
metamorphism s. metamorfismo.
metamorphosis s. (*pl.* -ses) metamorfosi.
metaphor s. metafora.
metaphoric(al) *agg.* metaforico.
metaphysic(al) *agg.* metafisico.
metaphysics s. metafisica.
metapsychic(al) *agg.* metapsichico.
metapsychics s. metapsichica.
metastasis s. (*pl.* -ses) metastasi.
metayage s. mezzadria.
metayer s. mezzadro.
mete s. segno di confine || *metes and bounds* (*giur.*), limiti e confini.
metempsychosis s. metempsicosi.
meteor s. meteora.
meteoric *agg.* 1. meteorico 2. transitorio.
meteoroid s. meteorite.
meteorologic(al) *agg.* meteorologico.
meteorologist s. meteorologo.
meteorology s. meteorologia.
meter s. 1. contatore 2. tassametro.
methane s. metano.
method s. metodo.
methodic(al) *agg.* metodico.
methodist s. metodista.
methodological *agg.* metodologico.
methodology s. metodologia.
meticulosity s. meticolosità.
meticulous *agg.* meticoloso.
metre s. 1. metro 2. (*mus.*) tempo.
metrical *agg.* metrico.
metrics s. metrica.
metronome s. metronomo.
metropolis s. metropoli.
metropolitan *agg.* metropolitano.
♦ metropolitan s. abitante di una metropoli.
mettle s. tempra.
mettled, mettlesome *agg.* focoso.
mew[1] s. gabbiano.
mew[2] s. miagolio.
to mew[1] *vt.* rinchiudere in gabbia.
to mew[2] *vi.* miagolare.
to mewl *vi.* vagire.

Mexican *agg.* e s. messicano.
mezzanine s. mezzanino.
miaul s. miagolio.
mice V. *mouse.*
microbe s. microbo.
microbial *agg.* microbico.
microbiology s. microbiologia.
microcosm s. microcosmo.
micrometer s. micrometro.
micrometry s. micrometria.
micro-organism s. microorganismo.
microphone s. microfono.
microphotography s. microfotografia.
microscope s. microscopio.
microscopic(al) *agg.* microscopico.
microscopy s. microscopia.
mid *agg.* medio, mezzo.
midday s. mezzogiorno.
middle *agg.* medio || *Middle Ages*, medioevo; — *-aged*, di mezza età.
♦ middle s. 1. mezzo 2. cintola.
middle class s. borghesia.
middleman s. intermediario.
middling *agg.* medio.
midge s. moscerino.
midget s. nano.
midland *agg.* centrale. ♦ midlands s. *pl.* regione centrale (*sing.*).
midnight s. mezzanotte.
midriff s. 1. diaframma 2. costume da bagno a due pezzi.
midshipman s. guardiamarina.
midst s. mezzo.
midsummer s. solstizio d'estate.
midway *agg.* e *avv.* a mezza strada.
mid-week *agg.* di metà settimana.
midwife s. (*pl.* -wives) levatrice.
midwinter s. solstizio d'inverno.
mien s. portamento.
might s. potenza.
might V. *may.*
mighty *agg.* potente.
migrant *agg.* e s. migratore.
to migrate *vi.* (e)migrare.
migration s. (e)migrazione.
migratory *agg.* migratore.
milady s. nobildonna.
mild *agg.* dolce.
mildew s. muffa.
mildness s. dolcezza.
mile s. miglio.
milestone s. pietra miliare.
milfoil s. millefoglio.
miliary *agg.* migliare.
militant *agg.* militante. ♦ militant s. attivista.

militarily avv. militarmente.
militarism s. militarismo.
militarist s. militarista.
militarization s. militarizzazione.
to **militarize** vt. militarizzare.
military agg. e s. militare.
militiaman s. milite.
milk s. latte || — -jug, lattiera.
to **milk** vt. mungere. ♦ to **milk** vi.
1. produrre latte 2. mungere.
milker s. 1. mungitore 2. mucca da
latte.
milking s. mungitura.
milkmaid s. mungitrice.
milkman s. lattaio.
milky agg. 1. latteo 2. (fig.) genti-
le || the Milky Way, la Via Lat-
tea.
mill s. 1. mulino 2. macinino 3. fab-
brica || saw- —, segheria.
to **mill** vt. 1. macinare 2. segare 3.
frullare.
millenary agg. millenario. ♦ millenary s. 1. millennio 2. millenario.
millennium s. millennio.
millepede s. millepiedi.
miller s. 1. mugnaio 2. fresatore 3.
fresa.
millet s. (bot.) miglio.
milliard s. 1. miliardo 2. (amer.)
bilione.
milligram(me) s. milligrammo.
millimetre s. millimetro.
milliner s. modista.
millinery s. modisteria.
milling s. 1. macinatura 2. fresa-
tura.
million s. milione.
millionaire s. milionario.
millstone s. macina.
mime s. mimo.
to **mime** vi. e vt. mimare.
to **mimeograph** vt. ciclostilare.
mimetic agg. mimetico.
mimic agg. imitativo || — art, mi-
mica. ♦ **mimic** s. imitatore.
to **mimic** (**mimicked, mimicked**)
vt. imitare.
mimicry s. 1. imitazione 2. mimetismo.
minaret s. minareto.
minatory agg. minatorio.
mince s. carne tritata.
to **mince** vt. 1. tritare 2. tagliuzzare
3. mitigare. ♦ to **mince** vi. camminare, parlare in modo affettato.
mincer s. tritacarne.
mincing agg. affettato.

mind s. 1. mente 2. opinione.
to **mind** vt. 1. badare a 2. spiacere
|| never —!, non importa!; I do
not —, non mi preoccupo di.
minded agg. incline || broad- —, di
larghe vedute; narrow- —, di idee
ristrette || if you are so —, se la
pensate così.
mindful agg. memore.
mindless agg. 1. disattento 2. stupido.
mine[1] pron. poss. il mio, la mia, i
miei, le mie || a friend of —, un
mio amico.
mine[2] s. 1. miniera 2. mina || —
-sweeper, dragamine.
to **mine** vt. 1. scavare 2. estrarre 3.
minare.
miner s. minatore.
mineral agg. e s. minerale.
to **mineralize** vt. mineralizzare.
mineralogy s. mineralogia.
to **mingle** vt. mescolare. ♦ to **mingle** vi. mescolarsi.
miniature agg. in miniatura. ♦
miniature s. miniatura.
to **miniature** vt. e vi. fare miniature.
miniaturist s. miniaturista.
minim s. 1. (mus.) minima 2. quantità minima 3. inezia.
minimal agg. minimo.
to **minimize** vt. minimizzare.
minimum s. (pl. -ma) minimo.
mining s. minerario. ♦ mining
s. 1. scavo 2. estrazione 3. posa
di mine.
minion s. favorito.
miniskirt s. minigonna.
minister s. ministro.
to **minister** vi. assistere.
ministerial agg. ministeriale.
ministry s. ministero.
mink s. visone.
minor agg. minore. ♦ **minor** s.
minorenne.
minority s. 1. minoranza 2. età minore.
minstrel s. menestrello.
mint[1] s. zecca.
mint[2] s. menta.
to **mint** vt. coniare.
mintage s. conio.
minuend s. minuendo.
minuet s. minuetto.
minus s. e prep. meno.
minute agg. minuto, minuscolo.
minute s. 1. minuto 2. nota || —
-hand, lancetta dei minuti.

minutely[1] *avv.* minutamente.
minutely[2] *avv.* di minuto in minuto.
minuteness *s.* **1.** minutezza **2.** minuziosità.
miracle *s.* miracolo.
miraculous *agg.* miracoloso.
mirage *s.* miraggio.
mire *s.* fango.
to **mire** *vt.* infangare. ◆ to **mire** *vi.* infangarsi.
mirror *s.* specchio || *driving- —,* specchietto retrovisore.
to **mirror** *vt.* rispecchiare.
mirth *s.* allegria.
mirthful *agg.* allegro.
mirthless *agg.* triste.
miry *agg.* fangoso.
misadventure *s.* disavventura.
misanthrope *s.* misantropo.
misanthropy *s.* misantropia.
misapplication *s.* applicazione erronea.
to **misapply** *vt.* applicare erroneamente.
misapprehension *s.* malinteso.
misbehaviour *s.* cattivo contegno.
misbelief *s.* falsa credenza.
to **misbelieve** *vi.* avere una falsa credenza.
misbeliever *s.* miscredente.
misbelieving *agg.* eretico.
to **miscalculate** *vt.* e *vi.* calcolare male.
miscarriage *s.* **1.** disguido **2.** fallimento **3.** aborto.
to **miscarry** *vi.* **1.** smarrirsi **2.** fallire **3.** abortire.
miscellaneous *agg.* miscellaneo.
miscellany *s.* miscellanea.
mischance *s.* sfortuna.
mischief *s.* **1.** danno, male **2.** malizia **3.** birichinata.
mischievous *agg.* **1.** nocivo **2.** malizioso.
misconduct *s.* cattiva condotta.
miscount *s.* conteggio errato.
misdeed *s.* misfatto.
misdemeanour *s.* misfatto.
to **misdirect** *vt.* mandare in direzione sbagliata.
misdirection *s.* indicazione sbagliata.
misdoing *s.* misfatto.
miser *s.* avaro.
miserable *agg.* **1.** triste **2.** miserabile.
miserliness *s.* avarizia.
miserly *agg.* avaro.

misery *s.* **1.** miseria **2.** sofferenza.
misfire *s.* cilecca.
misfit *s.* **1.** cosa che si adatta male **2.** *(fig.)* pesce fuor d'acqua.
misfortune *s.* sventura.
to **misgive (misgave, misgiven)** *vt.* preoccupare. ◆ to **misgive (misgave, misgiven)** *vi.* preoccuparsi.
misgiving *s.* **1.** presentimento **2.** timore.
to **misgovern** *vt.* governare male.
misgovernment *s.* malgoverno.
to **misguide** *vt.* **1.** guidare male **2.** traviare.
to **mishandle** *vt.* maltrattare.
mishap *s.* infortunio.
to **misinform** *vt.* informare male.
misinformation *s.* informazione sbagliata.
to **misinterpret** *vt.* interpretare male.
misinterpretation *s.* interpretazione errata.
to **misjudge** *vt.* giudicare male.
misjudgement *s.* giudizio erroneo.
to **mislay (mislaid, mislaid)** *vt.* smarrire.
to **mislead (misled, misled)** *vt.* **1.** traviare **2.** ingannare.
misogamy *s.* misogamia.
misogynist *s.* misogino.
misogyny *s.* misoginia.
misoneism *s.* misoneismo.
to **misplace** *vt.* collocare male, fuori posto.
misplacement *s.* spostamento.
misprint *s.* errore di stampa, refuso.
to **misprint** *vt.* stampare con errori.
to **mispronounce** *vt.* pronunciare male.
mispronunciation *s.* pronuncia scorretta.
misquotation *s.* citazione erronea.
to **misquote** *vt.* citare erroneamente.
to **misread (misread, misread)** *vt.* leggere erroneamente.
mesreading *s.* falsa interpretazione.
to **misrepresent** *vt.* travisare.
misrepresentation *s.* travisamento.
miss[1] *s.* **1.** colpo mancato **2.** difetto.
miss[2] *s.* signorina: *Miss Jane Smith,* la signorina Jane Smith.
to **miss** *vt.* **1.** mancare (*il colpo*) **2.** perdere **3.** notare, sentire la man-

canza di **4.** evitare.

missal s. messale.

missile s. missile.

missing agg. mancante || the —, i dispersi.

mission s. missione.

missionary agg. e s. missionario.

missioner s. missionario.

to **misspell** vt. sbagliare l'ortografia.

mist s. **1.** bruma **2.** pioggerella **3.** appannamento.

to **mist** vt. appannare. ♦ to **mist** vi. appannarsi.

mistakable agg. suscettibile d'errore.

mistake s. errore.

to **mistake (mistook, mistaken)** vt. **1.** sbagliare **2.** scambiare **3.** non capire. ·

mistaken agg. **1.** in errore **2.** erroneo.

mister s. signore: Mr. Brown, il signor Brown.

mistletoe s. vischio.

mistook V. to mistake.

mistral s. maestrale.

mistranslation s. traduzione errata.

mistress s. **1.** signora: Mrs. Brown, la signora Brown **2.** insegnante **3.** amante.

mistrust s. diffidenza.

to **mistrust** vt. e vi. diffidare di, sospettare.

mistrustful agg. diffidente.

misty agg. **1.** nebbioso **2.** confuso.

to **misunderstand (misunderstood, misunderstood)** vt. e vi. fraintendere.

misunderstanding s. **1.** malinteso **2.** disaccordo.

misunderstood V. to misunderstand.

misusage, misuse s. **1.** cattivo uso **2.** maltrattamento.

to **misuse** vt. **1.** usar male **2.** maltrattare.

to **miswrite (miswrote, miswritten)** vt. scrivere scorrettamente.

mithridatic agg. immunizzante (contro veleni).

mithridatism s. immunizzazione (contro un veleno).

to **mitigate** vt. mitigare.

mitigation s. mitigazione.

mitral agg. mitrale.

mitre s. **1.** (eccl.) mitra **2.** giunto ad angolo.

mitt(en) s. manopola, guantone.

to **mix** vt. mescolare || to — up, confondere. ♦ to **mix** vi. mescolarsi.

mixed agg. misto, eterogeneo.

mixer s. (mecc.) mescolatore.

mixing s. mescolanza.

mixture s. **1.** mescolanza **2.** miscela.

mizzen s. (mar.) mezzana.

mnemonic agg. mnemonico.

mnemonics s. mnemonica.

moan s. gemito.

to **moan** vt. e vi. gemere.

moanful agg. lamentoso.

moaning s. lamento.

moat s. fossato.

mob s. **1.** folla **2.** plebaglia.

to **mob** vt. **1.** assalire **2.** affollare.

mobile agg. **1.** mobile **2.** mutevole.

mobility s. **1.** mobilità **2.** mutevolezza.

mobilization s. mobilitazione.

to **mobilize** vt. mobilitare.

moccasin s. mocassino.

mock agg. **1.** ironico **2.** finto || — -heroic, eroicomico. ♦ **mock** s. **1.** derisione **2.** imitazione.

to **mock** vt. e vi. beffare, prendersi gioco di.

mocker s. burlone.

mockery s. **1.** derisione **2.** contraffazione.

mocking agg. beffardo.

modal agg. modale.

modality s. modalità.

model agg. modello. ♦ **model** s. **1.** modello **2.** copia.

to **model** vt. modellare.

modeller s. **1.** modellatore **2.** modellista.

modelling s. **1.** modellatura **2.** creazione di modelli.

moderate agg. e s. moderato.

to **moderate** vt. moderare. ♦ to **moderate** vi. moderarsi.

moderateness s. moderatezza.

moderation s. moderazione.

moderator s. moderatore.

modern agg. e s. moderno.

modernism s. modernismo.

modernist s. modernista.

modernity s. modernità.

modernization s. **1.** rimodernamento **2.** aggiornamento.

to **modernize** vt. modernizzare. ♦ to **modernize** vi. modernizzarsi.

modest agg. **1.** modesto **2.** pudico.

modesty s. 1. modestia 2. pudore.
modifiable agg. modificabile.
modification s. modificazione.
modifier s. modificatore.
to **modify** vt. modificare.
to **modulate** vt. e vi. modulare.
modulation s. modulazione.
modulator s. modulatore.
mofette s. mofeta.
Mohammedan agg. e s. maomettano.
moist agg. umido.
to **moisten** vt. inumidire. ♦ to **moisten** vi. inumidirsi.
moistness s. umidità.
moisture s. vapore umido.
molar agg. e s. molare.
molasses s. melassa.
mole[1] s. neo.
mole[2] s. talpa.
mole[3] s. molo.
molecular agg. molecolare.
molecule s. molecola.
moleskin s. 1. pelle di talpa 2. fustagno. ♦ **moleskins** s. pl. calzoni di fustagno.
to **molest** vt. molestare.
molestation s. molestia.
molester s. molestatore.
to **mollify** vt. addolcire.
mollusc s. mollusco.
molybdenum s. molibdeno.
moment s. 1. momento 2. importanza.
momentary agg. momentaneo.
momentous agg. importante.
monachal agg. monacale.
monad s. monade.
monarch s. monarca.
monarchic(al) agg. monarchico.
monarchist s. monarchico.
monarchy s. monarchia.
monastery s. monastero.
monastic(al) agg. monastico.
Monday s. lunedì.
monetary agg. monetario.
monetization s. monetazione.
to **monetize** vt. monetizzare.
money s. denaro ‖ — -bag, portamonete; — -order, vaglia; earnest —, caparra; paper —, valuta cartacea; ready —, contanti.
moneyed agg. 1. di, in denaro 2. ricco.
moneyless agg. squattrinato.
monger s. mercante ‖ fish —, pescivendolo.
Mongolian agg. e s. mongolo.
mongolism s. mongolismo.

mongoloid agg. e s. mongoloide.
mongrel agg. misto. ♦ **mongrel** s. 1. bastardo 2. incrocio.
monism s. monismo.
monition s. 1. ammonizione 2. (giur.) citazione.
monitor s. 1. consigliere 2. capoclasse 3. dispositivo di controllo.
monitory agg. ammonitore.
monk s. monaco.
monkey s. scimmia.
monkeyish agg. scimmiesco.
monkhood s. monacato.
monkish agg. monastico, manacale.
monochromatic agg. monocromatico.
monochrome s. monocromia.
monocle s. monocolo.
monody s. monodia.
monogamist s. monogamo.
monogamy s. monogamia.
monogram s. monogramma.
monograph s. monografia.
monographic(al) agg. monografico.
monolith s. monolito.
monolithic agg. monolitico.
monologue s. monologo.
monometallic agg. monometallico.
monomial s. monomio.
monomolecular agg. monomolecolare.
monoplane s. monoplano.
monopolist s. monopolista.
to **monopolize** vt. monopolizzare.
monopoly s. monopolio.
monorail s. monorotaia.
monosyllabic agg. monosillabico.
monosyllable s. monosillabo.
monotheism s. monoteismo.
monotheist s. monoteista.
monotheistic(al) agg. monoteistico.
monotone s. tono uniforme.
monotonous agg. monotono.
monotony s. 1. tono uniforme 2. monotonia.
monotype s. monotipo.
monsoon s. monsone.
monster agg. colossale. ♦ **monster** s. mostro.
monstrance s. ostensorio.
monstrosity s. mostruosità.
monstrous agg. mostruoso.
montage s. montaggio.
month s. mese.
monthly agg. e s. mensile. ♦ **monthly** avv. mensilmente.
monument s. monumento.
monumental agg. monumentale.

mood s. 1. umore 2. (gramm.) modo.
♦ **moods** s. pl. capricci.
moodily avv. di malumore.
moodiness s. malumore.
moody agg. di malumore.
moon s. luna.
to moon vi. 1. gingillarsi 2. allu-
nare || to — about, bighellonare.
mooncalf s. (pl. -lves) idiota.
mooning s. vagabondaggio.
moonlight s. chiaro di luna.
moonlit agg. illuminato dalla luna.
moonshine s. V. moonlight.
moonshiny agg. V. moonlit.
moony agg. 1. lunare 2. distratto.
Moor s. moro.
moor s. brughiera.
to moor vt. e vi. ormeggiare.
moorage s. ormeggio. ♦ **moor-
ings** s. pl. 1. gomena (sing.) 2.
ormeggi.
mop[1] s. 1. scopa 2. zazzera.
mop[2] s. smorfia.
to mop[1] vt. 1. pulire 2. asciugare ||
to — up (mil.), rastrellare.
to mop[2] vi. fare smorfie.
mope s. 1. persona avvilita 2. tristezza.
to mope vt. avvilire. ♦ **to mope**
vi. avvilirsi.
mopish agg. avvilito.
moraine s. morena.
moral agg. morale. ♦ **moral** s.
1. morale 2. principio morale. ♦
morals s. pl. costumi.
morale s. il morale.
moralism s. moralismo.
moralist s. moralista.
moralistic agg. moralistico.
morality s. moralità.
moralization s. moralizzazione.
to moralize vt. moralizzare. ♦ **to
moralize** vi. trarre la morale.
morass s. palude.
moratory agg. moratorio.
moratorium s. (pl. -ria) moratoria.
moray s. murena.
morbid agg. 1. morboso 2. patologico.
morbidity s. 1. morbosità 2. stato
patologico.
mordacity, mordancy s. mordacità.
mordant agg. e s. mordente.
more (comp. di much, many) agg.,
pron. e avv. più, di più, maggior-
mente || — and —, sempre più;
once —, ancora una volta.
moreover avv. inoltre.

morganatic agg. morganatico.
morgue s. obitorio.
Mormon agg. e s. mormone.
morning s. mattino.
Moroccan agg. e s. marocchino.
moron s. deficiente.
morose agg. tetro.
morphia, morphine s. morfina.
morphinomaniac agg. e s. morfi-
nomane.
morphologic(al) agg. morfologico.
morphology s. morfologia.
morsel s. boccone.
mortal agg. e s. mortale.
mortality s. mortalità.
mortally avv. mortalmente.
mortar[1] s. mortaio.
mortar[2] s. calcina.
mortgage s. ipoteca.
to mortgage vt. ipotecare.
mortagagee s. creditore ipotecario.
mortgager s. debitore ipotecario.
mortification s. mortificazione.
to mortify vt. 1. mortificare 2. incancrenire. ♦ **to mortify** vi. 1.
mortificarsi 2. incancrenirsi.
mortuary agg. mortuario. ♦ **mortuary** s. camera mortuaria.
mosaic agg. musivo. ♦ **mosaic** s.
mosaico.
Moslem agg. e s. mussulmano.
mosque s. moschea.
mosquito s. zanzara || — -net, zan-
zariera.
moss s. 1. acquitrino 2. muschio.
mossy agg. muscoso.
most agg. e pron. (superl. di much,
many) il più, la maggior parte di,
il massimo. ♦ **most** avv. 1. il più
2. molto 3. maggiormente.
mostly avv. per lo più.
mote s. particella.
moth s. 1. falena 2. tignola.
mother s. madre || — -country, ma-
drepatria; — -in-law, suocera.
motherhood s. maternità.
motherless agg. senza madre.
motherly agg. materno.
mothproof agg. inattaccabile dalle
tarme.
motif s. motivo.
motion s. 1. moto, movimento 2.
mozione || — -picture, film.
motionless agg. immobile.
to motivate vt. 1. motivare 2. stimolare.
motivation s. 1. motivazione 2.
stimolo.
motive agg. motore. ♦ **motive** s.

motivo, movente.

motley *agg.* **1.** screziato **2.** eterogeneo. ♦ **motley** *s.* miscuglio.

motor *agg.* e *s.* motore || — -*cycle*, motocicletta; — -*car*, automobile, — -*boat*, motobarca; — *ship*, motonave.

to **motor** *vi.* andare in automobile.

motoring *s.* automobilismo.

motorist *s.* automobilista.

motorization *s.* motorizzazione.

to **motorize** *vt.* motorizzare.

mottle *s.* chiazza.

to **mottle** *vt.* chiazzare.

moufflon *s.* muflone.

mould[1] *s.* stampo.

mould[2] *s.* muffa.

mould[3] *s.* terriccio.

to **mould**[1] *vt.* modellare.

to **mould**[2] *vi.* ammuffire.

moulding *s.* **1.** il modellare **2.** cornice **3.** fusione.

mouldy *agg.* ammuffito.

mound *s.* monticello.

mount[1] *s.* monte, montagna.

mount[2] **1.** cavalcatura **2.** intelaiatura **3.** affusto di cannone **4.** montatura.

to **mount** *vt.* salire. ♦ to **mount** *vi.* **1.** montare **2.** ammontare.

mountain *s.* montagna.

mountaineer *s.* **1.** montanaro **2.** alpinista.

mountaineering *s.* alpinismo.

mountainous *agg.* montuoso.

mountebank *s.* ciarlatano.

mounter *s.* montatore.

to **mourn** *vt.* e *vi.* piangere.

mourner *s.* chi è in lutto.

mournful *agg.* lugubre.

mourning *s.* **1.** dolore **2.** lutto: *to go into* —, mettere il lutto.

mouse *s.* (*pl.* mice) topo.

moustache *s.* baffi (*pl.*).

mouth *s.* bocca.

to **mouth** *vt.* declamare. ♦ to **mouth** *vi.* fare smorfie.

mouthful *s.* boccone.

mouthpiece *s.* **1.** bocchino **2.** portavoce.

movable *agg.* mobile.

movables *s. pl.* beni mobili.

move *s.* **1.** movimento **2.** mossa **3.** trasloco.

to **move** *vt.* **1.** muovere **2.** commuovere. ♦ to **move** *vi.* **1.** muoversi

movement *s.* **1.** movimento, moto. **2.** traslocare **3.** commuoversi.

mover *s.* promotore.

movie *s.* film. ♦ **movies** *s. pl.* cinema (*sing.*).

moving *s.* **1.** spostamento **2.** trasloco.

mow *s.* covone.

to **mow** (mowed, mown) *vt.* falciare.

mower *s.* falciatore.

mowing *s.* falciatura.

mown V. *to mow.*

much (more, most) *agg.*, *s.* e *avv.* molto || *so* —, tanto; *too* —, troppo; *as* — *as*, tanto quanto; *how* —?, quanto?

muck *s.* letame.

mucous *agg.* mucoso.

mucus *s.* muco.

mud *s.* fango || — -*guard*, parafango.

to **mud** *vt.* infangare.

muddle *s.* confusione, pasticcio.

to **muddle** *vt.* confondere.

muddleheaded *agg.* confusionario.

muddler *s.* confusionario.

muddy *agg.* **1.** fangoso **2.** torbido **3.** infangato.

to **muddy** *vt.* infangare.

muff[1] *s.* manicotto.

muff[2] *s.* **1.** colpo mancato **2.** babbeo.

to **muffle** *vt.* **1.** avvolgere **2.** smorzare.

muffler *s.* **1.** sciarpa **2.** guantone **3.** silenziatore.

mug *s.* (*fam.*) faccia || — *shot* (*tv*), primo piano.

mulberry *s.* mora || — (-*tree*) gelso.

mule *s.* mulo.

mulish *agg.* (*fig.*) testardo.

muller *s.* pestello.

multiform *agg.* multiforme.

multimillionaire *s.* multimilionario.

multiple *agg.* e *s.* multiplo.

multiplicable *agg.* moltiplicabile.

multiplicand *s.* moltiplicando.

multiplication *s.* moltiplicazione.

multiplicity *s.* molteplicità.

multiplier *s.* moltiplicatore.

to **multiply** *vt.* moltiplicare. ♦ to **multiply** *vi.* moltiplicarsi.

multitude *s.* moltitudine.

multitudinous *agg.* **1.** innumerevole **2.** vasto.

mumble *s.* borbottio.

to **mumble** *vt.* e *vi.* borbottare.

mumbling *s.* V. *mumble.*

mummer *s.* guitto.

mummification s. mummificazione.
to **mummify** vt. mummificare.
mummy[1] s. mummia.
mummy[2] s. mammina.
mumps s. pl. orecchioni.
to **munch** vt. e vi. biascicare.
municipal agg. municipale.
municipality s. municipalità.
municipalization s. municipalizzazione.
to **municipalize** vt. municipalizzare.
munificence s. munificenza.
munificent agg. munifico.
munitions s. pl. munizioni.
mural agg. murale. ♦ **mural** s. affresco.
murder s. assassinio.
to **murder** vt. assassinare.
murderer s. assassino.
murderous agg. omicida.
muriatic agg. muriatico.
murky agg. tenebroso.
murmur s. **1.** mormorio **2.** brontolio.
to **murmur** vt. mormorare. ♦ to
murmur vi. brontolare.
murmuring s. V. *murmur*.
muscat(el) s. moscato.
muscle s. muscolo.
muscled agg. muscoloso
muscular agg. **1.** muscolare **2.** muscoloso.
musculature s. muscolatura.
Muse s. musa.
to **muse** vi. meditare.
museum s. museo.
mushroom s. fungo.
mushy agg. infrollito.
music s. musica.
musical agg. **1.** musicale **2.** appassionato di musica.
musicality s. musicalità.
musician s. musicista || *street —,*
suonatore ambulante.
musicologist s. musicologo.
musicology s. musicologia.
musing agg. meditabondo. ♦ **musing** s. meditazione.
musk s. muschio.
musket s. moschetto.
musketeer s. moschettiere.
musky agg. muschiato.
Muslim agg. e s. mussulmano.
muslin s. mussola.
muss s. stato di confusione.
mussel s. mitilo.
must[1] s. mosto.
must[2] s. muffa.

must v. dif. (*pres. ind.*) dovere ||
be — return here, deve ritornare
qui, *it — be true*, deve essere vero;
you — know him!, non puoi non
conoscerlo!
mustard s. senape.
muster s. adunata.
to **muster** vt. adunare. ♦ to **muster** vi. adunarsi.
mutability s. mutabilità.
mutable agg. mutevole.
mutation s. cambiamento.
mute agg. muto. ♦ **mute** s. **1.** muto **2.** sordina.
to **mutilate** vt. mutilare.
mutilation s. mutilazione.
mutineer s. ammutinato.
mutinous agg. ammutinato, ribelle.
mutiny s. ammutinamento.
to **mutiny** vi. ammutinarsi.
mutism s. mutismo.
to **mutter** V. to *murmur*.
mutton s. montone.
mutual agg. **1.** reciproco **2.** comune.
muzzle s. **1.** muso **2.** museruola **3.**
bocca (*di arma*).
to **muzzle** vt. mettere la museruola a.
my agg. poss. mio, mia, miei, mie.
mycosis s. (pl. -ses) micosi.
myocardial agg. miocardico.
myocarditis s. miocardite.
myocardium s. miocardio.
myopia s. miopia.
myopic agg. miope.
myosote s. miosotide.
myriad s. miriade.
myriagram s. miriagrammo.
myriametre s. miriametro.
Myriapoda s. pl. miriapodi.
myrrh s. mirra.
myrtle s. mirto.
myself pron. r. io stesso, me stesso,
mi.
mysterious agg. misterioso.
mystery s. mistero.
mystic agg. e s. mistico.
mystical agg. mistico.
mysticism s. misticismo.
mystification s. mistificazione.
mystifier s. mistificatore.
to **mystify** vt. **1.** disorientare **2.**
avvolgere nel mistero.
myth s. mito.
mythic(al) agg. mitico.
to **mythicize** vt. volgere in mito.
mythologic(al) agg. mitologico.
to **mythologize** vi. studiare i miti.
mythology s. mitologia.

mythomania s. mitomania.
mythomaniac agg. e s. mitomane.

N

nabob s. nababbo.
nacre s. madreperla.
to nag vt. e vi. brontolare.
naiad s. naiade.
nail s. 1. unghia, artiglio 2. chiodo.
to nail vt. 1. inchiodare 2. munire di chiodi.
nailer s. fabbricante di chiodi.
naïve agg. ingenuo, semplice.
naïveté s. ingenuità.
naked agg. 1. nudo, spogliato 2. spoglio, indifeso.
nakedness s. nudità.
name s. 1. nome 2. fama, reputazione || — -day, onomastico; full —, generalità.
to name vt. 1. nominare, dare un nome 2. designare.
nameless agg. 1. senza nome 2. innominabile.
namely avv. cioè.
nanny s. bambinaia, balia.
nap[1] s. siesta, sonnellino.
nap[2] s. pelo (di stoffe).
to nap vi. schiacciare un sonnellino, sonnecchiare.
nape s. nuca.
naphtha s. nafta.
napkin s. 1. tovagliolo: — -ring, anello per tovagliolo 2. pannolino.
narcissism s. narcisismo.
narcosis, narcotism s. narcosi.
narcotic agg. s. narcotico.
narcotization s. narcotizzazione.
to narcotize vt. narcotizzare.
to narrate vt. narrare.
narration s. narrazione, racconto.
narrative agg. narrativo. ♦ **narrative** s. resoconto, narrazione.
narrator s. narratore.
narrow agg. 1. stretto, angusto, ristretto (anche fig.) 2. esatto, minuzioso || — -minded, di idee ristrette. ♦ **narrow** s. stretto, strettoia.
to narrow vt. stringere, ridurre. ♦ **to narrow** vi. stringersi, contrarsi.
narrowness s. strettezza, limitatezza.
narwhal s. narvalo.
nasal agg. nasale. ♦ **nasal** s. 1.

suono nasale 2. osso nasale.
nascent agg. nascente.
nastily avv. 1. sgradevolmente 2. con cattiveria.
nastiness s. 1. cattivo gusto 2. cattiveria.
nasty agg. 1. sporco, sgradevole 2. cattivo, tempestoso (di tempo).
natal agg. natale.
natality s. natalità.
natant agg. natante.
natation s. nuoto.
natatorial agg. natatorio.
nation s. nazione.
national agg. nazionale.
nationalism s. nazionalismo.
nationalist s. nazionalista.
nationality s. 1. nazionalità 2. patriottismo.
nationalization s. 1. nazionalizzazione 2. naturalizzazione.
to nationalize vt. 1. nazionalizzare 2. naturalizzare.
native agg. 1. innato 2. natio, indigeno. ♦ **native** s. indigeno, nativo.
nativity s. nascita, natività.
natural agg. 1. naturale, fisico 2. spontaneo 3. istintivo, innato.
naturalism s. naturalismo.
naturalist s. naturalista.
naturalistic agg. naturalistico.
naturalization s. 1. naturalizzazione 2. acclimatamento.
to naturalize vi. 1. naturalizzare 2. acclimatare.
nature s. 1. natura 2. carattere, temperamento || good —, bontà.
natured agg. di natura, per natura || good —, buono, di buon carattere.
naturism s. naturismo, nudismo.
naturist s. naturista.
naughtily avv. con cattiveria.
naughtiness s. cattiveria.
naughty agg. cattivo, impertinente.
to nauseate vt. nauseare, disgustare. ♦ **to nauseate** vi. avere la nausea, disgustarsi.
nauseating agg. nauseabondo.
nautical agg. nautico.
naval agg. navale.
nave[1] s. mozzo di ruota.
nave[2] s. navata centrale (di chiesa).
navel s. 1. ombelico 2. (fig.) centro.
navigability s. navigabilità.
navigable agg. navigabile.
to navigate vt. e vi. 1. navigare 2. regolare la rotta.

navigation s. 1. navigazione 2. rotta.

navigator s. navigatore, ufficiale di rotta.

navvy s. sterratore.

navy s. marina da guerra, flotta.

nay avv. anzi, non solo.

Nazi agg. e s. nazista.

Neapolitan agg. e s. napoletano.

near agg. 1. vicino, prossimo 2. affine, intimo 3. fedele, esatto. ♦ **near** prep. vicino a, presso a. ♦ **near** avv. vicino, presso, accanto.

to **near** vt. e vi. avvicinarsi (a).

nearby agg. avv. prep. assai vicino.

nearly avv. quasi.

neat agg. 1. pulito, lindo 2. grazioso, di buon gusto 3. chiaro, conciso.

neatly avv. 1. lindamente, ordinatamente 2. con semplicità, con buon gusto 3. concisamente.

neatness s. 1. pulizia, ordine 2. grazia, armonia 3. semplicità 4. concisione.

nebula s. nebulosa.

nebular agg. nebulare.

nebulosity s. nebulosità.

nebulous agg. nebuloso, vago.

necessary agg. necessario.

to **necessitate** vt. 1. rendere necessario 2. obbligare.

necessity s. necessità.

neck s. collo || stiff —, torcicollo.

neckerchief s. fazzoletto da collo.

necklace s. collana, vezzo.

neckline s. scollatura.

necktie s. cravatta.

necrology s. necrologia.

necromancer s. negromante.

necromancy s. negromanzia.

necropolis s. necropoli.

necrosis s. (pl. -ses) necrosi.

nectar s. nettare.

need s. necessità, bisogno.

to **need** vt. e vi. essere necessario, occorrere, abbisognare, mancare di.

needful agg. necessario, indispensabile.

neediness s. bisogno, povertà.

needle s. 1. ago 2. puntina di grammofono.

to **needle** vt. 1. cucire, pungere (con un ago) 2. irritare.

needleful s. gugliata.

needless agg. inutile, superfluo.

needlewoman s. cucitrice.

needlework s. lavoro ad ago.

needs avv. necessariamente.

needy agg. povero, indigente.

ne'er avv. (contrazione di never) mai.

negation s. diniego.

negative agg. negativo. ♦ **negative** s. 1. negazione 2. qualità negativa.

neglect s. negligenza, trascuratezza.

to **neglect** vt. trascurare.

neglectful agg. negligente, noncurante.

negligence s. negligenza, trascuratezza.

negligent agg. negligente, trascurato.

negligible agg. trascurabile.

negotiable agg. negoziabile.

to **negotiate** vt. e vi. negoziare, trattare.

negotiation s. trattativa.

negress s. negra.

negro agg. e s. negro.

negroid agg. negroide.

neigh s. nitrito.

to **neigh** vi. nitrire.

neighbour s. vicino.

to **neighbour** vi. essere vicini di casa.

neighbourhood s. 1. i vicini, vicinato 2. paraggi, dintorni (pl.).

neighbouring agg. vicino, contiguo.

neither[1] agg. né l'uno né l'altro.

neither[2] avv. né, neppure, nemmeno: ... nor, né ... né.

nemesis s. (pl. -ses) nemesi.

neo-classic(al) agg. neoclassico.

neo-classicism s. neoclassicismo.

neo-criticism s. neocriticismo.

neolithic agg. neolitico.

neologism s. neologismo.

neology s. neologia.

neon s. neon.

neophyte s. neofito.

neoplatonic agg. neoplatonico.

Neoplatonism s. neoplatonismo.

neopositivism s. neopositivismo.

neorealism s. neorealismo.

neorealist s. neorealista.

nephew s. nipote (di zio).

nephritic agg. nefritico.

nephritis s. nefrite.

nepotism s. nepotismo.

nerve s. 1. nervo 2. nervatura 3. forza, energia, sangue freddo.

to **nerve** vt. tonificare, rinvigorire.

nerveless agg. snervato, inerte.

nervous agg. 1. nervoso 2. forte, vigoroso 3. timido, apprensivo.

nervously avv. 1. nervosamente 2.

timidamente.

nervousness s. 1. nervosismo, irritazione 2. timidezza.

nervy agg. 1. muscoloso, forte 2. nervoso.

nescient agg. ignorante.

nest s. 1. nido 2. (fig.) covo, tana 3. colonia (di uccelli, insetti ecc.).

to **nest** vi. fare il nido, nidificare.

to **nestle** vt. ospitare. ♦ to **nestle** vi. annidarsi, rifugiarsi.

nestling s. uccellino di nido.

net[1] agg. e s. netto.

net[2] s. 1. rete 2. (fig.) trappola.

to **net** vt. 1. coprire con reti 2. pescare con reti.

netful s. retata.

netting s. rete, reticolato.

nettle s. ortica || — rash, orticaria.

to **nettle** vt. pungere (di ortica).

network s. rete, reticolato.

neuralgia s. nevralgia.

neuralgic agg. nevralgico.

neurasthenia s. nevrastenia.

neurasthenic agg. nevrastenico.

neuritis s. nevrite.

neurologist s. neurologo.

neurology s. neurologia.

neuropathic agg. neuropatico.

neuropathology s. neuropatologia.

neurosis s. (pl. -ses) nevrosi.

neurotic agg. neuropatico.

neuter s. parola neutra, neutro.

neutral agg. neutrale.

neutralism s. neutralismo.

neutralist s. neutralista.

neutrality s. neutralità.

neutralization s. neutralizzazione.

to **neutralize** vt. neutralizzare.

neutron s. neutrone.

never avv. mai, giammai || — again, mai più; — mind, non importa; now or —, ora o mai più; —-ending, eterno.

nevermore avv. mai più.

nevertheless avv. nonostante, ciò nondimeno.

new agg. nuovo, recente || —-born, neonato; — -comer, nuovo venuto; — -made, appena fatto.

newish agg. piuttosto nuovo.

newly avv. recentemente.

news s. notizia, notizie || — -man, strillone (di giornali); — -reel, cinegiornale.

newsmonger s. persona pettegola e curiosa.

newspaper s. giornale, quotidiano.

New Zealander s. neozelandese.

next agg. 1. prossimo, vicino, il più vicino 2. futuro, venturo 3. primo contiguo. ♦ **next** avv. dopo, in seguito, poi. ♦ **next** prep. presso, accanto.

nib s. pennino.

nibble s. morso.

to **nibble** vt. 1. mordicchiare, sgranocchiare 2. abboccare.

nibbler s. roditore.

nice agg. 1. piacevole, bello, simpatico 2. buono, gustoso 3. accurato, minuzioso.

nicely avv. 1. amabilmente, piacevolmente 2. esattamente.

nicety s. 1. finezza, precisione. ♦ **niceties** s. pl. minuzie.

niche s. nicchia.

nick s. tacca, intaccatura || in the — of time, al momento giusto.

to **nick** vt. 1. intaccare 2. colpire, afferrare al momento opportuno.

nickel s. nichel.

to **nickel** vt. nichelare.

nickname s. soprannome, nomignolo.

to **nickname** vt. soprannominare.

nicotine s. nicotina.

niece s. nipote (femmina) (di zio).

niggard agg. spilorcio.

niggardliness s. spilorceria.

niggardly agg. avaro, spilorcio.

nigger s. (spreg.) negro.

night s. 1. notte, sera 2. buio, oscurità || by —, di notte, good —, buona notte; — -bird, uccello notturno, nottambulo; — -dress, camicia da notte; — -shift, turno di notte.

nightcap s. berretto da notte.

nightfall s. tramonto.

nightingale s. usignolo.

nightly agg. notturno. ♦ **nightly** avv. di notte.

nightmare s. incubo.

nightpiece s. « notturno » (dipinto che rappresenta una scena notturna).

nihilism s. nichilismo.

nihilist s. nichilista.

nimble agg. 1. agile, leggero 2. acuto, sveglio.

nimbleness s. 1. agilità 2. prontezza, acutezza.

nimbly avv. 1. agilmente, leggermente 2. prontamente.

nine agg. nove.

ninepins s. pl. birilli.

nineteen agg. diciannove.

nineteenth agg. e s. diciannovesimo.

ninetieth agg. novantesimo.

ninety agg. novanta.

ninth agg. nono.

nip s. 1. pizzicotto, morso 2. stretta, presa 3. morso (di freddo, gelo ecc.).

to **nip** vt. 1. pizzicare, mordere (anche di freddo ecc.) 2. stroncare.

nipple s. capezzolo.

nitrate s. nitrato.

nitric agg. nitrico.

nitrite s. (chim.) nitrito.

nitroglycerin(e) s. nitroglicerina.

no agg. nessuno. ♦ **no** avv. 1. no 2. in nessun modo.

nobiliary agg. nobiliare.

nobility s. nobiltà (anche fig.).

noble agg. 1. nobile (anche fig.) 2. superbo, grandioso. ♦ **noble** s. nobile.

nobleman s. nobiluomo.

nobleness s. nobiltà (anche fig.).

noblewoman s. nobildonna.

nobly avv. nobilmente.

nobody pron. indef. nessuno.

nocturnal agg. notturno.

nocturne s. (pitt.; mus.) notturno.

nod s. 1. cenno del capo 2. ordine, comando.

to **nod** vt. e vi. 1. annuire col capo 2. assopirsi, chinare il capo dal sonno 3. inclinarsi (di edifici ecc.).

nodding agg. chinato, inclinato. ♦ **nodding** s. cenno del capo.

nodose agg. nodoso.

nodosity s. nodosità.

nodular agg. a forma di nodo.

nodule s. nodulo.

noise s. rumore, fragore, chiasso.

noiseless agg. senza rumore, silenzioso.

noisily avv. rumorosamente.

noisy agg. 1. rumoroso, turbolento 2. (fig.) vistoso, chiassoso.

nomad agg. e s. nomade.

nomadism s. nomadismo.

nomenclature s. nomenclatura.

nominal agg. nominale.

nominalism s. nominalismo.

nominalist s. nominalista.

nominalistic agg. nominalistico.

nominative agg. e s. nominativo.

nominator s. nominatore.

nonagenarian agg. e s. nonagenario.

non-aligned agg. non allineato.

non-alignment s. non allineamento.

non-appearance s. contumacia.

non-attendance s. assenza.

non-commital agg. evasivo.

non-conducting agg. isolante, non conduttore.

non-conductor s. isolante.

nonconformist agg. e s. anticonformista.

nonconformity s. anticonformismo.

non-delivery s. mancata consegna.

none pron. sing. e pl. nessuno, non uno. ♦ **none** avv. affatto, niente affatto.

nonentity s. 1. cosa o persona insignificante 2. inesistenza.

non-existence s. inesistenza.

non-resistance s. resistenza passiva.

nonsense s. assurdità, sciocchezza.

nonsensical agg. assurdo, sciocco.

non-stop agg. continuo, senza fermate. ♦ **non-stop** avv. di continuo, senza fermate.

non-transferable agg. non trasferibile.

noodle agg. sciocco, gonzo.

nook s. 1. cantuccio, angolo 2. ripostiglio.

noon s. mezzogiorno.

noose s. 1. nodo scorsoio 2. tranello.

nor cong. né, neppure || neither I — he, né io né lui.

normal agg. 1. normale, regolare 2. perpendicolare.

normality s. normalità.

normalization s. normalizzazione.

to **normalize** vt. normalizzare.

Norman agg. e s. normanno.

normative agg. normativo.

north s. nord, settentrione || — wind, vento di tramontana.

north-east s. nord-est.

northerly agg. del nord, settentrionale. ♦ **northerly** avv. verso il nord.

northern agg. nordico, settentrionale.

northerner s. abitante del nord.

northward(s) agg. e avv. verso nord.

Norwegian agg. e s. norvegese.

nose s. 1. naso 2. muso (di animali) 3. prua (mar.).

to **nose** vt. e vi. 1. fiutare 2. indagare 3. ficcare il naso.

nostril s. narice.

not avv. non || — at all, niente affatto.

notability s. notabilità.
notable agg. degno di nota, notevole.
notarial agg. notarile.
notary s. notaio.
notation s. 1. (mus.) notazione 2. (mat.) numerazione.
notch s. tacca, dentellatura.
to notch vt. 1. intaccare 2. intagliare.
note s. 1. (mus.) nota, tono 2. marchio, segno 3. nota, appunto, commento 4. (comm.) cedola, acconto 5. banconota.
to note vt. notare.
notebook s. taccuino.
notehead s. intestazione.
noteless agg. privo di interesse.
noteworthiness s. importanza.
noteworthy agg. notevole.
nothing pron. indef. nulla, niente, nessuna cosa.
nothingness s. 1. il nulla 2. nullità.
notice s. 1. avviso, avvertimento 2. (giur.) intimazione 3. licenziamento 4. attenzione, cura 5. recensione || — -board, cartello pubblicitario, tabella.
to notice vt. 1. osservare, fare attenzione a 2. recensire.
noticeable agg. notevole.
notifiable agg. da denunciarsi.
notification s. notifica.
to notify vt. notificare; far sapere.
notion s. 1. nozione 2. idea, teoria.
notional agg. 1. immaginario 2. speculativo.
notoriety s. notorietà.
notorious agg. 1. noto, conosciuto 2. famigerato.
notoriously avv. notoriamente.
notwithstanding prep. nonostante, malgrado.
nougat s. torrone.
nought s. 1. nulla 2. (mat.) zero.
noumenon s. (pl. -ena) noumeno.
noun s. (gramm.) nome, sostantivo.
to nourish vt. nutrire (anche fig.).
nourishing agg. nutriente.
nourishment s. nutrimento.
novel s. romanzo.
novelist s. romanziere.
to novelize vt. romanzare.
novelty s. novità.
November s. novembre.
novice s. 1. (eccl.) novizio 2. apprendista.
novitiate s. noviziato.

now avv. 1. ora, adesso, subito, al presente 2. allora 3. a dire il vero. ♦ **now** cong. ora che. ♦ **now** s. ora, il presente.
nowadays avv. al giorno d'oggi.
nowhere avv. in nessun luogo.
noxious agg. nocivo, dannoso.
nozzle s. becco, beccuccio (di teiera, pompa ecc.).
nuclear agg. nucleare.
nuclein s. nucleina.
nucleonics s. pl. fisica nucleare.
nucleus s. (pl. -ei) 1. nucleo 2. nocciolo, centro.
nude agg. 1. nudo 2. (fig.) semplice. ♦ **nude** s. (pitt.; scult.) nudo.
nudism s. nudismo.
nudist agg. e s. nudista.
nugget s. pepita.
nuisance s. 1. noia, seccatura 2. danno.
null agg. nullo.
nullification s. annullamento.
to nullify vt. annullare.
nullity s. 1. nullità 2. il non essere valido.
numb agg. 1. intorpidito, intirizzito 2. tramortito, intontito.
to numb vt. 1. intorpidire, intirizzire 2. (fig.) istupidire.
number s. 1. numero, cifra 2. numero, quantità 3. numero di giornale.
to number vt. 1. contare, numerare 2. annoverare 3. ammontare.
numberless agg. innumerevole.
numbness s. torpore (anche fig.).
numerable agg. numerabile, calcolabile.
numeral agg. e s. numerale.
numerator s. numeratore.
numerical agg. numerico.
numerically avv. numericamente.
numerous agg. numeroso.
numismatic agg. numismatico.
numismatics s. numismatica.
numismatist s. numismatico.
numismatology s. numismatica.
nun s. 1. monaca, suora 2. piccione dal cappuccio.
nuncio s. (eccl.) nunzio.
nunnery s. convento (di suore).
nuptial agg. nuziale.
nuptials s. pl. nozze, sponsali.
nurse s. 1. nutrice, balia 2. infermiera.
to nurse vt. 1. allattare, nutrire 2. allevare 3. curare (ammalati).
nursling s. lattante.

nursery s. **1.** camera dei bambini **2.** scuola materna **3.** vivaio || — *rhyme*, filastrocca per bambini.
nursing agg. **1.** che allatta, nutre **2.** che cura || — *home*, casa di cura. ♦ **nursing** s. **1.** allattamento **2.** il curare **3.** professione di infermiera.
nurture s. vitto, nutrimento.
to **nurture** vt. nutrire, allevare.
nut s. **1.** noce **2.** (*mecc.*) dado.
nutcracker s. schiaccianoci.
nutmeg s. noce moscata.
nutrition s. nutrizione.
nutritive agg. nutritivo.
nutshell s. guscio di noce.
nylon s. nailon.
nymph s. ninfa.

O

oak s. quercia.
oakum s. stoppa.
oar s. remo || — *-blade*, pala di remo.
to **oar** vi. remare.
oarsman s. rematore.
oasis s. (*pl.* -ses) oasi.
oats s. *pl.* avena (*sing.*).
oath s. **1.** giuramento **2.** bestemmia.
obduracy s. **1.** inesorabilità **2.** ostinazione.
obdurate agg. **1.** inesorabile **2.** ostinato.
obedience s. ubbidienza.
obedient agg. ubbidiente.
obeisance s. riverenza.
obelisk s. obelisco.
obese agg. obeso.
obesity s. obesità.
to **obey** vt. e vi. ubbidire.
to **obfuscate** vt. **1.** offuscare **2.** confondere.
obituary s. necrologio.
object s. oggetto.
to **object** vt. e vi. obiettare.
objectification s. oggettivazione.
to **objectify** vt. oggettivare.
objection s. **1.** obiezione **2.** avversione.
objectionable agg. **1.** biasimevole **2.** sgradevole.
objective agg. oggettivo. ♦ **objective** s. obiettivo.
objectiveness s. oggettività.

objectivism s. oggettivismo.
objectivity s. oggettività.
objector s. oppositore || *conscientious* —, obiettore di coscienza.
obligation s. obbligo.
obligatoriness s. obbligatorietà.
obligatory agg. obbligatorio.
to **oblige** vt. **1.** obbligare **2.** fare un favore a.
obliging agg. cortese.
oblique agg. obliquo.
obliqueness, obliquity s. obliquità.
to **obliterate** vt. cancellare.
obliteration s. cancellatura.
oblivion s. oblio || *Act of* —, amnistia.
oblivious agg. dimentico.
oblong agg. **1.** oblungo **2.** rettangolare. ♦ **oblong** s. (*geom.*) rettangolo.
obnoxious agg. odioso.
obscene agg. osceno.
obscenity s. oscenità.
obscurantism s. oscurantismo.
obscurantist agg. e s. oscurantista.
obscuration s. oscuramento.
obscure agg. oscuro. ♦ **obscure** s. oscurità.
to **obscure** vt. oscurare.
obscurity s. oscurità.
obsecration s. supplica.
obsequies s. *pl.* esequie.
obsequious agg. ossequioso.
observable agg. **1.** visibile **2.** notevole.
observance s. **1.** osservanza **2.** (*relig.*) regola.
observant agg. osservante.
observation s. osservazione.
observatory s. osservatorio.
to **observe** vt. e vi. osservare.
observer s. osservatore.
observing agg. attento.
to **obsess** vt. ossessionare.
obsession s. ossessione.
obsessive agg. ossessivo.
obsolescence s. disuso.
obsolescent agg. che sta cadendo in disuso.
obsolete agg. **1.** antiquato **2.** scaduto (*di prezzi*).
obstacle s. ostacolo.
obstetric(al) agg. ostetrico.
obstetrician s. ostetrico.
obstetrics s. ostetricia.
obstinacy s. ostinazione.
obstinate agg. ostinato.
to **obstruct** vt. **1.** ostruire **2.** ri-

tardare **3.** intasare.

obstruction s. ostruzione, ostacolo.

obstructionism s. ostruzionismo.

obstructionist s. ostruzionista.

to obtain vt. ottenere. ♦ **to obtain** vi. prevalere.

obtainable agg. ottenibile.

to obtrude vt. imporre. ♦ **to obtrude** vi. **1.** imporsi **2.** intromettersi.

obtruder s. **1.** intruso **2.** importuno.

obtrusion s. intrusione.

obtrusive agg. **1.** intruso **2.** importuno.

obtrusiveness s. **1.** intrusione **2.** invadenza.

to obtund vt. ottundere.

obtundent agg. ottundente.

to obturate vt. otturare.

obturation s. otturazione.

obturator s. otturatore.

obtuse agg. **1.** ottuso **2.** sordo.

obtuseness s. ottusità.

to obviate vt. ovviare.

obvious agg. ovvio.

obviousness s. chiarezza.

occasion s. **1.** occasione **2.** motivo.

occasional agg. occasionale.

occident s. occidente.

occidental agg. occidentale.

occidentalism s. occidentalismo.

to occidentalize vt. occidentalizzare.

occidentally avv. all'occidentale.

occipital agg. occipitale.

occiput s. (pl. -pita) occipite.

to occlude vt. occludere.

occlusion s. occlusione.

occlusive agg. occlusivo.

occult agg. occulto.

to occult vt. occultare. ♦ **to occult** vi. occultarsi.

occultation s. occultamento.

occultism s. occultismo.

occultist s. occultista.

occupant s. occupante.

occupation s. occupazione.

occupational agg. professionale.

occupier s. occupante.

to occupy vt. occupare: to — oneself with, occuparsi di.

to occur vi. **1.** accadere **2.** venire in mente **3.** ricorrere.

occurrence s. avvenimento.

ocean s. oceano.

oceanic agg. oceanico.

oceanography s. oceanografia.

ocellus s. (pl. -li) ocello.

ochre s. ocra.

octagon s. ottagono.

octagonal agg. ottagonale.

octahedron s. ottaedro.

octane s. ottano.

octave s. ottava.

October s. ottobre.

octogenarian agg. e s. ottuagenario.

octonarian agg. e s. ottonario.

octonary agg. di otto in otto. ♦ **octonary** s. strofa di otto versi.

octopus s. (pl. -pi) polipo, piovra.

octosyllabic agg. ottosillabico.

octosyllable s. verso, parola di otto sillabe.

ocular agg. e s. oculare.

oculate(d) agg. maculato.

oculist s. oculista.

oculistic agg. oculistico.

odalisque s. odalisca.

odd agg. **1.** dispari **2.** scompagnato **3.** in più **4.** occasionale **5.** bizzarro. ♦ **odd** s. cosa extra.

oddity, oddness s. stranezza.

odds s. pl. **1.** differenza **2.** disaccordo **3.** pronostico || — and ends rimanenze.

ode s. ode.

odious agg. odioso.

odontological agg. odontoiatrico.

odontologist s. odontoiatra.

odontology s. odontoiatria.

odoriferous agg. odorifero.

odorous agg. odoroso.

odour s. odore.

odourless agg. inodoro.

oedema s. edema.

oenologist s. enologo.

oenology s. enologia.

oesophagus s. (pl. -gi) esofago.

of prep. **1.** di **2.** (tempo) a, in **3.** da parte di: very kind — you, molto gentile da parte vostra || — late, ultimamente.

off avv. **1.** lontano, via **2.** completamente || to be —, essere finito, fermo, in libertà. ♦ **off** prep. **1.** lontano, via da **2.** giù da. ♦ **off** agg. **1.** destro **2.** esterno **3.** lontano **4.** secondario **5.** libero || — day, giorno di libertà.

offence s. **1.** offesa **2.** colpa, delitto **3.** scandalo.

offenceless agg. **1.** inoffensivo **2.** innocente.

to offend vt. offendere. ♦ **to offend** vi. **1.** peccare **2.** violare la legge.

offender s. **1.** peccatore **2.** colpevole.

offensive agg. 1. offensivo 2. sgradevole. ♦ **offensive** s. offensiva.
offensiveness s. aggressività.
offer s. offerta.
to offer vt. offrire. ♦ **to offer** vi.
offrirsi.
offerer s. offerente.
offering s. offerta.
offertory s. offertorio.
offhand agg. 1. improvvisato 2.
spontaneo. ♦ **offhand** avv. lì
per lì.
office s. ufficio, carica || box- —,
botteghino.
officer s. ufficiale, funzionario ||
non-commissioned —, sottufficiale.
official agg. ufficiale. ♦ **official** s.
funzionario.
officiant s. ufficiante.
to officiate vi. 1. esercitare le funzioni di 2. (relig.) ufficiare.
officious agg. 1. ufficioso 2. intrigante.
offing s. (mar.) largo.
offscourings s. pl. rifiuti, scarti.
offset s. 1. compenso 2. sperone (di
monte) 3. germoglio, progenie 4.
(tip.) fotolito.
offshoot s. 1. germoglio 2. ramo.
offshore agg. 1. di terra 2. lontano
dalla costa. ♦ **offshore** avv. al
largo.
offside s. (sport) fuori gioco.
offspring s. 1. prole 2. frutto.
often avv. spesso || how —?, quan-
te volte?
ogive s. ogiva.
oil s. 1. olio 2. petrolio || — cloth,
tela cerata; — field, giacimento petrolifero; — -mill, frantoio; —
paper, carta oleata; — pipeline,
oleodotto.
to oil vt. ungere, oliare.
oiler s. oliatore.
oily agg. oleoso, untuoso.
ointment s. unguento.
O.K. avv. bene: to be —, andar
bene.
old (**elder, older; eldest, oldest**)
agg. vecchio || how — are you?,
quanti anni hai?; — -fashioned,
antiquato. ♦ **old** s. passato.
oldish agg. attempato.
oleander s. oleandro.
oleograph s. oleografia.
oleographic agg. oleografico.
olfactory agg. olfattivo.
oligarch s. oligarchia.
oligarchic(al) agg. oligarchico.

oligarchy s. oligarchia.
olive agg. 1. d'oliva 2. olivastro. ♦
olive s. 1. oliva 2. (-tree) olivo.
Olympiad s. olimpiade.
Olympian agg. olimpico, olimpionico. ♦ **Olympian** s. olimpionico.
Olympic agg. V. Olympian.
omelet(te) s. frittata.
omen s. auspicio.
ominous agg. di cattivo augurio.
omission s. omissione.
to omit vt. omettere.
omnipotence s. onnipotenza.
omnipotent agg. e s. onnipotente.
omnipresent agg. onnipresente.
omniscience s. onniscienza.
omniscient agg. e s. onnisciente.
omnivorous agg. onnivoro.
on prep. 1. su 2. a, in, di, per || on
purpose, apposta. ♦ **on** avv. 1. su,
indosso 2. (in) avanti || to be —,
essere in funzione, essere rappre-
sentato; and so —, eccetera.
once avv. una volta || at —, subito;
all at —, improvvisamente. ♦
once cong. una volta che.
on-coming agg. prossimo.
one agg. 1. uno 2. uno solo. ♦ **one**
pron. 1. (dimostr.) questo, quello
2. (indef.) (l') uno || — by —, uno
a uno. ♦ **one** s. uno || — John
Brown, un certo John Brown.
one-eyed agg. guercio.
oneness s. unità, unicità.
onerous agg. oneroso.
oneself pron. r. se stesso.
one-sided agg. unilaterale.
one-sidely avv. unilateralmente.
oneway agg. a senso unico.
ongoings s. pl. avvenimenti.
onion s. cipolla || spring- —, cipol-
lina.
onlooker s. spettatore.
only agg. e avv. solo.
onomastic agg. onomastico.
onomatopoeia s. onomatopeia.
onomatopoeic agg. onomatopeico.
onset s. 1. attacco 2. inizio.
onto prep. su, in cima a.
ontological agg. ontologico.
ontology s. ontologia.
onus s. onere.
onward agg. avanzato.
onward(s) avv. avanti.
onyx s. onice.
to ooze vt. e vi. stillare || to — out,
trapelare.
oozy agg. melmoso.
opacity s. opacità.

opal *s.* opale.

opalescent *agg.* opalescente.

opaque *agg.* opaco.

open *agg.* aperto || *wide* —, spalancato; *in the* — *air*, all'aperto.

to open *vt.* aprire. ♦ **to open** *vi.* aprirsi.

open-handed *agg.* generoso.

opening *s.* 1. apertura 2. radura.

openly *avv.* apertamente.

open-minded *agg.* di larghe vedute.

open-mindedness *s.* larghezza di vedute.

openness *s.* 1. apertura 2. franchezza.

opera *s.* opera lirica || — *-house*, tèatro dell'opera; — *glass*, binocolo.

to operate *vt.* 1. operare 2. far funzionare 3. gestire. ♦ **to operate** *vi.* 1. operare 2. funzionare.

operatic *agg.* di opera.

operation *s.* 1. operazione 2. funzionamento 3. azione.

operative *agg.* 1. attivo 2. operatono, operaio (*meccanico*). sentenza. ♦ **operative** *s.* artigianista, telegrafista.

operator *s.* 1. operatore 2. teleforio || — *part*, dispositivo di una

ophthalmia *s.* oftalmia.

ophthalmic *agg.* oftalmico.

ophthalmology *s.* oftalmologia, oculistica.

ophthalmoscopy *s.* oftalmoscopia.

opiate *agg.* 1. oppiato 2. soporifero. ♦ **opiate** *s.* narcotico.

opinion *s.* opinione.

opinionated, opinionative *agg.* ostinato.

opium *s.* oppio.

opponent *s.* avversario.

opportune *agg.* opportuno.

opportunism *s.* opportunismo.

opportunist *s.* opportunista.

opportunist(ic) *agg.* opportunistico.

opportunity *s.* occasione.

opposable *agg.* opponibile.

to oppose *vt.* opporre. ♦ **to oppose** *vi.* opporsi.

opposed *agg.* 1. opposto 2. ostile.

opposer *s.* oppositore.

opposite *agg.* e *s.* opposto. ♦ **opposite** *avv.* di fronte. ♦ **opposite** *prep.* di fronte a, dirimpetto a.

opposition *s.* opposizione.

to oppress *vt.* opprimere.

oppression *s.* oppressione.

oppressive *agg.* opprimente.

oppressor *s.* oppressore.

opprobrious *agg.* obbrobrioso.

to opt *vi.* optare.

optic(al) *agg.* ottico.

optician *s.* ottico.

optics *s.* ottica.

optimism *s.* ottimismo.

optimist *agg.* e *s.* ottimista.

optimistic(al) *agg.* ottimistico.

option *s.* opzione.

optional *agg.* facoltativo.

opulence *s.* opulenza.

opulent *agg.* opulento.

or *cong.* o, oppure || *either*... —, *sia*... *sia*.

oracle *s.* oracolo.

oracular *agg.* profetico.

oral *agg.* e *s.* orale.

orange *s.* 1. arancia 2. arancio.

orangeade *s.* aranciata.

orangery *s.* aranceto.

oration *s.* discorso.

orator *s.* oratore.

oratorical *agg.* oratorio.

oratory¹ *s.* oratorio.

oratory² *s.* oratoria.

orb *s.* 1. cerchio 2. sfera.

orbit *s.* orbita.

orbital *agg.* orbitale.

orchard *s.* frutteto.

orchestra *s.* orchestra.

orchestral *agg.* orchestrale.

to orchestrate *vt.* orchestrare.

orchestration *s.* orchestrazione.

orchid, orchis *s.* orchidea.

to ordain *vt.* ordinare (*anche eccl.*).

ordeal *s.* 1. ordalia 2. dura prova.

order *s.* 1. ordine 2. classe || *in* — *that*, affinché; *in* — *to*, allo scopo di; *postal* —, vaglia postale; *made to* —, eseguito su ordinazione. ♦ **orders** *s. pl.* (*relig.*) ordini: *to take* —, farsi prete.

to order *vt.* 1. ordinare 2. riordinare.

ordering *s.* ordinamento.

orderly *agg.* ordinato. ♦ **orderly** *s.* 1. (*mil.*) ordinanza 2. (*mil.*) attendente.

ordinal *agg.* e *s.* ordinale.

ordinance *s.* 1. ordinanza 2. (*relig.*) rito.

ordinary *agg.* ordinario. ♦ **ordinary** *s.* 1. condizione ordinaria 2. pranzo a prezzo fisso.

ordinate *s.* ordinata.

ordination s. 1. ordine 2. (*relig.*) ordinazione.

ore s. minerale.

organ s. organo || *barrel-* —, organetto; *mouth-* —, armonica.

organic agg. organico.

organism s. organismo.

organist s. organista.

organizable agg. organizzabile.

organization s. organizzazione.

to **organize** vt. organizzare. ♦ to **organize** vi. organizzarsi.

organizer s. organizzatore.

organzine s. organzino.

orgasm s. orgasmo.

orgeat s. orzata.

orgiastic agg. orgiastico.

orgy s. orgia.

orient s. oriente.

to **orient** vt. 1. orientare 2. volgere verso oriente.

oriental agg. e s. orientale.

orientalist s. orientalista.

orientation s. orientamento.

orifice s. orifizio.

origan s. origano.

origin s. origine.

original agg. e s. originale.

originality s. originalità.

originally avv. 1. originalmente 2. originariamente.

to **originate** vt. dare origine. ♦ to **originate** vi. aver origine.

originator s. iniziatore.

ornament s. ornamento.

ornamental agg. ornamentale.

ornamentation s. decorazione.

ornate agg. ornato.

ornithological agg. ornitologico.

ornithologist s. ornitologo.

ornithology s. ornitologia.

orographic(al) agg. orografico.

orography s. orografia.

orphan agg. e s. orfano.

orphanage s. 1. la condizione di orfano 2. orfanotrofio.

orthodox agg. ortodosso.

orthodoxy s. ortodossia.

orthogonal agg. ortogonale.

orthographic(al) agg. 1. ortografico 2. ortogonale.

orthography s. 1. ortografia 2. (*geom.*) proiezione ortogonale.

orthop(a)edic(al) agg. ortopedico.

orthop(a)edics s. ortopedia.

orthop(a)edist s. ortopedico.

to **oscillate** vi. oscillare.

oscillation s. oscillazione.

oscillator s. oscillatore.

oscillatory agg. oscillatorio.

oscillograph s. oscillografo.

osier s. vimine.

osmose, osmosis s. osmosi.

osseous agg. osseo.

ossification s. ossificazione.

to **ossify** vt. ossificare. ♦ to **ossify** vi. ossificarsi.

ostensible agg. apparente.

ostensory s. ostensorio.

ostentation s. ostentazione.

ostentatious agg. ostentato.

osteological agg. osteologico.

osteology s. osteologia.

ostracism s. ostracismo.

to **ostracize** vt. dare l'ostracismo a.

ostrich s. struzzo.

other agg. e pron. altro || *each* —, l'un l'altro; *every* — *day*, un giorno sì e un giorno no. ♦ **others** pron. pl. altri || *some...* —..., gli uni... gli altri.

otherwise agg. diverso. ♦ **otherwise** avv. altrimenti.

otherworld s. mondo ultraterreno.

otitis s. otite.

otorhinolaryngologist s. otorinolaringoiatra.

otter s. lontra.

Ottoman agg. e s. ottomano.

ought s. zero.

ought v. dif. (*condiz.*) dovere: *you* — *to wait*, dovresti aspettare.

ounce s. oncia.

our agg. poss. nostro, nostra, nostri, nostre.

ours pron. poss. il nostro, la nostra, i nostri, le nostre.

ourselves pron. r. pl. noi stessi.

out agg. esterno. ♦ **out** avv. fuori. ♦ **out** (*of*) prep. 1. fuori (*di*) 2. senza 3. per || —*of-date*, fuori moda; — *-of-work*, disoccupato; — *-of-the-way*, remoto.

to **outbid** (**outbade, outbidden**) vt. offrire di più.

outboard agg. e avv. fuoribordo.

outbreak s. 1. scoppio 2. sommossa.

outburst s. scoppio.

outcast s. proscritto.

to **outclass** vt. surclassare.

outcome s. risultato.

outcry s. grido, scalpore.

outdid V. *to outdo*.

to **outdistance** vt. distanziare.

to **outdo** (**outdid, outdone**) vt. superare.

outdoor agg. all'aperto.

outdoors avv. all'aperto.

outer *agg.* esteriore.

outfit(ting) *s.* equipaggiamento.

to **outfit** *vt.* rifornire di equipaggiamento. ♦ to **outfit** *vi.* rifornirsi di equipaggiamento.

outfitter *s.* fornitore.

to **outfly** (**outflew, outflown**) *vt.* sorpassare nel volo.

outgone V. *to* **outgo**.

outgo *s.* uscita.

to **outgo** (**outwent, outgone**) *vt.* sorpassare.

outgoing *agg.* uscente, in partenza.

to **outgrow** (**outgrew, outgrown**) *vt.* **1.** diventare troppo grande per **2.** sorpassare (*in statura*).

outgrowth *s.* **1.** escrescenza **2.** risultato.

outhouse *s.* **1.** tettoia **2.** dipendenza.

outing *s.* escursione || — *clothes*, abiti sportivi.

outlandish *agg.* **1.** strano **2.** remoto.

outlaw *s.* fuorilegge.

outlawry *s.* (*giur.*) proscrizione.

outlay *s.* spesa.

outlet *s.* **1.** sbocco **2.** cortile.

outline *s.* **1.** contorno **2.** schema **3.** lineamento.

to **outline** *vt.* **1.** delineare **2.** abbozzare.

outliner *s.* bozzettista.

to **outlive** *vt.* sopravvivere a.

outlook *s.* **1.** veduta **2.** prospettiva **3.** vigilanza.

to **outnumber** *vt.* superare numericamente.

outpost *s.* avamposto.

outpour *s.* **1.** scroscio di pioggia **2.** (*fig.*) sfogo.

output *s.* produzione, rendimento.

outrage *s.* oltraggio.

to **outrage** *vt.* oltraggiare.

outrageous *agg.* **1.** oltraggioso **2.** violento.

outrageousness *s.* **1.** oltraggio **2.** violenza.

outran V. *to* **outrun**.

to **outrange** *vt.* avere una portata maggiore di.

to **outreach** *vt.* sorpassare.

outrider *s.* battistrada.

outright *agg.* **1.** franco **2.** completo. ♦ **outright** *avv.* **1.** francamente **2.** completamente.

outrightness *s.* **1.** immediatezza **2.** franchezza.

outroar *s.* fracasso.

to **outrun** (**outran, outrun**) *vt.* oltrepassare.

outrush *s.* fuga.

to **outsell** (**outsold, outsold**) *vt.* **1.** vendere in quantità superiore **2.** vendere a prezzo superiore.

outset *s.* esordio.

to **outshine** (**outshone, outshone**) *vt.* eclissare (*anche fig.*).

outside *agg.* e *s.* **1.** esterno **2.** massimo. ♦ **outside** *avv.* **1.** all'esterno **2.** all'aperto. ♦ **outside** *prep.* fuori di.

outsider *s.* **1.** profano **2.** estraneo **3.** (*sport*) non favorito.

outsize *agg.* fuori misura. ♦ **outsize** *s.* taglia fuori misura.

outskirt *s.* orlo. ♦ **outskirts** *s. pl.* periferia (*sing.*).

outsold V. *to* **outsell**.

outspoken *agg.* franco.

to **outspread** (**outspread, outspread**) *vt.* spiegare. ♦ to **outspread** (**outspread, outspread**) *vi.* spiegarsi.

outstanding *agg.* **1.** prominente **2.** resistente **3.** in sospeso.

to **outstretch** *vt.* distendere.

to **outstrip** *vt.* superare (*in velocità*).

outward *agg.* e *s.* esterno. ♦ **outward(s)** *avv.* esternamente.

outwent V. *to* **outgo**.

oval *agg.* e *s.* ovale.

ovary *s.* ovaia.

ovation *s.* ovazione.

oven *s.* forno.

over *avv.* **1.** di sopra **2.** eccessivamente || *to be* —, essere finito; — *and* — *again*, più e più volte. ♦ **over** *prep.* **1.** su **2.** più di **3.** durante || — *there*, dall'altra parte; — *and above*, oltre a.

overalls *s. pl.* tuta da lavoro (*sing.*).

overate V. *to* **overeat**.

to **overbear** (**overbore, overborne**) *vt.* dominare, sopraffare.

overbearing *agg.* imperioso.

overbearingness *s.* imperiosità.

overboard *avv.* in mare.

overbore V. *to* **overbear**.

overborne V. *to* **overbear**.

to **overburden** *vt.* sovraccaricare.

overcame V. *to* **overcome**.

overcast *agg.* scuro, nuvoloso.

to **overcast** (**overcast, overcast**) *vt.* oscurare. ♦ to **overcast** (**overcast, overcast**) *vi.* oscurarsi.

overcharge s. 1. sovraccarico 2. sovrapprezzo.

to **overcharge** vt. 1. sovraccaricare 2. far pagare troppo caro.

to **overcloud** vi. rannuvolarsi.

overcoat s. soprabito.

to **overcome** (**overcame, overcome**) vt. superare, vincere.

overcoming s. superamento, vittoria.

overconfident agg. troppo sicuro di sé.

overcredulity s. credulità eccessiva.

overcrowded agg. sovraffollato.

overcrowding s. sovraffollamento.

to **overdo** (**overdid, overdone**) vt. 1. esagerare 2. stancare.

overdone agg. troppo cotto.

overdose s. dose eccessiva.

overdrank V. to overdrink.

to **overdraw** (**overdrew, overdrawn**) vt. 1. esagerare 2. scoprire il conto in banca.

to **overdrink** (**overdrank, overdrunk**) vi. bere troppo.

overdue agg. scaduto.

to **overeat** (**overate, overeaten**) vi. mangiare troppo.

to **overestimate** vt. sopravvalutare.

overexcitability s. sovreccitabilità.

overexcitable agg. sovreccitabile.

to **overexcite** vt. sovreccitare.

overexcitement s. sovreccitazione.

to **overexert** vt. stancare.

to **overexpose** vt. sovresporre.

overfeeding s. superalimentazione.

overflew V. to overfly.

to **overflow** vt. inondare. ♦ to **overflow** vi. traboccare.

overflowing s. inondazione.

to **overfly** (**overflew, overflown**) vt. 1. sorvolare 2. superare in volo.

overfond agg. troppo appassionato.

to **overgrow** (**overgrew, overgrown**) vt. 1. coprire 2. superare. ♦ to **overgrow** (**overgrew, overgrown**) vi. 1. coprirsi 2. crescere troppo.

overgrowth s. 1. crescita eccessiva 2. vegetazione sovrabbondante.

overhang s. sporgenza, aggetto.

to **overhang** (**overhung, overhung**) vt. 1. sovrastare 2. ornare con tendaggi ecc.

to **overhaul** vt. 1. revisionare 2. sorpassare.

overhaul(ing) s. revisione.

overhead agg. 1. alto 2. (comm.) generale. ♦ **overhead** avv. in alto.

to **overhear** (**overheard, overheard**) vt. 1. udire per caso 2. origliare.

to **overheat** vt. surriscaldare. ♦ to **overheat** vi. surriscaldarsi.

overheating s. surriscaldamento.

overhung V. to overhang.

overindulgence s. eccessiva indulgenza.

overladen agg. sovraccarico.

overland avv. via terra.

overlap s. sovrapposizione.

overlay s. copertura.

to **overleap** vt. saltare di là da.

overload s. sovraccarico.

to **overload** vt. sovraccaricare.

to **overlook** vt. 1. guardare dall'alto 2. trascurare 3. ispezionare.

overlooker s. ispettore.

overnight agg. 1. compiuto durante la notte 2. per una notte. ♦ **overnight** avv. durante la notte.

overpaid V. to overpay.

to **overpass** vt. 1. attraversare 2. sorpassare 3. trasgredire.

overpast agg. passato.

to **overpay** (**overpaid, overpaid**) vt. pagare più del dovuto.

overpayment s. pagamento eccessivo.

overpeopled agg. sovrappopolato.

overplus s. soprappiù.

overpopulated agg. sovrappopolato.

overpopulation s. sovrappopolazione.

to **overpower** V. to overbear.

overpowering agg. 1. schiacciante 2. prepotente.

overpressure s. sovrapressione.

to **overprint** vt. sovrastampare.

to **overprize** vt. sopravvalutare.

to **overproduce** vt. produrre in eccesso.

overproduction s. sovraproduzione.

overproud agg. troppo orgoglioso.

overran V. to overrun.

to **overrate** vt. sopravvalutare.

to **overreach** vt. 1. oltrepassare 2. imbrogliare.

to **overrule** vt. 1. dirigere 2. annullare 3. dominare.

to **overrun** (**overran, overrun**) vt. 1. invadere 2. devastare 3. oltrepassare.

oversaw V. *to oversee.*

oversea(s) *agg.* e *avv.* d'oltremare.

to oversee (oversaw, overseen) *vt.* ispezionare.

overseer *s.* 1. ispettore 2. capo squadra.

to overset (overset, overset) *vt.* rovesciare. ♦ to overset (overset, overset) *vi.* rovesciarsi.

to overshadow *vt.* 1. ombreggiare 2. adombrare 3. proteggere.

overshoe *s.* soprascarpa.

to overshoot (overshot, overshot) *vt.* lanciare di là da ‖ *to — the mark,* passare i limiti.

overside *avv.* lungo il fianco.

oversight *s.* 1. svista 2. sorveglianza.

to oversleep (overslept, overslept) *vi.* dormire oltre l'ora fissata.

to overspread (overspread, overre. ♦ to overspread (overspread, overspread) *vi.* spargersi.

to overstate *vt.* esagerare.

to overtake (overtook, overtaken) *vt.* 1. cogliere 2. superare.

overtaking *s.* sorpasso: *no —,* divieto di sorpasso.

overthrew V. *to overthrow.*

overthrow *s.* 1. rovesciamento 2. disfatta.

to overthrow (overthrew, overthrown) *vt.* 1. rovesciare 2. sconfiggere.

overtime *s.* straordinario (*orario di lavoro*).

overtook V. *to overtake.*

to overturn V. *to overthrow.*

overturnable *agg.* rovesciabile.

overturn(ing) *s.* rovesciamento.

overweary *agg.* stremato.

overweight *agg.* che supera il peso. ♦ overweight *s.* sovraccarico.

to overwhelm *vt.* 1. sommergere 2. sopraffare.

overwhelming *agg.* schiacciante.

overwork *s.* 1. lavoro eccessivo 2. straordinario.

to overwork *vt.* 1. far lavorare troppo 2. far eccessivo uso di. ♦ to overwork *vi.* lavorare troppo.

to overwrite (overwrote, overwritten) *vi.* scrivere troppo.

overwrought *agg.* 1. esausto 2. ricercato (*di stile*).

ovine *agg.* ovino.

oviparous *agg.* oviparo.

ovulation *s.* ovulazione.

ovule *s.* ovulo.

to owe *vt.* dovere, essere debitore di ‖ *you must pay what is owing,* dovete pagare il vostro debito.

owing *agg.* dovuto.

owing to *prep.* a causa di.

owl *s.* gufo.

own *agg.* e *pron.* proprio.

to own *vt.* 1. possedere 2. ammettere ‖ *to — to,* confessare.

owner *s.* proprietario ‖ *shipowner,* armatore.

ownership *s.* proprietà.

ox (*pl.* oxen) *s.* bue.

oxidation *s.* ossidazione.

oxide *s.* ossido.

oxidizable *agg.* ossidabile.

to oxidize *vt.* ossidare. ♦ to oxidize *vi.* ossidarsi.

oxygen *s.* ossigeno ‖ *— tent,* tenda ad ossigeno.

to oxygenate *vt.* ossigenare.

oxygenation *s.* ossigenazione.

to oxygenize *vt.* ossigenare.

oxyhydrogen *agg.* ossidrico: *— blowpipe,* cannello ossidrico.

oyster *s.* 1. ostrica 2. persona silenziosa, riservata.

ozone *s.* ozono.

to ozonize *vt.* ozonizzare.

P

pace *s.* passo.

to pace *vi.* andare al passo. ♦ to pace *vt.* percorrere. ♦ to pace *vi.* andare al passo, marciare.

paced *agg.* misurato (*a passi*) ‖ *slow- —,* a passi lenti.

pachyderm *s.* pachiderma.

pacific *agg.* pacifico.

to pacificate *vt.* pacificare.

pacification *s.* pacificazione.

pacificator, pacifier *s.* pacificatore.

pacificatory *agg.* conciliante.

pacifism *s.* pacifismo.

pacifist *agg.* e *s.* pacifista.

to pacify *vt.* pacificare.

pack *s.* 1. pacco, balla, fagotto 2. carico 3. imballaggio 4. muta (*di cani*) 5. (*med.*) impacco ‖ *— -ice,* banchisa; *— -saddle,* basto.

to pack *vt.* 1. impacchettare 2. im-

ballare 3. raggruppare. ♦ to pack
vi. raggrupparsi || to — up, fare
i bagagli.
package s. 1. imballaggio 2. pacco.
to package vt. 1. imballare 2. impacchettare.
packer s. 1. imballatore 2. impacchettatrice (macchina).
packet s. 1. pacchetto 2. (mar.) —
(-boat), postale.
packing s. 1. imballaggio 2. (mecc.)
guarnizione 3. (mar.) baderna ||
— -free, franco d'imballaggio.
pact s. patto.
pad[1] s. 1. imbottitura 2. zampa (di
cane, lupo, volpe) 3. (med.) tampone.
pad[2] s. rumore sordo.
to pad vt. imbottire.
paddle s. 1. pala 2. pagaia.
to paddle vi. remare con pagaie.
paddy s. risaia.
padlock s. lucchetto.
to padlock vt. chiudere con lucchetto.
paediatric agg. pediatrico.
paediatrician s. pediatra.
paediatrics s. pediatria.
paediatrist s. pediatra.
pagan agg. e s. pagano.
paganism s. paganesimo.
page[1] s. paggio.
page[2] s. pagina.
to page vt. 1. (tip.) impaginare 2.
numerare le pagine.
pageant s. 1. (teat.) scena (di sacra rappresentazione) 2. parata,
corteo.
pageantry s. 1. pompa, fasto 2.
ostentazione.
to paginate vt. V. to page.
pagination s. 1. paginatura 2. impaginazione.
paid V. to pay.
pail s. secchio.
paillasse s. pagliericcio.
pain s. 1. pena 2. dolore, sofferenza.
♦ pains s. pl. doglie.
to pain vt. far male, far soffrire.
painful agg. penoso.
painless agg. indolore.
painstaking agg. diligente. ♦
painstaking s. cura.
paint s. 1. pittura 2. belletto.
to paint vt. dipingere. ♦ to **paint**
vi. imbellettarsi.
painter s. 1. pittore 2. imbianchino.
painting s. 1. pittura 2. dipinto,
quadro.

paintress s. pittrice.
pair s. paio, coppia.
to pair vt. accoppiare. ♦ to **pair**
vi. accoppiarsi.
palace s. palazzo.
paladin s. paladino.
palatable agg. 1. gustoso 2. (fig.)
gradevole.
palatal agg. e s. palatale.
palatalization s. palatalizzazione.
palate s. palato.
pale[1] agg. pallido.
pale[2] s. 1. palo 2. palizzata.
to pale vt. far impallidire. ♦ to
pale vi. impallidire.
paleness s. pallore.
paleochristian agg. paleocristiano.
paleographer s. paleografo.
paleography s. paleografia.
paleolithic agg. paleolitico.
paleologist s. paleologo.
paleology s. paleologia.
paleontologic(al) agg. paleontologico.
paleontologist s. paleontologo.
paleontology s. paleontologia.
paleozoic agg. paleozoico.
palette s. tavolozza.
palfrey s. palafreno.
palinode s. palinodia.
palisade s. palizzata.
pall s. 1. drappo funebre 2. (eccl.)
pallio.
to pall[1] vt. coprire con un drappo.
to pall[2] vt. saziare. ♦ to **pall** vi.
saziarsi.
pallet[1] s. pagliericcio.
pallet[2] s. 1. paletta 2. tavolozza.
to palliate vt. 1. attenuare 2. scusare.
palliation s. 1. attenuazione 2. scusante.
palliative agg. e s. palliativo.
pallid agg. pallido.
pallor s. pallore.
palm[1] s. palma (anche fig.).
palm[2] s. (anat.) palmo.
to palm vt. toccare con la mano.
palmaceous agg. (bot.) di palma.
palmar agg. palmare.
palmate, palmated, agg. palmato.
palmiped agg. e s. palmipede.
palmistry s. chiromanzia.
palmy agg. 1. coperto di palme 2.
prosperoso, vittorioso.
palpability s. palpabilità.
palpable agg. palpabile.
to palpate vt. palpare.
to palpitate vi. palpitare.

palpitation s. palpitazione.
palsy s. paralisi.
to **palsy** vt. paralizzare.
to **palter** vi. tergiversare.
paltriness s. meschinità.
paltry agg. meschino.
to **pamper** vt. viziare.
pamphlet s. opuscolo.
pamphleteer s. autore di opuscoli.
pan s. 1. padella 2. vaschetta 3. bacino 4. piatto di bilancia || *baking-* —, teglia.
pancake s. frittella.
panchromatic agg. pancromatico.
pancreatic agg. pancreatico.
pandemonium s. pandemonio.
pander s. mezzano, ruffiano.
to **pander** vi. fare il mezzano.
pane s. 1. lastra di vetro 2. (*edil.*) pannello 3. faccia (*di brillante*).
panegyric s. panegirico.
panegyric(al) agg. laudativo.
panel s. 1. pannello 2. (*neol.*) commissione, comitato 3. (*giur.*) lista di giurati.
pang s. 1. fitta 2. (*fig.*) stretta al cuore.
panic agg. e s. panico.
panicky agg. allarmato.
panicle s. pannocchia.
panification s. panificazione.
pannier s. paniere.
panoramic agg. panoramico.
pansy s. viola del pensiero.
pant s. 1. palpito 2. ansito.
to **pant** vi. 1. palpitare 2. ansimare.
pantagruelian agg. pantagruelico.
pantheism s. panteismo.
pantheist s. panteista.
pantheistic(al) agg. panteistico.
panther s. pantera.
panties s. pl. (*fam.*) mutandine.
panting s. 1. palpitazione 2. ansito 3. ansia.
pantograph s. pantografo.
pantomime s. pantomima.
pantry s. dispensa.
pants s. pl. (*fam.*) mutande.
pap s. pappa.
papacy s. papato.
papal agg. papale.
paper s. 1. carta 2. prova d'esame
paper s. 1. carta 2. certificato, documento 3. prova d'esame 4. giornale || — *back*, libro in brossura; — *board*, cartone; — *hanger*, tappezziere; — *hanging*, tappezzeria.
to **paper** vt. 1. incartare 2. tappezzare.

papery agg. cartaceo.
papillary agg. papillare.
papism s. papismo.
papist s. papista.
papyrology s. papirologia.
papyrus s. (*pl.* -ri) papiro.
parable s. parabola.
parabolic(al) agg. 1. parabolico 2. di parabola.
paraboloid s. paraboloide.
parachute s. paracadute.
to **parachute** vt. paracadutare. ♦ to **parachute** vi. paracadutarsi.
parachutism s. paracadutismo.
parachutist s. paracadutista.
parade s. 1. (*mil.*) parata 2. mostra, sfoggio 3. viale, passeggiata.
to **parade** vt. disporre in parata. ♦ to **parade** vi. marciare in parata.
paradigm s. paradigma.
paradisaic(al) agg. paradisiaco.
paradise s. paradiso.
paradisiac(al) agg. paradisiaco.
paradox s. paradosso.
paradoxical agg. paradossale.
paraffin s. paraffina.
paragon s. modello (*di perfezione ecc.*).
paragraph s. paragrafo.
to **paragraph** vt. dividere in paragrafi.
parallel agg. parallelo. ♦ **parallel** s. 1. parallelo 2. parallela.
to **parallel** vt. 1. mettere in posizione parallela 2. paragonare.
parallelepiped s. parallelepipedo.
parallelism s. parallelismo.
parallelogram s. parallelogramma.
paralogism s. paralogismo.
to **paralyse** vt. paralizzare.
paralysis s. (*pl.* -ses) paralisi.
paralytic agg. e s. paralitico.
parameter s. parametro.
paramount agg. supremo. ♦ **paramount** s. capo supremo.
paramour s. amante.
paranoia s. paranoia.
paranoiac agg. e s. paranoico.
paranymph s. paraninfo.
parapet s. parapetto.
paraphrase s. parafrasi.
to **paraphrase** vt. e vi. parafrasare.
parasite s. parassita.
parasitic(al) agg. parassitico.
parasitism s. parassitismo.
parasol s. parasole.
paratrooper s. paracadutista.
paratyphoid s. paratifo.

parcel 496

parcel s. 1. pacco 2. lotto, appezzamento di terreno 3. gruppo.
to parcel vt. spartire.
parcelling s. spartizione.
parcener s. coerede.
to parch vt. 1. arrostire 2. disseccare. ♦ **to parch** vi. 1. bruciarsi 2. disseccarsi.
parchment s. pergamena.
pardon s. perdono.
to pardon vt. perdonare.
pardonable agg. perdonabile.
to pare vt. 1. tagliare 2. sbucciare.
parenchyma s. parenchima.
parent s. 1. genitore 2. causa, origine.
parentage s. 1. discendenza 2. nascita.
parental agg. paterno, materno.
parenthesis s. (pl. -ses) parentesi.
parenthetic(al) agg. parentetico.
parenthood s. paternità, maternità.
parentless agg. orfano.
paresis s. paresi.
pariah s. paria.
parietal agg. parietale.
parish s. parrocchia || — priest, parroco.
parishioner s. parrocchiano.
Parisian agg. e s. parigino.
parisyllabic agg. e s. parisillabo.
parity s. parità.
park s. 1. parco 2. posteggio.
to park vt. 1. adibire a parco 2. parcheggiare.
parking s. parcheggio || no —, divieto di sosta.
parkway s. (amer.) viale.
parley s. colloquio.
to parley vi. parlamentare.
parliament s. parlamento.
parliamentarian s. parlamentare.
parliamentarianism s. parlamentarismo.
parliamentary agg. parlamentare.
parlour s. 1. salotto 2. parlatorio || beauty —, istituto di bellezza.
Parmesan agg. parmigiano.
parochial agg. 1. parrocchiale 2. (fig.) ristretto.
parochialism s. ristrettezza di vedute.
parodist s. parodista.
parody s. parodia.
to parody vt. parodiare.
parole s. 1. parola d'onore 2. parola d'ordine.
paroxysm s. parossismo.
parricidal agg. parricida.

parricide s. 1. parricidio 2. parricida.
parrot s. pappagallo.
to parrot vt. ripetere pappagallescamente.
parry vt. parare, schivare.
parsley s. prezzemolo.
parson s. parroco (anglicano).
parsonage s. (eccl.) canonica, parrocchia.
part s. parte.
to part vt. dividere. ♦ **to part** vi. dividersi.
to partake (partook, partaken) vi. partecipare, prendere parte.
parthenogenesis s. partenogenesi.
partial agg. parziale.
partiality s. parzialità.
partially avv. parzialmente.
participant agg. e s. partecipante.
to participate vi. 1. partecipare 2. condividere.
participation s. partecipazione.
participial agg. participiale.
participle s. participio.
particle s. particella (anche gramm.).
particular agg. 1. particolare 2. particolareggiato 3. esigente. ♦ **particular** s. particolare.
particularism s. particolarismo.
particularist s. particolarista.
particularity s. 1. particolarità 2. meticolosità.
to particularize vt. e vi. dettagliare.
parting s. separazione.
partisan agg. e s. partigiano.
partition s. 1. divisione 2. tramezzo.
to partition vt. dividere.
partitive agg. e s. partitivo.
partly avv. in parte.
partner s. 1. socio 2. coniuge.
partnership s. 1. associazione 2. (comm.) società.
partook V. to partake.
partridge s. pernice.
parturient agg. partoriente.
parturition s. parto.
party s. 1. parte 2. partito 3. brigata 4. trattenimento 5. pattuglia.
pasha s. pascià.
pass¹ s. 1. passo, gola.
pass² s. 1. passaggio 2. trapasso 3. promozione 4. lasciapassare.
to pass vt. e vi. passare || to — away, sparire; to — by, passar oltre.

passable *agg.* passabile.
passage *s.* 1. passaggio 2. corridoio 3. brano.
passementerie *s.* passamaneria.
passenger *s.* passeggero.
passer *s.* — *-by*, passante.
passible *agg.* passibile.
passing *agg.* 1. passeggero 2. casuale. ♦ **passing** *s.* passaggio.
passion *s.* passione || — *-flower*, passiflora.
passional *agg.* passionale.
passionate *agg.* appassionato, passionale.
passionless *agg.* impassibile.
passive *agg.* e *s.* passivo.
passivism, passivity *s.* passività.
passport *s.* passaporto.
password *s.* parola d'ordine.
past *agg.* passato. ♦ **past** *s.* passato. ♦ **past** *avv.* vicino. ♦ **past** *prep.* al di là di.
paste *s.* pasta || *tooth* —, dentifricio.
to paste *vt.* 1. incollare, appiccicare 2. (*gergo*) attaccare.
pasteboard *agg.* di cartone. ♦ **pasteboard** *s.* cartone.
pastel *s.* pastello.
pasteurization *s.* pastorizzazione.
to pasteurize *vt.* pastorizzare.
pastime *s.* passatempo.
pastoral *agg.* e *s.* pastorale.
pastry *s.* dolci (*pl.*).
pasture *s.* pascolo.
to pasture *vt.* e *vi.* pascolare.
pasty *agg.* pastoso. ♦ **pasty** *s.* (*cuc.*) pasticcio.
pat *agg.* adatto. ♦ **pat** *avv.* esattamente. ♦ **pat** *s.* 1. colpetto 2. panetto di burro.
to pat *vt.* battere leggermente.
patch *s.* 1. pezza, toppa 2. macchia.
to patch *vt.* aggiustare, rattoppare, raffazzonare.
patching *s.* rattoppo.
patchy *agg.* 1. rappezzato 2. a macchie.
patent *agg.* 1. chiaro, manifesto, evidente 2. brevettato. ♦ **patent** *s.* brevetto.
to patent *vt.* brevettare.
patentee *s.* detentore di brevetto.
paternal *agg.* paterno.
paternalism *s.* paternalismo.
paternalistic *agg.* paternalistico.
paternity *s.* paternità.
path *s.* 1. sentiero 2. pista 3. percorso, traiettoria.
pathetic *agg.* patetico.
pathfinder *s.* esploratore.
pathless *agg.* 1. senza sentieri 2. inesplorato.
pathogenic *agg.* patogeno.
pathologic(al) *agg.* patologico.
pathologist *s.* patologo.
pathology *s.* patologia.
pathway *s.* sentiero.
patience *s.* pazienza.
patient *agg.* 1. paziente 2. suscettibile. ♦ **patient** *s.* paziente.
patriarch *s.* patriarca.
patriarchal *agg.* patriarcale.
patriarchate *s.* patriarcato.
patrician *agg.* e *s.* patrizio.
patricide *s.* V. *parricide*.
patrimonial *agg.* patrimoniale.
patrimony *s.* patrimonio.
patriot *s.* patriota.
patriotic *agg.* patriottico.
patriotism *s.* patriottismo.
patrol *s.* pattuglia, ronda.
to patrol *vt.* e *vi.* pattugliare, fare la ronda.
patron *s.* patrono.
patronage *s.* patronato.
patronal *agg.* patronale.
patroness *s.* patronessa.
to patronize *vt.* 1. patrocinare 2. trattare con condiscendenza.
patronizing *agg.* 1. protettivo 2. condiscendente.
patter[1] *s.* gergo.
patter[2] *s.* picchiettio.
to patter *vi.* picchiettare.
pattern *s.* 1. modello, campione 2. disegno (*di stoffa ecc.*).
to pattern *vt.* modellare (su).
paunch *s.* pancia.
pauper *s.* povero.
pauperism *s.* povertà.
pause *s.* pausa.
to pause *vi.* 1. fare una pausa 2. esitare, indugiare.
pauseless *agg.* incessante.
to pave *vt.* 1. pavimentare 2. (*fig.*) appianare.
pavement *s.* 1. pavimentazione 2. marciapiede.
paver *s.* lastricatore.
pavilion *s.* padiglione.
paving *s.* pavimentazione.
paw *s.* zampa.
to paw *vt.* dare zampate. ♦ **to paw** *vi.* scalpitare (*di cavalli*).
pawn *s.* 1. pegno 2. pedina (*di scacchi*).

to **pawn** vt. impegnare (dare in pegno).

pawnbroker s. prestatore su pegno.

pawnbroking s. il prestare su pegno.

pawner s. chi dà qualcosa in pegno.

pawnshop s. agenzia di prestiti su pegno.

pay s. paga.

to **pay (paid, paid)** vt. e vi. 1. pagare 2. rendere, fruttare || to — off, liquidare.

payable agg. 1. pagabile 2. redditizio.

payee s. creditore.

payer s. pagatore.

paying out s. esborso.

payment s. pagamento.

payoff s. 1. giorno di paga 2. liquidazione.

payroll s. libro paga.

pea s. pisello || chick —, cece.

peace s. pace.

peaceable agg. pacifico.

peaceful agg. pacifico, tranquillo.

peacefulness s. pace, calma.

peaceless agg. agitato.

peacemaker s. pacificatore.

peach s. (bot.) pesca.

peach-tree s. pesco.

peachy agg. simile a pesca.

peacock s. pavone.

to **peacock** vi. pavoneggiarsi.

peak s. 1. picco 2. punta 3. visiera.

peaky agg. appuntito.

peal s. 1. scampanio 2. scoppio, fragore, scroscio (di risa, applausi).

to **peal** vi. scampanare. ♦ to **peal** vt. far rimbombare.

peanut s. arachide.

pear s. pera.

pear-tree s. pero.

pearl s. perla.

to **pearl** vt. imperlare, ornare di perle. ♦ to **pearl** vi. imperlarsi.

pearly agg. 1. perlaceo 2. ricco di perle.

peasant s. contadino.

peasantry s. 1. condizione di contadino 2. i contadini (pl.).

peat s. torba || — -bog, torbiera.

pebble s. 1. ciottolo 2. cristallo di rocca.

to **pebble** vt. coprire con ciottoli.

peccary s. pecari.

peck s. beccata.

to **peck** vt. e vi. beccare.

pectoral agg. e s. pettorale.

peculation s. peculato.

peculiar agg. 1. particolare 2. strano.

peculiarity s. 1. particolarità 2. bizzarria, eccentricità.

pecuniary agg. pecuniario.

pedagogic(al) agg. pedagogico.

pedagogics s. pedagogia.

pedagogist s. pedagogista.

pedagogue s. pedagogo.

pedagogy s. pedagogia.

pedal s. pedale.

to **pedal** vt. e vi. pedalare.

pedant s. pedante.

pedantic agg. pedante.

pedantry s. pedanteria.

pedestal s. piedistallo.

pedestrian agg. pedestre. ♦ **pedestrian** s. pedone.

pediatrics ecc. V. paediatrics ecc.

pediment s. (arch.) frontone.

pedlar s. venditore ambulante.

peel s. buccia.

to **peel** vt. sbucciare. ♦ to **peel** vi. sbucciarsi.

peeling s. buccia.

peep[1] s. 1. sguardo furtivo 2. fessura.

peep[2] s. pigolio.

to **peep**[1] vi. 1. guardare furtivamente 2. far capolino.

to **peep**[2] vi. pigolare.

peeper[1] s. ficcanaso, persona curiosa.

peeper[2] s. piccioncino.

peer s. 1. pari 2. Pari, membro della Camera dei Lord.

to **peer** vt. uguagliare. ♦ to **peer** vi. 1. scrutare 2. far capolino.

peerage s. 1. i Pari 2. nobiltà.

peerless agg. senza pari.

peevish agg. irritabile.

peg s. piuolo.

to **peg** vt. fissare.

pejorative agg. e s. peggiorativo.

pelagic agg. oceanico.

pelican s. pellicano.

pellet s. 1. pallottolina (di carta ecc.) 2. pallottola 3. pillola.

pellucid agg. trasparente.

pelt[1] s. colpo (di proiettile ecc.).

pelt[2] s. pelle (di animale).

to **pelt** vt. colpire.

pelvic agg. pelvico.

pelvis s. bacino.

pen[1] s. penna || -nib, pennino; fountain- —, penna stilografica.

pen[2] s. recinto (per animali).

to **pen**[1] vt. scrivere.

to **pen**[2] vt. rinchiudere animali in un recinto.

penal *agg.* penale.

to **penalize** *vt.* (*sport.*) penalizzare.

penalty *s.* penalità, punizione.

penance *s.* penitenza.

pence *s.* V. *penny*.

pencil *s.* matita.

pendant, pendent *agg.* e *s.* pendente.

pending *prep.* **1.** durante **2.** fino a.

pendular *agg.* pendolare.

pendulous *agg.* pendulo.

pendulum *s.* pendolo || — -*clock*, pendola.

penetrable *agg.* penetrabile.

to **penetrate** *vt.* e *vi.* penetrare.

penetration *s.* penetrazione.

penetrative *agg.* penetrante.

penguin *s.* pinguino.

penicillin *s.* penicillina.

peninsula *s.* penisola.

peninsular *agg.* peninsulare.

penis *s.* pene.

penitence *s.* penitenza.

penitent *agg.* e *s.* penitente.

penitential *agg.* penitenziale.

penitentiary *agg.* penitenziale. ♦ **penitentiary** *s.* (*eccl.*) penitenziere **2.** riformatorio **3.** (*amer.*) penitenziario.

penknife *s.* (*pl.* -knives) temperino.

pennant *s.* (*mar.*) pennone.

penniless *agg.* senza un soldo.

pennon *s.* pennone.

penny *s.* (*numero delle monete*), **pence** (*loro valore*) *s.* "penny".

pension *s.* pensione.

to **pension** *vt.* pensionare.

pensionable *agg.* pensionabile.

pensioner *s.* pensionato.

pensive *agg.* pensoso.

pent *agg.* chiuso.

pentagon *s.* pentagono.

pentagonal *agg.* pentagonale.

pentagram *s.* pentagono.

pentahedron *s.* pentaedro.

pentameter *s.* pentametro.

pentane *s.* pentano.

pentathlon *s.* pentatlon.

Pentecost *s.* Pentecoste.

Pentecostal *agg.* pentecostale.

penthouse *s.* tettoia.

pentode *s.* (*elettr.*) pentodo.

pentose *s.* pentosio.

penult(imate) *agg.* e *s.* penultimo.

penury *s.* povertà.

peony *s.* peonia.

people *s.* (*costruzione al pl.*) **1.** popolo **2.** gente **3.** folla.

to **people** *vt.* popolare.

pepper *s.* pepe || — -*mill*, macinapepe.

to **pepper** *vt.* condire con pepe.

peppercorn *s.* grano di pepe.

peppermint *s.* menta peperita.

peppery *agg.* **1.** pepato **2.** collerico.

pepsin(e) *s.* pepsina.

per *prep.* per: — *cent*, per cento.

peracid *s.* peracido.

to **perambulate** *vt.* **1.** attraversare **2.** ispezionare. ♦ to **perambulate** *vi.* passeggiare.

perambulation *s.* **1.** ispezione **2.** passeggiata.

perambulator *s.* carrozzella per bambini.

percale *s.* percalle.

perceivable *agg.* percettibile.

to **perceive** *vt.* percepire, scorgere. ♦ to **perceive** *vi.* accorgersi.

percentage *s.* percentuale.

perceptible *agg.* percettibile.

perception *s.* percezione.

perceptive *agg.* percettivo.

perch[1] *s.* gruccia.

perch[2] *s.* pesce persico.

to **perch** *vi.* appollaiarsi.

perchlorate *s.* perclorato.

percipience *s.* percezione.

to **percolate** *vt.* e *vi.* filtrare, colare.

percolator *s.* filtro.

percussion *s.* percussione || — -*pin*, percussore.

perdition *s.* perdizione.

perdurable *agg.* durevole.

to **peregrinate** *vi.* peregrinare.

peregrination *s.* peregrinazione.

peremptory *agg.* perentorio.

perennial *agg.* perenne.

perfect *agg.* perfetto.

to **perfect** *vt.* perfezionare.

perfectibility *s.* perfettibilità.

perfectible *agg.* perfettibile.

perfecting *s.* **1.** perfezionamento **2.** completamento.

perfection *s.* **1.** perfezione **2.** perfezionamento.

perfectionism *s.* perfezionismo.

perfectionist *s.* perfezionista.

perfectly *avv.* perfettamente.

perfidious *agg.* perfido, sleale.

perfidy *s.* perfidia, slealtà.

to **perforate** *vt.* perforare.

perforation *s.* perforazione.

to **perform** *vt.* **1.** eseguire **2.** (*teat.*) rappresentare.

performable *agg.* **1.** eseguibile **2.** rappresentabile.

performance s. 1. esecuzione 2. atto 3. (*teat.*) rappresentazione.
performer s. 1 esecutore 2. attore.
performing agg. ammaestrato.
perfume s. profumo.
to **perfume** vt. profumare.
perfumer s. profumiere.
perfumery s. 1. profumeria 2. profumi.
perfunctory agg. superficiale.
to **perfuse** vt. aspergere.
perfusion s. aspersione.
perhaps avv. forse.
pericardium s. pericardio.
perigee s. perigeo.
peril s. pericolo.
perilous agg. pericoloso.
perimeter s. perimetro.
period s. 1. periodo 2. ora di lezione 3. stadio, fase (*di una malattia*) 4. (*gramm.*) punto.
periodic agg. periodico.
periodical agg. e s. periodico.
periodicity s. periodicità.
peripheral agg. periferico.
periphery s. 1. perimetro 2. superficie.
periphrase, periphrasis s. (*pl.* -ses) perifrasi.
periphrastic agg. perifrastico.
periscope s. periscopio.
to **perish** vi. perire.
perishable agg. 1. deperibile 2. mortale.
perishables s. pl. merci deteriorabili.
peristyle s. peristilio.
peritonitis s. peritonite.
periwig s. parrucca.
periwigged agg. imparruccato.
periwinkle s. pervinca.
to **perjure** vt. giurare falsamente.
perjurer, perjury s. spergiuro.
permanence s. permanenza.
permanent agg. permanente.
permanganate s. permanganato.
permeability s. permeabilità.
permeable agg. permeabile.
to **permeate** vt. permeare. ♦ to **permeate** vi. permearsi.
permission, permit s. permesso.
to **permit** vt. e vi. permettere.
to **permute** vt. permutare.
pernicious agg. pernicioso.
to **perorate** vi. perorare.
peroration s. perorazione.
peroxid(e) s. perossido || *hydrogen* —, acqua ossigenata.
to **peroxide** vt. ossigenare.

perpendicular agg. perpendicolare.
♦ **perpendicular** s. 1. perpendicolare 2. filo a piombo.
perpendicularity s. perpendicolarità.
to **perpetrate** vt. perpetrare.
perpetration s. perpetrazione.
perpetual agg. perpetuo.
to **perpetuate** vt. perpetuare.
perpetuity s. 1. perpetuità 2. rendita vitalizia.
to **perplex** vt. 1. rendere perplesso 2. complicare.
perplexed agg. perplesso.
perplexity s. 1. perplessità 2. complicazione.
to **persecute** vt. perseguitare.
persecution s. persecuzione.
persecutor s. persecutore.
perseverance s. perseveranza.
to **persevere** vi. perseverare.
Persian agg. e s. persiano.
persimmon s. (*bot.*) cachi.
to **persist** vi. persistere.
persistence s. persistenza.
persistent agg. persistente.
person s. persona.
personable agg. ben fatto.
personage s. personaggio.
personal agg. personale.
personality s. personalità.
personalization s. personificazione.
to **personalize** vt. personificare.
personally avv. personalmente.
personification s. personificazione.
to **personify** vt. personificare.
personnel s. personale.
perspective agg. prospettico. ♦ **perspective** s. prospettiva.
perspicacious agg. perspicace.
perspicacity s. perspicacia.
perspicuity s. perspicuità.
perspicuous agg. perspicuo.
perspiration s. traspirazione.
to **perspire** vt. e vi. sudare, trasudare.
to **persuade** vt. persuadere.
persuasion s. 1. persuasione 2. credenza.
persuasive agg. persuasivo.
pert agg. impertinente.
to **pertain** vi. appartenere.
pertinacious agg. pertinace.
pertinacy, pertinacity s. pertinacia.
pertinence s. pertinenza.
pertinent agg. pertinente.
pertly avv. insolentemente.
pertness s. insolenza.

to **perturb** *vt.* perturbare.
perturbation *s.* perturbazione.
perusal *s.* lettura attenta.
to **peruse** *vt.* leggere attentamente.
to **pervade** *vt.* pervadere.
pervasion *s.* penetrazione.
pervasive *agg.* penetrante.
perverse *agg.* **1.** perverso **2.** errato **3.** ostinato.
perversion *s.* perversione.
perversity *s.* perversità.
pervert *s.* **1.** pervertito **2.** apostata.
to **pervert** *vt.* pervertire.
pessimism *s.* pessimismo.
pessimist *s.* pessimista.
pessimistic *agg.* pessimistico.
pessimistically *avv.* in modo pessimistico.
pest *s.* peste (*anche fig.*).
to **pester** *vt.* importunare.
pestiferous *agg.* pestifero.
pestilence *s.* pestilenza.
pestilent *agg.* **1.** nocivo **2.** molesto.
pestilential *agg.* pestilenziale.
pestle *s.* pestello.
pet *agg.* e *s.* favorito || — *name*, vezzeggiativo.
to **pet** *vt.* vezzeggiare.
petal *s.* petalo.
petard *s.* petardo.
petition *s.* petizione, istanza.
to **petition** *vt.* e *vi.* fare una petizione (a).
petitioner *s.* postulante.
to **petrify** *vt.* pietrificare. ♦ to **petrify** *vi.* pietrificarsi.
petrography *s.* petrografia.
petrol *s.* benzina.
petticoat *s.* sottoveste.
pettifogger *s.* azzeccagarbugli.
petty *agg.* **1.** meschino **2.** subalterno.
petulant *agg.* petulante.
pew *s.* banco (*di chiesa*).
pewter *s.* peltro.
phagocyte *s.* fagocita.
phalanstery *s.* falansterio.
phalanx *s.* (*pl.* -ges) falange.
phallic *agg.* fallico.
phantasm *s.* fantasma.
phantasmagoria *s.* fantasmagoria.
phantasmagorial, phantasmagoric(al) *agg.* fantasmagorico.
phantom *s.* **1.** fantasma **2.** apparizione.
Pharaoh *s.* faraone.
Pharisee *s.* fariseo.
pharmaceutic(al) *agg.* farmaceutico.

pharmaceutics *s.* farmaceutica.
pharmacology *s.* farmacologia.
pharmacopoeia *s.* farmacopea.
pharmacy *s.* farmacia.
pharyngitis *s.* faringite.
pharynx *s.* (*pl.* -ges) faringe.
phase *s.* fase.
pheasant *s.* fagiano.
phenic *agg.* fenico.
phenol *s.* fenolo.
phenomenal *agg.* **1.** fenomenico **2.** fenomenale.
phenomenalism *s.* fenomenismo.
phenomenology *s.* fenomenologia.
phenomenon *s.* (*pl.* -na) fenomeno.
phial *s.* fiala.
to **philander** *vi.* fare il cascamorto.
philanderer *s.* cascamorto.
philanthrope *s.* filantropo.
philanthropic(al) *agg.* filantropico.
philanthropism *s.* filantropia.
philanthropist *s.* filantropo.
philanthropy *s.* filantropia.
philatelic(al) *agg.* filatelico.
philatelist *s.* filatelico.
philately *s.* filatelia.
philharmonic *agg.* filarmonico.
philippic *s.* filippica.
Philippine *agg.* filippino.
philologian, philologist *s.* filologo.
philology *s.* filologia.
philosopher *s.* filosofo.
philosophic(al) *agg.* filosofico.
philosophist *s.* pseudofilosofo.
to **philosophize** *vi.* filosofare.
philosophy *s.* filosofia.
phlebitis *s.* flebite.
phleboclysis *s.* fleboclisi.
phlegm *s.* flemma.
phlegmatic(al) *agg.* flemmatico.
phlegmon *s.* flemmone.
phlogistic *agg.* flogistico.
phobia *s.* fobia.
phoenix *s.* fenice.
phone *s.* V. *telephone*.
phones *s. pl.* cuffie.
phoneme *s.* fonema.
phonetics *s.* fonetica.
phonogram *s.* fonogramma.
phonograph *s.* fonografo.
phonology *s.* fonologia.
phosphate *s.* fosfato.
phosphor *s.* fosforo.
phosphorescence *s.* fosforescenza.
phosphorescent *agg.* fosforescente.
phosphoric *agg.* fosforico.
phosphorous *agg.* fosforoso.

photo 502

photo s. foto.
photocell s. cellula fotoelettrica.
photocopy s. fotocopia.
photoelectric(al) agg. fotoelettrico.
photogenic agg. fotogenico.
photograph s. fotografia.
to **photograph** vt. fotografare.
photographer s. fotografo.
photography s. fotografia (come arte).
photometry s. fotometria.
photomontage s. fotomontaggio.
phrase s. 1. locuzione, frase 2. stile.
to **phrase** vt. esprimere.
phraseology s. fraseologia.
phrenetic(al) agg. frenetico.
phrenologist s. frenologo.
phrenology s. frenologia.
phthisiology s. tisiologia.
phthisis s. tisi.
phylloxera s. fillossera.
physic s. medicina.
physical agg. fisico.
physician s. medico.
physicist s. fisico.
physics s. fisica.
physiognomist s. fisionomista.
physiognomy s. fisionomia.
physiologic(al) agg. fisiologico.
physiologist s. fisiologo.
physiology s. fisiologia.
physiotherapy s. fisioterapia.
physique s. fisico.
pianist s. pianista.
picaresque agg. picaresco.
pick[1] s. 1. piccone 2. colpo di piccone || tooth —, stuzzicadenti.
pick[2] s. scelta, il meglio (di qc.).
to **pick** vt. 1. scavare 2. pulire 3. raccogliere 4. rubare.
pickax(e) s. piccone.
picker s. 1. piccone 2. zappatore 3. raccoglitore.
picket s. 1. piolo, palo 2. (mil.) picchetto.
pickle s. 1. salamoia 2. sottaceti (pl.).
to **pickle** vt. mettere in salamoia, sotto aceto.
picklock s. 1. scassinatore 2. grimaldello.
pickpocket s. borsaiolo.
pickup s. 1. raccolta 2. (mecc.) accelerazione 3. fonorivelatore.
pictorial agg. 1. illustrato 2. pittorico. ♦ **pictorial** s. giornale illustrato.
picture s. 1. quadro, dipinto, ritrat-

to 2. illustrazione. ♦ **pictures** s. pl. cinema (sing.) || — fook, libro illustrato.
to **picture** vt. dipingere || to — to oneself, immaginarsi, figurarsi.
picturesque agg. pittoresco.
pidgin agg. — English, inglese scorretto (usato tra cinesi ed europei).
pie[1] s. pica, gazza.
pie[2] s. torta, pasticcio.
pie[3] s. (tip.) refuso.
piece s. 1. pezzo 2. pezza (di tessuto) || by the —, a cottimo.
to **piece** vt. rappezzare, raggiustare.
piecemeal avv. pezzo per pezzo. ♦ **piecemeal** agg. frammentario.
piecework s. (lavoro a) cottimo.
pieceworker s. cottimista.
pied agg. screziato.
pier s. 1. molo 2. pilone || — -glass, specchiera.
to **pierce** vt. 1. forare 2. trafiggere.
piercer s. 1. punzone 2. punzonatore.
piercing agg. penetrante. ♦ **piercing** s. perforamento.
pietism s. pietismo.
piety s. pietà, reverenza.
pig s. 1. maiale 2. (metal.) lingotto.
pigeon s. piccione || — -house, piccionaia; carrier —, piccione viaggiatore.
pigeonhole s. 1. colombaia 2. casella 3. (giur.) casellario.
to **pigeonhole** vt. incasellare.
piggish agg. porcino.
pigheaded agg. testardo.
pigment s. pigmento.
pigmentation s. pigmentazione.
pigmy agg. e s. pigmeo.
pigsty s. porcile.
pike[1] s. picca.
pike[2] s. (amer.) pedaggio.
pilaster s. pilastro.
pile s. 1. mucchio 2. fabbricato 3. rogo 4. (elettr.) pila 5. (fig.) gruzzolo.
to **pile**[1] vt. ammucchiare. ♦ to **pile** vi. ammucchiarsi.
to **pile**[2] vt. conficcare pali in, fare palizzate.
piles s. pl. emorroidi.
to **pilfer** vt. e vi. rubacchiare.
pilferer s. ladruncolo.
pilgrim s. pellegrino.
pilgrimage s. pellegrinaggio.
piling[1] s. ammucchiamento.
piling[2] s. palificazione di sostegno.

pill s. pillola: *contraceptive (pill)*, pillola anticoncezionale.
pillage s. 1. saccheggio 2. bottino.
to pillage vt. saccheggiare.
pillar s. colonna, guanciale || — -box, cassetta delle lettere.
pillory s. berlina.
to pillory vt. mettere alla berlina.
pillow s. cuscino, guanciale || — -case, federa.
pilot s. pilota.
to pilot vt. pilotare.
pilotage s. pilotaggio.
pimple s. foruncolo.
pin s. 1. spillo 2. perno || *pins and needles*, formicolio.
to pin vt. 1. puntare 2. (*fig.*) inchiodare.
pinafore s. grembiulino.
pinaster s. pinastro.
to pincer vt. attanagliare.
pincers s. pl. tenaglie.
pinch s. 1. pizzico, pizzicotto 2. (*fig.*) angustia.
to pinch vt. 1. pizzicare 2. stringere 3. causare dolore. ♦ **to pinch** vi. essere avaro.
pinchbeck s. princisbecco.
pincushion s. puntaspilli.
Pindaric agg. pindarico.
pine s. pino || — -apple, ananasso; — -cone, pigna; — -wood, pineta.
to pine vi. struggersi.
pinion[1] s. penna remigante.
pinion[2] s. (*mecc.*) pignone.
to pinion vt. tarpare le ali a.
pink agg. rosa. ♦ **pink** s. 1. colore rosa 2. garofano 3. (*fig.*) quintessenza.
to pink vt. 1. traforare 2. trafiggere.
pinky agg. roseo.
pinnacle s. 1. pinnacolo 2. sommità.
pinpoint s. capocchia di spillo.
pint s. pinta.
pioneer s. pioniere.
pious agg. 1. pio 2. pietoso.
piousness s. pietà.
pip s. seme di frutto.
to pip vi. pigolare.
pipage s. 1. tubatura 2. trasporto per tubatura.
pipe s. 1. tubo 2. pipa 3. strumento a fiato 4. condotta.
to pipe vi. 1. suonare (*piffero ecc.*) 2. stridere. ♦ **to pipe** vt. 1. suonare 2. trasportare con tubature 3.

fornire di tubature.
pipeline s. oleodotto.
piper s. pifferaio.
pipet(te) s. (*chim.*) pipetta.
piping agg. 1. flautato 2. acuto. ♦ **piping** s. 1. suono (*di piffero ecc.*) 2. suono acuto 3. tubatura.
piquancy s. gusto piccante.
piquant agg. piccante.
pique s. ripicco, risentimento.
piracy s. 1. pirateria 2. plagio.
pirate s. 1. pirata 2. plagiario.
pirogue s. piroga.
pirouette s. piroetta.
to pirouette vi. piroettare.
pistil s. pistillo.
pistol s. pistola.
piston s. pistone.
pit s. 1. fossa 2. cavità 3. platea.
to pit vt. 1. bucare 2. mettere in una fossa.
pitch[1] s. 1. lancio 2. beccheggio 3. (*mecc.*) passo 4. (*mus.*) intonazione 5. inclinazione.
pitch[2] s. pece, bitume || — -dark, nero come la pece.
to pitch[1] vt. 1. sistemare 2. gettare 3. intonare. ♦ **to pitch** vi. 1. beccheggiare 2. (*aer.*) picchiare.
to pitch[2] vt. impeciare.
pitcher s. brocca.
pitchfork s. forcone.
to pitchfork vt. 1. rimuovere 2. spingere (*col forcone*).
pitching s. beccheggio.
pitchy agg. 1. impeciato 2. simile a pece.
piteous agg. pietoso.
pitfall s. trappola.
pith s. 1. midollo 2. (*fig.*) essenza.
pithy agg. (*fig.*) vigoroso.
pitiable, pitiful agg. pietoso.
pitiless agg. spietato.
pittance s. poco denaro.
pitted agg. butterato.
pity s. pietà || *what a* —!, che peccato!
to pity vt. aver pietà di, compatire.
pitying agg. pietoso.
pivot s. cardine.
to pivot vt. montare su cardini. ♦ **to pivot** vi. girare su cardini.
placable agg. placabile.
placard s. manifesto.
to placate vt. placare.
placatory agg. conciliante.
place s. 1. posto 2. brano || *to take* —, aver luogo, accadere.

to **place** vt. mettere, porre, situare.
placement s. collocamento.
placid agg. placido.
placidity s. placidità.
placing s. sistemazione.
plagiarism s. plagio.
plagiarist s. plagiario.
to **plagiarize** vt. plagiare.
plagiary s. 1. plagio 2. plagiario.
plague s. peste.
to **plague** vt. affliggere.
plaguer s. tormentatore.
plaid s. 1. mantello scozzese 2. tessuto a quadri.
plain agg. 1. piano, chiaro, evidente 2. semplice 3. comune, scialbo. ♦ **plain** s. pianura. ♦ **plain** avv. 1. chiaramente 2. semplicemente.
plain-clothes s. pl. abiti borghesi.
plainness s. 1. chiarezza 2. semplicità 3. aspetto scialbo.
plaint s. 1. lamento, lagnanza 2. (giur.) querela.
plaintiff s. (giur.) attore (nei processi civili).
plaintive agg. lamentoso.
plait s. 1. piega (di abiti) 2. treccia.
to **plait** vt. 1. pieghettare 2. intrecciare.
plan s. 1. piano, progetto 2. pianta (di una città).
to **plan** vt. progettare.
plane[1] agg. piano. ♦ **plane** s. 1. piano 2. aereo.
plane[2] s. pialla.
plane[3] s. — -tree, platano.
to **plane**[1] vi. volare.
to **plane**[2] vt. piallare.
planer s. (mecc.) piallatrice.
planet s. (astr.) pianeta.
planetary agg. planetario.
planimetric(al) agg. planimetrico.
planimetry s. planimetria.
planisphere s. planisfero.
plank s. tavola, asse.
to **plank** vt. coprire di tavole.
planking s. tavolato.
plankton s. plancton.
planner s. progettista.
planning s. progettazione.
plant s. 1. pianta 2. impianto, apparato 3. fabbrica, stabilimento.
to **plant** vt. (im)piantare.
plantation s. piantagione.
planter s. 1. piantatore 2. colonizzatore.
plantigrade agg. e s. plantigrado.
plaque s. placca.
plash s. pozzanghera.

plaster s. 1. cerotto 2. gesso 3. intonaco.
to **plaster** vt. 1. incerottare 2. ingessare 3. intonacare 4. ricoprire.
plastering s. 1. intonacatura 2. ingessatura.
plastic agg. plastico, malleabile.
plasticine s. plastilina.
plasticity s. plasticità.
to **plasticize** vt. rendere plastico.
plastics s. pl. materie plastiche.
plate s. 1. lastra, lamina 2. piatto 3. tavola fuori testo 4. targa 5. squama 6. vasellame.
to **plate** vt. 1. placcare 2. rivestire di piastre.
plateau s. altipiano.
platen s. 1. piastra metallica 2. rullo di macchina da scrivere.
platform s. 1. piattaforma 2. (ferr.) marciapiede 3. impalcatura 4. (amer.) programma politico.
plating s. 1. placcatura 2. rivestimento metallico.
to **platinize** vt. platinare.
platinum s. platino.
platitude s. banalità.
Platonic agg. platonico.
Platonism s. platonismo.
platoon s. plotone.
plausibility s. plausibilità.
plausible agg. plausibile.
play s. 1. gioco 2. dramma 3. (mus.) esecuzione 4. azione || — bill, cartellone teatrale; — -time, ricreazione.
to **play** vt. e vi. 1. giocare 2. recitare 3. agire 4. suonare || to — down, dare poca importanza a.
playboy s. (fam.) gaudente.
player s. 1. giocatore 2. attore 3. suonatore.
playful agg. giocoso.
playfulness s. allegria.
playground s. terreno di giochi.
playhouse s. teatro.
playing s. 1. gioco 2. rappresentazione 3. (mus.) esecuzione.
plaything s. giocattolo.
playwright, playwriter s. commediografo.
plea s. 1. giustificazione 2. (giur.) eccezione difensiva.
to **plead** vt. 1. patrocinare 2. addurre a pretesto 3. (giur.) perorare (una causa). ♦ to **plead** vi. 1. difendersi 2. supplicare.
pleader s. patrocinatore.
pleading agg. supplichevole. ♦

pleading s. difesa. ♦ **pleadings** s. pl. comparse.

pleasant agg. piacevole.

pleasantry s. piacevolezza.

to please vt. e vi. piacere (a) || — God, a Dio piacendo.

pleased agg. lieto.

pleasing agg. piacevole.

pleasure s. piacere.

pleat s. piega (di abiti ecc.).

to pleat vt. pieghettare.

plebeian agg. e s. plebeo.

plebiscitary agg. plebiscitario.

plebiscite s. plebiscito.

plectrum s. plettro.

pledge s. 1. pegno 2. promessa 3. brindisi.

to pledge vt. 1. impegnare 2. brindare a.

pledgee s. (giur.) creditore pignoratizio.

plenary agg. plenario || — session, seduta plenaria.

plenilune s. plenilunio.

plenipotentiary agg. e s. plenipotenziario.

plentiful agg. abbondante.

plenty s. abbondanza, quantità.

pleonasm s. pleonasma.

pleonastic agg. pleonastico.

plethora s. pletora.

plethoric agg. pletorico.

pleurisy s. pleurite.

plexus s. plesso.

pliability s. pieghevolezza.

pliable agg. pieghevole.

pliancy s. V. pliability.

pliant s. V. pliable.

pliers s. pl. pinze.

plight[1] s. situazione critica.

plight[2] s. impegno, promessa.

to plight vt. impegnare, promettere.

plod s. 1. passo pesante 2. lavoro faticoso.

to plod vt. e vi. 1. camminare faticosamente 2. sgobbare.

plodder s. 1. chi cammina faticosamente 2. sgobbone.

plot s. 1. appezzamento 2. trama 3. congiura.

to plot vt. e vi. 1. fare la pianta di 2. tramare.

plotter s. cospiratore.

plough s. aratro.

to plough vt. e vi. 1. arare 2. solcare.

ploughing s. aratura.

ploughman s. aratore.

ploughshare s. vomere.

plover s. piviere.

pluck s. 1. strappo 2. coraggio.

to pluck vt. 1. strappare 2. spennare 3. tirare || to — up, sradicare.

plucky agg. coraggioso.

plug s. 1. tappo (di lavandino ecc.) 2. (elettr.; tel.) spina || spark(ing)- — (mecc.), candela.

to plug vt. 1. tappare 2. tamponare || to — in, inserire la corrente; to — away, sgobbare:

plugging s. chiusura.

plum s. 1. prugna, susina 2. uva passa 3. (fig.) il meglio.

plumage s. piumaggio.

plumb agg. 1. a piombo 2. completo. ♦ **plumb** s. 1. filo a piombo 2. scandaglio. ♦ **plumb** avv. 1. a piombo 2. esattamente.

to plumb vt. 1. rendere verticale 2. scandagliare 3. impiombare.

plumber s. idraulico.

plumbery s. negozio di idraulico.

plumbing s. 1. piombatura 2. lavori idraulici.

plumbum s. piombo.

plume s. piuma, penna.

plummet s. piombino.

plump[1] agg. grassottello.

plump[2] agg. brusco, netto. ♦ **plump** avv. 1. improvvisamente 2. direttamente.

to plump vt. 1. ingrassare 2. far cadere. ♦ **to plump** vi. 1. ingrassare 2. cadere.

to plunder v. depredare.

plunderer s. saccheggiatore.

plunge s. tuffo.

to plunge vt. tuffare. ♦ **to plunge** vi. tuffarsi.

plunger s. 1. tuffatore 2. stantuffo.

plunk s. colpo metallico.

to plunk vt. far cadere pesantemente. ♦ **to plunk** vi. cadere pesantemente.

plural agg. e s. plurale.

pluralism s. pluralismo.

plurality s. pluralità.

plus agg. 1. in più 2. (elettr.) positivo || — value, plusvalore. ♦ **plus** s. 1. più 2. quantità positiva. ♦ **plus** prep. più.

plush s. « peluche », felpa.

plutocracy s. plutocrazia.

plutocrat s. plutocrate.

ply s. piega || — -wood, compensato.

to ply vt. 1. maneggiare 2. importunare. ♦ **to ply** vi. 1. lavorare as-

siduamente **2.** fare la spola.
pneumatic *agg.* e *s.* pneumatico.
pneumonia *s.* polmonite.
pneumothorax *s.* pneumotorace.
to **poach** *vt.* **1.** calpestare **2.** cacciare di frodo **3.** interferire.
poacher *s.* bracconiere.
poaching *s.* bracconaggio.
pocket *s.* **1.** tasca **2.** buca (*di biliardo*) || — -*book*, libro tascabile.
to **pocket** *vt.* **1.** intascare **2.** nascondere, soffocare (*sentimenti ecc.*).
pocketful *s.* tascata.
pod *s.* **1.** baccello **2.** gruppetto.
poem *s.* **1.** poesia **2.** poema.
poet *s.* poeta.
poetic(al) *agg.* poetico.
poetic(s) *s.* poetica.
poetry *s.* poesia.
poignant *agg.* **1.** pungente **2.** commovente.
point *s.* **1.** punto **2.** punta, estremità **3.** caratteristica.
to **point** *vt.* **1.** indicare, segnare a dito **2.** appuntire **3.** dirigere || *to — out*, indicare, porre in rilievo.
point-blank *agg.* diretto. ♦ **point-blank** *avv.* direttamente.
pointed *agg.* **1.** appuntito **2.** mordace **3.** evidente.
pointer *s.* **1.** indicatore **2.** lancetta (*di orologio*).
pointless *agg.* **1.** spuntato **2.** inutile, senza scopo.
pointsman *s.* (*ferr.*) deviatore.
poise *s.* equilibrio.
to **poise** *vt.* bilanciare. ♦ to **poise** *vi.* bilanciarsi.
poison *s.* veleno.
to **poison** *vt.* avvelenare.
poisoning *agg.* velenoso. ♦ **poisoning** *s.* avvelenamento.
poisonous *agg.* velenoso (*anche fig.*).
poke *s.* spinta, urto.
to **poke** *vt.* e *vi.* **1.** spingere **2.** andare a tastoni.
poker *s.* attizzatoio.
poky *agg.* meschino.
polar *agg.* polare.
polarity *s.* polarità.
polarization *s.* polarizzazione.
to **polarize** *vt.* polarizzare.
pole[1] *s.* palo.
pole[2] *s.* polo.
Pole[3] *s.* polacco.
polecat *s.* puzzola.
polemic *s.* **1.** polemica **2.** polemista.
polemic(al) *agg.* polemico.

polemi(ci)st *s.* polemista.
to **polemize** *vi.* polemizzare.
police *s.* polizia || — -*force*, corpo di polizia.
police court *s.* pretura.
policeman *s.* poliziotto.
policy[1] *s.* **1.** linea di condotta **2.** sagacia.
policy[2] *s.* polizza.
polio(myelitis) *s.* poliomielite.
Polish[1] *agg.* polacco.
polish[2] *s.* **1.** lucidatura **2.** lucido **3.** raffinatezza || *shoe* —, lucido per le scarpe.
to **polish** *vt.* **1.** lucidare **2.** raffinare. ♦ to **polish** *vi.* **1.** divenire lucido **2.** raffinarsi.
polisher *s.* **1.** lucidatore **2.** lucido.
polishing *s.* lucidatura.
polite *agg.* cortese.
politeness *s.* cortesia.
politic *agg.* abile.
political *agg.* politico.
politician *s.* uomo politico.
politics *s.* politica.
poll *s.* **1.** votazione, scrutinio **2.** referendum.
to **poll** *vt.* radere. ♦ to **poll** *vi.* votare, raccogliere voti.
pollen *s.* polline.
to **pollinate** *vt.* impollinare.
pollination *s.* impollinazione.
to **pollute** *vt.* contaminare.
pollution *s.* contaminazione.
polyandry *s.* poliandria.
polychrome *agg.* policromo.
polychromy *s.* policromia.
polyclinic *s.* policlinico.
polygamist *s.* poligamo.
polygamous *agg.* poligamo.
polygamy *s.* poligamia.
polyglot *agg.* e *s.* poliglotta.
polygon *s.* poligono.
polyhedral *agg.* poliedrico.
polyhedron *s.* poliedro.
polymerization *s.* polimerizzazione.
polymorphic *agg.* polimorfo.
polymorphism *s.* polimorfismo.
polyp *s.* polipo.
polyphonic *agg.* polifonico.
polyphony *s.* polifonia.
polysyllabic(al) *agg.* polisillabico.
polysyllable *s.* polisillabo.
polytechnic *agg.* e *s.* politecnico.
polytheism *s.* politeismo.
polytheist *s.* politeista.
polytheistic(al) *agg.* politeistico.
polyvalent *agg.* polivalente.

pomade s. pomata.
to **pomade** vt. impomatare.
pomegranate s. 1. melagrana 2. melograno.
pomp s. pompa, fasto.
pomposity s. pomposità.
pompous agg. pomposo.
pond s. stagno.
to **pond** vt. e vi. stagnare.
to **ponder** vt. e vi. ponderare.
ponderable agg. ponderabile.
ponderous agg. ponderoso.
pontiff s. pontefice.
pontifical agg. pontificio. ♦ **pontifical** s. pontificato.
pontificate s. pontificato.
to **pontificate** vi. pontificare.
pontoon s. pontone.
pony s. « pony », piccolo cavallo.
poodle s. barboncino.
pool[1] s. 1. stagno 2. pozza || swimming —, piscina.
pool[2] s. (comm.) 1. fondo comune 2. (comm.) consorzio, sindacato.
poor agg. povero.
poorly avv. male.
poorness s. povertà.
pop s. scoppio.
to **pop** vi. scoppiare. ♦ to **pop** vt. 1. far scoppiare 2. ficcare.
popcorn s. fiocco di granoturco.
pope s. papa.
popery s. papismo.
poplar s. pioppo.
poppied agg. coperto di papaveri.
poppy s. papavero.
populace s. plebaglia.
popular agg. popolare.
popularity s. popolarità.
popularization s. popolarizzazione.
to **popularize** vt. popolarizzare.
to **populate** vt. popolare.
population s. popolazione.
Populism s. populismo.
Populist s. populista.
populous agg. popoloso.
porch s. portico.
porcupine s. porcospino.
pore s. poro.
to **pore** vi. esaminare.
pork s. carne di maiale.
pornographic agg. pornografico.
pornography s. pornografia.
porosity s. porosità.
porous agg. poroso.
porphyry s. porfido.
port[1] s. porto.
port[2] s. 1. (mecc.) apertura, foro 2. (mar.) portello.

port[3] s. fianco sinistro di nave.
portable agg. portatile.
portal s. portale.
portcullis s. saracinesca (di fortezza).
to **portend** vt. preannunciare.
portent s. 1. presagio 2. portento.
portentous agg. 1. sinistro 2. portentoso.
porter[1] s. facchino.
porter[2] s. custode, portiere.
porter[3] s. birra scura.
portfolio s. 1. cartella, busta 2. (pol.) portafoglio.
porthole s. 1. (mar.) portello 2. feritoia.
portion s. porzione, parte.
to **portion** vt. dividere, distribuire.
portrait s. ritratto.
portraitist s. ritrattista.
to **portray** vt. ritrarre.
portrayal s. ritratto.
portrayer s. ritrattista.
Portuguese agg. e s. portoghese.
pose s. posa.
to **pose**[1] vt. proporre.
to **pose**[2] vi. posare.
poser s. posatore.
position s. posizione.
positive agg. 1. positivo 2. sicuro. ♦ **positive** s. 1. realtà 2. (foto) positiva.
positivism s. positivismo.
positivist s. positivista.
positivistic agg. positivistico.
posology s. posologia.
to **possess** vt. possedere.
possessed agg. indemoniato.
possession s. possesso.
possessive agg. possessivo.
possessor s. possessore.
possibility s. possibilità.
possible agg. possibile.
possibly avv. possibilmente.
post[1] s. posta, corrispondenza || — card, cartolina; by return of —, a giro di posta.
post[2] s. 1. palo, sostegno, puntello 2. stipite || sign- —, indicatore stradale.
to **post**[1] vt. imbucare, inviare per posta.
to **post**[2] vt. affiggere.
postage s. spese postali (pl.).
postage stamp s. francobollo.
postal agg. postale.
to **postdate** vt. posdatare.
poster s. 1. affisso 2. attacchino.
poste-restante s. fermo posta.

posterior *agg.* posteriore.
posterity *s.* posterità.
postern *s.* postierla.
post-free *agg.* franco di porto.
posthumous *agg.* postumo.
postil(l)ion *s.* postiglione.
postman *s.* postino.
postmark *s.* timbro postale.
postmaster *s.* direttore di ufficio postale.
to postpone *vt.* rimandare.
postponement *s.* rinvio.
to post-score *vt.* (*cine*) sonorizzare.
postscript *s.* poscritto.
postulate *s.* postulato.
to postulate *vt.* 1. porre come postulato 2. chiedere.
postulator *s.* postulante.
posture *s.* posizione.
to posture *vi.* assumere una posizione.
post-war *agg.* postbellico.
posy *s.* mazzolino di fiori.
pot *s.* 1. recipiente 2. pentola || — -bellied, panciuto.
to pot *vt.* conservare (*in vaso*).
potable *agg.* potabile.
potash *s.* potassa.
potassic *agg.* potassico.
potassium *s.* potassio.
potato *s.* patata.
potent *agg.* potente.
potential *agg.* e *s.* potenziale.
potentiality *s.* potenzialità.
potion *s.* pozione.
potter *s.* vasaio.
pottery *s.* 1. terraglie 2. fabbrica di terraglie.
pouch *s.* borsa.
to pouch *vt.* intascare.
poulterer *s.* pollivendolo.
poultry *s.* pollame.
pounce *s.* balzo.
to pounce *vi.* avventarsi su, contro.
pound[1] *s.* 1. libbra 2. sterlina.
pound[2] *s.* recinto.
to pound[1] *vt.* e *vi.* pestare.
to pound[2] *vt.* rinchiudere.
pour *s.* acquazzone.
to pour *vt.* versare. ♦ **to pour** *vi.* 1. versarsi 2. diluviare.
pout *s.* broncio.
to pout *vi.* fare il broncio.
poverty *s.* povertà.
powder *s.* 1. polvere 2. cipria, talco.
to powder *vt.* 1. polverizzare 2. incipriare. ♦ **to powder** *vi.* 1. pol-

verizzarsi 2. incipriarsi.
powdery *agg.* 1. friabile 2. polveroso.
power *s.* potenza, potere || *horse* —, cavallo vapore; — *-station*, centrale elettrica.
to power *vt.* motorizzare.
powerful *agg.* potente.
powerless *agg.* debole.
pox *s.* sifilide || *chicken-* —, varicella, *small-* —, vaiolo.
practicability *s.* praticabilità.
practicable *agg.* 1. praticabile 2. fattibile.
practical *agg.* pratico.
practicality *s.* praticità.
practice *s.* 1. pratica 2. abitudine, regola 3. esercizio 4. professione 5. (*coll.*) clienti (*di medico ecc.*).
to practise *vt.* 1. praticare 2. esercitare. ♦ **to practise** *vi.* esercitarsi.
practitioner *s.* professionista.
praetorian *s.* pretoriano.
pragmatic(al) *agg.* prammatico.
pragmatism *s.* pragmatismo.
pragmatist *agg.* e *s.* pragmatista.
prairie *s.* prateria.
praise *s.* lode.
to praise *vt.* lodare.
praiser *s.* lodatore.
praiseworthy *agg.* lodevole.
prance *s.* impennata.
prank *s.* monelleria.
to prank *vt.* ornare, agghindare vistosamente. ♦ **to prank** *vi.* mettersi in mostra.
prate *s.* chiacchiera, sproloquio.
to prate *vi.* chiacchierare, proferire parole senza senso.
prattle *s.* balbettio.
to prattle *vt.* e *vi.* balbettare.
praxis *s.* prassi.
to pray *vt.* e *vi.* pregare.
prayer *s.* preghiera.
to preach *vt.* e *vi.* predicare.
preacher *s.* predicatore.
to preachify *vi.* predicare in modo noioso.
preaching *s.* predicazione.
preachy *agg.* (*fam.*) incline a far prediche.
to pre-announce *vt.* preannunziare.
to prearrange *vt.* predisporre.
prearrangement *s.* predisposizione.
prebend *s.* prebenda.
prebendary *s.* prebendario.
precarious *agg.* precario.

precariousness s. precarietà.
precatory agg. supplichevole.
precaution s. precauzione.
precautional agg. precauzionale.
to **precede** vt. e vi. precedere.
precedence s. precedenza.
precedent agg. e s. precedente.
preceding agg. precedente.
precept s. precetto.
preceptive agg. istruttivo.
preceptor s. precettore.
precession s. precessione.
precinct s. 1. recinto 2. limiti 3. vicinanze (pl.).
preciosity s. preziosità.
precious agg. prezioso.
preciousness s. preziosità.
precipice s. precipizio.
precipitate agg. e s. precipitato.
to **precipitate** vt. e vi. precipitare.
precipitation s. precipitazione.
precipitous agg. ripido.
précis s. riassunto.
precise agg. preciso.
precision s. precisione.
to **preclude** vt. precludere.
precocious agg. precoce.
precociousness, precocity s. precocità.
preconceived agg. preconcetto.
precursor s. precursore, predecessore.
precursory agg. 1. preliminare 2. premonitore.
predaceous agg. rapace.
to **predate** vt. predatare.
predatory agg. rapace.
to **predecease** vt. premorire a.
predecessor s. predecessore.
to **predesignate** vt. predesignare.
predestination s. predestinazione.
to **predestine** vt. predestinare.
predetermination s. predeterminazione.
to **predetermine** vt. predeterminare.
predicable agg. asseribile.
predicament s. situazione scabrosa.
predicate agg. e s. predicato.
to **predicate** vt. 1. asserire 2. implicare.
predication s. affermazione.
predicative agg. 1. predicativo 2. affermativo.
predicatory agg. predicatorio.
to **predict** vt. e vi. predire.
prediction s. predizione.
predilection s. predilezione.

to **predispose** vt. predisporre.
predisposition s. predisposizione.
predominance s. predominanza.
to **predominate** vi. predominare.
pre-eminence s. preminenza.
pre-eminent agg. preminente.
pre-emption s. prelazione, priorità.
to **pre-engage** vt. impegnare in anticipo.
to **pre-establish** vt. prestabilire.
to **pre-exist** vi. preesistere.
pre-existence s. preesistenza.
to **prefabricate** vt. prefabbricare.
prefabricated agg. — house, casa prefabbricata.
preface s. prefazione.
to **preface** vt. 1. fare una prefazione a 2. iniziare.
prefatory agg. introduttivo.
prefect s. prefetto.
prefecture s. prefettura.
to **prefer** vt. 1. preferire 2. promuovere, elevare.
preferable agg. preferibile.
preference s. preferenza.
preferential agg. preferenziale.
preferment s. avanzamento, promozione.
prefiguration s. prefigurazione.
to **prefigure** vt. prefigurare.
prefix s. prefisso.
pregnancy s. 1. gravidanza 2. (fig.) significato, importanza.
pregnant agg. 1. incinta 2. significativo, importante 3. fecondo.
prehension s. 1. prensione 2. apprendimento.
prehistoric(al) agg. preistorico.
prehistory s. preistoria.
prejudice s. pregiudizio.
to **prejudice** vt. 1. pregiudicare 2. influenzare.
prejudicial agg. pregiudizievole.
prelate s. prelato.
prelatic(al) agg. prelatizio.
preliminary agg. preliminare. ♦ **preliminaries** s. pl. preliminari.
prelude s. preludio.
to. **prelude** vt. preludere. ♦ to **prelude** vi. eseguire un preludio.
premature agg. prematuro.
to **premeditate** vt. premeditare.
premeditation s. premeditazione.
premier s. primo ministro.
premise s. 1. premessa 2. stabile con terreni annessi.
to **premise** vt. premettere.
premolar agg. e s. premolare.
premonitory agg. premonitore.

preoccupation s. preoccupazione.
to preoccupy vt. 1. preoccupare 2. occupare in precedenza.
preparation s. preparazione, preparativo.
preparative, preparatory agg. preparatorio.
to prepare vt. preparare. ♦ **to prepare** vi. prepararsi.
preponderance s. preponderanza.
preponderant agg. preponderante.
preposition s. preposizione.
prepositional agg. di preposizione.
to prepossess vt. 1. occupare in precedenza 2. influenzare.
prepossessing agg. attraente.
prepossession s. prevenzione.
preposterous agg. assurdo.
prepotence s. predominio.
prepotent agg. predominante.
Pre-Raphaeli(ti)sm s. preraffaellismo.
prerogative agg. privilegiato. ♦ **prerogative** s. prerogativa.
presage s. presagio.
presbyope s. presbite.
presbyopic agg. presbite.
Presbyterian agg. e s. presbiteriano.
Presbyterianism s. presbiterianismo.
presbytery s. presbiterio.
prescience s. prescienza.
to prescribe vt. prescrivere.
prescript s. ordinanza.
prescription s. prescrizione.
presence s. presenza.
present[1] agg. presente || — -day, contemporaneo. ♦ **present** s. presente, tempo presente || at —, attualmente. ♦ **presents** s. pl. (giur.) documento (sing.).
present[2] s. dono, regalo.
to present vt. 1. presentare 2. regalare.
presentable agg. presentabile.
presentation s. 1. presentazione 2. dono.
presenter s. 1. presentatore 2. donatore.
presentiment s. presentimento.
presently avv. presto, quanto prima.
presentment s. presentazione.
preservable agg. conservabile.
preservation s. conservazione.
preservative agg. e s. preservativo.
preserve s. 1. riserva 2. conserva (di pomodoro, frutta ecc.).
to preserve vt. 1. preservare 2. conservare 3. mettere in conserva.

to preside vi. presiedere.
presidency s. presidenza.
president s. presidente.
presidential agg. presidenziale.
press s. 1. stretta, pressione 2. pressa 3. (fig.) stampa 4. calca, ressa || — conference, conferenza stampa.
to press vt. 1. premere, comprimere 2. costringere. ♦ **to press** vi. affollarsi.
pressing agg. 1. urgente 2. insistente.
pressman s. 1. cronista (di giornale) 2. (tip.) stampatore.
pressure s. pressione || — -cooker, pentola a pressione.
to pressurize vt. pressurizzare.
prestige s. prestigio.
presumable agg. presumibile.
to presume vt. e vi. 1. presumere 2. avere la presunzione di.
presuming agg. presuntuoso.
presumption s. 1. presunzione 2. supposizione.
presumptive agg. presunto.
presumptuous agg. presuntuoso.
presumptuousness s. presunzione.
to presuppose vt. presupporre.
presupposition s. presupposizione.
pretence s. 1. pretesa 2. pretesto 3. simulazione.
to pretend vi. 1. pretendere 2. fingere.
pretender s. 1. pretendente 2. simulatore.
pretension s. 1. pretesa 2. presunzione.
pretentious agg. pretenzioso.
preternatural agg. soprannaturale.
pretext s. pretesto.
prettiness s. grazia.
pretty agg. grazioso. ♦ **pretty** avv. abbastanza.
to prevail vi. prevalere.
prevailing agg. 1. prevalente 2. efficace.
prevalence s. prevalenza.
to prevaricate vi. 1. tergiversare 2. mentire.
prevarication s. 1. tergiversazione 2. menzogna.
prevaricator s. 1. chi tergiversa 2. mentitore.
to prevent vt. impedire.
prevention s. 1. impedimento 2. prevenzione.
preventive agg. preventivo.

preview s. anteprima.
previous agg. precedente.
prevision s. previsione.
pre-war agg. prebellico.
prey s. preda.
to **prey** vi. 1. (de)predare 2. (fig.) consumare.
price s. prezzo, costo.
to **price** vt. fissare il prezzo di.
priceless agg. inestimabile.
prick s. 1. punta 2. puntura 3. (fig.) pungolo, rimorso.
to **prick** vt. 1. pungere 2. segnare 3. rizzare le orecchie. ♦ to **prick** vi. 1. formicolare 2. pungersi.
prickle s. 1. spina 2. pungiglione.
prickly agg. pungente.
pride s. orgoglio.
to **pride** vt. to — oneself upon, essere orgoglioso di.
priest s. prete.
priesthood s. 1. clero 2. sacerdozio.
prig s. presuntuoso.
prim agg. affettato.
primary agg. primo, primario.
primate s. (eccl.) primate.
prime agg. 1. primo 2. di prima qualità. ♦ **prime** s. 1. principio 2. (fig.) fiore.
to **prime** vt. caricare, innescare.
primer[1] s. sillabario.
primer[2] s. innesco.
primeval agg. primordiale.
primigenial agg. primigenio.
priming s. 1. innesco 2. prima mano (di vernice ecc.).
primitive agg. e s. primitivo.
primitiveness s. primitività.
primogeniture s. primogenitura.
primordial agg. primordiale.
primrose s. primula.
prince s. principe.
princely agg. principesco.
princess s. principessa.
principal agg. principale. ♦ **principal** s. 1. principale, direttore 2. (edil.) trave maestra 3. (comm.) mandante.
principality s. principato.
principle s. principio.
print s. 1. impronta 2. stampa 3. stampatello 4. (foto) copia.
to **print** vt. 1. stampare 2. scrivere a stampatello 3. imprimere.
printer s. 1. tipografo 2. (mecc.) stampatrice.
printing s. 1. stampa 2. tiratura || — -press, pressa tipografica.
prior agg. precedente. ♦ **prior** s.

priore. ♦ **prior** avv. prima.
priorate s. priorato.
prioress s. priora.
priority s. priorità.
prism s. prisma.
prismatic(al) agg. prismatico.
prison s. prigione.
prisoner s. prigioniero.
privacy s. 1. intimità 2. riserbo.
private agg. 1. privato 2. appartato 3. segreto, riservato, personale. ♦ **private** s. soldato semplice.
privation s. privazione.
privative agg. privativo.
privilege s. privilegio.
to **privilege** vt. privilegiare.
privy agg. 1. nascosto 2. al corrente di.
prize s. premio.
to **prize** vt. stimare.
probabilism s. probabilismo.
probability s. probabilità.
probable agg. probabile.
probate s. omologazione.
probation s. prova.
probative agg. probativo.
probatory agg. probatorio.
probe s. sonda.
to **probe** vt. sondare.
probity s. probità.
problem s. problema.
problematic(al) agg. problematico.
procedural agg. procedurale.
procedure s. 1. procedimento 2. procedura.
to **proceed** vi. 1. procedere 2. provenire.
proceeding s. V. procedure.
proceeds s. pl. profitto (sing.).
process s. 1. procedimento 2. processo.
to **process** vt. 1. processare 2. (chim.) trattare.
procession s. processione.
processionary s. (zool.) processionaria.
proclaim s. proclama.
to **proclaim** vt. proclamare.
proclamation s. proclama(zione).
proconsul s. proconsole.
to **procrastinate** vt. e vi. procrastinare.
procrastination s. procrastinazione,
to **procreate** vt. procreare.
procreation s. procreazione.
procreator s. procreatore.
proctor s. 1. censore 2. (giur.) procuratore.

procurator s. procuratore.
to **procure** vt. 1. procurare, procurarsi 2. adescare.
procurer s. mezzano.
prod s. pungolo.
to **prod** vt. pungolare.
prodigal agg. e s. prodigo.
prodigality s. prodigalità.
prodigious agg. 1. prodigioso 2. enorme.
prodigiousness s. prodigiosità.
prodigy s. prodigio.
produce s. prodotto || farm —, prodotto agricolo; raw —, materia prima.
to **produce** vt. 1. produrre 2. presentare.
producer s. 1. produttore 2. (teat.) regista.
product s. prodotto.
production s. 1. esibizione 2. produzione.
productive agg. produttivo.
productivity s. produttività.
proem s. proemio.
profanation s. profanazione.
profane agg. 1. profano 2. empio.
to **profane** vt. profanare.
profaner s. profanatore.
profanity s. 1. profanità 2. empietà.
to **profess** vt. 1. professare 2. pretendere.
profession s. professione.
professional agg. professionale || — man, professionista. ♦ **professional** s. professionista.
professionalism s. professionismo.
professor s. professore (d'università).
professorial agg. professorale.
proficiency s. competenza || — in English, buona conoscenza dell'inglese.
proficient agg. e s. esperto, competente.
profile s. profilo.
to **profile** vt. 1. profilare 2. tracciare il profilo di.
profit s. profitto, guadagno.
to **profit** vt. giovare. ♦ to **profit** vi. approfittare.
profitable agg. vantaggioso.
profiteer s. profittatore.
profligacy s. 1. sregolatezza 2. spergero.
profligate agg. e s. 1. dissoluto 2. scialacquatore.
profound agg. profondo.

profuse agg. 1. abbondante 2. prodigo.
profusion s. 1. profusione 2. prodigalità.
progenitor s. progenitore.
progeny s. progenie.
prognathism s. prognatismo.
prognathous agg. prognato.
prognosis s. (pl. -ses) prognosi.
prognostic agg. rivelatore. ♦ **prognostic** s. 1. pronostico 2. sintomo.
prognostication s. 1. pronostico 2. prognosi.
program(me) s. programma.
to **program(me)** vt. programmare.
programming s. programmazione.
programmist s. programmista.
progress s. 1. progresso 2. avanzata 3. sviluppo 4. andamento, corso.
to **progress** vi. 1. progredire 2. avanzare 3. svilupparsi.
progression s. 1. progressione 2. avanzamento.
progressive agg. progressivo, progressista. ♦ **progressive** s. progressista.
to **prohibit** vt. proibire.
prohibition s. 1. proibizione 2. proibizionismo.
prohibitionist s. proibizionista.
prohibitive agg. proibitivo.
project s. progetto.
to **project** vt. 1. progettare 2. proiettare. ♦ to **project** vi. sporgere.
projectile s. proiettile.
projection s. 1. progetto 2. proiezione.
projector s. 1. progettista 2. proiettore.
proletarian agg. e s. proletario.
proletariat s. proletariato.
to **proliferate** vt. proliferare. ♦ to **proliferate** vi. moltiplicarsi.
proliferation s. proliferazione.
prolific agg. prolifico.
prolix agg. prolisso.
prolixity s. prolissità.
prologue s. prologo.
to **prolong** vt. 1. prolungare 2. (comm.) prorogare.
promenade s. passeggiata, passeggio pubblico, lungomare.
prominence s. prominenza.
prominent agg. prominente.
promiscuity s. promiscuità.
promiscuous agg. promiscuo.
promise s. promessa.
to **promise** vt. e vi. promettere.

promissory *agg.* contenente una promessa || — *note* (*comm.*), pagherò cambiario.

promontory *s.* promontorio.

to **promote** *vt.* **1.** promuovere **2.** dare impulso, favorire.

promoter *s.* promotore.

promotion *s.* **1.** promozione **2.** incoraggiamento.

prompt *agg.* **1.** sollecito **2.** (*comm.*) in contanti. ♦ **prompt** *s.* **1.** (*comm.*) termine di pagamento **2.** suggerimento.

to **prompt** *vt.* **1.** spingere **2.** suggerire.

prompter *s.* suggeritore.

promptness *s.* prontezza.

to **promulgate** *vt.* promulgare.

promulgation *s.* promulgazione.

promulgator *s.* promulgatore.

prone *agg.* prono.

prong *s.* **1.** dente (*di forca*) **2.** forca.

pronominal *agg.* pronominale.

pronoun *s.* pronome.

to **pronounce** *vt.* **1.** pronunciare **2.** dichiarare. ♦ to **pronounce** *vi.* pronunciarsi.

pronouncement *s.* dichiarazione.

pronouncing, pronunciation *s.* pronuncia.

proof *agg.* a prova di. ♦ **proof** *s.* **1.** prova **2.** bozza **3.** gradazione alcoolica || — *-reader*, correttore di bozze; *burden of* — (*giur.*), onere della prova.

prop *s.* puntello.

to **prop** *vt.* **1.** sostenere **2.** appoggiare.

propaedeutic(al) *agg.* propedeutico.

propaedeutics *s.* propedeutica.

propagandist *s.* propagandista.

to **propagandize** *vt.* propagandare.

to **propagate** *vt.* propagare. ♦ to **propagate** *vi.* propagarsi.

propagation *s.* **1.** propagazione **2.** (*bot.*; *zool.*) riproduzione.

propagator *s.* propagatore.

propane *s.* propano.

to **propel** *vt.* spingere avanti.

propellent *agg.* e *s.* propulsore, propellente.

propeller *s.* propulsore || (*screw-*) —, elica.

propensity *s.* propensione.

proper *agg.* **1.** proprio **2.** adatto **3.** corretto **4.** propriamente detto.

property *s.* **1.** proprietà **2.** (*teat.*) costumi, arredi per la scena (*pl.*) ||

real —, beni immobili (*pl.*).

prophecy *s.* profezia.

to **prophesy** *vt.* e *vi.* profetizzare.

prophet *s.* profeta.

prophetic(al) *agg.* profetico.

prophylactic *agg.* e *s.* profilattico.

prophylaxis *s.* profilassi.

to **propitiate** *vt.* propiziare.

propitiation *s.* propiziazione.

propitiator *s.* propiziatore.

propitiatory *agg.* propiziatorio.

propitious *agg.* propizio.

proportion *s.* **1.** proporzione **2.** parte. ♦ **proportions** *s. pl.* dimensioni.

to **proportion** *vt.* **1.** proporzionare **2.** dividere in parti proporzionate.

proportional *agg.* proporzionale.

proportionality *s.* proporzionalità.

proportionate *agg.* proporzionato.

to **proportionate** V. *to proportion*.

proportioning *s.* proporzionamento.

proposal *s.* proposta.

to **propose** *vt.* proporre. ♦ to **propose** *vi.* **1.** prefiggersi, intendere **2.** fare richiesta di matrimonio || *to* — *the health of so.*, bere alla salute di qu.

proposition *s.* **1.** proposta **2.** proposizione **3.** asserzione **4.** problema.

proprietary *agg.* di proprietà. ♦ **proprietary** *s.* proprietario || — *rights*, diritti di proprietà.

proprietor *s.* proprietario.

propriety *s.* **1.** proprietà **2.** opportunità **3.** decoro, decenza. ♦ **proprieties** *s. pl.* convenienze.

propulsion *s.* propulsione.

propulsive *agg.* propulsivo.

propylaeum *s.* (*pl.* -laea) propileo.

propylene *s.* propilene.

prosaic *agg.* prosaico.

prosaism *s.* prosaicità.

proscenium *s.* (*pl.* -nia) proscenio.

to **proscribe** *vt.* **1.** bandire **2.** vietare.

proscription *s.* **1.** proscrizione **2.** proibizione.

prose *s.* **1.** prosa **2.** prosaicità || — *writer*, prosatore.

prosecutable *agg.* perseguibile.

to **prosecute** *vt.* **1.** proseguire **2.** perseguire.

prosecution *s.* **1.** proseguimento **2.** processo **3.** (*giur.*) accusa.

prosecutor *s.* **1.** prosecutore **2.** accusatore || *Public* — (*giur.*), l'accusa pubblica.

proselyte *s.* proselito.
proselytism *s.* proselitismo.
prosiness *s.* **1.** prosaicità **2.** banalità.
prosody *s.* prosodia.
prospect *s.* **1.** panorama **2.** prospettiva **3.** speranza, aspettativa.
to prospect *vt.* **1.** esplorare **2.** ricercare.
prospecting *s.* ricerca.
prospective *agg.* **1.** futuro **2.** eventuale.
to prosper *vt.* far prosperare. ♦ **to prosper** *vi.* prosperare.
prosperity *s.* prosperità.
prosperous *agg.* prospero.
prostate *s.* prostata.
prostatic *agg.* prostatico.
prosthesis *s.* (*med.*) protesi.
prostitute *s.* prostituta.
to prostitute *vt.* prostituire.
prostitution *s.* prostituzione.
prostrate *agg.* prostrato.
to prostrate *vt.* prostrare.
prostration *s.* **1.** prostrazione **2.** prosternazione.
prostyle *agg.* e *s.* prostilo.
prosy *agg.* **1.** prosaico **2.** noioso.
protagonist *s.* protagonista.
to protect *vt.* proteggere.
protection *s.* **1.** protezione **2.** salvacondotto.
protectionism *s.* protezionismo.
protectionist *s.* protezionista.
protective *agg.* protettivo.
protector *s.* protettore.
protectorate *s.* protettorato.
protectory *s.* patronato.
protein *s.* proteina.
protest *s.* **1.** protesta **2.** (*comm.*) protesto.
to protest *vt.* e *vi.* protestare.
protestant *agg.* e *s.* protestante.
Protestantism *s.* protestantesimo.
protestation *s.* dichiarazione.
protocol *s.* protocollo.
proton *s.* protone.
protoplasm *s.* protoplasma.
prototype *s.* prototipo.
Protozoa *s. pl.* protozoi.
to protract *vt.* **1.** protrarre **2.** rilevare.
protraction *s.* **1.** protrazione **2.** rilievo.
protractor *s.* **1.** protrattore **2.** goniometro.
to protrude *vt.* **1.** sporgere **2.** imporre. ♦ **to protrude** *vi.* **1.** sporgersi **2.** imporsi.

protrusion, protuberance *s.* protuberanza.
proud *agg.* orgoglioso, superbo.
to prove *vt.* **1.** provare, verificare **2.** omologare. ♦ **to prove** *vi.* risultare.
provender *s.* foraggio, biada.
proverb *s.* proverbio.
proverbial *agg.* proverbiale.
to provide *vi.* **1.** provvedere **2.** premunirsi **3.** stabilire (*di leggi*). ♦ **to provide** *vt.* **1.** procurare **2.** rifornire.
provided *cong.* purché, a patto che.
providence *s.* **1.** provvidenza **2.** previdenza.
provident *agg.* **1.** provvido **2.** previdente.
providential *agg.* provvidenziale.
province *s.* **1.** provincia **2.** (*fig.*) sfera, campo d'attività.
provincial *agg.* e *s.* provinciale.
provincialism *s.* provincialismo.
provision *s.* **1.** preparativo **2.** provvedimento **3.** clausola **4.** (*giur.*) disposizione. ♦ **provisions** *s. pl.* provviste.
to provision *vt.* approvvigionare.
provisional *agg.* provvisorio.
provisioning *s.* approvvigionamento.
provocation *s.* provocazione.
provocative *agg.* **1.** provocante **2.** stimolante.
provocativeness *s.* provocazione.
to provoke *vt.* **1.** provocare **2.** irritare.
provoker *s.* provocatore.
provost *s.* prevosto.
prow *s.* prora.
prowess *s.* prodezza, valore.
proximity *s.* prossimità.
proxy *s.* **1.** procura **2.** procuratore.
prude *s.* persona eccessivamente pudica.
prudence *s.* prudenza.
prudent *agg.* prudente.
prudential *agg.* prudenziale.
prudentials *s. pl.* provvedimenti precauzionali.
prudery *s.* ritrosia eccessiva.
prudish *agg.* pudibondo.
prune *s.* prugna secca.
to prune *vt.* potare.
pruner *s.* potatore.
pruning *s.* potatura || — -*book*, falcetto.
prussic *agg.* prussico.
pry[1] *s.* ficcanaso.

pry² s. leva.
to pry¹ vi. indagare.
to pry² vt. muovere con una leva.
psalm s. salmo.
psalmody s. salmodia.
pseudonym s. pseudonimo.
psyche s. psiche.
psychiatric(al) agg. psichiatrico.
psychiatrist s. psichiatra.
psychiatry s. psichiatria.
psychic s. 1. medium 2. psicologia.
psychic(al) agg. psichico.
psychoanalysis s. psicanalisi.
psychoanalyst s. psicanalista.
psychoanalytic(al) agg. psicanalitico.
to psychoanalyze vt. psicanalizzare.
psychologic(al) agg. psicologico.
psychologist s. psicologo.
psychology s. psicologia.
psychometry s. psicometria.
psychopathic agg. e s. psicopatico.
psychopathology s. psicopatologia.
psychopathy s. psicopatia.
psychosis s. psicosi.
psychotherapy s. psicoterapia.
ptisan s. tisana.
pub s. bar (in Gran Bretagna).
puberty s. pubertà.
pubis s. (pl. -bes) pube.
public agg. e s. pubblico || the reading —, i lettori (pl.).
publican s. 1. oste 2. (stor.) pubblicano.
publication s. pubblicazione.
publicity s. pubblicità.
to publish vt. 1. pubblicare 2. divulgare.
publishable agg. pubblicabile.
publisher s. editore.
pucker s. ruga, grinza.
to pucker vt. raggrinzare, corrugare. ♦ to pucker vi. raggrinzarsi, corrugarsi.
pudding s. 1. budino 2. pasticcio || black —, sanguinaccio.
puddle s. 1. pozzanghera 2. malta.
to puddle vt. 1. infangare 2. coprire di malta.
puerility s. puerilità.
Puerto Rican agg. e s. portoricano.
puff s. 1. soffio, sbuffo 2. piumino.
to puff vi. 1. sbuffare 2. gonfiarsi. ♦ to puff vt. 1. soffiare 2. gonfiare.
puffy agg. 1. gonfio 2. ansimante 3. paffuto, grasso.
pugilist s. pugile.

pugnacious agg. pugnace.
pugnacity s. combattività.
puke s. vomito.
to puke vt. e vi. vomitare.
pull s. 1. strappo 2. sforzo, tensione 3. maniglia (di cassetto).
to pull vt. 1. tirare 2. strappare || to — down, demolire. ♦ to pull vi. 1. trascinarsi 2. remare || to — back, ritirarsi; to — up, fermarsi.
puller s. (mecc.) estrattore.
pulley s. puleggia.
pulmonary agg. polmonare.
pulp s. polpa.
to pulp vt. ridurre in polpa. ♦ to pulp vi. diventare polposo.
pulpit s. pulpito.
pulpy agg. polposo.
pulsation s. pulsazione.
pulsatory agg. pulsante.
pulse s. 1. pulsazione, polso, battito 2. (radio) impulso.
to pulse vi. pulsare.
to pulverize vt. polverizzare. ♦ to pulverize vi. polverizzarsi.
pumice s. pomice.
pump s. pompa || petrol —, distributore di benzina.
to pump vt. e vi. pompare || to — up, gonfiare.
pumpkin s. zucca.
pun s. gioco di parole.
punch¹ s. punzone.
punch² s. pugno.
punch³ s. « punch » (bevanda alcoolica).
to punch¹ vt. (per)forare.
to punch² vt. prendere a pugni.
punching s. perforazione.
punctilio s. meticolosità.
punctilious agg. meticoloso.
punctual agg. puntuale.
punctuality s. puntualità.
punctually avv. puntualmente.
to punctuate vt. 1. punteggiare 2. (fig.) sottolineare.
punctuation s. punteggiatura.
puncture s. 1. puntura 2. foratura.
to puncture vt. 1. pungere 2. forare.
pungency s. 1. asprezza 2. acutezza (di dolore).
pungent agg. 1. pungente 2. acuto, cocente 3. piccante.
to punish vt. punire.
punishable agg. punibile.
punishment s. punizione.
punitive, punitory agg. punitivo.
punt s. chiatta.

punter *s.* puntatore (*di corse ecc.*).

puny *agg.* sparuto.

pup *s.* cucciolo.

pupil[1] *s.* 1. allievo 2. (*giur.*) pupillo.

pupil[2] *s.* pupilla.

pupil(l)age *s.* (*giur.*) minorità: *child in —*, bambino sotto tutela.

pupil(l)ary *agg.* (*giur.*) pupillare.

puppet *s.* burattino || *— show*, spettacolo di burattini; *— player*, burattinaio.

puppy *s.* cucciolo.

purchase *s.* acquisto.

to purchase *vt.* acquistare.

purchaser *s.* acquirente.

purchasing *s.* acquisto || *— power*, potere di acquisto.

pure *agg.* puro, schietto, casto.

purely *avv.* puramente, semplicemente.

purgative *agg.* purgativo. ◆ **purgative** *s.* purgante.

purgatory *s.* purgatorio.

purge *s.* 1. purga 2. epurazione.

to purge *vt.* 1. purgare 2. epurare. ◆ **to purge** *vi.* purgarsi.

purification *s.* purificazione.

purificatory *agg.* purificatore.

to purify *vt.* purificare.

purism *s.* purismo.

purist *s.* purista.

Puritan *agg. e s.* puritano.

Puritanism *s.* puritanismo.

purity *s.* purezza.

to purloin *vt.* rubare.

purloiner *s.* frodatore.

purple *agg.* 1. purpureo, paonazzo 2. ornato. ◆ **purple** *s.* porpora.

to purple *vt.* imporporare. ◆ **to purple** *vi.* imporpòrarsi.

purport *s.* significato.

to purport *vt.* 1. significare 2. pretendere.

purpose *s.* 1. intenzione, scopo 2. fermezza || *on —*, di proposito.

to purpose *vi.* proporsi (*di*).

purposeful *agg.* 1. premeditato 2. avveduto.

purposefully *avv.* intenzionalmente, espressamente.

purposeless *agg.* 1. inutile 2. senza intenzione.

purpurin *s.* porporina.

to purr *vi.* fare le fusa.

purse *s.* borsellino.

to purse *vt.* contrarre. ◆ **to purse** *vi.* incresparsi, contrarsi.

purser *s.* commissario di bordo.

pursuant *agg.* conforme.

to pursue *vt.* 1. (in)seguire 2. continuare.

pursuer *s.* 1. inseguitore 2. continuatore.

pursuit *s.* 1. inseguimento 2. occupazione, impiego.

purulence *s.* suppurazione.

purulent *agg.* purulento.

push *s.* 1. spinta, influenza, pressione 2. bisogno 3. (*elettr.*) pulsante.

to push *vt.* 1. spingere, incalzare, fare pressione 2. lanciare (*una moda, un articolo ecc.*) ◆ **to push** *vi.* spingersi.

pusher *s.* chi, ciò che spinge.

pusillanimity *s.* pusillanimità.

pusillanimous *agg.* pusillanime.

puss(y) *s.* micino.

pustule *s.* pustola.

to put (put, put) *vt.* 1. mettere, porre 2. esporre, sottoporre || *to — off*, rimandare, togliere (*vestiti ecc.*); *to — on*, indossare, accendere; *to — through*, mettere in comunicazione telefonica; *to — up*, alzare. ◆ **to put (put, put)** *vi.* dirigersi.

putative *agg.* putativo.

putrefaction *s.* putrefazione.

to putrefy *vt.* putrefare. ◆ **to putrefy** *vi.* putrefarsi.

putrescence *s.* putrescenza.

putrescible *agg.* putrescibile.

putrid *agg.* putrido.

putridness *s.* putridità.

puttees *s. pl.* mollettiere.

putty *s.* mastice, stucco.

puzzle *s.* 1. enigma 2. imbarazzo 3. intrigo.

to puzzle *vt.* imbarazzare. ◆ **to puzzle** *vi.* essere imbarazzato.

pygmy *agg. e s.* pigmeo.

pyjamas *s. pl.* pigiama (*sing.*).

pylon *s.* pilone || *steel —*, traliccio.

pylorus *s.* piloro.

pyorrh(o)ea *s.* piorrea.

pyramid *s.* piramide.

pyramidal *agg.* piramidale.

pyre *s.* pira.

pyrites *s.* pirite.

pyrography *s.* pirografia.

pyromancy *s.* piromanzia.

pyromaniac *s.* piromane.

pyrope *s.* piropo.

pyrotechnic(al) *agg.* pirotecnico.

pyrotechnics *s.* pirotecnica.

Pythagorean *agg. e s.* pitagorico.

python *s.* pitone.

pyx *s.* pisside.

Q

quack[1] *s.* ciarlatano.

quack[2] *s.* schiamazzare (*di anitra*).

to **quack**[1] *vi.* fare il ciarlatano.

to **quack**[2] *vi.* schiamazzare (*di anitra*).

quadrangle *s.* quadrangolo.

quadrangular *agg.* quadrangolare.

quadrant *s.* quadrante.

quadrennial *agg.* quadriennale.

quadrilateral *agg.* e *s.* quadrilatero.

quadrille *s.* quadriglia.

quadrumane *s.* quadrumane.

quadrumanous *agg.* quadrumane.

quadruped *agg.* e *s.* quadrupede.

quadruple *agg.* e *s.* quadruplo.

to **quadruple** *vt.* quadruplicare. ♦ to **quadruple** *vi.* quadruplicarsi.

quagmire *s.* pantano.

quail *s.* quaglia.

to **quail** *vi.* avvilirsi, sgomentarsi.

quaint *agg.* strano, bizzarro.

quake *s.* scossa, tremito.

to **quake** *vi.* 1. avere i brividi 2. tremare (*anche di terra*).

Quaker *s.* Quacchero.

quaky *agg.* tremante.

qualifiable *agg.* qualificabile.

qualification *s.* 1. qualificazione, capacità, requisito 2. condizione, riserva 3. qualifica.

qualified *agg.* 1. qualificato, competente 2. limitato || — *acceptance* (*comm.*), accettazione con riserva.

qualifier *s.* (*gramm.*) parola che modifica.

to **qualify** *vt.* 1. qualificare, definire 2. abilitare 3. (*giur.*) autorizzare. ♦ to **qualify** *vi.* 1. qualificarsi 2. abilitarsi.

qualitative *agg.* qualitativo.

quality *s.* qualità, caratteristica.

qualm *s.* 1. nausea 2. scrupolo.

qualmish *agg.* 1. soggetto a nausee 2. nauseante 3. scrupoloso.

quantitative *agg.* quantitativo.

quantity *s.* quantità.

quarantine *s.* quarantena.

quarrel *s.* lite, contesa.

to **quarrel** *vi.* litigare, venire a contesa.

quarreller *s.* attaccabrighe, contendente.

quarrelsome *agg.* attaccabrighe, rissoso.

quarry[1] *s.* 1. cava 2. (*fig.*) fonte d'informazione.

quarry[2] *s.* selvaggina, preda.

to **quarry** *vt.* 1. cavare (*pietre, marmo ecc.*) 2. ricavare informazioni da.

quarter *s.* 1. quarto: *a — of an hour*, un quarto d'ora 2. quartiere, rione. ♦ **quarters** *s. pl.* 1. alloggio 2. (*mil.*) acquartieramento.

to **quarter** *vt.* e *vi.* 1. dividere in quattro parti 2. alloggiare 3. (*mil.*) acquartierarsi.

quarterly *agg.* trimestrale. ♦ **quarterly** *s.* pubblicazione trimestrale. ♦ **quarterly** *avv.* trimestralmente.

quartermaster *s.* 1. commissario 2. quartiermastro.

quartet *s.* quartetto.

quartz *s.* quarzo.

to **quash** *vt.* (*giur.*) annullare.

quaternary *agg.* quaternario.

quatrain *s.* quartina.

quaver *s.* trillo, vibrazione.

to **quaver** *vt.* e *vi.* 1. vibrare, tremare (*di voce*) 2. gorgheggiare.

quay *s.* banchina, molo.

queasy *agg.* 1. nauseabondo 2. schizzinoso.

queen *s.* regina.

queenlike *agg.* regale.

queenly *agg.* regale, da regina.

queer *agg.* strano, eccentrico.

to **queer** *vt.* mettere in ridicolo.

queerly *avv.* stranamente.

to **quench** *vt.* 1. spegnere, estinguere 2. calmare.

quencher *s.* estintore.

quenchless *agg.* inestinguibile.

querulous *agg.* querulo, gemebondo.

query *s.* domanda, quesito.

to **query** *vt.* e *vi.* 1. chiedere, indagare 2. mettere in dubbio.

quest *s.* ricerca.

to **quest** *vt.* e *vi.* cercáre, far ricerche.

question *s.* 1. domanda, interrogazione 2. dubbio, obiezione 3. questione, problema || — *mark*, punto interrogativo.

to **question** *vt.* 1. interrogare 2. mettere in dubbio.

questionable *agg.* incerto, discutibile.

questionably *avv.* discutibilmente.

questionary *s.* questionario.

queue *s.* 1. coda 2. fila di persone: *to stand in a —*, fare la coda.

to **queue** *vt.* e *vi.* fare la coda, mettere in coda.

quibble s. giuoco di parole, doppio senso.

to quibble vi. 1. fare giuochi di parole 2. cavillare.

quibbling agg. a doppio senso.

quick agg. 1. rapido, veloce 2. pronto, intelligente, acuto || — -eyed, dagli occhi penetranti; — -eared, dall'orecchio fino; — -lime, calce viva; — -sighted, dalla vista acuta; — -tempered, irascibile.

to quicken vt. 1. affrettare 2. animare. ♦ **to quicken** vi. 1. affrettarsi 2. animarsi.

quickly avv. rapidamente, prontamente.

quickness s. 1. rapidità 2. vivacità, acutezza.

quicksand s. sabbia mobile.

quickset s. siepe di sempreverdi.

quicksilver s. mercurio, argento vivo (anche fig.).

quickstep s. passo cadenzato.

quickthorn s. biancospino.

quiescence s. quiescenza.

quiescent agg. quiescente.

quiescently avv. tranquillamente.

quiet agg. 1. quieto, tranquillo 2. sobrio, tenue (di colore) 3. docile, dolce.

to quiet vt. acquietare. ♦ **to quiet** vi. acquietarsi.

quietism s. quietismo.

quietist s. quietista.

quietly avv. tranquillamente, con calma.

quietness s. quiete, tranquillità.

quill s. 1. penna, penna d'oca 2. piccolo galleggiante (per canna da pesca).

to quill vt. pieghettare, increspare.

quilt s. trapunta.

to quilt vt. trapuntare.

quince s. cotogna || — jam, marmellata di cotogne.

quinine s. chinino.

quinquennial agg. quinquennale.

quintal s. quintale.

quintessence s. quintessenza.

quintet s. quintetto.

quintuple agg. e s. quintuplo.

to quintuple vt. quintuplicare. ♦ **to quintuple** vi. quintuplicarsi.

quisling s. collaborazionista.

to quit vt. 1. abbandonare, lasciare 2. quietanzare, saldare.

quite avv. 1. completamente, interamente 2. piuttosto, abbastanza || — young, giovanissimo; to be

— well, stare proprio bene.

quiver s. fremito, brivido.

to quiver vt. e vi. 1. tremare, fremere 2. palpitare.

quivering agg. fremente, tremolante. ♦ **quivering** s. tremolio.

quixotic agg. donchisciottesco.

quiz s. (pl. quizzes) burlone.

to quiz vt. burlare.

quotation s. 1. citazione 2. (comm.) quotazione.

quote s. (fam.) citazione. ♦ **quotes** s. pl. virgolette.

to quote vt. 1. citare 2. (comm.) quotare (in borsa).

quotidian agg. quotidiano.

quotient s. quoziente.

R

rabbi s. rabbino.

rabbit s. coniglio.

rabble s. plebaglia.

to rabble vt. assaltare, linciare.

rabid agg. 1. rabbioso 2. irragionevole 3. idrofobo.

rabidity s. 1. rabbia 2. fanatismo.

rabies s. idrofobia.

race[1] s. 1. corso 2. corsa || — -meeting, concorso ippico.

race[2] s. razza.

to race vi. 1. correre 2. imballarsi (di motori) 3. prendere parte a una corsa 4. allevare cavalli da corsa.

racecourse s. ippodromo.

racehorse s. cavallo da corsa.

racer s. 1. corridore 2. cavallo da corsa 3. mezzo da corsa.

racial agg. razziale.

racialism s. razzismo.

racialist s. razzista.

racially avv. dal punto di vista razziale.

racily avv. vivacemente.

raciness s. vivacità.

racing s. corsa || — car, automobile da corsa.

racism s. razzismo.

racist s. razzista.

rack[1] s. 1. rastrelliera 2. reticella portabagagli 3. (mecc.) cremagliera || clothes —, attaccapanni.

rack[2] s. ruota, strumento di tortura.

rack[3] s. nembo, nuvolaglia.

rack[4] s. rovina, distruzione.

to **rack**[1] *vt.* **1.** torturare **2.** pretendere troppo.

to **rack**[2] *vi.* fuggire (*di nubi*).

racket[1] *s.* racchetta.

racket[2] *s.* **1.** fracasso **2.** baldoria **3.** (*gergo*) associazione a delinquere.

racy *agg.* **1.** genuino **2.** vivace, pungente.

radial *agg.* radiale.

radiance *s.* radiosità.

radiant *agg.* **1.** radiante **2.** raggiante.

to **radiate** *vt.* e *vi.* irradiare.

radiation *s.* (ir)radiazione.

radiator *s.* radiatore.

radical *agg.* e *s.* radicale.

radicalism *s.* radicalismo.

radio *s.* radio || — *-beacon*, radiofaro; — *-control*, radiocomando; — *-operator*, radiotelegrafista.

radioactive *agg.* radioattivo.

radioactivity *s.* radioattività.

radioengineering *s.* radiotecnica.

radiogoniometer *s.* radiogoniometro.

radiogram *s.* **1.** marconigramma **2.** radiogrammofono.

radiograph *s.* radiografia.

radiography *s.* radiografia.

radiologist *s.* radiologo.

radiology *s.* radiologia.

radioscopy *s.* radioscopia.

radiostatics *s. pl.* disturbi atmosferici.

radiotelegraphy *s.* radiotelegrafia.

radiotelephony *s.* radiotelefonia.

radiotherapeutics *s.* radioterapia.

radish *s.* ravanello.

radium *s.* radio.

radius *s.* raggio.

raffia *s.* rafia.

raft *s.* zattera || — *-bridge*, ponte di barche.

rag *s.* straccio.

ragamuffin *s.* pezzente.

rage *s.* **1.** furore **2.** passione.

to **rage** *vi.* infuriare || *the plague raged*, la peste infieriva.

ragged *agg.* **1.** lacero **2.** frastagliato **3.** spettinato **4.** rozzo.

raggedly *avv.* **1.** a brandelli **2.** in modo non uniforme.

raggedness *s.* **1.** cenciosità **2.** ineguaglianza.

raging *agg.* furioso.

raid *s.* incursione, scorreria.

to **raid** *vt.* e *vi.* fare un'incursione.

rail, railing *s.* **1.** sbarra **2.** ringhiera **3.** rotaia || *to go by* —, viaggiare per ferrovia.

raillery *s.* canzonatura.

railroad, railway *s.* ferrovia || — *companies*, società ferroviarie.

railwayman *s.* ferroviere.

rain *s.* pioggia || *it looks like* —, vuol piovere; *to be drenched with* —, essere inzuppato || — *-glass*, barometro.

to **rain** *v. imp.* piovere. ♦ to **rain** *vt.* far piovere.

rainbow *s.* arcobaleno.

raincoat *s.* impermeabile.

rainfall *s.* **1.** piovosità **2.** scroscio di pioggia.

rainproof *agg.* impermeabile.

rainy *agg.* piovoso.

raise *s.* aumento.

to **raise** *vt.* **1.** alzare **2.** innalzare **3.** allevare **4.** coltivare **5.** (*mil.*) arruolare.

raisin *s.* uva passa.

raising *s.* **1.** innalzamento **2.** aumento **3.** allevamento **4.** coltivazione **5.** educazione.

rake[1] *s.* rastrello.

rake[2] *s.* inclinazione.

rake[3] *s.* libertino.

to **rake**[1] *vt.* **1.** rastrellare **2.** raschiare || *to* — *up*, ammucchiare.

to **rake**[2] *vi.* essere inclinato.

rally[1] *s.* riunione, raduno.

rally[2] *s.* canzonatura.

to **rally**[1] *vt.* raccogliere. ♦ to **rally** *vi.* rianimarsi.

to **rally**[2] *vt.* canzonare.

ram *s.* **1.** ariete **2.** (*mar.*) sperone.

to **ram** *vt.* **1.** (*mar.*) speronare **2.** conficcare **3.** comprimere.

ramble *s.* vagabondaggio.

to **ramble** *vi.* **1.** vagare **2.** divagare.

rambler *s.* **1.** vagabondo **2.** rampicante.

rambling *agg.* **1.** errante **2.** sconnesso || — *thoughts*, divagazioni.

ramification *s.* ramificazione.

to **ramify** *vt.* ramificare. ♦ to **ramify** *vi.* ramificarsi.

rammer *s.* (*mil.*) pestello.

ramp[1] *s.* rampa.

ramp[2] *s.* (*gergo*) truffa.

rampage *s.* contegno iroso.

rampant *agg.* **1.** rampante **2.** violento **3.** predominante **4.** lussureggiante.

rampart *s.* bastione.

to **rampart** *vt.* fortificare.

ramshackle *agg.* sgangherato, che cade in rovina.

ran V. *to run*.
rancid *agg.* rancido.
rancour *s.* rancore.
rand *s.* soletta (*di scarpa*).
random *agg.* fatto a caso || *at* —, a casaccio.
rang V. *to ring*.
range *s.* 1. fila 2. catena (*di monti*) 3. spazio 4. sfera, raggio 5. gamma 6. fornello 7. (*aer.*) autonomia.
to range *vt.* 1. allineare 2. classificare 3. puntare. ◆ to range *vi.* 1. vagare 2. avere una portata di 3. oscillare (*di prezzi*).
ranger *s.* 1. guardia forestale 2. vagabondo.
rank *agg.* 1. rigoglioso 2. volgare 3. puzzolente. ◆ rank *s.* 1. fila 2. rango, grado 3. truppa.
to rank *vi.* 1. schierarsi 2. essere classificato.
to ransack *vt.* 1. frugare 2. saccheggiare.
ransom *s.* riscatto.
to ransom *vt.* riscattare.
to rant *vt. e vi.* declamare.
rap *s.* colpo.
to rap *vt. e vi.* 1. battere 2. bussare.
rapacious *agg.* rapace.
rapacity *s.* rapacità.
rape[1] *s.* violenza carnale.
rape[2] *s.* rapa.
to rape *vt.* violentare.
rapid *agg.* rapido. ◆ rapid *s.* rapida.
rapidity *s.* rapidità.
rapt *agg.* rapito.
raptorial *agg.* rapace.
rapture *s.* rapimento.
rare *agg.* 1. raro 2. rarefatto.
rarefaction *s.* rarefazione.
to rarefy *vt.* 1. rarefare 2. raffinare. ◆ to rarefy *vi.* rarefarsi.
rarely *avv.* 1. raramente 2. in modo eccellente.
rareness, rarity *s.* 1. rarità 2. rarefazione.
rascal *s.* furfante.
rascalism, rascality *s.* furfanteria.
rash *agg.* avventato. ◆ rash *s.* eruzione cutanea.
rashness *s.* avventatezza.
rasp *s.* 1. raspa 2. stridore.
to rasp *vt.* 1. raspare 2. irritare.
raspberry *s.* lampone.
rasping *agg.* stridente.
rat *s.* 1. topo 2. (*fig.*) traditore.
rate *s.* 1. tasso, quota 2. tassa 3. prezzo, tariffa 4. ritmo, andamento

|| *first* —, di prim'ordine; — *of discount*, tasso di sconto.
to rate[1] *vt.* 1. stimare 2. tassare 3. classificare.
to rate[2] *vt.* redarguire.
rateable *agg.* soggetto ad imposta.
ratepayer *s.* contribuente.
rather *avv.* piuttosto || *I had* —, preferirei; *I would* — *not*, non ci tengo.
ratification *s.* ratifica.
to ratify *vt.* ratificare.
rating[1] *s.* 1. stima 2. tassa 3. classificazione.
rating[2] *s.* sgridata.
ratio *s.* rapporto.
ration *s.* razione.
to ration *vt.* razionare.
rational *agg.* razionale.
rationalism *s.* razionalismo.
rationalist *s.* razionalista.
rationality *s.* razionalità.
to rationalize *vt.* 1. razionalizzare 2. spiegare razionalmente.
rationally *avv.* razionalmente.
rattle *s.* 1. sonaglio 2. rantolo 3. tintinnio.
to rattle *vt.* far risuonare. ◆ to rattle *vi.* 1. risuonare 2. cianciare.
rattling *agg.* 1. vivace 2. tintinnante.
ravage *s.* rovina.
to ravage *vt.* devastare.
rave *s.* delirio.
to rave *vt.* declamare. ◆ to rave *vi.* delirare || *to* — *about sthg.*, andar pazzo per qc.
ravel *s.* 1. groviglio 2. lembo sfilacciato.
to ravel *vt.* ingarbugliare. ◆ to ravel *vi.* sfilacciarsi.
raven *s.* corvo.
to raven *vt. e vi.* saccheggiare.
ravenous *agg.* vorace.
ravine *s.* burrone.
raving *agg.* delirante. ◆ raving *s.* delirio.
to ravish *vt.* 1. rapire 2. violentare.
ravisher *s.* rapitore.
ravishing *agg.* (*fig.*) affascinante.
ravishment *s.* 1. rapimento 2. stupro.
raw *agg.* 1. crudo 2. greggio 3. inesperto 4. a nudo. ◆ raw *s.* punto vivo.
rawness *s.* 1. crudezza 2. rozzezza 3. inesperienza 4. escoriazione.
ray[1] *s.* 1. raggio 2. lampo.

ray² s. (zool.) razza.
to ray vt. irradiare. ♦ **to ray** vi. irradiarsi.
to raze vt. radere al suolo.
razor s. rasoio || — -blade, lametta.
to reabsorb vt. riassorbire.
reach s. 1. portata 2. penetrazione || beyond my —, irraggiungibile.
to reach vt. 1. raggiungere 2. porgere. ♦ **to reach** vi. estendersi.
to react vi. reagire.
reaction s. reazione.
reactionary agg. e s. reazionario.
reactive agg. reattivo.
read agg. colto. ♦ **read** s. lettura.
to read (read, read) vt. 1. leggere 2. interpretare 3. segnare || to — over, rileggere; to — through, esaminare.
readable agg. 1. leggibile 2. interessante.
reader s. 1. lettore 2. libro di lettura.
readily avv. prontamente.
readiness s. prontezza.
reading s. 1. lettura 2. interpretazione || — -desk, leggio.
to readjust vt. riaggiustare.
readjustment s. riordinamento.
to readmit vt. riammettere.
readmittance s. riammissione.
ready agg. pronto || — -made, confezionato; — money, contanti; — -made clothes, abito preconfezionato; — -built, prefabbricato.
to ready vt. preparare.
to reaffirm vt. riaffermare.
reafforestation s. rimboschimento.
reagent s. reagente.
real agg. e s. reale || — estate, beni immobili (pl.).
realism s. realismo.
realist s. realista.
realistic agg. realistico.
reality s. 1. realtà 2. realismo.
realizable agg. realizzabile.
realization s. 1. realizzazione 2. percezione.
to realize vt. 1. accorgersi di 2. realizzare 3. capire.
really avv. realmente.
realm s. reame.
realty s. beni immobili (pl.).
ream s. (tip.) risma.
to reap vt. 1. mietere 2. fare il raccolto (anche fig.).
reaper s. mietitore.
reaping s. mietitura.

to reappear vi. riapparire.
to reappoint vt. rinominare.
rear agg. posteriore. ♦ **rear** s. 1. retroguardia 2. retro.
to rear vt. 1. alzare, innalzare 2. allevare 3. coltivare.
to rearm vt. riarmare.
rearmament s. riarmo.
to rearrange vt. riordinare.
rearrangement s. riordinamento.
reason s. 1. ragione 2. causa, motivo 3. raziocinio.
to reason vt. e vi. 1. ragionare 2. persuadere || to — about a subject, discutere di un argomento.
reasonable agg. ragionevole.
reasonableness s. ragionevolezza.
reasonably avv. ragionevolmente.
reasoning s. ragionamento.
to reassert vt. riasserire.
reassurance s. rassicurazione.
to reassure vt. rassicurare.
to reawaken vt. risvegliare. ♦ **to reawaken** vi. risvegliarsi.
rebate s. riduzione, sconto.
rebel agg. e s. ribelle.
to rebel vi. ribellarsi.
rebellion s. ribellione.
rebellious agg. ribelle.
to rebind (rebound, rebound) vt. rilegare (un libro).
rebirth s. rinascita.
reborn agg. rinato.
rebound¹ V. to rebind.
rebound² s. rimbalzo.
to rebound vi. rimbalzare.
rebuff s. diniego, mortificazione.
to rebuild (rebuilt, rebuilt) vt. ricostruire.
rebuke s. rimprovero.
to rebuke vt. rimproverare.
to rebut vt. respingere, rifiutare.
recalcitrant agg. recalcitrante.
to recalcitrate vi. recalcitrare.
recall s. 1. richiamo 2. revoca.
to recall vt. 1. richiamare 2. rievocare, far tornare alla memoria.
to recant vt. e vi. ritrattare.
recantation s. ritrattazione.
to recapitulate vt. e vi. ricapitolare.
recapitulation s. ricapitolazione.
recapture s. riconquista.
to recapture vt. riconquistare.
recast s. nuova forma.
to recast (recast, recast) vt. 1. rifondere 2. rimaneggiare.
to recede vi. 1. indietreggiare 2. diminuire.

receding agg. 1. rientrante 2. sfuggente.

receipt s. 1. ricevimento 2. ricevuta 3. ricetta.

to receipt vt. quietanzare.

to receive vt. 1. ricevere 2. accettare.

receiver s. 1. ricevitore 2. (giur.) ricettatore.

receiving s. ricezione.

recension s. revisione.

recent agg. recente.

receptacle s. ricettacolo.

reception s. 1. ricevimento 2. ricezione 3. accoglienza.

receptive agg. ricettivo.

receptivity s. ricettività.

recess s. 1. intervallo 2. rientranza 3. recesso.

recession s. 1. ritiro 2. recessione.

recessive agg. retrocedente.

recharge s. ricarica.

to recharge vt. ricaricare.

to rechristen vt. ribattezzare.

recidivism s. recidività.

recipe s. ricetta.

recipient agg. e s. ricevente.

reciprocal agg. reciproco. ♦ **reciprocal** s. (mat.) numero reciproco.

to reciprocate vt. 1. contraccambiare 2. muovere alternativamente. ♦ **to reciprocate** vi. muoversi alternativamente.

reciprocating agg. (mecc.) alternativo.

reciprocation s. 1. moto alterno 2. scambio.

reciprocity s. reciprocità.

recital s. 1. relazione 2. recitazione.

recitation s. 1. recitazione 2. recita 3. narrazione.

recitative agg. e s. recitativo.

to recite vt. 1. recitare 2. riferire.

reckless agg. incurante.

recklessness s. noncuranza.

to reckon vt. 1. contare, computare 2. considerare.

reckoner s. calcolatore.

reckoning s. conto.

reclaim s. rivendicazione.

to reclaim vt. 1. redimere 2. bonificare 3. rivendicare.

reclamation s. 1. redenzione 2. bonifica 3. rivendicazione.

to recline vt. chinare. ♦ **to recline** vi. chinarsi.

reclining agg. chinato.

recluse agg. recluso. ♦ **recluse** s. eremita.

reclusion s. 1. reclusione 2. eremo.

recognition s. riconoscimento.

recognizable agg. riconoscibile.

to recognize vt. riconoscere.

recoil s. 1. il ritrarsi 2. rinculo.

to recoil vi. 1. ritrarsi 2. ricadere 3. rinculare.

to recollect vt. 1. raccogliere 2. ricordare || to — oneself, riaversi.

recollection s. ricordo.

to recommence vt. e vi. ricominciare.

to recommend vt. raccomandare.

recommendation s. raccomandazione.

recommendatory agg. raccomandatorio.

recompense s. 1. ricompensa 2. risarcimento.

to recompense vt. 1. ricompensare 2. risarcire.

to recompose vt. ricomporre.

recomposition s. ricomposizione.

to reconcile vt. (ri)conciliare || to — oneself, rassegnarsi.

reconcilement s. 1. riconciliazione 2. rassegnazione.

reconnaissance s. ricognizione.

to reconnoitre vt. e vi. perlustrare.

to reconquer vt. riconquistare.

reconquest s. riconquista.

to reconsider vt. riconsiderare.

reconsideration s. revisione.

reconstitute vt. ricostituire.

to reconstruct vt. ricostruire.

reconstruction s. ricostruzione.

reconversion s. riconversione.

to reconvert vt. riconvertire.

record s. 1. registrazione 2. documento 3. passato 4. disco || — player, giradischi.

to record vt. registrare.

recorder s. 1. cancelliere 2. registratore 3. archivista || tape —, magnetofono.

recording s. registrazione.

recordist s. (cine) tecnico del suono.

recourse s. ricorso.

to recover vt. ricuperare, riacquistare, riscoprire. ♦ **to recover** vi. ristabilirsi.

recoverable agg. 1. ricuperabile 2. guaribile.

recovery s. 1. recupero 2. guarigione 3. (giur.) rivendicazione.

to recreate vt. divertire. ♦ **to recreate** vi. divertirsi.

to re-create vt. ricreare.

recreation s. ricreazione.

recreative *agg.* ricreativo.

to recriminate *vi.* recriminare.

recrimination *s.* recriminazione.

recrudescence *s.* recrudescenza.

recrudescent *agg.* che rincrudisce.

recruit *s.* recluta.

to recruit *vt.* 1. reclutare 2. rinforzare. ◆ to recruit *vi.* ristabilirsi.

recruitment *s.* reclutamento.

rectangle *s.* rettangolo.

rectangular *agg.* rettangolare.

rectification *s.* rettificazione.

rectifier *s.* (*mecc.*) rettificatrice.

to rectify *vt.* rettificare.

rectilineal *agg.* rettilineo.

rectitude *s.* rettitudine.

rector *s.* 1. rettore 2. parroco.

rectorate *s.* rettorato.

rectorship *s.* rettorato.

rectory *s.* 1. presbiterio 2. (*eccl.*) beneficio.

to recur *vi.* ritornare.

recurrence *s.* ricorso.

recurrent *agg.* ricorrente.

recusant *agg.* e *s.* dissidente.

red *agg.* e *s.* rosso || — -*hot*, rovente; — -*lead*, minio; — -*letter day*, giorno festivo. ◆ Reds *s. pl.* comunisti.

to redact *vt.* 1. redigere 2. revisionare.

redactor *s.* redattore.

to redden *vt.* arrossare. ◆ to redden *vi.* arrossire.

reddish *agg.* rossiccio.

to redeem *vt.* 1. riscattare 2. ricuperare 3. estinguere: *to — a mortgage*, estinguere un'ipoteca.

redeemable *agg.* 1. riscattabile 2. ricuperabile.

redeemer *s.* redentore.

redemption *s.* 1. redenzione 2. (*comm.*) rimborso 3. (*giur.*) riscatto.

redness *s.* rossore.

to redouble *vt.* e *vi.* raddoppiare.

redress *s.* riparazione.

to redress *vt.* riparare, rimediare.

redskin *agg.* e *s.* pellerossa.

to reduce *vt.* 1. ridurre 2. degradare.

reduced *agg.* ridotto.

reducer *s.* riduttore.

reduction *s.* 1. riduzione 2. degradazione.

redundance *s.* sovrabbondanza.

redundant *agg.* ridondante.

redwood *s.* sequoia.

to re-echo *vt.* e *vi.* riecheggiare.

reed *s.* canna || *broken* —, persona infida; — -*pipe*, zampogna.

re-edification *s.* riedificazione.

to re-edify *vt.* riedificare.

to re-educate *vt.* rieducare.

reef *s.* secca || *coral-* —, banco di coralli.

to reek *vi.* puzzare. ◆ to reek *vt.* trasudare.

reel *s.* 1. bobina 2. giro vorticoso || *news-* —, cinegiornale.

to reel *vt.* avvolgere || *to — off*, snocciolare. ◆ to reel *vi.* girare.

to re-elect *vt.* rieleggere.

to re-emerge *vi.* riemergere.

to re-enact *vt.* richiamare in vigore (*una legge*).

to re-enter *vt.* rientrare.

re-entrance *s.* rientro.

re-entry *s.* 1. rientro 2. nuova registrazione.

to re-establish *vt.* ristabilire.

re-establishment *s.* ristabilimento.

re-examination *s.* riesame.

to re-examine *vt.* riesaminare.

refectory *s.* refettorio.

to refer *vt.* 1. attribuire 2. rimandare. ◆ to refer *vi.* 1. riferirsi 2. rivolgersi.

referable *agg.* riferibile.

referee *s.* arbitro.

to referee *vt.* e *vi.* arbitrare.

reference *s.* 1. riferimento 2. consultazione 3. referenza 4. (*giur.*) rinvio.

referential *agg.* riferentesi a.

refill *s.* ricambio.

to refill *vt.* riempire di nuovo.

to refine *vt.* raffinare. ◆ to refine *vi.* raffinarsi.

refined *agg.* 1. raffinato 2. colto.

refinement *s.* 1. raffinamento 2. raffinatezza.

refiner *s.* raffinatore.

refinery *s.* raffineria.

refit *s.* riparazione.

to refit *vt.* riparare.

to reflect *vt.* e *vi* 1. riflettere 2. meditare.

reflection *s.* 1. riflessione, riflesso 2. biasimo || *to cast reflections on so.*, criticare qu.

reflective *agg.* riflessivo.

reflector *s.* riflettore.

reflex *agg.* e *s.* riflesso.

reflorescence *s.* rifioritura.

reflux *s.* riflusso.

reform *s.* riforma.

to reform *vt.* riformare.

reformation *s.* riforma.

reformational agg. di riforma.

reformatory agg. riformativo. ◆ **reformatory** s. riformatorio.

reformer s. riformatore.

to **refract** vt. rifrangere.

refraction s. rifrazione.

refractivity s. rifrangibilità.

refractor s. rifrattore.

refractory agg. 1. refrattario 2. ostinato.

refrain s. ritornello.

to **refrain** vi. trattenersi, astenersi.

to **refresh** vt. 1. rinfrescare 2. rinvigorire. ◆ to **refresh** vi. 1. rinvigorirsi 2. rifornirsi.

refreshment s. ristoro. ◆ **refreshments** s. pl. cibo, bevanda (sing.).

refrigerant agg. e s. refrigerante.

to **refrigerate** vt. refrigerare.

refrigeration s. refrigerazione.

refrigerator s. frigorifero.

refrigeratory agg. refrigerante.

to **refuel** vt. rifornire di carburante. ◆ to **refuel** vi. rifornirsi di carburante.

refuge s. rifugio.

refugee s. rifugiato, profugo.

refulgence s. fulgore.

refulgent agg. rifulgente.

refund s. rimborso.

to **refund** vt. rimborsare.

refusable agg. rifiutabile.

refusal s. 1. rifiuto 2. diritto di opzione.

refuse s. rifiuto.

to **refuse** vt. rifiutare. ◆ to **refuse** vi. rifiutarsi.

refuser s. ricusante.

refutal s. confutazione.

to **refute** vt. confutare.

to **regain** vt. riguadagnare.

regal agg. regale.

regality s. regalità.

regally avv. regalmente.

regard s. 1. considerazione 2. sguardo || **with — to**, riguardo a. ◆ **regards** s. pl. saluti.

to **regard** vt. 1. considerare 2. riguardare 3. osservare.

regardful agg. 1. attento 2. rispettoso.

regardless agg. senza riguardo. ◆ **regardless** avv. senza riguardo a, senza badare a.

regatta s. regata.

regelation s. ricongelamento.

regency s. reggenza.

to **regenerate** vt. rigenerare. ◆ to **regenerate** vi. rigenerarsi.

regeneration s. rigenerazione.

regenerative agg. rigeneratore.

regenerator s. rigeneratore.

regent agg. e s. reggente.

regicide s. 1. regicida 2. regicidio.

regimen s. regime.

regiment s. reggimento.

to **regiment** vt. 1. irreggimentare 2. disciplinare.

regimental agg. reggimentale.

regimentals s. pl. (mil.) uniforme (sing.).

region s. regione.

regional agg. regionale.

register s. registro.

to **register** vt. registrare, iscrivere. ◆ to **register** vi. iscriversi.

registrar s. 1. segretario 2. ufficiale di stato civile.

registration s. registrazione, iscrizione.

registry s. 1. registrazione 2. ufficio del Registro.

regnant agg. regnante.

regress s. retrocessione.

to **regress** vi. retrocedere.

regression s. regresso.

regressive agg. regressivo.

regret s. rammarico.

to **regret** vt. 1. rimpiangere 2. rammaricarsi di.

regretful agg. pieno di rammarico.

regular agg. e s. regolare.

regularity s. regolarità.

regularization s. regolarizzazione.

to **regularize** vt. regolarizzare.

regularly avv. regolarmente.

to **regulate** vt. regolare.

regulation s. 1. regolamento 2. regolazione.

regulative agg. e s. regolatore.

regulator s. regolatore.

to **rehabilitate** vt. 1. riabilitare 2. ripristinare.

rehabilitation s. 1. riabilitazione 2. ripristino.

rehearsal s. 1. ripetizione 2. (teat.) prova.

to **rehearse** vt. 1. ripetere 2. provare.

reign s. regno.

to **reign** vi. regnare.

to **reimburse** vt. rimborsare.

reimbursement s. rimborso.

rein s. redine.

to **rein** vt. tenere a freno.

to **reincarnate** vt. reincarnare.

reincarnation s. reincarnazione.

reindeer s. renna.

to **reinforce** *vt.* rinforzare.
reinforce(ment) *s.* rinforzo.
to **reinstate** *vt.* ristabilire.
to **reintegrate** *vt.* reintegrare.
reinvestment *s.* nuovo investimento.
to **reinvigorate** *vt.* rinvigorire.
reinvigoration *s.* rinvigorimento.
to **reiterate** *vt.* reiterare.
reiteration *s.* reiterazione.
reject *s.* persona, cosa rifiutata.
to **reject** *vt.* rifiutare.
rejection *s.* rifiuto.
to **rejoice** *vt.* rallegrare. ♦ to **rejoice** *vi.* rallegrarsi.
rejoicing *s.* **1.** allegria **2.** festa.
rejuvenation *s.* ringiovanimento.
relapse *s.* ricaduta.
to **relapse** *vi.* **1.** ricadere **2.** avere una ricaduta.
to **relate** *vt.* **1.** narrare **2.** mettere in relazione. ♦ to **relate** *vi.* aver rapporto con.
relater *s.* narratore.
relation *s.* **1.** relazione **2.** parente.
relationship *s.* **1.** relazione **2.** parentela.
relative *agg.* relativo. ♦ **relative** *s.* parente.
relativism *s.* relativismo.
relativity *s.* relatività.
to **relax** *vt.* **1.** rilassare **2.** allentare. ♦ to **relax** *vi.* rilassarsi.
relaxation *s.* **1.** rilassamento **2.** svago **3.** mitigazione.
relay *s.* **1.** turno **2.** ricambio **3.** (*radio*) collegamento.
to **relay** *vt.* (*radio*) collegare.
release *s.* **1.** liberazione **2.** quietanza **3.** cessione **4.** scarico.
to **release** *vt.* **1.** liberare **2.** cedere.
releasee *s.* cessionario.
to **relegate** *vt.* **1.** relegare **2.** rimettere.
relegation *s.* relegazione.
relentless *agg.* inflessibile.
to **relent** *vi.* impietosirsi.
relevance *s.* **1.** relazione **2.** pertinenza.
relevant *agg.* **1.** relativo **2.** pertinente.
reliability *s.* attendibilità.
reliable *agg.* attendibile, fidato.
reliance *s.* **1.** fede **2.** persona, cosa di fiducia.
relic *s.* reliquia.
relief[1] *s.* **1.** sollievo **2.** aiuto **3.** esenzione **4.** cambio.
relief[2] *s.* **1.** rilievo **2.** (*pitt.*) pro-

spettiva.
to **relieve** *vt.* **1.** alleviare, sollevare **2.** aiutare **3.** dare il cambio a **4.** dare rilievo a.
reliever *s.* soccorritore.
relieving *agg.* **1.** che allevia, soccorre **2.** (*mil.*) che dà il cambio.
religion *s.* religione.
religiosity *s.* religiosità.
religious *agg.* e *s.* religioso.
to **relinquish** *vt.* abbandonare.
relinquishment *s.* abbandono.
reliquary *s.* reliquario.
reliques *s. pl.* resti.
relish *s.* **1.** gusto **2.** sapore, profumo, aroma **3.** condimento.
to **relish** *vt.* **1.** gustare **2.** insaporire.
to **relive** *vt.* e *vi.* rivivere.
to **reload** *vt.* ricaricare.
to **reluct** *vi.* essere riluttante.
reluctance *s.* riluttanza.
reluctant *agg.* riluttante.
reluctantly *avv.* con riluttanza.
to **rely** *vi.* fidarsi.
remade V. to **remake**.
to **remain** *vi.* rimanere, restare.
remainder *s.* resto, avanzo, rimanenza.
remains *s. pl.* resti.
to **remake (remade, remade)** *vt.* rifare.
remark *s.* nota, osservazione, commento.
to **remark** *vt.* e *vi.* osservare.
remarkable *agg.* notevole.
remarkableness *s.* ragguardevolezza.
remarkably *avv.* notevolmente.
to **remarry** *vt.* risposare. ♦ to **remarry** *vi.* risposarsi.
remediable *agg.* rimediabile.
remedy *s.* rimedio, cura.
to **remedy** *vt.* rimediare.
to **remember** *vt.* ricordare. ♦ to **remember** *vi.* ricordarsi.
remembrance *s.* ricordo.
to **remind** *vt.* ricordare (*qc. a qu.*), far ricordare, rammentare.
reminder *s.* ricordo, promemoria.
remindful *agg.* **1.** memore **2.** che fa ricordare.
reminiscence *s.* ricordo.
reminiscent *agg.* che ricorda.
remise *s.* (*giur.*) cessione.
to **remise** *vt.* (*giur.*) rinunciare a, cedere (*diritti ecc.*).
remiss *agg.* negligente.
remissible *agg.* remissibile.

remission s. **1.** remissione **2.** esonero, annullamento **3.** (*med.*) remissione.

remissive *agg.* indulgente.

to **remit** *vt.* rimettere. ♦ to **remit** *vi.* diminuire, mitigarsi.

remittal s. (*giur.*) remissione (*condono*).

remittance s. rimessa (*di denaro*).

remittent *agg.* (*med.*) intermittente.

remnant *agg.* rimanente. ♦ **remnant** s. resto, rimanenza, avanzo.

to **remodel** *vt.* rimodellare.

remonstrance s. rimostranza.

to **remonstrate** *vi.* protestare.

remonstration s. rimostranza.

remorse s. rimorso.

remorseful *agg.* pieno di rimorso.

remorseless *agg.* senza rimorsi.

remote *agg.* remoto.

remoteness s. distanza, lontananza.

remotion s. rimozione, allontanamento.

remount s. rimonta (*di cavalli*).

to **remount** *vt.* e *vi.* **1.** rimontare (*a cavallo, in bicicletta*) **2.** risalire.

removable *agg.* rimovibile.

removal s. **1.** rimozione **2.** trasferimento, trasloco.

remove s. **1.** trasferimento **2.** grado (*di parentela*).

to **remove** *vt.* rimuovere. ♦ to **remove** *vi.* trasferirsi.

removed *agg.* lontano.

remover s. chi, ciò che toglie.

to **remunerate** *vt.* rimunerare.

remuneration s. rimunerazione.

remunerative *agg.* rimunerativo.

renaissance s. rinascimento.

renal *agg.* renale.

to **rename** *vt.* rinominare.

to **rend (rent, rent)** *vt.* lacerare. ♦ to **rend (rent, rent)** *vi.* lacerarsi.

to **render** *vt.* **1.** rendere **2.** consegnare.

rendering s. **1.** restituzione **2.** resa.

renegade s. rinnegato.

to **renew** *vt.* rinnovare. ♦ to **renew** *vi.* rinnovarsi.

renewable *agg.* rinnovabile.

renewal s. **1.** rinnovo **2.** ripresa.

renewer s. rinnovatore.

renitency s. riluttanza.

renitent *agg.* renitente, riluttante.

rennet s. ranetta.

to **renounce** *vt.* **1.** rinunciare a **2.** ripudiare.

renouncement s. rinuncia.

to **renovate** *vt.* rinnovare.

renown s. rinomanza, fama.

renowned *agg.* rinomato, famoso.

rent[1] s. affitto.

rent[2] s. **1.** strappo, squarcio **2.** spaccatura.

rent[3] V. to *rend*.

to **rent** *vt.* affittare. ♦ to **rent** *vi.* essere affittato.

rental s. affitto.

renunciation s. rinuncia.

to **reoccupy** *vt.* rioccupare.

to **reopen** *vt.* riaprire. ♦ to **reopen** *vi.* riaprirsi.

reopening s. riapertura.

reorganization s. riassetto, riorganizzazione.

repaid V. to *repay*.

repair s. **1.** riparazione, restaurazione **2.** stato, condizione.

to **repair** *vt.* riparare, restaurare.

repairer s. riparatore.

reparation s. riparazione.

repartee s. replica arguta.

repartition s. ripartizione.

to **repatriate** *vt.* e *vi.* rimpatriare.

repatriation s. rimpatrio.

to **repay (repaid, repaid)** *vt.* ripagare.

repayable *agg.* ripagabile.

repeal s. revoca.

to **repeal** *vt.* revocare.

repealer s. revocatore.

repeat s. ripetizione.

to **repeat** *vt.* ripetere. ♦ to **repeat** *vi.* ripetersi.

repeater s. **1.** ripetitore **2.** ripetente **3.** arma a ripetizione.

repeating *agg.* **1.** a ripetizione **2.** periodico (*di numero*).

to **repel** *vt.* respingere.

repellent *agg.* repellente.

to **repent** *vt.* e *vi.* pentirsi.

repentance s. pentimento.

repentant *agg.* pentito.

repenter s. penitente.

repercussion s. ripercussione.

repercussive *agg.* ripercussivo.

repertoire s. repertorio.

repertory s. **1.** repertorio **2.** raccolta.

repetition s. ripetizione.

to **repine** *vi.* lamentarsi.

to **replace** *vt.* **1.** ricollocare **2.** rimpiazzare, sostituire.

replaceable *agg.* sostituibile.

replacement s. **1.** ricollocamento **2.** sostituzione.

replete *agg.* pieno.
repletion *s.* pienezza.
replication *s.* replica.
reply *s.* risposta.
to **reply** *vi.* rispondere.
report *s.* **1.** diceria **2.** reputazione **3.** rapporto **4.** scoppio.
to **report** *vt.* riportare. ♦ to **report** *vi.* **1.** stendere rapporto **2.** fare il cronista **3.** presentarsi.
reporter *s.* cronista (*di giornale*).
to **repose** *vt.* porre. ♦ to **repose** *vi.* riposare.
to **reprehend** *vt.* rimproverare.
reprehensible *agg.* biasimevole.
reprehension *s.* biasimo.
to **represent** *vt.* rappresentare, raffigurare.
representation *s.* **1.** rappresentazione **2.** rappresentanza.
representative *agg.* rappresentativo. ♦ **representative** *s.* rappresentante.
to **repress** *vt.* reprimere.
repressed *agg.* represso.
repressible *agg.* reprimibile.
repression *s.* repressione.
repressive *agg.* repressivo.
reprimand *s.* rimprovero.
reprint *s.* ristampa.
to **reprint** *vt.* ristampare.
reprisal *s.* rappresaglia.
reproach *s.* **1.** rimprovero **2.** discredito.
to **reproach** *vt.* **1.** rimproverare **2.** discreditare.
reproachable *agg.* riprovevole.
reproachful *agg.* di rimprovero.
reprobate *agg.* corrotto. ♦ **reprobate** *s.* reprobo.
to **reprobate** *vt.* **1.** riprovare **2.** dannare.
reprobation *s.* **1.** riprovazione **2.** dannazione.
to **reproduce** *vt.* riprodurre. ♦ to **reproduce** *vi.* riprodursi.
reproducer *s.* riproduttore.
reproducible *agg.* riproducibile.
reproduction *s.* riproduzione.
reproductive *agg.* riproduttivo.
reproof *s.* rimprovero.
to **reprove** *vt.* rimproverare.
reptile *agg.* strisciante. ♦ **reptile** *s.* rettile.
republic *s.* repubblica.
republican *agg.* e *s.* repubblicano.
republication *s.* ripubblicazione.
to **republish** *vt.* ripubblicare.
to **repudiate** *vt.* ripudiare.

repudiation *s.* ripudio.
repugnance *s.* **1.** ripugnanza **2.** incompatibilità.
repugnant *agg.* **1.** ripugnante **2.** incompatibile.
repulse *s.* ripulsa, rifiuto.
to **repulse** *vt.* respingere.
repulsion *s.* repulsione.
repulsive *agg.* ripulsivo.
reputable *agg.* onorato.
reputation *s.* reputazione.
repute *s.* fama.
to **repute** *vt.* reputare.
reputed *agg.* **1.** supposto **2.** putativo.
request *s.* richiesta.
to **request** *vt.* (ri)chiedere.
to **require** *vt.* **1.** richiedere **2.** ordinare, obbligare.
requirement *s.* **1.** richiesta **2.** requisito.
requisite *agg.* richiesto. ♦ **requisite** *s.* requisito.
requisition *s.* **1.** richiesta **2.** requisito **3.** requisizione.
to **requisition** *vt.* requisire.
requital *s.* **1.** contraccambio **2.** ricompensa.
to **requite** *vt.* **1.** ricompensare **2.** contraccambiare.
to **reread** (**reread, reread**) *vt.* rileggere.
to **rescind** *vt.* rescindere.
rescission *s.* rescissione.
rescue *s.* **1.** liberazione **2.** soccorso.
to **rescue** *vt.* **1.** liberare **2.** riacquistare **3.** soccorrere.
research *s.* ricerca || — **work**, lavoro di ricerca.
to **research** *vi.* fare ricerche.
researcher *s.* ricercatore.
to **resell** (**resold, resold**) *vt.* rivendere.
resemblance *s.* rassomiglianza.
to **resemble** *vt.* assomigliare a.
to **resent** *vt.* risentirsi di.
resentful *agg.* **1.** risentito **2.** permaloso.
resentment *s.* risentimento.
reservation *s.* **1.** riserva **2.** prenotazione.
reserve *s.* **1.** riserva **2.** riserbo.
to **reserve** *vt.* riservare.
reservoir *s.* serbatoio.
to **reset** (**reset, reset**) *vt.* **1.** rimettere a posto **2.** (*tip.*) ricomporre.
to **resettle** *vt.* risistemare. ♦ to **resettle** *vi.* risistemarsi.
resettlement *s.* risistemazione.

to **reshape** vt. dare nuova forma a.
to **reside** vi. risiedere.
residence s. residenza.
resident agg. e s. residente.
residential agg. residenziale.
residual agg. residuo. ♦ **residual**
s. 1. residuo 2. resto.
residue s. residuo, avanzo.
to **resign** vt. 1. consegnare 2. ri-
nunciare || to — oneself, rasse-
gnarsi. ♦ to **resign** vi. dimettersi.
resignation s. 1. dimissioni (pl.)
2. rinuncia 3. rassegnazione.
resigned agg. rassegnato.
resilience, resiliency s. elasticità.
resilient agg. elastico.
resin s. resina.
resinous agg. resinoso.
resipiscence s. resipiscenza.
resipiscent agg. resipiscente.
resist s. sostanza protettiva.
to **resist** vt. e vi. resistere.
resistance s. resistenza.
resistant, resistent agg. resistente.
resistive agg. resistente.
resold V. to **resell**.
to **resole** vt. risolare.
resolubile agg. (ri)solubile.
resolute agg. risoluto.
resoluteness s. risolutezza.
resolution s. 1. risolutezza 2. risoluzione 3. scissione.
resolutive agg. risolutivo.
resolvable agg. risolvibile.
resolve s. risoluzione.
to **resolve** vt. 1. risolvere 2. scindere. ♦ to **resolve** vi. risolversi.
resolvent agg. e s. solvente.
resonance s. risonanza.
resonant agg. risonante.
to **resorb** vt. riassorbire.
resorbent agg. riassorbente.
resort s. 1. ricorso 2. risorsa 3. ritrovo 4. luogo di soggiorno.
to **resort** vi. 1. ricorrere 2. recarsi.
to **resound** vi. risonare. ♦ to **resound** vt. proclamare.
resource s. risorsa.
resourceful agg. pieno di risorse.
resourceless agg. senza risorse.
respect s. 1. rispetto, stima 2. aspetto 3. punto di vista.
to **respect** vt. rispettare.
respectability s. 1. rispettabilità 2.
convenzioni sociali (pl.).
respectable agg. rispettabile.
respectful agg. rispettoso.
respecting prep. rispetto a.
respective agg. rispettivo.

respiration s. respirazione.
respirator s. respiratore.
respiratory agg. respiratorio.
respite s. 1. dilazione 2. tregua.
to **respite** vt. concedere una dilazione, una tregua a.
resplendent agg. risplendente.
respond s. responsorio.
to **respond** vi. rispondere.
respondence s. rispondenza.
respondent agg. 1. rispondente 2.
sensibile. ♦ **respondent** s. (giur.)
convenuto.
response s. risposta.
responsibility s. responsabilità.
responsible agg. 1. responsabile 2.
di responsabilità.
responsive agg. rispondente.
responsory s. responsorio.
rest[1] s. 1. riposo 2. appoggio.
rest[2] s. resto, residuo.
to **rest** vt. 1. riposare 2. appoggiare.
♦ to **rest** vi. 1. riposarsi 2. appoggiarsi.
to **restate** vt. riesporre.
restaurant s. ristorante || — -car,
vagone ristorante.
restful agg. tranquillo.
restfulness s. tranquillità.
resting-place s. luogo di riposo.
restitution s. restituzione.
restive agg. 1. restio 2. irrequieto.
restless agg. 1. irrequieto 2. incessante.
restlessness s. irrequietezza.
restorable agg. 1. restituibile 2. re-
staurabile.
restoration s. 1. restituzione 2. re-
stauro 3. restaurazione 4. ricostruzione.
to **restore** vt. 1. restituire 2. restaurare 3. ricostruire 4. ristabilire.
to **restrain** vt. 1. trattenere 2. confinare.
restrainable agg. reprimibile.
restraint s. 1. freno 2. detenzione.
to **restrict** vt. limitare.
restrictedly avv. limitatamente.
restriction s. restrizione.
restrictive agg. restrittivo.
result s. risultato.
to **result** vi. 1. risultare 2. risolversi.
resultant agg. e s. risultante.
resultful agg. utile, efficace.
resultless agg. inutile, inefficace.
to **resume** vt. riprendere.
resummons s. nuova convocazione.
resumption s. ripresa.

resurgent *agg.* risorgente.

to **resurrect** *vt.* (*fam.*) risuscitare.

resurrection *s.* risurrezione.

resurrectional *agg.* di risurrezione.

to **resuscitate** *vt.* e *vi.* risuscitare.

resuscitation *s.* risuscitamento.

to **ret** *vt.* macerare.

retail *s.* vendita al minuto || *by* —, al minuto.

to **retail** *vt.* e *vi.* vendere al minuto.

retailer *s.* dettagliante.

to **retain** *vt.* trattenere, conservare.

retainable *agg.* trattenibile, conservabile.

retainer *s.* caparra, anticipo.

retaining *agg.* — *wall*, muro di sostegno.

retake *s.* (*cine*) replica di una ripresa.

to **retake** (**retook, retaken**) *vt.* 1. riprendere 2. (*cine*) ripetere una ripresa.

to **retaliate** *vi.* far rappresaglia.

retaliation *s.* rappresaglia.

retaliative, retaliatory *agg.* vendicativo.

retard *s.* ritardo.

to **retard** *vt.* e *vi.* ritardare.

to **retaste** *vt.* riassaggiare.

to **retch** *vi.* avere conati di vomito.

to **retell** (**retold, retold**) *vt.* ripetere.

retention *s.* 1. ritenzione 2. memoria.

retentive *agg.* 1. che trattiene 2. tenace (*di memoria*).

reticence, reticency *s.* reticenza.

reticent *agg.* reticente.

reticle *s.* (*ott.*) reticolo.

reticular *agg.* reticolare.

reticulate *agg.* reticolato.

reticulum *s.* (*pl.* -la) reticolo.

retinue *s.* seguito.

to **retire** *vt.* ritirare. ◆ to **retire** *vi.* ritirarsi.

retired *agg.* 1. ritirato 2. a riposo, in ritiro.

retirement *s.* 1. ritiro 2. collocamento a riposo 3. (*mil.*) ritirata.

retiring *agg.* 1. riservato 2. che si ritira, uscente.

retold V. *to retell.*

retook V. *to retake.*

retorsion *s.* ritorsione.

retort *s.* storta.

to **retort** *vt.* ritorcere. ◆ to **retort** *vi.* ribattere.

retort(ion) *s.* ritorsione.

retouch *s.* ritocco.

to **retouch** *vt.* ritoccare.

to **retrace** *vt.* ripercorrere, risalire.

to **retract** *vt.* 1. ritrarre 2. ritrattare. ◆ to **retract** *vi.* ritrarsi.

retractable *agg.* ritraibile 2. ritrattabile.

retractation *s.* ritrattazione.

retractile *agg.* retrattile.

retractor *s.* (*med.*) divaricatore.

to **retread** (**retrod, retrodden**) *vt.* ripercorrere.

retreat *s.* eremo, luogo appartato.

to **retreat** *vi.* ritirarsi, retrocedere.

retreating *agg.* sfuggente. ◆ re**treating** *s.* (*mil.*) ritirata.

retribution *s.* punizione.

retrievable *agg.* 1. ricuperabile 2. riparabile.

retrieval *s.* 1. ricupero (*di beni*) 2. riparazione.

to **retrieve** *vt.* 1. ricuperare 2. riparare.

retroaction *s.* 1. reazione 2. azione retroattiva.

retroactive *agg.* retroattivo.

to **retrocede**[1] *vi.* retrocedere.

to **retrocede**[2] *vt.* restituire.

retrocession[1] *s.* retrocessione.

retrocession[2] *s.* restituzione.

retrod V. *to retread.*

retrodden V. *to retread.*

retrospect(ion) *s.* sguardo retrospettivo.

retrospective *agg.* retrospettivo.

retroversion *s.* retroversione.

return *s.* 1. ritorno 2. restituzione 3. guadagno, profitto 4. relazione || — *journey*, viaggio di ritorno; *election returns*, risultati elettorali.

to **return** *vi.* 1. ritornare 2. rispondere, ricambiare, replicare. ◆ to **return** *vt.* 1. restituire, rimandare 2. produrre, fruttare 3. (*pol.*) eleggere.

reunion *s.* riunione.

to **reunite** *vt.* riunire. ◆ to **reunite** *vi.* riunirsi.

revaluation *s.* rivalutazione.

to **revalue** *vt.* rivalutare.

to **reveal** *vt.* rivelare.

revel *s.* baldoria.

to **revel** *vi.* far baldoria.

revelation *s.* rivelazione.

reveller *s.* chi fa baldoria.

revelry *s.* baldoria.

revenge *s.* vendetta.

to **revenge** *vt.* vendicare. ◆ to **revenge** *vi.* vendicarsi.

revengeful *agg.* vendicativo.

revenger s. vendicatore.
revenue s. 1. entrata 2. fisco.
to **reverberate** vt. e vi. riverberare.
reverberation s. riverberazione, riverbero.
to **revere** vt. riverire.
reverence s. riverenza.
to **reverence** vt. riverire.
reverend agg. reverendo.
reverent(ial) agg. riverente.
reverie s. fantasticheria.
reversal s. 1. rovesciamento 2. (giur.) annullamento.
reverse agg. e s. rovescio || — gear, retromarcia.
to **reverse** vt. rovesciare. ◆ to **reverse** vi. innestare la retromarcia.
reversibility s. reversibilità.
reversible agg. reversibile, rovesciabile.
reversion s. reversione.
to **revert** vi. ritornare.
review s. 1. revisione 2. recensione 3. rivista, periodico 4. (mil.) rivista.
to **review** vt. 1. rivedere 2. recensire 3. (mil.) passare in rivista.
reviewal s. revisione, recensione.
reviewer s. recensore, revisore.
to **revile** vt. e vi. ingiuriare.
to **revise** vt. rivedere, modificare.
reviser s. revisore.
revision s. revisione, correzione.
revival s. 1. ripristino 2. ripresa 3. rinascita.
to **revive** vt. e vi. resuscitare.
reviver s. chi, ciò che rinvigorisce.
revivification s. rinascita.
to **revivify** vt. ravvivare.
revocable agg. revocabile.
revocation s. revoca.
revocatory agg. revocatorio.
to **revoke** vt. revocare.
revolt s. rivolta.
to **revolt** vt. disgustare. ◆ to **revolt** vi. rivoltarsi.
revolution s. rivoluzione.
revolutionary agg. e s. rivoluzionario.
to **revolutionize** vt. rivoluzionare.
to **revolve** vt. meditare. ◆ to **revolve** vi. girare, rotare.
revolver s. rivoltella.
revolving agg. 1. rotante 2. rotativo.
revulsion s. 1. revulsione 2. mutamento.
revulsive agg. revulsivo.

reward s. ricompensa.
to **reward** vt. ricompensare.
rewarding agg. rimunerativo. ◆ **rewarding** s. rimunerazione.
to **rewrite** (**rewrote, rewritten**) vt. riscrivere.
rhagades s. pl. ragadi.
rhapsody s. rapsodia.
rheostat s. reostato.
rhetoric s. retorica.
rhetorical agg. retorico.
rhetorician s. retore.
rheumatic agg. e s. reumatico.
rheumatism s. reumatismo.
rhinitis s. rinite.
rhinoceros s. rinoceronte.
rhizome s. rizoma.
rhododendron s. rododendro.
rhomb s. rombo.
rhombic(al) agg. rombico.
rhombohedron s. (pl. -dra) romboedro.
rhomboid agg. e s. romboide.
rhubarb s. rabarbaro.
rhyme s. rima.
to **rhyme** vt. far rimare. ◆ to **rhyme** vi. rimare.
rhymer s. rimatore.
Rhynchota s. pl. rincoti.
rhythm s. ritmo.
rhythmic(al) agg. ritmico.
rib s. 1. costola 2. costa, nervatura 3. stecca.
to **rib** vt. 1. munire (di coste ecc.) 2. scanalare.
ribbing s. 1. nervatura 2. rigatura.
ribbon s. nastro.
rice s. riso || —-field (o —-swamp), risaia.
rich agg. ricco.
richly avv. riccamente.
richness s. ricchezza.
rick s. bica.
ricket(s) s. rachitismo.
rickety agg. 1. rachitico 2. malsicuro.
to **rid** (**rid, rid**) vt. liberare || to get — of, sbarazzarsi di.
ridden V. to ride.
riddle[1] s. indovinello.
riddle[2] s. vaglio, crivello.
to **riddle**[1] vt. risolvere.
to **riddle**[2] vt. 1. vagliare 2. setacciare.
ride s. passeggiata, percorso (a cavallo, su un veicolo).
to **ride** (**rode, ridden**) vt. 1. montare (cavallo, bicicletta) 2. percorrere (a cavallo, su un veicolo) 3.

(*fig.*) opprimere. ◆ to **ride** (rode, ridden) *vi.* andare (*a cavallo, su un veicolo*).

rider *s.* cavaliere, fantino.

ridge *s.* cresta, catena di monti.

ridicule *s.* ridicolo.

to **ridicule** *vt.* schernire.

ridiculous *agg.* ridicolo.

riding *s.* corsa (*a cavallo, in veicolo*).

rifle *s.* fucile.

rifleman *s.* fuciliere.

rift *s.* crepa.

rigging *s.* attrezzatura.

right[1] *agg.* 1. giusto 2. (*geom.*) retto 3. destro.

right[2] *s.* 1. il giusto, il bene 2. diritto 3. destra, mano destra, lato destro.

right[3] *avv.* 1. giustamente, bene 2. direttamente 3. proprio 4. a destra.

righteous *agg.* giusto.

righteousness *s.* rettitudine.

rightful *agg.* 1. legittimo 2. giusto.

rightly *avv.* 1. rettamente 2. esattamente.

rigid *agg.* rigido.

rigidity, rigor *s.* rigidità.

rigorism *s.* rigorismo.

rigorist *s.* rigorista.

rigorous *agg.* rigido.

rigour *s.* rigore.

rim *s.* bordo, orlo.

to **rim** *vt.* bordare, cerchiare.

rind *s.* 1. buccia 2. corteccia 3. crosta 4. cotenna.

to **rind** *vt.* 1. sbucciare 2. scortecciare.

ring[1] *s.* 1. anello, cerchio 2. pista.

ring[2] *s.* 1. scampanellata 2. (*fig.*) accento, tono.

to **ring**[1] *vt.* circondare.

to **ring**[2] (rang, rung) *vt.* suonare || to — up, telefonare. ◆ to **ring** (rang, rung) *vi.* risuonare.

ringleader *s.* capobanda.

rink *s.* pista di pattinaggio.

to **rinse** *vt.* sciacquare.

rinsing *s.* risciacquatura.

riot *s.* 1. rivolta 2. gazzarra.

to **riot** *vi.* 1. tumultuare 2. gozzovigliare.

rioter *s.* rivoltoso.

riotous *agg.* 1. tumultuante 2. sregolato.

rip *s.* lacerazione, scucitura, strappo.

to **rip** *vt.* lacerare. ◆ to **rip** *vi.* lacerarsi.

ripe *agg.* maturo.

to **ripen** *vt.* e *vi.* maturare.

ripeness *s.* maturità.

ripple *s.* 1. increspatura, ondulatura 2. gorgoglio.

to **ripple** *vt.* increspare, ondulare. ◆ to **ripple** *vi.* incresparsi, ondularsi.

rise *s.* 1. il sorgere 2. salita, ascesa 3. aumento 4. sorgente.

to **rise** (rose, risen) *vi.* 1. sorgere 2. aumentare.

riser *s.* chi si alza.

risible *agg.* risibile.

rising *s.* 1. sorgere 2. salita, ascesa 3. aumento 4. rivolta.

risk *s.* rischio.

to **risk** *vt.* rischiare.

risky *agg.* rischioso.

rissole *s.* polpetta.

rite *s.* rito.

ritual *agg.* e *s.* rituale.

rival *agg.* e *s.* rivale.

to **rival** *vt.* rivaleggiare.

rivality, rivalry *s.* rivalità.

river *s.* fiume.

riverside *s.* lungofiume.

to **rivet** *vt.* 1. ribadire 2. fissare.

rivulet *s.* fiumicello.

road *s.* strada || — -bed, fondo stradale; — sign, cartello stradale.

roadstead *s.* (*mar.*) rada.

roadway *s.* carreggiata.

to **roam** *vt.* e *vi.* vagare (*per*).

roar *s.* 1. ruggito 2. rombo.

to **roar** *vt.* e *vi.* 1. ruggire 2. tuonare || to — with laughter, ridere fragorosamente.

roaring *agg.* 1. rumoroso 2. ruggente, mugghiante. ◆ **roaring** *s.* V. roar.

roast *agg.* e *s.* arrosto.

to **roast** *vt.* 1. arrostire 2. tostare ◆ to **roast** *vi.* arrostirsi.

roasting *agg.* rovente. ◆ **roasting** *s.* 1. arrostimento 2. torrefazione.

to **rob** *vt.* derubare. ◆ to **rob** *vi.* rubare.

robber *s.* ladro.

robbery *s.* furto.

robe *s.* 1. toga 2. vestiti (*pl.*).

to **robe** *vt.* vestire. ◆ to **robe** *vi.* vestirsi.

robin *s.* pettirosso.

robust *agg.* 1. robusto 2. faticoso.

robustness *s.* robustezza.

rock[1] *s.* 1. roccia 2. rocca.

rock[2] *s.* dondolio.

to **rock** *vt.* cullare, dondolare. ◆

to **rock** vi. dondolarsi, oscillare, barcollare.

rocker s. 1. chi culla, dondola 2. dondolo (di sedia ecc.) 3. (mecc.) bilanciere.

rocket s. razzo.

rocking agg. 1. a dondolo 2. vacillante. ♦ **rocking** s. oscillazione, dondolio.

rocky agg. roccioso.

rod s. verga || fishing- —, canna da pesca.

rode V. to ride.

rodent agg. e s. roditore.

roe[1] s. capriolo maschio.

roe[2] s. uova di pesce.

rogue s. briccone.

roguery s. bricconeria.

roguish agg. bricconesco.

role s. 1. (teat.) ruolo, parte 2. funzione.

roll[1] s. 1. rotolo 2. elenco, lista 3. rullo, cilindro.

roll[2] s. 1. (mar.; aer.) rollio 2. rullo (di tamburo).

to **roll** vt. 1. far rotolare 2. arrotolare 3. spianare. ♦ to **roll** vi. 1. rotolare 2. arrotolarsi 3. ruotare 4. rollare 5. rullare.

roller s. 1. rullo, cilindro 2. cavallone || — skates, schettini.

rolling s. (ar)rotolamento || — -mill, laminatoio; — pin, matterello.

Roman agg. e s. romano.

Romance agg. romanzo, neolatino.

romance s. 1. poema cavalleresco, racconto fantastico 2. avventura romanzesca 3. idillio 4. poesia 5. (mus.) romanza.

Romanesque agg. e s. romanico.

Romanian agg. e s. romeno.

Romanic agg. romanico.

Romanist s. romanista.

Romansh agg. e s. ladino.

romantic agg. e s. romantico.

romanticism s. romanticismo.

to **romanticize** vt. romanzare.

to **romp** vi. giocare rumorosamente.

rompish agg. chiassoso.

rood s. croce.

roof s. tetto || — -garden, giardino pensile.

to **roof** vt. 1. coprire con un tetto 2. ospitare.

rook s. cornacchia.

room s. 1. stanza 2. spazio 3. possibilità.

to **room** vt. e vi. (amer.) alloggiare.

roomy agg. spazioso.

root s. radice.

to **root**[1] vt. piantare || to — away, out, up, sradicare. ♦ to **root** vi. mettere radice.

to **root**[2] vt. e vi. grufolare.

rope s. fune, corda || — -dancer, funambolo.

to **rope** vt. legare.

rosary s. 1. roseto 2. (eccl.) rosario.

rose agg. e s. rosa || — -bush, rosaio; — -diamond, rosetta; — -window, rosone.

rose V. to rise.

rosemary s. rosmarino.

roseola s. rosolia.

rosery s. roseto.

rosette s. 1. rosetta 2. (arch.) rosone 3. coccarda.

rosewood s. palissandro.

rosin s. pece greca.

rostrum s. (pl. rostra o rostrums) rostro.

rosy agg. roseo.

rot s. putrefazione.

to **rot** vt. e vi. imputridire.

rotary agg. rotante. ♦ **rotary** s. — (press), rotativa.

to **rotate** vt. e vi. rotare.

rotation s. rotazione.

rotative, **rotatory** agg. rotatorio.

rote s. abitudine, memoria meccanica.

rotogravure s. rotocalco.

rotor s. rotore.

rotten agg. marcio.

rottenness s. marciume.

rotund agg. 1. rotondo 2. enfatico.

rouble s. rublo.

rouge s. rossetto.

rough agg. 1. irregolare, ruvido, scabro 2. tempestoso 3. rozzo.

to **rough** vt. irruvidire || to — it (fam.), vivere primitivamente.

to **roughen** vt. irruvidire. ♦ to **roughen** vi. irruvidirsi.

to **rough-hew** vt. abbozzare.

roughly avv. ruvidamente.

roughness s. 1. ruvidezza 2. rudezza 3. inclemenza (di tempo).

round agg. 1. rotondo 2. intero 3. franco 4. vigoroso 5. considerevole. ♦ **round** s. 1. cerchio 2. sfera 3. ciclo 4. giro, ronda.

round avv. intorno. ♦ **round** prep. intorno a.

to **round** vt. arrotondare. ♦ to **round** vi. 1. arrotondarsi 2. girare

3. svilupparsi.

roundabout *agg.* indiretto. ♦
roundabout *s.* giostra.

roundly *avv.* **1.** vigorosamente **2.**
francamente.

roundness *s.* **1.** rotondità **2.** scorrevolezza **3.** franchezza.

to **rouse** *vt.* (ri)svegliare (*anche fig.*).
♦ to **rouse** *vi.* (ri)svegliarsi.

rouser *s.* ridestatore.

rousing *agg.* stimolante.

rout *s.* **1.** plebaglia **2.** tumulto **3.**
rotta.

to **rout** *vt.* sconfiggere.

route *s.* via, rotta.

routinist *s.* abitudinario.

rove *s.* vagabondaggio.

to **rove** *vt.* e *vi.* vagare.

rover *s.* **1.** vagabondo **2.** pirata.

roving *s.* vagabondaggio.

row[1] *s.* fila.

row[2] *s.* remata, gita in barca.

to **row** *vt.* trasportare (*remando*). ♦
to **row** *vi.* remare.

rowdy *agg.* e *s.* turbolento.

rower *s.* rematore.

rowlock *s.* scalmo.

royal *agg.* regale, reale.

royalist *s.* realista.

royalty *s.* **1.** regalità **2.** i reali **3.** diritto d'autore.

rub *s.* **1.** fregata, grattata **2.** ineguaglianza **3.** ostacolo, difficoltà.

to **rub** *vt.* fregare. ♦ to **rub** *vi.* fre-
garsi.

rubber *s.* **1.** massaggiatore **2.** stro-
finaccio **3.** gomma || — *-solution*,
mastice.

rubbish *s.* rifiuti (*pl.*).

rubble *s.* pietrisco.

ruby *s.* rubino.

rucksack *s.* zaino.

rudder *s.* timone.

ruddy *agg.* rosso, rubicondo.

rude *agg.* **1.** rude, violento **2.** rudimentale **3.** grezzo.

rudeness *s.* **1.** rozzezza **2.** violenza.

rudiment *s.* rudimento.

rudimentary *agg.* rudimentale.

ruffian *agg.* brutale. ♦ **ruffian** *s.*
ribaldo.

ruffle *s.* **1.** increspatura **2.** sconvolgimento **3.** tumulto.

to **ruffle** *vt.* **1.** increspare **2.** arruffare
3. agitare.

rug *s.* **1.** coperta **2.** tappetino.

rugged *agg.* **1.** ruvido **2.** scompiglia-
to **3.** austero **4.** rozzo.

ruggedness *s.* **1.** ruvidezza **2.** auste-

rità **3.** rudezza.

ruin *s.* rovina.

to **ruin** *vt.* e *vi.* rovinare.

ruinous *agg.* **1.** rovinoso **2.** in rovina.

rule *s.* **1.** regola **2.** dominio **3.** riga
da disegno.

to **rule** *vt.* **1.** governare, dominare **2.**
rigare.

ruler *s.* **1.** dominatore **2.** regolo.

ruling *s.* **1.** governo **2.** decisione.

Rumanian *agg.* e *s.* romeno.

rumble *s.* **1.** rombo **2.** brontolio.

to **rumble** *vt.* e *vi.* **1.** rombare **2.**
brontolare.

rumbling *s.* V. *rumble*.

rumen *s.* rumine.

ruminant *agg.* e *s.* ruminante.

to **ruminate** *vt* e *vi.* ruminare.

rummage *s.* ricerca, perquisizione.

to **rummage** *vt.* e *vi.* **1.** rovistare
2. perquisire.

rumour *s.* diceria.

to **rumour** *vt.* far correre la voce.

rump *s.* **1.** posteriore **2.** resto.

to **rumple** *vt.* **1.** spiegazzare **2.** arruffare.

run *s.* **1.** corsa **2.** percorso, giro **3.**
andamento **4.** periodo **5.** richiesta.

to **run** (ran, run) *vi.* **1.** correre **2.**
colare **3.** diventare **4.** estendersi **5.**
essere in vigore, durare. ♦ to **run**
(ran, run) *vt.* **1.** far funzionare
2. dirigere **3.** seguire **4.** passare ||
to — in, rodare; *to — over*, investire.

runaway *agg.* **1.** fuggitivo **2.** decisivo. ♦ **runaway** *s.* **1.** fuggitivo
2. fuga.

rung[1] *s.* **1.** piolo **2.** raggio (*di
ruota*).

rung[2] V. *to ring*.

runnel *s.* ruscello.

runner *s.* **1.** corridore **2.** messo **3.**
passatoia **4.** pattino **5.** carrello.

running *s.* **1.** corsa **2.** esercizio **3.**
flusso || — *-in*, rodaggio.

runway *s.* pista.

rupture *s.* rottura.

rural *agg.* rurale.

rush[1] *s.* giunco.

rush[2] **1.** attacco **2.** impeto **3.** afflus-
so || — *-hours*, ore di punta.

to **rush** *vt.* spingere. ♦ to **rush** *vi.*
precipitarsi.

rushy *agg.* **1.** di giunchi **2.** folto di
giunchi.

Russian *agg.* e *s.* russo.

rust *s.* ruggine.

to **rust** *vt.* arrugginire. ♦ to **rust** *vi.* arrugginirsi.

rustic(al) *agg.* rustico. ♦ **rustic(al)** *s.* campagnolo.

rustle *s.* fruscio, stormire (*di foglie*).

to **rustle** *vt.* far frusciare. ♦ to **rustle** *vi.* frusciare.

rusty *agg.* 1. rugginoso 2. (*fig.*) ombroso.

ruthless *agg.* spietato.

ruthlessness *s.* crudeltà.

rye *s.* segale.

S

Sabbath *s.* il giorno della settimana dedicato al riposo.

sable *s.* zibellino.

sabot *s.* zoccolo.

sabotage *s.* sabotaggio.

to **sabotage** *vt.* e *vi.* sabotare.

saboteur *s.* sabotatore.

sabre *s.* sciabola || — *-cut*, sciabolata.

to **sabre** *vt.* sciabolare.

saccharin(e) *s.* saccarina.

saccharose *s.* saccarosio.

sacerdotal *agg.* sacerdotale.

sack[1] *s.* 1. sacco 2. (*gergo*) licenziamento.

sack[2] *s.* (*mil.*) sacco, saccheggio.

sack[3] *s.* vino bianco delle Canarie.

to **sack**[1] *vt.* 1. insaccare 2. (*gergo*) licenziare.

to **sack**[2] *vt.* (*mil.*) saccheggiare.

sacking[1] *s.* tela da sacco.

sacking[2] *s.* saccheggio.

sacral[1] *agg.* (*anat.*) sacro.

sacral[2] *agg.* rituale.

sacrament *s.* sacramento.

sacramental *agg.* sacramentale.

sacred *agg.* 1. sacro, religioso 2. consacrato, dedicato.

sacrifice *s.* 1. sacrificio 2. abnegazione.

to **sacrifice** *vt.* e *vi.* 1. sacrificare, immolare 2. rinunziare.

sacrilege *s.* sacrilegio.

sacrist *s.* sagrestano.

sacristy *s.* sagrestia.

sacrosanct *agg.* sacrosanto.

sad *agg.* triste, mesto || *to make so.* —, rattristare qu.

to **sadden** *vt.* rattristare. ♦ to **sadden** *vi.* rattristarsi.

saddle *s.* 1. sella, sellino 2. giogaia.

to **saddle** *vt.* sellare, mettere in sella.

saddler *s.* sellaio.

sadism *s.* sadismo.

sadist *s.* sadico.

sadistic *agg.* sadico.

sadly *avv.* tristemente, mestamente.

sadness *s.* tristezza, mestizia.

safe *agg.* 1. sicuro, al riparo 2. salvo, intatto 3. innocuo || — *and sound*, sano e salvo; — *-conduct*, salvacondotto; — *-deposit*, cassetta di sicurezza. ♦ **safe** *s.* 1. cassaforte 2. sicura (*di armi*).

safeguard *s.* salvaguardia.

to **safeguard** *vt.* salvaguardare, difendere.

safekeeping *s.* custodia.

safety *s.* sicurezza, salvezza, scampo || — *belt*, cintura di sicurezza; — *device*, dispositivo di sicurezza; — *pin*, spilla di sicurezza.

saffron *s.* zafferano.

sag *s.* 1. abbassamento, cedimento 2. (*mar.*) scarroccio.

sagacious *agg.* acuto, sagace.

sagaciousness, **sagacity** *s.* sagacia, perspicacia.

sage[1] *s.* salvia.

sage[2] *s.* saggio, dotto.

said *V. to say.*

sail[1] *s.* vela, velatura || *to set* (*v. irr.*) —, spiegare le vele, salpare; *to strike* (*v. irr.*) —, ammainare le vele.

sail[2] *s.* gita su imbarcazione a vela.

to **sail** *vt.* e *vi.* 1. veleggiare, navigare, costeggiare 2. salpare 3. volare, veleggiare (*di uccelli, nuvole ecc.*).

sailer *s.* veliero.

sailing *s.* 1. navigazione, traversata 2. partenza (*di navi*).

sailor *s.* marinaio.

sailplane *s.* veleggiatore.

saint *agg.* e *s.* santo.

to **saint** *vt.* canonizzare, santificare.

sainthood, **saintliness** *s.* sanità.

saintly *agg.* santo, di santo.

sake *s.* 1. amore, interesse 2. riguardo, rispetto || *for God's* —, per l'amor di Dio.

salaam *s.* riverenza, salamelecco.

salacious *agg.* salace, lascivo.

salad *s.* insalata || *fruit* —, macedonia di frutta.

salamander *s.* salamandra.

salariat *s.* categorie salariate.

salary *s.* stipendio.

sale *s.* **1.** vendita || *bill of* —, fattura; *on* —, in vendita **2.** asta: — *by auction*, vendita all'asta **3.** liquidazione, svendita.

sal(e)able *agg.* vendibile, commerciabile.

salesman *s.* venditore, commesso.

saleswoman *s.* venditrice, commessa.

salicylate *s.* salicilato.

salient *agg.* **1.** sporgente, prominente **2.** saliente, notevole.

saline *agg.* salino, salso.

salinity *s.* salsedine, salinità.

saliva *s.* saliva.

salivary *agg.* salivare.

salivation *s.* salivazione.

sallow *agg.* giallastro.

sally *s.* **1.** (*mil.*) sortita **2.** escursione.

to sally *vi.* fare una sortita || *to* — *forth*, uscire (*per una passeggiata*).

salmon *s.* salmone.

saloon *s.* salone || *dancing* —, sala da ballo.

salt *s.* sale. ♦ **salt** *agg.* **1.** salato **2.** sotto sale **3.** (*fig.*) amaro, piccante || — *-cellar*, saliera; — *-mine*, salina.

to salt *vt.* **1.** salare, cospargere di sale **2.** rendere piccante (*anche fig.*).

salting *s.* palude costiera.

saltish *agg.* salmastro, salaticcio.

saltness *s.* salsedine.

saltpetre *s.* salnitro.

salty *agg.* **1.** sala:o, salmastro **2.** piccante (*anche fig.*).

salubrious *agg.* salubre.

salutary *agg.* salutare.

salutation *s.* saluto.

salute *s.* saluto, gesto di saluto || *to fire a* —, salutare a salve.

to salute *vt.* salutare, dare il benvenuto.

salvage *s.* salvataggio (*di navi, carico ecc.*).

salvation *s.* salvezza (*anche relig.*).

salve *s.* unguento, balsamo.

same *agg.* medesimo, stesso, uguale || *at the* — *time*, allo stesso tempo. ♦ **same** *pron.* lo stesso, il medesimo.

samely *agg.* monotono, uniforme.

sameness *s.* **1.** somiglianza **2.** monotonia.

sample *s.* campione, modello, esemplare || — *book*, campionario.

sanatorium *s.* sanatorio.

sanatory *agg.* curativo.

sanctification *s.* santificazione.

to sanctify *vt.* santificare.

sanction *s.* **1.** autorizzazione, approvazione **2.** (*giur.*) ratifica **3.** sanzione.

to sanction *vt.* **1.** autorizzare **2.** (*giur.*) ratificare **3.** aggiungere sanzioni penali (*ad una legge*).

sanctity *s.* santità.

sanctuary *s.* **1.** santuario **2.** asilo, rifugio.

sand *s.* sabbia, rena || — *-bath*, bagno di sabbia. ♦ **sands** *s. pl.* spiaggia (*sing.*).

to sand *vt.* **1.** coprire di sabbia **2.** arenare **3.** smerigliare.

sandal *s.* sandalo.

sandpaper *s.* carta vetrata.

sandstone *s.* arenaria.

sandy *agg.* sabbioso.

sane *agg.* sano di mente, sensato.

saneness, sanity *s.* sanità (*di mente*), equilibrio.

sang V. *to sing*.

sanguinary *agg.* sanguinario, crudele.

sanguine *agg.* sanguigno.

sanguineous *agg.* del sangue, sanguigno.

sanitarian *s.* igienista. ♦ **sanitarian** *agg.* igienico.

sanitarist *s.* igienista.

sanitary *agg.* igienico, sanitario.

sanity *s.* V. *saneness*.

sank V. *to sink*.

Sanscrit, Sanskrit *agg. e s.* Sanscrito.

santon *s.* santone.

sap *s.* **1.** linfa, succo **2.** (*fig.*) vigore.

sapful *agg.* **1.** succoso **2.** vigoroso.

sapid *agg.* sapido, gustoso (*anche fig.*).

sapient *agg.* pedante.

sapless *agg.* **1.** secco, avvizzito **2.** fiacco.

saponification *s.* saponificazione.

to saponify *vt.* saponificare.

Sapphic *agg.* saffico.

sapphire *s.* zaffiro.

saraband *s.* sarabanda.

Saracen *agg. e s.* saraceno.

sarcasm *s.* sarcasmo.

sarcastic *agg.* sarcastico.

sarcophagus *s.* (*pl.* -gi) sarcofago.

sardine s. sardina.
sardonic agg. sardonico.
sash[1] s. fascia, cintura.
sash[2] s. telaio scorrevole (di finestra).
sat V. to sit.
satanic(al) agg. satanico.
satchel s. cartella (di scolaro).
to sate vt. saziare.
satellite s. satellite.
satiable agg. saziabile.
to satiate vt. saziare, satollare.
satiety s. sazietà.
satin s. raso.
satire s. satira.
satiric(al) agg. satirico.
satirist s. autore di satire.
to satirize vt. satireggiare.
satisfaction s. 1. soddisfazione 2. riparazione 3. (giur.) estinzione.
satisfactory agg. soddisfacente.
satisfiable agg. che può essere soddisfatto.
to satisfy vt. soddisfare, appagare || to — a claim, accogliere un reclamo. ♦ to satisfy vi. fare ammenda.
satrap s. satrapo.
saturate agg. saturo.
to saturate vt. saturare, impregnare.
saturation s. saturazione.
Saturday s. sabato.
satyr s. satiro.
satyric agg. satiresco.
sauce s. salsa, intingolo.
saucepan s. casseruola.
saucer s. piattino, sottocoppa.
saucily avv. sfacciatamente.
saucy agg. sfacciato, insolente.
sauerkraut s. crauti.
to saunter vi. bighellonare.
saunterer s. bighellone.
sausage s. salsiccia, salame.
savage agg. 1. selvaggio, barbaro 2. feroce, crudele. ♦ savage s. selvaggio.
savagely avv. selvaggiamente, barbaramente.
savannah s. savana.
save prep. salvo, tranne, eccetto.
to save vt. e vi. 1. salvare, difendere 2. conservare, risparmiare.
saving s. liberazione, salvezza. ♦ savings s. pl. risparmi.
saviour s. salvatore, redentore.
to savour vi. aver sapore.
savoury agg. saporito, piccante.
saw s. sega || — -mill, segheria.
to saw (sawed, sawn) vt. e vi.

segare.
saw V. to see.
sawdust s. segatura.
sawn V. to saw.
sawyer s. segatore.
Saxon agg. e s. sassone.
saxophone s. sassofono.
say s. il dire, detto, parola.
to say (said, said) vt. e vi. 1. dire, affermare 2. esprimere un'opinione || to — out, dire apertamente.
saying s. proverbio, massima: as the — goes, come dice il proverbio.
scabbard s. fodero.
scabby agg. coperto di croste.
scabies s. scabbia.
scaffold s. 1. impalcatura 2. patibolo, forca.
to scaffold vt. erigere impalcature.
scaffolding s. impalcatura.
scald s. scottatura.
to scald vt. 1. scottare 2. sterilizzare con acqua bollente. ♦ to scald vi. scottarsi.
scale[1] s. piatto (di bilancia). ♦ scales s. pl. bilancia (sing.).
scale[2] s. scaglia.
scale[3] s. scala, misura, gradazione.
to scale[1] vt. e vi. pesare.
to scale[2] vt. squamare, scrostare. ♦ to scale vi. squamarsi, scrostarsi.
to scale[3] vt. 1. scalare 2. graduare || to — down, diminuire; to — up, aumentare.
scalene agg. e s. scaleno.
scallop s. 1. conchiglia 2. dentellatura, festone, smerlo (di stoffa).
to scallop vt. 1. tagliare a festone 2. cuocere pesce in conchiglia.
scalp s. 1. cranio, cuoio capelluto 2. scalpo.
to scalp vt. 1. scalpare 2. criticare aspramente.
scalpel s. bisturi.
to scan vt. e vi. 1. scandire (versi) 2. esaminare, scrutare.
scandal s. 1. scandalo 2. maldicenza 3. (giur.) diffamazione.
to scandalize vt. scandalizzare.
scandalous agg. scandaloso.
Scandinavian agg. e s. scandinavo.
scanning s. 1. scansione (di versi) 2. osservazione || — -line, (tv), linea di scansione.
scansion s. scansione.
scantily avv. debolmente, scarsamente.
scantiness s. insufficienza, scarsezza.

scanty *agg.* **1.** scarso, insufficiente **2.** esiguo, angusto.

scapegoat *s.* capro espiatorio.

scapegrace *s.* **1.** scapestrato **2.** monello.

scapular *agg.* scapolare.

scar *s.* cicatrice, sfregio.

to scar *vt.* **1.** cicatrizzare **2.** sfregiare. ♦ **to scar** *vi.* cicatrizzarsi.

scarab *s.* scarabeo.

scarce *agg.* insufficiente, scarso.

scarcely *avv.* appena, a fatica, a malapena.

scare *s.* terrore, sgomento.

to scare *vt.* spaventare, sgomentare.

scarecrow *s.* **1.** spaventapasseri **2.** spauracchio.

scarf *s.* sciarpa, fascia.

to scarify *vt.* scarificare.

scarlet *agg.* scarlatto, porporino || — *-fever*, scarlattina.

scarp(e) *s.* scarpata.

to scatter *vt.* **1.** spargere **2.** mettere in fuga, disperdere. ♦ **to scatter** *vi.* spargersi, diffondersi.

scattered *agg.* sparso, disseminato.

scattering *s.* sparpagliamento, dispersione.

scenario *s.* sceneggiatura || — *writer*, sceneggiatore.

scene *s.* **1.** scena **2.** episodio **3.** scenario, quinta **4.** vista, panorama || — *-painter*, scenografo.

scenery *s.* **1.** scenario **2.** prospettiva, veduta.

scenographer *s.* scenografo.

scenographic *agg.* scenografico.

scenography *s.* scenografia.

scent *s.* **1.** odore, profumo **2.** traccia, pista (*anche fig.*).

to scent *vt.* **1.** fiutare, seguire la traccia **2.** profumare.

scented *agg.* profumato.

scentless *agg.* inodoro.

sceptical *agg.* scettico.

scepticism *s.* scetticismo.

sceptre *s.* scettro.

schedule *s.* **1.** catalogo, distinta, elenco **2.** (*amer.*) orario **3.** inventario.

to schedule *vt.* comporre una lista, un catalogo.

schematic(al) *agg.* schematico.

schematism *s.* schematismo.

scheme *s.* **1.** schema **2.** piano, progetto.

to scheme *vt.* e *vi.* **1.** progettare, fare un piano **2.** tramare.

schism *s.* scisma.

schismatic(al) *s.* scismatico.

schizophrenic *agg.* e *s.* schizofrenico.

scholar *s.* studioso, letterato.

scholarly *agg.* dotto, istruito.

scholarship *s.* **1.** dottrina, sapere **2.** borsa di studio.

scholastic *agg.* **1.** scolastico, pedante **2.** (*fil.*) scolastico.

scholastically *avv.* scolasticamente, secondo la scolastica.

scholasticism *s.* (*fil.*) scolastica.

school *s.* **1.** scuola, classe **2.** lezione, ora di lezione || — *-book*, libro di testo; — *-mate*, compagno di scuola; — *-report*, pagella; — *-term*, trimestre; — *-time*, periodo scolastico; *boarding-* —, collegio; *grammar-* —, ginnasio; *night-* —, serale.

to school *vt.* **1.** istruire **2.** controllare, disciplinare.

schoolboy *s.* scolaro.

schoolfellow *s.* compagno di scuola.

schoolmaster *s.* maestro, insegnante.

schoolmistress *s.* maestra, insegnante.

schoolroom *s.* aula scolastica.

schooner *s.* (*mar.*) goletta.

science *s.* scienza || — *fiction*, fantascienza; *man of* —, scienziato.

scientific *agg.* scientifico.

scientifically *avv.* scientificamente.

scientism *s.* scientismo.

scientist *s.* scienziato.

scimitar *s.* scimitarra.

scion *s.* **1.** germoglio **2.** rampollo, discendente.

scission *s.* scissione, divisione.

scissors *s. pl.* forbici, cesoie.

sclerosis *s.* (*pl. -ses*) sclerosi.

sclerotic *s.* sclerotico.

scoff *s.* derisione, scherno.

to scoff *vt.* e *vi.* deridere, schernire || *to* — *at so.*, farsi beffe di qu.

scold *s.* donna bisbetica.

to scold *vt.* sgridare, rimproverare. ♦ **to scold** *vi.* essere adirato.

scolding *s.* sgridata, rimprovero.

scoliosis *s.* scoliosi.

scooter *s.* **1.** monopattino **2.** motoretta.

scope *s.* **1.** portata, possibilità **2.** prospettiva, sfera, campo.

scorbutic *agg.* e *s.* scorbutico.

scorch *s.* bruciatura, scottatura.

to scorch *vt.* e *vi.* **1.** bruciacchiare **2.** inaridire (*di sole, gelo ecc.*).

scorching agg. 1. bruciante, ardente 2. (fig.) caustico, mordace.

score s. 1. tacca, scanalatura 2. linea, segno, linea di partenza, limite (in corse, giuochi ecc.) 3. (sport) punteggio 4. (mus.) spartito.

to score vt. e vi. 1. intaccare, intagliare 2. marcare, segnare 3. (sport) segnare il punteggio 4. (mus.) orchestrare || to — up, mettere in conto.

scorer s. (sport) marcatore.

scorn s. 1. disprezzo, disdegno 2. scherno.

to scorn vt. disprezzare, disdegnare.

scornful agg. sprezzante, sdegnoso.

scorpion s. scorpione || — -fish, scorfano.

Scot s. scozzese.

Scotch agg. scozzese.

Scotsman s. (uomo) scozzese.

Scottish agg. scozzese.

scoundrel s. furfante, farabutto.

scourge s. (fig.) flagello.

to scourge vt. sferzare, flagellare.

scout s. esploratore, ricognitore.

to scout vi. andare in esplorazione, in ricognizione. ♦ to scout vt. perlustrare.

scowl s. cipiglio, sguardo torvo.

to scowl vt. e vi. aggrottare le ciglia, guardare torvamente.

scramble s. 1. arrampicata 2. contesa, gara.

to scramble vt. 1. arraffare 2. mescolare alla rinfusa. ♦ to scramble vi. 1. inerpicarsi 2. gareggiare 3. (cuc.) strapazzare (le uova).

scrap s. pezzetto, frammento || — -heap, mucchio di rifiuti. ♦ scraps s. pl. rimasugli, scarti.

scrape s. 1. graffio, scalfittura 2. raschio.

to scrape vt. e vi. 1. raschiare, grattare 2. levigare 3. sfregare, strisciare || to — a living, sbarcare il lunario.

scraper s. 1. raschietto 2. strimpellatore.

scraping s. raschiatura.

scratch s. 1. graffiatura, graffio 2. grattata 3. colpo fortunato (al giuoco).

to scratch vt. e vi. 1. graffiare 2. (fig.) scalfire 3. grattare.

scrawl s. scarabocchio, sgorbio.

to scrawl vt. e vi. 1. scarabocchiare 2. scribacchiare.

scrawler s. chi scarabocchia.

scrawly agg. scarabocchiato || — writing (fam.), scritto a zampe di gallina.

scream s. grido acuto, strillo.

to scream vt. e vi. 1. gridare, strillare 2. fischiare (di locomotiva).

screamer s. strillone.

screaming agg. 1. strillante, urlante 2. sguaiato.

screech s. 1. grido, strillo acuto 2. stridore.

screen s. 1. paravento 2. (cine; tv) schermo 3. (mil.) scorta.

to screen vt. e vi. 1. riparare, schermare 2. vagliare.

screenings s. pl. materiale vagliato (sing.).

screenplay s. (cine) sceneggiatura.

screenwriter s. sceneggiatore.

screw s. 1. vite 2. cavatappi, succhiello 3. elica.

to screw vt. 1. avvitare, stringere 2. torcere. ♦ to screw vi. torcersi || to — out, svitare.

screwdriver s. cacciavite.

screwy agg. 1. brillo 2. tirchio, spilorcio.

scribble s. sgorbio, scarabocchio (anche fig.).

to scribble vt. e vi. scarabocchiare.

scribe s. copista.

scriber s. punta a tracciare.

scrip[1] s. 1. pezzo di carta 2. frammento di uno scritto.

scrip[2] s. certificato provvisorio, cedola.

scripture s. la sacra Scrittura.

to scrounge vt. e vi. rubacchiare.

scrounger s. ladruncolo, scroccone.

scrub s. 1. boscaglia 2. povero diavolo (fam.).

to scrub vt. e vi. sfregare.

scrubby agg. esile, debole.

scruff s. nuca, collottola.

scruple s. scrupolo.

scrupolosity s. scrupolosità.

scrupulous agg. scrupoloso.

to scrutinize vt. scrutinare, esaminare.

scrutiny s. 1. esame minuzioso 2. scrutinio 3. esame (di una legge).

scuffle s. zuffa, tafferuglio.

to scuffle vi. azzuffarsi.

scullery s. retrocucina || — -boy, -maid, sguattero, sguattera.

sculptor s. scultore.

sculptress s. scultrice.

sculptural agg. scultorio, statuario.

sculpture *s.* scultura.

to **sculpture** *vt.* e *vi.* scolpire.

scum *s.* 1. schiuma, spuma 2. feccia (*anche fig.*).

to **scum** *vt.* e *vi.* 1. schiumare, far schiuma 2. produrre feccia.

scummer *s.* schiumarola.

scurf *s.* 1. squama, forfora 2. incrostazioni (*pl.*).

scurrility *s.* scurrilità, volgarità.

scurrilous *agg.* scurrile, triviale.

to **scurry** *vi.* precipitarsi.

scurvy *agg.* spregevole, meschino.

scuttle[1] *s.* recipiente per carbone.

scuttle[2] *s.* 1. (*mar.*) portellino 2. botola.

scuttle[3] *s.* fuga precipitosa.

to **scuttle**[1] *vt.* produrre falle (*in una nave*).

to **scuttle**[2] *vi.* correre via precipitosamente.

sea *s.* mare ‖ — *-bear*, orso polare; — *-biscuit*, galletta; — *calf*, foca; — *fight*, battaglia navale; — *food*, frutti di mare; — *front*, lungomare; — *quake*, maremoto; — *storm*, mareggiata.

seacoast *s.* costa, spiaggia.

seafarer *s.* navigante, navigatore.

seafaring *s.* viaggi per mare.

seahorse *s.* ippocampo.

seal[1] *s.* foca.

seal[2] *s.* 1. sigillo, timbro 2. (*fig.*) suggello, vincolo.

to **seal**[1] *vi.* andare a caccia di foche.

to **seal**[2] *vt.* 1. sigillare 2. suggellare ‖ *to — one's fate*, decidere la propria sorte.

sealing *s.* suggellamento ‖ — *-wax*, ceralacca.

seam *s.* 1. cucitura 2. sutura.

to **seam** *vt.* 1. unire con cucitura 2. rigare, segnare.

seamen *s. pl.* equipaggio (*di una nave*).

seamanship *s.* arte della navigazione.

seamless *agg.* senza cucitura.

seamstress *s.* cucitrice.

seaplane *s.* idrovolante.

seaport *s.* porto marittimo.

search *s.* 1. ricerca, indagine 2. perquisizione, visita doganale ‖ — *warrant*, mandato di perquisizione.

to **search** *vt.* e *vi.* cercare, perlustrare, perquisire ‖ *to — out*, rinvenire, scovare.

searcher *s.* ricercatore.

searching *agg.* indagatore, inquisi-

torio. ♦ **searching** *s.* 1. ricerca, esame 2. sondaggio.

searchlight *s.* riflettore.

seashore *s.* spiaggia, lido.

seasickness *s.* mal di mare.

seaside *s.* spiaggia, riva.

season *s.* stagione, epoca ‖ — *bill* (*teat.*), cartellone; — *ticket*, abbonamento stagionale.

to **season** *vt.* 1. stagionare 2. acclimatare 3. condire. ♦ to **season** *vi.* 1. stagionarsi 2. invecchiarsi (*di vino*).

seasonable *agg.* 1. di stagione 2. opportuno.

seasonal *agg.* stagionale.

seasoned *agg.* 1. stagionato 2. condito.

seasoning *s.* 1. stagionatura 2. condimento.

seat *s.* 1. sedile, posto 2. seggio 3. sede.

to **seat** *vt.* 1. mettere a sedere 2. insediare, collocare.

seaward *agg.* che va verso il mare.

seaweed *s.* alga marina.

sebaceous *agg.* sebaceo.

secant *agg.* e *s.* secante.

to **secede** *vi.* separarsi, ritirarsi.

seceder *s.* secessionista, separatista.

secession *s.* secessione, scissione.

secessionism *s.* secessionismo.

to **seclude** *vt.* 1. appartare, isolare 2. rinchiudere.

secluded *agg.* appartato, isolato, solitario.

seclusion *s.* 1. isolamento 2. solitudine.

seclusive *agg.* che serve ad isolare.

second[1] *s.* minuto secondo.

second[2] *agg.* secondo.

secondary *agg.* secondario.

secrecy *s.* 1. segretezza 2. riserbo.

secret *agg.* 1. segreto 2. nascosto, intimo. ♦ **secret** *s.* segreto.

secretariat(e) *s.* 1. segretariato 2. segreteria.

secretary *s.* 1. segretario 2. ministro (*preposto ad un dicastero*).

to **secrete**[1] *vt.* secernere.

to **secrete**[2] *vt.* occultare, nascondere.

secretion *s.* secrezione.

secretly *avv.* 1. segretamente 2. in modo reticente.

sect *s.* setta.

sectarian *s.* settario.

sectarianism *s.* spirito di setta.

sectary *s.* settario.

section s. 1. sezione, parte 2. paragrafo 3. regione, quartiere.
to **section** vt. sezionare.
sectional agg. 1. parziale, di classe 2. a sezioni.
sector s. settore.
secular agg. 1. secolare 2. laico 3. mondano, profano. ♦ **secular** s. laico.
secularism s. secolarismo.
secularist agg. e s. laico.
to **secularize** vt. laicizzare.
secure agg. 1. sicuro, certo 2. salvo.
to **secure** vt. 1. assicurare, salvaguardare 2. (giur.; comm.) garantire 3. mettere al sicuro.
security s. 1. sicurezza, protezione 2. certezza, garanzia, cauzione. ♦ **securities** s. pl. titoli, valori.
sedan s. — (-chair), portantina.
sedate agg. 1. posato, composto 2. grave, serio.
sedative agg. e s. sedativo.
sedentary agg. e s. sedentario.
sediment s. sedimento.
sedimentary agg. sedimentario.
sedimentation s. sedimentazione.
sedition s. sedizione.
seditious agg. sedizioso.
to **seduce** vt. sedurre, corrompere.
seduction s. seduzione.
sedulous agg. assiduo.
to **see** (saw, seen) vt. e vi. 1. vedere, scorgere 2. capire, rendersi conto di 3. esaminare, giudicare 4. fare in modo che || to — about, assumersi l'incarico di; to — off, accompagnare (alla partenza); to — over, ispezionare; to — through (fig.), indovinare, penetrare.
see s. (eccl.) sede, diocesi.
seed s. 1. seme, semenza 2. (fig.) principio, germe 3. stirpe.
seedy agg. pieno di semi.
to **seek** (sought, sought) vt. e vi. 1. cercare, andare alla ricerca di 2. ottenere 3. chiedere, ricorrere a || to — for sthg., ricercare qc.
seeker s. cercatore.
to **seem** vi. sembrare, apparire.
seeming agg. apparente, esteriore.
seemliness s. decenza, decoro.
seemly agg. decoroso, decente.
seen V. to see.
segment s. segmento, sezione.
segmentation s. segmentazione.
to **segregate** vt. segregare, separare. ♦ to **segregate** vi. separarsi, scindersi.

segregation s. segregazione.
seismograph s. sismografo.
seismologist s. sismologo.
seismology s. sismologia.
seizable agg. afferrabile.
to **seize** vt. e vi. 1. afferrare, prendere 2. capire, comprendere 3. (giur.) avere in possesso, sequestrare.
seizing s. 1. atto dell'afferrare 2. conquista, cattura.
seizure s. 1. (giur.) confisca, sequestro 2. conquista, cattura.
seldom avv. raramente.
select agg. 1. scelto, selezionato 2. schizzinoso.
to **select** vt. selezionare.
selection s. selezione, scelta.
selective agg. selettivo.
selectivity s. selettività.
selector s. selettore.
self s. (pl. selves) l'io, l'individuo. ♦ **self** agg. 1. della stessa materia 2. uniforme.
self-conceit s. presunzione.
self-control s. autocontrollo.
self-defence s. legittima difesa.
self-denial s. abnegazione.
self-determination s. autodeterminazione.
self-educated agg. autodidatta.
self-examination s. esame di coscienza.
self-government s. (pol.) autogoverno.
self-help s. (giur.) legittima difesa.
selfish agg. egoistico.
selfishness s. egoismo.
self-portrait s. autoritratto.
sell s. (fam.) delusione.
to **sell** (sold, sold) vt. e vi. 1. vendere 2. (fig.) vendere, tradire || to — off (comm.), liquidare.
seller s. 1. venditore 2. articolo che si vende.
selling s. vendita, smercio || — up, vendita fallimentare.
selves V. self.
semantic agg. semantico.
semantics s. semantica.
semester s. semestre.
semi prefisso semi, mezzo, metà.
semicircle s. semicerchio.
semicircular agg. semicircolare.
semicolon s. punto e virgola.
semifinal agg. e s. semifinale.
seminar s. seminario (d'università).
seminarist s. seminarista.
seminary s. seminario.
semination s. semina.

Semite *agg.* e *s.* semita.

Semitic *agg.* semitico.

Semitism *s.* semitismo.

semitone *s.* semitono.

semivowel *s.* semivocale.

senate *s.* senato.

senator *s.* senatore.

senatorial *agg.* senatoriale.

to send (sent, sent) *vt.* e *vi.* mandare, inviare, spedire || *to — away*, congedare; *to — back*, rinviare; *to — for*, mandare a chiamare; *to — off*, inviare (*per lettera*); *to — out*, emettere.

sender *s.* **1.** mandante, mittente **2.** (*comm.*) spedizioniere **3.** (*radio, tv.*) emittente.

sending *s.* **1.** invio **2.** (*comm.*) spedizione **3.** (*radio, tv.*) trasmissione.

senescence *s.* senescenza.

senile *agg.* senile.

senility *s.* senilità.

senior *agg.* **1.** più vecchio, più anziano **2.** più ragguardevole, che ha più anzianità. ♦ **senior** *s.* **1.** decano, anziano **2.** il superiore.

seniority *s.* anzianità (*d'anni, di grado*).

sensation *s.* **1.** senso, sensazione **2.** colpo, impressione.

sensational *agg.* **1.** che dipende dai sensi **2.** sensazionale.

sense *s.* **1.** senso, sensazione, impressione **2.** conoscenza **3.** significato || *common —*, buon senso. ♦ **senses** *s. pl.* facoltà mentale (*sing.*).

senseful *agg.* significativo.

senseless *agg.* **1.** inanimato **2.** insensato.

sensibility *s.* **1.** sensibilità, sensitività **2.** emotività.

sensible *agg.* **1.** sensato, giudizioso **2.** percettibile **3.** notevole, considerevole **4.** consapevole.

sensibly *avv.* **1.** assennatamente **2.** percettibilmente.

sensism *s.* sensismo.

sensist *s.* sensista.

sensitive *agg.* **1.** sensitivo, sensibile **2.** suscettibile, impressionabile.

sensitively *avv.* sensibilmente.

sensitiveness *s.* **1.** sensibilità **2.** suscettibilità.

to sensitize *vt.* sensibilizzare.

sensitizer *s.* (*foto*) sensibilizzatore.

sensorial *agg.* sensorio.

sensory *agg.* sensoriale.

sensual *agg.* sensuale.

sensualism *s.* sensualismo.

sensuality *s.* sensualità.

sensually *avv.* sensualmente, voluttuosamente.

sensuous *agg.* sensoriale, voluttuoso.

sent V. *to send.*

sentence *s.* **1.** giudizio, sentenza **2.** (*gramm.*) frase || *to pass a —*, pronunciare una sentenza.

to sentence *vt.* giudicare, pronunciare una sentenza contro.

sententious *agg.* sentenzioso.

sententiously *avv.* sentenziosamente.

sentient *agg.* senziente, sensibile.

sentiment *s.* **1.** sentimento **2.** opinione, parere.

sentimental *agg.* sentimentale, romantico.

sentimentalism *s.* sentimentalismo.

sentimentalist *s.* persona sentimentale.

sentimentality *s.* sentimentalità.

sentinel *s.* sentinella, guardia.

sentry *s.* sentinella, guardia, scolta || *— box*, garitta.

separate *agg.* separato, staccato.

to separate *vt.* separare. ♦ **to separate** *vi.* separarsi.

separately *avv.* separatamente.

separation *s.* separazione, divisione.

separatism *s.* separatismo.

September *s.* settembre.

septicaemia *s.* setticemia.

septuagenarian *agg.* e *s.* settuagenario.

septuagenary *agg.* settuagenario.

septum *s.* (*pl.* -ta) diaframma.

sepulchral *agg.* sepolcrale.

sepulchre *s.* sepolcro.

sequacious *agg.* pedissequo, servile.

sequel *s.* **1.** conseguenza **2.** seguito.

sequence *s.* **1.** successione, sequela **2.** sequenza.

to sequestrate *vt.* sequestrare, confiscare.

sequestration *s.* sequestro, confisca.

sequin *s.* lustrino.

seraphic(al) *agg.* serafico.

serenade *s.* serenata.

serene *agg.* **1.** sereno, senza nubi **2.** calmo, tranquillo.

serenely *avv.* serenamente.

serenity *s.* **1.** serenità, limpidezza **2.** tranquillità.

sergeant *s.* **1.** sergente **2.** brigadiere.

serial *s.* romanzo a puntate, pubblicazione periodica.

serially *avv.* **1.** in serie **2.** periodicamente.

sericulture *s.* sericoltura.

sericulturist *s.* sericoltore.

series *s.* serie, successione.

serigraphy *s.* serigrafia.

serious *agg.* **1.** serio, pensieroso **2.** grave, importante.

seriousness *s.* **1.** serietà **2.** gravità.

sermon *s.* sermone, predica.

serotherapy *s.* sieroterapia.

serous *agg.* sieroso.

serpent *s.* serpente.

serum *s.* siero.

servant *s.* servo, servitore.

to serve *vt.* e *vi.* **1.** servire, essere al servizio di **2.** servire, essere utile **3.** essere sotto le armi **4.** (*giur.*) notificare (*di atti*) || *to — out*, distribuire.

server *s.* **1.** chi serve **2.** chierico **3.** vassoio.

service *s.* **1.** servizio (*anche militare*) **2.** servigio, favore **3.** funzione religiosa **4.** (*giur.*) notifica. ◆ **Services** *s. pl.* forze armate.

serviceable *agg.* utile, pratico.

serviette *s.* tovagliolo.

servile *agg.* servile.

servilism *s.* servilismo.

servility *s.* servilità.

serving *s.* **1.** il servire **2.** servizio (*di tavola*).

servitude *s.* servitù, schiavitù.

session *s.* sessione, seduta. ◆ **sessions** *s. pl.* (*giur.*) udienze.

set[1] *agg.* **1.** fermo, fisso **2.** stabilito, prestabilito **3.** studiato, preparato. ◆ **set** *s.* **1.** il solidificarsi **2.** forma, serie **3.** gruppo **4.** direzione, corso **5.** (*poet.*) tramonto **6.** serie completa, insieme: *a — of teeth*, una dentiera; *the complete — of Shakespeare's works*, la raccolta completa delle opere di Shakespeare.

to set (set, set) *vt.* e *vi.* **1.** mettere, porre, collocare **2.** sistemare, mettere a punto **3.** tramontare (*anche fig.*) || *to — about*, accingersi; *to — back*, impedire; *to — in*, incominciare; *to — out*, esporre; *to — up*, fissare, installare; *to — aside* (*giur.*), annullare; *to — off*, compensare.

set-back *s.* contrattempo.

set-down *s.* rimprovero.

set-off *s.* **1.** contrasto **2.** compensazione.

setting *s.* **1.** messa in opera, mon-

taggio **2.** ambiente **3.** scenario, messa in scena **4.** incastonatura.

to settle *vt.* e *vi.* **1.** fissare, decidere, determinare **2.** saldare, liquidare (*conti, questioni ecc.*) **3.** sistemare, sistemarsi **4.** stabilire **5.** calmare, calmarsi **6.** depositare, depositarsi (*di sedimenti ecc.*) || *to — down*, stabilirsi (*in un luogo*).

settled *agg.* fissato, stabilito.

settlement *s.* **1.** determinazione **2.** saldo, liquidazione **3.** sistemazione **4.** lo stabilirsi (*in un luogo*) **5.** colonia, distretto **6.** (*giur.*) transazione || *financial —*, regolamento di conti.

settler *s.* **1.** chi decide **2.** colonizzatore.

settling *s.* **1.** stabilizzazione **2.** saldo, pagamento.

set-to *s.* zuffa.

setup *s.* disposizione, organizzazione.

seven *agg.* sette.

sevenfold *agg.* settuplo. ◆ **sevenfold** *avv.* sette volte tanto.

seventeen *agg.* diciassette.

seventeenth *agg.* diciassettesimo.

seventh *agg.* settimo.

seventieth *agg.* settantesimo.

seventy *agg.* settanta.

to sever *vt.* staccare, dividere. ◆ **to sever** *vi.* staccarsi, dividersi.

several *agg.* **1.** parecchi, diversi (*pl.*) **2.** separato, distinto. ◆ **several** *pron.* alcuni, diversi (*pl.*) || *— of them*, alcuni di loro.

severally *avv.* separatamente, individualmente.

severe *agg.* **1.** severo, austero **2.** violento, forte **3.** rigido (*di clima*).

severely *avv.* **1.** severamente **2.** violentemente.

severity *s.* **1.** severità, durezza **2.** violenza.

to sew (sewed, sewn) *vt.* e *vi.* cucire.

sewage *s.* acque di scolatura.

sewer[1] *s.* chi cuce, cucitrice.

sewer[2] *s.* **1.** canale artificiale di drenaggio **2.** fogna.

sewing *s.* **1.** il cucire **2.** lavoro di cucito.

sewn V. *to sew.*

sex *s.* sesso.

sexagenarian *agg.* e *s.* sessagenario.

sextet(te) *s.* sestetto.

sexton *s.* sagrestano.

sextuple *agg.* e *s.* sestuplo.

sexual *agg.* sessuale.

shabbiness s. 1. l'essere male in arnese 2. meschinità.

shabby agg. 1. male in arnese, cencioso 2. meschino, gretto.

shackles s. pl. 1. manette, ceppi 2. (fig.) impedimenti.

shade s. ombra (anche fig.) 2. sfumatura (di colore, significato ecc.) 3. spirito, ombra 4. schermo, riparo ‖ eye- —, visiera.

to shade vt. e vi. 1. ombreggiare, riparare (da luce, calore) 2. velare, oscurare (anche fig.).

shadiness s. ombrosità.

shading s. 1. l'ombreggiare 2. ombreggiatura, sfumatura.

shadow s. ombra (anche fig.). ♦ **shadows** s. pl. oscurità.

to shadow vt. pedinare, seguire come un'ombra.

shadowy agg. 1. ombroso, ombreggiato 2. indistinto, vago.

shady agg. ombreggiato, all'ombra.

shaft[1] s. 1. lancia, giavellotto 2. fulmine 3. gambo, stelo 4. asta, bastone 5. (mecc.) albero.

shaft[2] s. sfiatatoio, condotto.

shaggy agg. 1. ispido, irsuto 2. peloso (di tessuto) 3. incolto.

Shah s. scià.

shake s. 1. scossa, scuotimento 2. tremore, tremito 3. frullato.

to shake (shook, shaken) vt. e vi. 1. scuotere, agitare (liquidi) 2. tremare, far tremare 3. turbare 4. indebolire.

shakily avv. instabilmente.

shaking agg. tremante, vacillante. ♦ **shaking** s. scossa, scuotimento.

shaky agg. 1. instabile, tremolante 2. malsicuro.

shall v. dif. 1. (aus. per le prime pers. del fut. predicente) I — go to England next summer, andrò in Inghilterra l'estate prossima; we — work next week, lavoreremo la prossima settimana 2. (aus. per le seconde e terze pers. del fut. volitivo) you — go to bed!, andrai a letto! 3. dovere: you — wait for me, devi aspettarmi.

shallow agg. 1. poco profondo, basso 2. (fig.) superficiale.

sham s. 1. finta, inganno 2. ipocrita.

shaman s. sciamano.

shambles s. pl. 1. mattatoio (sing.) 2. carneficina (sing.).

shame s. 1. vergogna, pudore 2. disonore.

to shame vt. 1. svergognare, far arrossire 2. disonorare.

shamefaced agg. 1. vergognoso 2. timido.

shameful agg. vergognoso, disonorevole.

shameless agg. svergognato, sfacciato.

shamelessly avv. sfacciatamente.

shank s. 1. gamba, stinco 2. gambo, stelo 3. fusto (di colonna) ‖ — -bone, tibia.

shape s. forma, figura.

to shape vt. e vi. creare, dar forma a.

shapeless agg. informe.

shapely agg. ben fatto.

share s. 1. parte, porzione 2. (comm.) azione, titolo.

to share vt. dividere, spartire. ♦ **to share** vi. partecipare, condividere.

shareholder s. azionista.

share-out s. distribuzione.

shark s. 1. squalo, pescecane 2. (fig.) profittatore.

sharp agg. 1. tagliente, affilato 2. aguzzo 3. scosceso, ripido 4. netto, chiaro 5. intelligente, acuto.

sharp avv. puntualmente, in punto.

to sharpen vt. 1. affilare, aguzzare 2. (fig.) rendere più acuto.

sharper s. imbroglione.

sharply avv. acutamente.

sharpness s. 1. filo, affilatura 2. acutezza 3. vivacità, intelligenza.

sharp-sighted agg. dalla vista acuta.

to shatter vt. frantumare. ♦ **to shatter** vi. frantumarsi.

shattering s. disintegrazione.

shave[1] s. il radersi, rasatura.

shave[2] s. pialla.

to shave[1] vt. radere. ♦ **to shave** vi. radersi.

to shave[2] vt. piallare.

shaven agg. 1. rasato 2. (eccl.) tonsurato.

shaving s. 1. il radersi 2. truciolo.

shawl s. scialle.

she pron. pers. f. ella, lei, colei. ♦ **she** attr. indicante il sesso degli animali: a — -bear, un'orsa.

sheaf s. (pl. sheaves) 1. fascio, covone 2. (geom.) fascio (di rette ecc.).

to shear (sheared, shorn) vt. 1. cesoiare, tranciare 2. tosare.

shearing s. recisione, taglio.

shears s. pl. cesoie, forbici.

sheath s. guaina, fodero.

to **sheathe** vt. **1.** mettere nel fodero **2.** rivestire di.

sheaves V. sheaf.

to **shed** (**shed, shed**) vt. **1.** versare, spandere **2.** lasciar cadere.

shed s. tettoia, capannone.

shedding s. **1.** spargimento **2.** perdita, caduta (di foglie ecc.).

sheen s. splendore, lucentezza.

sheep s. (anche pl.) **1.** pecora, ovino **2.** (fig.) persona debole, timorosa.

sheepish agg. timido, impacciato.

sheepskin s. **1.** pelle di pecora **2.** cartapecora.

sheer[1] agg. **1.** puro, semplice, mero **2.** liscio, non diluito (di bevande).

sheer[2] s. virata, cambiamento di rotta.

sheet s. **1.** lenzuolo **2.** foglio **3.** lamina, lamiera.

sheik(h) s. sceicco.

shelf s. (pl. shelves) mensola, scaffale.

shell s. **1.** conchiglia, guscio **2.** involucro, carcassa **3.** bossolo (di cartuccia) **4.** (fig.) apparenza.

to **shell** vt. e vi. sgusciare, sgranare.

shelter s. **1.** riparo, rifugio **2.** pensilina.

to **shelter** vt. riparare. ◆ to **shelter** vi. ripararsi.

to **shelve** vt. **1.** provvedere di scaffali **2.** mettere negli scaffali.

shelves V. shelf.

shelving s. scaffalatura.

shepherd s. pastore, pecoraio.

sherbet s. sorbetto.

shield s. **1.** scudo **2.** (fig.) protezione.

to **shield** vt. proteggere, difendere.

shift s. **1.** cambiamento, sostituzione **2.** risorsa, espediente **3.** turno (di lavoro).

to **shift** vt. **1.** spostare **2.** cambiare. ◆ to **shift** vi. **1.** spostarsi **2.** arrangiarsi.

shilling s. scellino.

to **shilly-shally** vi. tentennare.

to **shimmer** vi. luccicare, mandare bagliori.

to **shine** (**shone, shone**) vt. e vi. **1.** splendere, brillare (anche fig.) **2.** essere brillante.

shine s. **1.** splendore, luminosità **2.** luce del sole.

Shintoist s. scintoista.

shiny agg. splendente, rilucente.

ship s. nave, bastimento ‖ convoy-—, nave scorta; flag-—, nave ammiraglia; landing-—, nave da sbarco.

to **ship** vt. **1.** imbarcare **2.** (comm.) spedire. ◆ to **ship** vi. imbarcarsi.

shipboard s. bordo.

shipboy s. mozzo.

shipbuilder s. costruttore navale.

shipmate s. compagno di bordo.

shipment s. imbarco, spedizione di merci.

shipping s. **1.** forze navali (pl.) **2.** imbarco, spedizione.

shipwreck s. naufragio.

to **shipwreck** vi. naufragare.

shipyard s. cantiere navale.

shirker s. scansafatiche.

shirt s. camicia (da uomo).

shiver[1] s. scheggia.

shiver[2] s. brivido, fremito.

to **shiver**[1] vt. frantumare. ◆ to **shiver** vi. frantumarsi.

to **shiver**[2] vt. e vi. rabbrividire, tremare.

shivering s. V. shiver.

shivery agg. **1.** fragile **2.** tremante.

shoal[1] s. secca, bassofondo.

shoal[2] s. banco (di pesci).

shock s. **1.** urto, collisione **2.** forte impressione, violenta emozione.

to **shock** vt. **1.** colpire, disgustare **2.** provocare un collasso. ◆ to **shock** vi. **1.** scandalizzarsi **2.** scontrarsi.

shocking agg. **1.** che colpisce **2.** disgustoso.

shoe s. scarpa, calzatura ‖ horse-—, ferro di cavallo.

shoeblack s. lustrascarpe.

shoemaker s. calzolaio.

shoe-string s. laccio (da scarpe).

shone V. to shine.

shook V. to shake.

shoot s. **1.** spedizione di caccia **2.** virgulto **3.** puntura, fitta.

to **shoot** (**shot, shot**) vt. e vi. **1.** lanciare **2.** sparare, uccidere sparando **3.** cacciare **4.** fare un'istantanea.

shooter s. cacciatore.

shooting s. **1.** tiro, sparo **2.** caccia **3.** il fotografare, il girare un film.

shop s. **1.** bottega, negozio **2.** officina, laboratorio ‖ — -assistant, commesso; — -book, libro dei conti; — -lifter, taccheggiatore; — -window, vetrina.

shopkeeper s. negoziante.

shopman s. commesso di negozio.

shopping s. compere, acquisti (pl.).

shore s. spiaggia, lido.

shorn V. to shear.

short agg. 1. corto, breve 2. basso, piccolo (di statura) 3. conciso 4. brusco, rude. ♦ **short** s. 1. compendio 2. (cine) cortometraggio.

short avv. 1. bruscamente, improvvisamente 2. (comm.) allo scoperto.

shortage s. mancanza, carenza.

short-circuit s. corto circuito.

short-cut s. scorciatoia.

short-dated agg. (comm.) a breve scadenza.

to shorten vt. accorciare, abbreviare.

shortening s. accorciamento, abbreviazione.

shorthand s. stenografia.

shortly avv. 1. fra breve 2. brevemente.

shortness s. brevità.

short-sighted agg. miope.

shot[1] V. to shoot.

shot[2] s. 1. sparo, colpo 2. proiettile 3. ripresa cinematografica.

shotgun s. fucile da caccia.

should s. dif. 1. (aus. per le prime pers. del condiz.) I — be very happy, sarei felicissimo 2. dovere: it — be so, dovrebbe essere così.

shoulder s. spalla.

to shoulder vt. e vi. 1. spingere con le spalle 2. portare sulle spalle.

shout s. grido, chiasso.

to shout vt. e vi. gridare, urlare.

shove s. spinta, urto.

to shove vt. spingere. ♦ **to shove** vi. spingersi.

shovel s. pala.

to shovel vt. spalare.

shoveller s. spalatore.

show s. 1. mostra, esibizione 2. apparenza 3. pompa, ostentazione || — case, bacheca; — down, chiarificazione; —-off, esibizionismo.

to show (showed, shown) vt. e vi. 1. mostrare, far vedere 2. rappresentare, indicare 3. dimostrare, provare 4. apparire, farsi vedere || to — down, mettere le carte in tavola; to — off, darsi delle arie.

shower s. acquazzone, rovescio.

showman s. presentatore.

shown V. to show.

showy agg. fastoso, appariscente.

shrank V. to shrink.

shred s. brandello, frammento.

shrew s. bisbetica.

shrewd agg. sagace, accorto.

shrewdly avv. sagacemente.

shrewdness s. sagacia, accortezza.

shrewish agg. brontolone.

shriek s. grido, strillo, suono lacerante.

to shriek vt. e vi. gridare, stridere.

shrill agg. stridulo, acuto.

to shrill vt. e vi. strillare, stridere.

shrimp s. gamberetto.

shrine s. reliquiario.

shrink s. restringimento.

to shrink (shrank, shrunk) vt. e vi. 1. restringere, restringersi, contrarre 2. indietreggiare.

shrinkable agg. restringibile.

shrinkage s. 1. diminuzione, restringimento 2. (comm.) deprezzamento.

shrinking s. contrazione, ritiro.

shroud s. sudario.

shrub s. arbusto, cespuglio.

shrubbery s. boscaglia d'arbusti.

shrug s. spallucciata.

to shrug vi. alzate le spalle.

shrunk V. to shrink.

shudder s. brivido.

to shudder vi. rabbrividire.

shuffle s. 1. passo strascicato 2. scompiglio 3. il mescolare (le carte).

to shuffle vt. e vi. 1. muoversi a fatica 2. mescolare, scompigliare.

to shun vt. sfuggire, scansare.

shunt s. 1. (elett.) derivazione 2. (ferr.) scambio.

to shunt vt. e vi. 1. (elett.) inserire in derivazione 2. (ferr.) smistare, smistarsi.

shut agg. ben chiuso.

to shut (shut, shut) vt. e vi. chiudere, serrare || shut up!, tacil

shutter s. imposta, persiana.

shuttle s. spola, navetta.

shy agg. riservato, timido.

to shy vt. spaventare. ♦ **to shy** vi. scartare (di cavallo).

shyly avv. timidamente.

shyness s. timidezza, scontrosità.

Siberian agg. e s. siberiano.

sibilant agg. e s. sibilante.

Sibylline agg. sibillino.

Sicilian agg. e s. siciliano.

sick agg. 1. ammalato 2. nauseato || to fall —, ammalarsi.

to **sicken** vt. e vi. **1.** far ammalare, ammalarsi **2.** sfiorire **3.** sentir nausea.

sickening agg. nauseabondo, rivoltante.

sickle s. falce.

sickly agg. **1.** malaticcio **2.** pallido, debole **3.** nauseante.

sickness s. malattia.

side s. **1.** lato, fianco **2.** parte, partito, fazione **3.** discendenza || — -door, porta laterale; — -face, profilo; — -look, occhiata in tralice; — -note, nota marginale; — -post, stipite.

sideboard s. credenza.

sidecar s. motocarrozzetta.

sidelong agg. laterale, obliquo.

sidereal agg. sidereo.

sideways avv. lateralmente, obliquamente.

to **sidle** vi. camminare di fianco, andare a sghembo || to — up to so., avvicinarsi furtivamente a qu.

siege s. assedio.

sieve s. setaccio, crivello.

to **sieve** vt. setacciare, crivellare.

to **sift** vt. e vi. setacciare **2.** filtrare (di luce, polvere ecc.).

sigh s. sospiro.

to **sigh** vt. e vi. **1.** sospirare **2.** sibilare.

sight s. **1.** vista, visione **2.** veduta, panorama **3.** colpo d'occhio **4.** mirino.

to **sight** vt. e vi. **1.** avvistare **2.** prendere la mira.

sighted agg. **1.** fornito di vista || long- —, presbite; short- —, miope.

sightless agg. senza vista.

sign s. **1.** segno, cenno **2.** indicazione, traccia || traffic —, segnale stradale.

to **sign** vt. e vi. firmare, segnare, sottoscrivere.

signal s. segnale, segno.

to **signal** vt. segnalare. ♦ to **signal** vi. far segnali.

signalman s. segnalatore.

signatory s. firmatario.

signature s. **1.** firma, sigla **2.** (tip.) segnatura.

signboard s. insegna (di albergo, negozio ecc.).

significant agg. espressivo, significativo.

to **signify** vt. e vi. **1.** significare, voler dire **2.** denotare, indicare, presagire **3.** importare.

silence s. silenzio.

to **silence** vt. far tacere, imporre il silenzio.

silencer s. silenziatore.

silent agg. **1.** silenzioso, taciturno **2.** muto.

silently avv. silenziosamente.

silhouette s. profilo, contorno.

silica s. silice.

silicate s. silicato.

silicon s. silicio.

silicosis s. silicosi.

silk s. seta.

silken agg. serico, di seta.

silkworm s. baco da seta || — breeding, sericoltura.

silky agg. di seta, serico.

sill s. basamento, soglia.

silliness s. stupidità, sciocchezza.

silly agg. sciocco, stupido.

to **silo** vt. conservare, mettere in silo.

silt s. melma.

silver s. argento, argenteria || — -plate, argenteria; — -plating, argentatura || quick —, mercurio.

to **silver** vt. inargentare. ♦ to **silver** vi. inargentarsi.

silverware s. oggetti d'argento.

silvery agg. argenteo.

similar agg. simile, analogo.

similarity s. somiglianza, similitudine.

similitude s. **1.** similitudine **2.** somiglianza.

simoniac agg. e s. simoniaco.

simony s. simonia.

to **simper** vi. parlare in modo affettato.

simple agg. **1.** semplice, elementare **2.** sincero **3.** autentico.

simpleton s. semplicotto.

simplicity s. semplicità, candore.

simplification s. semplificazione.

to **simplify** vt. semplificare.

simply avv. semplicemente.

simulation s. simulazione.

simulator s. simulatore.

simultaneity s. simultaneità.

simultaneous agg. simultaneo.

sin s. **1.** peccato, colpa **2.** offesa.

to **sin** vi. peccare.

since avv. da allora, da allora in poi || long —, molto tempo fa. ♦ since cong. **1.** da quando **2.** poiché. ♦ since prep. da, fin da.

sincere agg. sincero, schietto.

sincerely avv. sinceramente || yours —, cordialmente vostro (nelle lettere).

sincerity s. sincerità.

sinew s. 1. tendine, nervo 2. (fig.) vigore, nerbo.

sinful agg. peccaminoso, colpevole.

sinfully avv. peccaminosamente.

to **sing** (sang, sung) vt. e vi. cantare.

to **singe** vt. bruciacchiare, strinare (anche fig.). ♦ to **singe** vi. bruciarsi.

singer s. cantante.

singing s. 1. canto 2. fischio (del vento ecc.).

single agg. 1. solo, unico 2. individuale, particolare 3. celibe ‖ every — day, tutti i giorni.

to **single** vt. distinguere, scegliere: to — out sthg., scegliere qc.

singleness s. 1. unicità 2. sincerità.

singly avv. 1. separatamente, ad uno ad uno 2. da solo, senza aiuto.

singsong s. cantilena, canto monotono.

singular agg. 1. singolare, solo 2. eccezionale 3. bizzarro, strano.

singularity s. 1. singolarità, rarità 2. particolarità 3. stranezza.

singularly avv. singolarmente.

sinister agg. sinistro, funesto, di cattivo augurio.

sink s. 1. lavandino, acquaio 2. scolo.

to **sink** (sank, sunk) vi. 1. affondare, andare a fondo 2. sprofondare 3. abbassare, abbassarsi, calare 4. cadere, cedere (di terreno, muro ecc.).

sinner s. peccatore.

sinuous agg. sinuoso.

sinus s. 1. cavità 2. seno.

sip s. sorso.

to **sip** vt. e vi. sorseggiare.

siphon s. sifone.

sir s. 1. (vocativo) signore 2. « sir » (titolo).

siren s. sirena.

siroc s. scirocco.

sirup s. sciroppo.

sister s. 1. sorella 2. suora ‖ — -in- -law, cognata.

sisterhood s. congregazione religiosa di suore.

sisterly avv. da sorella, amorevolmente.

to **sit** (sat, sat) vt. e vi. 1. sedere, stare seduto, far sedere 2. essere in seduta 3. appollaiarsi, posare 4. covare ‖ to — out, rimanere fino alla fine; to — up, rimanere al-

zato.

site s. area fabbricabile.

sitting s. 1. posa, seduta 2. adunanza ‖ —-room, stanza di soggiorno. ♦ **sittings** s. pl. sessioni (di una Corte).

situated agg. 1. situato, collocato 2. in una certa situazione (di persona).

situation s. 1. situazione, posizione 2. stato, circostanza 3. posto, impiego: to apply for a —, fare una domanda di impiego.

six agg. sei.

sixfold agg. sestuplo. ♦ **sixfold** avv. sei volte tanto.

sixpence s. moneta da sei « pence », mezzo scellino.

sixpenny agg. del valore di sei « pence ».

sixteen agg. sedici.

sixteenth agg. sedicesimo.

sixth agg. sesto.

sixtieth agg. sessantesimo.

sixty agg. sessanta.

size s. 1. grandezza, misura, dimensione 2. formato, taglia 3. colla.

to **size** vt. allineare ‖ to — up, valutare.

sizzle s. sfrigolio.

skate s. pattino ‖ roller —, pattino a rotelle.

to **skate** vi. pattinare.

skating s. pattinaggio.

skein s. matassa.

skeleton s. scheletro (anche fig.).

to **skeletonize** vt. scheletrire. ♦ to **skeletonize** vi. scheletrirsi (anche fig.).

skeptic agg. e s. scettico.

skeptical agg. scettico.

skepticism s. scetticismo.

sketch s. 1. schizzo, abbozzo 2. scenetta.

to **sketch** vt. abbozzare, schizzare.

skewness s. asimmetria.

ski s. sci ‖ — -lift, sciovia.

to **ski** vi. sciare.

skier s. sciatore.

skiff s. (mar.) schifo.

skilful agg. abile, esperto.

skilfully avv. abilmente.

skilfulness s. abilità.

skill s. abilità, destrezza.

skilled agg. esperto, abile, versato ‖ — worker, operaio specializzato.

to **skim** vt. e vi. 1. schiumare, scremare 2. rasentare, sfiorare.

skimmer s. schiumarola.

skimming s. scrematura.
skin s. pelle, cute.
to **skin** vt. e vi. scuoiare || to — over, rimarginarsi (di ferite).
skinny agg. magro, scarno.
to **skip** vt. e vi. fare un balzo, saltare alla corda || to — a few pages, saltare qualche pagina.
skirmish s. scaramuccia.
skirt s. 1. sottana, gonna 2. orlo, lembo.
to **skirt** vt. e vi. orlare, costeggiare.
skittish agg. capriccioso, frivolo.
skittles s. pl. birilli.
skull s. cranio, teschio || — -cap, papalina.
sky s. cielo, firmamento.
skylark s. allodola.
skylight s. lucernario.
skyline s. linea, profilo (di montagne ecc.).
skyman s. paracadutista.
skyscraper s. grattacielo.
skyward agg. e avv. verso il cielo.
slab s. 1. lastra, piastra 2. pezzo, fetta.
slack agg. 1. molle, allentato 2. debole, fiacco 3. (comm.) calmo, stagnante, debole. ♦ **slack** s. (comm.) stagione morta.
to **slacken** vt. 1. allentare, mollare 2. diminuire. ♦ to **slacken** vi. 1. allentarsi 2. smorzarsi.
slacker s. fannullone.
slain V. to slay.
slam s. sbatacchiamento.
to **slam** vt. sbattere, chiudere violentemente. ♦ to **slam** vi. chiudersi violentemente.
slander s. 1. calunnia 2. (giur.) diffamazione.
to **slander** vt. 1. calunniare 2. (giur.) diffamare.
slanderer s. 1. calunniatore 2. (giur.) diffamatore.
slanderous agg. calunnioso, maldicente.
slang s. gergo.
slant s. pendenza, inclinazione.
to **slant** vt. e vi. essere in pendenza, inclinare.
slanting agg. inclinato, obliquo, sghembo.
slap s. schiaffo, ceffone.
to **slap** vt. 1. schiaffeggiare 2. sbattere.
slash s. 1. taglio, sfregio 2. frustata.
to **slash** vt. tagliare, fendere.

slate s. ardesia, tegola d'ardesia.
slaughter s. 1. macello 2. carneficina, massacro.
to **slaughter** vt. 1. macellare 2. massacrare.
slaughterer s. 1. macellatore 2. massacratore.
slaughterhouse s. mattatoio.
Slav agg. e s. slavo.
slave s. schiavo.
slaver[1] s. schiavista.
slaver[2] s. saliva, bava.
slavery s. schiavitù.
to **slay** (**slew, slain**) vt. ammazzare.
sleek agg. lucido, levigato.
sleep s. sonno, dormita || — walker, sonnambulo.
to **sleep** (**slept, slept**) vt. e vi. 1. dormire, riposare 2. passare la notte.
sleeper s. 1. dormiente, dormiglione 2. (ferr.) traversina 3. (ferr.) vettura letto.
sleepily avv. con aria assonnata.
sleeping agg. dormiente, addormentato || — bag, sacco a pelo; — -berth, cuccetta; — -car, vagone letto; — -draught, sonnifero.
sleepless agg. insonne.
sleeplessness s. insonnia.
sleepy agg. assonnato, sonnolento.
sleet s. nevischio.
sleeve s. manica.
sleeved agg. con maniche.
sleigh s. slitta.
slender agg. 1. magro, snello 2. debole, fiacco.
slenderness s. 1. snellezza, magrezza 2. debolezza.
slept V. to sleep.
slew V. to slay.
slice s. pezzo, fetta, porzione.
to **slice** vt. affettare.
slicer s. affettatrice.
slid V. to slide.
slide s. 1. scivolata 2. pendenza 3. scivolo 4. (mecc.) carrello, pattino.
to **slide** (**slid, slid**) vt. e vi. 1. scivolare, far scivolare, scorrere, far scorrere 2. sfuggire.
sliding agg. scorrevole.
slight agg. 1. esile, minuto, magro 2. leggero, scarso.
slim agg. 1. magro, sottile 2. debole.
slime s. melma, limo.
slimy agg. fangoso, viscoso.
sling[1] s. fionda.

sling² s. cinghia.

to **sling¹** (**slung, slung**) vt. scagliare con la fionda.

to **sling²** vt. sospendere, appendere.

to **slink** (**slunk, slunk**) vi. sgattaiolare.

slip¹ s. 1. innesto 2. (tip.) bozza in colonna.

slip² s. 1. scalo, molo 2. guinzaglio 3. sottoveste 4. scivolone 5. papera, lapsus.

to **slip** vt. e vi. 1. scivolare, inciampare 2. entrare, uscire furtivamente 3. sgusciare, liberarsi ‖ to — away, scorrere (di tempo).

slipper s. pantofola.

slippery agg. sdrucciolevole, viscido (anche fig.).

slipshod agg. 1. scalcagnato 2. trasandato.

slit s. fessura, fenditura.

to **slit** (**slit, slit**) vt. fendere.

slope s. pendenza, pendio.

to **slope** vi. essere in pendenza, inclinarsi.

sloping agg. inclinato, obliquo.

slot s. fessura, scanalatura ‖ -machine, distributore automatico a gettoni.

sloth s. pigrizia, indolenza.

slothful agg. pigro, indolente.

slouch s. andatura dinoccolata.

slouching agg. dinoccolato, goffo.

slovenliness s. sciatteria, sporcizia.

slovenly agg. sciatto, sudicio.

slow agg. 1. lento 2. tardo, ottuso ‖ — -down, rallentamento; — -match, miccia.

to **slow** vt. e vi. to — up o down, rallentare.

slowly avv. lentamente.

slowness s. lentezza, pigrizia.

sluggish agg. pigro, tardo, indolente.

sluggishness s. pigrizia, indolenza.

slum s. vicolo, tugurio. ♦ **slums** s. pl. quartieri poveri (di una città).

slumber s. dormiveglia, assopimento.

to **slumber** vt. e vi. dormire, dormicchiare.

slung V. to sling.

slunk V. to slink.

slush s. poltiglia, fango.

sly agg. 1. astuto, malizioso 2. infido.

smack s. 1. sapore, aroma 2. schiocco 3. schiaffo.

to **smack** vt. e vi. 1. schioccare 2. schioccare baci 3. schiaffeggiare.

small agg. 1. piccolo, minuto 2. leggero, debole 3. poco, scarso 4. di poca importanza.

small-arms s. pl. armi portatili.

smallness s. piccolezza.

smallpox s. vaiolo.

smart agg. 1. acuto, pungente 2. vivace, sveglio 3. elegante.

to **smarten** vt. e vi. abbellire ‖ to — up, rianimarsi, farsi bello.

smartness s. 1. acutezza, vivacità, brio 2. eleganza.

smash s. 1. urto, scontro 2. rovina.

to **smash** vt. 1. frantumare, fracassare 2. sconfiggere, annientare. ♦ to **smash** vi. 1. frantumarsi 2. sfasciarsi 3. crollare.

smasher s. 1. chi frantuma 2. (fam.) caso eccezionale.

smear s. macchia, imbrattatura.

to **smear** vt. macchiare, imbrattare.

smell s. 1. odorato, olfatto 2. odore.

to **smell** (**smelt, smelt**) vt. e vi. 1. fiutare, sentire l'odore 2. avere odore ‖ to — of, sapere di; to — out, scovare.

smile s. sorriso.

to **smile** vt. e vi. sorridere ‖ fortune smiled on you, la fortuna ti fu favorevole.

smiling agg. sorridente, sereno.

smirch s. onta, macchia.

to **smite** (**smote, smitten**) vt. e vi. 1. colpire, percuotere 2. sconfiggere, sgominare ‖ to — down, abbattere.

smith s. fabbro.

smitten V. to smite.

smoke s. 1. fumo 2. fumata ‖ -stack, fumaiolo.

to **smoke** vt. e vi. 1. fumare 2. affumicare.

smoker s. fumatore, fumatrice.

smoking s. il fumare. ♦ **smoking** agg. fumante.

smoky agg. 1. fumoso 2. affumicato, annerito dal fumo 3. che sa di fumo.

smooth agg. 1. liscio, levigato 2. omogeneo 3. armonioso (di suono) 4. mellifluo 5. calmo, tranquillo (di mare).

to **smooth** vt. 1. lisciare, spianare 2. appianare.

smoothing s. lisciatura, spianatura.

smoothly avv. 1. pianamente 2. armonicamente 3. in modo mellifluo.

smoothness s. 1. levigatezza 2. armonia (di verso, suono) 3. affabilità.

smote V. *to smite*.

to **smother** *vt.* e *vi.* 1. soffocare, opprimere 2. ricoprire.

to **smoulder** *vi.* ardere sotto la cenere.

to **smuggle** *vt.* e *vi.* contrabbandare.

smuggler *s.* contrabbandiere.

smuggling *s.* contrabbando.

smut *s.* fuliggine.

snack *s.* 1. boccone, porzione 2. spuntino || — *-bar*, tavola calda.

snail *s.* chiocciola, lumaca.

snake *s.* serpente.

snakily *avv.* 1. tortuosamente 2. (*fig.*) slealmente.

snaky *agg.* serpentino.

snap *s.* 1. colpo secco, morso, schiocco 2. scatto 3. fermaglio, fibbia.

to **snap** *vt.* e *vi.* 1. schioccare, far schioccare 2. aprirsi di colpo, spezzare con un colpo secco 3. (*foto*) scattare un'istantanea.

snapshot *s.* (*foto*) istantanea.

snare *s.* 1. trappola, rete 2. insidia, tentazione.

to **snare** *vt.* prendere in trappola, al laccio (*anche fig.*).

snarl *s.* ringhio.

to **snarl** *vi.* ringhiare.

snatch *s.* 1. strappo, strattone 2. brano, frammento.

to **snatch** *vt.* e *vi.* afferrare, ghermire || *to — off*, strappare.

sneak *s.* persona malfida.

sneer *s.* sogghigno beffardo.

to **sneer** *vt.* e *vi.* sorridere beffardamente, schernire.

sneeze *s.* starnuto.

to **sneeze** *vi.* starnutire.

to **sniff** *vt.* e *vi.* fiutare || *to — at sthg.* annusare qc.

snip *s.* 1. ritaglio, scampolo 2. forbiciata.

to **snip** *vt.* tagliuzzare.

snobbery *s.* snobismo.

to **snore** *vi.* russare.

snort *s.* sbuffo, rumore sbuffante.

to **snort** *vt.* e *vi.* sbuffare.

snout *s.* muso, grugno.

snow *s.* neve, nevicata || — *plough*, spazzaneve; — *-slide*, valanga.

to **snow** *v. imp.* nevicare || *it is snowing*, nevica.

snowfall *s.* nevicata.

snowflake *s.* fiocco di neve.

snowy *agg.* 1. nevoso, coperto di neve 2. niveo.

snuff *s.* 1. l'aspirare col naso 2. tabacco da fiuto || — *-box*, tabacchiera.

to **snuff**[1] *vt.* e *vi.* 1. annusare aspirando 2. fiutare tabacco.

to **snuff**[2] *vt.* e *vi.* smoccolare (*una candela*).

to **snuffle** *vt.* e *vi.* pronunciare con tono nasale.

snug *agg.* 1. comodo 2. confortevole 3. nascosto.

to **snuggle** *vi.* 1. rannicchiarsi 2. accoccolarsi.

so *avv.* così, tanto, talmente || — *far*, fino ad ora; — *long as*, a patto che; *if* —, in tal caso; *that being* —, stando così le cose.

to **soak** *vt.* 1. immergere 2. bagnare. ♦ to **soak** *vi.* 1. inzupparsi, imbeversi 2. bagnarsi.

soaking *agg.* 1. che bagna, che inzuppa 2. bagnato. ♦ **soaking** *s.* immersione, bagnatura.

soap *s.* sapone || — *dish*, portasapone.

to **soap** *vt.* insaponare. ♦ to **soap** *vi.* insaponarsi.

soapbox *s.* 1. cassa per sapone 2. (*fam.*) palco improvvisato per oratori (*da strada*).

soapsuds *s. pl.* saponata (*sing.*).

soapwort *s.* saponaria.

sob *s.* singhiozzo.

to **sob** *vt.* e *vi.* singhiozzare.

sober *agg.* 1. sobrio (*nel bere*) 2. calmo, composto.

sobriety *s.* 1. sobrietà (*nel bere*) 2. moderazione, calma.

so-called *agg.* cosiddetto.

sociability *s.* socievolezza.

sociable *agg.* socievole.

social *agg.* 1. sociale 2. socievole.

socialism *s.* socialismo.

socialist *s.* socialista.

sociality *s.* socievolezza.

to **socialize** *vt.* socializzare.

society *s.* 1. società, compagnia 2. strato sociale 3. associazione.

sociological *agg.* sociologico.

sociologist *s.* sociologo.

sociology *s.* sociologia.

sock *s.* 1. calzino, calza corta 2. soletta.

socket *s.* 1. cavità 2. (*elett.*) presa di corrente, portalampada 3. (*anat.*) orbita.

Socratic *agg.* e *s.* socratico.

sod *s.* zolla erbosa.

soda *s.* carbonato di sodio.

sodium s. sodio.

soft agg. 1. molle, tenero 2. liscio, morbido, soffice 3. dolce, mite || — -boiled (egg), uovo alla coque.

to **soften** vt. 1. ammollire, ammorbidire 2. calmare, raddolcire. ◆ to **soften** vi. 1. ammorbidirsi 2. intenerirsi.

softening agg. che rende molle. ◆ **softening** s. 1. ammorbidimento 2. intenerimento.

softly avv. 1. teneramente 2. sommessamente 3. pian piano.

softness s. 1. morbidezza 2. dolcezza, mitezza.

soil s. 1. suolo, terreno 2. macchia (anche fig.).

to **soil** vt. macchiare. ◆ to **soil** vi. macchiarsi.

sojourn s. soggiorno.

to **sojourn** vi. soggiornare.

solace s. sollievo, conforto.

to **solace** vt. consolare.

solar agg. solare.

sold V. to sell.

solder s. lega per saldatura.

to **solder** vt. saldare.

soldering s. saldatura.

soldier s. 1. soldato 2. stratega || foot- —, soldato di fanteria; horse- —, soldato di cavalleria.

soldierlike agg. militaresco.

soldiery s. coll. soldatesca, truppe.

sole[1] agg. solo, unico.

sole[2] s. suola, pianta del piede.

sole[3] s. sogliola.

solecism s. solecismo.

solely avv. solamente.

solemn agg. solenne, serio, grave.

solemnity s. solennità.

to **solemnize** vt. solennizzare.

solemnly avv. solennemente.

sol-fa s. solfeggio.

to **sol-fa** vt. e vi. solfeggiare.

to **solicit** vt. 1. sollecitare 2. adescare. ◆ to **solicit** vi. fare sollecitazioni.

solicitation s. 1. sollecitazione 2. invito, adescamento.

solicitor s. 1. sollecitatore 2. procuratore legale.

solicitous agg. 1. sollecito 2. ansioso, desideroso.

solid agg. 1. solido, compatto 2. reale, fondato. ◆ **solid** s. solido.

solidarity s. solidarietà.

solidary agg. solidale.

solidification s. solidificazione.

to **solidify** vt. solidificare. ◆ to **so-**

lidify vi. solidificarsi.

solidity s. 1. solidità 2. (comm.) solvenza.

solidly avv. 1. solidamente 2. all'unanimità.

soliloquy s. soliloquio.

solitaire s. solitario (pietra preziosa e giuoco delle carte).

solitary agg. 1. solo, unico 2. solitario 3. isolato, romito.

solitude s. solitudine, isolamento.

soloist s. solista.

solstice s. solstizio.

solubility s. solubilità.

soluble agg. 1. solubile 2. scomponibile 3. risolvibile.

solution s. 1. (chim.) soluzione 2. risoluzione.

solvability s. 1. (comm.) solvibilità 2. solubilità 3. risolvibilità.

solvable agg. 1. (comm.) solvibile 2. solubile 3. risolvibile.

to **solve** vt. risolvere, chiarire.

solvency s. (comm.) solvibilità.

solvent agg. 1. (comm.) solvibile 2. solvente. ◆ **solvent** s. solvente.

somatic(al) agg. somatico.

somatology s. somatologia.

sombre agg. 1. fosco, scuro 2. (fig.) tetro, triste.

some agg. 1. qualche, alcuni, certi 2. un certo, qualsiasi 3. (partitivo) un po' di, del, della, dei, degli, delle. ◆ **some** pron. 1. alcuni, alcune 2. un po'. ◆ **some** avv. circa.

somebody pron. indef. qualcuno.

somehow avv. in qualche modo, in un modo o nell'altro.

someone pron. indef. qualcuno: — else, qualcun altro.

somersault s. 1. salto mortale, capriola 2. (aer.) capottamento 3. (auto) ribaltamento.

to **somersault**, to **somerset** vi. 1. fare salti mortali 2. (aer.) capottare 3. (auto.) ribaltare.

something pron. indef. qualche cosa.

sometime avv. 1. un tempo 2. presto o tardi, in un giorno o l'altro.

sometimes avv. qualche volta, alcune volte.

someway avv. in un modo o nell'altro.

somewhat pron. ind. un poco.

somewhere avv. in qualche luogo.

somnambulism s. sonnambulismo.

somnambulist s. sonnambulo.

somnolent *agg.* **1.** sonnolento **2.** assopito.

son *s.* figlio, figliolo || — *-in-law,* genèro.

song *s.* canto, canzone.

songbook *s.* canzoniere.

songful *agg.* **1.** melodioso **2.** che ama cantare.

songster *s.* cantante (*uomo*).

sonnet *s.* sonetto.

sonority *s.* sonorità.

sonorous *agg.* sonoro, risonante.

sonorously *avv.* sonoramente.

soon (*comp. di* sooner) *avv.* presto, tra poco || *the sooner the better,* prima è meglio è; *sooner or later,* presto o tardi; *I had sooner,* preferirei; *as* — *as,* non appena.

soot *s.* fuliggine.

to soot *vt.* macchiare, sporcare di fuliggine.

to soothe *vt.* calmare, placare.

soothsayer *s.* indovino.

sooty *agg.* fuligginoso.

sophism *s.* sofisma.

sophist *s.* sofista (*anche fig.*).

sophistic(al) *agg.* sofistico, pedante.

sophisticated *agg.* **1.** sofisticato, raffinato **2.** adulterato.

sophistry *s.* sofisma.

sorcerer *s.* stregone, mago.

sorceress *s.* strega, maga.

sorcery *s.* stregoneria, sortilegio.

sordid *agg.* **1.** sordido, avaro **2.** vile, meschino.

sore *agg.* **1.** doloroso, dolorante, infiammato **2.** triste, addolorato **3.** estremo, intenso.

sorrel *s.* sauro.

sorrow *s.* **1.** dispiacere, dolore **2.** rincrescimento **3.** sventura.

to sorrow *vi.* affliggersi, addolorarsi.

sorrowful *agg.* **1.** triste, infelice **2.** penoso, doloroso.

sorry *agg.* spiacente, dolente || *sorry!,* scusate!; *to be* —, dispiacersi.

sort *s.* sorta, specie.

to sort *vt.* raggruppare, selezionare. ♦ **to sort** *vi.* accordarsi, adattarsi.

sought V. *to seek.*

soul *s.* **1.** anima, animo, spirito **2.** essenza, personificazione.

sound[1] *avv.* profondamente.

sound[2] *agg.* **1.** sano, intero, in buono stato **2.** buono, solido **3.** profondo, completo || — *-headed* equilibra-

to, — *-minded,* di buon senso.

sound[3] *s.* suono, rumore || — *wave,* onda sonora.

sound[4] *s.* sondaggio.

sound[5] *s.* braccio di mare, stretto.

to sound[1] *vt. e vi.* **1.** suonare, risuonare **2.** sembrare, aver l'aria di.

to sound[2] *vt. e vi.* sondare, scandagliare.

sounding *agg.* sonoro, sonante, risonante.

soundless *agg.* muto, senza suono.

soundly *avv.* **1.** sanamente **2.** profondamente.

soundness *s.* **1.** buona condizione (*di salute*) **2.** solidità (*di argomento*).

soup *s.* zuppa, minestra.

sour *agg.* **1.** acido, aspro, acerbo **2.** bisbetico.

to sour *vt. e vi.* **1.** inacidire **2.** inasprire, esacerbare.

source *s.* **1.** fonte, sorgente **2.** origine.

sourdine *s.* (*mus.*) sordina.

sourish *agg.* acidulo.

sourness *s.* acidità.

south *s.* sud, mezzogiorno.

southern *agg.* del sud, meridionale.

southerner *s.* abitante del sud, meridionale.

southward *avv.* verso sud.

sovereign *s.* sovrano.

sovereignty *s.* sovranità.

sow *s.* scrofa.

to sow (**sowed, sown**) *vt. e vi.* seminare, piantare.

sowing *s.* seminagione.

sown V. *to sow.*

spa *s.* sorgente minerale.

space *s.* spazio || — *-ship,* astronave.

to space *vt.* spaziare, disporre ad intervalli.

spaceman *s.* astronauta.

spacesuit *s.* tuta spaziale.

spacial *agg.* spaziale.

spacing *s.* spaziatura, interlineatura.

spacious *agg.* spazioso, ampio.

spade *s.* vanga, badile.

span V. *to spin.*

span *s.* **1.** spanna, palmo **2.** breve spazio di tempo.

to span *vt.* **1.** misurare a spanne **2.** attraversare.

spangle *s.* lustrino.

Spaniard *s.* spagnolo.

Spanish *agg.* spagnolo.

to spank *vt.* (*fam.*) sculacciare.

spar¹ s. (*mar.*) antenna.

spar² s. incontro di pugilato.

spare agg. 1. parco, frugale 2. d'avanzo, disponibile, in più || — *room*, camera in più (*per gli ospiti*); — *time*, tempo disponibile; — *wheel*, ruota di scorta.

to spare vt. 1. economizzare, risparmiare 2. privarsi, fare a meno di. ♦ **to spare** vi. essere frugale.

sparing agg. 1. parco, frugale 2. limitato, moderato.

spark s. 1. scintilla, favilla 2. (*fig.*) lampo, barlume.

to spark vi. scintillare, emettere scintille.

sparkle s. scintilla, favilla.

to sparkle vi. 1. emettere scintille (*di fuoco*) 2. sfavillare, brillare, risplendere (*anche fig.*).

sparkler s. stella filante.

sparkling agg. scintillante, vivace (*anche fig.*).

sparrow s. passero || — -*hawk*, sparviero.

Spartan agg. e s. spartano.

spasm s. 1. spasmo 2. attacco, spasimo (*anche fig.*).

spasmodic(al) agg. spasmodico.

spastic agg. spastico.

spat V. *to spit*.

spatial agg. spaziale.

spatiality s. spazialità.

spatter s. 1. schizzo 2. sgocciolio.

to spatter vt. e vi. 1. schizzare, inzaccherare 2. gocciolare.

to speak (**spoke, spoken**) vt. e vi. 1. parlare 2. esprimere, rivelare || *to* — *at*, alludere a; *to* — *out*, parlare francamente; *to* — *to*, garantire; *to* — *up*, alzare la voce.

speaker s. parlatore, oratore, annunciatore || *the* — *of the House of Commons*, il Presidente della Camera dei Comuni.

speaking agg. parlante, espressivo, eloquente. ♦ **speaking** s. 1. il parlare, discorso 2. eloquenza, declamazione.

spear s. 1. lancia, alabarda, asta 2. fiocina.

to spear vt. 1. trafiggere (*con lancia*) 2. fiocinare.

special agg. 1. speciale, particolare 2. eccezionale, straordinario.

specialist s. specialista.

speciality s. specialità, particolarità.

to specialize vt. specializzare. ♦ **to**

specialize vi. specializzarsi.

specially avv. specialmente, soprattutto.

specialty s. 1. (*comm.*) specialità 2. (*giur.*) contratto sigillato.

species s. 1. specie, classe 2. sorta, genere, tipo.

specific agg. specifico, particolare.

specification s. 1. specificazione 2. descrizione dettagliata.

to specify vt. specificare, precisare.

specimen s. modello, esemplare.

speck s. 1. macchiolina, punto 2. granello (*di polvere ecc.*).

speckled agg. macchiato, screziato.

speckless agg. senza macchia (*anche fig.*).

spectacle s. spettacolo, vista. ♦ **spectacles** s. pl. occhiali: *to put on one's* —, mettersi gli occhiali.

spectacled agg. che porta gli occhiali.

spectacular agg. spettacolare.

spectator s. spettatore.

spectral agg. spettrale.

spectre s. spettro, fantasma.

specular agg. speculare.

to speculate vt. e vi. 1. meditare, considerare 2. (*comm.*) speculare.

speculation s. 1. speculazione, meditazione 2. (*comm.*) speculazione.

speculative agg. contemplativo, speculativo (*anche comm.*).

speculator s. 1. spirito speculatore 2. (*comm.*) speculatore.

sped V. *to speed*.

speech s. 1. parola, favella 2. discorso, arringa 3. linguaggio.

speechless agg. senza parola, muto (*anche fig.*).

speed s. velocità, rapidità.

to speed vi. affrettarsi. ♦ **to speed** (**sped, sped**) vt. 1. aiutare 2. affrettare 3. regolare la velocità || *to* — *up the work*, affrettare i lavori.

speedometer s. tachimetro.

speedway s. pista, circuito (*di autodromo*).

speedy agg. rapido, pronto.

spell¹ s. incantesimo.

spell² s. 1. turno di lavoro 2. intervallo.

to spell (**spelt, spelt**) (*anche reg.*) vt. e vi. compitare, sillabare.

to spellbind (**spellbound, spellbound**) vt. incantare, affascinare.

spelling s. 1. compitazione 2. ortografia.

spelt V. *to spell.*

to spend (spent, spent) *vt.* e *vi.*
1. spendere, sborsare 2. dedicare, impiegare 3. passare, trascorrere.

sperm *s.* sperma.

sphenoid *agg.* e *s.* sfenoide.

sphere *s.* sfera, globo.

spheric(al) *agg.* sferico.

sphericity *s.* sfericità.

sphincter *s.* sfintere.

Sphinx *s.* sfinge (*anche fig.*).

spice *s.* 1. aroma 2. (*fig.*) sapore, gusto 3. spezie (*pl.*).

to spice *vt.* 1. condire con spezie 2. (*fig.*) dar gusto a, rendere interessante.

spicery *s.* spezie, aromi (*pl.*).

spicily *avv.* 1. aromaticamente 2. (*fig.*) gustosamente.

spiciness *s.* 1. aroma, profumo 2. (*fam.*) arguzia.

spick-and-span *agg.* (*fam.*) lindo, lucente.

spicy *agg.* 1. aromatico, piccante 2. (*fig.*) arguto, mordace.

spider *s.* ragno.

spidery *agg.* 1. simile a ragno 2. infestato da ragni.

spike[1] *s.* punta, aculeo.

spike[2] *s.* spiga.

to spike *vt.* inchiodare ‖ *to — so.'s guns*, guastare i piani di qu.

to spill (spilt, spilt) *vt.* 1. versare 2. disarcionare. ♦ **to spill (spilt, spilt)** *vi.* versarsi, traboccare.

spin *s.* (*aer.*) avvitamento.

to spin (span, spun) *vt.* e *vi.* 1. filare (*cotone ecc.*) 2. (*mecc.*) lavorare al tornio 3. girare, far girare.

spinach *s.* spinacio.

spinal *agg.* spinale.

spindle *s.* 1. fuso, fusello 2. (*mecc.*) asse, mandrino.

spine *s.* 1. spina, lisca 2. spina dorsale.

spineless *agg.* 1. senza spine 2. senza spina dorsale 3. (*fam.*) debole, molle.

spinner *s.* 1. ragno filatore 2. (*aer.*) ogiva 3. filatore.

spinning *s.* 1. filatura, filato 2. movimento rotatorio ‖ *— -mill*, filanda.

spinster *s.* 1. filatrice 2. donna nubile, zitella.

spiral *agg.* spirale, a spirale. ♦ **spiral** *s.* spirale.

spire[1] *s.* guglia, cuspide.

spire[2] *s.* spira, spirale.

spirit *s.* 1. spirito, anima 2. folletto, fantasma 3. genio, intelletto 4. coraggio, vigore.

spirits[1] *s. pl.* umore, stato d'animo (*sing.*).

spirits[2] *s. pl.* bevande fortemente alcooliche.

spirited *agg.* brioso, vivace ‖ *high- —*, fiero; *poor- —*, depresso.

spiritism *s.* spiritismo.

spiritual *agg.* spirituale.

spiritualism *s.* 1. spiritualismo 2. spiritismo.

spiritualist *s.* 1. spiritualista 2. spiritista.

spirituality *s.* spiritualità.

spit *s.* sputo, saliva.

to spit (spat, spat) *vi.* sputare.

spite *s.* dispetto, ripicco: *out of —*, per dispetto; *in — of*, a dispetto di.

spiteful *agg.* dispettoso.

spittle V. *spit.*

spittoon *s.* sputacchiera.

splash *s.* 1. schizzo, spruzzo 2. tonfo.

to splash *vt.* e *vi.* 1. schizzare, spruzzare 2. inzaccherare, infangare. ♦ **to splash** *vi.* 1. spruzzare 2. cadere con un tonfo.

splashy *agg.* bagnato, fangoso.

splay *agg.* largo e piatto. ♦ **splay** *s.* (*arch.*) strombatura.

to splay *vt.* (*arch.*) strombare. ♦ **to splay** *vi.* essere in posizione obliqua.

spleen *s.* 1. milza 2. (*fig.*) malumore, umore nero.

splendid *agg.* splendido, magnifico.

splendour *s.* splendore, lustro.

splenetic *agg.* e *s.* splenetico, bilioso.

splinter *s.* scheggia, frantume.

split *agg.* spaccato, diviso. ♦ **split** *s.* 1. fessura, crepaccio 2. scissione.

to split (split, split) *vt.* 1. fendere 2. spaccare, frazionare ‖ *to — hairs*, spaccare un capello in quattro; *to — one's sides (with laughing)*, ridere a crepapelle. ♦ **to split (split, split)** *vi.* fendersi.

splitting *agg.* che si fende, che fende. ♦ **splitting** *s.* fessura, spaccatura.

spoil(s) *s.* spoglia, preda.

to spoil (spoilt, spoilt) (*anche reg.*) *vt.* e *vi.* **1.** rovinare, alterare, sciupare, viziare **2.** saccheggiare, predare.

spoilt *agg.* **1.** guasto, avariato **2.** viziato.

spoke *s.* **1.** raggio (*di ruota*) **2.** piolo (*di scala*).

spoke V. *to speak.*

spoken V. *to speak.*

spokesman *s.* portavoce.

spoliation *s.* ruberia, saccheggio.

sponge *s.* spugna, colpo di spugna.

to sponge *vt.* **1.** pulire, lavare con la spugna **2.** fare spugnature **3.** (*fig.; fam.*) scroccare.

sponger *s.* **1.** pescatore di spugne **2.** scroccone.

spongy *agg.* spugnoso, poroso.

sponsor *s.* **1.** padrino, madrina **2.** (*giur.*) garante, mallevadore.

to sponsor *vt.* **1.** essere garante di **2.** offrire (*programmi radio, tv*).

sponsorial *agg.* **1.** di garanzia **2.** di padrino, di madrina.

sponsorship *s.* **1.** garanzia **2.** qualità di padrino, di madrina.

spontaneity *s.* spontaneità.

spontaneous *agg.* spontaneo.

spontaneously *avv.* spontaneamente.

spool *s.* rocchetto, bobina.

spoon *s.* cucchiaio.

to spoon *vt.* prendere con un cucchiaio.

spoon-fed *agg.* coccolato, viziato.

spoonful *s.* cucchiaiata.

sporadic *agg.* sporadico, raro.

sport *s.* **1.** giuoco, divertimento **2.** scherzo **3.** sport. ♦ **sports** *s. pl* gare, incontri.

to sport *vi.* **1.** scherzare **2.** giocare **3.** fare dello sport.

sporting *agg.* sportivo.

sportive *agg.* **1.** gioviale **2.** sportivo.

sportsman *s.* **1.** sportivo **2.** uomo animato da spirito sportivo.

sportsmanlike *agg.* caratteristico di uno sportivo.

sportswoman *s.* donna sportiva.

spot *s.* **1.** luogo, località **2.** macchia (*anche fig.*) || on the —, sul colpo.

to spot *vt.* macchiare, punteggiare. ♦ **to spot** *vi.* macchiarsi.

spotless *agg.* senza macchia, immacolato (*anche fig.*).

spotlight *s.* riflettore, luce della ribalta.

spotty *agg.* macchiato, chiazzato.

spout *s.* **1.** tubo di scarico, grondaia **2.** getto, colonna (*d'acqua*).

to spout *vt.* scaricare, emettere. ♦ **to spout** *vi.* scaturire, zampillare.

sprain *s.* distorsione, strappo muscolare.

to sprain *vt.* storcere, slogare.

sprang V. *to spring.*

to sprawl *vi.* sdraiarsi in modo scomposto.

spray *s.* **1.** spruzzo, schiuma **2.** getto vaporizzato (*di acqua ecc.*) **3.** spruzzatore.

to spray *vt.* **1.** polverizzare, vaporizzare **2.** aspergere, spruzzare.

sprayer *s.* spruzzatore.

spread *agg.* steso, aperto, spiegato.

to spread (spread, spread) *vt.* **1.** stendere, spiegare, spalmare **2.** (*fig.*) spargere, diffondere. ♦ **to spread (spread, spread)** *vi.* stendersi, spiegarsi.

spreader *s.* spruzzatore.

spreading *agg.* che si propaga. ♦ **spreading** *s.* (*fig.*) propagazione.

spree *s.* baldoria.

sprig *s.* **1.** ramoscello **2.** (*fig.*) rampollo.

spring *s.* **1.** sorgente, fonte **2.** primavera **3.** salto, balzo **4.** molla, elasticità || — -board, trampolino; — -head, fontana; — -mattress, materasso a molle.

to spring (sprang, sprung) *vi.* **1.** nascere, discendere, scaturire (*di acqua*) **2.** saltare **3.** scattare || *to* — up, crescere (*di piante*). ♦ **to spring (sprang, sprung)** *vt.* **1.** far scattare (*con una molla*) **2.** far brillare (*una mina*) **3.** saltare.

springiness *s.* elasticità.

springy *agg.* **1.** pieno di sorgenti **2.** elastico.

sprinkle *s.* aspersione, spruzzatina.

to sprinkle *vt.* e *vi.* spruzzare, aspergere.

sprinkler *s.* **1.** spruzzatore, innaffiatoio **2.** aspersorio.

sprint *s.* (*sport*) scatto finale.

to sprout *vi.* germogliare. ♦ **to sprout** *vt.* far germogliare.

to spruce *vt.* adornare, agghindare.

sprung V. *to spring.* ♦ **sprung** *agg.* **1.** a molla **2.** spaccato.

spun V. *to spin.*

spur *s.* **1.** sperone **2.** (*fig.*) sprone.

to spur *vt.* **1.** spronare **2.** (*fig.*) incitare.

to **spurn** *vt.* e *vi.* disdegnare, trattare con disprezzo.

spurt *s.* getto, vampata.

spy *s.* spia.

to **spy** *vt.* e *vi.* spiare, fare la spia.

squabble *s.* battibecco, lite.

to **squabble** *vi.* accapigliarsi, venire a parole.

squad *s.* squadra, plotone.

squalid *agg.* squallido, miserabile.

squall *s.* urlo, strepito.

squalor *s.* squallore.

to **squander** *vt.* sprecare, scialacquare.

squanderer *s.* sciupone, sperperatore.

square *agg.* 1. quadrato 2. robusto, massiccio 3. perpendicolare. ◆ **square** *s.* 1. quadrato 2. piazza 3. squadra || — -*built*, tarchiato; — -*root*, radice quadrata; — -*shouldered*, dalle spalle larghe e diritte. ◆ **square** *avv.* ad angolo retto, in squadra.

to **square** *vt.* e *vi.* 1. quadrare, squadrare 2. pareggiare un conto 3. elevare al quadrato.

squared *agg.* 1. squadrato, quadrato 2. elevato al quadrato.

squash *s.* 1. cosa schiacciata 2. spremuta (*di frutta*): *orange*— , spremuta d'arancio.

to **squash** *vt.* 1. schiacciare, spiaccicare 2. spremere.

squat *s.* rannicchiato, accoccolato.

to **squat** *vi.* accovacciarsi, accoccolarsi.

squatter *s.* pioniere.

squeak *s.* 1. grido acuto 2. pigolio, squittio, guaito 3. cigolio.

to **squeak** *vt.* e *vi.* 1. strillare in tono acuto 2. squittire, guaire 3. cigolare.

squeaky *agg.* 1. che strilla 2. che guaisce, squittisce 3. cigolante.

squeamish *agg.* 1. soggetto a nausee 2. schizzinoso.

squeeze *s.* 1. compressione 2. spremitura 3. stretta, abbraccio.

to **squeeze** *vt.* 1. spremere 2. stringere, abbracciare. ◆ to **squeeze** *vi.* accalcarsi.

squeezer *s.* 1. ciò che preme 2. (*mecc.*) torchio.

squid *s.* seppia.

squint *agg.* strabico. ◆ **squint** *s.* strabismo.

to **squint** *vi.* essere strabico. ◆ to **squint** *vt.* guardare di traverso.

squire *s.* gentiluomo, nobiluomo (*di campagna*).

squirrel *s.* scoiattolo.

stab *s.* coltellata, pugnalata.

to **stab** *vt.* pugnalare, accoltellare.

to **stabilize** *vt.* stabilizzare.

stabilizer *s.* stabilizzatore.

stable[1] *agg.* stabile, permanente.

stable[2] *s.* scuderia, stalla.

stack *s.* mucchio, cumulo || *chimney*- —, ciminiera.

to **stack** *vt.* ammucchiare, accumulare.

staff *s.* 1. bastone, sostegno (*anche fig.*) 2. stato maggiore 3. personale (*di ufficio ecc.*) || *editorial* —, corpo redazionale; *flag* —, asta della bandiera.

stag *s.* cervo.

stage *s.* 1. piattaforma 2. palcoscenico 3. (*fig.*) campo d'azione, scena 4. stadio, grado 5. tappa || — -*direction*, didascalia; — -*director*, regista (*teat.*); — -*effect*, effetto scenico; — -*name*, nome d'arte; *landing*- — (*mar.*), pontile.

to **stage** *vt.* 1. mettere in scena 2. inscenare (*una dimostrazione ecc.*).

stagger *s.* barcollamento, andatura a zig-zag.

to **stagger** *vi.* 1. vacillare 2. dubitare, esitare. ◆ to **stagger** *vt.* far vacillare.

staginess *s.* teatralità.

staging *s.* 1. (*teat.*) messa in scena 2. (*edil.*) impalcatura.

stagnancy *s.* ristagno.

stagnant *agg.* stagnante.

to **stagnate** *vi.* ristagnare.

stagnation *s.* ristagno, stasi.

staid *agg.* posato, serio.

stain *s.* 1. scolorimento, macchia 2. (*fig.*) taccia, onta.

to **stain** *vt.* 1. macchiare 2. tingere. ◆ to **stain** *vi.* macchiarsi, sporcarsi.

stained *agg.* macchiato, sporco.

stainless *agg.* senza macchia.

stair *s.* scalino, gradino. ◆ **stairs** *s. pl.* scale || *winding*- —, scala a chiocciola; *flight of* —, rampa di scale.

staircase *s.* 1. scala, scalone 2. tromba delle scale.

stairway *s.* scalinata.

stake[1] *s.* 1. palo, paletto 2. piccola incudine.

stake[2] *s.* posta, scommessa || *at* —, in giuoco. ◆ **stakes** *s. pl.* (*ippica*) premio, corsa.

to **stake**[1] *vt.* cintare, chiudere (*con una palizzata*).

to **stake**[2] *vt.* mettere in giuoco, scommettere.

stale *agg.* 1. vecchio, stantio 2. (*fig.*) trito, caduto in disuso.

stalk[1] *s.* stelo, gambo.

stalk[2] *s.* andatura rigida e maestosa.

stall *s.* 1. stalla 2. bancarella, chiosco.

stammer *s.* balbuzie, balbettamento.

to **stammer** *vt.* e *vi.* 1. balbettare 2. farfugliare.

stammering *agg.* balbuziente. ◆ **stammering** *s.* balbuzie.

stamp *s.* 1. impronta, segno 2. francobollo, bollo 3. stampo || – *-collector*, filatelico; — *-paper*, carta bollata.

to **stamp** *vt.* 1. imprimere, incidere 2. (*fig.*) dare l'impronta 3. timbrare || *to* — *down*, calpestare. ◆ to **stamp** *vi.* battere i piedi.

stamping *s.* 1. scalpitio 2. timbratura.

stand *s.* 1. pausa, fermata 2. punto di vista 3. posizione, luogo (*d'appostamento*) 4. palco, tribuna 5. bancarella, chiosco || *test-* —, banco di prova.

to **stand** (**stood, stood**) *vi.* 1. essere, stare in piedi 2. stare, trovarsi 3. fermarsi, indugiare 4. conservarsi, rimaner valido || *to* — *by*, stare accanto, restare fedele a; *to* — *for*, significare, implicare; *to* — *out*, resistere, tener duro, spiccare. ◆ to **stand** (**stood, stood**) *vt.* sopportare, resistere.

standard *s.* 1. stendardo, bandiera 2. modello, campione 3. livello, qualità 4. supporto, base 5. tipo.

standardization *s.* standardizzazione.

stand-by *s.* scorta, riserva.

standing *agg.* 1. eretto, che sta in piedi 2. fermo, inattivo 3. fisso, immutabile. ◆ **standing** *s.* 1. posizione eretta 2. posizione, rango 3. periodo di tempo.

standoffish *agg.* riservato, altezzoso.

standpoint *s.* 1. luogo di osservazione 2. punto di vista.

standstill *agg.* in riposo, fermo. ◆ **standstill** *s.* arresto, fermata.

stank V. *to* **stink**.

staple *s.* 1. prodotto principale (*di un paese ecc.*) 2. (*fig.*) argomento principale (*di una conversazione*).

star *s.* 1. stella, astro 2. (*fig.*) fortuna, destino 3. (*tip.*) asterisco.

to **star** *vt.* 1. costellare 2. segnare con un asterisco. ◆ to **star** *vi.* (*cine, teat.*) avere il ruolo di protagonista.

starboard *agg.* di dritta. ◆ **starboard** *s.* (*mar.*) dritta.

starch *s.* 1. amido 2. (*fig.*) rigidezza, formalismo.

to **starch** *vt.* 1. inamidare 2. (*fig.*) rendere formale.

starchiness *s.* 1. inamidatura 2. (*fig.*) formalismo, rigidità.

stardom *s.* divismo.

stare *s.* sguardo fisso.

to **stare** *vt.* guardare intensamente, fissare. ◆ to **stare** *vi.* sgranare gli occhi.

starfish *s.* stella di mare.

staring *agg.* 1. fisso, stupefatto 2. sgargiante, vistoso.

staringly *avv.* fissamente, con occhi sbarrati.

stark *agg.* 1. rigido, duro 2. completo, vero e proprio.

starless *agg.* senza stelle.

starlet *s.* 1. piccola stella 2. (*cine*) stellina.

starlight *agg.* stellato, stellare. ◆ **starlight** *s.* luce stellare.

starlike *agg.* simile a stella.

starlit *agg.* illuminato dalle stelle.

starred *agg.* 1. stellato, adorno di stelle 2. a stella.

starry *agg.* stellato, trapunto di stelle, brillante come una stella.

start *s.* 1. inizio, partenza 2. soprassalto || *by fits and starts*, irregolarmente 3. vantaggio dato all'inizio di una corsa 4. (*mecc.*) avviamento.

to **start** *vi.* 1. partire, mettersi in viaggio 2. cominciare 3. trasalire || *to* — *out*, aver intenzione di; *to* — *up*, spuntare all'improvviso. ◆ to **start** *vt.* 1. cominciare 2. far trasalire.

starter *s.* 1. iniziatore, fondatore 2. (*sport*) "starter", mossiere.

starting *s.* 1. inizio, partenza 2. debutto 3. (*mecc.*) messa in moto, avviamento.

startle *s.* trasalimento.

to **startle** *vt.* spaventare, far trasalire. ◆ to **startle** *vi.* spaventarsi, trasalire.

startling *agg.* impressionante, sorprendente.

starvation *s.* inedia, fame.

to **starve** *vi.* **1.** morire di fame **2.** (*fig.*) bramare. ♦ to **starve** *vt.* far morire di fame.

state *s.* **1.** stato, condizione **2.** governo, nazione **3.** rango, dignità || — *-control*, statalizzazione; — *-documents*, documenti ufficiali; — *-prisoner*, prigioniero politico; — *-trial*, processo politico.

to **state** *vt.* **1.** affermare, dichiarare **2.** stabilire.

stateless *agg.* **1.** senza patria **2.** senza pompa **3.** apolide.

stately *agg.* nobile, signorile.

statement *s.* **1.** esposto, relazione **2.** asserzione, affermazione **3.** (*giur.*) deposizione, esposizione dei fatti.

statesman *s.* statista.

static(al) *agg.* statico.

statics *s.* statica.

station *s.* **1.** posto, luogo, base **2.** stazione **3.** condizione sociale || *petrol* —, stazione di rifornimento; *through* —, stazione di transito.

stationary *agg.* stazionario.

stationer *s.* cartolaio || —*'s (shop)*, cartoleria.

stationery *s.* articoli di cancelleria.

station house *s.* guardina.

stationmaster *s.* capostazione.

statist *s.* statista.

statistic(al) *agg.* statistico.

statistically *avv.* statisticamente.

statistics *s.* **1.** scienza della statistica **2.** statistiche (*pl.*).

statuary *agg.* statuario, scultorio.

statue *s.* statua.

statuesque *agg.* statuario.

stature *s.* statura.

status *s.* **1.** stato, condizione sociale **2.** situazione.

statute *s.* statuto, regolamento.

statutory *agg.* statutario.

to **staunch** *vt.* **1.** arrestare **2.** stagnare. ♦ to **staunch** *vi.* stagnarsi.

stave *s.* **1.** dòga (*di botte*) **2.** piolo (*di scala*) **3.** strofa.

stay¹ *s.* **1.** soggiorno **2.** pausa.

stay² *s.* **1.** sostegno, supporto **2.** (*mecc.*) puntello.

to **stay¹** *vi.* **1.** fermarsi, sostare, soggiornare **2.** resistere || *to — away*, essere assente; *to — in*, stare in casa, (*mil.*) essere consegnato; *to*

— *up*, vegliare. ♦ to **stay** *vt.* **1.** arrestare, fermare **2.** resistere.

to **stay²** *vt.* (*mecc.*) puntellare.

steadfast *agg.* fermo, risoluto.

steadfastly *avv.* stabilmente, fermamente.

steadfastness *s.* fermezza, tenacia.

steadily *avv.* **1.** saldamente, fermamente **2.** costantemente.

steadiness *s.* **1.** fermezza, sicurezza **2.** assiduità, perseveranza.

steading *s.* tenuta agricola.

steady *agg.* **1.** fermo, saldo **2.** equilibrato **3.** continuo, regolare **4.** fedele, assiduo.

to **steady** *vt.* rafforzare, rendere fermo, equilibrato. ♦ to **steady** *vi.* rafforzarsi.

steak *s.* bistecca.

to **steal** (**stole**, **stolen**) *vt. e vi.* rubare || *to — along*, camminare furtivamente; *to — away*, svignarsela; *to — upon*, avvicinarsi pian piano.

stealing *s.* furto || *cattle (o horse)- —*, abigeato.

stealthily *avv.* furtivamente.

stealthy *agg.* furtivo.

steam *s.* vapore: — *-engine*, macchina a vapore.

to **steam** *vt.* **1.** esporre al vapore **2.** cucinare al vapore. ♦ to **steam** *vi.* emettere vapore.

steamboat *s.* imbarcazione a vapore.

steamer *s.* nave a vapore.

steamship *s.* piroscafo.

steamtight *agg.* a tenuta di vapore.

steamy *agg.* **1.** che esala vapore **2.** appannato, umido.

stearic *agg.* stearico.

steel *s.* **1.** acciaio **2.** arma, spada **3.** acciarino || — *cap*, elmetto; — *company*, acciaieria || *stainless —*, acciaio inossidabile.

steelwork *s.* lavoro, struttura in acciaio.

steelwork *s. pl.* acciaieria (*sing.*).

steely *agg.* **1.** di acciaio, simile ad acciaio **2.** (*fig.*) severissimo.

steelyard *s.* stadera.

steep¹ *agg.* **1.** ripido, scosceso **2.** (*fig.*) ambizioso, arduo **3.** esorbitante (*di prezzi*).

steep² *s.* macerazione, l'inzuppare.

to **steep** *vt.* immergere (*anche fig.*), inzuppare.

steeple *s.* guglia, campanile.

steeplechase *s.* (*ippica*) corsa ad

ostacoli.

steer *s.* bue giovane, manzo.

to steer *vt.* 1. governare, manovrare 2. dirigere. ♦ **to steer** *vi.* 1. dirigersi 2. (*auto*) sterzare.

steering *s.* guida, governo (*dello sterzo, del timone*).

stem *s.* 1. tronco, gambo, stelo 2. cannello (*di pipa*) 3. (*mar.*) prua.

to stem *vt.* arrestare, arginare.

stench *s.* puzzo, tanfo.

step *s.* 1. passo (*anche fig.*), andatura 2. orma, impronta 3. provvedimento 4. gradino || *to be in — with so.*, tenere il passo con qu.; *— by —*, gradualmente; *in —* (*elett.*), in fase.

to step *vi.* camminare || *to — aside*, farsi da parte; *to — forward*, avanzare; *to — in*, montare (*su un veicolo*). ♦ **to step** *vt.* misurare a passi.

stepbrother *s.* fratellastro.

stepchild *s.* (*pl.* -children) figliastro.

stepdaughter *s.* figliastra.

stepfather *s.* patrigno.

stepmother *s.* matrigna.

stepsister *s.* sorellastra.

stepson *s.* figliastro.

stereophonic *agg.* stereofonico.

stereophony *s.* stereofonia.

stereoscope *s.* stereoscopio.

stereotype *s.* stereotipo.

sterile *agg.* sterile.

sterility *s.* sterilità.

to sterilize *vt.* rendere sterile, sterilizzare.

stern[1] *agg.* severo, austero.

stern[2] *s.* (*mar.*) poppa.

sternly *avv.* severamente.

sternness *s.* severità, austerità.

stethoscope *s.* stetoscopio.

stevedore *s.* scaricatore (*di porto*).

stew *s.* (*cuc.*) umido, stufato.

to stew *vt.* e *vi.* cuocere in umido.

steward *s.* 1. amministratore, intendente 2. (*aer., mar.*) cameriere di bordo.

stewardess *s.* 1. dispensiere 2. (*aer., mar.*) cameriera di bordo.

stick *s.* 1. bastone 2. bastoncino 3. barra, stecca.

to stick (**stuck, stuck**) *vt.* 1. ficcare, conficcare 2. infilare 3. incollare, appiccicare. ♦ **to stick** (**stuck, stuck**) *vi.* 1. fissarsi, conficcarsi 2. incollarsi.

stickiness *s.* viscosità, adesività.

sticky *agg.* 1. appiccicaticcio, visco-

so 2. poco accomodante.

stiff *agg.* 1. rigido, duro 2. (*fig.*) inflessibile 3. indolenzito, intorpidito 4. freddo, riservato || *— collar*, colletto duro; *— -neck*, torcicollo.

to stiffen *vt.* 1. indurire 2. indolenzire, intorpidire 3. rassodare. ♦ **to stiffen** *vi.* 1. indurirsi, irrigidirsi (*anche fig.*) 2. rassodarsi.

stiffness *s.* 1. durezza, rigidezza 2. intorpidimento.

to stifle *vt.* 1. soffocare 2. (*fig.*) reprimere. ♦ **to stifle** *vi.* sentirsi soffocare.

stifling *agg.* soffocante.

to stigmatize *vt.* 1. marchiare 2. stigmatizzare.

stile *s.* scaletta.

still[1] *agg.* tranquillo, calmo, silenzioso || *— -life* (*pitt.*), natura morta.

still[2] *avv.* 1. ancora, tuttora 2. tuttavia, nondimeno.

still[3] *s.* alambicco.

to still *vt.* acquietare, calmare. ♦ **to still** *vi.* acquietarsi, calmarsi.

stillness *s.* calma, quiete.

stilt *s.* trampolo.

stimulant *s.* 1. stimolante 2. bevanda alcolica.

to stimulate *vt.* stimolare, incitare.

stimulus *s.* (*pl.*- li) stimolo, incentivo.

sting *s.* 1. pungiglione, aculeo 2. puntura d'insetto 3. dolore acuto 4. pungolo, stimolo.

to sting (**stung, stung**) *vt.* e *vi.* 1. pungere 2. colpire, ferire (*anche fig.*).

stinginess *s.* avarizia, spilorceria.

stinging *agg.* pungente, mordace.

stingy *agg.* avaro, taccagno.

stink *s.* puzzo, fetore.

to stink (**stank, stunk**) *vt.* e *vi.* puzzare, riempire di puzzo.

stinking *agg.* puzzolente, fetido.

to stipulate *vt.* e *vi.* stipulare.

stipulation *s.* stipulazione, patto.

stir *s.* 1. il rimescolare, l'attizzare || *to give a —*, dare una rimescolata 2. animazione, tumulto.

to stir *vt.* 1. rimescolare 2. muovere, agitare. ♦ **to stir** *vi.* muoversi, agitarsi.

stirabout *agg.* indaffarato.

stirrer *s.* incitatore, istigatore.

stirring *agg.* eccitante.

stirrup *s.* staffa.

stitch *s.* 1. punto 2. maglia.

stock s. 1. rifornimento, provvista || to be out of —, essere sprovvisto 2. titoli, azioni (pl.) 3. tronco, ceppo 4. (fig.) stirpe.

to stock vt. 1. approvvigionare 2. tenere in magazzino.

stockbroker s. agente di cambio.

stockbroking s. professione dell'agente di cambio.

stock company s. società per azioni.

Stock Exchange s. Borsa valori.

stockfish s. stoccafisso.

stockholder s. azionista.

stocking s. calza lunga.

stoic agg. e s. stoico.

stoicism s. stoicismo.

stoker s. fuochista.

stole V. to steal.

stolen V. to steal.

stolid agg. 1. imperturbabile 2. sciocco.

stolidity s. flemma.

stomach s. stomaco: — -ache, mal di stomaco.

stomatitis s. stomatite.

stomatology s. stomatologia.

stone s. 1. pietra, ciottolo, sasso 2. nocciolo 3. (med.) calcolo || — -blind, completamente cieco; — -breaker, spaccapietre; — cutter, tagliapietre.

to stone vt. 1. lapidare 2. rivestire di pietra 3. snocciolare.

stoneless agg. senza nocciolo.

stoneware s. ceramica.

stony agg. 1. pietroso, sassoso 2. (fig.) duro, insensibile.

stood V. to stand.

stool s. sgabello, seggiolino.

stoop s. curvatura, inchino.

to stoop vi. 1. curvare, inchinarsi 2. (fig.) accondiscendere, abbassarsi.

stop s. 1. sosta, arresto 2. segno di punteggiatura || — watch, cronometro.

to stop vt. 1. fermare 2. turare, otturare 3. impedire. ♦ to stop vi. fermarsi.

stopper s. 1. tappo, turacciolo 2. otturatore.

stopping s. 1. otturazione 2. (comm.) cessazione, sospensione (di pagamenti ecc.).

storage s. 1. immagazzinamento 2. deposito, magazzino.

store s. 1. provvista, riserva 2. magazzino || — -keeper, magazziniere; — -ship, nave da carico.

to store vt. 1. fornire, rifornire 2. immagazzinare, mettere da parte (anche fig.).

storehouse s. magazzino, deposito.

storey s. piano (di edificio).

stork s. cicogna.

storm s. 1. tempesta, temporale 2. tumulto, agitazione.

to storm vi. 1. infuriare, scatenarsi 2. (fam.) adirarsi. ♦ to storm vt. attaccare.

stormy agg. tempestoso, burrascoso.

story s. storia, racconto, novella, favola || to tell stories, contar frottole.

stoup s. acquasantiera.

stout agg. 1. forte, robusto, resistente 2. fermo, risoluto 3. grosso, tozzo.

stove s. 1. stufa 2. cucina economica: gas— —, cucina a gas.

to stove vt. mettere in forno, stufa.

to stow vt. stivare, riempire.

stowage s. (mar.) stivaggio.

straddle s. posizione a gambe divaricate, il mettersi a cavalcioni.

to straddle vt. stare a cavalcioni di. ♦ to straddle vi. mettersi a gambe divaricate.

straight[1] agg. 1. diritto, rettilineo 2. onesto, retto 3. ordinato || a — whisky, un whisky liscio.

straight[2] s. 1. posizione diritta 2. (fig.) condotta onesta.

straight[3] avv. 1. diritto, in linea retta 2. direttamente.

to straighten vt. raddrizzare. ♦ to straighten vi. raddrizzarsi.

straightforward agg. 1. diritto, diretto 2. schietto, leale.

straightforwardly avv. 1. in linea retta 2. francamente, schiettamente.

strain s. 1. tensione (anche fig.) 2. sforzo, fatica 3. distorsione, strappo muscolare.

to strain vt. 1. sottoporre a tensione 2. sforzare. ♦ to strain vi. sforzarsi.

strained agg. 1. teso 2. indebolito 3. non spontaneo, forzato.

strainer s. colino, filtro.

strait s. (geogr.) stretto. ♦ to strand vi. incagliarsi.

stranding s. incagliamento (di una nave).

strange agg. 1. strano, bizzarro 2. estraneo, sconosciuto.

stranger s. estraneo, sconosciuto, forestiero.

to **strangle** vt. strangolare.

strangling s. strangolamento.

strap s. 1. cinghia, correggia 2. maniglia a pendaglio (su tram ecc.).

to **strap** vt. legare con cinghia.

stratagem s. stratagemma.

strategic(al) agg. strategico.

strategist s. stratega.

strategy s. strategia.

stratification s. stratificazione.

to **stratify** vt. stratificare.

stratosphere s. stratosfera.

stratospheric agg. stratosferico.

stratum s. (pl. -ta) 1. strato 2. strato sociale.

straw s. 1. paglia 2. fuscello, cannuccia || — (-hat), paglietta; — -colour, giallo paglierino.

strawberry s. fragola.

stray agg. 1. smarrito, randagio 2. casuale. ◆ **stray** s. animale domestico smarrito.

to **stray** vi. vagare, vagabondare (anche fig.).

streak s. 1. striscia, striatura 2. vena (anche fig.).

to **streak** vt. 1. striare 2. venare.

stream s. 1. corso d'acqua, ruscello 2. flusso, fiotto 3. corrente (anche fig.).

to **stream** vi. 1. scorrere, fluire 2. ondeggiare || to — out, effondersi. ◆ to **stream** vt. far scorrere.

street s. via, strada || one-way —, strada a senso unico.

streetwalker s. passeggiatrice.

strength s. 1. forza, vigore 2. solidità, tenacia.

to **strengthen** vt. rafforzare, irrobustire. ◆ to **strengthen** vi. rafforzarsi, irrobustirsi.

strengthening agg. fortificante.

strenuous agg. strenuo, energico.

strenuously avv. strenuamente.

strenuousness s. vigore.

streptococcus s. (pl. -cci) streptococco.

streptomycin s. streptomicina.

stress s. 1. sforzo, pressione 2. enfasi 3. accento tonico.

to **stress** vt. 1. forzare 2. accentuare 3. porre in rilievo.

stretch s. 1. stiramento, tensione 2. spazio di tempo 3. distesa, estensione.

to **stretch** vt. tirare, tendere, stendere. ◆ to **stretch** vi. estendersi.

stretcher s. 1. tenditore 2. lettiga.

to **strew** (**strewed, strewn**) vt. spargere, sparpagliare.

strict agg. 1. preciso, esatto 2. (fig.) severo, rigido.

strictly avv. 1. esattamente 2. severamente.

stridden V. to **stride**.

stride s. passo lungo, andatura || to make great strides, avanzare a grandi passi.

to **stride** (**strode, stridden**) vi. camminare a grandi passi.

strident agg. stridente.

strife s. contesa, lotta.

strike s. 1. sciopero 2. scoperta (di giacimento) 3. attacco aereo.

to **strike** (**struck, struck**) vt. e vi. 1. battere, colpire 2. (fig.) impressionare, colpire 3. suonare le ore 4. accendere (un fiammifero) 5. scioperare || to — down, abbattere; to — in, frapporsi.

striker s. 1. scioperante 2. (mecc.) percussore.

striking agg. sorprendente.

string s. 1. spago, cordicella 2. laccio 3. (mus.) corda.

to **string** (**strung, strung**) vt. e vi. 1. legare con corde 2. accordare (uno strumento) || to — up, impiccare.

strip s. striscia, nastro.

to **strip** vt. svestire. ◆ to **strip** vi. svestirsi.

stripe s. striscia, lista.

to **stripe** vt. rigare, listare.

striped agg. a righe, a strisce.

to **strive** (**strove, striven**) vi. sforzarsi.

strode V. to **stride**.

stroke s. 1. colpo, percossa 2. movimento 3. bracciata (al nuoto), remata, battuta (al tennis) 4. tratto (di penna ecc.) 5. rintocco (d'orologio) 6. (med.) colpo 7. carezza.

to **stroke**[1] vi. vogare in cadenza.

to **stroke**[2] vt. accarezzare, lisciare.

stroll s. passeggiatina, quattro passi.

to **stroll** vi. gironzolare.

strolling agg. errante, girovago.

strong agg. forte, robusto, energico.

stronghold s. roccaforte.

strontium s. stronzio.

strove V. to **strive**.

struck V. to **strike**.

structural agg. strutturale.

structure s. 1. struttura 2. costruzione.

struggle s. 1. lotta, combattimento 2. sforzo || *hand-to-hand* —, lotta corpo a corpo.

to **struggle** vi. 1. lottare, divincolarsi 2. (*fig.*) sforzarsi.

struggler s. contendente, chi lotta.

to **strum** vt. e vi. strimpellare.

strumpet s. prostituta.

strung V. *to string*.

strut s. andatura solenne.

to **strut** vi. incedere con sussiego.

stub s. 1. ceppo 2. mozzicone.

stubble s. stoppia.

stubborn agg. ostinato, cocciuto, tenace, ribelle.

stubbornness s. caparbietà, tenacia.

to **stucco** vt. stuccare.

stuck V. *to stick*.

stud s. 1. chiodo a capocchia larga 2. bottoncino (*da camicia*).

to **stud** vt. guarnire di borchie.

student s. studente.

studentship s. borsa di studio.

studied agg. 1. studiato, ricercato 2. colto.

studio s. 1. studio (*d'artista*) 2. teatro di posa.

studious agg. studioso, diligente.

study s. 1. studio 2. esame attento, investigazione.

to **study** vt. e vi. 1. studiare 2. esaminare attentamente.

stuff s. 1. sostanza, materia prima 2. cosa, roba 3. stoffa, tessuto.

to **stuff** vt. 1. imbottire 2. (*cuc.*) farcire 3. rimpinzare.

stuffing s. 1. imbottitura 2. (*cuc.*) ripieno.

stuffy agg. afoso || — *air*, aria viziata.

to **stumble** vi. 1. inciampare 2. (*fig.*) fare passi falsi.

stump s. 1. ceppo, tronco 2. radice (*di dente*) 3. piattaforma, podio.

to **stun** vt. stordire, tramortire.

stung V. *to sting*.

stunk V. *to stink*.

stunt s. (*gergo*) 1. bravata, esibizione 2. trovata pubblicitaria, notizia sensazionale.

stupefaction s. 1. stupore 2. torpore provocato da stupefacenti.

to **stupefy** vt. 1. istupidire 2. abbrutire. ♦ to **stupefy** vi. 1. istupidirsi 2. abbrutirsi.

stupendous agg. splendido, stupendo.

stupid agg. stupido, ottuso.

stupidity s. stupidità.

stupidly avv. stupidamente.

sturdy agg. 1. vigoroso, forte 2. risoluto.

to **stutter** vt. e vi. balbettare.

stuttering s. balbuzie.

sty s. porcile.

style s. 1. stile (*anche fig.*) 2. modello, genere 3. moda.

to **style** vt. chiamare, denominare.

stylist s. stilista.

stylistic agg. stilistico.

stylization s. stilizzazione.

to **stylize** vt. stilizzare.

stylographic agg. stilografico.

stylus s. stilo.

subalpine agg. subalpino.

subaltern s. subalterno.

subaquatic agg. subacqueo.

subclass s. sottoclasse.

subcommission s. sottocommissione.

subcommissioner s. vice-commissario.

subcommittee s. sottocomitato.

subconscious agg. e s. subcosciente.

subcutaneous agg. sottocutaneo.

subdeacon s. suddiacono.

to **subdivide** vt. suddividere. ♦ to **subdivide** vi. suddividersi.

subdivisible agg. suddivisibile.

subdivision s. suddivisione.

subdual s. 1. soggiogamento 2. attenuazione.

to **subdue** vt. 1. conquistare, soggiogare 2. ridurre, attenuare.

subgovernor s. vicegovernatore.

subject[1] agg. 1. soggetto, assoggettato 2. sottoposto, esposto a.

subject[2] 1. argomento, materia di studio 2. (*gramm.*) soggetto 3. suddito.

to **subject** vt. 1. assoggettare 2. esporre.

subjection s. 1. assoggettamento 2. dipendenza.

subjective agg. soggettivo.

subjectivism s. soggettivismo.

subjunctive s. congiuntivo.

sublease s. subaffitto.

to **sublease** vt. subaffittare.

to **sublet (sublet, sublet)** vt. subaffittare.

sublieutenancy s. grado di sottotenente.

sublieutenant s. sottotenente.

sublimate agg. e s. sublimato.

to **sublimate** vt. sublimare.

sublime agg. e s. sublime.

sublimity s. sublimità.

submarine agg. subacqueo. ♦ **submarine** s. sommergibile.

submariner s. sommergibilista.

to **submerge** vt. immergere, sommergere. ♦ to **submerge** vi. immergersi.

submergence s. sommersione.

submersible agg. affondabile.

submersion s. immersione.

submission s. sottomissione, docilità.

submissive agg. remissivo, docile.

submissively avv. in modo remissivo.

submissiveness s. sottomissione.

to **submit** vt. sottomettere, sottoporre. ♦ to **submit** vi. sottomettersi, assoggettarsi.

submultiple agg. e s. sottomultiplo.

subnormal agg. al di sotto della norma.

subordinacy s. subordinazione.

subordinate agg. subordinato. ♦ **subordinate** s. subalterno, inferiore.

to **subordinate** vt. subordinare.

subordination s. subordinazione.

to **suborn** vt. subornare, corrompere.

subornation s. subornazione.

subplot s. trama secondaria.

to **subscribe** vt. e vi. 1. sottoscrivere, firmare 2. aderire, trovarsi d'accordo 3. abbonarsi.

subscriber s. 1. the —, il sottoscritto 2. abbonato.

subscription s. 1. sottoscrizione 2. abbonamento 3. consenso.

subsequence s. susseguenza.

subsequent agg. successivo, ulteriore.

subsequently avv. successivamente.

to **subside** vi. 1. calare, decrescere 2. quietarsi 3. cadere (sul fondo), depositare (di liquidi).

subsidiary agg. sussidiario, supplementare, ausiliario.

to **subsidize** vt. sussidiare.

subsidy s. sussidio.

to **subsist** vt. e vi. sussistere.

subsistence s. esistenza, sussistenza.

subsistent agg. sussistente.

subsoil s. sottosuolo.

subspecies s. sottospecie.

substance s. 1. sostanza, essenza 2. contenuto, l'essenziale 3. solidità, fondamento.

substantial agg. 1. sostanzioso, solido 2. importante, notevole.

substantialism s. sostanzialismo.

substantiality s. 1. sostanzialità 2. concretezza.

substantially avv. sostanzialmente.

substantive agg. considerevole, reale. ♦ **substantive** s. (gramm.) sostantivo.

substitute s. 1. sostituto 2. surrogato, imitazione.

to **substitute** vt. e vi. sostituire.

substitution s. sostituzione.

substratum s. (pl. -ta) 1. sostrato (anche fig.).

subtenancy s. subaffitto.

subtenant s. subaffittuario.

subterfuge s. sotterfugio.

subterranean agg. sotterraneo.

sub-title s. sottotitolo, didascalia.

subtle agg. 1. penetrante, acuto, sottile 2. elusivo, indefinibile.

subtleness s. 1. sottigliezza, acutezza 2. carattere elusivo.

subtlety s. sottigliezza.

subtly avv. 1. acutamente, sottilmente 2. elusivamente.

to **subtract** vt. sottrarre, detrarre.

subtraction s. sottrazione.

subtractive agg. sottrattivo.

subtrahend s. sottraendo.

suburb s. sobborgo. ♦ **suburbs** s. pl. periferia (sing.).

suburban agg. suburbano, periferico.

subversion s. sovversione.

subversive agg. sovversivo.

to **subvert** vt. sovvertire.

subway s. 1. sottopassaggio 2. (amer.) metropolitana.

to **succeed** vt. succedere a, seguire, subentrare a. ♦ to **succeed** vi. 1. succedere, seguire 2. riuscire, aver successo.

success s. successo, riuscita.

successful agg. che ha successo.

successfully avv. con successo.

succession s. successione, serie.

successive agg. successivo, seguente.

successively avv. successivamente.

successor s. successore.

succinct agg. succinto, conciso.

succulent agg. succulento.

to **succumb** vi. soccombere, soggiacere.

succursal s. succursale.

such agg. tale, simile: — that, — as, tale che, tale da. ♦ **such** pron. tale, tali, questo, quello, questa, quella, questi, quelli, queste, quelle.

suchlike agg. simile, dello stesso genere.

suck s. succhiata, poppata.

to suck vt. e vi. 1. succhiare, poppare 2. assorbire.

sucker s. 1. (mecc.) pistone 2. ventosa.

to suckle vt. allattare.

suckling s. lattante.

sudden agg. improvviso, inaspettato.
◆ **sudden** s. evento improvviso.

suddenly avv. inaspettatamente.

suddenness s. subitaneità.

to sue vt. e vi. 1. ricorrere in giudizio 2. sollecitare.

to suffer vt. e vi. 1. subire, patire 2. tollerare 3. soffrire.

suffering s. 1. sofferenza, pena 2. tolleranza.

sufficiency s. sufficienza.

sufficient agg. sufficiente.

suffix s. (gramm.) suffisso.

to suffocate vt. e vi. soffocare.

suffocation s. soffocamento.

suffrage s. 1. suffragio, diritto di voto 2. preghiera.

to suffuse vt. coprire, cospargere.

sugar s. 1. zucchero 2. (fig.) atteggiamento mellifluo || — -beet, barbabietola da zucchero; — -cane, canna da zucchero; — -tongs, mollette per lo zucchero; lump —, zucchero in zollette.

to sugar vt. 1. inzuccherare 2. (fig.) addolcire, adulare.

sugariness s. 1. dolcezza 2. mellifluità.

sugary agg. 1. zuccheroso, zuccherino 2. (fig.) mellifluo.

to suggest vt. 1. suggerire 2. far nascere un'idea 3. insinuare.

suggestible agg. suggeribile, suggestionabile.

suggestion s. 1. suggerimento 2. suggestione 3. associazione di idee.

suggestive agg. stimolante, che ispira.

suggestiveness s. carattere allusivo.

suicidal agg. suicida, che ha tendenze al suicidio.

suicide s. 1. suicidio 2. suicida.

suit s. 1. domanda, preghiera 2. (giur.) causa 3. abito completo (da uomo) || — -case, valigia.

to suit vt. adattare, convenire a, far comodo a. ◆ **to suit** vi. essere conveniente, accordarsi, adattarsi.

suitability s. convenienza.

suitable agg. adatto, idoneo.

suitably avv. appropriatamente.

suite s. 1. seguito, corteo 2. serie.

suitor s. 1. postulante 2. corteggiatore.

sulkiness s. malumore.

sulks s. pl. malumore, broncio (sing.).

sulky[1] agg. 1. imbronciato, scontroso 2. tetro.

sulky[2] s. "sulky", sediolo.

sullen agg. 1. accigliato 2. tetro.

sullenly avv. accigliato, di malumore.

sulphate s. solfato.

sulphide s. solfuro.

sulphite s. solfito.

sulphonamide s. sulfamidico.

sulphur s. zolfo || — -mine (o — -pit), solfatara.

to sulphur, **to sulphurate** vt. solforare.

sulphuric agg. solforico.

sulphurous agg. solforoso.

sultan s. sultano.

sultanate s. sultanato.

sultriness s. afa, caldo soffocante.

sultry agg. afoso, soffocante.

sum s. 1. somma, quantità (di denaro) 2. addizione.

to sum vt. e vi. sommare, addizionare || to — up, riassumere.

summarily avv. sommariamente.

to summarize vt. e vi. riassumere.

summary s. sommario, ricapitolazione.

summer s. estate.

to summer vi. trascorrere l'estate.

summertime s. stagione estiva.

summit s. 1. cima, vetta 2. (fig.) culmine || at the — (pol.), al vertice.

to summon vt. 1. chiamare, mandare a chiamare 2. convocare 3. (giur.) citare.

summons s. 1. (giur.) citazione, ingiunzione 2. convocazione.

sumptuous agg. sontuoso.

sumptuously avv. sontuosamente.

sumptuousness s. sontuosità.

sun s. sole || — -bath, bagno di sole; — -glasses, occhiali da sole.

to sun vt. esporre al sole. ◆ **to sun** vi. esporsi al sole.

to sun-bathe vi. fare i bagni di sole.

sunbeam s. raggio di sole.

sunbow s. arcobaleno.

sunburn s. 1. abbronzatura 2. scottatura (solare).

sunburnt *agg.* **1.** abbronzato **2.** scottato dal sole.

sunburst *s.* sprazzo di sole.

Sunday *s.* domenica.

to **sunder** *vt.* separare, recidere. ◆ to **sunder** *vi.* separarsi, scindersi.

sundry *agg.* parecchi, vari.

sunflower *s.* girasole.

sung V. *to sing.*

sunk V. *to sink.*

sunlight *s.* luce del sole.

sunlit *agg.* soleggiato.

sunny *agg.* luminoso, soleggiato.

sunproof *agg.* inalterabile al sole.

sunrise *s.* il sorgere del sole.

sunset *s.* tramonto (*anche fig.*).

sunshade *s.* parasole.

sunshine *s.* luce del sole.

sunspot *s.* macchia solare.

sunstroke *s.* insolazione.

sun-worship *s.* culto del Sole.

sup *s.* sorso, goccia.

to **sup¹** *vt.* e *vi.* sorseggiare.

to **sup²** *vi.* cenare.

superable *agg.* superabile.

to **superabound** *vi.* sovrabbondare.

superabundance *s.* sovrabbondanza.

superabundant *agg.* sovrabbondante.

superb *agg.* superbo, magnifico.

superciliary *agg.* sopracciliare.

supercilious *agg.* altero.

superelevation *s.* sopraelevazione.

superficial *agg.* superficiale, poco profondo.

superficiality *s.* superficialità.

superfluous *agg.* superfluo.

superhuman *agg.* sovrumano.

to **superimpose** *vt.* sovrapporre.

superintendence *s.* sovrintendenza.

superintendent *s.* sovrintendente.

superior *agg.* superiore.

superiority *s.* superiorità.

superlative *agg.* superlativo.

superman *s.* superuomo.

supermarket *s.* supermercato.

supermundane *agg.* ultraterreno.

supernatural *agg.* soprannaturale.

supernutrition *s.* supernutrizione.

to **supersede** *vt.* rimpiazzare.

supersensitive *agg.* ipersensibile.

supersensitiveness *s.* ipersensibilità.

supersession *s.* sostituzione.

supersonic *agg.* ultrasonoro, supersonico.

superstition *s.* superstizione.

superstitious *agg.* superstizioso.

superstructure *s.* sovrastruttura.

supertax *s.* soprattassa.

superterrestrial *agg.* ultraterreno.

to **supervise** *vt.* e *vi.* sovrintendere.

supervision *s.* sorveglianza, sovrintendenza.

supervisor *s.* sovrintendente.

supervisory *agg.* di controllo.

supine *agg.* supino (*anche fig.*).

supinely *avv.* supinamente.

supper *s.* cena || *to have* —, cenare; — *-time,* ora di cena.

to **supplant** *vt.* soppiantare.

supple *agg.* **1.** pieghevole, flessibile **2.** elastico (*anche fig.*).

supplement *s.* supplemento.

supplementary *agg.* supplementare.

suppliant *agg.* supplichevole. ◆ **suppliant** *s.* supplicante.

supply *s.* **1.** rifornimento, approvvigionamento **2.** (*comm.*) fornitura **3.** sostituto, supplente.

to **supply** *vt.* fornire, rifornire. ◆ to **supply** *vi.* fare da sostituto.

support *s.* sostegno, appoggio || *in* — *of,* in favore di.

to **support** *vt.* **1.** sostenere, reggere **2.** dare appoggio a **3.** mantenere.

supportable *agg.* sostenibile, sopportabile.

supporter *s.* **1.** sostegno **2.** fautore, sostenitore.

to **suppose** *vt.* supporre, presupporre, presumere.

supposed *agg.* presunto, supposto.

supposition *s.* supposizione, ipotesi.

suppository *s.* (*med.*) supposta.

to **suppress** *vt.* **1.** sopprimere, reprimere **2.** (*fig.*) soffocare, trattenere.

suppression *s.* **1.** soppressione **2.** il mettere a tacere.

to **suppurate** *vi.* suppurare.

suppuration *s.* suppurazione.

suprarenal *agg.* surrenale.

supremacy *s.* supremazia.

supreme *agg.* sommo, supremo.

surcharge *s.* **1.** sovraccarico **2.** soprattassa **3.** sovrapprezzo.

sure *agg.* sicuro, certo, fidato.

surely *avv.* sicuramente, certamente.

surety *s.* garanzia, pegno.

suretyship *s.* garanzia.

surf *s.* **1.** risacca **2.** spuma dei marosi.

surface *s.* superficie (*anche fig.*).

surfeit *s.* **1.** eccesso **2.** sazietà. ◆ to **surfeit** *vt.* saziare. ◆ to **sur-**

feit *vi.* saziarsi.
surge *s.* **1.** maroso, cavallone **2.** (*fig.*) impeto.
to surge *vi.* gonfiarsi, sollevarsi, tumultuare.
surgeon *s.* chirurgo.
surgery *s.* chirurgia.
surgical *agg.* chirurgico.
surlily *avv.* sgarbatamente.
surly *agg.* sgarbato.
to surmount *vt.* sormontare, superare.
surname *s.* **1.** cognome **2.** soprannome.
to surname *vt.* soprannominare.
to surpass *vt.* sorpassare, superare.
surpassing *agg.* superiore, eccellente.
surpassingly *avv.* straordinariamente.
surplus *s.* **1.** sovrappiù, eccedenza **2.** residuati di guerra.
surprise *s.* **1.** sorpresa **2.** stupore, meraviglia.
to surprise *vt.* **1.** sorprendere, cogliere all'improvviso **2.** stupire.
surprisedly *avv.* con sorpresa.
surprising *agg.* sorprendente.
surrealism *s.* surrealismo.
surrealist *agg. e s.* surrealista.
surrender *s.* **1.** resa, capitolazione **2.** abbandono, cessione.
to surrender *vt.* cedere, consegnare. ♦ **to surrender** *vi.* arrendersi.
surreptitious *agg.* clandestino, furtivo.
surrogate *s.* sostituto, supplente.
surround *s.* bordura, bordo.
to surround *vt.* **1.** circondare **2.** accerchiare.
surrounding *agg.* circostante. ♦ **surroundings** *s. pl.* dintorni.
survey *s.* esame, sguardo generale.
to survey *vt. e vi.* esaminare, fare rivelazioni.
surveyor *s.* ispettore.
survival *s.* **1.** sopravvivenza **2.** avanzo, reliquia.
to survive *vi.* sopravvivere. ♦ **to survive** *vt.* vivere più a lungo di.
survivor *s.* superstite.
susceptibility *s.* suscettibilità.
susceptible *agg.* **1.** suscettibile **2.** impressionabile.
suspect *agg.* sospetto. ♦ **suspect** *s.* persona sospetta.
to suspect *vt.* sospettare. ♦ **to suspect** *vi.* essere sospettoso.
to suspend *vt.* **1.** appendere, tenere

sospeso **2.** sospendere.
suspender *s.* giarrettiera, bretella.
suspense *s.* incertezza, attesa ansiosa.
suspension *s.* sospensione.
suspensive *agg.* sospensivo.
suspicion *s.* sospetto, dubbio.
suspicious *agg.* sospettoso, diffidente.
suspiciously *avv.* sospettosamente.
to sustain *vt.* **1.** mantenere, sostenere **2.** prolungare **3.** reggere.
sustainable *agg.* sostenibile.
sustenance *s.* mezzi di sussistenza (*pl.*).
suture *s.* sutura.
to suture *vt.* suturare.
swab *s.* **1.** strofinaccio **2.** (*mar.*) radazza **3.** (*med.*) tampone.
to swab *vt.* pulire, strofinare.
swag *s.* movimento ondeggiante.
swagger *agg.* sgargiante.
to swagger *vi.* **1.** pavoneggiarsi **2.** gloriarsi.
swallow[1] *s.* rondine.
swallow[2] *s.* **1.** baratro **2.** deglutizione.
to swallow *vt. e vi.* **1.** deglutire, inghiottire **2.** (*fig.*) ingoiare.
swam V. *to swim.*
swamp *s.* palude || — *-fever*, febbre malarica.
to swamp *vt.* inondare, inzuppare. ♦ **to swamp** *vi.* affondare (*anche fig.*).
swan *s.* cigno || — *song*, canto del cigno.
swarm *s.* sciame, folla.
to swarm *vi.* **1.** sciamare **2.** pullulare, brulicare, essere affollato.
swash *s.* **1.** sciacquio **2.** gradassata.
to swash *vi.* **1.** spruzzare, sguazzare **2.** turbinare, infrangersi. ♦ **to swash** *vt.* far sguazzare.
to swat *vt.* colpire, schiacciare (*mosche ecc.*).
swathe *s.* benda, fascia.
to swathe *vt.* bendare, fasciare.
sway *s.* **1.** oscillazione **2.** potere, potenza, preponderanza.
to sway *vt.* **1.** sballottolare **2.** dominare, influenzare **3.** maneggiare, impugnare **4.** (*mar.*) issare. ♦ **to sway** *vi.* **1.** ondeggiare **2.** propendere **3.** predominare.
swear *s.* bestemmia, imprecazione.
to swear (swore, sworn) *vt. e vi.* **1.** giurare, far giurare **2.** imprecare, bestemmiare.

sweat s. sudore, traspirazione.

to **sweat** vt. e vi. traspirare, sudare, sfacchinare.

sweater s. **1.** chi suda **2.** maglione di lana.

sweating s. sudore || — -*bath*, bagno turco.

sweaty agg. **1.** sudato **2.** che fa sudare.

Swede s. svedese.

Swedish agg. svedese.

sweep s. **1.** scopata **2.** movimento circolare **3.** curva, distesa.

to **sweep** (swept, swept) vi. **1.** spazzare, scopare **2.** muoversi rapidamente **3.** estendersi. ◆ to **sweep** (swept, swept) vt. **1.** spazzare **2.** sfiorare.

sweeping agg. **1.** vasto **2.** completo **3.** rapido, impetuoso (*di corrente*). ◆ **sweepings** s. pl. rifiuti.

sweet agg. **1.** dolce, amabile **2.** piacevole, gentile. ◆ **sweet** s. **1.** dolce, torta **2.** caramella.

to **sweeten** vt. **1.** zuccherare **2.** addolcire. ◆ to **sweeten** vi. addolcirsi.

sweetening s. **1.** addolcimento **2.** sostanza che addolcisce.

sweetheart s. innamorato.

sweetly avv. dolcemente.

sweetmeat s. dolciumi; frutta candita.

sweetness s. **1.** sapore dolce **2.** dolcezza, amabilità.

swell s. **1.** rigonfiamento **2.** il gonfiarsi (*dell'acqua ecc.*).

to **swell** (swelled, swollen) vi. **1.** gonfiarsi **2.** crescere, aumentare. ◆ to **swell** (swelled, swollen) vt. gonfiare.

swelling s. rigonfiamento, ingrossamento.

swept V. to *sweep*.

to **swerve** vt. deviare. ◆ to **swerve** vi. fare uno scarto.

swift agg. rapido, veloce.

swim s. nuotata.

to **swim** (swam, swum) vi. nuotare. ◆ to **swim** (swam, swum) vt. attraversare a nuoto.

swimmer s. nuotatore.

swimming s. nuoto || — -*belt*, salvagente; — -*pool*, piscina.

swindle s. truffa, frode.

to **swindle** vt. e vi. truffare.

swindler s. truffatore.

swine s. maiale, porco || — -*herd*, porcaro.

swing s. **1.** oscillazione **2.** libertà d'azione **3.** altalena.

to **swing** (swung, swung) vt. **1.** dondolare, oscillare **2.** ruotare **3.** camminare dondolandosi. ◆ to **swing** (swung, swung) vt. **1.** far dondolare **2.** far ruotare.

swinging s. dondolio.

swish s. **1.** sibilo **2.** sferzata.

Swiss agg. svizzero.

switch s. **1.** verga, frustino **2.** (*elett.*) interruttore.

to **switch** vt. e vi. **1.** colpire con un frustino **2.** muovere bruscamente **3.** (*ferr.*) smistare || to — *off*, spegnere (*la luce*); to — *on*, accendere (*la luce*).

swollen V. to *swell*.

swoon s. svenimento.

to **swoon** vi. svenire.

to **swoop** vi. calare improvvisamente, abbattersi.

sword s. spada.

swore V. to *swear*.

sworn V. to *swear*.

swum V. to *swim*.

swung V. to *swing*.

sycamore s. sicomoro.

syllable s. sillaba.

syllogism s. sillogismo.

syllogistic agg. sillogistico.

to **syllogize** vt. e vi. sillogizzare.

sylph s. silfo, silfide.

sylvan agg. silvano, silvestre.

symbiosis s. simbiosi.

symbol s. simbolo.

symbolic(al) agg. simbolico.

symbolism s. simbolismo.

to **symbolize** vt. simboleggiare.

symmetric(al) agg. simmetrico.

symmetry s. simmetria.

sympathetic agg. **1.** sensibile, comprensivo **2.** congeniale, adatto.

to **sympathize** vi. condividere i sentimenti altrui.

sympathizer s. **1.** chi è comprensivo **2.** simpatizzante (*di un partito ecc.*).

sympathy s. **1.** comprensione, partecipazione **2.** condoglianze (*pl.*).

symphonic agg. sinfonico.

symphony s. sinfonia.

symposium s. simposio, banchetto.

symptom s. sintomo.

symptomatic(al) agg. sintomatico.

synagogue s. sinagoga.

synchronism s. sincronismo.

synchronization s. sincronizzazione.

to **synchronize** *vt.* e *vi.* sincronizzare.

to **syncopate** *vt.* sincopare.

syncope *s.* sincope.

syndicalism *s.* sindacalismo.

syndicate *s.* sindacato.

synod *s.* sinodo.

synonym *s.* sinonimo.

synonymous *agg.* sinonimo.

synonymy *s.* sinonimia.

synovitis *s.* sinovite.

syntactic(al) *agg.* sintattico.

syntax *s.* sintassi.

synthesis *s.* (*pl.* -ses) sintesi.

to **synthesize** *vt.* sintetizzare.

synthetic(al) *agg.* sintetico.

syntony *s.* sintonia.

syphilis *s.* sifilide.

syphilitic *agg.* sifilitico.

Syrian *agg.* e *s.* siriano.

syringe *s.* siringa.

syrup *s.* sciroppo.

syrupy *agg.* sciropposo.

system *s.* 1. sistema 2. metodo || *railway* —, rete ferroviaria.

systematic(al) *agg.* sistematico, metodico.

systematically *avv.* sistematicamente, metodicamente.

systematization *s.* sistemazione.

to **systematize** *vt.* ridurre a sistema.

T

tab *s.* 1. linguetta (*di scarpa*) 2. (*mil.*) mostrina 3. talloncino.

tabernacle *s.* 1. tabernacolo 2. tempio.

table *s.* 1. tavola 2. tavolata 3. tabella || —*cloth*, tovaglia; *time*—, orario.

tablet *s.* 1. tavoletta 2. pastiglia, compressa.

tabloid *s.* pasticca.

taboo *agg.* e *s.* tabù.

tabular *agg.* 1. a forma di tabella 2. catalogato 3. piano, piatto.

tabulate *agg.* piano.

to **tabulate** *vt.* disporre in tabelle.

tabulation *s.* classificazione.

tabulator *s.* tabulatore.

tachometer *s.* tachimetro.

tachycardia *s.* tachicardia.

tacit *agg.* tacito.

taciturn *agg.* taciturno.

tack *s.* 1. chiodo 2. imbastitura 3. bordata 4. (*fig.*) linea di condotta.

to **tack** *vt.* 1. inchiodare 2. imbastire. ♦ to **tack** *vi.* 1. bordeggiare 2. virare.

tacking *s.* 1. l'inchiodare 2. imbastitura 3. bordeggio.

tackle *s.* 1. arnesi (*pl.*) 2. (*mar.*) paranco.

to **tackle** *vt.* 1. afferrare 2. affrontare (*difficoltà ecc.*).

tacky *agg.* viscoso.

tact *s.* tatto.

tactful *agg.* pieno di tatto.

tactical *agg.* tattico.

tactician *s.* tattico.

tactics *s.* tattica.

tactile *agg.* 1. tattile 2. tangibile.

tactility *s.* 1. tattilità 2. tangibilità.

tactless *agg.* senza tatto.

tactlessness *s.* mancanza di tatto.

tactual *agg.* tattile.

tadpole *s.* (*zool.*) girino.

tag *s.* 1. lembo pendente 2. cartellino 3. aggiunta 4. luogo comune || *licence* —, bollo di circolazione.

to **tag** *vt.* mettere cartellini a.

tail *s.* coda || — *-coat*, marsina.

to **tail** *vt.* munire di coda. ♦ to **tail** *vi.* 1. essere in coda 2. seguire da presso || *to* — *away*, affievolirsi.

tailor *s.* sarto || — *-made costume*, tailleur.

to **tailor** *vi.* fare il sarto. ♦ to **tailor** *vt.* fare un abito.

taint *s.* 1. infezione 2. tara 3. marchio.

to **taint** *vt.* guastare. ♦ to **taint** *vi.* guastarsi.

taintless *agg.* incontaminato.

take *s.* 1. presa 2. incasso 3. (*cine*) ripresa.

to **take** (**took**, **taken**) *vt.* 1. prendere 2. portare 3. accompagnare 4. necessitare || *to* — *after*, assomigliare; *to* — *in*, ricevere, ridurre, capire; *to* — *off*, togliere, decollare; *to* — *on*, assumere; *to* — *to*, darsi a.

take-off *s.* (*aer.*) decollo.

taking *agg.* 1. attraente 2. contagioso. ♦ **taking** *s.* 1. presa 2. incasso.

talc(um) *s.* talco || *talcum powder*, talco in polvere.

tale *s.* racconto, storia, novella.
talent *s.* talento.
talented *agg.* che ha talento.
talentless *agg.* senza talento.
tales *s. pl.* (*giur.*) giudici supplenti.
talisman *s.* talismano.
talk *s.* **1.** conversazione **2.** chiacchiera.
to talk *vt.* e *vi.* parlare, conversare, discutere || *to — out*, discutere a fondo.
talkative *agg.* loquace.
talkativeness *s.* loquacità.
talker *s.* **1.** parlatore **2.** chiacchierone.
talkies *s. pl.* (*gergo*) film sonoro (*sing.*).
talking *s.* conversazione.
talky *agg.* loquace.
tall *agg.* **1.** alto **2.** incredibile.
tallness *s.* altezza, statura.
tallow *s.* sego.
tally *s.* **1.** tacca **2.** cartellino, talloncino, etichetta.
to tally *vt.* registrare. ◆ **to tally** *vi.* combaciare.
tallyshop *s.* negozio che vende a rate.
talon *s.* **1.** artiglio **2.** (*mecc.*) dente **3.** (*comm.*) matrice.
tamarind *s.* tamarindo.
tambourine *s.* tamburello.
tame *agg.* **1.** addomesticato **2.** mansueto **3.** insipido, banale.
to tame *vt.* domare, addomesticare. ◆ **to tame** *vi.* ammansirsi.
tameable *agg.* addomesticabile.
tameless *agg.* indomito.
tamely *avv.* docilmente.
tameness *s.* **1.** docilità **2.** banalità.
tamer *s.* domatore.
taming *s.* addomesticamento.
to tamp *vt.* pigiare.
tamper *s.* pestello.
to tamper *vi.* **1.** manomettere **2.** immischiarsi: *to — with*, immischiarsi in **3.** corrompere.
tamperer *s.* **1.** falsificatore **2.** corruttore **3.** ficcanaso.
tampering *s.* **1.** manomissione **2.** corruzione.
tampon *s.* tampone.
tan *agg.* marrone rossiccio. ◆ **tan** *s.* **1.** tannino **2.** concia **3.** abbronzatura.
to tan *vt.* **1.** conciare **2.** abbronzare. ◆ **to tan** *vi.* abbronzarsi.
tanning *s.* abbronzatura.

tang[1] *s.* **1.** punta **2.** odore, sapore penetrante.
tang[2] *s.* suono acuto.
to tang *vt.* far risuonare. ◆ **to tang** *vi.* risuonare.
tangency *s.* tangenza.
tangent *agg.* e *s.* tangente.
tangential *agg.* tangenziale.
tangerine *s.* mandarino.
tangibility *s.* tangibilità.
tangible *agg.* tangibile.
tangle *s.* groviglio.
to tangle *vt.* **1.** aggrovigliare **2.** intrappolare. ◆ **to tangle** *vi.* aggrovigliarsi.
tanglesome, tangly *agg.* ingarbugliato.
tank *s.* **1.** serbatoio, cisterna **2.** carro armato || *— -truck*, autobotte.
tankard *s.* boccale.
tanker *s.* nave cisterna || *air —*, aerocisterna; *oil —*, petroliera.
tanner *s.* conciatore.
tannery *s.* conceria.
tannin *s.* tannino.
tanning *s.* concia.
to tantalize *vt.* tormentare.
tantalizing *agg.* allettante.
tantamount *agg.* equivalente.
tap[1] rubinetto, spina.
tap[2] *s.* colpetto.
to tap[1] *vt.* **1.** spillare **2.** forare.
to tap[2] *vt.* battere leggermente.
tape *s.* nastro || *— -recorder*, magnetofono; *recording —*, nastro magnetico.
to tape *vt.* **1.** legare con un nastro **2.** misurare con un nastro **3.** incidere su nastro magnetico.
taper *agg.* conico, rastremato ◆ **taper** *s.* **1.** candela **2.** conicità, rastremazione.
to taper *vt.* assottigliare. ◆ **to taper** *vi.* assottigliarsi, restringersi.
tapestry *s.* arazzo.
tapeworm *s.* tenia.
tapir *s.* tapiro.
tar *s.* catrame.
to tar *vt.* incatramare.
tardiness *s.* **1.** lentezza **2.** indolenza.
tardy *agg.* **1.** lento **2.** svogliato.
tare *s.* tara.
target *s.* bersaglio.
tariff *s.* tariffa.
tarnish *s.* **1.** appannamento **2.** macchia.
to tarnish *vi.* **1.** appannarsi **2.** macchiarsi. ◆ **to tarnish** *vt.* **1.** mac-

chiare 2. inquinare.
tarpaulin s. telone impermeabile.
tarry agg. 1. catramato 2. simile a catrame.
to **tarry** vi. indugiare.
tart agg. aspro.
tart s. torta di frutta, crostata.
tartan[1] s. tessuto scozzese.
tartan[2] s. (mar.) tartana.
tartar agg. e s. tartaro.
tartaric agg. tartarico.
tartlet s. pasticcino.
tartly avv. in modo acido.
task s. compito, dovere, impresa.
to **task** vt. 1. assegnare un compito a 2. affaticare.
task-work s. lavoro a cottimo.
tassel s. 1. nappa 2. segnalibro.
to **tassel** vt. adornare di nappe.
taste s. 1. gusto 2. assaggio.
to **taste** vt. 1. gustare 2. assaggiare. ♦ to **taste** vi. sapere di.
tasteful agg. raffinato.
tastefulness s. buon gusto.
tasteless agg. 1. insipido 2. di cattivo gusto.
tastelessness s. 1. scipitezza 2. mancanza di gusto.
taster s. assaggiatore.
tasty agg. 1. saporito 2. (gergo) di buon gusto.
tatter s. cencio.
to **tatter** vt. stracciare. ♦ to **tatter** vi. cadere a pezzi.
tattery agg. stracciato.
tattle s. chiacchiera.
to **tattle** vi. chiacchierare.
tattler s. chiacchierone.
tattoo[1] s. tatuaggio.
tattoo[2] s. (mil.) 1. ritirata 2. carosello militare.
to **tattoo**[1] vt. tatuare.
to **tattoo**[2] vi. tamburellare.
taught V. to teach.
taunt s. sarcasmo.
to **taunt** vt. 1. rimproverare 2. schernire.
taunting agg. beffardo. ♦ **taunting** s. rimprovero sarcastico.
taut agg. 1. teso 2. in ordine.
to **tauten** vt. tendere. ♦ to **tauten** vi. tendersi.
tautness s. tensione.
tautologic(al) agg. tautologico.
tautology s. tautologia.
tavern s. taverna || — -keeper, oste.
taw s. biglia.
tawdry agg. sgargiante.
tawny agg. bruno fulvo.

tax s. 1. tassa 2. peso || — -payer, contribuente.
to **tax** vt. 1. tassare 2. accusare.
taxability s. tassabilità.
taxable agg. tassabile.
taxation s. tassazione.
taxi s. tassì || — -driver, tassista; (aer.) — track, pista di rullaggio.
to **taxi** vi. (aer.) rullare.
taxicab s. autopubblica.
taximeter s. tassametro.
tea s. tè || — -pot, teiera; high —, cena fredda; — -set, servizio da tè.
to **teach (taught, taught)** vt. insegnare.
teachable agg. 1. che apprende facilmente 2. che si insegna facilmente.
teacher s. insegnante.
teachership s. insegnamento.
teaching agg. che insegna. ♦ **teaching** s. insegnamento.
teacup s. tazza da tè.
team s. 1. squadra 2. tiro (di cavalli).
to **team** vt. aggiogare, accoppiarsi, raggrupparsi. ♦ to **team** vi. accoppiarsi, associarsi.
tear[1] s. 1. lacrima 2. goccia || — -gas, gas lacrimogeno.
tear[2] s. strappo, lacerazione.
to **tear (tore, torn)** vt. strappare, lacerare. ♦ to **tear (tore, torn)** vi. strapparsi.
tearful agg. lacrimoso.
tearing agg. violento. ♦ **tearing** s. strappo, lacerazione.
tear-off s. parte da staccare.
tease s. chi stuzzica.
to **tease** vt. 1. stuzzicare 2. cardare (lana ecc.).
teaser s. 1. seccatore 2. cardatore 3. questione difficile.
teaspoon s. cucchiaino da tè.
technical agg. tecnico.
technicality s. tecnicismo.
technician s. tecnico.
technique s. tecnica.
technological agg. tecnologico.
technology s. tecnologia.
tectonics s. 1. edilizia 2. tettonica.
tedious agg. tedioso.
tediousness s. tedio.
to **teem** vi. brulicare.
teen-ager s. adolescente.
teens s. pl. età da tredici a diciannove anni.
teeth V. tooth.
teething s. dentizione.

teetotal(l)er s. astemio.
telecast s. teletrasmissione || — *news*, telegiornale.
to **telecast (telecast, telecast)** vt. teletrasmettere.
telecommunication s. telecomunicazione.
telecontrol s. telecomando.
telegram s. telegramma.
telegraph s. telegrafo.
to **telegraph** vt. e vi. telegrafare.
telegraphic agg. telegrafico.
telegraphist s. telegrafista.
telegraphy s. telegrafia.
telemeter s. telemetro.
telepathy s. telepatia.
telephone s. telefono || — *booth*, cabina telefonica; — *-book*, elenco telefonico.
to **telephone** vt. e vi. telefonare.
telephonist s. telefonista.
telephony s. telefonia.
telephoto s. telefoto.
telephotograph s. telefotografia.
telescope s. telescopio.
to **telescope** vi. incastrarsi.
teletype s. telescrivente.
teletyper s. telescriventista.
teletypewriter s. telescrivente.
to **teleview** vt. e vi. guardare la televisione.
televiewer s. telespettatore.
to **televise** vt. riprendere con la televisione.
television s. televisione || — *set*, televisore.
televisional agg. televisivo.
to **tell (told, told)** vt. e vi. 1. dire 2. raccontare 3. distinguere.
teller s. 1. narratore 2. (*comm.*) cassiere.
telling agg. efficace. ♦ **telling** s. 1. il raccontare 2. rivelazione.
telltale s. 1. chiacchierone 2. (*tec.*) controllore.
telluric agg. tellurico.
telpher s. cabina di funivia.
telpherage s. trasporto per teleferica.
temper s. 1. indole 2. umore 3. collera 4. moderazione.
to **temper** vt. temperare.
temperament s. temperamento.
temperamental agg. capriccioso.
temperance s. temperanza.
temperate agg. 1. temperato (*di clima*) 2. moderato.
temperature s. temperatura || *to have a* —, avere la febbre.

tempered agg. 1. temprato 2. moderato 3. di indole, umore || *quick* —, irritabile.
tempest s. tempesta.
temple[1] s. tempio.
temple[2] s. (*anat.*) tempia.
temporal agg. temporale.
temporariness s. temporaneità.
temporary agg. temporaneo.
temporization s. temporeggiamento.
to **temporize** vi. temporeggiare.
to **tempt** vt. tentare.
temptation s. tentazione.
tempter s. tentatore.
tempting agg. seducente.
ten agg. e s. dieci.
tenacious agg. 1. tenace 2. viscoso.
tenacity s. tenacia.
tenancy s. locazione.
tenant s. 1. proprietario 2. locatario.
to **tend**[1] vt. curare, badare a, custodire.
to **tend**[2] vi. tendere.
tendency s. tendenza.
tendential, tendentious agg. tendenzioso.
tender[1] agg. tenero || — *of*, sollecito verso.
tender[2] s. 1. guardiano, custode 2. nave di appoggio.
tender[3] s. offerta, proposta.
to **tender** vt. offrire, presentare.
tenderness s. 1. tenerezza 2. delicatezza.
tendon s. (*anat.*) tendine.
tendril s. viticcio.
tenebrous agg. tenebroso.
tenement s. 1. podere 2. abitazione.
tenor s. 1. tenore (*di vita ecc.*) 2. (*giur.*) copia esatta 3. (*mus.*) tenore.
tense[1] agg. teso.
tense[2] s. (*gramm.*) tempo.
to **tense** vt. tendere. ♦ to **tense** vi. tendersi.
tension s. tensione.
tent s. tenda.
tentacle s. tentacolo.
tentative agg. sperimentale. ♦ **tentative** s. tentativo, prova.
tenth agg. e s. decimo.
tenuity s. 1. tenuità 2. rarefazione 3. fluidità.
tenuous agg. 1. tenue 2. rarefatto 3. fluido.
tenure s. 1. possesso 2. gestione.

tepid agg. tiepido.
tepidity s. tepidezza.
tercet s. terzina.
tergal agg. dorsale.
to tergiversate vi. tergiversare.
tergiversation s. tergiversazione.
term s. 1. termine 2. (scol.) trimestre 3. (giur.) sessione 4. condizione. ◆ **terms** s. pl. rapporti.
to term vt. definire.
terminable agg. terminabile.
terminal agg. estremo. ◆ **terminal** s. 1. estremità 2. stazione di testa, capolinea 3. (elettr.) morsetto.
to terminate vt. 1. limitare 2. terminare. ◆ **to terminate** vi. 1. essere limitato 2. terminare.
termination s. 1. termine 2. (gramm.) desinenza.
terminator s. 1. chi termina 2. limite.
terminology s. terminologia.
terminus s. (pl. -ni) 1. capolinea 2. meta.
termite s. (zool.) termite.
tern s. terno.
ternary agg. ternario.
terrace s. 1. terrapieno 2. terrazzo (sul tetto) 3. fila di case.
terraqueous agg. terracqueo.
terrestrial agg. e s. terrestre.
terrible agg. terribile.
terrific agg. 1. spaventoso 2. (fam.) straordinario.
to terrify vt. atterrire.
territorial agg. territoriale.
territory s. territorio.
terror s. terrore.
terrorism s. terrorismo.
terrorist s. terrorista.
terroristic agg. terroristico.
to terrorize vt. terrorizzare.
terse agg. conciso.
terseness s. concisione.
tertiary agg. e s. terziario.
test s. 1. prova, esperimento, saggio 2. "test", reattivo psicologico || — driver, collaudatore; — film, provino; — -tube, provetta.
to test vt. 1. controllare 2. mettere alla prova 3. analizzare.
testament s. testamento.
testamentary agg. testamentario.
tester s. 1. collaudatore 2. apparecchio di misura 3. baldacchino.
testicle s. testicolo.
to testify vt. e vi. testimoniare.
testimonial s. 1. benservito 2. dono.
testimony s. testimonianza.

testing s. collaudo, prova.
tetanic(al) agg. tetanico.
tetanus s. tetano.
tetchy agg. stizzoso.
tetrahedron s. tetraedro.
tetralogy s. tetralogia.
Teutonic agg. teutonico.
text s. 1. testo 2. argomento.
textile agg. e s. tessile.
textual agg. testuale.
texture s. trama, tessuto.
thallium s. tallio.
than cong. che, di, di quello che (non), di quanto (non): be is older — you, è più vecchio di te.
to thank vt. ringraziare || — you!, grazie!
thankful agg. riconoscente.
thankfulness s. riconoscenza.
thankless agg. ingrato.
thanks s. pl. grazie, ringraziamenti.
thanksgiving s. ringraziamento.
that agg. (pl. those) quello, quella. ◆ **that** pron. dimostr. quello, questo, ciò. ◆ **that** pron. rel. che, il quale, la quale, i quali, le quali.
that cong. 1. che 2. affinché 3. purché.
thatch s. copertura di paglia (per tetti).
to thatch vt. coprire con paglia.
thaumaturge s. taumaturgo.
thaumaturgic(al) agg. taumaturgico.
thaw s. sgelo, disgelo.
to thaw vt. sgelare. ◆ **to thaw** vi. sgelarsi.
the art. il, lo, la, i, gli, le.
theatre s. teatro.
theatrical agg. teatrale.
theft s. furto.
their agg. poss. loro.
theirs pron. poss. il, la loro; i, le loro.
theism s. teismo.
them pron. loro, li, le, sé.
thematic agg. tematico.
theme s. tema.
themselves pron. r. 1. se stessi, se stesse, sé, si 2. essi stessi, esse stesse.
then avv. 1. allora 2. poi.
theocracy s. teocrazia.
theocratic(al) agg. teocratico.
theologian s. teologo.
theologic(al) agg. teologico.
theology s. teologia.
theorem s. teorema.

theoretic(al) *agg.* teorico.
theoretics *s.* teoretica.
theorist *s.* teorico.
to **theorize** *vi.* teorizzare.
theory *s.* teoria.
therapeutic(al) *agg.* terapeutico.
therapeutics *s.* terapeutica.
therapy *s.* terapia.
there *avv.* 1. là, lì 2. ci, vi 3. in
   ciò. ♦ **there** *inter.* ecco! su!
thereabout(s) *avv.* 1. là vicino 2.
   all'incirca.
thereby *avv.* per mezzo di, perciò.
therefore *avv.* quindi, dunque.
thereupon *avv.* al che, tosto.
thermal *agg.* termico, termale.
thermic *agg.* termico.
thermionic *agg.* termoionico.
thermodynamics *s.* termodinamica.
thermoelectric *agg.* termoelettrico.
thermometer *s.* termometro.
thermonuclear *agg.* termonucleare.
thermostat *s.* termostato.
these (*pl. di* this), questi, queste.
thesis *s.* (*pl.* -ses) tesi, dissertazione.
thews *s. pl.* muscoli.
they *pron. pers.* 1. essi, esse, loro
   2. (*in costruzioni impersonali*) si:
   — *say*, si dice.
thick *agg.* 1. spesso, grosso: *a —
   book*, un grosso libro 2. fitto, folto
   3. denso, torbido.
to **thicken** *vt.* ispessire, addensare.
   ♦ to **thicken** *vi.* ispessirsi, addensarsi.
thickening *s.* ispessimento.
thicket *s.* boschetto.
thickly *avv.* fittamente, densamente.
thickness *s.* 1. spessore, grossezza
   2. densità 3. strato.
thickset *agg.* 1. fitto, spesso 2. tarchiato.
thief *s.* (*pl.* thieves) ladro.
to **thieve** *vt.* e *vi.* rubare, essere
   ladro.
thievish *agg.* ladresco.
thigh *s.* coscia || — *bone*, femore.
thimble *s.* ditale.
thin *agg.* 1. sottile 2. magro, snello
   3. rado, raro 4. fluido, rarefatto
   5. debole, fiacco.
to **thin** *vt.* e *vi.* 1. assottigliare, assottigliarsi, dimagrire 2. diradare,
   sfoltire. ♦ to **thin** *vt.* 1. assottigliare 2. diradare, sfoltire. ♦ to
   thin *vi.* 1. assottigliarsi 2. diradarsi.
thing *s.* 1. cosa, oggetto 2. argomen-

to, soggetto.
to **think** (**thought**, **thought**) *vt.* e
   vi. 1. pensare, riflettere 2. ritenere,
   considerare 3. credere, aspettarsi
   || *to — of*, pensare, avere in ani-
   mo di; *to — ill of so.*, avere una
   cattiva opinione di qu.; *to — out*,
   escogitare; *to — over*, riflettere.
thinkable *agg.* concepibile, immaginabile.
thinker *s.* pensatore.
thinking *agg.* pensante, ragionevole
   ♦ **thinking** *s.* pensiero, riflessione, opinione.
thinness *s.* sottigliezza, tenuità, magrezza, radezza.
third *agg.* e *s.* terzo.
thirdly *avv.* in terzo luogo.
third-rate *agg.* di terz'ordine.
thirst *s.* 1. sete, arsura 2. (*fig.*)
   avidità.
thirsty *agg.* assetato || *to be* —,
   aver sete; *to be — for* (*fig.*), bramare.
thirteen *agg.* tredici.
thirteenth *agg.* tredicesimo.
thirtieth *agg.* trentesimo.
thirty *agg.* trenta.
this *agg.* e *pron. dimostr.* (*pl.* these)
   questo, questa.
Thomism *s.* tomismo.
thomist *s.* tomista.
thorax *s.* torace.
thorn *s.* spina (*anche fig.*).
thorny *agg.* spinoso (*anche fig.*).
thorough *agg.* 1. completo, totale
   2. perfetto, esperto 3. meticoloso.
thoroughbred *agg.* 1. purosangue
   (*di cavallo*) 2. di antico lignaggio. ♦ **thoroughbred** *s.* purosangue.
thoroughfare *s.* arteria di grande
   traffico || *no* —, passaggio vietato.
those (*pl. di* that) quelli, quelle.
though *avv.* comunque, tuttavia. ♦
   though *cong.* benché, sebbene.
thought V. *to* **think**.
thought *s.* 1. pensiero, riflessione
   2. idea, parere 3. concezione.
thoughtful *agg.* 1. pensoso, pensieroso 2. sollecito.
thoughtless *agg.* sconsiderato, sventato, negligente.
thoughtlessness *s.* sconsideratezza,
   negligenza.
thousand *agg.* mille. ♦ **thousand**
   s. migliaio.
thrall *s.* schiavo.
to **thrash** *vt.* e *vi.* 1. battere, sfer-

zare **2.** (*mar.*) navigare contro vento **3.** trebbiare **4.** bastonare || *to — out*, dibattere.

thrasher *s.* trebbiatore.

thrashing machine *s.* trebbiatrice.

thread *s.* **1.** filo (*anche* fig.) **2.** vena, filone.

to thread *vt.* **1.** infilare **2.** far passare attraverso.

threadbare *agg.* **1.** consumato, consunto **2.** (*fig.*) vieto, trito.

threading *s.* filettatura.

threadlike *agg.* filiforme.

threat *s.* minaccia.

to threaten *vt.* e *vi.* minacciare.

threatening *agg.* minaccioso.

three *agg.* e *s.* tre.

threescore *agg.* sessanta.

to thresh *vt.* e *vi.* trebbiare.

threshold *s.* **1.** soglia, limitare **2.** (*fig.*) esordio, inizio.

threw V. *to throw.*

thrice *avv.* tre volte.

thriftiness *s.* economia, parsimonia.

thrifty *agg.* frugale, economo.

thrill *s.* brivido, palpito.

to thrill *vt.* far fremere, elettrizzare. ♦ **to thrill** *vi.* fremere, vibrare, emozionarsi.

thriller *s.* (*gergo*) storia, film sensazionale, poliziesco.

thrilling *agg.* **1.** sensazionale, emozionante **2.** penetrante.

to thrive (**throve, thriven**) *vi.* **1.** prosperare, fiorire **2.** crescere vigorosamente.

thriving *agg.* **1.** prospero, fiorente **2.** rigoglioso.

throat *s.* gola || *— wash*, gargarismo; *sore —*, mal di gola.

throaty *agg.* gutturale.

throb *s.* battito, pulsazione, fremito.

to throb *vi.* battere, pulsare, fremere.

throbbing *agg.* palpitante, vibrante (*anche* fig.).

thrombosis *s.* trombosi.

throne *s.* trono.

throng *s.* folla, moltitudine.

to throng *vt.* affollare, stipare. ♦ **to throng** *vi.* affollarsi, affluire.

to throttle *vt.* strozzare, strangolare.

through *avv.* **1.** attraverso, da una parte all'altra **2.** (*ferr.*) direttamente || *— train*, treno diretto. ♦ **through** *prep.* **1.** attraverso, per **2.** durante, per tutta la durata di

3. per mezzo.

throughout *avv.* da un capo all'altro, dal principio alla fine. ♦ **throughout** *prep.* in ogni parte di, durante tutto il, dal principio alla fine di.

throve V. *to thrive.*

throw *s.* lancio, gittata (*di missile ecc.*), tiro.

to throw (**threw, thrown**) *vt.* e *vi.* **1.** gettare, scagliare, proiettare **2.** atterrare, rovesciare || *to — away*, buttar via; *to — off*, buttar fuori; *to — out* espellere.

throwback *s.* **1.** movimento brusco all'indietro **2.** ostacolo.

thrown V. *to throw.*

thrush *s.* tordo.

thrust *s.* **1.** colpo, botta **2.** colpo con arma appuntita.

to thrust (**thrust, thrust**) *vt.* e *vi.* **1.** spingere, ficcare **2.** frapporre **3.** forzare.

thud *s.* tonfo, rumore sordo.

to thud *vi.* fare un rumore sordo.

thumb *s.* pollice.

to thumb *vt.* **1.** lasciare ditate su (*un foglio ecc.*) **2.** strimpellare.

thump *s.* rumore sordo.

to thump *vt.* battere, percuotere, dar pugni.

thumping *agg.* pesante.

thunder *s.* **1.** tuono: *a peal of —*, un colpo di tuono **2.** scoppio, rombo **3.** fulmine (*anche* fig.).

to thunder *vt.* e *vi.* **1.** tuonare, rimbombare **2.** minacciare.

thunderbolt *s.* fulmine, saetta (*anche* fig.).

thundering *agg.* **1.** tonante, fulminante **2.** (*fam.*) straordinario.

thundery *agg.* minaccioso.

Thursday *s.* giovedì.

thus *avv.* così, in questo modo.

to thwart *vt.* opporsi a, ostacolare.

thyme *s.* timo.

thyroid *s.* tiroide.

tibia *s.* tibia.

tick *s.* tic-tac, ticchettio (*di orologio*).

to tick *vt.* e *vi.* ticchettare.

ticket *s.* **1.** biglietto, tessera, scontrino **2.** (*mil.*) congedo || *— -collector*, bigliettario; *— -inspector*, controllore; *single —*, biglietto di andata.

to ticket *vt.* **1.** mettere il cartellino del prezzo a **2.** fornire di biglietto.

ticking s. traliccio.
tickle s. solletico.
to **tickle** vt. fare il solletico, solleticare (anche fig.). ♦ to **tickle** vi. prudere.
tickler s. 1. chi solletica 2. questione delicata.
ticklish agg. 1. sensibile al solletico 2. scabroso.
tide s. 1. marea 2. (fig.) corrente, corso ‖ — -gauge, mareografo.
to **tide** vi. salire, crescere come la marea.
tidily avv. lindamente.
tidings s. pl. novità.
tidy agg. ordinato, preciso, pulito.
to **tidy** vt. riordinare, mettere in ordine.
tie s. 1. laccio, legaccio 2. cravatta 3. (fig.) legame 4. (ferr.) traversina.
to **tie** vt. 1. legare, allacciare, congiungere (anche fig.) 2. annodare.
tied agg. vincolato, schiavo.
tier s. ordine, fila (di posti).
to **tier** vt. allineare.
tiff s. stizza, bisticcio ‖ to be in a —, essere in collera.
to **tiff** vi. essere stizzito.
tiger s. tigre.
tight agg. 1. impermeabile, a perfetta tenuta 2. teso, tirato 3. stretto, aderente, attillato 4. scarso, a corto di denaro 5. (gergo) ubriaco.
♦ **tight** avv. 1. ermeticamente 2. in maniera tesa.
to **tighten** vt. 1. serrare 2. tirare, tendere. ♦ to **tighten** vi. 1. serrarsi 2. tendersi.
tightly avv. ermeticamente, strettamente.
tightness s. 1. impermeabilità, tenuta 2. tensione 3. (gergo) ubriachezza.
tights s. pl. calzamaglia.
tigress s. tigre (femmina).
tile s. 1. tegola, mattonella, piastrella 2. (fam.) cappello a cilindro.
to **tile** vt. coprire di tegole, piastrelle.
tilemaking s. fabbricazione di tegole.
tilery s. fabbrica di tegole.
tiling s. tegolato, piastrellatura.
till[1] prep. fino a: — now, fino ad ora. ♦ **till** cong. finché, fino al momento in cui.
till[2] s. cassetto in cui si custodisce il denaro.

to **till** vt. dissodare, arare.
tillage s. 1. dissodamento, aratura 2. terreno coltivato.
tiller s. 1. aratore 2. (mar.) barra del timone.
tilt[1] s. tenda, tendone.
tilt[2] s. 1. torneo, giostra 2. contesa, disputa 3. inclinazione, pendenza.
to **tilt** vt. 1. inclinare 2. rovesciare. ♦ to **tilt** vi. 1. oscillare 2. (mar.) beccheggiare.
timber s. 1. legname da costruzione 2. bosco con alberi d'alto fusto 3. trave 4. (fig.) tempra, carattere 5. (mar.) costola ‖ — -work, costruzione in legno.
to **timber** vt. rivestire di legno.
timbre s. timbro (di suoni).
time s. 1. tempo, periodo di tempo, circostanza, epoca, età 2. volta, volte 3. orario, ora ‖ with —, col passar del tempo; from — to —, di tanto in tanto; as times go, coi tempi che corrono; at times, a volte; in good —, per tempo; what — is it?, che ore sono?
to **time** vt. fissare l'orario di. ♦ to **time** vi. tenere il tempo.
timekeeper s. 1. cronometro 2. cronometrista.
timeliness s. tempestività.
timely agg. opportuno, tempestivo.
timepiece s. orologio (da tavolo).
timer s. cronometrista.
time-study agg. — engineer, analista tempi.
timid agg. timido.
timidity s. timidezza.
timing s. 1. calcolo del tempo (di pose fotografiche ecc.) 2. (mecc.) messa in fase.
timorous agg. timoroso.
tin s. 1. stagno, latta 2. recipiente.
to **tin** vt. 1. stagnare 2. conservare in scatola.
tincture s. 1. (chim.) tintura, soluzione alcoolica 2. tinta 3. sfumatura, traccia 4. gusto, aroma.
to **tincture** vt. 1. tingere, colorare 2. aromatizzare.
tinder s. esca (per fuoco).
tinge s. 1. sfumatura, tocco 2. (fig.) pizzico.
to **tinge** vt. dare una sfumatura a (anche fig.).
to **tingle** vt. 1. pizzicare 2. far tintinnare. ♦ to **tingle** vi. arrossire (di guance).
tink s. tintinnio.

tinker s. calderaio (*ambulante*), stagnino.

to **tinker** vt. rabberciare, riparare.

tinkle s. tintinnio.

to **tinkle** vt. far tintinnare. ♦ to **tinkle** vi. tintinnare.

tinkling s. tintinnio.

tinsel agg. vistoso, sgargiante. ♦ **tinsel** s. orpello (*anche fig.*).

tint s. tinta, colore delicato, sfumatura.

to **tint** vt. colorire, tinteggiare.

tiny agg. minuscolo.

tip[1] s. 1. punta, cima 2. puntale.

tip[2] s. 1. immondezzaio 2. inclinazione.

tip[3] s. mancia.

to **tip**[1] vt. toccare, battere leggermente.

to **tip**[2] vt. 1. rovesciare 2. inclinare. ♦ to **tip** vi. 1. rovesciarsi 2. inclinarsi.

to **tip**[3] vt. e vi. 1. dare la mancia 2. (*gergo*) dare, passare.

tippet s. mantellina.

tipsy agg. ubriaco.

tiptoe s. punta dei piedi: *on* —, in punta di piedi.

to **tiptoe** vi. camminare in punta di piedi.

tire s. 1. cerchione di ruota 2. pneumatico || *flat* —, gomma a terra.

to **tire**[1] vt. stancare, annoiare. ♦ to **tire** vi. stancarsi, annoiarsi.

to **tire**[2] vt. fornire di cerchione, di pneumatico.

tired agg. stanco, affaticato, esausto || *to be* — *out*, essere stanco morto.

tireless agg. instancabile.

tiresome agg. faticoso, stancante, noioso.

tissue s. tessuto || — *paper*, carta velina.

Titan s. titano, gigante.

titanic agg. titanico (*anche fig.*).

title s. 1. titolo 2. titolo, grado, qualifica.

to **title** vt. 1. intitolare, intestare 2. conferire un titolo.

titular s. titolare.

to prep. 1. (*con verbo di moto*) a, in, da 2. verso, per 3. (*di tempo*) fino a 4. (*paragone, rapporto*) contro a 5. riguardo a || — *all appearances*, stando alle apparenze; — *my despair*, con mia disperazione; — *this end*, a questo scopo.

toad s. rospo.

toady s. adulatore.

to **toady** vt. adulare, comportarsi servilmente.

toast[1] s. pane abbrustolito, crostino.

toast[2] s. brindisi.

to **toast**[1] vt. abbrustolire, tostare.

to **toast**[2] vt. e vi. fare un brindisi.

toaster s. tostapane.

tobacco s. tabacco || — *-box*, tabacchiera.

tobacconist s. tabaccaio || —*'s shop*, tabaccheria.

tocsin s. segnale d'allarme.

today s. oggi. ♦ **today** avv. oggigiorno.

toddle s. andatura incerta, vacillante.

to **toddle** vi. camminare a passi incerti, passeggiare.

toe s. dito del piede.

together avv. assieme, insieme, unitamente.

toil[1] s. fatica, duro lavoro || — *-worn*, sfinito dalla fatica.

toil[2] s. laccio, trappola (*anche fig.*).

to **toil**[1] vi. faticare, lavorare duramente.

to **toil**[2] vt. prendere in trappola (*anche fig.*).

toilet s. 1. toletta, pulizia 2. abbigliamento 3. bagno, gabinetto || — *-paper*, carta igienica.

toilsome agg. faticoso, laborioso.

token s. 1. segno, simbolo 2. prova, pegno, ricordo.

tolerable agg. 1. tollerabile 2. discreto.

tolerance s. tolleranza.

tolerant agg. tollerante.

to **tolerate** vt. tollerare, sopportare.

toleration s. tolleranza.

toll[1] s. pedaggio, dazio, gabella.

toll[2] s. rintocco (*di campana*).

to **toll** vt. suonare. ♦ to **toll** vi. rintoccare.

tomato s. pomodoro.

tomb s. tomba.

tomboy s. ragazza indiavolata.

tome s. tomo, volume.

tomfool agg. e s. sciocco, banale.

tommy s. 1. pane, pagnotta 2. provviste (*che l'operaio porta da casa*) (*pl.*).

tommy-gun s. fucile mitragliatore, mitra.

tomorrow s. e avv. domani.

ton s. tonnellata.

tonality s. tonalità.

tone s. tono, timbro, accento.

to **tone** vt. e vi. 1. (mus.) dare il tono, intonare, accordare 2. (pitt.) sfumare.
toneless agg. inespressivo, privo di colore, senza vigore.
tongs s. pl. pinze, molle, tenaglie.
tongue s. 1. lingua 2. lingua, linguaggio 3. lingua (di terra, fuoco) || — -tied, muto, taciturno; — -twister, scioglilingua.
to **tongue** vt. leccare, lambire.
tonic agg. tonico, corroborante. ◆ **tonic** s. (med.) tonico, energetico.
tonight avv. e s. stanotte, stasera.
tonnage s. tonnellaggio, stazza.
tonsil s. tonsilla.
tonsillitis s. tonsillite.
tonsure s. tonsura.
to **tonsure** vt. tonsurare.
too avv. 1. troppo 2. anche, pure 3. inoltre.
took V. to take.
tool s. 1. arnese, attrezzo, utensile 2. (fig.) strumento.
tooth s. (pl. teeth) 1. dente, zanna 2. dente (di pettine, forchetta ecc.) || — -paste, dentifricio; — -pick, stuzzicadenti.
toothache s. mal di denti.
toothbrush s. spazzolino da denti.
toothing s. dentatura, dentellatura.
toothless agg. sdentato.
toothy agg. dai denti sporgenti.
top[1] s. 1. cima, sommità 2. (fig.) apice 3. parte superiore, "capote" di automobile.
top[2] s. trottola.
topaz s. topazio.
topic s. argomento, soggetto.
topical agg. d'attualità.
topographer s. topografo.
topographic(al) agg. topografico.
topography s. topografia.
topology s. topologia.
toponymy s. toponomastica.
topsail s. vela di gabbia.
topsyturvy agg. sottosopra, capovolto. ◆ **topsyturvy** s. capovolgimento, disordine, scompiglio. ◆ **topsyturvy** avv. sottosopra.
to **topsyturvy** vt. mettere sossopra.
toque s. berretto, tocco.
torch s. torcia, fiaccola || electric —, lampadina tascabile.
torchlight s. luce di fiaccole, torce || — procession, fiaccolata.
tore V. to tear.
torment s. tormento, tortura.
to **torment** vt. tormentare.

torn V. to tear.
tornado s. ciclone.
torpedo s. 1. (zool.) torpedine 2. (mar.) siluro || — -boat, torpediniera; — boat destroyer, cacciatorpediniere.
to **torpedo** vt. silurare.
torpid agg. torpido, apatico.
torpor s. torpore.
torrefaction s. torrefazione.
to **torrefy** vt. torrefare.
torrent s. torrente (anche fig.).
torrential agg. torrenziale.
torrid agg. torrido.
torsion s. torsione.
tortoise s. tartaruga.
torture s. tortura, tormento (anche fig.).
to **torture** vt. torturare, tormentare.
torturous agg. tormentoso.
toss s. 1. lancio 2. movimento del capo.
to **toss** vt. 1. gettare, lanciare 2. agitare, scuotere 3. disarcionare. ◆ to **toss** vi. 1. agitarsi, smaniare 2. tirare a sorte 3. (mar.) beccheggiare.
total agg. totale, completo. ◆ **total** s. totale.
totalitarian agg. totalitario.
totalitarianism s. totalitarismo.
totality s. totalità.
totalizator s. totalizzatore.
to **totalize** vt. e vi. totalizzare.
totalizer s. totalizzatore.
to **totter** vi. camminare barcollando.
tottering agg. vacillante, malsicuro.
touch s. 1. tocco, colpetto 2. tatto 3. contatto, rapporto.
to **touch** vt. 1. toccare 2. sfiorare 3. (fig.) colpire, commuovere. ◆ to **touch** vi. essere in contatto, confinare.
touchiness s. suscettibilità.
touching agg. toccante, commovente. ◆ **touching** prep. riguardo a.
touchstone s. pietra di paragone.
touchwood s. esca (per accendere il fuoco).
touchy agg. permaloso.
tough agg. 1. duro 2. forte, robusto 3. (fig.) inflessibile 4. difficile 5. violento.
to **toughen** vt. indurire. ◆ to **toughen** vi. indurirsi.
toughness s. 1. durezza 2. inflessibilità.
tour s. giro, viaggio, escursione.
to **tour** vt. e vi. fare un viaggio.

tourism s. turismo.
tourist s. turista.
tourmalin(e) s. tormalina.
tournament s. torneo.
to **tousle** vt. scompigliare, arruffare.
tow s. rimorchio.
toward(s) prep. **1.** verso, in direzione di **2.** riguardo a **3.** verso, circa (di tempo).
towel s. asciugamano || — -horse, porta-asciugamano.
tower s. torre.
to **tower** vi. torreggiare.
towing s. rimorchio.
town s. **1.** città **2.** cittadinanza || — -council, consiglio comunale; — -planning, piano regolatore; chief —, capoluogo.
townhall s. municipio.
townhouse s. residenza di città.
townscape s. veduta (di città).
townsfolk s. abitanti di una città.
township s. territorio, giurisdizione di una città.
townsman s. cittadino.
townspeople s. cittadinanza.
townward(s) avv. verso la città.
toxic(al) agg. tossico.
toxicity s. tossicità.
toxicologist s. tossicologo.
toxicology s. tossicologia.
toxin s. tossina.
toy s. **1.** giocattolo **2.** bazzecola, storiella.
to **toy** vi. giocherellare, trastullarsi.
toyish agg. **1.** simile a giocattolo **2.** insignificante.
toyshop s. negozio di giocattoli.
trabeation s. trabeazione.
trace s. traccia, orma.
to **trace** vt. **1.** tracciare **2.** seguire le tracce **3.** rintracciare || to — back, risalire.
traceable agg. **1.** rintracciabile **2.** che si può tracciare.
trachea s. trachea.
tracheal agg. tracheale.
tracheitis s. tracheite.
trachyte s. trachite.
tracing s. **1.** tracciato **2.** calco, ricalco.
track s. **1.** traccia, orma **2.** sentiero, corso (anche fig.) **3.** (sport) pista **4.** (ferr.) binario || sound — (cine), colonna sonora.
to **track** vt. **1.** inseguire, pedinare **2.** tracciare un sentiero. ♦ to **track** vi. posare i binari.
tract[1] s. periodo, tratto, spazio.

tract[2] s. opuscolo.
tractability s. arrendevolezza.
tractable agg. arrendevole.
traction s. **1.** trazione **2.** contrazione.
tractor s. trattore.
trade s. **1.** mestiere **2.** commercio, traffico **3.** commercianti (pl.) || — bank, banca commerciale; — -dispute, vertenza sindacale; — -mark, marchio di fabbrica; — -show (cine), anteprima per la critica; free- —, libero scambio.
to **trade** vt. e vi. commerciare, negoziare.
trader s. **1.** commerciante **2.** nave mercantile.
trading s. commercio.
tradition s. tradizione.
traditional agg. tradizionale.
traditionalism s. tradizionalismo.
traditionalist s. tradizionalista.
to **traduce** vt. calunniare.
traffic s. **1.** traffico, commercio **2.** traffico, circolazione || — lights, semaforo; — jam, ingorgo stradale.
tragedian s. **1.** tragediografo **2.** attore tragico.
tragedy s. tragedia.
tragic(al) agg. tragico.
tragicomedy s. tragicommedia.
tragicomic(al) agg. tragicomico.
trail s. **1.** traccia, striscia **2.** pista, orma **3.** cammino, sentiero.
to **trail** vt. **1.** trascinare **2.** seguire le tracce di. ♦ to **trail** vi. trascinarsi.
trailer s. **1.** inseguitore, cacciatore **2.** rimorchio **3.** (cine) film di prossima programmazione.
train s. **1.** treno: express — (o fast —), rapido; slow —, accelerato **2.** seguito, corteo **3.** serie, successione, fila.
to **train** vt. **1.** allevare, educare **2.** esercitare, allenare, addestrare. ♦ to **train** vi. **1.** esercitarsi, allenarsi **2.** viaggiare in ferrovia.
trainer s. istruttore, allenatore.
training s. educazione, ammaestramento, allenamento.
trait s. tratto, fattezza, caratteristica.
traitor s. traditore.
trajectory s. traiettoria.
tram s. **1.** tram **2.** carrello da miniera || — -conductor, tranviere.
trammel s. **1.** tramaglio **2.** intoppo.
tramp s. **1.** calpestio **2.** viaggio a piedi.

to **tramp** *vt.* **1.** camminare pesantemente **2.** viaggiare a piedi **3.** vagabondare.

trample *s.* calpestio.

to **trample** *vt.* **1.** calpestare **2.** (*fig.*) offendere. ♦ to **trample** *vi.* camminare pesantemente.

tramway *s.* tranvia.

to **tranquillize** *vt.* tranquillizzare.

tranquillizer *s.* (*med.*) tranquillante.

to **transact** *vt.* e *vi.* negoziare, trattare affari.

transaction *s.* **1.** affare, operazione **2.** (*giur.*) transazione **3.** atti (*di congresso ecc.*) (*pl.*).

transactor *s.* negoziatore.

transalpine *agg.* e *s.* transalpino.

transatlantic *agg.* transatlantico.

to **transcend** *vt.* trascendere, superare.

transcendence *s.* trascendenza.

transcendent *agg.* trascendente.

transcendental *agg.* trascendentale.

transcendentalism *s.* trascendentalismo.

transcontinental *agg.* transcontinentale.

to **transcribe** *vt.* trascrivere.

transcript *s.* riproduzione, copia.

transcription *s.* trascrizione.

transept *s.* transetto.

transfer *s.* **1.** trasferimento, cessione **2.** (*giur.*) trapasso **3.** decalcomania.

to **transfer** *vt.* trasferire, cedere.

transferable *agg.* trasferibile.

transfiguration *s.* trasfigurazione.

to **transfigure** *vt.* trasfigurare.

to **transfix** *vt.* trafiggere.

transfocator *s.* (*cine*) teleobiettivo.

to **transform** *vt.* trasformare.

transformable *agg.* trasformabile.

transformation *s.* trasformazione.

transformer *s.* trasformatore.

transformism *s.* trasformismo.

to **transfuse** *vt.* **1.** travasare **2.** fare una trasfusione (*di sangue*).

transfusion *s.* trasfusione.

to **transgress** *vt.* trasgredire. ♦ to **transgress** *vi.* commettere una violenza, peccare.

transgression *s.* trasgressione.

transgressor *s.* trasgressore.

transient *agg.* passeggero, transitorio.

transistor *s.* (*radio*) transistor.

transit *s.* **1.** transito, passaggio **2.** trasporto.

transition *s.* transizione.

transitive *agg.* transitivo.

transitory *agg.* transitorio.

translatable *agg.* traducibile.

to **translate** *vt.* tradurre.

translation *s.* **1.** traduzione **2.** trasferimento, assunzione (*al cielo*).

translator *s.* traduttore.

translucent *agg.* traslucido, diafano, trasparente.

to **transmigrate** *vi.* trasmigrare.

transmigration *s.* trasmigrazione.

transmissible *agg.* trasmissibile.

transmission *s.* trasmissione.

to **transmit** *vt.* trasmettere.

transmitter *s.* trasmettitore.

transoceanic *agg.* transoceanico.

transparence *s.* trasparenza.

transparent *agg.* **1.** trasparente, limpido **2.** chiaro, evidente.

to **transpire** *vt.* e *vi.* traspirare.

to **transplant** *vt.* trapiantare.

transplantation *s.* trapianto.

transport *s.* **1.** trasporto (*anche fig.*) **2.** mezzo di trasporto.

transportable *agg.* trasportabile.

transposal *s.* trasposizione.

transposition *s.* trasposizione (*di parole, cifre ecc.*).

transubstantiation *s.* transustanziazione.

transversal *agg.* e *s.* trasversale.

trap *s.* trappola || — -*door*, botola.

to **trap** *vt.* prendere in trappola.

trapezium *s.* trapezio.

trapper *s.* chi tende trappole.

trash[1] *s.* rifiuto.

trash[2] *s.* guinzaglio.

to **trash** *vt.* sfrondare.

trashy *agg.* senza valore.

traumatic *agg.* traumatico.

travel *s.* **1.** viaggi (*pl.*): — *agency*, agenzia di viaggi **2.** (*mecc.*) corsa.

to **travel** *vi.* viaggiare.

traveller *s.* viaggiatore.

travelling *agg.* **1.** viaggiante **2.** di, da viaggio **3.** mobile. ♦ **travelling** *s.* il viaggiare.

traverse *agg.* trasversale. ♦ **traverse** *s.* **1.** trasversale **2.** traversata.

to **traverse** *vt.* **1.** traversare **2.** muovere lateralmente. ♦ to **traverse** *vi.* **1.** fare una traversata **2.** muoversi lateralmente **3.** girare su un perno.

travertin(e) *s.* travertino.

travesty *s.* parodia.

trawl *s.* (*mar.*) strascico.

trawler s. peschereccio a strascico.
tray s. vassoio || *ash* —, portacenere.
treacherous agg. traditore, sleale.
treacherousness, treachery s. tradimento, slealtà.
tread s. 1. passo 2. suola 3. battistrada.
to tread (trod, trodden) vt. e vi. camminare. ♦ **to tread** (trod, trodden) vt. 1. percorrere 2. calpestare.
treadle s. pedale.
treason s. tradimento.
treasure s. tesoro.
to treasure vt. 1. ammassare 2. custodire gelosamente.
treasurer s. tesoriere.
treasury s. 1. tesoreria 2. Ministero del Tesoro.
treat s. festa.
to treat vt. 1. trattare 2. offrire.
treatise s. trattato.
treatment s. 1. trattamento 2. (*med.*) cura.
treaty s. trattato.
treble agg. 1. triplo, triplice 2. (*mus.*) di soprano, parte di soprano.
to treble vt. triplicare. ♦ **to treble** vi. triplicarsi.
tree s. 1. albero 2. trave || — *-frog*, raganella.
trefoil s. trifoglio.
trellis s. graticcio.
tremble s. tremore.
to tremble vi. tremare.
trembling agg. tremante, tremolante. ♦ **trembling** s. tremito.
tremendous agg. tremendo.
tremor s. tremore.
tremulous agg. tremulo.
trench s. 1. fosso 2. trincea.
to trench vt. e vi. scavare, solcare, scavare trincee.
trenchant agg. tagliente, incisivo, efficace.
trencher s. tagliere.
trend s. direzione, orientamento, tendenza.
to trend vi. tendere.
trepan s. trapano.
to trepan vt. trapanare.
trepidation s. 1. tremito 2. trepidazione.
trespass s. 1. trasgressione 2. violazione.
to trespass vi. 1. commettere una violazione 2. peccare.

trespasser s. 1. trasgressore 2. peccatore.
trestle s. 1. cavalletto 2. intelaiatura.
trial s. 1. processo 2. prova, esperimento.
triangle s. triangolo.
triangular agg. triangolare.
triangulation s. triangolazione.
tribal agg. tribale.
tribe s. tribù.
tribune[1] s. tribuno.
tribune[2] s. tribuna.
tributary agg. e s. tributario.
tribute s. tributo.
trichromatic agg. tricromico.
trick s. 1. trucco 2. imbroglio 3. mania.
to trick vt. ingannare.
trickery s. inganno.
trickish agg. scaltro.
trickle s. gocciolio.
to trickle vi. gocciolare.
tricky agg. 1. scaltro 2. intricato.
tricolour agg. e s. tricolore.
tricycle s. triciclo.
trident s. tridente.
tridimensional agg. tridimensionale.
triennial agg. triennale.
trifle s. sciocchezza.
to trifle vi. scherzare.
trifler s. persona leggera.
trifling agg. 1. insignificante 2. frivolo.
trigeminal agg. e s. trigemino.
trigeminus s. trigemino.
trigger s. grilletto.
trigonometry s. trigonometria.
trihedron s. triedro.
trill s. trillo.
to trill vt. e vi. trillare.
trillion s. 1. trilione 2. (*amer.*) bilione.
trilogy s. trilogia.
trim agg. ordinato. ♦ **trim** s. 1. ordine 2. assetto 3. (*cine*) taglio.
to trim vt. 1. ordinare 2. tagliare.
trimester s. trimestre.
trimmer s. decoratore.
trimming s. 1. guarnizione 2. bastonatura.
trinity s. trinità.
trinket s. ninnolo.
trinomial s. trinomio.
trip s. 1. gita, viaggio 2. passo agile 3. passo falso.
to trip vi. 1. saltellare 2. inciampare. ♦ **to trip** vt. 1. far inciam-

pare 2. (*mecc.*) liberare.

tripartite *agg.* tripartito.

tripartition *s.* tripartizione.

tripe *s.* 1. trippa 2. (*gergo*) ciarpame, sciocchezze (*pl.*).

triple *agg.* triplo.

to **triple** *vt.* triplicare. ♦ to **triple** *vi.* triplicarsi.

triplicate *agg.* triplicato. ♦ **triplicate** *s.* triplice copia.

to **triplicate** *vt.* triplicare.

tripod *s.* 1. treppiede 2. tripode.

tripper *s.* gitante.

triptych *s.* trittico.

trisyllabic(al) *agg.* trisillabico.

trite *agg.* trito.

to **triturate** *vt.* triturare.

triumph *s.* trionfo.

to **triumph** *vi.* trionfare.

triumphant *agg.* trionfante.

triumvir *s.* triumviro.

triumvirate *s.* triumvirato.

trivalent *agg.* trivalente.

trivial *agg.* banale.

triviality *s.* banalità.

trod V. to tread.

trodden V. to tread.

troglodyte *s.* troglodita.

troglodytic(al) *agg.* trogloditico.

trolley *s.* carrello || — *bus*, filobus; — *line*, linea tranviaria.

troop *s.* 1. gruppo 2. truppe (*pl.*).

to **troop** *vi.* 1. radunarsi 2. sfilare.

trophy *s.* trofeo.

tropic *agg.* tropico.

tropical *agg.* tropicale.

tropism *s.* tropismo.

troposphere *s.* troposfera.

trot *s.* trotto.

to **trot** *vt.* far trottare. ♦ to **trot** *vi.* trottare.

trotter *s.* trottatore.

trouble *s.* guaio, disturbo.

to **trouble** *vt.* disturbare. ♦ to **trouble** *vi.* preoccuparsi.

troublesome *agg.* fastidioso.

trough *s.* 1. truogolo 2. condotto, solco 3. depressione (*atmosferica*).

trousers *s. pl.* calzoni

trout *s.* trota.

trowel *s.* cazzuola.

truce *s.* tregua.

truck[1] *s.* baratto, scambio.

truck[1] *s.* 1. carrello 2. (*amer.*) autocarro.

to **truck**[1] *vt.* barattare.

to **truck**[2] *vt.* trasportare (*su carrello*).

trucker *s.* camionista.

truculent *agg.* truculento.

to **trudge** *vi.* camminare faticosamente.

true *agg.* vero, esatto || *ouf of* —, sfasato.

truffle *s.* tartufo.

truly *avv.* 1. veramente 2. esattamente.

to **trump** *vt.* ingannare || *to* — *up a charge*, inventare un'accusa.

trumpery *agg.* illusorio. ♦ **trumpery** *s.* orpello.

trumpet *s.* tromba.

to **trumpet** *vi.* 1. suonare la tromba 2. barrire. ♦ to **trumpet** *vt.* strombazzare.

trumpeter *s.* trombettiere.

truncate *agg.* tronco, troncato.

truncheon *s.* manganello.

trunk *s.* 1. tronco 2. baule 3. proboscide || — -*call*, comunicazione interurbana. ♦ **trunks** *s. pl.* calzoni corti.

truss *s.* 1. fascio 2. (*arch.*) capriata.

trust *s.* 1. fede, fiducia 2. incarico di fiducia 3. (*econ.*) "trust", consorzio monopolistico.

to **trust** *vt.* e *vi.* confidare, fidarsi di, dar credito || *to* — *so. with sthg.*, affidare qc. a qu.

trustee *s.* 1. (*comm.*) fiduciario 2. (*giur.*) curatore.

truster *s.* chi si fida.

trustful *agg.* fiducioso.

trustworthy *agg.* degno di fiducia.

truth *s.* verità.

truthful *agg.* 1. vero 2. fedele.

try *s.* tentativo || — -*on*, prova (*di abiti*); — -*out* (*mecc.*), prova.

to **try** *vt.* provare, tentare || *to* — *for sthg.*, cercare di ottenere qc.; *to* — *on*, provare (*di abiti*); *to* — *out*, sottoporre a dura prova.

trying *agg.* 1. difficile 2. difficilmente sopportabile.

tub *s.* tinozza, vasca.

tube *s.* 1. tubo 2. camera d'aria 3. (*fam.*) ferrovia sotterranea.

tuber *s.* 1. tubero 2. tubercolo.

tubercular *agg.* 1. tubercolare 2. tubercoloso.

tuberculosis *s.* tubercolosi.

tuberculous *agg.* tubercoloso.

tubing *s.* tubatura.

tubular, tubulous *agg.* tubolare.

tuck *s.* piega (*di abito*).

to **tuck** *vt.* 1. (ri)piegare 2. pigiare || *to* — *up*, rimboccare.

Tuesday *s.* martedì.

tuff *s.* tufo vulcanico.

tuft *s.* **1.** ciuffo **2.** fiocco **3.** cespuglio.

tug *s.* strappo || — *-of-war*, tiro alla fune.

to tug *vt.* e *vi.* **1.** tirare **2.** dare strattoni.

tugboat *s.* (*mar.*) rimorchiatore.

tuition *s.* istruzione.

tulip *s.* tulipano.

tumble *s.* **1.** caduta **2.** confusione.

to tumble *vi.* **1.** cadere **2.** agitarsi **3.** precipitarsi **4.** fare acrobazie. ♦ **to tumble** *vt.* **1.** far cadere **2.** scompigliare.

tumble-down *agg.* in rovina.

tumbler *s.* **1.** acrobata **2.** bicchiere (*senza piede*).

tumefaction *s.* tumefazione.

to tumefy *vt.* tumefare. ♦ **to tumefy** *vi.* tumefarsi.

tumescence *s.* tumescenza.

tumescent *agg.* gonfio.

tumid *agg.* tumido.

tumidity *s.* gonfiore.

tumour *s.* tumore.

tumult *s.* tumulto.

tumultuous *agg.* tumultuoso.

tumulus *s.* (*pl.* -li) tumulo.

tun *s.* botte.

tuna *s.* tonno.

tune *s.* **1.** tono **2.** accordo **3.** motivo || *in* —, intonato; *out of* —, stonato.

to tune *vt.* (*mus.*) accordare || *to* — *up*, mettere a punto. ♦ **to tune** *vi.* essere in armonia.

tuneful *agg.* armonioso.

tuner *s.* **1.** (*mus.*) accordatore **2.** (*radio*) sintonizzatore.

tungsten *s.* tungsteno.

tunic *s.* tunica.

Tunisian *agg.* e *s.* tunisino.

to tunnel *vi.* costruire un tunnel. ♦ **to tunnel** *vt.* perforare.

tunny *s.* tonno.

turban *s.* turbante.

turbid *agg.* torbido.

turbidity *s.* torbidezza.

turbine *s.* turbina.

turbojet *s.* turbogetto || — *engine*, turboreattore.

turbulence *s.* turbolenza.

turbulent *agg.* turbolento.

tureen *s.* zuppiera.

turf *s.* **1.** zolla erbosa **2.** torba **3.** campo da corse || — *-accountant*, allibratore.

turgid *agg.* turgido.

turgidity *s.* turgidezza.

Turk *agg.* e *s.* turco.

turkey *s.* tacchino.

Turkish *agg.* turco.

turmoil *s.* agitazione.

turn *s.* **1.** giro **2.** curva **3.** turno **4.** servizio **5.** attitudine || — *-out*, assemblea, sciopero, produzione; — *-table*, piattaforma girevole, giradischi.

to turn *vi.* **1.** girarsi, volgersi **2.** diventare. ♦ **to turn** *vt.* **1.** girare, volgere **2.** mutare **3.** tornire || *to* — *off*, chiudere, spegnere; *to* — *on*, aprire, accendere; *to* — *down*, abbassare; *to* — *out*, scacciare, produrre, spegnere, risultare; *to* — *over*, rovesciare.

turnabout *s.* **1.** giostra **2.** inversione (*di rotta*).

turncoat *s.* voltagabbana.

turner *s.* tornitore.

turning *s.* **1.** giro, svolta **2.** tornitura.

turning-point *s.* svolta decisiva, momento critico.

turnip *s.* rapa.

turnkey *s.* secondino.

turnout *s.* **1.** folla **2.** equipaggio.

turnover *s.* **1.** rovesciamento **2.** (*comm.*) giro **3.** torta.

turnpike *s.* strada a pedaggio.

turnspit *s.* girarrosto.

turpentine *s.* trementina.

turpitude *s.* turpitudine.

turquoise *s.* turchese.

turret *s.* torretta.

turtle *s.* **1.** tartaruga **2.** — (*-dove*), tortora.

Tuscan *agg.* e *s.* toscano.

tusk *s.* zanna.

tussle *s.* zuffa.

to tussle *vi.* azzuffarsi.

tutelar(y) *agg.* tutelare.

tutor *s.* istitutore.

to tutor *vt.* **1.** istruire **2.** controllare.

tutorial *agg.* di istitutore.

tutorship *s.* mansione di istitutore.

twang *s.* **1.** suono acuto **2.** suono nasale.

to twang *vi.* **1.** avere un suono acuto **2.** parlare con voce nasale.

tweet *s.* cinguettio.

to tweet *vi.* cinguettare.

tweezers *s. pl.* pinzette.

twelfth *agg.* e *s.* dodicesimo.

twelve *agg.* e *s.* dodici.

twentieth *agg.* e *s.* ventesimo.

twenty *agg.* e *s.* venti.

twice *avv.* due volte.
twig *s.* ramoscello.
twilight *s.* 1. crepuscolo 2. luce fioca.
twin *agg.* e *s.* gemello.
to **twin** *vt.* accoppiare. ♦ to **twin** *vi.* accoppiarsi.
twine *s.* 1. spago, corda 2. groviglio.
twinge *s.* fitta, dolore.
twinkle *s.* 1. scintillio 2. ammicco || *in a* —, in un batter d'occhio.
to **twinkle** *vi.* 1. scintillare 2. ammiccare.
twinkling *s.* balenio.
twirl *s.* piroetta, rotazione.
to **twirl** *vt.* e *vi.* girare, roteare.
twist *s.* 1. filo ritorto 2. torsione 3. curva.
to **twist** *vt.* 1. torcere 2. travisare. ♦ to **twist** *vi.* 1. torcersi 2. serpeggiare.
twister *s.* 1. torcitore 2. truffatore.
twisty *agg.* 1. tortuoso 2. disonesto.
to **twit** *vt.* biasimare.
twitch *s.* 1. strattone 2. tic nervoso.
twitter *s.* 1. pigolio 2. agitazione.
to **twitter** *vi.* 1. pigolare 2. essere ansioso.
two *agg.* e *s.* due.
twofold *agg.* doppio. ♦ **twofold** *avv.* doppiamente.
twopence *s.* due penny (*valore*).
tycoon *s.* (*amer.*) magnate.
type *s.* 1. tipo 2. simbolo 3. (*tip.*) carattere tipografico || — *-setting* (*tip.*), composizione.
to **type** *vt.* 1. rappresentare 2. dattilografare.
   written) *vt.* e *vi.* dattilografare.
to **typewrite** (**typewrote, typewritten**) *V. to typewrite*.
typewriter *s.* dattilografo.
typewriting *s.* dattilografia.
typewritten V. *to typewrite*.
typewrote V. *to typewrite*.
typhoon *s.* tifone.
typhus *s.* tifo.
typic(al) *agg.* tipico.
to **typify** *vt.* 1. incarnare 2. esemplificare.
typist *s.* dattilografo.
typographer *s.* tipografo.
typographic(al) *agg.* tipografico.
typography *s.* tipografia.
tyrannic(al) *agg.* tirannico.
tyrannicide *s.* 1. tirannicida 2. tirannicidio.
to **tyrannize** *vt.* e *vi.* tiranneggiare.
tyrannous *agg.* tirannico.

tyranny *s.* tirannia.
tyrant *s.* tiranno.
tyre *s.* V. *tire*.
Tyrrhene, Tyrrhenian *agg.* e *s.* tirreno.
Tzigane *agg.* e *s.* tzigano.

U

ubication *s.* ubicazione.
ugliness *s.* bruttezza.
ugly *agg.* 1. brutto 2. vile, turpe.
ulcer *s.* ulcera, piaga (*anche fig.*).
to **ulcerate** *vt.* ulcerare. ♦ to **ulcerate** *vi.* ulcerarsi.
ulceration *s.* ulcerazione.
ulcerous *agg.* ulceroso.
ulna *s.* (*pl.* -ae) (*anat.*) ulna.
ultimate *agg.* ultimo, finale, definitivo.
ultra *agg.* ultra, estremo, eccessivo. ♦ **ultra** *s.* estremista.
ultramarine *agg.* oltremarino.
ultramontane *agg.* e *s.* oltremontano.
ultramundane *agg.* oltremondano.
ultra-red *agg.* infrarosso.
ultrasonic *agg.* ultrasonico.
ultraviolet *agg.* ultravioletto.
umbilical *agg.* ombelicale.
umbrella *s.* ombrello || — *-stand*, portaombrelli.
umpire *s.* (*giur.; sport*) arbitro.
unabashed *agg.* imperturbato.
unabated *agg.* non diminuito, non scemato.
unable *agg.* incapace, inabile.
unabridged *agg.* non abbreviato, completo || — *edition*, edizione integrale.
unacceptable *agg.* inaccettabile.
unaccomplished *agg.* incompleto, incompiuto.
unaccountability *s.* inesplicabilità.
unaccountable *agg.* inesplicabile.
unaccustomed *agg.* non abituale, insolito.
unachievable *agg.* ineseguibile.
unacquainted *agg.* 1. ignaro di, non al corrente di 2. sconosciuto, poco familiare.
unacquired *agg.* non acquisito, innato.
unactive *agg.* inattivo.
unadapted *agg.* inadatto.

unadorned *agg.* disadorno.

unadvisable *agg.* non consigliabile, inopportuno.

unaffected *agg.* 1. senza affettazione, semplice 2. insensibile.

unafraid *agg.* impavido.

unalienable *agg.* inalienabile.

unallied *agg.* senza relazione, senza connessione.

unalterable *agg.* inalterabile.

unamendable *agg.* incorreggibile.

to unanchor *vi.* toglier l'ancora. ◆ **to unanchor** *vt.* disancorare.

unanimated *agg.* inanimato.

unanimity *s.* unanimità.

unanimous *agg.* unanime.

unannounced *agg.* non annunciato, imprevisto.

unanswerable *agg.* 1. a cui non si può rispondere 2. irrefutabile.

unanswered *agg.* senza risposta.

unappealable *agg.* inappellabile.

unappeasable *agg.* implacabile.

unappeased *agg.* insoddisfatto.

unapplied *agg.* non impiegato, inapplicato.

unappreciated *agg.* non apprezzato, incompreso.

unapprehensive *agg.* 1. lento nell'apprendere 2. non apprensivo.

unapproachable *agg.* inaccessibile.

unapt *agg.* 1. inadatto 2. inetto.

unargued *agg.* indiscusso.

to unarm *vt.* disarmare.

unarmed *agg.* disarmato, inerme.

unartful *agg.* privo di artifici, ingenuo.

unascertainable *agg.* non verificabile.

unascertained *agg.* sconosciuto, non accertato.

unasked *agg.* non richiesto.

unaspiring *agg.* senza ambizione.

unassailable *agg.* inattaccabile.

unassailed *agg.* inattaccato.

unasserted *agg.* non asserito.

unassuming *agg.* modesto, senza pretese.

unattackable *agg.* inattaccabile.

unattainable *agg.* inaccessibile.

unattempted *agg.* intentato.

unauthorized *agg.* 1. non autorizzato 2. illecito.

unavailable *agg.* 1. inutile, vano 2. non disponibile.

unavenged *agg.* impunito.

unavoidable *agg.* inevitabile.

unaware *agg.* inconsapevole, inconscio.

unawareness *s.* inconsapevolezza.

unawares *avv.* inconsapevolmente, inconsciamente.

unbalance *s.* squilibrio.

to unbalance *vt.* sbilanciare.

to unbandage *vt.* sbendare.

unbearable *agg.* insopportabile.

unbeaten *agg.* 1. insuperato, non battuto 2. non frequentato.

unbecoming *agg.* disdicevole.

unbelief *s.* incredulità, scetticismo.

unbelievable *agg.* incredibile.

unbelieving *agg.* incredulo, scettico.

to unbend (unbent, unbent) *vt.* 1. raddrizzare 2. allentare, slegare. ◆ **to unbend (unbent, unbent)** *vi.* raddrizzarsi.

unbias(s)ed *agg.* imparziale, senza preconcetti.

to unbind (unbound, unbound) *vt.* sciogliere, slegare.

to unbolt *vt.* disserrare, aprire.

unborn *agg.* non nato, nascituro, che deve venire.

to unbosom *vt.* rivelare, confidare. ◆ **to unbosom** *vi.* sfogarsi: *to — oneself to so.*, aprirsi con qu.

unbound V. *to unbind.*

unbreakable *agg.* infrangibile.

unbreathable *agg.* irrespirabile.

to unbreech *vt.* togliere i calzoni.

to unbridle *vt.* sbrigliare, dare libero corso a (*anche fig.*).

unbridled *agg.* incontrollato, senza briglia.

unbroken *agg.* 1. intatto, intero, inviolato 2. incessante.

unbruised *agg.* non ammaccato, illeso.

to unbuckle *vt.* sfibbiare, slacciare.

to unburden *vt.* 1. scaricare, alleggerire 2. (*fig.*) alleviare.

unburied *agg.* insepolto.

to unbury *vt.* disseppellire.

to unbutton *vt.* sbottonare. ◆ **to unbutton** *vi.* sbottonarsi.

uncalled *agg.* non chiamato, non invitato: — *for*, superfluo, gratuito.

uncanny *agg.* misterioso, irreale.

uncared-for *agg.* negletto, abbandonato.

unceasing *agg.* incessante.

uncensurable *agg.* incensurabile.

uncertain *agg.* 1. incerto, malsicuro 2. irresoluto.

uncertainty *s.* 1. incertezza 2. irresolutezza.

to unchain *vt.* sciogliere da catene.

unchanged *agg.* immutato.

uncharged *agg.* 1. non carico 2. non incriminato.

uncharitable *agg.* poco caritatevole.

to **uncharm** *vt.* liberare da un incantesimo.

unchaste *agg.* impuro.

unchecked *agg.* sfrenato.

uncivil *agg.* 1. scortese, maleducato 2. indecoroso.

uncivilized *agg.* non civilizzato.

to **unclasp** *vt.* slacciare. ♦ to **unclasp** *vi.* allentare la stretta.

uncle *s.* zio.

uncombed *agg.* spettinato.

uncomely *agg.* 1. sgraziato 2. sconveniente.

uncomfortable *agg.* 1. scomodo, a disagio 2. spiacevole.

uncommon *agg.* insolito, raro.

uncompared *agg.* incomparato.

uncompelled *agg.* non costretto, spontaneo.

unconcerned *agg.* indifferente, noncurante.

unconcerning *agg.* irrilevante, che non interessa.

unconditional *agg.* incondizionato.

uncongenial *agg.* 1. antipatico, spiacevole 2. non congeniale.

unconquerable *agg.* invincibile, indomabile.

unconquered *agg.* invitto, indomito.

unconscionable *agg.* 1. irragionevole 2. senza scrupoli.

unconscious *agg.* 1. inconscio, ignaro 2. privo di sensi. ♦ **unconscious** *s.* inconscio.

unconsciousness *s.* 1. inconsapevolezza 2. stato di incoscienza.

unconsolable *agg.* inconsolabile.

unconstitutional *agg.* incostituzionale.

unconstrained *agg.* 1. non costretto, libero 2. disinvolto.

unconstraint *s.* 1. assenza di costrizione, libertà 2. spontaneità.

uncontrollable *agg.* incontrollabile.

uncontrolled *agg.* senza controllo, sfrenato.

unconventional *agg.* non convenzionale, disinvolto.

unconvertible *agg.* inconvertibile.

unconvincing *agg.* non convincente.

to **uncork** *vt.* sturare, stappare.

uncountable *agg.* innumerevole.

to **uncouple** *vt.* 1. sguinzagliare 2. staccare.

uncouth *agg.* 1. ordinario, rozzo 2. desolato.

to **uncover** *vt.* 1. scoprire 2. spogliare. ♦ to **uncover** *vi.* togliersi il cappello.

uncovered *agg.* 1. scoperto, senza tetto 2. spogliato 3. senza cappello.

unction *s.* 1. unzione 2. unguento.

unctuous *agg.* grasso, untuoso (*anche fig.*).

uncultivable *agg.* non coltivabile.

uncultivated *agg.* incolto, non coltivato.

uncut *agg.* intonso, non tagliato.

undaunted *agg.* intrepido, impavido.

to **undeceive** *vt.* disingannare.

undecided *agg.* 1. indeciso, non risolto 2. indefinito 3. irresoluto.

undeclinable *agg.* indeclinabile.

undecomposable *agg.* indecomponibile.

undefended *agg.* 1. indifeso 2. (*giur.*) non assistito da difesa legale.

undeniable *agg.* innegabile.

under *prep.* 1. sotto, al di sotto di 2. in corso di 3. meno di. ♦ **under** *avv.* sotto, al di sotto || —-age, minorenne.

underbrush *s.* sottobosco.

to **undercharge** *vt.* far pagare troppo poco.

underclothes *s. pl.* biancheria intima (*sing.*).

undercover *agg.* segreto.

undercurrent *s.* 1. corrente sottomarina 2. (*fig.*) attività, tendenza nascosta.

to **underdo (underdid, underdone)** *vt.* e *vi.* 1. agire in modo insufficiente 2. cuocere poco.

underdone V. to *underdo.* ♦ **underdone** *agg.* poco cotto.

to **underestimate** *vt.* sottovalutare.

underfed *agg.* denutrito.

to **underfeed (underfed, underfed)** *vt.* nutrire insufficientemente.

to **undergo (underwent, undergone)** *vt.* 1. subire, essere sottoposto a 2. sopportare.

undergraduate *s.* studente universitario.

underground *agg.* sotterraneo. ♦ **underground** *s.* 1. sottosuolo 2. metropolitana.

underground *avv.* 1. sottoterra 2. (*pol.*) clandestinamente.

underhand *agg.* 1. clandestino, segreto 2. furbo, astuto. ♦ **underhand** *avv.* segretamente, clandestinamente.

to underline *vt.* sottolineare.

underlining *s.* sottolineatura.

undermentioned *agg.* sottoindicato.

to undermine *vt.* 1. minare, scalzare 2. (*fig.*) indebolire, insidiare.

underneath *avv.* di sotto, al di sotto.

to underpay (underpaid, underpaid) *vt.* pagare inadeguatamente.

to underrate *vt.* sottovalutare.

underscriber *s.* sottoscrittore.

undersea *agg.* sottomarino.

to undersell (undersold, undersold) *vt.* svendere.

undershrub *s.* sottobosco.

undersignature *s.* firma in calce.

undersold V. *to undersell.*

to understand (understood, understood) *vt.* e *vi.* 1. capire, comprendere 2. dedurre, supporre 3. sentir dire.

understandable *agg.* comprensibile.

understanding *s.* 1. comprensione 2. patto, intesa || *on this —,* a queste condizioni.

to understate *vt.* minimizzare.

understatement *s.* attenuazione del vero.

understood V. *to understand.*

to undertake (undertook, undertaken) *vt.* e *vi.* 1. intraprendere 2. incaricarsi di 3. prendere in appalto.

undertaker *s.* 1. impresario 2. imprenditore di pompe funebri.

undertaking *s.* 1. l'intraprendere 2. (*comm.*) impresa 3. (*giur.*) promessa, obbligazione.

undertook V. *to undertake.*

undervaluation *s.* 1. scarsa stima 2. svalutazione.

to undervalue *vt.* sottovalutare.

underwater *agg.* subacqueo || *fishing —,* pesca subacquea.

underwent V. *to undergo.*

underworld *s.* 1. bassifondi (*pl.*) 2. oltretomba.

to underwrite (underwrote, underwritten) *vt.* e *vi.* 1. sottoscrivere, firmare 2. (*comm.*) assicurare.

undeserved *agg.* immeritato.

undeserving *agg.* immeritevole.

undesirable *agg.* indesiderabile.

undestroyable *agg.* indistruttibile.

undetected *agg.* non scoperto.

undetermined *agg.* 1. indeterminato 2. indeciso.

undid V. *to undo.*

undies *s. pl.* biancheria intima (*sing.*).

undine *s.* ondina.

undisciplined *agg.* indisciplinato.

undiscriminating *agg.* che non distingue, che non fa distinzioni.

undiscussed *agg.* indiscusso.

indisputed *agg.* incontestato.

undissembled *agg.* non dissimulato.

undistinguished *agg.* indistinto.

undisturbed *agg.* indisturbato.

undividable *agg.* indivisibile.

to undo (undid, undone) *vt.* 1. disfare, sciogliere 2. annullare, rovinare.

undoing *s.* 1. disfacimento 2. rovina.

undone[1] V. *to undo.* ♦ **undone** *agg.* disfatto, rovinato.

undone[2] *agg.* incompiuto.

undoubtable *agg.* indubitabile.

undoubted *agg.* indubbio.

undreamed *agg.* non sognato, impensato.

to undress *vt.* svestire. ♦ **to undress** *vi.* svestirsi.

undue *agg.* 1. non dovuto, indebito 2. inadatto.

to undulate *vi.* 1. ondeggiare 2. essere ondulato.

undulation *s.* ondulazione.

undulatory *agg.* ondulatorio.

unduly *avv.* indebitamente.

to unearth *vt.* 1. dissotterrare, portare alla luce 2. far uscire dalla tana (*un animale*).

unearthly *agg.* ultraterreno || *— hour,* ora impossibile.

uneasily *avv.* 1. a disagio, con difficoltà 2. con ansia.

uneasiness *s.* 1. disagio, pena 2. ansia.

uneasy *agg.* 1. a disagio 2. ansioso, inquieto.

uneatable *agg.* immangiabile.

uneducated *agg.* rozzo, ignorante.

uneffected *agg.* non effettuato.

unembarrassed *agg.* a proprio agio, disinvolto.

unemployed *agg.* 1. disoccupato 2. non usato.

unemployment *s.* disoccupazione

|| — *benefit,* sussidio di disoccupazione.

unending *agg.* eterno, senza fine.

unequal *agg.* 1. ineguale 2. inadeguato, incapace.

unequalled *agg.* ineguagliato.

unerring *agg.* infallibile, sicuro.

uneven *agg.* 1. ineguale, irregolare 2. ruvido, non livellato.

unevenness *s.* 1. disuguaglianza, irregolarità 2. dislivello.

uneventful *agg.* pacifico, senza avvenimenti importanti.

unexceptionable *agg.* ineccepibile.

unexhausted *agg.* inesausto.

unexpected *agg.* inatteso.

unexpensive *agg.* poco costoso.

unexplored *agg.* inesplorato.

unextinguishable *agg.* inestinguibile.

unfadable *agg.* 1. che non può appassire 2. solido (*di colore*).

unfading *agg.* 1. che non appassisce 2. che non sbiadisce.

unfailing *agg.* 1. infallibile, sicuro 2. immancabile.

unfair *agg.* sleale: — *competition,* concorrenza sleale.

unfairness *s.* slealtà, ingiustizia.

unfaithful *agg.* 1. infedele, sleale 2. inesatto.

unfaithfulness *s.* 1. infedeltà 2. inesattezza.

unfaltering *agg.* fermo, non esitante.

unfamiliar *agg.* poco familiare.

unfashionable *agg.* fuori moda.

to **unfasten** *vt.* slacciare, slegare. ♦ to **unfasten** *vi.* slacciarsi, slegarsi.

unfathomable *agg.* insondabile.

unfavourable *agg.* sfavorevole.

unfeeling *agg.* insensibile, spietato.

unfinished *agg.* 1. incompleto 2. non rifinito.

unfit *agg.* 1. inadatto, disadatto 2. inabile.

unfitness *s.* 1. inidoneità 2. debole costituzione.

to **unfold** *vt.* 1. aprire, schiudere 2. svelare. ♦ to **unfold** *vi.* 1. aprirsi, schiudersi 2. svelarsi.

unforbearing *agg.* insofferente, impaziente.

unforeseeing *agg.* imprevidente.

unforeseen *agg.* imprevisto.

unforgettable *agg.* indimenticabile.

unforgiving *agg.* senza misericordia.

unforgotten *agg.* inobliato.

unfortunate *agg.* sfortunato.

unfortunately *avv.* sfortunatamente.

unfounded *agg.* infondato.

to **unfreeze** (**unfroze, unfrozen**) *vt.* disgelare, scongelare. ♦ to **unfreeze** (**unfroze, unfrozen**) *vi.* disgelarsi.

unfrequent *agg.* infrequente.

unfriendly *agg.* poco amichevole.

to **unfrock** *vt.* spretare.

unfroze V. to *unfreeze.*

unfrozen V. to *unfreeze.*

unfruitful *agg.* infruttuoso.

unfruitfulness *s.* infruttuosità.

to **unfurl** *vt.* e *vi.* spiegare, spiegarsi (*di bandiere ecc.*).

unfurnished *agg.* 1. non ammobiliato 2. sfornito.

ungainly *agg.* goffo, maldestro.

ungentlemanlike *agg.* indegno di un gentiluomo.

ungirt *agg.* senza cintura.

to **unglue** *vt.* scollare. ♦ to **unglue** *vi.* scollarsi.

ungodly *agg.* 1. empio 2. malvagio.

ungraceful *agg.* sgraziato.

ungrammatical *agg.* sgrammaticato.

ungrateful *agg.* ingrato.

ungrounded *agg.* 1. infondato 2. senza preparazione.

unguarded *agg.* sguarnito, senza difesa.

unguent *s.* unguento.

unhandy *agg.* 1. maldestro 2. poco maneggevole.

unhappiness *s.* infelicità.

unhappy *agg.* infelice, triste.

unharmed *agg.* intatto, illeso.

unharmful *agg.* innocuo.

unhealthily *avv.* in modo malsano, poco igienicamente.

unhealthy *agg.* 1. malsano, insalubre 2. (*fig.*) dannoso 3. malaticcio.

unheard *agg.* 1. non udito 2. non ascoltato 3. sconosciuto, strano || — -*of,* inaudito.

to **unhinge** *vt.* scardinare.

unholy *agg.* profano, empio.

to **unhook** *vt.* sganciare. ♦ to **unhook** *vi.* sganciarsi.

unhoped *agg.* insperato, inatteso.

to **unhorse** *vt.* 1. disarcionare 2. staccare i cavalli da.

unhuman *agg.* sovrumano.

unhurt *agg.* illeso, incolume.

unhurtful *agg.* innocuo.

unicellular *agg.* unicellulare.
unification *s.* unificazione.
uniform *agg.* uniforme, costante. ◆
  uniform *s.* uniforme, divisa.
to **uniform** *vt.* uniformare.
uniformity *s.* uniformità.
to **unify** *vt.* unificare.
unilateral *agg.* unilaterale.
unilaterally *avv.* unilateralmente.
unimaginable *agg.* inimmaginabile.
unimpaired *agg.* inalterato, intatto.
unimpassioned *agg.* spassionato,
  calmo.
unimpeachable *agg.* incensurabile.
unimportance *s.* scarsa importanza.
unimportant *agg.* privo d'importanza.
unimposing *agg.* poco imponente,
  che non fa soggezione.
uninhabitable *agg.* inabitabile.
uninhabited *agg.* disabitato.
uninominal *agg.* uninominale.
unintelligent *agg.* stupido.
unintelligible *agg.* inintelligibile.
unintended *agg.* **1.** involontario **2.**
  (*giur.*) non intenzionale.
uninteresting *agg.* non interessante.
uninviting *agg.* poco attraente.
union *s.* unione, associazione, lega
  || (*trade*) —, sindacato; *the Union
  Jack*, la bandiera del Regno Unito.
unionism *s.* tendenza ad unirsi.
unionist *s.* unionista.
uniparous *agg.* uniparo.
unique *agg.* **1.** unico, solo **2.** eccezionale.
uniqueness *s.* unicità.
unisexual *agg.* unisessuale.
unison *s.* **1.** (*mus.*) unisono **2.** (*fig.*)
  concordia.
unit *s.* **1.** unità, unità di misura **2.**
  complesso, insieme.
unitary *agg.* unitario.
to **unite** *vt.* unire. ◆ to **unite** *vi.*
  1. unirsi **2.** mettersi d'accordo.
united *agg.* unito, collegato.
unity *s.* **1.** unità **2.** armonia.
universal *agg.* universale.
universality *s.* universalità.
to **universalize** *vt.* universalizzare.
universe *s.* universo.
university *s.* università.
univocal *agg.* univoco, non ambiguo.
to **unjoint** *vt.* disgiungere.
unjust *agg.* ingiusto.
unjustifiable *agg.* ingiustificabile.
unjustified *agg.* ingiustificato.
unkempt *agg.* trascurato, sciatto.

unkind *agg.* **1.** sgarbato, scortese **2.**
  crudele.
unkindness *s.* scortesia.
unknown *agg.* sconosciuto, ignoto.
unlawful *agg.* illegale.
to **unlearn** (**unlearnt, unlearnt**)
  (*anche reg.*) *vt.* disimparare.
unleavened *agg.* non lievitato || —
  bread, pane azzimo.
unless *cong.* a meno che, salvo che.
unlike *agg.* dissimile, diverso. ◆
  unlike *avv.* diversamente. ◆ **unlike** *prep.* diversamente da.
unlikelihood *s.* inverosimiglianza,
  improbabilità.
unlikely *agg.* inverosimile, improbabile.
unlimited *agg.* illimitato, sconfinato.
to **unline** *vt.* sfoderare.
unlined[1] *agg.* senza fodera.
unlined[2] *agg.* senza rughe.
unliterary *agg.* non letterario.
to **unload** *vt.* **1.** scaricare **2.** (*fig.*)
  alleggerire.
to **unlock** *vt.* aprire (*con chiave*).
unlooked-for *agg.* imprevisto.
to **unloose** *vt.* slegare.
unlosable *agg.* che non può essere
  perso.
unlovable *agg.* poco amabile, antipatico.
unlucky *agg.* **1.** sfortunato **2.** di
  cattivo augurio.
to **unman** *vt.* **1.** evirare **2.** abbrutire **3.** togliere forza.
unmarred *agg.* non sciupato.
unmarried *agg.* non coniugato.
to **unmask** *vt.* togliere la maschera
  (*anche fig.*). ◆ to **unmask** *vi.* togliersi la maschera.
unmatched *agg.* senza rivali.
unmentionable *agg.* innominabile,
  irripetibile.
unmerciful *agg.* spietato.
unmethodical *agg.* non metodico.
unminded *agg.* negletto.
unmindful *agg.* **1.** immemore **2.** incurante.
unmistakable *agg.* indubbio, ine-
  quivocabile.
to **unmoor** *vt.* e *vi.* togliere gli ormeggi a.
to **unnail** *vt.* schiodare.
unnatural *agg.* innaturale, contro
  natura.
unnavigable *agg.* non navigabile.
unnecessary *agg.* non necessario.
unneeded *agg.* inutile, non neces-

sario.

to **unnerve** *vt.* snervare.

unnoticed *agg.* inosservato.

unobjectionable *agg.* ineccepibile.

unobliging *agg.* poco compiacente.

unobservant *agg.* 1. inosservante 2. distratto.

unobserved *agg.* inosservato.

unobtrusive *agg.* discreto, modesto.

unoffending *agg.* inoffensivo.

unofficial *agg.* ufficioso.

to **unpack** *vt. e vi.* 1. disfare (*le valigie*) 2. disimballare.

umpalatable *agg.* di gusto sgradevole.

unpardonable *agg.* imperdonabile.

unpaved *agg.* non lastricato.

unperceivable *agg.* impercettibile.

unperceived *agg.* inavvertito.

unperishable *agg.* duraturo, imperituro.

unpleasant *agg.* spiacevole, sgradevole.

umpliable *agg.* poco piacevole.

unpoetic(al) *agg.* poco poetico.

to **unpoison** *vt.* svelenire.

unpolluted *agg.* incontaminato.

unpopular *agg.* impopolare.

unpopularity *s.* impopolarità.

unprecise *agg.* impreciso.

unpredictable *agg.* imprevedibile.

unpredicted *agg.* imprevisto.

unpremeditated *agg.* non premeditato.

unprepared *agg.* impreparato.

unpreparedness *s.* impreparazione.

unprepossessed *agg.* senza prevenzioni.

unprepossessing *agg.* senza attrattive, antipatico.

unpresentable *agg.* impresentabile.

unpriestly *agg.* che non si addice a un prete.

unprincely *agg.* che non si addice a un principe.

unprintable *agg.* non adatto ad essere pubblicato.

unproductive *agg.* improduttivo.

unprofitable *agg.* poco vantaggioso.

unprofitableness *s.* infruttuosità.

unpronounceable *agg.* impronunciabile.

unprovable *agg.* indimostrabile.

unpublished *agg.* inedito.

unqualified *agg.* 1. incompetente 2. non abilitato 3. (*giur.*) senza restrizioni.

to **unqualify** *vt.* 1. inabilitare 2. squalificare.

unquenchable *agg.* inestinguibile, insaziabile (*anche fig.*).

unquestionable *agg.* incontestabile, indiscutibile.

unquestioned *agg.* indiscusso.

unquiet *agg.* inquieto.

unquoted *agg.* 1. non citato 2. (*comm.*) non quotato (*di titoli*).

to **unravel** *vt.* districare. ♦ to **unravel** *vi.* districarsi.

unreachable *agg.* irraggiungibile.

unready *agg.* 1. impreparato 2. tardo, lento.

unreal *agg.* irreale.

unreality *s.* irrealtà.

unrealizable *agg.* irrealizzabile.

unreasonable *agg.* irragionevole.

unrecognizable *agg.* irriconoscibile.

unredeemed *agg.* 1. irredento 2. non controbilanciato 3. (*comm.*) non estinto.

unrelated *agg.* senza rapporti, senza legami.

unreliable *agg.* 1. non fidato 2. inattendibile.

unrepealed *agg.* (*giur.*) non abrogato.

unrequired *agg.* non richiesto.

unrest *s.* inquietudine.

unrestrained *agg.* non represso.

unrestricted *agg.* senza limitazioni.

unrevenged *agg.* invendicato.

unripe *agg.* immaturo, acerbo (*anche fig.*).

unrivalled *agg.* impareggiabile.

to **unroll** *vt.* svolgere. ♦ to **unroll** *vi.* svolgersi.

unruly *agg.* sregolato, indisciplinato.

to **unsaddle** *vt.* dissellare, disarcionare.

unsafe *agg.* malsicuro.

unsatisfied *agg.* 1. insoddisfatto 2. non convinto.

unsavoury *agg.* insipido, scipito.

unscholarly *agg.* 1. indegno di un letterato 2. non erudito.

to **unscrew** *vt.* svitare.

unscriptural *agg.* non conforme alle Sacre Scritture.

to **unseal** *vt.* dissigillare.

unseasonable *agg.* 1. fuori stagione 2. (*fig.*) intempestivo.

unseemliness *s.* indecenza

unseemly *agg.* sconveniente, indecente.

unseizable *agg.* inafferrabile.

unselfish *agg.* disinteressato.

unselfishness *s.* disinteresse.

unsettled *agg.* **1.** disordinato **2.** sconvolto, turbato **3.** mutevole, indeciso.

to **unsew** (**unsewed, unsewn**) *vt.* scucire.

unshaken *agg.* non scosso, fermo.

to **unsheathe** *vt.* sguainare.

to **unshoe** (**unshod, unshod**) *vt.* **1.** togliere le scarpe **2.** togliere i ferri a (*un cavallo*).

unshrinkable *agg.* irrestringibile.

unskilfulness *s.* incapacità, imperizia.

unskilled *agg.* inesperto, inabile.

unsocial *agg.* asociale.

unsold *agg.* invenduto.

to **unsolder** *vt.* dissaldare.

unsolved *agg.* insoluto.

unsound *agg.* **1.** malsano, malato **2.** guasto, avariato.

unspeakable *agg.* **1.** inesprimibile **2.** inqualificabile.

unstable *agg.* **1.** instabile **2.** (*fig.*) mutevole.

unsteadiness *agg.* incostanza, volubilità.

unsteady *agg.* instabile, incostante.

unsubstantial *agg.* **1.** inconsistente **2.** illusorio.

unsuccessful *agg.* mal riuscito, sfortunato.

unsuitable *agg.* inadatto, non appropriato.

unsure *agg.* **1.** malsicuro, precario **2.** incerto.

unsurpassed *agg.* insorpassato.

unsuspected *agg.* insospettato, non sospetto.

unsustainable *agg.* insostenibile.

untamable *agg.* indomabile.

untame *agg.* selvaggio, non addomesticato.

untaught *agg.* poco istruito, ignorante.

unteachable *agg.* **1.** difficile da insegnare **2.** non educabile.

unthinkable *agg.* inimmaginabile.

to **unthread** *vt.* sfilare, togliere il filo a.

untidily *avv.* disordinatamente.

untidy *agg.* disordinato, trasandato.

to **untie** *vt.* slegare. ♦ to **untie** *vi.* slegarsi.

until *prep.* fino a. ♦ **until** *cong.* finché.

untimeliness *s.* intempestività, inopportunità.

untimely *agg.* **1.** prematuro **2.** inopportuno. ♦ **untimely** *avv.* **1.** pre-

maturamente **2.** inopportunamente.

untiring *agg.* instancabile.

untitled *agg.* senza titolo.

to **untomb** *vt.* dissotterrare.

untouchable *agg.* **1.** intoccabile **2.** (*fig.*) irraggiungibile.

untouched *agg.* **1.** non toccato, intatto **2.** illeso, indenne.

untoward *agg.* **1.** restio, caparbio **2.** infausto.

untranslatable *agg.* intraducibile.

untravelled *agg.* che non ha viaggiato.

untrodden *agg.* non calpestato, non battuto.

untrue *agg.* **1.** falso, menzognero **2.** infedele.

untrustworthy *agg.* indegno di fiducia.

to **untune** *vt.* scordare (*uno strumento musicale*).

unusable *agg.* inutilizzabile.

unusual *agg.* insolito, inusitato.

unutterable *agg.* indescrivibile, impronunciabile.

unvarying *agg.* invariabile.

to **unveil** *vt.* **1.** togliere il velo a **2.** (*fig.*) rivelare.

unwary *agg.* incauto, sconsiderato.

unwatchful *agg.* non vigilante, disattento.

unweaned *agg.* non svezzato.

unweary *agg.* non stanco, indefesso.

unwell *agg.* indisposto, ammalato.

unwieldy *agg.* **1.** ingombrante **2.** impacciato.

unwilling *agg.* **1.** riluttante **2.** involontario.

unwillingly *avv.* malvolentieri.

unwillingness *s.* **1.** riluttanza **2.** malavoglia.

to **unwind** (**unwound, unwound**) *vt.* srotolare. ♦ to **unwind** (**unwound, unwound**) *vi.* srotolarsi.

unwise *agg.* malaccorto.

unwitting *agg.* inconsapevole.

unworldly *agg.* spirituale, non mondano.

unworthy *agg.* indegno, spregevole.

unwound *V.* to **unwind**.

to **unwrap** *vt.* disfare, svolgere.

unwritten *agg.* non scritto || — *law*, legge tramandata oralmente.

unwrought *agg.* **1.** non lavorato **2.** grezzo.

up[1] *avv.* **1.** su, in su, in alto **2.** in piedi || — *to*, fino a; *hurry* —, spicciati; *the game is* —, tutto è perduto. ♦ **up** *prep.* su, su per, in cima a || — *now*, fino ad ora.

up² *agg.* ascendente, che va verso l'alto || — *-train*, treno per Londra.

up-and-down *agg.* **1.** che va in su e in giù **2.** oscillante.

to **upbraid** *vt.* rimproverare.

upheaval *s.* **1.** sollevamento **2.** agitazione.

uphill *agg.* **1.** in salita **2.** (*fig.*) difficile. ♦ **uphill** *avv.* in salita. ♦ **uphill** *s.* salita.

to **uphold** (**upheld, upheld**) *vt.* **1.** sostenere, sorreggere **2.** (*fig.*) appoggiare, patrocinare.

to **upholster** *vt.* tappezzare, imbottire.

upholsterer *s.* tappezziere.

upholstery *s.* tappezzeria, imbottitura.

upkeep *s.* mantenimento, manutenzione.

upland *agg.* montuoso. ♦ **upland** *s.* zona montuosa.

upon *prep.* V. *on.*

upper *agg.* **1.** superiore, più alto **2.** più lontano (*dall'ingresso ecc.*) || *the Upper House*, la Camera dei Lords.

uppercut *s.* (*sport*) "uppercut", colpo dal basso in alto.

upright *agg.* **1.** ritto, diritto, eretto **2.** retto, integro. ♦ **upright** *avv.* in piedi, perpendicolarmente.

uprightness *s.* **1.** perpendicolarità **2.** rettitudine.

uproar *s.* tumulto, chiasso.

uproarious *agg.* tumultuoso, chiassoso.

to **uproot** *vt.* sradicare, svellere.

ups and downs *s. pl.* **1.** ondulazioni (*del terreno*) **2.** (*fig.*) vicissitudini, alti e bassi.

to **upset** (**upset, upset**) *vt.* **1.** rovesciare **2.** disturbare, sconvolgere. ♦ to **upset** (**upset, upset**) *vi.* rovesciarsi, capovolgersi.

upset *agg.* **1.** rovesciato, capovolto **2.** (*fig.*) sconvolto, turbato. ♦ **upset** *s.* **1.** rovesciamento **2.** disordine.

upshot *s.* esito, risultato.

upside-down *avv.* capovolto, sottosopra.

upstairs *agg. e avv.* al piano superiore, di sopra.

upstanding *agg.* **1.** eretto, diritto **2.** (*fig.*) franco, leale.

up-to-date *agg.* aggiornato, all'ultima moda.

upward(s) *agg.* ascendente, rivolto verso l'alto. ♦ **upward** *avv.* **1.** in su, in alto **2.** al di sopra.

uranium *s.* uranio.

urban *agg.* urbano, di città.

urbane *agg.* urbano, cortese.

urbanity *s.* urbanità, cortesia.

urbanization *s.* urbanizzazione.

to **urbanize** *vt.* urbanizzare.

urchin *s.* monello.

uretic *agg. e s.* diuretico.

urge *s.* **1.** impulso, stimolo **2.** spinta, sprone.

to **urge** *vt. e vi.* **1.** spingere, stimolare **2.** consigliare, raccomandare.

urgency *s.* **1.** urgenza, premura **2.** bisogno urgente, necessità.

urgent *agg.* urgente, pressante.

uric *agg.* urico.

to **urinate** *vi.* orinare.

urine *s.* orina.

urn *s.* **1.** urna **2.** bricco.

us *pron. pers. compl. pl.* ci, noi: *three of* —, tre di noi.

usable *agg.* usabile, servibile.

usage *s.* **1.** uso, trattamento, impiego **2.** usanza.

use *s.* **1.** uso, impiego **2.** utilità, vantaggio **3.** (*giur.*) usufrutto.

to **use** *vt.* **1.** usare, adoperare **2.** trattare || *to* — *up*, consumare.

used *agg.* **1.** usato, adoperato **2.** abituato || — *-up*, esaurito.

useful *agg.* utile, pratico.

usefulness *s.* utilità, vantaggio.

useless *agg.* inutile, vano.

uselessness *s.* inutilità.

user *s.* **1.** utente **2.** (*giur.*) usufruttuario.

usher *s.* usciere.

to **usher** *vt.* precedere (*in qualità di usciere*).

usual *agg.* usuale, abituale || *as* —, come al solito.

usually *avv.* di solito, abitualmente.

usufruct *s.* (*giur.*) usufrutto.

usufructuary *agg. e s.* usufruttuario.

usurer *s.* usuraio.

to **usurp** *vt.* usurpare.

usurpation *s.* usurpazione.

usurper *s.* usurpatore.

usury *s.* usura (*anche fig.*).

utensil *s.* utensile, arnese.

uterine *agg.* uterino.

uterus *s.* (*pl.* -ri) utero.

utilitarian *s.* utilitarista.

utilitarianism *s.* utilitarismo.
utility *s.* utilità, vantaggio.
utilizable *agg.* utilizzabile.
utilization *s.* utilizzazione.
to utilize *vt.* utilizzare.
utmost *agg.* e *s.* 1. estremo, ultimo 2. massimo, sommo ‖ *to do one's* —, fare del proprio meglio.
Utopian *s.* utopista.
utter *agg.* completo, totale.
to utter *vt.* 1. emettere 2. esprimere, pronunciare.
utterable *agg.* esprimibile.
utterance *s.* espressione, sfogo.
uttering *s.* 1. messa in circolazione 2. spaccio (*di assegni ecc.*).
utterly *avv.* completamente, totalmente.
uttermost *agg.* e *s.* V. *utmost.*
uxoricide *s.* 1. uxoricida 2. uxoricidio.

V

vacancy *s.* 1. vuoto, lacuna 2. posto vacante ‖ *no* —, completo (*di alberghi ecc.*).
vacant *agg.* 1. vuoto, vacante 2. non occupato.
to vacate *vt.* lasciar vacante, sgomberare ‖ *to* — *a seat,* dare le dimissioni.
vacation *s.* 1. il ritirarsi, il lasciar libero 2. vacanze: *long* —, vacanze estive (*pl.*).
to vaccinate *vt.* e *vi.* vaccinare.
vaccination *s.* vaccinazione.
vaccine *s.* vaccino.
to vacillate *vi.* 1. vacillare 2. (*fig.*) esitare.
vacillating *agg.* 1. vacillante 2. incostante, irresoluto.
vacillation *s.* 1. vacillamento 2. esitazione.
vacillatory *agg.* V. *vacillating.*
vacuity *s.* vacuità (*anche fig.*).
vacuous *agg.* 1. vacuo, vuoto 2. sciocco, ozioso.
vacuum *s.* vuoto pneumatico ‖ — *cleaner,* aspirapolvere.
vagabond *s.* viandante, vagabondo.
vagary *s.* fantasticheria, capriccio.
vagrancy *s.* vagabondaggio, accattonaggio.
vagrant *agg.* e *s.* vagabondo.

vague *agg.* vago, impreciso.
vaguely *avv.* vagamente.
vagueness *s.* indeterminatezza.
vain *agg.* 1. vano, inutile 2. vanitoso.
vainglorious *agg.* vanaglorioso.
vainglory *s.* vanagloria.
vainly *avv.* 1. inutilmente 2. vanitosamente.
valance *s.* 1. drappeggio 2. cortina (*di un letto*).
valediction *s.* addio, commiato.
valedictory *agg.* d'addio, di saluto. ♦ **valedictory** *s.* discorso d'addio.
valence *s.* (*chim.*) valenza.
valerian *s.* valeriana.
valet *s.* valletto.
valiant *agg.* valoroso, prode.
valid *agg.* valido, legittimo.
to validate *vt.* render valido, convalidare.
validity *s.* validità.
validly *avv.* validamente.
valley *s.* valle, vallata.
valorization *s.* valorizzazione.
to valorize *vt.* valorizzare.
valour *s.* valore.
valuable *agg.* 1. di valore, prezioso 2. valutabile.
valuation *s.* 1. valutazione, stima 2. considerazione.
value *s.* 1. valore, prezzo 2. (*fig.*) pregio, importanza ‖ — *in exchange,* valore effettivo.
to value *vt.* 1. valutare, stimare 2. considerare, dar valore.
valueless *agg.* di nessun valore.
valuer *s.* estimatore.
valve *s.* 1. valvola 2. valva.
vamp[1] *s.* 1. rappezzamento 2. (*mus.*) accompagnamento.
vamp[2] *s.* (*gergo*) donna fatale.
vampire *s.* vampiro.
van *s.* 1. furgone 2. vagone ferroviario ‖ *luggage* —, bagagliaio; *prison* —, cellulare.
Vandal *agg.* e *s.* vandalo.
Vandalic *agg.* vandalico.
vandalism *s.* vandalismo.
vane *s.* 1. banderuola 2. pala (*di mulino a vento ecc.*).
vanguard *s.* avanguardia (*anche fig.*).
vanilla *s.* vaniglia.
to vanish *vi.* svanire, sparire.
vanishing *s.* il dileguarsi, lo sparire.
vanity *s.* vanità ‖ — *-case,* borsetta col necessario per il trucco.

to **vanquish** *vt.* vincere, conquistare.

vanquisher *s.* conquistatore

vantage *s.* vantaggio.

vapid *agg.* insulso.

vaporization *s.* evaporazione.

to **vaporize** *vt.* far evaporare. ♦ to
vaporize *vi.* 1. evaporare 2. *(fig.)*
volatilizzarsi.

vaporizer *s.* vaporizzatore.

vaporous *agg.* vaporoso.

vapour *s.* vapore, esalazione.

to **vapour** *vi.* 1. evaporare 2. *(fig.)*
vantarsi.

vapouring *agg.* che evapora. ♦ **vapouring** *s.* vanteria.

vapourish *agg.* 1. pieno di vapori
2. depresso.

vapours *s. pl.* depressione *(sing.)*,
allucinazioni.

variability *s.* variabilità, mutevolezza.

variable *agg.* variabile, incostante.

variance *s.* 1. variazione 2. disaccordo.

variant *agg.* differente, contrastante.
♦ **variant** *s.* variante.

variation *s.* variazione, modificazione. ♦ **variations** *s. pl.* *(mat.)* va-
riazioni.

varicoloured *agg.* variopinto.

varicose *agg.* varicoso.

varied *agg.* 1. vario, variato 2. variopinto.

to **variegate** *vt.* variegare, screziare.

variegated *agg.* variegato, screziato.

variegation *s.* screziatura.

variety *s.* varietà, diversità || —
show *(teat.)*, spettacolo di varietà.

various *agg.* alcuni, molti *(pl.)*.

variously *avv.* variamente.

varnish *s.* 1. vernice, lacca 2. *(fig.)*
apparenza, aspetto esteriore || *nail*
—, smalto per unghie.

to **varnish** *vt.* 1. verniciare, laccare
2. *(fig.)* mascherare.

varnishing *s.* verniciatura, laccatura.

to **vary** *vt.* variare, cambiare. ♦ to
vary *vi.* essere differente.

vase *s.* vaso.

vaseline *s.* vaselina.

vassal *s.* vassallo.

vassallage *s.* vassallaggio.

vast *agg.* ampio, immenso, vasto.

vastness *s.* vastità.

vat *s.* tino, tinozza.

vault¹ *s.* 1. volta, soffitto a volta
2. cantina 3. sepolcro 4. *(fig.)* volta celeste.

vault² *s.* volteggio.

to **vault** *vi.* volteggiare. ♦ to **vault**
vt. saltare.

vaulting *s.* 1. il costruire volte 2.
costruzione a volta.

to **vaunt** *vt.* vantare. ♦ to **vaunt**
vi. vantarsi.

veal *s.* *(cuc.)* vitello.

vector *s.* vettore.

vectorial *agg.* vettoriale.

veer *s.* 1. cambiamento di direzione
2. *(mar.)* virata.

to **veer** *vi.* 1. cambiare direzione 2.
(mar.) virare.

vegetable *agg.* vegetale. ♦ **vegetable** *s.* 1. vegetale 2. ortaggio. ♦
vegetables *s. pl.* verdura *(sing.)*.

vegetal *agg.* vegetale.

vegetarian *agg. e s.* vegetariano.

to **vegetate** *vi.* vegetare *(anche fig.)*.

vegetation *s.* 1. vegetazione 2. il
vegetare.

vegetative *agg.* vegetativo.

vehemence *s.* veemenza.

vehement *agg.* veemente, impetuoso.

vehicle *s.* veicolo.

veil *s.* 1. velo, cortina 2. *(fig.)* apparenza, pretesto.

to **veil** *vt.* 1. velare, coprire 2. *(fig.)*
dissimulare, nascondere.

veiling *s.* 1. il velare 2. velo, schermo.

vein *s.* 1. *(anat.; geol.; fig.)* vena
2. venatura, nervatura.

to **vein** *vt.* venare, coprire di ve-
nature.

veined *agg.* 1. venato 2. con vena-
ture, nervature.

velleity *s.* velleità.

velocipede *s.* velocipede.

velocity *s.* velocità.

velvet *agg.* di velluto, vellutato. ♦
velvet *s.* velluto.

velvety *agg.* vellutato, morbido.

venal *agg.* venale.

venality *s.* venalità.

to **vend** *vt.* vendere.

vendor *s.* venditore.

to **veneer** *vt.* 1. impiallacciare 2.
(fig.) mascherare.

veneer, veneering *s.* 1. impiallac-
ciatura 2. *(fig.)* maschera, vernice.

venerable *agg.* venerabile.

to **venerate** *vt.* venerare.

veneration *s.* venerazione.

venereal *agg.* venereo.

Venetian *agg. e s.* veneziano || —

blinds, shades, persiana alla veneziana.

vengeance s. vendetta || *to take — on so.,* vendicarsi di qu.

vengeful agg. vendicativo, vendicatore.

venial agg. veniale.

venom s. veleno (*di animali*).

venomous agg. velenoso.

venous agg. 1. venoso 2. con nervature.

vent[1] s. spacco, apertura (*di abito*).

vent[2] s. 1. sbocco, apertura, foro 2. (*fig.*) sfogo || *to give — to,* dar libero corso a.

to vent vt. 1. svuotare, esalare 2. (*fig.*) sfogare.

to ventilate vt. 1. ventilare 2. (*fig.*) discutere, rendere manifesto.

ventilation s: 1. ventilazione 2. discussione.

ventral agg. ventrale, addominale.

ventricle s. ventricolo.

ventriloquism s. ventriloquio.

ventriloquist s. ventriloquo.

venture s. 1. avventura, azzardo 2. (*comm.*) speculazione.

to venture vt. avventurare, arrischiare. ♦ **to venture** vi. avventurarsi, arrischiarsi.

venturer s. avventuriero.

venue s. sede giurisdizionale.

veracious agg. verace.

veracity s. veracità.

veranda(h) s. veranda.

verb s. verbo.

verbal agg. 1. verbale 2. orale, a parole.

verbally avv. verbalmente, oralmente.

verbiage s. verbosità.

verbose agg. verboso, prolisso.

verdant agg. verdeggiante.

verdict s. verdetto.

verdigris s. verderame.

verge s. 1. orlo, limite || *on the — of,* sul punto di 2. bacchetta, verga.

to verge vi. 1. confinare, essere contiguo, adiacente 2. (*fig.*) rasentare: *to — on madness,* rasentare la pazzia.

verifiable agg. verificabile.

verification s. verifica.

verifier s. verificatore.

to verify vt. 1. verificare, controllare 2. (*giur.*) autenticare.

verily avv. in verità.

verisimilar agg. verosimile.

verisimilitude s. verosimiglianza.

verism s. verismo.

veritable agg. vero, genuino.

verity s. verità, realtà.

vermiform s. vermiforme.

vermin s. *coll.* insetti parassiti.

verminous agg. infestato da parassiti.

vernacular s. vernacolo, dialetto nativo. ♦ **vernacular** agg. vernacolo, nativo.

versatile agg. versatile, multiforme.

versatility s. versatilità.

verse s. 1. verso 2. strofa 3. componimento in versi.

versification s. versificazione.

to versify vt. e vi. 1. comporre in versi 2. narrare in versi.

version s. versione, traduzione.

vertebra s. (*pl.* -ae) vertebra.

vertebral agg. vertebrale.

vertebrate agg. e s. vertebrato.

vertex s. (*pl.* -tices) vertice, apice, sommità.

vertical agg. verticale. ♦ **vertical** s. piano verticale, verticale.

verticality s. posizione verticale, perpendicolarità.

very agg. 1. vero e proprio, autentico 2. (*uso enfatico*) esatto, stesso: *at that — moment,* in quello stesso istante. ♦ **very** avv. molto, assai.

vessel s. 1. vaso, recipiente 2. nave, vascello.

vest s. 1. panciotto 2. camiciola, davantino.

to vest vt. 1. conferire, investire 2. (*giur.*) assegnare 3. parare (*di altari ecc.*). ♦ **to vest** vi. passare per eredità.

vestal s. vestale.

vestibule s. vestibolo, entrata, portico di chiesa.

vestige s. vestigio, traccia.

vestment s. veste (*spec. liturgica*).

vestry s. 1. sagrestia 2. assemblea parrocchiale.

vesture s. rivestimento, veste.

veteran agg. e s. veterano.

veterinary agg. e s. veterinario.

to vex vt. 1. vessare, opprimere 2. irritare.

vexation s. 1. vessazione, oppressione 2. irritazione.

vexatious agg. 1. irritante, fastidioso 2. (*giur.*) vessatorio.

vexed agg. 1. vessato, oppresso 2. irritato.

via *prep.* per, via, attraverso: — *air mail*, per via aerea.
viability *s.* vitalità.
viable *agg.* vitale.
viaduct *s.* viadotto.
vial *s.* fiala.
viand *s.* vivanda, cibo.
vibrant *agg.* vibrante, tremante.
to vibrate *vi.* vibrare, risuonare. ♦ **to vibrate** *vt.* far vibrare.
vibration *s.* vibrazione, tremolio.
vibrator *s.* vibratore.
vibratory *agg.* 1. vibratorio 2. vibrante.
vicar *s.* 1. curato (*nella Chiesa d'Inghilterra*) 2. vicario (*Chiesa Cattolica*).
vicariate *s.* vicariato.
vice[1] *s.* 1. immoralità, depravazione 2. vizio.
vice[2] *s.* (*mecc.*) morsa.
vice[3] *s.* sostituto, vice.
vice[4] *prep.* in luogo di.
viceroy *s.* viceré.
vicinity *s.* 1. vicinanza, prossimità 2. affinità.
vicious *agg.* 1. vizioso, immorale 2. maligno 3. bizzarro (*di animali*) 4. difettoso, scorretto.
vicissitude *s.* vicissitudine.
victim *s.* vittima.
victor *s.* vincitore.
victorious *agg.* vittorioso.
victory *s.* vittoria.
to victual *vt.* vettovagliare, approvvigionare. ♦ **to victual** *vi.* approvvigionarsi.
victualling *s.* vettovagliamento, approvvigionamento.
victuals *s. pl.* vettovaglie, viveri.
to vie *vi.* gareggiare.
view *s.* 1. vista, sguardo 2. veduta, panorama 3. opinione 4. scopo, mira 5. (*giur.*) sopralluogo || *point of* —, punto di vista; — *-finder* (*foto*), mirino.
to view *vt.* 1. guardare attentamente 2. esaminare.
viewer *s.* 1. chi guarda 2. telespettatore 3. ispettore.
viewless *agg.* 1. senza vista (*di casa ecc.*) 2. invisibile.
viewpoint *s.* punto di vista.
vigil *s.* veglia.
vigilance *s.* vigilanza.
vigilant *agg.* vigilante, vigile.
vigorous *agg.* vigoroso, forte.
Viking *s.* vichingo.
vigour *s.* vigore, energia.

vigorously *avv.* vigorosamente.
vile *agg.* vile, spregevole.
vileness *s.* viltà, bassezza.
to vilify *vt.* diffamare.
villa *s.* villa.
village *s.* villaggio, paese.
villager *s.* abitante di villaggio.
villain *s.* furfante, scellerato.
villainous *agg.* scellerato, infame.
villainy *s.* scelleratezza.
to vindicate *vt.* 1. rivendicare 2. giustificare, difendere.
vindication *s.* 1. rivendicazione 2. giustificazione, difesa.
vindictive *agg.* vendicativo.
vine *s.* vite || — *-leaf*, pampino; — *-dresser*, vignaiuolo.
vinegar *s.* aceto.
vinery *s.* serra per viti.
vineyard *s.* vigneto, vigna.
vintage *s.* 1. vendemmia 2. annata.
vintager *s.* vendemmiatore.
vintner *s.* vinaio.
to violate *vt.* 1. violare, trasgredire 2. profanare.
violation *s.* 1. violazione, trasgressione 2. profanazione.
violator *s.* 1. violatore, trasgressore 2. profanatore.
violence *s.* violenza, veemenza.
violent *agg.* violento, impetuoso.
violet *agg.* violetto, viola. ♦ **violet** *s.* viola mammola.
violin *s.* violino.
violoncellist *s.* violoncellista.
viper *s.* vipera (*anche fig.*).
virgin *agg. e s.* vergine.
virginal *agg.* verginale.
virginity *s.* verginità.
virile *agg.* virile.
virility *s.* virilità.
virtual *agg.* virtuale, effettivo.
virtuality *s.* potenzialità, virtualità.
virtue *s.* 1. virtù, moralità, forza d'animo 2. qualità, merito.
virtuosity *s.* virtuosismo.
virtuous *agg.* virtuoso, morale.
virulence *s.* virulenza.
virulent *agg.* virulento.
virus *s.* virus.
visa *s.* visto consolare.
to visa *vt.* vistare (*un passaporto*).
visceral *agg.* viscerale.
viscid *agg.* viscido.
viscidity *s.* viscidità.
viscose *s.* viscosa.
viscosity *s.* viscosità.
viscount *s.* visconte.
viscous *agg.* viscoso.

visibility *s.* visibilità.
visible *agg.* visibile, evidente, manifesto.
vision *s.* 1. visione, immaginazione 2. vista, capacità visiva.
visional *agg.* irreale.
visionary *s.* visionario.
visit *s.* visita: *to pay a* —, fare una visita.
to visit *vt. e vi.* visitare, fare una visita.
visitation *s.* 1. visita ufficiale 2. castigo divino.
visitor *s.* visitatore, ospite.
visor *s.* visiera.
visual *agg.* visuale, visivo.
to visualize *vt.* 1. rendere visibile 2. prospettare. ♦ **to visualize** *vi.* diventare visibile.
vital *agg.* vitale, essenziale.
vitality *s.* vitalità.
to vitalize *vt.* vivificare.
vitals *s. pl.* organi vitali.
vitamin *s.* vitamina.
to vitiate *vt.* 1. viziare 2. *(giur.)* invalidare.
vitiation *s.* 1. corruzione 2. *(giur.)* l'invalidare.
viticulture *s.* viticoltura.
vitreous *agg.* vitreo.
vitrifiable *agg.* vetrificabile.
vitrification *s.* vetrificazione.
to vitrify *vt.* vetrificare. ♦ **to vitrify** *vi.* vetrificarsi.
vitriol *s.* vetriolo.
to vituperate *vt.* vituperare.
vituperation *s.* invettiva, biasimo.
vivacious *agg.* vivace, vispo.
vivacity *s.* vivacità, brio.
vivid *agg.* 1. vivace, vigoroso 2. vivido, colorito.
to vivify *vt.* vivificare, animare.
viviparous *agg.* viviparo.
vivisection *s.* vivisezione.
vixen *s.* 1. volpe femmina 2. megera.
vocabulary *s.* vocabolario.
vocal *agg.* vocale.
vocalization *s.* vocalizzazione.
to vocalize *vt. e vi.* vocalizzare.
vocation *s.* 1. vocazione 2. attitudine, inclinazione 3. professione.
vocational *agg.* professionale.
vocative *agg. e s.* vocativo.
vociferous *agg.* clamoroso, vociferante.
vogue *s.* voga, moda.
voice *s.* voce || *with one* —, all'unanimità.

to voice *vt.* esprimere, dire.
voiced *agg.* 1. dalla voce: *deep-* —, dalla voce profonda 2. sonoro.
voiceless *agg.* senza voce, muto.
void *agg.* 1. vuoto 2. privo 3. *(giur.)* nullo. ♦ **void** *s.* il vuoto.
to void *vt.* 1. vuotare, liberare 2. abrogare.
volatile *agg.* 1. volatile, alato 2. *(fig.)* incostante. ♦ **volatile** *s.* 1. volatile 2. *(chim.)* sostanza volatile.
to volatilize *vt.* volatilizzare. ♦ **to volatilize** *vi.* volatilizzarsi.
volcano *s.* vulcano.
volley *s.* 1. scarica, raffica, salva || — *-ball*, palla a volo.
voltage *s.* *(elettr.)* voltaggio, tensione.
voltameter *s.* voltametro.
volubility *s.* speditezza *(di eloquio)*, loquacità.
voluble *agg.* spedito *(di eloquio)*, loquace.
volume *s.* 1. volume 2. tomo, libro 3. massa.
volumetric(al) *agg.* volumetrico.
voluminous *agg.* 1. in molti volumi 2. *(fig.)* fecondo *(di scrittore)* 3. voluminoso.
voluntarily *avv.* volontariamente.
voluntary *agg.* 1. volontario, spontaneo 2. voluto, fatto di proposito 3. mantenuto da contributi non statali. ♦ **voluntary** *s.* azione volontaria.
volunteer *s.* volontario.
to volunteer *vi.* 1. offrirsi volontariamente 2. arruolarsi volontario.
voluptuary *agg.* 1. voluttuario 2. voluttuoso.
voluptuous *agg.* voluttuoso, sensuale.
voluptuousness *s.* voluttà, sensualità.
volute *s.* voluta, spirale.
vomit *s.* vomito.
to vomit *vt. e vi.* vomitare *(anche fig.)*.
voracious *agg.* ingordo, vorace.
vortex *s.* vortice, gorgo.
vortical *agg.* vorticoso.
votary *s.* seguace, devoto.
vote *s.* voto, votazione.
to vote *vt. e vi.* votare.
voter *s.* elettore.
votive *agg.* votivo.
to vouch *vt. e vi.* 1. attestare, garantire 2. *(giur.)* citare come garante.

voucher s. 1. testimone 2. documento giustificativo.
to **vouchsafe** vt. concedere.
vow s. voto.
to **vow** vi. fare un voto.
vowel s. vocale.
voyage s. viaggio (*spec. per via d'acqua*) || *outward* —, viaggio di andata; *bome* —, viaggio di ritorno.
to **voyage** vi. fare una traversata, navigare.
vulcanization s. vulcanizzazione.
vulgar agg. volgare, triviale.
vulgarism, vulgarity s. volgarità.
to **vulgarize** vt. 1. rendere volgare 2. divulgare.
vulnerability s. vulnerabilità.
vulnerable agg. vulnerabile.
vulture s. avvoltoio.

W

to **wabble** vi. vacillare, traballare.
wad s. 1. tampone 2. imbottitura 3. rotolo (*di banconote*).
to **wad** vt. 1. tamponare 2. imbottire.
wadable agg. guadabile.
wadding s. ovatta.
waddle s. andatura ondeggiante.
to **waddle** vi. camminare ondeggiando.
wade s. guado.
to **wade** vt. guadare. ♦ to **wade** vi. procedere faticosamente.
wader s. 1. chi passa a guado 2. (*zool.*) trampoliere. ♦ **waders** s. pl. stivaloni impermeabili.
wading s. il guadare.
wafer s. 1. cialda 2. disco adesivo.
waft s. soffio.
to **waft** vt. sospingere. ♦ to **waft** vi. fluttuare.
wag s. 1. cenno 2. scodinzolio.
to **wag** vt. scuotere. ♦ to **wag** vi. scuotersi || *to have a wagging tongue*, avere la lingua troppo lunga.
to **wage** vt. intraprendere (*guerra*).
to **wager** vt. e vi. scommettere.
wages s. pl. salario (*sing.*) || — -*earner*, salariato.
to **waggle** V. *to wag*.
wag(g)on s. carro || *tea*- —, car-

rello da tè.
waif s. relitto (*anche fig.*).
wail s. gemito.
to **wail** vt. e vi. gemere.
wainscot s. rivestimento in legno.
to **wainscot** vt. rivestire in legno.
waist s. cintola.
waistband s. cintura.
waistbelt s. cinturone.
waistcoat s. panciotto.
wait s. 1. attesa 2. agguato.
to **wait** vt. e vi. (*for so., sthg.*) aspettare (*qu., qc.*) || *to* — *on*, servire.
waiter s. 1. cameriere 2. vassoio.
waiting s. attesa || — -*room*, sala d'aspetto; *to keep* —, fare aspettare.
waitress s. cameriera.
to **waive** vt. rinunciare a, mettere da parte.
wake[1] s. 1. scia 2. pista.
wake[2] s. 1. risveglio 2. veglia (*funebre*).
to **wake** (**waked** e **woke, waked, woke(n)**) vt. svegliare. ♦ to **wake** (**waked** e **woke, waked, woke(n)**) vi. svegliarsi.
wakeful agg. sveglio.
wakefulness s. veglia.
to **waken** V. *to wake*.
wakening s. risveglio.
waking agg. sveglio. ♦ **waking** s. 1. risveglio 2. veglia.
walk s. 1. passeggiata 2. andatura 3. (*fig.*) rango || *to take a* —, fare una passeggiata.
to **walk** vi. passeggiare, andare a piedi || *to* — *off*, andarsene.
walker s. camminatore.
walkie-talkie s. (*radio*) trasmettitore-ricevitore portatile.
walking s. il camminare || — *tour*, escursione a piedi.
walkover s. facile vittoria.
wall s. muro || — *paper*, carta da parato; *main* —, muro maestro.
to **wall** vt. circondare di mura || *to* — *up*, murare.
wallet s. portafoglio.
wall-eye s. glaucoma.
Walloon agg. e s. vallone.
to **wallop** vt. 1. bastonare 2. percuotere, sculacciare.
wallow s. pantano.
to **wallow** vi. sguazzare.
walnut s. noce.
walrus s. tricheco.
waltz s. valzer.

to **waltz** vi. ballare il valzer.
wan agg. pallido.
to **wan** vi. impallidire.
wand s. bacchetta magica.
wander s. vagabondaggio.
to **wander** vi. 1. vagare 2. vaneggiare.
wanderer s. vagabondo.
wandering agg. 1. errante 2. delirante. ♦ **wandering** s. 1. vagabondaggio 2. delirio.
wane s. declino.
to **wane** vi. 1. declinare 2. decrescere 3. essere in fase calante.
to **wangle** vt. ottenere con intrighi.
want s. 1. mancanza 2. bisogno: to be in — of, aver bisogno di.
to **want** vt. 1. volere 2. aver bisogno di 3. mancare.
wanted agg. ricercato: to be — by the police, essere ricercato dalla polizia.
wanting prep. senza, in mancanza di.
wanton agg. 1. licenzioso 2. capriccioso 3. arbitrario 4. lascivo.
to **wanton** vi. 1. scherzare 2. comportarsi dissolutamente.
wantonness s. 1. dissolutezza 2. capriccio.
war s. guerra: — Office, Ministero della Guerra.
to **war** vi. guerreggiare.
warble s. trillo.
to **warble** vt. e vi. trillare.
warbling agg. melodioso. ♦ **warbling** s. gorgheggio.
ward s. 1. guardia 2. reparto 3. rione 4. tutela 5. pupillo.
to **ward** vt. parare: to — off a blow, parare un colpo.
warden s. 1. guardiano 2. direttore 3. governatore.
wardenship s. carica di direttore, governatore.
warder s. 1. guardiano 2. carceriere.
wardrobe s. guardaroba.
wardroom s. (mar.) quadrato ufficiali.
wardship s. tutela.
ware agg. conscio, circospetto.
to **ware** vt. fare attenzione a.
wares s. pl. 1. articoli 2. vasellame (sing.).
warehouse s. magazzino.
to **warehouse** vt. depositare in magazzino.
warehouseman s. 1. magazziniere 2. commerciante all'ingrosso.

warfare s. operazione bellica.
warfaring agg. bellicoso.
warily avv. cautamente.
wariness s. cautela.
warlike agg. guerriero.
warlikeness s. bellicosità.
warlock s. stregone.
warm agg. 1. caldo 2. animato.
to **warm** vt. 1. scaldare 2. animare. ♦ to **warm** vi. 1. scaldarsi 2. animarsi.
warmer s. riscaldatore.
warm-hearted agg. bonario, cordiale.
warming s. riscaldamento.
warmonger s. guerrafondaio.
warmth s. calore.
to **warn** vt. avvertire || to — off, invitare ad allontanarsi.
warning s. (pre)avviso || — light, spia luminosa.
warp s. 1. ordito 2. deformazione.
to **warp** vt. 1. curvare 2. (fig.) alterare. ♦ to **warp** vi. 1. curvarsi 2. (fig.) alterarsi.
warpath s. sentiero di guerra.
warping s. deformazione, pervertimento.
warrant s. 1. garanzia, garante 2. (giur.; comm.) ordine, autorizzazione.
to **warrant** vt. 1. garantire 2. giustificare.
warrantable agg. 1. giustificabile 2. legittimo.
warrantee s. chi riceve una garanzia.
warranter, -tor s. garante.
warranty s. 1. garanzia 2. autorizzazione.
warrior s. guerriero.
warship s. nave da guerra.
wart s. verruca.
wartime s. tempo di guerra.
wary agg. cauto.
was V. to be.
wash s. 1. lavata 2. bucato 3. sciacquio 4. brodaglia 5. mano (di colore).
to **wash** vt. 1. lavare 2. bagnare 3. gettare. ♦ to **wash** vi. 1. lavarsi 2. essere lavabile || to — up, rigovernare (le stoviglie); to — over, sommergere.
washable agg. lavabile.
washbasin s. catino.
washboard s. asse per lavare.
washer s. 1. lavandaio 2. (mecc.) lavatrice 3. (mecc.) rondella.

washerwoman s. lavandaia.

washhouse s. lavanderia.

washing s. 1. lavaggio 2. bucato 3. risciacquatura || — -*machine*, lavatrice.

whashout s. erosione, dilatamento.

washroom s. 1. lavanderia 2. gabinetto.

washstand s. lavabo.

washy agg. 1. annacquato 2. scialbo.

wasp s. vespa.

waspish agg. pungente.

waspishness s. irascibilità.

wastage s. logorio.

waste agg. 1. deserto 2. di scarto. ♦ **waste** s. 1. spreco 2. scarto 3. deserto || — -*basket*, cestino per rifiuti; — -*paper*, carta straccia.

to **waste** vt. 1. consumare 2. sprecare 3. rovinare. ♦ to **waste** vi. 1. consumarsi 2. rovinarsi.

wasteful agg. 1. rovinoso 2. prodigo.

waster s. dissipatore.

wasting agg. 1. logorante 2. devastante. ♦ **wasting** s. 1. sciupio 2. deperimento 3. devastazione.

watch s. 1. orologio (*da polso*) 2. guardia || — -*fire*, fuoco di bivacco; *to be on the* —, stare in guardia.

to **watch** vt. 1. osservare 2. stare a guardia di. ♦ to **watch** vi. 1. vegliare 2. aspettare.

watcher s. 1. spettatore 2. sorvegliante.

watchful agg. attento.

watchfulness s. 1. vigilanza 2. cautela.

watchmaker s. orologiaio.

watchman s. guardia (*notturna*).

watchword s. parola d'ordine.

water s. acqua || *to hold* —, non fare acqua, (*fig.*) essere logico; — -*bottle*, borraccia; — -*colour*, acquarello; — -*colourist*, acquarellista; — -*closet*, gabinetto; — -*gate*, chiusa; — -*line*, linea di galleggiamento; — -*meadow*, marcita; — -*polo*, pallanuoto; *drinking* —, acqua potabile.

to **water** vt. 1. bagnare 2. diluire 3. abbeverare 4. secernere || *to make one's mouth* —, far venire l'acquolina in bocca. ♦ to **water** vi. 1. abbeverarsi 2. riempirsi di acqua.

waterfall s. cascata.

watering s. 1. annaffiamento 2. diluizione 3. abbeverarsi 4. rifornimento d'acqua 5. secrezione || — -*can*, — -*pot*, annaffiatoio.

waterman s. (*pl.* -men) barcaiolo.

watermark s. 1. filigrana 2. indicatore di livello 3. livello d'acqua.

watermelon s. anguria.

waterproof agg. e s. impermeabile.

to **waterproof** vt. impermeabilizzare.

watershed s. 1. spartiacque 2. bacino idrico.

watertight agg. stagno.

waterway s. canale navigabile.

waterworks s. pl. impianto idrico (*sing.*).

watery agg. 1. acquoso 2. lacrimoso.

wattle s. 1. fascina 2. vimine.

wave s. 1. onda, ondata 2. cenno (*della mano*).

to **wave** vi. 1. ondeggiare 2. far cenno (*con la mano*). ♦ to **wave** vt. 1. far ondeggiare 2. ondulare 3. chiamare (*con un cenno di mano*).

waved agg. ondulato.

wave-length s. lunghezza d'onda.

waveless agg. liscio.

wavelet s. piccola onda.

wavelike agg. ondeggiante.

to **waver** vi. vacillare.

wavering s. 1. oscillazione 2. esitazione.

wavily avv. a onde.

waviness s. ondulazione.

waving s. 1. ondeggiamento, ondulazione 2. sventolio 3. cenno.

wavy agg. 1. ondulato 2. ondeggiante.

wax s. 1. cera 2. paraffina.

to **wax**[1] vt. incerare.

to **wax**[2] vi. 1. crescere 2. aumentare.

waxen agg. di, come cera.

way s. 1. via 2. maniera 3. punto di vista 4. stato || *to make* —, far posto; *this* —, per di qua; *in a* —, in un certo senso; *by the* —, tra parentesi; *one-* —, senso unico; *out of the* —, fuori mano.

waybill s. lista dei passeggeri.

wayfarer s. viandante.

to **waylay** vt. tendere un agguato a.

wayside s. margine della strada.

wayward agg. 1. indocile 2. capriccioso.

waywardness s. ostinazione.

we pron. sogg. noi.

weak agg. 1. debole 2. diluito.
to **weaken** vi. indebolirsi. ♦ to **weaken** vt. indebolire.
weakling s. persona debole.
weakly agg. debole.
weakness s. debolezza.
weal[1] s. benessere, prosperità.
weal[2] s. livido.
wealth s. ricchezza.
wealthy agg. ricco.
to **wean** vt. 1. svezzare 2. togliere il vizio a.
weaning s. svezzamento.
weapon s. arma.
wear s. 1. uso, usura 2. durata 3. abbigliamento.
to **wear (wore, worn)** vt. 1. indossare 2. logorare 3. stancare || to — out, logorare, stancare. ♦ to **wear (wore, worn)** vi. 1. logorarsi 2. stancarsi 3. durare || to — out, logorarsi, stancarsi.
wearily avv. stancamente.
weariness s. 1. stanchezza 2. tedio.
wearing agg. 1. logorante 2. da indossare. ♦ **wearing** s. 1. logorio 2. l'indossare.
wearisome agg. 1. faticoso 2. tedioso.
weary agg. 1. stanco 2. annoiato.
to **weary** vt. 1. affaticare 2. annoiare. ♦ to **weary** vi. 1. affaticarsi 2. annoiarsi.
weasel s. donnola.
weather s. tempo (atmosferico) || — -glass, barometro; — -report, bollettino meteorologico.
to **weather** vt. 1. esporre all'aria 2. superare || to — a storm, resistere a una burrasca. ♦ to **weather** vi. alterarsi.
weathercock s. banderuola.
weathering s. alterazione (di tempo).
weave s. tessuto.
to **weave (wove, woven)** vt. 1. tessere, intrecciare 2. (fig.) ideare.
weaver s. tessitore.
weaving s. 1. tessitura 2. orditura.
web s. 1. tela 2. (fig.) trama 3. membrana || cob- —, ragnatela.
to **wed** vt. sposare. ♦ to **wed** vi. sposarsi.
wedding s. nozze (pl.) || — -breakfast, rinfresco di nozze; — -ring, fede nuziale.
wedge s. cuneo.
to **wedge** vt. 1. incuneare 2. fendere con cunei.

wedlock s. vincolo matrimoniale.
Wednesday s. mercoledì.
wee agg. minuscolo || a — bit, un tantino.
weed s. erbaccia. ♦ **weeds** s. pl. gramaglie.
to **weed** vt. 1. sarchiare 2. estirpare.
weeding s. sarchiatura.
week s. settimana || today —, oggi a otto; — in — out, una settimana dopo l'altra.
weekday s. giorno feriale.
week-end s. fine settimana.
weekly agg. e s. settimanale. ♦ **weekly** avv. settimanalmente.
weep s. pianto.
to **weep (wept, wept)** vt. e vi. 1. piangere 2. trasudare || to — out, piangere disperatamente.
weeper s. 1. chi piange 2. velo, nastro di lutto.
weeping s. 1. pianto 2. trasudamento.
weft s. trama (di tessuto).
to **weigh** vt. e vi. 1. pesare 2. (fig.) ponderare || to — down, piegare; to — anchor (mar.), levar l'ancora.
weigh-house s. pesa pubblica.
weighing s. pesatura || — -machine, pesa.
weight s. 1. peso 2. importanza || to put on —, ingrassare
to **weight** vi. appensantire, caricare.
weightiness s. 1. pesantezza 2. (fig.) importanza.
weightless agg. senza peso.
weighty agg. 1. pesante 2. (fig.) importante.
weir s. chiusa, diga.
weird agg. 1. fatale 2. misterioso.
welcome agg. gradito. ♦ **welcome** s. benvenuto.
to **welcome** vt. dare il benvenuto a, gradire.
to **weld** vt. saldare. ♦ to **weld** vi. saldarsi.
welding s. saldatura.
welfare s. benessere || — contributions, oneri previdenziali; — state, stato assistenziale; — work, assistenza sociale.
well[1] s. 1. fonte, pozzo 2. tromba delle scale.
well[2] avv. e s. bene || as —, pure; as — as, oltre a, oltre che; to be —, star bene; to get —, guarire.
to **well** vi. sgorgare.
well-advised agg. saggio.
well-being s. benessere.

well-bred *agg.* educato.
well-doing *s.* buona condotta.
well-done *agg.* (*cuc.*) ben cotto.
well-meaning *agg.* ben intenzionato.
well-off *agg.* agiato.
well-read *agg.* colto, ben educato.
well-timed *agg.* opportuno,
well-to-do *agg.* agiato.
Welsh *agg.* gallese.
Welshman *s.* gallese.
went V. *to go.*
wept V. *to weep.*
were V. *to be* ‖ *as it* —, per così dire.
west *agg.* occidentale. ♦ **west** *avv.* a, verso ovest. ♦ **west** *s.* ovest.
westerly *agg.* 1. dall'ovest 2. verso ovest. ♦ **westerly** *avv.* verso ovest.
western *agg.* occidentale.
westerner *s.* occidentale.
to westernize *vt.* occidentalizzare. ♦ **to westernize** *vi.* occidentalizzarsi.
westward *agg.* e *avv.* verso ovest.
westwards *avv.* verso ovest.
wet *agg.* 1. umido 2. piovoso ‖ — *blanket*, guastafeste. ♦ **wet** *s.* 1. umidità 2. tempo piovoso.
to wet *vt.* bagnare. ♦ **to wet** *vi.* bagnarsi.
wet-nurse *s.* nutrice.
wetting *s.* bagnatura.
whale *s.* balena ‖ — *-boat*, baleniera.
to whale *vi.* andare a caccia di balene.
whalebone *s.* stecca di balena.
whaler *s.* 1. baleniere 2. baleniera.
wharf *s.* banchina.
to wharf *vt.* attraccare.
what *agg.* 1. (*int.*) quale? quali? che? 2. (*rel.*) (quello) ... che 3. (*escl.*) che! ♦ **what** *pron.* 1. (*int.*) che?, che cosa? 2. (*rel.*) ciò che 3. (*escl.*) quanto! ‖ — *for?*, perché mai?; — *is he?*, che cosa fa? ♦ **what** *inter.* come!
whatever *agg.* qualunque. ♦ **whatever** *pron.* qualunque cosa. ♦ **whatever** *avv.* affatto.
whatsoever V. *whatever.*
wheat *s.* grano.
to wheedle *vt.* lusingare.
wheel *s.* 1. ruota 2. volante ‖ *wheels within wheels*, retroscena.
to wheel *vt.* 1. far ruotare 2. spingere (*su un veicolo a ruote*). ♦

to wheel *vi.* ruotare.
wheelbarrow *s.* carriola.
wheeze *s.* respiro affannoso.
to wheeze *vi.* ansimare.
whelp *s.* cucciolo.
when *avv.* e *cong.* quando.
whence *avv.* da dove.
whenever *avv.* tutte le volte che.
where *avv.* dove.
whereabout(s) *avv.* e *cong.* dove. ♦ **whereabout(s)** *s.* luogo.
whereas *cong.* mentre.
whereby *avv.* 1. (*int.*) come? 2. (*rel.*) per cui.
wherefore *avv.* 1. (*int.*) perché 2. (*rel.*) perciò.
wherein *avv.* 1. (*int.*) come? dove? 2. (*rel.*) in cui.
whereof *avv.* 1. (*int.*) di che? 2. (*rel.*) di cui.
whereon *avv.* 1. (*int.*) su che? 2. (*rel.*) su cui.
whereto *avv.* 1. (*int.*) verso dove? a che scopo? 2. (*rel.*) a cui.
whereupon *avv.* 1. (*int.*) su che? 2. (*rel.*) dopo di che.
wherever *avv.* dovunque.
whet *s.* 1. affilatura 2. (*fig.*) stimolante.
to whet *vt.* 1. affilare 2. stimolare.
whether *cong.* se ‖ — ... *or*, o...o.
whey *s.* siero (*del latte*).
which *agg.* 1. (*int.*) quale?, quali? 2. (*rel.*) il, la quale, i, le quali. ♦ **which** *pron.* 1. (*int.*) quale?, quali?, chi? 2. (*rel.*) il, la quale, i, le quali; il che ‖ *I cannot tell* — *is* —, non so distinguerli l'uno dall'altro.
whichever *agg.* qualunque. ♦ **whichever** *pron.* qualunque cosa.
whiff *s.* 1. soffio 2. sbuffo.
to whiff *vt.* e *vi.* 1. soffiare 2. emettere sbuffi.
whig *agg.* e *s.* (*pol. inglese*) liberale.
while *cong.* 1. mentre 2. sebbene. ♦ **while** *s.* momento ‖ *once in a* —, una volta tanto; *the* —, frattanto.
to while *vt.* *to* — *away the time*, ammazzare il tempo.
whilst V. *while.*
whim *s.* capriccio.
whimper *s.* 1. piagnucolio 2. uggiolio.
to whimper *vi.* 1. piagnucolare 2. uggiolare.
whimsical *agg.* stravagante.

whimsicality s. stravaganza.
whimsy agg. capriccioso. ♦ **whimsy** s. capriccio.
whine s. piagnisteo.
to **whine** V. to whimper.
whinny s. nitrito.
to **whinny** vi. nitrire.
whip s. frusta.
to **whip** vt. 1. frustare 2. frullare. ♦ to **whip** vi. precipitarsi || to — away, partire improvvisamente; to — out, pronunciare con violenza, tirar fuori.
whipper-snapper s. gradasso.
whirl s. 1. vortice 2. (fig.) confusione.
to **whirl** vt. 1. far roteare 2. trascinare. ♦ to **whirl** vi. 1. roteare 2. correr via 3. (fig.) esser confuso.
whirligig s. giostra.
whirlpool s. gorgo.
whirlwind s. turbine.
whir(r) s. 1. ronzio 2. frullio (d'ali) 3. rombo (di motore).
to **whir(r)** vi. 1. ronzare 2. frullare (d'ali) 3. rombare (di motore).
whisk s. 1. scopino 2. frullino 3. movimento rapido.
to **whisk** vt. 1. spazzare 2. (cuc.) frullare 3. agitare. ♦ to **whisk** vi. guizzare via.
whisker s. 1. basetta 2. baffo.
whisper s. 1. mormorio 2. diceria.
to **whisper** vt. e vi. mormorare, bisbigliare.
whistle s. fischio.
to **whistle** vt. e vi. 1. fischiare 2. chiamare con un fischio.
whistler s. 1. chi fischia 2. marmotta canadese.
whit s. 1. inezia 2. atomo.
Whit agg. di Pentecoste.
white agg. e s. bianco || — feather, viltà; — -livered, codardo.
to **whiten** vt. e vi. imbiancare.
whitener s. 1. imbianchino 2. candeggiante.
whiteness s. bianchezza.
whitening s. 1. imbiancamento 2. candeggiamento.
whitesmith s. lattoniere.
whitethorn s. biancospino.
whitewash s. 1. calce 2. (fig.) riabilitazione.
to **whitewash** vt. 1. imbiancare 2. (fig.) riabilitare.
whitewasher s. imbianchino.
whitewashing s. 1. imbiancatura 2. riabilitazione.

whiting s. calce.
whitish agg. biancastro.
whitlow s. patereccio.
Whitsunday s. Pentecoste.
whiz s. sibilo.
who pron. 1. (int.) chi? 2. (rel.) il, la quale, i, le quali.
whoever pron. chiunque.
whole agg. tutto, intero. ♦ **whole** s. 1. il tutto, l'intero 2. il complesso || as a —, nell'insieme; on the —, nel complesso.
wholeness s. totalità.
wholesale agg. e avv. all'ingrosso. ♦ **wholesale** s. vendita all'ingrosso.
to **wholesale** vt. e vi. vendere all'ingrosso.
wholesaler s. venditore all'ingrosso.
wholesome agg. salutare.
wholly avv. totalmente.
whom pron. compl. di who.
whomever pron. compl. chiunque.
whomsoever V. whomever.
whoop s. ululato.
whooping-cough s. pertosse.
whorl s. spirale.
whose pron. 1. (int.) di chi? 2. (rel.) del, della quale, dei, delle quali.
whosever pron. di chiunque.
whosoever V. whoever.
why avv. 1. (int.) perché? 2. (rel.) per cui. ♦ **why** cong. perché. ♦ **why** inter. perbacco.
wick s. lucignolo.
wicked agg. malvagio.
wickedness s. malvagità.
wicker s. vimine.
wicket s. 1. sportello 2. cancelletto.
wide agg. 1. largo 2. alto (di tessuto) 3. spalancato: — open, spalancato. ♦ **wide** avv. largamente.
wide-awake agg. 1. completamente sveglio 2. (fig.) vigilante.
widely avv. largamente.
to **widen** vt. allargare. ♦ to **widen** vi. allargarsi.
widespread agg. esteso.
widow s. vedova.
widower s. vedovo.
widowhood s. vedovanza.
width s. 1. larghezza 2. altezza (di stoffa).
to **wield** vt. 1. brandire 2. esercitare (autorità ecc.).
wife s. (pl. wives) moglie.
wig s. (fam.) sgridata.

wild agg. 1. selvaggio, selvatico 2. agitato 3. pazzo 4. avventato 5. disordinato. ♦ **wild** s. deserto. ♦ **wild** avv. 1. selvaggiamente 2. impulsivamente 3. sfrenatamente.

wilderness s. deserto.

wild-goose chase s. impresa vana, impossibile.

wildness s. 1. selvatichezza 2. furore.

wile s. astuzia.

wilful agg. 1. ostinato 2. premeditato.

wilfulness s. 1. ostinazione 2. premeditazione.

will s. 1. volontà 2. testamento || free —, libero arbitrio.

will v. ausiliare (usato per il futuro) he — be, egli sarà 2. v. dif. volere: I — go, io voglio andare, io andrò (futuro volitivo).

to **will** vt. e vi. 1. disporre 2. lasciare per testamento.

willed agg. strong —, di forte volontà.

willing agg. 1. volonteroso 2. disposto || — or not, volente o nolente.

willingly avv. volentieri.

willow s. —(tree), salice: weeping —, salice piangente.

willy-nilly agg. e avv. volente o nolente.

wily agg. astuto.

wimple s. 1. soggolo 2. arricciatura.

to **win** (won, won) vt. e vi. vincere || — back, riconquistare.

wince s. sussulto.

to **wince** vi. trasalire.

winch s. 1. argano 2. manovella.

wind[1] s. 1. vento 2. respiro || to get — of, aver sentore di; —-breaker, giacca a vento; —-cone, manica a vento.

wind[2] s. 1. svolta, curva 2. giro di carica.

to **wind**[1] vt. 1. fiutare 2. sfiatare.

to **wind**[2] (wound, wound) vt. 1. avvolgere 2. (una molla) caricare 3. girare || to — off, svolgere. ♦ to **wind** (wound, wound) vi. 1. serpeggiare 2. avvolgersi || to — off, svolgersi.

windbag s. 1. otre (di cornamusa) 2. (fig.) parolaio.

winder s. 1. manovella 2. avvolgitore.

winding agg. tortuoso. ♦ **winding** s. 1. tortuosità 2. tornante 3. spira

4. caricamento 5. ritorcitura.

windlass s. argano.

windmill s. mulino a vento.

window s. finestra, finestrino || — -dresser, vetrinista; French- —, porta finestra.

windpipe s. trachea.

windscreen s. parabrezza || — wiper, tergicristallo.

windshield s. (amer.) parabrezza.

windward agg. contro vento. ♦ **windward** s. sopravvento.

windy agg. 1. ventoso 2. verboso.

wine s. vino.

wing s. 1. ala 2. battente (di porta) 3. (teat.) quinta || on the —, in volo; to take —, spiccare il volo.

winged agg. alato.

wink s. 1. battito di palpebre 2. ammicco 3. (fig.) istante.

to **wink** vi. 1. battere le palpebre 2. ammiccare 3. scintillare.

winner s. vincitore.

winning agg. 1. vincitore 2. suadente. ♦ **winning** s. vittoria.

to **winnow** vt. e vi. vagliare.

winsome agg. incantevole.

winter s. inverno. ♦ **winter** agg. invernale.

to **winter** vi. svernare.

wintered agg. gelato.

winterly V. wintry.

wintriness s. rigore invernale.

wintry agg. invernale, freddo.

wipe s. 1. asciugatura 2. spolverata.

to **wipe** vt. 1. asciugare 2. strofinare || to — off, cancellare.

wiper s. 1. chi pulisce 2. strofinaccio.

wire s. 1. filo metallico 2. telegramma || — netting, rete metallica; barbed —, filo spinato.

to **wire** vt. e vi. 1. legare con filo metallico 2. prendere in trappola 3. telegrafare.

wired agg. munito di filo metallico, di rete metallica.

wireless agg. senza fili. ♦ **wireless** s. radiotelegrafia.

to **wireless** vt. e vi. radiotelegrafare.

wire-puller s. intrigante, eminenza grigia.

wiry agg. 1. di, simile a filo metallico 2. (fig.) resistente.

wisdom s. saggezza.

wise agg. 1. saggio 2. edotto, informato.

wise s. modo, maniera.

wiseacre s. saccente.

wisely *avv.* saggiamente.

wish *s.* **1.** desiderio **2.** augurio: *best wishes,* i migliori auguri.

to **wish** *vt. e vi.* **1.** desiderare **2.** augurare || *I wish I were,* vorrei essere; *I wish I had,* vorrei avere; *I wish I could,* vorrei potere.

wisher *s.* **1.** chi desidera **2.** chi augura.

wishful *agg.* desideroso.

wishing *agg.* desideroso. ♦ **wishing** *s.* desiderio.

wistaria *s.* glicine.

wistful *agg.* **1.** desideroso **2.** pensoso.

wistfully *avv.* **1.** con desiderio **2.** pensosamente.

wistfulness *s.* **1.** bramosia **2.** raccoglimento.

wit *s.* **1.** ingegno **2.** spirito **3.** persona di spirito || *to live by one's wits,* vivere di espedienti; *to be at one's wits' end,* non saper più cosa fare.

witch *s.* strega.

to **witch** *vt.* stregare.

witchcraft *s.* **1.** stregoneria **2.** fascino.

witch-doctor *s.* stregone.

witchery *s.* V. *witchcraft.*

witching *agg.* magico.

with *prep.* **1.** con **2.** presso **3.** a causa di, per, da.

to **withdraw** (**withdrew, withdrawn**) *vt.* ritirare. ♦ to **withdraw** (**withdrew, withdrawn**) *vi.* ritirarsi.

withdrawal *s.* **1.** ritirata, ritiro **2.** ritrattazione.

withdrawn V. *to withdraw.*

withdrew V. *to withdraw.*

withe *s.* vimine.

to **wither** *vt. e vi.* avvizzire.

withering *s.* avvizzimento.

to **withhold** (**withheld, withheld**) *vt.* **1.** trattenere **2.** rifiutare **3.** nascondere.

within *prep.* entro. ♦ **within** *avv.* dentro.

without *prep.* senza, senza di. ♦ **without** *cong.* senza (che). ♦ **without** *avv.* fuori.

to **withstand** (**withstood, withstood**) *vt.* resistere a, fronteggiare.

withstander *s.* oppositore.

withstood V. *to withstand.*

witness *s.* **1.** testimone: *eye- —,* testimone oculare **2.** testimonianza.

to **witness** *vt.* **1.** essere testimone a **2.** mostrare. ♦ to **witness** *vi.* testimoniare.

witticism *s.* arguzia.

wittily *avv.* spiritosamente.

wittiness *s.* spirito.

wittingly *avv.* consapevolmente.

witty *agg.* spiritoso.

wives V. *wife.*

wizard *s.* mago.

to **wobble** V. *to wabble.*

woe *s.* dolore.

woeful *agg.* doloroso.

woke V. *to wake.*

woken V. *to wake.*

wolf *s.* (*pl.* wolves) lupo || *she- —,* lupa.

to **wolf** *vt.* divorare.

wolfish *agg.* da lupo.

woman, *s.* (*pl.* women) donna.

womanhood *s.* **1.** femminilità **2.** maturità (*della donna*) **3.** condizione di donna.

womanish *agg.* **1.** effeminato **2.** femminile.

womankind *s.* le donne (*in genere*).

womanlike *agg.* femminile. ♦ **womanlike** *avv.* femminilmente.

womanliness *s.* femminilità.

womanly *agg.* femminile.

womb *s.* **1.** ventre **2.** grembo **3.** utero.

women V. *woman.*

won V. *to win.*

wonder *s.* **1.** prodigio **2.** meraviglia.

to **wonder** *vi.* **1.** domandarsi **2.** stupirsi.

wonderful *agg.* meraviglioso.

wonderingly *avv.* con meraviglia.

wonderland *s.* paese delle meraviglie.

wondrous *agg.* mirabile.

wont *agg.* abituato. ♦ **wont** *s.* abitudine.

wonted *agg.* abituato, abituale.

to **woo** *vt.* corteggiare.

wood *s.* **1.** bosco **2.** legno || *— -cutter,* boscaiolo.

woodcock *s.* beccaccia.

woodcut *s.* **1.** incisione su legno **2.** xilografia.

wooden *agg.* di legno.

woodiness *s.* **1.** boscosità **2.** legnosità.

woodland *s.* terreno boscoso.

woodman *s.* **1.** guardaboschi **2.** taglialegna.

woodpecker *s.* picchio.

woodwork s. lavoro in legno.
woody agg. 1. boscoso 2. legnoso.
wooer s. corteggiatore.
wool s. 1. lana 2. peluria di animale || cotton —, ovatta.
wool(l)en agg. di lana. ♦ **wool(l)en** s. stoffa di lana.
woolly agg. 1. di lana, lanoso 2. (fig.) confuso.
word s. parola || by — of mouth, oralmente.
to word vt. esprimere.
wordiness s. verbosità.
wording s. espressione.
wordy agg. verboso.
wore V. to wear.
work s. lavoro || out of —, disoccupato. ♦ **works** s. pl. 1. meccanismo (sing.) 2. fabbrica, officina (sing.).
to work vt. 1. lavorare 2. far funzionare 3. dirigere || to — in, introdurre; to — off, liberarsi di; to — out, calcolare; to — up, elaborare. ♦ **to work** vi. 1. lavorare 2. funzionare 3. agitarsi.
workable agg. 1. eseguibile 2. lavorabile.
workaday agg. lavorativo.
workday s. giorno feriale.
worker s. lavoratore || skilled —, operaio qualificato.
workhouse s. ospizio di mendicità.
working agg. 1. laborioso 2. funzionante. ♦ **working** s. 1. lavorio 2. funzionamento 3. lavorazione || -clothes, abiti da lavoro; — expenses, spese d'esercizio.
workless agg. senza lavoro.
workman s. operaio.
workmanship s. 1. abilità 2. fattura.
workroom s. laboratorio.
workshop s. officina.
workwoman s. operaia.
world s. mondo: all over the —, in tutto il mondo.
worldliness s. 1. condizione terrena 2. mondanità.
worldly agg. 1. terreno 2. mondano.
world-wide agg. diffuso, noto in tutto il mondo.
worm s. verme || — -screw, vite senza fine.
to worm vt. carpire || to — one's way, insinuarsi.
wormwood s. assenzio.
worn V. to wear. ♦ **worn** agg. 1.

consumato 2. indebolito || — -out, logoro, (fig.) esausto.
worried agg. 1. preoccupato 2. tormentato.
worrier s. seccatore.
worrisome agg. 1. irritante 2. preoccupato.
worry s. 1. ansia 2. guaio.
to worry vt. tormentare. ♦ **to worry** vi. preoccuparsi.
worrying agg. 1. preoccupante 2. tormentoso.
worse agg. (comp. di bad e ill) peggiore, peggio. ♦ **worse** avv. e s. peggio || all the —, tanto peggio; so much the — for, tanto peggio per; none the —, ugualmente; — and —, di male in peggio.
worship s. adorazione.
to worship vt. e vi. adorare, venerare.
worshipper s. 1. adoratore 2. fedele.
worst agg. (superl. di bad e ill) peggiore, pessimo. ♦ **worst** avv. e s. peggio || at (the) —, nella peggiore delle ipotesi.
worsted agg. di lana pettinata.
worth agg. degno. ♦ **worth** s. valore.
worthily avv. degnamente.
worthiness s. 1. valore 2. dignità.
worthless agg. 1. senza valore 2. indegno.
worthlessness s. 1. mancanza di valore 2. indegnità.
worthy agg. degno, meritevole. ♦ **worthy** s. persona illustre.
would v. dif. 1. (ausiliare del condiz.) he — go, egli andrebbe 2. (passato ind. imperfetto, congiuntivo, condiz.) volere 3. (imperfetto ind.) solere: he — come every day, soleva venire ogni giorno.
would-be agg. sedicente.
wound s. ferita.
to wound vt. ferire.
wound V. to wind.
wove V. to weave.
woven V. to weave.
wrack s. distruzione, rovina.
to wrangle vi. discutere.
wrangler s. attaccabrighe.
wrap s. sciarpa, coperta, mantello.
to wrap vt. avvolgere || to — up, impacchettare. ♦ **to wrap** vi. avvolgersi.
wrapper s. 1. imballatore 2. carta da imballo 3. copertina.

wrapping s. involucro || — *paper*, carta da imballaggio.
wrath s. ira.
wrathful *agg.* irato.
wrathfulness s. ira
wreath s. ghirlanda.
to **wreathe** vt. 1. intrecciare 2. inghirlandare 3. attorcigliare. ♦ to **wreathe** vi. innalzarsi in spire.
wreathy *agg.* 1. inghirlandato 2. a forma di ghirlanda.
wreck s. 1. naufragio (*anche fig.*) 2. relitto.
to **wreck** vt. rovinare. ♦ to **wreck** vi. naufragare.
wreckage V. *wreck*.
wren s. scricciolo.
wrench s. 1. strappo 2. (*mecc.*) chiave inglese.
to **wrench**, to **wrest** vt. 1. strappare 2. torcere.
wrestle s. lotta.
to **wrestle** vi. lottare.
wrestler s. lottatore.
wrestling s. (*sport.*) lotta.
wretch s. disgraziato.
wretched *agg.* 1. disgraziato 2. scadente.
wretchedness s. 1. disgrazia 2. squallore.
wriggle s. contorsione.
to **wriggle** vt. contorcere. ♦ to **wriggle** vi. 1. contorcersi 2. (*fig.*) dar risposte evasive.
wring s. 1. torsione 2. dolore acuto.
to **wring** (wrung, wrung) vt. 1. torcere 2. estorcere 3. stringere || *to* — *out*, spremere, (*fig.*) strappare.
wringer s. 1. torcitore 2. torchio.
wringing *agg.* lancinante (*di dolore*). ♦ **wringing** s. torcitura.
wrinkle[1] s. 1. ruga 2. grinza.
wrinkle[2] s. stratagemma.
to **wrinkle** vt. 1. corrugare 2. spiegazzare. ♦ to **wrinkle** vi. corrugarsi.
wrinkled, wrinkly *agg.* 1. corrugato 2. rugoso.
wrinkledness s. rugosità.
wrist s. polso.
wristband s. polsino.
to **write** (wrote, written) vt. scrivere || *to* — *back*, rispondere; *to* — *down*, annotare, descrivere; *to* — *off*, cancellare; *to* — *out*, copiare, emettere un assegno.
writer s. scrittore.
writhe s. contorcimento.

to **writhe** vt. contorcere. ♦ to **writhe** vi. 1. contorcersi 2. (*fig.*) fremere.
writing s. 1. lo scrivere 2. scrittura 3. scritto || — *-desk*, scrivania; — *-paper*, carta da lettere.
written V. *to write*.
wrong *agg.* 1. sbagliato 2. ingiusto 3. illegale. ♦ **wrong** *avv.* 1. erroneamente 2. ingiustamente.
wrong s. 1. torto 2. male || — *-doer*, peccatore, offensore; — *-doing*, peccato, offesa.
to **wrong** vt. 1. far torto a 2. imbrogliare.
wrongful *agg.* V. *wrong*.
wrongfulness s. ingiustizia.
wrongly *avv.* V. *wrong*.
wrote V. *to write*.
wrought *agg.* lavorato || — *-iron*, ferro battuto.
wrung V. *to wring*.
wry *agg.* storto.
to **wry** vt. contorcere. ♦ to **wry** vi. contorcersi.
wryly *avv.* per traverso.

X

xenophobe s. xenofobo.
xenophobia s. xenofobia.
xerophilous *agg.* xerofilo.
Xmas s. Natale.
X-ray *agg. attr.* a, di raggi X.
to **X-ray** vt. sottoporre a raggi X.
X-rays s. pl. raggi X.
xylograph s. xilografia.
xylographer s. xilografo.
xylographic(al) *agg.* xilografico.
xylography s. xilografia.
xylophone s. xilofono.
xylophonist s. xilofonista.

Y

yacht s. panfilo.
to **yacht** vi. fare crociere su panfilo.
yachtsman s. (*pl.* -men) proprietario di panfilo.
to **yank** vt. e vi. strappare, dare uno

strattone.
yap s. guaito.
to yap vi. guaire.
yard s. 1. iarda 2. cortile 3. cantiere: ship- —, cantiere navale.
yarn s. 1. filo 2. (fig.) storia.
yawl s. (naut.) iole, piccola imbarcazione.
yawn s. 1. sbadiglio 2. apertura.
to yawn vi. 1. sbadigliare 2. aprirsi.
yawning agg. 1. sonnolento 2. spalancato.
yea avv. sì.
year s. anno: — by —, di anno in anno; all the — round, per tutto l'anno; New Year's Day, Capodanno.
yearbook s. annuario.
yearling agg. di un anno d'età. ♦ **yearling** s. animale di un anno.
yearlong agg. che dura un anno.
yearly agg. annuale. ♦ **yearly** avv. annualmente.
to yearn vi. languire || to — for, after sthg., bramare qc.
yearning s. brama. ♦ **yearning** agg. bramoso.
yeast s. 1. lievito 2. fermento.
to yeast vi. 1. lievitare 2. fermentare.
yell s. urlo.
to yell vt. e vi. urlare.
yeller s. urlatore.
yellow agg. e s. giallo.
to yellow vt. e vi. ingiallire.
yellowish agg. giallastro.
yelp s. guaito.
to yelp vi. guaire.
yeoman s. piccolo proprietario terriero.
yes avv. sì.
yesterday avv. e s. ieri: the day before —, l'altro ieri; — week, ieri a otto.
yet avv. 1. ancora 2. già || as —, finora. ♦ **yet** cong. tuttavia.
yew s. — (-tree) tasso.
yield s. 1. produzione 2. (comm.) rendita.
to yield vt. e vi. 1. produrre, rendere 2. cedere || to — oneself up, arrendersi.
yielding agg. 1. pieghevole 2. docile.
yoke s. 1. giogo 2. barra (del timone) 3. coppia (di animali).
to yoke vt. aggiogare.
yolk s. tuorlo.

yonder agg. quello là, di laggiù. ♦ **yonder** avv. là.
you pron. pers. 1. tu, te, ti 2. voi, ve, vi 3. (forma di cortesia) Lei, Loro.
young agg. giovane || — people, i giovani (in genere).
youngster s. giovanetto.
your agg. poss. 1. tuo 2. vostro 3. (forma di cortesia) Suo.
yours pron. poss. 1. tuo 2. vostro 3. (forma di cortesia) Suo, Loro || — truly, — faithfully, distinti saluti.
yourself pron. r. 1. tu stesso, ti, te, te stesso 2. (forma di cortesia) Lei stesso.
yourselves pron. r. 1. voi stessi, vi 2. (forma di cortesia) Loro stessi.
youth s. 1. gioventù 2. ragazzo.
youthful agg. 1. giovane 2. giovanile.
youthfulness s. aspetto giovanile.
Yugoslav agg. e s. iugoslavo.

Z

zeal s. zelo.
zealot s. fanatico.
zealous agg. zelante.
zed s. zeta.
zenith s. zenit.
zephyr s. zeffiro.
zero s. 1. zero 2. (fig.) nullità.
zest s. 1. gusto 2. aroma.
zigzag agg. e avv. a zigzag.
to zigzag vi. andare a zigzag.
zinc s. zinco.
to zinc vt. zincare.
zincking s. zincatura.
zincograph s. zincografia.
to zincograph vt. imprimere su lastre di zinco.
zincographer s. zincografo.
zincography s. zincografia.
Zionism s. sionismo.
Zionist s. e agg. sionista.
zip s. fischio || — (-fastener), cerniera lampo.
to zip vi. sibilare.
zipper s. cerniera lampo.
zircon s. zircone.
zirconium s. zirconio.
zodiac s. zodiaco.
zodiacal agg. zodiacale.

608

zonal, zonary *agg.* zonale.
zonate(d) *agg.* a zone.
zonation *s.* zonatura.
zone *s.* zona.
zoo *s.* zoo.
zoological *agg.* zoologico.
zoologist *s.* zoologo.
zoology *s.* zoologia.
zoom *s.* **1.** rombo **2.** (*aer.*) salita a candela.
to **zoom** *vi.* **1.** rombare **2.** (*aer.*) salire a candela.

zoomorphic *agg.* zoomorfo.
zoomorphism *s.* zoomorfismo.
zoophilist *s.* zoofilo.
zoophilous *agg.* zoofilo.
zoophily *s.* zoofilia.
zoophobia *s.* zoofobia.
zootechnic *agg.* zootecnico.
zootechnics, zootechny *s.* zootecnica.
zootomic(al) *agg.* zootomico.
zouave *s.* zuavo.
zygoma *s.* (*pl.* zygomata) zigomo.